DONALD SASSOON wa... is, Milan
and London. He teaches ... College,
University of London an... cluding
Contemporary Italy: Politics ... 945 (1986). *One
Hundred Years of Socialism* ... Deutscher prize in 1996.

Further praise for *One Hundred Years of Socialism*:

'[An] extraordinary achievement . . . Sassoon constantly stresses, with
an amazing and enviable width of scholarship, how the pre-existent
cultures of different countries made the socialist project so different in
each . . . this book is a small masterpiece. It is vastly informative . . .
and wise in its conclusions . . . I have not felt so sure that a work
would be a standard book for a long time.'   BERNARD CRICK

'An astonishing achievement. *One Hundred Years of Socialism* is so
learned and wide-ranging, so densely packed and yet so readable,
so subtle and refined in its judgements and scholarship, it is a
constant source of inspiration.'   HUGO YOUNG

'I read it with unflagging interest and appetite never wishing it a page
shorter. After reading Sassoon's enthralling account, glib capitalist
triumphalism seems as historically misconceived as the naive socialist
millenarianism of an earlier generation.'

PETER CLARKE, author of *Liberals and
Social Democrats* and *A Question of Leadership*

'Donald Sassoon tells his kaleidoscopic story with ease and urbanity as
he guides his readers, with great skill, through the complex issues of
ideology and industrial development, diplomacy and war, which have
shaped one hundred years of European socialism.'

PAUL PRESTON, author of *Franco* and
A Concise History of the Spanish Civil War

MORE REVIEWS OVERLEAF

ONE HUNDRED YEARS
OF SOCIALISM

THE WEST EUROPEAN LEFT IN
THE TWENTIETH CENTURY

Donald Sassoon

FontanaPress
An Imprint of **HarperCollins***Publishers*

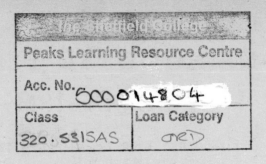
Fontana Press
An imprint of HarperCollins*Publishers*
77–85 Fulham Palace Road
Hammersmith, London, W6 8JB

This paperback edition, with line corrections, 1997
3 5 7 9 8 6 4 2

First published in Great Britain by I. B. Tauris 1996

ISBN 0 00 686376 0

Set in Monotype Garamond

Printed and bound by
Caledonian International Book Manufacturing Ltd, Scotland

Contents

Tables

Figures

Acknowledgements

I am very grateful to Eric Hobsbawm for reading large sections of this work, and for his advice and encouragement.

My debt to Jill Tilden, who read the entire manuscript, and to her enviable editing skills, is immense.

I shall always be grateful to Anna Coote, who read and commented on every word I wrote, discussed many of the issues raised, gave me invaluable encouragement and precious advice.

Gregory Elliott also read the entire text and gave me the inestimable benefit of his thirty-page critical, yet enormously constructive, report. I wish every author had a reader like him.

I wish to thank the following friends who read and commented on various aspects of this work: Nina Fishman, University of Westminster, for chapters 1–5 and 13, and various illuminating conversations; Mike Newman, University of North London, for chapters 1–3 and 5; Monica Threlfall, Loughborough University, for chapter 15; Diana Coole, Queen Mary and Westfield College, University of London, for chapter 15; Vassilis Fouskas, QMW College, for the section on Greece in chapter 21; Ilaria Favretto, QMW College, for chapter 10; Daniel Pick and Peter Hennessy, both at QMW, for help with the epilogue.

I wish to thank my old friend George Brennan, one of the finest minds in the country, for help with chapters 1 and 11–15.

I have been fortunate in having I.B.Tauris as my publisher; few houses would have had the temerity to back such a lengthy tome. I particularly thank Emma Sinclair-Webb for championing the project and Sian Mills for seeing it to its completion.

I thank the staff of the University of London Library (Senate House), of the British Library of Political and Economic Science, of the library of the Friedrich Ebert Stiftung in Bonn (especially Herr Ziska), of the Arbetar-rörelsens Archiv och bibliotek in Stockholm, of the Gramsci Institute of Bologna, and of the Bibliothèque de la Fondation Nationale des Sciences Politiques in Paris.

I also wish to thank Pia Locatelli, Vice-President, Socialist International Women, for help with material from the PSI and the SI; Angela Vegliante of the Italian Institute of London for help with the cover illustration; Helga May of the Friedrich Ebert Stiftung for helping me during my visit to Bonn; Sven Olsson for doing the same when I was in Stockholm; David Kirby of the School of Slavonic and Eastern European Studies, University of London, for help over Finland; Tanya Sassoon for statistical help with chapter 22. For helping me with party programmes in Spanish and German, I thank Angelica Sodupe, Gabriele Madsen and Arne Hoffmann.

I also thank those I have consulted – especially Susanne Miller, Bonn; Gösta Rehn, SOFI (Stockholm); David Miliband (IPPR), Walter Korpi, SOFI (Stockholm); Wolfgang Berner, formerly deputy director of the Bundesinstitut fur Ostwissenschaftliche und internationale Studien; Heinz Timmermann, of the same institute; Veronica Isenberg, International Affairs, SPD; Klas Eklund, Ministry of Industry, Sweden; Beatrix Wrede-Bouvier, Friedrich Ebert Stiftung, Bonn; Herbert Joos, Secretary of the Labour Committee, SPD, John Jungclaussen (QMW), and Catherine Hakim of the LSE.

I also wish to thank the British Academy for a grant which enabled me to visit Bonn and Stockholm in 1991; Westfield College for a grant to visit Paris in 1988; and the Central Research Fund of the University of London for a small grant for photocopying expenses.

Abbreviations

ACLI	Associazioni Cristiane Lavoratori Italiani
ADGB	Allgemeiner Deutscher Gewerkschaftsbund (general German trade union federation)
AES	Alternative Economic Strategy
AP	Alianza Popular (Spain)
CBI	Confederation of British Industry (UK)
CC.OO.	Comisiones Obreras (Spanish trade union federation)
CDS	Centro Democrático Social (Portugal)
CDU	Christlich Demokratische Union (German Christian Democratic Party)
CFDT	Confédération Française Démocratique du Travail
CFTC	Confédération Française des Travailleurs Chrétiens
CGIL	Confederazione Generale Italiana del Lavoro (Italian trade union confederation)
CGT	Confédération Générale du Travail (French trade union federation)
CHU	Christelijk-Historische Unie (Holland, Christian Historical Union)
CISL	Confederazione Italiana Sindacati Lavoratori (Italian Catholic trade union confederation)
CND	Campaign for Nuclear Disarmament
COMECON	Council for Mutual Economic Assistance
COMISCO	Comité de Défense Socialiste Internationale
CPGB	Communist Party of Great Britain
CPSU	Communist Party of the Soviet Union
CSC	Confédération des Syndicats Chrétiens (Belgium)
CSCE	Conference on Security and Co-operation in Europe
CSU	Christlich-Soziale Union (Christian-Social Union, Bavaria)
CVP-PSC	Christelijke Volkspartij – Parti Social Chrétien (Belgium)
DC	Democrazia Cristiana (Italy)
DGB	Deutscher Gewerkschaftsbund (German trade union federation)
DKP	Deutsche Kommunistische Partei (German Communist Party)
DNA	Det Norske Arbeiderparti (Norwegian Labour Party)
EAM	National Liberation Front (Greece)
ECSC	European Coal and Steel Community
EDA	Eniaia Dimokratiki Aristera (United Democratic Left, Greece)
EDC	European Defence Community

EFTA	European Free Trade Association
ELAS	National Popular Liberation Army (Greece)
EURATOM	European Atomic Energy Community
FDP	Freie Demokratische Partei (German Free Democratic Party)
FEN	Fédération de l'Education Nationale (French teaching union)
FGDS	Fédération de la Gauche Démocratique et Socialiste (France)
FGTB	Fédération Générale du Travail de Belgique
FIM	Federazione Italiana Metallurgici (Italian engineering union)
FIOM	Federazione Impiegati Operai Metallurgici (engineering union, Italy)
FO	Force Ouvrière (French trade union)
FPÖ	Freiheitliche Partei Österreichs (Austrian Freedom Party)
GATT	General Agreement on Tariffs and Trade
GAZ	Grüne Aktion Zukunft (Germany)
ICBM	Inter-Continental Ballistic Missiles
ILP	Independent Labour Party (UK)
IRI	Istituto per la Ricostruzione Industriale (Italy)
KKE-es	Kommounistiko Komma Elladas-esoterikou (Communist Party of Greece-Interior)
KKE	Kommounistiko Komma Elladas (Greek Communist Party)
KPD	Kommunistische Partei Deutschlands (Communist Party of Germany)
KPÖ	Kommunistische Partei Österreichs (Austrian Communist Party)
KSC	Czechoslovak Communist Party
LO	Landsorganisationen (Swedish trade union confederation)
LRC	Labour Representation Committee (UK)
MFA	Movimento das Forças Armadas (Armed Forces Movement, Portugal)
MRP	Mouvement Républicain Populaire (France)
MSI	Movimento Sociale Italiano (Italy)
NATO	North Atlantic Treaty Organization
ND	Nea Dimokratia (New Democracy, Greece)
NEB	National Enterprise Board (UK)
NUM	National Union of Mineworkers (UK)
OPEC	Organization of Petroleum Exporting Countries
ÖVP	Österreichs Volkspartei (Austrian People's Party)
PASOK	Panellinio Sosialistiko Kinima (Pan-Hellenic Socialist Movement)
PCdI	Partito Comunista d'Italia (later PCI)
PCE	Partida Comunista de España
PCF	Parti Communiste Français (originally Parti Communiste de France)
PCI	Partito Comunista Italiano (Italy)
PCP	Partido Comunista Português (Portugal)
PDS	Partito Democratico della Sinistra (Democratic Party of the Left, Italy)
PDS	Partei des Demokratischen Sozialismus (Democratic Socialist Party, Germany)

PLP	Parti de la Liberté et du Progrès (Belgium)
POB	Parti Ouvrier Belge (in Flanders, Belgische Werklieden Partij – BWP)
POF	Parti Ouvrier Français (pre-1905, led by Jules Guesde)
PPI	Partito Popolare Italiano (Italy)
PS	Partido Socialista Português (Portugal)
PSB/BSP	Parti Socialiste Belge/Belgische Socialistische Partij (Belgium)
PSD	Partido Social Democrata (Portugal)
PSDI	Partito Social Democratico Italiano (Italy)
PSI	Partito Socialista Italiano (Italy)
PSIUP	Partito Socialista Italiano di Unità Proletaria (Italy)
PSOE	Partido Socialista Obrero Español (Spain)
PSU	Parti Socialiste Unifié (France)
PvdA	Partij van de Arbeid (Labour Party, Holland)
SAF	Svenska Arbetsgivareföreningen (Swedish Employers' Association)
SAP	Socialdemokratiska Arbetarepartiet (Swedish Social Democratic Party)
SDAP	Sociaal Democratische Arbeiders Partij (Dutch Social Democratic Party)
SDF	Social Democratic Federation (UK)
SDP	Social Democratic Party
SDS	Sozialistische Deutscher Studentenbund
SED	Sozialistische Einheitspartei Deutschlands (Socialist Unity Party, German Democratic Republic)
SF	Socialistisk Folkeparti (Socialist People's Party, Denmark)
SFIO	Section Française de l'Internationale Ouvrière (France)
SKDL	Finnish People's Democratic League
SKP	Suomen Kommunistien Puolue (Finnish Communist Party)
SPD	Sozialdemokratische Partei Deutschlands (German Social Democratic Party)
SPÖ	Sozialistische Partei Österreichs (Austrian Socialist Party)
SSTP	Suomen Sosialistinen Työväenpuole (Finnish Socialist Workers' Party)
SV	Socialistisk Venstreparti (Socialist Left Party, Norway)
TGWU	Transport and General Workers' Union (UK)
UC	Enosis Kentrou (Union of the Centre, Greece)
UCD	Unión Centro Democrático (Spain)
UDI	Unione Donne Italiane (Union of Italian Women)
UGT	Unión General de Trabajadores (trade union federation, Spain)
UIL	Unione Italiana del Lavoro (left of centre trade union confederation)
UNRRA	United Nations Relief and Rehabilitation Administration
USPD	Unabhängige Sozialdemokratische Partei Deutschlands (Independent SPD, Germany)
VVD	Volkspaztij voor Vrijheid en Democratie
WEU	Western European Union
WSPU	Women's Social and Political Union

Introduction

ON 14 JULY 1889, as France celebrated the centenary of the Revolution, socialists from all over Europe gathered in Paris. Their purpose was to launch a new organization to replace the First International, defunct since 1876.

The delegates who met on that day in rue Rochechouart, near Pigalle, considered themselves the true heirs of the 1789 revolutionaries. That epic uprising, they believed, had been the first stage of a great social revolution for the emancipation of humanity. The ruling bourgeoisie had appropriated the memory of 1789 and some of its symbols, but not its true spirit. Liberty, equality and fraternity could become a reality only if social wealth and economic power were transferred from the control of the few to the sovereignty of the whole people.[1]

Monarchist, Catholic, traditional France had little to celebrate: the empire had vanished, ignominiously defeated. Socialist France had been taught a lesson it would not forget: in 1871 the Commune of Paris had been crushed in a bloodbath. Political power was now in the hands of 'bourgeois' France. The Third Republic, however, was less than twenty years old, and not yet consolidated. All its neighbours, except Switzerland, were monarchies. Only in 1880 did the National Assembly decide that 14 July 1889 should become a day of celebration. It was a choice dictated by caution. The government of the time had no wish to multiply its enemies by unnecessarily offending the still strong royalists. Thus, there was no question of celebrating the Terror and Jacobinism by holding the festivities on 2 June 1893, the centenary of the Jacobin Republic. The National Assembly could have erred on the side of moderation by opting for 5 May 1789, when Louis XVI opened the Etats Généraux at Versailles, or 17 June, when the third estate turned itself into the National Assembly. It could have chosen 26 August, the anniversary of the Declaration of the Rights of Man and Citizen. It was decided that the fall of the Bastille offered a suitable 'revolutionary' moment which, while not specifically republican, was still popular and heroic enough to satisfy radical feelings.[2]

When a tradition is created, it is essential to make clear what is actually being celebrated: not only a past event, but a contemporary reality in search of legitimation. France, bourgeois and self-satisfied, may have been applauding liberty, equality and fraternity but, in practice, what was being consecrated was commerce and trade, modernity and the wonders of technology exhibited in the *Galerie des machines*, in a word: capitalism. This, as the socialist paper

Le cri du peuple commented bitterly, 'is the kind of fête which the bourgeoisie prefers. As they are our masters we will have to be content with the entertainment prescribed by their taste.'[3] No monument was erected in homage to the martyrs of the Revolution. Instead, the centrepiece of the *Exposition universelle* and its lasting icon was a huge metallic tower bearing the name of its creator, Gustave Eiffel, which has dominated the Parisian landscape ever since.[4] Under the banner of modernity, progress and the peaceful pursuit of wealth, the French people would regain national pride and unity after the humiliating defeat of 1870 by the new Germany.[5] The newspaper *Le Temps* caught the mood of the time; its leading article, commenting on the inauguration of the Eiffel Tower (held on 5 May, the anniversary of the convening of the Etats Généraux), patriotically exclaimed: 'France, proud of herself, head held high, celebrates the economic as well as the political centenary of 1789.'[6] In 1889 France was celebrating the capitalist outcome of the Revolution. This was not lost on the mainly Marxist founders of the Second International. These enemies of capital, as they met in its shadow, declared:

> The capitalists have invited the rich and powerful to the *Exposition universelle* to observe and admire the product of the toil of workers forced to live in poverty in the midst of the greatest wealth human society has ever produced. We, socialists, have invited the producers to join us in Paris on 14 July. Our aim is the emancipation of the workers, the abolition of wage-labour and the creation of a society in which all women and men (*toutes and tous*) irrespective of sex or nationality will enjoy the wealth produced by the work of all workers.[7]

Among the signatories were August Bebel and Wilhelm Liebknecht from Germany, William Morris from England, Keir Hardie from Scotland, Victor Adler from Austria, Amilcare Cipriani from Italy. Also present were the old Engels, Marx's comrade-in-arms, Edouard Vaillant and Jules Guesde from France, Georgii Plekhanov from Russia, César De Paepe from Belgium, Pablo Iglesias from Spain, and nearly four hundred other delegates representing the socialist organizations of nineteen countries including Austria, Italy, Norway, Sweden, Britain, Belgium, Greece, Spain and Portugal. A rival congress of more moderate socialists, the so-called *possibilistes*, was held at the same time in rue Lancry. It was less important than that of the Marxists and none of its resolutions differed significantly from those approved in rue Rochechouart.[8]

What did these socialists want? The first resolutions of the Marxist congress demanded legislation to protect workers (particularly women workers), the eight-hour day, the abolition of child labour. Prominence was given to sexual equality:

> Congress declares it is the duty of male workers to admit female workers as equal in their ranks on the basis of the principle of 'equal work, equal pay' for workers of both sexes without discrimination of nationality.[9]

The delegates decided that the First of May would be designated 'workers' day' and condemned war as 'the inevitable product of present economic conditions', asserting with confidence that it 'will disappear for ever when the capitalist order itself has disappeared, the workers have been emancipated and socialism [is] triumphant throughout the world'.[10] Finally, Congress noted that, as the possession of political power was what enabled capitalists to rule, workers in countries where they had the vote should join the socialist parties and elect them to office. Elsewhere, workers should use all possible means to obtain the suffrage. The use of force by the ruling class to prevent this peaceful evolution towards a society based on co-operation (i.e. socialism) would be a crime against humanity.[11]

This founding congress of the socialist parties of Europe – all committed to Marxism – established a set of principles which they have upheld, not always consistently, for these last one hundred years: the extension of democracy, the peaceful evolution towards political power, the regulation of the labour market, the end of sexual and other forms of discrimination. These principles set a wide agenda which no political force in Europe could subsequently ignore. As the socialist parties emerged, their aristocratic and bourgeois opponents, while attempting to repress them, adopted some of their ideas (e.g. Bismarck's plans for accident, sickness and old-age insurance in 1883–89). Even the Roman Catholic church shifted ground and, with Leo XIII's papal encyclical *Rerum Novarum* (1891), laid the foundation for what came to be known as the 'social' doctrine of the church.

The history I present here is the history of the socialist organizations which modified the trajectory of European society. When I speak of 'the Left', I speak of these traditional socialist parties. The term 'Left', of course, predates socialism. It originated with the French Revolution. When Louis XVI convened the Etats Généraux, the members of the first and second estates, the aristocracy and the church, elected to sit to the right of the presiding chair; the representatives of the 'people' – in reality, the middle classes, or third estate – took their place on the left.[12] This was where, throughout the revolutionary period, the most intransigent anti-royalist upholders of the principle of popular sovereignty sat. Biblically speaking, the left is hardly the most propitious place: 'Then he will say to those at his left hand: "Depart from me, you cursed, into the eternal fire prepared for the devil and his angels"' (Matthew 25:41). One might say that at its very birth the Left looked askance at the world of tradition and established convention.

I have chosen, not entirely arbitrarily, to begin the story of the socialist Left in those days of 1889 – exactly half-way between the great liberal-democratic revolution whose language has marked the course of the twentieth century, and the final collapse of the communist revolution against capitalism; poised, equidistantly, between the fall of the Bastille and that of the Berlin Wall.

In the rue Rochechouart the representatives of labour gathered in the shadow of the celebration of capital as the ghost stalking it. One part of it old, the other still unborn, the socialist movement turned, Janus-like, simultaneously towards the past, the unfulfilled ideals of the French Revolution, and towards a future when these ideals would be realized.

Born within the interstices of the advanced industrial societies of Western Europe, the rising socialist movement had, as its long-term goal, the destruction of capitalism and the establishment of a society where production would be subjected to the associated control of the producers, and not left to the mercy of the spontaneous decisions of millions of consumers and the calculations of thousands of capitalists. In the meantime, they believed, much could be done. The reforms advocated by the Second International were expected to make working-class life under capitalism endurable and dignified, and to enable the workers themselves to organize freely and independently. But the more successful the socialists became, the more dependent they found themselves on the prosperity of capitalism. Though they dreamt of its final crisis, they gradually realized how dangerous a moribund social system could become. We now know that the first political casualties of capitalist crises in Western Europe would be the parties of the Left – as was the case in the 1930s – while their greatest successes occurred during the thirty glorious years of capitalist growth (1945–75) – the Golden Age of Capitalism.

Capitalism was, in turn, dependent on the social and political institutions of the state. Consequently, socialists had no alternative but to organize themselves accordingly, that is, as national parties. Thus, even though they had created an international organization, socialists were, from their inception, circumscribed by the political framework of what is conventionally, if misleadingly, called the 'nation-state' – misleadingly, because no state's territory can precisely enclose all and only the members of a 'nation', however defined.

Capitalism, of course, changed considerably over the course of the next hundred years. In the USA, unchallenged by socialism, helped by two world conflicts which debilitated European rivals, it became the cornerstone of the international economic system. The elements of constriction and regulation which were in their infancy in the nineteenth century (tariffs, factory legislation and laws governing joint-stock companies) expanded substantially. The nation-state consistently co-operated with capitalists, protected them when necessary, regulated their activities where desirable, and favoured this or that enterprise. Many capitalists lost out and fell by the wayside. But capitalism lived on and conquered the globe. At the end of the twentieth century, the fundamental political conflict in democratic capitalist countries was over the extent and form of the regulation of capitalism. Its abolition was no longer sought. Beyond the advanced countries where capitalism appears to be firmly implanted, conflicts concern nationalism, religion and the speed or form of capitalist development. No one, any longer, anywhere, pursues a non-capitalist path.

From Western Europe, socialism followed capitalism across the world –

a source of inspiration for many struggling against exploitation and dis-crimination, tyranny and injustice (including the not infrequent tyranny and injustice exercised in the name of socialism). Yet one should bear in mind that the idea of socialism was not born among the most wretched of the earth. It was born in *Western* Europe, in industrial societies or societies on the verge of industrialization. It was born among skilled workers, not the *lumpenproletariat*. It was born inside capitalism, in the midst of the great wealth produced by the workers themselves. However, though intrinsically linked to the industrial working class, socialism attracted all those who wanted to change the world and who refused to accept distress as the fated condition of human beings. This moral appeal was its strongest point. On this terrain, liberalism, in its pure individualistic form, stripped of its social content, was never a match for socialism, while nationalism, unless harnessed to socialism, could never free itself sufficiently of its backward glance to inspire those who sought to move forward.

Outside Western Europe, socialism – especially, but not exclusively, in its communist version – became a force for modernization, agrarian reform, decolonization, nationalism. It was embraced by Africans fighting against apartheid, by Latin Americans struggling against foreign multinationals or local landed interests. In China socialism inspired the organization of the most massive peasant revolution in recorded history. In India it was a part of the widest non-violent movement that ever existed. In Russia socialists launched the most daring, longest and most disastrous experiment in social engineering of the twentieth century. By the end of the twentieth century, socialism has been rejected as an instrument of modernization throughout most of the Third World. In what used to be called the Soviet Union it subsists, so far, only as a rallying call for those looking nostalgically to past certainties. In China and Vietnam, whose socialism had inspired the young in the 1960s and 1970s, capitalism, albeit of a special type, is being rapidly developed under the guidance of communist parties. Only in Western Europe does socialism appear to survive, battered by electoral defeats, uncertain of its future, suspicious of its own past.

Whether socialism is in its death throes, or poised on the threshold of an era of renewal, is not a question historians can answer. This book is neither a protracted obituary, nor an optimistic 'upbeat' account comforting to the remaining supporters of socialism.

Although it cannot be classified as a short work, I am only too aware that much has been left out. In particular, I should warn the potential reader that this is not a history of socialist ideas, a survey of the thinkers who have ceaselessly tried to renew values and strategies by adapting them to the development of capitalism. Nor is it the history 'from below' of the socialists themselves, of the men and women who joined the movement, who were inspired by it and who fought for it. It is a comparative history of socialist *parties* in the context of the constraints they faced: capitalist development, the nation-state, the international system, dominant ideologies, the past. I have refrained from using any particular definition of socialism to adjudicate which parties are 'worthy' of being called socialist. Historians who do not wish to be judges have no alternative but to use the parties' own definition of themselves. I have, consequently, included all self-styled socialist, social-democratic, labour and workers' parties. I have not confined myself to the social-democratic tradition. When size or the particular conjuncture warranted, I have dealt with the communist parties of Western Europe – particularly those, like the Italian and French communist parties, which have been for a long time the principal party of the Left in their country.

Having taken seriously the historicist dictum that all history is the history of the present, I have written these pages because I wanted to put the apparent decline of the idea of socialism, and the difficulties faced by the socialist parties in the last twenty years or so, into historical perspective. This may account for the structure of the book, which resembles that of an inverted pyramid: the closer we get to the present, the more detailed becomes the account. Though I proceed sequentially, the volume grows exponentially. The years up to the Second World War are dealt with swiftly and somewhat perfunctorily, in just over one-tenth of the book. Half of what is left covers the 'Thirty Glorious Years' of capitalism, the years up to 1973–75; the remainder probes the subsequent two decades. The story stops in the middle of the 1990s when past and present become indistinguishable and when, denied the advantage of even limited hindsight, historians can only write as contemporaries. The book ends without concealing the fact that the closing years of the millennium are marked by unparalleled uncertainties. In these circumstances predictions are no more than informed guesswork.

Most of the book, then, explores the problems and constraints of political power, and the demands of electoral politics, which the main parties of the Left have faced in Western Europe since 1945 – the period when the socialist parties could truly aspire to power and encountered the formidable limitations of democratic politics. Small organizations and sects have the unenviable luxury of the powerless: the programmes they concoct are directed at the loyal few, not the indifferent many; their unsullied ideological purity can be more easily maintained far from the exigencies of practical politics. They play no part in this history.

My territorial focus, inevitably, is 'Western Europe' where the conjunction between democracy, capitalism and socialism has arisen. To some extent, 'Western Europe' is purely a geographical expression given political meaning by the division resulting from the Second World War. Now that the Cold War is over, a social-democratic Left may arise in Eastern and Central Europe and thus contribute to a political unification of the continent without historical precedent. Be that as it may, Western Europe's distinctiveness is not defined simply in terms of the territory unoccupied by the Red Army in 1945. Eastern and Western Europe have had different histories for centuries.[13] The West has had a history marked by the stubborn growth of 'liberties' – though usually limited to certain groups which exploited others.[14] This is where serfdom was first abolished, where the 'rights of man' were first promulgated, where the ideas of the Enlightenment first manifested themselves. This is where industrialization and modernization – in a word, capitalism – originated, beginning with Britain, Belgium and the Rhineland, though often using technologies which arose as far east as China.[15] That Western Europe, never under the rule of a single power, produced ideas used to subject others – including nearly all non-Europeans – to new forms of despotism and exploitation is undeniable. But so is the fact that those who fought against Europeans did so largely on the basis of concepts of freedom which also originated in Western Europe.

The boundaries of this territory are not precise: west of the river Elbe down to Venice on the Adriatic may be a useful approximation. This is the setting for our story. Within this area, the treatment of the various parties is unavoidably uneven: large countries – France, Great Britain, Germany and Italy – are covered in greater detail, but so is Sweden, in spite of its small population, because of the importance of its social-democratic party. Because the focus of the book is the parties of the Left in a democratic and electoral context, the examination of the socialist and communist parties of Spain, Portugal and Greece – except for a few pages on the Spanish and Greek civil wars – has focused on the transition from authoritarianism and its aftermath. Finally, I have not considered the vicissitudes of the Left in the very small countries of Western Europe such as Iceland and Luxemburg, or in countries, such as Switzerland and Ireland, where the Left does not play a leading role either in government or in opposition.

Outside these considerable and self-imposed restrictions, the book seeks to examine everything significant in the history of Europe that has had an impact on the history of the Left: from economic development to international relations, from elections to coalition-building, from trade unions to feminism and ecology. Whenever possible I have tried to distinguish the parties' conception of themselves from the circumstances surrounding them.

Gramsci once explained that to write the history of a party is like writing the history of a country from a monographic point of view. I had not fully comprehended the truth of this proposition until I realized, half-way through my work, that I was writing the history of Western Europe from the perspective of the history of the Western European Left. This was unavoidable: the history of a party is inseparable from the history of the economic and social structures which shape it and against which it strives. The tension which has inspired this book, like those which preceded it, is the age-old question of structural constraints on human actions, the restraint imposed by reality on our dreams of freedom.

Book One
Expansion

PART ONE

The Hard Road to Political Power

CHAPTER ONE

The Establishment of Socialism
Before 1914

BY 1914 A sizeable labour or working-class movement existed in virtually all European countries. Although its politics was for the most part inspired by socialism, socialism was not its necessary precondition. Both within and beyond Europe there would have been an organized labour movement even without socialism. Prior to the First World War, Britain had no significant socialist party. In the last quarter of the twentieth century, Japan has emerged as, arguably, the most successful capitalist country of the world, but has so far produced only a weak and ineffectual socialist party.

Contrary to what virtually all socialists believed at the time, there was no necessary causal link between the rise of an organized labour movement and the ideology of socialism. As for the conjunction between socialism and industrialization, this was characteristic of only a fairly limited geographical area: continental Europe. Its subsequent diffusion outside Europe has been confined to countries without a significant industrial base and, hence, without a significant working-class movement (Australia and New Zealand provide the main exceptions). In continental Europe socialism was, so to speak, 'captured' by Marxism which, at the turn of the century, dominated the labour movement. I am concerned here not with Marx's Marxism but with the interpretations of his doctrine which came to prevail in the socialist and social-democratic parties, i.e. what is sometime referred as 'vulgar Marxism' or the 'Marxism of the Second International'. The interpretation of 'Marxism' I am interested in is the one which strongly appealed to the leaders of the working-class movement and the activists who followed them. It was obviously a simplified version of Marx's work. Otto Bauer, the main theoretician of what would later be called 'Austro-Marxism', was quite candid about the necessity of such adaptation:

> From the history of the natural sciences and of philosophy many examples could be provided which show that the simplification and vulgarization of a new doctrine is nothing but a stage of its victorious advance, of its rise to general acceptance.[1]

The popular rendering of the new doctrine was diffused through the works of Kautsky and Bebel, which were read and distributed more widely than Marx's own works.[2]

In essence, pre-1914 vulgar Marxism, condensed into its essential outline, consisted of the following fairly simple propositions:[3]

PROPOSITION ONE   The present capitalist system is unfair. Its fundamental relation, the wage relation, is based on a contract between juridically equal parties, but this disguises a real inequality: the capitalists 'cheat' the workers by appropriating far more than they pay in wages and other necessary production costs. This special and statistically unquantifiable appropriation, called 'surplus-value' by Marxists, gives the owners of capital great wealth and control over the economic development of society. They thus appropriate not simply wealth but also power.

PROPOSITION TWO   History proceeds through stages. Each stage is characterized by a specific economic system to which corresponds a particular system of power and hence a specific ruling class. The present capitalist stage is not everlasting, but a transient historical phenomenon: the present ruling class will not rule for ever.

PROPOSITION THREE   Workers are a fundamentally homogeneous class, regardless of differences which may exist among them. All workers are united 'in essence' by similar interests: to improve their conditions of life under capitalism; to struggle against the existing social order; and to overcome it by bringing about a new stage of history in which there can be 'real', and not merely formal, equality. It follows that workers must organize themselves into political parties and trade unions and reject any attempt to divide them.

The first proposition embraces the Marxist economic theory of exploitation; the second is the so-called materialist conception of history; while the third, not really elaborated by Marx, was the product of the ideas and political practice of the leaders of European socialism (especially in Germany) after Marx's death.

On one level of analysis these propositions express a simple 'trinity': (1) a statement on the present: 'the existing social order is unfair'; (2) a statement on the future: 'the existing social order can be changed'; (3) a strategic statement on the transition from (1) to (2): 'fate alone will not bring about this transition, we must organize and act.' Belief in this 'trinity' (the religious expression is rather appropriate) is a necessary requirement for any social movement, socialist or otherwise, whose aim is to change the status quo. What gave the socialist movement its winning edge over other rivals within the working-class movement (e.g. anarchism) was that it had more powerful ideas regarding the third proposition of the trinity, the question of 'what is to be done?' – that is, the strategic aspect. Socialism appeared to be better adapted than its rivals to the mode of organization of the working class into ever larger units of production and the forms of combination of workers, such as trade unions. Socialism distinguished itself from potential rivals (such as utopian movements) by looking frankly to the future and not harking back to an idealized past; though as regards the future nothing more definite than vague generalities was ever said about the end of class society and the withering away of the state. Only after the Soviet Revolution would it be possible to point to a model of 'actually existing' socialism.

All this was not enough to guarantee the ideological supremacy of socialist ideology within the working-class movement. This supremacy was largely due to the far-sighted political work of socialist activists. Like earlier revolutionaries and reformers they wanted to change society. They believed the fundamental agency of change to be the working class, and in a sense this act of identification was also one of creation. The socialist activists understood, more or less instinctively, that the working class represented a social subject with tremendous political potentialities. In today's language we could say that the great intuition of the first socialist activists was that they had identified a 'new political subject' with definite potential aspirations, able to produce a coherent set of political demands for both the short and the long term. If politics is an art, then this was one of its masterpieces. Socialist politics and the socialist movement could comprehend the most varied issues: short-term demands such as an improvement in working conditions; national reforms such as pension schemes; comprehensive schemes such as economic planning and a new legal system; major political changes such as expansion of the suffrage; utopian projects such as the abolition of the state, etc. All these demands could be embodied into a single overarching project in spite (perhaps because) of their contradictory nature.

By thinking of the working class as a political class, ascribing to it a specific politics and rejecting the vaguer categories ('the poor') of earlier reformers, the pioneers of socialism thus virtually 'invented' the working class. Those who define, create. 'Democratic' politics, that is, modern mass politics, is a battlefield in which the most important move is that which decides what the battle is about, what the issue is. To be able to define the contending parties, name them and thus establish where the barricades should go up, or where the trenches should be dug, gives one a powerful and at times decisive advantage. This is what all major movements for social change have had to do. Although Marxism attempted to elaborate a theoretical definition of the working class – propertyless producers of surplus separated from the means of production – in practice this was never seriously used to define the proletariat politically. Self-definition was always more important. For example, on 19 April 1891 in Castelfiorino, a small town in the heart of Tuscany, where the prevailing social group was made up of sharecroppers, a group of 'workmen' signed a May Day manifesto in which they invited the local population to join them in a banquet to celebrate May Day, the feast day designated 'exclusively' for workers, under the banner of 'unity makes us strong'.[4] The workmen who signed this appeal, and who identified themselves completely with the cause of the working class, were not factory workers, producers of surplus value, exploited by capital-owning entrepreneurs. They were a blacksmith, a printer, a bricklayer, a shoe-maker, a carpenter, and so forth. All were self-employed, all were their own bosses, all – in Marxist terms – petty bourgeois. Nevertheless, they remained certain that their cause was the same as that of the workers, indeed that they were workers.

To say that the working class was 'invented' is not to claim that its members did not exist. Practically 'all observers of the working class were agreed that "the proletariat" was very far from being a homogeneous mass, even within single nations.'[5] What existed was a vast array of different occupations ranked by skills, divided by territories, separated by nationalities, often segregated sexually or racially, secluded from each other by religion, traditions, prejudice, constantly reorganized by technological developments. These fragments were given an ideological cohesion and an organizational unity. Class consciousness was constructed by political activists, just as nationalism was constructed by nationalists, feminism by feminists, racism by racists.[6] This process does not, of course, depend solely on activism. For the activists to be successful, they must build on real foundations, not on thin air. The appeal must be recognized and interiorized. As Machiavelli explained, the Prince, to be successful, must rely not only on his own skills, his *virtù*, but also on objective circumstances, on his *fortuna*.

If the hegemony achieved by socialism was due in decisive part to its superior understanding of Proposition Three of the 'trinity' (strategy), the victory of Marxism in the socialist movement of continental Europe was almost certainly due to its superior handling of Propositions One and Two – that is, to the fact that it had the best available theory of exploitation and the best available theory of history. These theories gave powerful intellectual backing to the moral outrage arising from the iniquities of capitalism and to the hope that a system which ought to disintegrate would eventually do so. It was important that the theories provided by Marxism should be strong and sophisticated enough to appeal to the intellectual-minded, while being amenable to simplification and diffusion at a mass level by the socialist activists who were the real NCOs of the movement. The fact that the 'theory of history' of Marxism (the succession of stages, the inevitability of socialism) could be presented in a positivist light – that is, as a science on a par with Darwinism – contributed considerably to its success. Those who detested capitalism could not avoid being encouraged by reading in Kautsky's *The Class Struggle* that 'Irresistible economic forces lead with the certainty of doom to the shipwreck of capitalistic production.'[7] Most radical intellectuals at the end of the nineteenth century were totally committed to the positivist notion that the only true knowledge was scientific and that the methods of the natural sciences could be imported into the study of society. They would not have taken so readily to an overtly anti-positivist doctrine.

Of course, the diffusion of Marxism towards the end of the last century was helped by other factors. The prolonged crisis of profitability which caused such doom-laden predictions about the destiny of capitalism between 1873 and 1896 (the putative 'Great Depression') encouraged its enemies. However, more important must have been the relative success of socialism in organizing a significant sector of the working class, thereby forcing its opponents to view it seriously or make attempts either to suppress it, or to offer concessions. Often they were forced to do both.

Marxism expanded rapidly throughout the European Left after it became, in 1891, the official ideology of the most successful socialist party of the time, the German Sozialdemokratische Partei Deutschlands (SPD). The diffusion of Marxism in the SPD was in part a response to Bismarck's anti-socialist legislation (1878), while its official 'adoption' occurred immediately after the German Reich had more or less been forced to withdraw in 1890.[8]

In 1895 Engels congratulated the SPD for the intelligent way in which it used universal (manhood) suffrage ('a new weapon, and one of the sharpest'), resulting in a remarkable expansion of the social-democratic vote: 'they have used the franchise in a way which has paid them a thousandfold and has served as a model to the workers of all countries.' 'The irony of world history turns everything upside down,' Marx's old friend added. 'We the "revolutionaries", the "rebels" – we are thriving far better on legal methods than on illegal methods and revolt.'[9]

The success of the SPD had been decisive. It initiated a phase in which most European socialist parties were formed and expanded rapidly. Most were founded between 1890 and 1900, but their electoral strength varied considerably. Neither the date of creation of the socialist party, nor its electoral strength correlates with the level of industrialization or the size of the working-class electorate. In fact, the statistical correlation is negative (see Table 1.1). Italy's socialist party, established in 1892, had conquered one-fifth of the electorate by 1904, while Great Britain, with a far stronger industrial base, a more developed and more ancient trade union movement, had no significant socialist party until 1900 (or even 1918) and its pre-1918 electoral peak was a paltry 7 per cent (1910). Clearly, a more important determinant of electoral strength than the level of industrialization was the introduction of universal manhood suffrage or competition from parties which could, conceivably, promote some of the demands of the working class (e.g. the British Liberals). This suggests that the key factors in the development of socialist parties were political, rather than social or economic. Table 1.1 gives a general comparative perspective of the expansion of socialist parties before 1918.

The 'hegemonic' role of the German SPD in the European socialist movement cannot be attributed solely to its great electoral success. As the figures show, the socialist parties of Belgium, Sweden, Finland and Denmark were as strong or stronger than the SPD; but parties in small and politically peripheral countries can never hope to play an international role. Had the first communist revolution occurred in, say, Bulgaria, it would never have become the first great international model for the construction of socialism

Table 1.1 Socialist parties, basic data, c. 1880–1918

	Year founded	Universal manhood suffrage	Workforce engaged in industry (%)	Pre-1900 electoral peak (%)	Pre-1918 electoral peak (%)
Austria	1889	1907[a]	23.5 (1910)	n/a	25.4 (1911)
Belgium	1885	1893[b]	45.1 (1910)	8.5 (1896)	30.3 (1914)
Denmark	1876–8	1901	24.0 (1911)	19.3 (1901)	29.6 (1913)
Finland	1899	1906[d]	11.1 (1910)	n/a	47.3 (1916)
France	1905[c]	1848	29.5 (1906)	n/a	16.8 (1914)
Germany	1875[e]	1871	39.1 (1907)	19.7 (1890)	34.8 (1912)
Holland	1894	1917	32.8 (1909)	3.0 (1897)	11.2 (1905)
Italy	1892	1919[f]	26.8 (1911)	6.8 (1895)	21.3 (1904)
Norway	1887	1898[g]	26.0 (1910)	0.3 (1894)	32.1 (1915)
Sweden	1889	1907	24.7 (1910)	3.5 (1902)	36.4 (1914)
UK	1900–6	1918[b, h]	44.6 (1911)	1.3 (1900)	7.0 (1910)

Notes: [a] In the German-speaking parts of the Austro-Hungarian Empire (roughly corresponding to modern Austria). [b] Some double votes. [c] In 1905 various socialist groupings formed the SFIO. [d] Suffrage was granted to men and women, thus making Finland the first country in Europe to achieve true universal suffrage even though it was a Grand Duchy of the Tsar. [e] Year in which the Social-Democratic Workers' Party (the so-called Eisenachers), led by W. Liebnecht and A. Bebel, joined forces with the General Association of German Workers (which had been founded by Lassalle) to form the SPD. [f] The 1912 law enfranchised all men over 30, all those who completed military service and all literate men over 21. [g] Those in receipt of public assistance could not vote. [h] Women over 30 were enfranchised if they (or their husbands) were householders. Note that the 1884 legislation enfranchised five-sixths of the adult male population.

Sources: Year of foundation of the various socialist parties and organizations in Stefano Bartolini, 'I primi movimenti socialisti in Europa. Consolidamento organizzativo e mobilitazione politica', in *Rivista italiana di scienza politica*, Vol. XXIII, no.2, August 1993, p. 245. Electoral data in Thomas T. Mackie and Richard Rose, *The International Almanac of Electoral History*, Macmillan, London 1974. Data on industrial workforce in Peter Flora et al., *State, Economy and Society in Western Europe 1815-1975. A Data Handbook*, Campus Verlag, Macmillan Press and St James Press, Frankfurt, London and Chicago 1987, Vol. 2, chapter 7.

even if it had, improbably, survived. This is not to deny the important role the Swedish 'model' of socialism or the Cuban 'model' of communism have played in their respective geographical areas.

The emergence of the SPD as the key party of the Second International was due to a unique combination of circumstances: the SPD operated in what was by then the strongest country in Europe, having more steel and more soldiers than Britain. Germany thus became a 'model' of development for other countries. Culturally, and especially in the social sciences and

philosophy, Germany had no rivals. The SPD was unquestionably the best
organized socialist party in Europe. It was electorally stronger than most
other socialist parties at an earlier stage; in fact, in the same year as the
Reichstag refused to renew the anti-socialist laws (1890), the SPD had become,
in percentage terms, the largest party in Germany (due to the first-past-the-
post system, it became the first party in the Reichstag with 110 seats only in
1912). The rapid development of the SPD as a mass party was not only due
to the ability of its leaders or the size of the working class. Its mass basis
was connected to specific German factors which also led to the formation
of a mass party of the Catholics, the Zentrumspartei (Centre Party). Both
these parties 'considered themselves largely outside the course of political
life in Imperial Germany'.[10] By 1914 the SPD had one million members, but
the Centre Party was not far behind with 850,000.[11] By contrast, the French
SFIO was not a mass party; but then there were no mass parties in France.

During the period of anti-socialist legislation many of its leaders and
intellectuals operated from Zurich, which was then the foremost meeting
place for exiled radical students and thinkers from the Tsarist Empire, from
the Balkans and even from the USA. They were thus ideally situated for an
accelerated diffusion of SPD ideas.[12] Zurich is where Karl Kautsky had moved
in 1880. There he started working with Eduard Bernstein who, in 1881,
became the editor of the SPD's monthly, the *Sozialdemokrat*.[13] The programme
of the SPD, the Erfurt Programme, jointly drafted by Kautsky and Bernstein
and adopted in 1891, became one of the most widely read texts of socialist
activists throughout Europe. Kautsky's commentary, *The Class Struggle*, was
translated into sixteen languages before 1914 and became the accepted popular
summa of Marxism. Editor-in-chief and founder of *Neue Zeit*, the monthly
theoretical organ of the SPD, Kautsky enjoyed incomparable prestige and
was much admired by Lenin. As Haupt has written: 'In Budapest, Kautsky
was called "the revered old master", and the further one went into South
Eastern Europe, the more admiration turned into infatuation and even into
a cult.'[14]

Most social-democratic parties were created after the German SPD and
followed its lead as a 'model' – for instance, the Austrian (1889), the Swedish
(1889) and the Swiss parties (1888). At its Tenth Congress (25–26 March
1894), the Parti Ouvrier Belge (POB) adopted the *Charte de Quaregnon*, a
programme drafted by Emile Vandervelde, which would remain its basic
manifesto until the end of the following century. It was as influenced by
German social democracy as by French radicalism. It began with a general
statement of values, rather than with a Marxist-style analysis of capitalist
society as did the Erfurt Programme.[15] Its Walloon members were particularly
influenced by the French revolutionary tradition of Fourier, Blanc and
Proudhon.[16] The fundamental trait which united this party was a staunch
anti-clericalism. This led Belgian social democracy, after the war, to forge
links with the pro-capitalist Liberal Party, otherwise quite distant (especially

in economic policy), while confessional Christian parties (especially in Flanders) developed a social outlook and a solid base in the working class. The Norwegian Labour Party (founded in 1887) – like its Danish counterpart – took its programme straight from the SPD. Even the Finnish Social-Democratic Party, which might have been expected to be somewhat influenced by Russian Marxism (Finland being under the rule of the Tsar), drew its main inspiration from the Germans.[17] The small parties of south-east Europe were the most loyal disciples of the SPD. Their socialist intellectuals, seduced by the scientific claims of Marxism, were attracted by the rigorous exposition of it provided by Kautsky's SPD.[18]

There are good reasons why the French socialists could not offer a model to rival the SPD, in spite of the French revolutionary tradition.[19] They were weak in theory and organizationally divided. The painful and difficult revival of working-class activity in France after the crushing of the Paris Commune, and the persecutions which followed, failed to help the socialist movement to cohere and develop.[20]

French socialism was chronically split along organizational and ideological lines. There was little ground between the followers of Fourier (utopian socialists), Saint-Simon (technocrats), Louis Blanc (reformists) and Auguste Blanqui (insurrectionists).[21] By 1911 France had only one million organized workers, while the German and British trade unions had around three million members. The real 'magnetic pole' (both repelling and attracting) round which the French socialist party eventually emerged was the Parti Ouvrier Français (POF), founded in 1879 by Jules Guesde with a vulgarized Marxism as its guide and German social democracy as its model.[22] Other tendencies joined forces with it under the banner of the SFIO (Section Française de l'Internationale Ouvrière). To the 'Guesde-style' Marxism, with its emphasis on the revolutionary overthrow of the capitalist state, was added the French revolutionary tradition, with its pronounced distrust of organization, strong taste for direct democracy and virulent anti-clericalism.[23]

The outlook of the two main figures of the new socialist party, Guesde and Jean Jaurès, differed sharply in many respects, though, like many French socialists, they had both come to politics through the ranks of free-thinking (and Freemason) radicalism.[24] Jaurès had been a *dreyfusard*, while Guesde and his POF remained neutral during the entire Dreyfus affair on the grounds that this was merely a dispute within the ranks of the bourgeoisie. Unlike Guesde, Jaurès felt that socialism had to be adapted to 'our political and economic conditions, to the traditions, ideas and spirit of our country'. Only after it had become organizationally united as a single party under Jaurès did French socialism acquire some standing *vis-à-vis* its more influential German 'rival'.[25] Such prestige owed more to its being *French* than to its effective strength: unlike the SPD, the SFIO was organized on a local basis, had no factory groups and was more an electoral front than a party. Factionalism was so rife that the first law on workers' pensions was supported by twenty-five socialist deputies (led by Jaurès), while twenty-seven opposed it, and the rest (including Guesde and Vaillant) abstained.

In these years French socialism made no contribution to Marxism at all; few of Marx's works had been translated and the socialist press hardly ever discussed them.[26] It was its lack of theoretical distinction which prevented the expansion of French socialism even into countries profoundly influenced by French culture, such as Romania.[27] Why France, which has contributed so much to political thought, did not produce Marxist theorists of any calibre, not even of the level of Kautsky and Bernstein, is an unanswered question. Some argue that an obstacle to the diffusion of Marxism was that it gave excessive priority to the factory proletariat; this could not appeal to the largely urban petty bourgeoisie and craft artisans who still made up the French 'working class'.[28] However, as we have seen, the fact that Italy was even less developed than France did not prevent the development of a thriving Italian Marxism. There is no strong correlation between theoretical and economic developments. Others suggest that French Marxists were disadvantaged because – unlike those of Germany – they had to compete with a vibrant radical republican tradition.[29] However, on the same grounds Britain – as deprived as Germany – should have produced leading Marxist theorists. Portelli has argued that the weakness was due to the organizational split between the SFIO and the trade unions (the CGT).[30] That being deprived of a union base leads to theoretical weakness remains to be proven. This, however, highlights one of the most striking specificities of the French Socialist Party: it never had any close links with the trade unions because the CGT, imbued with revolutionary syndicalism, had rejected formal links with organized political parties.

In spite of this, elsewhere in Southern Europe the French pattern (though not necessarily French socialist thought) did have some importance. In Spain the Partido Socialista Obrero Español (PSOE), founded in 1879, was heavily influenced by Guesdism, taken to be orthodox Marxism. Revolutionary rhetoric, as usual, gave way to practical reformism, especially after the success in the municipal elections of 1890 and the parliamentary elections of 1910 (in alliance with the republicans).[31] Like the French party (but unlike the Italian), the PSOE would never produce a socialist thinker of any stature. In fact, the Marxist parties of the Second International were not, on the whole, led by intellectuals and paid little attention to theorists. Outside the German-speaking world and the Russian empire, socialist leaders were content with reproducing the main tenets of the doctrine.

Italian socialism, however, did produce a notable thinker, Antonio Labriola. But his influence on the new socialist party, founded in Genoa in 1892, was minimal, which is probably why he refused to join it. There were deep cultural differences between him and most of the socialist leadership group around Filippo Turati. Labriola was a southern intellectual, whose theoretical mentors were Hegel and Herbart, while Turati and company were pragmatic northerners and convinced positivists (Labriola held the not unreasonable view that modern positivism was a form of bourgeois cretinism), who took their lead from the German socialists.[32] Labriola understood the prominence of the 'Southern Question'. The others, like their bourgeois opponents, did not.

As elsewhere, the main disputes within the party arose not from theoretical questions, but from practical issues and particularly whether socialists should co-operate with non-socialist forces in order to extract reforms and concessions. At the Eighth Congress of the Italian Socialist Party (1904), the majority motion declared: 'the class struggle does not permit supporting any governmental initiative or sharing in political power.'[33] In reality, Italian socialists co-operated in varying degrees with other parties. The justification was that the peculiar complexity of the Italian social structure (backwardness of the south, feudal residues, divisions within the other classes, the radical nature of some segments of the petty bourgeoisie, etc.) was such that a totally intransigent line was unrealistic.[34] This appeal to an alleged Italian specificity runs throughout the history of the Italian Left.

The political strategy of Italy's ruling class and its ablest leader, Giovanni Giolitti, included attempting to involve the socialists in the existing system of power. This could be achieved by adopting some of the 'more reasonable' (Giolitti's words) aspects of the socialist party's minimum programme, as well as abandoning repression.[35] A similar tactic of co-optation (what Antonio Gramsci would later call a 'passive revolution') had been tried by other far-sighted representatives of the bourgeois order: Bismarck, Disraeli and Gladstone. What was special about the Italian case was that its bourgeoisie was chronically weak and internally divided. Thus it could not hope to co-opt the labour movement by welfare policies (like the British Liberals), or by anti-clerical radical politics (like the French). The socialists could not openly accept Giolitti's deal: they were not strong enough to compromise effectively. But they were not weak either: underdeveloped Italy could boast a socialist party with three million votes, an unusually strong influence, comparatively speaking, among land labourers, a well-developed complex network similar to that of the SPD and, unlike the British and French Left, trade unions, Chambers of Labours, *case del popolo* or 'people's homes', and co-operatives, in addition to a flourishing 'municipal socialism' which led to the conquest, by 1914, of major cities such as Bologna and Milan.[36]

Practically every section of the European Left could invoke some national peculiarity to explain its own deviancy from what was thought to be the norm. Marx's analysis of capitalism provided an abstract model of which all capitalist countries were but an approximation, and the socialist movement had produced a number of demands uniformly applicable to all countries such as the eight-hour day (which in turn assumed standardization of labour) and universal suffrage. But no existing country was purely capitalist and no socialist movement could have emerged fully armed and fully grown outside the specific national tradition which, in reality, had shaped it. Thus, in the world of the empirical as opposed to that of the theoretical, deviancy and abnormality were the norm. Europe was full of special cases. Germany was not the only one to have had a *Sonderweg*; the English were not alone in musing on their peculiarities.[37]

While the Italians were preoccupied with proclaiming their peculiarities at every congress, the Finns might well have pointed out that their socialist party was largely developed from a temperance movement which at the beginning of the century still had a larger mass base than the party. Furthermore, the Finnish Social Democratic Party, although formally adhering to the strictest of Marxist views and incorporating all the concrete demands of the SPD Erfurt Programme into its own, never discussed the major issues of interest to European Marxists such as militarism, war and imperialism.[38] It was in fact a party of agrarian socialism: at the first general election (1907) it obtained a higher percentage of the rural vote (38 per cent) than of the urban (34 per cent).[39]

The leading candidate for the position of 'most anomalous Left' in Europe was and has perhaps remained the British. Prior to 1914, socialism itself did not achieve much popularity among the working class and it took longer to become accepted as the ideology of the labour movement than anywhere else in Europe. Those who were in favour of socialism were reluctant to call themselves socialists for fear of being unpopular. Thus the first socialists, who were overwhelmingly middle-class and included some notably eccentric characters, remained few and their organizations tiny, in spite of powerful trade unions (which were led, on the whole, by non-socialist trade unionists of impeccable proletarian extraction).[40] H. M. Hyndman, a stockbroker, started the Democratic Federation in 1881 on 'Marxist' lines. Hyndman himself was a jingoist, an anti-Semite and an imperialist.[41] This did not prevent his group from becoming Britain's first socialist party in 1884 when it changed its name to the Social Democratic Federation (SDF). It achieved very little other than providing a training for a succession of gifted working-class activists – an achievement not to be disparaged – and acting as the main progenitor of the British Communist Party.[42] William Morris, the wealthy writer and artist, had joined Hyndman at first, but then left to found the Socialist League, an organization which did not survive Morris's death in 1896. The Fabian Society, founded in 1884, was an entirely middle-class intellectual organization which drew its main inspiration from the British radical utilitarian tradition, was never Marxist and opposed the formation of an independent socialist party. The report it presented to the 1896 Congress of the International (drafted by George Bernard Shaw) asserted that the Society cared 'nothing by what name any party calls itself, or what principles, Socialist or other, it professes, but [has] regard solely to the tendency of its actions, supporting those which make for Socialism and Democracy, and opposing those which are reactionary', thus siding explicitly with those socialists who were prepared to support progressive 'bourgeois' reforms. Like Bernstein (who was certainly influenced by the Fabians, and formulated his so-called 'revisionism' while living in London between 1888 and 1901), they did not believe in any inevitable collapse of capitalism: 'The Fabian Society therefore begs those Socialists who are looking forward to a sensational historical crisis, to join some other Society.'[43] The Scottish Labour Party, founded by the miner Keir Hardie in 1888, was not at first socialist. It was one of the constituent groups of the Independent Labour Party (ILP), at whose founding conference (1893) a proposal to include the term socialist in the title was rejected, because it was felt that neither the electorate nor the trade unions would approve.

In 1900 the unions, together with the ILP, the SDF and the Fabians, set up the Labour Representation Committee: 'Yet the trade unionists who accepted the LRC were in the main at heart still Liberals not socialist.'[44] It was not until February 1918 that a Labour Party was constituted on a solid national basis with an unambiguously socialist, though appropriately vague, indication of the final aim of the movement: 'To secure for the producers by hand or by brain the full fruits of their industry, and the most equitable distribution thereof that may be possible, upon the basis of the common ownership of the means of production and the best obtainable system of popular administration and control of each industry and service' – the famous fourth paragraph of Clause Four of the party statute drafted by Sidney Webb. It was only then that the British labour movement entered the mainstream of European socialism. Its singularity was that, while its continental counterparts had revolutionary goals co-existing with a reformist practice, the Labour Party was born with reformist goals. It adopted the post-capitalist aim of common ownership in 1918 partly as a radical response to the birth of Soviet communism, partly as an afterthought.[45]

The prestige of German social democracy meant that its internal theoretical disputes would be a matter for debate throughout European socialism just as, years later, the internal vicissitudes of the Bolsheviks would have a correspondingly wide impact on the rest of the international communist movement. The co-ordinates of 'vulgar' Marxism delineated at the beginning of this chapter define in rough outline Kautsky's Marxism, i.e. the ruling orthodoxy. Bernstein's challenge occurred at precisely the moment when the SPD had successfully emerged from the period of anti-socialist legislation and was developing into a formidable force in German politics. Bernstein's position, expressed between 1896 and 1898 in articles in *Neue Zeit* (published in 1899 in *Die Voraussetzungen des Sozialismus und die Aufgaben der Sozialdemokratie*, 'The preconditions for socialism and the tasks of social democracy'; the title of the English edition was *Evolutionary Socialism*), advanced a substantial modification of hitherto existing socialist positions, on the grounds that capitalism had reached a new stage which had not been foreseen by Marx. This situation required not just adaptation of the current doctrine, but a drastic change.

Bernstein's denunciation of armed struggle was not the main focus of his attack on orthodoxy. Far more important was his critique of the two theses which were closely associated with Kautsky's Marxism and which were pivotal to the Erfurt Programme, namely the 'collapse theory' and the 'pauperization thesis'.[46]

What was particular about the new stage of capitalism? The system, claimed Bernstein, had developed a structure capable of self-regulation; in other words, it was able to avoid crises. Secondly, the development of parliamentary democracy enabled the working class to struggle against the bourgeoisie in conditions of legality and equality; power could thus be achieved peacefully and within the existing state. Finally, Bernstein identified new tendencies: the development of a complex banking system, the growth of monopolies (cartels), and the vast development in communications. He noted that even though there was a growing concentration in the industrial, distribution and agricultural sectors, there was also a parallel expansion of small and medium-sized firms everywhere in Western Europe and North America, contrary to what Marxist doctrine had projected.[47] There was also a growth of inter-mediate social groups – which, he claimed, had a stabilizing function – rather than a rapid polarization of society.

Bernstein further maintained, wrongly, as it turned out, that capitalism had somehow succeeded in avoiding crises: 'Signs of an economic world-wide crash of unheard-of violence have not been established, nor can one describe the improvement of trade in the intervals between the crises as particularly short-lived.'[48] The expansion of international trade, the growth in com-munication and the improvement in transportation increased the chance of avoiding prolonged economic disequilibria. It was Bernstein's view that the great wealth of European industrial states, the flexibility of credit systems and the birth of industrial cartels had the effect of restricting the impact of local crises, making future economic crises unlikely.[49]

Bernstein's attack on Marxism challenged the relationship between theory and practice as it had hitherto been understood. The theory had linked the distant goal of socialism to the critique of present-day society by postulating a strategy which required the coupling of the everyday struggle for political improvements with the longer-term strategy. It was felt that only the final aim, the *Endziel,* could define the operating principles for current political practice. Bernstein sought to break this coupling. Not only did the everyday struggle not require a long-term perspective, but to hold on to such an irrelevancy would endanger or weaken the everyday struggle. Socialism was not a goal but a never-ending process. As he put it in his much-quoted phrase:

> I frankly admit that I have extraordinarily little feeling for, or interest in, what is usually termed 'the final goal of socialism'. This goal, whatever it may be, is nothing to me, the movement is everything. And by movement I mean both the

general movement of society i.e. social progress, and the political and economic agitation and organisation to bring about this progress.[50]

Bernstein and his doctrine were roundly condemned at the 1899 and 1903 SPD conferences and, shortly afterwards, by virtually all parties of the International convened at the Amsterdam Congress (August 1904). This, however, did not reflect the ambivalence many felt towards the orthodox position. The 'practical men of the party', i.e. the trade union leaders, were Bernstein's main supporters.[51] They were just beginning to establish themselves 'as the full equals of the party leaders and soon began to apply pressures on the party to curb its left-wing radicals'.[52]

Socialists in other countries were more gradualist à la Bernstein than their rhetoric appeared to indicate. For example, when the Swedish Social Democratic Party adopted its first independent programme in 1897, Bernstein's criticisms of the doctrine of pauperization – according to which the majority of workers would grow poorer and the wealthy richer – were not entirely ignored. The programme seems at first sight a faithful copy of the Erfurt Programme, which is not surprising because since 1886 the Swedish leader, Hjalmar Branting, had accepted wholesale the materialist conception of history, the labour theory of value, the doctrine of capital concentration and the theory of pauperization. The programme eventually adopted, however, coming as it did in the middle of the *Bernstein-Debatte*, contains no clause on pauperization.[53] In France Jaurès sided with neither Kautsky nor Bernstein. Although he had much in common with the latter, he remained firmly of the opinion that the final goal of the movement had to be maintained as a symbolic guide to practical action.[54] In Italy the majority took the side of Kautsky, but the pro-Bernstein reformist minority was influential. Its leading lights, Ivanoe Bonomi and Leonida Bissolati, wanted the total abandonment of the ideological tradition of the party: Marxism, and perhaps even socialism, belonged to the past. They were, declared Bissolati at the Eighth Party Congress (1904), 'old formulae overtaken by events'.[55] Socialism had accomplished its historical task. This was not the establishment of a socialist society, but the conquest of citizenship rights (achieved – so they thought – with the introduction of universal manhood suffrage).[56]

Contrary to general belief, the question of armed insurrection was less significant than these doctrinal disputes. Armed insurrection was not systematically advocated as a strategy by any of the leading members of social democracy in countries in which legal work was possible. Even those who did subscribe to violent revolution regarded it as a tactic for the future, on the grounds that the bourgeoisie would not give up power without a struggle. In other words, violent revolution was not required by anything inherent in capitalism. Its adoption as a road to power would be determined by the political conditions prevailing at the time. Kautsky had gradually come to the conclusion that violent revolution depended on the particular situation, and especially on whether there existed legal and peaceful means to achieve the conquest of power.[57] Before 1917 Marxists never ruled out the possibility of the state in the period of transition to socialism – the famous, much debated and ill-defined concept of 'the dictatorship of the proletariat' – assuming the parliamentary form. Kautsky, writing on parliamentarism in 1893, declared: 'a genuine parliamentary regime can be just as good an instrument for the dictatorship of the proletariat as it is an instrument for the dictatorship of the bourgeoisie.'[58]

In France, too, the main dispute within the SFIO was never over the question of armed insurrection. As elsewhere, the major arguments were over whether socialists should participate in government at local or central levels with other political parties, or over the socialists' attitude to war.[59] On the first question the decision of Alexandre Millerand to participate in the Waldeck-Rousseau government of 1899 was eventually opposed even by his supporters, such as Jaurès. As to war, the traditional Jacobin view, epitomized by Guesde, that socialists had to be ready to fight in defence of the French Republic, was accepted by Jaurès who, while believing that 'war is evil', rejected the Marxian idea that workers had no country: 'If our country were threatened,' he said, 'we would be the first at the border to defend France whose blood runs through our veins.'[60] The irony is, of course, that in 1914 French socialism had to perform a *volte-face*: to support the war it entered the government.

Until then, however, non-involvement in government was a strongly held view throughout European socialism. In Holland, by 1913 the socialists had a chance to participate in government but they deliberately refused to take it.[61] In Sweden the social-democratic leader was able to enter Parliament in 1897 with Liberal support (he was the sole socialist deputy until 1903, when he was joined by three others) and, in 1914, the party agreed to support the neutralist policies of the Liberal government. But it entered the coalition in 1917 with great reluctance.[62] By then, of course, the taboo had been broken by the active involvement of French and German socialists in the war coalition.

Violent revolution did not become a matter of principle even in countries where the socialist movement operated in conditions of illegality. In the Tsarist empire the Bolsheviks were prepared to use all available legal forms as well as extra-legal ones. Lenin, often seen as an intransigent proponent of violent revolution, never advocated it as a matter of principle or at all times. When, in 1904, the then Menshevik paper *Iskra* called on the workers 'to seize the branch offices of the State Bank and the munition stores and arm the people', Lenin disagreed: 'if Social Democracy sought to make the socialist revolution its immediate aim, it would assuredly discredit itself.'[63] The image of Lenin as a fundamental insurrectionist is quite false. For him (as for Kautsky) questions of violence, preventive civil war, etc. could not be decided in advance.[64] He rejected Vaillant's and Keir Hardie's proposal for a general strike to prevent war, scorned the insurrectionary tactics of Gustave Hervé, the leader of the near-syndicalist wing of the SFIO, for their adventurism and 'imbecility', and attacked the German extreme Left (Karl Radek). His position in 1907 was that the aim was not only 'to prevent war from breaking out, but to use the crisis caused by the war to accelerate the fall of the bourgeoisie'.[65]

Before 1914 there was very little difference between the orthodox Marxist position represented by Kautsky and those, such as Lenin, who, after 1914, would denounce him as a social-patriot and renegade. The story of the pre-1914 rupture between Lenin and Kautsky was largely invented by official Comintern historiography, beginning with Gregori Zinoviev in the 1920s and vigorously continued by Stalin in 1930.[66] The only serious theoretical opponent of Kautsky from the left before 1914 was Rosa Luxemburg. Her 1910 break with him anteceded Lenin's by four years.[67]

What a post-revolutionary society would look like was hardly ever discussed. Between 1882 and 1914 there was only one article on the subject in Neue Zeit. Socialists did not appear to be much interested in socialism. Even the revolution itself was little discussed.[68]

Of far greater importance than the issue of revolutionary violence was the debate over the uses of the general or 'mass' strike as a political weapon. Here there was a genuine dispute, but it did not constitute the demarcation line between revisionists and the orthodox. The most vociferous opponents of mass strikes in all countries were the trade union leaders, while few people advocated them as a substitute for legal and parliamentary work, not even Rosa Luxemburg, the most distinguished theorist of the mass political strike. The SPD debated the issue repeatedly, in 1905–16, 1908 and 1910. But nothing was done because its leaders were afraid that they would be unable to control the movement and that the state would destroy it.[69] The leaders of German socialism were cautious people. They believed in discipline and organization. They were most unwilling to lead a strike, any strike, unless they believed that there was a high probability of victory. They even ignored the resolutions of the Second International enjoining them to celebrate May Day on the first day of the month (instead of the first Sunday), because it was too radical.[70] The leaders of the SPD had an 'almost instinctive distrust of mass enthusiasm ... and a contempt for noisy demagogues'.[71] Kautsky, for all his caution, did not reject the mass strike in principle, though he set so many preconditions for its justified use as to make the eventuality highly unlikely.[72] Bernstein, for all his 'revisionism', was in favour of political strikes, provided they had very specific short-term aims and also had the support of some groups within the bourgeoisie.[73]

The International as a whole could not ignore the fact that the use or threatened use of the general strike had resulted in some major victories in the sphere of electoral reform. In Belgium, in order to head off an anarchist challenge, the POB opted to accept the tactics of the mass strike and forced a reluctant Constituent Assembly to concede universal manhood suffrage after repeated general strikes in 1893, 1902 and 1913.[74] It was a general strike and mass demonstration of 1905 (in turn sparked by the October 1905 revolution in Russia) which led to the replacement of the old Finnish Diet by a unicameral assembly (the *Eduskunta*) of 200 members elected by all Finns, men and women, over the age of twenty-four, using a system of proportional representation.[75] In Austria, without the November 1905 mass strike for voting rights, the 1907 electoral reforms would have been unlikely.[76] In Sweden there had been a brief general strike in 1902, 'People's Parliaments' were organized, petitions signed. The threat of a general strike in 1907 finally secured universal manhood suffrage.[77]

The main strategic disputes dividing the socialist movement in the pre-1914 period (and later) were concerned with the nexus between the immediate tasks of the movement and its longer-term goals. This argument was in turn connected to what were, and have remained, the critical questions facing socialists: what are the central co-ordinates of the present situation? What are its underlying tendencies? Where is capitalism going? Are the changes which seem to be occurring fundamental enough to warrant a change in strategy?

It is commonly believed that the main dividing line between the Russian Mensheviks and Bolsheviks was the question of organization, between the former's 'open', more 'democratic' concept of a political party, and the Leninist precept that only a clandestine organization of professional revolutionaries could lead the Russian masses towards socialism. In fact, the evidence shows that the Mensheviks were as keen as anyone on centralized leadership and very unwilling to abandon illegality (an understandable position given the highly restricted freedom granted by the Tsarist authorities).[78] Before 1912, when the final organizational split occurred, the differences between Bolsheviks and Mensheviks — apart from Lenin's militaristic conception of how the Russian party should develop — were mainly of emphasis: the Bolsheviks were far more pessimistic than the Mensheviks regarding the willingness of the liberals to struggle for constitutional reforms; the Mensheviks were readier to co-operate with the bourgeoisie. Mensheviks and Bolsheviks agreed (against the socialist revolutionaries) that the advance of capitalist relations in Russia was unstoppable and that, from an economic point of view, no stage could be skipped. They both agreed that the Russian bourgeoisie was inept and weak as a class, and would be unwilling and/or unable to lead a bourgeois-democratic revolution. It followed that, as the democratic stage could not be skipped, the proletariat, in alliance with other social forces, would have to struggle for the establishment of democracy. Such differences were not sufficient to force either faction out of the Russian Social Democratic Labour Party.

Subsequently, it became apparent that the contrast between the two centred on a difference of views regarding the possibility of survival of the capitalist order and the imminence of the socialist revolution. Both expected capitalism to end, but for the Mensheviks this end was not in sight. The Mensheviks were thus more in tune with twentieth-century European social democrats for whom the tocsin of capitalist society never seems to ring out.

The third major component of the Russian revolutionary movement was the socialist revolutionaries: the heirs of the Narodniks, the Russian populists, who are known for their terrorist activities. But the true importance of their ideas resides in the fact that they embodied in a revolutionary form the slavophile distrust for capitalism, regarded as a Western construct. The political expression of this distrust was the refusal to accept the inevitability of capitalist advance in Tsarist Russia and denial of the extent of the transformation which was occurring.

With the benefit of nearly one hundred years of hindsight, a modern socialist might be tempted to adjudicate between these positions. But what matters here is to establish that in the development of the Russian labour movement three broad tendencies had emerged:

1. An *intransigent* position which denied that any ongoing changes in the economic and social structure dictated a change in one's chosen strategy. This was the fundamentalism of the populists and their successors.
2. A position, that of the *renovators*, which understood the changeable nature of the socio-economic system and realized that strategy would have to be adapted to these changes, but which sought to preserve the visibility of the final aim of the movement: socialism. This was the position of Lenin and the Bolsheviks.
3. A *pragmatist* position which shared with the renovators an understanding of the nature of ongoing transformations, but which deduced from this that the 'final aim' of the movement belonged to such a distant future that any attempt to maintain a strategic link between the immediate tasks of the movement and the final goal would be disastrous for the movement itself. This was the position held by many Mensheviks.

Of course, the three tendencies sketched above cannot be mapped neatly on to the three political movements and, in any case, populists (i.e. the Socialist Revolutionary Party), Bolsheviks and Mensheviks often changed position in the years leading to the revolution. It is also clear that my proposed taxonomy is hardly comprehensive. Other categories could be devised and real-life demarcation lines are never clear-cut or all-encompassing: for some purposes a whale may count as a fish. Nevertheless, this classification may be useful as a descriptive tool rather than an analytical one, as an instrument which enables us to understand various positions adopted by the Left on a more fundamental level than that of organizational differences, or differences over purely conjunctural or tactical matters. In politics it is very often the case that an apparently nominalistic dispute, over a certain slogan, a symbol, a word, a controversy which leaves outsiders baffled as to its meaning, hides a more important controversy. As the situation changes, controversies arise; these inevitably tend to converge on the extent to which the situation has changed and, secondly, on whether the changes require the revision of one's goals. The first point demarcates the intransigents from the others; the second demarcates the renovators from the pragmatists.

Intransigence and pragmatism could and did co-exist, as the history of the SPD demonstrates. This political party combined a revolutionary rhetoric with a reformist practice. Merle Fainsod's description of Kautsky fits the party as a whole: 'The verbiage breathes fire; the tactics are tame.'[79] That the SPD was, underneath its revolutionary language, reformist was recognized by the shrewder members of the party such as Ignaz Auer, who wrote to Bernstein: 'My dear Ede, one doesn't formally decide to do what you ask, one doesn't say it, one *does* it. Our activity ... was the activity of a Social Democratic reforming party. A party which reckons with the masses simply cannot be anything else.'[80]

The split between 'the final aim' and the 'everyday struggle', between the short-term and the medium- to long-term, existed throughout the socialist movement. Bernstein's polemic had centred almost entirely on the general perspective. As he said in March 1899: 'I have no objection to the practical aspect of the Social Democratic programme with which I am entirely in agreement.'[81] The crux of the matter, as both Luxemburg and Lenin recognized immediately, was the attitude to theory.[82] Lenin's famous rebuttal, *What is to be Done?*, usually taken to be only a defence of a tightly organized and disciplined party, was also a defence of the role of theory as a guide to action. Lenin borrowed explicitly from Kautsky's doctrine, which asserted that socialist consciousness could not be a spontaneous development out of the everyday struggle. The assumption underlying this conception is that, without a political party, the working class could not become a political subject.

If Lenin and Kautsky were right in their belief that socialist theory and consciousness cannot be produced spontaneously by everyday struggles, it does not follow that only the 'correct' theory will produce 'correct demands'. It is perfectly possible to arrive at a compilation of short-term tasks without a 'general theory' or a long-term perspective. Here Bernstein is right. Un-theoretical socialist parties, non-socialist labour parties and unpolitical trade unions have often produced a list of demands not so dissimilar from that of Marxist theorists. The problem lies elsewhere, namely in the connections between the general analysis of the current situation, the changes occurring, social and economic trends and the short-term demands advanced. A reading of the Erfurt Programme will show that the connecting line between principles and demands is fairly tenuous.[83]

The first part of the programme describes the situation thus: current developments are leading to the end of small enterprises and the gradual division of society into two mutually hostile camps, an ever-expanding working class and an ever-shrinking élite of capitalists. Only the latter benefit from this trend; for the proletarianized masses conditions constantly deteriorate. Economic crises inevitably cause more and more hardship, while becoming steadily more and more destabilizing. Given this situation, the long-term goal of the movement is the transformation of private property in the means of production into 'social' or 'common' ownership, whose goal is 'socialist production', i.e. production 'for the benefit of society'. To achieve 'common ownership', it is necessary to acquire political power. This is the mission of the Social Democratic Party.

Then follow two distinct lists of demands. The first consists of demands which are not class-specific: they clearly relate to 'the people' in general. The second is made up of explicitly working-class demands, i.e. measures 'to safeguard the working class'. The first list amounts to a programme for a major reform of the state, that is, constitutional reform, a 'Bill of Rights' and a welfare state; while the second constitutes a plan for a drastic change in the conditions of the working class. This is how the political part of the Erfurt Programme would appear today after some reorganization and judicious renaming:

SECTION 1: THE REFORM OF THE STATE

i. The Constitution: universal adult (i.e. including female) suffrage under pro-portional representation, the right of referendum, the election of judges, the separation of Church and State especially in education, parliamentary control over foreign policy.

ii. The Bill of Rights: devolution of power, a citizen army, freedom of association and opinion, repeal of all laws discriminating against women, equal rights.

iii. The Welfare State: legal aid, a free medical service, free burial, free education at all levels, including higher education. All of this to be paid for by graduated income and property taxes and death duties. Abolition of all indirect taxes.

SECTION 2: THE CONDITIONS OF THE WORKING CLASS

Length of working day fixed at eight hours, regulations on the conditions of work, right to form trade unions, labour insurance paid by the State and administered by the workers.

The implication is clear: in 1891 the SPD had already formulated the core demands which in one form or other would constitute the central co-ordinates of virtually all programmes of West European social democracy in the twentieth century: the democratization of society, the welfare state and the regulation of the labour market. What is less clear is the relationship between the practical demands – all of which can be accommodated within a much reformed capitalist state, based on commodity production and private owner-ship of the means of production – and the scenario sketched in the first part of the programme. The point is not whether the scenario was right, but whether it is related to the demands. In his own analysis of Erfurt, Carl

Schorske writes that the programme represented a compromise between revolutionaries and reformists.[84] That both trends were present in the SPD as a whole is true, but one must not assume that the 'practical' demands had been grudgingly accepted by the Marxists. They had appeared in the same form in the Gotha Programme of 1875, and Marx's famous *Critique* was substantially directed at the theoretical section.

Here it should be noted, *en passant*, that not a bit of notice was taken of Marx's criticism of the draft version. As for Engels' own objections to the Erfurt Programme, they were not published for ten years. Unlike everyone else, Engels had concentrated his fire on the political section because it had left out an essential part of socialist policy: the establishment of a democratic republic, which he called 'the specific form of the dictatorship of the proletariat which was seen as long ago as during the great French revolution'.[85] On the whole the disputes which ensued over Erfurt appeared only to involve theory, whereas in fact they were concerned with the main question of the *connection* between the two parts of the programme.

There is no necessary theoretical or analytical relation between the two sections, since to reach an agreement on the practical demands it is not necessary to accept the 'theoretical section'. Moreover, it was never clearly established whether socialists, by achieving their immediate demands, would delay the crisis of capitalism, by making it more acceptable, or hasten it. Kautsky, who happened to be the author of the theoretical section, never disputed the validity of the practical demands (drafted by Bernstein). There was in fact considerable unanimity on the practical tasks. Luxemburg, whose polemic against Bernstein was merciless, indicated that she disagreed with him only on what he had to say about the objective development of capitalism, not on the practical tasks confronting the SPD.[86]

If there is no connection between the principles and the tasks, it does not necessarily follow that either or both are 'wrong'. It simply means that the interpretation of their respective roles, the answer to the question, what is their function?, cannot be found in the programme itself. The consensus which existed on the programme simply defined the boundary within which the contending parties would fight it out. For Kautsky and most of the orthodox group, both parts of the programme were totally consistent. This unity was not due to the fact that the practical demands could be deduced from the theory, but to the fact that both served the same function: to inspire and organize the movement, to build it up so that it would become strong enough to take advantage of the eventual collapse of capitalism. Both 'theory' and 'practice' were a fundamental constitutive element of the SPD; they were the indispensable cement holding the party together in an inclement environment. Kautsky did not assume that the movement could or should hasten the collapse of capitalism. This would eventually occur and it was important to be ready for it. He wrote in 1910: 'The task of Social Democracy does not consist in hastening the inevitable catastrophe, but in holding it

back for as long as possible; that is to say, to avoid carefully anything that
might look like a provocation.'[87]

In the final analysis, Kautskyist Marxism resolved itself not so much as a
strategy for the long haul, but as a passive strategy whereby the movement
might find ways of growing and expanding without ever posing the question
of what to do when the crisis arrived. Thus it was never ready for it and,
consequently, always wished to delay it. There were only two avenues leading
away from this theoreticized inactivity. One, that of Lenin or Luxemburg,
tried to devise strategies which would hasten the collapse of capitalism such
as the mass strike or revolutionary wars. The other (Bernstein's) assumed
that, because capitalism would be able to restructure itself and continue to
develop, a collapse would not occur for the foreseeable future. It followed
that the movement had to devise strategies capable of securing immediate
political and social benefits within the existing order.

Bernstein had thus become convinced that significant advances could be
achieved within capitalism. He still agreed with the practical tasks of the
movement, but wished to redefine their function. Reforms were no longer to
be purely propagandistic objectives but real targets. The new boundaries
within which socialists pursued their arguments had to be the 'realism' of the
demands. Once the question of the fatal hour of capitalist collapse had
become a secondary issue, the general principles embodied in Section 1 of
Erfurt would lose their main *raison d'être*. Bernstein's approach made it possible
to direct all efforts towards the immediate aims of the movement, but his
optimistic view of capitalist development entailed the acceptance of so
complete 'a dependence of the proletariat upon the capitalist economy ... as
to preclude any major action to upset it'.[88]

CHAPTER TWO

From War to War (1914–40)

The War

BEFORE 1914 not a single socialist anywhere in Europe served in any government with the endorsement of his party. Otherwise divided in political practice, and wrecked by ideological conflicts, the European Left stood unsullied in its radical opposition to the governments of the bourgeois world, though in some cases, as in Britain, there were deals on electoral and parliamentary tactics.

The war changed all this. In most of the belligerent countries, socialists joined governments. Their purpose in doing so was not to obtain the political and economic reforms they had been fighting for, but simply to defend the existing state. The result of this was that many became legitimized, though at the cost of the *de facto* destruction of the International. After the Bolshevik Revolution and the war, the reconstituted Socialist International amounted to very little. By 1933, as G. D. H. Cole wrote, it consisted only in a loose federation of the British and French parties with those of some of the states of Western Europe.[1]

At the the founding congress of the Second International (July 1889) and at the Stuttgart Congress of 1907, the vast majority of member parties committed themselves to averting war by all possible means and, should war nevertheless erupt, to using the crisis to bring about a social revolution. However, on 3 August 1914 the SPD parliamentary group in the Reichstag stood unanimously behind the German Kaiser and *his* war by voting for the war credits. Karl Kautsky, Rosa Luxemburg, Franz Mehring, none of whom was in the Reichstag, and a minority of the parliamentary group (fourteen out of seventy-eight), had opposed this policy. Eduard Bernstein at first sided with the 'pro-war' faction, but later changed his mind.

In Austria the Socialist Party also approved the war credits, opposed by a dissident faction led by Friedrich Adler (whose assassination of the prime minister in October 1916 won him great popularity among the workers). Only in the autumn of 1917 did the party turn sharply to the left and reverse its previous patriotic stand.[2]

The Czech and the Hungarian socialists similarly acquiesced in the war effort, as did Polish social democrats residing in Austria, who were enthusiastically pro-war, hoping that a Russian defeat would induce the birth of an independent Poland.

The attitude of the French socialists (the SFIO) was, at first, strongly pacifist. They assumed that their comrades in Germany would actively seek to stop the war, and were also convinced that their bourgeois government had genuinely tried to prevent a conflict. A few days before the declaration of war, Jaurès could still maintain that 'the French government wants peace and is working for the maintenance of peace'.[3] However, when war was finally declared, the SFIO supported the war credits unanimously and agreed to enter the government. The Belgian socialists did the same. By the end of the war, 'they were more fully integrated into the government than any other European socialist party'.[4] In Great Britain the bulk of Labour MPs and the overwhelming majority of the trade unions adopted a vigorous patriotic position. However, some of their most important leaders, such as Keir Hardie, Ramsay MacDonald, Tom Richardson and F. W. Jowett and, outside Parliament, the British Socialist Party (one of the future constituent pillars of the Communist Party), remained strongly opposed to the war.

In neutral countries such as Sweden, Holland, Denmark and Italy the socialist parties held out against entering the conflict. When in 1915 the Italian government joined the war against Germany and Austria, the Socialist Party remained opposed but an important interventionist faction emerged. Earlier in 1914, the editor of the socialist paper L'Avanti, Benito Mussolini, had resigned and started his own interventionist group. In Portugal the socialists were at first in favour of neutrality, but when the government decided to enter the war to support its traditional ally (Great Britain), the socialists concurred. Although Spain was not involved in the war, the PSOE decided to follow the lead of the SFIO and did not condemn the war. On the whole the socialist parties followed a patriotic line. The most important exception was Russia. There all the factions of the Social Democratic Labour Party, i.e. both the Mensheviks and the Bolsheviks, were against the war: they walked out of the Duma without voting for war credits. Kerensky's Labour Party did the same. Among the exiles, however, the 'Father of Russian Marxism', Plekhanov, and the leading Russian anarchist, Pietr Kropotkin, supported the war.[5] In the belligerent countries, only the Serbian socialists stood out against the war as their Russian counterparts had done.

Most European socialists supported the war for a multiplicity of reasons. Their political stance was one of pacifism and they had fought for peace. Once it was clear hostilities could not be avoided, they came to feel there was little alternative but to support their own country; patriotism may not have been their first reflex, but it emerged when their pacifism failed. An understandable element of opportunism also entered into this. It would have been very difficult for any mass organization to resist pressure from below, particularly from its own supporters. There is in fact little doubt that although the majority of activists were against the war, the majority of the working class was, like the rest of the population, in favour of it, at least initially. German workers felt that 'Germany was morally in the right and that its very

existence was threatened.'⁶ With the war they felt they had finally been
accepted as true citizens of imperial Germany. The socialist parties of Europe
had failed to convince their respective working class of the necessity of
international solidarity before 1914. They could hardly hope to convince
them of it in the fiery days of August 1914.

The socialist leaders had, in any case, been taken by surprise. They believed
war was not a possibility and never seriously prepared a policy to deal with
it.⁷ Their understanding of international affairs was minimal. Their internationalism was a façade, not in the sense that they were opportunists as the
Leninists believed, but in the sense that they did not imbue it with any
strategic content. Internationalism was just a word, not a key component of
a coherent strategic line. It was a feature of the verbal radicalism which was
one of the most characteristic traits of the movement. As Georges Haupt
put it, socialist leaders 'found refuge in short-term solutions and compromises,
thereby avoiding the issues that would have forced them to take a stand'.⁸

Had the German Social Democratic Party called upon the workers to join
in a general strike against the war (an unlikely event), then perhaps the other
socialist parties might have taken a less aggressive stance. But the representatives of the German workers decided to throw in their lot with the hated
bosses in defence of the Fatherland. This was no temporary aberration. It
was consistent with the party's symbiosis with the German state both in its
political development – the creation of the Reich – and in its economic
growth.

The Reich had enfranchised the people, thus enabling the SPD to flourish
even when the very same Reich had attempted to weaken it with anti-socialist
legislation. By 1890 the SPD had become legitimized – not in the sense of
being able to take power, of course, but merely in the sense of being allowed
to *exist* within the German empire. The SPD saw itself as an alternative state,
but in so doing mirrored the organization of the very state it sought to
destroy.⁹ Its fate had become entwined with the Reich it so ardently despised.
SPD influence grew as German industry grew. SPD prestige flourished as
German prestige flourished.¹⁰ The SPD was also imbued with many of the
political values of the 'West'. The fear of Russia, of being engulfed by Asian
barbarism, was common among all shades of the political spectrum and was
particularly pronounced among liberals and socialists. Throughout the nineteenth century Tsarist absolutism had been the *bête noire* of the progressive
movements. Marx and Engels themselves considered the Russian empire to
be the principal threat to Western civilization. Enmity towards Russia was
thus a common factor which linked the SPD with the German military
establishment. It would not be the last time that the threat from the East
would unite social democrats and their conservative opponents.

The SPD could not have remained indifferent to the dangers which in
August 1914 threatened the country itself. The Reich had become *its* state.
It is true that right up to 1914 the SPD had always maintained that it would

have no truck at all with the bourgeois state or any of its institutions. Its practice, of course, was somewhat different. After 1912, in the Reichstag the SPD was increasingly, and inevitably, involved in the legislative process. In the parliamentary leadership, 'the isolation of the SPD was becoming imaginary rather than real'.[11] In states where the situation was far more liberal than in oppressive Prussia and Saxony, such as Baden, Hesse, Bavaria and Württemberg, the SPD developed a constructive opposition, entering into electoral pacts, voting the budget, and so forth.[12] In a 'free' city like Hamburg, the social democrats identified quite strongly with the free-trading ideology which dominated civic consciousness. Even in 1918, when the SPD had a majority in Hamburg, they spontaneously assumed that the best man to lead the city was a member of one of the old liberal families.[13]

A similar process had taken place in a rather different setting. Until the beginning of the century, the British labour movement was organized not as a party but in trade unions. It adapted itself to British capitalism through a lengthy process of negotiation which required a strong sense of class identity. Such class consciousness was directed not towards the destruction of the capitalist state, but towards the integration of the working class within it. Thus in Britain, as in Germany, working-class militancy contributed to the creation of a national consensus which incidentally coincided with the aim of the ruling classes. In Britain, as Hobsbawm has remarked:

> the further we progress into the imperialist era, the more difficult does it become to put one's finger on groups of workers which did not, in one way or another, draw some advantage from Britain's position ... Or ... on workers who could not be made to feel that their interests depended on the continuance of imperialism.[14]

By the outbreak of war the old pre-1850 Chartist demands of the organized British labour movement – republicanism, secularism and internationalism – had 'expired from sheer inanition'.[15] The wave of syndicalist unrest in the years leading up to the First World War did not make any serious inroad into the 'social-patriotic' mentality of most British workers.[16]

With greater speed and enthusiasm than their counterparts elsewhere, French socialists participated in the *Union Sacrée* to save the republic, thus demonstrating the strength of Jacobin nationalism, of 'this idea of France, blessed land of revolution and socialism'.[17] Most of the other socialist parties, having prospered in the conditions of the 1890–1914 period, followed the lead of their own state. Italian socialists were ambivalent about the war, as was the Italian government itself. In Italy the divisions between neutralists and interventionists were more pronounced and would last longer than anywhere else.

The war divided the SPD more than any of the other main belligerent socialist parties. The split led to the formation of the Independent (*Unabhängige*) SPD, the USPD. For the first time the SPD was no longer the sole representative of the German working class.

In Russia alone the socialist movement remained solidly against the war. It owed nothing at all to 'its' state. Tsardom was owed no loyalty, deserved no support and obtained none.

Roughly speaking, the war divided the socialists into three camps:[18]

1. The patriotic socialists: Vaillant and Guesde in France, Scheidemann in Germany, Vandervelde in Belgium, Plekhanov among the Russians, Hyndman, former leader of the BSP, in Britain and Bissolati in Italy. Originally this was the strongest group.

2. The centre or pacifist socialists: they were against the war and in favour of some kind of neutrality, though initially they did not wish to break ranks with the pro-war majority. They included people like Kautsky and Bernstein in Germany, MacDonald and Hardie in Britain, Bourderon and the trade unions in the Confédération Générale du Travail (CGT) in France. This was the position of the Italian, Swiss, Dutch and Scandinavian socialist parties.

3. Finally, there was the anti-war Left, or revolutionary socialists eager to turn the war into an opportunity for revolution. They included Karl Liebknecht and Rosa Luxemburg in Germany, Lenin in Russia, Amadeo Bordiga as well as the Turin group of the *Ordine nuovo* led by Antonio Gramsci in Italy.

The Birth of Modern Communism

If the outbreak of war was the first body-blow to the pre-1914 European socialist movement, October 1917 was the *coup de grâce*.

The split which had occurred in the European Left had been threatening for a long time. The tension between reformism and revolutionism epitomized by disputes over programmes and strategies had characterized the International since its inception, but the movement had maintained a loose organizational structure. The war ended this fictitious unity. Finally, the Russian Revolution provided the Left with a fundamental reference point. Thereafter, until the collapse in 1989–91, every single European socialist group or faction faced the continuous necessity of defining its position not only on the revolution itself, but on each of its subsequent stages. Both revolutionaries and reformists now had a model, positive for the former, negative for the latter. Those who were hesitant could not afford to remain so for long. The Soviet decision in 1919 to form a new international organization, the Third International (the Comintern), forced everyone to take a stand.

The birth of the Communist International occurred in a unique conjuncture. The three imperial eagles – the Russian, the Prussian and the Austrian – had been annihilated. In the land of the Hohenzollern a democratic republic had emerged out of the National Constituent Assembly meeting at

Weimar in February 1919. The empire the Habsburgs once ruled had disintegrated and Vienna had been reduced to the capital of a tiny alpine republic. In Russia the Bolsheviks (to quote Vladimir Mayakovsky) 'spat out the two-headed, hook-beaked eagle of the Romanov dynasty like the chewed stump of a cigar'. After the acquiescence exhibited during the war, the workers appeared to be on the move. The degree of working-class unrest and revolutionary potential smouldering between 1918 and 1920 has remained unparalleled in the twentieth century. It was probably the only period during which it was not unrealistic to assume that a 'revolution in the West' was on the agenda. This was the era which spawned virtually all the communist parties of Western Europe. Thereafter, in one of those ironies of which history seems to be composed, the parties born to make the revolution failed to lead a single one – at least in Europe. They were condemned to grow and develop (or not, as the case may be) in the cold climate of non-revolutionary situations. The reformists, for whom socialism was a distant goal, did not fare much better, at least in the short term. The threat of revolution did not make major reforms possible. Charles Maier, in his magisterial account of the reorganization of bourgeois power in Europe after the First World War, wrote:

> Late 1920 and early 1921 ... saw the end of the postwar working class offensive throughout Europe. In France and Italy the unions had suffered or were shortly to suffer serious setbacks; in Germany their Republic seemed stalemated and in bourgeois custody. Major changes in the ownership or control of the economy had failed to come about: French railroad nationalisation was a dead letter; German coal mines remained under private auspices (as did English [sic] ones). Workers' councils ... had lost their radical impetus, and Italian labor had given up its hold on the nation's factories for the promise of a study committee ... With the exception perhaps of Weimar's Labor Ministry, the organized working class did not even have the protection of a social Maginot line by the end of 1920.[19]

Lenin, undaunted, had drafted the 'Twenty-one Conditions' (originally there were nineteen) of membership of the Third International at the Second Congress held in July–August 1920. By then the post-war situation had been stabilized, Soviet Russia effectively quarantined, and the revolution in the West defeated. The result of the Twenty-one Conditions was the permanent division of the West European Left. In retrospect the Comintern was a major political error.[20] This, however, was not yet apparent. The Red Army had recovered Ukraine and was marching on Warsaw, hoping to provoke a communist uprising in Poland.[21] A few weeks later, this advance was stopped, but, for a brief moment, the delegates to the Second Congress had believed that the day of reckoning was about to dawn.

The Twenty-one Conditions demanded little in terms of ideology and next to nothing in terms of strategy. However, they were harsh on organizational matters. They could be paraphrased thus: expel all reformists and centrists, accept the discipline which the new international organization will demand, support the Soviet Republic, be prepared for illegal political work and call yourselves communists. Socialist parties such as the Italian, which had joined the new organization, now demurred. The Comintern, unlike the Second Socialist International, aimed to be a super-party, a centralized body – as, indeed, each separate social-democratic party had been before the war. Karl Marx's First International never really existed; the Second International had been little more than an information bureau; but the Third International was to become the only centralized international organization of the Left in history. It could do so only because it was supported by an authentic state. Lenin himself was well aware in 1920 of how difficult it would be to establish communist parties in the West and 'to be a revolutionary when the conditions for direct, open, really mass and really revolutionary struggle *do not yet exist* ...'[22]

The years 1918–21 had seen a major crisis of socialist ideas. The leadership of those parties which had supported the war was locked into a defence of its position. The activists who had at first supported them had become increasingly alienated as the war dragged on. The Russian Revolution was the catalyst for a move towards radicalism. It could be taken as a demonstration that Lenin had been right all along – and not just about the war, but also about the final goals of the movement. Gradualist socialism had led to an acceptance of the war; the 'maximalist' position (as Lenin's stance was commonly described) had proved that there really was a final goal and that the revolution was possible.

Socialists reacted to this in a variety of ways. Inside each party there was a faction of some significance which supported the aims and methods of the Bolshevik Revolution and was ready to take it as a model applicable to their own countries. However, in most cases the majority of the rank and file expressed solidarity without going further.

On the whole communist parties were formed as a result of a minority split from the socialist parties, as was the case in Spain and Italy. There were, however, various exceptions to this rule. In Norway, for instance, the Labour Party – hitherto fairly moderate, now radicalized by the war – joined the Comintern in 1919 and accepted the Twenty-one Conditions. Its moderate wing split and organized a reformist 'Social Democratic Party' which gained 9.3 per cent in the 1921 elections to the Storting against 21.3 per cent for the Labour Party. By 1923 the extent of Comintern control had become excessive and the Labour Party left the communist movement while retaining its maximalist programme. A left-wing faction split to form the Communist Party of Norway.[23] In Great Britain the Communist Party of Great Britain (CPGB) was formed as a result of the coming together of groups already outside the Labour Party which suffered no split as a result of the October Revolution.

The Communist Party of Holland, like the CPGB, was the result of the evolution of political groupings already outside the mainstream socialist party, the Sociaal Democratische Arbeiders Partij (SDAP). In 1909 the SDAP had expelled a vociferous Marxist faction, the De Tribune group led by David Wijnkoop, which then assumed the name of Sociaal Democratische Partij. However, in spite of its commitment to Kautskyist orthodoxy, it was never recognized by the other parties of the International. It was this organization which became the Communist Party of Holland.[24]

In France, at the Eighteenth Congress of the SFIO (Tours, 1920) a majority voted to join the newly formed Third International and to become a communist party. According to Judt,[25] three factors contributed to transforming the wartime minority of leftists into a majority: the radicalizing effects of the Russian Revolution, disillusion with Parliament after the 1919 elections and the government repression of 1919–20. None of these explains why the SFIO was the only major socialist party with a pro-Soviet majority; similar factors were at stake in the Italian case, for example, with the added dimension of a major working-class upheaval and the occupation of the factories (the *biennio rosso*), yet only a minority of Italian socialists opted for Lenin's Twenty-one Conditions.

The SFIO, like the majority of the Italian and Spanish socialist parties, was reluctant to join the reconstructed Second International dominated by the 'rightist' SPD. It preferred, at first, to support the Austrian socialists' proposal to work for a new international organization – promptly nicknamed the Second-and-a-Half International – whose aim was to build bridges between the Bolsheviks and social-democrat reformists.[26] The attempt (1921–23) failed and the bridge-builders merged with the Second International to form the Socialist International at Hamburg in May 1923.

October 1917, like all great turning-points, was interpreted in a variety of ways. Within the new French Communist Party the differing traditions of French socialism found a novel unity by stressing this or that aspect of Leninism. The Blanquists emphasized insurrection and the dictatorship of the proletariat; the Guesdists were impressed by the Soviet decrees nationalizing the major banks and enterprises; the 'red' small peasantry of southern France was pleased with the agrarian reform. There was little, however, the French communists could do to influence events in France. They had captured a majority of the old SFIO cadres, but had the support of only a fraction of the SFIO electorate.

In Germany the situation was quite different. In the first place the socialist party had emerged from the war already split. There were the so-called Majority Social Democrats (the MSPD), the Independent Social Democrats (the USPD), and the Spartacus League dominated by Luxemburg and Liebknecht. Secondly, in 1918, they had a revolutionary situation on their hands. The old imperial state was in ruins. Socialists could fight for one of two alternatives: either a parliamentary republic or a state based on directly elected councils – the new Soviet model of direct democracy. The Spartacus League embraced this second option, but the General Congress of Workers' and Soldiers' Councils (16–20 December 1918) decided to call for an election to a national assembly. A few days later the Spartacists formed the Kommunistische Partei Deutschlands (KPD). In November 1918, the MSPD – *de facto* in control, insofar as any one party could be said to be in control of Germany at the time – had implemented some of the main demands of the old Erfurt Programme – votes for women, proportional representation, freedom of expression, the eight-hour day – and promised a national assembly, thus reaffirming its commitment to the parliamentary form of state. The subsequent elections (19 January 1919) resulted in a clear victory for the MSPD (37.9 per cent) with the USPD obtaining 7.4 per cent. Thus by the time the Comintern was formed and Lenin's twenty-one demands were advanced a communist party already existed in Germany that was committed to Council (Soviet) democracy, and a Social Democratic Party that was not only unmistakably 'reformist' but clearly tainted, not least for having allowed the murder of Rosa Luxemburg and Karl Liebknecht, the communist leaders. The majority of the USPD decided to join the KPD (October–December 1920) while the rest merged with the MSPD to reconstitute the old SPD (September 1922).

Condition 16 of the Twenty-one Conditions of the Comintern (number 17 in the original nineteen) established that the new communist parties would have to draw up new programmes in conformity with 'the special conditions of the country' and 'the resolutions of the Communist International'. However, it was the Communist International and its executive committee which had to decide what these 'special conditions' were.[27] From the beginning it was widely assumed that the interests of the Soviet regime and those of the communist parties totally coincided. Attempts to challenge such assumptions were silenced. By 1928 the Comintern was entirely controlled by the Soviet Communist Party. The concept of special national conditions – what would later be called 'national roads to socialism' – was partially and temporarily reintroduced in the mid-1930s when 'national conditions' (the struggle against fascism) and Soviet foreign policy (the end of Soviet diplomatic isolation) coincided. This permitted the development of an anti-fascist popular front strategy aimed at renewing the link between communists and socialists. This connection was again broken by an act of Soviet foreign policy (the Molotov–Ribbentrop pact of 23 August 1939), only to be re-established as the result of an act of German foreign policy (the Nazi invasion of the USSR on 22 June 1941). Thus communist parties had very little control over their fate.

The Third International was dissolved in May 1943 as a gesture of reassurance on the part of the USSR towards its wartime allies. During its twenty-four years of existence the main turning-points of the Comintern were thus all fundamentally determined either by the struggle for control within the Soviet Communist Party or by questions of Soviet foreign policy. The Comintern was supposed to guide the international working class towards revolution, but during all the years of its existence not a single socialist or quasi-socialist regime was established anywhere in the world, with the exception of the Mongolian People's Republic in 1924 – an event which owed nothing at all to the Comintern. This was, to say the least, a dismal result for an organization based on the principles of *Weltklasse*, *Weltpartei* and *Weltrevolution* (world class, party and revolution). Having failed in the business of revolution, the Comintern also failed in electoral politics. Some parties were more influential than their share of the poll might indicate (the British Communist Party, for example); nevertheless, electorally weak communist parties have had very little significance in the national politics of their countries.

On the whole the communist parties, with some significant exceptions, emerged on the losing side in all electoral battles of the inter-war years. This may explain the endurance of their anti-parliamentarian ideology. In Italy the Communist Party was only able to fight a single election in 1924 before being banned along with all other parties. In Britain the Communist Party oscillated between 0.1 and 0.3 per cent of the poll, though one might argue that under a different electoral system it would have done better (but not that much better). In Holland the Communist Party progressed from a low of 1.2 to a high of 3.4 per cent in 1937, but in Norway the process was reversed, from 6.1 per cent in 1924 to 0.3 per cent in 1936. The Danish peaked in 1939 (2.4 per cent), but previously had remained below 1.6 per cent. In Austria the Communist Party was never able to break the one per cent barrier. Communists did better, comparatively speaking, in Sweden, where they achieved 6.4 per cent in 1928, but settled at around 3 per cent in the 1930s; and in Belgium, with less than 2 per cent in the 1920s, but 6.1 per cent in 1936.

At the Eighteenth Congress of the Soviet Communist Party held in March 1939 in Moscow, Dmitri Manuilsky gave this depressing account of the organizational strength of communism in capitalist Europe: 300,000 Spanish communists, 270,000 in France, 60,000 in Czechoslovakia, 19,000 in Sweden, 18,000 in Great Britain, 10,000 Dutch, 7,000 Belgian, 3,000 Yugoslavs.[28] The three strongest parties were about to face their major ordeals: the Spanish Communist Party was about to be destroyed in the civil war, those of Czechoslovakia and France forced into clandestinity by the Nazi invasion. Italian and German communists had been in this predicament for some time.

During the whole of the inter-war period only two Western European communist parties did develop a significant electoral base: the KPD in Germany and the Parti Communiste de France (PCF). Throughout the 1920s the KPD was the main communist party in Western Europe. In the 1930s this role was assumed by the PCF. Neither, however, was able to overtake their socialist rivals. During the years of crisis which led to the establishment of the Weimar system (1919–20), the KPD was little more than a splinter party.[29] It soon benefited, however, from the indecision of the SPD and from the economic crisis. Its share of the vote increased steadily from 9 per cent (December 1924) to 10.6 per cent (May 1928), 13.1 per cent (September 1930), 14.3 per cent (July 1932), 16.9 per cent (November 1932 – only 3.5 per cent less than the SPD), and still gathered 12.3 per cent in the last elections (March 1933), mainly from the unemployed. The advent of Nazism destroyed it along with all the other parties.

The problem was that KPD electoral strength was never translated into appropriate political action and that at no stage was the KPD a protagonist in the political life of Weimar. Its votes were in a way 'subtracted' from politics altogether in a way the Nazi vote, equally anti-Weimar, was not. The Nazis used their electoral strength to destabilize Weimar in favour of an authoritarian alternative. The KPD oscillated between putschism (the ideology of 'now is the time for armed insurrection') and preparation for a putsch. Its insurrectionist strategy never allowed any of its activities to be directed to winning immediate reforms.[30] It refused to have anything to do with the institutions of Weimar and was repaid in kind: the Law for the Protection of the Republic (July 1921) was used far more against the Left than against the Right (which, like the KPD, had voted against it).[31] In its misconceived notion that Leninism amounted to pinpointing the existence of revolutionary conditions, the KPD reduced strategic debates to tactical ones. All issues were subsumed by the overarching belief that the road to revolution was an insurrectionary one. Thus, all one needed to decide was whether the time was ripe. If it was, then a precise demarcation line had to be drawn in order to separate the revolutionaries from all others. If the time was not ripe, then various types of alliances could be entertained, but all were temporary adjustments to be rescinded when the revolutionary hour struck. Thus, after 1923, during the years of 'capitalist stabilization', the KPD made demands very similar to those of the socialists.[32]

The Comintern encouraged this Janus-like attitude: any communist leader who envisaged a more flexible conception of politics was open to the charge of opportunism. Events in Saxony in 1922 and 1923 epitomized the situation.[33] The SPD, under pressure from its left wing, opened negotiations with the KPD for a coalition government. The SPD was not prepared to accept all demands laid down by the Saxon KPD. The KPD leaders Ernst Meyer and August Thalheimer were willing to compromise, but the Comintern forced the KPD to break off negotiations. Had these been successful, they would have paved the way for the first practical experiment in government for West European communism. When, in 1923, the KPD did enter the Saxon government it was purely in order to prepare for an insurrection. Once this failed, the chances of a revolutionary situation developing again dwindled and the party began to lose members.

In 1921, following its amalgamation with the left wing of the USPD, the KPD had nearly half a million members. By 1924 it had 121,000. Only in

1930 did it begin to recover lost ground and it gradually climbed back to over 330,000 at the beginning of 1933.[34] By the late 1920s, in spite of being the main European communist party, the KPD, like the rest of the communist movement, was totally under the thumb of the Comintern. Leaders like Thalheimer had been forced to resign. The line of 'class against class' adopted by the Comintern was another variation on the insurrectionary model. It defined social democrats as 'social-fascists' and as 'the main enemy', thus making the constitution of a broad anti-Nazi front impossible. The increase in the communist vote thus contributed to the destabilization of the Weimar Republic. In an economically disastrous situation, in which no single party was strong enough to stage a coup or obtain a parliamentary majority, what was at stake was the strategic ability to make alliances. The SPD had tried to forge alliances with the centre and the constitutional Right, and in so doing had found itself politically paralysed. The KPD did not even try, quietly confident that its hour would come. Its political ghettoization was paralleled by the social conditions of those who supported the KPD: the unemployed. Far from being the party of the organized working class, for this was the prerogative of the SPD, the KPD overwhelmingly represented the un-employed; indeed, a special term was coined to designate an *employed* party member. The jobless were a consequence of the rationalization and modern-ization policies of the Weimar state. They were isolated not only from the world of production, but also from the organizational and cultural traditions of the social-democratic labour movement. They were attracted by the voluntarism of the KPD, which provided them with the cathartic vision of a sudden and apocalyptic change – the revolution which would alter, once and for all, their conditions of existence.[35] The isolation and division of the Left made it possible for the Nazis to work out their own alliances on their own terms. The German Left was wiped out. Only much later did German communists find the way open to power, after 1945, and then solely by virtue of the victories of the Red Army in the eastern part of Germany. In the western part the SPD had to wait until 1966 before entering government again.

By the 1930s only in France were the communists still doing reasonably well. Until 1932 they oscillated around the 10 per cent mark. By 1934 the PCF had dropped the sectarian anti-socialist 'class against class' line, and in the elections of 1936, fighting under the banner of democracy and anti-fascism, it increased its share of the vote to 15.3 per cent, with 1.5 million votes (a gain of 800,000) and seventy-two seats (a gain of sixty-one).[36] It subsequently refused to join the socialist-led government, but supported it in Parliament until the end of the year. This, apart from the Spanish case (see below), was the nearest a West European communist party ever came to sharing in the responsibility of running a country.

The road, however, had been hard. By 1922–23, after its failure to conquer the majority of the socialist electorate, the PCF was as isolated as the other communist parties. This isolation increased with the general Bolshevization of European communism from 1924 onwards. It reached it apex at the end of the 1920s when the sectarian policy of the 'Third Period' was adopted. Any form of alliance strategy (from above or from below) was abandoned. It was assumed that conditions for an armed insurrection were rapidly developing and that capitalism would soon collapse. Social democrats were viciously labelled 'social fascists', the 'left wing of the bourgeoisie'. The Wall Street crash (1929) seemed to confirm the widely held belief (on the Left) that capitalism was doomed. During this period the overall membership of the PCF decreased, but while many intellectuals left the party, many prominent ones joined, including André Breton, Louis Aragon, Paul Eluard (all surrealists), Henri Lefebvre, Paul Nizan and Georges Politzer.[37] This had very little to do with the strategic line of the party. Whatever the causes of the PCF's attraction for intellectuals, it neither courted them nor knew how to use them. The leaders were usually of working-class extraction and suspicious of intellectuals.

It was only in 1934 that the line changed: sectarianism was dropped in favour of a united front with all other anti-fascist forces. This change had some real political significance in only two countries: France and Spain. The causes of the change of line were manifold: the lessons drawn from the Nazi accession to power; the USSR's fear of being isolated and facing a hostile capitalist world (which led to a rapprochement with France embodied in the Stalin–Laval anti-German pact of May 1935); pressures from other Western communist parties; the obvious dead-end into which the 'Third Period' policies had led. Communists everywhere began to work for an alliance with socialists and social democrats. This eventually expanded to include antifascist centre parties and crystallized in the shape of the Popular Front.

The Popular Front was welcomed with particular enthusiasm by French communists. The party borrowed the revolutionary and patriotic rhetoric of French radicals in order to 'nationalize' itself by association with the Jacobin tradition. It could do so without fear of ideological contamination. The Bolsheviks liked to compare themselves to the Jacobins and the years after 1917 were full of references back to revolutionary France.[38] But it was only in the 1930s that 'French communism made its peace with French political traditions. The Popular Front brought together communism and the Third republic.'[39] To signify its renewal, the party changed its name from Parti Communiste de France to Parti Communiste Français.

This exaltation of Frenchness and French history was to be long-lasting. The party never really abandoned it. The rapport which existed between the French communists and their country's history is peculiarly French. Not many other socialist forces in other countries have a historical past which so readily provides justification and legitimacy for a revolutionary language structured by anti-clericalism and populism. The French communists could write – as did their leader, Maurice Thorez – 'In the name of the working class, the Communists claim the heritage of the Encyclopedists of the eighteenth century, d'Alembert, Diderot, Voltaire, Montesquieu, Rousseau etc.'[40] Fusing the Stalinist vulgate with Gallic populism, they could rally round Jeanne d'Arc, the Jacobins, 1848 and the Commune of Paris; sing the Marseillaise with tears in their eyes, and drape themselves in the tricolour with reasonable credibility.[41] Their British or German (or even Italian) comrades never had so fertile a field of radical national traditions to plough.

All in all, the French communists improved their prospects significantly during the period of the Popular Front. The party's membership was up from 32,000 in 1932 to 290,000 at the end of 1936, again overtaking the socialists. The fourteen National Assembly deputies of 1928 had become seventy-two in 1936. Its vote rose from 800,000 in 1932 to nearly 1.5 million in 1936. In 1932 the PCF had only 8 per cent of the vote; in 1936 it had 15 per cent. By contrast, the radicals receded from 19 per cent in 1932 to 14 per cent in 1936, while the SFIO remained stationary at around 20 per cent.[42]

As in Spain, the French Communist Party's strategy aimed to bring about an anti-fascist government with the paramount goal of stopping fascism. It would not be a government expected to initiate sweeping reforms (capitalism could not be reformed), and it would not be revolutionary (this could only be achieved by following the Bolsheviks, that is, through armed insurrection). The paradoxical consequence was that the PCF fought for a government which would be neither revolutionary nor reformist. It excluded itself from the government and did everything it could to avoid frightening the middle classes and the centrist parties (in France the radicals, in Spain the republicans).[43] In fact, on 6 August 1936, after the victory of the Popular Front, Maurice Thorez advocated a wider alliance, the Front Français, which would be purely defensive: defence of republican legality, of the national economy and of the international status quo (i.e. an anti-German collective security system).[44] Six months earlier, at the Eighth Party Congress (January 1936), Thorez had defined the Popular Front government as an anti-fascist government that would 'make the rich pay' and that would be the 'preface to armed insurrection for the dictatorship of the proletariat'.[45] There are no inconsistencies: the PCF still held the view that reforms within capitalism were impossible, and that everything which was done was done in view of an armed insurrection. The PCF could be as moderate as the radicals, while maintaining its Bolshevik credentials intact. But the intellectual poverty of this mode of thinking could not but prevent all further thought: 'words without thoughts never to heaven go.'

The radical party too did not want a reformist or a revolutionary programme, but was quite ready to adopt the revolutionary rhetoric of the communists. The PCF programme was anti-capitalist in words only: inveighing against the minority of 'parasites' in society, the 'Council of Regents of the Banque de France', the 'kings of commerce', and the 'two-hundred families' which ruled the country.[46]

By the eve of the war the PCF was the only communist party left in Europe with a substantial electoral following. Elsewhere it was banned, crushed or electorally insignificant.

Clearly, by any reasoned judgement, the record of pre-war communism in Europe must be described as one of failure. But this should not obscure the positive political contributions it nevertheless made. In some cases – Great Britain, for instance – communist parties provided the terrain for the training of an entire generation of political activists, intellectuals and trade unionists.[47] In others it provided a nucleus of dedicated activists who would form the backbone of the resistance movement to Nazism during the Second World War, as in Italy and France. In most instances, through the policy of popular frontism, they provided much of the impetus for the anti-fascist struggle. In a few rare cases communist parties provided the only terrain for an original development of Marxist theory (e.g. the Italian Communist Party, with Antonio Gramsci and Palmiro Togliatti). It is thus perfectly possible to produce a more favourable balance-sheet than may be deduced from the electoral and political results. However, this cannot alter the overall negative judgement on the paucity of communist achievements. The purpose of forming communist parties was not to train trade unionists, advance Marxism, or even fight against fascism to restore parliamentary democracy. Communist parties were formed to lead the world revolution. This they did not do. Their positive achievements were, in some cases, in areas where others had done as well, if not better. When they approached power (as in France and Spain), their belief that reforms within capitalism were impossible or counter-productive led them to side with the least reformist wing of the anti-fascist coalition.

The Socialists: Nordic Success and Spanish Failure

The belief that capitalist society could not be reformed into socialism was not, however, peculiar to communist revolutionaries. Socialists shared it too. Their reformism did not entail a belief that it was possible to introduce elements of socialism into the body of capitalist society. Unlike the followers of Bolshevism, they believed that socialism could be introduced peacefully following an electoral victory which would give them control over Parliament and the machinery of government. They would then use this machinery to bring about a permanent redistribution of power by eliminating private ownership of the principal means of production and exchange. Thus, they were working with a conception of socialism as a 'model of society', that is, a 'final goal' to be attained.

The communists believed that 'liberal' democratic institutions could not be fully utilized for the seizure of power and that they were incompatible with the establishment of a socialist society (that is, a society in transition towards communism). For their part, the socialists did not really contemplate any changes in the political organization of society except in the sense that they would eventually abolish undemocratic relics (unelected upper chambers, monarchy, restrictions on the suffrage if any).

On the whole the communist parties failed to establish themselves as leading contenders for power. Conversely, the socialist parties in almost all cases emerged as one of the two main political parties. In all cases they became the main party of the working class and were able to form a government in many countries of Western Europe between the wars – for example, in Sweden, Great Britain, Germany and Spain. The First World War, the Bolshevik Revolution and the ensuing collapse of the Second International had clearly not done any harm to the electoral strength of the socialist parties, which generally achieved between a quarter and a third of the vote, as can be seen from Table 2.1.

The war contributed to the growth of the socialist parties. Change and innovation – as so often happens – were immeasurably accelerated by the war. The 'mass society' which was just beginning to emerge at the turn of the century had finally been established. The new situation favoured 'new' political parties: old conservative parties had to be 'born again' (the British Conservatives – as did the Labour Party – stole the clothes of the Liberals and became an unambiguously pro-capitalist party); new authoritarian parties emerged (Italian Fascists and German National Socialists). Socialist parties, unlike the communists, had surfaced from the war as legitimate 'national' forces. This brusque transition to political legitimacy, objectively ratified by electoral success, meant that many socialist parties were propelled in a short space of time towards an active share in governmental power though, on the whole, very few were prepared for it. The French socialists found themselves in *de facto* alliance with the radicals, the British with the Liberals, the Spanish with the republicans, the Swedish with the Liberal Party (1917) and then with the Agrarian Party (1936), the Norwegian with the Farmers' Party (1935), the German with the Centre Party (among others). In most cases, the experience was not happy: the combined pressure of facing unforeseen problems (such as a world economic collapse), having to negotiate with a governmental partner usually able to switch sides by turning to the parties to their right, and trying to satisfy the aspirations of its voters and the often immoderate expectations of its rank and file, proved too much.

There were exceptions, notably in Scandinavia and especially in Sweden. The Swedish social democrats were able to combat unemployment more effectively than the German SPD and the British Labour Party. In so doing, between 1932 and 1938 they laid the foundation for what would become the modern West European conception of social democracy after the Second World War: the compromise between labour and capital, with a welfare state and full employment.[48]

Between the war and 1932 the Swedish Social Democratic Party (Social-

Table 2.1 Socialist, social-democratic and labour parties' share of the vote, 1918–40 (%)

	Aus	Bel	Dnk	Fin	Fra	Ger (SPD)	Ger (USPD)	Hol	Ita	Nor	Swe	UK
1918	–	–	28.7	–		–	–	22.0	–	31.6	–	21.4
1919	40.8	36.6	–	38.0	21.2	37.9	7.6	–	32.3	–	–	–
1920	36.0	–	32.2^a	–	–	21.6	17.9	–	–	–	29.7	–
1921	–	34.8	–	–	–	–	–	–	–	21.3	36.2	–
1922	–	–	–	25.1	–	–	–	19.4	–	–	–	29.7
1923	39.6	–	–	–	–	–	–	–	–	–	–	30.7
1924	–	–	36.6	29.0	b	26^c	–	–	e	18.4	41.1	33.3
1925	–	39.4	–	–	–	–	–	22.9	–	–	–	–
1926	–	–	37.2	–	–	–	–	–	–	–	–	–
1927	42.3	–	–	28.3	–	–	–	–	–	36.8	–	–
1928	–	–	–	–	18.0	29.8	–	–	–	–	37.0	–
1929	–	36.0	41.8	27.4	–	–	–	23.8	–	–	–	37.1
1930	41.1	–	–	34.2	–	24.5	–	–	–	31.4	–	–
1931	–	–	–	–	–	–	–	–	–	–	–	29.3
1932	–	37.1	42.7	–	20.5	20.3^d	–	–	–	–	41.7	–
1933	–	–	–	37.3	–	18.3	–	21.5	–	40.1	–	–
1934	–	–	–	–	–	–	–	–	–	–	–	–
1935	–	–	46.1	–	–	–	–	–	–	–	–	38.1
1936	–	32.1	–	38.6	19.9	–	–	–	–	42.5	45.9	–
1937	–	–	–	–	–	–	–	21.9	–	–	–	–
1938	–	–	–	–	–	–	–	–	–	–	–	–
1939	–	30.2	42.9	39.8	–	–	–	–	–	–	–	–
1940	–	–	–	–	–	–	–	–	–	–	53.8	–

Notes: ^{a} This is the result of the third election of 1920. The socialists obtained 29.3 per cent in the first and 29.9 per cent in the second. ^{b} Socialists fought the elections in alliance with radicals and others resulting in about one hundred socialist deputies. In 1919 68 SFIO deputies had been elected. ^{c} Results of second election of that year. The SPD obtained 20.5 per cent in the first. ^{d} Results of second election of that year. The SPD obtained 21.6 per cent in the first. ^{e} There were elections in Italy in 1924 but because of widespread violence and intimidation they cannot be considered valid.

demokratiska Arbetarepartiet – SAP) had repeatedly been in government, either in coalition with the Liberal Party (October 1917 to March 1918), or as a minority government (March–October 1920, October 1921 to April 1923, and October 1924 to June 1926). Coalition with a bourgeois party had become acceptable to most social democrats on the grounds that Sweden was politically backward and that its bourgeoisie could not be relied upon to carry out the democratization of society: 'we have acquired a strong and large Social Democratic Party that must carry out the work accomplished by the bourgeoisie in other nations.'[49]

Although the Swedish social democrats did not officially abandon their original Marxism (i.e. the theory of exploitation and the demand for the collectivization of the means of production), they did not put forward any plans for institutional reform: the state machinery was to be left intact under a monarchy. There were to be no major nationalizations. Instead, the SAP established a successful 'corporative' structure for permanent negotiations between employers, trade unions and government on labour market and social policies.[50]

In the 1920s the SAP introduced the pre-1914 social-democratic demand for the eight-hour day, while at the same time shedding traditional pre-war social-democratic ideology by turning down proposals for widespread nationalization advanced by its left-wing tendency.[51] By then, the SAP was left with no distinct programme for an overall reform of society. The great radical plans of 1920 had disappeared and after 1924 the question of industrial democracy (which had never seriously interested the unions) was, in practice, dropped.[52] The social democrats developed an analysis which correlated progress with the growth of economic concentration.[53] This view, akin to Hilferding's theory of 'organized capitalism', signalled the acceptance of the 'class compromise' between labour and capital, keystone of Swedish social democracy.

In 1932 the first social-democratic government to possess a majority in Parliament was elected in Sweden. For the first time the labour movement was in the business of formulating policy. Both the Trade Union Confederation (the Landorganisationen – LO) and the social-democratic government gave priority to economic growth. In so doing, they accepted that the Depression which ensued from the 1929 crash did not constitute *the* crisis of capitalism and could not be an occasion for implementing the vast socialization measures which had been reiterated in various programmes. In any case, the party had dropped from its 1932 electoral manifesto all references to socialism and to socialization of the means of production. It had become necessary to manage capitalism and to manage it differently. The LO entered into a pact (the so-called Saltsjöbaden Agreement) with the employers' association (Svenska Arbetsgivareföreningen – SAF) in 1938, which established collective bargaining and a code of practice for the regulation of industrial relations.[54] The actual content of the agreement was not as important as its symbolic significance.[55] Nevertheless, it reinforced the centralized nature of the LO and was based on two principles. The unions accepted the management's right to manage, while the SAF recognized the unions' right to represent the workers. It survived as the basis of industrial relations in Sweden until the 1970s.

Other factors helped the Swedish social democrats: their native bourgeois opponents were weak, uncertain, vacillating and disunited. The unity between the industrial wing of the labour movement (the unions) and the political wing (the party) was exceptionally solid, unlike in Germany or France.[56]

Furthermore, while other social-democratic parties – such as the SFIO, the SPD and the Labour Party – acceded to power only through an alliance with the 'bourgeois' centre, the SAP, in May 1933, found its strongest ally in the Agrarian Party when they signed the so-called Crisis Agreement.[57] The SAP and the Agrarian Party governed together – with one minor interruption – from 1933 to 1939, then in a wartime coalition with all the other parties (except for the communists), and then between 1951 and 1957. The parties of the bourgeoisie had thus to face a 'united front' of parties representing not only the traditional labour movement, but also a politically well-organized farming sector committed to protectionism (against the import of wheat) and market regulation to ensure the price stabilization of dairy products. This unique pattern of a 'worker–peasant' alliance led by social democracy was reproduced only in the other Nordic countries: in Denmark (January 1933), Norway (1935) and Finland (1937).[58] In Norway, as in Sweden, the compromise between farmers and workers which gave rise to the minority Labour Government of 1935 led by Johan Nygaardsvold, involved social welfare legislation, unemployment insurance, old-age pensions, and a minimum wage for the workers as well as new or greatly increased price stabilization subsidies to farmers and fishermen.[59]

Between 1933 and 1938 the SAP-led government introduced employment creation programmes, a housing programme to the benefit of large families, indexation of pensions, near-universal maternity benefits, paid holidays and state loans to newly married couples.[60] The Swedish social democrats used new counter-cyclical policies, developed by home-grown economists (Wicksell and the Stockholm School), to fight unemployment. One of the leading social-democratic thinkers and future minister of finance, Ernst Wigforss, adopted an underconsumptionist theory and a plan against unemployment based on the active intervention of the state (not dissimilar from policies later advocated by Keynes and others in Britain). The Swedish social democratic government, unlike the left-wing governments in Britain (1929–31), France (1936–37) and Spain (1936–39) and the Weimar coalition (1928–30), presided over a successful economic recovery which lasted well into the late 1930s (unlike the New Deal which, by 1937, was in difficulties). While, in July 1933, there were 139,000 unemployed, by August 1937 this had been reduced to 9,600.[61] Was this entirely due to the government's use of the state budget as an instrument of recovery? Retrospective attempts to trace the origins of a 'Swedish model' to the 1930s tend to conceal Swedish exceptionalism.

Sweden's export-led, post-1932 recovery was helped by the fact that most of its exports were forest products (four-fifths of the total), and the rest were iron ore, iron and steel. Being vital to the rest of the world, these products were little affected by the growth of protectionism in the 1930s. Exports were boosted by rearmament and by the huge British housing programme, for which Sweden was a major supplier of raw materials.[62]

Nevertheless, from 1934 onwards Swedish recovery was based on the growth of domestic demand due to the huge expansion in the building industry (which accounted for one-third of all industrial employment). Such expansion was facilitated by the enormous increase in state investment. Further growth in domestic demand was achieved thanks to the government's agricultural policy (the SAP's coalition partners, the Agrarian Party, played a central role in this), which boosted the purchasing power of farmers. Finally, it should be noted that, unlike their comrades in Britain and France (not to speak of Germany and Spain!), and unlike the New Dealers in the USA, the Swedish social democrats were able to pursue their expansionist policy without encountering any serious opposition from the industrialists.[63] The weakness of the Right as a political and social force – a weakness which led to the employers' acceptance of the Saltsjöbaden Agreement – must stand as one of the fundamental reasons for the success of the Swedish Left. The SAP kept to its side of the *de facto* compromise with the bourgeoisie. Moreover, there were no constitutional barriers to the rule of the Left: the first socialist–liberal coalition of 1917 had democratized the Upper Chamber by having it elected by local authorities, while removing all property qualifications for local elections.[64]

By 1940 the last paragraph of the preamble to the party programme contained a statement which declared social democracy 'to be one with the Swedish nation', rather than 'with Social Democracy in other countries' as in the previous programme. The welfare state was the new goal; nationalization and class conflict had been dropped; democracy was valued for itself rather than as a tactic; the national road, based on a relatively insulated national economy, had come to prevail over internationalism. The Swedish model had come into being.[65]

Arguably, one could speak in broader terms of a Nordic model, since the itinerary of the Danish social democrats was not very different. They were part of the national coalition formed in 1916 (Denmark was neutral). The social-democratic leader Thorvald Stauning was prime minister of a minority government between 1924 and 1926. This failed, unable to stabilize an economy hurt by the previous government's premature withdrawal of wartime controls. In 1929 the social democrats returned to power with 42 per cent of the vote. When the world crisis hit Denmark (1933), the employers, confident that the unions were too weak to resist, wanted to cut wages. The government intervened, banning strikes *as well as* lockouts, and extending wage agreements. The social democrats invited the agrarian party, Venstre, to enter into a pact, later known as the Kanslergade Agreement, whereby the currency would be devalued, taxation on farms reduced, public works started and a social reform programme implemented.[66] As in Sweden, there were no nationalizations, but, given the relation of forces between employers and employees, the intervention of the government in farm prices and industrial wages was *de facto* pro-labour even though it appeared impartial.[67]

Other socialist parties, even when they shared power, did not produce anything remotely resembling a model or a credible alternative to capitalism. This is not difficult to understand, given that in virtually all cases socialist parties appeared to enter government without knowing what do to. It was as if, because the time had not come for a socialist government, they felt they should not be in power at all. It was as if they felt History had somehow cheated them by giving them power prematurely, when they still had little idea of what should be done. Like their communist rivals, the socialists had a notion of what the final goal might look like. Unlike them, their political strategy to get there involved winning an election when the situation was ripe, i.e. with the country solidly behind them, and the capitalists quiescent, paralysed by fear. What one was supposed to do between winning the election and reaching the final goal was a matter of intense speculation and utter uncertainty.

Nevertheless, comparatively speaking, the inter-war years witnessed a hardening of the North–South division in the socialist movement, already apparent at the turn of the century. In Nordic Europe socialists were laying the foundation of the most successful welfare states in Europe. In the South the situation was dismal. There was no socialist party to speak of in Greece. Portugal was ruled by a traditional clerical regime destined to last fifty years. In Italy fascism had triumphed. Only in Spain could socialists nurture some hopes. They were tragically frustrated. At first, however, the situation appeared promising. A limited corporatist experience, involving socialist participation, occurred in Spain in 1923, when the Primo de Rivera dictatorship, influenced by Catholic social doctrines, obtained the co-operation of the trade union federation (the UGT) and of the Spanish Socialist Workers' Party (PSOE). One of its main representatives, Largo Caballero, became a member of the Council of State and trade unionists sat with employers' representatives on some of the new corporate bodies.[68]

No significant social reforms were achieved in this experiment. The formal justification for socialist co-operation was the need to accelerate the end of the monarchical regime. Those who were in favour of collaboration acted on the basis of the Kautskyist–Marxist doctrine of the two stages: first bourgeois democracy, then socialism. This theory, however, purported to describe a whole process of historical development and consequently no specific tactics necessarily followed from it. Participation in a bourgeois government could be justified on the grounds that it was necessary to enable it to carry out its 'historical task', namely the construction of bourgeois democracy. Conversely, the theory could be used to support abstentionist tactics on the grounds that the socialist party had to wait until the bourgeois-democratic stage was completed. In fact, 'theory' was used as a peg on which to hang whatever tactics – intervention or inaction – seemed suitable.[69] The use of theory as a substitute for strategic thinking, rather than as an instrument for the analysis of reality, disguised a paucity of ideas on what to do with political power.

The Spanish Socialist Party used the two-stage theory to justify its acceptance of the apparent inevitability of a bourgeois-democratic phase prior to the 'real' socialist revolution. In reality, it seems that the internal disputes of this party were far more attributable to the rivalries between personalities and disagreements over organizational questions than to any marked ideological conflict.[70]

Collaboration with Primo de Rivera, though much criticized, was part of the process of political legitimation of the PSOE. This led to the formation in 1931 of a government in coalition with the republicans. Caballero was minister for labour and used the post to achieve pro-worker legislation, including the eight-hour day, which enhanced the influence of the UGT. The socialists were able in addition to obtain a progressive constitution. The 1931 coalition was defeated in the elections of 1933 and much of its legislation was not implemented by the incoming conservative coalition which ruled Spain until the victory of the Popular Front in 1936.

The Spanish Popular Front was at first a republican–socialist coalition, in which socialist participation was supported by the communists, then a minor force in Spanish politics. The socialists wanted social reforms, but the communists, envisaging the Front as broadly anti-fascist, wished to keep as many (non-socialist) republican forces in it as possible, since they did not really think that the new republic had much chance of developing in a socialist direction. Because the communists had limited goals, they tended to support the 'centre-right' of the coalition, though they were reluctant to enter the government.[71] The same situation was developing in France, where radicals and communists coalesced against attempts to elaborate a detailed programme of social reforms. Unlike its French equivalent, however, the Spanish Popular Front was brought down by a long civil war whose crucial cause was the threat of agrarian reform.[72] The war seemed to confirm that in particular circumstances even reformist policies might lead to a violent reaction and that gradual, peaceful and legal transformations might not always be possible. The war showed how pivotal the international context had become in the chances of the Left acceding to power. The Western democracies simply looked on, unwilling to act. Soviet help had been significant in altering the power balance within the Spanish Left to the advantage of the communists, while German and Italian intervention were in turn determinant in ensuring Franco's victory.

The German Social Democrats

Unlike most other socialist parties in the immediate post-war period the German Social Democratic Party (SPD) faced a particular dilemma: it was in power in a period which approximated to a revolutionary situation: 1918–20. I say 'approximated', because, with hindsight, few of the necessary pre-conditions for a German version of the Bolshevik Revolution existed.[73] Like the Bolsheviks, the revolutionaries were in a minority, but, unlike them, they were very far from being able to mobilize armed forces. In other words, neither a majority revolution (e.g. a situation in which those who take to the streets to force a rupture with the old regime have the clear backing of a majority of the population), nor a minority coup, were possible (the latter was tried by the Spartacists in 1919 and ended in utter failure).

The realistic alternative, a democratically elected left-wing government, able to neutralize the opposition by legal means, would have necessitated an agreement between the old SPD and the USPD. But the two social-democratic parties did not have a majority and the USPD was unwilling to serve with bourgeois parties. What followed was a coalition in which the SPD shared power with the parties of the centre (the Centre Party and the German Democratic Party).

The SPD found itself paralysed in this coalition, unable to modify the fundamental structures of power of the old regime: the army, the civil service and the judiciary. What is at issue is the extent to which the SPD compromised, and particularly whether it went further than necessary in preserving the old social order. What is clear is that when it took charge of the government, the SPD was completely devoid of any concrete plan for a radical reform of the economy.

The real achievement of the SPD was the creation of the Weimar Republic. Considering its tragic end, however, one should say that the SPD had handed itself a poisoned chalice. The new democratic constitution had established the republic and extended social rights (universal suffrage, basic freedoms, education for all, etc.). But the economic and social order had remained unreformed. The SPD identified with the new constitution completely and was virtually its only true supporter.[74]

It can be argued that little could be done given the real relations of forces which prevailed in and out of Parliament, and that the constitution, because it contained clauses committing the state to what was in effect a welfare state, established a legal framework for future struggles. The SPD could and did claim that the Erfurt Programme had been incorporated in the new constitution.[75]

What policies did the SPD have? How did it conceive of the tasks of socialists? In the programme adopted at Görlitz in 1921, it stated quite categorically that the essentially *political* transformation had been accomplished: '[The party] considers the democratic republic to be the form of government irrevocably given by historical development.'[76] The consolidation of this political revolution required little more than 'the creation of a uniform system of local government'.[77] The political road to socialism was thus opened. What was still required was 'the progressive transformation of the *entire* capitalist economy into *a Socialist economy operated for the common good*'.[78] The first steps in this direction, according to the programme, would be anti-trust legislation and nationalizations.

If the SPD had simply assumed that constitutional and parliamentary struggle contained all the necessary conditions for social transformation, then it could be legitimately accused of 'parliamentary cretinism'. But that was not the case. The party accepted that the constitutional compromise had to be underpinned by a compromise between capital and labour in the form of a pact between the trade unions and the employers' association (the Stinnes–Legien Pact of November–December 1918).

It follows that what really governed the evolution of the system in a progressive direction was the circumstances prevailing at the time. In the period prior to 1923 these tended to favour the labour movement (even though the SPD was out of government after 1920). In 1918 and 1919 measures benefiting the working class were introduced: the eight-hour day, unemployment benefits, and the institutionalized system of wage regulation and arbitration.[79] This was not accomplished simply because of the strength of the socialists in Parliament, but because of the power of the working class as manifested in, for instance, the number of strikes, including political strikes in defence of the republic against attempted coups by the Right. The massive inflation of 1923–24 ended the phase of working-class advance. Inflation in Austria had similar effects on the socialists: the stabilization policies which followed the period of inflation forced the Austrian socialists out of government.[80]

The trade unions pushed for wage protection instead of fiscal reform. The resulting unemployment 'allowed industry to renegotiate with Labour the terms of the social partnership that had been accepted five years earlier only under menace of revolution'.[81] The employers regained confidence: lockouts prevailed over strikes, which became increasingly defensive. The eight-hour day was abandoned.[82]

The SPD (now reunited with the USDP) produced a new programme at its Congress of Heidelberg in 1925. It was closer to the old Erfurt Programme in its insistence that 'The proletarians are growing ever more numerous, the antagonism between exploiters and exploited ever more marked, and the class struggle ... ever more bitter.'[83] Support for the democratic republic was reiterated ('the most favourable basis for the working-class struggle for emancipation and hence for the realization of Socialism'), as was belief in nationalization and anti-trust legislation. The only real novelty was an appeal specifically directed at the middle classes: 'Not only the proletarians but also the middle classes are being denied a full share in the material and cultural progress that the enhanced productive forces make possible.'[84] This could have been the basis for the construction of an anti-monopolistic coalition, by giving German socialism what it had always lacked: a populist anti-big-business perspective.

However, this kind of perspective was alien to the more novel aspects of SPD thinking, of which Rudolf Hilferding was a leading exponent.[85] In his keynote address to the 1927 Party Congress in Kiel, 'The Task of Social

Democracy', he developed the concept of 'organized capitalism' which he had begun to analyse in 1915. This term defined the existing stage of capitalist development as the effective end of the free-market system and the definitive establishment of an economy dominated and regulated by cartels and trusts, organized internationally by growing monopolies:

> Organised capitalism thus means in effect the replacement of the capitalist principle of free competition by the socialist principle of planned production. This planned, deliberately managed form of economy is much more susceptible to the conscious influence of society, which means to the influence of the *sole institution capable of the conscious*, compulsory organisation of the whole society, the state.[86]

But this 'collectivized' and 'organized' economy was still led by the capitalists. It followed that the task of social democrats was to use the state (now democratized) to guide the economy. The growth of monopolies and cartels had led to the end of *laissez-faire* capitalism. The road to a planned organization of society was now open. The sole remaining problem was that control was still in the hands of capitalist private interests. The installation of the state at the helm of the economy, and the consequent assumption of political and social goals in economic management, would pave the way for the transition to socialism. Hilferding's work can be thus considered a compelling conceptualization of one of the central co-ordinates of the economic thinking of West European social democracy in its most *statist* expression.

Between 1920 and 1928 the SPD was out of office, although it frequently took part in coalition governments in some of the *Länder* (especially in Prussia). It was back in office in a *Grosse Koalition* in 1928. But now it was trapped. Though in government, the SPD could do little to gain control over the economy. The growth of unemployment, the 'investment strike' of the employers, and the concomitant fiscal crisis 'combined to negate the victories of the preceding years'.[87] By then the situation was, if anything, a counter-revolutionary one. Like the Labour Party in Britain, the SPD (with Hilferding as minister of finance) approved a severely deflationary package. The fear of a return to the hyperinflation of 1923–24 – what came to be known *Angst vor der Inflation* – had paralysed even the social democrats.[88] The labour movement was already in full retreat more than three years before the actual Nazi takeover. The employers, compelled by economic circumstances to contain wages, had nothing to offer the unions. These, in turn, could not be expected to 'abandon positions which had been won previously or to guarantee extensive material concessions to the employers'.[89] Weimar had reached a state of deadlock. The conciliatory strategy of the SPD had failed – as had that of its communist rivals, who had mistaken the crisis of Weimar for that of capitalism in general. The pro-Weimar basis of Parliament had been further reduced by the electoral advances of the Nazi party. The SPD was on the retreat, desperately bent on making any compromise with the conservative Right to preserve the republic. As we know, this strategy did not work and

German social democracy was destroyed by Nazism and, at least temporarily, eradicated from the face of Europe. The reconciliation of capital and labour, which had been the *de facto* policy of the SPD, had failed. The compromise between capital and labour had made Weimar possible; its failure almost inevitably led to Weimar's collapse.[90] The social democrats' first experience of a 'parliamentary road to socialism' was extremely inauspicious and, in Germany, quite tragic. Fascists, on the other hand, at least judging from their successes in Germany and Italy, found that the 'parliamentary road to fascism' paid off handsomely.

The Popular Front in France

French socialism, though it suffered a less dramatic fate, was nevertheless also a substantial failure. Unlike the SPD, the French Socialist Party played a very small role in shaping post-war France. The country had emerged victorious from the war, with its bourgeois establishment intact and the consensus which underlay the Third Republic much enhanced. The SFIO had surfaced rather weakened from the Tours Congress (1920), where the pro-Bolshevik majority had split to form the PCF. The consequence was that the French labour movement was more than ever consigned to a ghetto within the political system of the Third Republic.[91] The socialists very soon recouped the lost ground and, in terms of members and votes, overtook the French Communist Party for the rest of the inter-war years, even though the party lost most of its proletarian base to the PCF. It had few workers, few trade unionists, a feeble press and no party apparatus.[92]

In 1924 just over one-third of SFIO parliamentarians were of working-class extraction. By 1936 out of its 146 MPs only sixteen were workers, while teachers formed the largest single professional group. The socialist parliamentarians now, more than ever, reflected *la France moyenne*. Outside its strongholds in the Department of the Nord, the SFIO had become the party of rural, agricultural, southern France.[93]

In fact, in terms of its personnel, organization, membership and electoral basis, the SFIO had become indistinguishable from the Radical Party. It needed a strong ideological profile to maintain its identity, which is probably why, in spite of its increasingly reformist political practice, it retained a formal attachment to Marxism and the ideals of constructing a socialist society. It should be added, however, that – as explained in the preceding chapter – the ideological profile of the SFIO had never been high, that it was imbued with the vague ideology of French radicalism from the very beginning, and that (due to the anti-party, syndicalist orientation of the main trade union confederation, the CGT) it had a much smaller proletarian base than other socialist parties.

Nevertheless, its size and power, as well as the fragmented nature of French politics, prevented the SFIO from remaining a purely opposition party. To avoid a repeat of the electoral defeat of 1919, it sought an electoral alliance with the Radical Party in 1924 (the Cartel des Gauches). Between 1924 and 1926 it supported a government whose policies it could do little to influence, then in 1926 it withdrew again into opposition.

Léon Blum, the acknowledged leader of the reformist wing after 1928, insisted, like Jaurès, on the 'national road' to socialism, except that now the reference to a national road had a distinctly anti-Soviet ring to it. Blum's socialism, like that of most SFIO members, was formally based on Marxism, though in fact it was a mixture of enlightened rationalism, humanism, anti-clericalism and internationalism.[94]

Between 1922 and 1926 Blum developed a conceptual distinction between the *conquest of power* and the *exercise of power*.[95] The *conquest of power* was a revolutionary, though not necessarily violent, act, which led to a new social order based on new property relations. This could occur only under determinate conditions: a mass party, an advanced culture, a strong economy and international peace. It would be the culmination of a lengthy evolutionary period.

The second concept – that of the *exercise of power* – was developed at a special party congress in January 1926, as a response to a new situation brought about by the 1924 Cartel des Gauches. The new concept would function as a theoretical justification should the SFIO be 'forced' into government before the conditions for the conquest of power were ripe. Until capitalism collapsed, all socialists could hope for was to 'exercise' power, which meant pursuing limited reformist goals. During the exercise of power, there would be no major change in property relations.

This 'theory' reproduced in a very slightly modified version the dichotomy between the 'final goal' and the 'practical tasks', between the 'day of the revolution' and the 'tasks of the present'. The purpose of this distinction was to preserve the 'end-state' aspect of socialism, while allowing the party the possibility of following practical policies. In the Erfurt Programme of pre-1914 days, these policies took the form of demands social-democratic parties made on established governments. Blum's SFIO remained ideologically very much in this pre-war mould, and did not take advantage of its post-Tours rebirth to adapt to the new post-war situation (unlike, for instance, the Swedish social democrats). Now, with Blum's distinction, the socialists could envisage the possibility of exercising power in a non-revolutionary situation. This would be a 'socialist management of capitalism'. Socialism itself was relegated to a distant future, 'nebulous and mythical'.[96]

One should note that these preoccupations were not uncommon within the European Left. Socialists often reflected on the problems of having political power thrust on an unprepared socialist party. In October 1928 John Strachey warned that a future Labour government 'would have to rule largely at the mercy of the capitalist classes'. All that Labour supporters could hope for from this government was 'to secure certain things, some of which would be of definite material benefit to the workers ... and some of which ... would be of the greatest assistance to the workers in their further struggle'.[97] In reality, the Labour government of 1929–31 was not able to deliver either.

By 1934 the threat of fascism had forced the Comintern to abandon its sectarian policy. This created the conditions for a realignment of the Left. In France this led to the reunification of the trade union movement and an alliance of radicals, socialists and communists under the banner of the Popular Front. Blum's theoretical justification for a future government based on this alliance was the concept of the *occupation of power*. This was, clearly, not the 'conquest' of power; but it was not an exercise of power either, because it was not meant to prepare the way for a social revolution. The occupation of power – in practice an occupation of office – was a strategy aimed at denying the forces of fascism access to power. In this sense it was a defensive strategy.[98]

It should be noted, however, that the SFIO programme demanded structural reforms, including nationalizations. The PCF programme was more moderate because it could not conceive of gradual progress towards socialism within capitalism. It was content to unite as many voters as possible against fascism. Its fear of alienating the middle classes was such that it was a contributory factor to Maurice Thorez's decision not to seek cabinet posts for the communists.[99] As it turned out, the only nationalization promised in the final programme agreed by the three parties was that of the Banque de France and of the armament industries. The programme sought to restore purchasing power, establish a fund for the unemployed, the rapid execution of public works and support for farming communities (such as a National Wheat Marketing Board).[100]

The programme was overtaken by events. In 1936 the most massive and unexpected wave of strikes in the history of the Third Republic forced employers and unions to the negotiating table. The left-wing government, caught by surprise, had to be more radical than it had anticipated. On 7 June, at the Hotel de Matignon, with Blum presiding, the employers agreed to collective bargaining and to an increase in wages of between 7 and 15 per cent (more for those on lower incomes). A few days later, the government introduced legislation establishing the forty-hour week, paid holidays and arbitration by the Ministry of Labour in industrial disputes. It encountered very little opposition.[101] The bill passed on 21 June, instituting, among other things, the *congé payé*, had not been part of the electoral programme of 1935. It was the direct product of workers' militancy, but also of a wider consensus supported by the Catholics, for whom this measure signified more family leisure.[102] The Communist Party played its role by urging the workers to accept the agreement; Thorez said that there could be no question of an escalation towards a social revolution.[103] The strikes of May–June had panicked the *patronat*, the employers, into making concessions. They had also alarmed communists and socialists, who did not believe that this spontaneous unrest could be channelled into revolution.[104] It should be noted that what historians consider to be the lasting achievements of the Popular Front government (paid holidays and arbitration) were not so dissimilar in kind to what was obtained in other countries in the same period. Legislation providing for paid holidays had existed before the mid-1920s in Germany, Austria, Denmark, Norway, Finland, Italy, Czechoslovakia and Poland. Between 1926 and 1934 similar legislation was enacted in Luxemburg, Greece, Romania, Chile, Mexico, Spain, Peru, Brazil and Portugal and, after 1936, in Ireland, Iraq, Belgium and Bulgaria.[105] In the United Kingdom, home of the oldest labour movement in the world, this did not occur. Under the inspiration of Ernest Bevin, the TUC obtained representation on a government-appointed committee of inquiry into the claim for an annual holiday with pay and, as a direct result, in 1938 a law was passed extending paid holidays from three million workers to eleven million – a 'minor social revolution', writes Allan Bullock.[106] Bevin failed, however, to obtain the eight-hour day. Opposition was not limited to the government and employers; trade unionists objected on the grounds that it would interfere with the opportunity to earn overtime pay.[107] This is probably why the eight-hour day was never instituted in Britain while, in the aftermath of the First World War, this demand, sustained by workers' militancy, swept its way throughout Europe: it had been proclaimed in Russia after 1917, then in 1918–19 in Finland, Norway, Germany, Italy, Poland, France, Spain, Czechoslovakia, Austria, Holland, Portugal and Sweden.[108]

The international situation, and British pressures in particular, led the Popular Front government to tone down its anti-fascist stance by adopting a policy of non-intervention in the Spanish Civil War – a policy which was not modified even after Germany and Italy had intervened directly. Domestically, the economic record of the Popular Front was a failure. Blum had to wait until September to ensure that the inevitable devaluation of the franc would not bring about British and American retaliation.[109] Like so many before them, Blum's economic ministers and advisers were ill-prepared to provide an alternative to the orthodoxy of Finance Ministry officials.[110] Blum later claimed that he had wanted to be the 'loyal manager of capitalism'.[111] The capitalists responded with a massive flight of capital. Blum sought special powers to counteract this, but failed to obtain the approval of the Senate which, dominated by conservatives, was the main source of parliamentary opposition to the government.

Here all the limits of the 'occupation of power' strategy came to the surface. Blum backed down even though his constitutional position was far from unsound: he had the backing of the Chamber of Deputies and it was not certain whether the Senate had the constitutional power to overthrow a government.[112] He was prisoner of the reform–revolution dilemma and assumed that any attempt to resist would cause grave unrest and throw the economy into chaos. As Joel Colton shrewdly noted, Lloyd George and Franklin Roosevelt did not hesitate to take on, respectively, the House of

Lords and the Supreme Court.[113] Blum, like MacDonald before him, simply capitulated, accepting the entire institutional framework as an immovable constraint. This capitulation was compounded by his agreeing to serve in the successor government led by the radical Camille Chautemps. Chautemps did obtain from the Senate the powers which had been denied to Blum, but he used them for a conventional deflationary programme.[114] It was not only the economy which defeated the first Popular Front government, but its inability to reform the state. It was also a lack of foresight: had these special powers been solicited in June–July 1936, when the strike movement was still strong, the Senate would have readily granted them.[115]

If the French Popular Front developed a mythology of its own, this was a phenomenon that fed more on the importance of France itself, than on any major achievements of the socialist-led government. Although the PCF remained outside the government, it was nevertheless reckoned to be of fundamental importance by communists everywhere. With the Spanish Popular Front, it represented the most important instance of co-operation between the communist and socialist wings of the movement. But it is difficult to argue convincingly that without it fascism would have taken over in France. It is even more implausible to maintain, as some have done retrospectively (including supporters of Trotsky), that the Popular Front prevented a spontaneous workers' revolution.[116]

If there is one single thread in the evolution of Western Europe from 1917 to date, it is the marked absence of *any* possibility of a working-class revolutionary insurrection on the Bolshevik pattern. Those who failed to appreciate this fundamental fact were condemned to the most complete political insignificance, or to utter defeat, as subsequent events in Greece (1944–48) and Portugal (1974–75) demonstrate.

The Failure of the British Labour Party

In one other country there occurred a situation in which a 'socialist management of capitalism' was thinkable: Great Britain.

At the 1923 elections the Conservatives had emerged as the main party, but without a majority in the House of Commons. The Labour Party was therefore able to rule, but its dependence on the parliamentary support of the Liberals made it impossible to contemplate implementing any of the distinctive measures of the Labour manifesto such as the nationalization of the mines, railways and electric power stations.[117] Though the party had no plans for dealing with unemployment, Labour made important contributions to housing and education reforms. Defeated at the 1924 elections (Liberal losses tipped the balance in the Conservatives' favour), 'Labour had proven its responsibility. It had supplanted the Liberals as the alternative government.'[118]

Labour returned to power in 1929 to head another Liberal-supported minority government, though, for the first time, it had more seats than the Conservatives (288 to 260); the Liberals trailed behind with 59 seats. The Labour manifesto contained few specific proposals for dealing with unemployment: housing and slum clearance, land drainage, road building. It was not clear how these schemes would be financed. Everyone agreed that unemployment was the main problem. Roughly speaking, there were two views: that of the Treasury, which suggested that nothing could be done; and that of a wide spread of opinion, which included the Liberals, John Maynard Keynes, David Lloyd George, Oswald Mosley (then a Labour minister), the Trades Union Congress (TUC), Ernest Bevin's Transport and General Workers' Union, all proposing various versions of public works programmes. Mosley presented a memorandum to deal quickly and effectively with unemployment. This required an injection of cash into the economy by expanding credit, increasing purchasing power through higher social benefits and pensions, and some protectionist measures.[119] These measures, influenced by Keynes, drew considerable support from the Left of the Labour Party and from the Liberal Party.[120] The Labour leadership, however, decided that a sense of economic responsibility entailed following the 'Treasury view'. The Mosley plan was rejected and Mosley himself abandoned Labour and committed political suicide by embracing a ludicrous British version of Italian fascism, including all its paraphernalia complete with black shirts and street thuggery. Thereafter, Labour's financial policies bore 'the depressing imprint of Snowden' (the chancellor of the exchequer), who 'accepted the "Treasury view" in all its essentials'.[121]

The Labour government did not produce any further original thoughts on the economy. Its policies became indistinguishable from those of the Conservatives. It was only when faced with the Labour chancellor's suggestion that unemployment benefit be cut that the cabinet split. The resulting crisis led to the formation of a 'National Government' dominated by the Conservatives, but led by the former Labour prime minister, Ramsay MacDonald. The Labour Party remained in opposition until 1940.

Robert Skidelsky has argued convincingly that Labour's insistence that only a socialist society could resolve the basic evils of capitalism blocked it from dealing effectively with unemployment through Keynesian techniques: 'The Labour Party's commitment to a nebulous Socialism made it regard the work of the "economic radicals" such as Keynes as mere "tinkering".'[122] Ross McKibbin has pointed out that while Labour was in office, there were no relevant foreign examples to follow.[123] Britain faced specific international constraints which made any serious counter-cyclical budgeting problematic.[124] Keynes himself (in his Addendum to the Report of the Macmillan Committee on Finance and Industry) was rather vague both as to the size of the budget deficit required and to the speed of the predicted economic recovery.[125] This suggests that the Labour government was not free to choose between alternatives. What had to happen happened.

This is not the place to arbitrate in the controversy, or to speculate on the kind of alternative policies Labour should have developed. What is clear, however, is that – like its socialist and communist counterparts on the continent – the Labour Party had been unable to develop an analysis of the problems it was likely to face when in power. Furthermore, the Labour Party had not thought through the relationship between its international outlook and its domestic plans. In terms of foreign policy Labour internationalism amounted to a commitment to the League of Nations, international arbitration, conciliation, disarmament, an extension of the economic functions of the League, an international solution to the problem of currency stability, and so on. As Robert Boyce has pointed out, the Labour aim of a nationally planned economy had to be reconciled with the extension of international interdependence, and yet 'it was clear that senior Ministers ... had devoted little if any thought to the matter'.[126]

Thus, when it achieved power, Labour had neither immediate practical plans nor a medium-term strategy. It seems to me that the cause of this was the adoption of contradictory political assumptions. While in opposition, Labour's fundamental assumption had been that government policies were by and large determined by the will of the government; in other words, that the constraints which existed were not so much economic as institutional (e.g. the House of Lords, the abolition of which appeared in virtually all Labour programmes). In opposition Labour thus accepted in its entirety the doctrine of the sovereignty of Parliament (and of national sovereignty): once in power with a parliamentary majority, anything was possible.

In government, Labour abandoned this assumption posthaste in favour of its opposite: under capitalism fundamental economic and political constraints are such that nothing is possible (pending socialism) and therefore nothing of a socialist nature can be achieved. Skidelsky has written of Labour's attitude: 'Socialism was impossible and capitalism was doomed: there was nothing to do but govern without conviction a system it did not believe in but saw no real prospect of changing.'[127] It is not unsurprising that, in spite of the wealth of left thinking in the 1930s on planning and social reorganization, there was a conspicuous silence on reorganization of the state. For instance, Attlee's *The Labour Party in Perspective* (1937), which has the undoubted merit of being, almost certainly, the only manifesto by a socialist leader with a chapter on beauty – 'One of the heaviest indictments against the Capitalist system is that it is destructive of beauty'[128] – was completely supportive of the existing machinery of government: 'It is my belief that with this machinery we can bring about the fundamental changes which we desire.' The sole changes advocated ('reforms' would be too grand a word), apart from the ritual demand for the abolition of the House of Lords, were a speeding-up of parliamentary procedure and a reorganization of cabinet functions.[129] Evidently, to be electable it was believed that it was necessary to be committed to the existing institutional arrangements.

Between the wars European socialism had advanced remarkably. In many cases it had indeed demonstrated itself to be an electable political force. Before the First World War some socialist parties had succeeded in becoming the main opposition force and the repositories and focus of demands for change. Between the two wars this trend had become universal, blocked only by the establishment of a non-democratic authoritarian regime (as in the case of Germany and Italy). As the history of the post-1945 *Western* European system demonstrates, the downfall of authoritarianism, in *all* cases, produced a political system in which the Left was the main force either in government or in opposition (i.e. in Italy, Germany, Spain, Portugal and Greece). Only countries with a particular history dominated by unresolved national questions – of which Ireland remains the outstanding instance – failed to conform to the trend. So much for the achievements of the Left. On the negative side of the balance-sheet the organized Left seldom succeeded in producing novel ideas which would match the economic developments of inter-war Europe, particularly the downfall of *laissez-faire* capitalism after 1929.

Once again we should not be too dismissive: real attempts were nevertheless made to develop new strategies. We have mentioned Hilferding's elaboration of the concept of 'organized capitalism' and Blum's distinction between conquest, exercise and occupation of power. In both cases the thinkers involved were trying to map out the necessary preconditions for some sort of collective control of the economy, or to develop a theory of intermediate phases.

Other attempts were made to abandon the Kautskyist straitjacket of revolutionary verbiage and day-to-day reformist practice. Three are worth mentioning at this stage: an amorphous tendency of 'neo-socialist planners' who were interested in a socialist use of planning under capitalism; and the attempts to rethink a strategy for the Left in the non-revolutionary conditions of advanced capitalist societies associated, on the one hand, with the Italian communists, Antonio Gramsci and Palmiro Togliatti, and, on the other, with Otto Bauer and 'Austro-Marxism'. In the next chapter I will limit myself to brief outlines so that the reader can be in possession of at least a rudimentary (albeit incomplete) map of some of these unsuccessful alternatives, before proceeding to explore the Left during and after the Second World War.

CHAPTER THREE

Thwarted Alternatives

The 'Neo-Socialist' Planners

NO SINGLE definition would do justice to the multifarious diversity of this catch-all category. Its most enthusiastic proponents tended to be on the margins of power: either outside the main parties of the Left, or unheeded minorities within them, or they were in the trade unions. Mario Telò has persuasively argued that the protagonists of the socialist rethinking of the 1930s could only be outsiders.[1] What united this group was the recognition that, following the 1929–31 crisis and the ensuing Depression, the capitalist state had been forced to abandon the traditional role of 'nightwatchman' – one limited to law and order and defence and regulating competition, while showing some concern for social questions such as conditions of work in factories, strikes, the consequences of unemployment. The new state had to take into account the fact that the economy was increasingly directed by a few large firms and that it was, to that extent, a regulated economy. At the same time what was evolving was increasingly a mass society with collective needs which, in conditions of democracy (or aspiring democracy), had to be met. In other words, the new capitalist society had specific collectivist traits which favoured the formation of modern non-individualist ideologies.

It was widely felt that, alongside formal political institutions such as parliaments and governments, the co-operation of the main social forces, especially the employers' associations and trade unions, was required. A 'corporatist' position along these lines could be found in most European political parties. Under the threat of working-class unrest or, more usually, as a consequence of wartime co-operation, the inter-war years witnessed a blossoming of employer–union pacts (some of which were mentioned in chapter 2): from the Stinnes–Legien pact of 1918, which established the joint labour–management board for economic regulation (the *Zentralarbeitsgemeinschaft* or ZAG) in Germany, to the largely ineffectual 'Whitley Councils' in Britain, the Matignon Accords of 1936 following the victory of the Popular Front in France, the National Recovery and Wagner Acts of 1933 and 1935 in the USA, the employer–employee pacts in the Nordic countries such as the Saltsjöbaden Agreements in Sweden (1938), and the so-called Main Agreement between the LO and the NAF in Norway (1935).[2]

Even the British trade unions, notoriously hostile to any corporatist approach, began, under the dominant influence of Ernest Bevin, to be systematically included in Royal Commissions and committees of inquiry alongside employers and government representatives, thus becoming an 'estate of the realm'.[3]

In substance what all this meant was the recognition that the formal aspects of democratic life (i.e. elections to an assembly which would validate and legitimize the decisions of the executive) did not provide sufficient powers for effective control over society. The whole complexity of the state could not be controlled by the liberal institutions democratic theory had developed.

That some sort of agreement between employers and trade unions was necessary had already been recognized by the SPD in the Weimar Republic during the 1920s. The Swedes institutionalized the principle when the trade unions (the LO) signed the Saltsjöbaden Agreements with the employers. What this pact amounted to was a 'class compromise' in which the organizations of the working class agreed to accept the capitalist definition of growth and productivity in exchange for social reforms and full employment, though it did not necessarily follow that growth and productivity would always be achieved by private capital. In other words, while the economy would still be 'capitalist', it would be regulated towards some politically defined social goals.

The starting-point of many 'alternativist' proposals was often a public works programme against unemployment. By itself this was not necessarily linked to planning, but in practice it was seen as a state-initiated mechanism which would increase employment and growth – in other words a public intervention where the private sector had failed. In 1932 three leading German trade unionists, Wladimir Woytinski, Fritz Tarnow and Fritz Baade, put forward a large-scale public works programme with counter-cyclical aims, to be financed by deficit spending.[4] This plan (named the WTB after the initials of the three unionists) met some resistance in the German trade unions (Allgemeiner Deutscher Gewerkschaftsbund – ADGB). By intervening with concrete legislative proposals, the WTB Plan contravened one of the principles of the division of labour between the SPD and the unions. Hilferding opposed it because it was 'unMarxist' – in reality, because the SPD was by then committed to deflationary policies, was afraid that the plan would antagonize the Chancellor, Brüning, and did not wish to upset the French authorities unnecessarily by appearing to promote economic autarchy.[5] The relative indifference of the SPD to the plight of the unemployed can be partly explained in terms of the support enjoyed by the communists among them.[6] The employers opposed the WTB plan too because they feared inflation more than unemployment. Ironically, Gregor Strasser, a Nazi leader, thought that it was a good idea and incorporated much of it in his own public works programme.[7] Needless to say, these sympathies further alienated social democrats from the WTB Plan.

These ideas about 'planning the economy' did not come out of thin air.

Ever since the 1914–18 war years there had been a growing interest in planning in both 'bourgeois' and social-democratic circles, but, on the whole, it was disregarded by most of the SPD.[8]

In Britain, public works schemes were far more the domain of the Liberal Party and those who were close to Keynes' positions than of orthodox Labourites. Within the Labour government (see chapter 2) Mosley was one of the few people who fought the battle for a nationally co-ordinated public works programme before his withdrawal into the politics of the absurd.[9] Others like him – for instance, John Strachey – turned instead to communism (in Strachey's case without becoming a party member), dismissing as irrelevant the imaginative reformism he had hitherto supported.[10] Later, however, in his 1940 'socialist-Keynesian' *A Programme for Progress* and, much later and more theoretically, in his *Contemporary Capitalism* (1956) he attempted the integration of Marxism into what he called the 'Western cultural tradition'.[11]

Others stayed within the confines of Labour politics and tried to examine practical policies which could resolve the unemployment problem. It is worth emphasizing the extent to which the British Left, in the 1930s, was seriously trying to devise an anti-unemployment strategy. The only parallel was in Scandinavia. In France the Left did not consider unemployment to be the most prominent issue. In other countries, such as Germany and Italy, there was, of course, no longer a Left to speak of.

However, in Britain, it was only when Labour was in opposition that Keynes' ideas on the causes of unemployment became influential within the Labour Party. For this to happen Keynes had to be dressed up in socialist language, a task attempted with varying degrees of success by Hugh Dalton and Douglas Jay.[12] Keynes, who was no socialist, did not assume that his employment policies would pave the way towards socialism. If anything, they were supposed to save capitalism from the dangers of the free market. Socialists, however, did not see themselves as being in the business of saving capitalism. Once again the conception of socialism as an 'end-state' stood in the way of developing an intermediate strategy. Socialism was always something which would occur in the future. But politics was always something which dealt with the present, a subject on which Labour had little to say.

'Little', not 'nothing'. What it did have to say was mainly embodied in documents such as the party's programme, *For Socialism and Peace*, approved at its Southport Conference of 1934. This document made a sharp distinction between 'full and rapid socialist planning' (described as 'the only sane alternative' to competition) and 'economic reorganization' by privately owned monopolistic capital.[13] 'Real' economic reorganization could occur only under socialism. In the meantime, through public ownership and the control of fundamental industries (public utilities, transport, banking, coal, iron and steel), planning would introduce rationality into the economy on the supply side ('The organization of efficient methods of production ... the organized purchase of raw materials'), and do the same on the distribution side by establishing marketing boards on the basis of 'reasonable' wages and prices.[14] Finally, a National Development Programme (in effect a public works programme) would tackle unemployment.[15]

At no stage in the Labour Party's rethinking during the 1930s was there a serious attempt to understand why such a programme of economic reorganization and development had not even been attempted in 1929–31. The only explanatory category which was used was that of 'betrayal': Labour failed to advance towards socialism because it was betrayed by its leaders – MacDonald and Snowden. This explanation, by ascribing the sole responsibility for the Labour rout of 1929–31 to its leaders, prevented further thought. All that was necessary was for the Labour Party to be led by good and consistent socialists.

In the 1930s, as well as failing to produce new socialist ideas, let alone a socialist strategy, the Labour Party was not even able to exploit the divisions existing in the other parties, nor the considerable amount of innovative work on planning socialist thinkers were producing, both in Britain and on the Continent. Paralysed by its consistent refusal to try anything new, its overall political role remained a minor one.[16]

Throughout this period others were working on alternatives. For example, G. D. H. Cole, even before the crisis of 1931, produced a constitutional plan, the *Labour Programme of Action*, based on the assumption that it was impossible to have an effective transition to socialism within the traditional limits of parliamentary procedure. Included in his plan was not only the abolition of the House of Lords, but a proposed Emergency Powers Act which would give the government powers of nationalization (or 'socialization' as it was called) in accordance with the needs of a socialist plan, institute special tribunals with powers to examine compensation claims, and, while leaving Parliament to deal with the general principles of legislation, would place the real task of administration in the hands of statutory commissions. Predictably, there was a political storm, and the Labour leadership denounced the plan, reaffirming its commitment to parliamentary democracy. Cole's 'constitutional revolution, however, did represent a genuine attempt to think out the conditions for radical socialist advance in a non-revolutionary situation'.[17] At the Labour Party Conference at Hastings in 1933, Stafford Cripps (supported by Clement Attlee and other 'moderates') put forward a resolution along the same lines: immediate abolition of the Lords, an Emergency Powers Act, and a revision of the procedure of the House of Commons. He also included the demand for an economic plan designed to 'end the present system and thus abolish unemployment and poverty'. It took Bevin and the bloc vote of the unions to send back the resolution to the National Executive Committee for further consideration.[18]

In the 1930s the New Fabian Research Bureau produced detailed studies on economic policy, emphasizing social control of industry as the distinguishing feature of socialism. Cole himself went further than any other

Labour Party thinker towards adopting central planning as the fundamental element of socialism. Crucial to this process was the adoption by the USSR of a command economy. It was this and not Keynesianism which provided the Labour Party with a distinctive socialist reference point. A generally pro-Soviet attitude was common currency in official Labour circles. Beatrice and Sidney Webb returned from the USSR in the mid-1930s thoroughly convinced of the superiority of the Soviet planning system and said so in their book *Soviet Communism: A New Civilization?*, published in 1935 (and republished in 1937 without the question mark).[19] Hugh Dalton too was impressed and included in his book *Practical Socialism for Britain* a long section on planning.[20] Unlike the communists, however, the Labour supporters of the Soviet planning system were no friends of the Soviet political system and had to find ways of reconciling central planning with political democracy. This is the context within which Cole's 'constitutional revolution' and Cripps' proposal must be read. In the 1920s Cole had already toyed with different concepts of representation, especially corporate-functional ones based on each industry (the idea of Guild Socialism). In 1935, in *The Principles of Economic Planning*, he stressed, in designing the machinery for planning, workers' control and participation.[21] The Webbs, realizing that British parliamentary institutions were not appropriate to a planned economy, envisaged – as early as 1920 – a 'social parliament' working alongside the political one and elected in the same way, though they proposed that its operations should be conducted by standing committees. Such schemes had some influence abroad, particularly among some of the 'Austro-Marxists'.[22] In Britain in the 1930s neither the Webbs nor Cole were particularly influential with the leadership of the Labour Party, though the latter was close to Bevin. Attlee was not interested in analyses and was suspicious of concepts, thinkers and thoughts.

Resistance to planning from within the labour movement could also be expected for objective structural reasons, and not just ideological ones. One of the younger socialist theorists of the period, Evan Durbin, was well aware of this. Along with many of the planners, he agreed that there should be some kind of central authority with powers over industry and finance, but added that the 'most important requirement of efficient Planning is ... the suppression in the Trade Union and Labour Movement in practice as well as in theory of the last element of Syndicalism'.[23] Durbin had expressed openly what others only thought: trades union practices would be a real problem for socialist planning. To strike for higher wages against private capitalists could be subsumed under a socialist ethos; to strike for the same reasons against a planning authority deemed to be acting on behalf of collective welfare, could not.

In France the SFIO paid very little attention to the whole issue of planning which was at the centre of so much intellectual ferment. The French communists were, of course, in favour of planning. But to them planning meant Soviet planning – a system of managing the economy which required the prior establishment of the dictatorship of the proletariat. As in Germany, the only significant section of the French labour movement in favour of planning under capitalism was the trade unions, (the non-communist CGT). Continental unions were never as strong as the British ones and never relied so consistently on their strength as wage bargainers. They were also more political, in the sense that they believed they would be able to get through political means what they were unable to achieve through economic strikes. As early as 1918–19 the French unions lobbied in favour of a corporatist National Economic Council, a demand promptly turned down by the government as well as by the SFIO.[24] In 1934 the CGT approved the *Plan du travail* boycotted by all three Popular Front parties.[25] Others in favour of planning were maverick or nonconformist intellectuals, who wanted to replace liberal capitalism with a 'self-conscious economy', and Catholics who followed *L'Esprit*'s definition of capitalism as 'usury erected into general laws'.[26] Within the SFIO the planners' group was made up mainly of young intellectuals. The central figures here were Jules Moch, who in 1931 had prepared a scheme to nationalize the railways, and André Philip, a student of Taylorism and Fordism.[27] Moch was the author of *Socialisme et rationalisation*, in which he maintained that socialists must embrace the concept of rationalization and use it to the benefit of all.[28]

The other group of planners within the SFIO was centred round Marcel Déat. Kuisel argues that Déat's proposals were so vague and ill-thought-out as to approach quackery, and that their net effect was to handicap the 'true Socialist *planistes*' (i.e. Moch and Philip) who were trying to get the SFIO to adopt their ideas in 1934–35.[29] Others are less severe.[30] There is a thread linking Bernstein to Déat which emerges when considering the latter's three central ideas, as expressed in his *Perspectives socialistes* (1930):

1. Ownership of the means of production was an obsession to be abandoned. What mattered was the state's *control* over the economy. The development of joint-stock companies had brought about the separation of ownership and management (as Bernstein had pointed out forty years earlier and Crosland would repeat twenty years later: see chapter 10). The possibility of state regulation made nationalization irrelevant.

2. The state was not something that socialists should seek to curtail or abolish. On the contrary, they should reconcile themselves to it and use it to best advantage.

3. Socialism insisted far too much on the proletariat as the leading class. Déat was much more concerned to appeal to the middle classes.

In fact the 'Bernsteinian' confidence of Déat and other *planistes* like him that capitalism was able to overcome economic crises by rationalization convinced them of the superiority of capitalism. Accordingly, they called for an alliance with the capitalist élites around a programme of rationalization, modernization and increased productivity.[31]

None of the *planistes* had any decisive impact on the leading politicians of the Left and, anyway, Blum and the SFIO were far more interested in party unity than doctrinal disputes.[32] As it turned out, of all the planners' proposals Blum accepted only nationalization, dressing it up in anti-fascist clothes, but rejecting the concept of the *économie dirigée*. The communists made common cause with the radicals against all the CGT's planning schemes. In the Popular Front programme there was a reference to public works, but none to planning.[33] The PCF leader, Maurice Thorez, explicitly rejected the plans of the so-called *néo-socialistes* (Déat's), of the CGT and the 'Anti-fascist Intellectuals' (a plan inspired by the Belgian de Man), of the Catholics of *L'Esprit* (labelled a 'fascist plan'), and supported only that put forward by the CGTU, which was not a plan at all but simply the Communist Party's programme.[34]

In 1933 the neo-socialists around Déat broke with the SFIO. They formed a new party, the Parti Socialiste de France – Union Jean Jaurès, with Déat as leader. After the failure of the Popular Front (whose anti-fascism had left Déat indifferent), Déat found himself increasingly attracted, like Mosley before him and Hendrik de Man later, by the fascist emphasis on action and will, its apparent commitment to a rational and planned organic state and its recognition of the need for authority and corporatism.[35] By 1940 Déat was hailing the Nazi armies marching into France as a harbinger of a revolution comparable to that of 1789.[36]

In the 1930s the journey from left to far right was not unusual. The best-known pioneer of this voyage had been Benito Mussolini, a leading socialist before the First World War. Anti-socialist polemicists find in this evidence of a convergence between two forms of modernist collectivism, two aspects of a totalitarian mind.[37] This conveniently overlooks not only the absence of similar cases in Weimar Germany, where no leading social democrat or communist joined the ranks of the Nazis, but the fact that the overwhelming majority of the leaders of fascist movements came from the traditional Right.[38] Nevertheless, that some of the more stimulating minds of socialism started with a critique of traditional Marxism or socialist orthodoxy and ended up as fascists remains a still 'insufficiently lit danger spot' which one should visit and explore.[39]

Many of the 'planners' felt as if they were in some sort of internal exile within the Left. Those unable to find an audience in the established socialist movement made their home elsewhere, some turning to the Right having become convinced that 'doctrinaire socialism neglected man's vitalist drives. … From Michels to de Man and then to Emil Lederer … the disillusion with social democracy dominated sociological discourse.'[40]

Planning obviously required a strong and efficient state. Conservatism, right-wing authoritarianism, the new technocratic liberalism of Keynes and Lloyd George, and all shades of socialism converged on this. The only main ideology still defending the minimal state, classical liberalism, was on the run even in its Anglo-Saxon heartlands after the collapse of 1929. A common problem – mass unemployment – led to an unusual cross-fertilization of ideas. In France the principal source of inspiration to neo-socialist planners was unquestionably the works of Hendrik de Man, the Belgian socialist.[41] His *Plan du Travail*, or, to use its more appropriate Flemish title, the *Plan van den Arbeid*, adopted by the Belgian socialists in 1933, was the most coherent neo-socialist project of the decade for the management of capitalism. It advocated a mixed economic system, including, in addition to a private sector, a nation-alized sector consisting of credit institutions and former private monopolies. The private sector would be controlled indirectly by fiscal and monetary means. The national economy would then be reorganized for the welfare of all.[42] De Man was convinced that the success of the Nazis made it imperative for the working class to join forces with the middle classes in order to isolate and defeat finance capital, which he described as the oligarchy of bankers. In his view capitalism had exhausted its course and no longer had the potential for reform.

De Man understood that economic control and power would be of far greater significance than the ownership of the means of production.[43] He wrote:

> The essence of nationalisation is less the transfer of ownership than the transfer of authority ... the problem of administration takes precedence over that of possession, and changes in the property system are functions of changes in the system of authority required by the managed economy.

In his address to the Maison du Peuple of Brussels (21 June 1927) on the 'crisis of socialism', he argued that the messianic faith in the imminence of the Great Day had to be disposed of:

> The Great Day has not come, and one does not believe in its imminence, nor in its certainty, as much as hitherto. The motives of practical action bear on much less ambitious goals, in large part defensive or indeed conservative ones; one *defends* democracy, the mark, the franc, the eight-hour day, the unions, reforms already won and vested interests.[44]

The echoes of Bernstein are unmistakable here, but de Man explicitly denied the parallel: 'I do not say that the goal is nothing. On the contrary I say: no movement without a goal, but the goal exists and is valid only by reason of the movement and has no reality whatsoever outside of it.'[45] Here as elsewhere, de Man was influenced by the Austrian socialist leader Otto Bauer (see below). The convergence centred on one fundamental point: the transi-tion from *laissez-faire* to organized capitalism forced the entire socialist movement to rethink everything. The end of a phase in the history of socialism had been reached.[46]

In 1933 de Man's plan was adopted by the Parti Ouvrier Belge. It aimed to provide a programme against unemployment combined with *réformes des structures* (structural reforms) – a term which we will find promoted again by

Italian communists and socialists in the late 1950s – see chapter 10). The aim was to escape the traditional dilemma of 'reforms or revolution', and to isolate an economic terrain where a common front could be developed with the Catholic unions.[47] De Man believed that this front could provide the basis for an alliance with the middle classes. This productivist and anti-deflationary plan, similar to proposals advanced by Keynes, the Swedish social democrats and the New Dealers in the USA, can be seen as a variant of the compromise between labour and capital attempted with so little success in Weimar Germany. Indeed, de Man, who had taught at Frankfurt (1929–33), had been influenced by the WTB trade union plan.[48] He in turn influenced the Swiss Socialist Party, which accepted a similar plan in 1935, and the French *planistes*. The *Plan van den Arbeid* was also published in England as a Fabian pamphlet, with an introduction by G. D. H. Cole.[49]

De Man's ideas had a particular influence on the Sociaal Democratische Arbeiders Partij in neighbouring Holland. The SDAP had become interested in the *Plan van den Arbeid* as a result of electoral defeat.[50] The unions backed it with considerable enthusiasm. The party leadership hoped that the adoption of the plan, in 1935, would help the SDAP to win the election. The mood of the country appeared ready for some bold initiative. Even the Anti-Revolutionary Party had produced a similar plan in 1934, known as the *Werkfonds* or Labour Funds. Nevertheless, the SDAP never had the opportunity of implementing the plan. It did not win the election. It did not succeed in mobilizing the support of the so-called 'new middle classes'. In Holland, as in Belgium, these emergent social groups either flirted with fascism, or remained loyal to the traditional bourgeois parties.[51]

The situation in Belgium initially appeared more promising. The POB (or, in Flemish, Belgische Werklieden Partij – BWP) was one of the strongest socialist parties in Europe. It had recognized the enormity of the crisis of the 1930s and was rethinking its socialism. More specifically, it was seeking to transform itself from a class party to a people's party by abandoning revolutionary slogans and the rhetoric of internationalism in favour of what it called (in 1933!) *le socialisme national*. The idea was that it was perfectly possible to mobilize the 'bourgeois state' on behalf of its programme. Most of this rethinking was due to the personal drive of Hendrik de Man.[52]

The chances of implementing the plan seemed, at first, quite promising. Belgium was an ideal setting for an experiment in planning. It was a small country, the oldest industrial country of the continent, highly urbanized, with a marked concentration of industry.[53] Moreover, in 1935 the POB had been able to achieve what the SDAP had not: office in coalition with the Catholic party led by Paul Van Zeeland. De Man became minister of public works and, in later governments during the next few years, minister of finance. The plan, however, was not implemented. The government dropped all the new planning projects of structural reforms, even though it followed an anti-deflationary policy of public works programmes.[54] The Belgian government failed to deliver because, in reality, once it was in office, there was little backing for the plan. The POB's working-class supporters wanted immediate concrete benefits. After the wave of strikes of June 1936, the government established paid holidays and a minimum wage. The Socialist Party's Christian and bourgeois allies in the coalition turned out not to have any intention of adopting the plan. The POB leader himself, Emile Vandervelde, a traditional socialist, was unenthusiastic and never defended the plan with conviction, preferring instead more conventional social-democratic policies.[55] The 1936 election resulted in losses for all government parties, while the far Right gained considerably. By 1937, the POB had run out of steam and had withdrawn from the government. De Man, having succeeded Vandervelde, was soon supporting a policy of appeasement towards Nazi Germany. Later he accepted Leopold II's decision to surrender to the invading German army. He then became a collaborator and, like other 'revisionists' of the 1930s, became a supporter of Nazi ideology, announcing that Nazism was 'the German form of socialism'.[56] He died in exile in Switzerland in 1953, having been convicted *in absentia* of treason by a Belgian court.[57]

Conceived as a practical application of socialist principles, neo-socialist planning was never implemented and thus remained an untested assumption of what might have been possible. The ideas of de Man and many of those he inspired were an expression of the crisis of socialism in the West in the 1930s. The attraction towards planning, due, as we noted, to the crash of 1929, was magnified by the fact that the economic crisis had had no effect on the USSR. As capitalism appeared to be ineffective and Soviet socialism was engaged in a gigantic planning experiment whose outcome was not yet clear, countless intellectuals began to look towards the USSR as the repository of an enticing economic model. Nevertheless, the most obvious motivation behind the pro-Sovietism of much of the progressive intelligentsia was the desire to play a role in the struggle against fascism. Alongside this, there was also an unmistakable desire to achieve some form of political certainty in an uncertain world. The idea of participating in, perhaps even guiding, a collective will shaping the destiny of society cannot but have had the strongest attraction, particularly to those intellectuals without roots in the traditional labour movement.

Planning, as we have seen, was far from being the prerogative of the Left. It had hardly been considered, let alone theorized, by Marx and Engels. It had not been part of the ideological armoury of the Second International: introduced in the USSR more than ten years after the revolution (and against much opposition), it was not really fought for in Western Europe either by social democrats or by communists. A technocratic-corporatist version of planning was attempted more or less seriously only in authoritarian countries, such as Salazar's Portugal, Dollfuss' Austria and Mussolini's Italy. It is not so surprising, therefore, that so many of the disillusioned planners turned to the authoritarian Right.

Austro-Marxism and Otto Bauer

The term Austro-Marxism describes the thought and politics of Austrian socialists leaders from the beginning of the century down to the defeat of the First Austrian Republic in 1934. The main exponents were Otto Bauer, the party leader (1918–34), Max Adler, Karl Renner (twice president of the Austrian republic), and Rudolf Hilferding (eventually minister of finance for the SPD in Weimar Germany). Space here prevents me from dealing with more than a few of the main aspects of Bauer's thought.

Bauer's magisterial appraisal of the causes of fascism, by far the most outstanding of all the left-wing analyses of fascism in the inter-war period, is devoted to identifying the fundamental feature of the 'revolution in the West'.

Austro-Marxism is a purely descriptive term, and therefore does not denote a consistent 'monolithic' theory which can be easily counterposed to Leninism or Kautsky's Marxism. As characterized by Otto Bauer, it denotes a specific feature of post-1918 Austrian socialism, namely the fact that it refused to choose between the reformism of the defunct Second International and the revolutionism of the Third, seeking instead a 'third way' (see chapter 2). Bauer believed that this position had enhanced the radical image of the Austrian socialists, thus preventing the development of a credible communist alternative. As Bauer himself wrote, in an unsigned leading article in 1927:

> where the working class is divided, one workers' party embodies sober, day-to-day *Realpolitik,* while the other embodies the revolutionary will to attain the ultimate goal. Only where a split is avoided are sober *Realpolitik,* and revolutionary enthusiasm united in *one* spirit.[58]

The central strategic concept of the politics of Austro-Marxism was that of the 'slow revolution', or the gradual construction of a socialist society from within the entrails of capitalism. In *Der Weg zum Sozialismus* (1919), Bauer wrote:

> We must construct socialist society gradually, by planned organizing activity, proceeding step by step towards a clearly conceived goal. Each one of the successive measures which are to lead us to a socialist society needs to be carefully considered. It must not only achieve a more equitable distribution of goods, but also improve production; it should not work to destroy the capitalist system of production without establishing at the same time a socialist organization which can produce goods at least as effectively.[59]

Bauer maintained that this 'social revolution' (his term) could occur only *after* the seizure of power (the 'political' revolution). This assumes that there is no rigid separation between socialism and capitalism, that it is possible for 'elements of socialism' to co-exist within capitalism. In the first year of the Austrian Republic, when the working-class movement was dominant, social legislation was extended. This and other reforms 'actually transformed the capitalist mode of production in a fundamental way and introduced into it new elements, the nucleus of the socialist organization of the future'. [60]

This led to recognition of the paramount importance of majority support in the development of socialist institutions; socialists were required to involve themselves in a politics of alliances aimed at achieving some sort of unity not only within an increasingly fragmented working class, but also with the peasantry and the emergent middle classes. Bauer reasoned that a proletarian revolution in 1918 (on the Soviet model) would have led to a suicidal civil war:

> It was impossible to govern the industrial district in opposition to the workers ... it was equally impossible to govern the great agrarian districts in opposition to the peasants. The economic structure of the country therefore created a balance of power between the classes which could only have been abolished by force in a bloody civil war ... Large sections of the proletariat did not realize these dangers, but it was the duty of Social Democracy to see them. [61]

The avoidance of civil war was one of the two tasks of social democracy. The other was 'to capture for the proletariat strong and permanent positions in the state and in the factories, in the barracks and in the schools'. [62] Similarly, at the Linz Congress of 1926, Bauer warned the Viennese workers not to assume that to have great power and influence in Vienna was sufficient for ruling Austria: 'most of Austria is agricultural ... no form of proletarian rule can last more than a couple of weeks unless we can establish strong support in the tranquil valleys and their towns.' [63] He then added, explicitly, 'the fight within democracy is necessarily a fight for the intermediate middle classes.' [64]

This is clearly evident in Bauer's analysis of the defeat of Austrian social democracy in 1933–34, when Engelbert Dollfuss established his authoritarian regime. Some analysis was indeed necessary: in 1931 the socialists commanded over 41 per cent of the vote, were the strongest single party, had an armed force at their disposal (the *Shutzbund*), and had controlled Vienna for most of the 1920s though they had not been in government since 1920. The Linz declaration of 1926 had made it clear that the Socialist Party would use force only if the Right abandoned the terrain of democracy. Yet, when the time came, the socialists were entirely unprepared. [65]

In his compelling analysis of this historic defeat, Bauer rejected the view that it had been caused by the party's excess of moderation at the beginning of the crisis, its strict adherence to the constitution, or by its resort to armed force at their disposal (the *Schutzbund*), and had controlled Vienna for most deeper than in the tactics of its parties or than in this or that tactical mistake.' [66] The authoritarian takeover that followed was facilitated by the fact that – at a time of economic crisis – the system of social protection established in the immediate post-war period and the achievements of Red Vienna had become an intolerable burden for the middle classes, who saw in the Socialist Party an 'establishment party': 'The economic crisis had involved the proletarian-isation of the lower middle classes and the peasants.'[67] Embittered and impoverished, these social groups thus became ripe for fascism. One is reminded of Coriolanus: 'when two authorities are up,/Neither supreme, how soon confusion/May enter 'twixt the gap of both and take/The one by th' other.' A unique balance of forces had been reached between the bourgeoisie and the working class. The former could no longer impose its will on the proletariat in a democratic context, while the latter was not strong enough to overturn capitalism:

> The result of this balance of forces, or rather of the weakness of both classes, is the triumph of fascism, which serves the capitalists by crushing the working class, and yet, despite being in their pay, so far outgrows them that they cannot help making it the undisputed master over the whole people, themselves included.[68]

Recent historiography largely confirms Bauer's account. Jill Lewis's work on *Rote Vienna* demonstrates that the social welfare programme undertaken by Vienna city council greatly improved the lot of the working class, while scrupulously adhering to the terms of the capitalist economy down to a balanced budget. While not materially affected by the changes to the same degree as the bourgeoisie, the petty bourgeoisie experienced a massive loss of power: the council was seen as uncompromisingly pro-working class, 'in complete contrast to the central role which the Viennese petty bourgeoisie had previously played in city politics'. This is not to say that the administration of welfare in Red Vienna was not exercised paternalistically, from the top down.[69] The fears of the middle classes were heightened in July 1927, after violent working-class demonstrations had taken place (in spite of attempts by the socialists to prevent them).[70]

Reformist socialism, in Bauer's analysis, had established a protective net-work (we would now say: the welfare state) around the class it 'represented'. This had a dual effect: it created an objective obstacle to the continuous reorganization of capitalism and was, consequently, objectively anti-capitalist. At the same time, it could not produce a strategy of advance beyond capitalism itself, since one of the conditions of the reformists' popularity was capitalist growth and success.

Bolshevism, on the other hand, had no strategy for co-existing with capitalism, and therefore had little to offer to advanced societies in which democracy had become well established and co-existed with capitalism. The importance of the concept of 'integral' socialism advocated by Bauer is that it recognized the failure of both Bolshevism and traditional social-democratic reformism as strategies for advancing to socialism – an intuition which would be confirmed by the subsequent development of the socialist movement in Eastern and Western Europe in the second half of the twentieth century.

Bauer's 'integral' socialism acknowledged 'the full historical, social and cultural significance of bourgeois democracy, as the product of decades of successful class struggles by the working class and the fertile soil for its economic, social and intellectual development'.[71] At the same time he – like de Man – saw it as the duty of socialists to defend the USSR, the first workers' state (though not a model to be imitated by Western socialists), from fascist aggression. He hoped that the Second and Third Internationals would join forces to fight fascism and looked forward to the day when the transformation of Soviet dictatorship into a socialist democracy would overcome the split between Western democratic socialism and socialism in the East.[72]

No novel, fully worked out strategy automatically flows from Bauer's analysis. But its central assumption is clear: if the socialist party follows a purely corporative strategy, designed to protect and advance the working class with little consideration for middle-class aspirations, it will be unable to rely on sufficiently ample support to move beyond the horizons of capitalism. Furthermore, in times of economic crisis, the separation of the working class from the middle classes will benefit pro-capitalist parties seeking a clear anti-working class outcome to the crisis. These parties would take advantage of the situation and offer the middle classes the prospect of an improvement in their conditions of life in exchange for the termination of welfare constraints designed to protect the working class.

These problems of socialist parties' representativeness would become central to the travails of West European socialism after the Second World War. But neither its communist nor its social-democratic wings would acknowledge the contribution of the Austro-Marxists to strategy. Bauer had concluded his last important work, *Between Two World Wars?*, with a proud appraisal of the contribution of Austrian socialism to the movement: 'To reformist socialism we have bequeathed the great achievement of Red Vienna, to revolutionary socialism the heroic deeds of the insurrection of February.'[73] Both, of course, ended in utter defeat. Both are now half-forgotten. Otto Bauer died in 1938. Austro-Marxism resurfaced briefly in the 1970s when, once again, a 'third way' between Soviet-style communism and reformist social democracy was being sought. This search was actively encouraged by younger intellectuals in the SPD, the Austrian Socialist Party and advocates of Eurocommunism in Italy and France. In retrospect, it appears to have been a passing fashion rather than a real revival.

Italian Communism and Gramsci

Of the multiplicity of factions which made up the Partito Socialista Italiano (PSI) in 1920, four can usefully be distinguished here: the reformists led by Filippo Turati, the 'maximalists' led by Giacinto Serrati, the communists led by Amadeo Bordiga, and the 'culturalist' or 'workers' councils' wing around the Turin journal *L'Ordine nuovo* (Antonio Gramsci, Angelo Tasca, Umberto Terracini and Palmiro Togliatti).

Though it will be necessary briefly to discuss the first three, it is only the fourth which is of interest here, and then only after it dropped the problematic of workers' councils. The Turatian reformists, world war and Russian Revolution notwithstanding, had not modified their fundamental strategic views. They supported in 1920 what they had advocated since at least 1900: an alliance between modern capitalism (represented by Giovanni Giolitti) and the working class.[74]

But in the meantime everything had changed: Italian capitalism had been consolidated by the war effort; a Catholic party (the Partito Popolare Italiano – PPI) had been created in January 1919; the Socialist Party itself had become a powerful force under the new 'maximalist' leader, Giacinto Serrati, capturing the party from the reformists in 1918.[75] By 1920, the PSI had 216,000 members and 151 representatives in the Chamber of Deputies. The previous year (Sixteenth Congress, Bologna, October 1919) it had joined the Comintern enthusiastically and had included in its programme the tactics of armed insurrection and the goal of the dictatorship of the proletariat. But the widespread occupation of the factories of 1919–20 (the *biennio rosso*, 'the two red years') resulted in defeat. The PSI and the unions proved themselves quite unable to use the movement either for revolutionary purposes, as did the Bolsheviks, or for reformist ones, as did the German social democrats or the Austrian socialists.

Serrati and his group, in spite of their avowed pro-Bolshevik sympathies, refused to accept Lenin's Twenty-one Conditions (see chapter 2) for continuing membership of the Comintern. In particular, they refused to expel the reformist wing of Turati and to adopt the name of Communist Party. Accordingly, at the Leghorn Congress of the PSI (January 1921), they rejected the 'communist' left-wing motion which represented the Comintern position. Serrati's position was understandable: when Italy entered the war in 1915, the Turati reformists, unlike their German and French counterparts, did not 'capitulate to chauvinism' and nationalism; virtually alone in Europe, they had stood against the war. For Lenin, of course, the expulsion of the reformists was a necessary political and organizational requirement for the construction of a highly disciplined Bolshevik-type party, though this did not prevent a subsequent alliance with Turati and his followers.[76]

At Leghorn Bordiga and the supporters of the pro-Lenin motion, including the *Ordine nuovo* group led by Gramsci, left the hall where the congress was taking place and moved to a previously booked one to form the Partito Comunista d'Italia (PCdI). Like all the other European communist parties, it was born too late to take advantage of the post-war wave of working-class unrest. The timing of the split and of subsequent events reveals something of the disarray of the socialist movement in Italy. What Serrati could not do in 1921, he did a year later, at the Rome Congress of the PSI (October 1922), when he finally expelled Turati and the other reformists. Now Serrati was ready to join the PCdI. But he encountered the opposition of the ever more sectarian Bordiga leadership group still in charge of the party. Eventually

(1924), the Comintern intervened, removed Bordiga, enabled Gramsci's group to take over the new executive and the merger took place. While all these events were taking place, Benito Mussolini had become prime minister (October 1922), changed the electoral law (1923), rigged the subsequent elections (April 1924), and accepted responsibility in January 1925 for the murder of the reformist socialist Matteotti the previous June. Shortly afterwards, in 1926, he banned all parties and, having established a Special Tribunal, sent to prison or to confinement under police surveillance most of the communist and anti-fascist leaders still operating in Italy.

Like Turati's reformism, Serrati's brand of maximalism was solidly anchored in the pre-war tradition of Italian socialism: it was a matter of certainty that the revolution would eventually take place and that it would be generated by the fury of proletarian violence. The party 'makes the revolution' by intervening in an existing revolutionary situation and shaping it to its advantage in the direction of socialism. Leadership is thus something which can occur only after the 'masses' are in movement.[77] This conception of revolutionary practice owes more to Kautsky's 'wait-and-see' attitude than to Lenin's voluntarism. It is also at variance with the position of the Austro-Marxists, for whom a spontaneous mass movement was not a necessary or sufficient condition for revolution. Serrati's attempt at strategic mediation between the Comintern's supporters and those of the Socialist International in Italy should not therefore be confused with that of the Austrians, otherwise superficially similar.

Amadeo Bordiga belonged to that generation of communists who had assumed that the post-war wave of social unrest had signalled the general applicability of the Bolshevik model to the rest of Europe. The fact that no revolution occurred was due to the betrayal of the reformist leadership and the lack of an authentically revolutionary party. Once this analysis was made, there was no need for further thought: iron discipline, agitation and propaganda, avoidance of compromise and doctrinal purity were all that was required. Eventually, a new crisis would come about and the party, a true vanguard led by an intransigent leadership inspired by the correct line, would finish the job. In practice Bordighism also resolved itself into a wait-and-see attitude not so dissimilar from that of Serrati and Kautsky.

Its theoretical antecedents, if we can speak of theory in this case, derived from Blanqui in France. In Risorgimento Italy this élitist vanguardism was common currency, as was the case with the failed Pisacane expedition of 1857, one of Gramsci's illustrations of erroneous insurrectionary strategy.[78] There was in Leninism a strong Blanquist component, but there was much else besides.

Lenin himself conducted (1920) a celebrated battle against the far Left, though he castigated Bordiga only for his anti-parliamentarianism.[79] Bordiga complied by toning down his distaste for 'bourgeois legality', though he later also opposed the united front policies pursued by the International in 1921.[80]

The intervention of the International had been decisive in the removal of Bordiga in June 1924, though most of the party was still Bordighist at heart. At this stage it was, after all, little more than a persecuted sect and it stayed in this state until the Resistance. Its new leader, Antonio Gramsci, was condemned to prison and confinement in 1926 and died in 1937. His successor, Palmiro Togliatti, remained in exile abroad until 1944.

In the years 1924–26 Gramsci laid down in a more directly political form the basis for some of the theoretical work which he would undertake in jail. It is here that one can find the origins of his analysis of fascism in terms of a 'passive revolution' and a re-examination of the course of Italian unification in terms of the construction of a specific 'historic bloc'.[81] In 1926 he included some of the results of these analyses in the programme of the Italian Communist Party known as the Lyons Theses, which he drafted with Togliatti.[82]

In the historical and theoretical sections of the theses, Gramsci and Togliatti used a language and a subtlety of analysis uncommon in the communist movement. In the more immediately political sections, however, they rarely diverged from mainstream Comintern thought. They exhibited a chronic underestimation of fascism ('the party today finds itself in the phase of political preparation of the revolution'),[83] an unswerving belief in the necessity of 'Bolshevizing' the Communist Party,[84] and an unmitigatedly sectarian attitude towards social democracy, labelled the 'left-wing of the bourgeoisie' – a terminology later used throughout the 'Third Period' phase of the Comintern.[85] They described the policy of the united front and the presentation of intermediate demands in tactical and instrumental terms. These demands were supposed to prepare the ground for a civil war waged by the proletariat, rather than being genuinely transitional objectives around which a broad anti-fascist opposition could develop.[86]

After Gramsci's arrest, when the fascist dictatorship had been consolidated, Togliatti announced a new transitional goal, a 'Republican Assembly on the basis of peasants' and workers' committees'. By then the Comintern, now under complete Stalinist control, had moved sharply against Bukharin and, on the assumption that capitalism would collapse imminently, had become suspicious of any slogan other than one calling for a socialist insurrection. Togliatti, who was dangerously close to Bukharin (as indeed Gramsci had been, especially on the agrarian question),[87] capitulated, and in July 1929 at the Tenth Plenum of the Executive Committee of the Communist International declared:

> If the Comintern tells us that this [i.e. the transitional slogan of the Republican Assembly] is not right, we shall no longer pose these questions; we shall all think these things but we shall not speak of them; we shall only say that the anti-fascist revolution and the proletarian revolution are one and the same thing.[88]

Togliatti went on 'thinking these things', but did not begin to say them until the more favourable climate of the Popular Front allowed him to characterize the civil war in Spain (where he was the Comintern's main envoy) as a struggle for a 'new type of democratic republic', i.e. an intermediate form of state between a bourgeois and a socialist republic.[89]

Togliatti had to submit or allow himself to be removed from the leadership of the PCdI in favour of someone more malleable and less astute. He chose to submit and lived to fight another day. Gramsci, however, owed his freedom of expression to his incarceration. What he could not have written, unpunished, in Stalin's Russia, he could, undetected, in Mussolini's prison.

It is impossible in a few pages to do justice to the complexity of Gramsci's thought. He is, arguably, the most sophisticated Marxist theorist of politics of the inter-war period. Furthermore, the particular conditions under which he wrote his prison works – the fear of the censor, the fact that he was writing in the uncertainty of ever being read, his poor health – make his scattered words rather difficult to decode and interpret, particularly as he is not always consistent in his terminology. Here we can focus on only one central aspect of his thought: like his contemporary Otto Bauer, Gramsci was a theorist of the defeat of the working-class movement in the post-1918 period when bourgeois Europe was 'recast'.

His starting-point was this: the direct assault on the state which had been the primary aspect of the Bolshevik struggle in October 1917 was not an option open to those operating in the West. Lenin had hinted at this as early as March 1918: 'the world socialist revolution cannot begin so easily in the advanced countries as the revolution began in Russia – in the land of Nicholas and Rasputin.'[90] Gramsci assumed that a strong civil society enveloped the state in the West and protected it. This civil society, 'at least in the case of the most advanced States', had become a 'very complex structure and one which is resistant to the catastrophic "incursions" of the immediate economic element (crises, depressions, etc)'.[91] In the East (i.e. in Russia),

> the State was everything, civil society was primordial and gelatinous; in the West, there was a proper relation between State and civil society, and when the State trembled a sturdy structure of civil society was at once revealed. The State was only an outer ditch, behind which there stood a powerful system of fortresses and earthworks: more or less numerous from one State to the next, it goes without saying – but this precisely necessitated an accurate reconnaissance of each individual country.[92]

It matters little that Gramsci was wrong in considering Russian civil society 'primordial and gelatinous'. What matters is the distinction he made between the state in the narrow sense – 'an outer ditch' – and the complex system which results from the accumulation of habits and traditions, conventions and customs, from the intertwining of layers of relations between the élite groups (the 'leaders') and the fragmented mass of the population ('the led'). Power does not reside in a unitary control room which, once stormed, yields all the mechanisms necessary for the exercise of power. Political power rests, in the final analysis, on its fragmentary and disjointed nature, on its very diversification. Those who are formally in command exercise real power, but are themselves subject to manifold constraints which do not vanish suddenly when the previous holders of power are removed.

Throughout civil society everyone has roles and functions, the crucial ones being held by a veritable army of intermediaries whose task it is to organize work, culture, religion and leisure (Gramsci called these – misleadingly – the 'intellectuals'). The ideological capture of this group is central to the conquest of power. No complex social system can survive or be constructed without them. They are the educators, the journalists, the clergy, the communicators, the artists, the advertisers, the disseminators of popular culture, the technical cadres, etc. In other words, all those who translate, modify and adapt and, therefore, constantly *alter* the dominant and accepted ideas of the existing order so that they can be understood, internalized and accepted by all. In this way, what is historically determined and hence transient appears just, natural and eternal. These intellectual 'functionaries' define what is normal and hence what is 'deviant'; they distinguish the acceptable from the unacceptable in all areas, including production and work, everyday life and the assumption of what is 'common sense'. And as everyone is, at least some of the time, an 'educator' or 'organizer' in this Gramscian sense, everyone is, some of the time, an 'intellectual'. Reciprocal socialization is the business of all humans.

If this is true, then it follows (at the cost of dilating the concept of 'political' to everyday life) that those who seek to establish an entirely new social order cannot limit themselves to 'politics' in the old sense – that is, the determination of political tactics and strategies required for storming the citadel of the state (in the narrow sense). The tasks are far more formidable. They require the establishment of a new kind of consensus. Yet consensus is not a static state of affairs, but a battlefield where various conceptions constantly vie with each other. To obtain hegemony, it is necessary to be the force which dominates this battlefield.

What Gramsci called the 'war of movement or manoeuvre' was the storming of the citadel of the state (in the narrow sense), as in the 1848 revolutions (which resulted in the defeat of the revolutionaries) and October 1917. He considered a particular text, Luxemburg's *The General Strike* (1906), to be 'one of the most significant documents theorizing the war of manoeuvre in ... political science'.[93] But the accolade ended here, because Gramsci went on to stigmatize her strategy of the revolutionary mass strike as a form of iron economic determinism thus: an economic crisis produces a phenomenon (the strike) which 'in a flash' throws the enemy into disarray, causes them to lose faith in their future, enables one to organize one's own troops, create the necessary cadres and bring about the required ideological concentration on the common objective to be achieved. This, according to

Gramsci, is 'out and out historical mysticism, the awaiting of a sort of miraculous illumination'.

Whether Gramsci was a fair critic of Luxemburg's pamphlet is beside the point here. What matters is the unmistakable rejection of the war of movement as a strategy for power. This war is at best a tactic to be used if and when necessary, and which, in any case, only enables one to win 'positions which are not decisive'.[94] The royal road to power requires a different strategy: the war of position. This 'demands enormous sacrifices by infinite masses of people' (it is, in other words, a long-term mass event): 'an unprecedented concentration of hegemony is necessary ... since in politics the "war of position", once won, is decisive definitively.'[95]

In another notebook Gramsci pointed out that a 'social group ... must exercise leadership before winning governmental power (this is indeed one of the principal conditions for the winning of such power); it subsequently becomes dominant when it exercises power, but even if it holds it firmly in its grasp, it must continue to "lead" as well.'[96] This could be interpreted as a chronological prescription: first, sufficient hegemony is required to seize the state machine; then the actual seizure; then hegemonic consolidation. Elsewhere, however, Gramsci wrote: 'The truth is that one cannot choose the form of war one wants, unless from the start one has a crushing superiority over the enemy.'[97] It follows that in reality the 'moment' of seizing state power is precisely this: only a moment in a revolutionary process. Paradoxically, seizing it at the wrong moment may precipitate defeat in the longer term. What matters above all else is an accurate understanding of the enemy, because in politics (i.e. in positional warfare) 'the siege is reciprocal'.[98] The enemy too fights a war of position in what is a 'passive revolution' – that is, the gradual modification of its own power system by reorganizing hegemony. This reorganization is achieved by 'molecular changes which in fact progressively modify the pre-existing composition of forces, and hence become the matrix of new changes'.[99]

Thus, in Gramsci's view, the Italian Risorgimento was won by the moderates (i.e. Camillo Cavour and Piedmont) because Cavour, in adopting the principles of the war of position, understood not only his own role but also that of his opponent, Giuseppe Mazzini, who, on the contrary, 'does not seem to have been aware either of his own or Cavour's'.[100] Cavour was able to absorb elements from the Mazzinian camp by modifying his strategy and marshalling international support. Cavour's superiority did not rest only on his greater understanding of the national terrain, but also of the international relation of forces (in so far as Italian unification was made possible by the interplay of European power politics) and the fact that, after 1848, Europe had entered a period in which the war of movement would only lead to defeat.

It is important to realize that this kind of analysis holds as long as one goes beyond the military metaphors which permeated Gramsci's political discourse. These seem to suggest that everything is in the hands of the superior strategist who could be perceived as some sort of 'man of destiny', able to shape events more or less at will though within determinate historical constraints. It is true that Gramsci analysed fascism in terms of the intervention of a 'man of destiny' (Mussolini). But he saw Mussolini very much as the result of a particular equilibrium of forces (in the Italian case, the form assumed by the political crisis was a parliamentary stalemate), which required a solution to 'unblock' the system – in this case, an 'extra-parliamentary' solution.[101]

Fascism was the form which the 'passive revolution' had taken in Italy as a result of the post-war crisis. The rise of Mussolini was evidence of the weakness of the Italian ruling establishment. But it was the entire capitalist world which was undergoing a 'passive revolution', a reorganization of power necessitated by the requirements of the passage from 'the old economic individualism', that is, *laissez-faire*, to 'the planned economy', that is, managed capitalism.[102]

Gramsci used his main categories to analyse the development of American capitalism ('Fordism and Americanism'). America's favourable economic position was traced back to the absence of a feudal past and its consequently more 'rational demographic composition'. It benefited from not having numerous classes with no essential function in the world of production – i.e. purely parasitic classes made up of aristocrats, rentiers and their innumerable hangers-on. European 'tradition', European 'civilization', was, conversely, characterized precisely by the existence of such classes, created by the 'richness' and 'complexity' of past history.[103] Because it did not have 'this leaden burden to support', 'hegemony' in the USA 'is born in the factory and requires for its exercise only a minute quantity of professional political and ideological intermediaries'.[104] The high level of wages characteristic of Fordist production was the 'ideological' means whereby the compliance of the workers was obtained.[105] It is perhaps in this passage, more than elsewhere, that one can feel the *materiality* of Gramsci's concept of hegemony: it is far more than a mere matter of propaganda and instilling the 'right' ideas, a sort of unremitting global brainwashing. It is something which includes conditions of existence, such as a desirable standard of living, as well as the development of a 'well-articulated skilled labour force'.

Where Gramsci innovated little was in the concept of the party: having expanded the concept of hegemony well beyond the old Leninist notion of the ideological battle, he gave the party tasks which such an organization was simply unfit to perform. The old Leninist party was supposed to be the vanguard of the revolution. The old (Kautskyist) social-democratic party was supposed to await the moment of the capitalist crisis. But Gramsci's party had a far more formidable task: it had to construct a new state in the enlarged sense. It fell to Gramsci's successor, Togliatti, in the much more favourable conditions of post-war Italy, when democracy had been established, to attempt to construct a *partito nuovo*, a new mass party organizationally and ideologically better equipped than either the Leninist party or the old workerist SPD. Gramsci had explained what the tasks of this party, this 'new prince' (after Machiavelli), were to be. He did not provide an indication of what it should be. There are, of course, passages in his writings where the word 'party' is used loosely (e.g. a newspaper can be a 'party').[106] But by decoding it thus, the concept becomes so general as to be either virtually meaningless, or it implodes into its reverse: the tasks of the revolution cannot belong to a party or parties, but are devolved to a multiplicity of terrains and struggles. Such an interpretation, so subversive of the Leninist concept of the party, is possible and legitimate; but it does not belong to the historical Gramsci.

The central merit of *this* Gramsci (if we can talk of 'centrality' in a thought which is so diffuse) is that, not unlike Otto Bauer, he abandons the dilemma 'reform or revolution' in the only possible way: by going beyond it. The concept of revolution can refer either to the seizure of state power, or to the whole process of transition from one society to another. In the first case, revolution is only an aspect of a much longer process in which reforms prevail. In the second case, i.e. 'revolution as a process' or establishment of a new hegemony, there is no definitive single act of seizure: it is a war of position. Revolutions in the traditional sense thus do not resolve anything on their own, though they may re-open possibilities which had previously been foreclosed. The central task remains – namely, that of creating a new form of society in which the prevailing social relations are significantly different from those prevailing hitherto.

By the end of the 1930s the Left in Western Europe was as far from this goal as it had ever been. It was underground and persecuted in Germany, Austria and Italy; defeated and decimated in Spain; excluded from power in Great Britain; and marginalized in France. Only in the Nordic periphery, in some of the Scandinavian countries, did the Left possess strength and power. Authoritarian and semi-authoritarian governments of the Right held sway nearly everywhere else.[107] In Bulgaria, a military putsch in 1923 paved the way for the royal dictatorship of King Boris in 1934. In Albania, Ahmed Zogu established his dictatorship in 1924 and turned himself into King Zog in 1928. In Poland, the hero of the war against the Bolsheviks, General Josef Pilsudski, took over in 1926. In Lithuania, Antanas Smetona established a dictatorial regime after 1926 which led to the establishment of a one-party system in 1932. In 1929 King Alexander established an authoritarian regime in Yugoslavia. In Romania, thanks to a royal *coup d'état* in 1938, King Carol II had full powers. In 1934, in Estonia, Konstantin Päts established his dictatorship. In the same year, in Latvia, Karlis Ulmanis had staged his *coup d'état*. Throughout the inter-war period up to 1944, Hungary was ruled by the relatively benign dictatorship (by the standards of the time) of Admiral Miklos Horthy. In Greece General Joannis Metaxas became the *de facto* dictator after 1936. In Finland in 1930, under pressure from the semi-fascist Lapua movement, the government promulgated a series of anti-communist bills banning communist publications, arresting all communist and left-socialist members of parliament, and making all legal activity by the communists impossible.[108]

In the Soviet Union the construction of socialism in a form which most of the West European Left would, sooner or later, reject totally, proceeded at precipitous speed amid heroic deeds and unspeakable crimes.

The approaching war recast Europe once again, splitting it apart and exacerbating the divisions of the Left. With no noteworthy exceptions, however, the Left in Western Europe – both communists and social democrats – forswore all insurrectionary conceptions where democratic conditions prevailed, and committed itself to a reformist path. How 'revolutionary' or radical these reforms would be, remained a matter for debate and analysis. One thing was certain: the form of the October Revolution (and, further away in history, the Paris Commune or the barricades of 1848) came to be seen as unrepeatable, if not undesirable.

CHAPTER FOUR

The War, Resistance and Its Aftermath: The Rise and Fall of West European Communism 1939–48

IN 1917 THE First World War had engendered the first communist state and in 1919 an international communist movement. With the exception of the People's Republic of Mongolia, no new communist regimes emerged between the wars. The Second World War provided European communism with a second chance to establish itself as a significant political force. In the aftermath of the conflict the Soviet model was extended to much of Eastern Europe, while in the West communism reached the zenith of its influence and power in 1945–46. When the dust had settled, Europe, and with it socialism, had become effectively divided. In Eastern and parts of Central Europe a form of authoritarian socialist society was created, only to be bitterly denounced by the social-democratic majority of the Western labour movement. This lasted until 1989–90, when each of the socialist states collapsed under the weight of internal dissent following the revocation of Soviet control. By 1991, when the USSR itself imploded, it had become apparent that no novel socialist phoenix would arise from the ashes of over forty years of authoritarian left-wing rule – at least for the foreseeable future.

In Western Europe, with the exception of France (until the end of the 1970s) and Italy (until the decision of the Italian Communist Party in 1990–91 to 'reconstitute' itself as a non-communist party), the dominant voice on the Left in democratic Europe was that of the heirs to the Second International – the socialist or social-democratic parties. Thus this book, which is solely concerned with Western Europe, will of necessity deal principally with the social-democratic tradition which, after 1945, prevailed in an even more dominant manner than it had done between the wars.

Why did social democracy predominate? Fundamentally, it was due to the fact that once the war was over and normality re-established, the socialist parties reassumed their previous positions of influence, immensely helped by the rapidly developing Cold War. Their prestige had not been seriously damaged during the war, even though, as we shall see, they had not covered themselves in glory: in none of the countries ruled by the Nazis or their allies had the socialists been in the vanguard of the struggle. This remarkable continuity should cause no surprise. The Second World War, arguably the most devastating international war in the history of humanity, resulted in minimal changes in the European state system such as the incorporation of the Baltic republics into the USSR, the westward shift of Poland's borders, and the division of Germany – puny changes when compared to the comprehensive restructuring that followed the Napoleonic wars or, indeed, the First World War.

If the war had shattered anything, it was the already damaged belief that capitalism, if left to its own devices, would be able to generate the 'good society'. By extension the war had also hurt pro-capitalist parties: in the first post-war elections they were in retreat everywhere. To achieve creditable results, pro-capitalist conservatives had to resurface and reconstruct themselves within confessional Christian democratic parties, strongly imbued with populism and committed to social reforms, as in Italy and West Germany. The débâcle of the non-fascist Right in the first post-war elections even affected conservatives with an excellent war record, such as Winston Churchill's Tories, who suffered in 1945 a shattering and humiliating defeat. The reconstruction of Europe after the war required parties committed to a fair measure of state intervention aimed at achieving social equality and the redistribution of wealth. The agenda had shifted to a more statist form of politics and hence – at least for the immediate post-war period – to the Left. In a continent shattered by war and haunted by memories of the Depression of the 1930s, there was no room for unreconstructed conservatism.

The role played by social democracy in the post-war period of reconstruction will be the subject-matter of subsequent chapters. Here I want to examine what the war meant to the Left in general and trace the vicissitudes of the main Western communist parties up to 1948.

The beginning of the Second World War, like the outbreak of the First, shattered the European Left, dividing communists from socialists as severely as in the 1920s. The immediate cause was the non-aggression pact entered into by the USSR and Germany on 23 August 1939. Not having been consulted or informed beforehand, all communist parties in the world were taken by surprise: the twin pillars of their policy – defence of the first socialist state and anti-fascism – were now mutually inconsistent. At first the contradiction was glossed over by rationalizing the pact – not unjustifiably – as the inevitable Soviet response to the appeasement policies of Britain and France, perceived (by Moscow) as a strategy to steer Nazi aggression towards the East.[1] Not a single communist party failed – in this first phase – to denounce Nazi Germany as the principal enemy.[2] For example, on 4 September, the day after the Anglo-French declaration of war, the Dutch Communist Party declared that 'Barbaric German fascism has unleashed a rapacious war in Europe'.[3] The French communists voted in favour of the war credits. The headline of the PCF paper L'Humanité on 26 August 1939 was 'Union of the French nation against the Hitlerite aggressor', and it urged a rapprochement between Paris and Moscow.[4] The French government refused and, instead, began a full-scale persecution of the PCF, banning *L'Humanité*, arresting communist deputies, dissolving the party and sending leading militants to prison camps.[5]

Until 24 September, when the Communist International declared that the war was imperialist rather than anti-fascist, the Communist Party of Great Britain (CPGB) had taken an intransigent anti-Nazi stand and had even published its views in 50,000 copies of a penny pamphlet by Harry Pollitt, its leader. Until then only Palme Dutt had opposed this policy. It took a week of tormented discussions before, on 3 October 1939, the Central Committee of the CPGB announced its support for the Moscow line by twenty-one votes to three.[6]

Between 17 and 28 September the secret protocols of the Soviet-German Pact dividing north-eastern Europe into Soviet and German spheres of influence were applied in full.[7] Soviet troops occupied the Ukraine and Western Byelorussia, re-establishing the pre-1920 Russian frontiers, the first of a sequence of events which would lead to the Soviet occupation of the Baltic states of Estonia, Latvia and Lithuania, part of Poland and the invasion of Finland. The USSR and Germany entered a new agreement, this time a veritable friendship pact, not a non-aggression treaty. Ambiguity was no longer a possible option. Communists had to choose: internationalism (in practice, defence of the motherland of socialism) or patriotism. In what might be described as a direct response to the 'social-patriotism' of most socialists in 1914, they hoped, however, perversely, for 'internationalism'. As Hobsbawm has written:

> There is something heroic about the British and French CPs in September 1939. Nationalism, political calculation, even common sense, pulled one way, yet they unhesitatingly chose to put the interests of the international movement first. As it happens, they were tragically and absurdly wrong.[8]

French and British communists followed the Comintern line by declaring that the war was not anti-fascist but imperialist, and attributed to France and Britain the responsibility for its continuation. The damage this new policy caused Western communism and its credibility was severe in the extreme. The persecuted German communists, many of whom were in a concentration camp at Dachau, found themselves in the grotesque position of condemning British imperialism and suggesting that Germans would gain nothing if they escaped Nazism in order to become subject to the British.[9] Others were less preposterously servile: the Italian Communist Party never stopped identifying fascism and Nazism as the main enemy, even though it abandoned the line of anti-fascist unity. Thus the PCI declared in June 1940 (after Mussolini's entry into the war): 'The Italian people has but one enemy, fascism.'[10]

When on 22 June 1941 Germany invaded the Soviet Union, the situation was totally changed. The 'imperialist' war had been transformed into an anti-fascist one. On 13 July Britain and the USSR became allies. This time there was no need of instructions from Moscow: the new line was spontaneously adopted by all communists and, once again, the defence of the socialist motherland and anti-fascism became part of the same struggle. From then on until the end of the war, the communist parties played a considerable, often a leading role in the Resistance against Nazism. In Britain the only fully legal West European communist party in a non-neutral country supported the war effort unreservedly and patriotically.[11] In neutral Sweden the communists unsuccessfully strove for a so-called 'active' neutrality, i.e. one which would favour the anti-Nazi forces. In Spain the (illegal) PCE sought to avoid the entry of Spain into the war alongside the Axis powers.[12] The Comintern directive of 22 June 1941 established quite clearly that the final aim of the movement, the achievement of socialism, was to be put into abeyance: absolute priority had to be given to the anti-fascist effort. This precept was taken to its extreme conclusion when the USSR decided to disband the Comintern, presumably to improve its relations with the Allies, and to leave each communist party free from any formal control and obligation.[13] Thus ended the less than glorious history of Lenin's Communist International.

The entry of the USSR into the war led to a considerable rapprochement between socialists and communists. Because the communists played a greater role in the Resistance against Nazism than did the socialists, and because they seemed less concerned to ensure that post-war reconstruction should proceed along socialist lines, their priority being the defence of the USSR, they were better able to forge links with all other anti-fascist parties. In the majority of cases this reciprocal respect would last only until the end of the hostilities or, at most, the commencement of the Cold War. On the whole there remained an unalterable, and usually well-founded, distrust between the communists and all the other parties.

European socialists reacted to the vicissitudes of war in a less uniform way than the communists. Much depended on the situation facing their respective countries. Of the neutral countries, the socialists were insignificant in Switzerland and Ireland and banned in Spain. But in neutral Sweden the record of the SAP, now in a coalition of national unity even though it had an absolute majority, was rather mixed. Like the USSR in 1939, and with as much justification, the SAP wanted to avoid being dragged into the war. As a result, it co-operated fully with Germany in all aspects of trade and commerce and regarded the Swedish communists as a much greater security risk than the Swedish Nazis.[14] Sweden supplied Germany with almost all the iron ore and timber required, and from June 1940 to August 1943 Swedish railways ferried more than two million German soldiers to and from Narvik in Norway and Rovaniemi in Finland – a shameful episode partially redeemed by Sweden's refusal to sign a treaty with Germany or to stop providing asylum to Jews and resisters.[15]

In unvanquished Britain the Labour Party had returned to government in May 1940 in the national coalition led by Winston Churchill; it was thus the only socialist party in power in the whole of belligerent Europe. This unique position would enable the British Labour Party to tackle the tasks of post-war reconstruction with an unequalled experience of government. As for the war, Labour had no major strategic decision to take once it had thrown in its lot with the national coalition.

The situation facing socialists was totally different in the Axis countries, their allies and the countries subject to their rule (virtually the rest of continental Europe). Here the choice facing the Left was either passivity and acceptance of the situation, or active armed resistance.

In two of the occupied countries, Denmark and France, some (in Denmark virtually all) socialists co-operated, though unenthusiastically, with Nazism. In Denmark the government (a coalition of radicals and socialists) resolved 'to place its neutrality under the protection of the Germans' and to form a wider national government with the other two main parties.[16] The government agreed to ban the Danish Communist Party (June 1941) and to adhere to the Anti-Comintern Pact (November 1941), while the social democrat Vilhelm Buhl became prime minister in May 1942. Nazi–socialist co-operation came to a virtual end after the communist-organized wave of strikes of July 1943. The Nazis unsuccessfully tried to coerce the government into instituting a state of emergency and were forced to control Denmark directly.[17] The only open gesture of defiance outside the ranks of the Communist Party came from Danish diplomats in London and Washington who formed the Free Danish movement.[18] Danish co-operation never extended to complicity in the destruction of Danish Jews. On the contrary, when, after August 1943, the Nazis planned to deport all Danish Jews to Germany, a daring rescue operation – unparalleled in Europe – was mounted with the full co-operation of the population: 95 per cent of the 7,800 Jews were hidden and then transported to safety in Sweden. Thus, one of the most glorious pages of Danish history was written.[19]

The Nazis were less successful in Holland, where their attempt to 'de-marxify' the SDAP failed against the intransigent opposition of most of the membership and their leader, Koos Vorrink.[20] In Belgium, as we saw in chapter 3, the socialist leader Hendrik de Man enthusiastically collaborated with the Germans. In Norway the socialist cabinet opposed the archetypal Nazi collaborator and head of the puppet regime, Vidkun Quisling (whose unpopularity was such that the Germans were forced to rule Norway directly), and eventually went into exile with the king. They joined the Dutch and Belgian governments in London and became utterly dependent on British initiatives.[21]

In Austria, part of Germany since the *Anschluss* of March–April 1938, the remnants of the socialist movement were not able to generate significant clandestine activity. The only serious political force in the underground was the Kommunistische Partei Österreichs (the KPÖ) which, after the *Anschluss*, had improved its position within the Left. The socialists' failure to organize a Resistance movement probably spared them from complete annihilation, thus preserving their strength for the post-war period.[22]

Like most of the population, the Austrian socialists had supported the principle of a Greater Germany. They accepted that post-war Austria would be a separate state again only after the Moscow Declaration of November 1943 in which the Allied foreign ministers designated Austria, schizophrenically but correctly, as both a victim and an accomplice of Nazi Germany to be 're-established', consequently, as an independent state after the war.

In Czechoslovakia the leading force in the Resistance was the Czech Communist Party and not groups associated with the British-backed government-in-exile of Eduard Benes, which included the socialists.[23] Finland was a special case. Invaded by the USSR in 1940, its government, led by the Social Democratic Party, welcomed the Nazi invasion of the USSR. The socialist speaker of the Finnish Parliament declared on 20 July 1941: 'We are not alone, that nation in Europe which is the most fit for battle and the most efficient, the German nation, is now crushing with its steel army our traditional, ever treacherous and ever deceitful enemy.'[24] In so saying, the social democrats were at one with public opinion: as late as the autumn of 1942 a clear majority, including a majority of social democrats, were in favour of a final German victory.[25]

In Italy there was no armed resistance to speak of until 1943. It was preceded by strikes in some of the main northern cities in March 1943. These and the decisive advance of the Allies in the south precipitated the decision of the Grand Fascist Council to force Mussolini to resign (25 July). This led to the ignominious flight of the king, his court and his new prime minister, General Pietro Badoglio, who all ran away to the south, leaving the Italian people and the Italian army in disarray – a textbook case, if ever there was one, of a spineless and wretched 'ruling' class.

The Partito Socialista Italiano di Unità Proletaria (PSIUP) joined forces with the more numerous communists in the left-wing Garibaldi brigades of partisans which formed the backbone of the armed Italian Resistance, although, as elsewhere, Allied drops of weapons and food tended to favour the pro-monarchist groups, or those of the Catholics or even the radical Action Party brigades (the group Giustizia e Libertà). Even in the liberated areas at the end of 1944 (i.e. south of Florence), the membership of the PSIUP was not only inferior to that of the Christian democrats (not surprisingly: the socialists were never strong in the south outside some parts of the Apulia), but also to that of the communists.[26]

In politics as in military matters, the Italian socialists never had the initiative, while the communists knew precisely what to do, though only after the return of Togliatti from the USSR in March 1944. The PCI broke the political stalemate caused by the anti-fascist parties' refusal to recognize the monarchist government. The communists agreed to co-operate with it and to postpone all constitutional questions to the post-war period. The other parties followed the communist lead. On 21 April Italian communists were, for the first and only time in their history (and for only three years), in government.

On 6 June, in his *Instructions to All Comrades and to All Party Cadres*, Togliatti declared:

> Always remember that the aim of the insurrection is not the imposition of political and social transformations in the socialist or communist sense. Its aim is national liberation and the destruction of fascism. All other problems will be solved by the people through free popular consultation and the election of a Constituent Assembly once the whole of Italy is liberated.[27]

Even though 'all problems' were to be solved later, the thoughts of Togliatti, in reality, were directed towards the post-war period. His party would then need to consolidate the position of prestige it was bound to acquire during the Resistance. It had to become a 'national' party just as the German SPD had done during the First World War, and the French communists during the heyday of the Popular Front. National symbols, such as the tricolor flag, Garibaldi and the Risorgimento tradition would have to be woven into communist discourse, alongside the red flag. The post-war party statute established that at the end of party meetings and demonstrations, the participants would have to sing the national anthem (though, musically speaking, it is quite unworthy of the land of Vivaldi and Verdi), along with the *Internationale* and *Bandiera Rossa*.

Like the PCI, the Italian Socialist Party fought in the Resistance with an eye to the post-war period, though this eye was both wandering and unfocused. Pietro Nenni, the PSIUP leader, tried to outflank the communists from the left when, on 3 September 1944, at the party congress, he came out in favour of a socialist republic as the immediate goal of the struggle.[28] The impression gained abroad was negative, as evidenced by an internal Foreign Office memo which noted with uncanny accuracy: 'This is very silly ... but then the Italian Socialist Party is a remarkably silly party. It is living in a world of its own making, using language coined in the '20s and doomed to be eaten up by the much more astute Communist Party.'[29] Nenni had an additional problem: even during the war his party suffered from traditional factional infighting, which was further exacerbated by the fact that his right-wing opponents within the party were receiving funds from the USA (especially from the American Federation of Labor).[30]

In Italy at least, the situation facing the socialists had been clear-cut from the beginning: they were never in a position to consider any form of compromise with fascism. Their anti-fascist record remained unsullied. In France this was not the case. In 1940 the country had been defeated, but not completely occupied. In Vichy France there was a semblance of autonomy under Marshal Pétain. The French socialists of the SFIO were unsure what to do when the country surrendered to Germany in 1940.

Against Léon Blum's advice, a majority of socialist deputies and senators (90 out of 168) led by Paul Faure voted to hand over all powers to Pétain, thus accepting the German *diktat*. Only thirty-six voted against it.[31] The SFIO collaborators justified their action, which was overwhelmingly determined by their anti-communism, on pacifist grounds.[32] They were, by and large, the representatives of socialist notables for whom the party often represented little more than a means to acquire and maintain positions of power. The new situation had opened the way for further personal advancement and they were loath to let it pass. They were in the majority: only eighty parliamentarians voted against Pétain in a parliament which, having been elected in 1936 when the Popular Front triumphed, was probably the most left-wing National Assembly France had elected since 1848. One should add, however, that this Pétainist majority was truly representative of French public opinion. In July 1940 the vast majority of the French were in no mood for resistance.

Blum's followers started the Comité d'Action Socialiste (CAS), reorganized the party as a fighting force and, in the spring of 1943, reacquired the label of SFIO. Of course, many who regarded themselves as socialists joined whatever form of local resistance they could find, irrespective of what the leadership said or did. Many of these activists tended, not unjustifiably, to remain suspicious of party labels and began to join the SFIO only later, when liberation was in sight and the contours of peacetime politics (and the prospects of a strong PCF) began to be discernible.[33]

In devising its programme and its strategy, the SFIO meticulously followed the guidelines laid down by Blum, who had been arrested in September 1940 by the Vichy authorities, handed over to the Gestapo in March 1943 and sent to Buchenwald concentration camp, where he remained until the end of the conflict. Blum's most important directive was to recognize Charles de Gaulle as the sole leader of the Resistance. In a note of November 1942 to de Gaulle (written at his behest), to be forwarded to Roosevelt and Churchill, he was full of praise for the general, whom he described as the incarnation of French unity, adding that 'without him nothing would have been possible.'[34] In reality, the French socialists needed de Gaulle to retrieve some of their lost legitimacy.[35] Unlike the communists, they did not have their own Resistance organizations and, consequently, their distinctive contribution did not emerge as limpidly.[36]

The socialists distinguished themselves from the communists in many other important respects, especially in their considerably greater output of programmes and policy documents.[37] The communists were anxious, as they had been during the debates leading to the formation of the Popular Front, to keep in abeyance any discussion of radical change in the post-war era for fear of weakening the unity of the anti-fascist front or hindering Allied victory over Germany. The socialists had no such qualms.

All the SFIO projects for social reform were marked by the conviction that there could not be a return to the capitalism of the 1930s. The bourgeoisie, having lost its will to command, could no longer be a ruling class. Social emancipation was inevitable. The *Projet de Charte économique et sociale* and the document *Réformes économiques de structure* (both drafted in 1944) declared that full employment would be one of the goals of the post-war state. Wealth would be redistributed, planning instituted. The coalmines, the chemical and metal industries, would be taken into public ownership alongside insurance firms, banks and all public utilities. The country would be thoroughly modernized: 'France cannot remain a country of artisans and farmers as in Pétain's reactionary romantic dreams.'[38] The social reforms of 1936 would be protected and developed and some system of workers' participation would be introduced.[39] A new deal would be offered to the people of France's colonies. Full decolonization was not mentioned; it was assumed that it would eventually come about after a lengthy process of education and emancipation.

These proposals made no difference at all to the conflict, or to the relation of forces within the Resistance, or to the extent to which any of these proposals were implemented after the war. As Andrew Shennan notes: 'The study of postwar reforms was dismissed by the majority of resisters as irrelevant to the main aim of carrying on the struggle against Germany.'[40] The main function of these schemes, if any, was to demarcate factions and currents of ideas within the party itself. What the French socialists said or thought mattered very little during the war. There were really only three forces of any significance within the French Resistance. The first was de Gaulle and his supporters in London and throughout France. The second was the so-called Mouvements Unis de la Résistance (MUR), the organized resistance of those without parties who, by the end of 1942, had accepted Gaullist political leadership.[41] The third was the PCF.

Ideologically poles apart, de Gaulle and the communists otherwise had much in common: they were both apparently unconcerned with plans of post-war reconstruction and felt that the main thing was to get on with the war. Thus, the PCF had no hesitation in accepting the crisp and succinct programme that the intrepid Jean Moulin, on behalf of de Gaulle, had proposed to the first meeting of the Conseil National de la Résistance. The first paragraph elegantly and concisely said: *Faire la guerre* (make war), while those that followed were generic commitments to a return to republican democracy and French prestige. Jean Moulin then explained that de Gaulle's position was that, though political parties were necessary in a democracy, the parties of post-war France did not have to be the same as those of pre-war France; they should reflect the main ideological blocs (*les larges blocs idéologiques*). The communists agreed heartily.[42] The general and the communists, for entirely different reasons, were both highly suspicious of their Anglo-Saxon allies. For the communists they were the 'capitalist' side of the anti-fascist alliance: temporary companions and future foes. For de Gaulle, the Allies, and the detested Churchill in particular, were guilty of taking full advantage of the intolerably humiliating position in which his conditions of exile and his lack of political power had placed him – the living embodiment of France. This led de Gaulle to have far more sympathy for the USSR and its friends than he would have otherwise had. The sympathy was reciprocated: the USSR recognized de Gaulle's Free French committee before Britain did; de Gaulle adopted, word for word, the PCF's slogan: 'national liberation cannot be separated from national insurrection.'[43]

There were, of course, several occasions on which de Gaulle and the communists clashed: de Gaulle wanted to choose which communists should join his government (the PCF wanted party appointees); de Gaulle was reluctant to purge Vichy collaborators from the administration of liberated Algeria.[44] Nevertheless, there was much to unite Gaullists and communists who were both equally distrustful of other parties: the communists, because they were not communist; de Gaulle, because he had an intense loathing for political parties, which he regarded as squabbling associations of petulant and flatulent politicians seeking their own aggrandizement rather than that of France – a fairly accurate assessment of Third Republic politics. Of course, the PCF too was a party. But at least for the time being, it appeared to have put aside its aberrant and unpatriotic ideology to devote itself to the salvation of the nation. .

The socialists, like de Gaulle, toned down their anti-communism as the war proceeded. Thus, after the Soviet entry into the war, Blum described the PCF in his self-critical book *A l'Echelle humaine*, written in jail in 1941, as a 'foreign nationalist party', because of its attachment to the USSR. Less than two years later (15 March 1943), however, in a letter to de Gaulle he said that a 'French nation without the participation of the Communist Party would be neither complete nor viable', just as 'no international community without the USSR would be complete or viable'.[45] This was not reciprocated by the communists who, as liberation approached, became more critical of the socialists.[46]

Not only in France but also in Yugoslavia, Greece, France, Czechoslovakia, Italy and elsewhere, the communists were 'the bravest of the brave'.[47] That had been the case even where bravery was most difficult: Germany. The activities of narrow conservative anti-Nazi circles, which culminated in the generals' bomb plot of 20 July 1944, have tended to obscure the daring and heroism of left-wing activists and of the communists in particular.[48]

The war turned out to afford Western communists their finest hour. They could fight fascism and Nazism, be true internationalists, defend the USSR, be flawless patriots and all without inconsistency. Instead of being reviled in a ghetto of their own, they were praised by all: by Churchill, by Roosevelt and by de Gaulle. The world had finally become black and white, with clearly defined battlelines: on one side there were the forces of darkness, fascism and Nazism; anyone willing and able to fight them belonged to the other side, to the forces of light, democracy and social progress. The strategy was equally clear: armed combat and insurrectionary tactics, the political means which they had always considered superior to all others. The organizational form this combat required approximated to that of an army and consequently to that of the Leninist party with its top-to-bottom command structure and its iron military discipline. The revolutionary communist parties which the Comintern had set up between 1920 and 1922, when it was assumed that Europe was on the brink of revolution, were ill-suited to electoral politics, but turned out to be the best organizational weapon for the conduct of disciplined and intrepid partisan warfare.

The communists did not forcefully advance the issue of the reshaping of post-war society. Most of the militants believed that raising this too early would simply weaken the anti-fascist coalition by introducing divisive concerns. In any case, there could not be any doubt: the future was bound up with socialism. Fascism and Nazism had been the most naked expression of capitalist violence, towards whose destruction the motherland of socialism, the USSR, had contributed in a decisive and unquestionable fashion. Between 1943 and 1946 Soviet prestige was at its highest. Planning and collectivization, communist leadership and Stalin's guidance, had demonstrated the superiority of the Soviet system. In the rest of Europe the Depression of the 1930s had confirmed that capitalism could offer only unemployment and misery, while in Germany and Italy it had produced monsters. It was thus simply inconceivable to most communists and many socialists that the peoples of liberated Europe, once free to choose their own destinies, would not rally round the red flag.

Though the Resistance did not provide the communists with the possibility of a socialist insurrection at the end of the war, at least in the western part of Europe, it went a very long way towards legitimizing them. Having fought bravely, they could no longer be excluded from politics on the grounds that they were not patriotic. The communists would thus be able to participate in the establishment of the new post-war order which, it was generally agreed, would have to be radically different from the pre-war era.

For the communists, as for all other forces involved in it, the importance of the Resistance was essentially political. For many of the participants, however, the Resistance was a great moral quest, a way of redeeming their country and their fellow citizens from a collective guilt: the stigma of having allowed the establishment of repressive and war-mongering regimes (Italy, Germany), or of not having been able to keep them at bay. This moral and psychological dimension cannot be ignored. It enabled a whole people, not just those few who did resist, to claim that they were not passive objects of history, at first enslaved by Nazism, then liberated by others, but that they deserved their freedom because they had fought for it. This recovered national pride was a powerful element in the establishment of democratic rule in

Western Europe after the war. A sense of one's worth and dignity, and the self-confidence which goes with it, are indispensable ingredients of democratic politics.

The historiographical debate on whether or not the Resistance had a military importance, interesting as it is, misses out the central features delineated above. Only Albania and Yugoslavia were actually liberated by the Resistance. In some countries (for instance, Italy and Greece, and to a much lesser extent France), the Resistance almost certainly prevented greater casualties among the Allies, but was not decisive. In others, such as Norway, the German forces were more firmly in control of the country when Berlin fell to the Red Army than after the first months of occupation.[49] In some instances, a general attitude of non-co-operation, such as the one reported in a German survey on French railways, was so effective that the Nazi authorities could not use the network effectively.[50]

The Resistance was the key factor determining the balance of forces between the socialist and communist components of the traditional Left in Western Europe after the war. There is some correlation between the magnitude of the Resistance and communist political successes immediately after the war. In countries which had not been occupied by the Germans, such as Britain or neutral Sweden, or which either had an insignificant Resistance movement, as in Denmark, or one largely controlled from London, as in Belgium and Holland, the communist parties, after an initial electoral spurt (see Table 4.1 below), remained as politically negligible as during the inter-war period, while the socialist and social-democratic forces virtually monopolized the Left.

Leaving aside the territories liberated by the Red Army, there was an armed resistance of some significance only in Albania, Yugoslavia, Greece and Italy, and, more debatably, in France. In all these countries the communist parties, whose role in the struggle had been preponderant, increased their influence and prestige more than elsewhere. In Albania and Yugoslavia, the communists were able to acquire a monopoly of power, establish a one-party regime and a non-capitalist economic system, while remaining altogether independent of the USSR, unlike the other states of Eastern Europe.

Greece was a special case. The Kommounistiko Komma Ellados (KKE) tried to follow the Yugoslav and Albanian road of an armed route to power, but was prevented by a combination of conservative forces and Allied intervention. The KKE dominated the National Liberation Front (EAM) and its military wing, the National Popular Liberation Army (ELAS), which, between 1942 and 1943, had become mass organizations. By the time Greece was liberated, the KKE, an insignificant party prior to the war, had 300,000 members and EAM/ELAS two million members, almost 30 per cent of the population.[51] By 1944 EAM/ELAS was at war with its main rivals, the resistance movement EDES, which was backed by Churchill, determined to prevent the communists from obtaining political influence commensurate

Table 4.1 Communist parties' share of the vote in the first post-1945 election (%)

Austria	1945	5.4
Belgium	1946	12.7
Denmark	1945	12.5
Finland	1945	23.5
France	1945	26.0
Holland	1946	10.6
Italy	1946	19.0
Norway	1945	11.9
Sweden	1944	10.3
West Germany	1949	5.7

with their role in the Resistance. The KKE eventually agreed to sign an armistice in January 1945.[52] In the elections held on 31 March 1946, 40 per cent of the electorate abstained and the pro-monarchist parties won the day. The subsequent referendum on the monarchy, held on 1 September 1946, was rigged, and the monarchy won with two-thirds of the vote.[53] These events and the unchecked development of right-wing terror convinced the KKE that the parliamentary road to socialism all Western communists had been advocating (with Moscow's sanction) was no longer viable in Greece. They reorganized and launched an insurrection. Some communists, for instance the Yugoslav Edvard Kardelj, reprimanding the French and Italian communists in 1947 for their legalism, thought that the KKE, not so encumbered, faced a situation 'incomparably better than that which prevails in France and Italy'.[54] What he failed to realize was that the international situation had changed utterly. A Cold War had begun. The USA took over the guardianship of the West and, under the banner of the Truman Doctrine, promised to 'support free peoples who are resisting subjugation by armed minorities or outside pressures'.[55] Greece had become a 'hot' battlefield of the Cold War. With substantial American assistance, the Greek regular army crushed the KKE after bitter fighting throughout 1948 until the summer of 1949. The consequence of these events was that communism remained effectively banned in Greece (it was compelled to fight elections under other names and symbols), while socialists failed to become a credible force until the mid-1970s, when the Communist Party too was legalized. The practical elimination of the Greek Left from mainstream politics was one of the most important consequences of the Greek Communist Party's singular peculiarity: it was the only party which attempted to follow the insurrectionary route in the Western sphere of influence.

The two remaining countries where there had been some armed resistance were Italy and France. Here and only here Western communist parties managed to supplant the socialist parties as the main force of the Left for many years to come. This statement nevertheless needs qualifying. In France the PCF was larger than the Socialist Party from the very first post-war elections to the mid-1970s only. In Italy the PCI was just beaten by the socialists in the 1946 elections to the Constituent Assembly but, by the end of the year, it had overtaken them for good.

In Finland too, as in France, the communists, in spite of the Soviet invasion of 1940, emerged as the main party of the Left in 1945, but they were overtaken by the social democrats at the subsequent elections in 1948. The French and Italian anomaly of having communist parties with wider support than the socialists was linked to another: France and Italy remained the only democratic countries in Western Europe in which no left-wing government came to power. The Left achieved power in France only in 1981, when the PCF was no longer the main party of the Left.

With the exception of Italy (and France, where the communists peaked in the second elections in 1946 at 28.6 per cent), the first post-war results were also the communists' historical best. Never again would they achieve such a degree of popular support.

The principal cause for the popularity of communism in the West was the Soviet Union – also the principal cause for its subsequent unpopularity. Forty-five years of authoritarian regimes in Eastern Europe must not obscure the historical fact that the relative good fortune of communism in the West on the morrow of the war was due to the universal recognition of the pre-ponderant and determinant role of the USSR in the defeat of Nazi Germany. The Russo-German campaigns constituted 'the most terrible war that has ever been waged'.[56] While Great Britain, France and Italy suffered fewer military casualties than during the First World War, and the mainland of the USA stood untouched by destruction of any kind, the Soviet Union lost twenty million lives – more than all the dead of all the nations in the entire course of the Great War of 1914–18.[57] It is another strange irony of history that Western Europe was made free for democracy by the relentless advance of Stalin's Red Armies from the bloody furnaces of Stalingrad and the salient of Kursk to the bunker in Berlin, where the itinerary of the Third Reich was completed.

After the initial communist successes of 1945–46, decline rapidly set in. By 1948 communism ceased to have any political significance as an independ-ent force in Denmark and Norway, in Austria and West Germany, in Belgium and Holland, as well as in Britain (where, in 1945, the CPGB had obtained its only two post-war parliamentary seats).[58] In Sweden the Communist Party would eventually serve as a prop for the main party of the Left. Only in countries under right-wing authoritarian regimes, such as Spain and Portugal, did the communists remain the chief opposition force, a role they relinquished on the advent of democracy.

Why was initial growth never consolidated, and why did the respectable post-war results achieved by communists in, say, Belgium, Denmark and Norway not lead to a decisive advance? Many factors precipitated this stillbirth, the most significant being the Cold War and the division of Europe.

The communists had assumed a correspondence between international and national politics. They believed that the international entente between the 'progressive' capitalist countries (the USA and its allies) and the USSR would continue. This broad international anti-fascist coalition, they believed, would sanction the growth and development of other similar national coalitions. The assumption that there was such a correspondence was correct, but it worked in the opposite direction: the break-up of the international anti-fascist alliance and the beginning of the Cold War made it impossible for national coalitions to continue to include the communists. Nineteen forty-seven was the *annus horrendus* of communism. They were ousted or withdrew from the ruling coalitions of France, Italy, Norway, Belgium, Luxemburg and Austria. The Danish communists had already departed from government in 1945, while the Finns left in 1948. The Dutch communists had refused to take part in the national coalition because of the continuing Dutch colonial wars.

The other main factor which spelled the doom of communism in most of Western Europe was that, in peacetime, the demarcation between communist and social-democratic political demands had become obfuscated. The communists could offer only a more militant form of social democracy and, consequently, restricted the support obtained to the most class-conscious workers and the most committed intellectuals.

A hard core of militants organized along Leninist lines might have been all that was required to exploit a revolutionary situation. But since the goal pursued was electoral advancement in a non-revolutionary situation, it was necessary to appeal to a wide section of the population without alarming them with militancy of any sort. If the terrain for electoral competition was one in which only limited advances towards greater social progress were permissible, then social democracy offered the best chance for an electorate already alarmed by communist repression in Eastern Europe. Of course, some communist leaders understood that the tightly-knit Leninist party had to be superseded. In Italy Palmiro Togliatti advocated a *partito nuovo*, a new party, less centralized and more open than the traditional vanguard. He argued that now the party had to 'become an organization which is in the midst of the people and satisfies all their needs as they appear to the mass of the people. This is the great transformation that our party must carry through.'[59]

In the western part of Europe most communist parties were too weak even to consider a violent takeover. Those who were strong enough to consider it, such as the Finns, the French and the Italians, did not.[60] Few Western communists – apart from the PCI – understood that an overall restructuring of the party organization had to accompany a change in strategy. But even those leaders less far-sighted than Togliatti understood that they had little choice: there could be no return to the insurrectionary road advocated in the 1920s – a policy which had been a dismal failure. Thus the end of the Second World War signalled the definitive abandonment by West

European communism of the insurrectionary road as a viable route to power in a liberal democracy. This was certainly the prevailing view among the majority of the leadership, even though many rank-and-file militants harboured dreams of a Soviet-style takeover.

The very failure of the Greek insurrection may have influenced the communists to recognize the need for change, but the crucial factors in the abandonment of an insurrectionist strategy must be sought elsewhere. In the first place, there were obvious geopolitical considerations: the Americans and their allies were in control and had both the will and the strength to prevent a communist takeover. No help could be expected from the USSR: even the Greek communists of the KKE did not expect any, though they thought, mistakenly, that Tito's Yugoslav partisans might lend a hand.[61] Moreover, everywhere in Europe the communists had achieved some popular support under the banner of the struggle for democracy and the return to electoral politics. They could not count on the same degree of popular support following any decision to start an armed struggle for power.

Finally, the remote possibility of insurrection would only ever be worth considering in areas of strong communist presence: in France, Italy and Finland. Elsewhere, the relation of forces between the communists and the other political parties was just too unfavourable to the former. Even the USSR had given up on Western communism outside Italy and France, as became obvious later, when, in September 1947, at Szklarska Poreba in Poland, the USSR launched the Communist Information Bureau (the Cominform), a slimmer and less grandiose version of the Comintern, restricting its membership only to the communists that really mattered – that is, those still in power plus the French and Italian.

Having abandoned the road of insurrection and armed struggle, European communism adopted the strategy of capture of state power via participation in a coalition government. The survival of the wartime coalitions became one of the main aims of communist parties. Even in the United Kingdom the communists campaigned for the continuation of the national coalition, even though they were not in it, only to abandon this line once the election was called.

This 'coalitionist' strategy was based on the assumption that there would be considerable continuity between wartime and peacetime politics, and that the political understanding which had prevailed during the war would persist into the post-war period. Co-operation with other anti-fascist parties would continue, it was thought, and the communists would gradually emerge as the dominant political force. By legislative means such as nationalization, post-war governments would weaken the economic foundations of large-scale capital, thus depriving the conservative groups of their basis of support. However, as the preservation of coalition governments had become the primary goal, it was necessary to contain, to some extent, the front-line tactics of economic class struggle, such as strikes and factory occupation, since these would only destabilize the economy and frighten the middle classes. During the inter-war period, the communists had learned the importance of avoiding isolation and, during the war, the significance of being a national force.

The term 'people's democracy' was coined precisely to denote a form of state or regime led by a coalition government in which the communist party would have a significant share of power. The policies of this regime would be the enlargement of the public sector through nationalization of the most important enterprises, strengthening of the trade unions, development of organs of 'direct democracy' (vaguely defined), and a foreign policy generally oriented towards friendship with the USSR. With the development of the Cold War, 'people's democracy' became a euphemism designating communist regimes in Eastern Europe. But it originally represented a new departure in communist nomenclature. It was an attempt to go beyond the stark dichotomy in which all non-socialist regimes were simply 'bourgeois' and all socialist regimes the dictatorship of the proletariat.

The strategy of 'people's democracy' required for its success the continuation of the national and international wartime coalitions. It also involved the discovery of an autonomous and 'national road to socialism', different from the route taken in 1917 by the Bolsheviks. The communists now saw what they continued to call 'the revolution' as part of a developmental process, a continuation of indigenous radical bourgeois traditions whose symbols they could appropriate, and no longer as a dramatic rupture in the life of the nation. The antecedents of this national strategy were the Popular Fronts of the 1930s with the difference that, while at that time the communist parties had been reluctant to enter government (as in France and, initially, in Spain), they were now impatient to have as large a share as possible in ruling the country. Whenever they could, they developed an alliance strategy which would buttress their presence in the coalition. This had two aspects:

1. As far as their social-democratic rivals were concerned, the communists would seek to develop maximum unity with them, perhaps even leading to amalgamation. Although in Western Europe nothing came of it, the question of a socialist–communist merger had been posed by both Thorez and Togliatti. In November 1946, in an interview with *The Times*, Thorez declared: 'The French workers' party which we wish to create by the fusion of communists and socialists would be a guide towards this democracy, *nouvelle et populaire*.'[62] Togliatti was more cautious. Speaking in Florence on 3 October 1944, he broached the question of merging with the socialists: 'we shall have to wait for the liberation of the North [of Italy] before trying to bring about the creation of a single party.'[63] Amalgamation was, in fact, virtually imposed by the more powerful communists in some of the newly emergent people's democracies in Eastern and Central Europe, such as Czechoslovakia, Poland and East Germany. In the West, to achieve this aim it would have been necessary to isolate the anti-communist wing of social democracy.

2. As far as the 'bourgeois' parties of the centre were concerned, it was necessary to compromise as much as possible on traditional socialist demands in order to ensure that there could be no grounds for a break-up of the coalition (just as, during the war, socialist demands were dropped for the sake of national unity and the war effort).

The aim of this strategy was the permanent insertion of the communist party into the arena of legitimate national politics. This required the total removal of traditional anti-communism from 'normal' political discourse. The new ideological bond which would maintain unity among the 'democratic' parties of a people's democracy would be anti-fascism. In other words, the legitimation of communism required the delegitimation of anti-communism and of anti-communist parties. This, in turn, meant that to be anti-communist was incompatible with being a true anti-fascist.

As we have seen, this 'national road' strategy failed throughout Western Europe. The communists' claim that a people's democracy would be a more advanced form of bourgeois democracy was not credible. They were expelled from coalition governments or put in a position where they had no alternative but to leave. In all cases except Italy, the socialist or social-democratic parties remained in the coalition or became the main legitimate opposition. The entire direction of Western communist strategy had been aimed at establishing anti-fascism as the key concept for distinguishing the politically legitimate from the unacceptable. This failed utterly. The precondition for access to power in the West turned out to be anti-communism, that is, the acceptance of 'Western' values defined in Cold War terms.

The justification later offered for expelling the communists from coalition governments throughout Western Europe was the communist takeover of Czechoslovakia, which was regarded as demonstrating their unreliability as coalition partners. This was very much a *post facto* explanation, because the expulsion of communists from government in the West had occurred in 1947, while the takeover in Czechoslovakia took place in 1948; nevertheless, the justification did contain much that was valid. The successful strategy adopted by the Czech Communist Party resembled that of its (albeit unsuccessful) Western counterparts, and should be described briefly.

At its 1946 Congress the Czechoslovak Communist Party (the KSC) had emphasized that the current phase was that of a national-democratic, rather than socialist, revolution. It accepted, like other communist parties including the French and the Italian, that there could be different roads to socialism. It was a leading party in the national coalition. It was also the main force in the mass organizations which had sprung up in the country (the trade unions, the youth movement, the farmers' and women's organizations).[64]

In the 1946 elections the KSC obtained 38 per cent of the vote and 114 out of the 300 seats in the National Assembly; with its social-democratic allies, it had 153 seats, a clear majority. Klement Gottwald, the Czech communist leader and prime minister, had taken the people's democracy strategy so seriously that he had even been in favour of the Marshall Plan until he was dissuaded by the Soviet Union. Thus, the Czech communists found themselves in a position not unlike that of their French and Italian counterparts, similarly ensconced in coalition governments which included non-left-wing parties. The Cold War made these coalitions untenable. In 1947 the French and Italian communists were expelled from the national government of their respective countries and, later that year at the founding meeting of the Cominform, were upbraided for having allowed themselves to be evicted from power.[65]

The criticisms were harsh. The Soviet delegate, Andrei Zhdanov, urged the representative of the PCI, Luigi Longo, to go on the offensive.[66] The Yugoslav delegate, Kardelj, attacked the coalition strategy of the PCI and its commitment to a peaceful road to socialism, adding that 'The Italian leading comrades did not make sufficient and consistent use of our experiences.'[67] Milovan Djilas, who must have had time to reflect on this incident when he, in turn, became a victim of Titoist repression, chastised the French comrades for their opportunism and urged them to 'draw lessons from their work and the mistakes they have made'.[68] The Italians and French, thus rebuked, accepted the criticisms. Jacques Duclos, the PCF envoy, somewhat more unreservedly than Longo, added that there had been on their part 'obviously excessive respect for legalism and parliamentarism'.[69]

Unlike its Western counterparts, however, at the end of 1947 the KSC was still in power, controlled the main ministries and could form, in February 1948, a government without the parties of the centre and the Right. Having done so, with considerable popular support, it suppressed all other parties except the social democrats, whom it anyway swallowed up a few months later. Unlike the Italian or French communists, the KSC was able to mobilize, for the purposes of remaining in government, the strength of the organized working class.[70]

This road to power, the Czech road, was taken to be the strategic model for Western communism and the reason why communists could not be trusted. Communists – it was said – only pretend to follow the democratic road; covertly, they prepare the subversion of democracy; they appear to seek allies and seem willing to share power, but in reality they consider them 'useful idiots' to be discarded when the time comes; they proclaim their patriotism, while supporting the interests of the Soviet Union over and above those of their own countries, as had been evident after the Nazi–Soviet pact of 1939. Each of these affirmations and many like them could be backed (and were backed) by examples from recent political history. No ruling communist party offered itself for re-election in a genuine contest until 1990. In any case, no one-party system can be established democratically because no majority, however large, can bind future generations of voters.

Western communists could offer no reasoned argument to counter this. Their prudent and democratic behaviour, their moderation, their recognition of constitutional guarantees, their defence of civil rights, were no proof against the conviction that this was all a deception. Their credibility would have been enhanced by a refusal to give uncritical and systematic support to Soviet foreign policy and by a critique of the practices of socialism in Eastern Europe and in the USSR. This was not an option which really presented itself to the Western communists immediately after the war. The leadership of these parties could not ignore their own supporters, who believed that what was being constructed in the USSR and in the other countries of Eastern Europe was socialism; and, generally speaking, this belief was shared by rank and file and leaders alike.

Furthermore, to denounce Soviet socialism would break down the main demarcation line between social democracy and communism: it would thus have been tantamount to dissolving the party and joining social democracy. And the communist activists, so distrusted by social democrats, did not trust them in their turn: they were always talking about socialism while in reality compromising with capitalism.

In Western Europe, the main requirement for a regime of 'people's democracy', namely a strong communist party, existed only in Italy, France and Finland. In these countries the communists found themselves in coalition with a socialist or social-democratic party and a party of the Centre: in France with the Catholic-based Mouvement Républicain Populaire (the MRP); in Italy with the Democrazia Cristiana (DC – Christian Democratic Party), and in Finland with the Agrarian Party. These coalitions survived until 1947 or 1948. In these three countries the communists obtained, in this period, around one-quarter of the vote, more than twice the average of the communist vote in Belgium, Denmark, Holland, Sweden and Norway.

In electoral terms the strongest communist party was undoubtedly the French. The PCF obtained around 26 per cent of the vote in the two elections of 1945 and 28.6 per cent in 1946, thus becoming the largest French party both in the country and in the National Assembly. It had also become a truly national party with at least one deputy returned in virtually each *département*, making it the most nationally established of all French parties.[71] In all elections it was stronger than the SFIO. By comparison, the PCI was weaker. In the elections to the Italian Constituent Assembly (1946) it obtained 19 per cent, while the PSIUP just overtook it with 20.7 per cent, well behind the leading party, the DC, which had 35.2 per cent. Later, in 1948, the socialists and communists fought the elections together in a single electoral list, obtaining 31 per cent, a loss of 8 percentage points on their 1946 results. In Finland the communists obtained 23.5 per cent in 1945 and were second to the social democrats, who had 25.1 per cent; in 1948 they obtained 20 per cent to the 26.3 per cent of the social democrats and 24.2 per cent of the Centre Party.

The comparative electoral weakness of the PCI *vis-à-vis* the PCF was partly compensated for by its greater membership. By the end of 1946 the PCI had nearly two million members against 800,000 for the PCF. To some extent this gap was the result of differing policies. Togliatti's goal was the largest possible membership and he was not too worried about the ideological credentials of new recruits. The French communists were more careful, but they could also afford to have a smaller party than the Italians. In France there was no tradition of mass parties: neither the Catholics of the MRP nor the socialists of the SFIO had an organization remotely comparable to that of the communists. In Italy the DC had emerged – with the substantial help of the church – as a mass party at the centre of a network of associations and 'fronts' not unlike the Italian communists.

Both French and Italian communists consistently pursued the coalition strategy of 'people's democracies'. Both were eager to demonstrate their statesmanlike qualities and their sense of national responsibility. Both were intent on appeasing and winning over the middle classes and isolating what they called *les trusts* (PCF) or *i monopoli* (PCI). Accordingly, they discouraged strikes and high wage demands in favour of a policy favouring high industrial productivity. This was obviously the right policy given the low level of industrial output of the two countries. The containment of strikes demonstrated that both parties were determined to become national parties and not the representatives of the narrow corporate interests of the working class.

Thus Thorez, on 21 July 1945, told the miners of Waziers that to produce more coal was their class duty,[72] while Gaston Monmousseau, a veteran communist trade unionist, declared that 'strikes are a weapon of the trusts'.[73] In his famous Waziers speech, Thorez insisted on discipline, suggested that workers might consider giving up their holidays, and castigated absenteeism ('those who are lazy will never be good Communists or good revolutionaries, never, never'). But he also insisted that working conditions had to be improved, that coalmining should be made attractive in order to increase the number of miners, that women should be encouraged to work in the industry (in spite of the 'reactionaries who espouse the view that women should stay at home. There will not be any emancipation of women unless women achieve it for themselves').[74] Nevertheless, there is no question that production had become the top priority; thus the PCF's *Programme d'action gouvernementale* of November 1946, in its chapter on industry, placed much greater emphasis on the needs of production than on nationalization, while it did not mention workers' control or industrial democracy.[75] In spite of their radical rhetoric, the French communists courted the middle classes in an even more uninhibited way than the PCI, by declaring that they stood for the maximum of individual initiative and by blocking the Mendès-France plan to enforce an exchange of banknotes in circulation. The aim of this was to tax illicit wartime cash profits hoarded in mattresses.[76] In Italy a similar plan had been initiated by the communist minister of finance, Mauro Scoccimarro, only to be blocked by the Christian democrats, more consistent protectors of middle-class economic interests.

In August 1945, at a special economic conference called by the PCI, Palmiro Togliatti opposed subsidies, national economic planning ('utopian'), Soviet-type control over the economy, and called for increased production, British-type wartime controls, an anti-inflationary policy to protect small savers ('if they were ruined by inflation,' he said, 'they would be thrown into the arms of reactionaries and fascists'). Finally, he warned the trade unions to be more concerned with increasing production than wages.[77]

It should be said that in both France and Italy this attitude did not bring any benefits to the communists. On 19 February 1947, a few months before the break-up of the tripartite coalition, Togliatti complained bitterly:

> In the last years no political strike has taken place in Italy ... This is a country where the unions have signed a wage truce ... This is the surprising and absurd feature of the present economic situation: the working class and the unions are giving the best example and taking the necessary steps to preserve production, order and social peace to enable reconstruction to take place. On the other side a pack of political and economic speculators are taking advantage of the situation.[78]

In both France and Italy the two parties were responding not only to the objective economic requirements of the post-war situation, but also to the need for an alliance with the middle classes. The crucial difference between them was that for the French communists such an alliance did not entail a compact with middle-class parties. On the contrary, their policy, especially their pro-middle-class policy, sought to isolate the party with the widest middle-class appeal, the centre-left Catholic MRP, and to block any rapprochement between it and the SFIO. Throughout this period the PCF was working towards a left coalition between itself and the SFIO, thus still assuming that it was possible for the traditional Left to represent a significant section of the middle classes. This is why the 1945–47 period was punctuated by the PCF's repeated appeals to the SFIO to form a government without the MRP. When the crunch of the Cold War came, and the SFIO was forced to choose between the unreliable communists on their left and the safe and internationally respectable MRP on their right, they opted for the latter and the PCF found itself outside the governing coalition.

The Italian communists were equally unsuccessful in remaining in government, but their alliance strategy was markedly different from that of their French counterparts. It is true that, like the PCF, they sought to appeal directly to the middle classes, but they also recognized the central role of the DC in representing these groups. Consequently, all their efforts were directed towards maintaining the tripartite coalition of socialists, communists and Christian democrats. The compromise they pursued with the middle classes was deliberately broadened to include Christian democracy (even though this allowed the socialists to challenge them from the left). Of course, it can be argued that in Italy, unlike France, the Left did not have a majority, and that the PCI did not therefore have the option of fighting for a Left government;

the difference in strategy reflected a disparity in electoral strength. Nevertheless, it is equally clear that Togliatti hoped that such a compromise with the Catholics might keep the DC on a reformist course, and hinder the reconstitution of a conservative power bloc.

Togliatti was well aware of the complex social composition of Christian democracy and of its strength. In a major speech in Florence on 3 October 1944, he emphasized the vitality of Catholic organizations, which had been able 'to exist legally ... for nearly twenty years under the fascist regime, and therefore have many cadres who are at this moment going back into political life and are able to work to organize a large party quickly.' In this party there would be not only bourgeois property-owners, but also 'working people, even workers, but most of all peasants'.[79] Togliatti was trying to develop what political scientists would later refer to as a consociational democracy, a semi-permanent grand coalition, whose central axis would be left of centre. Thorez's project was far closer to the British model: a polarized two-party system with clear Left vs. Right ideological demarcations.

The difference in the tactics of the French and Italian parties can be better understood by comparing their approach to constitutional issues. In 1945 it was generally agreed that there could be no return to the previous constitutional regime: the Third Republic in France, the pre-fascist liberal state in Italy. Both countries therefore faced the question of drafting a new constitution. For the first time in their history, communist parties were called upon to share in the determination of the constitutional form of a non-socialist state. Both the PCF and the PCI were in favour of a single representative assembly with substantial powers, unhindered by a second chamber, a strong president, a powerful executive, or a supreme court. In practice, they both envisaged a system in which the main form of organization of politics would be through free and powerful political parties, which would be fully in control of the decision-making process.

This position coincided with an optimistic assessment of the electoral chances of communist parties and of the Left in general. The more restrained the system of constitutional checks and balances, the more easily could a left-wing parliamentary majority transform the social and economic landscape of the country.

In France the PCF was able to convince a very reluctant and badly divided SFIO to support it on the principle of a strong single-chamber legislature against the opposition of the MRP, and to incorporate it in the constitutional draft of May 1946 which was put to a referendum. The strategy was a disaster. The electorate, including, it appears, 600,000 socialist voters, rejected the draft.[80] An amended constitution, which provided for a second chamber, was narrowly approved, with the communists forced into diffident support. A little over one-third of the electorate voted for it, slightly less than one-third were against; and 31.1 per cent abstained. The new constitution contained many progressive clauses, such as sex equality, full employment, the right to strike, the right to education, the nationalization of monopolies, a social security service, and the institution of joint management–worker workplace committees.[81] But the PCF's intransigence over the political battle for the constitution had resulted in its isolation and the much feared rapprochement between the SFIO and the MRP.

The Italian communists, though starting with constitutional plans similar to those of their French counterparts, soon sacrificed them in order to ensure the stability of the entente with the Christian democrats. They even went as far as voting with the DC (in spite of strong socialist pressures) to enshrine in the constitution the 1929 Concordat with the church and to accept the Christian democrats' ideas for a regional devolution of power. The resulting constitution included traditional liberal principles and social and economic rights, such as the right to strike and to form trade unions. It also included a remarkably progressive clause (the second paragraph of Article 3), which asserted that 'It is the task of the Republic to remove obstacles of an economic and social nature which, limiting in fact the liberty and equality of citizens, prevent the full development of the human personality and the effective participation by all workers in the political, economic and social organization of the country.'[82]

Even though the political strategy of the Italian communists failed, because they were not able to remain in government with the Christian democrats, their constitutional strategy succeeded. The form of regime which they helped to establish survived the whole course of the Cold War, unlike the French Fourth Republic. With much justification, they could claim to be the main defenders of the Italian constitution and hence a constitutional party, and to have contributed decisively to the consolidation of democracy in Italy.[83] The electoral system of proportional representation, though not enshrined in the constitution, guaranteed them a parliamentary weight commensurate with their popular support, support which increased uninterruptedly until 1979. The form of organization they had chosen – that of the mass party supported by a network of collateral associations – enabled them to become established as an enduring feature of the political panorama. Their alliance with the Socialist Party lasted into the late 1950s. They never became a ghetto party cut off from power, in constant wait for the *dénouement* of a political drama in which they played no role. The massive popular support they obtained in the central territories of Italy, and especially in the cities and towns of the Emilia region, enabled them to develop a form of municipal socialism which was much admired and much studied.[84]

Compared with this, the record of the French Communist Party is less than brilliant. The constitution it had grudgingly accepted lasted little over ten years. At the moment when the communists had become its enthusiastic defenders, the Algerian crisis returned de Gaulle to power and led directly to the demise of the Fourth Republic and to a new constitution, which gave major executive powers to the president.

The trajectory described by the Finnish communists bears considerable similarity to those of the French and the Italian, although, as always, Finland constitutes a special case. In terms of its post-war electoral record, the Finnish Communist Party (SKP) ranks as a strong communist party along with the Italian and French, and it did surprisingly well in the 1945 elections. Unlike its French and Italian counterparts, however, it could not attribute this success to armed struggle, since there had been no major armed resistance against the Germans. The people of Finland had little reason to be grateful to the USSR: Soviet aggression had led to the Winter War of 1939–40, while the Continuation War of 1941–44 found Finland making common cause with Nazi Germany.

When the war began the SKP, already banned, was still a tiny group with no influence. The suggestion that it had underground mass support able to surface only after 1945 is probably unjustified.[85] However, the SKP had inherited a hard core of activists from the Suomen Sosialistinen Työväenpuole (SSTP), the Finnish Socialist Workers' Party, which was, between 1919 and 1923, the main left-wing alternative to the social democrats, and which represented an entirely indigenous brand of left-radicalism.[86] Moreover, the SKP was the sole beneficiary of the general post-war shift to the Left. Its nearest rival, the Social Democratic Party, bore the stigma of having been a member of a government which fought on the same side as the Nazis.

At its first legal congress, held on 4 and 5 October 1944, the SKP decided to follow the 'people's democracy' strategy developed elsewhere. Accordingly, it dropped its revolutionary programme and committed itself to a constitutional politics on the basis of a broad popular front.[87] It sought unity with the social democrats and an understanding with the Agrarian Party. However, the goal of creating a single party of the Left was thwarted by the expulsion from the Social Democratic Party of the pro-communist Vapaa Sana group, led by Karl Wiik. In its place the Finnish People's Democratic League (SKDL), an electoral alliance between the SKP, the Vapaa Sana group and other leftists, was established.[88]

The SKDL was dominated by the communists, but not overwhelmingly. It has been estimated that 130,000 of the 398,618 votes cast for it in 1945 belonged to the Vapaa Sana group and other left-social democrats. These two groups had nine of the forty-nine MPs gained by the SKDL. Though the key post of secretary-general was held by communists until 1965, when the independent socialist Ele Alenius was elected, throughout the post-war period the presidency of SKDL was not held by a communist.[89]

The League's electoral programme conformed to the people's democracy strategy: it sought the maintenance of anti-fascism as a unifying ideology, and the consequent banning of fascist organizations; a foreign policy in accordance with the principles of the United Nations; and a special relationship with the USSR.[90]

The positive electoral results of 1945, in which the SKDL obtained 23.5

per cent of the vote and emerged as the largest group in Parliament, encouraged the communist leaders to discuss a joint programme with the two other major parties. An agreement was concluded in April 1945. The communists and their allies obtained nearly one-third of the cabinet posts including, as in Czechoslovakia, the Ministry of the Interior, which naturally led to their control of the police. A pattern not dissimilar to the events in Czechoslovakia ensued. In the spring of 1946 the SKP launched a broad mass movement, backed by demonstrations, calling for social reform and the democratization of the army and the civil service. Unlike the Prague movement, this failed, and the social democrats were able to fight back. They succeeded in postponing internal trade union elections by alleging irregularities, and when the elections were finally held in 1947 the social democrats won a majority on an anti-communist platform.[91]

By May 1948, the agreement between the three main parties was virtually dead. Anti-communism had now re-emerged as an election issue. The SKDL, which had obtained forty-nine seats in 1945 in a 200–seat Chamber, now had only thirty-four seats and was offered a smaller role in government. The SKDL refused, left the government, and remained in opposition until 1966.[92]

Why the Communist Party in Finland did not follow the road taken by the Czech Communist Party has remained controversial.[93] Those who seek to explain the communist takeover in Eastern and Central Europe in purely geopolitical terms face a challenge here: the geopolitical position of both countries was strikingly similar in that neither was under the Western sphere of influence or under Red Army occupation. It is clear that in Finland the Soviets were quite content to have a situation in which friendship with the USSR was accepted by all the main political parties, including the conservatives. It had sought and obtained a purge of all those who had collaborated with the Germans (especially social democrats like Väinö Tanner, who had been foreign minister during the war), as a symbol of atonement for the past. A shift of Finland into the Soviet sphere might have had more negative international repercussions than the Prague coup: it might alarm the Swedes sufficiently to lead them to abandon their position of neutrality. Finally, the Soviets and their Finnish followers would also have taken into account the different national characteristics ascribed to Finns and Czechs: the anti-communist Finns might resist a communist takeover with force while the Czechs – never keen to wear the crown of martyrdom – would tolerate it. Thus, Finland remained the only illustration that it was perfectly possible to be anti-communist at home, without being anti-Soviet in foreign affairs.

The most striking differences between the two countries were internal. The Czech communists had 40 per cent of the vote, the Finns only twenty-25 cent. Between 1947 and 1948, national coalitions throughout Europe which included communists and anti-communists had to adapt to the break-up of the international anti-fascist coalition, that is, to the Cold War. In most cases the anti-communists were strong enough to expel the communists from any share in government. This was true of Italy and France, not to speak of all West European countries where the communists represented 10 per cent or less of the popular vote. In Finland they were strong enough to humiliate the communists and force them out of office. In Czechoslovakia alone the communists were too strong to be expelled. Had there been parliamentary elections, they would probably have attained an absolute majority since they had the support of the majority of the industrial working class, large sections of the intelligentsia, and many small farmers.[94]

The role of the socialists or social democrats was crucial in accounting for the end of communist participation in government in the West. In France, the socialists were not afraid to fight the communists and had strong allies in the centre. In Italy, only a minority in the Socialist Party chose to side with the anti-communists, but this was sufficient to provide Christian democracy with the necessary strength to evict the Left from office. Again, Czechoslovakia was different. Though the right wing of the Social Democratic Party fought hard, it lost to a majority which was genuinely willing to continue to co-operate with the communists.[95] In Finland during the war, the social democrats had fought alongside the Germans and, after the war, had agreed to co-operate with the communists only with great reluctance. Moreover, once the Vapaa Sana group had been expelled from the Finnish Social Democratic Party, the SKP could no longer count on having a friend in it.[96] In reality, in spite of its electoral achievements, the Finnish Communist Party was too weak either to take over the country through armed struggle (which it had no intention of doing), or to become a permanent participant in a governing coalition. Thus, its situation was far more similar to that of its French and Italian counterparts than to that of the Czechoslovaks.

The overall balance-sheet of Western communism, a few years after its electoral zenith, can be rapidly drawn. Outside France, Italy and Finland, it ceased to exist as a significant force in national politics.

In Eastern Europe, thanks to indirect or direct Soviet intervention or pressure, communism triumphed. For years Soviet pronouncements would remind the world that whatever was being built in Eastern Europe was the only form of 'actually existing socialism'. The territories under this regime were situated, with some exceptions, in areas which in the previous century had been subjected to the rule of Prussia and of the Tsarist, Austrian and Turkish empires – all lands which had been the focus of hostility for nineteenth-century liberal and progressive Europe. It was in this area, historically so impervious to the flowering of a robust democratic tradition, that socialism was implanted, constrained within a relatively monolithic bloc, stultified into an official ideology, and unable to develop, adapt or change.

Thus, not only was the social-democratic tradition destroyed, but so was the possibility of a genuine development of the communist one. What occurred was the superimposition of a more or less uniform Soviet model of socialist construction on countries which were significantly different from each other and from the USSR.

The Sovietization of Eastern and Central Europe cannot be separated from the particular revolutionary conjuncture which emerged between 1917 and 1920. The creation of the Comintern was based on the central hypothesis that the coming revolution would be international, consequently requiring international co-ordination. In this the Comintern was really a child of the twentieth century, not just because of its ideology, but because its fundamental assumptions were those of interdependence and globalism. These concepts were central to the communists' initial belief that the Soviet revolution could not survive without a revolution in other countries. Such events would be induced by a generalized crisis of capitalism creating relatively uniform conditions throughout Europe, dictating co-ordination of communist strategy in the different countries. But the modern assumption of interdependent globalism co-existed alongside a much older and more enduring framework of international affairs: the modern state system, which has come down in unbroken descent from eighteenth-century Europe – in other words, an association of states whose conflicting interests are resolved by diplomacy and/or force. Thus, the Bolsheviks found themselves not only in charge of *their* state – the Union of the Soviets, the land of a socialism yet to be invented – but also in possession of the successor state to the Tsarist Empire, a state with definite 'national' security interests which could not all change simply because a new ideology guided it. Like Tsarist Russia, the USSR needed secure boundaries, buffer states, safety belts, international treaties, secret diplomacy and so on. Anyone ruling the Soviet Union would have to face this reality.

By the mid-1930s there was an objective correlation between Soviet foreign policy interests and those of the communist movement in Western Europe: the threat of fascism was not just internal to each European state; it was also, because of German power and geopolitical position, a threat to the USSR. The Popular Front policy adopted by the Seventh Congress of the Comintern (1935) was the recognition that it was in the interest of the USSR for each communist party to develop its policies according to the national particularities of its country, because that was the best way of stopping fascism.

Once the principle of 'national roads' had been adopted, there was no reason for the Leninist and Comintern conception of a co-ordination of revolutionary activities to survive. The communist parties were ready to confront their socialist rivals on the basis of 'democratic politics' and, therewith, to enter into more or less temporary alliances with them. Once it had been accepted that a peaceful transition to socialism utilizing the possibilities of liberal democracy was possible, and once the political horizon was that of the national state, there was no need of a specific communist tradition. Had they survived, the communist parties might simply have come to represent a more radical strand of the national variety of socialism.

In the absence of a Cold War and fears of Soviet communism, communist parties might have developed instead of shrinking as they did, for example, in Belgium and Holland; or they would have merged with socialist parties to create a powerful radical force. Nor would they have been harassed and excluded from employment, as Dutch and Belgian former Resistance fighters were after the war.[97] In France, a united Left might have been possible. In Italy, where socialists and communists co-operated until the late 1950s, they might have been able to provide an alternative to the Christian democratic takeover of the state.

The process of gradual reconciliation of the two wings of socialism had started haltingly in the mid-1930s and continued more confidently during the war. The Cold War stopped it dead in its tracks. In the East, national roads to socialism were abandoned in favour of the Soviet road. In the West, national roads were an impossible or difficult strategy to follow, because all communists were seen – inevitably and, in the majority of cases, correctly – as substantially subordinate to the foreign policy interests of the USSR. Where communism survived, as in France, Finland and Italy, it did so by becoming the inheritor and representative of a strong national Left radical tradition at the expense of the social democrats. In the French case, it took over completely a strong workerist strand which, elsewhere (for example, in Britain or Germany), was present in the social-democratic parties. In Italy, the PCI took over much of the 'subversive' radical tradition, especially in Tuscany and the Emilia-Romagna.

In all cases Western communists lived the beginnings of the Cold War as events imposed upon them from the outside. The 'iron curtain', the Cominform, the Truman Doctrine, Marshall Aid, even their participation in government were all phenomena which found them – like Gabriel Garcia Marquez's General – at the mercy of a destiny that was not theirs. They became the target of frenzied propaganda and were held responsible for repressive acts which they had not initiated, but which they nevertheless found themselves compelled to justify. As a minority force, they stubbornly and consistently defended all the civil rights which Western democracy afforded them; as communists, they equally stubbornly defended all the infringements of these rights in the 'people's democracies' in Eastern and Central Europe. Seldom had a political force found itself so entangled in so schizophrenic a predicament. The development of the Cold War and the division of Europe sealed the fate of communists in the West in the most mortifying manner. They did not resist their expulsion from government – and for good reason. By 1947 they had come to realize that they were no longer able to influence events from inside the government and that, precisely because they were inside it, they could not rally the opposition. In France, in particular, they could not risk allowing Trotskyite activists to inspire working-class radicalism as had happened at two Renault plants in April 1947.[98] In government, West European communists were expected to continue supporting austerity programmes which weighed heavily on the working class. In France, the PCF could no longer support the war against the communist-led anti-colonial movement in Indochina.[99] At both the national and international level, the tendency was shifting back towards a restoration of capitalist ethos and values. The radical winds raised by the war, and upon whose strength Western communists had staked their political future, had abated.

The fate of socialists and social democrats in the West was entirely different. They could, and did, accede to power, availing themselves of the conditions of democracy and freedom which they had so decisively helped to establish in the face of opposition, or at best grudging acceptance, from the Right.

What the Cold War meant, however, was that the socialists could accede to power only once they had accepted the international hegemony of the USA, the only *capitalist* power devoid of a strong socialist party. Thus, West European socialism had to develop under the international protection of a country whose ethos, traditions and outlook were deeply hostile to socialism, and which could never offer the hope of producing a government friendly to a socialist project in any form. It was an international order which could tolerate socialism on certain conditions, but never encourage it.

This fundamental subordination of socialist ideas to the requirements of a bipolar world was an aspect of the decay of European power following the Second World War. The fate of socialism was inseparable from the political destiny of individual nation-states. With Europe divided and subject to outside constraints, socialists found themselves on hostile terrain. To them fell the painful task of living with a particularly grievous paradox: they must advance the cause of socialism, while fighting a 'cold war' against the only existing 'socialist' nation.

The conservative and confessional parties which were the socialists' main opponents were also constrained, of course, by European weakness; but this worked to their advantage. After all, they were natural allies of the American superpower. Unlike the socialists, they did not have to demonstrate their reliability in the shadows of American suzerainty.

Book Two
Consolidation

PART TWO

The Construction of Welfare
Socialism 1945–50

CHAPTER FIVE

The Socialists After 1945

IN THE FEW years following the end of the Second World War, many of the 'short-term' political objectives of the Second International, adopted at the beginning of the century, were implemented. True universal suffrage had become a reality in all countries enjoying free elections, with the exception of politically backward Switzerland where women obtained the vote only in 1971. Thus, full citizenship, once granted only to male property-owners, was now finally extended to women. The Finns had been the trail-blazers in 1907. They were followed by Denmark in 1918, Austria and Germany in 1919, Norway and Sweden in 1921, Hollland in 1922, Ireland in 1923 and Britain in 1928. Finally, after the Second World War, France (1945), Italy (1946) and Belgium (1948) completed the transition to democracy.

The eight-hour day had been adopted everywhere, if not *de jure*, at least *de facto*. This was no minor reform: Marx himself had called the legal restriction on the length of the working day 'an all-powerful social barrier' and 'a modest Magna Carta ... which shall make clear when the time which the worker sells is ended, and when his own begins.'[1] Later, in a passage which still deserves attention, he added:

> the realm of freedom actually begins only where labour ... ceases. ... Beyond (the realm of necessity) begins that development of human energy which is an end in itself, the true realm of freedom, which, however, can blossom forth only with this realm of necessity as its basis. The shortening of the working-day is its basic prerequisite.[2]

Leisure time, the authentic basis of freedom and the necessary precondition for political activity, was now protected by law.

With the introduction of genuine universal suffrage, the liberal-democratic principle of the formal equality of all had been firmly established. With the eight-hour day the principle of state regulation of the labour market had been further strengthened. Democratic rights were thus enhanced by social rights.

Electorally speaking, the socialist parties emerged from the war as major political forces (see Table 5.1). Virtually everywhere they had at least one-third of the vote. Where they had less than that (for example, in Finland, Italy and France), it was because the communists had 20 per cent or more of the vote. In all cases the balance of power lay with the Left.

Table 5.1 Socialist, social-democratic and labour parties' share of the vote, 1945–50 (%)

	1945	1946	1947	1948	1949	1950
Austria	44.6	–	–	–	38.7	–
Belgium	–	32.4	–	–	29.8	35.5
Denmark	32.8	–	40.0	–	–	39.6
Finland	25.1	–	–	26.3	–	–
France	23.8	21.1	–	–	–	–
		17.9[a]				
Holland	–	28.3	–	25.6	–	–
Italy	–	20.7	–	(31.0)[b]	–	–
Norway	41.0	–	–	–	–	–
Sweden	46.7[c]	–	46.1	–	45.7	–
UK	48.3	–	–	–	–	46.1
West Germany	–	–	–	–	29.2	–

Notes: [a] There were two elections in France in 1946. [b] Joint list with the communists. [c] The elections were held in 1944.

When the war was ended, socialist and social-democratic parties were in power in virtually the whole of democratic Western Europe, but only in Britain, Sweden and Norway were they clearly in charge. In other countries they shared power with non-socialist parties. In France and in Italy they found themselves squeezed between a powerful communist party to their left and an emerging Christian democratic party to their right. In the previous chapter we chronicled the diverging paths of the French and Italian socialists: in France socialists repudiated the communists and opted for a coalition with the centre (1947); in Italy they pinned their hopes on an alliance with the communists. Paradoxically, these diametrically opposed tactics produced the same negative result: alone in Western Europe, French and Italian socialists became electorally weaker than their communist rivals.

In France the socialists, no longer a radical force for change, became the upholders of an increasingly indecisive and visionless Fourth Republic. In Italy the Socialist Party was, until the late 1950s, politically subordinated to the PCI; then it shifted its strategy, broke with the communists and, in the early 1960s, entered into a coalition government with the Christian democrats.

The fate of socialists and social democrats in the rest of Western Europe was more fortunate than that of the French and the Italians – not to mention the Portuguese and Spanish Left still under dictatorial rule. This confirmed the continuing difficulties of socialists in much of Southern Europe. Where democracy had not been fully established – as in Greece, Spain and Portugal – the main operationally active clandestine forces were those of the communists. Where democracy had been re-established – as in France and in Italy – the communists soon emerged as the dominant party of the Left. To find clear instances of socialist successes we must turn to north-western Europe.

In Belgium there were seven coalition governments between 1945 and 1949, all led by a socialist. The all-party national unity government of 1945 gave way to socialist-led coalitions which included the communists and the Liberals, but excluded the Catholics of the CVP-PSC (Christelijke Volkspartij – Parti Social Chrétien). In 1947 the Communist Party and the Liberal Party were expelled from the government and the socialists went on ruling with the CVP-PSC. Thus the POB, now rechristened the Parti Socialiste Belge/ Belgische Socialistische Partij (PSB/BSP), although having only one-third of the vote, was able to dominate Belgian politics throughout the immediate post-war period by being continuously in government and deciding the shape of the coalition.

In Holland the Labour Party (now called the Partij van de Arbeid – PvdA), with much less than one-third of the vote, was present in all five coalition governments which ruled the country from the end of the war to 1958; furthermore, between 1948 and 1958 the prime minister was always the socialist Willem Drees.

In Austria the Socialist Party (Sozialistische Partie Österreichs – SPÖ) entered into a durable coalition in 1945 with the Austrian People's Party (Österreichs Volkspartei – the ÖVP), a party of farmers and clerical workers, successor to the pre-war Christian Social Party. With the brief exception of the Renner government in 1945, however, the ÖVP controlled the post of chancellor. This exceptionally long 'historic compromise', which deprived Austria of a meaningful opposition for over twenty years from 1945 to 1966, was, at least in part, due to the SPÖ's awareness 'of the dangers of class confrontation'.[3] But there were many other factors contributing to co-operation between the parties, such as the appalling economic situation and the fact that Austria was under foreign occupation. By co-operating, the SPÖ prevented the ÖVP from having to rely on the right-wing party which emerged in 1949, the Verband der Unabhängigen (after 1956 it became the Freiheitliche Partei Österreichs – FPÖ – or Freedom Party). The tragic lessons of the 1920s had led the SPÖ to adopt a remarkably cautious strategy which eschewed confrontation and the risks of isolation. It was the beginning of the most important model of so-called consociational democracy in Western Europe, object of many political science studies.

In Finland, as we saw in the preceding chapter, the socialists were engaged in a struggle against the Communist Party. Following the exclusion of the communists from the government in 1948, the socialists remained in the coalition with the Agrarian League and the smaller bourgeois parties.

In Denmark, the Social Democratic Party (Socialdemokratiet) emerged as the leading party, but it was not strong enough to form a government on its own. Furthermore, the 1945 elections had turned out to be one of the worst electoral defeats for Danish social democracy: they polled only 32.8 per cent of the vote and lost eighteen of the sixty-six parliamentary seats they held before. Their wartime collaboration with the Nazi occupation forces was probably the main reason for these losses and for the communist gains, which amounted to the eighteen seats vacated by the social democrats.[4]

Nevertheless the Socialdemokratiet led the all-party government of 1945, then was out of office until 1947. From 1947 to 1950 it led a minority government sustained by the communists and the neutralist Radical Liberal Party.

In the remaining two Nordic countries, Sweden and Norway, socialists ruled uninterruptedly throughout most of the post-war period: in Norway until the mid-1960s and in Sweden until the mid-1970s. In Norway, the Labour Party, thanks to an electoral system less proportional than the Swedish, obtained an absolute majority of the seats (76 out of 150 seats, with only 41 per cent of the vote) and ruled without allies. In Sweden, the SAP, though by far the largest party with 46.6 per cent of the vote, could not muster more than half of the seats in the Riksdag (115 out of 230), and had to rely on the support of the Communist Party until 1951 and then on the Agrarian Party until 1957.

In occupied Germany what had once been the most influential social-democratic party in the world, the SPD, resurfaced after thirteen years spent under the tragic interlude of Nazism. After May 1945 there was no German state and the occupying forces took all major decisions. In the western part of the country there were no general elections until 1949. By then the high tide of radicalism had subsided; the Christlich Demokratische Union (CDU – Christian Democratic Party) obtained a decisive victory and forced the Social Democrats into opposition where they remained for seventeen years.

The SPD was led by Kurt Schumacher, a self-righteous and strong-willed man who had lost his right arm in the First World War and spent virtually the entire Nazi period in the concentration camp at Dachau. Like all the German social democrats of his time, Schumacher, who always professed to be a Marxist (but, emphatically, not a Leninist), believed Germany to be on the verge of a socialist transformation. At the same time he was a committed anti-communist and a stalwart upholder of parliamentary democracy.[5] The SPD was then a party of 600,000 members, but it no longer possessed the vast organizational infrastructure, including two hundred daily papers and a wire service, which had been the basis of the party's power in Weimar and before. Nor could it count on the unquestioned support of the trade unions (as had been the case in the pre-Nazi period), or on their substantial financial contribution.[6] After 1945, the SPD could no longer offer its supporters a total environment as it had in the days of Weimar and imperial Germany: a Vaterhaus und Lebensinhalt (literally: Parental Home and Life Substance). In those far-off days a member could read the party's newspapers, borrow from its book clubs, drink in its pubs, keep fit in its gyms, sing in its choral societies, play in its orchestras, take part in the so-called people's theatre organizations, compete in its chess clubs, and join, if a woman, the SPD women's movement, and, if young, the youth organization. When members were ill, they would receive help from the Working Men's Samaritan Federation. When they died, they would be cremated by a social-democratic burial club (as an alternative to church burial).[7] In the 1930s all this had been destroyed by the devastating impact of the Nazi dictatorship; the formidable political machine of August Bebel and his successors could not be brought back to life after 1945. Such erosion of the cultural world of labour was not confined to Germany. But elsewhere, for instance, in France, Italy and Britain, it occurred more gradually. By the 1960s it had reached near-completion.[8]

At first the SPD grew more rapidly in the Soviet-occupied part of the country than in the western sectors. The effective leader of the SPD in the Soviet zone, Otto Grotewohl, was in favour of a close alliance with the communists (KPD). Schumacher made no effort to intervene. He was content to leave Grotewohl in charge of the party in the east as long as he could control it in the west from his Hanover headquarters. When Schumacher eventually tried to intervene to stop the impending merger with the KPD, it was only to advise Grotewohl to dissolve the party. By then it was too late. The fate of social democracy in the eastern zone was sealed. In 1946 Grotewohl merged his party with the KPD to form the Sozialistische Einheitspartei Deutschlands (Socialist Unity Party – SED), becoming its co-chairman and, in 1949, the first prime minister of the German Democratic Republic.[9] Initially, the new merged party was closer to the old SPD than to the KPD: Lenin ceased to be a reference point and there was no explicit endorsement of the Soviet system.[10] With the development of the Cold War, the SED quickly became a pro-Soviet communist party and its social-democratic component was obliterated. Once it had become clear that Grotewohl's party could not have any independence from the USSR (something which was not initially obvious), the fate of the SPD became closely bound up with the Cold War.

The revival of the fortunes of the Left in Western Europe after 1945 is not quite so sweeping when we see it in the context of the division of Europe, the split with the communists in France, the necessity of coalition politics in Denmark, Austria, Holland and Belgium, the electoral defeat in Italy in 1948 and in Germany in 1949.

This is the European context for the trajectory of the British Labour Party, from its historic victory in 1945 to its bizarre defeat in 1951. The victory *was* historic: never before had a socialist party in Britain been able to rule without being constrained by Liberal Party support, as had been the case in 1924 and 1929–31, or by coalition government, as during the war. Leaving aside the peripheral instance of Norway, this was the first time in European history that a socialist party was elected to power with an absolute parliamentary majority. The defeat *was* bizarre: the Labour Party 'lost' the 1951 elections because it obtained fewer *seats* than the Conservatives; however, it had secured more *votes*. In fact the 1951 results were, in percentage terms, the best results in the entire history of the Labour Party, including the 'historic' victory of 1945. It is, of course, fair to point out that Labour's absolute majority of the seats achieved in 1945 could not have been ensured without the vagaries of the first-past-the-post electoral system. The fact remains that, in spite of the many difficulties it had to face, the Labour Party left office with a greater share of the poll than when it came in. Socialist politics or, at least, the policies of the Labour government did not result in unpopularity.

Perry Anderson is right when he refers to the Second World War as Labour's 'historical windfall' because: 'The Party was initiated into power without having to mobilize for it; and it acquired a programme for government without having to originate the ideas behind it.'[11] But there is no reason to single out the Labour Party in this context. Wars have always been among the most formidable harbingers of vast social change: they have constituted a 'windfall' for socialists in the twentieth century, from the Bolsheviks in 1917 to virtually all the parties of the Left in 1945. The antagonism towards war which had often been so strong a component of socialist consciousness was always at odds with the recognition that a measure of social progress so often follows the most unbearable human suffering. This, of course, justifies nothing and offers no consolation.

The Labour Party prevailed in 1945 because, unlike its Conservative rivals, it expressed the mood of the time: the egalitarian ethos of the war, the solidaristic feelings enhanced by having to face a common enemy, the prestige of the USSR, the failure of the Conservatives to stop Hitler before 1939, the memories of the Depression of the 1930s, the readier recognition of the need for change.

To the new ethos should be added a second factor: the Labour Party's full-hearted participation in the war cabinet and their acceptance of governmental responsibilities had established the 'efficiency' criterion of politics. By this I mean that the party had succeeded in effecting the difficult transition from being a party of opposition to being a party of government. The former gathers support because of its antagonism to the existing system; it is a party of protest; it expresses outrage at current injustices. The key question, however, is: can it rule? To do so it must convince friends and foes that it possesses political competence. To some extent this is a question of image, although a credible programme based on policies which exhibit some degree of realism may help. It is important that some credibility should be established even among those who will not vote for the party. To govern effectively it is essential to have the consent of opponents who must assume that even undesired and unacceptable policies can be reversed. To be both credible and legitimate has always presented difficulties for parties which seek radical change, and therefore for parties of the Left. Nearly all of them have in fact been able to accede to power only through a period of apprenticeship in coalition with, or supported by, well-established and legitimized political forces. The Labour Party had had three previous periods in government, but only the war coalition qualifies as authentic apprenticeship: the 1924 and 1929–31 governments had been unsuccessful. What really legitimated Labour was the war coalition.

The war enabled Labour to acquire a further precious asset: a national–patriotic identity, though such excessive attachment to the empire turned into a liability. Whatever remained of its pacifism had been successfully confined to its fringes. The idea that internationalism meant that all wars were fought in the interests of the ruling class was discarded. It is difficult to imagine how this form of pacifism could ever have been abandoned in Britain without a war as politically 'acceptable' to the Left as the Second World War. This remains the most readily available and virtually unchallenged instance of the elusive concept of the 'just war'. In other countries, violent revolutions and wars of national liberation against foreign invaders or occupiers supply the Left with an acceptable array of national memories, traditions and myths which can be used to redefine its politics in national–patriotic terms. In Britain's case the traditional left-wing sentiment that 'all wars are the bosses' wars' had a basis in the history of an ancient imperial country whose history was one of plunder and conquest and of narrowly defined 'national' interest. The struggle against Nazi Germany provided a real rupture with this strong commitment to pacifism. In spite of occasional power politics rhetoric, the war could justifiably be seen as a war waged by an extreme and cruel right-wing regime against the British people as a whole, not just against its rulers or its empire. The ideological dimension of the war had been foreshadowed by its prelude, the Spanish Civil War, which pitted Left versus Right and in which the defence of democracy was identified with the Left.

In 1945, the Labour Party thus possessed virtually all the necessary attributes for its chrysalid-like metamorphosis into a party of government. It was this which enabled it to acquire the necessary support of many who did not identify with the working class: those nebulous and indistinct cohorts generically lumped in the all-embracing and ill-defined category of 'middle class', without whose support no one can rule in a democracy. The presumed acquisition of new middle-class voters should not disguise the fact that it also acquired, for the first time, the support of the majority of the working-class vote.[12]

The Labour Party was thus elected with a mandate for change. What this involved was not altogether clear. In broad outline, however, there can be no disputing that the Labour Party was expected to introduce a fairer society, one, that is, where excessive inequalities would be removed, and in which those which persisted (for there was no real support for massive levelling) would not deprive anyone of certain basic social rights, such as employment, health care and education. The presumption was that the citizenship rights which had been the rallying cry of the liberal-democratic tradition – the juridical equality of all – would be supplemented by new socio-economic rights. It was also expected that, in order to make these rights generally available, determinate economic conditions of growth and prosperity would have to be established and that, since the market would not be able to achieve this on its own, it would be necessary for the state to intervene in the economy.

In the rest of Europe confessional parties competed fairly successfully with the parties of the Left on the terrain of state-induced social change. Christian concern for the downtrodden and the poor, and the anti-individualistic and solidaristic basis of both the Protestant and Catholic churches, could be harnessed for a politics of social transformation. Indeed, thanks to Leo XIII's encyclical *Rerum Novarum* of 1891 – updated in 1931 with Pius XI's *Quadragesimo Anno* – the Roman Catholic church had rejected the individualist ethos of private capital accumulation in favour of social solidarity. In Britain, however, there were no confessional parties and little, if any, populist basis for conservative forces. Their nearest equivalent, Disraeli's 'one-nation' strand of Conservatism, was far too paternalistic and old-fashioned a framework for a modern conservative social policy and was, consequently, no match for the Labour Party. Furthermore, on the Continent anti-clericalism had been one of the most characteristic traits of socialist parties and one of the causes of their lack of support among religious people. The British Labour Party faced none of these problems: the strength of the nonconformist churches in British socialism had prevented the growth of anti-clericalism. The Conservatives in Britain had been deprived of one of the traditional weapons of the Right on the Continent: the political use of religion as an instrument to divide the potential supporters of the Left, and the dread that an incoming 'red' government would desecrate all that was hallowed.

The unique conjuncture which had produced a Labour government was itself the result of a set of highly singular circumstances. Once elected, the Labour government also had at its disposal a distinctive advantage which it has probably never fully appreciated. It was able to use, for the implementation of its policies, an uncommonly efficient administrative machine: the British civil service.

On the continent of Europe the administrative system of the various states, without whose support and efficiency no radical policies can be implemented, had been undermined in various ways. The German system was gravely impaired and needed to be reconstructed; like the Austrian and the Italian, it had been an accomplice of the previous authoritarian regimes. Elswhere, the civil servants had been guilty of over-enthusiastic and ultimately damaging co-operation with the occupying Axis powers (France, Belgium and Holland). The Italian bureaucracy was corrupt and inefficient; that of Greece was fundamentally not only anti-socialist, but also anti-democratic.

Outside Britain, most socialists had to deal with the fact that virtually the entire personnel of the state had been tainted with sympathies with anti-democratic forces.

In Austria the purge of former Nazis was half-hearted: 524,000 were barred from voting and holding office, but by 1949 most of them were back on the electoral registers willing and able to vote for the so-called Freedom Party.[13] Only the development of party patronage and many years of 'jobs for the boys' under the *Proporz* system after 1945 gave the socialists an uncommon degree of strength in public administration. After each election a 'Coalition Committee' composed of delegations from the main parties met to arrange a division of government jobs and patronage.[14]

It is not true, as some have claimed,[15] that 'The Austrians were almost alone in avoiding the politics of vengeance' by allowing those who col-laborated with the previous regime to remain *in situ*. After an initial brief period of vendetta, the general pattern was one of unavoidable forgiveness, as had been the case in Italy where the communist leader, Palmiro Togliatti, as minister of justice, granted an amnesty in June 1946.[16] Similar policies of leniency were followed in France, Belgium and Holland. As a result most of those who had faithfully served pro-Nazi and pro-fascist political systems were left unmolested and indeed were often employed in the services of the reconstructed democratic regimes. The ensuing interminable debate on the purges, and a naive fixation with the importance of the specific personnel managing the apparatuses of the state (as if the Holocaust could have been prevented had different bureaucrats been in charge), helped to avoid con-fronting the far more crucial issue of reforming the institutions themselves. The absence of reform ensured the continuation of unwieldy bureaucratic machine devoid of any sense of public service, whose main function was to provide employment.

The French, of course, had a great tradition of state service stretching back to the days of Louis XIV, but it was confined to the higher echelons, not to the all-important middle ranks. Consequently, instead of major institu-tional reforms there was the much-heralded revival of the Ecole Nationale d'Administration for the training of senior civil servants in 1945. With this, the tradition of élitism continued to prevail.

Britain, and consequently the British Labour Party, enjoyed the advantage of a politically reliable and efficient civil service which was not the property of any one political party. It is true that its highest levels were colonized by the scions of the upper classes who had frequented the same exclusive private schools and leading universities. The great reform of the civil service following the Northcote–Trevelyan Report of 1854 had eliminated parliamentary patron-age in favour of the meritocratic principle. This ensured that the top levels of public administration would remain in the possession of the aristocracy, the class which had a virtual monopoly on the educational system that defined and classified merit.[17] Together with other élites, these administrators constituted an elusive establishment which was prepared to accept that the 'national interest' – according to its own definition – could be adequately served, at least for the time being, by the party of the working class.

This 'national' ethos of the British civil service did not make it any less 'conservative' than its continental counterparts. Revolutionary radicalism and a penchant for insurgency are not among the most characteristic features of the senior civil servants of the British crown. But they were efficient, more so than those of the whole of Latin or Slavic Europe, and more loyal towards those who had passed the democratic test by winning elections than their colleagues in any other European country. Furthermore, during the years of war they had acquired a novel capacity and taste for planning and managing the economy. Outright sabotage of Labour measures was never seriously considered by malevolent administrators. Without them it is doubtful whether the welfare state would have been erected so swiftly and efficiently.[18] Thus, during the war it was the senior civil servants of the Ministries of Education and Health which set the agenda for the Education Act of 1944 and the post-war health-care reforms.[19]

The incoming Labour government had designs and schemes, but no detailed legislative programme. This meant that civil servants were in charge of what is often of more consequence than devising policies: implementing them. Subsequent complaints that 'socialist' legislation was watered down by pro-establishment civil servants belong to political mythology and are to be ascribed to the unremitting desire of some socialists to find scapegoats for the Left's own shortcomings. The resulting legislation was not significantly less 'socialist' than what had been originally proposed.

Because the British state had survived the war intact, the Labour Party inherited all its peculiarities: its bizarre and childish customs, its absurd invented traditions, its preposterous sense of hierarchy, its ludicrous rituals. All Labour leaders, left and right, accepted and reinforced all of these without apparent qualms. Republicanism never had the slightest foothold in the Labour Party. Labour leaders and supporters had sensed that what makes no sense rationally may often be politically perfectly possible, and that consequently the monarchy, although an absurd medieval relic, was nevertheless compatible not only with capitalist efficiency (Japan), but also with welfare socialism (the Scandinavian countries).

Labour's intentions on assuming office were limited to social reforms. There was no question even of minor changes in the political organization of the state. Thus, paradoxically, the existence of a complex charade of often ridiculous and, at times, mildly amusing establishment conventions helped the party of the working class in its quest for legitimacy. By embracing them and making them their own, Labour proved that it accepted the political system *en bloc*, including the institutions of the monarchy and even, eventually, the House of Lords. In so doing, it demonstrated its credentials as a respectable party of government, and, therefore, as a loyal opposition. The Labour

Party could be treated by the establishment as a not too distant relative who was acceptable, in spite of its manifestly subversive ideas, because it was quite willing to learn how to behave decorously at dinner.

Lenin, of course, might well have been right when he surmised that in order to revolutionize society, it was necessary to revolutionize the state by destroying its administrative and political machine. But the Labour Party did not want a revolution, only social reforms compatible with the existing state. As Morgan has written, any failures by the Labour government between 1945 and 1951 cannot be attributed to the institutional framework it inherited[20] – though it could be argued that its real failure was in the preservation of such a framework. The absolute power of Parliament, the prerogative of the monarchy now in the hands of a prime minister, the lack of a written constitution resulting in government having free reins, an electoral system which made coalitions unnecessary, all this meant that the Labour Party was much freer to do what it wanted than any of its continental counterparts. This must go a long way towards explaining why the Labour Party, throughout its existence, has paid only lip-service to any notion of drastic institutional reform and has, on the contrary, been a strong supporter of the central peculiarities of the British political system: the electoral system, the unwritten constitution and the virtual unfettered control enjoyed by the cabinet and its leader over Parliament as a whole.

In the institutional field the changes the Labour government brought about were infinitesimal: a Parliament Act in 1949 further to limit the right of the Lords to delay legislation; and a Representation of the People Act which eliminated absurdities like double-voting for university graduates and certain categories of businesspeople and landlords.

In the field of civil liberties no major progress was made. There was no separation of church and state (unlike in virtually the whole of Europe) and, consequently, the Church of England maintained its privileged position as the established church. Quaint relics from the past, such as the power of the Lord Chamberlain, an officer of the Royal Household, to censor theatrical performances, were left untouched with predictably philistine consequences. However, legal aid was introduced and corporal punishment abolished, though only for convicted criminals, not for children in schools. In England and Wales a boy could still be beaten for smoking at school, but not in later life for raping someone. Hanging was kept on the statute books.

That the 'establishment' had little to fear was further confirmed by Labour's astonishing timidity when it came to educational policy. The Labour government defended and upheld the 1944 Education Act, whose formal architect was the leading Conservative R. A. Butler, and the grammar school system as an avenue of improvement for the more academically gifted children of the working class. To the others, the overwhelming majority, it had nothing to offer. The 1944 Act contained no specific reference to training or vocational education, no plans to expand higher education, still narrow by comparison with other countries.[21] The Act set 1945 as the target date for raising the school-leaving age to fifteen. It took the determination of the education minister, Ellen Wilkinson, to convince her reluctant cabinet colleagues to implement the decision in January 1947.[22] This was her greatest success. It was also her last, for she died a few weeks later. However, Wilkinson was also committed to some form of comprehensive education but did not know how to proceed, as her sympathetic biographer admits.[23] Wilkinson's Emergency Training Scheme (ETS), which might have provided the basis for a thorough and modern training scheme, failed because it was understaffed and over-centralized.[24] Training was then a Conservative platform rather than a Labour one. A considerable expansion in technical and vocational training was recommended by the Conservative Party, but not by the Labour Party, at their respective 1945 conferences.[25] This was a warning which should have been heeded. Compared to other countries, British training was already seriously backward.[26]

At the time, socialist parties in general had no well-thought-out policies on education beyond a general belief that barriers to working-class advancement through education should be removed and that comprehensive schooling would facilitate this process. For example, in Sweden the School Commission produced a report in 1948 favouring a comprehensive school system, but it was not until 1962 that the Riksdag introduced comprehensive education for all children aged seven to sixteen.[27] In Austria the SPÖ had proposed, without much conviction, that the various *Mittelschule* should be abolished in favour of a common education until the age of fifteen, but nothing concrete happened. Instead, the party much preferred to fight the old battle over religious education with its social Christian rivals and allies.[28] The continental radical-republican hostility to clerical influence in schools never spread to Britain, where religious schools continued to be funded by taxpayers of all denominations and none. In the state schools of Britain the children of Christian, Jewish and atheistic parents assembled every morning for a formal act of (usually Christian) worship. This, in France or the USA, would have appeared as a profound breach of democratic values.

The British Labour government's reluctance to engage in any major institutional reform was not, however, a British peculiarity. The Swedish and Norwegian socialists solemnly stated in every programme they published that they aimed to install a republic, while not taking the slightest step towards it in all their years in power. The Left participated in institutional changes and constitution-making only in countries where it was necessary to do so because the previous regime had been totally discredited, as in Germany and Italy. The new constitution of the French Fourth Republic was very similar to that of the Third. The main concern of the French socialists had been to prevent political instability, rather than to reform the state in a new democratic direction. But the reverse happened: all the drafts and proposals which were significantly different from those of the defunct and much-reviled Third

Republic met strong opposition: Léon Blum's presidential system, Jules Moch's functional corporatist upper chamber, and Vincent Auriol's mildly federalist proposal of a regional chamber.[29] The fact was that, on the whole, constitutional reforms were not given a high priority by the socialists (or by the communists), in spite of all the drafting work done during the Resistance.

Austria readopted the constitution it had had prior to 5 March 1933, the date on which Parliament had been suspended.[30] In Holland there were no substantial political changes. In Belgium, socialist republicanism was directed against the collaborationist King Leopold III. Once Leopold abdicated in favour of his son Baudouin, the socialists ceased questioning the institution of the monarchy.[31] It was as if, throughout Western Europe, the socialist and social-democratic Left had accepted the Leninist view of politics with a special twist: the bourgeois state could not be reformed, it could only be smashed; as the socialists did not wish to smash it, they accepted it in its entirety.

In the defeated states, Italy and West Germany, the central issue was not whether to accept the rules of the game, but which rules to institute: constitution-making was on the agenda. Yet neither the SPD in Germany nor the PSIUP in Italy played the leading role. The fundamental principles of the Italian constitution were the result of a compromise between the Italian Communist Party and the left wing of the Christian Democratic Party, led by Giuseppe Dossetti. The socialists kept a low profile, occasionally trying to introduce more radical amendments. For Togliatti an acceptable constitution was the top priority, which is why he refrained from activating a potentially large mass movement to obtain social reforms. Dossetti thought along the same lines, leaving the conduct of day-to-day political affairs to the leader of the DC, Alcide De Gasperi. The result was that both Dossetti and Togliatti lost the immediate political battle: the PCI was expelled from the government in 1947, while Dossetti, a few years later, defeated and disappointed, left politics to enter the priesthood.

The constitution which had resulted from the Togliatti–Dossetti entente provided for extensive civil rights, for a strong degree of parliamentary sovereignty and a consequently weak executive, and ensured that any future radical programme of social reforms and nationalizations would not confront any notable constitutional impediments. Togliatti favoured a centralist state, but accepted the Christian democratic preference for a regional system. He also sanctioned the incorporation in the constitution of the 1929 Concordat with the church, against the wishes of the socialists and of his own supporters. In spite of such communist moderation, it appears that the resulting constitution was far too left-wing for the conservative DC governments in charge of the country after 1948. It was not fully implemented for many years. A constitutional court was not set up until 1956. The scope the constitution allowed for reforms was not utilized until the 1970s. Until then the traditional gap between the institutional, legal form of the state, the *pays légal*, and the policies in fact enforced, the *pays réel*, increased. However, defeated in the short term, Togliatti's party in fact gained the longer-term advantage of being able to be, in deed as well as in thought, a 'constitutional' communist party. Togliatti had had the foresight, rare in politicians, to accept a short-term loss in order to consolidate and fight another day. In the field of constitution-making, politics must be conceived in terms of decades. The drafter of constitutions must heed Dante's words and act

> come quei che va di notte,
> che porta il lume dietro e sè non giova,
> ma dopo sé fa le persone dotte. (*Purgatory* XXII, 67–9)

> (as one who, walking by night/carries a light behind him
> not for his own benefit/but to make wise those who
> come after him.)[32]

The Italian constitution came into being as the expression of the unity of the anti-fascist forces at the same moment as this unity was being irrevocably broken. Drafted by a specially convened Constituent Assembly, elected by universal suffrage, the constitution was the work of the Italians themselves. There were no outside constraints, and even the onset of the Cold War did not interrupt the co-operation between the Left and the Christian democrats, which led to a unanimous vote in favour of the final draft.

Matters proceeded quite differently in Germany. There, the constitution was drafted after the beginning of the Cold War and was an expression of it. The initiative was taken in 1948 by the three occupying powers of the western zone, who asked the eleven *Lander* governments (the only elected bodies in Germany) to set up a German parliamentary council, made up of representatives from the *Lander* assemblies in proportion to party strength, to draft a constitution. The Germans were reluctant to do so for the western zone only, fearing that it would perpetuate the division of their country. Furthermore, this constitution would have to be approved by the occupying powers who could suspend it at any time.[33] To underline the ephemeral nature of the new state, it was decided to draft a 'Basic Law' (*Grundgesetz*) rather than a constitution (*Verfassung*). The SPD, as *the* party of German unity, was the least willing to regard the new Basic Law as anything other than a purely temporary expedient. It assumed it would win the first elections and that after reunification it would be able to draft a new constitution.[34] Because of this it underestimated the importance of the constitutional battle and did not fight seriously for the inclusion of social rights such as the right to work and to welfare. The assumption of impending electoral victory also led the SPD to oppose the Christian democrats' demand for considerable decentralization. This, inevitably, would give the *Lander* governments substantial powers over education. To the (largely Protestant) social democrats this meant giving Catholic clericalism control over the schools in Bavaria and most of the Rhineland. The regionalists were in turn supported by the Americans and the French; the Americans because they thought federalism was best, the French because they thought that non-centralist states were weak states, and they wanted Germany to be weak. The SPD often joined forces with the centralist and pro-capitalist liberal Freie Demokratische Partei (the Free Democratic Party or FDP), to the extent of not insisting on the inclusion of a precise definition of social rights in order to neutralize the regionalists.[35] In the end both the SPD and the CDU voted in favour of the final draft, the communists and the Liberals voted against and so did most of the CDU's Bavarian ally, the Christlich-Soziale Union (CSU or Christian Social Union), which wanted a much more decentralized state.[36] The resulting system gave considerable powers to the chancellor (prime minister), a ceremonial role to the president, and a considerable advantage to the government of the day thanks to the constitutional device of the 'constructive vote of no-confidence', a provision that obliged the opposition to present its own alternative government whenever it called for a no-confidence vote.

Further examination of the attitude of the parties of the Left in Western Europe to constitutional questions confirms that virtually all of them were united in their unashamed centralism. They were all against federalism, regionalism, devolution of power. But they were all also 'parliamentarist': they were not in favour of presidential systems (with the exception of Léon Blum), nor were they in favour of a strong constitutional court or a second chamber which would weaken the powers of the main chamber. This is not surprising: the Jacobin tradition of the centralist state had been incorporated lock, stock and barrel to the continental socialist tradition. Socialists assumed that a move away from capitalism would require a firm use of the state machine: there was no point in limiting its powers. Constitutional courts gave power to senior judges and the Left – quite understandably – did not trust judges; upper chambers were a relic of the old regimes and a bastion of their privileges: they were either useless replicas of the main chamber or dangerous rivals. The allergy of the British Labour Party to any constitutionalism originated in the same fear: any obstacle to parliamentary sovereignty would be used by its opponents to block reforms and socialism.

There is little doubt that a centralized state was considered everywhere to be a useful instrument for the introduction of welfare socialism. The idea that the desired reforms would have to be introduced from above could co-exist perfectly well with the democratic rule which prescribed a prior electoral sanction. On the day of the elections the people would speak; thereafter politicians should implement their programme by using the state machine. Thus a *dirigiste* and *étatique* mentality (note the appropriately French origins of these words) suited social reformers, such as the Fabians in Britain, exceptionally well. The temptation of social engineering was seldom resisted, especially in countries where there was little upheaval, considerable continuity and where socialists could realistically aspire to government.

Among northern social democrats (including the British) social reformism and social engineering went hand in hand. For instance, in the 1930s the Swedish reformers Gunnar and Alva Myrdal were convinced that over-crowding in Gothenburg was not only the result of poverty but also of overspending and irrational consumer habits. Consequently, they preferred to provide benefits 'in kind' rather than in cash. Better to decide from the top what the workers should get, than allowing them to spend public cash (they might drink it away). The Myrdals also endorsed sterilization of the insane and prescribed in detail the correct clothes and equipment for the newly born.[37] This mentality found its way into the 1944 programme of the Swedish social democrats. Out of concern for the heavy work performed by women in the home, the programme promised not only the construction of dwellings provided with drains, running water, central heating, bathrooms, laundries and play centres for children, but also that after 'exhaustive studies into types of domestic utensils and articles of furniture', the state would make available to the public 'quality-guaranteed, practical domestic utensils, furniture and textiles'.[38] Further on, the document stated that 'In carrying out this programme the advice of experienced housewives should be sought.'[39] Those shocked rather than amused by the prospect of the state suggesting how someone's kitchen should be organized, should reflect that the idea of the kitchen as a domestic laboratory had been a frequent theme, at least since the 1920s, in Sweden, though the 'modern' or 'rational' kitchen became common only in the 1950s.[40] In Britain, during the collectivist war years, official propaganda had endlessly offered advice on what to eat, how to make clothes and decorate the home. In any case, socialists were not the only ones to proffer 'expert' advice on domestic consumption and organization; that had been (and still is) the staple diet of most women's magazines and radio programmes for many years. One should also recognize that at least the Swedish social democrats, unlike their comrades elsewhere, were trying to deal with the difficulties facing women working in the home.

The social engineering ethos of Swedish social democracy may have been particularly pronounced, but all the former members of the Second Inter-national had acquired an *étatique* dimension by the late 1940s by which time their identification with their own nation-state was complete. The development of mass democratic politics had led these parties to formulate appeals which included the whole people and were no longer directed towards the 'working class' as a separate group. The concept of 'working class' itself was dramatic-ally enlarged. It now included all 'working people' and thus also many members of the employed middle classes, without whose support electoral victory would be problematic. In the light of these advances it was impossible to disregard the powerful appeal of nationalism as a concept which could integrate the whole population. Of course, most Left parties had made their peace with nationalism well before 1945, but the aftermath of the Second World War sanctioned it. The Italian socialist and communist parties used the image of Giuseppe Garibaldi to adorn their banners when they jointly fought the 1948 election, rather than the hammer and sickle which they both used as their party symbols. The French communists had made use of all the national images of French patriotic history, including Joan of Arc, since the 1930s. In Germany the main upholders of German reunification were the social democrats. In Sweden, the SAP leader, Per Albin Hansson had used the national flag at rallies ever since the 1930s, and, in a speech on Swedish Flag Day 1934, he praised the enduring natural beauties of the motherland, while exalting the establishment of the objectives of full employment and social security as patriotic achievements.[41] Conservatives were no longer going to be allowed to be the sole defenders of nationalism. In embracing national-ism, the 'people' not 'the working class' inevitably would become the subject of History. Was socialism in any way redefined as a result of this?

In France Blum was among those who believed that official socialist doctrine had to be modified because too wide a gap had opened up between the socialist principles of class struggle, propounded by the party, and its frankly reformist practice. This early revisionist attempt failed miserably. The SFIO Congress of 1946 rejected all efforts to modify its commitment to the 'class struggle' into one for 'class actions', as Blum had advocated. A new leader, Guy Mollet, was elected. It was the victory of the 'hard' tradition of French socialism, that of Jules Guesde over the moderate Jaurès. Mollet appeared not to want any ideological compromise with the middle classes, wished to 'return' to Marxism (though Blum claimed to be merely re-interpreting Marx, not abandoning him), and to centralize further the SFIO. More realistically than Blum, Mollet, in 1946, was convinced that there was nowhere for the SFIO to go except towards an alliance with the PCF.[42] The truth was that the SFIO had been losing ground to the communists and was now the junior party of the French Left. It attempted to recover the radical working-class vote lost in the 1930s by refusing to tone down its anti-clericalism and, by doing so, it lost hopes of regaining the Catholic working class from the MRP. Having purged its ranks of many former Resistance fighters, the SFIO fell back on the traditional support of local notables.[43] Unlike the PSIUP leader, Pietro Nenni, who believed an alliance with the communists was the only way forward, Mollet sought to compete with the PCF by by-passing it from the left. His journal, La pensée socialiste, attacked Blum's revisionism, accused the communists of having sold out to the bourgeoisie, fought against any weakening of Marxist doctrine, celebrated Lenin and the October Revolution, and urged the smashing of the capitalist state.[44] This position coincided with that of some of the Trotskyist groups which had entered the party. It had little practical result, apart from enabling Mollet to oust Blum and his supporter Daniel Mayer from the leadership of the party.

Neither Blum nor Mollet ackowledged explicitly that what really worried them was not principles but the power of the PCF.[45] The real question was how to defeat the communists, not how to redefine socialism. It turned out that the Cold War intervened to enable them to unite on a staunchly anti-communist platform. Mollet discarded his radicalism with the nonchalance of the consummate politician and moved towards the centre, espousing all the values of Cold War anti-communism. He eventually supported the war in Algeria and the Gaullist takeover in 1958. As if exhausted by this ideological somersault, the SFIO ceased to think and produced not a single original idea, except perhaps an attempt at a socialist justification for European integration, until its unlamented death in 1969, prior to its rebirth as the Parti Socialiste.

In a less extreme form, all other left-wing parties in Western Europe were faced by the increasing contrast between their socialist rhetoric and their moderate practice, often made more evident by their growing responsibilities in government. None did anything about it explicitly. It was as if the more reformist their pratice became, the more necessary it was to remain anchored to some of the symbols of the past. One could really be a moderate as long as the followers of the party could be reassured that moderation was only for the present; the future would eventually bring the full application of the maximum programme. To have dropped the insignia at this stage would have signified a capitulation to the class enemy, eliminating from the horizon even the dream of a socialist future. For all continental socialists the signs of their commitment to the class struggle and the Marxist view of history were the proof of their deep-seated anti-capitalism. This was so even in the Nordic countries where Marxism had never been intellectually prominent.[46]

The economic programme of the SPD in 1946 spoke the traditional language of Marxists only in the general historical analysis section (as in the Erfurt Programme). The sections which dealt with immediate economic tasks already had strong Keynesian tones. The more thorough revision of traditional social-democratic theory which occurred at the 1959 Congress at Bad Godesberg had its origin in a passage in 1946 when the party announced that it did not consider 'a socialist planned economy as a goal in itself. This is why it demands that State activities be limited to what is necessary.'[47]

In Austria the Austro-Marxist tradition of Otto Bauer (see chapter 2) could not survive the war. The organization of the Austrian Revolutionary Socialist Party (Revolutionäre Sozialisten) of the pre-1945 period had been destroyed by the Gestapo.[48] Those surviving this struggle had joined forces with the pre-war socialists to form the Sozialistische Partei Österreichs from the merger of the pre-war Sozialdemokratische Partei and the Revolutionäre Sozialisten, under a leadership determined to end all ideological disputes.[49] Karl Renner, a contemporary of Otto Bauer, leader of the reformist wing of the SPÖ and now its foremost intellectual, became the first president of the new Austrian Republic.[50] Bauer's theory that there could be two distinct roads to socialism, one insurrectionary and one reformist, was abandoned. The democratic way of gradual evolution – the reformist path – had become the only way.[51] Bauer had believed that socialists should join a coalition with 'bourgeois' parties only in exceptional circumstances, but now the new party chairman, Dr Adolf Schärf, propounded the necessity of permanent coalition with the successor of the old Christlich-Soziale Partei, the Österreichs Volkspartei.[52]

In Italy the PSIUP had remained Marxist, declaring in 1946 that the party was 'a class party inspired by the economic and social principles of Marxism whose final aim is the downfall of capitalism'.[53] This entailed the continuation of the wartime alliance with the Communist Party and a neutralist foreign policy which, in the specific conjuncture of the post-war period, was objectively pro-Soviet. By 1947, this dual policy had become untenable in most of Western Europe. In Italy the situation was different: the Italian communists were strong and popular, and the socialists were afraid that they would be annihilated if they moved to the right. At the 1946 Congress of the PSIUP only 10 per cent voted for Giuseppe Saragat's 'social-democratic' faction, while the majority rallied round two motions, to any outsider indistinguishable from each other,[54] which reaffirmed their commitment to unity of action with the PCI. A year later, Saragat's faction, against the advice of the SFIO and the British Labour Party, decided to form what eventually came to be known as the Partito Social Democratico Italiano (PSDI), while the PSIUP changed its name to Partito Socialista Italiano (PSI). The split was favoured and financially subsidized by the USA in what has remained a classic case of interference in Italian domestic affairs.[55] Nevertheless, it was the PSDI which was recognized by all other social-democratic parties and admitted, after the expulsion of the PSI, into COMISCO (Comité de Défense Socialiste Internationale) which, created in 1946, would become in 1951 the new Socialist International.

Once again, as after 1917, social democracy clearly defined itself as 'non-communism', thus establishing the main point of demarcation to its left. To define itself in more positive terms, it had to produce a strategic framework to cope with three broad central issues: social reforms, capitalism and the international state system.

The traditional communist response to the above was that radical reforms under the private ownership of the means of production were impossible and that a stable international peace could occur only when capitalism had been eliminated globally. This communist politics, defeated in the West by 1948, prevailed in Eastern Europe for over forty years before falling in 1989–91, quite suddenly, like the House of Usher.

Social democrats and democratic socialists (as some preferred to call themselves), far less monolithically organized than their communist counterparts, faced these three central issues in many different ways. In the first few crucial years after the end of the Great European Civil War of 1914–45 (as it will probably be seen by later generations), they advanced and established a strategy of *welfare socialism*. This would be articulated within a reformed capitalist structure regulated by the state, often through a large and powerful public sector and a planning mechanism. Internationally, there was no cohesion at all among socialists and social democrats. Some wanted to be part and parcel of a powerful, internationally integrated, anti-Soviet military and ideological system. Others assumed that a non-aligned policy would prevent the emergence of serious international conflicts. It is to these three related dimensions of politics that we now turn.

CHAPTER SIX

Building Social Capitalism 1945–50

The Welfare State

THE IDEA OF the welfare state is irrevocably bound up with the post-war British Labour government, though the ideas and the practice of welfare did not originate in Britain or in the European socialist movement. The most important path-breakers were the Germans, who introduced a health insurance scheme in 1883 and a general pension scheme for old age and invalidity in 1889. The French instituted similar pension plans in 1910. In 1911 the British Liberal government initiated a national insurance system, old-age pensions on a non-contributory basis (unlike the German), and health and compulsory unemployment insurance systems (which the Germans did not introduce until the Weimar Republic). The Swedes, in 1913, introduced the first compulsory and universal pension system in the world, though there was still widespread means-testing, and pensions were low until the Pension Reform of 1946.[1] Table 6.1 illustrates the diffusion of welfare schemes in Europe.

Although most of the early schemes were insurance-based (more so in Germany and less so in Great Britain), it was at least the intention of radicals

Table 6.1 Introduction of social welfare schemes in Western Europe

	Occupational injuries	Health	Pensions	Unemployment
Austria	1887	1888	1927	1920
Belgium	1971	1944	1924	1944
Denmark	1916	1933	1922	none
Finland	1895	1963	1937	none
France	1946	1930	1910	1967
Germany	1884	1883	1889	1927
Holland	1901	1929	1913	1949
Italy	1898	1928	1919	1919
Norway	1894	1909	1936	1938
Sweden	1916	1953	1913	none
UK	1946	1911	1925	1911

Source: Peter Flora et al., *State, Economy and Society in Western Europe, 1815–1975. A Data Handbook*, Campus Verlag, Macmillan Press and St James Press, Frankfurt, London and Chicago 1983, p. 454.

like Lloyd George that there should develop, eventually, a 'social service state', that is, a state which would acknowledge full responsibility in matters of sickness and unemployment.[2]

Why were these first welfare systems built? Was it because the conservative and liberal forces which erected them intended to prevent the growth of socialist parties? The idea that the 'respectable' (i.e. skilled and relatively prosperous) working class could be bought off by reforms had considerable appeal for the more intelligent representatives of large middle-class parties. There have been numerous statistically based attempts to establish a correlation between the development of the welfare state and the political mobilization of the working class, in the hope of demonstrating that without the initiative of a strong labour movement or the threat of labour conflicts there would have been no welfare state.[3] Others have tried to demonstrate that, on the contrary, the distribution of political power is far from being the main variable influencing the spread of welfare. Harold L. Wilensky's research led him to maintain that: 'During the entire period since World War I or the shorter period after World War II, cumulative left power has had no effect on welfare effort or output.'[4] According to this view, politics does not really matter: it is the level of economic prosperity and the general culture of a country which determines the development of welfare provisions.[5] Esping-Andersen accepts that the demographic structure is the most powerful explanation of cross-national variations in social spending, but points out that the crucial issue is not the actual amount of money spent, but how it is spent.[6]

The welfare state can also be seen as a response to the needs of advanced capitalism and particularly to the fact that the private sector, on its own, is unable to ensure the reproduction of all the conditions of production, including the following: an ideologically non-hostile labour force able and willing to work without having to provide for its own health care and future pension needs out of wages; an efficient transport and educational infrastructure; and the provision of essential supplies, such as gas and electricity, at reasonably low costs.[7] Thus the welfare state, while it improves the standard of life of the workforce, simultaneously stabilizes the capitalist system from an economic, social and political point of view. Herein lies the inescapable dilemma which has faced the socialist movement ever since its origins: does the success obtained in forcing capitalism to reform itself and improve the conditions of the population also stabilize and legitimize capitalism itself? Do short-term achievements undermine the grounds for the eventual overthrow of the system?

In reality, practical socialists never seriously agonized over such dilemmas. They produced welfare schemes because this is what they and their followers wanted. The authorities could not avoid responding. These activities and the effects they produced cannot be separated from the fact that the European twentieth-century state is irreversibly interventionist. In a situation in which the state is seen to be responsible for welfare in its widest meaning, and in which democracy is either a reality or a real possibility, it would be surprising if the governing élites did not devise policies aimed at establishing norms and standards of living which could not be spontaneously arrived at by other means such as market relations, familial bonds and charitable efforts.

It is certain that a British Conservative government would have introduced some welfare measures between 1945 and 1950. The British Conservatives had committed themselves to social reforms ever since the Second World War, when, stung by the success of the Beveridge Report and convinced by a run of by-election defeats, Churchill told the nation (21 March 1943) that, after the war, unemployment would be abolished, state ownership should be extended, compulsory national insurance introduced 'for all purposes from the cradle to the grave', and that 'there was no finer investment ... than putting milk into babies'.[8] This is not to say that Churchill and the Conservatives had become supporters of the welfare state. They had not. They had understood that the mood of the country was shifting, and moved tentatively and without zeal towards the creation of a 'New Jerusalem'. The Beveridge Report caused enthusiasm in Labour's ranks, concern in those of the Tories who could not avoid jumping on the bandwagon, hoping it would not proceed too speedily.[9] At their 1945 Conference the Conservatives carried a resolution in favour of 'a vigorous policy of full employment' and a comprehensive national health service 'available to all', though Tory backbenchers systematically opposed Bevan's specific plans whenever they could. In 1948 the Conservative Conference 'expressed its satisfaction that the present government (Labour) has adopted the proposals made by the Coalition Government under Mr. Churchill for fuller social security'.[10] Standing up boldly against the welfare state after the war would have taken some guts and/or a strong urge to court unpopularity. The Conservative Party was too wise to have either. In analogous manner, its brethren in other countries (re)discovered their social conscience. In Norway, for example, the non-socialist parties voted in the Storting (Parliament) in favour of all welfare legislation, including the law on family allowances of 1946.[11] They could not have done otherwise: during the war they had accepted the basic proposals of the Norwegian Labour Party – the welfare state, full employment and a planned industrial expansion.[12] In Sweden, in the 1940s, the conservatives backed all major welfare reforms and were, arguably, keener on universal pension rights than either the social democrats or the liberals.[13]

Nevertheless, it is significant that everywhere in Europe it was the parties of the Left which were seen as best suited to carry out social reforms, to fight for them against vested interests, to make them a political priority, and to resist the inevitable compromises longer and more determinedly than others. In Britain, the electorate had little doubt that the Labour Party was the party of welfare reform and voted accordingly. People wanted better health care and job security, though they remained hostile to the prospect of increased state direction of their private life. There is no evidence that the demand for social reform was based on an ideological commitment to collectivism.[14]

The spirit of the time was on the side of social reformism. Only this can explain the Conservative Party's manifesto. This was called *Mr Churchill's Declaration of Policy to the Electors*, in an effort to avoid any reference to the party of the great war leader. Mr Churchill's declaration contained modified support for the same reform ideas as the Labour Party was advocating: a high and stable level of employment; a compulsory national insurance scheme; a comprehensive health service; and a massive housing programme.[15] It was the most left-wing Conservative manifesto ever.

This reflected the amazing unpopularity of capitalism everywhere in Europe immediately after the war. These years constituted the nadir of capitalist ideology. Everyone was in favour of state intervention and structural reforms; no one wanted to return to the bad old days of the 1930s. Everyone sought to appropriate left-wing credentials. Thus, the Italian Christian democrat leader Alcide De Gasperi, in a speech on 23 July 1944, claimed that Karl Marx and Jesus Christ, 'a Jew like Marx', shared the same message of equality and universal brotherhood, 'the true image of redemption'.[16] He was following in the footsteps of left-leaning French Catholic intellectuals who, in the period of the Popular Front, had tried to put a religious gloss on Marxism by using Marx's early works.[17]

The Ahlen Programme of the German Christian democrats (1947) declared that 'The new structure of the German economy must start from the realisation that the period of uncurtailed rule by private capitalism is over'; and even as late as 1949, its Düsseldorf Programme stated boldly in the opening paragraph that 'the capitalist economic system has not done justice to the vital interests of the German people'.[18]

In France, the newly constituted Catholic Mouvement Républicain Populaire (MRP) in its first manifesto (24 November 1944) declared itself in favour of 'a revolution' to create an economy directed by a state 'liberated from the power of those who possess wealth'; it committed itself to structural reforms and to economic planning to establish a real social and political democracy.[19]

The supporters of free-market capitalism, usually congregated under the banner of liberal parties, were everywhere severely penalized by the electorate. Between 1945 and 1950, not a single pro-capitalist liberal party succeeded in becoming the main party of government anywhere in Europe. Yet though capitalism was defeated, socialism did not triumph on the battlefield of ideas. The economic theory which would guide the construction of the West European welfare states was the achievement of a liberal, John Maynard Keynes; while the document which constituted the nearest approximation to a blueprint for the post-war welfare state – the Beveridge Report – was written by another liberal (who campaigned for the British Liberal Party in 1945). Socialist theorists contributed very little to an understanding of how to institute social reforms under capitalism, or of how to run the system. Much has been made of this apparent incongruity. Some, defensively, have correctly argued that there were other influences and that many of the proposals contained in the two Beveridge reports, *Social Insurance and Allied Services* (1942) and *Full Employment in a Free Society* (1944), had been discussed before the war, in the 1920s and 1930s.[20] The fact of the matter, however, is that the political affiliations of Beveridge and Keynes are important only to their biographers. The 800,000 people who bought the 1942 Beveridge Report, thereby making it an unusual bestseller, were concerned with the author's proposals, not his ideological ancestry. In the dunghills of politics, as opposed to the groves of academia, what is decisive in the final instance is not the writing of policies or even their commissioning. The quintessence of the game is to seize the appropriate policies and struggle for their implementation. Here there is no contest: Labour fought for Beveridge with minimum reservation and maximum credibility. The historical precedents for such poaching of ideas are as abundant as they are illustrious: Bismarck stole the nationalist programme of the German Liberals, Disraeli the extension of the suffrage from Gladstone, Lenin the agrarian programme of the populists. It is not such a bad enterprise to use other people's ideas, especially if you have no good ones of your own.

The electors who wanted a welfare state were right to vote Labour. As John Ramsden pointed out, the Tories lost, not because their policies were different from Labour's, but because the electorate believed more strongly in Labour's intention to implement them.[21] The Conservatives would probably have built a welfare state, but it would have been based on an extension of the widely criticized pre-war social services and public assistance. They would not have accepted the principle of a citizen's universal right of access to services of an equal standard regardless of income.

The principle of universality, crowned in Britain by the National Insurance Act of 1946 and the introduction of the National Health Service in 1948, was the radically distinguishing feature of the British and Scandinavian welfare state. By following Esping-Andersen's path-breaking classification, we can distinguish three types of welfare states: the bourgeois-liberal (prevailing in the USA) with its means-test, modest universal transfers and benefits being directed essentially to those on low incomes; the 'corporatist' (prevailing in Germany and Austria), which steps in only when the family's capacity to service its members is seriously impaired; and finally the social-democratic welfare state, which promotes 'equality of the highest standards, not an equality of minimal needs as pursued elsewhere'. These standards were to be commensurate with the discriminating tastes of the new middle classes.[22]

For a few years after the war this social-democratic welfare state prevailed mainly in Britain. It was the most advanced welfare state in the world. What would later become the showcase of social-democratic welfarism, Sweden, still in the first stages of the construction of the *Folkhemmet* (People's Home), had not yet reached British levels, though some of its post-war achievements were impressive: the National Pension Act of 1946 extended the 1939 universal coverage principle to an even greater degree than in Britain by completely severing the connection between financial responsibility and benefit eligibility.[23] However, the *folkpension* was not index-linked until 1950 and the housing supplement benefit, which raised Swedish pensions considerably, was means-tested and not available to a majority of pensioners even after the system had been in operation three years.[24] The great change in Swedish pension provision occurred only in 1959, with the much fought-over introduction of the supplementary pension system (ATP), a compulsory, earnings-related addition to the basic national pension which extended to blue-collar workers the pension protection enjoyed by clerical workers.[25] A compulsory national health insurance was enacted in 1947, but was implemented only in 1955 because of inflation, political disputes and the opposition of the Swedish medical profession. Dental insurance was not introduced until 1974. Other Swedish reforms date from the 1950s and 1960s.[26]

The Det Norske Arbeiderparti (Norwegian Labour Party – DNA), which, like its British counterpart, had an absolute parliamentary majority, lagged far behind the Swedes in introducing the universal coverage principle in pensions. This was adopted only in 1957, a year after the Danes.[27] However, the DNA pioneered a system of universal and equal child allowance in 1946, which the Danes and Swedes soon followed. This had originally been advocated in 1934 by the Swedish reformers Gunnar and Alva Myrdal to counter declining fertility.[28]

The Swedish social democrats shared with virtually all the other parties of the Left (and also with some liberal and conservative parties) the belief that there would be a post-war depression. This pessimistic and erroneous assessment was based on the assumption that the economic instability and stagnation of the inter-war years would recur unless something was done. Accordingly, the main objective of the Swedish social democrats was full employment – by then an aim of all the Swedish 'bourgeois' parties – while welfare reforms would be used to achieve a fairer distribution of income and a relative equality in living standards.[29] These demands were incorporated in the 1944 document, *The Post-war Programme of the Swedish Labour Movement*.

The British welfare system was certainly one of the chief influences on the development of the French system of *sécurité sociale*, though not the only one. There was in France a pronounced concern with the low birth rate, as there had been in Sweden in the 1930s. Traditionally, that had been an apprehension of the patriotic Right, who were worried that there were never enough Frenchmen to stand up against the German hordes. This concern could be used, and was used, to suggest that a social security system, particularly one based on family allowances, might encourage the French to have more children. The result of this was that while British welfare policies reflected a 'male breadwinner' logic, those of France expressed a 'parental' logic. Family policies remained more popular in France, even though the Left failed to achieve power for so long. In Britain family allowances remained a 'subordinate and contested part of a welfare system organized largely around the wage'.[30]

It must also be said that, in France, social security legislation was not among the chief preoccupations of the parties of the Left. They much preferred to fight for nationalization, against *les trusts*, for the restoration of trade union rights after the Vichy interlude, and for an increase in wages.[31] The initiative for reform came from the minister of labour, Alexandre Parodi, and his *directeur général de la sécurité sociale*, Pierre Laroque. The Parodi social security plan was submitted to the Consultative Assembly in July 1945 and was welcomed by the SFIO, which dropped its own very similar plan. The communists, who had at first been suspicious, as they always were of reforms within capitalism, became enthusiastic supporters once their own man, Ambroise Croizat, became minister of labour (October 1945). The Catholics of the MRP raised objections because the plan was too centralist and would weaken the existing religious-based social security and mutual aid societies. The Parodi plan, now the Croizat Law, had as its ultimate objective a universalist social security system which would cover the entire population after the Beveridge model. Initially, it would cover payments for sickness, maternity, temporary disability and family allowances, but not unemployment benefits; and at first, only wage-earners (and their families) would be covered, not the self-employed.

The initial enthusiasm soon evaporated. By 1947 reformism was a spent force in France. The communists were out of power, while the socialists had run out of ideas and strength. The social security system did not proceed to its planned development. The Croizat Law had established that everyone would eventually be covered, but this goal was not finally achieved until 1967.[32] As in Britain, the impetus for social reform had not originated within the Left but, once the plans were on the table, the Left fought for them. In France, however, though supportive of social reforms, the Left had preferred to throw its weight behind wage increases, thus favouring the ephemeral over the enduring. Between October 1944 and April 1948, hourly wages trebled but prices increased fivefold: the purchasing power of salaried workers dropped by 30 per cent.[33]

Unemployment benefits were not provided in France because no one fought for them. Here Shennan is probably right when he suggests that the reason was historico-cultural: during the 1930s the French, unlike the British, did not have mass unemployment. The memories of those years were of political weakness and economic backwardness. Furthermore, as Pierre Laroque himself wrote in 1971, the general assumption in the aftermath of the war was that the low level of unemployment was likely to persist in the future.[34]

In countries where the Left could aspire to power only as part of a coalition government, the welfare state immediately revealed a feature which was disguised in countries such as Britain and Sweden, where the Left had a working majority. This was that welfare reforms in fact represented a compromise by which the parties of the Left and the trade unions would renounce the more radical aim of intervening directly in the restructuring of the private sector. This compromise was explicit in Holland, where during and after the Second World War a broad coalition was established on the basis of policies in favour of full employment, economic growth and the welfare state.

A similar compromise was achieved in Austria by a coalition of socialists (SPÖ) and Christian democrats (ÖVP). The ÖVP wanted to build on the existing corporatist framework of the Austrian welfare state, whose origins can be traced to the 1880s and the government of Eduard von Taaffe. The inter-war years had brought about a plethora of social insurance programmes organized according to occupational status, such as private salaried workers, public sector employees, industrial workers, and workers in agriculture and industry. The ÖVP – not unlike the MRP in France – wanted to maintain and even expand this system, increasing the number of social insurance bodies from fifty-eight to eighty-three, while the SPÖ wanted to abolish them in favour of a single scheme which would provide equality between the rights of industrial and white-collar workers. Beyond this dispute lay the principle of universality which required, for its application, the establishment of equal rights irrespective of occupation. The resulting compromise simply halved the number of separate pension and accident insurance schemes. Thus, even though the Workers Vacation Act of 1947 equalized the length of holidays paid to manual and salaried workers, Austria did not adopt the egalitarian welfare concept based on need.[35]

In Finland the 1946 coalition of communists (SKDL), agrarians and social democrats maintained full employment without reducing purchasing power, introduced family allowances, and 'probably did more for the workers and the underprivileged in Finland than any other Finnish government'. But the communists' coalition partners blocked a purge of the civil service, nationalization and a radical land reform.[36] The communists had been outmanoeuvred.

No major breakthrough towards the development of the welfare state occurred in Italy, even though both socialists and communists shared power with Christian democracy (DC) until 1947. Neither of the two left-wing parties adopted a welfare strategy or demanded major social reforms. Of course, the DC might have initiated such policy even without being pressurized by the Left; after all, its own ideology was open to the idea of a compassionate state and to the concept of welfare, albeit of a paternalistic kind. Indeed, the Catholics had been in the forefront of debates on how to reform the health and pension systems, and in 1947 the DC had supported the inclusion in the constitution of Article 38 which stated that 'workers have a right to insurance provisions necessary to meet their needs in case of accident, sickness, disability, old age and involuntary unemployment'. Accordingly, the Ministry of Labour appointed Ludovico D'Aragona (a social democrat) to head a commission with the task of finding out how to implement Article 38. Any desire to do so, however, was abandoned after the victory of the anti-communist and anti-socialist DC-led coalition in April 1948.[37] All that occurred was an improvement of the provisions established by the fascist regime in the 1930s.[38] Instead of a 'welfare *state*', the Christian democrats preferred to continue the fascist system based on quasi-governmental public institutions, the so-called *enti* such as INPS for social security, INAM for health and INAIL for accidents at work.[39] These *enti* were also centres of political power and patronage. The DC used them to build up its own dominance as a party.[40] One of the functions of the welfare state was to widen the consensus and the legitimacy of the modern state, but in Italy this function became associated with the preservation of the hegemony of a party, the DC, which, after 1945, was in government without interruption until 1993 – longer than any other European party.

By 1948, the DC had thrown in its lot with a 'capitalist' reconstruction of the Italian economy. By this I mean the acceptance that the future of Italy was intrinsically bound up with the future of the Western economy, that its growth would have to be oriented towards international trade, and that Italy's main advantage over its international competitors would be cheap labour. Belt-tightening was necessary, declared Alberto Pirelli, one of the wealthiest men in Italy, thus approving the popular slogan of 1949, *più macchine e meno maccheroni* (more machines and less pasta).[41] But a badly paid workforce could not provide the fiscal basis for a developed welfare state, and thus Italy, for the sake of its international competitiveness, had to dispense with major welfare reforms. Employment would eventually eliminate poverty. In the meantime, those who could not find work could leave the country and find it elsewhere. The Left was not able to offer any economic alternative to this strategy, other than protests against the unfairness of it all. The DC was not self-evidently pro-capitalist, being a heterogenous coalition united by a commitment to Christianity. The DC's rejection of social reformism was, rather, the outcome of a battle in which the anti-capitalist forces lost. The losers were not only the socialists and the communists but also the left-wing forces within the DC.[42] Until 1947 the strategy of the Left, especially that of the Communist Party, was to give priority to the preservation of the government of national unity. It was thought that only an alliance between the DC and the Left would make possible an eventual policy of social reform. But in 1947 a government including two Marxist parties, the PCI and the PSI, both committed to a neutralist foreign policy, was unlikely to remain in power. Had the DC gone against the logic of the Cold War and refused to 'choose' the West against the Soviet Union, it would probably have split and a second Catholic party would have emerged under the twin sponsorship of the church and the USA.

At no stage did the PCI use its prestige among the working class to unleash a militant mass movement committed to fighting for political reforms. Had that occurred, would the DC, out of alarm if not conviction, have initiated reforms to steal the thunder of the communists? Some historians believe that this would have occurred, but it is not convincing. Further communist-inspired agitation would have been taken as evidence of a Moscow-inspired conspiracy to destroy Italian democracy and establish totalitarian communism. In fact, the Christian democrats used repressive policies against the working-class movement between 1948 and 1953.[43] They had opted for the stick instead of the carrot. No wonder; at the time, in Italy, sticks were much cheaper than carrots.

One of the pressures behind the introduction of welfare systems in Europe after the war was the impossibility of reproducing the American system of high wages. Between 1945 and 1950, most governments were forced to resort at some stage to a policy of controlling wages, and this was true even in countries where socialists were in government. Welfare policies were a necessary counter-balance to policies enabling entrepreneurs to compete internationally by keeping labour costs down. Welfare states expressed a political compromise between the two main industrial classes which would otherwise have been locked in a constant battle.

In Britain, with the National Insurance Act of 1946, entitlement to welfare provisions became a consequence of citizenship and was to be financed out of general taxation. It was universal: 'The insurance scheme is one for all citizens irrespective of their means.'[44] This Act, which remained the corner-stone of Labour's welfare scheme and the basis for the welfare state, commanding all-party support, removed any connection between the market and welfare provision.[45]

Commodities produced for the market can only be exchanged through the market: they are offered to all and thus appear to be universally available. But this, as Marx showed long ago, disguises the reality of exchange relations: the demand for a commodity is valid only if it is backed by money; needs can be satisfied only if services can be bought. The human fellowship implied by the existence of a mass of commodities available to all is torn asunder by the brute and banal fact that these goods are available only to those who can, cash in hand, enter the market; those who do not, stay outside. The power to possess, even in the era of mass consumerism, remains a private power. But when consumption is achieved because the recipient has a recognized need (and not because he or she owns money), it is no longer consumption but the exercise of a social right. The commodity, usually a service, has become 'de-commodified'.[46] The discourse of commerce must give way to another voice, to the language of rights and citizenship. Just as universal suffrage extended political rights to all citizens, universal social rights break down further barriers to full membership of a community. This is what T. H. Marshall was suggesting when he divided citizenship into three elements: civil, political and social.[47] As social rights to welfare, health, security and education developed, class distinction, he believed, would be eliminated except for those 'which have no appropriate economic function'.[48] In this sense universal rights extend citizenship, now no longer restricted to the few – for instance, to those who own property, or those who can pay, or who are male, or Christians, or white. Citizenship makes possible one of the goals of the French revolution: *fraternité*.

Does this principle of universality coincide with that of socialism? In theory, all the services provided by the welfare state could be provided by a free market in which consumers can purchase welfare services. Even in this case there would still be instances, such as blood transfusion services, in which altruistic non-market relations are a far safer, cheaper and more efficient system of allocation than market relations, as Richard N. Titmuss demonstrated in his now classic *The Gift Relationship: From Human Blood to Social Policy*.

For a market-based social service system to fulfil the criteria of universality, two conditions are required:

1. Full employment: all citizens between school-leaving age and retirement age must have the possibility of being gainfully employed.
2. High wages: minimum wages must be high enough to enable all citizens to purchase privately the necessary pension and insurance plans which would protect them against illness, disablement, temporary unemployment and old age.

If free-market capitalism were able to fulfil these two conditions, it would also fulfil, in practice, the criteria of universality: everyone would be able to obtain, through the market, all the social protection needed. The full employment condition precludes the formation of a group in the population excluded from the private market for social services, while the high wages condition enables all to purchase necessary goods; the sole effect of salary differentials would be on the apportioning of non-essential goods. However, the conjunction of high wages and full employment has seldom, if ever, occurred. Thus, it is possible to argue that the universal welfare principle has never been achieved in a society entirely determined by market relations. Its introduction in Western Europe after 1945 required parties biased against the 'free market'.

But to return to the question: is the introduction of the universal welfare principle socialism? If socialism is a state of affairs – an 'end-state' – which describes the overall organization of a particular social order, then the universal welfare principle is not socialism because it co-exists with a dominant capitalist production system. If socialism denotes a social relation, then the universal welfare principle whereby access to a service or a good is available to all members of the collectivity, irrespective of their incomes, signals the presence of an element of socialism co-existing with elements of capitalism.

It will be worth noting, *en passant*, that attempts to identify the 'end-state' conception of socialism as a peculiarity of Marxists and Leninists require a rather monolithic view of the actual works of Marx and Lenin. In reality, their writings are permeated by the same acute contradiction that pervades the whole of socialist thought: that between socialism-as-a-process and socialism-as-an-end-state. For instance, in *The German Ideology*, Marx and Engels wrote:

> Communism is for us not a stable state which is to be established, an *ideal* to which reality will have to adjust itself. We call communism the *real* movement which abolishes the present state of things.[49]

Even Lenin, arguably the chief strategist of the 'end-state', believed that embryonic elements of communism could begin to develop within the interstices of the capitalist order and that these 'shoots of communism', as he called them, were the public provision of social goods, such as nurseries. In a telling passage in which he admitted that, notwithstanding all the Bolshevik laws emancipating woman, she continues to be 'a domestic slave' stultified by the boring drudgery of housework, he added:

> Do we in practice pay sufficient attention to this question, which in theory every Communist considers indisputable? Of course not. Do we take proper care of the *shoots* of communism which already exist in this sphere? Again the answer is *no*. Public catering establishments, nurseries, kindergartens – here we have examples of these shoots ... which can *really emancipate women* .... These means are not new, they (like all the material prerequisites for socialism) were created by large-scale capitalism.[50]

If socialism is considered a process rather than an end, it can, in principle, begin to be implemented immediately. The expectation of momentous revolutionary breaks, historical ruptures and insurrectionary onslaughts can be disposed of. The terrain can be freed for more subtle, but also more nebulous, notions of progress. Social reforms acquire a new meaning. In the socialist movement prior to 1914, the prevailing view of social reforms was that they were temporary expedients designed to alleviate the conditions of existence of the toiling masses until an inevitable catastrophic crisis would project the social order into a new, socialist orbit. By 1945, social reforms were seen as elements of socialism to be introduced within capitalism; their eventual growth and extension would bring nearer the day when capitalism would no longer exist. Bernstein's old heresy had come to be accepted.

None of this was cogently theorized by the Left, either in wartime or in the period of post-war reconstruction. The socialist and social-democratic movement after 1945 lost interest more or less totally in theoretical approaches which had been a feature of the old German SPD of Kautsky and Bernstein and Hilferding, and of the Austro-Marxists such as Otto Bauer.

Nevertheless, the view of social reforms as elements of socialism growing within the interstices of capitalism presents considerable problems. Social reforms could be pursued for a variety of motives: because they benefit people; because they stabilize the system, thereby increasing the consensus it enjoys; because they enable citizens to obtain collectively by political means what they would not be able to obtain through the market; and so on. A specifically socialist justification for social reforms is that they empower ordinary people, by conferring upon them new rights of a social and economic nature. In so doing, socialism can present itself as the continuation and development of an older liberal-democratic process through which ordinary people had acquired the *political* rights which were once the prerogative of the few. Socialism would provide the majority with hitherto unattainable social rights. The Chinese wall between liberal 'bourgeois' democracy and socialist democracy, so forcefully stressed by Lenin, could give way to the idea of a continuum between liberalism and socialism, in which social reforms would redistribute power and hence bring about a drastic reduction in inequality.

It should be said that the proposition that the welfare state has led to considerable social equality begs many questions. Measuring inequality is no simple task. The available data are not satisfactory and there are also major conceptual problems: how to distinguish between lifetime and current income, for example, and what allowance to make for children of different ages.[51] What can be established is that in 1938, in Britain, the top 10 per cent of the population possessed 34.4 per cent of all post-tax income and in 1949 this percentage had been reduced to 27.1.[52] However, the main causes of this were the high levels of taxation and inflation during the Second World War, rather than full employment and the welfare state. The cost of welfare is such that it can be financed only by transfer of incomes within the middle- and lower-income groups, rather than from the rich to the poor: it cannot be otherwise, for there are never enough rich and the rich are never rich enough. Those who bemoan this should reflect that the point is not to make the rich poorer (though this would not be tragic), but to eliminate poverty and gross differentials which degrade the noble and revolutionary aim, *l'égalité*, which has inspired so many struggles. In the long run, the equality which is really worth pursuing is not levelling modest income differences, but the effective equalization of social as well as political rights in order to provide equal dignity for all. *That* is worth fighting for. The difference in income which allows the rich to purchase a diamond as big as the Ritz may be vexing to destitute diamond-lovers. But it is not as iniquitous as the private purchase of a life-saving operation to the exclusion of others who cannot afford it.

Controlling Capitalism: Nationalization and Economic Planning

In the late 1940s most socialists thought of socialism as an 'end-state', a final goal. Their gradualism led them to believe that this desirable state of affairs could be the result of the accumulation of reforms or else, perhaps, the outcome of a decisive legislative *fiat* executed at an appropriate moment when the time was ripe and the socialist parties had a substantial majority. This 'state of socialism' involved the end of capitalism and this, in turn, could only mean the abolition of the private ownership of the principal means of production. The introduction of the universal welfare principle was seen by many left-wing socialists as a major and important reform, but not quite as radical as state ownership of industry.

It is strange and perplexing that, given the importance of the policy of state ownership, no Left party in Western Europe (including communist parties) had detailed plans aimed at the abolition of the private property of at least some of the means of production. The general and vague anti-capitalist rhetoric which pervaded even some of the continental confessional parties disguised the evident shortage of ideas on how to abolish capitalism. Socialists knew, most of the time, what to do in the present; they knew what they wanted for the future. But how to establish the connection between today's reforms and tomorrow's socialism remained as mysterious as it had been at the end of the nineteenth century, when Bernstein had suggested, in effect, that socialists should abandon the future to concentrate on the present.

In Britain, the Labour Party found itself in a situation which would become increasingly familiar: the social reforms sought by the Left, for which it had gained electoral support and political power, had to be financed by a strong wealth-creating economy. Many socialists believed that this could be achieved through complete state control of industry. It was thought that centrally planned management would be more 'rational' and more efficient, and that the country as a whole would benefit from large-scale economies and from the adoption of scientific principles of management.

In reality, in 1945, the nationalization of the entire economy was not on the agenda anywhere in Western Europe. Where the Left was weak, it was impossible to convince reluctant coalition partners to proceed along such a radical road. Where the Left was strong, as in Britain or the Nordic countries, no visible minority, let alone a majority, emerged within it with plans for achieving such grandiose objectives.

In the absence of a plan for the elimination of the capitalist economy, the financial requirements for social reforms had to be provided by the capitalist economy itself. Socialist parties faced an unavoidable paradox: in order to pay for social welfare, it was imperative that the market be made as efficient as possible; to follow 'socialist' policies, it was essential to be pro-capitalist. If the private sector could not be abolished – at least in the immediate future

– then it had to be encouraged to produce as much wealth as possible and to be an efficient allocator of resources, so as to provide employment for all. Only when the private sector failed to function properly could the state be expected to step in through subsidies, encouragement, concessions, special help and, if necessary, nationalization.

Some socialists thought that the private sector could not perform its wealth-creating tasks adequately. Had it not brought about a massive depression in the 1930s? By 1945 it was widely assumed on the Left that capitalism would not be able to guarantee constant growth and economic development. It was thus necessary for the state to take over some of its key sectors through a policy of gradual nationalization. If priority had to be given to social reforms and their financing, it followed that the gradual transfer of segments of the private economy into public ownership should be determined by the following considerations:

1. Viability and efficiency: the least viable and hence more inefficient sectors of the capitalist economy should be nationalized first.
2. Strategic importance: the most strategic sectors of the capitalist economy (for example, banking or the power industry) should be nationalized and used as instruments to ensure that the remainder of the private sector followed an economically profitable and socially desirable path.

Either way, the results to be aimed for would be an increased level of efficiency in the private economy. Either way, the socialist motivation for partial and/or gradual nationalization coincided with the motivations of those who advocated it on the non-socialist grounds of capitalist rationalization. There were good 'managerial' grounds for nationalization: the new state-owned industry would become more efficient and would benefit the rest of the economy by ensuring an efficient supply of goods and services at reasonable prices, thus lowering average costs.

In practice the common goal of all post-1945 West European governments was an efficient capitalist economy and nationalizations were, generally speaking, conceived as part of this goal. In no instance, however, was the expanded state sector used in an organic or strategic manner. On the contrary, each nationalized industry was conceived as autonomous and instructed to fulfil its tasks separately from the others.

In Britain the nationalizations proposed in the Labour Party's 1945 manifesto *Let Us Face the Future* all had practical justifications. The state takeover of the Bank of England was supposedly designed to ensure full employment. The objective of nationalizing the coal, gas and electricity industries was to make it possible to modernize production, lower charges, prevent waste and increase efficiency.[53] Labour Party activists clamoured for public ownership for all sorts of reasons: because it was in Clause Four of the party's constitution; because it was the beginning of socialism; because it was imperative to give the state the necessary instruments of control and intervention. Yet in 1945 the party had no worked-out plans for nationalization, even though they had been frequently discussed in the 1930s. This was so even in the mining industry, where the pressures for public ownership from the unions were strongest and Conservative objections weakest.[54] Prior to 1945, peacetime nationalizations, as Peter Hennessy reminds us, had been resorted to more frequently by the Conservatives than by the Labour Party: Churchill, when First Lord of the Admiralty in 1912, bought the Anglo-Iranian Oil Company (BP), Stanley Baldwin took over the BBC in 1927, Neville Chamberlain created the British Overseas Airways Corporation in 1939.[55]

Between 1945 and 1949 the Labour government extended the boundaries of state property to include the Bank of England, civil aviation, telecommunications and coal in 1946; the railways, long-distance road haulage and electricity in 1947; gas in 1948; iron and steel in 1949.[56] All nationalizations received parliamentary approval before February 1947, less than two years after the Labour victory, except for the Gas Bill (February 1948) and the controversial nationalization of iron and steel (November 1948). These nationalized industries were either basic to the economy or public utilities or both. None was flourishing or particularly profitable, with the exception of road haulage and, possibly, iron and steel. Consumer interests were important, but capitalist firms were among the main purchasers of these services, and it was in their interests too to obtain coal, gas and electricity at reasonable prices and to have an efficient transport system. The idea of introducing greater industrial democracy or workers' control was never seriously considered.

Labour blueprints in the 1930s had emphasized the strategic importance of controlling the financial sector and establishing a National Investment Board. Bankers and financiers always had a special role in the demonology of the Labour movement. Consequently, one might have expected that the acquisition of the Bank of England would be used by the Labour government to control the City and the rest of the banking system. But the Bank was never employed to discipline, control, or dominate the banks. Labour missed this chance and never sought to explain why. Establishing a decisive measure of control over the banking system as a whole would not have been an exceptionally radical action. After all, this is what happened in Austria in the late 1940s under a coalition of socialists and Christian democrats, and in Italy under Mussolini in the 1930s.

In Labour Britain the nationalization of the Bank of England remained a purely technical and institutional act and was so designated by the chancellor of the exchequer, Hugh Dalton.[57] The case for it was so overwhelming that the Conservatives did not vote against it; some, for example Robert Boothby, Churchill's parliamentary private secretary, even voted in favour.[58] No subsequent Tory leader ever asked for its privatization.

The coalmining industry was backward, grossly inefficient, overmanned and plagued by bad industrial relations, except for some pits, such as Fife and Powell Dylfryn. No one seriously assumed that the private sector would be able to modernize it. Nationalization had been on the agenda since the findings of the Sankey Commission in 1919. Yet the Labour Party had never produced a plan for the industry, much to the surprise of the Minister of Fuel, the singularly obtuse and incompetent Emmanuel (later Lord) Shinwell. In fact, it was Shinwell who should have been expected to provide such a plan, for he had been a minister of mines in 1924 and again from 1929 to 1931 and represented a mining constituency.[59]

The railways, though in private hands, were heavily dependent on public subsidies. In their last year under private ownership, they lost £60 million. Huge sums were required to re-equip the industry and no private capital would have been forthcoming. The case for nationalization on practical grounds was exceptionally strong. Labour, however, nationalized long-distance road haulage as well. This, unlike the railways, was profitable and roused stiff Conservative and Liberal opposition.

The nationalization of electricity and gas had been recommended by the Heyworth Committee set up in 1944. Even so, the Conservatives fought against the nationalization of gas and disputed every part of the Bill.[60] Electricity was a different matter because 60 per cent of supply was already under municipal control and the McGowan Committee in 1936 had set out the case for public ownership on grounds of efficiency.[61]

Serious opposition arose in connection with the nationalization of iron and steel, the sole manufacturing industry to be subjected to a state takeover. The Labour Party had not been enthusiastic about it. Industrial relations were good and the unions did not fight for it. The cabinet was divided: those who were in favour of nationalization argued that state intervention was required to ensure the future of iron and steel. No one argued in favour of the takeover on ideological grounds. The Bill was the only measure in Labour's term of office which the Lords delayed, causing it to become law at the end of 1949 with its vesting date postponed until 1951. Soon afterwards, Labour lost the general election and the Conservatives privatized iron and steel, the only industry to be denationalized until the privatization of the 1980s.

It is not clear what nationalization achieved. No serious examination of alternative forms of control had ever been undertaken. Alec Cairncross doubts whether nationalization did much to ensure full employment, or to stabilize the economy, or had any impact on the distribution of income (since extremely generous compensation was paid to the owners).[62] Furthermore, as it was generally accepted that commercial profitability was the overall guiding criterion for the nationalized industries, it is not clear how there could be any significant change in management policy away from the system operating under private ownership.

In some instances, for example the coalmines and the railways, there had been pressure for nationalization from the workforce who, quite rightly considering the appalling behaviour of the owners in the 1920s, assumed that it would improve their working conditions and their wages. In the iron and steel sector, however, workers already enjoyed relatively good conditions, as well as satisfactory industrial relations, and were consequently indifferent to nationalization. The general assumption among many trade unionists was that the state would be a better and more enlightened employer than private capitalists. Others, less kindly, would observe that the state could absorb losses indefinitely and that nationalization was therefore a recipe for over-manning, restrictive practices, and a level of wages higher than productivity would warrant. From the point of view of the national economy, however, overmanning is counter-productive only in a situation of full employment, since it penalizes other industries which might require workers employed elsewhere and keeps wages artificially high. In a situation of unemployment, overmanning in one sector may be a rational policy because it reduces the need for welfare spending: those who might require benefits remain in employment.

In a mixed economy the public sector remains constrained by the over-arching requirement of maintaining an efficient and profitable private sector, though it does not follow that commercial criteria in the public sector must always be maintained. There are circumstances in which it may be advisable to pursue a policy of lower costs, rather than profitability – for instance, where a monopoly controls basic services such as gas and electricity. This would lower costs in the private sector, thereby making it internationally more competitive. In effect, this would amount to a taxpayers' subsidy to private enterprise.

By nationalizing public utilities the Labour government acquired a potenti-ally formidable weapon for restructuring the private sector. For example, by using differential prices it could have induced the location of industry in areas where it wished to increase employment and investment for social reasons, or helped export or import-substitution. As part of an overall plan, or at least a fairly comprehensive industrial policy, nationalization could have played a major role. The Labour government, however, had no industrial strategy, no comprehensive plan. It simply maintained the financial and physical controls it had inherited from the wartime coalition.[63] These cannot be considered to be the British equivalent of the French post-war planning policies established by Jean Monnet, let alone a precursor of the Japanese post-war system of collaboration between banks, industry and government through the Ministry of International Trade and Industry.[64] The most devastating criticism one can make of the Attlee government was that, at least until 1947, it produced nothing that remotely resembled a policy towards the private sector. In 1946, for instance, the government produced a Steel Plan aimed at rationalizing the industry but stopping short of outright nationalization. The plan failed partly because of the unco-operative attitude of many entrepreneurs, partly because the government quickly abandoned its long-term goals of restructuring in favour of immediate requirements such as maximizing exports and employment.[65] The main problem with Labour was not that it did not have policies for transforming the capitalist economy into a socialist one, but that it did not know how to run the capitalist economy.[66]

The standard and rather trite reply to the above observations is that businessmen, rather than politicians and civil servants, are best at running the economy. More than fifty years of British economic decline in the face of competition from countries equipped with planning mechanisms and/or some form of industrial policy such as Japan, Germany and France, ought to have exposed the utter bankruptcy of this position. But ideologies can usually withstand the onslaught of hard facts.

A slightly less insular and intellectually limited cabinet than Attlee's might have studied more thoroughly the far more convincing experiment in state planning that was under way in France. However, even the most entrenched provincialism has its limits: Stafford Cripps did cast a rapid glance across the Channel. In 1948 he asked Monnet to come to London with some of his advisers to explain to him the French modernization plan. In his memoirs Monnet wrote: 'These meetings were so interesting that Attlee and several of his ministers ... attended them.' Monnet, however, was trying to persuade the British of something they could not even begin to understand: the need to create a situation of profound economic interdependence between the two countries.[67] Monnet, unlike most other planners, always realized that a national plan, in order to succeed, had to be thought out within an international perspective. But the British were not ready to forge special links with the Continent. Their trade was still prevalently extra-European, their foreign policy still planetary.

According to Cairncross, there were really only two serious official attempts to explain what economic planning might involve. One was the preliminary section of *The Economic Survey of 1947* personally written by Stafford Cripps (when president of the Board of Trade); the other was a memorandum written by Gaitskell in 1949, when he was minister of fuel and power.[68] Neither minister ever succeeded, or indeed attempted, to put his thoughts into practice. Once they became Chancellor (Cripps in 1947–50 and Gaitskell in 1950–51), they instantaneously developed a belief in the supremacy of the Budget as the most powerful instrument of economic policy.

What induced the British government to try to do something with the private sector was not socialism, but the balance of payments crisis of 1947. This made production the main issue, supplanting unemployment.[69] Consumption was held back with singular severity, exports raced ahead and, by 1948, the balance of payments deficit was wiped out. The subsequent sterling devaluation of 1949 therefore had nothing to do with restoring British trade to balance, since it was in balance already. Britain's strong export performance was no mean achievement. In Cairncross's words, 'If the balance of payments is looked after ... industrial economies can recover very fast.'[70] There was much talk to the effect that 'planning' had done the trick. That was not quite true: much of the wartime control machinery was dismantled, thus (to use the language of today) 'deregulating' the private sector. The emphasis on export meant that domestic consumption had to be cut through rationing. Expenditure on social services, however, was not reduced. The policy followed could be characterized as one which favoured the export sectors of the economy − that is, the dominant part of private capitalism − and the poor, who gained from the stable level of social spending and from rationing (without which they would not have been able to pay the free-market price of the rationed goods).

What was not utilized was the very large public sector the state had just acquired. As the official historian of British nationalization wrote: 'Very little thought had been given to the organization of the nationalized industries either in the Labour movement or in Whitehall.'[71] Why, then, was there such a wide extension of public control if Labour did not know what to do with it?[72] The most obvious explanation is, quite simply, that the traditional left-wing bias against private ownership met with little resistance. Its logic seemed to be that because the state was, at least in formal terms, subject to demo-cratic political control through the electoral and parliamentary processes, everything subjected to state control was, directly or indirectly, democratic, while everything still in private hands remained 'outside democracy'. In other words, the extension of state ownership was good in itself, because it brought the 'end-state' of socialism that much nearer. When the order of priority of nationalizations came to be decided, pragmatism prevailed: the state initially extended its domain in those areas of the economy where there was little effective opposition to nationalization. The Conservatives, defeated and demoralized, wisely chose to put up resistance only in strategically selected instances, where the case for nationalization was at its most contentious. They knew they would live to fight another day. Of course, whether or not a nationalization measure was opposed is no indication of whether or not it represented a threat to private capital accumulation. The interests of capitalism 'in general' are as hard to locate as those of socialism. This calls for perplexing political calculations or for endlessly fascinating (or tedious) debates, depend-ing on one's point of view.[73]

The fact that the Labour Party did not seek to reform the private sector of industry, that it had no serious industrial policy or training programme, is evidence not of the purity of its socialism, but of its unconsciously reverential and touching faith in the capabilities of the capitalist system. In spite of its rhetoric, Labour assumed that capitalism would recover more or less spon-taneously and create the wealth required to pay for social reforms. Like all previous governments, Labour approached the private sector with a *laissez-faire* attitude at the micro-economic level. The most important thing the Labour government did between 1945 and 1950 was an act of omission: it did not reform capitalism. How this might have been achieved was not even considered. Thus, Labour observed to the letter the closing proposition of Wittgenstein's *Tractatus Logico-Philosophicus*: 'Whereof one cannot speak, thereof one must be silent.' Unasked questions will never find an answer.

In the rest of Western Europe nationalization became a strong priority only in France and Austria. In Norway, which, like Britain, had a Labour government with an absolute majority in Parliament, very little was nationalized. Railways and telecommunications were already under state ownership.[74] The Central Bank was taken over, as it was in Britain, France, Holland and other countries in Europe. The state also acquired as war compensation German assets including one of the biggest aluminium companies in Europe and most of the mines.[75] Otherwise, the pragmatic Norwegian social democrats (DNA) left their private sector intact, including the powerful shipbuilding interests, and concentrated on social reform and income redistribution. Even by 1960, after fifteen years of uninterrupted DNA administration, Norway's state sector was still proportionately smaller than that of Germany, which had not yet experienced a single year of social democracy.

In parallel with Norway, the Swedish Social Democratic Party (SAP), in its 1944 programme, dropped nationalization as an effective instrument of state policy and referred to 'the rights of determination over production', a coy formula vaguely equivalent to the British Labour Party's use of the term 'common ownership' in Clause Four of its constitution. It advocated the use of public works to compensate for any fall in employment in the private sector, and a wages policy aimed at levelling differences between agriculture and other branches of production.[76] The SAP declared that it did not intend all property to be in state hands or all economic activity to be directed by a central agency. It did, however, still intend to nationalize inefficient industries, oil importation and insurance companies, and to set up a state commercial bank.[77] There was a strong emphasis on the democratization of the economy and on planning, seen as a pragmatic, 'trial and error' policy greatly preferable to nationalization.[78]

The SAP was in an even better position than the Labour Party to implement a radical socialist programme. Sweden had emerged unscathed from the war, having refrained from taking part in it. It was – in per capita terms – the richest country in Europe after Switzerland, and was in a perfect position to meet the demands of reconstruction.[79] As elsewhere, the end of the war had found the country radicalized: the Swedish communists achieved their best electoral results ever (11 per cent) in the 1946 local elections.[80]

The conditions were thus favourable for implementing the more radical aspect of the SAP programme: the widely expected post-war recession had not materialized,[81] and unemployment had fallen 'spontaneously'. The nationalization proposals were passed on to royal commissions whose task it was to open wide consultations with interest groups. This approach entailed accepting an important general principle, namely, that a major transfer of privately-owned industry into the public domain would occur only if widely acceptable. The so-called 'bourgeois' parties launched a massive and ultimately successful campaign against public ownership. The commissions suggested that only a minor restructuring of the business sector was desirable and that only the oil importing and processing industry should be nationalized.[82] But not even this industry was taken over, and so even the limited nationalization promised by the 1944 programme was abandoned.

Once this had occurred, it followed, almost naturally, that the expansion of the Swedish social-democratic state would require the co-operation of the business sector. In the absence of a powerful public sector, any state policy of economic rationalization necessarily requires an overall agreement between the government and industry. Nationalizations were abandoned in Sweden not only because of widespread opposition, but also because there did not appear to be any obvious connection between an expanding state sector and the central aims of the SAP – namely, full employment and an increase in real wages to the level of 1939.[83]

In Holland state ownership was not conceived as an instrument of socialist reconstruction, but as an extension of the 'creeping' nationalizations which had begun even before the First World War 'from the bottom up', when much of the gas, electricity and transport industries had been municipalized. On the whole it was conceived as an attempt at economic rationalization, rather than as a step towards socialism. The new nationalized industries were expected to make a profit just as they had done under municipal control, in order to finance other local activities.[84] The requirements of coalition politics forced the Dutch Labour Party to abandon in 1936 its project of economic planning, the so-called *Plan Socialism*, as they conceded to their Christian democratic allies the control of the Ministry of Economic Affairs (see chapter 3).

Economic policy was developed on the basis of a system of formal compromises. During the war the trade unions and employers had formed the 'Foundation of Labour' and supported a succession of coalition governments whose core were the PvdA (the Labour Party) and the Katholieke Volkspartei (Catholic People's Party). These two parties governed together between 1946 and 1948, and then included in the coalition the Liberals and the Christelijk-Historische Unie (Christian Historical Union – CHU) until 1952. The same coalition, minus the Liberals but including the Anti-Revolutionaire Partij, ruled the country between 1952 and 1958. The unions agreed not to strike and to desist from demanding industrial democracy, while the employers committed themselves to full employment and recognized the unions. Wages were to be negotiated between the government and the Foundation of Labour (formalized in 1950 as the Social and Economic Council). Catholics and socialists rejected liberal economic policies and favoured various forms of corporatism, but disagreed on economic planning. This post-war settlement lasted until the end of the 1950s, permitting the PvdA to be in government for nearly fifteen years even though its share of the vote, less than 30 per cent, was low by the standards of West European social democracy.[85]

In West Germany, left-wing initiatives to reform the economy were considerably hampered by the policies of the American occupying forces. The SPD leader, Kurt Schumacher, demanded in 1945 the nationalization of the mines, the heavy goods industry, power, transport, insurance and banking. The SPD economic spokesman, Victor Agartz, declared at the Hanover Congress (1946) that the party rejected liberalism, monopoly capitalism, the corporate state, and was in favour of a planned economy and 'socialization' (this term was favoured over nationalization).[86]

Public ownership was advocated not only by the SPD, but also in the surprisingly left-wing 1947 Ahlen Programme of the Christian Democratic Union. The CDU became an explicitly pro-capitalist party only a couple of years later. Still unpopular were liberal views, such as those held by Alfred Müller-Armack, the little-known author of the formula of the *Soziale Marktwirschaft* (social market economy), whose suggestive ambiguity led to its eventual hijacking by an ever-increasing number of European political parties.

As early as October 1946, Ernest Bevin, then, as foreign secretary, in virtual control of the British zone of occupation, supported the nationalization proposed by both the SPD and the CDU.[87] Thus, public ownership was supported by the two main German parties and the main European occupying forces. That was not enough. Without a central authority over the whole country a nationalization programme could not be implemented. An attempt was made to insert into the regional constitutions of the new *Länder* the principle of state ownership. In Hesse the German Left scored a major success when, with the support of both the CDU and the communists (only the Liberals were against), the Constituent Assembly of that *Land* voted for Article 41 which would have made the nationalization of 169 firms inevitable. The US occupying forces, under General Lucius D. Clay, insisted that the article should be subjected to a referendum separately from the constitution as a whole. The results showed 76.8 per cent of the electorate to be in favour of the constitution and 71.9 per cent in favour of Article 41. In spite of this, the US military government forbade its implementation.[88] The USA put pressure on the British military government to desist from favouring nationalization policies in their zone. Similar left-leaning legislation establishing some form of industrial democracy in Hessen, Baden-Württemberg and Bremen was vetoed by the Americans either directly or through pressure on the French and the British. Communist newpapers were censored, protest strikes banned, and land reform plans drastically reduced.[89]

The US was able to shape the reconstruction of capitalism in West Germany to a far greater extent than in the rest of Western Europe, including Italy. Germany had been defeated and had no government. The only possible obstacles to US hegemony were the other forces of occupation, the French and the British (in Japan, the purest case of US hegemony, not even these hindrances existed).[90] Once the British and US zones were merged in the joint Bi-Zone (January 1947), the Americans took the lead and 'swarms of American "steel people" and lawyers arrived in Düsseldorf ... who had little sympathy for Britain's industrial plans for the Ruhr. The most they could conceive of was deconcentration, but strictly within the framework of private capitalism.'[91] The Germans had no choice but to co-operate. Those who favoured a clear-cut capitalist reconstruction did so with delight.

The picture was not one of unrelieved gloom for the forces of the Left. The SPD obtained the insertion into the Basic Law of the Federal Republic of Article 15, which stipulated that 'land, natural resources and means of production may be socialized and transformed into public ownership'. In the British zone the trade unions obtained special participation rights in coal and steel concerns. But this remained an anomaly: by the time free elections were held in 1949, resulting in the overwhelming victory of the CDU, Germany had not undergone any of the social and economic reforms which occurred in many other West European countries. Free elections in 1945 would probably have resulted in a left-wing majority or, at least, a government of national unity in which the strength of the SPD, coupled with the CDU's acceptance of nationalizations, would almost certainly have brought about the creation of a large public sector.

This is precisely what happened in Austria, where the relation of forces between the parties resembled that of Germany, but where two crucial variables, absent in Germany, led to the creation of a considerable state sector comparable to the British and the French. The two variables were early national elections (25 November 1945) and the favourable attitude of the USA towards Austrian nationalizations. The elections resulted in the 'Social Christian' ÖVP gaining an absolute majority of seats (85 out of 165), while the SPÖ had seventy-six and the communists four. Austria was then occupied in the east by the Red Army and in the west by the Anglo-American allies. Furthermore, the economic situation was disastrous. This is what led the three parties to form a national government.

The SPÖ was committed to achieving a maximum of socialization, partly out of ideology and partly to control the economy. The ÖVP, just like the German and Italian Christian democratic parties, was in favour of some measure of state intervention. It was widely assumed that priority would have to be given to the nationalization of basic industries which had been destroyed during the war and whose senior management had co-operated with the Nazis. There was also a widespread desire to establish an Austrian claim to the ownership of these firms in order to escape the compensation clauses agreed by the Allies at Potsdam. According to these clauses, all German property had to be considered as belonging to the Allies as war compensation. This would have involved much of Austria's basic industry, whose main shareholders were in fact Germans. Nationalization was thus a practical device to enable Austria to keep its industries.

The first Nationalization Act passed by the Austrian Parliament (1946) designated the following enterprises to be nationalized: the entire engineering metal industry, the Danube Shipping Company, the Austrian branches of the German electricity industry (AEG-Union, Siemens-Schukert Werke), the largest nitrogen plant, the entire oil refinery industry, and the three principal banks. The strongest objections to these state takeovers were registered by the USSR, still an occupying power and the main beneficiary of the Potsdam clauses. The Austrian Parliament overruled the Soviet objections; this was possible because the Allied Control Council could not reach unanimous agreement to veto the Act.[92] Thus, in Austria nationalizations were carried out against Soviet wishes and with US support! In 1947 a second Nationalization Act brought the large electricity industry within the public sector. By the early 1950s, 22 per cent of Austria's industrial output was in state hands. If firms controlled by the nationalized banks are included, the state sector would reach 70 per cent of industrial production.

As in Britain and France, Austrian nationalizations did not lead to a more 'social' or socialist way of running the economy. Managerial criteria of productive efficiency continued to dominate the state sector, with the object of making the Austrian economy competitive.[93] The SPÖ had, at least on paper, a strong commitment to planning, but the main impetus came from the Marshall Plan, which forced the government to produce a long-term programme for proposed investment in both the private and public sectors for the period 1949–53.[94] Much of this machinery was dismantled in the 1950s, when American aid dwindled. Nevertheless, the Marshall Plan was a decisive factor in the overall economic success of the Austrian nationalization programme: 50 per cent of Marshall funds were used to re-finance the state sector.[95]

The fact that the ÖVP controlled the Planning Ministry bound up this party with the entire development of the state sector, providing ample opportunities for the growth of an uninhibited patronage system. As in Italy with the Christian democrats, the ÖVP became a 'public sector party' rather than a British-style conservative party. It acquired a further stake in the economic organization of the country by obtaining virtual control of the network of chambers of commerce; these largely middle-class organizations monopolized the representation of employers' interests in the same way as the trade unions controlled working-class interests. Thus, the basis for the Austrian consociational model was laid. At the political level the SPÖ and the ÖVP were in charge of the government and of a vast state sector, while at the social level the associations representing the two sides of industry would negotiate policies the politicians would later have to accept.[96]

The third great pillar of Austrian society, the farmers – 20 per cent of the population in 1945 – readily supported the new social order: the new state would protect them from the perils of uncontrolled competition. Ten years previously, Otto Bauer had identified in the division between the urban and rural classes one of the causes of the defeat of Austrian socialism. Now this division, at least in its dangerous pre-war form, was no more. The result was not socialism, but a heavily bureaucratized consensual society where the new middle classes, comfortably ensconced in the public sector, had no reason to fear the state as an alien force: it had now become the source of their daily bread and the fountain of their power and social status.[97]

Any attempt to alter the delicate social equilibrium thus created was doomed to failure. In pursuit of industrial democracy, the SPÖ had drafted a Works Council Bill to give workers, through their elected councils, a voice in management decisions. Works councils were to be informed of company policy, entitled to participate in drawing up business plans, empowered to prevent dismissals. The resulting compromise embodied in the 1947 Act excluded agricultural workers and eliminated the workers' veto on dismissals. Thus enfeebled, the works councils remained almost exclusively grievance committees, concerned with individual complaints rather than with broad policy.[98]

After Austria and Britain, France was the country which saw the greatest extension of public ownership. The parties of the Left (PCF and SFIO) together had nearly 50 per cent of the vote. Employers were even more demoralized and on the defensive than in Britain. The state to which they had pledged their allegiance, the Vichy regime and its corporatist structures, had collapsed ignominiously. The PCF was the largest organization in the country. The principle of nationalization was popular with the French. It had been enshrined in the charter of the Resistance and also supported by the Catholic MRP and by de Gaulle himself.[99] Indeed, on this particular issue the general had no major ideological difference with the communists. For him nationalization was one of the instruments for the resurrection of France.[100] This generalized sentiment was not the result of a nationwide surge of socialist consciousness, although the popularity of socialism played a role in this, but of a deeper populist distaste for *les trusts*. Discontent with private monopolies, enmity towards what is large and powerful, a wish to protect and defend the 'little man' were more entrenched in the French lower middle classes than in the proletariat. Urban white-collar workers still had strong links with the countryside and kept more or less intact the populist instinct of farmers and shopkeepers. This populism may partly explain why the extension of public ownership in France was as radical as in Britain.[101]

French nationalization proceeded in three phases. During the first phase (December 1944 to the end of 1945), under considerable popular pressure, the coalmines in the *départements* of the Nord and of the Pas de Calais were nationalized, and the car manufacturer Renault and the engineering works of Gnome et Rhône were confiscated. During the second phase (end of 1945 to May 1946), the rest of the coal industry, some credit institutions, the major insurance companies, gas and electricity were brought under public control. During the third phase, which lasted until 1948, it was the turn of the merchant navy, Air France and other transport systems.[102] Given the limited scope of the third phase, we can conclude that French nationalizations were over by May 1946, which is when they began to be enacted in Britain. The difference is that in Britain nationalizations were part of a government programme of post-war reconstruction, while in France they were part of the liberation of the country and were profoundly marked by the ethos and climate of the Resistance.

What was their purpose? In the first place, they were regarded as punishment for the collaborationism exhibited by employers during the war – hence the punitive confiscation of Renault. In addition, there was, as in Britain, a general supposition that public services should be under public control and that nationalizations would make economic rationalization possible.

In France, as elsewhere, banks and insurance companies were the main targets of left-wing criticism: the least acceptable face of capitalism was shown by bankers and financiers. Not only was the central bank – the Banque de France – taken over but, in contrast to what happened in Britain, so were the four largest deposit banks and the largest insurance companies. All of them retained their corporate identity.[103] As in Britain, coal, gas and electricity had been inefficiently managed and nationalization was not seriously opposed. This newly created state system did not become, as some socialists had hoped it would, an integrated, powerful public sector, intelligently co-ordinated by a central plan devised by public-spirited planners and technocrats. What occurs in the frustrating domain of politics is often very different from what is conceived in the more congenial realm of ideas, and in this case it reflects the widely different motives of those who supported nationalizations.

The socialists were more eager than the communists to promote public ownership, though both were anxious to justify the course of action in non-socialist terms. In their joint text of 2 March 1945, the two parties offered three reasons for advocating nationalization: economic – private enterprise on its own would be unable to modernize the country; patriotic – to punish collaborators; and democratic – to break the power of *les trusts*, an allegedly homogeneous *patronat* able and willing to blackmail the Republic.[104]

The SFIO talked about 'socialization' (a word the PCF explicitly refused to use), meaning that nationalizations would be accompanied by some form of industrial democracy or workers' control.[105] The communists, however, remained committed to their pre-war conception. This held that socialist measures could be introduced only by a socialist government – that is, a government they controlled. As the coalition government in which they participated was not a socialist one, nothing enacted by the National Assembly could possibly be socialist. It was with simple, succinct and easily digestible formulae such as these that French communism intended to confront the challenges of the second half of the twentieth century. The third party, the MRP, was quick to chime with the times and supported nationalization, workers' control, planning and all policies aimed at subordinating the economy to the service of the community, rather than that of individuals.[106] Finally, the Gaullists promoted nationalizations for technocratic and *étatique* reasons: by then, de Gaulle was committed to a *dirigiste* notion of economic development. The result of all this was that the preamble of the French constitution of 1946 contained a clause which amounted to an obligation to nationalize: 'All property and all enterprises that now or subsequently shall have the character of a national public service or a monopoly in fact must become the property of the community.'[107] In France, unlike Germany, there was no occupying force to veto the incorporation of a pro-nationalization paragraph in the constitution.

A similar clause (Article 42, paragraph 3) was also inserted in the Italian constitution, drafted in 1946–47 and approved by Christian democrats, socialists and communists. It read: 'For reasons of general interest private property may be expropriated by law and with compensation.' The Italians had inherited from Mussolini's regime a vast public sector based on a distinctive conception of state ownership. Since the mid-1930s, state property was held through a holding company, the Istituto per la Ricostruzione Industriale (IRI), which was supposed to be run like a private investment trust except that its president and vice-president were appointed directly by the government. Through IRI, the largest employer in Italy, the state had effective control of iron and steel, gas production (AGIP), broadcasting (RAI), 60 per cent of the telephone system, 25 per cent of all bank deposits.

Of the three main 'nationalizing' countries – Austria, Britain and France – the latter made the most use of its public sector for the purposes of planning. While France had contributed little to the construction of a welfare state, it did make major progress towards economic planning, practically as well as theoretically. Just as in Britain the thinkers behind the welfare state and macro-economic management, Beveridge and Keynes, were not socialists, in France too the main architect of what may have appeared to be the 'socialistic' policy of planning, Jean Monnet, was no socialist. Monnet, of course, being a 'spontaneous' public relations man, presented his plan with a view to getting it accepted by as many shades of political opinion as possible. Given the left-wing ethos of the post-Resistance climate, he naturally stressed the democratic and co-operative nature of the plan. It would not be something imposed from on high; there would be widespread consultations; employers and employees working in every sector of the economy would be asked to establish their own targets.[108] All sides of the political spectrum supported this policy, including the communists and the unions they controlled, even when it was decided that the working week had to be lengthened from forty hours to forty-eight. Far from being any kind of attempt at socialist reconstruction, the plan was devised by Monnet as the best way to use American aid to renovate the economy.

The Americans were duly informed that the French intended to submit to them a programme of industrial re-equipment aimed at modernization.[109] By the time the Marshall Aid fund was established, the French, unlike most other countries, had already worked out all the data required of them by it, thus ensuring that by 1949 90 per cent of the modernization plan's resources came from Marshall.[110] By then, of course, the communists were out of power and had turned against the plan. Whether it was a mere capitalist exercise to be opposed, or a 'democratic' strategy to be supported, seemed to depend entirely on whether or not the PCF was in government.

The PCF adopted an increasingly anti-technocratic attitude. It thus joined forces in the battle of ideas with the Poujadists of the Right, for whom technocrats 'were heartless productivity maniacs who imposed their will on others, took orders from foreign trusts, blindly admired America, patronized supermarkets, knew only Paris, and drank whisky and Coca-Cola'.[111] There is much that is true in this caricature, though the adoption of these positions by the French communists led them to cede the crucial concept of modernity to their political opponents. To suggest, as they did, that the plan had not the slightest intention of abolishing capitalism is quite true, but that must have been clear to them from the beginning. Its chief aim was the modernization of French capitalism, universally judged to be lacking in the necessary competitive spirit with which to face a new era of free trade. The planners' central task was 'to threaten, conjure, and cajole the owners of French capital into adopting an aggressive marketing stance and into undertaking massive investments that might be risky but could pay dividends for the entire polity'.[112] Whether the rapid economic growth enjoyed by France in the successive decades was due to the establishment and development of a planning system – as some have claimed[113] – or whether it was largely determined by external circumstances such as the expansion of world trade, remains debatable. What is less controversial is that the weak French trade unions made them marginal to the system. The 'triangular' consultation machinery, established to involve the trade unions alongside the employers and the representatives of the state, was soon bypassed in favour of informal bilateral discussions between government and employers. Once they realized this, the unions – and not only the communist CGT, but also the anti-communist Force Ouvrière (FO) – withdrew from the planning machinery.

The pattern of nationalization, the paucity of planning, the absence of the most rudimentary forms of industrial democracy, demonstrate the massive failure of socialists throughout Europe to achieve even the semblance of a distinctive policy towards private capital. Unable to abolish capitalism, they were reduced to attempting, often unsuccessfully, to improve it by making it more efficient, more modern, more 'capitalist'.

Nationalization, the Left's favoured policy, was far from being a uniquely socialist policy. The evidence abundantly supports the view that nationalizations occurred for a whole variety of reasons: to modernize, to rationalize, to plan, to punish Nazi collaborators (France), to prevent the loss of a national asset (Austria), to protect employment, and so on. Achieving a socialist use of the private economy for political ends seemed to have been one of the least prominent aims of state ownership. Welfare reforms could be conceived as an end in themselves, but nationalizations had originally been envisaged as a tool with which to plan economic development. Yet where socialists were strong, as in the United Kingdom and the Nordic countries, there was little or no planning. In France, where the socialists were weak and the Left divided, there was a consistent attempt at planning. In the minds of many socialists, nationalizations were seen as the proverbial Good Thing, since they brought nearer the form of property relations which most closely approximated to socialism: public (state) ownership. For exactly the same reason, those on the 'free-market' and conservative side of the political spectrum opposed them. Yet the inescapable conclusion must be that nationalizations could be an instrument for the modernization and rationalization of capitalism: they contained costs, increased productivity, facilitated the elimination of excess labour. This positive assessment (which does not rule out a less sanguine and different one: an instrument for subsidizing high wages and high employment) provides no comfort to socialists who believed that any policy adopted would have to be justified in terms of whether or not, directly or indirectly, it would bring a socialist society nearer. Only those who believed in social reforms as an end in themselves had reason to rejoice at the recovery and reconstruction of capitalism. A highly efficient and profitable capitalist system would make possible a welfare state, redistribution of income and greater social opportunities for all. It would not bring any nearer a socialist society conceived of as an end-state. But, in 1948, socialism as the final aim of the movement was still the one idea which united the overwhelming majority of committed socialists and communists in Western Europe.

CHAPTER SEVEN

External Constraints: A Socialist Foreign Policy?

AFTER THE break-up of the international war coalition (1946–47) and the development of the East–West conflict, none of the socialist parties – with the exception of the German and Italian – had a significantly different foreign policy from that of the parties of the centre and centre-right. In 1945 there was no existing framework for conducting international relations. The war had destroyed the previous system and the new world had not yet emerged. It was not then possible to see what later became obvious – namely, that the European countries would become marginal in world affairs; that the USA would no longer be isolationist; and that the East–West conflict would assume the features of a 'Cold War'. The socialist parties could have perhaps tried to construct this new framework, but they had no international organization, no common foreign policy, no instrument of co-ordination. They were national parties struggling to make their mark in national politics. When they turned to foreign affairs, they embraced the prevailing ideas on the national interest. Their supporters clamoured for a 'socialist' foreign policy. But clamouring is never enough. There was never a 'socialist foreign policy' or, at least, no one knew where to find it or how to make it.

In theory, any one of three distinct positions could have been adopted: pro-Soviet, pro-American or 'bridge-building' neutralism. In reality, the USSR would have been content with a neutralist position, since it did not seriously expect outright pro-Sovietism. Neutralism prevailed among the socialist or social-democratic parties of Switzerland, Sweden, Finland, Austria, West Germany and Italy. In the first four countries neutralism was accepted by all the main political parties and was thus not a distinctly socialist position. In Austria and Finland neutralism was anyway buttressed by international treaties. In Sweden and Switzerland neutrality was the patrimony of all shades of opinion; having been maintained throughout two world wars, it was unlikely to be abandoned. The remaining two neutralist socialist parties, the Italian PSI and the German SPD, were in countries which joined the Atlantic Alliance. Thus, their foreign policy was at odds with those of the parties to their right. The PSI had adopted neutralism partly in order to strengthen its alliance with the communists, the SPD because it hoped it would facilitate the reunification of Germany. By the end of the 1950s, these illusions had dissipated, and both the PSI and the SPD submitted to the embraces of Atlanticism.

Denmark, Norway and Iceland broke with Nordic solidarity to side with 'the West' and enter the North Atlantic Treaty Organization (NATO). The pro-NATO attitude of their socialist parties was decisive. Opposition came mainly from the communist parties, the left within the socialist parties and, in Denmark, from neutralist, non-socialist parties. Danish and Norwegian membership of NATO caused such resentment inside the socialist parties that the anti-NATO Left eventually seceded in, respectively, 1960 and 1961.[1] In Norway membership of NATO was passed by the Storting virtually unanimously, with the exception of eleven communist and two Labour Party deputies.[2] Why the socialists of Denmark and Norway behaved so differently from those of Finland and Sweden is not easy to surmise. The different intensity of socialist anti-communism cannot have been a major factor: the Finnish social democrats were more anti-communist than all the others, yet remained neutralists. The decisive variable was almost certainly the enduring strength of the 'national' factor. Once again, the socialists upheld the prevailing view of what the national interest was. The specific geopolitical predicament of Finland; the strength of neutralism and the undamaged state of the economy in Sweden; the common predicament of Norway and Denmark during the war (both had been occupied by the Nazis) and their difficult post-1945 economic circumstances – these led the Nordic countries to take differing stands on the great ideological and political schism which pitted East against West. Nevertheless, prior to the Cold War, Denmark and Norway followed the so-called 'bridge-building' foreign policy option with Sweden and Finland. This was taken to mean the adoption of an equidistant position from the USA and the USSR in order to harmonize relations between the two great powers. The election of the Norwegian Trygve Lie as secretary-general of the UN was regarded as important international recognition of this role.[3] The assumption underlying the 'bridge-building' policy was that the international entente would last for a considerable period and that this would ensure the security of the Nordic countries. When the Cold War began, Sweden, which had never been invaded, assumed that its security was better served by neutralism. Finland assumed that its own security required it to have a cautious attitude towards the USSR. Norway and Denmark, both invaded in the past by the Germans in spite of their neutrality, abandoned this position in favour of Atlanticism. Thus, the origin of foreign policy options owes little either to American pressure[4] or to the ideology of the socialists in power. It is true that, at first, Norway would initially have preferred a Nordic alliance with a minimum of Western support, instead of direct NATO membership. But negotiations failed because Sweden could not accept even a modicum of Atlantic ties.[5]

Until the die was cast in 1947, and the Cold War had broken out, the socialists could still avail themselves of the luxury of considering alternative positions. After 1947, with the exception of West Germany and Italy, all countries which joined NATO did so with the positive encouragement of the socialist and social-democratic parties. The idea of a 'socialist' foreign policy remained embryonic.

Before the Cold War the British Labour Left as a whole insisted on what it called a 'socialist foreign policy', meaning a policy of friendship with the USSR and support for anti-colonialist movements.[6] After 1947, pro-Sovietism narrowed to become the prerogative of the 'fellow-travelling' fringes of the Left.[7] For instance, Leslie J. Solley MP wrote in the pages of the communist *Labour Monthly*: 'In my opinion the acid test of our policy is our attitude to the USSR.'[8] The vast majority of the Labour Left, however, 'were driven, often reluctantly and a step at a time, to take up anti-Soviet attitudes nearly indistinguishable from those of Ernest Bevin's'.[9] At first the *Keep Left* group led by Richard Crossman fought for the idea of a democratic-socialist 'Third Force', independent of both the USA and the USSR, comprising the Commonwealth and Europe – and with Britain, of course, at its centre, for these British neutralists shared with Churchill's Conservatives a vastly inflated view of the role and position of Britain in the world. Soon, however, the Labour Party, including most of the *Keep Left* group, rallied to an uncomplicated Atlanticism.

In Italy the majority of the PSI, in spite of repeated pressures from the USA and Britain, decided that their common front with the increasingly powerful Italian communists made it imperative that they should not adopt an anti-Soviet stand. They preferred to advocate Italian neutrality. A dissenting minority, led by Giuseppe Saragat and supported by American money, split from the party and formed the PSDI (see chapter 5). Clutching the 7 per cent of the vote obtained in 1948, it rapidly drifted towards the centre where it remained safely ensconced, protected by its anti-communism and its subordination to the DC, until engulfed by the corruption scandals of 1992–94.

In Germany the SPD leader, Kurt Schumacher, opted for a neutralist foreign policy, equidistant from both East and West. This equidistance was not ideological: the rejection of the values of Soviet communism had been made clear by his complete refusal to entertain any notion of a merger with the Communist Party in the Eastern zone. Schumacher's policy was based on the assumption that the division of Germany was a purely temporary phenomenon. The SPD thought it could aspire to become the party of German unity and reclaim the mantle of the nation, precisely because its tragic and tormented history made its own nationalism markedly different from that of German militarism. Schumacher believed that only through the socialism of the SPD could the Germans recover their national pride and regain the trust of the rest of Europe. This combination of socialism and nationalism was enshrined in the Hanover Party Congress of 1946 and became the bedrock of SPD foreign policy until the late 1950s.[10] The SPD argued for a distinctive and special role. It envisaged that Germany would assume an independent and mediating position between the big power blocs, thereby serving as a bridge between East and West.[11]

There is a remarkable contradiction between Schumacher's unquestioned commitment to German unity and his seeming lack of concern for the predicament of the SPD in East Germany at the time of its forced unification with the KPD. By not attempting to forge some sort of compromise, he in fact left the East German social democrats at the mercy of the communists. With hindsight we know that such a compromise would almost certainly not have worked, and that the SPD in the East was doomed. But Schumacher did not know that: his entire demeanour was based on the expectation that unification was possible.

Schumacher's nationalism was directed towards the restoration of Germany's 1937 borders, which meant including the Saarland, restoring Berlin as capital, and not recognizing the Oder–Neisse border with Poland. This nationalism may have been a reaction to the fate of the SPD in the Weimar period. Then, its practical acceptance of reparation and of the Versailles Treaty, as well as the very fact that it was socialist, had marked the party as 'un-German' in spite of its support for the 1914–18 war and the resolute manner in which it fought against separatist aspirations (such as those of the Bavarians) during the 1918 Revolution.[12] The SPD also had a powerful electoral reason to seek reunification: the bulk of its traditional support was in Prussia and most of Prussia was now in Poland.

The SPD, like all other socialist parties, assumed that any advance towards socialism had to be on the basis of the nation-state. Of course, Schumacher had a broad commitment to Europe. In 1945 he declared that 'Social Democracy cannot conceive of a new Germany as an isolated, nationalistic Germany. It cannot think of Germany as anything but a constituent part of Europe.'[13] But this Europe was one of strongly autonomous nation-states, not an integrated economic structure. The idea that post-war reconstruction would require a growing economic and political interdependence expressed through Atlanticism and a 'common market' could not have come from the Left.

The fact that a commitment to nationalism, even if in a clearly non-bellicose form, could be one of the chief components of post-war West German socialism, demonstrates how far these parties, previously members of an association called the International, had moved towards the conception of 'socialism in one country'. With the possible exception of the French, Dutch and Belgian socialists, early upholders of European unity, all the other major socialist parties, from Finland and the Scandinavian countries to Germany and Britain, were committed to a 'national road to socialism'. In this they were at one with all those West European communist parties which, at least until 1947, had also asserted their belief in a specific French or Italian, German or British 'national' – i.e. non-Soviet – road to socialism. By yet another irony of history, the banner of internationalism, or, at least, of an aspiration towards some form of supra-national system, had passed into the hands of the parties of the Right and the centre. The founding fathers of European unity were three conservative politicians, all Catholics and all from German-speaking provinces. They were Konrad Adenauer from the Rhineland; Robert Schuman, a Frenchman born in Luxemburg; and Alcide de Gasperi, an Italian from the South Tyrol. All of them, like all the other European saints, thought, first and last, of their own nation-state.[14]

The socialists did as their predecessors had done in those fateful summer days of 1914: they soldered their party to the fate of the nation. For Schumacher and the SPD there was a special problem: the nation in question had ceased to exist. By disregarding the depth of the East–West division, and assuming the partition of Germany to be ephemeral, they fought a battle they could not possibly win. Forty years later, in 1989, Schumacher's dream came true and Germany was united again; but by then the SPD had become the most Europeanist of the German parties and the least enthusiastic about national unity. Evidently, success in politics does not consist in having the right ideas, but in having them at the right time.

The socialist party best placed to develop a distinct foreign policy was the British Labour Party, not only because it was actually in government with an overall parliamentary majority, but also because it inherited the prestige that resulted from the war and a far-flung empire. Britain was neither a peripheral country, with merely sectoral foreign policy interests, such as Finland or Belgium; nor a defeated nation, with a problem of international credibility, such as Germany. The Labour government ruled over a nation still perceived as a world power. Beneath this image, however, there was another reality. The country resembled an enormous stately home, cold and draughty, which required for its upkeep great sacrifices and outside help. But the occupants, conscious of their past and of what they had been, preferred not to see what they had become, and were unable to imagine what life might be like without their possessions and the prestige that went with them.

Labour's leaders did not assume that their task was to dismantle this estate; they wanted to run it better for the benefit of all. They could not have had other concerns. Had they not felt a sense of kinship and ownership of the land they inherited and its history; had they felt distant and alienated from what Britain had come to represent these last three hundred years; had they not interiorized the imperial mentality of their predecessors, they probably would not have been at the helm of the nation in 1945. A party excessively in advance of its voters never wins elections.

Clement Attlee had told the war cabinet in June 1943 that he had no intention of presiding over the dissolution of the British Commonwealth, and intended to continue 'to carry our full weight in the post-war world with the US and the USSR'.[15] The consequence of this was that the construction of the welfare state would have to be constrained by the requirements of a world role. After Hiroshima such a role dictated the development and deployment of atomic weapons. The commitment to develop an independent atomic, and later nuclear, weapons system was undertaken by Attlee and Bevin in the utmost secrecy. Most of the cabinet ministers did not know anything about it. Those who did, such as Cripps and Dalton, objected on the grounds of cost, not principle.

Attlee's initial position on atomic weapons, expressed in a handwritten letter to Truman in September 1945, was that in the atomic age, lasting security meant mutual security, and that a new system of international relations would have to be developed in which a narrow view of the national interest should not prevail: if international affairs were conducted in the same old way, 'sooner or later these bombs will be used for mutual annihilation.'[16] This position was soon modified, first by the refusal to share atomic secrets with the USSR, then by the belief that only by possessing atomic weapons could Britain hope to exercise some influence on the USA and in the world at large. There was an implicit distrust of the USA in Attlee's and Bevin's belief that it would be politically undesirable to allow them the monopoly of such destructive weapons. Britain successfully sought to manufacture the bomb which the USA had attempted to deny it through the McMahon Act (which made it illegal to pass any classified information to any other country, including Britain). By 1949 the British Labour government was close to the United States on most issues, from NATO to the Marshall Plan. On atomic policy, however, as on British participation in an integrated Europe, they were far apart and there was no co-operation.[17]

The main justification for a British bomb was that it would act as a deterrent. This has remained the kernel of successive governments' nuclear strategies up to the present, but there is little doubt that the possession of the bomb was also a question of international prestige. The equation 'A-bomb equals world power status' worked both ways: a great power required atomic weapons; but if one had atomic weapons, then it necessarily followed that one was a great power. Ernest Bevin felt that it was important to have the Union Jack flying over the atomic bomb.[18] As Margaret Gowing put it, Britain's atomic role was an important factor in obscuring from Britain its changed status in the world.[19]

Another point needs to be made here: British atomic policy was one added obstacle to the Europeanization of Britain, for it prevented any possible Franco-British co-operation, and anything that was an impediment to this assisted the development of Franco-German co-operation.

The bomb acted as a screen against reality, a phallic symbol concealing an underlying inadequacy; the empire had no clothes but, thanks to the bomb, no one could see its emaciated limbs, let alone its empty stomach. Clearly this particular *forma mentis* was not conducive to a radical departure towards unexplored and possibly left-wing foreign policy horizons. While there was no socialist blueprint for economic and social policies, a rough strategic outline at least existed. In the field of foreign policy, however, there was a virtual void. In the Cold War, of course, Britain was a protagonist; it did not endure the situation passively. Ernest Bevin's anti-Sovietism was deeply felt. He was more hawkish than at least some of his Foreign Office subordinates and had the virtually unquestioned support of his colleagues, although initially Attlee himself had favoured a policy of co-operation with the USSR.[20] With the exception of a tiny pro-communist fringe, there was very little dissent within the Labour Party on the twin pillars of the Western alliance: the North Atlantic Treaty and the Marshall Plan.

Acceptance of the Marshall Plan was almost universal among the European socialist parties. This is hardly surprising. In 1945 there were perhaps forty million uprooted people in Europe.[21] Black markets flourished. The economic relations between town and country had broken down, one hundred million people were being fed at a level of 1,500 calories a day or fewer. Starvation in many German cities, as well as in Vienna, was not uncommon.[22] In these circumstances to reject American aid would have been – to say the least – politically foolish.

Marshall Aid gave the USA considerable leverage in European affairs. The USA not only had to agree with the European governments on the list of goods to be sent as gifts, but also on how the savings thus generated would be spent. To accept Marshall Aid meant to accept some form of American hegemony. This is why the USSR and its 'allies' could not take part in the plan.[23] Some, of course, attempted to disguise this reality under a flood of rhetoric. Thus, Léon Blum even declared that 'international socialism' should be in the forefront of public opinion in accepting the plan, because it brought the goal of supra-nationalism that much nearer.[24] At the outset, however, in spite of the considerable advantages of the plan, many socialists and not all communists reacted with some diffidence. The Norwegian Labour Party initially considered not taking part in the Marshall Plan because it feared that it would tie Norway too closely to the USA, while arousing the hostility of the USSR. The example of Labour Britain was one of the factors which convinced the Norwegians to accept; another was their dollar shortage.[25] The Finnish social democrats, unlike the Norwegians, wanted, at first, to accept the plan. They were backed in this by the Finnish communists through their daily paper, *Vapaa Sana*, which thus contradicted the stand taken by *Pravda*.[26] Soviet pressures forced both parties to reject US aid, which had initially been offered to all European countries, including the USSR. Other communist parties, such as the Czech and the Italian, were very tempted to accept. Luigi Longo, defending the PCI from Soviet criticisms at the first meeting of the Cominform, explained that 'our enemies wanted to present us as opponents of the granting of aid to Italy'.[27] After all, at first, even Vyacheslav Molotov, the Soviet foreign minister, did not reject the plan outright, but merely asked that the conditions for acceptance of the plan be redefined. It would have been a considerable embarrassment to the Americans if the Soviet Union had accepted it, since its political aim was to halt the advancement of communism in Western

Europe. They did not need to fear: all the countries under direct Soviet control, plus Finland, rejected Marshall Aid; however, Austria, under partial Soviet occupation, did not.[28]

The other aim of the plan was to stabilize the Western economies.[29] Whether the plan itself 'saved Europe' economically, as subsequent propaganda would have it, is doubtful. The benefits, economically speaking, are questionable and have indeed been considerably debated. According to Milward, it helped some countries, such as Holland and Austria, more than others, such as Belgium, Denmark, Sweden and West Germany (where the effects were minimal), with France, Italy and Great Britain in the middle. Milward adds: 'it can certainly be said that the idea that the gains achieved (by Marshall Aid) were so large as to have shaped the politico-economic future of Western Europe is nonsense.'[30] Charles Maier concurs: 'in quantitative economic terms American aid amounted to little.'[31]

Marshall Aid, however, presents a paradox for both socialists and free marketeers. Politically, its aim was the furthering in Europe of 'American values' of which 'free' enterprise is the most crucial. It would follow from this that it should have been welcomed by free marketeers. The plan, however, also implied that the European economies would not have survived had they been abandoned to the invisible hand of the market. It was, after all, a *plan*, launched by a state to help other states recover from the war and integrate their economies. The 'free market' may have been the desired end, but it was not the means. As Ellwood succinctly explained, there was even more than production and integration in the plan:

> [It] evolved into a complete model of investment, production and consumption. This would transform the ancient battle between reactionary capitalists and revolutionary workers into a constructive, dynamic relationship, uniting enlightened producers and contented consumers. Growth would resolve all the difficulties, overcome all the challenges, just as in America.[32]

Socialists and their opponents resolved the paradox by the unstated and informal agreement to drop their long-term goals – socialism and unregulated capitalism, respectively. The meeting-point was what Charles Maier has called the 'politics of productivity'.[33] It was as if both sides had agreed to work for growth in the immediate future, postpone conflict over the share of future output to the medium term, and let distant ideological goals remain ... distant ideological goals. As Keynes wisely reflected, 'in the long run we are all dead.'

Politically, however, Marshall Aid was part and parcel of the Cold War and, as such, represented another step in the long march of the West European Left towards making its peace with capitalism. Whether the policy of Cold War was right or wrong will be debated endlessly. Did it lengthen the period of Soviet rule in Eastern Europe? Would a more benign and less bellicose attitude have allowed the USSR to relax its grip over what it considered its 'safety-belt'? Did NATO really protect West European demo-cracy from the devastating embrace of Soviet communism? No conclusive evidence could ever be produced to answer these questions. We shall never know. History remains a highly speculative affair and, as the heroine of *Northanger Abbey* opines, it is odd 'that it should be so dull, for a great deal of it must be invention'. What is certain, however, is that on its own Britain was not in a position decisively to influence an alternative course for Europe. Perhaps a co-ordinated effort on the part of the main European countries might have been able to shape a route different from the bipolar road taken by the international system; but it is unlikely that these states could have found the foresight or the common purpose to undertake it.

This foresight was certainly not present in Britain and in the Labour Party. When it came to foreign policy, Bevin could provide an intelligent and competent understanding of the overall situation packaged in the no-nonsense, truculent attitude characteristic of British trade unionists (the proletarian equivalent of military bluster).[34] Not for nothing was it observed that Bevin acted as if he were under the misapprehension that the Union of Soviet Socialist Republics was a breakaway from the Transport and General Workers' Union which he had led before the war. Bevin's bullish persona disguised the fact that senior officials at the Foreign Office were the chief architects of Labour's foreign policy, especially in the early phase of the post-war period.[35] Bevin's successor at the Foreign Office, Herbert Morrison, was utterly ignorant of the outside world. The most knowledgeable foreign affairs man in the cabinet after Bevin, Hugh Dalton, was more imbued with prejudices about foreigners than is normally the case among ministers of the crown: not only did he hate all Germans (whom he usually referred to as 'the Huns'), but his suggested policy towards Palestine was to deport most of the indigenous Arab population, presumably by force. This astonishingly callous policy was approved by the 1944 Labour Party Conference without a squeak of protest. Dalton's ravings on the matter included 'throwing open Libya or Eritrea to Jewish settlement, as satellites or colonies to Palestine'.[36] The general assumptions in the Labour Party were the Churchillian ones that Atlanticism could be based on a special US–UK relationship, that no obstacle should be raised to European integration as long as Britain was not a part of it, and that the Empire-Commonwealth had to be preserved in some form or other. Bevin had the odd moment of uneasiness about the 'special relationship' with the USA; but it was based on national pride not on politics: 'We find ourselves at times irked at the role of junior partner ... nevertheless ... the partnership is worth the price', he claimed in February 1947.[37] Bevin's own global strategy was based on an imperial vision of Britain leading the colonies and a group of West European countries to act independently of the two superpowers.[38] The harsh realities of politics forced him to discard this aspiration. A small group of left-wingers, such as Barbara Castle, Michael Foot and Richard Crossman thought that the future lay in a socialist-led

Europe.[39] But the majority of the party either oscillated between little Englandism and imperialism, or were both little Englanders and imperialists. Others were just mindless patriots like the minister for fuel and power, and later minister of defence, Emmanuel Shinwell.

The twin pillars of Labour foreign policy were anti-Europeanism and pro-Americanism. The first was exemplified by Labour's scorn for the Schuman Plan (which would lead to the setting up of the European Coal and Steel Community, the first major step towards the EEC), condemned by the 'intellectual' organ of the Left, the *New Statesman*, as a conspiracy headed by French and German industrialists and the Pope.[40] The pro-American strand was typified by sending two brigades to back the US over Korea, and by increasing defence spending even though this could be met only by the introduction of prescription charges in the National Health Service.[41] As Gaitskell wrote in his diary, 'we could hardly start arguing with the Chiefs of Staff about what was essential and what was not essential.'[42] By 1950–51 Labour Britain was spending more per capita on defence than the USA.[43]

The commitment to a major international role for Britain was never really questioned by Labour leaders, or indeed anyone else, even abroad, with a very few exceptions. Left-wingers like Michael Foot, who never doubted that Great Britain was truly 'great', declared in the House of Commons in 1945: 'Britain stands today at the summit of her power and glory and we hold that position because today, following the election, we have something to offer.'[44] It was assumed that being a world power gave one the possibility of being also a welfare state. In reality, the world role constrained the welfare ambitions. Colonies, as long as they were quiet, could be profitable. To maintain troops in Germany and elsewhere was crippling. Those who, like Correlli Barnett, seek to demonstrate that the development of the welfare state was a luxury the country could not afford, and that its construction was the cause of Britain's subsequent decline and inability to keep up with its overseas competitors, fail to examine seriously the parallel case – namely that by the same token, Britain's imperial role had become too expensive for an offshore island in a world divided between two superpowers. While food was rationed in Britain (but not – for instance – in defeated Italy), the Labour government had to find the currency to pay for the British zones in Germany and Austria; the troops stationed in Egypt, Palestine, Trieste and Greece; the re-occupation of Burma, Malaya and Hong Kong; the contributions to pay for UNRRA work; and the financing of the large debts contracted abroad in the sterling area. It is only in the last page of his book that Correlli Barnett eloquently points out:

> [the] New Jerusalem was not the only wartime fantasy to beguile the British from a cold, clear vision of their true post-war priorities. Their political leaders and the governing Establishment ... simply could not accept that British power had vanished amid the stupendous events of the Second World War and that the era

of imperial greatness that had begun with Marlborough's victories had now ineluctably closed.[45]

That world role (Barnett calls it a 'hallucination') acted as a fundamental constraint which shaped both domestic policies through the balance of payments, and external policies by foreclosing the only real option the country had left: an uninhibited commitment towards Europe. The alternative was pursued by the other 'great' imperial country in decline, France, whose geographical position at the heart of the continent and on the borders with Germany made it necessary to temper whatever ambitions it still possessed in the colonies with a more realistic appraisal of its Europeanness. London was left pursuing a special relationship with the USA which Washington never took seriously, except in so far as the White House 'needed the evidence acceptable to Congress and the American public that the "free world" wanted to be saved'.[46] Great Britain appeared increasingly as a half-discarded mistress kept in genteel existence by the odd hand-out absentmindedly dispensed. Paris, on the other hand, while far less enlightened in its attitude to the colonies, and soon to be engaged in unwinnable colonial wars, was at least able to determine after 1948 that a special relationship with defeated Germany would be the basis of its future foreign policy. Labour's incapacity to delineate its own external relations became, with the passing of time, increasingly pronounced.

Trotsky's famous comment on becoming the first Soviet foreign minister ('I will issue a few revolutionary proclamations to the peoples of the world and then shut up shop'),[47] epitomizes the complacent attitude of many socialists in the delicate field of foreign policy. Of all terrains of political decision-making, foreign affairs is the one in which the government is least accountable, the opposition least effective, public opinion most ignorant, and secrecy most intense – the ideal situation for ministers. This is especially true of the stuff of which the fortunes of diplomatic historians are built: great international crises. However, tomorrow's international emergency is always the unforeseen result of earlier events which allowed the as yet unperceived crisis to develop and unfold. During the actual emergency it often appears as if politicians are in full control. Crisis-management thus becomes the business of the chosen few: the prime minister or president, the foreign secretary, one or two advisers, one or two envoys. Personalities dominate. They assemble, they confront each other, they decide, they respond, they negotiate. Or so it seems, because the reality, as usual, differs from appearances: nothing ever turns out the way one thought it should or would. There is little apprenticeship involved. One learns, if at all, on the job. The socialists who were in power had to learn the hard way how little they were in control of events – even, or especially, in the field of foreign affairs.

In August 1945, a few weeks after gaining office, the British Labour government was forced to confront this shocking truth, finding itself in a frightening economic situation. The assumption that the USA would prolong the Lend Lease agreement turned out to be mistaken. On 17 August 1945 President Truman, by abruptly terminating Lend Lease, left Britain almost bankrupt. During the war the UK had lost 28 per cent of its entire national wealth.[48] Keynes, in a memorandum to Dalton, wrote that the country needed over £1,000 million-worth of imports to maintain wartime consumption. Without a loan the welfare state promised by Labour could not be financed. A senior Treasury official, Richard W. B. Clarke, was commissioned in February 1946 to write a report on what to do if the US Congress rejected the loan. He concluded that 'it would force us willy-nilly to cut our overseas commitments which would radically affect the world political balance.'[49] Keynes added a minute to the report, which was sent to the cabinet on 22 February: 'I should be inclined to highlight still more than (Clarke) has that the main reaction of the American loan must be on our military and political expenditure overseas.' Rough calculations followed these words, and he then added:

> Thus, it comes out in the wash that the American loan is primarily required to meet the political and military expenditure overseas. If it were not for that, we could scrape through without excessive interruption of our domestic programme if necessary by drawing largely on our reserves ... The main consequence of the failure of the loan must, therefore, be a large-scale withdrawal on our part from international responsibilities.[50]

It appeared that the American loan could allow the Labour government to avoid having to decide between the welfare state and a world role. Keynes had naively and mistakenly assumed that the US would be generous; as if congressmen from the backwoods of Iowa and Idaho were likely to inform their electors that their tax money would finance the nationalization and welfare plans of a socialist government in far-away England.[51] After exasperating negotiations, instead of the virtually free gift expected, Keynes got less than he had hoped for – and at a price. Interests had to be paid, and Britain also agreed to reduce its imperial preference scheme and liberalize trade. In addition, there was to be an early return to sterling convertibility into dollars.[52] The likelihood of an independent foreign policy had dwindled to zero. By 1947 it had become apparent that Britain could not cope with the level of overseas commitments which had been expected of it. The ensuing cancellation of aid to Turkey and Greece compelled the USA to become the supreme bastion of Western interests against communism. This led directly to the promulgation of the Truman Doctrine, the cardinal policy statement of the *Pax Americana*.

The French too sought an American loan. Soon after the British delegation had returned to London clutching its borrowed dollars, the veteran socialist Prime Minister Léon Blum, accompanied by Jean Monnet, went to Washington. They knew they were going to get much less than the British. The

Americans had made it clear that the loan to the UK was to be treated as a special case because of the distinctive position of Britain in international trade.[53] The main US condition for the $650 million loan the French did obtain consisted in an undertaking to move rapidly towards free trade. The option of economic development under protective tariffs was now barred to France.[54] For France the only alternative was how to make a decisive move towards the policy of European economic interdependence Monnet had been advocating.

It is probably ahistorical to expect the Labour leaders to have had a distinctive 'socialist' foreign policy in a field so fraught with difficulties as that of the developing Cold War, though one might have expected them to devise a foreign policy which could somehow be distinguished from that of the Conservatives. When it came to the empire, however, it could reasonably be presumed that socialists would have held clear views. This was not so: neither the French nor the British Left had given the matter serious consideration. Their attitude towards the colonies seemed to be 'hold on to them if you can'. In France, the parties of the Left did not mention the question of the colonies in their manifestos for the general election of October 1945; the future of the empire seemed to concern only a few right-wingers and the occasional Christian democrat.[55] As if by common accord, the British Labour Party's election manifesto of 1945, Let Us Face the Future, was equally silent on the subject of the British Empire. Yet the years 1945–51 were a watershed in imperial history: the empire in the Indian subcontinent was dismantled, resulting in a change in the nature of the Commonwealth, and paving the way for later decolonization in Africa, the Caribbean and the Pacific.[56]

As far as the Labour Party's intentions could be judged from its conference resolutions and other statements, it appeared to oppose withdrawal from the colonies. Instead, it favoured preserving the Commonwealth in its traditional form – that is, the 'white' Commonwealth based on the Ottawa system of imperial preference. The colonies were to be developed or, in the case of India, allowed an indigenous government with close military and economic ties with the United Kingdom.[57] Not only did this ambition fail, but the Labour government continued to exploit colonies that were politically unable to defend their own interests, with serious repercussions for their economic and social welfare.[58] There was an unjust and unfair use of the sterling area to support the pound and the British balance of trade. The effect of this was that net dollar earners – such as the Gold Coast (now Ghana) and Malaya – could not use their dollars to buy the goods they wanted outside the sterling areas. As Britain was not able to supply them, these dependencies were forced to hold a large surplus of sterling balances. In practice this was the same as lending to Britain at low rates of interest.

The Labour government also succeeded in maintaining trading relationships which ensured that it could buy the produce of the colonies at below world prices. Finally, the manipulation of investment and development projects in the colonies was designed to suit British, rather than colonial, interests. The Labour government rationed all colonial borrowing in the City on the grounds that the British economy had to have priority because of the devastation it had suffered during the war – as if the three years of Japanese occupation in Malaya, and the scorched-earth policy Malaya had endured when the British pulled out in 1942, had not been far worse than anything suffered during the blitz.[59] The currency structure of the colonial territories was based on a 100 per cent reserve in London. Thus the colonies could not even use their own savings to finance their development.[60] In fact, the colonies became Britain's main source of 'dollar earning' and they were used to help overcome the two main financial crises of the 1940s: the convertibility crisis of 1947 and the devaluation crisis of 1949.[61] The government's use of colonial resources to resolve the country's financial crisis cannot be explained in terms of idealistic politicians being out-manoeuvred by hard-headed civil servants; those in favour of a coherent development policy which would benefit the economy of the colonies would have received the solid backing of the Colonial Office and its minister, A. Creech Jones. Creech Jones himself, it should be added, loyally justified what was obviously a sorry record in a collection of essays he edited. In his own contribution he explained that socialist colonial policies could not be implemented because, 'in practice a socialist Secretary of State is limited in his exercise of authority. His powers to export "socialism" were very restricted', and there were 'historic responsibilities', and 'treaty obliga-tions'. 'Clichés about imperialism and colonialism' were inadequate, because 'much of what is wrong in under-developed societies comes because of the poverty of nature and the backwardness of people.' And, anyway, 'colonies ... cannot be administered from London.' In 1945, 'conditions were not ripe' for British withdrawal. This veritable *apologia* by one of the weakest secretaries of state to run the Colonial Office[62] concluded by asserting – in defiance of the evidence he had offered in the preceding pages and the indictment made by Balogh in the very same collection which Creech Jones had edited, but perhaps not read – that Labour had a 'coherent' and 'remarkably consistent' colonial policy: 'Labour did not wait on events and stumble and fumble with no over-all conception of principle or purpose or of where it was going.'[63]

Rita Hinden, the formidable secretary of the Fabian Colonial Bureau, had understood that there was a structural contradiction between Labour's colonial policies of development prior to independence and domestic welfare policies. The British electorate wanted cheap food and hence cheap colonial imports at the expense of colonial standards of living. From the colonies' point of view, the best defence would have been autonomy or independence, but this was never on the cards.[64] The anti-colonialist feelings which prevailed in so much Labour Party rhetoric were not a cynical manoeuvre designed to disguise a policy of plunder. The words so ardently expressed were genuine but, on the whole, they emanated from internationalists who were neither in government, nor in charge of colonial policy. Devoid of contingency plans, the Labour government lurched from crisis to crisis. Attention was paid to colonial problems only when it was imperative to do so – that is, when there was an effective anti-colonial struggle. The consequence of not having any clear strategy is that one is propelled forward by events, as was the case with the decolonization of India; or kept within the confines of traditional policies, as was the case with the African and Caribbean colonies. The British did not leave India because the Labour government thought that this was what a socialist government should do. India obtained independence because it was far too expensive, both politically and economically, for the British to remain. This is not to refuse credit to Labour's policy. After all, as the French and the Americans proved in Indochina, politicians are at times willing to pay an astonishingly high political and economic price in pursuit of unattainable and undesirable ends. Attlee, one of his party's two experts on India – the other was Stafford Cripps – behaved, in the circumstances, in an extremely adroit manner. He may be criticized for the haste with which he accomplished his task, or for his underestimation of the strength of Islamic nationalism. But any other Labour leader would have made even greater mistakes.[65] Bevin, for instance, in full imperial flight of rhetoric, wrote to Attlee begging him not to 'knuckle under at the first blow'.[66] As for the Conservatives, it can be convincingly argued that, under Churchill, Britain would have taken much longer to extricate itself from the Indian imbroglio.

The French government, even when it contained both socialists and communists, had nothing remotely approaching an anti-colonial mentality. Though the claim that all French political parties were pro-imperialist may be an overstatement, decolonization was not their objective. It was recognized that the empire needed reforming for a number of reasons: there were nationalist movements which had to be placated, France was weak, and American anti-colonialist public opinion could not be ignored.[67]

The PCF tempered its anti-colonialism in order to establish its credentials as a patriotic party and thus declared, in January 1944, that the French Republic, with its metropolitan and overseas territories, is 'one and indivisible'.[68] The French communists remembered anti-colonialism only when they were out of power and at odds with the socialists – i.e. before 1936, between 1939 and 1941, and after 1947. As for the socialists of the SFIO, they justified their growing hostility towards Vietnamese nationalism with the excuse that it went against the new principles of internationalism and world federalism. From this grand vista the nationalism of the Vietnamese (but not that of the French) could be stigmatized, at the 1944 SFIO Congress, as an ideology which 'would keep the overseas peoples in the grip of backward feudalism or agitators in the pay of foreign powers',[69] and, at the 1947 Congress, as a reactionary position.[70]

For the French even more than for the British the preservation of the empire was a way of reasserting France's international role. The British could fool themselves with the idea of a special relationship with the USA. The French, Gaullists as well as socialists, could not hope or wish for a similar advantage; moreover, they were worried that there might really be an international entente between the Anglo-Saxon countries at their expense.[71] In France, anti-Americanism was not the prerogative of the socialist or communist Left. The most prestigious newspaper, the newly created *Le Monde*, was from the beginning staunchly neutralist.[72] The French suspected that they could not expect a return to the imperial *status quo ante bellum*, but they hoped that they could delay as long as possible, and by force if necessary, decolonization, ensuring that it would proceed at a snail's pace or not at all, and always in the interests of France.

The consequences were disastrous. The French socialists, almost uninterruptedly in government until 1951, found themselves entangled in a costly and lengthy war in Indo-China, whence France emerged defeated and humiliated in 1954, after General Nguyen Giap's Vietminh troops had routed the French forces at Dien Bien Phu.

Colonialism gripped Holland too, a country where imperial pretensions might appear even more ludicrous than those of France. At first, it looked as if American pressures might lead the socialist-led government to abandon the Dutch East Indies (Indonesia). The US were keen that the Dutch should not waste precious resources in Asia when they ought to be sharing responsibility for West European defence against the USSR. Then Washington began to relent: it appeared that the anti-colonialist movement in Java was communist-inspired. Perhaps Dutch colonial policies should be supported. When the Indonesian nationalists, led by Achmed Sukarno, brutally put down their communist allies in 1948, they acquired legitimacy in the eyes of the Americans. An anti-communist regime could be safely established in Djokjakarta, terminating Dutch imperial pretensions in Asia.[73] As R. F. Holland has pointed out, the Americans, by ensuring the ousting of the Dutch from their colonies in 1949, did them a favour, forcing them to concentrate on Europe.[74] This was done much more by the Catholic and Liberal members of the coalition government than by the Dutch socialists of the PvdA, who provided the prime minister, Willem Drees, from 1948 to 1958, but never the foreign minister.[75] For most of this time the PvdA – with the exception of a small group of advocates of federalism – took no interest in foreign affairs and was content to demonstrate its general reliability by a pronounced anti-communism.

Well after the sun had definitively set on their worldly empires, the British and French Left would remain divided on the issue of European integration. French socialists were quick to embrace the ideals of Europeanism, while the British joined them in the early 1990s, and even then with some reservations. But how 'European' were the French?

Every party has in its ideological armoury various ideals which it parades whenever they appear to be required. These ideals may be sincerely held by some of the leaders and activists but, as they are of little practical value, no one expects them to be implemented and therefore no one ever thinks them through. Occasionally, however, these views turn out to be exceedingly useful in providing the ideological backbone for policies which might otherwise not spark much enthusiasm. This was the case with the European ideal within French socialism. One of its antecedents was the world federalist view held by Léon Blum and others in the 1920s and 1930s, and reiterated during the war in Blum's celebrated book, *A l'échelle humaine*. As the vision of a world government receded, the European perspective grew in importance. By the end of 1943 the SFIO was increasingly committed to a united Europe with Germany as an acceptable member within a global security system. These ideas were firmly opposed by de Gaulle. He was joined in this by the French communists, who declared with Gaullist grandiloquence at their Central Committee meeting on 25 April 1944 that the United States of Europe would mean the abandonment of national sovereignty, and that 'the independence of France and the restoration of its *grandeur*, sacred vow of all our heroes, must be the leading principle of the future foreign policy of the country'.[76]

The SFIO approached the question of European unity not in order to overcome the narrow confines of the nation-state, but as the continuation of national French policy. After the 1914–18 conflict, the objective of French foreign policy was the isolation of Germany. In 1945 this had not changed. However, after the division of Germany and the beginning of the Cold War, the destruction of German industrial power and the establishment of French control over German steel by the economic annexation of the Saar were no longer possible. A strong West Germany was required for the containment of the USSR. Treating it as an outcast was now an impossible goal for any pro-Western party, including the SFIO. It is at this stage that the old Euro-peanist ideals were revived and given a new shape. France turned to Europe 'to escape from a situation in which she remained preoccupied with the German problem, subordinate to Britain and powerless *vis-à-vis* the USA'.[77]

Given these constraints, France agreed to surrender some of its sovereignty on political and military grounds. Its primary goal became that of achieving the largest possible measure of interdependence between Germany and its neighbours.[78] French economic policy went with the grain of its foreign policy. Monnet's modernization plan was not conceived in isolation from international economic relations. On the contrary, its chief aim was 'to create a framework for the European economy in which the reconstruction and modernization of France could be achieved'.[79] The Monnet Plan had tied the reconstruction of France to that of Germany. As Alan Milward has shrewdly put it, 'The Schuman Plan was called into existence to save the Monnet Plan.'[80] This is not surprising: the real originator of the Schuman Plan was Jean Monnet. The key to French recovery was access to the coal and coke resources of the Ruhr. This could be achieved either by a ferocious anti-German policy, which would deprive German industrialists of these resources, or by the revival of the German economy in the context of European economic interdependence. The second alternative – the integration of the French and German steel and coal industries – prevailed. The basis of the Paris–Bonn axis, and therefore of the European Community, thus rested on the recognition by France that Germany could not be destroyed.[81] The Franco-German entente remained the central co-ordinate of French foreign policy throughout the Fourth and Fifth Republics. European integration and interdependence owe their origin to the requirements of the nation-state, and to the tradition of the national interest, not to the ideals of socialist internationalism.

The British were never properly consulted over the Schuman Plan and were presented, much to their dismay, with a *fait accompli*, partly as retaliation by the French for having been kept in the dark over British devaluation, and partly because Monnet thought, rightly, that the British would block, delay or sabotage the proposals. Of course, there was no visible immediate British national interest in the integration of UK coal and steel. With hindsight it would have enabled Britain to participate in the construction of a European Community at its inception; but few people could have had such foresight at the time. The French and German interests in the matter were visible from the start: the French feared German recovery, the Germans wanted to establish an internationally acceptable context for economic recovery. Note, however, that the SPD too had rejected the Schuman Plan on the grounds that this measure, taken before the reunification of the country, would deepen its division.[82]

The Labour Party's overall coolness towards the Schuman Plan did not include any rejection of the idea of European unity. On the whole, European unity was seen as a Good Thing provided it did not include Britain which, not being 'in Europe', could not be part of any move towards European integration. That much transpired from the Labour Party pamphlet *The Labour Party and European Unity*, written by Denis Healey, then in charge of the International Department, which was directed against supra-nationalism and the Coal and Steel Community.[83] In fact, in 1950, both the Labour Party National Executive Committee and its annual Conference supported the Schuman Plan, with the proviso that it should be modified in a 'socialist direction', which meant public ownership of steel and full employment.[84] Since no concrete indication was ever given as to what such modifications might be, one is left to surmise that Conference's intentions, in this as in other matters, were not to be taken seriously.

As for the Labour government, as distinct from the Labour Party, rejection of British integration into Europe was justified in terms of nothing prejudicing the discharge of its responsibilities towards the Empire/Commonwealth.[85] Like the USA, the British Labour government had contradictory policies. The USA wanted a thriving, stable and *integrated* Western Europe able to stand up to communism. The UK wanted a special partnership with the

USA, but did not want to make European integration one of its foreign policy objectives. To do so would necessarily mean abandoning the empire. But the USA did not want Britain to dismantle its defence and imperial commitments: 'This would mean that serious vacuums would be created in other areas, which could be most embarrassing to us and cause us many headaches ... . Some of these vacuums are ones we might have to fill. This could cost far more than ... aid to Britain at this time.'[86]

There was only one specifically 'socialist' justification for Labour's anti-Europeanism, a succinct version of which can be found in a memorandum drafted by Ernest Davies, Bevin's parliamentary private secretary:

> Maintenance of the welfare state and a planned economy to ensure maximum production, full employment and a fairer distribution of the national income are among the chief aims of Labour's economic policy. There must therefore be complete freedom to plan, and power to control production, investment, prices and distribution of goods in short supply, all of which means that the preservation of Socialist democracy necessitates a closed economy.[87]

The belief that Britain was well advanced on the road to socialism, and that any supra-national constraints of a federalist nature would block further development, became the bedrock of Labour's foreign policy towards Europe. It would take well over thirty years and repeated electoral defeats to shake the Labour Party out of such absurdity. But in the rest of Western Europe no distinctive socialist foreign policy emerged. The possibility of a 'third way' Europe, which avoided subordination to the USA while remaining firmly opposed to the Soviet Union, was confined to the fringes and could be easily caricatured as 'the policy of a little grey home in the West for pinks scared white by the reds'.[88]

PART THREE

Towards Revisionism 1950–60

CHAPTER EIGHT

The Golden Age of Capitalism

IN 1945 capitalism in Europe appeared to be in mortal danger. It had been ousted by the Red Army in most of Central and Eastern Europe – including one-quarter of Germany. In Western Europe it seemed about to undergo a less painful but equally decisive dismissal at the hands of socialist parties. By 1949, however, capitalism in the West was well on the way to recovery even though socialist parties, on their own or with allies, were still in charge of the governments of all democratic West European states except for West Germany and Italy. By 1960 socialists were in power only in Norway and Sweden, and – in coalition with the Christian democrats of the ÖVP – in Austria.

In democratic Europe the configuration of socialist political influence in government throughout the 1950s can be broadly summarized as follows.

In four major countries – France, Germany, Italy and Great Britain – the Left wielded no power at all. In Britain the Labour Party was defeated in the elections of 1951, 1955 and 1959; in Germany the SPD suffered the same fate in 1953 and 1957. In Italy the PSI remained in opposition throughout the decade – as did, of course, the French and Italian communists – while the SFIO was in a coalition government only between July 1950 and July 1951 and again between 1956 and 1958.

In the three Scandinavian countries social democracy continued to dominate. In Norway the DNA ruled with an absolute majority in Parliament. In Sweden the SAP had the support of the Agrarian Party from 1951 to 1957 and was able to rule without it afterwards. In Denmark the social democrats depended on the votes of liberal parties of the centre, but continued to prevail as the leading government party.

In the remaining smaller countries, though the Left never dominated, it was seldom entirely excluded from power: as we have seen, the Austrian SPÖ was locked in coalition with the ÖVP. In Holland, Belgium and Finland socialists were in coalition for most of the 1950s, though by 1960 they were in opposition.

The performance of the communist parties everywhere was dismal except in Italy, France and Finland, where they retained a substantial following. Some of these parties showed minute electoral improvements: the PCI from 22.6 per cent in 1953 to 22.7 per cent in 1958; the Finnish communists from 21.6 per cent in 1951 to 23.3 per cent in 1958. But the PCF declined from

25.9 per cent in 1951 to 19.2 per cent in 1958. Put in perspective these results are fairly creditable: the 1950s was a period of great difficulty for what was left of West European communism: the crushing of the workers' unrest in the DDR (East Germany) and Poland, the invasion of Hungary, the denunciation of Stalin at the Twentieth Congress of the Soviet Communist Party were so many body-blows to the prestige of international communism. To these difficulties, mainly self-inflicted, should be added the discrimination and persecution communist parties suffered in most countries. In 1956 the West German Communist Party (Kommunistische Partei Deutschlands – KPD) was outlawed. In France demonstrations were frequently banned and, on one occasion in 1952, Jacques Duclos, the PCF's deputy leader, was arrested and spent two months in prison on trumped-up charges.[1] The French electoral system was modified in 1951 with the specific intention of discriminating against the communist and Gaullist opposition: the new law had 'only few and shamefaced defenders'.[2] The outcome was that in 1951 the PCF returned ninety-seven deputies to the National Assembly with over 25 per cent of the vote, while the socialists had ninety-four deputies with only 14.5 per cent and the MRP had eighty-two deputies with half the share of the vote of the PCF. In cantonal elections the PCF was even more grossly under-represented.[3] In Italy a similar attempt to modify the electoral system failed. But communist activists were sacked from factories or moved to the most unpleasant jobs, and hundreds of people were arrested and tried for selling communist newspapers on the streets.[4] The jaundiced view Western communists had of 'bourgeois' democracy had some substance.

As for the socialist parties, their marked decline in political power (as measured by their participation in government) cannot be attributed to the electorate's verdict. Indeed, as Table 8.1 demonstrates, support for the main parties of the Left remained remarkably steady.

The fundamental reason for the loss of power of the parties of the Left must be ascribed to their inability or unwillingness to enter into coalitions with the other parties. Loss of electoral support had very little to do with the passage to opposition at the end of the decade of the Belgian, Dutch, Finnish and French socialists. The British Labour Party's exclusion from power is only in part to be attributed to elections: they 'won' the 1951 elections in percentage terms and lost their majority in the House of Commons only because of an unfavourable distribution of votes. It is true that in Germany the SPD performed poorly, electorally speaking, but its main problem was that the other main parties did not regard it as sufficiently legitimate to become a coalition partner.

It was as if the *Zeitgeist* had moved away from the Left. The idea that post-war reconstruction would have to proceed along the strongly interventionist lines favoured by the Left had given way to far more widely held pro-market views.

This shift was only in part due to the ideology of the Cold War. The

Table 8.1 Social-democratic, socialist and labour parties' share of the vote, 1950–60 (%)

	1950	1951	1952	1953	1954	1955	1956	1957	1958	1959	1960
Austria	–	–	–	42.1	–	–	43.0	–	–	44.8	–
Belgium	35.5	–	–	–	38.7	–	–	–	37.1	–	–
Denmark	39.6	–	–	40.4ᵃ 41.3	–	–	–	39.4	–	–	42.1
Finland	–	26.5	–	–	26.2	–	–	–	23.2	–	–
France	–	14.5	–	–	–	–	14.9	–	22.8	–	–
Holland	–	–	29.0	–	–	–	32.7	–	–	30.4	–
Italy	–	–	–	12.7	–	–	–	–	14.3	–	–
Norway	–	–	–	46.7	–	–	–	48.3	–	–	–
Sweden	–	–	46.0	–	–	–	44.6	–	46.2	–	47.8
UK	46.1	48.8	–	–	–	46.4	–	–	–	43.9	–
West Germany	–	–	–	28.8	–	–	–	31.8	–	–	–

Note: ᵃ There were two elections in Denmark in 1953.

revival of pro-capitalist ideas in the 1950s had a clear material basis in the very considerable success of capitalism itself. A 'golden age' appeared to have dawned in which economic growth in the advanced countries surpassed all historical precedents. The sorry record of capitalism in the inter-war years receded from collective memory. Capitalism appeared to be able to deliver growth, employment and rising purchasing power. Angus Maddison has shown that the annual average growth rate in the period 1950–73 was more than twice as high as that of previous and subsequent periods (1820–70, 1870–1913, 1913–50 and 1973–79).[5] The main causes of this formidable growth were luck plus – as Maddison explains – the development of free trade in the international sphere, government policies that promoted domestic demand and held down inflation, and a backlog of growth possibilities which made the advanced economies highly responsive to high levels of demand.[6]

The development of free trade, actively pursued by the USA, encouraged export-led growth in the defeated countries of Germany, Italy and Japan. It facilitated the increase of American investment in Europe and the transfer of technology from the USA, the country which had, at the time, the highest level of productivity per capita.

The free movement of labour within and between countries was of decisive importance.[7] Labour migration permitted a large degree of flexibility in the labour force. Resident workers who had benefited from education and welfare policies and wanted to improve their expectations could move into higher productivity and better paid jobs. The positions they vacated could be filled by a migrant labour force far less demanding in terms of wages and working conditions. The existence of a large pool of migrant labour seeking employment was objectively anti-inflationary: it contained average wage increases not only in assembly-line manufacturing, but also in the 'infrastructure' sectors, such as transport and housing. This meant that overall costs (both social and private) were lower than they would otherwise have been. It permitted the pursuit of policies of 'full employment' (that is, the full employment of the resident labour force).

The new workers were overwhelmingly young males unencumbered by families. This made their demands on welfare services minimal in comparison with those of the resident labour force. They were not old and thus not in need of a pension; not disabled or chronically ill and thus not in need of medical care; not too young and thus not in need of special care or schooling. The first wave of immigrants contributed a great deal more to the national economy than they ever took from it.

As in previous 'golden ages' of capitalism, the growth of the late 1950s and 1960s was due in no small part to the transformation of rural workers into proletarians.[8] From the point of view of the capitalist order, this 'new' workforce, originating mainly from the former colonies, Southern Europe and the north of Africa, was ideal: its labour was cheap, its demand on the welfare state insignificant, its housing needs could be virtually ignored, and its political rights were inadequate. It is true these workers' presence eventually led to grave social tensions for which they bear little or no reponsibility. But this cannot disguise their contribution to the stabilization and success of capitalism. Finally, one should note that in the 1950s the major international source of migrant labour was Europe, and not what would later be called the Third World. Britain 'exported' 2.2 million people, Germany 1.5 million and Italy 1.3 million. In the 1950s just under five million people left Europe for the USA, Australia, Argentina and Brazil.[9] This meant that any excess of indigenous labour could be safely siphoned off to countries hungry for labour. The greatest beneficiary of this export/import of labour was West Germany. It was by far the largest net importer of labour, followed, at a great distance, by Sweden. West Germany was the recipient of the steady stream of highly skilled economic and political refugees from the DDR, and from the former German-speaking territories of Poland and Czechoslovakia. By 1950 there were eight million so-called *Heimatvertriebene* ('expelled from their homeland') in West Germany, of whom two million had come from Silesia, 1.4 million from East Prussia, one million from Pomerania and Brandeburg, two million from the Sudetenland, and 1.5 million from other parts of Europe. To these must be added 2.6 million refugees from the DDR.[10] This influx of labour kept German average wages well below what they would otherwise have been.

In other countries, the size of the foreign labour force grew, while that of indigenous labour diminished. This was due to the fact that more young people stayed in education and therefore delayed their entry into the work-force, while decent pensions ensured that the elderly would stop working at around sixty-five years of age. The main social transformation of the 1950s, namely the exodus from the countryside to the towns, also meant that the size of the female working population was almost certainly reduced since its participation rate in rural work was higher than in manufacturing; furthermore, the growth in the wages of the male industrial worker made it possible for his wife to dispense with paid employment. Welfare policy was not designed to modify the financial dependence of women, but was developed on the assumption that the husband would remain the main earner. As Beveridge said in his famous report: 'Very few men's wages are insufficient to cover at least two adults and one child'; and 'the attitude of the housewife to gainful employment outside the home is not and should not be the same as that of the solitary woman', because the married woman had 'other duties'.[11] Public policy could conceivably have been directed towards facilitating the entry of the female workforce into industry at the expense of migrant labour. This was not done because there were no significant pressures in that direction. As a consequence, the industrial labour force continued to be dominated by indigenous males, who retained the central role allotted them by socialist ideology at the beginning of the century. It is true, of course, that welfare measures, especially housing, were also vigorously pursued, and that these applied to the whole population, not exclusively to the male working class. Nevertheless, the social unit towards which welfare services were directed was the traditional family, organized on the basis of a division of labour between a male breadwinner and a female home carer. This had been made explicit by Beveridge himself:

> In any measure of social policy in which regard is had to facts, the great majority of married women must be regarded as occupied on work which is vital though unpaid, without which their husbands could not do their paid work and without which the nation could not continue.[12]

The family was also the basis of the consumption economy which was the 'demand' side of the boom of the 1950s : household goods and family cars. It was as if the supporters of welfare socialism and of consumer capitalism had come together in identifying the family as the central unit around which social welfare policies and markets should develop. This was far from being the only convergence of interests: the welfare/consumer society also required a constant increase in the average level of wages (which is what happened throughout the 1950s and 1960s, as Table 8.2 illustrates).

This spectacular growth provided both an ideal fiscal basis for the growth of the welfare system and the real foundation for the consumer society. What really legitimized capitalism was not growth *per se*, but its results: private mass consumption. This is what united most of Western Europe where economic experiences were otherwise rather varied: Britain did not really grow very much; inflation was well contained in Germany, but much less so in Italy; full employment existed in Britain throughout the 1950s, but not in Germany, and it only reached Italy in the early 1960s. Wages grew much

Table 8.2 Real wages per worker in selected countries, 1953–70

	1953	1960	1970
Belgium	53.5	64.3	100
France	55.5	61.9	100
Holland	40.2	54.9	100
Italy	37.5	52.5	100
Japan	38.2	50.9	100
UK	61.1	75.3	100
US	69.0	81.0	100
West Germany	41.8	55.8	100

Source: Herman Van der Wee, *Prosperity and Upheaval. The World Economy 1945–1980*, Penguin, Harmondsworth 1987, p. 237; original source: COMET-databank based on national accounts data.

more in Germany, Italy and France than in Britain, but then Britain had started at a higher level. Even though Britain was consistently at the bottom of the league table in terms of economic growth it was, as Kaldor has noted, 'at the top in terms of her *own* historical record'.[13] What all these countries shared was a consumption boom.

Under various forms of central planning, the societies of Eastern and Central Europe grew as well. Admittedly, statistics early on became a weapon in the Cold War and hence more unreliable than usual. But there is little doubt that in terms of quantitative growth, 'the socialist camp' did very well, even on the basis of Western estimates.[14] Between 1950 and 1955 the OECD countries grew by an average of 4.8 per cent a year: the socialist countries did better than this. with the exception of Czechoslovakia (3.4 per cent) and Yugoslavia (4.4 per cent). In the subsequent five years the OECD bloc grew as a whole by 3.3 per cent: the other side did much better, with Bulgaria leading the way with 7.2 per cent, Czechoslovakia achieving 6.4 per cent, and the DDR 5.1 per cent – not to mention Yugoslavia with 7.1 per cent. The USSR itself, according to estimates by the Central Intelligence Agency, scored 5.5 per cent for 1950–55 and 5.9 per cent for 1955–60.[15] This constituted an apparently commendable economic success, while being an astounding political failure, since the Soviet bloc proved to be utterly incapable of creating a consumer society. In the long term that was its undoing. The increase in growth was brutally quantitative. As Trotsky presciently pointed out in *The Revolution Betrayed*. 'It is possible to build gigantic factories according to a ready-made pattern by bureaucratic command ... But the farther you go, the more the economy runs into the problems of quality.'[16] People do not want to double steel output and treble iron production; they want comfortable houses and washing machines, and rightly so: the ideology of growth for growth's sake is the ideology of the cancer cell.

Of course people in Eastern and Central Europe were not asked what they wanted and the authorities could get on with 'the construction of socialism' without the bothersome requirements of electioneering. This could not be the case in the West: as a large proportion of the population of Western Europe benefited from the new consumer society, no political party intent upon achieving a majority could really afford to challenge the system as a whole, particularly when the only model of socialism available was not very alluring. In the West, capitalism had to accept welfare socialism and socialism had to adopt mass consumerism. The people as a whole, and not just the industrial working class, had to become the focus of attention of all mass parties. This was the basis for what was called in Britain and the Scandinavian countries the 'social-democratic consensus', and what social theorists identified as 'the end of ideology' (Daniel Bell) and the consequent transformation of the working-class party into a *Volkspartei*, or 'people's party' (Otto Kirchheimer).

The spirit of these new times was a consumer-oriented growth which originated in the USA in the inter-war period and which spread to Western Europe only in the 1950s. Its political umbrella was an international military organization centred on the USA and targeted against the USSR. Its ideological machine, unlike that of Soviet communism, was formidable and unparalleled: it consisted of a multinational and multidimensional advertising system and a mass cultural industry which required, for its diffusion, the possession of consumer goods (radios and, later, televisions) which everyone craved. Ideology was not imposed, it was purchased. The ensuing worldwide standardization of consumer taste made possible an international marketing strategy on the part of multinational corporations.

Conservative critics, like Edward Shils, writing in 1957, could now abandon élitism and celebrate the masses who had emerged from their 'immemorially old, clod-like existence' and achieved at least the 'possibility of becoming full members of their society, of living a human life with some exercise of cultural taste'.[17] Many writers on the Left castigated the consumer society as an 'admass' (the term was coined by J. B. Priestley), which stifled creativity and promoted conformity. Theorists such as Hannah Arendt saw it as a social mechanism from which escape seemed impossible:

> our whole economy has become a waste economy, in which things must be almost as quickly devoured and discarded as they have appeared in the world, if the process itself is not to come to a sudden catastrophic end.[18]

As Daniel Bell has pointed out, the first writers who used the term mass society – among them, Ortega y Gasset, Karl Jaspers and T. S. Eliot – were doing so from the point of view of an aristocratic or élitist conception of culture and had no wish to extend cultural rights to the masses.[19] Later on, 'progressive' intellectuals who wrote in the pages of left-wing journals were democrats who lambasted the consumer society of advertising and the debaucheries of mass culture, but could not provide any alternative except for various forms of avant-garde art which, far from being subversive, were often immediately acclaimed and successfully marketed.[20]

In Europe the left-wing struggle against the consumer society often took the form of a defence of national culture and sovereignty against the Americanization of society. Once again, socialist ideas had to seek the protection of nationalism in a battle which operated largely through modern symbols. The diffusion of Coca-Cola in Europe, for instance, provoked opposition almost everywhere – often, but not exclusively, led by the Left in semi-open alliance with local beer or wine interests. Maurice Thorez, leader of the French Communist Party, declared that 'in literature as elsewhere we must ensure that Coca-Cola does not triumph over wine'.[21] Attempts to ban the beverage were made in Belgium, Denmark, Switzerland and France. In Italy it was taxed to protect wine. Coca-Cola was seen as part and parcel of American neo-colonialist designs upon Europe. Coca-Cola self-consciously advertised itself as part of the American Way of Life, poised to become the Universal Drink.[22]

The left-wing battles of the 1950s against the consumer society were as hopeless as those of the Luddites of yesteryear against machines. In a society in which most people were powerless, as they had been since time immemorial, a new form of power, once the prerogative of the rich, had become the property of the many: the power to choose and purchase an ever-growing number of commodities. The drudgery of work could be tolerated because it was the royal road to the enchanted world of supermarkets and department stores: there one could lay claim to goods publicly exhibited and say, 'this is mine, it now belongs to me'. Language followed form: a word, 'sovereignty', once designating the unlimited and unchallengeable power of the monarch, was now used by economists who employed the term 'consumer sovereignty' to describe this novel individual power of private appropriation. A professor of marketing could write: 'Not the exploiter and not the robber baron but the *consumer* is king today ... And because of his "dollar ballots" the *consumer will continue to be king*. Every day he casts those ballots at the cash registers. Business has no choice but to discover what he wants and to service his wishes, even his whims.'[23] The parties of the Left, who competed for the votes of newly empowered consumers in an open political market, could neither ignore nor castigate the new 'admass' society.

Nor could they ignore the fact that the force and might of the USA was at the centre of a system which, in the West at least, required very little overt coercion. Like all successful politics, that of the consumer/welfare society was based on the willing participation of the overwhelming majority of those involved in it. The *Pax Americana*, though ultimately based on the most powerful military machine in human history, was really founded on the image of an American life-style endlessly adaptable to national and regional particularities which all could obtain. It should not be surprising if this engendered a deep conservatism in socialist parties, which became trapped in the defence of a generalized status quo. They defended the growth model of Western capitalism, which provided sought-after consumer goods and the necessary surplus with which to pay for the welfare state; they supported the Atlanticist international order, thus demarcating themselves from authoritarian forms of socialism in the East; they endorsed the liberal-democratic organization of the state, which provided the political conditions for their obtaining a parliamentary victory and/or participation in governmental power; they upheld the prevailing form of the family, with its peculiar division of labour, because it seemed best suited to existing conditions and was not overtly challenged by anyone. Consequently, many traditional socialist commitments were in practice abandoned or relegated to an ever-receding long term: the end of capitalism, universal peace, the reform of the state, the abolition of all forms of political and economic inequality between the sexes. Attention was entirely concentrated on the main short-term aims: full employment for all male workers and the provision of welfare services to meet needs not provided through the market.

This conservatism could easily be defended against radicals whose fundamentalist intransigence seemed to be out of touch with popular feelings: Atlanticism, the family, economic growth and parliamentary democracy were not imposed by some arcane outside force, but were fully legitimated. This was what the people wanted. If socialists wanted to keep in touch with their electorate, actual or potential, they would have to relinquish some of the primary features of their past radicalism. Those who did not paid the price, remaining tiny groups within the larger socialist parties, or marginal sects outside them.

Socialists became 'realists'. But like all those who no longer believe in dreams, socialist parties were doomed to be taken by surprise by all the changes which modernity thrust upon them over the following thirty years: the permissive society, pop culture, the revival of industrial conflicts of the late 1960s, student power, feminism, black consciousness, homosexual rights, the plight of the Third World, ecology, the end of ideology, European integration, the revival of ideology, the crisis of the family, the end of communism in Eastern Europe, the growth of nationalist separatism. Not one novelty worth writing or thinking about had been envisioned or predicted by the European socialist movement. Having given up much of their past in order to face the present, socialists became blind to the future.

Such an indictment cannot be made of the somewhat marginalized theorists and thinkers of Western socialism. On the whole, they did their thinking in isolation, often ignored if not ostracized by the socialist parties. Unlike the theorists of the past – Kautsky, Bernstein, Gramsci or Otto Bauer – they were not in positions of authority or political responsibility, but were mere academics who read each other's books.

The parties of the Right were no better than those of the Left in the arcane art of foretelling the future. But they were anyway not interested in it, much preferring to develop their skills at coping with the present.

The idea that some of the difficulties encountered by socialist parties in the 1950s (or later) had something to do with the changing size of the industrial working class should be dealt with briefly. In the first place, the size of the working class did not change dramatically during the period: on the contrary, with the exception of Belgium, the number of people employed in the manufacturing sector increased, as Table 8.3 demonstrates. In the second place, there is no correlation between changes in the size of the working class and the pattern of voting for socialist parties. In the third place, had socialists ever relied solely on the vote of the working class, they would never have won an election. In the fourth place, there was no significant overall decline in the percentage obtained by working-class parties in the 1950s. Finally, it should be added that, as far as the 1950s are concerned, the most important change in class composition which occurred in Western Europe affected the peasantry. This class, the supposed traditional backbone of conservative parties, shrank quite visibly. If there was a close connection between class composition and electoral fortunes, we should have expected the continental conservative parties to have had many more problems than those of the Left. They did not. The traditional conservatives held sway throughout most of Western Europe while the economy grew, modernization developed, the rural sector contracted, the consumer society advanced and traditional values retreated. No social theorist told them to change or adapt, let alone revise anything. The conservatives simply went on ruling with a characteristic nonchalance towards ideology and a pragmatism devoid of any existential *angst*.

The data in Table 8.3 conceal other profound modifications: there were changes in the school-leaving age; the tertiary sector expanded with entrants from the manufacturing sector who, in turn, absorbed many of those who had just left the rural sector. Yet the size of the electorate of the parties of the Left changed very little: the socialist parties of Austria, Belgium, Denmark, West Germany, Holland and Norway advanced slightly, those of Sweden and Britain retreated a little; in France and Italy the joint communist and socialist vote increased, while in Finland it declined. Nor was this peculiarity confined to the Left: the entire West European electorate was surprisingly stable in spite of the many social changes. Of the eleven democracies under consideration, only France underwent a change of regime (from the Fourth to the Fifth Republic); in retrospect, hardly a momentous transmutation.

In the Western Europe of the 1950s there did not seem to be widespread discontent; certainly nothing on the scale of the turmoil in East Germany (1953) and Poland (1956), not to speak of the Hungarian uprising; or even of the intensity of the student unrest and the industrial conflict of the late 1960s. One might, at most, single out the peace campaigns of the French and Italian communists in the early 1950s and the anti-nuclear marches in

Table 8.3 Percentage changes in the distribution of the labour force in selected West European countries in the 1950s: manufacturing and agriculture

Country	Period	Manufacturing industries	Agriculture, forestry and fishing
Austria	1951–61	+13.3	-29.3
Belgium	1947–61	-3.3	-40.2
Denmark	1950–60	+11.4[a]	-29.1
Finland	1950–60	+16.5	-20.9
France	1946–62	+15.5	-47.8
Holland	1947–60	+22.8	-40.1
Italy	1951–61	+25.48[a]	-31.5
Norway	1950–60	+ 0.8	-23.9
Sweden	1950–60	+13.6	-29.0
UK	1951–61	+ 1.9	-23.5
West Germany	1950–61	+37.22	-30.2

Note: [a] Includes mining and construction.

Source: my tabulation on the basis of data in B. R. Mitchell, 'Statistical Appendix 1920–1970', in Carlo M. Cipolla (ed.), *The Fontana Economic History of Europe, Contemporary Economies*, Vol. 2, Collins/Fontana, Glasgow 1976, pp. 657–64.

Britain at the end of the decade, not the last gasps of a backward-looking proletarian radicalism, but the harbinger of a nascent movement of middle-class social protest. The working class, the 'people' on whose discontent the socialists relied for their political progress, seemed to be quietly satisfied or, if not contented, fairly confident that their material life would improve in their lifetime. Of course, the supposition that 'things will get better' is, in principle, part of the conception of socialism, unlike the idea that the 'good life' is round the corner and that it can be obtained while the world is still full of capitalist tycoons. Socialists may be long-term optimists but are, perhaps unavoidably, short-term pessimists. The fundamental cause of the revisionism of some socialist parties in the late 1950s is therefore not hard to find: it lies in the conviction that the existing capitalist system of production, coyly rechristened 'the mixed economy', or the 'new capitalism', or the 'social market economy', was an adequate vehicle for the satisfaction of people's desires.

The preservation or acceptance of the status quo became the norm of politics. Like those of the Left, the parties of the centre and of the Right, in charge of governments in most West European countries, did their best to enhance social peace by not challenging any of the major welfare reforms, where these had been implemented, and by advancing their own social policies. Without exception they accepted the new consensus.

In Italy the Christian democrats promoted an agrarian reform in the south

(1949–50), and economic development in the north; meanwhile, however, they persecuted the left-wing trade unions mercilessly, in an effort to contain wages and favour the progress of Catholic unions.

In Britain the Conservatives launched a massive housing programme, pursued full employment policies, and limited privatization to the iron and steel industries and the introduction of a commercial television sector – an intelligent and popular move, which was opposed, at the time, by the entire Left, as well as the Archbishop of Canterbury and the churches, and by the university establishment.[24]

In France, given the lack of stable parliamentary majorities, state technocrats pursued their modernizing strategies through state agencies, achieving some social reforms, while the commitment to full employment enshrined in the preamble to the 1946 constitution was reaffirmed in that drafted by the Gaullists in 1958.[25]

In West Germany the conservative CDU passed legislation establishing some form of industrial democracy. That this should occur at all may seem surprising, given the weakness of the West German trade unions after the defeat of the SPD at the 1949 elections, the constant influx of 'expellees' from the territories of the former Reich which prevented a tight labour market, and the growing success of reconstruction. The unions had scored some notable successes between 1945 and 1947, when they had settled their religious and ideological differences to form a single trade union movement, the DGB (Deutscher Gewerkschaftsbund), founded at Bielefeld in 1947; and they had also achieved co-determination (*Mitbestimmung*) in the coal and steel industries, partly thanks to the British occupying authorities. On the wages front, however, the German trade unions had been unable to achieve significant gains: German wages remained at a relatively low level: 47 per cent of GNP, while in Britain they were 58 per cent of GNP.[26] This forced the DGB to seek in industrial democracy some compensation for what it had not been able to obtain in wage negotiations. The CDU government of Adenauer conceded three laws enacted between 1951 and 1955, the most important being the 1951 Co-determination Law in the Coal, Iron and Steel Industries, which was supported by over 90 per cent of the workers balloted. Henceforth all enterprises in the coal, steel and iron industries with over one thousand workers had to have employee representatives on the supervisory boards. A worker director was to be nominated to sit on the board of directors of each of these firms, with an equal vote in management affairs.[27] Claims were made that the law amounted to a revolutionary act, to be upheld or opposed according to which side of industry one was on.[28] The truth is that the legislation helped secure the long period of social peace and social partnership in the field of industrial relations which would be regarded in countries more prone to industrial conflicts (Britain, France and Italy) as the basis for German industrial growth and power. For the capitalist system, 'moderate' and 'reasonable' trade unions were worth more than ten Marshall Plans. The SPD had very little to do with the development of *Mitbestimmung*, though it did vote for the 1951 law (the free democrats and the communists voted against). The law would have had more impact if the principle of co-determination had been extended to the rest of industry, but this proved to be impossible and the resulting compromise – the Works' Constitution Law of October 1952 – failed to satisfy the trade unions, since the rights of participation in decision-making were granted to works councils and not to the unions themselves.[29] For most trade unionists at the time, in Germany as elsewhere, industrial democracy was synonymous with the extension of union power and was second best to wages militancy.

Conditions prevailing in the post-war European economies meant that capitalist growth could be promoted only if productivity grew faster than wages. From the political point of view, the crucial problem of achieving growth appeared, therefore, as a wages containment problem. The conservative and liberal parties in charge of state affairs throughout Europe could rely on the pool of unemployed labour (inside and/or outside the country) to stabilize wages, or on fiscal and monetary means. In some instances (France and Italy) the systematic persecution of the more militant (i.e. communist) trade unions was also functional to wages stabilization, as was their low level of unionization. Decentralized wage bargaining, as in Britain, enabled wage increases to be more closely tailored to the sectoral differences in productivity increases.

When in opposition, the parties of the Left were not faced with the growth versus wages issue. They could back, more or less on principle, any demand for an increase in wages. Where they were in government, they attempted, in almost all instances, to establish some form of accord (incomes policy) with the trade unions, so that wage increases did not outstrip productivity or cause a rise in unemployment.

Small countries heavily dependent on exports for their growth (e.g. Belgium and Holland), in particular, would have an inflation rate far more influenced by external factors than otherwise. But they would also need to keep their inflation under control to maintain international competitiveness. This is a constraint from which no party, whether of the Left or the Right, could escape. In these circumstances an incomes policy may become a national necessity. This was one of the most important factors influencing the growing involvement of governments, as well as trade unions and employers' associations, in what has been characterized as modern corporatism.[30]

For governments to become involved in wage determination, two conditions are necessary (though not sufficient): wage bargaining should be centralized (if the union leadership cannot deliver, there is little point in negotiating with it); and the 'social partners' – employers and employees – must be willing to enter into negotiations. Obviously, the more workers there were in trade unions, the greater the chances of success of an incomes policy. The presence of a socialist party in government usually provided the trade unions with an enhanced incentive to accept some centralized negoti-ations.

In six of the smaller countries of Europe (Austria, Belgium, Holland, Sweden, Norway and Denmark), some or all of these conditions were in existence in the 1950s. In the first place, the socialist or social-democratic parties were in power (on their own or in coalition) throughout the decade in Austria, Denmark, Sweden, Norway; in Holland until 1958 and in Belgium only between 1954 and 1957. Secondly, five out of the six countries exhibited a higher than average degree of centralization in collective bargaining; the exception, Belgium, was just below the medium point and well above France, the UK and Italy.[31] Finally, all six countries had a comparatively high degree of unionization.[32]

In all these countries some kind of anti-inflationary incomes policy was attempted. In some cases, as in Belgium, the government did not get involved because wages were determined by an agreement between a centralized trade union movement (though split on religious and linguistic lines) and a central-ized employers' association.

In Austria, after the strikes of 1951, trade union militancy had virtually disappeared and a highly effective centralized incomes policy continued to function.[33] This was formalized in 1957 in a joint wages and prices board, which brought together government, unions and employers. The Austrian wage–price agreement was not part of a grand idea for planning the economy. It was an *ad hoc* measure developed to contain inflation within supposedly acceptable limits. The wage agreements were always followed by price rises that outstripped the allegedly compensating increases in wages. Thus, workers lost in immediate monetary terms, though they presumably gained in social terms. The SPÖ and the trade unions were fully behind this anti-inflationary policy, whose success required wages to lag behind, although they were embarrassed to admit that wages had not kept up with rising prices, and accused all those who pointed it out of irresponsibility and of playing into the hands of communist propaganda.[34] Socialists, once in power, required wages to grow moderately but, somehow, unlike their conservative rivals, they could not yet openly boast of having achieved the desired objective.

In Holland, between the early 1950s and 1963, the process of wage determination was in effect channelled through various co-ordinated bodies which 'provided the most comprehensive centralized wage policy in Europe'.[35] In negotiations with the government, the Dutch Federation of Labour (the trade union federation) accepted cost-of-living adjustments in the immediate post-war years. And in 1951, during the Korean boom, when the terms of trade of Holland deteriorated, they even accepted a 5 per cent cut in real wages. This draconian incomes policy was accepted by all shades of trade union opinion – Catholic, Protestant and socialist.[36] As a result, the Dutch economy grew more rapidly than that of its Belgian rival, thus narrowing the gap between them.[37] The enhanced international competitiveness of Dutch industry was due to the fact that the Dutch had started out with lower prices than the Belgians and enjoyed lower costs. Dutch employers did well out of centralized bargaining, but the workers did not lose: full employment was reached by the late 1950s. Though the participation of socialists in government did not help the unions to achieve wage increases, there was a considerable increase in social spending and a massive housing programme designed to accommodate an expanding population.

In Norway, Denmark and Sweden agreements had existed between employers and employees since the 1930s (see chapter 3). In Norway the government (under DNA control throughout the 1950s) had price-control powers which were made permanent in 1953, and there was compulsory arbitration on wages.[38] But the most important and significant development was in Sweden, so often in the forefront of social engineering, and this must be examined at greater length.

Immediately after the end of the Second World War, Sweden's SAP government followed the expansionary policies advocated by the Myrdal commission report. These policies created a dangerous inflationary trend, as well as balance of payment difficulties. The government imposed wage freezes in 1949 and 1950 to curb inflation. The trade union federation, the LO, conceded that it was not possible to have free collective bargaining while at the same time containing inflation and pursuing full employment.[39]

An alternative to a straightforward incomes policy emerged from within the ranks of the LO. This was the report entitled *Trade Unions and Full Employment*, drafted by the LO economist Gösta Rehn with the assistance of Rudolf Meidner, presented to the 1951 LO Congress, and generally known as the Rehn–Meidner model.[40] The outstanding feature of this report was that it represented the most integrated strategic model for the social-democratic management of the capitalist economy, all the more remarkable as it was a product of the trade unions and not of the party. The model emerged from the labour movement with the longest experience of government in a West European democracy – further proof that the art of governing is learned in government. Rehn and Meidner had been working on this issue and producing position papers for a number of years. But it was only the necessity of dealing with inflation that motivated the trade union leadership to adopt their proposals.[41] It was an integrated strategy, because it set out clearly the primary and secondary objectives of the nation (and not merely those of the movement), allocated and delineated the respective roles of private enterprise, government and trade unions, and, in so doing, established the responsibilities of each side – in other words, the rules of the game.

The primary goal was clearly stated: full employment. This was to be made compatible with five secondary goals:

1. Wage determination by collective agreement without government interference.

2. Combating inflation.
3. Equality and fairness.
4. The preservation of trade union strength.
5. A rational allocation of resources to ensure maximum growth and productivity.

Control of inflation (goal 2), one of the key functions of governments, was to be pursued first and foremost by budgetary means.[42] When the economy overheated, the government was expected to tax purchasing power to dampen down demand. 'High' profits, defined as profit levels which no longer automatically ensure full employment and/or which could be used to grant inflationary wage increases, were to be taxed. The assumption was that taxation of profits would make entrepreneurs more reluctant to grant wage increases, especially those due to 'wage-drift' (that is, increases due to plant-level negotiation and other non-centralized forms of bargaining). In so doing, the government would also contribute to achieving goals 1 and 4.

Actual wage negotiation was to remain the prerogative of employers and trade unions, 'without any State intervention in the form of compulsory arbitration or wage legislation'.[43] This was because 'The trade union movement has a right to demand an economic policy which leaves the trade unions in undisturbed possession of their present role on the labour market and in society' (goal 4).[44] To ensure that the unions did not demand inflationary wages, it was necessary to adopt a principle for wage bargaining: the principle of equal pay for equal work performed (goal 3). This formed the basis of the so-called 'solidaristic wages policy'.[45] The entire conception of this wage policy seemed to be in accord with Marx's first stage of communism (to each according to the work performed), in his famous *Critique of the Gotha Programme*, though the report, prudently, did not mention Marx.

How was this to work in practice? A massive job evaluation scheme was to be carried out in each industry to grade and classify work. Negotiations were then to follow between employers and unions, to establish the 'fair' wages for each category, and all firms were to commit themselves not to deviate from it. Particularly efficient firms which could have afforded a bigger pay settlement would, of course, reap the reward of greater profits, though they would have to face a higher tax bill. Firms operating below average efficiency would be making a loss and would have an incentive to become more efficient (goal 5). They would no longer be able to rely on their own workers accepting lower pay and thus subsidizing their own firm's inefficiency. A certain number of bankruptcies or redundancies might well ensue. Here the government would intervene to pursue an active labour market policy, by offering incentives, financial and otherwise, as well as retraining and rehousing schemes, so that workers made redundant could find other jobs.[46] This would achieve flexibility in the labour market, while ensuring the preservation of full employment and an increase in productivity (goal 5).

Full employment was thus made compatible with the struggle against inflation, with productivity, equality and trade union independence. The model offered, in essence, a 'rational' wage structure, since differences in wages would be due solely to differences in skills, not to the degree of efficiency of the firm or to the demand for the firm's product. It offered a measure of price stability because the government would intervene to dampen down demand by fiscal means.[47]

The originality of the model was that it combined objectives which until then were normally seen as contradictory, or which generally had to be tackled separately. Active labour market policies had often been recommended in the past and a solidaristic wages policy was discussed as early as 1936 at the Congress of the LO.

The report was not implemented immediately. The employers resented giving so much power to the trade unions and feared the possibility of high company taxation. Unions representing the better paid workers in the expanding sectors of the economy were distinctly unenthusiastic about restraining their pay demands. The SAP government was reluctant to take action at the top of the boom to cool down a buoyant economy, as required by the model. It was only during the recession of 1957–59 that the Rehn–Meidner model began to be applied. The government adopted an active labour policy, employers accepted that a 'solidaristic wage policy' could be used as a wage restraint policy, and low-wage trade unions, strengthened by centralized wage bargaining, were able to impose a differential-reducing strategy on the LO as a whole. As Pontusson has noted, solidaristic wages policy evolved in a piecemeal way. The Rehn–Meidner model was adopted not because of its evident intellectual strength, but because it provided a strategy corresponding to the needs of the majority of the unions in the LO and acceptable to government and employers.[48] As Gösta Rehn himself explained in 1985:

> After some heated debates, the government was finally persuaded that the unions and their theorists were not trying to find pretexts for any populist inflationary wage policy, but were instead asking for an economic policy that would make it psychologically and politically possible for them to embrace a non-inflationary money-wage policy that would in turn foster optimal real-wage development.[49]

The model may have been conceived as a policy 'for socialism'. If so, it was only in the sense that it strengthened the hegemonic weight of the labour movement by emphasizing its capacity for government and its ability to manage the economy: the trade unions appeared in a novel role – namely, as guarantors of productivity. The results were undoubtedly positive: growth, full employment, increased prosperity, low inflation – though how much this was due to the model, and how much to structural factors, will long be debated. One of the results unintended by the Left was a consistent growth in the profitability of large firms operating in the exporting sector. This led to an excessive accumulation of profit and the consolidation of Swedish multinational firms, for which the solidaristic wages policy worked as a wage restraint mechanism as effective as any incomes policy. Twenty years after the report was originally presented, one of the co-authors, Rudolf Meidner wrote: 'the more successful the policy of solidarity proves to be, the greater are the undesirable side-effects in the form of ... extra profits'. And although it was desirable that companies should be financially sound, 'it was also essential for the community and the trade unions to acquire a greater say in the allocation of profits for investment purposes'.[50]

The solidaristic wages policy was of benefit to the workers, but also to the employers, whose power was not diminished. Nevertheless, the success of the policy demonstrated the innovatory capabilities of the SAP and the LO. However, political intelligence is not enough; a considerable amount of good fortune is required. Swedish social democracy was lucky to be in power when there was worldwide economic growth, leading to a period of unparalleled prosperity for the advanced economies. Its intelligence resided in its ability to go with the trend and exploit propitious circumstances.

Another special feature of Swedish social democracy was the comparatively high degree of co-operation attained by the three sectors of the labour movement, which are usually in constant conflict, especially when the socialists are in power: the party, the trade unions and the intellectuals. The trade unions owed their 'national' outlook partly to the fact that, to some extent, *they were* the nation: they represented a very large proportion of the population both because of their centralization and because most working Swedes were in trade unions. The innovatory role of the Swedish trade unions is particularly striking: they were in the forefront of the celebrated 1938 Saltsjöbaden Agreement with the employers' association, which established a collective bargaining agreement (discussed in chapter 2); in the 1950s they promoted the solidaristic wages policy; in the 1970s the wage-earner funds scheme (see chapter 23). They were also the foremost instigator of the supplementary pension reform of 1959. This measure led to the elimination of poverty, especially poverty in old age – something which had not been achieved either by the American model of high wages and private pension insurance, or by the British welfare system.[51] To clinch this reform, one of the most important in Swedish welfare history, considerable political activity had to take place: three state commissions; the break-up of the coalition between the SAP and the Agrarian Party; a referendum; a minority social-democratic government; and the decisive abstention in the final vote in the Lower Chamber of a Liberal MP (the only Liberal Christian worker), subsequently expelled from his party.[52] In real politics, policies are inevitably the outcome of a conglomeration of disparate circumstances; on its own the possession of an overall strategy never guarantees a favourable outcome, while the absence of such a strategy is always a liability.

We have taken the Swedish case as our instance of a 'successful' social-democratic party. But 'success' must be defined in the context within which it is produced. I would argue that, in the context of the 1950s, success for social democrats could only mean the ability of achieving 'American' goals – i.e. high productivity and high consumption, by social-democratic means and in social-democratic forms. The great dilemma of all European decision-makers was that their electorate aspired to American consumption levels, but these could not be achieved in the American way – that is, by high wages. Therefore the 'form' whereby Americanism could be implanted in Europe could not be American. Models of social organizations can never be successfully imported, though they can be adapted. Those who urge the adoption of this or that foreign example in reality seek the results, not the model itself. People want the omelette, not the broken eggs.

How to achieve the European version of the American consumer society was the real poiitical issue of the 1950s. The Swedish Left faced it. It accepted the laws of the market. It accepted that Sweden had to export or stagnate, and that it had to ensure the growth of a healthy and productive capitalist market. But it also sought to establish and impose its own terms and conditions in order to reach a working compromise. Elsewhere the pattern was different.

One section of the West European Left, made up of the surviving communist parties, was not in a situation where it could even contemplate adopting a social-democratic form of Americanism. The communists' problem was to survive and preserve their strength by holding high the vision and perspective of an entirely different social order. Of the two communist parties with which our story is chiefly concerned, the PCI used the opportunities available to distance itself, with great difficulty, many hesitations and over a considerable period of time, from its Leninist matrix, and move closer to the larger battalions of European social democracy; the PCF preferred the apparent security of allegiance to its past.

As for the major social-democratic and labour parties, they were simply not equipped or willing to face the issue of adapting their traditions to capitalist success, at least not in the early 1950s. It is easy to understand why. In the circumstances of the 'golden age' of capitalism, political realism could only mean divesting oneself of a substantial baggage of hopes and ideals which had taken a considerable history of struggles to build up.

Short-term realism is not always necessarily the most advantageous route. There are times when prudence dictates recognizing that one cannot win and that it is better to wait. Where there is no defence, valour lies in flight. But in politics one can seldom run away. Events impose themselves and compel choice. By the end of the decade, as we shall see in chapter 10, repeated electoral defeats led inexorably towards a more open revision of past positions.

Unlike the parties of the Left, those of the Right and the centre, which held sway in much of Western Europe, had a strategy: they would contain the welfare reforms of the immediate post-war period (where these had already taken place), but not to the extent of endangering social peace; they would use the state to promote the development of essential infrastructure (roads and houses); and they would seek to keep wages as low as possible. This last factor is the crucial one: it meant that wages could grow, but in an unequal manner, reflecting the productivity and profitability of firms. Income inequality would thus be dictated by the 'logic' of capital accumulation. The hierarchy of wages which would emerge from all this reflected the hierarchy of capitalism. The main determinant of high wages is greater profitability. Thus wages follow the rational logic of capital. It is a rationality which is identical to that of trade unions willing to put to one side (or to the long term – that is, to the day that never comes) any aspiration towards social reforms, and to dedicate themselves to a wages race perfectly in harmony with that celebrated by the upholders of capitalism. In such a race those at the top will enjoy salaries higher than average and enter spheres of con- sumption prohibited to others. Those in the middle or even at the bottom of the hierarchy will have to be satisfied with the knowledge that there exists a route to the nirvana of consumption: work harder and be lucky. The great achievement of capitalism in the late 1950s consisted in the very large number of those who could work, did work and were 'lucky' enough to see a constant improvement in their material wealth. In the 1960s the provisions of the welfare state became even more generous. The combination of a full employ- ment economy, rising wages and improved social protection characterized the Golden Age of Capitalism in Western Europe.

Trade union sectionalism, short-termism and blind determination to pre- serve existing differentials were the roads pursued by the strongest non- centralized trade union movement in Europe, the British. Here the 'tradition that they should bargain sectionally, each craft and trade for itself, is old and strong.'[53] The unheeded remedy suggested by Beveridge in his second report, *Full Employment in a Free Society* (1944), was a unified wages policy.[54] Sixteen years later, he counselled: 'Let our Government, whatever its colour make one more effort to secure freely, from organisations of employees and employers alike, co-operation in keeping our money sound and our prices stable.'[55] But it was not in Britain alone that much of the domestic politics of the subsequent twenty years would be troubled with this matter.

The dilemma of 'Americanism' suggested above was not concerned with economic policy alone. There was a foreign policy dimension of unparalleled importance: to what extent did having an 'American' society mean sharing the international values of the USA? Did it necessarily involve being a member of an international alliance led by the USA and aimed against the USSR? What was the real space for manoeuvre open to the European Left?

CHAPTER NINE

Between Neutralism and Atlanticism

IN THE 1950S the West European Left continued to have only two fundamental foreign policy alternatives: nationalist neutralism and supra-national
European Atlanticism. Neither was entirely thought out or internally consistent, or even mutually exclusive (there was a still embryonic European
anti-Atlantic neutralism among some socialists), and therefore should not be
accorded the dignity of an ample analytical treatment. Like most political
strategies, they developed as much in response to international events,
domestic considerations, concerns internal to the parties of the Left and
personality disputes, as from carefully constructed ideologies. In many instances, the proponents of one option simply opportunistically exploited any
theme which might strengthen their own side – a strategy which led them
to defend positions for which they had no natural sympathy. For example,
it was quite obvious that most communists intended to oppose any scheme
for West European rearmament as manifestly anti-Soviet; but since pro-
Sovietism could not rally anyone beyond their own ranks, other themes were
adopted, such as pacifism or nationalism. This does not mean that all or
even most communists were not sincerely committed to peace, or that pacifists
were communist stooges or political imbeciles. It simply means that in real
politics, those who seek an ample consensus often necessarily find themselves
with the strangest of bedfellows.

In this climate it was usual to attack an opinion not because it was believed
to be mistaken in itself, but because 'objectively' it gave comfort to the
'enemy'. Many of those who campaigned for peace in the 1950s were regularly
criticized thereafter, not on the grounds that pacifism was wrong, but on the
quite justifiable grounds that their position 'objectively' helped the foreign
policy aims of the USSR. Communists themselves had repeatedly used the
concept of 'objective error' to criticize and, as in Stalin's Russia, to execute
even those who were genuinely fighting for socialism. It was in the nature
of the Cold War, and of the division of the world into two camps, that any
attempt to weaken one of the two blocs 'objectively' helped the other side;
it was a 'zero-sum' game: one's loss became the opponent's gain. Trapped in
this logic, there was nothing the West European Left could do to disentangle
itself.

Virtually all 'neutralists' attempting to escape from the logic of the blocs tried to find a 'third way' between the USA and the USSR. This proved fruitless. Most of the left-wing socialists who sought to adopt a neutralist foreign policy had no quarrel with the command economy of the USSR or (until the invasion of Hungary in 1956) with its foreign policy; what they disapproved of was political repression. Their ideal 'third way' was a reformed and pluralist Soviet society, where the majority would always willingly vote for socialism.

The majority of socialists and social democrats in Western Europe were 'Atlanticists'. For all their differences, they were united by a commitment to liberal democracy. The only organizational form which could hold them together was a fairly loose association of independent parties. The Socialist International, which was revived in Frankfurt in June 1951, was based on an ideological declaration, *Aims and Tasks of Democratic Socialism*, mainly the work of the British Labour Party and Scandinavian social democrats, which emphasized the commitment to parliamentary democracy, civil liberties and the defence of the West. Attempts by some of the parties of Southern Europe – for example, the French – to inject some Marxist terminology were rebuffed, though there were some perfunctory positive references to Marxism as a method. When it was born, the Socialist International was a Cold War organization which did little else besides formulate compromise resolutions which never had the slightest importance. As is the case in many clubs, its only purpose was to provide its members with the respectability it denied others. Those parties of the Left too close to the communist position, such as the Italian socialists, were excluded until they repented.

What the socialist 'Atlanticists' called a 'third way' was simply a West European welfare state in a mixed economy. Their model was capitalism with as caring and human a face, and as few inequalities, as possible. In the final analysis, any liberal-democratic capitalist society was preferable to Russian socialism. As the Labour revisionists of the journal *Socialist Commentary* put it in August 1950: 'present-day American capitalism, for all our misgivings about it, at least leaves room for free institutions to flower and survive.'[1] Except in Italy, socialists tried to distance themselves from communists even when they had the same policies. For instance, in Austria, the neutralist SPÖ was embarrassed by the overt neutralism of the Austrian communists. Luckily for the socialists, their coalition partners, the ÖVP, had none of these problems – no one could accuse them of being crypto-communists. They advocated permanent neutrality along the Swiss model. This enabled the SPÖ to join the ÖVP in voting for the Neutrality Act in October 1955.[2]

Determined that neutrality should be confined to external affairs and eager to identify with the West, in the 1950s the Austrian socialists developed a positive view of the USA and depicted the New Deal as a decisive break with America's capitalist past. Nevertheless, in their 1958 programme, they sought to return to a position of equidistance by affirming that 'democratic socialism occupies a position between capitalism and dictatorship'.[3] Attempts to develop a pro-American socialism were made in other countries. In France the socialist E. Weill-Raynal wrote in 1955 that 'the USA were much nearer to a socialist regime than they imagine'.[4] Richard Crossman, who had once been the inspirer of the neutralist 'Third Force' group within the British Labour Party, did not go as far as this. But he was far from neutral: 'the USA is a better form of society than the USSR ... To reject America as a capitalist country and to treat the Soviet empire as an example of socialist planning is to make nonsense of every one of our ideals.'[5]

Tito's Yugoslavia which, alone in Eastern Europe, had stood up against Stalin and rejected the Soviet model, failed to provide a standard for a 'middle way' West European Left. Until the mid-1950s Yugoslavia was ostracized by all the communist parties without being supported by the socialists. Its foreign policy was often praised in the West, primarily because it was not pro-Soviet, not because it was neutralist. On the Left, some commended its system of workers' self-management, but mainly because it seemed to be the only instance of a non-centrally-planned socialist economy. The chief merit of the country was that it was a negative model. It was outside Europe, in the growing non-aligned movement, that Yugoslavia would have a wider impact. Neutralism – or rather, 'non-alignment', as it was called to distinguish it from strict Swiss-style non-involvement in any international dispute – turned out to be a seductive option for the emergent countries of the Third World. The programme of the Bandung movement of non-aligned countries (from the launching international conference held at Bandung in Indonesia in April 1955) provided a framework for international affairs which allowed them to keep some distance from superpower disputes. The Bandung movement insisted on equidistance but, even so, as with neutralism in Europe, it appeared more anti-Western than anti-Soviet. The hope that by refraining from taking sides they would be courted by both camps, while maintaining their independence, often proved illusory. The Third Worldism of a significant component of the West European Left received a notable impetus from the non-aligned position of many former colonies. They shared a common commitment to decolonization and a desire to escape from the vice of bipolar politics.

In Western Europe neutralism remained confined to the socialist parties of neutral countries, such as Austria, Finland and Sweden; to Left factions of most of the remaining socialist parties and to the German and Italian socialist parties. The communist parties too could be classified as neutralist, but only in the sense that the foreign policy they wished their own country to adopt was one of neutrality. Neutrality, however, was second best: on international affairs the communists supported all the main foreign policy initiatives of the USSR. This was true also of the Italian Socialist Party, for which there was no question of being 'equidistant' between 'Moscow, capital of the socialist revolution' and 'Washington, capital of imperialism', as the PSI leader Pietro Nenni declared at the Twenty-ninth Congress of his party

(January 1951), which unanimously approved a motion stating that 'American policy is the only threat to peace in Europe'.[6]

The neutralists tended to combine their position with a strong defence of national sovereignty. Atlanticism implied, after all, the integration or, at the very least, the co-ordination of military forces and a *de facto* subservience of Europe to the USA. Communist 'neutralists', in particular, were keen to promote the defence of national sovereignty, perhaps because they were particularly prone to the unfair, but not entirely undeserved, criticism that they were an extension of the Kremlin. Maurice Thorez declared on 22 February 1949 to the Central Committee of the PCF that 'The Soviet Union ... the country of socialism cannot, *by definition*, adopt aggressive or warlike policies.'[7] These pro-Soviet sentiments were usually combined with a defence of the French nation and accusations of selling out to foreign interests: 'the French bourgeoisie, as a class with interests opposed to those of the Nation, conducts and organizes the betrayal of the country.'[8] The PCF's pro-Sovietism persistently clashed with its assumption of the 'grandeur' of France and its belief that France was central to the future progress of humanity.[9]

In less extreme form, the idea that the interests of the nation corresponded to a position of pacifism and neutralism in foreign affairs united socialist parties which were otherwise very different, such as the Swedish, Italian and German. All were the object of serious American suspicions. It is worth remarking that the nationalism of some communist leaders on the other side of the 'Iron Curtain' equally irritated the Soviet authorities, who did their best to stamp it out, using show trials in which 'nationalist' communists such as Rudolf Slansky, the Czech deputy prime minister, were arraigned and executed (1952). Empires are usually better protected under the cover of universalism.

One social-democratic party – the Finnish – was more or less compelled to be neutralist. The Finnish social democrats were more hostile to the USSR than the parties of the centre and of the Right. They were considered by Soviet commentators as 'the American Party' in Finland; the USSR reacted strongly against the appointment of Väinö Tanner, the collaborationist wartime social-democratic leader, as prime minister in 1957.[10] There cannot be any parallel, however, between the more flexible political constraints on Finland and those facing the European NATO countries. In Finland, those who did not share the values of Soviet communism (i.e. all parties except for the SKDL) were often in government and Soviet pressure was not sufficient to persuade them to include the SKDL even when it obtained its greatest electoral victory in 1958, with 23.2 per cent of the vote, and became the largest parliamentary group.[11] In countries in the American sphere of influence those who did not share 'Western' values were relegated to a ghetto of their own.

All ensuing major developments, such as the American intervention in Vietnam or the installation of Pershing and Cruise missiles in the 1980s, would rekindle the contrast between neutralists and Atlanticists, though, as we shall see, parties changed side. The lines were never absolutely rigid, though they always became more sharply defined at a time of acute crisis. It often took a 'hot' war to clarify issues in the development of the Cold War. Thus the effects of the Korean War, though fought at a very great distance from Europe, had far greater implications for Europeans than for most of the rest of the world.

With the exception of the communists and the Italian socialists, the West was virtually unanimous in condemning the North Korean attack on the South in June 1950. Western anxiety can easily be explained: in August 1949 its atomic monopoly was ended when the first Soviet A-bomb was successfully detonated; in October 1949, on Tiananmen Square, Mao Zedong proclaimed the People's Republic of China. One-quarter of humanity was now under communist rule.

The Korean War showed that atomic supremacy did not deter aggressors and that the USA was not particularly good at fighting conventional land wars (as subsequent history would confirm). Washington concluded that atomic superiority was not a sufficient defence against a conventional Soviet attack on Europe. Before the Korean War it had been assumed that the USSR would not want to extend its empire in Western Europe. After Korea, this gave way to the opposite – with hindsight, highly dubious – assumption, namely, that the USSR was poised for a massive conventional attack on Western Europe.

Unable and unwilling to opt for an isolationist policy, the USA was faced with a particular dilemma: either it was prepared to finance and maintain a huge American army on European soil or it had to persuade the Europeans to do so. Dwight D. Eisenhower, who had been elected president in 1952, had promised deep defence cuts. The Europeans were most reluctant to spend money on armaments. It was difficult for democratically elected politicians to convince their electorates that they should tax themselves into poverty in order to contain the communist threat.[12] The main fascination of capitalism, after all, lies in the promise of the endless expansion of private consumption.

At the time, in defence terms, a European force meant in reality a Franco-British force. The other non-neutral countries were either too small (the Benelux countries), or too poor (Italy), or both (Greece and Portugal), to contribute significantly. Germany was not in NATO yet, and a rearmed Germany so soon after the war worried many people. Britain wanted to police its empire and could not afford a large standing army in Europe. All that was left was France and, on its own, France was not enough. It was therefore necessary to face the question of rearming Germany. For this to be acceptable to the French, it was essential to find a way of ensuring that the reconstituted German army would not be controlled from Bonn but under some sort of integrated High Command – in other words, that German soldiers would be taking orders from French generals. Fear of German rearmament was widespread throughout the European socialist Left and all communists were against it, as indeed for understandable reasons, was the USSR.[13]

In October 1950 the then French prime minister, René Pleven, proposed the creation of a European Defence Community (EDC), with a military force integrated down to the smallest unit, including West German troops. The Pleven Plan was the military equivalent of the Schuman Plan, which had established the European Coal and Steel Community (ECSC) and involved the same six countries. The two plans shared the same originator: the ubiquitous Jean Monnet, who was pursuing his long-term project for the creation of an interdependent and integrated Europe based on a French–German Axis. The EDC Treaty was agreed by the Bonn and Paris governments in 1952 and, by 1954, it had been ratified by all the parliaments concerned except the French, where it was defeated by 319 votes to 264.[14]

In effect, the majority of the French Left, that is, the communists and at least half of the socialist deputies, who defied the party whip, had succeeded in burying the EDC. The Gaullists, who had voted with the Left, objected to supra-nationalism and to the rearmament of Germany; the communists to the anti-Soviet aims of the treaty. The objections of the socialist dissidents were based on a mixture of nationalism and neutralism. The EDC turned out to be the only real ideological issue which divided the SFIO.[15]

The failure of the EDC led to the incorporation in 1954 of West Germany and Italy into the Brussels Treaty of 1948, now called the Western European Union (WEU) and the entry of West Germany into NATO in 1955 (Italy was an original signatory). The WEU was far more acceptable than the EDC because it did not involve the integration of European armed forces. The only concession to those who were worried about German rearmament was a clause in the WEU Treaty forbidding Germany to manufacture atomic, biological and chemical weapons.[16]

Through the WEU and, even more, through the military structure of NATO, the future of West Germany was now firmly and permanently linked to that of the West. The German army, the *Bundeswehr*, was equipped with delivery systems for nuclear warheads, the warheads remaining under American control. The German social democrats had failed to keep Germany neutral and de-militarized – the only way to achieve unification. Nevertheless, they remained hostile to NATO until 1960. By 1955 the militarization of the Cold War had been completed: less than a week after West Germany's entry into NATO, the USSR retaliated by establishing the Warsaw Pact with Poland, Hungary, the DDR, Czechoslovakia, Bulgaria, Romania and Albania.

This process of militarization did not begin in 1949, when NATO was created, but in 1951 when, under the impact of the Korean War, the US Senate endorsed the transfer of four divisions of ground troops to Europe and the principle of an integrated command.[17] The Americans would now be closely involved in the defence of Europe. They would not again arrive at the eleventh hour to rescue 'the West', as they had in two previous world wars. This was crucial in the atomic age, where hesitation and delay might well mean that there would be no one left to liberate in a third world war – or so ran the most alarmist scenarios. Now American military power was ensconced at the heart of the continent, in effective charge of a West European army, with the clear blessing of the socialist parties of Britain, France, Belgium, Holland, Norway, Denmark and Luxemburg. Those of West Germany and Italy would join the fold within a few years. Having accepted this defence system, most European socialists found it increasingly difficult to distance themselves from American foreign policy while firmly repudiating Soviet socialism.

In Britain membership of the EDC, like the membership of other European organizations such as the EEC, was not a party-political issue. Conservatives and Labour were equally opposed to it. The EDC, like all other European attempts at integration, was a matter for the Europeans and hence not for the British. Atlanticism, the special relationship, the empire and neutralism offered ample motivations for not even considering an integrated European defence system without the USA. Bipartisanship in foreign policy allowed the Labour Party to avoid developing its own view of international affairs.

There was no doubt that the USSR had been genuinely alarmed by the prospect of a West European defence bloc which included Germany. In his last theoretical work, *Economic Problems of Socialism in the USSR*, published in the spring of 1952, Stalin congratulated the European peace movement and sought to minimize the inevitably unfavourable echo of his support by recognizing that the movement did not have socialist aims.[18] At the same time he sought to strengthen the resolve of the neutralists by making, on 10 March 1952, the most advanced Soviet offer of the decade. The essential point of the Moscow Note was that Germany should be reunited within the 1945 Potsdam frontiers, i.e. with the Oder–Neisse line as its eastern frontier – something no German political party, including the SPD, was willing to consider then, though this turned out to be the only internationally acceptable border for post-1990 Germany.[19] This newly united German state would agree not to participate in any military pact directed against any of the belligerent parties of the Second World War; all foreign troops would withdraw from German soil within a year after the signing of the peace treaty, and the new state should be permitted limited rearmament.

It is very likely that Stalin was quite prepared to sacrifice his East German satellite in order to obtain a reduction of tension in Europe. This is certainly what the leaders of the DDR assumed would happen, aware that they would lose the first free elections and dismayed to see how dispensable Stalin considered them.[20] Schumacher wrote to Adenauer on 22 April 1952, urging him to explore all possibilities 'to determine whether the Soviet note offers an opportunity for finally reunifying Germany in peace'.[21] Luckily for the DDR, Adenauer did not want a neutral Germany. He, more than anyone else, was the principal obstacle to a dispassionate Western examination of Stalin's offer.[22] Probably Adenauer also feared that the Protestant and social-democratic eastern regions would, in subsequent elections, overwhelm his Catholic strongholds and drag the country towards the East. The West pretended that the Soviet offer was little more than an excuse to hold up or damage the EDC. In reality, they feared that the offer was serious and were afraid to take it up.[23] In France and Britain a united Germany inspired fear: better, perhaps, to leave some of it under Soviet control as long as the rest remained solidly in the Western sphere. His offer spurned, Stalin increased his hold over East Germany and completed its integration into the Soviet sphere. While it is impossible to establish what would have happened if the offer had been accepted, the fact remains that Germany had to wait a further thirty-eight years before being reunited.

This is, in fact, exactly what happened in Austria: the Red Army withdrew, free elections were held, and the country remained neutral *and* democratic. The USSR showed itself to be extremely pliable in order to ensure Austrian neutrality. They would have preferred it to be incorporated in the State Treaty of 1955, but the Austrian government, which had anyway decided to remain neutral, opted, with Russian consent, to insert the term 'perpetual neutrality' in the legislation, following the Swiss model.[24]

Disarmament proposals continued throughout the 1950s.[25] Not all came from the West European Left or from the East: in July 1955 Anthony Eden, arguably the least pro-American of post-war British prime ministers, proposed a plan which included a disarmament zone in Central Europe and the eventual reunification of Germany. But this was shot down by Adenauer, who did not want German unity and European security to be linked. A revised version of the plan assumed the possibility of continued NATO membership on the part of a reunited Germany, something the USSR could not countenance.[26]

In the spring of 1955 (Stalin died in 1953), the USSR launched another peace offensive 'which astonished even the most anti-communist in the West'.[27] They signed the peace treaty with Austria and withdrew the Red Army, returned a naval base to Finland and restored diplomatic relations with Yugoslavia. In November 1958 the Polish foreign minister Adam Rapacki, building on the Soviet offers of March and November 1956 and on his address to the UN General Assembly (October 1957), proposed a nuclear-free zone for the two Germanies, Poland and Czechoslovakia.[28] The Rapacki Plan clearly exemplified the fundamental problem of disarmament in Europe: the USSR and its allies wanted the removal of nuclear weapons from Central Europe, while the Atlantic Alliance wanted to keep them as a shield against Soviet superiority in conventional forces. In the context of deep reciprocal mistrust between the two great powers, such divergence made successful disarmament impossible, even though the Rapacki Plan evoked positive responses from some NATO countries, for example, Canada, Belgium and Norway, as well as from neutral countries such as Sweden.[29] The French and Dutch socialists had major reservations. In their view a nuclear-free zone was 'a zone from which atomic devices could not be launched, but where they could fall', as Christian Pineau sarcastically put it. Guy Mollet added: 'What threatens us are the rockets stationed in the Soviet Union. To prohibit their installation in Poland or East Germany would not alter the situation.'[30] The British Labour Party regarded the plan as 'an advance', although it contained certain 'weaknesses'.[31] The SPD was even more positive; the welcome it extended to the plan reflected German anxiety about the militarization of Central Europe. Even the German Federal government did not reject the plan outright, but only after protracted hesitation.[32]

Soviet and Soviet-backed proposals always had a propaganda advantage over those of the West. Public opinion invariably perceived nuclear weapons as a greater threat than conventional weapons. This was inevitable: nuclear weapons appeared, rightly, as weapons of mass civilian destruction from which there could be no escape, while it was felt that there was always a possibility of surviving even the most devastating conventional war.

One of the unavoidable effects of the various Soviet proposals – from the Stalin Note of 1952 to the Rapacki Plan – was to taint all plans to create a nuclear-free zone in Central Europe (i.e. in Germany) as 'pro-Soviet'. This particularly damaged the otherwise clearly anti-Soviet SPD, whose constant search for a way of reuniting Germany had led it, as we shall see, to make frequent suggestions about a neutralization of the country.

There are manifest reasons why the SPD was more active and gave more thought to foreign policy than any other socialist party in Western Europe. In a divided Germany the traditional distinction between domestic and foreign affairs was almost nullified. The division of Europe between East and West was not an issue external to the country as it was, for instance, in Britain or Hungary. The Cold War had sliced Germany in two and condemned it to remain divided for the duration of the East–West conflict. Furthermore, by the time the Berlin Wall was erected (1961), there were in West Germany more than ten million 'expellees' – Germans who had been forced to evacuate territories which had been ceded or returned to Poland and Czechoslovakia, or who had left the DDR. This vast mass constituted a formidable electorate which would always keep the issue of the division of Germany to the fore. At the state election in Schleswig-Holstein in July 1950, the 'Bloc of Expellees and Disenfranchised' received 23.4 per cent of the vote and was second only to the SPD. The three main spokesmen for this party of expellees were all ex-Nazis.[33] Clearly no German politician could afford to let the extremists of the Right monopolize the expellees' votes.

In all other fields of international affairs West Germany kept a low profile, especially when compared with France and Britain: it was, as has often been stated, an economic giant but a political dwarf. It could not be otherwise.

But such prudence did not entail an absence of internal debates on foreign affairs. On the contrary: in the 1950s the SPD and the CDU disagreed more on external matters (if we count the 'German Question' as 'external') than on internal ones, unlike most other West European countries, where foreign policy was not usually a partisan affair.

In spite of its *marxisant* rhetoric, the SPD was willing to co-operate with the CDU. It had even offered to enter the ruling coalition in 1949, though the offer was turned down by the CDU which preferred a coalition with the Free Democrats and the German Party (a minor conservative party of northern Germany, which disintegrated after 1960). But in North Rhine–Westphalia, the largest German *Land*, the CDU led by Karl Arnold was in coalition with the SPD until 1953.[34]

The SPD's insistence on being the party of German unity, and therefore a more national party than the CDU, probably had the positive effect of neutralizing the otherwise inevitable shift to the right of the expellees' vote. Schumacher's foreword to the SPD's Dortmund Programme of Action (1952) was imbued with national self-confidence. The SPD was the party of patriotism as well as international socialism, with unification as its most important national aim: 'For us the unification of Germany is a short-term not a long-term goal.'[35]

This nationalism, unlike that of the Labour Party or the French communists, was not anti-European: the SPD advocated greater European economic co-operation, including a reduction in national sovereignty unless it was specifically against German national interests.[36] Underlying this, however, was an unmistakable hostility to the actual process of European integration, on the part of much of the European Left. As Schumacher declared at the 1950 Hamburg Party Conference, this was a Europe of the 'Four Ks': *konservativ, klerikal, kapitalistisch* and *kartellistisch*.[37]

The 1952 action programme reaffirmed the SPD's opposition both to German rearmament, and to signing a treaty on West European defence, because it would have enshrined the division of Germany as permanent.[38] These positions had not substantially changed two years later, in 1954, when the SPD expounded its *Aktions-Programm* at the Berlin conference. There was the same insistence on German unity and the same conviction (which turned out to be correct) that only a policy of international détente would lead to the peaceful reunification of the country.[39] There was, however, a growing realization (which, in reality, Schumacher always had) that the fate of Germany was in the hands of the two superpowers, whose rivalry and struggle was – in the SPD's analysis – the principal cause for the continuation of the division.[40] In the meantime, no international treaty which was likely to prevent the unification of the country should be signed. Thus, the SPD was against both the Warsaw Pact and NATO (without naming them), as it was against any treaty signed by the Federal Republic which might involve military action. But the EDC treaty was particularly opposed on the grounds that it did not give Germany the same control over strategic decision-making as the other members.[41] This was not stated in the treaty itself, but no one seriously assumed that the French would accept a German general in charge of French troops.

The neutralism of the SPD did not represent the 'true' position of the party. In reality, the SPD was far from neutral between East and West, as its vociferous anti-communism made abundantly clear. Neutralism was rather the position which *the country* (as opposed to the party) should adopt in order to offer guarantees to the USSR and enable peaceful reunification to occur. Thus the SPD's policy was, so to speak, more pro-USSR than it would have been, had Germany been a 'normal' country.

Peace remained one of the most salient features of the SPD's foreign policy throughout the 1950s, though unlike the peace campaigners of France and Italy the SPD maintained its distinctively anti-Soviet outlook, blaming the Cold War on Moscow rather than Washington.

The SPD's manifest neutralism was further enhanced by the launching in March 1958 of a vast 'Campaign against Atomic Death' (*Kampf dem Atomtod*) which, like the British Campaign for Nuclear Disarmament (CND), was not officially sponsored, but was supported by the young, by intellectuals and theologians, and by the trade union confederation, the DGB, which even considered the possibility of calling a general strike.[42] The campaign was electorally unsuccessful: the elections of July 1958 for the largest *Land*, North Rhine–Westphalia, fought on the peace issue, resulted in a remarkable CDU victory, though this was largely at the expense of the FDP rather than the SPD, which did well.

This setback did not stop the SPD from persisting with a major (and final) neutralist document on foreign affairs: the famous *Deutschlandplan* (Plan for Germany) presented in March 1959. Similar to its own 1955 'German Manifesto', it was a positive response to previous Soviet proposals and to the Rapacki Plan, and therefore doomed from the beginning. It involved the creation of a denuclearized 'zone of détente' (*Entspannungszone*), which would initially include both parts of Germany, as well as Poland, Czechoslovakia and Hungary. Within it there would be no Warsaw Pact or NATO troops, and only limited national defence forces. This would create the precondition for a gradual and controlled disarmament of the two blocs within the framework of a collective security system which would include both the USA and the USSR. Once this was achieved, the countries comprising the *Entspannungszone* would leave NATO and the Warsaw Pact.[43] Only then, on the basis of consent, would there be a step-by-step unification of Germany through the development of contacts between the two parts of the country, including joint meetings of MPs from both the DDR and the Federal Republic.[44] The document made it clear that all existing international treaties would remain in existence until the final phase.[45]

The *Deutschlandplan* encountered the hostility of the CDU (but not of the free democrats, who had a similar plan of their own, having moved rapidly in the direction of neutralism in the course of 1956);[46] and it was ignored by the West (though the Labour Party, then in opposition, immediately adopted a similar plan – see below). The USSR was no longer interested in a neutral Germany, and this was made clear to the SPD envoys to Moscow, Fritz Erler and Carlo Schmidt. The Soviet Union now sought to defend the sovereignty of the DDR and was probably aware that neither Hungary nor Poland would remain communist for very long if allowed to be in a zone outside Soviet control.

Neutralism was now an option only for those countries already committed to it, and who therefore were outside a 'logic of the blocs' which had become totally impregnable. German unification, if it ever came, was going to be the product either of negotiations between the superpowers, or of a unilateral act by one of them. Either way, no West European country was going to be able to play more than a secondary role. When this was realized, only a year after the launching of the *Deutschlandplan*, Herbert Wehner, the SPD's deputy leader, stunned the party's supporters and opponents alike on 30 June 1960 by suggesting in the Bundestag that the CDU and the SPD should adopt a common, bipartisan foreign policy. The basis for this was the formal recognition by the SPD that 'the European and Atlantic Treaty system of which the Federal Republic is a part is the basis and framework for all German foreign and unification policy.'[47] The *Deutschlandplan* was a 'thing of the past', with the blame for its failure being firmly, and not entirely unjustly, pinned on the DDR.[48]

In the otherwise fairly grey politics of the Bundesrepublik, Wehner's speech quickly became a widely reported media event. There was, of course, some internal opposition, especially from Hesse, one of the bastions of the SPD Left, but there was also considerable public support.[49] The party had just gone through the lengthy discussions leading to the 1959 Bad Godesberg Programme: the idea of adopting a new party image had time to sink in. On the other hand, the surprise (and dismay) of many of the activists could be justified precisely because there had been no warning that changes in foreign policy were being considered. Bad Godesberg had not innovated in the field of foreign policy. It had not accepted NATO. It had restated its suspicions of the EEC: 'Regionally limited supranational association must not be allowed to result in "closed-door-policies".'[50] It had reaffirmed its aim of securing 'the inclusion of the whole of Germany in a European zone of reduced tensions'.[51] Now all this was changed and, soon, the party activists came to accept the changes as they usually do.

For years the SPD had been careful not to demand unilateral withdrawal from NATO and had already dropped its initial opposition to the EEC. But all its foreign policy initiatives assumed that Germany, and not the main victors of the Second World War, would have the leading role in the determination of its own future. The significance of Wehner's speech was the recognition that the consensus of the 'four occupying powers' (but Wehner here really meant the two superpowers) was the necessary condition for any eventual disarmament, and that this would occur prior to German unification and the creation of a 'neutral zone'.[52]

The SPD would contribute to the policy of détente by playing the role of constructive opposition. 'This is not a suggestion for a coalition. Do not be afraid', added Wehner, whose intention was rather to secure the official 'Western' legitimization of the SPD by being regularly consulted on foreign policy by the CDU. The most overt sign of the new constructive mood of the SPD was that it started to attend the meetings of the NATO parliamentary group.[53]

In divesting itself of its neutralist clothes and stressing once more that the party 'belongs spiritually to the West',[54] the SPD was in fact opening up the possibility of a coalition with the CDU, though no such offer would be made for another six years. The terrain was being prepared by the SPD through suggestions that the main difference between the two parties should be on domestic issues, rather than on foreign affairs.[55]

The acceptance of Atlanticism did not mean that the SPD had abandoned the idea of an active foreign policy, as most Atlanticist socialist parties had in fact done. Nor did it mean that bipartisanship in foreign policy entailed adopting all the positions of the CDU. On the contrary, in the 1960s and 1970s, with the development of Ostpolitik, the SPD left such a strong imprint on German external relations that it established a framework other parties had to follow. For once, some of the rules of the foreign policy game were drafted by the Left. The SPD had been the only major socialist party in a NATO country to support the European peace campaign. Now that it accepted Atlanticism, German pacifism was deprived of an organized political party. This left the communist parties as the most consistent West European campaigners for disarmament.

The French and Italian communists, who might otherwise have appeared to be quite isolated, succeeded in mobilizing and gaining the respect of many people. The peace campaigns of the 1950s were the most important early forays into a form of 'new politics', non-class-based and single-issue oriented, which would become familiar to the political activists of the 1960s and 1970s. In France and Italy, where the peace movement was strongest, it was virtually entirely communist dominated. Elsewhere it lacked strength and cohesion, with the possible exception of Germany.

The peace campaigns were directed against the new atomic weapons of mass destruction. The initial impetus came from the Stockholm Appeal launched by the World Congress of Partisans of Peace, a communist-sponsored body, in the Swedish capital on 19 March 1950, a few months before the outbreak of the Korean war. The text of the appeal demanded the banning of all atomic weapons and declared that first use of these weapons would constitute a crime against humanity.[56]

The movement collected 400 million signatures worldwide (including, obviously, the Soviet Union and the People's Republic of China) – or so it claimed. In Italy it allegedly gathered seventeen million signatures and in France fourteen million – though these figures almost certainly represent a 'creative' exaggeration and more sober estimates suggest a figure for France of 9.5 million (even then this was twice the number of communist electors).[57]

In France, the PCF could easily monopolize the peace movement since the socialists were aligned with Atlanticism, while in Italy Nenni's PSI was unable to galvanize a mass movement. Inevitably, the cause of peace and disarmament became associated with 'totalitarian' communism, yet the communist parties themselves used the issue to emphasize their national identity, patriotism and commitment to their country's independence from US imperialism. Thus Togliatti, protesting against the visit to Italy of US General Ridgway, who had allegedly used germ warfare in Korea, accused his Christian democratic opponents of selling the country to foreigners and of not being 'the true Italy ... victorious in 1945 against the fascists and the Germans'.[58]

While the French PCF was similarly anxious to stress its patriotism, it would nevertheless be wrong to conclude that the strategies and tactics of the two parties were identical. The Italian PCI eschewed street confrontations and distanced itself from violent demonstrations such as that organized by the PCF on the occasion of the visit of Ridgway to Paris on 28 May 1952, openly recognizing that they were not in a revolutionary or pre-revolutionary situation.[59] They also used the peace issue to begin to build bridges with the church. On 12 April 1954 Togliatti launched an appeal to Catholics to join with the communists in order to 'save human civilization'.[60] Togliatti's speech contained the familiar themes of anti-Americanism and pro-Sovietism, but there was a novel element – namely, an explicit request for a long-term alliance between communism and Catholicism on a non-class issue such as international peace.

Any goodwill acquired by either party on the peace front rapidly evaporated when they both supported the Soviet suppression of the Hungarian uprising in 1956. This signalled the end of the peace movement in Italy and France, while it began to develop elsewhere, particularly in Britain, largely outside the organized Left. This is hardly surprising: it had been the Labour Party, when in government, that had helped launch NATO, had been among the strongest supporters of the Cold War, and had developed and tested an atomic weapon.

The movement for British unilateral nuclear disarmament addressed itself to the Labour Party because its more realistic supporters successfully argued that there was no chance of unilateralism prevailing unless it became Labour policy. Thus, the British peace movement was from the very beginning quite different from those of France and Italy. In these two countries a strong communist party launched the movement, partly because peace was one of its foreign policy objectives, partly because it needed allies. In Britain the movement tried to force the issue on the Labour Party and the trade unions. 'Winning Over the Labour Party' has since then always been one of the chief goals of single-issue campaigns; while 'being inside the mass movement' has always been one of the main preoccupations of the communist parties of France and Italy and, to a lesser extent, of the SPD in Germany.

Accordingly, it is more plausible to argue that the origins of the British movement against nuclear weapons were to be found in the churches or even in the Golders Green Co-operative Women's Guild, led by ex-suffragette Gertrude Fishwick, rather than in the Labour Party.[61] The chief characteristic of this movement, apart from its evident ethical dimension, was its conviction that Britain's role was a global one, and that the actions of the United Kingdom mattered a great deal to the rest of the world.[62] The fact that France and China soon joined the nuclear club did not remove the belief that a unilateral British move to abandon nuclear armaments would have a great moral impact on other countries. This 'moral imperialism', as Richard Taylor aptly called it,[63] was epitomized by J. B. Priestley in the *New Statesman* of 2 November 1957; his 'Britain and the Nuclear Bomb', which launched CND, was full of nostalgia for Britain's 'former grandeur', for the days of the Second World War when Britain stood alone against fascism, and for a pre-Suez era when the country had some moral standing in the world.[64]

The Labour Party reacted coolly to all this. The recognized leader of the Labour Left, Aneurin Bevan, after briefly toying with unilateralism, denounced it mercilessly as 'an emotional spasm' at the 1957 Labour Party Conference (which rejected unilateralism by a resounding majority). His arguments were as 'imperial' as those of his opponents: the bomb gave Britain the prestige and international standing which would enable it to interpose itself between the two superpowers and act as a moderating influence.[65] This quite unrealistic assumption, redolent of imperial illusions, has remained at the very core of British defence policy for over thirty years – a powerful demonstration that political rationality and intelligence are not prerequisite in the formulation of foreign policy. The debate between unilateralists and those who wanted to keep a 'British' nuclear system continued for years, even after the decision to terminate the Blue Streak missile programme (for economic reasons) signified that the government had realized that the country could no longer support research and development in advanced weaponry. Britain had a bomb, but it could not deliver it without using American missiles. The 'British independent nuclear deterrent' was neither British nor independent: it had become inextricable from the US defence system. The fact is that possession of the bomb gave British public opinion the sense that the country mattered in world affairs: to be against the bomb was to alienate the electorate. This is not something political parties risk lightly. More or less unconsciously, politicians perceived that British possession of nuclear weapons made not the slightest difference –

one way or the other – to international peace. If that was the case, they might as well be retained and the people kept happy. Such views could not be held openly: an honest display of cynicism and electoral opportunism seldom wins votes.

Bevan's renunciation of unilateralism was almost certainly due to his belief that his post as shadow foreign secretary would never otherwise be translated into its equivalent in a Labour government.[66] If such was his thinking, he was certainly correct, since the unilateralist position was always seen, by friends and foes alike, as an 'oppositional' posture and/or, at best, as a symbolic gesture of the party's commitment to a 'third way' in foreign affairs.

The main practical effect of the CND on the Labour Party was to oblige it to develop a foreign policy somewhat different from that of the Conservative Party. This led to a new document, called *Disarmament and Nuclear War: The Next Step* (24 June 1959), which bore a striking similarity to the SPD's *Deutschlandplan*. It included the removal of foreign forces from Europe, the eventual reunification of Germany, its subsequent withdrawal from NATO, and the concurrent withdrawal of Poland, Czechoslovakia and Hungary from the Warsaw Pact. It also agreed that Britain would 'unilaterally' abandon nuclear weapons provided all other countries, except the USA and the USSR, agreed to ban them too.[67] There was never the slightest chance of this being acceptable to anyone, let alone the French and the Chinese who were well on the way to joining the nuclear club.

At the 1960 Conference the unilateralists won the vote on disarmament. Those whom Gaitskell had labelled 'pacifists, unilateralists and fellow travellers' trounced him. Even though CND was overwhelmingly a middle-class movement, Gaitskell was not beaten by the constituencies, two-thirds of which supported him, but by the bloc vote of the trade unions whose leaders objected to his attempt to abolish Clause Four of the party constitution (see chapter 10 for an extended discussion).[68] Gaitskell vowed to 'fight and fight and fight again'. And so he did and, a year later, having recouped the trade union vote (minus Frank Cousins's Transport and General Workers' Union), he overturned unilateralism. CND, which had not expected its 1960 victory, was defeated. Unilateralism became an important issue within the Labour Party only when used in internal factional struggles. Once the revisionist attempt to alter Clause Four had failed, unilateralism ceased to matter and remained dormant until the 1970s.

The dispute over the bomb barely disguised the far more controversial issue of Britain's membership of NATO. It could be argued that, to operate as an authentic international mediator, Britain would have had to leave NATO as well as disarm. But in so doing, it would automatically have weakened the West and strengthened the USSR, thus relinquishing whatever dubious authority it might have had as a mediator. No European socialist prime minister ever tried to take his country out of NATO's military structures. The only two leaders who did so, and did it successfully, were conservatives: Charles de Gaulle and Kostantinos Karamanlis, the Greek 'de Gaulle'. France, having become an atomic power in 1960, left the military structure of NATO in 1966, thus incurring the wrath of the USA. Greece followed France in 1974 in what were, however, quite different circumstances (see chapter 21). De Gaulle provided the most important argument for a West European independent nuclear force: the Soviet development of Inter-Continental Ballistic Missiles (ICBMs) and the successful launch of the first Sputnik meant that the USSR now had an effective deterrent against an American nuclear strike. In these circumstances US nuclear protection of Europe in the event of a Soviet conventional attack was less credible. It required the Europeans to trust that the Americans would risk the destruction of major East Coast cities in order to save Europe, and the Soviets to believe that the Americans would take such a risk. If such trust was lacking, and in France it certainly was, the logical consequence was that Europeans themselves had to possess a nuclear deterrent. West European nuclear disarmament made sense only if one believed that there were no circumstances which would lead to a Soviet attack, or that the defence of Europe would always be in the absolute national interest of the USA.

The French move was not destabilizing for the West because French nuclear weapons were obviously directed against the USSR, in spite of de Gaulle's claim that they were directed against any possible threat. The loss of France's membership of 'military' NATO had been more than compensated for by French deployment of nuclear weapons, which added to the West's system of deterrence. France acquired greater prestige in the non-aligned camp, but never became a mediator between East and West. Furthermore, France's withdrawal had been initiated by a man of the Right and had not been the outcome of pressure from a mass movement of the Left. The unwritten rules of the 'logic of blocs', which established that no country within a bloc could be ruled by politicians friendly to the other side, had been respected.

De Gaulle's foreign policy was inevitably rather problematic, not only for the USA but also for the French Left, especially the communists. De Gaulle sought a rapprochement with the USSR; he was anti-American, nationalistic, did not wish French armed forces to be under NATO (i.e. US) control, was suspicious of the EEC, and totally opposed to any form of supra-nationalism. In other words, there was no major foreign policy issue on which the PCF could disagree. At the same time, an alliance with Gaullism was unthinkable and impracticable. Anyway, de Gaulle did not need the communists. The entire French Left was condemned to have a strange love–hate relationship with the man who twice in his lifetime embodied France in a way unparalleled in the twentieth century. It was an entirely one-way relationship: de Gaulle ignored the Left while achieving, because he was not of the Left, what no socialist leader in a NATO country could: a shift towards national independence in foreign policy, a critical stance towards America's Vietnam policy, and recognition of France's role as a champion of the Third World among the advanced countries.

De Gaulle's foreign policy achievements contrasted sharply with the dismal failures of SFIO-led governments after 1956: Algeria and Suez. In Algeria the war was prosecuted with ferocity and a colonial mentality strongly imbued by a particular form of 'socialist' racism: at no stage were the interests of millions of Algerians allowed to prevail over those of less than a million working-class white settlers. Furthermore, the Algerian war led to the French socialists being dragged into the Suez affair, ostensibly to keep the canal in the hands of the West, in reality to weaken Arab nationalism as represented by Gamal Abdel Nasser.

The intervention in the Suez Canal and the Israeli invasion of the Sinai peninsula – jointly agreed with London and Paris – can be interpreted in a variety of ways. These events are usually considered to represent the last attempt on the part of the French and the British to hold on to their imperial roles and to intervene on the world stage without the prior support of the USA. This is certainly an accurate reading of the consequences of the Suez affair; but it is unlikely to have been one of the reasons for intervention. Illusions about imperial greatness, and Eden's fixation with equating Nasser with Hitler, account in part for British behaviour; SFIO leaders like Christian Pineau also had frequent recourse to the Hitler analogy, while sympathy for Israel and Nasser's support for the Algerian nationalists propelled the SFIO towards intervention. In intervening, however, the SFIO simply executed French foreign policy as any non-socialist government might have done. No specific view of the world informed its behaviour. A MRP-led government would have done exactly the same.

Suez was one of the very few international crises of the 1950s and 1960s which did not have an overt East–West dimension. True, the communist bloc took a clear pro-Egyptian stand, while the West European Left, including the British and excluding the French socialists, disapproved of the intervention. But the USA too was very critical. Gaitskell called the government's use of force in Suez an 'act of criminal folly'. He was backed by the whole of his party and by the TUC. Labour's stance was not motivated by any sympathy for Nasser and Egyptian nationalism, or any understanding of emergent nationalist Third World forces seeking to recover control over their own resources. Nor even was it prompted by the realization that any truly independent Egyptian government would sooner or later have done what Nasser had done. This unusual break with partisanship in foreign policy by the British Labour Party was due to distaste for the use of force, a commitment to the United Nations, perhaps a desire to unite the party, and, last but not least, to the conviction that Britain's place in the world was to march in step with the USA.[69]

Suez marked the only major disagreement between Labour and Conservatives on an international crisis in which British troops were used.

Subsequent military expeditions, such as the Falklands War in 1982 or the Gulf War of 1991, found Labour's leaders in complete agreement with the Conservative government. Suez also marked one of the few instances in British post-war history in which government foreign policy was sharply at odds with that of the USA, whose own UN resolution was vetoed by France and Britain. The whole expedition was mounted without American support and it was American financial retaliations against Britain through the IMF that led Harold Macmillan, Chancellor of the Exchequer, to change his originally hawkish position on Nasser. Thus Labour's stand, which occasioned some unpopularity with British public opinion, then in one of its periodic fits of mindless jingoism, was closer to that of the USA than the Conservatives.

The Suez crisis marked a historical turning-point in European attitudes towards the Middle East. After 1956 neither the French nor the British maintained a substantial interest in the Middle East, once their jealously guarded zone of influence. Arab nationalism became a force of growing political importance. Israel came to rely increasingly on American protection. The USSR, hitherto excluded from the area, became one of the principal players. The whole area, once removed from European imperialism, became caught up in the developing polarization of the international system between East and West.

Yet Suez had very little impact on the main parties of the European Left. The main significance was that the SFIO found itself isolated at a conference of the Socialist International held in Copenhagen (30 November to 2 December 1956). The delegates censured the invasion of Egypt by the UK and France. The French delegation walked out when the vote was taken and there were four abstentions – Belgium, Israel, Spain and the Jewish Labour Bund; otherwise it was unanimous.[70]

Mollet remained unrepentant, claiming his only regret was that he had been forced to stop the French intervention.[71] None of this seemed to matter: the French socialists were already unpopular and ineffective as a government and as a party. Even if Suez had not occurred, the Fourth Republic, with which they were so closely identified, would have collapsed. Similarly, the British Labour Party did not benefit from the Suez affair. It had warned against the intervention and had been proved right. Eden became a strong contender for the title of Britain's worst post-war prime minister. Yet this did not help Labour in the least. Eden resigned, Macmillan became prime minister, and the Conservatives went on in 1959 to win their third successive electoral victory. Foreign affairs, electorally speaking, mattered far less than the growing prosperity of consumers.

The other major crisis of that eventful year was the Soviet intervention in Hungary. This, as we shall see, considerably affected the West European communist parties, but not the socialists, who all responded with unequivocal condemnation. Only for the Italian Socialist Party was the Hungarian crisis of some significance. At the Turin Congress of 1955 the PSI had already begun to reconsider its policy of a united front with the PCI. There was a strong faction, led by Riccardo Lombardi, in favour of greater autonomy with respect to the PCI. During 1956 the denunciation of Stalin by the Soviet communists and, later, the invasion of Hungary, finally convinced the PSI leader Pietro Nenni that the time had come to renew its links with the centrist PSDI and re-examine its overall alliance strategy. So strong were the ties between the PCI and the PSI that even the invasion of Hungary was not condemned unanimously. Within the PSI, a small far left group led by Emilio Lussu supported the invasion and even the larger mainstream left faction, led by Lelio Basso and Tullio Vecchietti, could not bring themselves to condemn the presence of Soviet tanks in Budapest out of fear of helping the Right; both groups gained the epithet of 'tankist'.[72]

Hungary, however, acted as a catalyst for the divorce between the PSI and the PCI, an event of enormous importance for the subsequent course of Italian politics. The division of the Left was the single most important factor behind the persistence of Christian democratic power in Italy. By the time of its Venice Congress (1957), the PSI had denounced 'frontism' (the close alliance with the PCI) and had begun a rapprochement with the DC which would lead it into government six years later.

For the other European socialists, Hungary did not present any serious problems. They all worked on the assumption that the events occurring on the other side of the 'iron curtain' did not affect them. The fate of 'socialism' in Eastern Europe was not central to their concerns because it was not democratic socialism. In reality, Western socialists held some values in common with the ideology and practice of Soviet-type communism, such as an enmity towards capitalism, a belief in the historical inevitability of socialism and in the central role of the working class in progressive politics, and a generally collectivist outlook. This was often considered an inconvenient embarrassment, an association which would give solace to their conservative enemies. Once they had reiterated their not insignificant differences with communism, they remained content to disapprove when necessary and condemn if required. An ever increasing provincialism and the fear of being tainted by association with communism were sufficient to inhibit West European socialists from developing a distinct policy towards the 'socialist countries'. The only exception was the SPD in Germany; it did not have the option of ignoring the problem, at least not as long as communism ruled over East Germany.

In general, in the 1950s, the West European Left adopted foreign policy positions only when necessary – that is, when their own country had to have a position. Otherwise, all they seemed to think was needed was the adoption of a moral stance. The peculiarity of moral positions is that all they require is to identify the 'good' side. This often enables the parties concerned to refrain from engaging in any practical activity aimed at avoiding the recurrence of the problem. The problem-solving side of international affairs became of relevance to the parties of the West European Left only when they were in government, not a frequent occurrence in the 1950s. In opposition most of them were not expected to be particularly constructive and thus played a fairly insubstantial role in what, but only with considerable hindsight, turned out to be the most important event in Western Europe at the time: the creation of an European Economic Community between France, West Germany, Italy and the three Benelux countries. Not many people could foresee then that an economic pact which left out the majority of the countries of Western Europe, not to speak of the whole of Eastern Europe, could be seen as the possible foundation for the political and economic unification of the entire continent. In March 1957 the six founding member countries signed the Treaty of Rome, which established two organizations, the EEC and the European Atomic Energy Community (EURATOM), whose purpose was the promotion of nuclear power for peaceful purposes.

None of the socialist parties of the Six was opposed in principle to the construction of an integrated Europe; indeed, those of the Benelux countries were enthusiastic federalists. Nevertheless, there was no distinctive socialist input into the construction of the new European community. Its origins were firmly rooted in previous attempts at resolving the 'German question' – that is, the prevention of a revival of German military might – through the creation of a system of industrial economic interdependence, chiefly in steel and coal (the ECSC of the Schuman Plan), and through the integration of the German army in a European defence force (first the failed EDC, then the WEU and the inclusion of Germany in NATO). Furthermore, the EEC started life bearing the unmistakable marks of the free market. Its avowed objective was the removal of barriers to competition. Its ideology was one of liberalism allied to equivocal federalism. It made grandiloquent claims that it would prevent war breaking out in Western Europe as if, by 1957, there was the remotest possibility of such an eventuality. Its rationale was, of course, far more robust: the creation of a powerful zone of free exchange which would provide the basis for a large market. The USA was a staunch supporter of European integration and exercised constant pressure for the creation of an economically prosperous Europe, committed to Western values and the struggle against communism. This made it even more difficult to conceive of the EEC as a mechanism which would facilitate the development of socialism.

The EEC was then, as well as later, criticized for being a narrow-minded organization of inward-looking, prosperous countries. Though there is some truth in this, a less severe interpretation would also point out that the EEC was a European answer to the growing internationalization of the world economy, to the rise of two multinational world powers, to the development of a non-aligned movement. All these phenomena underlined how reduced the prospects for the traditional nation-state had become and how necessary it was to share sovereignty with other countries. This was happening precisely

at a time when the European socialist movement had made its peace with
the nation-state, and when West European communists were constructing a
'national' road to socialism grounded in the appropriation of patriotic sentiments. These and other political circumstances surrounding the birth of the
EEC, such as the Cold War, the weakness of social democracy, the successes
of capitalism, and the developing consumer society, account for the singular
absence of a significant 'social space' (as it would later be called) in the EEC.
Had the EEC been created in 1945, it would certainly have had a collectivistic
charter. This might not have made a great difference to its actual development
in the 1950s; but it would have provided the parties of the Left with a
socialist rationale for Europeanism and a continental framework for action.

Some may argue that the Treaty of Rome was not entirely silent on the
social dimension; no one could suggest that this was more than barely
perceptible. Article 119 established – at French insistence – the principle of
equal pay between men and women, but its impact was very small: the gap
did narrow a little, but this occurred throughout Europe and not just in the
Six. Articles 117 and 118 were vague and non-binding declarations of intention
to harmonise social policies. Article 120 aimed at not reducing paid holidays,
rather than increasing them. The only discernible meaning of Article 121 was
that the Commission could, if the Council so wished, help migrant workers.

The almost total exclusion from the Treaty of Rome of themes characteristic of welfare socialism confirms the view that its object was the creation
of a common market and not of an economic union. The difference between
the two is that a common market can be achieved by 'negative integration'
– that is, the removal of obstacles to competition – while economic union
also entails positive integration, that is, 'the formation and application of co-
ordinated and common policies in order to fulfil economic and welfare
objectives'.[73] At the time, 'economic union' was not really on the agenda.
The realistic alternatives seemed to be either a national sovereign state able
to define its own legislation on all matters, including welfare; or a common
market in which national welfare legislation would inevitably take second
place to the requirements of free competition. It is thus not surprising if, in
the circumstances, the more committed exponents of welfare socialism (such
as the British and the Scandinavian parties) turned out to be the least
'Europeanist' parties.

The socialist parties of the Benelux countries were left as the only ones
trying to inject some left-wing content into the process of European integration. The Belgian PSB/BSP tried to ensure that the EEC accepted the
principle of 'the common ownership of investments destined for public works
of an international utility'.[74] However, their chief negotiator, Paul-Henri Spaak,
one of the so-called 'founding fathers' of Europe, was far more interested in
establishing a large market than in any form of European public ownership.
The PSB/BSP became committed to rapid integration and many were already
looking beyond a mere common market to complete European unification.

The position of the Dutch PvdA was not very different. It too gradually became enthusiastically Europeanist. It was Johan Willem Beyen, the non-party affiliated foreign minister of a coalition government led by the PvdA leader, Willem Drees, who was the author of the main plan for the establishment of the EEC.[75]

In the three Benelux countries Europeanism remained a constant and unifying element in national politics. The differences between the parties were minimal. The Left never seriously tried to argue a distinctive socialist case for the EEC. Like the commitment to parliamentary democracy, it was not something to be questioned, but formed part of the common ground upon which political arguments could be advanced. Only the communists, who were outside the confines of 'normal' politics, systematically voted against European integration. All the main political parties assumed that the EEC would benefit their national economies which were, in any case, closely interconnected with those of Germany and France.

It should not be assumed, however, that because the socialist parties of the Benelux countries were Europeanist, Europe mattered a great deal to them.[76] European policy was in the hands of a small group of leaders, such as Spaak in Belgium and Beyen in Holland, while party activists moved slowly away from a position of diffidence to a cautious acceptance of the economic case for European integration.[77] On the whole, however, there was little debate since socialist activists were not interested in Europe and since all parties were in agreement.

The high degree of consensus over Europe achieved in the Benelux countries is hardly surprising, given that they were not seriously divided by political strife of the Left–Right kind, but by linguistic and/or religious matters. Furthermore, the Coal and Steel Community had already linked the economies of the Benelux countries to those of France and Germany, and the EEC was seen as a natural development of this process. Unlike the Scandinavian countries, which could look to further Nordic co-operation, the three small Benelux states had no other option but to turn towards Central and Southern Europe.

The SFIO contributed nothing at all to a European social space, which is hardly surprising given the consistent paucity of this party's welfare initiatives in France. The SFIO saw the EEC as the royal road towards the modernization of French capital. Only European integration, the SFIO believed, would compel France to modernize its economic structures and achieve the growth rates which would make higher social spending possible.[78] The emphasis here was on a 'common market' rather than a federal Europe. Even a pro-European 'revisionist' socialist like André Philip justified the EEC in largely economic terms: an expanded market would allow France to escape from the balance of payment constraints which turned every wage increase into a mechanism which sucked in imports and made French exports less competitive.[79] Justifications of the EEC couched in socialist terms were rare,

and limited to explaining that the Treaty of Rome was perfectly compatible
with socialism, that it would provide a favourable international context for
socialists, and that standards of living would improve.[80]

The French Communist Party's opposition to any supra-national organization was total. It expressed this in its usual extremely immoderate language:
Jean Monnet was accused of being an American agent, the Schuman Plan
had been described as the continuation of Hitlerism, and now the Adenauer
administration was referred to as the 'neo-Nazi' in Bonn, with the Mollet
government being assigned the role of the Vichy regime.[81] Yet the PCF was
consistent: like the SFIO, it accepted that the EEC could make possible the
modernization of French capitalism; but unlike the SFIO, it did not think
there was anything desirable in this. Capitalist modernization, in the PCF's
view, entailed an increase in productivity which would inevitably be achieved
by increasing the rate of exploitation of the workers. Georges Cogniot,
Thorez's main adviser on European matters, had no qualms: the EEC entailed
'a very serious abdication of national sovereignty'; it would deprive the French
Parliament of all powers over tariffs, prices, taxes and investments; France
would lose out economically to West Germany because investments would
go towards the Federal Republic rather than to France, and least of all to the
Midi and the west; French wages would sink to the level of those in Holland
and Italy.[82] The free movement of labour would lead to massive immigration
from Italy and would keep down the wages of French workers.[83] Furthermore,
modernization would require massive changes in French agriculture, the
closure of low productivity small farms, and a consequent exodus from the
countryside. The PCF was not just a working-class party. It had acquired a
sizeable following among the peasantry, especially in the south, and it wished
to expand it further.

The PCF was even outraged at the prospect of EURATOM, which was
expected to develop civilian nuclear energy, not because it had any objections
to nuclear power, but because the French would make a disproportionate
contribution (they were developing their own bomb), while the other five
would 'bring nothing' with them. It should be said that in France atomic
euphoria had started almost as soon as the news of the destruction of
Hiroshima was received. The promise of technological wonders, the belief in
a nuclear age based on an unlimited supply of clean, cheap and safe energy
had seized the country.[84] With pride, Cogniot reminded his readers that 'It
is in our country that atomic science was born. France has three thousand
nuclear specialists while in the rest of capitalist continental Europe you could
not find another thousand'.[85]

The PCF's nationalist appeal, couched in terms of defence of national
sovereignty against both the Americans and the supra-nationalism of the
EEC, could attract some sectors of the rural and urban petty bourgeoisie.
This reflected the fact that a nationalist discourse remained strong and
popular, and it is understandable that the PCF did not relinquish it. A few

months after the EEC Treaty became operational (1 January 1958), Charles
de Gaulle was called back to the helm of the country and developed further
a peculiarly national conception of European integration. As often happened,
the pessimistic predictions of the PCF were not fulfilled. German capital
went on growing but did not destroy France or the prosperity of the French
working class. French agriculture did undergo a massive transformation, since
EEC agricultural policy cushioned French farmers more than adequately.
The purpose of the PCF, however, was not the same as that of a forecasting
institute. The regular predictions of doom and gloom were part and parcel
of its electoral appeal: the PCF offered the sole opposition to 'the system',
to change, to technological progress; it rallied the discontented; it achieved
the remarkable objective of being at once a deeply conservative party and a
revolutionary one; all changes were for the worse, yet the future belonged to
socialism. Thus the PCF's ideological parameters were always contradictory:
it was a nationalist party subservient to a foreign power (the USSR) and a
revolutionary party eternally suspicious of novelty. This is not necessarily a
critical statement; ideologies often require contradictory elements. 'Pure'
ideologies which are internally consistent may be intellectually satisfying, but
they can only be the prerogative of negligible sects.

The PCI, apparently at one with the French in its opposition to the EEC,
had quite different ideological constraints. The fall of fascism had foreclosed
any further development of nationalist ideas. Nationalism was not used by
the ruling Christian Democratic Party, which relied, ideologically speaking,
on a contradictory commitment both to traditional values and to modernization – a characteristic of virtually all brands of post-1945 political catholicism.

The PCI, though always careful to stress its patriotic credentials, could
not play the national card in as truculent a manner as its transalpine counterpart. Furthermore, to appear to stand in the way of modernization in Italy
would have been political suicide. To be anti-modern is a luxury available
only in modern countries. Italy did not feel itself as yet to be in this category.
The Nazis could long for the good old days of rural Germany, but Mussolini's
fascists were clearly committed to modernity. Neither the Christian democrats nor the communists could seriously hope to make any advances on the
basis of 'the good old days'. Finally, the PCI of Togliatti, unlike the PCF of
Thorez, had a far more intelligent understanding of the strategy required by
Western communism if it was to survive in a hostile environment.

Two further elements led the PCI to have a less intransigent posture
towards the EEC than other communist parties: the first was the desire to
avoid antagonizing the PSI, which had already signified its positive view of
the EEC; the second was the pressure it was under from the main trade
union, the Confederazione Generale Italiana del Lavoro (CGIL), whose leader,
the communist Giuseppe Di Vittorio, was keen to preserve trade union unity
with the socialists. Thus the communiqué of the party's Executive Committee of 24 March 1957 simply called for a revision of the treaty (whose

contents had not yet been revealed), and stressed that it was 'understandable and correct' that narrow national markets should be enlarged and that new forms of international co-operation attempted: the working class should not in principle be against this.[86] Nevertheless, the PCI opposed the Treaty of Rome on the grounds that it would spell the ruin of Italian agriculture, that the EEC would be dominated by 'monopoly capital' and the USA, and that the division of Europe would become further entrenched. The PCI's opposition to the EEC increased rather than decreased in the following few years. But it tended to be motivated by catastrophic forecasts of the consequences of the EEC for the Italian economy, rather than by any principled animosity towards supra-nationalism.[87] The forecast was, of course, altogether mistaken: in that period Italy achieved an export-led boom of massive proportions, obtaining the fastest growth rate in its entire history. The PCI's pessimistic view of the chances of Italian capitalist development had, once again, turned out to be wrong. It was only in the 1960s that the party would eventually begin to adopt a Europeanist approach which would lead it, two decades later, to embrace an outspoken federalism.[88]

In the development of a policy towards the EEC, both Italian and French communists were hampered not only by their own analysis, but also by Soviet hostility towards all schemes for European integration. Such animosity was understandable. Both the superpowers had a perception of international affairs which was deeply influenced by the East–West dimension. Thus, the birth of the EEC, which might have been considered as the first phase in the self-emancipation of Western Europe from political dependency on Washington and/or as the creation of a trading bloc which would rival the USA, was in fact considered by both the USA and the USSR to be the economic dimension of Atlantic Europe. Consequently, the construction of the EEC was continually encouraged by the USA and disparaged by the USSR.

These reservations are not surprising. There has never been any certainty, before or since 1957, as to the course European integration might take. To attempt to discover what the EEC 'really is', by analysing the clauses of the Treaty of Rome, is a futile exercise. The nature of complex institutions, and the path of their eventual development, cannot be deduced from their legal framework. European integration should be seen as a territory in dispute, in which the contending participants vie to establish their own definition of what the process 'really' is. Differing meanings have been advanced, including: a large market necessary for further growth and prosperity; the long arm of the USA or 'Atlantic' Europe; the harbinger of everlasting peace in Europe; a rich men's club conspiring to defraud the Third World; a nightmare of bureaucratic centralization; the basis for a United States of Europe; the overcoming of petty and divisive nationalisms; a defence against 'the Anglo-Saxons'; an instrument with which to keep German militarism in its place; the gateway to modernization; a Roman Catholic plot for the domination of the continent; and so on.

In the mid-1950s, given the prevalent climate of the Cold War, the interpretations which prevailed were those of 'Atlantic Europe' and modernization. This is how the EEC was seen by much of the Left in continental Europe. Thus, when the PSI, the only pro-Soviet socialist party, resolved after the Hungarian revolt to distance itself from the Italian communists, it signalled the change by expressing itself favourably disposed towards the formation of a 'single European market' at its Venice Congress (February 1957) – with the face-saving proviso that 'the interests of the workers' and of the Italian south should be safeguarded.[89] The PSI, still an opposition party, could not go so far as to vote in favour of Italian participation. But, by abstaining, it gave a strong signal that it was moving away from pro-Soviet neutralism to Europeanism, and possibly Atlanticism, although it continued to abuse American imperialism. It was not by accident that the change of position *vis-à-vis* Europe coincided with the rise to eminence within the party of a group of modernizers, led by Riccardo Lombardi, who had a far less catastrophic view of modernity and capitalism than the old left majority of Pietro Nenni. The PSI, however, remained suspicious of the EEC for a long time: it was still attached to a national vision of the transition to socialism; it feared the alleged power of the Brussels bureaucracy; and it was alarmed by the dominance exercised by the Paris–Bonn axis.[90] The theme of European integration did not command much attention in the ranks or in the leadership of the PSI. It was used as a symbol of change but little thought was given to it. A book which purports to record the vicissitudes of post-war Italian foreign policy through the eyes of Nenni failed to include any information on how the birth of EEC was perceived by the socialists.[91]

What emerges so far is that, outside the narrow confines of the Benelux countries, the parties of the Left, unable to foresee the importance European integration would acquire, paid very little attention to it. In Northern Europe, Scandinavian co-operation was seen as a safer alternative. The Norwegian Labour Party thought that European integration might lead to a 'neutral' Europe, without American protection, at the mercy of the USSR. There was also the apprehension, shared by many outside Norway, that the new Europe would be dominated by Catholics.[92] In Britain the general assumption of both government and opposition was that the post-war impetus towards European integration had subsided.[93] Labour shared the Conservatives' general scepticism towards 'Europe', its distaste for supra-nationalism in any form, and an obsession with its 'kith and kin' in the white Commonwealth. The Labour Party, unable and unwilling to be *the* party of empire, could retain an 'imperial' stance by substituting the word 'commonwealth' – and this is what Harold Wilson did in 1956, when he announced to the House of Commons that the Labour Party had become the party of the Commonwealth.[94] The Kiplingesque ideology of the 'white man's burden' could be made acceptable from a socialist point of view: Labour's special international role was to help the peoples of the colonies on the road to political and economic emancipation. This is not to deny that the British imperial tradition had made the Labour Party particularly aware of the plight of the Third World. At a time when it was common to see evidence of blatant racial discrimination in the streets of London – 'coloureds need not apply' and 'sorry, no coloureds' – the Labour Party's 1959 election manifesto (*Britain Belongs to You*) denounced the 'vast problem of the hungry two-thirds of the world', declared that to 'solve this problem is the biggest task of the second half of the twentieth century', and warned that 'Two worlds, one white, well-fed and free, the other coloured, hungry and struggling for equality, cannot live side by side in friendship.'[95] Concern for the Third World was also manifested by the British Conservatives who argued, somewhat paternalistically but with justification, that the issues there were education, democracy and civil rights.[96]

Both parties assumed that, with the failure of the EDC, the high tide of Europeanism had receded. The chancellor of the exchequer, Harold Macmillan, was really speaking for both sides of the House when he declared in November 1956 that Britain would never agree, 'as a matter of principle', to enter an arrangement with European countries which would treat imports from the Commonwealth less favourably than those from the continent.[97] But a few years later, Macmillan himself as prime minister knocked in vain at the door of Europe in order to do precisely what – 'as a matter of principle' – he said Britain would never do. Bismarck put it well in a letter to his wife: 'One clings to principles only for as long as they are not put to the test; when that happens one throws them away as the peasant does his slippers.' Then the real, long and interminable Great British Debate on Europe began. But in the 1950s a supreme insouciance, bordering on complacency, dominated the country's two main parties. The EEC was scarcely mentioned at the Labour Party annual conferences of 1956, 1957 and 1958.

British indifference to the EEC cannot be attributed exclusively to vacuous dreams of imperial grandeur, narrow-minded provincialism, little England chauvinism, or irrational fear of continental involvement. All of these played a part, but there were also what seemed to be solid economic reasons. In 1958, the year in which the Treaty of Rome came into effect, British trade with the whole of Western Europe (i.e. imports plus exports) amounted to 30.2 per cent, while just four former colonies – Australia, Canada, New Zealand and South Africa – absorbed 21.2 per cent of total trade and the rest of the Third World (not including oil exporters) accounted for a further 25.6 per cent. The trend, of course, pointed towards Europe and away from the old and new Commonwealth, and one may reproach British political parties for not detecting it. But this trend was an historical novelty. In 1913 British trade with Europe was 37.2 per cent, much higher than it was in 1951.[98] The shared experience of all British politicians was of a long decline of British economic involvement with the Continent. It is therefore not surprising that so 'national' a party as British Labour should spend so little time discussing whether to join a community of six European countries, three of which had a market half the size of Britain's. The European issue was seen entirely as a question of economics, hence as a 'technical' question – which really amounted to working out whether the material benefits outweighed the disadvantages. Europeanism in the idealistic mode was the prerogative of small associations, such as the European Movement – 'prestigious but inert', as Robert Lieber put it.[99]

One of the minor paradoxes of the relationship between the British Labour Party and Europe was that its lack of interest in European integration, not to say its distaste for it, was matched by the desire of the social-democratic parties of the Continent to involve the British. In this strange saga, something approaching an unrequited love affair was being played out. British Labour Party supporters, if they were 'internationalists', had their eyes firmly fixed on the Commonwealth; otherwise they tended to avoid casting a glance at events beyond Dover. Beyond Dover they would have found Guy Mollet, the SFIO leader, opposing the development of a federal Europe as long as Britain did not join, on the grounds that this would cause too great a division in the Continent.[100] Further south, the Italian socialists longed for the British to come in to block the developing Paris–Bonn axis – a sentiment echoed by all the Benelux socialist parties.[101] In Germany, the only motion on Europe at the 1956 Munich Party Conference of the SPD called for the extension of the EEC to the UK.[102] The Danes and Norwegians had used British absence as one of the reasons for staying out. All this was to no avail. There were some lone voices, such as that of Richard Crossman when he wrote, with characteristic insistence, of the chances of British pre-eminence: 'If, deluding ourselves that the Commonwealth is an independent power bloc, we stand aloof from Europe, we forfeit the leadership of Europe, which could be ours.'[103] Apart from this, splendid isolation from continental affairs, once a tenet of British foreign policy, seemed to have become a principle of British socialism.

The Labour Party's great revisionist of the 1950s, Anthony Crosland, otherwise so open to innovatory ideas, did not mention the EEC either in the original 1956 edition of his celebrated *The Future of Socialism*, which is understandable; or in the revised edition of 1964, after Britain had applied to join and been vetoed by the French. Crosland and Gaitskell, unlike their followers, were never enthusiastic about the EEC and never thought the matter was particularly important. [104]

They were not alone. The SPD's revisionist Bad Godesberg programme of 1959, being primarily concerned with internal politics, was virtually silent on the European dimension. Nevertheless, the SPD, which had been critical of all previous integrationist efforts, such as the Schuman and Pleven plans, voted in favour of the EEC. It was the first time a major foreign policy initiative of the CDU had obtained the approval of the SPD.[105] This signified, among other things, that the SPD was beginning to distance itself from its previous commitment to unification, realizing that it would not occur in the foreseeable future. The Liberals (the FDP) voted against the ratification of the Treaty of Rome (as did the party of the 'expellees'), on the grounds that, being yet another step in the process of West Germany's integration with the West, it would constitute an obstacle to reunification.[106]

The motives for the SPD's turnaround are complex.[107] In the first place, it had become possible to argue that West Germany's membership of NATO had separated the issue of defence from that of economic integration. The SPD could remain opposed to the first (though not for long), while accepting the second. Furthermore, the SPD could not ignore the evident sympathy the majority of German trade unions felt for the EEC – an attitude shared by unions in other West European countries. In Italy and France even the communist-dominated unions looked towards European integration, if not in a positive way, at least without the animosity and pessimism of their respective parties. The DGB had accepted the Schuman Plan, though it had been rejected by the SPD, in return for Adenauer's assurance that he would secure the passage of co-determination legislation in the coal and steel industries. The German DGB was also particularly favourable towards EURATOM, and at its 1956 Munich convention the SPD discussed at length the problems of the second industrial revolution and the atomic age.[108] The civilian or peaceful use of nuclear energy was then something which appealed to the Left, since it appeared to incarnate the hope that the new source of energy which had been used to produce weapons of mass destruction could be harnessed for purposes of modernization and production. It must be added that support for civilian nuclear power was general. The Suez crisis and its effects on oil prices and supplies had also contributed to the popularity of nuclear power as a solution to oil dependency. Needless to say, EURATOM never worked effectively.

In the third place, the ideals of European unity greatly appealed to young Germans. Europe enabled them to disassociate themselves from the sins of their parents and to feel less German. The left-wing nationalism of Schumacher had not attracted them. Since Schumacher was dead, the SPD could distance itself from this part of his legacy.

Fourthly, the question of the Saarland had been satisfactorily resolved from the German point of view. France (between 1956–58 under a socialist prime minister, namely Mollet) had allowed a referendum to take place, which sanctioned its return to Germany. There were now no further outstanding disputes between the two countries and the SPD could view the developing Paris–Bonn axis with greater equanimity.

Finally, there was the economic issue. By the mid-1950s, the SPD had become increasingly committed, in practice at least, to the economic prosperity of Germany. It had rescinded its previously held pessimistic assumption regarding the fate of capitalism in Germany. Growth was clearly benefiting the German working class and the SPD was not prepared to disregard its pent-up desire to enjoy the fruits of economic development. This is understandable: in Germany the backlog of demand was particularly high. The population had suffered as their country fought and lost two world wars, went through a massive inflation (1923–24), the Depression, and a level of destruction of domestic property unparalleled in capitalist Europe.[109] The EEC offered the prospect of great export-led growth to a country which had lost all its potential extra-European markets (unlike the British and the French). It would have been suicidal for a political party of whatever persuasion to overlook this predicament. Obviously, this is largely a question of image: the connection between European integration and economic prosperity was firmly established in the popular imagination. Whether this was more than an image, and whether Germany would have prospered equally well outside the EEC, is something no one can tell. A counter-factual model of such dimensions would be difficult to construct.

As a socialist party, the SPD might have demanded the inclusion of some welfare targets in the Treaty of Rome. It did not do so. The SPD did not have a particularly high commitment to welfare reforms. On the contrary, it feared that any degree of social harmonization to the level of the French (whose insurance schemes were more advanced than those of the Germans) would weaken the competitive advantage of German industry. The SPD preferred, instead, to push for a common monetary, financial and investment policy. This made SPD views on the matter virtually indistinguishable from those of the CDU.[110] In any case, most laws passed by the Bundestag did so with SPD support.[111]

That the socialist parties of Western Europe showed a lack of conviction and originality in foreign policy during the 1950s cannot be disputed. Was this due to the obsolescence of the socialist tradition itself? The inevitable sclerosis which invades ideologies out of step with the times? This is unlikely. Social democracy was far from stagnant in this decade. These were the years of construction of the Scandinavian model, of ideological renewal in Germany and Austria, and, to a lesser extent, in Britain, and of regained independence from the PCI for the Italian Socialist Party. In the East, too, there were signs of renewal: in Hungary and Poland an ultimately unsuccessful attempt, but an attempt nevertheless, was made by independent-minded communists to regain autonomy from Moscow and go their own way; while in the USSR the Twentieth Congress of the CPSU condemned Stalin and inaugurated a long phase during which the system, though still unshakable in its authoritarianism, at least refrained from the gory terror of the preceding decades. And in Rome, though not in Paris, some Western communists began to free themselves from the shackles of Moscow and proceed, excruciatingly slowly, towards the mainstream of the European Left.

Stagnation cannot explain why the socialists did not develop their own distinctive view of foreign policy and international affairs. Nor can electoral defeat, for many were in government. Rather, their adoption of a non-socialist and fundamentally bipartisan concept of international political and economic relations provided the model for their ideological renewal. They accommodated their internal programme to the exigencies of a world economy. Once these parameters were established, all forms of renewal had to adapt to the dominant view of how basic property relations should be organized. In other words, the modernization of the socialist tradition became the form in which socialism renounced the ambition of developing non-capitalist economic relations. The constraints of a dominant and successful international capitalist economy appeared to make this imperative. To accept these constraints at the foreign policy level was one aspect of the problem. To be real 'innovators', it was necessary to adapt in domestic policy as well. Thus, it is in the 1950s and not in the 1980s or the 1990s that the revision of the socialist tradition effectively began.

This process was rarely overt and not always successful. It met strong resistance, which was accounted for not solely by the attachment to tradition of many activists and leaders, but also by the more or less conscious realization that authentic reformist politics, to be victorious, require sometimes – perhaps always – both revolutionary zeal and a radical perspective.

CHAPTER TEN

The Foundations of Revisionism

WHEN A number of socialists, notably in Germany and in Britain, tried to redefine what socialism should be, and what its supporters should do, they presented this revision as a necessary adaptation to modernity and altered circumstances. The growth of working-class affluence, the consumer society, the apparent levelling off of social groups, the undoubted prosperity which capitalism had brought about, the ostensible failure of nationalizations, even the successes of the welfare state were used to explain why the ideological armoury of socialist ideas needed a profound overhaul.

The new revisionism may appear as a striking reaction to successive electoral defeats. This was particularly true of the SPD in Germany and the Labour Party in Britain, which were out of office for the entire decade. It was not a marked feature of parties which were in power, either on their own or in coalition, such as the Scandinavian or the Belgian and Dutch. Revisionism, of course, was not a new phenomenon; as we saw in chapter 1, it originated at the end of the nineteenth century and developed alongside the organized socialist movement. The difference is that the early revisionism of Eduard Bernstein and his followers was denounced by all the parties of the Second International, while the revisionism of the 1950s was openly espoused by the leadership of most socialist parties in Western Europe and arguably had the support of the majority of the socialist electorate, as well as a strong following – in some instances, even a majority – of party activists.

What the new revisionism attacked was the view that socialism had as its goal the abolition of the private ownership of the fundamental means of production – in other words, of capitalism itself. This is less startling than may at first appear. The abolition of capitalism, after all, was hardly the only goal of socialism. It was considered a necessary and, for some, even a sufficient precondition for the achievement of other desirable objectives such as social equality, prosperity and happiness – all aims also pursued by many non-socialists. Unlike non-socialists, however, socialists maintained that these desirable goals could not be reached while large-scale private ownership prevailed. Thus, the establishment of collective ownership in some form or other, such as nationalization or, less frequently, workers' control, did not require any further justification: the abolition of private ownership was the precondition for public happiness.

The new revisionism, by demoting the importance of ownership, down-graded that of nationalization. State property no longer constituted the main road to socialism. The only remaining rationale for nationalization had to be couched entirely in practical terms; for example, that it abolished a private monopoly, protected employment, permitted greater investment, guaranteed essential services or supplies – all reasons which had been used by non-socialists. The consequence of this was that socialist revisionism quite deliberately obliterated the painstakingly established border between socialist and non-socialist thought.

It was believed that the loss in doctrinal purity would be more than amply compensated by greater strategic flexibility, increased electoral appeal and, for parties operating in circumstances which made coalitions necessary, a better chance of finding allies. The new revisionism prided itself on its pragmatism and realism while being, at the same time, deeply ethical: it constantly referred to the values of socialism and particularly to the struggle against inequality and poverty. This 'ethical pragmatism' (ethical ends and pragmatic means) deliberately rejected Marxism, its theoretical intransigence and its apparent disregard for the ethical dimension.

By the end of the 1950s, Marxist doctrine, which socialist parties, with the exception of the British, had formally adopted at the end of the nineteenth century, was abandoned – directly or indirectly – by almost all of them. The SPD's new Basic Programme, ratified at the Bad Godesberg Congress in November 1959, solemnly declared that 'Democratic Socialism' in Europe is 'rooted in Christian ethics, humanism and classical philosophy' – a general-ization difficult to take seriously.[1] There is not even the slightest suggestion that the views of Karl Marx may have had some influence on 'Democratic Socialism'. Anthony Crosland, writing from within the Labour Party, felt the need to distance British socialism from Marxism by listing – among the traditions of British socialism – no fewer than eleven other 'socialist doc-trines',[2] and by dismissing Karl Marx as the 'founder of the State or collectivist tradition in socialism'.[3]

There is no point trying to judge Crosland's Marxian scholarship, which appears to be based on ill-digested secondary sources. The target is not Marx's Marx, but two parallel interpretations of Marx. The first, embraced by the old Second International of Kautsky, enshrined in the Erfurt Programme, and criticized by Bernstein, propounded a catastrophic view of the destiny of capitalism: its ultimate collapse preceded by the growing pauperization of the working class.

The second interpretation of Marx attacked by Crosland was the 'collect-ivist' advocacy of a centrally planned economy, characterized by a formidable concentration of power in the hands of the state; a Marx far more easily detectable in the writings of the Fabians or in the practice of Stalin, than in *Das Kapital*. Neither Crosland nor the revisionist Bad Godesberg Programme, however, challenged Marx's conception of historical progress. Marx may have been pessimistic about the outlook for capitalism, but he had a deep philosophical commitment to the nineteenth-century idea of progress. This remained a strong and inescapable component of social-democratic thought and withstood all revisionism.

Belief in progress was compatible with the renunciation of a militant doctrinal commitment to anti-capitalism, for it is a position shared by all 'pro-industrial' ideologies. Liberalism is even more committed than Marxism to an optimistic view of the emancipatory potential of technical progress and science. By rejecting the most overtly anti-capitalist component of their ideological framework, the socialists had opened a route towards a more consequential alliance with liberalism. The revisionism of the late 1950s wished to tone down the differences with liberalism, while distancing itself not only from communism – repeatedly denounced since its inception – but also from traditional socialist anti-capitalism.

The new revisionists also tried to make their peace with religion. Anti-clericalism had been one of the driving forces of continental socialism. By the 1950s it had become apparent that this served no practical purpose bar antagonizing those with religious convictions. Hence the SPD reference in the Bad Godesberg Programme to its roots in Christianity. Not even this was new: the *Aktions-Programm* approved at the Berlin Congress of the SPD in 1954 contained positive remarks on the social message of Christianity.[4] The Austrian SPÖ declared in its 1958 programme that socialism and Christianity 'as the religion of neighbourly love are perfectly compatible with each other'.[5] In Holland where, prior to 1956, there were two Catholic and three Protestant parties, the socialists could attract only non-churchgoers: hence the attempt to eliminate anti-clericalism from the ideology of the party had obvious electoral purposes.[6] In Belgium the PSB/BSP toned down its anti-clericalism by compromising on the complex issue of religious schools with the confessional party, in the belief that 'we shall be able to win a working class majority only to the degree to which we remove the obstacles which exist in the religious and philosophic fields'.[7]

In Italy the PSI, traditionally far more anti-clerical than the PCI, had reached the conclusion that a rapprochement with the church could be a way of helping left-wing Catholics, such as Giovanni Gronchi, to stop the DC from becoming a right-wing party.[8] A 'dialogue with the Catholics' was the main theme of its Thirty-first Congress, held in Turin in 1955.[9] By then, 'talking with the Catholics' was no longer aimed at making the PSI more attractive to Catholic workers, as it had been in past.[10] It was clearly directed towards the Christian Democratic Party, with a view to participating in government. Though, as we shall see, nothing came of it until the early 1960s, this approach was a necessary rite of passage towards the legitimation of the PSI. The left-wing factions of the Socialist Party, loyal to the principle of a common front with the PCI, understood this perfectly well and fought back. Some (Tullio Vecchietti) called on left-wing Catholics to transform the

DC into a progressive Catholic party. Others (Emilio Lussu and Lelio Basso) simply continued to denounce the DC as the unredeemable servant of the church, capitalism and the USA.[11]

In Italy the encounter with religion had been pioneered by the PCI. Its new post-war constitution had been amended to delete any committment to Marxism as a condition of membership. Though Marxism was still the method guiding the party, anyone who accepted the programme could join it. In 1947, during the debate on the constitutional draft, the PCI had not hesitated to break ranks with the PSI and accept the incorporation of the Lateran Pacts of 1929 (in effect, the 'peace treaty' between the Italian state and the Vatican) into the Italian constitution (Article 7).[12] The communist dialogue with Catholics, somewhat unreciprocated, would be further intensified in the 1960s, under the reforming papacy of John XXIII and his successor Paul VI. Nevertheless, it received further impetus in 1954 when the PCI leader Palmiro Togliatti advocated a dialogue with the 'Catholic world' to establish a deeper co-operation on the issue of peace.[13] The PCI never ceased to seek this dialogue. At the Eighth Congress of 1956 Togliatti called for a 'political alliance with those Catholic forces which from a position of generic anti-capitalism aspire to subject Italy's capitalist structures to essential radical changes'.[14] By the Ninth Congress (1960), the PCI declared that 'the policy of entente with the Catholic world is part of the Italian Road to Socialism; we seek a long-term alliance not only with the Catholic masses but also with their organizations.'[15]

It is, of course, true that socialists, and a far from insignificant body of Christian opinion, share a commitment to social solidarity and altruism, a distaste for pecuniary greed, a repugnance for the single-minded accumulation of consumer goods, and a somewhat suspicious view of the effects of individualism on the general welfare. It may be thought that revisionist socialism was inconsistent in soliciting a more open relationship with the church, while embracing some of the fundamental principles of individualistic liberalism, such as the belief in the ultimately beneficial consequences of progress and material growth. Logic and politics have little in common. Successful political ideologies and parties are seldom consistent. The liberal parties themselves, in a minority throughout Western Europe, were quite content to share power whenever they could with confessional parties, while priding themselves on their anti-clerical roots. The new revisionism tried to find a way out of the impasse between a tradition which appeared to have come to a standstill (socialism) and a thriving reality (the popularity of capitalism); it did not seek to establish a rigorous doctrine but, rather, gloried in pragmatism.

In Britain the most important text of the new revisionism was un-questionably Anthony Crosland's *The Future of Socialism* (1956). Perhaps it was also the most important in Europe where, however, it had very little impact, notwithstanding the extravagant claims made on its behalf since: 'a towering castle', 'the greatest socialist thinker of all time'.[16] Most of what Crosland wrote was not very original, but it represented the best *summa* of the arguments put forward in an unsystematic way first by Evan Durbin and later by the Labour revisionists grouped around the journal *Socialist Commentary*.[17] One of them, Douglas Jay, had been a consistent upholder of a right-wing interpretation of social democracy and had frequently opposed public ownership as an aim of socialism.[18] Hugh Gaitskell, leader of the Labour Party after 1955, had previously shown impatience with Labour's fixation with nationalization.[19] In an essay on 'The Ideological Development of Democratic Socialism in Great Britain', published a few months before Crosland's book, Gaitskell relegated the Marxistic tradition of the Labour Party (John Strachey and Harold Laski) to brief unsympathetic comments, and highlighted J. M. Keynes's contribution instead.[20] The widespread acceptance of Keynes in the post-war period was very largely due to the fact that for social democrats he represented the possibility of regulating capitalism for social ends; and for moderate conservatives, the assurance that capitalism could survive and achieve a wide measure of social consensus.

In the 1964 preface to the second edition of his book, Crosland recognized that he had been too optimistic about the prospect of economic growth in 'the Anglo-Saxon economies'.[21] Yet the second edition is substantially the same as, though less complacent than, the first, as if his earlier supposition that there would be a continuous quantitative economic growth was peripheral to the main argument. This is not so. Crosland's *original assumption* of constant growth amounted to a recognition that capitalism had solved the problem of accumulation. This is no marginal admission: if capitalism can promote growth, then socialism can leave well alone and concentrate on its remaining priority: ensuring an equitable social division of the fruits of growth. In other words, belief in growth justified the greater significance placed by Crosland on the distribution of wealth at the expense of the struggle for the abolition of the private ownership of capital.

This belief was shared by all socialist revisionists throughout Europe in the 1950s, and was a necessary part of their new vision. It drastically revised the general view – held by many socialists immediately after the Second World War – that capitalism could not possibly recover successfully. Although the ideology of progress and the belief in constant growth can be easily traced back to the nineteenth century, it was only after the Second World War that this belief was translated into an overwhelming consensus, especially among economists. Writing in 1964, just before the popularization of the pessimistic predictions of doom-laden ecologists, Alec Cairncross could point out:

> Long after Adam Smith, the literature of economics is strewn with prophecies of a stationary state in which growth would finally cease under the influence of some limiting factor such as population growth, the law of diminishing returns, a fuel shortage or a chronic tendency to over-save ... The main shift of public opinion did not take place until the war and post-war years.[22]

The Marxist pioneers of the socialist movement did not believe that capitalism could grow constantly, but they believed in the inevitable improvement of society. Now the situation had almost reversed. There was faith in the strength of capitalism, but scepticism over the inevitability of social advance. The triumph of socialism was no longer believed to be inevitable, while barbarism had become possible. In the *New Fabian Essays* (1952) Richard Crossman clearly expressed what one might call 'the new pessimism', when he wrote:

> The evolutionary and the revolutionary philosophies of progress have both proved false. Judging by the facts, there is far more to be said for the Christian doctrine of original sin than for Rousseau's fantasy of the noble savage, or Marx's vision of the classless society ... modern civilisation ... enables us to cure sickness on a huge scale and to destroy each other on a huge scale. It enables us to liberate each other on a huge scale and to tyrannise each other on a huge scale ... there is no evidence of any continuous upward line of social progress.[23]

The paradox of the new revisionists was that while they were relinquishing belief in the 'continuous upward line of social progress', they were adopting a belief in the 'continuous upward line' of economic growth under capitalism. Thus Crosland criticized the negative view of capitalist development which, in the 1930s, had led socialists to assume that wealth distribution, full employment and other 'immediate objectives' could be implemented only after the abolition of capitalism.[24] Capitalism had now changed; indeed, it had become 'manifestly inaccurate to call contemporary Britain a capitalist society':[25] 'Today the business class has lost this commanding position', economic decisions were now in the hands of public industrial managers, and full employment had increased the power of organized labour.[26] The ownership of the means of production had become irrelevant.[27] Full employment had made the workers stronger. The social-democratic state, not the capitalists, was now in charge of the economy.

The idea that the control of large joint-stock companies had moved away from their owners, now a multitude of shareholders, to a class of managers, was not new. Keynes noted it as early as 1926.[28] It was widely discussed in the 1930s by de Man and other socialist revisionists of the time (see chapter 3). Other well-known theorists of the ownership–control divide were Adolf A. Berle and Gardiner C. Means, authors of *The Modern Corporation and Private Property* (1932). Subsequently, it was popularized by James Burnham, a former Trotskyist, who in his influential *The Managerial Revolution* (1941) argued that 'the *de facto* management of the instruments of production has ... (increasingly) ... got out of the hands of the capitalists'.[29] This argument was used not only by Crosland, but by virtually all other revisionists in Europe – the Austrians in particular – as an argument against nationalization.[30] In France Burnham's book was published in translation as *L'ère des organisateurs* with a preface by Léon Blum. The view that ownership had become immaterial was used by André Philip to suggest that the fundamental problem of socialism was now the distribution of power between social groups.[31] In 1952 Jules Moch, in a lengthy re-examination of the socialist tradition, came to similar conclusions: the evolution of capitalism meant that the 'socialization of profit' and a drastic alteration in the distribution of power could occur without necessarily modifying property relations.[32]

Nationalization – claimed Crosland – would not alter control, only owner-ship. Thus, it could not be among the ends of socialism, or a means to 'creating a socialist society, establishing social equality, increasing social welfare, or eliminating class distinctions'.[33] Crosland saw socialism as something to be achieved incrementally: 'since we could still have more social equality, a more classless society, and less avoidable social distress, we cannot be described as a socialist country.'[34] In this sense socialism was still seen as an 'end-state', though one which could not be reached by revolution or sudden legislative fiat, but only after a long process of molecular social and political change. Yet, in another context, socialism was not an 'end-state' at all, but a set of values held by socialists: 'Socialism is not an exact descriptive term, connoting a particular social structure ... it simply describes a set of values.'[35] The most important of these was that 'every individual should have an equal chance',[36] the state would ensure that the vigorous pursuit of equality would not lead to excessive élitism.[37] Personal consumption and a high wage eco-nomy should be promoted, not least in order to provide goods and services for all, which were broadly similar to those currently enjoyed by an élite.[38] Wealth and property should be redistributed.[39] The key to achieving this was 'A rapid rate of growth ... at least for the next decade', which, 'far from being inconsistent with socialist ideals, is a pre-condition of their attainment'.[40] Crosland added: 'So long as we maintain a substantial private sector, therefore, socialists must logically applaud the accumulation of private profit.'[41] This was the 'central economic dilemma facing contemporary social democracy', for the key question was what socialists should do to ensure that private profits were reinvested and therefore used as 'a source of collective capital accumulation and not as a form of personal income'.[42]

Crosland failed to provide concrete proposals as to how to achieve such a public-spirited and responsible capitalism. He recognized and accepted the division of labour between the economic and political levels of society: capital accumulates and the state spends. Socialism is about public spending and is thus dependent on capitalism's success for its own fortune. The enemy was not capitalism in general but a particular form of it: unregulated, *laissez-faire* capitalism. This enemy, however, had virtually vanished: 'private business now finds it quite natural that Whitehall should intervene in the economy to a degree which would have been thought outrageous a generation ago.'[43] A relatively new form of economic management had developed and this required a new form of socialist politics.

The argument was hardly unfamiliar. All 'revisionism' must necessarily be

based on the proposition that political doctrines need to be realigned with
the new realities that prevail. How this was to be done was far from clear.
Revisionism knew where not to go, but had not, as yet, discovered which
new route to follow outside the tested avenue of Keynesian macro-economic
management. Richard Crossman, the other main Labour Party thinker of the
1950s, admitted this: 'We are certainly not in a position as yet to map the
new route to socialism.' Apparently, some vital pieces of research were
required. Crossman's own list included a detailed assessment of the international balance of power, an analysis of the strength of Britain's position in
the world, and a fresh investigation of the changes in the structures of the
country since 1940.[44] In a similar vein Denis Healey lamented that 'the Party
as a whole lacks any systematic theory of world affairs.'[45] In the best academic
tradition the conclusion had to be that 'more research is needed'.

With hindsight, the most important and significant pages of Crosland's
book were not the first 517, but the last dozen or so. In these, with great
prescience, he suggested that as more and more socialist goals were achieved,
reformers would increasingly have to deal with issues which could not be
classified as specifically socialist or non-socialist, but which lay 'in other
fields altogether such as civil liberties, the sociological problems of mass
society, the freedom of personal and leisure life'.[46] With clarity and much
passion, taking issue explicitly with the Fabian tradition and, perhaps, his
upbringing (his parents were members of the Plymouth Brethren, a fundamentalist puritan Christian sect), Crosland called for a radical change in
cultural attitudes:

> much could be done to make Britain a more colourful and civilised country to
> live in. We need not only higher exports and old-age pensions, but more open-air
> cafés, brighter and gayer streets at night, later closing-hours for public houses,
> more local repertory theatres, better and more hospitable hoteliers and restaur-
> ateurs, brighter and cleaner eating-houses, more riverside cafés ... better design
> for furniture and pottery and women's clothes, statues in the centre of new
> housing-estates, better-designed street-lamps and telephone kiosks, and so on ad
> infinitum.

He then turned to the

> more serious question of socially-imposed restrictions on the individual's private
> life and liberty. There come to mind at once the divorce laws, licensing laws,
> prehistoric (and flagrantly unfair) abortion laws, obsolete penalties for sexual
> abnormality, the illiterate censorship of books and plays and the remaining restric-
> tions on the equal rights of women. Most of these are intolerable and should be
> highly offensive to socialists, in whose blood there should always run a trace of
> the anarchist and the libertarian, and not too much of the prig and the prude.[47]

This intimation remained quite unheeded in the socialist movement. The
prig and the prude prevailed. The peculiar blend of individualism and anarchism, and the longing for an alternative order of society which developed in

the 1960s were ostracized by both the revisionist and traditionalist wings of the organized Left.

Socialist revisionism remained firmly committed to politics in the narrow sense and ignored culture. It did not open new horizons. Perhaps this is inevitable under the conditions of democratic politics, where competition for votes acts as an obstacle to political innovation. This is confirmed by examining the most famous 'revisionist' manifesto of social democracy of the decade: the 1959 Bad Godesberg Programme of the German Social Democratic Party.

Like British Labour revisionism, that of the German social democrats was chiefly determined by what seemed an unstoppable series of electoral defeats. In 1957 the CDU/CSU had gained an absolute majority (50.2 per cent) and 270 seats out of 497. The SPD had increased its vote since 1953, but only from 28.8 to 31.8 per cent. This was all the more disappointing because in the second half of the 1950s the SPD was gaining ground in almost every election, and controlled major cities such as Berlin, Hamburg and Bremen. The problem was that the rival CDU was increasing its share of the vote as well, at the expense of the FDP.[48] The system was clearly becoming polarized.

Unlike Hugh Gaitskell in his attempt to alter Clause Four of the Labour Party constitution (see below), the SPD leadership met no serious resistance: the new programme was accepted by the delegates by 324 votes to 16. The Bad Godesberg Congress had been carefully prepared: thousands of activists attending hundreds of meetings discussed aspects of a new basic programme aimed at superseding the technically still valid Heidelberg Programme of 1925. With some exaggeration Bad Godesberg has been called the 'culmination of the almost one-hundred-year old process of deradicalizing socialism in Germany'.[49] Unlike the other two most important political programmes of German socialism – the *Communist Manifesto* of Marx and Engels and the Erfurt Programme of Kautsky and Bernstein – it was far more concerned with the image of the movement than its strategy. However, revisionism developed within an established German tradition of proceeding through the adoption of various 'fundamental programmes'.[50]

The most significant difference between Bad Godesberg and its predecessor of 1925 was not that Marxism went unmentioned – something most commentators emphasize – or that the party committed itself to growth (a commitment made in previous statements), or its acceptance of the market, but the merging of the party's immediate demands and its long-term aims. This classical distinction, readers will remember, enabled the party to advance virtually any reformist short-term goals provided the final aim – the abolition of capitalism – was regularly and resolutely reaffirmed. At Bad Godesberg short- and long-term aims were conflated. The forsaking of Marxism was the symbolic representation of the abandonment of socialism as an 'end-state'. The new goals were equally valid for both present and future: growth of prosperity, a just share of the national product, full employment, stable currency, increased productivity.[51]

The de-Marxification of the party was, in reality, the abandonment of Kautsky's Marxism, hitherto the dominant version of the doctrine in the SPD, and its belief in the inescapable laws of capitalism, the inevitable impoverishment of the working class, and the growing proletarianization of the middle classes. Against this, German social democrats, well into the 1970s, would read and revive Bernstein's Marxism.[52]

The other most heralded revision of Bad Godesberg was the alleged abandonment of nationalization. The *Aktions-Programm* of the Berlin Party Congress (1954) still explicitly advocated the nationalization of basic industries.[53] This was not to be found in Bad Godesberg. But it does not follow that nationalization was necessarily repudiated. A textual reading of the document discloses the enigmatic way in which the issue was dealt with. There was, at first, an apparently unambiguous statement to the effect that the SPD was against 'totalitarian' control of the economy and 'favours competition whenever free competition really exists'.[54] This was followed by the most frequently quoted words of the programme: 'As much competition as possible, as much planning as necessary.' These words were not new. The Dortmund *Aktions-Programm* of 1952 stated that the SPD supported real competition 'whenever it is appropriate'.[55] In 1954, at the Berlin Congress, the SPD was far from negative about the free market: it advocated an active competition policy and regulation against monopolistic and unfair competition; it maintained that planning for 'stability' would be in the interest of competition; and it championed help for small entrepreneurs to enable them to be more competitive.[56]

Though Bad Godesberg was not against free competition, it was hostile to large-scale enterprises on the grounds that these were incompatible with the free market.[57] This meant that the role allocated to planning ('as much as necessary') could be quite broad if one held the view that free competition, in advanced capitalist societies, was seriously limited by oligopolistic power. It may appear that the social democrats had joined the neo-liberals in assuming that capitalism functioned at its best under conditions of free competition – that is, in a golden and largely mythical age in which a wide array of small firms keenly competed and in which the consumer was sovereign. That may be so. But what is relevant here is that the SPD used the concept of 'free competition' as a justification for regulation of the 'new' capitalism, which was clearly large-scale and for which, so it followed, planning was necessary. Whether this may or may not have included nationalization is left to the readers to decide; the programme is diplomatically silent. There is nothing in Bad Godesberg to deter the supporters of nationalization. It is therefore not true – as some have asserted[58] – that this was necessarily 'a programme of "reformist liberalism" (in which) there was no longer any basic difference (with) the CDU social market philosophy' – though in practical terms (that is, when it came to legislating), many of the CDU proposals went through the Bundestag with the votes of the SPD.[59]

Bad Godesberg – like most party programmes – was an open text full of ambiguities. This is precisely why it could be acceptable to the overwhelming majority of the party. It followed the second principle of the Napoleonic dictum: 'constitutions should be short and obscure.' In this way it allowed for divergent interpretations and permitted the safeguarding of party unity.

To understand the Bad Godesberg Programme, it is necessary to go beyond the text and examine the context. It is the programme of a working-class party which no longer wished to represent itself as such, because this had become an obstacle to the securing of political power. This was not just electoral opportunism – although, after three defeats at the polls, it would have been quite understandable if the party had felt it necessary to divest itself of working-class 'signs' (language, programme, banners and images) in order to acquire non-working-class votes. The abandonment of the SPD's working-class identity and its transformation into a *Volkspartei* (a 'people's party'), were necessary in order to become acceptable to the whole of West German society, and not just to its own electorate. Thus the programme was more important for its silences (no mention of Marx or nationalization), and the accompanying symbolic changes, than for what it said.

In 1952, at Dortmund, the SPD had defined itself as the party of 'workers, civil servants, white-collar workers, intellectuals, middle classes, peasants and all the people who need to work', and not explicitly as a people's party.[60] Two years later, in the Berlin Action Programme, came the announcement that the SPD had changed from 'a party of the workers' to 'a party of the people' (*Partei des Volkes*) – though, schizophrenically, it reaffirmed that the working class remained the foundation of its membership and electorate.[61] By 1959, even these positive references to a working-class identity were abandoned for good.

The 'de-proletarianization' of the image of the party was a central feature of revisionism everywhere, including, as we shall see, the reform communism of Nikita S. Khrushchev in the Soviet Union. For example, the Austrian socialists, in their 1958 programme, relinquished the belief in the central role of the working class and dropped the expression 'working class', in favour of 'all the workers', in order to emphasize the community of interests which linked wage earners to salary earners.[62]

In Britain, Croslandism thought that shedding the 'proletarian' image of the party was a necessary precondition for electoral advance. The burgeoning of sociological studies which suggested that the working class was about to disappear or, if not the workers themselves, at least their consciousness of being such, reflected the widespread belief that Western European society was becoming less rigidly stratified in opposing classes. It was held that affluence was destroying class consciousness. Soon, as in the USA, the alleged model of the future, everyone would be middle class.

None of this was entirely new. The concept of the embourgeoisement of the working class and of the affluent worker, which became increasingly fashionable in the 1960s, was far from novel. It dated from Eduard Bernstein in the early days of socialist revisionism. Lenin himself, an innovator who disguised his ceaseless revisions in the language of fundamentalism and orthodoxy, produced a fully elaborated theory of embourgeoisement when he postulated that super-profits from the exploitation of the colonies enabled the capitalists to obtain the allegiance of better-off skilled workers, the so-called 'aristocracy of the proletariat'. The Belgian socialist Hendrik de Man, writing in 1926 in his *Psychology of Socialism*, noted that when he realized that it was impossible 'for the working class to attain more prosperity without undergoing embourgeoisement, I suffered one of the most grievous disappointments of my life'.[63]

By the early 1960s, Otto Kirchheimer had recognised that class parties, bourgeois as well as proletarians were everywhere transforming themselves into 'catch-all' parties and seeking the support of new social groups, while trying to hold on to their traditional ones. [64] For working-class parties, an appeal to the urban salary earning classes (civil servants, white-collar workers, etc.) was the most obvious avenue for electoral recruitment, because there was a considerable community of interest between these and blue-collar workers.[65] This transformation entailed further changes: a drastic reduction of the party's ideological baggage; a more electorally-oriented strategy; and a much higher profile and greater power for the leaders at the expense of the still too ideologically oriented individual members.

The abandonment of ideology had become a political necessity. Among committed intellectuals, affirmed Daniel Bell with over-hasty certainty, 'the old passions are spent' and he added, with more justification:

> The irony ... for those who seek 'causes' is that the workers, whose grievances were once the driving energy for social change, are more satisfied with the society than the intellectuals. The workers have not achieved utopia, but their expectations were less than those of the intellectuals, and the gains correspondingly larger.[66]

The assumption that working-class consciousness was being drastically altered by affluence is quite distinct from the supposition that the actual proportion of the working class in capitalist society had changed. The working class had not diminished in size; on the contrary, it had increased as we noted in chapter 8 (see Table 8.3). What occurred was a modification of the class structure due to the massive contraction in the size of the rural population and a corresponding expansion of the middle classes. Some of the new middle class came from the rural classes, but most were former workers or children of workers.

It is difficult to assess and generalize the ideological effects of such major changes. We know that religion had a greater hold among the rural than among the urban population. We also know that socialist ideology had

Table 10.1 France, 1956 elections: occupation of voters as a share of total party vote (%)

	PCF	SFIO	MRP	National average
Peasants and rural workers	5	8	7	22.5
Professionals and artisans	10	10	16	13.7
White-collar workers	17	23	20	13.4
Blue-collar workers	49	39	31	35.2
Pensioners	19	20	26	15.2
	100	100	100	100.0

Source: Adapted from *Sondages*, no. 4, 1960, p. 18; reproduced in Roger Martelli, 'L'année 1956', in Roger Bourderon et al., *Le PCF: étapes et problèmes 1920–1972*, Editions Sociales, Paris 1981, p. 443.

penetrated the working classes more than any other group. In the absence of reliable surveys, one can only surmise that the 'hold' of socialism among ex-members of the working class was less strong than the corresponding influence of religion among ex-rural dwellers. Socialism was specifically targeted at the working class, but religious appeal was always more universal. It follows that the new workers transferred from the countryside kept their religious ideology more than the new middle class which originated from the working class. If this is so, then the de-emphasis on working-class centrality by the socialist parties was a prudent strategy, and so was their toning down of anticlericalism.

Nevertheless, socialist parties did not wait until the 1950s to question their emphasis on the working class. They started doing so as soon as they became strongly engaged in electoral politics – in many instances, as far back as the 1920s – partly because the industrial working class is usually a minority of the population, partly because no socialist party could ever seriously hope to capture the allegiance of all workers.[67]

But was the appeal of the left parties so exclusively aimed at the working class? Even the most vociferously 'working-class' party in Europe, the PCF, had been quite successful in extending its influence from the working-class areas of northern France and the industrial belt around Paris to the rural societies of the south west and the Mediterranean. As a result, the PCF obtained a proportion of the non-working class vote not massively out of line with that obtained by its socialist rivals and the Christian democratic MRP.[68]

The Italian communists were far more aware of the need to capture the middle-class vote than the French had ever been. In 1946 Palmiro Togliatti, in a famous speech, had launched an appeal to the 'middle groups', suggesting that there was no fundamental contradiction of interests between the working class and the middle strata of society.[69] He had chosen to make this appeal in the central region of the Emilia, because it was the heartland of Italian communism and had been a staunchly socialist region in the pre-fascist period.

The Emilia was not the industrial and working-class centre of Italy. It was, on the contrary, a highly diversified and stratified society, which escaped the facile sociological determinism which assumes a close correlation between a party of the Left and a working-class presence. Italian communist leaders, like Pietro Ingrao, explicitly excluded such determinism: 'while we recognize ... the class origins of political parties we do not reduce every difference between parties to a class difference.'[70] Togliatti, in his report to the Eighth Congress of the Party (December 1956), hoped that 'the working class, the historical opponent of capitalism' would be joined by 'the broad peasant masses including the small and medium independent farmers, a very large productive urban middle class', as well as, he added rather optimistically, 'numerous small and medium industrialists'.[71] As we shall see later, these and other Italian communist revisions were not linked to a fundamental change of image. To have made this change would have entailed a radical break with the USSR, a move the leadership could not consider seriously.

In Germany the SPD did not have these problems. The belittling of the proletarian origin of the party, and its transformation into a *Volkspartei*, were accompanied by unmistakable symbolic changes aimed at eliminating the proletarian stigmata of the party: the colour of party membership books was changed from red to blue; the form of address among members was changed from 'comrade' to 'friend'; the national flag of the Federal Republic was now hoisted on the roof of the SPD headquarters in Bonn, next to the still traditionally red flag of the party.[72] The Bundesrepublik was finally accepted, even though Germany was still divided. The ghost of Schumacher was finally laid to rest.

Every single one of the great innovations of Bad Godesberg can be traced to a previous party statement. Even the 'opening to the Church' had an antecedent in the Berlin Action Programme of 1954, in which we find some positive remarks about the social message of Christianity.[73] Similarly, the celebrated 'dropping of Marxism' was preceded in 1954 by a recognition that although Marx and Engels had provided the scientific basis for socialism, so much had changed that, it was implied, the founding fathers were of limited use.[74]

It is rare for a party successfully to change its skin during relatively uneventful periods without careful preparation. Bad Godesberg was not a bombshell, but it was presented by the party as if it were. The party could have dropped nationalization quietly, tried to make its peace with the church, accepted the principle of national conscription, i.e. of German rearmament (the only serious foreign policy departure mentioned in the programme). Instead, it chose to highlight the change. With the hindsight gained from the development of 'image politics' commonplace and fashionable in the 1980s and 1990s, it is easy to see Bad Godesberg primarily as a major exercise in image construction. Susanne Miller, a perceptive observer and one-time participant in these great debates, suggested that on the whole Bad Godesberg summed up the principles that had guided the SPD since 1945, and that its greatest effect was to transform the SPD's public image, so creating the conditions in which it might achieve the goal of becoming a people's party attractive to various classes of voters.[75]

One must not assume that all parties of the Left embraced revisionism or seriously attempted it. Generally speaking, those that were successful left well alone. The Swedish SAP, in its 1960 programme, congratulated itself, quite justifiably, on all the measures undertaken to humanize society. It also found words of condemnation for capitalism and for the fact that, even in a welfare system, 'the larger part of the economy is still dominated by a minority of property owners'. Like the revisionists, the SAP accepted that economic power had passed from the shareholders to the managers, but this, it said, contrary to most revisionist arguments, made little difference: considerable power was still vested in a few private hands and this was 'incompatible with the principle of democratic equality'.[76]

In Norway, nothing remotely similar to Bad Godesberg occurred; the DNA commanded an absolute majority of the electorate and changed gradually, responding to circumstances. In Holland, the PvdA remained committed to Marxism, claiming for 'democratic socialism' the words of Karl Marx in a 'slightly changed form': 'The workers have more to lose than their chains but they still have a world to win.'[77] In its 1959 *Beginselprogram*, the PvdA restated its commitment to the socialization of the means of production, though this was carefully fudged: the mixed economy would be retained and nationalization would occur only to prevent excessive concentration of economic power and ensure efficiency.

In Belgium, the main issue confronting the socialists of the PSB/BSP, in government with the Liberal Party throughout most of the 1950s, was not revisionism but the traditional bourgeois radical battle aimed at removing church control over schools. This confrontation was concluded with a compromise, the so-called *Pacte scolaire* of November 1958. The main *raison d'être* for Catholic unity was eliminated; the church intervened less in elections; the Christian Social Party was more vulnerable to linguistic divisions.[78] Paradoxically, this eliminated the main bone of contention between Liberals and Social Christians, thus permitting them to join forces and keep the socialists out of government.[79] Even then, revisionism did not become the focus of attention for the party. On the contrary, during the celebrations for its seventy-fifth anniversary held on 29 May 1960, in which 100,000 people converged in a triumphant procession, many of the leading speakers insisted that the founding charter of the party, the *Charte de Quaregnon* of 1894, did not require any modification; while the PSB/BSP President, Léo Collard, declared that the 'final aim is not limited to reforming capitalist society'.[80] The Belgian socialists compared the revisionism of their British, Austrian and German counterparts unfavourably with the 'rigour and conciseness of the *Charte de Quaregnon*', arguing that the task facing socialists 'in 1960 as in 1894 is the collectivization of the means of production'.[81] Economic planning continued to be an important objective of the PSB/BSP, provided it was 'democratic and socialist', and not 'authoritarian or totalitarian' (i.e. communist); planning against the 'anarchic nature of capitalism' is what constituted the 'authentically socialist characteristic' of the party programme.[82] Finally, Léo Collard admitted that capitalism might be able 'to plan, organise and direct the economy' as well as eliminating its own crises, maintaining full employment, and achieving a high standard of living. But 'What distinguishes a socialist society from a capitalist one is the ultimate end to be served', that is, the emancipation of the workers in a full political and economic democracy.[83]

The Austrian SPÖ attempted a major revision of its programme in 1958. The situation facing the party, however, was quite different from that of most other Left parties. The SPÖ was in government, albeit in coalition with the ÖVP, and it operated in a neutral country.

The main thrust of the Austrian revisionists was the attempt to reject the class struggle and Marxist theory. This was particularly remarkable because the SPÖ had been, of all the socialist parties, the one which had contributed most to Marxism; one need go no further than to recall the Austro-Marxist school of Otto Bauer (see chapter 3). Yet revisionism had already been well established in the post-war party, thanks to Karl Renner, first president of the Second Austrian Republic, and one of the outstanding figures of twentieth-century pragmatic revisionism. Furthermore, the SPÖ had every reason to feel confident, sustained as it was by a genuine mass party with an enormous membership on a par with the SAP in Sweden: it had 700,000 members, 10 per cent of the population.

Why should the SPÖ leaders go out of their way to distance themselves from Marxism? The French SFIO, for example, whose practice was far more pragmatic than that of the SPÖ, never formally renounced Marxism. The theoretical review of that party, La revue socialiste, was replete with articles seeking to rescue Marx from the communists.[84] The SFIO 'needed' a rhetorical commitment to Marxism to maintain the 'left-wing' credibility of a party facing a powerful, more radical, rival: the PCF. In contrast, the SPÖ had no serious enemy on its left flank: after 1959 the communists were no longer represented in Parliament.[85]

What the SPÖ wanted was to become the senior partner in the coalition government and, eventually, to govern on its own. The 1956 elections had been disappointing for the SPÖ. Though they had added one percentage point to their 1953 result (a total of 43 per cent), and gained a further seat (a total of seventy-four), their coalition partners and rivals, the ÖVP, had done much better, from seventy-four seats and 41.3 per cent in 1953 to eighty-two seats and 46 per cent in 1956. This is why many Austrian socialists felt they had to review their position, and their commitment to Marxism. However, within the party an influential intellectual opposition led by Josef Hindels – a veteran Austro-Marxist – sought to keep the party committed to a radical perspective.

It was because of the strength of this faction that the commission in charge of preparing a new programme, chaired by Bruno Kreisky, was unable to alter the long-term pledge to an eventual classless society.[86] The original draft, presented at the Salzburg Party Congress of 1957, contained a sentence explicitly critical of Marxism: 'Modern society has developed quite differently from Marx's anticipation in the *Communist Manifesto*', and disparaged the allegedly poor predictive record of Marxism. This caused such an outcry that much of this was deleted from the final draft eventually accepted on 14 May 1958 by the Party Congress in Vienna. This fudged compromise allowed Hindels to declare that the new programme was 'permeated by the spirit of Austro-Marxism', and his opponents to say that 'it severed the tie with Marxism'.[87] Oscar Pollack, editor of the SPÖ organ, *Arbeiter Zeitung*, and member of the Executive Committee, was at pains to emphasize that if the party had grown from 'a narrow class party' to a 'mass party', it did not mean it had abandoned its belief in the class struggle or Marxism.[88]

In Britain, the revisionist ferment generated by Crosland and the Gaitskellites had become, after the second successive electoral defeat (1955), official Labour policy. The various party documents, *Industry and Society* (1957), *Plan for Progress: Labour's Policy for Britain's Economic Expansion* (1958), and Roy Jenkins' *The Labour Case*, written for the 1959 election, all presented, in substance, the case for a strong commitment to social reform, combined with a firm intention to preserve and develop a flourishing private sector of the economy.[89] The Labour Left, devoid of ideas, adequate leadership and, far more importantly, trade union support, had been thoroughly routed. The manifesto for the 1959 election, *Britain Belongs to You*, was a clear statement of revisionist policy. It included a generic commitment to 'a socialist ethics', a theme dear to Crosland; criticism of the Conservatives from a 'national' perspective: 'Britain in these last years has been outpaced by almost every other industrial nation' – a motif which would be repeated for the following thirty years; a promise that there would be no further nationalization, except for steel and road haulage (both recently privatized by the Conservatives), and that public ownership would be extended only if an industry could be shown 'to be failing the nation' (thus there was no ideological commitment to an extension of the public sector); an undertaking that social reforms would not be financed by increasing taxation, but by 'planned expansion'; a 'private sector' view of housing policy: 'Labour's housing policy has two aims: to help people buy their own homes and to ensure an adequate supply of decent houses to let at a fair rent.'[90]

No one could have argued that the manifesto was anything but moderate. It is not therefore surprising if the disappointment of Labour leaders was particularly intense when the Conservative Party emerged triumphant for the third consecutive time. Yet this defeat did not turn into a rout for the revisionists. The dominant position they had acquired in the party was reflected in their success in convincing the majority that the main cause of the defeat was the party's negative image, not its policies. This was sub-stantiated by a public relations firm which discovered what most people knew – namely, that the overwhelming majority of electors do not read party manifestos or the commentary these elicit in the quality press. Such surveys confirmed the revisionists' view: the Conservatives had succeeded in identifying themselves with the rising middle classes, youth and economic prosperity. The Labour Party appeared as a stuffy, bureaucratic party obsessed with nationalization, as a hopelessly divided force, and as an organization stubbornly identified with the pre-war working class and its so *démodé* cloth cap. The modern working class either no longer existed, as Douglas Jay claimed, or had become thoroughly *embourgeoisé*, as Crosland insisted. Crosland himself, in his Fabian pamphlet *Can Labour Win?* (1960), suggested the party should drop the idea of 'an ultimate goal', the source of much ineffectual internal wrangling, and concentrate on the all-important business of winning elections.[91] By now, the well-informed reader will have realized that the Labour Party revisionists of the 1950s had thoroughly ventilated most of the main themes and ideas of the future revisionists of the 1980s and 1990s. The main difference, however, is that Croslandite revisionism stressed the importance of social equality and the redistribution of wealth via taxation. Later modern-izers preferred to stress uncontroversial notions of 'community' and 'individual freedom'.[92] Perhaps history does repeat itself, after all, but only when those involved remain inattentive to the past: in politics Mnemosyne often prevails over Clio.

In one fundamental aspect Gaitskell differed from most of his revisionist successors: he attempted to modify Clause Four of the party constitution. Here the 'lessons of history' were well-grasped. For nearly thirty years, all Gaitskell's successors refrained from repeating what turned out to be a major tactical blunder. Only in April 1995, after four electoral defeats and sixteen years in the wilderness of opposition, did the Labour Party, led by Tony Blair, replaced the famous clause with another unlikely to arouse animosity except among some socialists.

All the surveys pointed out that, even though public ownership was barely mentioned in the party manifesto, public opinion closely identified Labour with nationalization and had a negative view of it.[93] Gaitskell became con-vinced that the best way to change this state of affairs was a highly publicized abandonment of the commitment to 'the common ownership of the means of production, distribution and exchange' embodied in the fourth paragraph of Clause Four. It must be assumed that Gaitskell wanted to win, not simply to raise the issue. His subsequent defeat must mean that he was not aware of the intensity of feeling within the party. Once conscious of it, he became hesitant and irresolute, compromised repeatedly, but to no avail.[94] Not only was Clause Four retained, but the crucial commitment to common ownership was printed thereafter on the back of the party's membership cards. It thus acquired a status it had never possessed. It became the symbol of Labour's commitment to socialism and, consequently, the target of all successive revisionists.

Gaitskell had not sought to remove Clause Four altogether. His plan was to include other statements of principle in the party constitution so that Clause Four would lose its pre-eminence as the party's sole definition of the final aim. Clause Four could then be 'amplified' and 'clarified' and become Clause Ten.[95] This would incorporate the old Clause Four and a new commitment to the mixed economy. It was an archetypal unsatisfactory compromise which displeased everyone. The trade unions, which had supported Gaitskell thus far, deserted him not just over Clause Four, but also over foreign policy, by espousing – albeit temporarily – the cause of unilateral nuclear disarmament. Gaitskell had misread the political ideology of the trade union leaders. He had assumed that their intense dislike of the Labour Left would lead them to abandon the ideology of the final goal. In fact, the trade union leaders wanted to preserve the contradiction at the heart of the Labour Party: a moderate, prudent and electorally sound practice with a socialist future on the distant horizon.

The immediate effect of this impasse was to widen the gap between the revisionists and their opponents. The former had come to regard public opinion as immutable; consequently, the party had to adapt itself to it. The latter believed that, sooner or later, public opinion would be won over to 'socialist objectives' and that the party would eventually win an election.[96] Michael Foot expressed this position with characteristic bluster: 'In order to win an election we have to change the mood of the people in this country, to open their eyes to what an evil and disgraceful and rotten society it is.'[97]

Gaitskell was eventually able to repair the damage he had inflicted on himself. In 1960 he had been defeated by the bloc vote of the unions on both Clause Four and unilateralism. In 1961 he convinced most of the unions (but not the mighty TGWU – the Transport and General Workers' Union – led by Frank Cousins) to abandon unilateralism and made no further attempts to drop Clause Four. It probably did not occur to him to do the opposite: Atlanticism prevailed over revisionism.

Gaitskell's ineffectual attempt to change the party, his 'imperfect appreciation of the function of symbols and myths within a political party',[98] provided the Labour Left with the victory they had unprofitably pursued throughout the 1950s. After the defeat of 1951, the Bevanites had concentrated on foreign not on domestic affairs, on technicalities (e.g. the size of the rearmament programme), rather than on substance (e.g. Britain's relationship with the USA). A qualification must be made to this exacting judgement: Bevan's proleptic realization of the importance of the plight of the Third World and of the dire consequences of the continuation of unequal exchange between rich and poor countries.[99] When Bevan renounced unilateralism, the Left was deprived of a leader.

The fundamental reason why Gaitskell could not win was that the Labour

Party was more organizationally divided than any other party of the Left in Europe. It consisted of a parliamentary leadership in charge of policy, but with little access to the membership; a National Executive Committee without effective power and therefore obliged to act as a pressure group; a rank and file devoid of any purpose except that of generating electoral enthusiasm; an affiliated trade union bloc united in little other than a vague commitment to socialism. Union leaders were deeply divided among themselves, not so much by ideology but by the fragmented nature of the trade union movement; in politics they were, at best, the expression of the small percentage of trade union activists involved in party politics. To make matters more complicated, the structure which held this amalgam together had to be ritually exposed to the gaze of all and sundry in an annual conference – an exhausting week of self-celebration and internecine warfare. To be kept on the road, this complex caravan required a judicious balancing act between the pledge to socialism's final aims and the longing for electoral victory.

Revisionism, to be successful, required considerable preparation, rather than shock therapy, and some understanding of party structure and party management. In most continental socialist parties – but not in the British Labour Party – this was the precondition for obtaining leadership. In Britain the road to the top party job was through the parliamentary group and the cabinet or shadow cabinet, not the party machine, which counted for little. Nevertheless, in spite of its organizational particularity, the British Labour Party conformed to the European pattern of revisionism in that similar issues were raised.

Revisionism was not confined to the socialist parties. One of the most significant shifts in programme occurred in the Italian Communist Party. Here, some of the items for revision were strikingly similar to those occurring in the socialist movement: the idea of socialism as an 'end-state', the relationship with religion, the question of capitalist growth and technical progress, the international role of the party, the central role of the working class. Two points need to be made at this stage:[100] First, the PCI, like the PCF, was tied to the USSR in ways which made uninhibited revisionism impossible. This dependency or attachment pervaded the entire party and, for most of the rank and file and many in the leadership, represented the assurance that an anti-capitalist transformation of society was possible. Such dependency provided the USSR with a potent instrument of control against any strong revisionist yearnings the leaders of the PCI might have had. The constraints were thus far more formidable and significant than those faced by social-democratic parties. To suggest that Togliatti could have done in the 1950s what Berlinguer did in the 1970s (see chapter 20), or Occhetto in the 1990s (see chapter 24) is to lack an elementary understanding of these constraints.

Secondly, in the PCI, but not in the PCF, adaptation to national circumstances had been on the agenda since the return of Togliatti from the USSR in 1944. The intervention of the Cold War made adaptation far more difficult and less overt. This created a highly ambiguous situation because it was never clear to the rank and file or anyone else whether the commitment to pluralism, Parliament, civil rights and freedom of worship was valid only under capitalism, or whether it would form part of a future socialist society. The commitment to a revolutionary tradition sharply distinguished from social democracy meant that every change had to be presented as perfectly congruent with the tradition and, in a sense, as never a change at all. This Togliattian insistence on 'renewal in continuity' unavoidably made revisionism difficult, while it reassured both the USSR and the party's traditional supporters.

Thus, the revisionism of the West European communists was dependent on an external impetus – a green light from the USSR – while that of the social democrats was essentially determined by national political and electoral issues.

The green light was given by the Soviet leader, Nikita Khrushchev, in his report to the Twentieth Congress of the Communist Party of the Soviet Union (CPSU) held in February 1956. The salient points were the acceptance of the principle of peaceful co-existence in international relations, the consequent abandonment of the doctrine of the inevitability of war with capitalist states, and the acceptance of 'national roads to socialism' different from the Soviet 'model' of the revolution of October 1917. This notion of nationally specific roads – originally advanced during the Second World War and its immediate aftermath – allowed the communist parties to reconcile supporting the CPSU – which was, after all, pursuing its own 'national road' – with a parliamentary and peaceful road congruent with Western traditions. With Khrushchev's report, it seemed that the era of monolithic communism had come to a close. It appeared that communist parties now had greater freedom in the elaboration of their own policies and that these could diverge from those elaborated in Moscow. What Khrushchev had not specified were the limits of this new freedom.

The non-official, secret part of Khrushchev's speech, leaked a few months later to the *New York Times*, went much further in 'revising' the established Soviet line, for it denounced Stalin's past deeds in a manner which remained unequalled among Soviet leaders until the advent of Mikhail Gorbachev. The revelations were embarrassing to all communists because all of them had, at one time or another, actively participated in the cult of Stalin. It was, however, an opportunity for a long overdue bout of communist revisionism.

Togliatti had two objectives. The first was to maintain the unity of his party; the second was to support Khrushchev's reformist policies in the belief that the main international precondition for an advance of communism in Italy was the success in the USSR of a new course under a new leadership. Both objectives required that traditional loyalty towards the USSR be firmly maintained, while making explicit the more gradualistic 'national' line Togliatti had started developing since the war. He allowed himself only two departures from pro-Sovietism: first, he disagreed with Khrushchev's use of the category of 'personality cult' to dispose of the question of Stalinism: 'At one time, all that was good was due to the superhuman positive qualities of a man; now all that is evil is attributed to the equally exceptional and staggering defects of the same man.'[101] He suggested instead that the problem was deeper and had to be traced to the 'limitations of Soviet democracy'.[102] Secondly, Togliatti took 'national roads to socialism' to mean that the USSR no longer had the leading role: 'The whole system is becoming polycentric. Within the Communist movement itself one cannot talk of a single guide, but of progress which is achieved by following roads which are often diverse.'[103]

Togliatti remained firmly in the 'socialist' camp. When Soviet troops invaded Hungary to quell what would inevitably have become an anti-communist revolution, he backed them with the substantial support of his entire party. All communist parties approved of the Soviet intervention in November 1956 – even the Yugoslav, newly reconciled with Moscow – though there were significant disagreements over the causes of the uprising and the justification for intervention. Hungary caused havoc among the pro-communist intelligentsia throughout Western Europe, and nowhere more so than in Italy. Characteristically, much of the debate among Italian intellectuals was not over Stalin, Hungary or foreign policy. The new dissidents concentrated their attacks on the excessive provincialism of the Italian communist tradition, the target being not so much its pro-Sovietism as its commitment to a Marxist-Crocean historicism and its rejection of modern social science. Condensed in a few words, the intellectuals' objections were that the PCI was too provincial, and that its outlook contained 'too much Italy and too little America, too much Southern Italy and too little of the North'. Italo Calvino attacked Italian culture in general for having 'given us so little with which to understand the world'. Alessandro Pizzorno complained that young scholars spent too many hours 'studying the Hegelian school of Naples or Piedigrotta, Engels' letters to Tom, Dick and Harry, or minor Sicilian writers'.[104]

The target of this attack was Togliatti's cultural policy. It attempted to provide the Italian road to socialism with an indigenous tradition by presenting Gramsci's Marxism as the inheritor of what was best in Italian culture. It had been devised – at least in part – as an implicit response to the inevitable Stalinization of the party. It was never able to develop a concept of modernity which could rival the dominant American model. Where the PCI failed was in harnessing images of modernity. These could not be found in the tradition of Italian historicism – hostile as it was to seemingly positivist conceptions of modernity. But neither could they be found in the USSR. Images of Russian steel workers were much too feeble to withstand the onslaught of the American way of life and the consumer society.

All this turmoil must have deeply disturbed Togliatti, whose exaggerated belief in the importance of intellectuals mirrored Thorez's contempt for them. Yet party unity remained his priority. He would have supported a mild form of reformed communism in Hungary. He could not support what was rapidly becoming a popular uprising against communism. In *L'Unità* of 26 October 1956, he wrote with unmistakable Stalinist accents:

> Tomorrow we may even discuss our differences ... Today we must defend the socialist revolution ... When the guns of the counter-revolutionaries are in operation one must be on one or the other side of the barricades. There is no third camp.[105]

Thus, the Hungarian events stopped in its tracks any chance of an emancipation of the Western communist parties from Moscow. They could not heed Denis Healey's painfully accurate prediction made in 1957: 'Within a generation at most, the French and Italian communist parties will either break their ties with Moscow or shrivel into insignificance.'[106]

It was easier for Togliatti and his closest advisers to revise the party line on pluralism and democracy than to distance themselves from the USSR. Here, it was not a question of innovating, but rather of restating more forcefully what had been official PCI policy: the commitment to a democratic road to socialism based on the Italian constitution, the central importance of a freely elected Parliament, the right of the minority to become the majority. At the same time, the traditional Marxist terminology of 'the dictatorship of the proletariat' was not explicitly abandoned, though it was used less frequently. The works of Antonio Gramsci, which had been published with the party's help immediately after the war, but which had not been adequately studied or well disseminated, became central to the future development of Italian communism.[107]

In adopting a less proletarian line, the PCI shared some of the principles of European revisionism. De-emphasizing the role of the working class was not the exclusive prerogative of social-democratic revisionism. It was the common property of all renovators and reformers of socialism, including those who sought to renew communism in the USSR. The history of socialism in the eastern part of Europe occasionally paralleled that of the western side. The late 1950s witnessed such a conjuncture: Khrushchev's ultimately unsuccessful attempt to modify the structures of the communist state converged strikingly with the great revisionist wave of the period.

After denouncing Stalin at the Twentieth Congress, Khrushchev launched a second revisionist offensive at the Twenty-second Congress (1961). This established two central principles:[108] first, communism could be built only on the basis of the effective development of the productive forces. The USSR had to become a science-oriented society; growth was more important than politics. This differed from the commitment to growth of the Stalin era, when modernization had to be propelled through sheer physical and quantitative effort and the hero was an 'ordinary' worker, Stakhanov, who, motivated by political devotion, inspired a massive collectivist commitment to economic development. This working-class-centred economic system had now to be replaced by a far more qualitative system, in which the new heroes would be the experts and the technical intelligentsia, the Soviet equivalent of Western managers: 'Not production for the sake of production, but production for the sake of Man is the sacred principle followed by the Party and the Soviet State in all activities.'[109]

Secondly, the 1961 Congress declared that the phase of the dictatorship of the proletariat had ended. The class nature of the USSR had to be redefined: the country was now a 'State of the whole people'.[110] Khrushchev had initially hoped to call the new phase the era of the 'withering away of the State' – Marx's own designation of post-capitalist society – but the anarchical undertones of the formula were resisted by Khrushchev's powerful opponents within the party. The phrase 'State of the whole people', used by the influential Finnish communist Otto Kuusinen a few years previously, was an acceptable compromise.[111]

The object of the Soviet reforms was the construction of a consumer society in peaceful competition with the USA. Khrushchev had realized that, unless communism offered the people it ruled the material benefits achieved by capitalism in the West, it would fail. In January 1961, Khrushchev called for a 'revolution' aimed at increasing the range of consumer goods produced, and attacked those still arguing in favour of priority for heavy industry. They were 'metal-eaters', as he called them, whose 'appetite for steel' would unbalance the Soviet economy to the detriment of pressing consumer needs. He warned that the failure to close the widening gap between consumer supply and demand would be 'fraught with dangerous consequences'.[112]

The wider role to be given to the technical intelligentsia, and the elimination of the central role of the working class in ideology, provided the starting-point for all subsequent attempts to reform communism, from the Prague Spring of 1968 to *perestroika* – attempts which all failed.

The PCF at first resisted following this trend. Unable and unwilling to criticize Khrushchev's 'revisionism', it eagerly distanced itself from that, more obvious, of its Italian counterparts. Roger Garaudy, the PCF delegate to the PCI's Eighth Congress (1956), wrote an attack of unusual severity in the theoretical monthly *Cahiers du communisme*, criticizing the whole conception of 'national roads to socialism', the PCI's insistence on the importance of the parliamentary road, and Togliatti's views on structural reforms.[113] Until the publication of Khrushchev's secret speech, the PCF barely reported even the veiled criticisms of Stalin which had begun to appear in the official Soviet press as early as 1953.[114] When Jacques Duclos, who had been at the Twentieth Congress of the CPSU with Thorez, and who was therefore acquainted with the secret speech, spoke about the Soviet Congress to communist activists assembled at the Salle Wagram in Paris on 9 March 1956, he concluded with overt praise of Stalin, 'whose achievements', he declared, amid enthusiastic applause, 'are inscribed in History and belong to the international working class movement'.[115] After the disclosure of the Secret Speech in the Western press, the PCF formally accepted both the veracity of Khrushchev's criticisms of Stalin (it could hardly have done otherwise), and their interpretative framework: that what went wrong was the cult of Stalin and the excessive power concentrated in his hands. The fundamental structures of Soviet society, however, continued to be regarded as healthy and stable.[116]

The PCF could be flexible on matters of tactics and strategy. When it came to ideology, however, it refused to yield to what it saw as a dangerous tendency towards innovation. It nailed its colours to the mast of rigid fundamentalism. This did not survive de-Stalinization: soon Garaudy was fronting an ideological revision, in the shape of Marxist humanism, in order to facilitate an alliance with the socialists and *la main tendue* to progressive Catholics. Garaudy himself turned, much later, to Christianity and, even later, to Islam. In the meantime, the PCF appeared resistant to change. The chosen ground for this was the great pauperization debate.[117]

This was a classic theme. Marx had explained that the workers were increasingly exploited as capitalism developed. Whether he meant that this determined a declining share of a growing national wealth for the workers, or that their poverty would increase in *absolute* terms, is a controversy I shall refrain from entering. Suffice it to say that all revisionist debates, beginning with Bernstein *contra* Kautsky, took this as one of their major themes.

Was it purely out of respect for tradition that the PCF sought to commit itself to the belief that the wages of workers under capitalism were declining in real terms? I think not. The commitment to socialism has to be based on the belief that capitalism could not resolve the fundamental problems of humanity; otherwise, a reformist strategy would be perfectly justified. The logic behind the PCF's position was that if it could be demonstrated that capitalism benefited the workers, though not as much as it benefited the capitalists, then any further political struggle could be limited to the distribution of resources. For the PCF, a quintessentially working-class party committed to revolution in the long term, it was important to believe and assert that the standard of living of the working class could not be secure under capitalism. To some extent, the context for this ideological struggle had already been established by the supporters of capitalism. Americanism, the consumer society, the glorification of free enterprise, were all grounded on the underlying assumption that 'things would get better and better'. Revisionists agreed that post-war capitalism, far from being stagnant, could deliver the goods. Some of the credit for this, they believed, belonged to the Left, without whose strength and vigilance a less than fair share of the national bounty would have been distributed to the majority of the population.

It was not just its retrograde ideology which led the PCF to believe that the absolute impoverishment of the working class was inevitable under capitalism. The real nucleus of the debate was the future of capitalism, its growth and development. This is why the PCF initiated and continued the pauperization debate, from its opening salvos in 1955 through to the late

1950s. The intervening events of 1956 – Khrushchev's speech and de-Stalinization, Suez and Hungary – did nothing to modify the line, though softer tones were adopted at the beginning of 1956, during the PCF's honeymoon with the Mollet government, and while the impact of the Twentieth Congress of the CPSU was still being digested – which is probably why pauperization was not mentioned at the central committee meeting of February 1956.[118] Though it is tempting to do so, one should not dismiss the position of the French communists as a mere reflection of their exceptional determination to ignore reality: inequalities in French society *were* very marked and one-quarter of French workers earned less than the official minimum wage.[119]

The journal of the SFIO, though not the party itself, took this apparently purely doctrinal controversy very seriously and devoted a series of articles to proving the opposite of what the PCF was asserting – namely, that the French working class *was* better off in absolute terms than *at the beginning of the century* (something even Thorez did not deny), and that the gap between rich and poor had narrowed (here the PCF disagreed).[120]

The divisions on this question reflected fairly accurately the divisions within the Left throughout Europe: on the whole socialists and social democrats, whether Marxist or not, abandoned any belief in inevitable misery; while Thorez's positions were supported by nearly all communists in Eastern and Western Europe. The most important exception was the Italian Communist Party, for which the pauperization thesis was an instance of obsolete thinking.

The rigidity manifested in the pauperization debate does not mean that the PCF was left totally unperturbed by Khrushchev's revelations or by the events of Hungary, not to speak of the advent of Gaullism in 1958. Concessions to de-Stalinization were made. Thus, towards the end of the 1950s, the 'aesthetic' theories of Andrei Zhdanov and his particular brand of socialist realism were repudiated, while, at its Fifteenth Congress (1959), the party called for unity of action with Catholics, though this was still couched in the unmistakably *ouvrièriste* and ornate language of the PCF: 'As previously, Communist workers offer the hand of friendship to the Catholic workers, their brothers in misery' – as if the French working class was still under the heel of nineteenth-century capitalism.[121]

In spite of these modifications, the Twentieth Congress of the CPSU impacted very little on the PCF, while it encouraged the PCI to develop its own variety of communism. It had no significant effect on the socialist parties, with one major exception: the Italian PSI. The invasion of Hungary and the de-Stalinization process convinced its leader, Pietro Nenni, that the time had come for a decisive break with the communists. The revisionism of the Italian socialists was therefore not determined by a succession of electoral defeats (as was the case with the British and the Germans), but by the realization that the alliance with the PCI was unprofitable from every point of view: it sentenced the socialists to being junior partners of the communists and, by separating them so clearly from the ruling Christian democrats, made their entry into a coalition almost impossible.

Looking back on these events from the vantage point of the present – the prerogative of historians and the source of their superiority over politicians – it becomes apparent that revisionism, at least in Italy and Germany, cannot be attributed solely to ideology or the pursuit of electoral gains. Its ultimate purpose was that of legitimizing the socialists and social democrats, so as to enable them to become coalition partners of their respective Christian-democratic parties. This was not so evident then; nor was it held to be desirable by a majority of socialists. Thus, among Italian socialists there was considerable opposition to any switch in alliance.

Nenni himself had played a double game for a number of years. He always sought to keep his alliance options open even while he published enthusiastic accounts of his trips to the Soviet Union, for which he obtained the Stalin Peace Prize in 1951. His commitment to the communists was based on his belief that it was the division of the Left which had permitted Mussolini to take over in the 1920s (belief which has little basis in historical evidence). Khrushchev's revelations led Nenni to seek to restore friendly relations with the breakaway Italian Social Democratic Party, a solid ally of the Christian democrats since 1947. The first step was made by meeting its leader, Giuseppe Saragat, at the Alpine resort of Pralognan on 25 August 1956. Breaking with the communists, however, took more than a few meetings. The PSI Central Committee of September 1956 rejected any moves towards reunification with the social democrats, thus dashing Nenni's efforts. Again, in October 1958, the Central Committee turned down Nenni's report, accepting instead that of Tullio Vecchietti, the leader of the party's Left faction. Only in 1959, at the Naples Congress, did Nenni finally prevail; the long march towards power could start. It took another four years before he could sit on the ministerial benches of the Chamber of Deputies.

This shift to the right was not associated with any formal revision of party doctrine. At an international socialist conference in March 1960, Nenni himself openly castigated the revisionism of the SPD at Bad Godesberg and Gaitskell's fight to replace Clause Four.[122] Nevertheless, there was an innovative flowering of intellectual life within the PSI, to which many ex-communist intellectuals contributed significantly. Antonio Giolitti, who had left the PCI in 1957, and Riccardo Lombardi, who had been a leader of the radical Action Party during the war, for instance, while using the Marxist language characteristic of the Italian Left, followed in the footsteps of other European revisionists. They dismissed the obsession with the ownership of the means of production, and criticized the Marxist definition of the state as the instrument of the ruling class. The state machine could be used to regulate the private sector of industry in the interests of the working class and the majority of the population.[123]

Italian PSI revisionists such as Lombardi and Giolitti, unlike those in the rest of Europe, belonged to the left wing of their party and advocated nationalization and planning. From the point of view of orthodox Marxism, their benchmark, this was a revision in its own right: nationalization and planning in a capitalist state entailed a belief in the possibility of reforming advanced capitalism. There was also an important 'national element'. Italian capitalism was seen as backward; socialist reformists wanted to transform Italy into a modern state. This did not mean just the development of a consumer society – something which was was occurring anyway – but the erection of proper educational and economic infrastructures, as well as a welfare system. Nationalization and planning were conceived as instruments for achieving these ends.

This was not very different from what the Italian communists were advocating, and both sides used the term 'structural reforms' to distance themselves from the reforms of mere reformists (this term was then being used in a pejorative sense in Italian political debates). The real difference was that the communists believed that 'real' structural reforms could not be achieved without their party in government. Pietro Ingrao insisted that structural reforms had to be 'organic', and attacked Giolitti and Lombardi for conceiving of reforms 'as so many "bits" separate or separable each from the other ... An action which remains sectoral, a single reform, even the most daring is destined to fail. What is necessary is *a policy of reforms*, gradual but organic.'[124] Lombardi and his comrades assumed that Italian society was made up of relatively distinct advanced and backward segments, a modern north and a undeveloped south: modernization would be achieved through a systematic attack on backwardness. The communists believed that there was an organic link between the two: the north was developed *because* the south was backward; the south funded northern growth by providing cheap labour and an open market:

> The devastation of agriculture and the South has been and is the first condition (and not a marginal and hence eliminable consequence) of a rapid process of capitalist concentration and centralization which has allowed monopoly capital to enlarge its economic and political dominance.[125]

The Italian communists turned out to be right in their intellectual critique, but were never able to produce a coherent plan of action. They wisely refrained from denouncing their former socialist comrades as traitors. Togliatti wanted to keep his options open. Should the PSI's march towards power fail to pay off, he wanted to leave open the possibility of a reconciliation. Should it succeed, it was important to have friends in government who could be influenced and prepare the terrain for eventual communist participation.

Such subtlety did not mark the policy of the French Communist Party; yet it is important to resist the temptation to dismiss it as dogmatic and sectarian. During the campaign against the EDC, the PCF was able to find allies and create a host of front organizations, even at the cost of resorting to a ludicrous juxtaposition of broad, general goals and immediate aims as in the *Comité national paysan pour la sauvegarde de la paix et de l'agriculture française* (National Farmers' Committee for the Defence of Peace and French Agriculture). The party, in spite of its overt working-class style and image, followed a policy of great ententes; promoted the massive peace campaigns of the early 1950s; and was the beacon round which the most distinguished French intellectuals rallied, from the once despised Sartre to Simone de Beauvoir, Frédéric Joliot-Curie, Paul Eluard and Pablo Picasso, to celebrities of the cinema such as Simone Signoret, Gérard Philippe and Yves Montand, to the cream of the elite Ecole Nationale d'Administration. Why was such an apparently undeserving party the receptacle of so much prestigious support?[126] Among the likely reasons canvassed are the latent anti-Americanism of the French intelligentsia, further strengthened by the humiliation of France's collapse in 1940 and its subsequent rescue by the 'Anglo-Saxons'.[127] This 'intellectual nationalism' must certainly have played a role, though it does not explain why Sartre and company opted for fellow-travelling on the Left rather than on the Right, where a cultural dislike for all things American happily co-existed with a pronounced anti-Sovietism. Could it be that the issue of international peace was believed to be of such importance that many intellectuals felt they had to support the only party ready to fight for it resolutely? Not only in France, but throughout Europe, intellectuals marched for peace and signed petitions and wrote articles: in Italy, Alberto Moravia, Italo Calvino and Danilo Dolci, in Britain Bertrand Russell, Sir Julian Huxley, J. B. Priestley and A. J. P. Taylor; in Germany, pastor Martin Niemöller, Heinrich Böll and Günter Grass. They were in the forefront of a mass radicalism of the middle classes, which would mark the organized Left for the rest of the century.

In Britain, or Germany, these radical intellectuals might have been able, with some difficulty, to find a home in the Labour Party or the SPD. But in France? In the France of the Fourth Republic a 'dissident' intellectual could not turn to the SFIO, which had more in common with the centre than with the Left. The Communist Party thus remained the only option. In the semi-clerical Italy of the 1950s, the situation was similar. The PSI, at least until 1956, was simply shadowing a large and self-confident Communist Party. It may not be so surprising, then, if politicized intellectuals – and it was difficult to be an apolitical one so soon after a world war against fascism – turned to the communists *faute de mieux*. In politics it is difficult to choose one's friends; even when, as in France, they were the same kind of angry prolet-arians who, in other countries, had made the life of dissident intellectuals miserable and, in some instances, shorter. In a series of articles in *Les Temps Modernes* (1952–54), Jean-Paul Sartre more than hinted that his admiration for the PCF (which would not outlast the Soviet invasion of Hungary) was partly a response to the shoddy quality of the other goods on offer:

In the France of today, the only class with a doctrine is the working class, the only one whose 'particularism' is in full harmony with the interests of the nation; a great party represents it, the only one which has included in its programme the safeguarding of democratic institutions, the re-establishment of national sovereignty, and the defence of peace, the only one which pays attention to economic rebirth and an increase in purchasing power, the only one, in fact which is *alive*, which crawls with life when the others are crawling with worms.[128]

The French Communist Party obtained the support of so many intellectuals because it was, unmistakably, the party of peace, rather than because it was the party of the working class. All this goodwill was lost after Hungary because, by supporting armed aggression against a country which sought independence, the PCF lost any credibility as the party of peace.

Though dogmatic and intransigent in matters of doctrine and in its support for the USSR, the PCF was able to be quite flexible in matters of tactics. It voted for the Mendès-France government in June 1954 and supported it on a number of occasions.[129] It did the same for the socialist leader Guy Mollet, a staunch anti-communist, when he became Prime Minister in January 1956 and, on 12 March, voted to accord him special powers over Algeria, to the dismay of many of its supporters.[130] This move was justified by the leadership as a tactic to prevent an understanding between Mollet and the Right.[131] Thorez himself explained in *L'Humanité* (27 March 1956) that, as support for the SFIO was the main priority, the party did not want 'to sacrifice the whole for the part'.[132] The PCF was genuinely ambivalent towards Algerian independence in a way it had not been towards the Vietminh in their struggle against French colonialism in Indo-China. It much preferred a formula whereby Algeria would have autonomy within the French Union to one providing outright independence.[133] This made it easier for national domestic consideration to prevail over anti-colonial principles. The PCF did not wish to become unpopular with the working class (which was patriotic), wanted to maintain some sort of relationship with the SFIO (which was deeply entangled in the Algerian tragedy), was, in any case, suspicious of Algerian nationalism and, after 1958, was reluctant to damage de Gaulle's international standing as a result of his anti-American policies.[134] Thorez, in his speech to the Fourteenth Congress of the PCF (July 1956), talked of rejecting 'colonial relations' in Algeria and the other colonies, but did not come out in clear favour of independence, though the right of Algeria to be independent was never denied.[135] It was only after 1959 that the PCF decisively supported the recognition of Algerian sovereignty, without ever offering the slightest explanation for its past wavering; but then political parties seldom do that. This is not to fail to recognize the merit of the PCF in being the only party to protest against the repressions and torture inflicted by the French authorities on the Algerians. It should not be invalidated because it chose to ignore similar events in Budapest, or, even worse, to justify them.

Throughout this period the French socialists behaved in a manner barely distinguishable from the mainstream centre parties of the Fourth Republic. Once it had adopted a position of equidistance from the extremism of 'Left' (the communists) and 'Right' (the Gaullists), it could not do otherwise. What it could have done, however, had it possessed intelligence and radicalism, was to support in a far more decisive manner the most reform-oriented French government of the 1950s: the Mendès-France government of 1954. This resolved the Indo-China conflict by withdrawing, and was envisaging major economic and social reforms. Mollet did not support Mendès-France for personal and sectarian political reasons: he feared his popularity and distrusted a radical who was not a socialist.[136] To consider the French Communist Party as 'the millstone around the neck of social progress in France', because of its obstructionist parliamentary tactics, as Maurice Larkin has written, is to discount the fact that the sectarianism of the communists was more than matched by that of the socialists.[137]

It would be a difficult task to trace the ideology of the SFIO. Unlike the Labour Party or the SPD, it had no strongly held views embedded in programmes or charters. By 1951 it was devoid of ideas.[138] Guy Mollet, who led the party for twenty-two years, left no work of political analysis. This would not be surprising in Britain or even Germany. It is in France, where politicians often wish to appear intellectual and publish volumes of political 'philosophy'. Mollet wisely resisted the temptation. His anti-communism was very strongly held: he would usually refer to communists in public as 'the Bolsheviks' and, in private, as *les cocos*.[139] It was easy for him to resist all the overtures of Thorez, thus further exacerbating the sectarianism of the PCF. No socialist revisionism of a Crosland, Gaitskell or Bad Godesberg type could be expected from Mollet. There were, of course, thinkers in the SFIO: for instance, Jules Moch, a former minister, follower of Léon Blum, anti-European, opponent of the EDC, pro-disarmament, who thought the SFIO should abandon its ideological commitment to the class struggle as it had done in practice; or André Philip, author of *Le Socialisme trahi* (1957) and *Les Socialistes* (1967), who advocated industrial democracy and self-management. Neither had much influence within the SFIO.[140] Philip, expelled in 1957, formed the small and electorally insignificant Parti Socialiste Autonome (later the Parti Socialiste Unifié). The SFIO allowed Moch to set up a 'Study Group on Doctrine' to bring the party 'face to face with the social evolution made possible by modern science and by the advance of socialism'. But nothing important came of it.[141]

One might have expected that a leadership such as that of Mollet, which piloted the SFIO downward from nearly one-quarter of the vote in 1945 to less than 13 per cent in 1962, would have had abundant cause for thorough-going revisionism. But the revisionist path was never followed. Those who wanted to renew the party found, very soon, that it was not a place for them. It remained curiously committed in theory to a staunchly Marxistic doctrine, inclusive of odd references to the dictatorship of the proletariat, while having very few workers among its members and pursuing a practice which seemed totally devoid of socialist content. Blum's old distinction between the 'exercise of power' and the 'seizure of power' (see chapter 3) was the ideological cover for this: power had to be exercised in whatever way was possible, while waiting for the time for the 'real' seizure.[142]

When Mollet became prime minister in 1956, he increased both pensions and the length of paid holidays, and introduced sweeping reforms in France's African colonies. In foreign relations, however, the Mollet government stepped up the war in Algeria and launched the insane Suez affair with relish. The official SFIO line was that Algeria was simply not ready for independence, and that the only alternative to the repressive measures undertaken by the socialist-appointed resident minister in Algeria, the notorious Robert Lacoste, was one of massive extermination, reprisals and napalm.[143] Initially, Mollet had looked favourably on Algerian independence. He changed his mind when he visited Algeria as prime minister and realized that the French *pieds noirs* were not rich colonialists, but ordinary working-class people (i.e. voters) – though, of course, being in Algeria they were, as André Philip put it, 'the top of the bottom' and had Arab women as domestic servants.[144]

Mollet's often reiterated comparison of Nasser with Hitler, subsequently used by innumerable others about countless others, served a dual purpose: it allowed the SFIO to avoid understanding Egypt, Nasser and Middle Eastern affairs generally; and it gave the appearance of a righteous anti-fascist struggle to what was in reality the shoddy conclusion of French and British imperial pretensions.

Algeria and Suez were the two most significant disasters of the contemptible history of the Fourth Republic. They also marked the end of the SFIO as a real political force, although its agony would last for years. After 1957, the party lost all effective political power – the only reason for its existence. When de Gaulle returned to power in 1958, the SFIO leadership, though it opposed him at first, promptly accepted ministerial positions and called on its supporters to rally round the general in the September 1958 referendum. After a four-year flirtation with Gaullism (the final break occurred in 1962), the SFIO relinquished power for ever. Only in the 1970s did French socialism re-emerge in an altered guise and with a new name.

At first, the PCF stood alone against Gaullism and what it called *le pouvoir personnel*, thus returning to the ghetto it had tried to leave. The political price paid was high: a significant proportion of the one and half million voters lost at the 1958 general election were *paysants* and women; this left the party a more male and working-class organization than before, at a time when a less narrowly proletarian approach was required.[145] Furthermore, the PCF was unable to understand the significance of the new Gaullist regime. For years the PCF had considered the French bourgeoisie as a mere appendage of US imperialism, as a class which had lost its sense of destiny, and as the betrayer of the nation. This was the ideological rationale behind the PCF's adoption of French nationalist rhetoric. But de Gaulle's antagonism towards *les anglo-saxons* was such that he could hardly be branded an American puppet. What was he, then? Initially, the party debated whether Gaullism was pure fascism or a dictatorship paving the way for fascism. Roger Garaudy wrote that 'Gaullism, like fascism before it, reinforces all the privileges of capitalism and disarms the working class ... Moreover, de Gaulle develops a national demagoguery typical of all forms of fascism.' [146] The PCF eventually settled for defining Gaullism as a modern form of non-fascist totalitarianism.[147] Its utter confusion before such a 'national' phenomenon as Gaullism stemmed, as its own historians later admitted, from a strategic and theoretical blindness.[148] This led the party to regard everything new as the repetition – in a somewhat distorted form – of something that had occurred in the past. By being above novelty, the PCF condemned itself to wallow in its own past mistakes.

Clearly, in the 1950s, France was badly served by its two Left parties. One, the PCF, was an ideologically sclerotic formation led by one of the most undiscerning communists in Europe, Maurice Thorez; the other, the SFIO, was distinguished, if that is the word, by a mixture of mindless moralism and opportunistic authoritarianism, without either the ethical dimension of Léon Blum or the shrewdness of François Mitterrand.

The disarray of the French Left at the close of the decade was, however, part of a more general phenomenon. Outside of its Scandinavian enclaves, European socialism seemed to have reached a dead end. By the end of the 1950s, Western Europe was dominated by Christian democracy and various forms of 'enlightened conservatism'. The diverse attempts at revisionism were the most obvious symptom of a major crisis of direction: even at its best (Bad Godesberg and Crosland), revisionism proceeded mainly in the negative – that is, by seeking to abandon ideological baggage which appeared to have become dysfunctional. While the defenders of orthodoxy remained committed to the vision of the final goal, no grand new ideas appeared on the horizon of European socialism. It was thus ill-equipped to meet the challenge of power which opened up in the 1960s in Britain, Germany and Italy; unprepared to face the strategic implications of the revival of working-class militancy; surprised at the reawakening of Marxism among the intelligentsia; disconcerted by the new radicalism expressed by feminism; and unaware of how the growth of interdependence was leading to the decline of the nation-state.

Revisionists could never understand the difference between watering down traditional socialism and establishing a new framework. Unable to achieve the latter, they remained content with the former. Over successive decades, the parties of the West European Left, socialists as well as communists, made no major conceptual advances.

PART FOUR

The Perplexing Sixties: 'Something in the Air'

CHAPTER ELEVEN

The Return of the Left

Prosperity

THROUGHOUT the 1960s capitalism continued its apparently unstoppable development. In comparison with the 1950s, productivity increased in all democratic Western European countries, with the exception of Austria (from 5.3 to 4.7 per cent) and West Germany (from 5.2 to 4.8 per cent), though they both retained a high rating. Italy had the highest growth in productivity (5.3 per cent) and Britain the lowest (2.5 per cent).[1] The growth of GDP per capita was even higher in the second half of the decade than in the first (except for Italy).[2]

Wages increased and so did profits. Workers, as well as capitalists, prospered. During the 1960s, full employment – one of the central goals of the Left, and once believed by socialists to be incompatible with capitalism – became a reality in all democratic West European countries (see Table 11.1). Unemployment was usually less than 2 per cent; it began to increase only after 1970. Italy, however, exhibited a very pronounced regional gap: by the early 1960s, the northern regions had reached full employment, but in the south there was still widespread poverty and joblessness. Japan, Australia and New Zealand conformed to the West European pattern, while the USA and Canada followed a distinct North American cycle, characterized by a much higher level of unemployment than in Europe (generally above 5 per cent).

Was this high level of employment due to the increased presence of socialists in government? Attempts to establish any correlation between growth, unemployment, productivity and the political weight of the Left in government have proved futile. Policies devised by one government may only have an impact later. It is not really possible to disentangle the percentage increase in growth due to government policies from that due to other factors. Political parties in government tend to claim for themselves the credit for positive economic indicators, while blaming international factors when the trend is negative. Furthermore, it is not certain that a country's prosperity can be measured in terms of growth and productivity (unemployment is a better indicator). Infant mortality rates provide a more satisfactory index of prosperity, on the grounds that the 'good society' is one which is at least able to ensure a high rate of survival to its newly born.

As Table 11.2 shows, the trend is almost uniform and long-term, though

Table 11.1 Unemployment as a percentage of the total labour force, 1960–73

	1960	1965	1970	1973
Austria	2.3	1.9	1.4	1.0
Belgium	3.3	1.5	1.8	2.2
Denmark	2.1	1.0	0.7	0.9
Finland	1.4	1.4	1.9	2.3
France	1.8	1.3	2.4	2.6
Holland	1.2	1.0	1.6	3.9
Italy	3.9	5.0	4.9	5.7
Norway	2.3	1.7	1.5	1.5
Sweden	1.7	1.2	1.5	2.5
UK	2.2	2.2	3.1	2.9
West Germany	1.0	0.5	0.6	1.0

Source: Angus Maddison, *Phases of Capitalist Development*, Oxford University Press, Oxford 1982, pp. 207–8.

Table 11.2 Infant mortality per 1,000 (including stillbirths)

	1935–39	1950	1960	1970	1975	Decrease 1960–75 (%)
Austria	87	88.0	52.7	36.1	29.0	-67.05
Belgium	83	76.9	46.3	32.7	24.4	-68.27
Denmark	64	48.2	34.1	23.0	17.1	-64.52
Finland	68	62.4	36.4	21.3	15.3	-75.48
France	70	72.0	45.0	31.7	24.9	-65.42
Germany	72	78.0	49.3	33.9	27.6	-64.62
Holland	–[b]	44.9	31.7	23.6	18.4	-59.02
Italy	103	97.1	69.0	44.8	31.8	-67.25
Norway	40	44.6	33.0	23.5	19.2	-56.95
Sweden	43	41.3	30.5	23.8	21.4	-48.18
UK[a]	56	52.9	42.0	31.4	25.7	-51.42

Notes: [a] England and Wales only. [b] Data not comparable.

Source: for 1935–9: B. R. Mitchell, 'Statistical Appendix 1920–1970', in Carlo M. Cipolla (ed.), *The Fontana Economic History of Europe, Contemporary Economies*, Vol. 2, Collins/Fontana, Glasgow 1976, pp. 648–53; for 1950–75; P. Flora et al., *State, Economy and Society in Western Europe 1815–1975. A Data Handbook*, Campus Verlag, Macmillan Press and St James Press, Frankfurt, London and Chicago 1987, Vol. 2, chapter 6.

it accelerates in the 1960–75 period. Infant mortality clearly declines in all eleven countries. It also declined in Spain, Portugal and Greece and, until the mid-1970s, in all communist states. The percentage decrease in infant mortality is obviously greater in countries which had a higher rate in 1950, such as

Table 11.3 Country ranking: lowest infant mortality, 1950–75

1950	1975
Sweden	Finland
Norway	Denmark
Holland	Holland
Denmark	Norway
UK	Sweden
Finland	Belgium
France	France
Belgium	UK
W. Germany	W. Germany
Austria	Austria
Italy	Italy

Italy and Austria. Table 11.3 shows that there are few significant changes in the league table, apart from the marked Finnish improvement. The general decline is due to a multiplicity of factors and unlikely to have been much affected by government policies. The obvious causes of a decline in infant mortality – better nutrition, improvements in hygiene, vaccination programmes – can be traced to growing economic prosperity, coupled with general welfare measures which were never the property of a single ideology.[3] It would be inconsistent to assert that the good performance of the Scandinavian countries was due to social democratic hegemony, the successes of Austria and Finland to consensual politics, and those of Italy to Christian democratic rule.

The recognition that 'the system' was able to deliver growth, jobs and a healthier environment constitutes the most cogent reason for the acceptance (in practice, if not in theory) by the parties of the Left that, at least for the short and medium term, there was no question of breaking with the capitalist system. When socialist parties talked about 'socialist policies' or 'socialist measures', they did not intend this to denote a strategy to bring about the downfall of capitalism. For nostalgic, ideological or political reasons, or in order to maintain party unity, some parties retained a formal commitment to Marxism or to the collective ownership of the means of production; or, at least, to the assumption that socialism was an end-state, a form of society which would be radically different from capitalism. For practical purposes, anti-capitalism was abandoned.

In the circumstances, it could not have been otherwise. Two fundamental political parameters circumscribed the Left: political democracy and economic prosperity.

POLITICAL DEMOCRACY During this period left-wing parties had no major demands for a radical transformation of political institutions. With universal suffrage they had achieved representative democracy. Vestiges of the past, such as monarchies and 'unfair' upper chambers, now devoid of major powers, seemed less important. In electoral politics, the long-term goal lost significance. The collective mind of all political parties had to be concentrated on winning elections, cementing alliances with other parties, and on convincing the electorate that they could resolve the immediate problems of the country. Once in power, a party had to prove itself to be an efficient administrator of what existed, and a reformer of what needed to be changed. These constraints proved to be formidable, more so for a radical party than for a conservative one. The latter is, by definition, a party of consolidation rather than change. Rapid *political* change tends to be supported only at a time of crisis, while at all other times prudence and caution are mandatory. Rapid *economic and social* change may occur, but usually not as the intended consequence of political decisions.

ECONOMIC PROSPERITY   Poverty or the expectation of poverty had become confined to a small and dwindling minority. The underclass, as a class, was expected to vanish. Full employment had become the norm. All parties were committed to it on principle and regarded it as a clear policy priority. The majority of the electorate could be enticed to vote for parties promising to protect and improve existing standards of living, but not for prophets who proclaimed that the situation was likely to deteriorate so far that some momentous political change would be necessary. 'Utopian catastrophism', or the belief in the inevitability of either disaster or revolution, had lost credibility. No party with a significant electoral following could hold this position any longer.

The result was the establishment of a 'conservative' consensus which held that the political system required no change and that the economic arrangements of society called for no fundamental reforms. This situation did not result from successful conservative policies, but from capitalism itself. High growth, by enabling an increase in the prosperity of the majority, diminished the demand for the redistribution of wealth and power. As Charles Maier noted: 'The concept of growth as a surrogate for redistribution is the great conservative idea of the last generation.'[4]

Socialist parties were thus in an impasse. They aspired to redistribute power away from the impersonal forces of the market towards ordinary people. They sought to help the poor, establish economic and social justice, expand opportunities for those who could not obtain them through the market. Little of this could be done without accepting economic growth – in other words, capitalist growth – as the overarching priority. The constraints of democratic electoral politics compelled them to do so.

The great political grievances of the beginning of the century – grinding poverty, brutal exploitation, lack of democracy – whose return was still feared

Table 11.4 Share of the vote of the main parties of the left in Western Europe, 1960–73

	1960	1961	1962	1963	1964	1965	1966	1967	1968	1969	1970	1971	1972	1973
Austria	—	—	44.0	—	—	—	42.6	—	—	—	48.4	50.0	—	—
Belgium	—	36.7	—	—	—	28.3	—	—	28.0	—	—	27.2	—	—
Denmark:														
SD	42.1	—	—	—	41.9	—	38.2	—	34.2	—	—	37.3	—	25.6
SPP	6.1	—	—	—	5.8	—	10.9	—	6.1	—	—	9.1	—	6.0
Finland:														
SD	—	—	19.5	—	—	—	27.2	—	—	—	23.4	—	25.8	—
SKDL	—	—	22.0	—	—	—	21.2	—	—	—	16.6	—	17.0	—
France:														
PS	—	—	20.3	—	—	—	—	–18.9	16.5	—	—	—	—	19.2
PCF	—	—	21.8	—	—	—	—	22.5	20.0	—	—	—	—	21.4
Holland	—	—	—	28.0	—	—	—	23.6	—	—	—	24.6	27.3	—
Italy:														
PSI	—	—	—	13.8	—	—	—	—	14.5	—	—	—	9.6	—
PCI	—	—	—	25.3	—	—	—	—	27.0	—	—	—	27.2	—
Norway:														
Lab	—	46.8	—	—	—	43.1	—	—	—	46.5	—	—	—	35.3
SPP	—	—	—	—	—	—	—	—	—	—	—	—	—	11.2
Sweden	47.8	—	—	—	47.3	—	—	—	50.1	—	45.3	—	—	43.6
UK	—	—	—	—	44.1	—	48.1	—	—	—	43.1	—	—	—
West Germany	—	36.2	—	—	—	39.3	—	—	—	42.7	—	—	45.8	—

Note: The results for Austria, Belgium, Denmark (SD), Finland (SD), France (PS), West Germany, Holland, Italy (PSI), Norway (Lab), Sweden, and the United Kingdom are for the socialist, social democratic or labour parties. In Denmark and Norway the SPP stands for the leftist Socialist People's Party; in Finland the SKDL is a coalition of Communists and their allies; in Italy the PSI results for the 1968 election are those for the Partito Socialista Unificato (the short-lived union of the PSI with the Social Democratic Party).

at the end of the Second World War, had been eliminated for the majority. Though difficult to establish with precision, it may nevertheless be argued that this success would not have been achieved without the pressures of socialists, communists, trade unionists and all those gathered under the banners of anti-capitalism. It does not follow, however, that the political beneficiaries of this process were the parties of the Left. Having been reformed, capitalism had become tolerable. The left-wing 'extremists' who argued that 'you cannot reform capitalism', remained a frustrated minority. Their vociferous agitation constituted, at best, simply another pressure towards the improvement of the system.

The authentically reformist majority of the socialist movement played according to the rules of the game. It acquired an optimistic belief in Keynesian 'fine-tuning' of the economy. In so doing, it forgot what 'both Marx and Keynes had known: that capitalism was a dangerous and untamable beast that needed to be handled with the utmost caution.'[5] Nevertheless, in the 1960s – in marked contrast to the 1950s – socialists were often successful in achieving political power. The downturn in the economic cycle, and the increased credibility of the Left, were often all it took to propel socialists towards political power under the banner of steering the capitalist system back to its growth-oriented course. Proximity to the trade unions, later considered one of the main liabilities of the parties of Left, even played to their advantage: in a situation in which the unions were considered a powerful and irremovable interest group, the socialist parties were often regarded as more electable *because* they would be able to appease or control them.

Elections

In the midst of these changes, how did the parties of the Left perform? Table 11.4 shows electoral gains and losses. Neither necessarily reflects reflect the strength or influence of left-wing ideas.

One of the few significant generalizations that can be made is that the West European Left was able to attract, on average, 40 per cent of the voters. The proportion of parliamentary seats obtained by the Left increased slightly, from 33.4 per cent in 1960 to 39.3 per cent in 1971.[6] All this is consistent with the overall electoral results for 1948–60 and, as we shall see, for 1973–92. Only in four elections out of the forty-five held in 1960–73 did a *single party* of the Left achieve an overall majority in the main legislative chamber: in Austria (1971) and in Sweden (1968), when the SPÖ and the SAP just broke through 50 per cent of the poll; and in Britain in 1964 and 1966, thanks to the first-past-the-post electoral system. Meanwhile, a clear Left majority of seats was achieved only in Sweden in all elections of this period, thanks to the Communist Party; and in Norway (1961 and 1973) and Denmark (1966), thanks to the smaller Socialist People's Party.

The overall pattern in the 1960–73 period was therefore as follows:

A. 'PURE' LEFT GOVERNMENTS in which the socialists were either in power on their own or as a minority government supported by smaller left-wing parties:

Austria: After 1971.
Denmark: In 1964–67 and (supported by the SPP) 1967–68 and 1971–73.
Norway: Until 1965 and in 1971–72.
Sweden: 1960–76.
UK: 1964–70.

B. 'LEFT–CENTRE' COALITIONS in which socialists were the senior part-ners in government or heading minority governments supported by non-socialists; in all these instances the prime minister was a socialist.

Austria: 1970–71.
Belgium: 1973–74.
Denmark: Until 1964 and after 1971.
Finland: 1966–71 (socialists and communists in coalition with others).
Germany: After 1969.

C. 'CENTRE' COALITIONS in which the socialists were the junior partner or played a subordinate role.

Austria: Until 1966.
Belgium: 1961–66 and 1968–73.
Finland: Socialists in government after 1971 without the communists.
France: Socialists in government until 1962.
Germany: Grosse Koalition, 1966–69.
Holland: 1965–66.
Italy: Socialists in 'Centre-Left' government, 1963–72.

This pattern is shown in Table 11.5, where 'AB' represents years in which the Left is in power either on its own or as the dominant force in government, 'C' where it is in government but not dominant and 'Out' when it is in opposition.

If taken too literally, this representation can be misleading. The role of the SPD in the Grosse Koalition of 1966–69 in Germany, or of the SPÖ in the Austrian equivalent until 1966 (both in category 'C'), was not as 'junior' as that of the Italian Socialist Party in a four-party coalition, in which the senior partner, the Christian democrats, had nearly three times the electoral weight of the socialists.

Initially, the decade saw the Left in power only in Scandinavia. Then there were significant breakthroughs all over Europe:

— In 1963 in Italy the socialists entered a centre–Left coalition with the Christian democrats.
— In 1964 the Labour Party won the British elections after thirteen years in opposition.

Table 11.5 Government participation of the parties of the Left, 1960–73

	1960	1961	1962	1963	1964	1965	1966	1967	1968	1969	1970	1971	1972	1973
Austria	C	C	C	C	C	C	C	Out	Out	Out	AB	AB	AB	AB
Belgium	Out	C	C	C	C	C	C	Out	C	C	C	C	C	AB
Denmark	AB	AB	AB	AB	AB	AB	AB	AB	AB	Out	Out	AB	AB	AB
Finland	Out	Out	Out	Out	Out	Out	AB	AB	AB	AB	AB	AB	C	C
France	C	C	C	Out	Out	Out	Out	Out	Out	Out	Out	Out	Out	Out
Holland	Out	Out	Out	Out	Out	C	C	Out	Out	Out	Out	Out	Out	Out
Italy	Out	Out	Out	C	C	C	C	C	C	C	Out	Out	Out	Out
Norway	AB	AB	AB	AB	AB	AB	Out	Out	Out	Out	AB	AB	AB	AB
Sweden	AB	AB	AB	AB	AB	AB	AB	AB	AB	AB	AB	AB	AB	AB
UK	Out	Out	Out	Out	AB	AB	AB	AB	AB	AB	Out	Out	Out	Out
West Germany	Out	Out	Out	Out	Out	Out	C	C	C	AB	AB	AB	AB	AB

Codes: AB = Left dominant in government; C = Left junior partner in government; Out = Left in opposition.

— In 1966 the SPD joined the government for the first time in the post-war period and, in 1969, Willy Brandt became prime minister of an SPD-dominated coalition with the FDP – the first social-democratic chancellor of Germany since Hermann Müller (1930).

— In 1966 in Finland a 'Popular Front' government was established with both social democrats and communists in power.

— In 1970 the Austrian socialists formed a government without the Christian democrats.

In some instances, notably in Britain and Austria, political power was the result of electoral gains. But on the whole the chief determinant of the advance of the Left lay in its ability to form alliances with other parties. Moderation in politics gained the parties of the Left allies as well as voters. The relatively proportional nature of most electoral systems compelled social-ist parties to seek an accommodation with the centre. But a 'convergence' towards the centre manifested itself even in Britain, where the electoral system presents an effective barrier to any aspiring new nationwide parties. This ensured that the Labour Party would not be by-passed to its left, leaving it free to pursue centrist voters without fear of being deserted by its leftist supporters. Thus, even the Labour Party, like its continental counterparts, was attracted towards the centre.

Opposition

Throughout the 1960s socialists in government effected no changes of great magnitude. Table 11.6, which lists the figures for central government taxation for 1960–75, may provide an illustration of this. The differences in taxation levels do not appear to correlate strongly with the presence of socialists in government: for instance, 'social-democratic' Sweden imposes high taxes, but so does relatively conservative Holland, where the Labour Party was out of power for virtually the whole of the 1960s. Perhaps the trend matters more than the level. Do taxes go up when the socialists are in power? Here too it is impossible to generalize. The entry of the PSI into the Italian government (in 1963) made no difference to the very low levels of taxation in Italy. As for the Belgian PSB/BSP, its presence or absence from power did not affect the rate of increase of taxation, the steepest in our table. The increase in Austrian taxation occurred mainly in the period of coalition, not in that of single-party government, whether of the Right (1966–70) or the Left (after 1970). In Norway taxation increased, though by a small proportion, when the Labour Party was out of power (1966–70). In Britain it was the reverse: taxation did increase under Labour, though to just below the level it had been under the Conservatives in 1957.

What matters, it could be argued, is whether the presence of socialists in power affects the distribution of government expenditure. Conservatives may

Table 11.6 General government taxes as a percentage of GDP

	1960	1965	1970	1975
Austria	17.9	20.4	21.4	21.9
Belgium	17.9	21.3	24.8	28.2
Denmark	18.7	22.8	30.3	26.7
Finland	17.1	16.8	19.4	20.6
France	20.8	22.7	22.3	21.9
Holland	22.2	23.3	25.2	26.8
Italy	16.9	16.6	16.4	16.6
Norway	18.2	18.9	19.2	20.6
Sweden	21.8	23.2	24.2	29.2
UK	23.2	22.7	31.0	27.4
West Germany	19.5	20.3	20.8	20.9

Source: Flora et al., *State, Economy and Society in Western Europe 1815–1975*, Vol. 1, p. 262.

spend more on law and order and defence, while socialists use public revenue for welfare services. Figure 11.1 shows the changes in the proportion of government expenditure upon defence and social services between 1960 and 1975. It illustrates quite clearly that expenditure on defence *as a proportion of total government spending* decreased in all countries, while expenditure on social services increased everywhere. The sharpest fall in percentage defence allocation occurred in (social-democratic) Sweden and Denmark, 'conservative' Holland and Belgium, Gaullist France, and in the United Kingdom (more in the seven years under Labour than in the eight under the Conservatives). Sweden easily topped the league for increase in proportion of social services expenditure, followed by conservative Holland and Gaullist France, as well as Belgium and Denmark. There is no significant relation between social-democratic hegemony and the increase or decrease in the proportion of money spent on the social services. This should not be a matter for perplexity: the political hue of the government is only one of many factors likely to influence the proportion of money spent on the social services. An increase in such spending is more likely to be related to the demand for social services than government ideology. Factors influencing this demand may range from the rise of novel social problems to changes in the demographic structure of the population.

Some social scientists have tried to use statistical methods to ascertain whether social-democratic governments make a difference. Douglas Hibbs has examined twelve European and North American nations and found that – in the 1960s – left-wing influence in governments brought about a situation of relatively higher inflation and lower unemployment than periods of conservative rule. His time series analyses of quarterly post-war unemployment

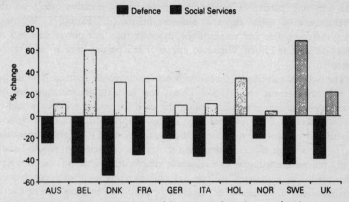

Note: For Italy and Norway the period is, respectively, 1960–73 and 1960–71.

Source: Figure drawn on the basis of figures in P. Flora et al., *State, Economy and Society in Western Europe 1815–1975. A Data Handbook*, Vol. 1: *The Growth of Mass Democracies and Welfare States*, Campus Verlag, Macmillan and St. James, Frankfurt, London and Chicago 1983, chapter 8.

Figure 11.1 Percentage change in public spending, 1960–75

data for the United Kingdom suggest that unemployment was driven downward by the Labour government of 1964–70.[7] None of this, however, holds true after 1973.

David Cameron, trying to account for the expansion of the 'public economy' (that portion of the nation's economic product which is consumed or distributed by all public authorities), has found that it positively correlated with the degree of left-wing control over the government and the degree of trade dependence of the economy.[8] Correlations are easily established; it is harder to explain them. The problem is that social democrats in the 1960s were stronger in many small countries than in big ones, and those small countries were more trade dependent than the big ones. Cameron tried to provide an overall explanation which rests on the following causal chain: small economies have a high degree of industrial concentration; this generates strong employers' associations as well as strong trade unions; strong trade unions lead to leftist governments.[9] This last claim is particularly implausible, and is implicitly recognized to be so by the author who adopts a fall-back position: whether or not social democrats are in power, what matters is whether the trade unions are strong; when this is the case, an unusually large increase in publicly funded income supplements will occur.[10] This may well be true, but it considerably weakens the case that parties make a difference, and suggests that what matters is the strength of the lobbies which put pressure on them.[11]

In Sweden, Walter Korpi provided statistical support for the assumption that left-wing parties in government have had a decisive effect on the development of social rights in sickness insurance.[12] Harold L. Wilensky, using different data and assumptions, asserted that 'left power' has had no effect on welfare effort: 'Whatever influence left parties have is indirect and weak.'[13]

The political sub-text of these controversies cannot be ignored: if welfarism or full employment are a Good Thing, and socialist governments are not instrumental in bringing them about, the case for voting socialist would be much weakened. I suspect that even if this proposition were to be demonstrated with the precision of the mathematical sciences – a highly improbable feat – not a single elector (other than the odd social scientist) would believe it and behave accordingly. The reason is simple: the parties of the Left have advocated and supported welfare reforms systematically and consistently, virtually from the moment of their birth. Nothing remotely similar can be said of conservative and liberal parties: no one would seriously suggest Bismarck's aim in uniting Germany was the development of a national insurance scheme. No one would suggest that Bismarck would have been interested in social insurance if the Left had not been a political threat. Catholic and Christian democratic parties are more credible 'welfare parties' than conservative ones, but even they do not match the consistency and coherence of the Left position on social spending and social rights. Thus, voters who decided to cast their ballot for a force committed to social welfare would almost certainly vote for a party of the Left. The more it is assumed that these voters are a sizeable proportion of the electorate, and not some charitable eccentrics or potential scroungers, the more *all* parties would accept some aspects of welfarism. It is the existence of a 'socialist-welfarist' ideology which may turn out to be the crucial factor in bringing about a welfare state, not the electoral victory of the most pro-welfare party.

Strong social-democratic parties and/or 'social' Christian parties provide some of the conditions favouring the development of such ideology. A given level of pre-existing social cohesion is another. In societies sharply divided into different classes, where the social risks facing one group are quite different from those facing another, the privileged groups would have little interest in universal provision. They would view the redistribution required as punitive. Their parties would oppose the welfare state ferociously. However, a given level of homogeneity would provide the middle classes with a direct stake in welfarism, particularly in those social provisions, such as health and education, which also affect them.[14] Old-fashioned Marxists are quite right to view the welfare state as an instance of class collaboration, forgetting, perhaps, that even communist revolutions require such alliances.

No volume of statistics could establish what would have happened if socialism had not become a powerful force in the advanced industrial states of Western Europe. Furthermore, it is impossible to establish what an alternative government might have done in any past political conjuncture.

Nor is it possible to establish with certainty what conservative governments would do if faced with a non-socialist opposition. What statistics show is that the advent of socialists in government in the 1960s induced no systemic changes – regardless of how one defines the system.

Few would argue that parties make no difference at all. Richard Rose, who comes close to this position, only goes so far as to argue, rather convincingly, that 'parties make less difference in reality than they claim in their rhetoric. The worst that parties threaten to do is unlikely to come to pass – as well as the best that they aspire to.'[15] The main reason is simply that 'the bulk of the resources crucial to the success and failure of policies are not altered by a general election ballot.'[16]

All this may explain why, in post-1945 Western Europe, Left governments have never caused a radical rupture with the existing order of things. Transitions were always smooth and orderly, with rules, conventions and traditions respected and followed. The only sharp discontinuities in democracies came from the Right, not from the Left. Since 1945, the only authentic *coup d'état* in a democratic West European country occurred in 1967 in Greece, where democracy had been less than consolidated. The only significant changes of regime were the advent of Gaullism in France in 1958, and the end of the DC-dominated 'First Republic' in Italy in 1994. Everywhere, state apparatuses remained unchanged, bureaucracies ever-powerful. At the time of writing, no Left government has carried out a major reform of the political institutions.

The suggestion, made in the preceding chapters, that the parties of the Left were increasingly satisfied with the organization of the political system in their respective countries is therefore further confirmed in the 1960s. It was as if social democrats agreed with Lenin's remark in *State and Revolution* that the democratic state was the best shell for capitalism and the shortest path to socialism.[17] The difference was that social democrats had no wish to get rid of such a comfortable shell and saw no sense in revolution.

Left-initiated constitutional reforms did occur, but they were not particularly radical. The reforms of the Swedish constitution in the early 1970s abolished the Upper Chamber, introduced a more strictly proportional election system, and stripped the monarchy of all its residual powers. None of this significantly altered Swedish political life. In embracing unicameralism, the Swedes had been preceded by the Danes, who had replaced the bicameral Rigsdag (Parliament) by a unicameral Folketing (People's House) in 1953.[18]

The adoption of regionalism in Italy in 1970, acclaimed by the Left, was in reality the rather late implementation of a constitutional requirement originally proposed by the Christian democrats. In spite of the rhetoric which accompanied its rise, regional reform caused no significant change in the Italian political system.

In Belgium, increasingly divided by linguistic nationalism, the PSB/BSP resisted demands for greater devolution of power throughout the 1960s. It was the left wing of the party, and many to its left, that pressed for a greater degree of federalism. This included André Renard, one of the leaders of the big trade union strikes of the early 1960s. The refusal of the PSB/BSP to adopt decentralization led Renard to form the Walloon Popular Movement. The mainstream socialists persisted for a long time in the defence of the traditional Belgian state, because, like the Belgian bourgeoisie, it had greater support in the dominant French-speaking and more secular Walloon areas – one of the earliest terrains of European industrialization – than in the monarchical, Catholic and more recently industrialized Flanders.[19] By 1967 the Belgian socialists had given up their losing battle against the linguistic fragmentation of the country: they resorted to holding separate and simultaneous congresses of their Walloon (or Parti Socialiste) and Flemish (or Socialistische Partji) sections.

In Britain the most important reform was the introduction in the House of Lords of the life peerage system alongside the hereditary one in 1958. This was neither radical nor democratic. Its obvious effect was to increase the powers of patronage of prime ministers, without lumbering future generations with an ennobled progeny. This occurred under a Conservative government. Labour governments left well alone. None of this can compare in importance to de Gaulle's establishment of the presidential system in France under a new constitution. Thus, when it came to changes in the functioning of established democracies, the socialist parties were, at most, timid reformists and, in most cases, intransigent upholders of the existing state of affairs.

Even left-wing parties which did not do well at elections opposed constitutional changes. The French communists, still committed, in the long term, to some unspecified termination of the capitalist state, proved to be the last defenders of the Fourth Republic which had excluded them from power in all possible ways. The Dutch Labour Party – out of power for virtually the entire period – opposed any changes in the 'informal' constitution, the so-called *Verzuiling* system, at least until 1971. Under the informal rules of this system, the whole of Dutch social life, from trade unions to amateur choirs, was organized on the basis of the main 'pillars' or blocs of society (*zuil* means 'pillars'): the Catholic, the Protestant (in its 'liberal' Calvinist and orthodox Calvinist forms), and the secular (i.e. socialist and liberals). The proportional representation system ensured that fourteen of the twenty-eight parties which fought the 1971 election had candidates elected, an exceptionally high level of fractionalism. Governments were formed after lengthy negotiations – in reality, a kind of secret summit diplomacy, in which the party leaders divided the spoils of power among themselves.[20]

Because the non-socialist confessional Dutch parties had a considerable following among low-income groups, and compromise was an accepted feature of political life, policies had no major anti-worker bias. The socialists could hope to win power only as coalition partners with some of the existing ruling parties; consequently, they refrained from demanding a thorough revision of the rules of the game. Aspiring radical reformers were forced to operate outside the existing party system and, eventually, to form their own parties, such as Democraten '66, with limited success. Their most drastic proposal called for the direct election of the prime minister. All they obtained was the formation of a constitutional commission, the Cals-Donner Commission, which made recommendations that were quickly shelved.[21]

Under pressure from Democraten '66 and a 'New Left' movement within the Party, the PvdA appeared to work towards the formation of a progressive alliance with all secular parties against the confessional ones. This strategy failed because of the success of Catholics and Protestants in holding on to a significant section of the low-income groups: until 1994 it proved impossible to form a coalition without the confessional parties.[22]

None of this means that, in Holland or elsewhere, the political system, as distinct from the constitution in the narrow sense, remained unaltered. Throughout the 1960s, there was a general trend towards greater state intervention in the economy; public spending increased; there was a greater preference for planning; trade unions were involved more closely in political affairs. But this occurred throughout Western Europe irrespective of the political parties in power.

Austria was the most significant illustration of the now dominant consensus which enveloped parties of the Left and Right. The SPÖ and the ÖVP shared power until 1966, managing the economy in relative harmony. At election time, though, they fought each other with amazing ferocity. The elections of 1966, in particular, showed that the intensity of ideological strife at such times bears no connection to 'normal' politics. In the course of a crude 'red scare' campaign, ÖVP posters depicted the SPÖ as a crypto-communist party, with the hammer and sickle in the background. Anonymous pamphlets branded the SPÖ leaders as agents of Tito and contained negative references to Bruno Kreisky's Jewish origins. Yet, once the battle was over, the victorious ÖVP, though it had obtained an absolute majority of seats, asked the SPÖ to continue in the coalition.[23] The conditions were too onerous and the offer was reluctantly rejected. For the first time since the war, a one-party government was established in Austria.[24] Thus, the SPÖ was indirectly responsible for what amounted to an informal 'reform' of the political system: the transition from a consensual model of power-sharing to an 'Anglo-Saxon' (i.e. British) two-party system. The significance of the SPÖ decision to leave the coalition amounted to a recognition that the ÖVP could be trusted to rule on its own, something which the SPÖ had not been prepared to acknowledge in 1945. This created the conditions for reciprocity in 1970–71, when electoral success provided the SPÖ with the opportunity to govern alone.

Even when in power on its own, the SPÖ (as did the ÖVP in 1966–70) continued the 'consociational' practice of the *proporz* system whereby the leading positions in the public sector are carved up between the main political parties in a ratio corresponding to their voting strength. Widespread consultations between the two main parties ensured that nearly 90 per cent of all legislation was passed without opposition. The informal adoption of the British two-party system did not extend to the espousal of adversarial politics.

Such broad parliamentary consensus was common currency in other countries too. In Denmark the majority of bills was passed by the Folketing more or less unanimously.[25] In Italy, voting in the committee stage of legislation indicated, even at the height of the Cold War, a surprising consensus between the government parties and the PCI. Three-quarters of all legislation passed between 1948 and 1968 had the approval of the PCI.[26]

The continuation of consensus politics in Austria did not prevent the SPÖ from conforming to the pattern of social democrats in opposition, particularly in attempting to develop a distinctive image which would make the party activists happy, while increasing its share of the electorate. It was virtually inevitable that the years of SPÖ opposition (1966–70) would witness a clash between fundamentalists and revisionists. The latter were now more vociferous than in the late 1950s, though most of their suggestions were rejected, including the proposal that the party should call itself 'social democrat' – only in 1991 did this occur. The revisionist offensive would have resulted in a radical overhaul of the party's image had the ÖVP government not run into economic difficulties. It was this, rather than the strength of those loyal to 'authentic socialism', which facilitated Kreisky's tactics. These amounted to equipping the party with a dynamic image without changing the vague, but dearly-held, commitment to the long-term socialist aims of the party.[27] In so doing, Kreisky was adopting the principle of Harold Wilson, Willy Brandt and other European social-democratic leaders: never kill a sacred cow when you can walk round it.

Electorally speaking, this strategy seemed to pay off. As Karl Czernetz, one of the party's leading theorists, recognized, Bruno Kreisky had succeeded where so many of his predecessors at the helm of the party had failed: he had established for himself a convincing image as a committed socialist within the party, while appearing to be a reliable pragmatic politician to moderate voters.[28]

The fortunes of the SPÖ did not just rest on Kreisky's personal image. In 1967–68 several committees were set up to discuss a new economic programme aimed at transforming Austria into a modern industrial state through planning and co-operation between the public and private sectors. At the same time, another commission was drafting new health, environmental and social welfare policies, resulting in a document known as the *Humanprogramm*, published in 1969. Both the economic and the welfare proposals were the product of wide consultation among economists, experts and doctors, without regard to their political affiliation.[29] This allowed the party to present itself before the electorate as an efficient and competent organization, supported by informed opinion, clearly able to run a capitalist system in a responsible way, while creating an environmental and welfare infrastructure on the basis of social justice. All this was done without rejecting the 1958 programme of the party; modernization went hand in hand with respect for traditions: the slogan used in the 1970 electoral campaign was 'For a Modern Austria'.[30]

Together with Holland and Switzerland, Austria has been singled out by political scientists as an instance of a 'consociational' society, defined, in the picturesque jargon of their discipline, as 'democracies with subcultural cleavages and with tendencies towards immobilism and instability which are deliberately turned into more stable systems by the leaders of the major subcultures'. In the late 1960s one of the leading exponents of this concept added to the list of 'consociational' democracies Columbia, Uruguay and, in those half-forgotten, halcyon days, the Lebanon.[31]

Since even political scientists are aware that the 'consociational' systems of Austria, Holland and Switzerland have more in common with those of Italy, Britain and France than with the Lebanon and Uruguay, 'consociational-ism' should really be considered a variant of a general form of Western governance where the political and economic constitution, the formal and informal institutional arrangements, 'the rules of the game', significantly constrain and limit the options of *all* parties of government, as well as their 'loyal' opposition. Consociational theory overemphasized the distinctiveness of Austria, Holland and Sweden. All opposition parties need to distinguish themselves from the government, but they can only do so within certain limits. They must avoid an excessively sharp contrast or any intimation of eventual wild and untested political experimentation; and yet excessive simil-arities might undermine their case for political change. In this delicate art of political fence-sitting, the slogan of modernity turned out to be a crucial weapon. The cause of change was no longer advanced on grounds of ideology, but because it was required by the situation, the changing times, the new environment.

In the late twentieth century the ancient category of 'modernity' acquired an increasingly favourable connotation. As the traditional concepts of class struggle and public ownership were gradually abandoned, modernity came to dominate the discourse of the Left. During the 1960s, the Left appeared to have appropriated this concept, while the Right had to make do with that of 'enlightened traditionalism'. Modernity had not yet obtained the general acceptance that democracy, the other central political concept of the century, had already secured. Conservatives and Christian democrats were not yet convinced that they could comfortably appropriate the notion of modernity and did not (yet) question the validity of the socialists' claim to be 'modern'. Both sides, however, were still fighting vigorously over democracy, denying the other's commitment to it, at least at election time. The Left–Right metaphor of politics facilitated this ritual infantile posturing: the socialists occasionally being accused of crypto-communism, while conservatives or Christian democrats were suspected of longing for a clerico-fascist or authoritarian regime. Such exchanges highlight the generalized commitment to democracy – once the prerogative of dangerous extremists and radicals, now universally praised.

Conservatives believed that traditional values should prevail in the construction of their image. Some socialists, and particularly trade unionists, were suspicious of a concept of modernity devoid of a strong class position: was not technical progress a threat to jobs? Did not modern techniques of production and industrial relations reduce workers to the status of machines? The task of the socialist revisionism of the late 1950s was to allay these fears by claiming that the concept of modernity could accommodate a 'new', reformed managerial capitalism. Modern capitalism – they explained – was dynamic and caring. The top-hatted capitalist owners who showed little concern for their workers, except in an unbearably paternalistic way, were virtually extinct. The energetic managers in charge of industry were willing to consult with the trade unions and, in joint partnership, invest in jobs and opportunities. Modern trade unionists understood that deciphering a balance-sheet was more important than decoding *Das Kapital*, never a bestseller among trade unionists. British revisionists, in particular, writing in a country with a conspicuous degree of class consciousness, were in the forefront of the attack on the 'old-fashioned' image of the working class.

Thus, in the 1960s the demarcation between Right and Left appeared to be moving well beyond the older dichotomy between capitalism and socialism. Both sides were increasingly involved in a dispute about how to organize capitalist societies, rather than about whether or not capitalism should be abolished. Socialists drew on their tradition, and advocated the rational development of the economy and insisted on the virtues of planning, the collectivist concern for the greater good, the enthusiasm for science and progress, the assumption of the perfectibility of human society. Of course, none of this was their exclusive patrimony and, in any case, the more traditional ideas of the nation and the national interest, which had become the property of conservatives, could be harnessed by socialists for the regulation of capitalism.

All this provided further ammunition for the view that the era of ideology had ended. The extent to which the Left was actually able to occupy the terrain of modernity depended, to some extent, on the policies of the Right. Where the image of the Right was strongly imbued with traditionalism, the Left could more easily appear modern. In Britain, in the mid-1960s, Harold Wilson's Labour Party could effectively challenge a still highly traditional-looking Conservative Party, led by a fourteenth Earl, Alec Douglas Home. However, Wilsonism, the particular breed of 'technocratic reformism' embraced by the Labour Party, bore some resemblance to the more successful policies of Gaullism. The Gaullist takeover of modernity – all the more effective as de Gaulle was deeply committed to the importance of traditions and the *grandeur* of France – pre-empted the French Left. In the absence of novel political ideas, socialists and communists were reduced to a rearguard action against the abuses of 'personal power' and the undemocratic nature of organized capitalism.

The French Left was further handicapped by the good performance of the French economy: this had been helped by the 17.5 per cent devaluation of December 1958 and the inflationary years of 1956–64, which led to sustained investment until the stabilization plan of Giscard d'Estaing.[32] Before the advent of Gaullism, French planners had kept a low profile, preferring to work in the background to such an extent that Shonfield's remark – that French planning amounted to 'a conspiracy in the public interest' – seems valid.[33] Under de Gaulle, planning became the establishment's doctrine. The general had succeeded in adopting a position which has often eluded the Left: an apparent indifference to, and even disdain for, short-term considerations (the business of petty politicians), and an Olympian and exclusive concern with the 'permanent' interest of the nation.[34] Here there is a striking contrast with Harold Wilson's famous quip: 'A week is a long time in politics.'

In neither France nor Britain was modernity a 'capitalist' creed. The entrepreneurs of both countries had, over the years, amply demonstrated their massive incompetence, their lack of foresight, and their unwillingness to modernize. Once they had lost the protected markets provided by their countries' empires, they would have been quite unable to face the competition of the Americans, the Japanese and the Germans. Left to their own limited perspicacity, they would have allowed their own national economy to flounder into underdevelopment.[35] This is arguably what occurred in Britain. But in France, de Gaulle could build on a *dirigiste*, technocratic tradition and impose on the employers the interventionist state they uncomprehendingly needed. Unable, for obvious reasons, to join forces with the Left, the employers could not oppose de Gaulle, who had no serious enemy on his right. Thus, they were left politically unrepresented. This turned out to be their good luck: *dirigiste* capitalism was preferable to the *laissez-faire* variety which employers atavistically preferred. De Gaulle had a further advantage: the French state officials who were in control of the complex machine of economic intervention had been well-trained for this task in prestigious institutions such as the ENA; while the trade unions were weak and, until May 1968, unable to impose wage increases in excess of productivity.

British capitalism did not enjoy these advantages. 'Managerial capitalism' could not really depend on the Conservatives who, as recent converts, were hesitant, embracing the principle openly only in 1962 when Macmillan set up the National Economic Development Council – the pale British version of the French *Commissariat du Plan*. As for the Labour Party, it was supposed to be against capitalism, managerial or otherwise, and in trying to make it work after 1964 had to face the opposition of the employers, backed by the Conservative Party (and the press). Moreover, in Britain, little expertise was available. The general education of senior civil servants had not equipped them for the tasks of planning capitalism, though they were intellectually superior to those who actually ran it – the private sector managers. But this was only part of the problem. Of greater relevance was the fact that the Treasury, which was in effective charge of the economy, was not concerned about production: its brief was sustaining the pound and the balance of payments, if necessary by repeated deflation.[36] Its attitude to industry was that of pre-modern doctors: if it hurts, bleed it.

The undoubted merit of Harold Wilson, as he prepared for the 1964 general election, was to have clearly articulated a widely recognized problem – namely, that what was required was a thorough modernization of the country's manufacturing capacity. The assumption of previous reformist socialists that somehow capitalism would grow, develop and produce a surplus which could be appropriated by a Left government, and spent on social services, was abandoned. It had become clear that capitalism, or at least British industry, if left to its own devices – that is, to its own managers – would never be able to extricate itself from the marshy bog it had wallowed in for so long. Of course, a large financial sector, by servicing the requirements of the international markets, would be able to survive; however, manufacturing, in decline for most of the century, required help. British socialists, erstwhile scourge of capitalism, became its presumptive saviours, and took a leaf out of the book of the French *dirigiste* tradition. The revitalization of British industry would occur from the top down, through the initiatives of two new ministries: the Ministry of Technology or (MinTech), in charge of the so-called scientific revolution whose 'white heat' represented the new challenge facing Labour; and the Department of Economic Affairs, whose national plan would drag British manufacturing into the second half of the twentieth century. Both enterprises failed.[37]

Compared to the British Left, however, the French Left suffered a double handicap: first of all, it was not united; and secondly, it could not adopt a programme of reforming capitalism, because that had been thoroughly appropriated by the Gaullists and was ideologically unacceptable to the communists.

From the early 1960s onwards, for nearly twenty years, the French Left was obsessed with the problem of unity, and understandably so: communists and socialists were condemned to ineffectual opposition as long as they were divided. In the course of the decade, they moved from bitter rivalry and hostility to the recognition that nothing would change unless they collaborated. Though flexibility was never a French communist characteristic, there is little doubt that it was the PCF, rather than the squabbling socialists, which worked hardest to achieve a unity of purpose within the Left as a whole. The SFIO appeared to be in the throes of terminal decline. It had less than 100,000 members, according to its own unreliably inflated figures. Its bureaucracy was top-heavy. Its internal life was as undemocratic as that of the PCF. The gulf between its daily practice as a party of the centre, devoid of the faintest whiff of radicalism, and its blood-curdling socialist rhetoric was enormous: its own parliamentary group, an assortment of mediocre Fourth Republic notables elected in 1962, defined itself as 'essentially a revolutionary party ... a party of the class struggle'.[38]

No realistic progress towards Left unity could commence without the prior termination of the Algerian War – the issue which divided the Left so bitterly – and recognition that Gaullism was the common enemy. The first condition was met by the Evian Agreement of March 1962 between de Gaulle and the Algerian nationalists, which effectively ended the war; the second by Guy Mollet's realization that without some electoral understanding with the communists, the SFIO would suffer pronounced losses. Mollet's anti-Gaullist remarks in a radio broadcast in 1962 were reprinted approvingly in *Cahiers du communisme*.[39] The PCF further responded by encouraging its supporters to vote in the second round of the 1962 elections for the best placed anti-Gaullist candidate.[40] This facilitated the election victory, among others, of the progressive Catholic priest and resistance hero Félix Kir, who became mayor of Dijon and after whom the rightly celebrated mixture of white Burgundy and cassis liqueur was named.

The overall results for both socialists and communists were a marked improvement on 1958, though the former gained far more in terms of seats. The PCF, with 21.8 per cent of the vote, gathered only 41 seats, while the socialists and their allies (radicals and left-wing 'clubs') collected 108 seats with 20.3 per cent. This did not unduly concern the PCF. A few weeks later, at its Central Committee meeting of 13–14 December 1962, it called on all 'republican forces' (code for anti-Gaullist) to work together around common demands and programmes. It even added, in an unusually conciliatory tone, that though real differences remained between the PCF and the socialists, particularly on the EEC and NATO, neither of these issues should be considered an obstacle to joint action.[41] This was ratified at the Seventeenth Congress of the PCF in 1964 and, after this, the PCF pursued, with remarkable coherence, a policy of unity with the socialists. It derived from an assessment of de Gaulle as the enemy to be beaten and against whom a broad coalition could be established. The theme of pauperization, so beloved of Thorez in the late 1950s (see chapter 10), was abruptly dropped with the PCF's characteristic lack of concern about theory when it stood in the way of practice. Thorez was probably encouraged by the fact that the 1962 programme of the CPSU had modified, without entirely abandoning, the official position on pauperization: it now held the view that living standards may drop during a crisis, but it was no longer a general law of motion of capitalist society.[42] Ideological and political concessions poured forth: 'dogmatism' (code for Stalinism) was condemned; the upholding of the party's monopoly of power under socialism was another of Stalin's 'mistakes'.[43]

On 14 June 1962 a conference of communist philosophers convened on the theme of *Les tâches des philosophes communistes et la critique des erreurs philosophiques de Staline* ('The Tasks of Communist Philosophers and Stalin's Philosophical Mistakes'). Thorez's opening remarks concentrated on Stalin's apparent failure to understand Hegel, not one of the crimes for which the Soviet leader is usually blamed.[44] Nevertheless, this was taken to be a significant start. Subsequent events seemed to confirm that something was changing in the PCF: Lucien Sève, a mainstream communist philosopher, wrote a sophisticated treatise called *Marxisme et la Théorie de la personnalité* which took Freud (hitherto a decadent exponent of degenerate petty bourgeois thought) seriously. Surprisingly, this text received the party's imprimatur and was printed by the PCF publishing house, Editions Sociales, in 1969. In March 1966 a Central Committee on ideology held at Argenteuil accepted the principle of letting a hundred flowers bloom: it looked, finally, as if a less illiberal conduct of affairs would prevail in French communism.

A few weeks later, in May 1966, at a conference at Choisy-le-Roi, a team of party economists produced a new theory of state monopoly capitalism (or *Stamocap*) which singled out the leading large firms as the opponents to be defeated, thus justifying the pursuit of alliances with virtually all other social groups. For a party so bereft of novel ideas *Stamocap* was an advance. Its principal proponent, Paul Boccara, traced it back to Lenin, as required, but also to Evgenij Varga, the Soviet economist of Magyar origin who had clashed with Stalin in the early 1930s. Even the help of Keynes, 'whose analysis, in essence, is not so distant from Marx's', was drafted.[45] Boccara stressed the connection between the state and capitalism, rather than the subordination of the state to capitalism; denounced the ideas, then prevalent in the PCF, of the inevitable crisis of capitalism ('catastrophism'); and emphasized that the new capitalist phase was characterized by a generalized intervention of the state, technical progress and globalization. More significantly, he sought to justify a strategy of 'capture' of the state (as opposed to the Leninist requirement that the bourgeois state must be destroyed): if the Left succeeded in wrenching political control from the 'monopolistic oligarchy', then it could use the state for a thorough democratization of the economy, paving the way for a 'democratic state capitalism' which would open a new 'revolutionary phase of peaceful transition to socialism'.[46]

The theory can justifiably be criticized for its crudity, and it was presented in the usual doctrinaire style of French and Soviet communism. Nevertheless, from the inside it was like a breath of fresh air. It taught activists that the enemy was a system, and not a sinister conspiracy of tycoons blinded by greed, and explained to them that the state and the economy were not the same thing.[47] It attracted the interest of economists and even obtained the mild praise of an editorial in the otherwise unfriendly weekly *L'Express*.[48] One should add, however, that the party leadership never took the doctrine of *Stamocap* seriously and made no use of it. By the 1970s, *Stamocap* was hardly discussed and had become little more than a 'sort of theoretical warranty backing up the anti-monopoly policy of the Common Programme'.[49]

Be that as it may, at the time it appeared as if the PCF had succeeded in replicating – with some modifications – the scenario of the Popular Front. Then, the main enemies were the notorious 'two hundred families' which allegedly owned the country. Now, instead, there was de Gaulle and State Monopoly Capitalism. Yet there were two major differences from the 1930s. The first was that the previous Popular Front had reflected the foreign policy interests of the USSR, whose objective was a friendly France, ready to stand up to Hitler. In the 1960s, however, de Gaulle had been pursuing a foreign policy of autonomy from the USA which no left-leaning government could have improved upon and which suited the USSR perfectly: after all, France had been the only country to withdraw from the military structure of NATO. The Soviet press even indicated openly in 1965 that they would welcome de Gaulle's re-election, rather than that of the joint candidate of the Left, François Mitterrand. The new PCF leader, Waldeck Rochet, understandably irate, wrote a letter to *Pravda* protesting. The letter was published but censored, as Mitterrand recollected with glee, attributing to his candidature the merit of having provoked the first serious dispute between the PCF and the USSR since 1921.[50] Thus this time, unlike the 1930s, the PCF's quest for Left unity had been entirely determined by genuine national domestic needs.

The other major difference with the Popular Front was that the PCF was now ready to join a coalition, instead of merely supporting a socialist-led government.[51] Once the PCF had taken the decision to pursue the path of unity with the socialists, it did not waver until, in the early 1970s, the long-sought-after Common Programme was finally drafted.

The main obstacle to Left unity in France was the non-communists. Even after the shift in the PCF, the old 'third force' SFIO ambition of rallying the so-called 'political centre' to the socialist cause was given another chance. The hope was to regroup in a single coalition the increasingly mythical progressive *'forces vives'* of Gaullism, the leftovers of radical Catholicism, the modernizers from the plethora of left-leaning political clubs – a feature unique to French political life – the residue of the Radical Party, assorted Freemasons of the Grand-Orient lodges, various semi-detached 'progressive', but ineffectual intellectuals, and the weekly news magazine *L'Express*.[52] This unlikely concoction, a veritable Barnum circus, was unable to impose Gaston Defferre as a candidate for president on the SFIO and on its leader, Mollet, who in turn was deeply vexed because he had not been involved in this scheme from its inception.[53]

Defferre's failure to be selected as candidate demonstrated that French political parties were not the moribund creatures the Gaullists assumed them to be. The fundamental assumption behind Defferrism was that modernity entailed an 'Americanization of politics' – that is, the belief that ideological political parties would shrink in importance as they had in the USA (the myth of Kennedy was widespread in France). If the end of ideology had finally arrived, what would keep political parties together except a shopping list of political issues, a network of clienteles, or a strong charismatic personality? This 'anti-party' theme developed powerfully in the 1960s on both sides of the political spectrum. From a different perspective – namely, that of a 'national interest' above party politics – de Gaulle had assumed the same stance. Neither de Gaulle's followers, nor those of Defferre, understood what became apparent much later: while it was true that political parties could no longer aspire to monopolize politics, and that extra-party political mobilization would become a common feature of West European societies, it did not follow that parties as such could be discarded. Modern parties would survive and develop, but only by finding ways of using, co-opting, manipulating or negotiating with non-party groups. When de Gaulle retired in 1969, he had changed the political face of France, but he took Gaullism with him, to Colombey-les-Deux-Eglises, and left behind a sturdy structure of political parties.

The misjudgement of Gaullists and Defferrists was understandable, however. In the mid-1960s, French political parties did appear to be doomed. On the Right there existed little more than a collection of camp followers of de Gaulle, stretching from the blindly devoted to the unreliably opportunistic, devoid of even the semblance of independent thought, content to gather the harvest of votes the General had sown. On the Left there were the familiarly intransigent PCF, the undecided SFIO, a small leftist clique, the Parti Socialiste Unifié, split six ways, and the proliferating clubs: the Club Jean Moulin (the main supporters of Defferre), Citoyens 60, the Cercle Tocqueville (Lyons), Démocratie Nouvelle (Marseille), etc.[54] In so far as they had anything in common, the clubs were against political parties and in favour of devolution of power, *la participation* and *la décentralisation*, the two central ideas which were to inspire the May events and the reconstructed Socialist Party of the 1970s.

In the meantime, the clubs had to accept that the defeat of Defferre had paved the way for François Mitterrand – himself an expression of the clubs – to become the sole representative of the Left at the 1965 presidential election. Under his impetus, the non-communist Left began the task of self-reconstruction under the banner of the Fédération de la Gauche Démocratique et Socialiste (FGDS), an electoral alliance which included the SFIO, the left-wing radicals, the clubs, but not the 'third force' Catholics of the MRP. The FGDS shunned the Marxist rhetoric of the SFIO and its anti-clericalism. It did not call for the establishment of a socialist society, or promise new nationalizations, instead emphasizing growth and equality.[55] All this was encapsulated in a lengthy programme of fifty pages which, as it served no real purpose, was quietly abandoned. What really mattered to the new organization was to obtain the support of the communists without becoming dominated by them, and without conceding what they wanted most: a common programme.

The dignified result Mitterrand obtained in the presidential elections of 1965 vindicated the pragmatic approach. By forcing a second ballot, he compelled de Gaulle to campaign like an ordinary politician, a role the general found profoundly distasteful. Mitterrand's 45 per cent in the second ballot was a victory for those, like himself, who had argued that only by co-operating with the PCF could one hope to rally the entire non-communist Left. Anti-communism could have no role in the realignment of the French Left. That may seem obvious, given that over half the Left electorate voted for the PCF, but it sometimes takes a little longer for politicians to draw the obvious consequences.

In 1966 the FGDS and the PCF made an electoral accord for the elections of 1967 and, only then, began to discuss what a common manifesto might contain. The road towards Left unity was tortuous and tormented. The precipitate resignation of de Gaulle in 1969 provided the old 'third force' option with its last chance. The Socialist Party presented its own candidate at the 1969 presidential election, the trusted Gaston Defferre, but did not seek the support of the communists. Defferre was eliminated in the first ballot with an ignominious 5.01 per cent, well behind the two conservative candidates, Alain Poher and Georges Pompidou, and the communist Jacques Duclos, an unrepentant but popular Stalinist, who obtained 21.5 per cent, a creditable result.

The rout of the old 'third force' component of the SFIO was a blessing in disguise for the longer-term prospects of French socialism. The final elimination of Defferrism permitted the overhaul of the Socialist Party and the creation of a framework of co-operation with the communists. In the final analysis, the traditional Left proved to be more resilient than the 'clubs'.

In France socialists had accepted that to become a credible government force they needed to unite the whole Left. In Italy too, the Left had been divided. But unlike the situation in France, the PSI had entered the government of the ruling Christian democrats in 1962–63, just when the SFIO was desisting from supporting de Gaulle. It was as if the two countries had inverted the position which had characterized much of the 1950s when both communists and socialists were in opposition to centrist governments in Italy, while in France the PCF was generally isolated.

The new Italian centre-left government – as the coalition of Christian democrats, socialists, social democrats and republicans was called – set itself a dual task: the reform of Italy's social structure and the isolation of the PCI. Togliatti's counter-strategy was to avoid being forced into a position of intransigent opposition. Togliatti had ruled out the possibility that a single party – even his own – could resolve the crisis of Italian society.[56] Under the system of proportional representation, the PCI's only hope of entering government was through an alliance with one or more of the governing parties. It was thus necessary to oppose them without causing excessive offence, to approve of their intentions for reforming the country while insisting that, without the communists and their supporters, no genuine reforms could be implemented. This delicate balancing act required considerable skill: the PCI had to preserve its radical image as the chief antagonist of 'the system', while displaying all the traits and characteristics of a 'loyal opposition'. The oft-repeated aim was to be 'a party of struggle and a party of government'.

Togliatti was helped in this by the international thaw in the Cold War, as well as by the new position adopted by the Roman Catholic church under the reforming papacy of John XXIII. In contrast to Pius XII, who had condemned modern ideologies, including existentialism, and 'erroneous' scientific doctrines, in his encyclical *Humani Generis* (1950), John XXIII proved to be far more open-minded towards new ideas. In his *Mater et Magistra* (1961), he accepted some of the views of reformist Catholic economists critical of neo-capitalism. In the 1963 encyclical, *Pacem in Terris*, the Pope suggested that Catholics could co-operate even with those inspired by 'false philosophical doctrines' because movements based on false ideological premises may, in some circumstances, represent positive and just human aspirations.[57] Togliatti responded along the same lines. In a major speech in Bergamo (John XXIII's birthplace), he declared that religion, far from being an obstacle to the development of a spiritually rich socialist society, could make a positive contribution.[58]

While relations with the church improved, the communists also tried to keep the door open to an understanding with both the Christian democrats (DC) and the PSI, by attacking only their right wing. The situation was complicated by the formation of a new leftist socialist party, the Partito Socialista Italiano di Unità Proletaria (or PSIUP), which had broken away from the mainstream PSI after it had decided to join forces with the ruling Christian democrats in a coalition government. As a result, the PSI and the right-wing social democrats (the PSDI) had moved closer together and begun to discuss reunification. Furthermore, in August 1964 Palmiro Togliatti, the last giant of Western communism, died, depriving the PCI of its most lucid strategist. His successor, Luigi Longo, was an interim leader, open-minded and respected, but set in the traditional communist mould. This was not the case with either of the two contenders for the succession: Giorgio Amendola and Pietro Ingrao.

Both took stock of the predicament of Western European communism. In two provocative articles in the party weekly *Rinascita*, Amendola drew up a balance-sheet of the negative achievements of the Left in the West. He made the obvious point that neither the social democrats nor the communists had succeeded in creating a socialist society in the previous fifty years. He declared that the reasons for the original split between the two were no longer valid. The time had come to reconstitute a single party of the working class. The implication of Amendola's proposal was that the Communist Party should cease to exist, merging in a wider Left which would embrace that '48 per cent' of the electorate who were against the Christian democrats.[59]

Amendola's perspective, closer to traditional European social democracy than Ingrao's, was that political parties were more reliable carriers of change than social movements; that Italy had to follow the path of development of the more advanced countries of the West – high productivity, full employment, welfare reforms; that socialism was not on the agenda anywhere in the West and that what really mattered was to avoid the emergence in Italy of authoritarian government. Finally, although Amendola's anti-Stalinist credentials were as strong as those of Ingrao, he assumed that the Soviet experience was valid for Eastern Europe and was therefore less harsh in criticizing it, though he believed that it was not applicable to the West. The more radical Ingrao advocated the development of a new historical bloc which would rest on the working class and the emerging social forces in civil society. He believed that the Left would win only if it provided a vision and a model for an alternative to capitalism and not just an improved version of it: 'An alliance with us is an alliance with a force which is opposed to the system; the other political forces know this very well,' he wrote in April 1964.[60] Ingrao relied far more than Amendola on the revolutionary potential of left-wing Catholicism, and on the possibility that political struggle within the Catholic world would bring about the disintegration of the Christian democrats.[61]

Both leaders expressed in differing ways a common understanding: Western communism had reached an impasse and could not develop without modifying itself drastically. Ingrao would become the most important reference point within the PCI for those leftist tendencies in Italian society which hoped that the Communist Party would eventually become a rallying point for all revolutionaries. In the years to come, student radicals, rank and file activists in the trade unions, socialist feminists, libertarians, ecologists, liberation theologians, in so far as they looked to the PCI at all, looked to Ingrao and his supporters as their companions in the struggle. Ingrao's role was to maintain a link between the Italian communist tradition and the new forces which emerged, from the 1960s onwards, in Italian society. Within the party, however, Ingrao lost virtually every battle. The Eleventh Congress of the PCI (1966) sanctioned the victory of the Amendoliani, and the party apparatus thereafter remained in the hands of the 'welfare reformists' of the central regions of Italy, the only communists in Western Europe who regularly engaged in the difficult art of governing. The majority of the trade union leadership (excepting the powerful engineering workers' union) continued to be staunchly 'rightist' – as the Amendola current was called in contrast to the Ingrao Left – and understandably so: it was of paramount importance that the divorce between socialists and communists over participation in government with the DC should not cause a break-up of the CGIL trade union confederation.

When Ingrao's closest supporters decided, against his better judgement, to start an internal 'dissident' magazine called *Il Manifesto*, inspired by the more egalitarian aspects of the Chinese Cultural Revolution, they were expelled from the party by the Central Committee by a near unanimous majority which included Ingrao himself. Amendola's victory, however, was never complete; he himself remained only the leader of a tendency. He knew he did not possess the temperament required for the top job: this larger-than-life (and large) man, the son of a Liberal cabinet minister and anti-fascist victim, had an authoritarian streak which often caused offence. A cautious party like the PCI always behaved like a 'broad church', reluctant to alienate an important minority, conscious that its internal unity was its strongest asset. Togliatti himself had always avoided defeating any internal opponent completely, on the Machiavellian grounds that, sooner or later, they might turn out to be useful allies when the situation changed.

Throughout the 1960s, the PCI opposed the centre-left government on the grounds that it did not fulfil its promises to modernize and reform Italy. Nevertheless, it strenuously avoided a head-on clash, continuing to co-operate with the socialists in local government and in trade unions. In Parliament it never used its voting strength or the superior discipline of its parliamentary group to block major legislation; on the contrary, in the less visible but all-important committees, communist benevolence ensured the smooth passage of many laws. Thus Italian politics, like those of many other West European countries, manifested a not insignificant degree of consensus, even though the opposition was represented by the largest communist party in the capitalist world. All-important party unity was preserved by ensuring that the succession to Longo was entrusted in 1969 to Enrico Berlinguer, a taciturn Sardinian with considerable strategic skills, who was not identified with either Amendola or Ingrao.

The behaviour of the Italian Communist Party in opposition was shaped by two contradictory, though mutually necessary, features: an enduring commitment to its own traditions; and a realistic adjustment to unfavourable circumstances – a position which even the more stubborn PCF was embracing. Not for nothing was 'Change in Continuity' one of the central slogans of the PCI.

A similar attitude was emerging in another opposition party otherwise quite different from the PCI: the British Labour Party. Gaitskell's defeat on Clause Four had signalled the limits of revisionist success. However, as long as no one openly challenged the socialist final aim of the party, it was possible for the revisionists to convince their comrades that the modernization of Britain should become its medium-term goal. At the 1961 Blackpool Conference a 'home policy statement' entitled *Signposts for the Sixties* was accepted 'by acclamation'.[62] This text, whose final draft was the product of a senior quartet of the party's leaders (Hugh Gaitskell, Harold Wilson, George Brown and Richard Crossman), constituted, in a minor key, the British equivalent of Bad Godesberg and should be considered, in its essential aspects, the central revisionist text of the modern Labour Party.

The original draft of *Signposts* had been pared down by the party's home policy committee and purged of all references to 'a socialist purpose'. The

word 'socialism' did not appear at all. All mention of an eventual democratization of society, and the paragraphs entitled 'Democracy in Local
Government', 'Democracy in Industry', 'Democracy and Bureaucracy' and
'Democracy and Minorities' were eliminated. Also excluded from the final
document were proposals to reform the laws on suicide, homosexuality,
abortion, prostitution, divorce, obscenity, censorship and Sunday observance,
and to improve the prisons and the treatment of criminals.[63]

Shorn of the cultural and libertarian ideas advocated both by the 'new'
Left and by revisionists like Crosland in his *The Future of Socialism*, *Signposts*
was presented as the way out of the decay and stagnation the Conservatives
were alleged to have induced. For the first time, Labour contrasted British
backwardness with advances in Europe. At Blackpool Gaitskell had dubbed
Britain 'the sick man of Europe', and in a television broadcast he denounced
the country's growing inability to produce and sell its products abroad.[64] The
country's economic decline was obvious to all: Britain's share of the world
market for manufacture had shrunk from 25.5 per cent in 1950 to 16 per
cent a decade later.

Signposts for the Sixties provided the basis for the wholesale and highly
effective adoption of the concept of modernity by the Labour Party and, in
particular, by Harold Wilson when he became party leader after Gaitskell's
death in January 1963. Its opening words were: 'We live in a scientific
revolution.' It then continued:

> In such an epoch of revolutionary change, those who identify *laissez-faire* with
> liberty are enemies, however unwitting, of democracy. The enlargement of free-
> dom which we all desire cannot be achieved by opposing State intervention but
> only by assuring that national resources are wisely allocated and community
> services humanely planned.[65]

Thus, a set of connecting themes was presented: the scientific revolution
required state intervention and a fair distribution of resources. Britain was
not faced with the prospect of sudden catastrophe, explained the document,
but of slow decay. The Conservatives had starved community services,[66] done
little about the growing transport problem,[67] while the economy was still run
by a small caste of old Etonians: six out of eighteen directors of the Bank
of England, eleven out of thirty-four Ministers, forty-four out of the 148
directors of the largest five banks.[68] *Signposts* contained a diagnosis: the main
cause of Britain's decline was the government's refusal to develop a strategy
for the capitalist economy. It also suggested a cure: first, an industrial policy
aimed at revitalizing the economy and a National Industrial Planning Board
to channel investment towards key sectors;[69] second, the encouragement of
science in industry through a revitalized National Research Development
Corporation, which would sponsor research and modernize backward industries;[70] third, a national plan for apprenticeship to compensate for the
failure of the private sector to provide training;[71] and, finally, a fairer taxation

system to achieve greater equality, and improved social services to provide a stronger safety net.

This regenerative strategy recognized, though only implicitly, that the aim of socialists was the modernization of capitalism. 'Modernization' provided the British Labour Party with an optimistic, future-oriented popular slogan. The Conservative Party's patrician image, enhanced by the succession to Harold Macmillan of a land-owning aristocrat, Alec Douglas Home, turned out to be an electoral liability. The card of prosperity, played so ably by Macmillan in the 'You never had it so good' election of 1959, could not be used in the less favourable climate of the early 1960s. Wilson took full advantage of this auspicious conjuncture.

A cursory reading of the Labour leader's 1964 speeches in preparation for the election provides the full flavour of Labour's rhetoric of modernity:

> I want to speak to you today about the new Britain and how we intend to bring home to our people the excitement there will be in building it. Since the war, the world has been rushing forward at an unprecedented and exhilarating speed ... Yet Britain lags behind, lacking the will or the plan which can bring this future within the reach of us all. We are living in the jet-age but we are governed by an Edwardian establishment mentality. Over the British people lies the chill frost of Tory leadership ... Tory society is a *closed* society, in which birth and wealth have priority. This is the time for a breakthrough to an exciting and wonderful period in our history ... We want the youth of Britain to storm the new frontiers of knowledge ... This is what 1964 can mean. A chance for change. More, a time for resurgence. A chance to sweep away the grouse-moor conception of Tory leadership.[72]

The co-ordinates of this appeal were an unproblematic optimism about scientific advance and technical progress, a conviction in the superiority of rule by the expert, and a belief in the importance for growth of education and training:

> Socialism ... means applying a sense of purpose to our national life ... Purpose means technical skill ... If you fly the Atlantic by jet, you want to be sure the pilot knows his job, that he's been trained for it.[73]

Britain's electoral system forces the opposition to present an image appreciably different from that of the government, while appearing reasonable and moderate enough to capture the middle ground. The obvious solution was for Labour to accept that although both parties now had similar objectives – namely, the prosperity and welfare of the nation – the government was incapable of meeting them. Thus, Labour's regular lambasting of the Conservatives could not entirely disguise the fact that they too were committed to full employment and the welfare state, if less wholeheartedly than Labour; conversely, Labour's plan presupposed the preservation of the capitalist economy, even if they were less enthusiastic about it than the Tories.

Thus, in Britain, as elsewhere, there existed a form of consensus politics behind the shadow-boxing of confrontational rhetoric. In Germany too, consensus displayed itself more clearly even when, as in Britain, the situation was becoming increasingly favourable to the Left. In the election of 17 September 1961, the SPD obtained 36.3 per cent against 31.8 per cent in 1957; the CDU lost its absolute majority (down from 50.2 to 45.3) while the Free Democrats did very well, improving from 7.7 per cent to 12.7 per cent.

The SPD had, of course, been moving closer to the government since the Bad Godesberg conference of 1959. After acceptance of a bi-partisan foreign policy in June 1960 (see chapter 10), there were few practical differences between social democrats and Christian democrats. The erection of the Berlin Wall in August 1961 demonstrated to the SPD that it was futile to develop a strategy based on the assumption that the reunification of Germany could be achieved in the short term. The East German state, the DDR, seemed there to stay, solid behind the Wall, protected by Russian tanks, ideologically confident of its own sovereignty.

In October 1961, in a move which startled the German political scene, the SPD parliamentary group suggested that a cabinet of 'national concentration' should be formed between all the parties.[74] There was surprisingly little opposition. At the end of 1962 further vague 'coalition talks' took place between Herbert Wehner of the SPD and the CDU/CSU deputies Paul Lücke and Karl-Theodor von Guttemberg. Nothing came of these. Germany seemed set to be ruled for a long time by a coalition of the CDU, the CSU (its Bavarian counterpart) and the FDP. Nevertheless, the SPD had put down a marker for the future by underlining its willingness to form a coalition government. Like the British Labour Party, it sensed that politics was turning its way. The party had grown confident. It had a strong leadership, which included a brilliant strategist like Herbert Wehner. Its *Kanzlerkandidat* was the charismatic and youthful-looking mayor of Berlin, Willy Brandt. On the government side, power was still in the hands of the intolerant and authoritarian Konrad Adenauer, eighty-four years old in 1960, whose political career had begun in 1907, and who still persisted in his dishonest denigration of his socialist opponents (frequently characterized as stalking horses for the communists – a position increasingly difficult to hold).[75] The SPD knew that even Adenauer would not live for ever: when it talked about coalition with the CDU, the general assumption was that it was necessary to await the post-Adenauer era. The new cult of youth was being born. It unmistakably favoured the Left: Brandt against Adenauer, Kennedy against Nixon (and Eisenhower), Wilson against Alec Douglas Home.

The SPD continued to cultivate carefully its own image of a *Staatenpartei*, a system-supporting party, but it could do no more than wait for developments in the new governing coalition. The entente between the CDU/CSU and the FDP was never a happy one. The free democrats succeeded in forcing the authoritarian and right-wing CSU defence minister, Franz-Josef Strauss, out of office in 1962 and obtaining the retirement of Adenauer in 1963.[76] The chosen successor was Ludwig Erhard, the former economics minister, commonly and disputably regarded as the father of the German economic miracle and the chief ideologue of the 'social market'. Erhard's economic philosophy was virtually identical to that of the FDP, the party of economic liberalism. Erhard, however, turned out to be the least inspiring of Germany's post-war chancellors. His luck had run out: the economic miracle had come to an end. The causes behind this are complex and cannot be satisfactorily dealt with here. Full employment, achieved in 1959, had strengthened the trade unions; the influx of labour from the East had been blocked by the Berlin Wall in 1961; productivity had started a slow decline; there was an unusually high level of labour conflict in 1963 (8,997 days lost per 100,000 non-agricultural workers, against 2,250 in 1962 and 339 in 1961).[77] Thus, gross wages rose faster than GNP between 1960 and 1966.[78] German workers began to enjoy the fruits of economic prosperity: their average working week was 2.5 hours shorter than that of their British counterparts, setting a pattern of high wages and short working days never subsequently altered – contrary to the cliché of hard-working Germans and lazy Brits.

Another stereotype frequently used by the ill-informed was that the German economy was run according to the strictest and most inflexible criteria of sound and austere economic management, and that this meant spending as little public money as possible. In reality, German Christian democracy was popular not only because of economic growth, but also because it was always willing to hand out plenty of public money: lavish pensions (60 per cent of final salary in many cases); large building subsidies; the subsidization of the West Berlin economy; generous compensation paid to those affected by the war (to prevent the growth of a right-wing war veterans' party); state sustenance to uneconomic industries such as textiles, coalmining and shipbuilding; and regular bribes to the electorate prior to elections, such as the tax-cutting budget of 1965. The German 'social market' economy was almost as much 'social' as it was 'market'.[79] This pattern explains why the SPD could contemplate what in Britain would have been unthinkable: an alliance with its sworn opponent, and why it could fight the 1965 election promising to do more or less what the government was already doing. The end of the economic miracle helped the SPD. It gained 3.1 per cent on the 1961 results, though the CDU did reasonably well too, gaining a further 2.2 per cent. The real losers, this time, were the winners of 1961: the FDP, which lost eighteen seats and 3.3 per cent of the vote.

The economic situation deteriorated further and so did relations between the FDP and the CDU. A third player intervened: the Bundesbank. The Federal Bank Act of 1957 had constituted it as the supreme guarantor of the currency and, consequently, as 'independent of instructions from the federal government in carrying out the duties assigned to it by law'.[80] Accordingly, the Federal Bank tried to impose on the government a balanced budget and to cut spending, not an easy task in a federal country where the regions have considerable spending power. The FPD sided with the Bank, unlike the more populist CDU, which was quite prepared to discard orthodox thinking and increase taxes to balance the budget.

The contrast between the two governing parties could not be resolved. The FDP, increasingly unwilling to be associated with what appeared to be a discredited government, smarting from heavy electoral losses in Bavaria and Hesse, began to extricate itself from office. The CDU rapidly got rid of the hapless Erhard in favour of a new chancellor, Kurt Kiesinger.[81]

It would be in coalition with this man, who had joined the Nazi Party in 1933 and remained a member of it throughout the Third Reich, that the SPD, led by Willy Brandt (who had been in exile while Kiesinger carried a swastika-adorned card in his back-pocket), returned to power for the first time since 1930. Kiesinger's past involvement in radio propaganda on behalf of Nazism was called an insult to the German people by intellectuals such as Heinrich Böll and Karl Jaspers, but to no effect.[82] The requirements of power lead even those of the highest integrity into the strangest of beds.

There was, of course, serious opposition to an entente with the CDU within the SPD and the trade union movement, though this occurred mainly after 1966, when the coalition actually came into being. At the 1968 party conference, the motion in favour of continuing the coalition obtained only 173 votes to 129.[83] At the top, however, the SPD was quite united and with Kiesinger as chancellor, Willy Brandt as foreign minister, and Karl Schiller (SPD) as economics minister, the *Grosse Koalition* began its three-year period of existence.

With socialists in government in London and Bonn, in Rome and Stockholm, the tide seemed to have turned once more towards the Left.

In Power

The contrast and parallels between the Labour Government which started life in 1964 and the German *Grosse Koalition* of 1966–69 offer some interesting comparisons.

During their years in opposition in the 1950s and early 1960s, both the Labour Party and the SPD had been immersed in revisionist debates. The result was that their policies were strikingly similar on many points. They were both committed to NATO and to solidarity with the West. They were both anti-communist. Neither had significant rivals to the left, for their respective communist parties lacked popular support (unlike their Finnish, Swedish, Italian or French equivalents), and neither of them was faced by radical leftist parties (unlike the Norwegian or Danish parties). Both enjoyed the support of the entire trade union movement. Both were seen as harbingers of change, youth and modernity. Both enjoyed a strong measure of support from the intellectual establishment. Their respective leaders, Harold Wilson and Willy Brandt, had a positive personal image and a commanding presence on television. They dominated their parties. They were backed by a competent team of ministers, albeit inexperienced in practical governmental matters due to their lengthy period in opposition.

The differences are equally compelling. Institutionally speaking, the British Labour Party was in a stronger position. It enjoyed an absolute, though small, majority in the House of Commons in 1964–66, and a massive and unchallengeable one after the successful 1966 general election. In contrast, the SPD was the junior partner in the 1966–69 coalition and, after 1969, was still forced to compromise with its Liberal allies, whose economic beliefs were more antagonistic to state intervention than those of the CDU. The Labour government was freer from institutional constraints than the SPD: it was not hampered by a constitution and hence did not have to worry about whether its legislation could be ruled unconstitutional by a supreme court. The second chamber, i.e. the House of Lords, though controlled by the Conservatives, had very limited powers; local government was no real challenge in what was in fact a highly centralized state.

In Germany, by contrast, the SPD was much more constrained. It faced a written constitution and hence an independent and strong supreme court. It operated in a federal system with powerfully established regional governments. The second federal chamber, the Bundesrat, represented the *Länder*, and therefore had more authority to veto legislation than the undemocratic British Lords. An independent central bank, the Bundesbank, was more or less in control of monetary policy. Furthermore, German membership of the EEC entailed commitments which reduced the powers available to a reforming government – or so the still anti-European Labour Party believed.

Accordingly, in terms of politico-institutional constraints, the Labour government was much freer than its German counterpart to pursue radical policies. On the simple theory of sovereignty, a party which had captured the majority of seats in the Commons could do whatever it wished. It could be, as Lord Hailsham's celebrated dictum had it, an elected dictatorship. In terms of economic and international realities, on the other hand, the Labour Party appears to have been far more constrained than the SPD. It was encumbered from the outset by Britain's expensive international commitments and large military expenditure, epitomized by the international role of sterling and the remains of the empire; by the country's economic backwardness; and by the existence of a decentralized trade union movement chronically unable to deliver a comprehensive wages policy on a continuous basis.

The SPD, for its part, enjoyed the advantage of having an economy with a strong manufacturing base, its defence expenditure underwritten by NATO (i.e. mainly by the USA and Great Britain), and a centralized and co-operative trade union organization. West Germany was not affected by most of the factors which have been invoked, correctly or otherwise, to explain Britain's systematically poor economic performance: a divisive class system; the lack of adequate financial support from the City to manufacturing industry; the anti-entrepreneurial bias of British culture; inadequate training; and so on. Most of these explanations have been arrived at by a simple operation: any features possessed by the more successful 'West German model' and not by Britain were deemed to provide the explanation for the latter's failure. Charles Feinstein proposed a more historical explanation when he suggested that countries such as Germany, Japan, Italy and France could grow faster than Britain and the USA because, around 1948, they found themselves acutely aware of the need for reform and sustained exertion: they were 'backward', they had suffered military defeat, their cities were ruined, their infrastructure in need of reconstruction, their previous political institutions discredited. They were not, however, backward in the sense that they lacked the cultural, political and administrative ability to catch up with their more satisfied and hence more lackadaisical competitors. Those starting from a position of inferiority 'inevitably approached the task of reconstruction with a great sense of urgency and determination and little prospect of early benefits. The (others) saw the course and outcome of the war as a triumph for which they could now expect to be rewarded.' [84] Whatever the reasons, it is clear that the Labour Party confronted economic disadvantages far more significant that those facing the SPD.

Did these economic constraints outweigh the institutional advantages which the Labour government enjoyed? Though this cannot be answered with precision, we attach greater importance to the economic factor, not out of some schematic belief in the primacy of economics, but because modern social democracy cannot accomplish its tasks without a thriving economic base. Reformist welfare and redistributive policies cannot be implemented without a growth economy operating at or near full employment. This requirement does not hold for conservative parties. Their main 'constraint' is the extent to which they are forced, for political reasons, to uphold social-democratic reforms and goals.

To suggest that the economic constraints faced by the British Labour government were prominent obstacles in the way of the implementation of its programme sets the proper context for what, on balance, was the less than memorable record of the 1964–70 experience. The government's policies failed to achieve the economic growth required to deliver the promised social reforms. The initial substantial increases in social expenditure (education, housing and pensions) were not paid for out of growth, but by foreign borrowing (though this was eventually paid back), or by diverting resources which could have been used for direct investment.[85]

In the early 1960s, the Labour Party had produced plans for the re-vitalization of the British economy, yet it failed to attain this goal or to promulgate major welfare reforms during its six years in office. Unlike the previous Labour governments of 1945–51, no major achievements can be inscribed to its credit, though the establishment of widows' pensions, the expansion of higher education, comprehensive schools, the founding of the Open University are not insignificant. The constraints Labour inherited may have been great, but it failed principally because – for the short term – it had neither a coherent strategy nor a sufficiently radical imagination. It inherited from the Conservatives a serious balance of payments problem which it could have tackled immediately by devaluing sterling – as de Gaulle had done with the franc as soon as he obtained office in 1958 – and giving up its overseas commitments. Both policies were eventually adopted, but too late. Both were viable, and were indeed debated in government circles. One of the obvious causes of Wilson's (and James Callaghan's) insistence that sterling and overseas commitments had to be upheld appears to reside in the domain of political psychology: both policies were powerful symbols of Britain's national past, a past to which Labour was as profoundly committed as the Conservatives. The Labour Party had not been elected to change anything seen as representing the 'essence' of the British nation, but to revitalize the economy, modernize the manufacturing bases, establish a fairer society, more equal, more just. The word 'more' epitomizes what was at stake: the same but better, quantitative not qualitative changes. To this should be added the historic problem afflicting Labour: once it accepted the 'nation' as it stood, it felt it had to demonstrate that it could be trusted as much as the Conservatives. Being trusted meant accepting as primary national objectives the maintenance of an extensive diplomatic and military role in the world, and retaining London as an international financial centre of the first rank; and that meant upholding sterling parity. The Labour Party was encumbered by the fact that, when it took office, sterling was still a major reserve currency whose defence had enormous domestic costs.[86] Other countries, especially the USA, did not want Britain to use devaluation to correct its balance of payments deficits, for this would have unsettled the international monetary system and put the dollar in the front line of speculative assaults. As a consequence, the USA, the City, and the Bank of England exercised constant pressure on Labour to avoid devaluation, and provided loans to help sustain sterling.[87]

Wilson and his principal ministers paid more attention to pressures from special interests than to their own advisers, who were divided among themselves. Labour did not want to be regarded as the party of devaluation and never established an alternative strategy. The party of planning had become the party of improvisation. As Cairncross and Eichengreen explained:

> The Labour Government, on taking office, came down firmly against devaluation. But it did so without giving much consideration to the alternative. It contented itself with ruling out devaluation as 'unmentionable' but devised no coherent strategy for avoiding it. Indeed, once it had taken this position, it neither embarked on any form of contingency planning nor sought to look beyond the various crises that seemed to succeed one another endlessly over the next few years. The focus throughout was extremely short-term.[88]

The defence of sterling was not cheap. In the 1960s the cost of remaining a world power had escalated. The terms of trade had moved heavily against overseas military expenditure. It required a much higher level of exports to support troops stationed abroad than had been the case in the 1940s and even in the 1950s.[89] In a country inhabited by a population imbued with national pride, no party could afford to be seen to be 'anti-national'.

The SPD was in a different situation. The German nation was accustomed to being redefined or reconstituted. As Oswald Spengler put it in 1927: 'The sense of German history ... is a constantly repeated attempt to find the beginning' (*On the German National Character*). There was no glorious past to live up to. Quite the contrary: there was a past to live down. This was where the SPD had fewer inhibitions than others. This does not mean that there were no psychologico-political constraints. The historical memory of the devastating inflation of 1923–24 (the purported cause of the destabilization of the Weimar Republic) meant that no politician could hope to last for very long in Bonn without pledging total commitment to stable prices. The fact that this 'memory' was carefully cultivated and cherished by fiscal conservatives does not make it any less powerful. That apart, there were fewer sacred cows – like sterling – in Brandt's way than in Wilson's. It takes considerable statesmanship to slaughter such cattle. Wilson, for all his cleverness and his tactical flair, could not bring himself to do it until it was far too late.

The opening page of Wilson's own account of his first period in office recognized that 'all but a year' in the life of the Labour government

> was dominated by an inherited balance of payments problem which was nearing a crisis the moment we took office ... the harsh measures which we had to take, and from which we did not shrink, bit deep. It was a Government which had faced disappointment after disappointment, and none greater than the economic restraints on our ability to carry through the social revolution to which we were committed at the speed we would have wished.[90]

In later years, analysts cast doubts over the seriousness of the crisis Britain was facing. Exports, it seems, were so under-recorded that Britain may have had a balance of payments surplus when sterling came under pressure and was devalued in November 1967.[91] While this may offer further evidence that politicians are too often expected to make momentous decisions on the basis of questionable information reliably conveyed by unreliable experts, it can be no consolation to learn that some of the unpopular policies to which Labour had to resort may have been unnecessary.

If we are to rely on Wilson's memoirs, from his earliest days in office the advice from financial circles was to adopt stringent policies in order to convince speculators that sterling was not in danger. On 24 November 1964, the governor of the Bank of England asked him to cut public expenditure regardless of the social consequences. Wilson wrote:

Not for the first time, I said that we had now reached the situation where a newly-elected Government with a mandate from the people was being told, not so much by the Governor of the Bank of England but by international speculators, that the policies on which we had fought the election could not be implemented; that the Government was to be forced into the adoption of Tory policies to which it was fundamentally opposed. The Governor confirmed that that was, in fact, the case ... He had to admit that that was what his argument meant, because of the sheer compulsion of the economic dictation of those who exercised decisive economic power.[92]

In its struggle to give absolute priority to the defence of the parity of sterling – the one 'great mistake of economic policy'[93] – the Labour administration was compelled to introduce a formidable array of dismal measures, listed in Table 11.7. They failed to achieve Labour's overall objectives, namely to achieve growth and employment while preventing devaluation. On 18 November 1967, Wilson and his ministers could no longer avoid the unavoidable. The pound was devalued by 14.3 per cent. Further austerity measures followed. The new chancellor, Roy Jenkins, produced in March 1968 what Wilson described as 'the most punishing Budget in Britain's peacetime history'.[94] Home consumption was reduced in an effort to shift resources into exports. An impressive range of goods and services was subjected to tax increases – betting tax, gaming duty, road tax, tobacco duties, taxes on wine, spirits, cars, refrigerators, luxury goods, tape recorders and so forth. But there was no increase in income tax. It would be, announced the chancellor, 'two years' hard slog'. He was right. By the first quarter of 1970, the balance of payments, and even the visible balance of trade, showed a surplus.

To achieve this result, the very foundations of Labour's industrial policy were systematically undermined. The Department of Economic Affairs (the DEA), forged to counter-balance the Treasury's alleged anti-production bias and revive the British economy, was divested of much of its remaining power. By prioritizing sterling, the Labour government gave primacy to the Treasury view. Wilson himself remained convinced that the DEA had been wrecked by a Treasury conspiracy, though, by then, his paranoia had increased – a common characteristic of British prime ministers.[95]

In Germany, the SPD was spared this trauma and angst. The recession of 1966–67 may be seen as a political turning-point in the history of post-war Germany, since it heralded the entry of the SPD into government. From an economic point of view it only signalled the end of the 'miracle' of a period of exceptionally fast growth. This is alarming only to those who assume miracles, economic or otherwise, can become routine. In reality, the 'crisis' was rather mild. In so far as the new government had a balance of payments problem at all, it consisted in being blessed with such a healthy surplus in 1966–69 that the Germans were regularly under pressure from their competitors, especially the French in 1968, to revalue the Deutsche Mark. The incoming SPD-led government finally complied in October 1969. The

Table 11.7 Labour government (UK) economic measures, 1964–67

Import surcharge of 15 per cent	Oct. 1964
National Insurance contributions increased	Nov. 1964
Petrol duty increased	Nov. 1964
Income tax increased	Nov. 1964
Bank Rate up (record 7 per cent)	Nov. 1964
Bank Rate up (record 8 per cent)	Nov. 1967
Public spending contained or cut	Feb. 1965, July 1966, July and Nov. 1967
Massive foreign loans to support sterling	Nov. 1964, Feb., May and Sept. 1965, July 1966, March, Oct. and Nov. 1967
Deflationary budget, HP regulation made more stringent, tax on alcohol, tobacco and cars increased	April 1965
Exchange control tightened	April 1965 July 1965
£50 maximum foreign travel allowance	Nov. 1966, renewed 1967
HP terms made more stringent	June and July 1965, Feb. and July 1966, Nov. 1967
Public authority investment cuts	July 1965
Budget: introduction of Selective Employment Tax	May 1966
Bank advances restrained	Dec. 1964, May and July 1965, January 1966
Sterling devalued	November 1967

German slowdown had been the product not of a structural decline – as in Britain – but of conjunctural factors, such as the Bundesbank's exercise of monetary restraint and increases in wages higher than the rate of growth of productivity.

The real problem facing the SPD, even when in coalition with the CDU, was to convince the trade unions to contain wages in exchange for some non-monetary benefits. The Labour Party too spent most of the 1964–70 period trying to convince the trade unions to adopt wage restraints, but in Britain this policy was deployed to eliminate a balance of payment deficit, rather then to achieve economic growth.

In Germany a medium-term stabilization policy was of at least as much importance as short-term measures. The *Stabilitäts-und-Wachstumsgesetz* (the Stability and Growth Law), passed by the Bundestag in June 1967, altered Article 109 of the Basic Law to decrease the fiscal sovereignty of the *länder*, compelling their budgets to be aligned with the federal government's so that they would meet the requirements of the economic cycle. Budgets had to conform, by law, to a balanced treatment of the *magisches Viereck* (magic square), the four key economic goals of full employment, steady growth, price stability and stable exchange rates. The government was also compelled to submit an annual economic report outlining the economic situation and setting out its economic and financial objectives.[96] The resources for anti-cyclical policy would come from increased state borrowing in periods of weakness and from a contingency fund built up during periods of high growth.[97]

The law also established that, should one of the four stated economic goals be endangered, the government 'will provide orientation data for simultaneous concerted action (*Konzertierte Aktion*) of local authorities, trade unions and employers' associations in order to achieve the goals'.[98] Many leading trade unionists welcomed the establishment of a formal consultative forum. They assumed that it would allow them to play a major role in the determination of national economic and social policy, which is what they had consistently advocated in their Basic Programme adopted at Düsseldorf in 1963. However, the key issue discussed in this forum turned out to be the increase in wages compatible with the government's macro-economic policies. Understandably, the unions became uneasy: *Konzertierte Aktion* was being reduced to an incomes policy forum.

During the first two years of this policy, 1966 and 1967, unions complied with the government's request to moderate their wage claims. There was a close match between the wages targets set by the government's 'orientation data' and the actual wage increases which, in any case, lagged behind the growth of the economy. Whether there was a direct causal relation between government wishes and union demands remained a matter of controversy, particularly as such apparent adherence to the guidelines did not occur after 1967.[99] The recession, and the attendant rise in unemployment, was the main ingredient in moderating union demands; and the *Konzertierte Aktion* forum was, at most, an additional contributing factor.[100] Moreover, the unions were more willing to co-operate because the SPD was in government, on the assumption that they would be able to obtain those social reforms which they (and the SPD) had long advocated.[101] Be that as it may be, the apparent success of the forum reinforced the prestige of the party which had championed it: the SPD. The policy which the social democratic minister of finance, Karl Schiller, had called Keynesian 'global steering' emerged triumphant. Unemployment fell. Growth picked up once more. The recession was over.

The ideological effects were notable. The macro-planning corporatist structure erected by Schiller, in his particular version of Keynesianism, became the dominant philosophy in German economic policy, thus marking a decisive break with the neo-liberal 'social market' policies of Erhard.[102] From an overall European point of view, this was hardly an innovation. Neo-Keynesianism had been dominant in Scandinavia and in Austria. Tripartite consultations existed even in conservative Britain through the National Economic Development Council set up by the Macmillan government. They were well established in Belgium, Holland and, of course, Austria. Nevertheless, in the context of German politics, the SPD had succeeded in engineering a major shift in policy and setting a new agenda. These are not puny results. A key purpose of politics is to establish a firm consensus on what is important, on what is not, on what must be done, on what must never be done, on what must be done first and how it must be done. Actually 'doing it' depends on many factors, most of which are outside the control of politicians. As for the overall effects of political actions, they are, mostly, unpredictable, in the lap of the gods.

'German' Keynesianism did not last in its 'pure', Schillerian form. Once the recession was over, the Bundesbank resumed its guardianship of a low-inflation Germany. The weakness of the pound and the 1971 devaluation of the dollar had produced an inflow of capital into Germany. The Bank abandoned its *laissez-faire* stance and advocated exchange controls, while Schiller lined up with those seeking to maintain the free market for capital. The SPD had to chose between its economics minister and the Bundesbank. It chose the Bank. The move looked 'pro-interventionist' enough to please the SPD Left, responsible enough to please the electorate and the FDP, the SPD's future ally.[103] In reality, it signified an expansion of the powers of the Bundesbank, which now effectively controlled the exchange rate as well as monetary policy.[104] Schiller resigned in July 1972 and was replaced by Helmut Schmidt. Schmidt was far less committed to *Konzertierte Aktion* and preferred to influence wages policy through fiscal measures and through a direct incomes policy in the public sector. When, in 1977, the DGB withdrew from *Konzertierte Aktion*, the government showed little concern.[105]

The verdict on *Konzertierte Aktion* must be that, in practical terms, it was a failure. It did not prevent strikes. It did not deter wage increases higher than productivity. It did not contribute to the further centralization of the trade union movement. However, it compelled the unions to appear consensus-seeking and moderate. Not that German trade unions went on strike as often or for as long as British or French or Italian trade unions. Clearly, this was not the case. In all probability, so-called trade union modera-tion, extolled by employers elsewhere, was the result of the higher German wages made possible by higher German rates of growth.

How did the *Grosse Koalition* fare in social policy? Many trade unions thought that, in exchange for moderation in wage demands, they would obtain long-awaited reforms: pension reform, reduction of working hours, and improvement in redundancy terms. None of this happened, even though the wage increases in 1967 and 1968 were well below productivity.[106]

The situation changed after 1969. The *Grosse Koalition* was never meant to be a permanent coalition. The FDP, which had been excluded from power by the entente between the two larger parties, began to stress what it had in common with the SPD: a policy of rapprochement with Eastern Europe and the reform of higher education.[107] In the elections of 1969, the CDU-CSU remained the largest party with 46.1 per cent of the votes; the SPD increased to 42.7 per cent; while the FDP, having lost its more conservative supporters to the CDU, had to be content with 5.8 per cent – just above the 5 per cent threshold required for representation in Parliament. This was enough to deprive the CDU of a working majority and pave the way for the SPD–FDP coalition, with Brandt as chancellor and Walter Scheel, the FDP leader, as foreign minister.

The new coalition embarked on a reform programme. University unrest facilitated commencement of a restructuring of all educational institutions. Marriage and family law was modernized, sickness benefits improved, family allowances reformed, co-determination for workers extended. Between 1969 and 1975 – all social-democratic years – expenditure for the three most important branches of the social insurance system – health, pensions and unemployment – grew faster than any other significant government outlay.[108] On the basis of the 1968 SPD document *Perspectives of Social Democratic Politics in Transition to the 1970s*, the SPD-controlled Ministry of Labour produced a new pension scheme incorporating flexible retirement age and a host of social reforms, including measures to help war veterans and mothers.[109] The transportation, education, housing and research budgets were expanded. In 1965 paid holidays were increased from eighteen days to twenty-four; by 1982, at the end of the social-democratic era, all West Germans had a right to six weeks' paid holidays.[110]

Much of this did not break new ground, but 'represented a logical continuation of the course pursued by the Great Coalition and to some extent by earlier governments as well'.[111] No major social welfare programmes were launched. Only in foreign policy, which Brandt prudently presented as the continuation of Adenauer's, was a real novelty introduced.

By 1973 Brandt had resigned, following a spy scandal, and the oil shock had destroyed one million jobs. The time for social reforms had come and gone. Nevertheless, the SPD had demonstrated its ability to govern, thus ensuring the continuation of the coalition until the early 1980s. However, as Table 11.8 shows, neither in electoral terms nor in length of office did it perform significantly better than the British Labour Party – at least until the Labour Party's electoral collapse of 1983.

Between 1964 and 1983, the SPD was in power for sixteen years, always in coalition, as against the Labour Party's eleven years in office. In the fifty years since 1945, each party has been in power for roughly sixteen years. Thus the SPD, while relatively more successful in the management of the nation's economy, was not much more electorally successful than Labour. And when all is said and done, there can be little doubt that managing the West German economy was an easier task than resolving the long-term economic problems of the British.

Labour had not achieved the modernization of the economy, the task it

Table 11.8 Labour Party (UK) and SPD percentage share of the vote, 1964–83

UK elections: Labour Party		W. German elections: SPD	
1964	44.1	1965	39.3
1966	48.1	1969	42.7
1970	43.1	1972	45.8
1974	37.2	1976	42.6
1974	39.2	1980	42.9
1979	37.0	1983	38.2

had set for itself. But it had doubled expenditure in the arts and had made major progress towards comprehensive schools – the basic educational system in all civilized, advanced and economically successful societies and a principle endorsed by all successive British governments. Furthermore, Labour, in its first foray into foreign affairs, established an arms embargo against the apartheid South African regime, a policy upheld by all its successors – a rare instance of the Left establishing a consensus in foreign policy. Labour introduced race relations legislation specifically aimed at outlawing racist practices, making Britain the first European country to do so and setting international standards not reached by others for years to come. Labour drafted the first comprehensive legislation establishing the principle of equal pay for women, enacted in 1970, to come into force in 1975.

None of these achievements could disguise the fact that, in the eyes of opponents and supporters alike, the 1964–70 Labour governments, unlike the 1945 Attlee administrations, had failed to transform society. It was no consolation for party activists to hear Roy Jenkins attempting to assuage them at a fringe meeting at the 1970 Conference at Blackpool, with the wary remark: 'We must not expect a full-scale peaceful revolution every time a Labour Government is elected.'[112]

How did other socialist parties score in government? A wider comparison is virtually impossible because, outside Sweden, no other socialist party was in an influential position of power similar to that enjoyed by the British and German parties in the second half of the 1960s. When they returned to power they were usually 'prisoners' in a coalition with non-socialists in which they were seldom the dominant partner. Peripheral Finland was the solitary exception: in 1966, for the first time since the 1940s, a communist party returned to power in a coalition with the agrarian Centre Party and the Social Democratic Party. But, although the Finnish situation was anomalous with respect to that of the other Western European countries, the actual policy content was hardly exceptional. As elsewhere, the new government faced a massive balance of payments crisis. Like Britain, it devalued its currency, though by a massive 31 per cent, in 1967. Like Germany, it promulgated a Stabilization Plan (March 1968) which restrained wages.[113]

This further demonstrated that there could not be *specific* communist policies in the governance of liberal democracies. The Finnish Communist Party had to choose between behaving like Western social democrats in government or 'real' communists in opposition. Predictably, they were divided between revisionists and traditionalists. The former, led by Aarne Saarinen and Erkki Salomaa, a trade unionist, took over the leadership from the traditionalists Aimo Aaltonen and Oiva Lehto. Both wings of the party had been in favour of joining the government coalition.[114] The growing un-popularity of the government strengthened the traditionalists, but what apparently split the party was not a question of domestic politics, but of the position to adopt over the Soviet invasion of Czechoslovakia in 1968. The revisionist leadership sided with Western communist parties, such as the Italian, condemning the Soviet Union. The result was that at the Party Congress held in April 1969 half the delegates walked out, in spite of Soviet pressure to find a compromise.[115] Pro-Sovietism was what marked out the communist traditionalists from all other political forces in Western Europe. In all domestic affairs, these pro-Soviet communists were indistinguishable from trade union militants in West European social democratic parties: they all espoused 'workerist' positions, rejected stabilization policies and urged a return to 'hard' wage bargaining.

Thus, even the Finnish Left, with its distinct history, operating in the only non-communist European country where the overall political consensus assumed the necessity of friendly relations with the USSR, could not avoid the common problems affecting the rest of the European Left: the same divisions, the same economic problems, and the constant clash between the requirements of capitalist growth and the ideals of socialist redistribution.

At the start of the 1960s, only the Swedish SAP appeared to be a positive model for West European socialism. A few years earlier, Sweden had been extolled by Crosland as the nearest approximation to a socialist society. The Austrian and German socialist leaders, Bruno Kreisky and Willy Brandt (the latter spent his wartime exile in Sweden), had acknowledged the political debt they owed the Swedes. Praise even came from more left-wing quarters. Sweden's clear stand against US intervention in Vietnam, and its policy of granting asylum to US deserters and draft-dodgers, its early concern for the plight of the Third World, and its hosting of the pacifist Congress for Peace provided Swedish social democracy with 'anti-imperialist' credentials able to satisfy many West European communists, as well as the 'dissident' Left within mainstream socialist parties. Even the intransigent PCF underwent a brief pro-Swedish phase to aid its rapprochement with the socialists: in 1970 a French communist journalist, Jacques Arnault, wrote a fair and non-polemical account of the achievements of Swedish social democracy, *Le Socialisme Suèdois*, published by Editions Sociales, the PCF publishers.[116] In fact, Sweden was singled out for various purposes. But, like most models, it could not be exported.

Swedish social-democratic success has several outstanding features: its uncanny ability to win elections; its welfare achievements and egalitarian outlook; its manifest moderation. The SAP had a distinct advantage: it was the overseer of one of the most efficient capitalist economies in the West which had turned the Swedes into the richest people in the world. By 1960, what was considered the most important piece of Swedish social welfare legislation – the pension scheme – was in operation. Its aim was the elimination of poverty after retirement. The connection between poverty and old age, a common feature of all advanced economies, was broken for the first time.

Swedish social welfare achievements could not fail to impress even the more radical representatives of the Left. One of the editors of the *New Left Review*, a journal whose ideological influence grew with its commitment to revolutionary politics, enthused, on his return from a fact-finding tour of Sweden, on a 'row of benefits with no real equivalent here at all':

> 10 day or more holidays for housewives under a certain income with 2 children of 15 or under, for a nominal fee ... free holiday transportation for children up to 14 anywhere in Sweden and back; free or fee-paid (according to income) domestic help; home furnishing loans up to £200 for the newly married ... removal allowances for the unemployed taking up work in new areas.[117]

The only other socialist party which could emulate the achievements of the Swedes was, after 1970, the Austrian SPÖ. Like Sweden, Austria was a small country, with a relatively homogeneous population, unencumbered by the requirements of belonging to an international alliance such as NATO. At the 1970 elections, the SPÖ, in opposition since 1966, had become the largest party, though without an absolute majority; the help of the small Freedom Party (the FPÖ) was obtained in return for a minor electoral reform which benefited small parties. The gamble paid off: at the elections of 1971 the SPÖ obtained an absolute majority and was able to rule on its own. The Kreisky government rationalized the public sector, especially the steel and iron industries, and, on the basis of the *Humanprogramm* of 1969 (discussed above), it created a new ministry for health and the environment, promulgated penal reform laws, introduced abortion legislation in 1974 (in spite of the strength of Catholic feelings and the power of the church), reduced military service, cut the age of majority from twenty-one to nineteen, and introduced free textbooks in schools.[118] Many of these important yet moderate reforms were an extension of previous policies, and much of the legislation was passed unanimously in the *Nationalrat*.[119]

In 1972 Bruno Kreisky launched what he hoped would become a grand intellectual debate on the future of social democracy and established a research centre, the Karl Renner Institute, in Vienna. Kreisky put forward the concept of 'permanent reforms', reforms aimed at modifying the existing system of power relations in an irreversible manner. This was similar to Palmiro

Togliatti's efforts between 1958 and 1964 to present structural reforms as something sharply different from reformists' reforms. It was also a return to what had been the central ambition of Austro-Marxism: to develop a way out of the traditional dichotomy of (communist) revolution and (social-democratic) reformism. Accordingly, the party became committed to economic democracy, co-determination in industry and the extension of the public sector.[120]

In spite of these efforts, Austrian socialism's main success was not the transformation of Austrian society, or the establishment of a model welfare state (as in Sweden), but the entrenchment of a commitment to full employment which lasted well into the 1980s, after it had been abandoned by much of mainstream social democracy.

Throughout Western Europe, a consensus was emerging in domestic affairs. This had a fundamental 'material' condition: relatively thriving economies. It was this which made possible the pursuit of full employment and social welfare. In the field of foreign policy, another consensus emerged: Atlanticism and Europeanism. Its foundations were equally 'material': the political organization of international affairs – the Cold War – appeared to be the reflection of an economic division of the world between successful market economies able to generate consumer goods for nearly everyone, and command economies increasingly directed towards catching up with the former. No one, even on the Left, could argue against the prevailing conviction that it was far better to model oneself upon the trailblazers than upon the laggards. As is often the case, the simplest solutions are the best. Nevertheless, explaining the growing foreign policy consensus, the task of the next chapter, may require more complex calculation than this.

CHAPTER TWELVE

The Establishment of a Foreign Policy Consensus

IN CHAPTER 7 I explored the question why, after the Second World War, in the midst of the reconstruction of Western Europe, socialist and social-democratic parties had not developed a 'socialist foreign policy'. With the exception of Germany and Italy, all had followed a 'national' or consensual foreign policy, neutral if their state was committed to neutrality (Sweden and Austria), otherwise aligned with 'the West' – that is, the Atlantic Alliance.

In the western half of divided Germany there had been no consensus. The SPD followed a national policy of reunification incompatible with the CDU's 'western' policy. The SPD had opted for neutrality on 'national' not 'socialist' grounds, because it believed that this was the best strategy for achieving German unification. By 1960 the SPD had reversed this policy and accepted NATO, thus opting for a bi-partisan foreign policy on the CDU's terms.

In Italy the Socialist Party – like the SPD – had initially embraced neutralism, aligning itself with its communist partner in what was the equivalent of a pro-Soviet policy. In the 1960s, it too, like the SPD, reversed this policy in favour of Atlanticism.

Neutralism remained the policy only of those socialist parties operating in countries which were neutral anyway, such as Sweden, Austria and Switzerland. Elsewhere, once neutralism had been defeated, what else could be the basis of a socialist foreign policy? Pacifism? Solidarity with the Third World? European integration?

By the early 1960s, nuclear disarmament, the modern form of pacifism, had been comprehensively repudiated by the leadership of the Left in the only two countries where there had been a serious mass movement backing it, Britain and Germany. In France an atomic armaments programme had been developed in the 1950s with the full co-operation of the socialists, as had been the case with Britain in the 1940s. The PCF opposed the programme only because it was targeted against the USSR.

Colonial empires were being more or less reluctantly disbanded without a coherent plan and regardless of socialist pressures. Pragmatic policies, rather than ideology, had been the dominant factor behind the British withdrawal from India; military defeat underlay the French evacuation from Indo-China.

Far from being in the vanguard of de-colonization, the French socialists resisted in Algeria and resorted to old-fashioned gunboat diplomacy in Egypt over Suez.

European integration, initiated by conservatives in Germany, France and Italy, provoked a response from the Left which ranged from the unenthusiastic to the downright hostile.

By the beginning of the 1960s, the elusive concept of a 'socialist foreign policy' had become even more vague. No doubt minority tendencies within each of the main parties of the Left thought they understood the nature of the beast: a socialist foreign policy was anti-Atlantic and in favour of non-alignment; it meant being on the side of decolonization and of all movements fighting for it, irrespective of the degree of communist influence exercised within them; it also meant being against all military or one-party dictatorships in the Third World which persecuted the Left and were supported by the USA. These leftist factions, which were usually neither communist nor stooges of Moscow, suffered an affliction: their policies, with rare exceptions, encountered the unconditional approval of the USSR.

There were at least two reasons why this could not be ignored. First, being associated with the USSR was deeply unpopular and led many voters to assume that the socialism advocated by this left-within-the-Left was, in the final analysis, not so different from the command economy overseeing the destinies of a quarter of humanity, from Vladivostock to Canton, from Prague to Ulan Bator. Second, policies never exist in a vacuum, never have a life of their own separated from the context which gives them meaning. This context was the Cold War and the division of the world. This, inevitably, was the fundamental framework for, and hence the fundamental constraint on, all foreign policy, including any hypothetical socialist variant. The fact that the Soviet Union did support many 'just' causes throughout the world obviously did not mean that these causes became less just. It meant that supporting them had repercussions wider than the issue itself. No one can ignore, in the name of principle, the effects of their policies.

To ask what a socialist foreign policy should be presupposes the possibility of distinguishing between what is impeccably socialist and what is not. The question harks back to a mythical period of uncomplicated politics where there was no grey in the sky, only black and white, day and night. This was never the case, especially for the socialist movement which had condemned war vociferously before 1914, when the world was at peace, and which turned to support the war when conflict erupted. There never was a period in which one could point to a socialist policy which simultaneously fulfilled two criteria: that it united all (or most) socialists and was clearly demarcated from non-socialist policies.

I have already alluded in the conclusion of chapter 4 to the fact that one of the fundamental paradoxes facing the non-communist Left was that it could not be neutral between the socialist East and the capitalist West. It had to condemn the authoritarian East, where the only existing form of socialism was to be found, and support the liberal West, where capitalism was triumphant. The form of government prevailing under the aegis of the Soviet system was completely inimical to Western socialism. The one-party state was not the appropriate political shell for the flowering of democratic socialism. What was required was precisely the institutional political system of liberal democracy which prevailed only where capitalism was at its most developed. Under the American umbrella, it was perfectly possible to be a socialist, win elections and form governments. Under the same umbrella, however, it might prove to be impossible to abolish capitalism. Where capitalism had been abolished, however, there was no democratic socialism.

By 1960, no socialist party seriously contemplated the abolition of capitalism in the foreseeable future; thus, commitment to 'the West' was absolute. In these circumstances it was virtually impossible to develop a 'socialist foreign policy'. The Left could never hope to match the Right on the terrain of anti-Sovietism. There were no compelling reasons for socialists to adopt pro-Sovietism, the prerogative of the communists. Non-alignment, the favoured third foreign policy option of many on the Left, required, for its implementation, conditions beyond the will of any single political party. It could be adopted only if particular geopolitical and historical circumstances prevailed, as in Finland, Sweden or Austria. There a neutral foreign policy co-existed perfectly well with a 'Western' economic and political system. Neutrality was highly popular with public opinion. It offered an ideal mix of consumer capitalism and a high-minded attitude in international affairs. It demonstrated that it was perfectly possible – contrary to a peculiar English saying – to have one's cake and eat it. This was so even in Austria which, unlike Sweden and Switzerland, had no tradition of neutrality and had been an active participant in most European wars. In 1973 an opinion poll revealed that 90 per cent of the population thought that there were more advantages than disadvantages in being neutral.[1]

Only one definition, and a tautologically vague one at that, could be used to describe a socialist foreign policy in a way which would satisfy most socialists: any policy conducive to an international framework more propitious for the development of socialism than the current situation.

The ending of the Cold War was considered to be just that kind of favourable international framework. It was generally assumed on the Left, and hardly questioned, that this would bring about a safer world system because it would end the nuclear escalation between the two superpowers. It would terminate the constant transformation of local disputes in the four corners of the globe into microcosms of the East–West confrontation. It would permit the softening of the repressive apparatus of the 'socialist' countries, leading, in the fullness of time, to internal reforms and, finally, to the end of the unfortunate but inevitable connection between the word 'socialism' and the unmitigated crucifixion of civil liberties in the East. The conclusion of the Cold War would permit a reduction of expenditure on defence and permit more spending on social reforms. Finally, it would deprive the warmongering Right of one of its best electoral cards. In the event, the end of the Cold War did not turn out as socialists expected. Saluted by the guns of free market capitalism, it appeared to represent the final nail in the coffin of all dreams of socialism, democratic or not. Whether this will also be the verdict of posterity we cannot tell.

The end of the Cold War leaves the central argument unaltered: if a socialist foreign policy is to be defined inductively – that is, by deriving it from the actual practices of socialist parties – then détente, international relaxation and the aim of ending the Cold War constitute its fundamental underpinnings. Indeed, many social-democratic leaders, such as the Austrian Bruno Kreisky, held the view that social democracy could be achieved only under conditions of détente.[2] Stated as a general goal, however, détente provided no clear guidelines for practical statecraft. Some pursued détente while arming themselves to the teeth, arguing that détente went hand in hand with deterrence. Others pleaded that only a non-aligned posture would create a favourable climate for détente. American and Soviet decision-makers understood détente as a situation in which local problems could be resolved through agreement between themselves. Others argued that bipolarism was itself the main problem and that multipolarism was the real purpose of détente. It is this last argument which is more in harmony with the grand goal of terminating the Cold War. A détente which froze the existing power relations between the superpowers, which carved up Europe and the rest of the globe into spheres of influence, and which constrained popular self-determination within the requirements of the national interests of the USSR and the USA, preserved the situation of undeclared warfare between East and West.

A policy which treated the power blocs as undesirable and temporary necessities to be phased out eventually was, ultimately, the only realistic goal for the forces of the Left, in Europe and elsewhere. Most, though not all, socialist and social-democratic parties, and many West European communist parties remained committed in principle, albeit in varying degrees, to this foreign policy. Some pursued it seriously in words and deeds. Others were content with merely enunciating it, while allowing themselves to be carried along by the flow of events, unwilling or unable to influence anything.

Foreign policy is the most constraining form of policy-making. The opposite appears to be the case, perhaps because it is frequently reported in highly personalized terms. Heads of state and government meet, stage summits, agree or disagree, make declarations, adopt positions, hold frank exchanges of views, send troops, withdraw them, sign treaties, move incessantly around the world, fly in supersonic planes, descend from helicopters, have banquets in exotic surroundings, are escorted in fast cars, and believe they make history. The journalists who follow them share in this excitement and legitimize this charade in written comments and televisual images. Observers and practitioners usually agree on this one point: foreign policy can be a wonderfully enjoyable form of political activity. This feeling of freedom from constraints is augmented by the fact that, in foreign policy, parliaments have little power and domestic opinion is often of marginal importance. A few salient foreign policy acts, usually of a spectacular kind, can be used to substantiate these impressions of personal power in action: John F. Kennedy's blockade of Cuba in October 1962; the 'ping-pong' diplomacy towards the USA initiated by Mao Zedong and Zhou Enlai in 1971; Anwar Sadat's visit to Israel in November 1977; the signing of the agreement between the Palestinians and Israelis on the lawn of the White House in September 1993 (carefully prepared by sensibly secret negotiations in Norway). These indisputably historical events are inseparable from the personalities who initiated them. Otherwise, the enormous burden of tradition, size, resources and geography weighs massively on the shoulders of all aspiring Talleyrands. Small countries with narrow interests can seldom play a role in the complex game of international diplomacy – except as a mediator. Some, such as Austria or Sweden, have great freedom to set an independent course on a wide range of issues, but this is because they count for very little. The USA could tolerate, albeit grudgingly, a Swedish government condemning their intervention in Vietnam because, in the final analysis, Sweden did not matter. It was mentioned only once in Henry Kissinger's 1,521 pages of memoirs, *The White House Years*. On the other hand, the US would have put enormous pressure on West Germany or even Italy had either tried to follow the Swedish path. It is, of course, dangerous to generalize: the instance of Israel's relation to the USA points to the possibility of small countries bullying big ones, of a client-state regularly biting the hand that feeds it.

The attitude towards the war in Vietnam illustrates the question of constraints. That the USA had blundered into Vietnam without a strategy or a clearly articulated goal; that the war, irrespective of the strong moral case against it, was a colossal mistake; and that it could not be won – these had become clear by 1968 even to Washington. Lyndon B. Johnson had decided not to seek re-election and his successor, Richard Nixon, realized that his main task was to extricate the USA from an unwinnable war. Unencumbered by Atlanticist ideology, as early as 1967, de Gaulle patiently explained to Harold Wilson that Ho Chi-Minh and the North Vietnamese would never yield because the future of their country was at stake; that the war would go on until the Americans left; that there was no purpose in further US escalation; that it was 'the greatest absurdity of the twentieth century'.[3]

In Sweden social democrats were overtly in sympathy with this position. On 15 November 1969, at an anti-war demonstration organized by the Swedish Vietnam Committee, the representative of the Social Democratic Party, Sten Andersson, declared: 'we support the National Liberation front … we condemn the meaningless war of the USA.'[4] Communists everywhere predictably felt no reluctance over criticizing the Americans. Students and other left-wing activists found in Vietnam a cause which united them just as much as the defence of the Spanish Republic had united their predecessors in the 1930s. Most activists in social-democratic parties throughout Europe, including the pro-American British Labour Party and German SPD, grew increasingly outraged at American involvement.

Nevertheless, pro-NATO socialists, along with a motley crowd of professional anti-communists and cold warriors, blindly defended American intervention even as the last CIA agent was boarding the last helicopter out of Saigon in 1975. The leadership of the socialist and social-democratic parties in NATO countries remained unswervingly loyal to the USA. They abstained from criticism, tried to mediate, as in the case of Harold Wilson, but did little else. Their abdication from international politics was complete. All were convinced that there was nothing they could do.

In the Cold War era of bipolarism, international diplomacy was mainly the business of the two superpowers, while growing economic interdependence had seriously narrowed foreign policy options for most countries. In Europe small countries, restricted by formal treaties, such as Belgium or Holland, stuck to their tried and tested Atlanticist Europeanism – an unassailable consensus to which all parties adhered. Italy followed a similar trajectory: once the twin pillars of its foreign policy – the European Community and the NATO alliance – were established, its foreign office could switch to automatic pilot and refrain from needless exertion. The PCI did not have this option and developed the most independent foreign policy of any communist party in the West – a policy I shall examine in detail alongside that of the Left in the three remaining middle-sized Western European powers, France, Great Britain and West Germany.

In France, de Gaulle was able and willing to manoeuvre himself into a distinctive independent position causing, as we shall see, considerable perplexity on the Left. In Britain, the Labour governments of 1964–70 remained anchored to a pristine pro-American policy. Their main foreign policy preoccupations were with trying to resolve the Rhodesian problem, an imperial remnant, and with convincing de Gaulle to let Britain into the EEC. Both policies were unsuccessful. At first the Labour government was determined to maintain what was called an 'East of Suez' role, that is, a presence in the Indian Ocean area and the Far East. As Wilson remarked, 'our frontiers are in the Himalayas' – a claim which, it has been pointed out, sounded less asinine at the time than it does now.[5]

While these commitments were loudly proclaimed, the arsenal with which they could be upheld – ships, planes and guns – was depleted or allowed to become obsolete. Military spending was slashed, programmes cancelled, cheaper American substitutes bought. In July 1967, the government announced that British forces would withdraw from Singapore and Malaysia by the mid-1970s.[6] This unheralded recognition that Britain had to abandon an international military role was arrived at grudgingly, though Labour incongruously maintained an 'independent' nuclear defence system. Harold Wilson, replying to left-wing critics and some pro-Europeans who were united in their insistence on a more radical withdrawal, declared: 'Perhaps there are some members who would like to contract out and leave it to the Americans and Chinese, eyeball to eyeball, to face this thing out. The world is too small for that kind of attitude today.'[7] Nevertheless, after the devaluation of 1967, things were really left to the Americans and the Chinese, as a new round of cuts was imposed by an alliance of pro-Europeans such as Roy Jenkins and left-wingers such as Crossman and Castle, supported by Wilson.

Britain's foreign policy could not yet be separated from the question of imperial remains. Germany's peculiarity was that its most obvious unresolved 'domestic' problem, the reunification of the country, was also a major international issue. Its own status of 'economic giant but political dwarf' did not prevent the SPD leadership from developing a complex strategy for the relative normalization of relations between the two German states and the pursuit of détente. With its 'eastern policy' or Ostpolitik, the SPD demonstrated that it was possible, with skill and flair, to follow an innovative course in foreign policy in the interests of all. The SPD succeeded where most of the West European Left failed: it linked the national interest to the cause of détente, the closest approximation to a 'socialist' foreign policy. The magnitude of this exploit can be accurately measured: for the first and only time since 1945, a party of the Left had successfully changed the foreign policy agenda of its country, imposed these changes, irreversibly, on its domestic opponents, while obtaining praise and consent from both East and West. Ostpolitik was an internationally acceptable German foreign policy, a rare phenomenon in a century in which Germany had twice unleashed a major European war. The SPD had redefined the national interest – an ideological construct and not an objective fact – in a direction which coincided with an international relaxation of tension, thus obtaining considerable domestic and international support. In a predictably ill-advised reflexive spasm, the CDU at first opposed Ostpolitik, then accepted it while in opposition, and finally pursued it vigorously when in government after 1982. Ostpolitik, the main achievement of German social democracy (perhaps its only achievement), had become the common patrimony of all German parties. Elsewhere in the West, the foreign policy agenda was always established by the Right, with the Left, sooner or later, complying.

Why did the SPD pursue Ostpolitik? What did it consist of? We noted that its previous policy of neutralism, aimed at achieving national reunification, had been repudiated in 1960 (Wehner's famous speech of 1960: see chapter 9). The SPD therefore found itself without a distinctive foreign policy. It could, of course, simply have adopted the Western-oriented Atlanticist/ Europeanist platform of Adenauer's CDU. It did not do so for two reasons. In the first place, the SPD had abandoned its policy of neutralism, but not entirely the purpose behind it: German reunification. Adenauer's Western policy pointed to a future with a permanently divided Germany. To accept it would mean abandoning reunification. In the second place, after Bad Godesberg, the SPD had already accepted much of the CDU's social market domestic agenda. To do the same with foreign policy would make the SPD indistinguishable from the CDU, not a condition an opposition aspiring to power could endure for long. In the short term, however, a toning down of differences worked to the SPD's advantage. Indeed, by 1966, the gap between the two parties had closed sufficiently to enable them to form a coalition government and to proceed towards the first stages of Ostpolitik by establishing diplomatic relations with Yugoslavia and Romania in 1967.

The origin of the SPD's Ostpolitik can be traced to the period 1961–63, after the erection of the Berlin Wall in August 1961. Willy Brandt was then mayor of West Berlin, heading a coalition which included the CDU and the FDP. As mayor he had to conduct negotiations with the East German authorities, hold discussions with the representatives of the three occupying Western powers (especially the Americans), and be fully conversant with matters of international diplomacy – skills not normally required of local politicians in other cities. Advised by Egon Bahr, and supported by Fritz Erler, leader of the SPD parliamentary group and a security specialist, Brandt actively supported John F. Kennedy, who projected a new, more flexible image of US foreign policy and who clearly intended to press for détente despite the division of Germany. During Kennedy's famous visit to Berlin, the media could not fail to underline the apparent similarities between Kennedy and Brandt, including their youthful good looks. Brandt came to be seen as the German Kennedy.[8] By 1969, Brandt's portrait was used on postcards, campaign buttons and television spots. American-style campaigning was beginning to have an impact in Europe: in Germany both parties had staff members who had been in the USA for the 1968 presidential elections and who attempted to transfer some of the techniques to the 1969 German elections.[9]

As in Italy, with the entry of the Socialist Party into the ruling coalition in 1962, in Germany too it was felt necessary to obtain Washington's seal of approval. The task was easier for Brandt than for the Italian socialists, since he was able to exploit the friction developing between the USA and Adenauer. The cause of this was Adenauer's friendship with de Gaulle, sanctioned by the Franco-German Treaty of 1963. Adenauer disliked de Gaulle's overtures to the USSR, but condoned them because he feared that détente, if left to the two superpowers, would result in a deal being reached at the expense of Germany. Also to Brandt's advantage was the split within the CDU between Erhard, who led the anti-Gaullist faction, and Adenauer. CDU divisions continued even after Erhard had become the Chancellor, for he remained at odds on foreign policy with Franz-Josef Strauss, the leader of the Bavarian sister-party of the CDU, the CSU.[10] There is little doubt that Brandt understood perfectly well that in order to adopt a more independent German policy, which is what Ostpolitik aimed to be, he had to appear the most 'American' German politician. He chose a series of lectures at Harvard in 1962 (*The Ordeal of Co-Existence*) to argue for the end of a policy of confrontation.[11] He followed this by declaring that he was ready to accept an invitation by Khrushchev to visit the USSR. Forced to decline by the West Berlin CDU, he broke the Berlin tradition of grand coalition government and formed a new coalition with the FDP after the elections of spring 1963.[12] In 1966 Brandt explained that German influence in Europe could increase only if it contributed towards a reduction of tension.[13]

In foreign policy the CDU was far from opposed to seeking a rapprochement with the USSR. Adenauer's policy towards the East was not as rigid as it is sometimes made out.[14] What Adenauer could not countenance was the idea of treating the East German regime as an acceptable partner with whom a deal could be made. The CDU's guiding principle in its own Ostpolitik was that the Federal Republic represented the whole of Germany (*Alleinvertretungsanspruch*), and that the USSR had to grant the Germans living in the East the right to free elections.[15] Only then could there be a rapprochement with the USSR. For Adenauer and his CDU successors, progress on the German question was a precondition of détente, not the key to it. The post-1969 Brandt government was willing to reverse this: détente came first. This was the basis of the new SPD-style Ostpolitik. On this terrain the SPD and the Liberals of the FDP had much in common, though they disagreed on domestic policy.[16]

It has been argued that Ostpolitik was successful because it served a number of purposes in domestic politics. It gave the FDP a solid reason to change coalition partners and return to government. Under the influence of the reformers Wolfgang Schollwer and Walter Scheel, the FDP, which had lost conservative voters to the CDU and the far Right, softened its anti-communism and became receptive to an opening to the East.[17] By January 1969, while still in opposition, the FDP submitted a plan for a treaty with the DDR which was included in the party's electoral platform.[18] Ostpolitik thus provided the new SPD–FPD coalition, established at the end of 1969, with a field for bold initiatives in foreign policy, where it was less fettered by its narrow parliamentary majority, while remaining cautious in domestic policies, where there was less internal governmental consensus.[19] Finally, the abandonment of German reunification as a possibility in the short term was made possible by changes in public opinion. Until 1964, reunification was the most salient 'foreign' affairs issue, with 41 per cent of respondents regarding it as 'the most important question facing Germany today'. By the late 1960s the economy was perceived as more important, and a general anxiety concerning Germany's probable obliteration in case of a world conflict was of central relevance to the electorate.[20] From the electoral point of view, Ostpolitik paid off handsomely: at the first elections following the Eastern treaties, the SPD emerged as the strongest party in the country, with 45.8 per cent of the vote against the CDU's 44.9 per cent – the only time in post-war German history it achieved this feat.

Domestic considerations, however, are not sufficient to explain the factors leading to the success of Ostpolitik. International circumstances were uniquely favourable. It would have been impossible for Bonn to deal directly with the Soviet Union without American consent. Kissinger attempted to exercise some control out of fear that Brandt might become over-dependent on the USSR, but the US realized that the most intelligent contribution they could make would be to accept the role of unenthusiastic spectators:

> Brandt did his part in assuaging anxiety by keeping in close touch. To be sure, the new German government informed rather than consulted. They reported pro-gress; they did not solicit advice. But this was also what we preferred. The last thing we wanted was to be held responsible for German negotiating positions that were turning into a bitter domestic issue in West Germany.[21]

In effect this was the ideal form of support. Too close an American involve-ment would have reduced the Germans, once again, to passive onlookers of decisions affecting their destiny. Had the USA and the other NATO allies not been consulted regularly, Ostpolitik could have been seen as yet further evidence of German unreliability and of the SPD's recurring neutralist tempta-tions. The SPD could not have conducted its own Ostpolitik had it not accepted NATO unconditionally. Thus, the abandonment of neutralism, which could have been taken as a move to the Right, turned out to be one of the essential preconditions for a move to the Left.

In practical terms, Ostpolitik amounted to the treaties signed by the Federal Republic with the USSR (August 1970), with Poland (December 1970), with the DDR (the Basic Treaty of 1972) and with Czechoslovakia (1973), as well as the Quadripartite Agreement on Berlin in 1971. The first of these treaties, that with the USSR, made everything else possible. By ratifying it, West Germany accepted all existing European frontiers, including the Oder–Neisse line between Poland and the DDR, and the frontier between the Federal Republic and the German Democratic Republic. In effect, the SPD had signed the equivalent of the peace treaty of the Second World War but, unlike the Versailles Treaty of 1919, which it had also underwritten, this one attracted no serious right-wing remonstrance, no nationalist cry of 'stab in the back'. This time the SPD had acted, and appeared to act, as the party of the German nation, while pursuing a policy which was in the interests of all. Brandt had seen this with remarkable lucidity before 1968:

> Germany has an interest in detente – for general, European, and national reasons. Here we are in accord not only with our allies … but with almost everyone. Here we join with the nations and governments of the uncommitted world. Here interests we have in common with the Communist-governed states also come to light in spite of some polemics.[22]

What did these treaties achieve? They established a framework for negotiations between NATO and the Warsaw Pact. As Wolfram Hanrieder explained, they 'became an important ingredient in an intricate set of dealings between and within the two alliances, cutting across several kinds of issues ... in which all parties involved sought to maximize their gains while hedging against possible losses.'[23] They stabilized the situation in West Berlin, whose special ties with the Federal Republic were now recognized by the USSR. They gave West Berliners the right (suspended following the erection of the Wall) to visit their relatives in East Berlin. The Eastern treaties brought into being by Ostpolitik were the signal for an expansion of trade and economic co-operation. This enabled West Germany to achieve an unbridgeable lead in Eastern markets well before the 1990s, when they unexpectedly became wide open to Western penetration. Ostpolitik gave the green light for the opening of the Helsinki talks under the auspices of the CSCE (Conference on Security and Co-operation in Europe), the first instance of multilateral East–West diplomacy.[24] Ostpolitik greatly increased the freedom of action of the Federal Republic *vis-à-vis* its allies in the West who, until then, always had the option, during negotiations, of hinting that they could seek an improvement in their own relations with the DDR independently of the FRG. After the recognition of East Germany, such blackmail among friends could no longer take place.[25]

Détente was not a finite goal, but a process susceptible to varying interpretations. As far as the USSR was concerned, the purpose of Ostpolitik was to validate the status quo in Europe, entrenching its own sphere of influence. The SPD had a quite different, dynamic conception of détente, entailing the overcoming of the rigid logic of the power blocs which had hitherto prevailed. The SPD hoped that a closer relationship would develop between the FRG and the DDR, that an entire network of economic, social, cultural as well as political transactions would emerge between Bonn and the other countries of Central and Eastern Europe. This did not occur on the expected scale. Relations remained politically limited. It was not in Moscow's interest, nor perhaps was it in Washington's, to promote or facilitate anything that might lessen the cohesion of the Warsaw Pact and the division of Europe.

Was Ostpolitik successful? If the aim was to lead to the removal of the power blocs in Europe, it was a failure. If, more modestly, it sought to contribute to détente, it was highly successful. Not much more could have been done by a political party such as the SPD, in coalition with liberals, and, with them, joint holders of a slim parliamentary majority facing the compact ranks of the CDU/CSU. The keys to the destiny of Europe were to be found in Moscow and Washington, not in Bonn, London or, notwithstanding de Gaulle, Paris. Nevertheless, Brandt never thought that delegation to the superpowers was the way forward for German foreign policy, even though he wrote that the security of Western Europe 'rests ultimately on the trustworthiness of the American commitment', while acknowledging that de Gaulle, 'in his own way is utilizing the political freedom of movement that has been won by the nuclear stalemate of the world powers'.[26]

It may appear as if the first phase of Ostpolitik (1967–71) had occurred at a most inauspicious time. The Soviet armed repression of the reformist Czechoslovak communists in 1968, and the constant military escalation of the USA in Vietnam, might be taken as aspects of the increasing bipolarity of the world. In reality, the opposite was the case. The 1960s witnessed the first systematic assaults on the rigidly bipolar US–USSR world condominium. In Asia the Chinese People's Republic was pursuing an independent foreign policy course after years of subservience to the USSR, and was acquiring its own nuclear weapons. In Europe, de Gaulle was emancipating France from too close an American embrace, while Britain was taking its first faltering steps towards the EEC. In Central Europe the Prague Spring, though ultimately unsuccessful, highlighted the presence of an exceptionally strong impulse for reform within communism. The most clear-sighted exponents of communism, Dubcek in Czechoslovakia and Togliatti and his successor Enrico Berlinguer in Italy, had become the champions of 'reform Communism' (later 'Eurocommunism'), by seeking some form of disengagement from Moscow. Even Romania, while maintaining unaltered the authoritarian structures of its despotic state, was following its own independent foreign policy by refusing to join the other Warsaw Pact forces in invading Czechoslovakia, and by welcoming Nixon in August 1969.

This new situation had been recognized, quite openly, by the USA. On 18 February 1970, Richard Nixon sent the US Congress a 40,000-word report, *United States Foreign Policy for the 1970s: A New Strategy for Peace*, which he described – with characteristic humility – as 'the most comprehensive statement on US foreign policy ever made this century', and which the US press dubbed a 'State of the World' address.[27] This report explained that a monolithic communist movement no longer existed; that the allies of the US would have to rely more on their own forces for their defence; that the end of the American nuclear monopoly had created a situation in which both sides could inflict unacceptable damage, no matter which struck first. The 'Nixon Doctrine', first outlined at Guam (25 July 1969), was now restated: the USA would no longer singlehandedly undertake the defence of the free world.[28]

The developing 'polycentric' nature of the world was thus increasingly recognized everywhere, except perhaps in Moscow. The pioneers of polycentrism had been the founders of the non-aligned movement, Gamal Abdel Nasser, Jawaharlal Nehru and Josip Broz Tito. In the West European Left the chief proponent of this trend was the PCI. We have noted in chapter 10 that, as early as 1956, Togliatti had eagerly anticipated the development of a polycentric communist world which would no longer be subject to a single hegemonic leadership. At first rebuffed by the USSR, he saw a new opportunity in the development of the EEC and the schism between China and the USSR. Although in complete disagreement with the Chinese communists, who had attacked him directly before starting their open polemic with Moscow,[29] Togliatti rejected all Soviet attempts to convene an international communist conference whose purpose would have been the excommunication of China from the international movement and the reaffirmation of Soviet leadership.[30] A few months later, in what turned out to be his last work, a memorandum written a few days before his death in August 1964 in Yalta and addressed to Khrushchev, he advocated an overall rethinking of major questions, from democratic planning to civil liberties:

> It is not right to speak of the Socialist countries (and even of the Soviet Union) as if everything always went well in them ... In actual fact, in all the Socialist countries, difficulties, contradictions and new problems, which must be presented in their effective reality, are arising all the time.[31]

The most relevant step suggested was an institutionalization, through meetings and discussions, of 'the different sectors of our movement, Western Europe, Latin America, the Third World ... People's Democracies, etc.'[32] The Yalta memorandum, though originally highly confidential, was quickly published by the PCI in its weekly journal and presented, as the years went by, as *the* manifesto of polycentrism. A close reading of the document shows this to be an exaggeration.[33] The point, however, is that Togliatti 'laid down the procedural ground rules for the new internationalism that his successors, Luigi Longo and Berlinguer, would pursue within and beyond the Communist movement'.[34] On the basis of the embryonic polycentrism contained in the memorandum, the PCI continued its practice of condemning Soviet cultural and religious policies and was – among communists – the most vociferous critic of the Soviet intervention in Czechoslovakia.[35] To the great irritation of the CPSU, the Moscow Conference of 1965, which was supposed to prepare an international gathering for the condemnation of the Chinese, ended with success for the PCI: the proposed meeting was postponed indefinitely. Instead, a conference of communist parties held in Moscow in June 1969 produced a final communiqué which accepted the demands of the PCI: it was non-binding on the participants and did not criticize the Chinese. For good measure, the PCI refused to sign even this document. Thus, while avoiding open rupture with Moscow, the PCI was able to restrain the CPSU, an unusual feat of diplomacy for a powerless opposition party.[36]

The most important foreign policy initiative of the PCI in this period, however, was achieved by acting secretly, as the chief mediator in the process of Ostpolitik between the SPD and the DDR. In 1967 Sergio Segre, foreign policy adviser to the PCI leader, Luigi Longo, acted as an intermediary between the DDR and the SPD during the entire first phase of Ostpolitik, thus contributing to a key phase of international détente. The PCI thus established useful contacts with a powerful European social-democratic party, earned its gratitude, succeeded in persuading the SPD to lift the ban on the

West German Communist Party (though on condition, for legal reasons, that the name be changed from KPD, Kommunistische Partei Deutschlands, to DKP, Deutsche Kommunistische Partei), and, by judicious leaking of details concerning its good offices, was able to present itself convincingly as a Western party able to pursue a responsible foreign policy.[37]

Meanwhile, under the influence of Giorgio Amendola, one of its leading reformists, the PCI abandoned its opposition to the European Community. As early as March 1962, Amendola had criticized the PCI's overestimate of the economic difficulties the EEC would cause Italy. He pointed out that the EEC had brought about technical progress and modernization.[38] The basis for the European policy of the Italian Communist Party had been established more than ten years before the birth of 'Eurocommunism'.[39]

In May 1966, the PCI's representative at the West European communist conference, held in Vienna, recognized that a new situation of economic interdependence had been reached in Western Europe, and that the simplistic condemnation and rejection of European integration was an unrealistic position to which 'for too long some sectors of the European working class have remained attached'.[40] In March 1969 the first Italian communist MPs joined the European Parliament. The ambitious goal was a revision of the Treaty of Rome, the phasing out of the two power blocs, and the affirmation of European autonomy. All this was to be achieved through the unity of the European Left, including the social-democratic parties.[41]

Though the PCI's conception of Europe was anti-Atlantic,[42] the Italian communists had now joined the pro-EEC consensus of the main parties of the Left in the member-states of the Community. The main exception remained the PCF. Even this party, however, had begun to change its position under pressure from its Italian comrades and the French socialists. Longo tried to involve the PCF in a joint initiative towards the EEC in successive meetings between the two parties in Geneva (1965) and San Remo (1966). At that time the PCF was going through one of its periodic bouts of political innovation. The new leader, Waldeck Rochet, was cautiously trying to change a party left unreformed by his predecessor, Maurice Thorez. This was not an easy task: Waldeck Rochet was surrounded by an old guard busily grooming their own candidate for the eventual succession, Georges Marchais.[43] Nevertheless, some timid advances were made in the direction of a less anti-EEC policy, mainly because the sought-after alliance with the socialists required them.

A new tone found its way into the pages of the PCF's official theoretical journal *Cahiers du communisme*: in April 1966 it printed an article calling for unity with the socialists on the issue of Europe;[44] a few months previously, it had published a reasonably objective explanation of the workings and development of the EEC, replete with useful data rejecting any autarchic economic strategy.[45] Browsing through the journal, one could even encounter a surprising distinction between Jean Monnet (until recently, regarded as a creature of European technocratic neo-capitalism) and Jean Lecanuet, the anti-Gaullist leader of the Christian Democrats: the former was praised for his recognition that the USSR was a force for peace and for his advocacy of détente; the second damned because of his repeated warnings of the need for eternal nuclear vigilance against the East.[46] Even more surprising was the conclusion, which admitted that in 'our new era' one could no longer develop an economic policy limited to the national framework, and that, though it 'would be unrealistic to deny the permanency of the national fact', the party now advocated 'a common European policy of the Left'.[47]

The PCF's flexibility on Europe never extended to embracing European integration. It accepted the EEC as a fact of life and no longer wished France to withdraw from it, but remained opposed to direct elections to the European Parliament, hostile to any extension of its powers, committed to defending national sovereignty, and convinced that any further integration would strengthen the powers of multinational companies.[48] On all these points the PCF diverged from the PCI, the SFIO – with which it wished to co-operate – and all the socialist parties in the other five EEC member-states. On all these points its views coincided with those of the anti-Europeans in the British Labour Party.

The PCF realized that European integration could no longer be ignored. Other Left parties in NATO countries were coming round to the same position. The Danish Socialdemokratiet realized full well the limitations of a small and relatively weak country. With Norway, it had broken with Nordic solidarity in the 1940s by joining NATO. In the 1960s it prepared, albeit unenthusiastically, to join the European Economic Community. As Jens-Otto Krag, the Danish social democrat foreign minister, explained without reticence, the reason was entirely pragmatic: Britain had applied to join; Denmark was very dependent on agricultural exports to Britain; therefore it had to follow Britain.[49] When Britain's application was vetoed, Denmark withdrew, even though de Gaulle offered full membership.[50] In Denmark the issue was entirely bi-partisan. When Edward Heath started the third and finally successful bid to enter the EEC in 1970, Denmark, Norway and Ireland reapplied. On this issue the Socialdemokratiet – by then out of power – backed the ruling 'bourgeois' parties. The legislation to join was passed by the Folketing on 7 September 1971 against the opposition of the seventeen MPs of the leftist Socialistisk Folkeparti (Socialist People's Party – SF), twelve dissident social democrats, four radicals and one Greenlander. The pro-EEC vote, however, had not reached the required five-sixths majority, and a mandatory referendum was held which was won by the pro-Europeans with 63.3 per cent.[51]

Ireland and Norway operated under constraints similar to those facing Denmark: their dependency on trade with the UK was very pronounced. Norway, however, was the most reluctant of the three. Unlike Denmark, its non-socialist parties were divided over the issue. The Centre Party (the farmers' party) was anti-European, and so were some factions in the Liberal and Christian People's parties. The trade unions were opposed and so was a majority of the population, including a majority of Labour supporters. In spite of this, all three applications to join the EEC received clear majorities in the Storting: 113 for and 37 against in 1962, 135 for and 14 against in 1967, and 132 for and 17 against in 1970.[52] The Norwegians, unlike the Danes, did not ratify the view of their Parliament in the referendum which followed the 1970 vote, and rejected entry with a 53.3 per cent majority. As in Denmark, the main force against membership came from the Left. Neither in Denmark nor in Norway did nationalist ideology play a significant role in the development of a leftist opposition to the EEC. In Norway the desire to protect some special groups – such as fishing communities – was sufficient to tip the balance against Europe even in 1994, when Norway once again rejected EC membership. In both Denmark and Norway, however, the main motive for the anti-EEC attitude was the fear that the welfare achievements of Nordic social democracy would be overwhelmed by the integrationist pace of a supra-national association whose stated purpose was the economic development of capitalist Europe. It followed inescapably from this, however, that, in spite of their repeated internationalist claims, the anti-Europeans remained anchored to a 'national' conception of socialism in one country: socialism would flower best, they thought, where outsiders trod the least.

Such fears were virtually non-existent among socialists and social democrats in the six countries which had founded the EEC. They all favoured an enlargement of the Community and hence British entry; wished to 'democratize' the EEC by making the European Parliament more accountable; criticized de Gaulle's concept of a *Europe des patries* and his obstructionism on EEC matters; and made vaguely positive remarks about greater co-operation.[53]

None of these parties, however, had succeeded in integrating its domestic policy with its Europeanism. They devised electoral programmes according to a national logic and took very little notice of any eventual constraints the Community might impose. To be a good European was a badge of respectability, responsibility and anti-chauvinism. Europeanism occupied the foreign policy void characteristic of this Left, with the important exception of the SPD. Had it been more than a rhetorical device to fill the void, these parties might have tried to devise and fight for a comprehensive plan of European reorganization, or might have had to ask themselves the key question: 'What should the European Community achieve?' In reality, there was no significant debate at all on the European Community among the socialist parties of the EC. Even the SPD, innovative on Ostpolitik (which was in any case a 'national' foreign policy), had very little to say on the EEC and remained cool towards supra-nationalism.[54]

Nevertheless, European socialists tried to justify the EEC in social-democratic terms. This was true even in countries which had not expressed any interest in joining the EEC, such as Austria. The new SPÖ leader, Bruno

Kreisky, asserted that social democracy could be achieved only in an integrated Europe. He divided the history of the socialist movement into three historical phases. In the first, the workers had acquired a consciousness of their historical role. In the second, social democrats constructed the welfare state. The purpose of the anticipated third phase was the democratization of all fields of social life and the construction of a wider European political unity.[55] This idea was directly borrowed from Per Albin Hansson's three stages of social democracy, devised in Sweden in the 1930s. In Britain, as we saw in chapter 6, the sociologist T. H. Marshall used a similar triptych in his differentiation between the political, social and economic rights constituting the modern meaning of citizenship.

In Denmark, the leader of Socialdemokratiert, Jens-Otto Krag, explained in 1971 to the Helsinki meeting of the Socialist International that the European Community was not a capitalist plot aimed at damaging the interests of social democrats; on the contrary, it could become a mechanism which would enable social democracy to expand into unconquered territories such as Italy.[56] At the same meeting, Willy Brandt welcomed the British application in the same spirit: the EEC must be 'directed towards shaping a political will … we are trying to create something more than just a Europe of business'.[57] Trygve Bratteli, prime minister of Norway and leader of the DNA, also insisted that European co-operation was not incompatible with the attainment of 'the long-term objectives which our parties have formulated for the individual countries'; and added that one of the main conditions for Norwegian participation in European integration 'should be that we maintain the possibility of developing a democratic socialist society'.[58]

At the Helsinki meeting none of these views was endorsed by the British Labour Party, then in opposition. Denis Healey made no comment on the EEC.[59] Harold Wilson explained that the parliamentary party had yet to make up its mind on it; he did not add that the party at large had already done so and was against it. Wilson's position was that two issues needed to be resolved – namely, Britain's contribution to the agricultural budget and a 'fair' deal for the countries of the Commonwealth.[60]

This ambivalence could not have surprised any of the delegates. In the 1960s the European Community had become one of the most fractious issues for the British Labour Party. No party of the Left has exhibited such profound uncertainty on the question of Europe. The saga could not have been more complicated. In 1962 Labour had united around Gaitskell with relish against the EEC, a time for unity after the bitter divisions over unilateral nuclear disarmament and Clause Four. In 1967 Harold Wilson unexpectedly launched Britain's second attempt to join the Community; de Gaulle vetoed it. Labour then lost the 1970 election and refused to support Edward Heath's third British attempt and voted against the terms of entry obtained. After the 1974 electoral victory, Wilson renegotiated the terms and submitted them to a national referendum in 1975 – Labour's first serious foray into constitutional reform, since nationwide referenda had never been used in British politics before. In the course of the referendum campaign, a majority of the party's National Executive Committee, together with a minority of the cabinet, joined forces to reject the renegotiated terms. By a crushing majority, the electorate sanctioned entry. Labour's 1983 election manifesto was decidedly anti-European, possibly the last gasp of the anti-EEC position before subsequent party programmes made a firm commitment to Europe, although sections of the Parliamentary Labour Party remained suspicious of the Community even in the early 1990s.

Labour leaders reflected this deep ambivalence. Gaitskell himself, before jumping on the anti-EEC bandwagon, performed a complex balancing act. As he put it to the arch pro-European Roy Jenkins in May 1962: 'it is not really a matter of what I think; it is a question of carrying the Party.'[61] By the time of the October 1962 Party Conference in Brighton, he had decided to oppose British entry not on principle, but because 'the terms were not right'. This was held to be the best device for obtaining the approval of all anti-EEC forces (the majority), without causing excessive grief among the pro-marketeers, his closest political supporters. 'The terms are not right' remained the standard objection to the EEC, opportunistically used even by those who opposed entry on principle.[62] Having united the party around a pragmatic rejection of entry, Gaitskell used demagogy to drive home his advantage. He concluded his speech by attacking the federalist dreams of the creators of the EEC: 'It would mean the end of Britain as an independent nation state ... the end of a thousand years of history.' Gaitskell received a rapturous welcome from the ranks of trade unionists and constituency activists who had mercilessly attacked him on defence and Clause Four in the previous two years; as his wife Dora warily but accurately remarked, 'all the wrong people are cheering'.[63]

De Gaulle's veto of Macmillan's application relegated the issue of British entry to the back burner. It did not loom large in the 1964 and 1966 general elections. Nevertheless, pro-Europeanism had become solidly entrenched in a significant minority of the Parliamentary Labour Party, probably one-third, most of whom belonged to the 'social-democratic' or Gaitskellite wing of the party. On the Left, anti-EEC feelings became one of the hallmarks of 'true' socialism. There were, however, a few exceptions: in 1967 a small group of MPs led by Eric Heffer argued for entry into the EEC as the first step towards a Socialist United States of Europe.[64] A few years later, Heffer and his friends changed their mind and became opponents of the EEC. The British Communist Party, the trade unions, the Labour Left around the magazine *Tribune*, and virtually all leftist sects, Trotskyist or otherwise, rallied against the Common Market and were joined by representatives of the Labour Right such as Peter Shore, Denis Healey and Douglas Jay. Supposed 'modernizers' in the trade unions such as Clive Jenkins coalesced with staunch traditionalists and communist trade unionists such as Ken Gill to defend

British national sovereignty from the European Community, often designated as a 'capitalist club', a French conspiracy, a springboard for Catholic hegemony, a German-dominated association.[65] Outside the Labour Party and the Left as a whole, it would have been necessary to travel to the far Right of British politics, to Enoch Powell and the nationalist ranks of Conservatism, to find kindred spirits.

Not surprisingly, the combination of petty provincial nationalism with intuitional 'gut' socialism and a sentimental attachment to the Commonwealth as a great multiracial family produced some entertaining silliness: 'Our type of beer might disappear if Britain joins the EEC ... we could not have our usual kippers because of their brown colouring ... British sausages also do not conform and would have to change.'[66]

The revival of the Labour debate on Europe was caused by the Wilson government's decision to launch Britain's second application to join the Community. Soon after the 1966 general election, Wilson announced that he would visit the capitals of the Six to ascertain the terms of entry should Britain decide to apply. In practice, Wilson embarked on informal negotiations with virtually no preconditions, though in March 1966 he had said that Britain had to continue to have access to cheap food from the Commonwealth and that there should be no supra-national control of foreign policy.[67] A few months later, he announced that he would apply to join. On 27 November 1967, before anti-EEC campaigners within the Labour Party had time to mobilize, de Gaulle renewed his veto. The official reasons given by the French were the rickety state of the British economy – in particular, the balance of payments – its preferential food imports from the Commonwealth, the restrictions imposed on exports of capital, and the international role of sterling.[68] No one could really be surprised. De Gaulle's press conference of 31 March 1967 at the Rome meeting of EEC leaders confirmed, if confirmation were needed, that his hostility towards the USA had increased.[69] From the general's point of view, France was the only EEC country truly willing to exercise an independent policy; without France, the Dutch, the Belgians, even the Germans, not to speak of the Italians, would simply fall into the seductive arms of the USA. British entry would compound these pressures.[70] Wilson's own accounts of his visits to de Gaulle in January and June 1967 show no signs of bitterness or anger against the general. On the contrary, as a mere politician Wilson was charmed by de Gaulle, the statesman, and overwhelmed by the general's aura and sense of being part of world history.[71]

De Gaulle's assumption that Britain was merely a vassal of the Americans appeared to be substantiated by Labour's foreign policy towards Vietnam. British defence of sterling as the second reserve currency was seen as a sign that it was playing second fiddle to the US. This accusation was particularly irksome to the British, as the French Treasury was busy accumulating gold and getting rid of its dollars – financially a shrewd move, considering that the dollar became non-convertible (i.e. devalued) in August 1971. Wilson was well aware that de Gaulle considered the role of sterling as an international reserve to be a critical indication of Britain's special relationship with the USA.[72] This view was also shared by some of the pro-Europeans within the Labour cabinet, such as George Brown, who, according to Richard Crossman and Barbara Castle, had come to the conclusion in 1966 that Harold Wilson would not consider floating the pound because he 'was now bound personally and irrevocably to President Johnson and had ceased to be a free agent'.[73] The irony was that Labour had devalued ten days before de Gaulle's veto.

Why did Wilson embark on a pro-EEC policy which he had previously rejected and which he knew would be so disruptive of party unity? A cluster of plausible reasons have been suggested: the inability of the European Free Trade Association (EFTA) to secure adequate access to the much larger EEC trading area; the decrease in importance of Commonwealth trade; America's blatant lack of interest in a 'special relationship' with Britain, and the obvious development of the EEC as the leading interlocutor of the USA in the GATT negotiating round.[74] In other words, the foreign policy based on a world role for the UK had collapsed. Wilson's undoubted merit was to have realized it and acted accordingly, by reducing overseas commitments 'East of Suez' and turning to Europe.

Moreover, Labour in government always found it difficult to resist the consensus constructed by the 'Establishment' which, by 1966, had become increasingly pro-EEC – a consensus which ranged from the City and the CBI to most of the press, including the pro-Labour *Daily Mirror*, and the civil service, especially the Foreign Office.[75] It should be added that public opinion was moving towards a more pro-EEC position; throughout the second half of 1966, at least two-thirds of respondents indicated that they would approve of British entry.[76] After the elections, which heralded the largest Labour parliamentary majority since 1945 – ninety-seven MPs overall – the new cohort turned out to be distinctly more pro-European, relatively speaking, than its predecessors.[77]

In his memoirs Wilson himself never explained why a second attempt to join the EEC was made. From his account Labour appeared simply to drift into it. Those who opposed membership did not strenuously resist the move, perhaps because they gambled, rightly as it turned out, that the French would do their work for them. The House of Commons approved the second application by a massive majority of 488 to 62.

The most plausible cause of Britain's second application, though difficult to verify, was that Wilson was simply acknowledging, at least implicitly and perhaps unconsciously, that Labour's domestic policy for economic recovery had been as unsuccessful as its foreign policy. The cabinet that decided to enter Europe did so in a half-hearted way because it somehow perceived that the decision was the result of a major domestic defeat.[78] Labour's domestic plans had been based on a modernized version of the idea of a national road to socialism, 'modernized' in the sense that while socialism may no longer have been the final destination of Labour's efforts, it evidently remained committed to a 'national' road – that is, a national solution to the century-old decline of the British economy. This vision, such as it was, had disintegrated. The 'technological revolution' had not produced a British economic miracle. The National Plan had folded. The management of the British economy had been reduced to defence of the currency.[79] Wilson's bid to enter Europe was a tacit acknowledgement that there were no national solutions to Britain's problems. It also reflected the growing importance of Europe for British trade, and the corresponding decrease in the relevance of the Commonwealth. As George Brown told the House of Commons in May 1967, British exports to Europe had doubled since 1958, but had remained static with the Commonwealth.[80]

This analysis highlights a crucial point. It confirms that the fortunes of socialism were inexorably bound up with those of the (capitalist) nation within which it operated. The fate of British capitalism and the destiny of British socialism were linked. These constraints affected all politicians. All British prime ministers since the early 1960s eventually accepted that there was no future for Britain outside the institutions of the European Community. Macmillan and then Wilson, Heath and then Wilson again, Callaghan and then, finally, the most 'nationalist' British prime minister of the post-war era, Margaret Thatcher, as well as her weak successor – all of them, irrespective of their ideological positions, of the promises made, of the internal party support required, of personal temperament, reluctantly or enthusiastically bowed their heads to Brussels. Not one of them failed to escape the integrationist course set by the irreversible growth of global interdependence. Over the thirty years following Britain's entry to the Community, these restraints would grow rather than abate, and would impact on all government leaders, however distasteful they personally may have found the idea of European unity.

Within the Labour Party, and especially within the Labour Left, a different analysis was produced to explain the failures of Wilsonism. According to this, the reason why state planning of the economy was dropped, the motive behind Britain's second application, the source of all U-turns, was the lack of courage of Labour leaders, their untrustworthiness, the ease with which the power of the City, international capitalism, multinational companies could bend the will of an elected Labour government. This naive analysis rested on an innocently idealist view of politics: the belief that once elected, politicians can do as they please so long as they have principles and trust the people who elect them.

The establishment of a consensus in domestic and foreign policy determined by objective circumstances does not necessarily lead to an identity of political views. Constraints establish what cannot be done. They do not dictate every detail of policy, only the broad guidelines. There can be different ways of 'being in Europe'. There can be different options for a European-wide management of national economies. It is only when one has understood the limits within which one must navigate that one can plot the course. Skilled politicians, like skilled downhill skiers, may not know every bump or dip in the terrain and may not be sure where they will end up. But they know where not to go and how to exploit the thrust of their descent at each bend. Of course, skiers, when they reach the valley, stop and catch their breath. In politics there are no resting places.

The necessity of supporting the US war in Vietnam was seen by virtually all socialist parties in NATO as part of the foreign policy consensus and hence as a constraint. America's lengthy entanglement in Vietnam traversed the entire course of the 1960s. The unpopularity of the war grew, among the American public, in synchrony with the increase in American casualties. It concluded with the comprehensive humiliation of Washington. Neither the intense bombing of 1972, nor the protracted negotiations, nor the face-saving device of an American withdrawal in 1973, and the consequent 'Vietnamization' of the war, could obliterate the glaring realization that the result had been a total victory for the communists. Vietnam had become the rallying call of the radical Left throughout Europe and North America. Demonstrations, teach-ins (or public debates), university occupations, protests of various sorts accompanied the growing American involvement. The leadership of the socialist and social-democratic parties remained apparently unmoved by all this. Their allegiance to Atlanticism was so solid and unquestionable that the issues posed by America's unwinnable Asian war were neither considered nor analysed. When it came to Vietnam, the two most important leaders of European social democracy, Willy Brandt and Harold Wilson, simultaneously decided that the best course to follow was unenthusiastic endorsement. Wilson, while never reneging on his general support for American policies, dissociated himself from the bombing of Hanoi and Haiphong in June 1966, and generally from any extension of US bombing to heavily populated cities.[81] When still in opposition and positioning themselves for power, the German social democrats were more supportive of the USA than even the German conservatives. In 1966, *Bild Zeitung*, the bestselling mass circulation daily owned by the ferociously anti-communist Springer Press, ran a surprisingly peace-oriented editorial, which reminded the Americans that 'in Vietnam also the right to self-determination applies even if free elections should turn out to be unfavourable to the Americans.' This prompted the irritation of the second-in-command of the SPD, Fritz Erler, who wrote to Axel Springer, outraged: 'I think it is terrible that … the last bit of confidence in our nation by its ally is being destroyed.' Having by-passed Springer on the right – no mean achievement – Erler and Brandt flew to Washington in April 1966 and publicly proclaimed their support for US foreign policy.[82] In his memoirs Brandt explained that he did not wish to interfere with the US 'in an area it said was vital' – a standard justification on both sides of the Cold War. He then added: 'I swallowed my grave doubts and held my tongue where it might have been better to make my opposition explicit.'[83]

In Atlanticist socialist circles, strong in Belgium and Germany, slightly less so in Holland and Italy, the general feeling was that the war was embarrassing; it put the USA in an unacceptable position. Yet it was America's war and no good would come of opposing it, since American support for more important and relevant policies such as Ostpolitik (for German social democrats), or supporting sterling (for Wilson's beleaguered cabinet), was required.

Be that as it may, the utter docility of the West European Left surprised even the USA. Henry Kissinger, in his unusually self-serving memoirs – even by the low standards of politicians – recorded it thus:[84]

> Strangely, Vietnam played a minor role in the visits of European leaders. European public opinion, at least as represented by the media, opposed the war. But European leaders registered no objection. During the entire period of the war I recall no criticism by a European leader in even the most private conversation ... Brandt and Wilson volunteered no comment and made sympathetic noises when Nixon outlined our Vietnam strategy.[85]

Earlier, when describing Michael Stewart, Wilson's rather incompetent Foreign Secretary, a man who liked the idea of occupying the moral high ground in international affairs – if only he could find it – Kissinger wrote: 'Despite his many doubts, he defended our position in Vietnam in a debate at the Oxford Union with more vigour and skill than was exhibited by many of the Americans who had made the decision to send our troops there; he never expressed his qualms to outsiders.'[86]

The problem with foreign policy constraints is that once they are accepted they are seldom questioned again. In the maelstrom of politics, as one limps from crisis to crisis, it is always comforting to have a set of apparently immutable parameters. They remove the need for much agonizing indecision. The logic of syllogism replaces analysis of the concrete situation: the war in Vietnam is part of the West–East conflict; we are on the side of the West; therefore we support the USA. By 1972 support had turned into silence. Kissinger grumbled: 'Not one NATO ally supported us or even hinted at understanding of our point of view.'[87] By then, as the USA was savagely bombing Hanoi, most of the mainstream USA press had risen in moral indignation. But there was no outright condemnation from socialist leaders in NATO countries.

The socialist supporters of the USA abdicated responsibility in decision-making by uncritically accepting the claim of the US administration that this Asian war was the main battlefront between the West and the East. Yet in the West, the powerful symbolism which came to dominate popular perception of the war was not that it was East versus West, but that it was a struggle between some of the most destitute people in the world and the most technologically advanced state in history; that it was a battle between the will, the spirit of the Vietnamese and advanced weaponry. Little could be more compelling than the stark difference between the two modes of warfare: on the one hand, the characteristically overfed, jargon-replete US pilots bombing the Vietnamese back to the stone age, from on high, in a scientifically directed campaign of saturation bombing; on the other, the undernourished and simply-clad Vietnamese guerrilla, able to walk for days with the sustenance of a miserly bowl of rice, archaically waging revolutionary war against the full fury of unlimited technological power.[88] These images were far more powerful than the clash between totalitarian communism and Western democracy, because the Saigon regime being defended by the Americans could not conceivably be labelled democratic. The strength of individual will (so much praised by Western liberalism) was far better embodied in the heroic guerrilla wading through the jungle's marshes than in the robotized John Wayne figure calmly and repeatedly pushing the death button from the relative security of his B-52 bomber. In a paradoxical reversal of roles, the Vietnamese communists represented the triumph of modern individualism against the human automatons deployed by a military-industrial complex. This powerful symbolism, and the objective reality which sustained it, escaped the leaders of European social democracy, yet it captured the imagery of the 'perplexing sixties' and its libertarian spirit. By uncritically following the American lead in Asia, the socialist and social-democratic parties signalled their refusal to engage with this problematic. In so doing, they lost contact with a crucial generation.[89] The political price paid remains unknown.

Willy Brandt's Social Democrats had a strategic justification for this major lapse. They were trying, with their Ostpolitik, to establish a new *modus vivendi* with the USSR. For this strategy to work, it was necessary that the resulting international scenario should be more secure for both East and West. In this way, Ostpolitik would create no losers, only winners. For this to occur, it was imperative that the foreign policy of the Bonn government should not be construed as being in any way anti-American: to criticize Washington's Vietnamese policy would inevitably be seen as a return to the SPD neutralism of the 1950s; Ostpolitik would acquire a pro-Soviet label and fail.

Such special pleading cannot be invoked on behalf of Harold Wilson's Labour government. The argument that Wilson's support for the Americans' Vietnamese policies was dictated by the need to receive US financial help, especially in order to defend sterling, is unconvincing.[90] The defence of sterling was in the interest of the USA, which had applied pressure in this direction, quite independently of Vietnam, in order to stem the possibility of speculators concentrating their fire on the dollar. British support over Vietnam did not waver even after 1967, when sterling, having been devalued, required less active international support. As Wilson himself has since implied, Labour's Vietnamese policies were a major factor in convincing de Gaulle that, irrespective of which government was in charge, Britain was an American

Trojan horse to be kept out of the EEC.[91] Thus, Wilson sacrificed his European policy on the altar of the special relationship. In so doing, he repeated the pattern of Macmillan's bungling of the first British application to join the EEC. In 1962, unable to fund the British 'independent' nuclear programme after the Skybolt air-to-ground missile had been cancelled by the Americans, Macmillan went to Nassau to meet Kennedy. An alternative solution was found: Britain would purchase the Polaris submarine missile instead. De Gaulle had hoped that the failure of Skybolt would offer Britain the opportunity to embark upon a Franco-British joint nuclear venture, instead of opting for a course of action which would make British nuclear defence almost completely dependent on American goodwill. A shrewd observer of the international scene would have known that the Polaris deal would incite the implacable hostility of de Gaulle. Not surprisingly, on 14 January 1963, the general angrily vetoed British entry. Later, in his final retirement, he confided to André Malraux: 'England's drama is to be forced to choose between the remains of her Empire at the price of American hegemony and a loyal commitment to the Continent.'[92]

Thus, from Macmillan to Wilson there was no departure from the curious idea that it was imperative for the United Kingdom to pursue the famous 'special relationship', a policy whose benefits for Britain were so intangible. Some Machiavellian US foreign policy decision-makers thought that the termination of the 'special relationship' would actually be in Britain's interests, for it would smooth its path into the European Economic Community. In his memoirs, Kissinger explained that such a termination was impractical and impossible: successive British governments had stood by it and it had cost America nothing. In a memo to Nixon he added: 'My own personal view on this issue is that we do not suffer in the world from such an excess of friends that we should discourage those who feel that they have a special friendship for us.'[93] It is worth noting that Kissinger's words made it clear that the relationship was one-way: the British felt a special friendship; the Americans did not need to reciprocate and accepted what was given to them. They were the sovereign on the throne, not the courtiers on their knees. The Labour government's slavish adherence to the USA on virtually all matters outraged the Labour Left. But it also caused puzzlement among commentators who could not be suspected of *a priori* anti-Americanism. For instance, writing in 1970, Samuel Brittan noted that 'During all the negotiations on international liquidity and in the various financial crises of the sixties, it was an occasion for remark if the British representative differed from the American.'[94]

Many of these constraints were of Labour's own making. Such pronounced subservience to the USA was unnecessary. Of course, it might have been unrealistic to expect from the Labour government an outright condemnation of the US, Swedish-style, as Wilson's leftist critics advocated; nevertheless, to suggest that there were no alternatives to Wilson's policies is to take the concept of foreign policy constraints too far. Wilson's foreign policy made the Labour government more committed to Washington than the Conservatives were under Heath, after their 1970 electoral victory. As Kissinger discovered to his surprise, Edward Heath was the British politician 'least emotionally committed to the United States', immune to the 'sentimental ... attachment forged in two wars', and convinced that 'the "special relationship" was an obstacle to Britain's European vocation. Heath was content to enjoy no higher status in Washington than any other European leader. Indeed, he came close to insisting on receiving no preferential treatment.'[95] But Heath, unlike Wilson, had a long-term strategy. Describing Heath's visit to Washington in December 1970, Kissinger ruminated: 'He stressed that his overriding goal was Britain's entry into the Common Market.' Heath did not wish

> to appear as – or, for that matter, to be – America's Trojan Horse in Europe. No previous British Prime Minister would have considered making such a statement to an American President ... we were witnessing a revolution in Britain's postwar foreign policy ... Heath was a new experience for American leaders: a British Prime Minister who based his policy towards the United States not on sentimental attachments but on a cool calculation of interest.[96]

It would have been hard for much of the 'NATO' West European Left other than the communists to pursue a similar quasi-Gaullist policy. In Italy, for instance, the Italian Socialist Party had been a strenuously anti-American party for much of the 1950s. Its participation in government in 1963 had required the concomitant decision to accept NATO. Yet, as in other parties, the majority of the activists did not wholeheartedly accept the shift towards 'Atlantic' socialism. At the Thirty-fifth Congress of the party in October 1963, Pietro Nenni explained that he no longer wished to 're-open the question of Italy's membership of NATO', because the international situation was far less tense than previously – a justification which might equally well have been invoked for leaving NATO.[97] By 1965 the main socialist justification for remaining in NATO was that a unilateral withdrawal of Italy would be dangerous for world peace – the identical justification the PCI would give, ten years later, when it in turn accepted NATO. In the same year (i.e. 1965), the new PSI leader, Francesco de Martino, warned the party Congress that the idea that the entire responsibility for the Vietnamese situation lay with the USA was 'simplistic'; nevertheless, the PSI Congress proceeded to condemn American intervention.[98]

Throughout the 1960s Italian socialist cabinet ministers continued, however unenthusiastically, to support American foreign policy in all its manifestations. Vietnam, however, was clearly too emotive an issue for the rank and file and the party leadership had to refrain from ever endorsing the US. There was little shift towards the USA even at the 1966 'unification congress' held to merge the PSI with the staunchly pro-American Social Democratic Party. Francesco de Martino avoided mentioning NATO in his main report, condemned US bombing of Vietnam, but blamed equally 'the West', the USSR and China, and the 'militaristic clique of South Vietnam'.[99] To signify its general mood of displeasure with the USA, the 1966 PSI Congress also voted unanimously to accept a motion on Vietnam which highlighted 'the indiscriminate massacre of civilians due mainly to the massive American bombings'.[100] Vietnam itself was not mentioned in the final motion of the joint conference held immediately after the Thirty-seventh Congress, in which the two parties officially joined forces. NATO membership was accepted, but only in the context of a policy of détente and multilateral disarmament, and strictly limited to 'defensive purposes and within its own geographical areas'. Enthusiasm was reserved for the United Nations and the European Economic Community.[101]

The unification of the Italian socialist and social-democratic parties proved to be short-lived. Less than three years later, the Partito Socialista Unificato again divided into its two original component parts. By then, however, the PSI had entered the Socialist International and had virtually buried its previous anti-Atlantic past. A consensus had been finally established in foreign policy among all socialist and social-democratic parties in NATO Europe.

In the communist camp too there were some timid moves towards this consensus. We have discussed the changes in communist perception of the EEC. Further moves towards 'the West' were accelerated by the dramatic events which surrounded the failure of the reform of communism in Czechoslovakia.

At the beginning of 1968, a group of reformers with considerable popular backing had wrested the leadership of the Czech Communist Party from the pro-Soviet group of Antonin Novotny. On 5 April 1968 an Action Programme had been drafted by the Central Committee. This offered a thorough critique of the preceding twenty years of communist rule and undertook to promulgate major reforms – in particular, a wider scope for market relations, a diminution of the role of the Communist Party in favour of more representative political institutions, and a respect for minority opinions. The Czech Communist Party prudently reaffirmed its loyalty to the 'Soviet Union and the other socialist states', adding 'we shall contribute more actively ... to the joint activities of the Council of Mutual Economic Aid (COMECON) and the Warsaw Treaty.'[102] In spite of these precautions, aimed at avoiding a repetition of the Hungarian events of 1956, Soviet troops backed by other Warsaw Pact members (but not by Romania) marched into Czechoslovakia on 20 August and re-established a pro-Soviet administration. In the West there was, as might be expected, widespread condemnation of the Soviet intervention.

The Italian PCI had been particularly scarred by these events. Its entire foreign policy, and the distant objective of gradually phasing out the two blocs, had been predicated on the assumption that, sooner or later, the communist regimes of Eastern Europe would undergo reform and democratization. The Italian communists assumed that the process of détente was closely related to the advance of the reformers in the East. The downfall of

Khrushchev in 1964 had been a blow to their hopes – in spite of his unpredictability. Thus, when Dubcek emerged armed with a programme of substantial reforms, the Italian communists enthusiastically backed him. The party weekly, *Rinascita*, devoted a multitude of articles to mapping out the itinerary and the successes of the reformers. The PCI Central Committee supported them unreservedly and without dissent. After the invasion (27 August), the PCI was unequivocal. Unlike the PCF, which simply 'disapproved', the PCI condemned the invasion, declaring that the USSR had no right to intervene militarily in any circumstances. But schizophrenia in politics, especially in communist politics, is an enduring disorder and, while condemning the CPSU, the PCI also reaffirmed 'the deep, fraternal and genuine ties that unite the Italian Communists to the Soviet Union and the CPSU'.[103]

The PCI had hoped that the 'Prague Spring' would herald a process which would transform the reality and image of communism. Leading Czech reformers thought it inevitable that radical changes in the communist system in Czechoslovakia would have a massive impact, if not on the USSR itself, then certainly on Poland and the DDR.[104] Even among German social democrats, always very attentive to signs of progress in Central Europe, the Prague experiment had given rise to expectations. Its principal analyst of communist affairs, Richard Löwenthal, in a study of the relations between social democracy and communism written at the request of the Presidium of the SPD, wrote that the advent of Dubcek suggested that there could have been a development towards 'real' socialism even where there was state property. The central difference between social democracy and communism was over the question of democracy, not property relations.[105]

The Soviet intervention had destroyed the possibility of 'socialism with a human face'. It had become clear that any eventual reform of communism could originate only from within the Soviet Union. Togliatti's old dream of a pluralist, polycentric Europe had been dealt a severe blow. De Gaulle, the other great supporter of a gradual European emancipation from the asphyxiating embrace of the two superpowers, had been defeated too. Still reeling from the shock of May 1968 (see chapter 14), the old general had to watch helplessly as the bipolarization of Europe reasserted itself. He resigned a year later, after a referendum defeat over a minor issue. He died in 1970, taking with him his dreams of *grandeur*, while routine politicians, like Georges Pompidou, returned to manage French politics.

The French Communist Party too, or at least its reforming wing and its leader, Waldeck Rochet, had suffered a serious reverse. Like the general, though for different reasons, they were recovering from the turmoil of May. Waldeck Rochet himself had offered his good offices to mediate between Alexander Dubcek and Leonid Brezhnev. He flew to Moscow and Prague, and even offered to organize a conference of all European communist parties. He had become convinced that the USSR would not invade, that there would not be a repetition of Hungary. The intervention was therefore a personal shock from which Waldeck Rochet never really recovered. Those who saw him a fortnight after the invasion remarked that he seemed to have aged considerably.[106] A year later, he fell seriously ill. The old guard did not miss its chance and Georges Marchais took over.

The reformers in the PCF however, had succeeded in obtaining, if not an outright condemnation of the Soviet invasion, at least a statement of 'disapproval'. This was not enough to satisfy the ultra-reformers such as Roger Garaudy, who resigned with others. But it was sufficiently strong to cause the resignation from the Politburo of Jeannette Vermeersch, widow of Thorez, and the most fervent Soviet supporter in the leadership.

In Bonn, the SPD, still trapped in the *Grosse Koalition*, was forced to reassess its Ostpolitik. This had originally been conceived in terms of courting Eastern Europe first and then the USSR. After the Soviet intervention, the policy could no longer be pursued in this way. August 1968 signified that Bonn would have to deal directly with Moscow.[107] There, and nowhere else, the keys to détente and Ostpolitik were kept. The tanks of the Red Army had not simply crushed the aspirations of Dubcek and his supporters. They had reasserted the primacy of bipolar politics. European autonomists, whether of the Right, like de Gaulle, or of the Left, like the German social democrats and Italian communists, had been dealt a devastating blow.

Atlanticists, including, of course, those in the socialist and social-democratic parties, took a general moral stand in support of democratization and reform in Czechoslovakia. Their policies had emerged more entrenched and triumphant than ever. NATO and the Warsaw Pact, the Iron Curtain and nuclear weapons, eternal suspicion and constant vigilance: these remained their watchwords.

For most socialist parties, unlike the SPD and the PCI, the Prague crisis turned out to be of little importance. These events expressed verities which they had ceased to question. No serious effort was made to assess the possibility of a reform of communism, or to determine what the policy of socialists should be towards such a possibility. It may be argued, quite legitimately, that there was very little West Europeans could do. An excess of enthusiasm in supporting the Czech reformers might not have been welcome even in Prague and might have alarmed the USSR.

In a previous era, the logic of 'spheres of influence' had constrained policy-makers, but ideology and even religion played little or no part. Alliances could be built and destroyed with relative ease. The logic of the blocs during the years 1947–91 was made of much firmer stuff. The parties of the Left were far more constrained in government than when in opposition. At no stage could they pose – or were they willing to pose – a threat to the stability of the Atlantic alliance comparable to that posed by the circumspect and cautious Czechs with respect to the Warsaw Pact.

The attitude of the British Labour government towards the Cold War, or even towards the possession of nuclear weapons, was not significantly different from that of the Conservatives, in spite of Labour's pacifist ethos, its tradition of disarmament and its strong anti-nuclear pressure group. Labour found it impossible to abandon nuclear weapons for two reasons: first because a majority of the country and, possibly, its own electorate objected to such unilateralism; second, because this would weaken the defence of the West and upset the USA. A British 'independent' nuclear weapons system had become a political sacred cow in Britain only in the 1960s. As late as 1962, several senior Conservatives had seriously considered abandoning a nuclear role: R. A. Butler, Iain Macleod, Reginald Maudling and Edward Heath, while Peter Thorneycroft and Julian Amery had been exploring the possibilities of an *entente nucléaire* with France.[108] Labour in power never seriously entertained the possibility of becoming non-nuclear, so great was the urge for respectability. It even refused to cancel the Polaris programme it had bitterly criticized when in opposition, on the specious grounds that it would be too costly to do so because its development was so far advanced.[109] Being respectable, and being well thought of in Washington, appeared to be one and the same thing.

The French socialists and communists had fewer such problems. Upsetting the USA was official French foreign policy. The equation, however, was complicated by the fact that the *force nucléaire stratégique* was presented by de Gaulle as a necessary symbol of French independence from the unreliable 'Anglo-Saxons', and as the inescapable consequence of French disengagement from the integrated military command of NATO. Nevertheless, for the PCF what really mattered was that these weapons were directed towards the USSR, even though de Gaulle's own position was that they were aimed in all directions (the so-called *à tous azimuts* strategy); consequently, the communists proposed their removal.

The socialists had a problem producing a coherent defence policy, since they were deeply divided between pro-American factions, pacifists and neutralists, and a left-wing tendency convinced that the priority was to obtain the support of communist voters for a socialist presidential candidate. This was the background to Mitterrand's 1965 presidential programme, which promised to disband the independent French nuclear force on the widely accepted grounds that it was ineffectual, costly and dangerous.[110]

De Gaulle's foreign policy challenged the idea that Atlanticism constituted the immutable framework of foreign policy for Western countries. To Britain and to the British Labour Party, de Gaulle indicated that it was possible to follow a policy of *grandeur*, the French equivalent of Britain's world role, while remaining in the European Community; that one could establish closer links with the USSR while developing nuclear weapons; that abandoning NATO's military structure was compatible with staying in the alliance and criticizing American intervention in Vietnam; that it was possible to leave Algeria in spite of French settlers' protests, and to become a champion of the Third World in spite of having been a major colonial power.

De Gaulle's foreign policy feat had, from his point of view, the added bonus of dividing the opposition between pro-Atlanticist socialists and pro-Soviet communists.[111] In 1966, when de Gaulle withdrew from the military framework of NATO, French foreign policy was endorsed by more communist supporters (48.7 per cent) than socialist (47.7 per cent).[112] So perplexed were the French communists that they chose to regard Gaullist foreign policy as hopelessly contradictory. An article in the PCF house journal described de Gaulle's foreign policy as 'fundamentally imperialistic' and unrealistic, because he sought to establish French national independence against the wishes of the other imperialist powers, the USA, Britain and Germany.[113]

De Gaulle was supported not because he was anti-American, but because he appeared to his electorate to be a traditional conservative anti-communist who could guarantee political stability in France. This enabled him to follow an independent foreign policy which appealed more to communist voters than to his own supporters. In so doing, de Gaulle created the framework for a wide consensus in foreign policy among all French political parties. By the time he left office, his foreign policy had become a fact of life, a new agenda and, for the first time, France's foreign policy no longer divided France.[114]

The parties of the Left – in France and in most of Western Europe – could not create their own foreign policy. Constrained by their nation-states, they could not hope to develop a common European policy, partly because they were not united over Europe, partly because they were never simultaneously in power. They reflected the disarray of Europe, its political irrelevance, its divisions. The era of superpower politics seemed destined to last for ever. The avoidance of a conflict between East and West remained the main task ahead.

If we take European social democracy as a whole, the balance-sheet for the 1960s was mixed. Its most positive accomplishment was to demonstrate that, in spite of the vitality, growth and popularity of capitalism, the Left was able to win elections, return to power, govern. For most of the decade it remained the main focus of the hopes and aspirations of all those who wanted to change society in a radical, non-capitalist manner. The revisionism of the late 1950s, whether or not it had been successful, contributed to the aura of modernity which still surrounded the socialist project. The working class, whose allegedly radical essence and centrality had been dismissed by revisionists and sociologists, turned out to be a force to be reckoned with. With or even without the support of the trade unions, workers throughout Europe were able by strike action to modify one of the main features of post-war capitalist success: the expansion of productivity at a higher rate than the growth in wages. Because they required capitalist growth to fund their welfare programmes, all governments found themselves under challenge. Socialists were caught in a difficult dilemma: strikes – so often seen as a manifestation of working-class consciousness against capitalist accumulation

– were clearly not aimed at obtaining social reforms for all workers. The obvious goal of industrial militancy was the acquisition of greater purchasing power to enable the individual worker to participate more fully in consumer capitalism. Wages growing faster than productivity caused a profit squeeze which made further capitalist growth more problematic. Yet constant growth was necessary to develop further welfare capitalism – at least for social democrats and all those who had given up the idea of overcoming capitalism.

The surge of industrial militancy was the first and most important challenge the organized Left had to face in the closing years of the 1960s. The second challenge was the revival of socialist ideology effected by the educated younger generation. The much-heralded 'end of ideology', which had convinced revisionists of the need for pragmatism, had not yet come. Far from dying or ending, 'ideology' came to dominate the social sciences. From their 'red' bases in the universities, the young radicals launched an incessant ideological critique of social democrats, socialists and communists. Social democracy's espousal of modernity was dismissed as mere pandering to neo-capitalism, its championing of pragmatism as a visionless form of technocratic authoritarianism.

Reeling under the impact of the two-pronged attack of militant workers and radical students, social democracy had to confront a third challenge, at this stage still embryonic: the growth of a multifaceted women's movement. The new feminists, like the socialist movement, had both an immediate practical political programme and a longer-term aim. In the short term, it sought to modify existing legislation to ensure a more equitable distribution of power between the sexes, and the institution of rights (such as to abortion) which recognized the distinctiveness (whether biologically determined or socially constructed) of being a woman. Its more complex, long-term aim was the emancipation of women from the domination of men, a goal which required a radical and reciprocal modification in the attitudes of both sexes.

The socialist movement had always had a formal commitment to the emancipation of women although, in practice, this had never held pride of place in its activities. The movement itself had always appealed to men far more than to women. It was based on overwhelmingly male organizations (the trade unions), and had originated in the world of industrial production, from which women had been excluded more thoroughly than in any previous system of production.

It is to this triple challenge emanating from workers, students and women that we now turn.

PART FIVE

The Great Contestation

CHAPTER THIRTEEN

The Revival of Working-class Militancy 1960–73

BETWEEN 1960 and 1973 there were two distinct cycles of strikes throughout most of Europe; the first, which occurred between 1960 and 1964, did not affect Belgium and occurred later than elsewhere in Sweden (1966). All countries, except Austria, participated in the second cycle, which occurred around 1968–72. As the eleven graphs (Figures 13.1 to 13.11) below indicate, the first cycle was far less marked than the second. In Holland, the upsurge in strikes took place in 1973, later than elsewhere, but it was the most pronounced since 1946. Not all countries were equally affected by the work stoppages whose intensity varied considerably: there were proportionately more strikes in the 'calmer' years of Italian industrial conflict than in the 'turbulent' 1971 in Sweden. In France, in May–June 1968, there was an unparalleled wave of strikes; the exact intensity is impossible to establish because it is futile to try to distinguish between those who were on strike voluntarily and those who could not go to work because of the strikes of others, the lack of transport, or the shut-down of plants due to the un-availability of energy. This may explain why there are no official government strike statistics for May–June 1968. The most plausible statistical analysis suggests that six or seven million people went on strike at the time.[1]

The following graphs plot the intensity of strikes in eleven West European countries. Note that, even though the absolute figures vary widely between countries, the shape of the strike curves is fairly similar. Most countries exhibit a revival of strike activity in the first part of the 1960s, followed by a period of apparent respite. All display a pronounced revival of working-class industrial unrest between 1968 and 1972.

The existence of a European-wide strike cycle, and the marked upswing in the late 1960s and early 1970s in so many countries, suggest that nationally-based interpretations are insufficient: there must be some overarching trend which explains the international increase in industrial conflict. A study made by the Frankfurter Institut für Sozialforschung argues, plausibly, that wage conflicts coincided with phases of cyclical downswing. This works well for the German downswings of 1962–63, 1967 and 1971, but only comparative studies over a long period of time (and the Frankfurt study is not one of them) can demonstrate a general causal relationship between cyclical

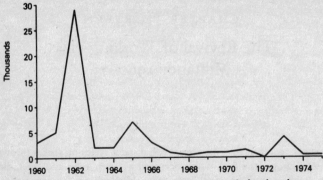

Figure 13.1 Austria: days lost per 100,000 non-agricultural workers

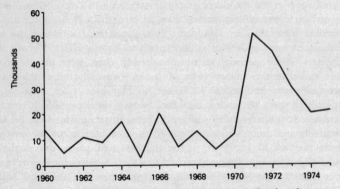

Figure 13.2 Belgium: days lost per 100,000 non-agricultural workers

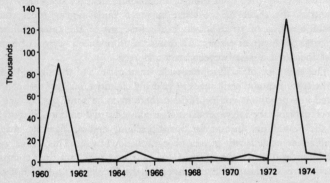

Figure 13.3 Denmark: days lost per 100,000 non-agricultural workers

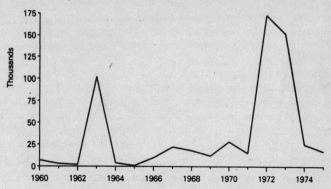

Figure 13.4 Finland: days lost per 100,000 non-agricultural workers

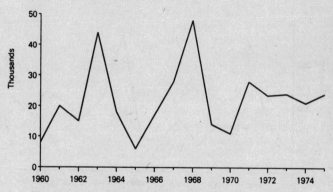

Figure 13.5 France: days lost per 100,000 non-agricultural workers
(no reliable data available for 1968)

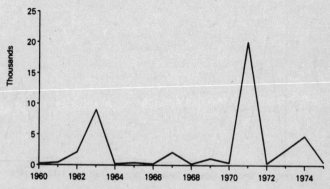

Figure 13.6 West Germany: days lost per 100,000 non-agricultural workers

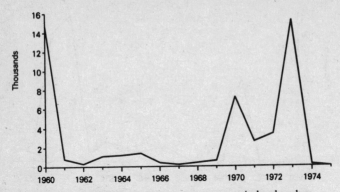

Figure 13.7 Holland: days lost per 100,000 non-agricultural workers

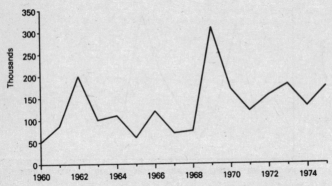

Figure 13.8 Italy: days lost per 100,000 non-agricultural workers

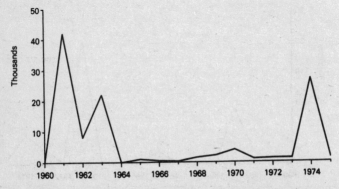

Figure 13.9 Norway: days lost per 100,000 non-agricultural workers

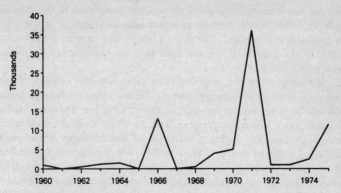

Figure 13.10 Sweden: days lost per 100,000 non-agricultural workers

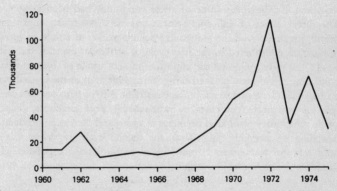

Figure 13.11 United Kingdom: days lost per 100,000 non-agricultural workers

Graphs constructed on the basis of data in Peter Flora et al., *State, Economy and Society in Western Europe 1815–1975. A Data Handbook*, cit., Vol. 2, pp. 688–753.

movements and the frequency of strikes.[2] Economic explanations for the strikes of the second half of the 1960s can tell only part of the story. Single-cause explanations which may be applicable to one country often do not apply to another. Thus, rising unemployment may explain the Belgian strikes of the winter and spring of 1970, but not those in the public sector in France in May 1968 (such as the shut-down at Renault). Lack of public spending on infrastructure may explain the Italian protest strikes of the 'hot autumn' of 1969, but not the German ones of September 1969. While the causes of the revival of working-class militancy are obviously multifarious, the main underpinning factor was the economic situation. Working-class earnings were frustrated as employers attempted to contain wage increases below the productivity level, which in turn was lower than in the preceding decade. In other words, workers expected wages to grow at a rate higher than productivity permitted. The cost of wages had become a fundamental variable in the growth of the economy and the containment of wages a central policy issue.

By the early 1960s the long boom of capitalism had brought about a situation of generalized full employment in Western Europe. Foreign workers could still be imported for low-paid, unskilled jobs, but the main 'internal' sources of spare labour, the 'reserve army of workers', could no longer be activated. In Italy, the apparent saturation of the northern labour market discouraged southern migrants, while in Germany the erection of the Berlin Wall in 1961 effectively blocked the flow of skilled workers from East Germany. The obvious remaining reserve of spare labour, women, could not be used without a substantial modification in the domestic division of labour, in the size of families, in childcare arrangements, and in cultural gender stereotyping. By the 1980s some of these conditions had been created.

The direct effect of full employment was to make trade unions more powerful, for they found themselves in a seller's market at a time of growth. This situation contributed to the first cycle of strikes. It explains the Italian strikes of the early 1960s and the important miners' strike of 1963 in France. The resulting inflationary pressure led governments and/or the central banks (as in Italy and Germany) to adopt wage restraint and/or deflationary policies. Employers sought to cut costs by rationalizing work practices, reducing allegedly inflationary plant-level payments systems, and increasing productivity by speeding up assembly lines. Thus, the second cycle of strikes was the delayed reaction by workers to widespread anti-inflationary policies.[3] This explanation assumes that the original inflation of the early 1960s (which started the process) was caused by higher wages.

An alternative, though not incompatible, explanation suggests that both waves of strikes were the result of inflation, rather than its cause: workers simply responded to higher prices. In this case, the origin of the European inflation of the mid-1960s must be traced, exogenously, to the overheating of the American economy. Here the causal chain would start with the massive increase in US government expenditure required to fund both the domestic welfare programme known as 'the Great Society', and the escalation of the war in Vietnam. In any other country this would have required the central authorities to increase taxes or, failing that, to devalue the currency in order to counteract the negative effects of inflation on the balance of payments. The USA, however, unlike any other country, was not afraid of exhausting its reserves and could run large balance of payments deficits because its own currency, the dollar, was a reserve currency 'as good as gold', being convertible at the fixed rate of thirty-five dollars per ounce of gold.[4] The hegemonic position of the USA in the international financial system had allowed it to unload its inflationary problems on to Western Europe.

These two possible explanations assume different causal processes: either inflation was of the cost-push type, originating in an increase in costs (here mainly the cost of labour, i.e. wages); or it was of the demand-pull variety, and hence caused by an increase in demand. We shall keep well away from this chicken-and-egg argument, which has disturbed the sleep of generations of economists, and simply note that both explanations caused considerable anguish to the parties of the Left. In politics, which of the two explanations is the 'true' one is not quite as important as their respective political implications.

By adopting the cost-push explanation, socialists would commit themselves to the containment of wages and prices. Restraining wages would bring them into a clash with trade unionists, while restraining prices would squeeze the profitability of private industry and damage investment. It was clear that an incomes policy would have a better chance of success if it were part of a package in which there would also be control of prices. Indeed, for 'presentational' purposes, the containment of the one was often couched in terms requiring the containment of the other. In reality, the control of prices in a market economy is virtually impossible even in an emergency – as the rapid growth of a black market in wartime demonstrates. Incomes are marginally easier to control, provided unions are weak or accept an incomes policy and can effectively carry their members with them. But for how long could unions deliver? It would be necessary to ensure that prices did not rise excessively, even though, as I have indicated, they could not easily be controlled directly. Even fanatical anti-trade unionists would accept that there were other factors, apart from wages, leading to a rise in prices and that by controlling wages one was really controlling only the wage cost aspect of a cost-push inflation.

By embracing the demand-pull explanation, socialists would commit themselves to cutting demand and hence to unpalatable policies, ranging from curtailing public spending (particularly of the redistributive kind), to increasing taxes and accepting more unemployment.

Either explanation, and the strategy it implies, brought to the fore a central issue: wages were not an independent variable which could be left outside the scope of government intervention. Once in government, at the helm of a capitalist economy, socialists could not consistently support trade union militancy (or 'the economic class struggle' in Marxist parlance). The short-term interests of some workers in increasing their wages might clash with the interest of other workers and groups. This was hardly a new dilemma: conflicts between socialists in government and workers on strike had occurred before, particularly during the period of post-war reconstruction. In the 1960s, however, industrial conflicts reached a much higher level of intensity than ever before, just at a time when socialists and social democrats were becoming reconciled to the 'mixed' economy and were in power. Furthermore, their being in power throughout most of Europe served to encourage the trade unions to step up militancy.

The wave of strikes also posed internal ideological problems for the parties of the Left. The unresolved dispute between revisionists and 'traditionalists' was intensified. As we saw in chapter 10, many socialists had come to terms with the idea that the era of working-class conflicts had come to an end, and had accepted some variant of the embourgeoisement thesis. They urged relinquishing an excessively strong class identity and transforming the socialist parties into 'people parties'. But the revival of working-class militancy seemed to challenge socialist revisionism. It appeared that embourgeoisement may have been overestimated and that the fighting spirit of the proletariat had only temporarily abated in the 1950s. In the 1960s, workers appeared more than ever willing to challenge capitalist development and capitalist work practices. The socialist parties, the traditionalists claimed, had been blinded by the uninterrupted growth of capitalism and the apparent success of the consumer society, and had thus stumbled into abandoning their traditional values.

However, an entirely opposite reading of the strikes can be given: the revival of working-class militancy can be seen as evidence that the workers were eager to obtain more of the fruits of capitalism. A strike seeks a modification of the distribution of the surplus produced, not the abolition of the system which produces it in the first place. To strike to obtain higher wages or longer holidays or better working conditions, or (more rarely) to obtain social reforms and social rights, does not necessarily challenge the stability of capitalism. Nor are strikes an indicator of a sweeping conviction that socialism is inevitable. To want a larger share of the cake is not to deny that it should be baked in the first place.

In practice, however, industrial militancy could not simply be written off by the revisionists in this way. Strikes had to be dealt with practically: by the late 1960s many socialist parties were not bystanders in opposition, but had ministers in government. Industrial militancy affected economic performance, creating a problem of crisis management, not merely of ideological interpretations.

The graphs above give an indication of the problem, but reveal little else. Comparing strikes is not a straightforward affair. What constitutes a strike is a matter of debate; there needs to be a common definition of the length of the dispute and the number of people involved. It may be necessary to distinguish between strikes involving the country as a whole (a general strike), a region, an entire industry, a branch of industry, a firm, a plant, a section of a plant. Furthermore, strikes can have different objectives: working conditions, pay levels, social reforms, protest against closures or redundancies. The most relevant distinction turned out to be between strikes called by trade union leaders at national or local level (so-called official strikes), and strikes called by workers' representatives elected at the shop-floor level (so-called unofficial or wildcat strikes).[5]

In the course of the 1968–72 cycle of industrial conflict, there was a marked increase in unofficial strikes. These adopted an entire galaxy of novel forms of struggle with fanciful names. These included sit-ins; *grèves-bouchon* or production stoppages, where strategically placed groups of workers downed tools; industrial sabotage; the *grèves perlées* or go-slows; the British work-to-rule in which a pedantic and meticulous implementation of the company rule-book ensures total paralysis; sector by sector strikes known as *grèves tournantes* in France, and *sciopero a singhiozzo* (hiccup strikes) or *a scacchiera* (chessboard) in Italy.[6] These new forms of industrial conflict caused considerable problems for employers: wages had to be paid to those still available for work, even though the disruption caused by others forced the entire plant to come to a standstill. Negotiating with delegates who had to report continuously to an entire group of workers was more arduous than dealing with a small committee representing a single union.

Socialist parties were often negatively affected by this. When in government, they had to deal with the economic implications of the stoppages and often had to confront their most loyal electorate. Strikes in the public sector were a particular problem: unanticipated delays in public transport and a sudden suspension of services created hostility towards the public sector as a whole and, by implication, towards the socialist parties which were identified with it. Where strikes were unofficial, union leaders faced great difficulties: their position was weakened and they lost credibility with their own members. If they granted recognition to shop-floor militancy, they widened the gap between themselves and the socialists in government.

Successful strikes compounded the problems facing the socialist parties. Their potential inflationary effects led the monetary authorities of Italy, Germany and France to respond by deflating the economy, not a policy which could appeal to socialists. The alternative to deflation was co-operation with the trade unions. Where the unions were strong, this was also the preferable course of action, though the socialist parties never had a monopoly on co-operation. In many instances, conservative parties were willing to seek union support. The Gaullist government attempted to do so in 1964, though nothing came of it because the unions were weak and ineffective, and the government was unwilling to grant concessions it did not have to make.[7] In 1962, the British Conservatives, responding to the increase in strikes, established the National Economic Development Council, a precursor of the German *Konzertierte Aktion* (examined in chapter 11), in which employers and trade unions could discuss issues under the benevolent eye of the government.

In reality, wage containment was the main – perhaps the only – reason why governments everywhere in Western Europe were keen to talk to the trade unions. Socialists in government needed union acquiescence more than other parties: the alternative to a so-called 'voluntary incomes policy' was either a compulsory one or deflation.

On the surface the question appeared simple. It involved a straight political deal between government and unions. The unions would convince their members to contain wage demands and, 'in exchange', the government would pursue policies of social reform. But the assumptions behind an agreed incomes policy presented numerous problems to socialists.

In the first place, the very necessity of a 'contract' of this kind weakened two cherished beliefs: that strikes were always justified, because they sought to reduce the exploitation of workers by capitalists; and that socialist governments would *always* seek to pursue the policy of social reform they had campaigned for, and been elected to implement, and that trade unions would *automatically* support this policy. Hence the bizarre nature of the negotiation: socialist trade unionists forgoing wage increases in order to obtain what they had always wanted – socialist reforms. Bizarre in appearance only, though, for the 'contract' tended to recast the old 'final aims'/minimum programme dichotomy and endow it with a new tension: this time, the longer-term aims – social reforms – could be achieved only by forgoing the short-term ones – higher wages – while, in earlier times, the short-term improvements were supposed to pave the way for the 'final aim'.

The second main problem with the co-operative approach was that it gave trade unions an official political role for which there was never formal popular and democratic assent. Democratic principles, to which trade unions and socialist parties were equally committed, established that governments had a popular mandate to do what they said they would do. Why then negotiate the programme again, once elected, with unions which at best represented only a sector of society?

In the third place, the implication of government–trade union negotiations was that working-class wage militancy was the only real obstacle to social reform or, at least, the main one. This was a strange belief for socialists to hold, and indeed went against the grain of socialist history. The development of trade unions was based on the belief that only unity of action would enable otherwise powerless workers to secure better working conditions and higher wages. Correspondingly, socialist parties had appealed to the working-class electorate on a similar basis of self-interest, even though, of course, committed socialists aspired to a wider final aim. Even the promise of social justice held out by socialist parties had a monetary appeal: it usually involved a fairer distribution of wealth. Throughout the history of the socialist movement, it was always assumed that wages were too low. For the capitalist economy wages were of central importance. Not only were they a key variable in the composition of costs, and hence in the determination of prices and profits; they were also the central mechanism which provided the working class with access to consumption, and hence to security, to the satisfaction of many needs, and to status. In a market economy, personal dignity, the cardinal pillar of civilization, is difficult to achieve in conditions of indigence.

This brings us closer to the key paradox of West European trade unions, strikingly illustrated by the debate on incomes policy: politically, the socialist sympathies of most trade unionists led them to desire a society regulated for the common welfare. Their trade unionism, however, required a 'free' labour market, without government interference, in which the price of labour was the result of unimpeded collective bargaining. However, market forces in the labour market determined different wages among different occupations and sections of the working class, resulting in inequalities which owed nothing to criteria of 'fairness' or utility independent of market forces. One of the reasons why some footballers and fashion models earn more than teachers and nurses lies in the scarcity of good footballers and top fashion models relative to the demand for their services. Issues of social need or fairness have no place in market-determined wages calculations, even though most people would readily agree that, if it came to a choice, a society without fashion models and footballers is preferable to one without nurses and teachers, lamentable as this may seem to the unsophisticated hedonist.

To reject any form of incomes policy as a matter of principle amounts to accepting the primacy of market preference over social needs in the determination of wages: a hard principle to justify if you are a socialist and insist that all major economic variables must be regulated. Only true economic liberals, committed to the efficiency of the market and its ultimately superior distributive effects, can declare themselves foes of incomes policies with unequivocal consistency.

Where unions are strong, governments need to seek their support for an incomes policy. Thus, a wages policy can be a sign of great union strength and may show that there is a mature and confident working class willing to forgo immediate monetary gains for more distant political ones. Militant trade unionists, who always reject incomes policies, naively confuse wages militancy with political militancy. It was the merit of Lenin, on the basis of Kautsky's work, to have stressed the distinction between economic and political militancy in his celebrated pamphlet *What is to be Done?* (March 1902). Few of his communist and radical followers took the necessary implications of this position seriously.

Over the long or medium term an incomes policy may be acceptable to workers if the eventual distribution of income is considered to be fair. However, the criteria of fairness used by workers are unlikely to correspond to those used by entrepreneurs, because each class has quite different points of reference. For employers, 'fair wages' must be low enough to guarantee an adequate return on investments and are linked to variables such as relative international prices, productivity and profitability; for employees, a concept of 'fair wages' is linked to past purchasing power, expectations, and wages in comparable sectors. Furthermore, top-earning skilled workers, whether or not inclined towards socialism, might accept an incomes policy as an anti-inflationary instrument. But there is no obvious way to convince them – without an appeal to altruism or political expedience – that it should be used in a redistributive manner, if the effect would be to reduce their differentials.

The central condition of an agreed and co-ordinated approach to wage rises involving unions, employers and government, must be that increases in wages decided and agreed at the top correspond to the real increases in wages obtained by workers on the shop floor. This is not always the case. Centrally agreed wages are treated as general guidelines for local bargaining. The imagination of trade unionists and employers is sufficiently fertile to produce an ever-widening array of reasons for extra payments: Christmas bonuses, marriage gifts, bonuses for being punctual, for not being ill, extra holiday money, interest-free loans, allowances for children, piece-rate schemes, shift-work additional payment, payments under job revaluation schemes, and so on. This phenomenon of wage-drift, widespread throughout Europe, is a working-class equivalent of the 'perks' to which middle and higher management in the private sector – the nomenklatura of capitalist societies – have become increasingly addicted: cars, numerous and unnecessary free lunches in expensive restaurants, travel for spouses, exotic holidays disguised as training seminars, free shirt-laundering service, concert and opera seats for performances sponsored by the firm – an entire cornucopia of tax-free and largely undeserved gratuities. This custom is far less prevalent in the state sector and, alas, totally unknown in the universities, with the possible exception of Oxford and Cambridge.

The problems of incomes policies are further compounded in that they are far more necessary in economies whose growth is export-led – such as those of many European countries – and financed largely by reinvested profits – as is the case, for instance, in Britain. Under a regime of fixed exchange rates, high wages, if passed on in prices, make one's exports less competitive; if absorbed, they cause a squeeze on profits and leave less available for re-investment.

Wage restraint is less important in a large, rich and mainly non-export-oriented national economy – such as that of the USA – where growth is generated by internal demand, where wage increases can simply be eaten away by inflation without having a significant negative effect on the balance of payments. If bank borrowing finances long-term investments – as in Germany – then high profits are not required for reinvestment and a profit squeeze caused by high wage demands would have less effect on investment. Britain happened to be in the category of countries which depended on international trade and whose banking system was relatively ineffective in providing finance for industry; therefore wage increases had an immediate impact on export prices and profits.

This in part explains why for most of the 1960s and 1970s Britain was virtually the only country which systematically attempted to resolve its economic difficulties by resorting to an incomes policy.

There were no wages policies in France and Italy during this period, because the union movement was divided into three confederations which would not have been able to impose wage restraint on their membership which, in turn, represented only a minority of the working class. In these two countries anti-inflation policies were therefore conducted by monetary

and fiscal means. Generally speaking, this is the strategy which is adopted
where the trade unions are politically weak and incomes policies unnecessary.

The workers' unrest which developed in such a pronounced way in Italy
and France was only partly due to the deflationary policies of their respective
governments. The general strike which followed the student unrest in Paris
in May 1968 was called by the Communist Party through the CGT. The mass
demonstration of 13 May, marking the entry of the organized working class
into what had hitherto been a conflict between the authorities and the
students, exhibited the following characteristics. It was a bid by the communists to establish or re-establish themselves at the head of the anti-Gaullist
movement, a position which was being challenged by the student leaders –
an uneasy coalition of non-affiliated leftists, Maoists, Trotskyists and anarchists
on whom the communists piled predictable insults: 'scions of big bourgeois',
'pseudo-revolutionaries', 'adventurists', 'provocateurs'.[8] It was a bid by the
student leaders to forge links with 'the working class', and to wrest it from
the pernicious influence of *les crapules staliniennes* – the Stalinist creeps, to use
Cohn-Bendit's insulting phrase chanted by thousand of students. Both
strategies failed. The students made no inroads at all into the working class,
while the PCF became increasingly unpopular with the students. The demonstration of workers and students of 13 May revealed the cultural chasm
between them, even though the students, led by Jacques Sauvageot, Alain
Geismar and Daniel Cohn-Bendit, were allowed to march at the head of the
entire procession. Students walked with students, unable to mingle with the
proletarians whose support they sought, chanting their own distinctive slogans,
insulting the communists, and mocking Mitterrand's socialists. The workers,
somewhat amused by the anarchistic humour of the students, marched,
disciplined as ever, under the banners of their traditional organizations, the
PCF and the CGT.

What had not been foreseen by the PCF and the CGT was that the workers
who had come out on strike in solidarity with the students would remain on
strike for weeks. As in the days of May–June 1936, the workers' radicalism had
taken the unions by surprise. Unprompted by the trade union leadership,
workers occupied the plants of Sud-Aviation in Nantes and those of Renault
at Cleon and Flins and, eventually, with the CGT's approval, the vast Renault
works of Boulogne Billancourt, the red bastion of communist France. The
conjuncture which made this possible was highly complex: many workers took
advantage of the apparent weakness of the political establishment, and the
panic spreading among the employers, to put forward substantial wage
demands; the communists made the strikes official in order to be able to
remain at the helm of the movement – a tactic modelled after Ledru-Rollin's
famous utterance of 1848: 'I am their leader. I must follow them.'

The May events, like a semiotician's 'open text', became the subject of a
formidable array of interpretations. They are called 'the events', *les événements*,
precisely because no one is sure what kind of events they were. Among the

contending explanations can be found alienation, frustration, boredom with Gaullism, relative deprivation, protest against the dehumanization of the work process, reaction against powerlessness, greed, desire for higher wages, the aspiration to increase the political weight of the workers, gallic bloody-mindedness and other similar stereotypes.

Leaving the question of causes aside, it is clear that the core demands of all the strikes which followed 13 May were for higher wages, shorter working time and improved working conditions. Surrounding these core demands there was a wider, more political, but vaguer set of issues, open to interpretation. The trade unions, especially the CGT, could not abstain from entering into formal negotiations with employers and politicians. Since negotiations must involve tangible, quantitative aspects, the unions dealt with the concrete – that is, with the core demands: the minimum wage, the percentage increase, the length of the working week. The popular slogan 'workers' participation', much favoured by the students and the trade unionists of the CFDT (Confédération Française Démocratique du Travail), was sufficiently vague to enable even de Gaulle to embrace it with apparent enthusiasm. Shop-floor issues, such as the question of workers' control – especially over the work process and the speed of assembly lines – were probably more important than the question of wages, but far less amenable to central negotiations.[9] Thus, it was inevitable that the main actors – unions, employers, government and political parties – concentrated on what could be negotiated at the top. There was no mechanism for a negotiation from below.

France offered perhaps the best demonstration of how the way in which the organizations of the labour movement, parties and unions, were ideologically structured, made it virtually impossible to deal with the demands of an unstructured movement such as a generic student or worker movement, especially when its most innovatory 'demands' could not be met within the established institutions. In other words, no socialist party operating within the confines of representative democracy could respond to the new political language manifested by working-class militancy (or feminism or student radicalism), without recasting *ab initio* its own view of politics.

Such momentous reorganization cannot possibly be achieved in a short space of time in response to rapidly moving events, particularly as these, to some extent, constituted a threat to what the 'institutional' Left had achieved over the years. Parties of the Left have rarely been endowed with an organizational framework enabling them to monitor molecular changes in society. Mass parties have often been surprised by a rapidly developing mass movement. Ideally, there should always be a systematic and constant restructuring of the party organization in the light of social changes, while the organization itself should be used as a mechanism with which to gather information about society. This, I believe, is at the root of Gramsci's injunction that the party should become 'a collective intellectual'. But this is more easily said than done.

The injunction was partly fulfilled, and only intermittently, in Gramsci's own country by the Italian Communist Party, though even the PCI was taken by surprise by the revival of working-class militancy in 1969, and even more so, understandably enough, by student unrest and the development of feminism.

The 'hot autumn' of 1969 saw the most acute and prolonged social conflict in post-war Italian history. As in other European countries, many of the strikes started out as 'wildcat' strikes, though the unions soon made them official. The consequences were more profound in Italy than elsewhere and they included, among other things, a considerable change in the structure of the trade union movement. This became more politically united, although the centralist structure of each of the three federations was significantly undermined by the growth of the Factory Councils, shop-floor organizations of all workers in a factory.[10] In 1980, Bruno Trentin, then the leader of the FIOM (Federazione Impiegati Operai Metallurgici: the communist-led engineering workers), could declare, with visible satisfaction, that the councils were an example of industrial democracy 'without precedent in our past', involving the participation in the elections of factory delegates of far more workers than in the previous decades (up to 80 per cent in the larger plants).[11] Another feature of the Italian strike movement was its distinctive insistence on wage equality, successfully advocated by the lowest paid workers who were at the helm of the movement. On this point workers and students shared, albeit temporarily, one of the strongest 'ethical' dimensions of 'Sixtyeight' – namely, a pronounced distrust of any form of hierarchy in terms of skills, rank, merit, achievements, status and pay. Workers in factories asked for 'the same salary for all', while students in universities demanded (and occasionally obtained) the same examination mark – the top one, naturally.

The communist-led unions, such as Trentin's FIOM, opposed these egalitarian demands, which undermined differentials based on skill; while the Catholic engineering unions (Federazione Italiana Metallurgici – FIM) supported them, appearing to by-pass the Communists on the Left. As Robert Lumley explains, these responses were due more to organizational and membership differences than to ideological ones.[12]

Similarly, the protracted industrial conflicts of the 'hot autumn' were due not to overtly ideological or political causes, but to concrete factors such as the speed-up of assembly lines and the intensification of the work process. There was also general dissatisfaction with the quality of life outside the factories: the congestion of urban centres; the paucity of adequate infrastructure to cope with the massive internal migration of the previous decade; the poor quality of the health system; the inferior calibre of education in working-class areas. The Italian state had visibly failed to resolve any of these problems in spite of the many promises made by the parties of the ruling centre-left coalition. The growth in public spending was badly administered and had taken the form of subsidies, an extension of bureaucracy and payments to clienteles. Attempts at planning had failed. Economic policy was hampered by the existence of four decision-making centres: the ministries of Finance, Treasury, Budget and the Bank of Italy. Entrepreneurs, so much admired during the years of the economic miracle, were now reviled and accused of being greedy and irresponsible: they exported capital from a country which exported labour. Most of all, there was a clear popular perception that economic growth had not been matched by a corresponding increase in social provision.

Italy was approaching the prosperity levels of other European countries without the welfare system of Britain, France and Germany. In the popular consciousness of the time, 'modernity' meant America plus Sweden – that is, high levels of private consumption and an efficient welfare state. What was missing to make Italy truly 'modern' was the 'social' half of the celebrated 'social market'. This explosive mixture of motivations gave the Italian strike movement a distinctive political flavour.

Paradoxically, the markedly political character of Italian industrial conflict, compared with that of other countries (except for France in May–June 1968), depended on the relative weakness of the trade unions. A stronger and more entrenched union movement would have exercised a greater measure of restraint and control over the workers, partly in order to protect vested interests, partly so as not to jeopardize existing power relations (of which they would have been a part). It was their weakness that led the unions to recognize the rank-and-file factory council movement. Had they been stronger, they might have tried to co-exist alongside this grassroots movement.[13] Instead, the unions decided to declare the factory council (elected by all workers irrespective of union membership) the *de facto* organ of the trade union on the factory floor. Given that the factory councils, unlike the unions, were not split on political lines, this decision had the effect of generating a unitary structure at the shop-floor level. Luciano Lama, a communist leader of the CGIL, always stressed that it was the CGIL which first insisted on the recognition of the factory councils as the only expression of the unions inside the factory, and that the main reason was the desire to reconstruct the unity of the trade union movement from the bottom up as well as from the top down.[14] Such aspirations required the growing independence of the unions from the political parties and hence the eventual abandonment of all links between the CGIL and the PCI. Consequently, in the few years after the 'hot autumn', all CGIL leaders who were in Parliament or on their parties' executive committees resigned their seats and posts to dedicate themselves to trade union work. This dissociation from formal party politics occurred throughout the trade unions and at all levels: even branch trade union secretaries could not simultaneously hold any elected office in their local party. Similar moves took place in the other two trade union federations.

The autonomy of trade unions from party politics was part of the strategy of the PCI. It thought that the unity of the entire trade union movement would provide a major foundation for its central political aim – namely, the formation of a government of national unity with the socialists and the Christian democrats similar to the 1944–47 coalition, a new 'historic compromise'.

Yet the growing necessity for trade unions to distance themselves from party politics was not an Italian prerogative. During periods of recession, in which the party of the Left, if in power, attempts to convince the unions to exchange wage increases for political gains, trade unions are inevitably politicized whatever their response.[15] Such developments lead inexorably to greater trade union autonomy, because an authentic bargaining relationship requires the genuine, reciprocal independence of the two sides.

This occurred even in Italy, because none of the government parties was in a position to be anti-trade unionism. Christian Democracy had close ties with the second largest union, the Catholic CISL (Confederazione Italiana Sindacati Lavoratori). The CISL did not want to antagonize the newly radicalized workers, many of whom were recent migrants from the south who had not joined a union. In the 1950s the links between the CISL and the DC had been useful to both: they delivered working-class votes to the DC and governmental access to the CISL. Now the CISL began to find these links dysfunctional.

The position of the socialists and the communists was more complex. The Communists were in opposition, but constituted the majority of the CGIL, while the socialists, whose party was in government, were in the minority. Socialist trade unionists were under pressure from the Social Democratic Party and the Republican Party to break with the communists and join the third trade union federation, the UIL (Unione Italiana del Lavoro). To keep the Socialists inside the CGIL, the communist trade unionists had to avoid using their majority to ride roughshod over the Socialist minority, while the Communist Party could not use working-class unrest in an overtly anti-government way, because their own chances of entering a government required some understanding with the socialists and, possibly, with the Christian democrats.

In a similar way, in Germany it was important for the main union federation, the DGB, not to antagonize its own CDU trade unionists by being too close to the SPD.[16]

Thus, even though working-class militancy was at an exceptionally high level, Italian political parties were forced on to a terrain of reciprocal compromise. The government was too weak for a frontal attack upon militant workers. The communists could not use their strength for radical purposes. The specific features of the Italian situation – divided Left, strong communist party, virtual impossibility of an alternation of parties in power – instead of leading Italy away from the European norm, fostered convergence towards it. In Italy, as elsewhere, government and opposition agreed that in order to rule it was necessary to come to some understanding with the trade union movement. This created the basis for the growing 'neo-corporatism' of the

1970s, that is, the development of a triangular relationship between governments, trade unions and employers.

In Italy working-class unrest resulted in a legal enshrinement of extensive working-class rights. The Statuto dei Lavoratori, which became law in May 1970, made it illegal for employers to discriminate against workers engaged in trade union activity, banned company trade unionism, and gave workers unfairly dismissed the right to be reinstated. It also gave unions the legal right to post union bulletins and to hold meetings in the workplace and in company time, for up to ten hours a year. It allowed workers the right to receive 150 hours of education a year during company time. A general amnesty was promulgated for all those charged with offences connected with labour disputes prior to passage of the Bill.[17] The Statuto dei Lavoratori was proposed by communists and socialists, and grudgingly accepted by the parties of the centre as a way of forestalling further unrest. It gave legal form to Article 39 of the constitution, which guaranteed workers the right to form trade unions.

This extension of political rights to the organized working-class movement as a whole was accompanied by the promulgation of legislation extending the devolution of power to Italy's regions. However, no major social reforms in health, education and social security were achieved. The Italian state became, on paper, one of the most advanced in Europe from the point of view of 'social rights'. In practice, its welfare system was inchoate and primitive. Some rights come cheap; social reforms are expensive.

In Sweden the social democrats responded to working-class militancy as the Italian trade unions had done: by embracing egalitarianism. However, this occurred in the context of the most advanced welfare state in Europe.

In December 1969, an unofficial strike spread from the largest state-owned enterprise in the country, the LKAB iron mines of Kiruna, in northern Lapland, beyond the Arctic Circle.[18] The reation of the social-democratic government was to treat the strike as a symptom of workers' alienation, rather than a question of wages, and to build on the report of the Working Group on Equality headed by Alva Myrdal, which had been set up by the party and the trade unions. Much of the report was dedicated to a balance-sheet of the achievements of the SAP. Its novelty lay in a commitment to altering the structural conditions of wages inequality. Labour market policy should be directed to reducing differentials by restructuring the tax system, i.e. by making it more progressive.[19] Priority would be given to improving the opportunities of the least privileged groups: women workers, the old, the less educated, workers in depressed regions, and immigrants. Many of these proposals were not carried out. Redistribution can be popular in conditions of growth – when a generalized increase in income makes a decrease in differentials more acceptable – or of acute national crisis, when solidarity can enhance the sense of community required for redistribution. Neither scenario obtained in Sweden in the decade that followed.

The other Swedish response to workers' alienation was to find ways of empowering the workforce by introducing greater consultation and shop-floor democracy. In 1971 the Congress of the largely blue-collar trade union federation, the LO, which had previously opposed the idea of workers' participation in management in principle, now endorsed a programme for employees' co-determination, *Industrial Democracy*. This followed a trend, started in Norway, and followed in most European countries.[20] It was a reaction against the classic Taylorist model of the highly hierarchical and authoritarian organization of factory work, which reduced workers to a mere extension of the machine.[21] It was not until 1976 that legislative action ensued to strengthen the right of trade unions to influence work organization in the factories. Whether this reduced the degree of alienation felt by the workers depended on the extent of workers' participation in trade union affairs or the degree of representativeness of the unions themselves. In Sweden, as in other countries, there were already Works Councils, but their operation was largely confined to consultation; they had made no noticeable inroads into management's rights.[22] The Swedish 'official' strikes of 1971, much wider than the wildcat ones of 1969, provided the LO with the impetus to examine the constitution of wage-earner funds which would be used to purchase a growing share of the private sector so as to subject it to closer worker (i.e. trade union) control. This paved the way for the Meidner Plan, which will be discussed in chapter 23.

To demand some form of industrial democracy became a common reaction to the high level of unofficial strikes in countries with a centralized trade union movement. It was an implicit recognition that such strikes were not simply a challenge to the employers, but also to the established trade unions and their political allies, the parties of the Left. The call for industrial democracy was a 'constructed' response to a phenomenon of factory-level discontent which had no straightforward explanation. Left-wing revolutionaries viewed such discontent as an expression of latent socialist consciousness. Sociologists resorted to the category of alienation. Less sympathetically, shop-floor militancy was viewed by anti-trade unionists (and by some not so anti-) as a form of working-class acquisitiveness, the mirror-image of middle-class greed, whereby one's position in the production process could be used to extract as many concessions as possible, without any regard for the welfare of others or the prosperity of society as a whole. From the point of view of the established socialist parties, industrial democracy represented a threat to the traditional organization of the working class and had to be stamped out or dealt with. In this context, the call for industrial democracy was a way of re-establishing some order in industrial relations so as to reassert the authority of the trade unions: nearly all proposals for greater industrial democracy gave a major role to trade unions. It is no surprise that this was taken seriously mainly in countries such as Sweden and Germany, where a tradition of co-operation existed between government and a centralized trade union movement. In Britain, France and Italy, among others, industrial democracy remained a demand articulated by a minority. In Belgium both main unions adopted the principles of *autogestion* in 1971, but little was done to find ways of implementing it and the idea remained as vague as it did elsewhere.[23]

In Belgium, as in France and Italy, the trade union movement was divided. Though formally independent of political parties, the Fédération Générale du Travail de Belgique (FGTB) was in fact the union which socialist workers joined, while Catholics, who supported the Christian Social Party, were to be found in the Confédération des Syndicats Chrétiens (CSC) which, in the 1960s, had become larger than the FGTB. Even the Liberal Party, the Parti de la Liberté et du Progrès (PLP), had a corresponding union.[24] However, these trade union divisions – later multiplied by the increasing weight of the linguistic conflict between Flemish and Walloon – had less effect than those in France and Italy, because the political allies of the unions were in power in coalition for the best part of the 1960–71 period. Industrial relations, in spite of trade union divisions, were highly centralized, as in Austria and Sweden, and wage-drift was not as extensive as in Britain. A tripartite organization of employers, unions and government, the National Committee for Economic Expansion, dealt with hours of work and working conditions in general. Pay negotiations were handled through industry-wide bargaining sessions. The result was that, despite rising concern about inflation, no Belgian government attempted to introduce an incomes policy.[25]

In Britain, on the contrary, incomes policy was chosen by the Labour government as the method for dealing with inflation and industrial relations. Historical precedents could be found in the pay pauses of the Attlee governments of 1945–51 and the Conservative administration of 1959–64. At the very outset, the Wilson government assumed that it could not fulfil its economic and social objectives (as embodied, for instance, in the National Plan) without some agreement on wages. In reality, wage control very soon became part of the economic armoury deployed to prevent devaluation and defend sterling.[26]

Neither incomes policy nor the defence of sterling was a major success. The ineffective 1964 agreement between the government and the TUC, with the National Board for Prices and Incomes, was followed by the equally ineffective TUC–government agreement of 1965. In 1966 the government decreed a statutory pay freeze and imposed further pay norms through to 1969. Whether or not these policies had a significant effect on the movement of wages and prices is difficult to establish. Computations hinge on unverifiable estimates of the extent to which wages would have increased in their absence. Moreover, one would need to ascertain which alternative policies would have been implemented, as well as their intended and unintended effects. For instance, had deflation been used instead of an incomes policy, it would almost certainly have caused an increase in unemployment which, in turn, would have brought about a containment of demand with negative effects on investment and wage demands.

Uncertainty surrounds the economic effects of incomes policies; but the speculative historian need not remain silent as to their political and social consequences. The incomes policy saga contributed to the systematic deterioration of the relationship between the Labour government and the trade union movement. The long-term effects are more difficult to judge, though it is legitimate to suggest that the insistence on incomes policy helped to fix 'the union problem' in the public consciousness as one of the major obstacles to the regeneration of British industry, even if very few professional economists saw it that way. As trade unionism was usually associated with socialism, there emerged a popular view which assumed that socialist methods and principles were incompatible with economic prosperity.

There were no planners in the Labour government ready to argue for an incomes policy which would regulate the growth of wages according to criteria of equity (i.e. in the direction of a narrowing of differentials). Had such a policy existed, the unions would have fought tooth and nail against it except, of course, for those whose members were among the low paid. From the point of view of the Labour government, such a division might have been preferable to having the entire movement solidly against it. It is true that each successive incomes policy statement after 1966 provided that the lower paid should receive preferential treatment, but there was never any agreed definition as to what constituted low pay.[27] Moreover, incomes policies tended to favour productivity agreements as the main justification for a wage increase. This quickly became a loophole, and an unfair one, since an increase in productivity generally has little to do with workers and much to do with productive techniques and investments in plants and machinery. Consequently, differentials widened simply because some workers were lucky enough to find themselves in fast-growing firms whose productivity growth could easily be measured.[28] This excluded many deserving public sector categories such as refuse collectors, miners, firefighters and academics.

The peculiarity of the British situation was that there existed two systems of industrial relations operating side by side: a formal system, in which agreement was arrived at through industry-wide or national negotiation, and which established the broad guidelines for pay and conditions; and an informal one, operating at the local level where actual pay and conditions were ultimately set. It was the view of many industrial relations experts that over the years the formal system had become a sham, while the informal one had achieved dominance. This view was embodied in the report produced by the Royal Commission on Trade Unions and Employers Associations (the Donovan Commission), which had been established in 1965 by Harold Wilson.[29] The view that Britain was especially strike-prone was not widely held among specialists, though it certainly held sway among the public at large. It was generally supposed that British workers went on strike more frequently than in other countries, and for trivial reasons such as tea-breaks (though only those who have done a day's back-breaking work on a building site – as I have – realize that a tea-break, in certain circumstances, is a fundamental human right and also an aid to productivity).[30]

The Donovan Report suggested that the time had come to redress the balance between the formal and informal systems. In practice, this would have entailed the centralization of the system of collective bargaining. But there was no reason *a priori* why a centralized system should be more efficient in the determination of wages than a highly decentralized one; and, in principle, there were no strong empirical grounds for preferring one system to the other. Controversy raged, though it was not always a clear-cut issue of Right versus Left: 'revolutionary' supporters of rank-and-file action joined forces (in theory) with neo-liberal economists in extolling the superiority of flexible, locally determined pay agreements over anything determined at the top. Many experts, however, believed that the more decentralized a wages bargaining system was, the faster wages were likely to move in whatever direction they were moving anyway. The consequence of this was that in an inflationary situation wages would increase faster in a decentralized system than in a centralized one, and so the level of unemployment required to check wages would have to be higher.[31] In the absence of a consensus among specialists, political considerations prevailed over economic ones, as is usually the case. The understandable, though controversial, social-democratic policy to follow was therefore towards centralizing the trade unions. Those who opposed this could be found throughout the political spectrum: from the Labour left to the Communist Party (small but influential in the unions), the trade unions, the Labour right, and the neo-liberals of the Conservative Party (whose hour had not yet arrived). A common leftist cliché was that shop-floor activists were 'spontaneous' socialists, while union leaders were dreary and unimaginative bureaucrats.

Whatever the truth of this, it was clear that in order to achieve a political understanding with the union leadership, it was necessary to strengthen their hands and move towards centralization. This is why the Labour government's new first secretary of state for employment and productivity, Barbara Castle, produced a White Paper in January 1969 which sought to embody some of the main suggestions of the Donovan report: *In Place of Strife*, an unhappily named document which, far from encouraging peace, provoked the hostility of the trade unions and a significant section of the party, including some of the most powerful members of the cabinet. What Castle tried to do was to centralize the British trade union movement – an essential precondition for the development of a more political role for British unions. The chances of success were considerable. Castle was a stalwart of the Labour left. The new generation of trade union leaders were more left-inclined than ever before. By 1967, four of the five largest unions affiliated to the Labour Party had elected left-wing leaders: Hugh Scanlon led the engineers, Jack Jones, the Transport and General Workers' Union, Lawrence Daly was in charge of the miners, and Richard Seabrook of the shopworkers.[32] Unfortunately for Castle, these leaders had the 'wrong' left ideology. They believed in rank-and-file power and militancy. This, after all, was where their own power effectively resided. The TUC mobilized its nominee MPs across the political spectrum: fifty-three voted against *In Place of Strife* and forty abstained – the largest rebellion of the 1966–70 Parliament.[33]

More important than the ideology of these 'left' trade union leaders was the fact that the structure of the labour movement – the multiplicity of craft unions, loosely linked by membership of the TUC – made it impossible to develop anything remotely resembling a coherent trade union policy. Inter-union rivalry, union leaders' fear of being forced into unpredictable compromises, the short-sightedness of politicians such as Jim Callaghan (the most senior minister to side against Castle), the conviction of modernizers such as Tony Crosland that the Bill could not be made to work,[34] and the predictable reflexes of much of the traditional Labour left, all coalesced to defeat *In Place of Strife*. Never again would the Labour Party seek to legislate a framework for industrial relations. The task of reforming the trade unions would be left to the Conservative Party, with limited success between 1970 and 1974, and with stunning success after 1979. Its aim, of course, was the very opposite of Barbara Castle's: the obliteration of trade unionism as a political force – the termination of its status as 'an estate of the realm', to use Middlemas's felicitous phrase.[35]

The phenomenon of shop-floor industrial unrest did not spare Germany, one of the least strike-prone countries of Western Europe. In September 1969, widespread unofficial strikes caught most observers by surprise. 'Mainstream' (i.e. non-Marxist) social scientists had emphasized the integration of the working class in the Germany of the economic miracle; student protestors inspired by Herbert Marcuse's thesis of the development of 'one-dimensional' man concurred: the working class could be written off as a force for change.[36] A popular explanation of these strikes was that they were the direct result of the German miracle: full employment had strengthened job security and heightened expectations. Workers were more likely to be militant under a social-democratic government than a conservative one committed to monetarism and indifferent to greater unemployment.[37]

The significance of the German strikes of September 1969 – the *Septemberstreiks* – was not that they were massive, but that they were unofficial. More days were lost in strikes and more workers had been involved in 1963, and in the recession of 1966–67, than in 1969.[38] The strikes of 1963 were disciplined affairs, concentrated in one industry (engineering) and directed by one big and centralized union (IG-Metall). The strikes of 1969, like those of 1966–67, 'seemed to represent a challenge to the cohesion and consensus which had been the outstanding feature of West German industrial relations and economic development since the early 1950s'.[39] More specifically, they were a reaction against the government's attempt to establish a new incomes policy through the *Konzertierte Aktion* procedure established in 1966–67, 'one of the first fruits of the labour movement's increasing participation in economic planning'.[40] During the recession of 1967, nominal earnings, as opposed to real wages, had risen by only 3.2 per cent. Workers in the steel industry felt they deserved more than that. This was understandable given that productivity in general, in the steel industry especially, had increased considerably.[41]

Whatever the causes, the *Septemberstreiks* enabled IG-Metall to renegotiate the 8 per cent increase achieved in August and obtain a better deal, while re-establishing the importance of this union as the wage locomotive of German industry. This enabled other unions to follow suit in obtaining higher wages, although, as a result, the union leadership relinquished some of its central control over wage bargaining to regional representatives.[42]

As in France with *autogestion* (see below), and in Norway and Sweden with *Industrialt Demokrati*, the West German political response to working-class unrest was the promise, made in 1972, to extend co-determination in industry to match the system which had operated in the coal and steel industries since the early 1950s. On the shop floor there had been little demand for this. The law (passed only in 1976) was the result of pressure from union leaders, with backing from the SPD. Pressure from below was not significant. Frequent surveys showed that only a small percentage of workers in the steel and coal industries had personally benefited from it.[43] The most notable achievement of the co-determination legislation in the 1970s was at the enterprise level: it allowed a smooth evolution of industrial change, i.e. redundancies and rationalization with little unrest. It had no effect on wages, for which it was not designed anyway, but was not very effective in inducing a growth of shop-floor control, which it was meant to do.[44] Far more significant for industrial relations was the *Arbeitsförderungsgesetz* (Employment Promotion Law) of 1969, which provided funds for the retraining of workers, the basis of an active labour market policy.

In France, the largest strike wave in modern history had a relatively modest impact on industrial relations.[45] Nevertheless, it facilitated the unity of the trade unions and of the parties of the Left. As elsewhere, the vicissitudes of a divided Left were paralleled by developments in the unions. Thus, in France, the long and painful march towards communist–socialist unity required some major shifts in union alignment. As the leaders of the CGT, the largest trade union federation, were also in the leadership of the PCF, it could be assumed that the union would follow it in its political strategy, in line with the Leninist principle that the unions are the 'transmission belts' of the party. The CFTC (Confédération Française des Travailleurs Chrétiens), the second union federation, used to be close to the Catholic party, the old MRP; in 1964 it transformed itself into an independent, lay and left-wing trade union association, the CFDT. While an intransigent minority remained in the old CFTC (with government support), the CFDT moved closer to the Socialist Party and reached an accord with the communist CGT in January 1966, leaving to the third trade union federation, Force Ouvrière (FO), the monopoly of anti-communist trade unionism.[46] Thus, in the early 1970s there was considerable entente between the CFDT and the CGT.[47]

The May events had pushed the CFDT to the left and, at its Thirty-fifth Congress in May 1970, it gave primacy to the class struggle, proclaimed its commitment to *autogestion*, and claimed to belong to the 'socialist family'.[48] As if to dumbfound the naive observer, the CFDT, whose image was closely identified with modern and forward-looking unionism, revived the class slogans of the socialist tradition with ardour; while the communist CGT, widely regarded as being led by hard-core unreconstructed Stalinists (a not unfair description), followed the PCF in supporting representative democracy and the French motherland.

With fewer inhibitions than the CGT, the CFDT looked with benevolence on spontaneous strikes (which tended to occur where it was weak anyway), was more ready to defend the rights of marginal workers, and was more tolerant of *gauchistes*.[49] Its less centralized structures and looser ideology (compared to the CGT) made the CFDT the natural home for disaffected Trotskyists and assorted *soixante-huitards* ('68ers).[50] This was not unique to France: parallel developments occurred elsewhere. In Italy many *sessantottini* found refuge and work in the Catholic union, the CISL; and in Germany many former student agitators got jobs in the unions, to the distress of some union leaders who tried to weed them out.[51]

In Britain, although student unrest had been a rather muted affair, the largely middle-class unions ASTMS and TASS had a left-wing leadership more in tune with the radical 1960s than that of most industrial unions. What was exclusive to French trade unionism was that it was not particularly concentrated on blue-collar workers. Not only had the *cadres* – that is, the supervisors and managerial staffs – been unionized for over forty years, but, by the early 1970s, the teachers' union (the FEN: *Fédération de l'Education Nationale*) was the largest in the country, recruiting from all sectors of education, from primary schools to universities. This union, organized separately from the three major confederations, had more members than all the engineering workers' unions combined.[52]

Notwithstanding this, middle-class radicalism never succeeded in its grand design, that of rallying 'ordinary working people' to its own brand of politics. As we have noted, encouraged by the wave of working-class militancy, many *gauchistes* joined the traditional organizations of the labour movement. But this compounded the problems of the socialist parties. While more workers than ever before were expressing their discontent, fewer and fewer socialist activists belonged to the working class. By the early 1960s, de-proletarian-ization was already evident in the French and Italian socialist parties, both outflanked on their left by important communist parties with stronger roots in the working class. A similar trend towards the embourgeoisement of activists and leaders – though not necessarily of electoral supporters – was confronting other well-entrenched socialist parties. In Britain the decline of working-class representation was one of the most striking characteristics of the evolution of the British political élite.[53] While half of the members of the Labour government of the 1940s were working-class, this proportion had dwindled to almost zero in the Labour cabinet of 1969.[54]

The revival of working-class radicalism had one striking effect: it increased the intellectual plausibility of its middle-class counterpart by providing sound empirical ammunition to those who argued that the era of class politics was far from over. The renewed vigour of Marxism in the West (it had been abundantly discredited in the East by its transformation into a state religion) owed much of its impulse to the fact that authentic proletarians, their hands soiled by the 'real' work of manufacturing (as if scholarly travails cannot be stressful), were not just drinking their pay-packets, watching, in semi-stupefied slumber, the mindless parade of the cultural products of advanced capitalism on television. They had taken to the streets (to use a favourite image of the time), and were plunging Europe into a maelstrom of industrial unrest. ·

This unrest, like all historical processes, lent itself to a multiplicity of interpretations, not all of them comforting to socialists. However, what it unquestionably did was to bring back to the fore an issue which many socialists thought belonged to the past: can the working class still be a revolutionary class? Among those who asked this with particular energy were neither the workers, nor their leaders, but the educated youth of the 1960s.

CHAPTER FOURTEEN

The Revival of Ideology and the Student Contestation

IN THE *annus mirabilis* of 1968, students were in the forefront of political struggles in the most disparate settings. In China they were in the vanguard of the Great Proletarian Cultural Revolution called by Mao Zedong under the slogan of 'Bombard the Headquarters', with the apparent purpose of blocking the 'capitalist roaders' in the Chinese Communist Party. In Czechoslovakia the students took a leading role during the Prague Spring, on behalf of a non-Soviet, libertarian and pluralistic 'socialism with a human face'. This was the most important attempt at a reform of established communist rule until the advent of Mikhail Gorbachev in the 1980s. In Mexico the students marched against a corrupt one-party system. In the resulting repression, more than twenty of them were killed and seventy-five wounded by the police in the course of demonstrations and riots preceding the Mexico City Olympic Games in September–October 1968. In many Latin American countries, such as Columbia, universities had been turned into no-go areas for the police or the armed forces. In the USA the struggles against an unwinnable war in South East Asia, against militarism, for civil rights, were overwhelmingly dominated by student activists. In Japan, otherwise obedient and deferential students exploded in a display of street violence unseen elsewhere.

In Europe, the student movement was strongest in West Germany, France, Italy, Holland and Sweden. It was more subdued in Norway, Denmark and in Great Britain. In Southern European authoritarian states, such as Spain and Portugal (and Greece after the 1967 military coup), students constituted one of the most vociferous anti-government groups, in spite of the far more overt repression they encountered.

This movement was unanticipated and more puzzling than the revival of working-class militancy. Contrary to expectation, among those born during or immediately after the war, the so-called 'baby-boomers', there was a renewed interest in socialism and a wider commitment to values which can only be generally described as 'anti-establishment'. The most visible form of this movement was the student 'revolt' – in reality, little more than occupations of university buildings and largely peaceful street demonstrations – which punctuated the final years of the decade. Much of this contradicted the general assumption behind the socialist revisionism of the 1950s, namely, that the era of ideology had come to an end, that anti-capitalism had to be replaced by a commitment to the mixed economy and piecemeal reforms, and that the overarching categories of Marxism had become anachronistic and irrelevant to the political struggle of advanced capitalist societies.

Most of the parties of the Left did not take the students seriously. In Europe their 'revolts' were actually fairly low-key – with the exception of those that took place in France and Italy. In spite of the strong emphasis on the war in Vietnam, the challenge was in fact cultural rather than narrowly political; and modern socialist parties took little notice of culture. In his 800-page memoirs of 1964–70, Harold Wilson mentions student unrest once and then only because his car was blocked by students in Cambridge while he was going to address the Eastern Regional Council of the Labour Party.[1] His secretary of state for education, Edward Short, a former schoolmaster, was less temperate. In a speech to the House of Commons on 29 January 1969, he attributed the occupation of the London School of Economics (supported by a large proportion of the student body) to a 'tiny handful of people – fewer than one-half of 1 per cent of the 3,000 at the LSE. Of these, at least four are from the United States.' Having branded such an obviously less than fully British cohort as the 'thugs of the academic world ... not even respectable Marxists', Short added, somewhat contradictorily: 'I hope no-one in this House or outside will underestimate the long-term effect of this kind of activity. It can only result in the slow rotting of institutions like the London School of Economics.'[2] How so much could be achieved by a tiny handful of 'academic thugs' is still an unsolved mystery. Short had tried to appear sympathetic to what was a genuine student commitment to action against racism and the war in Vietnam, and for the democratization of the universities; yet his 'academic thugs' remark was remembered as the characteristically pompous retort of a dull and second-rate politician.

In Germany the reaction from the SPD to much more serious student unrest was not systematically hostile: Gustav Heinemann, minister of justice and later president of the Federal Republic, kept his distance from the more intemperate proponents of a tough approach.[3]

In Italy, where the unrest had become serious, the leading Italian politician of the time, the Christian Democratic leader Aldo Moro, interpreted it in the following sensitive, if tortuous way: 'the fact that the young, perceiving themselves to be at a turning-point in history, do not feel at home in this society and wish to challenge it, (is) a sign of portentous changes and of the difficult travails within which a new humanity is born.' [4]

In France, by contrast, the PCF felt sufficiently threatened by student criticism to respond in kind. It claimed that the young and the students were not a homogeneous class, and therefore could not lead the revolution; that their *gauchisme* was of unmistakable petty-bourgeois origin; and that they were manipulated by Gaullism.[5]

What was certainly new, in England, Italy and elsewhere, was that a significant minority, not just a handful, of young intellectuals from the middle classes had adopted a style of political behaviour which was different from that of the rest of society: they emphasized new issues, such as direct participation and involvement in their immediate affairs, and used methods of struggle which were new or had not been used for a long time. Many rediscovered, adapted and even gave a new lease of life to an invigorated form of Marxism.

It is true that in some Left parties aspects of Marxist terminology had survived the onslaught of revisionism. But the status of this semi-official Marxism was increasingly symbolic and represented little more than a vague commitment to the 'final aim'. Only in the remaining communist parties were Marxist categories still used to construct a strategy. Otherwise, Marxism as a system of thought had become increasingly divorced from political practice. It tended to be confined to intellectual circles and dominated by philosophers rather than economists or political theorists.[6]

Many of the Marxist intellectuals active in Germany and Britain in the 1960s had no impact at all on the mainstream social-democratic parties. Usually communists, ex-communists, or 'dissident' intellectuals, they were, however, disproportionately influential among younger intellectuals, and some of them achieved national and international renown. In Britain, Marxist historians such as Christopher Hill, E. P. Thompson and Eric J. Hobsbawm had considerable prestige and following, and enjoyed a solid professional standing. In France and in Italy the central categories used to interpret, respectively, the French Revolution and the Italian Risorgimento were those elaborated by Marxist historians. Italian Marxism was substantially a monopoly of Communist Party intellectuals, at least until the mid-1960s, even though many intellectuals who had left the party after the revelation of the crimes of Stalinism and the Soviet invasion of Hungary in 1956, remained Marxist and committed to the Left.

The new generation of Marxists also reappraised Marxist works which had been little studied in the past or half-forgotten, either because they did not conform to the official views of communist parties or because they had fallen victim to the social-democratic insouciance towards Marxist theory. This led to a flowering of studies on the works of the young Marx, Rosa Luxemburg, Antonio Gramsci, Georg Lukács, Karl Korsch and many others. Of enormous though temporary influence were the writings of Louis Althusser, especially *Pour Marx* and *Lire le Capital* (1965). In the Anglo-Saxon world these developments had two consequences: a close study of Marx and the German classical tradition which had been totally ignored by academic philosophy; and an interest in social theory. This paved the way for the growing influence of French thinkers in American and British universities: Roland Barthes, Michel Foucault, Jacques Derrida, Jacques Lacan and others. The subsequent and paradoxical outcome of this importation was the eventual disengagement of many intellectuals from Marxism.

The term 'revival of Marxism' is inadequate to explain the growing fascination for the doctrine among so many student activists. The new Marxism differed considerably from that of the Second and Third Internationals. Much of it was based on texts written or conceived in the 1950s which could hardly be considered 'Marxist': Herbert Marcuse's *One-Dimensional Man* (1964) and *Eros and Civilization* (1955); Erich Fromm's *The Art of Loving* (1956); Frantz Fanon's *The Wretched of the Earth* (1961). The young Marxists and their older teachers took issue with what had hitherto been the two main models of socialism: that developed by Stalin and his successors; and the gradualist Bernsteinian model. Unlike the older form of Marxism which, in its heyday, had captured the imagination of many working-class activists, the new Marxism remained confined to the intellectuals. While it never realized its objective – to become the dominant ideology of a renewed working-class movement – neo-Marxism succeeded in establishing itself as a serious intellectual force in the advanced capitalist countries. By the 1980s, while socialism appeared to have become a spent force in much of Western Europe, and while even liberal progressivism was on the retreat in the United States, a critical 'anti-bourgeois' attitude, directly or indirectly inspired by some version or other of Marxism, was present throughout the humanities and social sciences faculties of most Western universities. This was true even in countries, such as the United States and Britain, which never had a powerful tradition of political Marxism.

It was not just Marxism which was revived in the 1960s, but a distinctly anti-establishment culture. The economic successes of consumer capitalism, buttressed by the welfare state and legitimized by representative democratic institutions, had not generated a placated and satisfied intelligentsia. In Germany left-wing and liberal intellectuals challenged the unwillingness of the complacent Bundesrepublik to look critically at its past. The historian Fritz Fischer attributed the causes of the First World War to German militarism. The playwright Rolph Hochhuth wrote a play in 1963, *The Deputy*, in which he accused the Pope of not having used his influence to condemn the genocide of the Jews – an accusation directed by extension against all those who remained silent during the Holocaust. A moral avant-garde, spearheaded by writers such as Günter Grass and Heinrich Böll of Gruppe 1947, sought to become the moral conscience of Germany. The group had been created in 1947 – hence its name – with the declaration:

> Let those who want to hide their faces hide them when they learn our history. We did not survive the collapse of a sham world only to create another world of illusions on the ruins of this one. Only he whose knowledge of the most recent past has burdened him has the right today to write and to come before the public.[7]

Such moral affirmations from an élite began to have an impact only in the 1960s, when meetings of Gruppe 47 became media events and the group in turn became a target of student demonstrations for having failed to become politically involved in the anti-Vietnam War movement. By that time, many German intellectuals had become convinced that the political system of the Federal Republic of Germany was 'beyond repair'.[8] In 1968 only 32 per cent of students were satisfied with the German political system.[9]

In Italy, too, the majority of important writers and film-makers belonged to the 'Left'. This term needs qualifying. To be 'left' in Italy in the 1960s meant to be strongly anti-fascist, not anti-communist, resentful of the influence of the Roman Catholic hierarchy, hostile towards the ruling Christian Democratic Party, and generally alienated from the provincialism of Italy. Above all, it meant to be 'modern'. The list of those who fit this particular bill includes much of what was best in post-war Italian culture: Alberto Moravia, Italo Calvino, Elsa Morante, Natalia Ginzburg, Giorgio Bassani, Franco Fortini, Pier Paolo Pasolini, Federico Fellini, Mario Monicelli, Michelangelo Antonioni. Similar claims can be made for writers and film-makers in France and other countries. These oppositional intellectuals, unlike their predecessors or their contemporaries in Eastern Europe, were usually respected and fêted. There was an established left-wing culture which could nourish and sustain the new 'counter-culture' developing within the younger generation.

As new forms of mass youth culture were being created, they were promptly marketed and distributed by the same capitalist system which attracted so much odium: distinct hairstyles, clothes 'for the young', and popular music which only the young (and the young at heart) enjoyed. It seemed as if the entire purpose of these new cultural forms was to establish the identity, and hence the separate nature, of the category of 'youth'. By itself this was not new: in late-nineteenth-century Manchester, the young street fighter or 'scuttler' 'had his own style of dress – the union shirt, bell-bottomed trousers, the heavy leather belt ... and the thick, iron-shod clogs. His girl-friend commonly wore clogs and shawl and a skirt with vertical stripes.'[10] Dora Russell, recollecting her quite different youth during the First World War, wrote:

> Life in Chelsea suited me. I had begun to abandon bourgeois style of dress. The modern hippies are no pioneers in marking themselves out by unusual apparel ... We made our own clothes, at this time peasant-style pinafore dresses of vivid cretonne, over a very bright coloured blouse.[11]

These early forms of 'youth culture' had been highly localized. In the 1950s and 1960s it cut across classes and nations, spread by the worldwide diffusion of US popular music and films.

In this sphere the British and the Americans reigned supreme, though the British were less advanced than the Germans, the French or the Italians in avant-garde culture. Youth and pop culture emanated from the United States, but an original native British version seized the imagination of youth throughout Europe. How and why this occurred has remained unexplained. The celebrated clothes designer, Mary Quant, whose audacious mini-skirts became the symbol of the swinging London of the 1960s, captured the *Zeitgeist* perfectly when she modestly explained that she did not cause the new climate, but caught (before other designers) 'an intangible "something in the air"'. What designers had to do, she stressed, was to 'catch the spirit of the day and interpret it in clothes'.[12] Some of the attitudes, peculiarities and eccentricities which, at the beginning of the century, had been the prerogative of the unconventional bohemian, the half-invented literary dweller of Montmartre and Chelsea, the debauched frequenter of Berlin cabarets, became a mass phenomenon. In the 1960s, all those who wanted to could distinguish themselves. The paradox of mass eccentricity became possible.

It is in the interplay of this twin-faceted phenomenon – an anti-establishment culture with an élitist and avant-garde profile, resting on popular foundations – that the student movement developed. It should not be thought, however, that student activism ever 'dominated' the universities, or that student activists were ever in the majority, or that Marxism became the uncontested ideology of the student movement. The single most important strand of the activists' ideology was a strong anti-authoritarianism. This was accompanied by a dislike of rules and bureaucracy, a suspicion of representative and delegated authority, and a strong sympathy for the oppressed, especially those oppressed by racial discrimination. Apart from such descriptive enunciations, it is difficult to provide an adequate analysis of the phenomenon of student and youth protest. Even though its protagonists operated mainly in institutions of higher education, and even though many of them became teachers and educators themselves, this remains a much under-researched area.

There is as yet no comprehensive explanation of why, towards the end of the 1960s, so many students in so many countries took part in political activities of a pronounced left-wing nature. In so far as there was a 'movement', it was never coherent, never united and always impervious to easy categorization. For instance, the central importance of the war in Vietnam as a strong – perhaps the strongest – catalyst of the student protests of 1967–72, should not lead anyone to suspect them of cultural anti-Americanism. The movement always distinguished between the activities of the US government – for which there was an attitude of total contempt – and 'America', which still provided the model for modernity. European students who marched against the war in Vietnam in fact had considerable sympathy for American students, who were liable to be drafted. The civil rights and anti-war movements of the USA were a source of inspiration. Radical students in Europe enjoyed the rhythm of American music, adopted American terminology and drugs, sang American protest songs, wore American clothes. Neither Soviet nor Chinese culture had the slightest impact on student protestors. 'Sex, drugs and rock-and-roll' were more central to student culture than the works of Karl Marx; the former, of course, did not exclude the latter.

What baffled and still baffles scholars is that, under the cover of a great similarity in behaviour, style, fashion and action, the trend displayed a complex array of contradictory values. Hard-core young Stalinists or Trotskyists went round with long hair and in tight jeans. Maoists enjoyed listening to the Rolling Stones' 'I Can't Get No Satisfaction'. Defence of individualism and distaste for bureaucracy went hand in hand with staunch advocacy of state or collective action against racism and poverty. Avowed libertarians urged withdrawing free speech from supporters of far-right groups. In the name of liberalism, student radicals defended the autonomy of the universities against the encroachments of capitalism, and condemned any funding from private enterprise or government departments connected to the police and the armed forces. At the same time, they criticized the liberal, élitist and allegedly 'irrelevant' nature of much academic research, demanded that the universities should no longer be ivory towers and a preserve for the few, and should instead serve society and the people.

Profound dislike for a consumer society capable of brainwashing its citizens was allied to an irrepressible consumerism and support for mass and 'pop' culture. The young were the children of growth, development, technical progress; yet many despised it, and became fascinated by the idea of a return to nature, to communal life, to uncomplicated religious certainties. It was as if the children of mass society turned against it, yet could not really escape it; no wonder the Freudian metaphor of 'killing the father' was often invoked to explain the apparently aberrant behaviour of the young.

Some student activists claimed that the working class should be written off as the principal agency of social change. The evidence seemed to be before their eyes: the workers had become Marcuse's 'one-dimensional men' and were content to stay at home and allow the bourgeoisie to brainwash them with television. The new revolutionary class was 'youth', or 'the students', or a new class of technicians, or the peoples of the Third World. Others, however, refused to write off the workers. The unofficial strikes erupting throughout Europe, May '68 in France, and the 'hot autumn' of 1969 in Italy, proved, on the contrary, that the class struggle was reviving. Far from being co-opted, the working class had become the spearhead of the struggle for a new social order – or so it seemed.

The student demand for a democratization of all institutions assumed that the majority of those involved in the process would want some form of socialism: everyone's 'true' consciousness was socialist, at least potentially. If required, consciousness could be 'raised' by example, education or personal experience.

Though the students were keen to break with the old and espouse the new, there was a great deal of curiosity about the past, as long as it was a 'new', regained past, rescued from the clutches of a bourgeois class whose paid agents, the bourgeois historians, had kept it under wraps. There was a robust identification with the 'losers' in history, and a haunting search for the opportunities and chances missed by the revolutionaries of yesteryear. The new 'subversives', like all subversives, needed their present to be firmly anchored in the past. Myth-making is a universal necessity.

It may be impossible to demonstrate the beneficial impact of the cultural unrest of the 1960s on the decades that follow. It is difficult to minimize its importance: it contributed, directly and indirectly, to the birth of mass feminism, to the ecological movement, to the growth, expansion and diffusion of the importance of subjectivity and consciousness, to the recognition of the existence of institutionalized and disguised forms of racism and repression. In academia, the movement directly or indirectly led to a revolution in the humanities and the social sciences: the development and spread of social history in all its forms, the growth of sociology, the flowering of inter-disciplinary approaches, the evolution of increasingly sophisticated theoretical methods. University reforms in Germany and France are directly attributable to student radicalism.

In politics the effects appeared negligible. No political party of any major weight developed out of the organizational structures devised by the student activists. No established party suffered unduly, or prospered particularly, as a consequence of the movement. All attempts to construct a more or less revolutionary party in opposition to the traditional socialist and communist organizations utterly failed, and all efforts to capture these organizations and subvert them were successfully repelled. Yet some of the long-term influence of the 1960s on politics manifested itself in unlikely quarters in the 1980s and 1990s: some of the individualism and anti-state rhetoric of the period was captured by a reconstructed conservatism with its emphasis on 'getting the state off the backs of the people' – a far more 1960s' slogan than anything subsequently invented by the parties of the Left. To some extent, May 1968 was the first step towards the dissolution of the Jacobin language of revolutionary politics which had for so long prevailed in France.[13]

The extraordinary concurrence of student unrest in Tokyo and Mexico City, Prague and Berkeley, Paris and Peking may be explained by identifying some common factors. For instance, the internationalization of mass media made it possible for students of the Bocconi University of Milan to know at once of the demands and actions of students three thousand miles away, at Columbia University in New York, for all of them to read the same books, see the same films, sing the same songs. Peasants in revolt in years gone by could never be members of this new global village. The student unrest, though anti-capitalist in its values, could only have occurred once capitalist develop-ment had finally brought about that mass society which had been discussed for more than half a century. What was once a consumption market of the few had become the consumer society for the majority. What had been an élite education system had expanded access to hundreds of thousands. The circula-tion of ideas which had for so long remained enclosed among the privileged few had become the 'mass media' available even to the few remaining illiterates.

The expansion of education, the growth in the number of students in higher education, the consequent increase in the gap between childhood and adulthood, were all contributing factors. Full employment and financial prosperity gave the youth of the 1960s a sense of confidence and certainty in their economic future, which permitted them to concern themselves with wider, non-material issues. The contrast between the élitist and liberal nature of higher education, and the increasingly technical requirements of mass schooling, also played a role in the growth of student radicalism. The overt commitment to popular rule and the democracy of Western societies some-how clashed with the obvious fact that most people felt they had very little real power over their environment. The basis of the Western conception of democracy remained the electoral process, defined as the designation of representatives. Examined from a different perspective, this, however, could be seen as a process whereby citizens were required to divest themselves of the main powers of decision-making in favour of representatives who would exercise them on the citizens' behalf. To be able to choose the powerful is better than having them imposed by *fiat*; but it is not the same as having power oneself.

Some journalistic explanations invoked a then fashionable term: the 'aliena-tion of youth in modern society' – though why that occurred in the 1960s rather than in the 1950s or the 1980s, why in France more than in Germany, why in Germany more than in England, remains unclear. Others, equally vaguely, refer to the alleged cultural sclerosis of advanced industrial society. Logically, this would require at least a comparison of France in turmoil with unruffled England, and hence the scarcely defensible claim that France – the France of Malraux, Sartre, the *Nouvelle Vague* film-makers, Georges Brassens, Simone de Beauvoir – was more culturally sclerotic than the England of Kingsley Amis and John Osborne.

Alain Touraine, one of the main writers on 'new social movements', argued in 1968 that the May movement in France was not a rejection of industrial society and its culture, but the unveiling of the contradictions which are at its heart; that it provoked a profound crisis of the state; and that it expressed a desire for change 'on behalf of society and of the people' against the state.[14] With hindsight, such statements appear vague. The belief that students could constitute a new and essentially radical social class, or that they were the equivalent of the developing proletariat of the nineteenth century – potentially revolutionary and central to the post-industrial world (as pro-fessionals and technicians) – turned out to be based on sociological guess-work – a good hunch which has not stood the test of time.

These and other *post factum* explanations contain important nuggets of sociological interpretation, but they are far from providing a satisfactory explanation. Spontaneous movements of the past are difficult to investigate, because the participants tended to be illiterate and inarticulate, and thus did not provide historians with 'proper' sources. Those who participated in the spontaneous movements of the 1960s were a quite different breed from the turbulent peasants of the past: familiar with the most recent sociological concepts and explanations, adept at examining their own activities in intellectual terms, radical students left behind them a superfluity of verbiage and sources which, however, left historians just as perplexed.[15]

While I share such bafflement, my task, fortunately, is not to analyse 1968. What matters here is that the parties of the Left, like the scholars, were surprised and puzzled by the events. The radicalism of students everywhere took the form of a deep hostility towards the parties of the Left; some of the values it exhibited were distant from, or quite external to, the tradition of socialism. For example, the new youth culture expressed a profound individualism, epitomized by the phrase 'doing my own thing', and a pre-occupation with the self which were quite alien to the more regimented traditions of social democracy. When youth culture – through the student Left – embraced a political-collective approach of the 'united we stand, divided we fall' variety, it tended to identify as 'youth' or 'students' the group to be united, rather than the working class. When the young radicals sought a privileged role for the working class, they believed that 'youth' would assume a leadership role, or, at least, that of the spark which started the prairie fire (to use one of Mao's expressions). When civil rights issues were embraced – such as the struggle against racial discrimination or against excessive police powers – they were always approached from a libertarian standpoint which intersected, but never merged, with that of the organized Left.

In challenging the alleged moral strictness of the establishment and of the older generation, the young activists were also in direct confrontation with the puritanical values enshrined in much working-class respectability, and to which the parties of the Left always paid lip-service. According to the ethos of traditional socialism, permissiveness was associated with bourgeois libertines. The dominant and dubious assumption of social-democratic and communist leaders was that their working-class supporters – had they been asked – would have expressed a strong contempt for sex, drugs and rock-and-roll.

The more socialist of the student activists attempted to involve workers in their struggle, but very few workers joined anti-Vietnam or anti-racist demonstrations, unless they were called by *their* trade unions or *their* parties. The chant, 'Workers! students! unite and fight!', remained an invitation uttered by students and unheeded by workers. Some students joined older leftist organizations, usually Trotskyist, or formed new ones inspired by the thought or life of celebrated socialists such as Rosa Luxemburg, Chè Guevara or Mao Zedong. None of these organizations, however, developed a significant working-class membership anywhere in the world.

Fewer workers were now participating in traditional socialist politics, but nor were they joining any of the new organizations or movements. It appeared that politics was becoming a more middle-class affair, though it is important to remember that the middle class was now large, not the small élite it was at the beginning of the century. Students themselves belonged in origin to this enlarged middle class. There was no major proletarian influx into higher education in the 1960s. Student unrest was not particularly concentrated in faculties or universities with a higher proportion of working-class students. If anything, the opposite seems to have been the case.

The expansion of education was the most significant change affecting the young. In the 1960s the overall European trend was towards a lengthening of the period at school, a unification of school experience across classes by reducing the element of separation or 'streaming' in secondary education, and an expansion of access to higher education. These three aspects of educational policy were central to the programmes of virtually all parties of the Left and came to be adopted by most European countries.

Before 1945, the majority of children left school after their primary years. In the 1960s the school-leaving age was increased to sixteen in Britain by the Labour government, though immediate implementation was postponed because of lack of funds. In Italy the school-leaving age was increased to fourteen, though the law was ignored by an estimated one in four of the age group.[16] Even in Sweden there was a marked divergence between the legal and the actual situation: in 1963 only 88 per cent of fourteen-year-olds were in school.[17]

Nevertheless, the standard left-wing position on education – longer schooling, comprehensive education and greater access – became the universally accepted agenda. Thus, the Gaullist regime in France legislated in 1959 the increase of the school-leaving age to sixteen by 1967, but the original proposal had been made by René Billères, education minister in the SFIO-led government of Guy Mollet (1956–7).[18] By 1965, the school-leaving age had been increased to sixteen in Sweden, to fifteen in Britain and most of West Germany, to fourteen in Belgium, Denmark, Italy and Norway.[19]

Similarly, a policy of comprehensivization (i.e. introducing a single school system throughout compulsory education) became a common feature of the educational system of Western Europe, although, once again, implementation was far more complex than policy-making. In Germany, the Brandt government produced enabling legislation for the establishment of comprehensive schools (*Gesamtschulen*) and left it to the *Länder* to introduce them: the SPD-controlled ones did so rapidly; the others delayed it as long as possible.[20] In Britain some Conservative-controlled local authorities defended to the very last the élite grammar school attended by the children of their most loyal voters. In France, in 1963, the junior classes of the élite *lycées* were merged with junior secondary schools into a network of comprehensive schools for pupils in the eleven to fifteen age group.[21] The Education Act introduced in Italy in 1962 fulfilled a long-standing left-wing demand, by abolishing the distinction between the élite *scuola media* and the *scuola di avviamento professionale*, which provided low-level training to the mass of eleven- to fourteen-year-olds.

Table 14.1 Expansion of university students, 1949–69

	Number of students			Percentage change	
	1949	1959	1969	1949–59	1959–69
Austria	28,000	36,000	54,000	+28.5	+ 50.0
Belgium	20,000	29,000	70,000	+45.0	+141.4
Denmark	9,200	10,000	35,000	+ 2.2	+250.0
Finland	12,000	17,000	51,000	+41.6	+200.0
France	137,000	202,000	615,000	+47.4	+204.4
Greece	14,000	16,000	50,000	+14.3	+212.5
Holland	29,000	38,000	94,000	+31.0	+147.4
Italy	146,000	176,000	488,000	+20.5	+177.3
Norway	5,300	6,100	20,000	+15.1	+227.9
Portugal	13,000	22,000	46,000	+69.0	+109.1
Spain	50,000	64,000	150,000	+28.0	+134.4
Sweden	15,000	33,000	115,000	+120.0	+248.5
UK	103,000	120,000	243,000	+16.5	+102.5
West Germany	105,000	196,000	376,000	+86.6	+91.8

Notes: The 1949 and 1959 figures for France include the University of Algiers. The figures for Sweden include all institutions of higher education.

Source: Mitchell, 'Statistical Appendix 1920–1970', in Cipolla (ed.), *The Fontana Economic History of Europe. Contemporary Economies*, Vol. 2, Fontana, London 1976, pp. 736–7.

The inevitable consequence of this was an unparalleled expansion of the university system throughout Western Europe, as Table 14.1 illustrates.

Between 1959 and 1969, the number of students in higher education doubled or trebled virtually everywhere except Austria. But clearly there is no correlation between this increase and the intensity of student unrest; otherwise, there would have been a much more severe disruption of the universities in Norway, Sweden, Finland and Greece than elsewhere. Nor is there a significant correlation between the weight of the Left in government and the expansion: France under de Gaulle, Spain under Franco, Greece under conservative and then authoritarian governments all did better than Britain under Labour or predominantly social-democratic Austria. A better correlation would probably be obtained if one used an index of university overcrowding. In France, Germany and Italy, anyone with the appropriate school-leaving certificate could enter a university. By the end of the 1960s, the University of Rome had 60,000 students, though its structures could cope with at best a few thousand. The result was chronic overcrowding. Higher education became a question of being lectured at (assuming one could gain access to the lecture theatres) and passing the relevant examinations. Students in Germany and Italy could stay at university as long as they liked, until they dropped out or graduated. Teachers had little or no contact with them. By 1968, in France, 95 per cent of those who passed the *baccalauréat* entered the universities. Fifty per cent of these were eliminated by the first-year examination, as an education minister remarked: 'It is as if we organized a system of shipwreck in order to pick out the best swimmers.'[22] It is thus not far-fetched to suggest, as Walter Laqueur has done, that 'The student protests in the 1960s were partly the outcome of this hypertrophy of the university and the resulting shortcoming in higher education.'[23]

Whatever the reasons behind student unrest, it is evident that the position of the Left on secondary and higher education could be reduced to a simple proposition: education should be expanded as economic resources allowed; secondary education should be reformed so that more people could have access to universities. Of course, this position was shared by many conservative parties. Politicians were evidently responding to popular pressures on the basis of the general recognition that a university education was the passport to a better job. On the Left, there was greater enthusiasm for this than on the Right, mainly because left-wing values clashed with the élitism of traditional university culture. However, the overall political strategy towards higher education was brutally quantitative: more was thought to mean better. In the absence of adequate funding, such expansion inevitably led to a relatively devalued qualification. In these circumstances, the losers, generally speaking, could be found among those who were expected to benefit the most – those least endowed 'with the inherited means of exploiting their qualifications', in other words, the children of the lower-income groups.[24]

Popular pressure for access was not the only factor behind the expansion. There was also a growing understanding that developed capitalism, modernization, high technology, and the scientific revolution, required highly qualified personnel. Had this been thought through, it would have resulted in a demand for greater planning – that is, matching the expansion to the required growth and, more importantly, establishing which disciplines needed expanding more than others. Such planning, which might have served capitalist growth better, would have been highly controversial. It would have required the establishment of social priorities by politicians. This was anathema to the Right, whose simplistic answer, had it asked itself the question, would have been that the market should decide: it would provide better paid jobs, and more of them, to the graduates in subjects it needed; students would flock to these faculties in greater numbers and all would be well.

This, of course, never really occurred. Students entered in greater numbers into so-called 'soft' disciplines taught in the faculties of humanities and social sciences – above all, sociology – and from there launched their protest. From the point of view of the authorities, these faculties had the immeasurable advantage of being cheap: one could cram a very large number of human bodies into a history lecture without spending an extra penny in expensive technical equipment (the teaching of this particular subject not having changed much, at least in its form, since the days of Thucydides). A planner's conception of higher education in terms of priorities would have also been anathema to student radicals, who were appalled at the very notion that universities were expected to meet the requirements of capitalism.

Anti-capitalism was in fact the most obvious ideological basis of the student movement, but its most salient feature was the assumption that politics could be based on semi-permanent mobilization. When the German 'Extra-Parliamentary Opposition' or APO (Ausserparlamentarische Opposition) advocated direct democracy, democratic councils, rule by the assembly of students (or workers in factories), rather than by delegates, it made demands which ran counter to the fundamental principles of Western representative democracy, and *hence* against those of all the political parties of the Left throughout Europe. It seemed clear to these parties that the historical models from which one could draw analogies with the forms of direct democracy advocated by the students – the Paris Commune, the Russian Soviets, the Italian occupation of the factories in 1920 – belonged to a rejected insurrectionary past, probably unrepeatable and certainly unsustainable.

Though it failed to offer a credible political alternative, the student movement expressed a global and radical critique of society and its institutions which could not be so easily dismissed. Such a critique had, of course, previously been expressed by individual theorists, writers and artists. What was new in the 1960s was that this was voiced, more or less spontaneously, by a mass movement.

Its cultural underpinnings were virtually ignored by the traditional Left, partly because socialist parties had little understanding of cultural politics, partly because it involved concepts which were outside the socialist tradition. What was this cultural substructure? Social theorists have described it as 'post-materialist', an expression which suggests the search for the politics appropriate to an age of abundance. Socialist and capitalist politics, in spite of their differences, shared a common terrain: if resources were scarce, the question was how to distribute them. For post-materialists this assumption did not hold. In an era of abundance, politics must, inevitably, acquire a different form.

Politicians of the Left (and the Right) could fairly retort that the assumption that a post-scarcity age had been reached could only be entertained by privileged students, temporarily removed from the world of gainful employment, detached from its competitive ethos and unencumbered by family responsibilities. The real electorate had mortgages or rent to pay, children to feed and clothe, jobs to obtain or preserve. The student radicals arrogantly or childishly ignored these fundamental truths. They were right, however, when they held that human dignity should not be satisfied merely with the riches available on the shelves of supermarkets and department stores; they were wrong when they believed themselves to be the first to hold these views.

Nevertheless, there was something new. The new politics, as Christopher Lasch has pointed out, can take manifold and contradictory forms: radical feminism, environmentalism, pacifism, nihilism, a cult of revolutionary violence:

> But in spite of its anti-intellectualism, the infantile insurgency, and the taste for destruction so often associated with cultural politics, it addresses issues ignored by the dominant political tradition: the limits of reason; the unconscious origins of the desire for domination; the embodiment of this desire in industrial techno-logy, ostensibly the highest product of the rational intelligence.[25]

In the 1960s the political importance of 'the private', of the self, of subjectivity acquired a mass following. Freud joined Marx as an unlikely ideological sponsor of the politics of the young generation: sexual desire seemed to go in hand in hand with revolutionary aspirations, sexual liberation with political liberation.[26] As Jürgen Habermas pointed out in 1969:

> Today, difficulties that a mere two or three years ago would have passed for private matters – for conflicts between students and teachers, workers and employers, or marital partners, for conflicts between individual persons – now claim political significance and ask to be justified in political terms. Psychology seems to turn into politics – perhaps a reaction to the reality that politics, insofar as it relates to the masses, has long been translated into psychology.[27]

The celebrated slogans of the Parisian days of May 1968 suggest both the limitations and the novelty of this 'new' politics: 'Be a realist, demand the impossible'; 'I take my desires for reality because I believe in the reality of my desires'; 'It is forbidden to forbid'; 'I have something to say but I don't know what'; 'Ce n'est qu'un début.' In his study of the Italian protest movement, Tarrow, when comparing the students' specific demands with those of the other groups, pointed out that students far more often demanded new rights, rather than 'more of X'.[28]

The parties of the Left could react only by ignoring these 'cultural under-pinnings', and attempting to appropriate specific demands which could be transformed into the terminology of established political discourse. It was not possible to accept the demands of the students without fundamentally changing the established Left's own attitude that politics was something best left to professional politicians.

The students, however, had asked not only for the 'impossible', but also for reform of higher education and for greater democracy in the universities. This was the language communists and socialists recognized. It was the language of 'normal' politics. Trade unions, the bureaucratic institutions so despised by the students, came out in support of these not impossible demands. Exploiting the palpable embarrassment of the government, the French workers added their own demands in the course of the longest general strike in European history. They did not demand the impossible either: a real forty-hour week, a significant increase in wages, and an extension of trade union rights at the workplace. Thus, the events of May proceeded almost from the beginning on two levels: a utopian-subjective level (whose long-term effects are still to be studied) and a practical-political one. But often – as is generally the case in times of acute political crisis – the two levels appeared to be intertwined. On Monday 27 May workers at the Renault-Billancourt near Paris rejected the accord of the rue de Grenelle negotiated by their own once-trusted communist union leaders. The settlement, when it was eventually revised and accepted, involved a commitment to a reduction of the working week, a 35 per cent increase in the minimum wage (this was of importance only for half a million workers), and other increases ranging from 18 per cent in the clothing industry to 7 per cent for the chemical workers.[29] However, all this must have seemed rather mundane on that fateful Monday morning. At this stage, for a few days, the prevailing impression was that anything could happen, that the workers too had started to demand the impossible, that there were no longer 'normal' political solutions.

In these unforeseen circumstances what did the official Left do? Very momentarily, the initiative passed to the Socialists. On Tuesday 28 May Mitterrand, assuming that de Gaulle would resign, announced his candidature for the presidency of the Republic and proposed that a caretaker government headed by Pierre Mendès-France be formed immediately. Mendès-France, because of the support he received from the small pro-student Parti Socialiste Unifié, was the 'establishment' personality most acceptable to the activists of May. Underlying this call was the assumption that elections would have to be called fairly soon. In other words, Mitterrand's strategy consisted of demanding that Parliament support an 'exceptional' government, pending elections. This was very similar to the strategy adopted by de Gaulle in May 1958 when he took over. The official Left's response had been the mirror-image of that of its opponent. Its legality was tenuous: constitutionally speaking, the Parliament elected in 1967 was the only legitimate forum for approving a new government. Had de Gaulle resigned, the existing government headed by Georges Pompidou would have had to remain in charge until a new president had been chosen. Legalistic as ever, the PCF was not enthusiastic about Mitterrand's proposal, but its Left unity strategy allowed it no alternative but to support Mitterrand. Paradoxically, when it looked as if the revolutionary crisis had come, it was Mitterrand's 'respectable' socialists who seemed to be prepared to act extra-constitutionally, not the formerly insurrectionary communists.

On Wednesday 29 May, de Gaulle disappeared for five hours to consult his generals, giving the impression that no one was in effective control of the country. He reappeared the following day, Thursday 30 May, having decided not to resign. Instead, he dissolved Parliament (a presidential prerogative) and called for elections. Five hundred thousand people demonstrated on that day on de Gaulle's behalf; it was the largest demonstration of May 1968. The PCF responded in the only way it could: by agreeing to fight the elections. This was not unreasonable: in 1967 the Left had obtained over 40 per cent.

It could expect that the radical winds of May would deliver a left-wing majority.

Elections were the only realistic means by which to resolve the situation. All the established political forces – Gaullists, communists and socialists – were for different reasons committed to an electoral solution. The PCF defended this by claiming that an insurrection was impossible. The workers would have been defeated. There would have been a massacre, perhaps a bloody civil war. In reality, an insurrection was impossible since no one, students included, had ever seriously considered the possibility of staging one. Insurrectionary politics, so often celebrated in chants, slogans and speeches, was no more than a cathartic hope for the future, an expression of a desire to escape from the constraints of electoral politics. Leninists of the Trotskyist variety, such as Ernest Mandel, a fierce critic of the PCF's reformism, accepted that the conditions for an armed insurrection did not exist.[30] Mandel's unimaginative and predictable alternative was the adoption by the France of the 1960s of Leon Trotsky's transitional programme of 1938. More significantly, Daniel Cohn-Bendit, the student 'leader' whose voice was nearer to the authentic spirit of May than that of Mandel, never really believed that there would be an insurrection. On 20 May, the weekly *Nouvel Observateur* carried an interview with Cohn-Bendit by Sartre. The philosopher-interviewer asked what effects the present movement would achieve. Cohn-Bendit lucidly replied:

> The workers will obtain the satisfaction of a number of material demands, and the moderates in the student movement and the teachers will put through important university reforms ... There will be some progress, of course, but nothing basic will have changed and we shall continue to challenge the system as a whole ... Besides, I don't believe the revolution is possible overnight like that, I believe that all we can get are successive adjustments of more or less importance, but these adjustments can only be imposed by revolutionary action.[31]

The 'revolutionary crowd' itself – the students demonstrating in the Latin Quarter – lacked the necessary anger which could turn protest into a civil war. May 1968, far from being the proof that a violent revolution in the West was possible, confirmed what had become evident since 1945, namely that it was inconceivable. Years later, the fantasy of May '68, *La Révolution*, had become the object of ironic advertising; a 1986 publicity slogan to launch IKEA (the Swedish furniture suppliers) in France proposed: *Mai 68, on a refait le monde; Mai 86, on refait la cuisine* (in May '68 we redesigned the world, in May '86 we'll redesign the kitchen).

It was in the nature of student unrest that it could not produce a new image of society around which to mobilize a majority. Anarchy can never be hegemonic. Anarchists can occasionally topple crowns, but never enjoy the results. Revolutionaries were as baffled by the events, which had caught them unprepared, as the non-revolutionaries: prior to the May events, an editorial in *Le Monde* lamenting the unexciting political stability of Gaullist France was entitled *La France s'ennuie*. The exceptional crisis was resolved conventionally – that is, by an electoral contest between Left and Right, both equally committed to electoral politics. Routine politics was re-established. Imagination once again abdicated. *L'ennui* returned.

Some contemporaries concluded that it was not possible to examine the May events in a rationalist manner: 'It cannot be seen with the eyes, only with poetry and the most abstract of thoughts, and these are the two muses invoked here ... Revolutions are the ecstasy of history: the moment when social reality and social dream fuse (the act of love).'[32] Medical students in Paris wrote:

> We don't want a revolution because we are fed up with others and with ourselves, but because we want to find each other again. We want to talk about medicine around a drink in the faculty and we want our patients to be something more than social security matriculation numbers.[33]

Raymond Aron, one of the most lucid representatives of conservative France, wrote that May 1968 was 'one of those strange national crises of which France holds the secret'.[34] Bewildered by it all (he was hardly the only one), Aron resorted to dotty comparisons: the May events had been a 'psycho-drama', he told his listeners on Radio-Luxembourg on 1 June,[35] 'a verbal delirium[36] possibly caused by overcrowding, for there were in fact too many students in the universities and they probably suffered from a neurosis of over-population which, as biology had demonstrated, affects 'rats and other animals ... when faced by an extremely high density'.[37]

François Mitterrand had a more perceptive self-criticism: 'the Left was taken by surprise ... The movement of May was an original event ... My generation ... has been blind and deaf. If I am more critical towards the Left to whom I belong and with whom I continue to express my solidarity, it is because it is the vocation of the Left to represent what is new and just.'[38] Yet he poured scorn upon the leaders of the movement: 'when they wanted to explain the motivations behind their demonstrations ... what a mish-mash of quasi-Marxism, what hotch-potch, what confusion!'[39]

Commenting soon after the events, two French writers listed no fewer than eight interpretations: it was a plot, a communist conspiracy (a view favoured by de Gaulle and Pompidou), though most commentators agreed that if the PCF had contributed to anything at all, it was to a return to law and order; it was the result of a crisis in the university, of the old-fashioned and sclerotic teaching of French academics; it was the result of a 'fever' among the young, the result of an Oedipal desire to kill the father (i.e. de Gaulle or the old generation); it was a spiritual revolt against a decaying civilization; it was a traditional class conflict (the view of the PCF); it was a political crisis due to the lack of a left-wing alternative and the excessive longevity of Gaullism; it was due to an unforeseeable chain of circumstances, a momentous bungle: if only the police had not been called to the Sorbonne, if only Pompidou had not been abroad at the beginning of May, if only . . .[40]

The elections of 1968 were a serious blow for the PCF and the socialists. Mitterrand's FGDS lost sixty-one seats, with 16.5 per cent of the votes; the PCF lost thirty-nine seats, obtaining 20 per cent. The entire Left now held only ninety of the 487 seats in the National Assembly. There is little doubt that this result represented a vote for law and order. The Gaullists made inroads among industrial workers, obtaining more working-class votes than the communists.[41]

Co-operation between the FGDS and the PCF was at a low ebb. Like all previous blows, the *coup de grâce* for the PCF was delivered from the USSR, when it invaded Czechoslovakia in August 1968. At first the PCF expressed 'its surprise and reprobation' at Moscow's action – an unprecedented reproach.[42] Then it pretended to believe in the agreement the Czech leader had been forced to sign with the occupying forces. This pusillanimous attitude was sufficient to provide the supporters of Mollet and Defferre with the excuse required to break the unity pact with the PCF. The renewal of anti-communism in the SFIO was marked by an apparent return to fundamentalist socialist rhetoric. In an address to the National Council of the SFIO, Mollet urged his followers to reject any deviation from the 'basic principles of socialism' and, in January 1969, the SFIO changed its name to Parti Socialiste and nominated Gaston Defferre as its candidate for the forthcoming election.[43]

Thus, initially it looked as if the effect of 1968 was a complete return to 'normalcy'. Gaullism was back at the helm. The Left was as divided as ever, with socialists and communists content to wallow in outdated thinking. Some argued that what was needed was a new political party to recast the socialist tradition in the light of the May events. This hope had parallels in other countries, where new left-wing parties had distanced themselves from both moderate social democracy and orthodox communism. In Denmark the 1960s saw the ascent of what might be called a 'spoiler' party: the SF (Socialistisk Folkeparti). This had been formed in 1958 by the then president of the Communist Party, Aksel Larsen, who, as a consequence of Khrushchev's speech at the Twentieth Congress of the CPSU, wanted to form a party which would reject both Stalinism and social democracy. The SF quickly became the main leftist alternative to the traditional social democrats. In 1966 the two Danish parties of the Left, the SF and the social democrats had, between them, a majority of the seats in Parliament. Consequently, the SF temporarily had the power to deprive a social-democratic government of its majority. Responsibility of this nature, in practice, always creates a dilemma for leftist parties, and the SF never had the political daring or the factionalist mentality to damage the social democrats in power. The SF, a true sixties party, differed from the mainstream social democrats principally on foreign affairs, defence and membership of the EEC, not on social welfare.[44] The significance of this is that domestic economic reforms, welfarism, progressive taxation, redistribution, trade union strength – in short, all the so-called 'working-class' issues – did not act as the 'signifier' of the distinction between radical socialism and revisionist social democracy as much as did the symbolic importance of militarism, or acceptance of European interdependence as represented by membership of the EEC.

A virtually identical situation occurred in Norway with the formation in 1961 of the Socialist People's Party (SPP), whose main difference with the DNA was on foreign policy (NATO and, later, the EEC). The SPP was a minor party for most of the 1960s, obtaining 2.4 per cent in 1961, 6 per cent in 1965, and 3.5 per cent in 1969. In 1973, however, the SPP, in alliance with left-wing anti-marketeers and the communists, managed to attract 11.2 per cent of the electorate at the 1973 Storting election. Communists and SPP together had only 4.5 per cent in 1969.[45] This election marked an electoral earthquake for the hitherto dominant Norwegian Labour Party: its vote fell from 46.5 to 35.2 per cent. Labour improved its position in the mid-1970s only when the leftist coalition began to disintegrate.

The nearest French and Italian counterparts to these Scandinavian leftist parties were the small technocratic Parti Socialiste Unifié (PSU) – formed in 1960 from various socialist groups disaffected with the SFIO because of its support for the Algerian War – and the Partito Socialista Italiano di Unità Proletaria (PSIUP), which had split from the mainstream PSI in 1963. These new leftist parties were ideally situated to capitalize on the student unrest. They offered those who had become radicalized in 1968 a more secure and permanent home, a structure for a longer-term form of political commitment.

In Britain, various Trotskyist sects were given an unexpectedly long lease of life by the after-effects of student unrest. In Italy, those who thought that the PSIUP or the ex-communist Manifesto Group were too tame could opt for new groups: Avanguardia Operaia (Trotskyist), Lotta Continua (anarcho-libertarian), or Potere operaio, from whose entrails many terrorist organizations would issue.

In France, the PSU made the clearest bid for the support of student activists, claiming that it accepted the ideology and message of May 1968. At the June election it polled 4 per cent, lost one-third of its traditional electorate, but gained new supporters among the educated and the young, thus becoming an overwhelmingly middle-class party.[46] The PSU appeared to remain unsullied by compromises because, under the leadership of Michel Rocard, it had staunchly refused to be associated with Mitterrand's FGDS and the PCF. Its rhetoric was well to the left of the PCF, though its ideology, until a few months before May 1968, was identified with the technocratic tradition of West European revisionism. Like other similar leftist parties in the rest of Europe, the PSU acquired an importance totally out of proportion to its real electoral force (it failed to win any seats in the 1968 elections).[47] Like so many before, it sought a 'third way' between communism and social democracy. Rocard claimed that the PSU was a revolutionary party in the sense that it wanted to revolutionize society, not in the sense that it sought an armed insurrection.[48] The Seventeen Theses approved at its Dijon Congress (March 1969) asserted that capitalism was in crisis;[49] that it faced insurmountable contradictions;[50] that under capitalism, universal suffrage did not accurately reflect the interests of the people;[51] and that the Left needed to be completely overhauled, since none of the existing major organizations was able to undertake successfully the momentous tasks ahead. By rejecting alliances and denouncing the reformism of the communists and socialists, the PSU believed that it could become a rallying point for the revolutionaries of May 1968. The strategic perspective was, of necessity, nebulous: it offered a structure for radicals without the need for compromise with the two main reformist parties. Because it rejected the facile sloganeering of the Marxist-Leninist groups and the dogmatism of the PCF, it provided an ideologically congenial format for the more thoughtful survivors of '68; by insisting on the need for analysis and theory, it appealed to intellectuals and theorists who would have felt ill at ease among the pragmatic politicians of the SFIO. It should be added, however, that the traditionally hyperbolic rhetoric of the French socialists acquired, thanks to 1968, a further lease of life: in presenting his winning motion at the Party Congress of November 1968, Mollet declared that 'it was not a question of ameliorating the system, but of substituting a better one. It is in this sense that the Socialist Party is revolutionary.'[52]

Many of the new PSU recruits were talented young members of the middle class, able and willing to use the media in an imaginative way. To these, the PSU offered an indispensable training for an eventual career in politics. Of course, the claim that a small élite organization such as the PSU (or the Manifesto Group in Italy, or the various New Left parties in the rest of Europe) could reform, regroup and realign the traditional Left was quite absurd, though, like many absurdities, it took a few years for this to become obvious to all clear-headed observers. By 1974, having been badly beaten at the 1973 elections, Michel Rocard and others had left the PSU and joined Mitterrand's new Parti Socialiste, carrying with them the staunch anti-communism which had served them well in the PSU, as well as a strong commitment to the principle of *autogestion* or (self-management). This much-abused concept was used, not for the first time, as the socialists' distinctive final aim, against the incorrigibly statist goal of the communists, bent on comprehensive nationalization. By the 1970s, the idea of *autogestion* had become so diffuse on the Left that support for it came from the most unlikely sources, from Defferre to the PCF.[53] Both *autogestion* and extensive nationalization symbolized one of the final goals of socialism. Once enunciated, it could be forgotten. Concepts such as these can be useful to politicians who wish to avoid the charge of being unprincipled or pragmatic.

Modernization, an aim shared by all parties, including conservative ones, was seldom an adequate substitute for ideological goals. In Germany, where student unrest never reached the same levels as in France or Italy, the leadership of the SPD had to face a constant barrage of criticism from its articulate youth section, the *Jusos*. The criticism was predictable: the party was silent on long-range goals and was no longer using the terms 'socialism' or even 'democratic socialism'.[54]

Not surprisingly, the socialist student organization, the SDS (Sozialistische Deutsche Studentenbund) had been excluded from the party and had become the organizing centre of the protest in the universities. Most left-wing parties had 'problems' with their youth sections. Even the centralized and highly disciplined PCF could never adequately control the Union des Etudiants Communistes, which was constantly influenced by the 'wrong people', such as the Italian communists in the early 1960s, then Ernest Mandel's Trotskyists and, later, Althusserian Maoists.[55] The British Labour Party never had a similarly important youth section (what it had tended to be infiltrated by Trotskyists and was not taken seriously by the party or anyone else); consequently, the leftist critique originated from New Left groups, organized around projects such as the May Day Manifesto, journals such as *New Left Review*, and single-issue campaigns around the Vietnam War or nuclear disarmament.

In Italy, young Catholics contributed at least as much as socialist or communist students to the creation of a student movement. The universities of Trento (the first in the country to train sociologists) and the Catholic university of Milan were among the first to be occupied by protestors.[56] The Italian student movement shared many of the features of the French: libertarianism, an even more pronounced commitment to sexual liberation (a consequence of the unbearably stultifying bigotry and provincialism of Italian society), the rejection of representative democracy, the cult of Third World revolutionary experiences, and intransigent criticism of the organized Left and, above all, of the Italian Communist Party.

The response from the PCI, however, was not uniformly hostile. Togliatti's successor as leader, Luigi Longo, a veteran of the Spanish Civil War and the Resistance, was far more positive towards the students than were other communists and socialists at the time. In an important article, written before the May events, he mercilessly criticized his own party for failing to understand the wider political implications of student unrest and for being too preoccupied to refute attacks and criticisms from the students. The PCI, he wrote, had become too bureaucratic, too immersed in routine activity and hence unable to understand what was new in society.[57] From the right of the party, however, Giorgio Amendola accused the students of being irrational and nihilistic, and demanded a 'battle on two fronts' against both the extreme Left and the government.[58] This position, similar to that of the PCF, was accepted by only a minority of Italian communists. Longo's 'soft' line prevailed.

The clearest sign of novelty in the policy of the Italian Communist Party was the recognition of the 'autonomy' of the students' movement. The PCI accepted that it could not hope to organize, co-ordinate and lead the student movement, subsuming it under its overall guidance. This negation (or, at the very least, redefinition) of the traditional communist ambition to be the 'vanguard-party' of society, is crucial to an understanding of the subsequent relationship between the PCI and later, more important 'new political subjects', such as the women's movement of the 1970s or the peace campaign of the 1980s. Breaking with communist tradition, the party now accepted that the students (and other movements in 'civil society') had a legitimate and important role to play in the 'revolutionary process' – as the party called the presumed development of Italian society towards post-capitalism. The recognition of autonomy had another implication: a distinction between the student movement as such and the numerous political organizations and 'vanguard-parties' (mainly Maoist and Trotskyist) which had sprung up everywhere, and which were attempting to take over the movement.[59]

In Western Europe, none of the established political parties of the Left succumbed to the activism of the student Left. None was taken over, or seriously split. Traditional organizations such as these could be perturbed by the far Left's critique and agitation, but their party machines were too well-oiled and their electorate too entrenched to imperil their political existence. In the USA, where presidential politics depend on complex *ad hoc* coalitions, rather than on a stable political machine, the young radicals virtually took over the Democratic Party and installed the only aspirant they trusted, George McGovern, as the presidential candidate for the 1972 election.[60] His disastrous performance in the polls was the most evident sign that radical politics had failed to capture middle America. Henceforth Democratic candidates would range from the colourless to the safe. In old Europe this saga of rapid success, followed by resounding failure, was not reproduced. Nevertheless, at least in France and Italy, politics was recast: de Gaulle lost a referendum in 1969 and resigned as he had threatened to do. Those who had supported him in 1968 as the guarantor of law and order had realized that the institutions of the Fifth Republic were just as safe in the hands of the uncharismatic Georges Pompidou. The French socialists began a process of internal restructuring which enabled them to achieve power in 1981, at the expense of their troubled allies, the PCF. In Italy, 1968 signalled a new phase marked by substantial reforms in 1970 (regional devolution of power, Workers' Charter), the defeat of Christian democracy in the divorce referendum of 1974, and the considerable advance of the PCI in 1975 and 1976.

Politics changed, but without a revolution – as the students themselves soon realized. A small minority of militants misread the *Zeitgeist* and degenerated into terrorism or wasted the rest of their lives in the dead-end politics of sectarian revolutionary organizations.

Alhough sufficient evidence will never be available, it could be argued that the complex and contradictory values of 1968 helped to change the shape of politics in the 1980s and 1990s. Whether the libertarian and permissive values of 1968 were a product of the young generation itself is impossible to determine. As Mary Quant put it, there was 'something in the air' in the early sixties. Much was changing. The Roman Catholic church, led by John XXIII (who was over eighty and who did not have the reputation of being an innovator), was in the midst of its Second Vatican Council under the banner of *aggiornamento* ('updating'). In the USA, the brief presidential term of John F. Kennedy seemed to herald a modern approach to statesmanship – in style, if not substance. In the USSR Khrushchev attempted to lead the country towards economic reforms and consumerism. Under the impact of Maoism, the international communist movement was irrevocably split. The 'winds of change' of decolonization (to quote Harold Macmillan) were creating a politically independent Third World, at least in appearance.

Was the student unrest anything more than the mere reflection of sections of a post-war generation coming of age? To what extent did it prepare the ground for the anti-state neo-liberalism of the 1980s? Did this rebelliousness achieve anything more than weakening the traditional Left, without leading to any alternative? As Zhou Enlai is supposed to have remarked about the effects of French Revolution: 'It is too soon to say.'

CHAPTER FIFTEEN

The Revival of Feminism

IN 1966, in Britain, a group of socialist intellectuals led by Raymond Williams, E. P. Thompson and Stuart Hall formed the May Day Manifesto Committee to draft a political declaration for the developing New Left. In 1968 a longer version of the initial draft was published as a 190-page book and was widely read. Critical of the Labour Party, the Manifesto dealt with all the important issues of the day: poverty, housing, education, inequality, communications and advertising, the economy, international capitalism, US imperialism, the technology gap, multinational companies, militarism, the Cold War, the Third World, the decline of British industry, the role of the state, the problems of the Labour Party, trade unions and so on.

This book, the product of the most alert minds among the British left-wing intelligentsia, did not contain a single reference to the position of women in society.[1] At the time this was not surprising. The *May Day Manifesto* might have had a longer shelf life if the drafters had taken more seriously a ground-breaking article by Juliet Mitchell published in 1966 in what had been their *de facto* house journal, the *New Left Review*.[2]

With remarkable insight Mitchell had identified the four themes around which the subsequent movement for the liberation of women would be structured: women's role in economic production; the domain of reproduction, including birth control and abortion; socialization, including the role of the family and education; and, finally, the realm of sexuality.[3] In 1968 the organized Left, new and old, had not yet confronted these questions. In the absence of a women's movement, there were no women's issues.

It is not surprising, therefore, if to many observers and participants the revival of feminism towards the end of the 1960s seemed to constitute a new phenomenon, distinct from the earlier battle for the suffrage, much of which had been forgotten. Once the vote had been secured, the British and North American suffragette movements subsided and for a while the struggle of women to free themselves from patriarchal forms of oppression appeared to be suspended. Initially, the new feminists of the late 1960s had little knowledge of their past history. In fact, one significant part of their endeavour precisely consisted in recapturing the origin of a movement which had been 'hidden from history': 'At regular intervals throughout history, women rediscover themselves.'[4]

As the past began to be rescued, it became apparent that many of the central features of the new, or 'second-wave' feminism had been present all along, in the aspirations of the first – hence the characterization of the phase discussed here as a 'revival'. To understand how the resurgence of feminism marked the Left in the late 1960s and 1970s it will be necessary to follow the trail of the new feminists into the forgotten past and to describe the old, uneasy relation between the proponents of female emancipation and those of socialism.

A study of leading British feminists in the 1850–1930 period – when feminism emerged as an organized movement – lists the following major campaigns: women's suffrage; the repeal of the Contagious Diseases Acts (which, in effect, controlled prostitutes); legal rights for married women; better educational and employment opportunities; birth control; trade union-ization; and family allowances.[5] Even though the intensity of these campaigns differed over time, they were all a struggle for equal rights, or against a double standard. 'First wave' feminism was essentially concerned with the extension to women of rights which had been conferred on men or obtained by them.

Among the earliest trail-blazers was, in France, Olympe de Gouges who, in her *Déclaration des droits de la femme et de la citoyenne* (September 1791), demanded complete equality between the sexes, including the redefinition of marriage as a new social contract between men and women.[6] In a forceful introduction to her *Déclaration*, she cross-examined 'Man' thus:

> who gave you the sovereign right to oppress my sex? ... blind, bloated with science yet wallowing in crass ignorance, in this century of Light and Wisdom, Man yearns to rule like a despot over a sex which possesses all the faculties of the intellect while pretending to support the revolution and claiming to stand for equality.[7]

Olympe de Gouges, who gallantly dedicated her book to Marie Antoinette as a demonstration of female solidarity, and who was not an aristocrat but the autodidact daughter of a butcher, suffered the same fate as the unfortunate queen: she was executed on 3 November 1793. The previous year, she had declared: *La femme a le droit de monter sur l'échafauld; elle doit avoir également celui de monter à la tribune* (women have the right to mount the scaffold; equally, they must have the right to mount the public platform).[8]

In England, in *A Vindication of the Rights of Woman* (1792), Mary Wollstone-craft expressed similar views, arguing that society, by forcing women into a condition of passivity and dependency, had made them inferior: 'how can women be generous when they are the slaves of injustice?'[9] The feminine condition is the result of man's dominance: 'From the tyranny of man, I firmly believe, the greater number of female follies proceed'; 'Let woman share the rights', she concluded 'and she will emulate the virtues of man.'[10]

Under the impact of the Enlightenment and the French Revolution, some men were in the same camp as the first feminists: in France, Antoine Caritat de Condorcet formulated the most developed, early protest of the revolutionary period on behalf of women's rights.[11] Writing shortly before de Gouges and Wollstonecraft, Condorcet argued in his essay 'On Giving Women the Right of Citizenship' (*Sur l'admission des femmes au droit de cité*, 3 July 1790) that the principles of the rights of man should be extended to women, and that no society which discriminated against women could be truly civilized, since there were no rational grounds for doing so. The arguments used by the detractors of women – including some which, though refuted for two centuries, re-emerge with tiresome frequency – were surveyed by Condorcet with refreshingly modern wit: 'Why should people who experience pregnancies and monthly indispositions be unable to exercise rights we would never refuse to men who have gout every winter, or who catch cold easily?'[12]

In Germany, Theodor von Hippel published a polemical work entitled *Über die bügerliche Verbesserung der Weiber* ('On the Civic Advancement of Women', 1792), in which he argued that in an age 'when human rights are preached loudly from the rooftops', women had to be accepted as equals and allowed to 'think and act in their own interests and by their own efforts'.[13]

It is evident from this that feminism was, from the very beginning, part and parcel of that liberal and democratic movement which might be said to constitute 'the Left' in the nineteenth century: Wollstonecraft herself had entered the English debate against Burke's *Reflections on the Revolution in France* by writing and anonymously publishing her *Vindication of the Rights of Men* in 1790, *before* turning to women's rights.[14] The most important feminist text of the nineteenth century, John Stuart Mill's *The Subjection of Women*, was the offspring of the radical-liberal tradition.[15] Mill did not question the competitive and individualistic nature of the existing social order, but challenged the 'legal subordination of one sex to the other' on two grounds: first, that it is 'wrong in itself' and, secondly, that 'it is one of the chief hindrances to human improvement.'[16] The struggle to repair this injustice could not be the work of women alone; it would not succeed 'until men in considerable number are prepared to join them in the undertaking'.[17]

Mill's courageous book was received with profound hostility by his enemies and with embarrassment by his friends. It failed commercially, 'the only book on which Mill's publishers ever lost money'.[18] It remained a relatively isolated example of male pro-feminist liberalism. It cannot be therefore surprising if mainstream liberalism had, in the view of feminists, a fundamental flaw: the category of citizen which was at the centre of its conceptual framework was not gender-neutral. The citizen whose rights were proclaimed by liberals and democrats was a *male* citizen still able to arrogate to himself the patriarchal prerogatives and privileges of the *ancien régime*.

A not dissimilar analysis was conducted by the first theorists of the socialist movement, particularly Karl Marx: the labour contract which brought juridically equal citizens face to face disguised a real inequality of power; a citizen owner of capital faced another – a worker – possessor only of his labour.

Both the feminist and the socialist movements, whose respective development would be unthinkable without the catalytic force of liberalism, challenged it on the same territory: the separation, established by liberalism, between the political sphere and civil society. Liberals held the view that citizens should be able to participate freely and equally in political society, while in civil society they were to be protected from interference from the political level, that is, from the state. This formulation implies that the only serious inequality is political. Once all citizens had established their political equality before the law, they could be left free to compete in civil society. The only thing that would preclude the poor from entering the Ritz would be the lack of ready cash, not the laws of the state or aristocratic privilege. The reforming zeal of liberalism left untouched the disequilibrium of power in civil society. Mainstream liberalism did not accept that to grant equal political rights to unequal persons perpetuates significant inequalities. True egalitarianism could not be indifferent to substantive social inequality between persons – as Jean-Jacques Rousseau, Mary Wollstonecraft's great mentor and interlocutor,[19] had indicated in his *Social Contract* and the *Discourse on Inequality*.[20]

Socialists and feminists did not simply denounce the duplicity and incompleteness of the liberal revolution – the citizenry whose power it sought to enhance excluded the propertyless worker and the female, both equally disenfranchised. They also sought to reveal the uneven distribution of power in civil society. It was at this point that the two traditions, the socialist and the feminist, diverged: socialists – of the post-utopian variety – concentrated their attacks on socio-economic inequality and its political repercussions; feminists focused on the systematic gender inequality which pervaded all spheres, from family life to the most elemental interpersonal associations, including the relationship between men and women. This 'private' sphere – especially the family – was more densely political than a constituent assembly, for it was the locus in which the most complex system for the formation and distribution of power, or the assignment of roles (which is the same thing), was endlessly being constructed and reconstructed. This awareness had been reached by feminists as early as Wollstonecraft.[21] Though generally regarded as the leading advocate of the extension of liberal rights to women, Wollstonecraft was far more than this. Above all, as Barbara Taylor has suggested,[22] she was one of the first theorists of sexual differentiation, who posed the key questions: 'How are women made?' and 'What does it mean to be a woman now?' – questions which have haunted feminism these past two hundred years and which will probably remain unanswered unless the analogous questions: 'How are men made?', 'What does it mean to be a man now?' are finally posed with similar force and urgency.

Wollstonecraft had the merit of opening up this dangerous field of human inquiry – before Freud – and contrasting the corrupt and debased relationship prevailing between the sexes to a pure, natural union between equals.[23] In this sense she was well in advance of J. S. Mill, who was mainly concerned with the legal, not the sexual, subjection of women. Mill remained a stereotypical 'Victorian' unconcerned with sexual passion, sex itself being an 'animal passion' which men inflicted on women.[24]

Some of the more perceptive socialists of the nineteenth century dimly grasped the importance of sexual equality. The young Marx, not yet a Marxist, attacked unilateral sexual relations (that is to say, person-to-object), whether under the conventions of bourgeois marriage (where women constituted, in his view, a form of private property); or under its mirror-image, collectivist 'crude' communism which views 'woman as the prey and the handmaid of communal lust', thus expressing 'the infinite degradation in which man exists for himself'. This is contrasted to the non-alienated, other-directed, person-to-person, equal sexual relationship in which 'man' (meaning the species – in German, *Mensch*) can become truly human: 'From this relationship man's whole level of development can be assessed ... It also shows how far man's needs have become human needs, and consequently how far the other person, *as a person*, has become one of his needs, and to what extent he is in his individual existence *at the same time* a social being.' In the true love relation of equal to equal, Marx finds the embryonic fragment of the society of the future which, by abolishing human self-alienation, signals the 'definitive resolution of the antagonism between man and nature and between man and man'. This society is communism, the self-conscious 'solution of the riddle of history'.[25]

Soon Marx abandoned all this and turned to his analyses of capitalism. Many years later, in 1884, Friedrich Engels developed his critique of the family, an institution, he wrote, 'based on the open or disguised enslavement of the woman ... In the family, he is the bourgeois; the wife represents the proletariat.'[26] 'Woman was the first human being that tasted bondage. Woman was a slave before the slave existed', August Bebel had written a few years earlier in *Die Frau und der Sozialismus* (1879), one of the fundamental texts of German social democracy and one of the most popular expositions of socialism, translated into many languages.[27]

By then, the connection between female emancipation and general emancipation had become widely accepted – at least in principle – in the socialist movement. The earliest formulation of this position, in France in 1808, was by Charles Fourier, one of the most feminist of the first socialists, who had argued in his *Théorie des quatre mouvements et des destinées générales* that 'The extension of rights to women is the general measure of all social progress.'[28] Sixty years later, this was echoed by Marx in a letter to Kugelmann: 'Social progress can be measured exactly by the social position of the fair sex.'[29]

It should be said that the emancipation of women is an imperfect index of socio-economic advance. For instance, in the quality and range of women's higher education, retrograde Tsarist Russia had no peer in Europe, and was second only to the USA; Russian wives could own property, while in 'advanced' Victorian Britain they were entirely propertyless until the Married

Woman's Property Act of 1882.[30] The University of Calcutta gave degrees to women in 1883, decades before Oxford and Cambridge.[31]

Nevertheless, by the end of the nineteenth century it was an axiom uncontested among all educated progressives that economic and technological growth brought with it social progress. By and large, reactionaries too subscribed to this determinism, though for them, of course, social progress was a poisoned chalice.

In socialist discourse, the link between social emancipation and the liberation of women developed into a language of priority and preconditions: the eventual destruction of 'sex slavery' could not occur until capitalism had been dismantled. The 'complete solution of the Women's Question is as unattainable as the solution of the Labour Question under the existing social and political institutions'.[32] This was so widely accepted that the twenty-two-year-old Bertrand Russell turned to socialism because he believed that this was the secure path to female emancipation. As he wrote to his fiancée, Alys Pearsall Smith: 'I feel that *the* thing I have learnt this year is that any improvement in the condition of the great mass of women is only possible through Socialism, and it is this discovery which has made me a Socialist.'[33]

The liberation of women was widely seen as inextricably linked with the liberation of labour. It provided women with a powerful ally – the labour movement – but at the price of subordination to it. Since the labour movement was a masculine guild, this was not entirely consistent with a movement which aimed at emancipating women from subordination to men. But it was certainly coherent with social-democratic ideology, according to which no major social question could be resolved under capitalism. Pending the socialist millennium, of course, much could be done; accordingly, the SPD's Erfurt Programme of 1891 committed the party to universal suffrage, equal rights and, consequently, to the repeal of all laws discriminating against women. No other party in Wilhelmine Germany raised such egalitarian demands.[34] Nevertheless, women remained marginal to the politics of the SPD, even when, as during the Weimar Republic, they had acquired formal equality and the right to vote.[35]

By the turn of the century, socialism and independent feminism had gone their separate ways. The former rose powerfully, a men's movement in a man's world. Feminism struggled to surface. It was forced to resort to symbolic politics. It was squeezed between the paternalism of its few male sympathizers, the hostility of the majority of men, and the indifference of too many women. The disjuncture between feminism and socialism occurred when the socialist movement became organized as a mass movement, when factory workers became overwhelmingly male, and when the universalist and arguably utopian objective of 'total' emancipation gave way to a more concrete and more reformist practice. This disjuncture had occurred in Britain much earlier than elsewhere, with the rise of an independently organized working-class movement, Chartism. In her magisterial analysis of Owenite socialism,

Barbara Taylor has documented the transition from a joint socialist–feminist vision of a world turned upside down, to one in which women's rights became a narrower issue, divorced from a revolutionary perspective and, consequently, more acceptable to middle-class women who could organize reform campaigns without being constantly accused of 'socialistic aims or immoral sexual intentions'.[36]

Socialist women had to distance themselves both from sexually emancipatory feminism and its reformist middle-class variant. To be accepted into the ranks of socialists they had to accept the prevailing view that sexual liberation was of interest only to a small minority of emancipated middle-class women. They had to distinguish themselves from those 'bourgeois' feminists who fought for the extension of liberal freedoms to women, while leaving the capitalist relations of production unchanged. Yet at the time feminists were turning to the socialist movement. Socialists appeared to be more consistent than liberals in their support for the extension of equal rights to women. Socialist parties were seen by many middle-class women activists as the best instrument with which to reach working-class women. Socialism accepted, in principle, even if only for the distant post-capitalist future, the idea of complete female emancipation. There was a further powerful ideological synchrony: both movements were children of the modern world. At the time, feminist women, like socialist men, stood in radical opposition to traditions. Unlike millenarian movements, feminism could not hark back to a mythical past. Even in the Garden of Eden woman was the inferior creature. Where were the 'good old days' for women, if the origin of their subjection was lost in unreconstructable myths? What was the past for the proletariat, a new class which had no history outside that of capitalism? In the domain of tactics, socialism and feminism often compromised, vacillated or turned moderate. But in the kingdom of principles, their hostility to the world of traditions was implacable. The past had to become scorched earth.

To be a feminist meant to be a 'modern' woman; socialism, still a radical creed, appeared equally modern, requiring new men, unencumbered by old prejudices and deference. The world of work, the centre of socialist organization, for all its alienating and brutalizing features, appeared to many feminists as an instrument of emancipation; in it, women could aspire to be 'like men', to earn a salary and secure a modicum of financial independence. By the turn of the century, in Western Europe, the working class had established some dignity, had acquired the consciousness of its own rights, had developed powerful trade unions and political parties, was feared and respected by the powers that be. Thus feminists assumed that emancipation required women to enter the mainstream of the new labour force, in factories and offices, not because it was desirable to submit to the same form of wage slavery and drudgery as men, but because this was the avenue for female emancipation, for the elimination of a division of labour which had restricted woman's work to the home, while designating 'real' – that is, remunerated –

work as the province of men. Socialist feminists such as Olive Schreiner believed that the march of technological progress and modernity offered the possibility of a new deal between men and women. In her *Woman and Labour* (1911), she wrote:

> The past material conditions of life have gone for ever; no will of man can recall them; but *this* is our demand: We demand that, in that strange new world that is arising alike upon the man and the woman, where nothing is as it was, and all things are assuming new shapes and new relations, that in this new world we also have our share of honoured and socially useful human toil, our full half of the labour of the Children of Woman. We demand nothing more than this, and we will take nothing less. This is our 'Woman's Right!'[37]

Such sentiments were not the prerogative of socialist feminists. The first Russian woman economist, Mariya Vernadskaya, a supporter of free trade liberalism, stressed the liberating possibility of work, and urged women to abandon their exclusive role as wives and mothers, explaining that the husband's power derived from his role as sole breadwinner.[38] The assumption that technology would release women from the drudgery of household chores was part of the optimistic view socialists and progressives had of the liberating potentiality of technical progress. Bebel himself was much impressed by the use of technology in the preparation of food and cited the Americans, who 'have made the common sense discovery' that it is inefficient for women 'to bake their own bread and brew their own beer' when the lot can be produced, more cheaply, by 'the co-operative cooking establishment'.[39] In future, mass catering would liberate women from the drudgery of the private kitchen, which was 'an obsolescent institution', in which time, power and material were thoughtlessly and extravagantly wasted. 'Chemistry', Bebel added, 'will teach us how to prepare new and better articles of food in the future to an extent quite unknown at present.'[40] As Diana Coole has pointed out, it was seldom suggested that women's drudgery could be decreased in the meantime by the simple expedient of sharing it with men.[41]

Some socialist parties continued to advocate protective legislation which would prohibit women working in physically demanding occupations, and even, as in the 1880 programme of the Spanish socialists, in jobs contrary to 'good morals'.[42] By the beginning of the twentieth century, however, it was widely held by socialists that entry into the labour force (though not necessarily in all occupations) was the key to female emancipation. In a speech delivered at the founding congress of the Second International in 1889, and entitled 'The Liberation of Women', Clara Zetkin pressed for the end of all restrictions upon female employment outside the family. Economic independence was one of the preconditions for women's social emancipation, even though, like Bebel, Zetkin agreed that no major gains could be achieved under capitalism. Nor was she under any illusion that the struggle for women within the organizations of the working class would be easy. Consequently, she explained to her followers that it would be necessary to fight against the men in the party who wished their women to stay at home.

Bebel too had realized the importance of convincing socialist men of the importance of female participation: 'Every Socialist recognizes the dependence of the workman on the capitalist, and cannot understand that others ... should fail to recognize it also; but the same Socialist often does not recognize the dependence of women on men because the question touches his own dear self more or less nearly.'[43]

However, socialists did not only demand the proletarianization of woman; they also fought for her to acquire citizenship rights and, above all, the right to vote. True universal suffrage, already established in the SPD's Erfurt Programme, was accepted by the Socialist International at the Stuttgart Congress of 1907. It had been approved unanimously, apart from the isolated opposition of the Fabian delegate, a woman who wanted female suffrage to be restricted to those owning property. In spite of the position officially adopted at Stuttgart, however, many social democrats, particularly in Austria, Belgium, France and Holland, feared that an extension of the suffrage to women would increase the vote of clerical parties. The Belgian socialist leader Emile Vandervelde, for instance, though upholding the principle of female suffrage, had declared that women were not yet intellectually mature enough to be given political rights – meaning, one presumes, that they would not vote for the socialists.[44] Even after the war, when women gained the vote in many countries, the Belgians extended it only to those who had distinguished themselves during the conflict, or who had lost a husband or a son during the war.[45]

This was not the position of the SPD. Bebel had been unequivocal: universal suffrage was a matter of principle.[46] Karl Liebknecht had promptly expressed his outrage at Vandervelde's position. Lenin, particularly shocked by the opportunistic behaviour of the Austrian socialists, readily agreed.[47]

That women should be able to work 'just like men', and vote 'just like men', might appear an emancipatory idea, were it not for the fact that it involved the acceptance of a male model of social organization. There was no question of a specifically feminist politics, but only of a socialist politics for women.

To succeed in the socialist movement, socialist feminists had to de-feminize themselves, or, at least, sharply demarcate themselves from feminism. The leaders of the Belgian socialist women's group, mainly middle class, thought like Vandervelde: women's role was to support the political activity of men.[48] Rosa Luxemburg, one of the leading socialist theoreticians of her day, took no interest in 'the woman question', and thought it was all 'old ladies' nonsense'.[49] Even Clara Zetkin, who considered the question of crucial importance to the destiny of socialism, was so hostile towards feminism that she thought Bebel had been too sympathetic to it. She instructed socialist women to avoid co-operating with feminist groups, and poured scorn on all those who thought that the war between the sexes was more important than the class struggle.[50] At the First International Congress of Socialist Women in 1907 – organized by Zetkin in conjunction with the Stuttgart Congress of the Second International – she reaffirmed her belief that 'The female proletariat cannot count on the support of the bourgeois women'. Nevertheless, for *class* reasons she believed that they ought to

> march separately but fight together ... But the female proletarians must know that they cannot acquire the right to vote in a struggle of the female sex without class distinctions against the male sex. No, it must be a class struggle of all the exploited without differences of sex against all exploiters no matter what sex they belong to.[51]

The essential difference between bourgeois feminists and socialist women, maintained Zetkin, was that 'For us Socialists ... women's suffrage cannot be the "final goal" as it is for bourgeois women.' It was only 'one phase of the battle towards our final goal'.[52]

The real aim of Zetkin's speech, however, was not to lambast bourgeois feminism, but to obtain the support of all socialist parties for real universal suffrage. In the first place, she had to establish that this was a question of principle against the waverers who argued that women would vote for the conservative parties. Secondly, she was arguing against those who were prepared to compromise by accepting the concession of limited suffrage to women of property, pointing out that this disadvantaged social democrats electorally, and that in addition it was essential to keep all women united in the battle for universal suffrage. Conceding the suffrage to women of property would allow 'the pacified bourgeois women to drop out of the battle for political equality of the entire female sex'.[53] Zetkin obtained what she wanted. The Congress passed a strong resolution in favour of universal suffrage, but added that 'socialist women must not ally themselves with the feminists of the bourgeoisie, but lead the battle side by side with the socialist parties'.[54] To obtain this Zetkin had been forced into a somewhat ambiguous position: class was always more important than gender, yet it was vital to keep all women, regardless of class, united in the struggle.

The General Austrian Women's Association (the Allgemeiner Österreich-ischer Frauenverein) was representative of the feminist organizations which had developed in most European countries by the end of the century. It was vastly outnumbered by anti-feminist women's associations, such as the rabidly anti-Semitic Viennese Christian Women's League.[55] It considered Karl Lüger's Social Christian Party to be the chief enemy. It had campaigned for the socialist leader Victor Adler in 1901, but refused to join his party. The Association's leader, Auguste Fickert, propounded views which became common currency among second-wave feminists: 'The women's movement ... does not need a political party, it is itself a driving force in political life and perhaps destined not only to transform party politics but to fill politics altogether with a different content.'[56] The Association had proclaimed as early as 1894 that 'The women's movement is at its heart revolutionary for it aims at a fundamental reorganization of all forms of human living together, a reorganization that perhaps Social Democracy does not even dream of.'[57] Nevertheless, social-democratic women continued to consider the Association to be reformist and not revolutionary. Class, not gender, was the driving force of history.

Denouncing feminism had become virtually obligatory for socialist women. Those who wanted to have some influence in the socialist movement had to understand the language of socialist priorities. The histories of some of the most important socialist women active between 1880 and 1920 are exemplary: in Italy Anna Kuliscioff, in France Madeleine Pelletier and Hubertine Auclert, in Russia Alexandra Kollontai.

Anna Kuliscioff, a Russian revolutionary who became one of the most influential personalities in Italian socialism, in her lecture *Il monopolio dell'uomo* (1890), had started out by following the official Bebel–Zetkin line, insisting that the class struggle was the main road leading to economic emancipation. Later in the lecture, however, she explained that 'as long as men, even socialist men, even the best men in the world, make laws these will be to their advantage and to our disadvantage.'[58] With views like these, it was impossible to have any significant influence in the PSI. Kuliscioff was compelled to relinquish her feminism. In 1897 she wrote in the party journal that 'the present feminism of the middle class is merely a replica of the revolutionary movement of the male middle class a century ago. Freedom for woman ... can only be freedom for the middle-class woman ... Socialism and feminism, if they can be parallel social tendencies, cannot be one cause.'[59]

By 1905, Kuliscioff had come out against the extension of the suffrage to women (for tactical reasons); and, later, when she (and the Socialist Party) demanded it, this was on class not on feminist grounds, as a reaction against its proposed extension only to women of property.[60] Kuliscioff directly experienced the contradiction between class and gender, and that between political involvement and personal life: in 1910 she was in open conflict with her companion of forty years, the leader of the PSI, Filippo Turati, who did not understand the urgency of fighting for universal suffrage. Her polemic blazed across three consecutive issues of *Critica Sociale* in 1910.[61] Her defence of universal suffrage for all women, regardless of class, had to rest on essentially class grounds, the only language acceptable to socialists.

In France, the political itinerary of Madeleine Pelletier, one of the first woman doctors, was similar to that of Kuliscioff. Pelletier started her political life as a feminist and joined the French socialists with the avowed purpose of using the Socialist Party on behalf of the feminist cause.[62] In outlook, Pelletier was closer to second-wave feminism than many of her contemporaries: she despised the institution of the family; was in favour of a free sexuality on equal terms with men; advocated the legalization of abortion;

and believed children should be brought up in common.[63] However, she soon discovered – and accepted – that in order to remain inside the SFIO, and wield some influence, she would have to temper her demands and accept the complete separation of socialist women from bourgeois feminists.[64]

Hubertine Auclert refused this constraint. Speaking at the Socialist Workers' Congress in Marseille in October 1879, she made it clear that she was speaking as a woman and not as a worker. She explained that she was reluctant to merge her demands with those of socialist men, because she feared that human equality 'will again be only the equality of men among themselves, and that women will be duped by the men of the proletariat as the proletarians were by the bourgeois'.[65] Nevertheless, her motion guaranteeing women equal rights with men in all spheres of social and political life won the day:

> in all circumstances, women will have their freedom of action like men. The congress, considering that a role must depend on the choice of the individual who fills it, if it is to be fulfilled, assigns no special role to women, they will take the roles and the places in society to which their vocations call them.[66]

Accepting resolutions, however, seldom changes the world. As Auclert suspected, the French socialists, though more advanced than all other parties in France, were never, in spite of the resolutions they regularly endorsed at their various congresses, wholeheartedly in favour of the extension of the suffrage to women. As Sowerwine explains, 'in 1906 ... the party voted to present a bill for women's suffrage which was never written and ... in 1907 the SFIO deputies named a sub-committee on women's rights which never met.'[67] Magraw concurs, pointing out that less than 3 per cent of SFIO members were women, and adds that 'There was an abject failure to mobilize female participation. Party congresses paid lip service to women's rights. But Jaurès failed to keep his promise, made to feminist delegations who came to lobby him, to give such questions priority.'[68] French trade unionists were deeply imbued with an archaic Proudhonian view of women, and were inordinately fond of the virtues of feminine domesticity, the idyllic image of the glow of the 'woman by the hearth'.[69] On the other hand, the Belgian socialists of the POB/BWP, fairly backward on women's issues, elected a genuinely revolutionary feminist, Emilie Claeys, to the Central Committee (1893).[70] Inconsistencies aside, in all countries the main reason behind the socialist ambiguity on the question of universal suffrage was a profound pessimism about the voting intentions of women. It was widely assumed that they would be the prey of the conservative parties and that they would be influenced by the local priest. This assumption was probably true, though, as we have seen, Bebel had insisted that there should be no compromise on universal suffrage.

The polemic against bourgeois feminists continued unremittingly even in the Russian Empire, where bourgeois democracy had yet to come. Thus, in 1908 Alexandra Kollontai – who became the only woman in the first

Bolshevik government – and a small group of social-democratic women argued at the All-Russian Congress of Women against 'bourgeois' feminists who held the view that women had specific interests which bound them together across class lines. Having made this necessary gesture of homage to the official view, Kollontai later argued that women workers were doubly oppressed, by capitalism and by the men in their lives, and advocated separate women's groups within the party. By 1917, all Russian socialist groupings – Mensheviks, Bolsheviks and socialist revolutionaries – and even the Liberals (the Kadets) had accepted the principle of separate organizations.[71]

At least on paper, the realization that working women suffered under a double oppression, as workers and as women, was common currency. Thus, no one was surprised when Lenin, in celebrating International Woman's Day in March 1921 wrote in *Pravda* that

> under capitalism the female half of the human race is doubly oppressed ... firstly ... because the law does not give them equality with men; and secondly – and this is the main thing – they remain in 'household bondage', they continue to be 'household slaves', for they are overburdened with the drudgery of the most squalid, backbreaking and stultifying toil in the kitchen and the family household.[72]

That feminism had a preferential relationship with the Left, that Left parties upheld women's demands for political and social equality more consistently and more vigorously than other parties, is difficult to deny. Nevertheless, the alliance between feminism and socialism was fundamentally unequal. It was accepted by socialists only on their own terms, namely that the social struggle between capital and labour was to be recognized as fundamental; the emancipation of women as women depended on the victory of the working class. Feminists who refused the terms of this alliance had to be content with demanding the extension to women of liberal or 'bourgeois' rights, assuming that social and economic emancipation would somehow ensue from political freedom. According to the canon of the established Left, once true universal suffrage was achieved, liberal feminists would rest on their laurels. Those who still felt dissatisfied could opt to join the socialist movement, whose aims were still far from being achieved. It seemed, in other words, that women had to follow, whether the liberals or the socialists, but they had to follow.

Most first-wave feminists, especially socialist feminists, were isolated from other women. This is a price often paid by those who belong to a vanguard movement. As recently as 1989, an editorial in a special issue of the *Feminist Review* marking twenty years of second-wave feminism, accepted that 'Many women have little access, or are indeed profoundly hostile to the social forms and political practices of the women's movement avant-garde.'[73] To this continuing problem had to be added – at the turn of the century – a particularly pronounced class dimension. Most of the male activists in the socialist movement were working-class men, while most of the women who fought for the suffrage were middle- or upper-class.[74] For instance, women members of the Russian Social Democratic Labour Party comprised between 11 and 15 per cent of the total, but they came prevalently from the intelligentsia, unlike the men who were mainly unskilled workers and artisans.[75] This class difference is hardly surprising: poor women, unlike their working-class husbands, had no organizational framework enabling them to participate in politics. They did not belong to the skilled, craft-based working class which had provided the trade unions with their best cadres. They were excluded from large-scale industrial plants where solidarity and brotherhood sprang from shared struggle and shared oppression. It was mainly self-confident and educated women from a privileged background who could have the intellectual courage, fortitude and determination to confront phalanxes of men whose attitudes – with some honourable exceptions – ranged from the condescendingly patronizing to the viciously hostile. Thus, socialist feminists had to fight their lonely battle within masculine organizations, speaking on behalf of working-class women with whom they had little in common and whom they could not organize. As if these handicaps were not enough, they were prevented from co-operating with their obvious allies, bourgeois feminists. The few socialist women who rose to the top in working-class parties did so by demonstrating that they were 'as good as men'. This meant putting class first and being women second, thus becoming even less representative of ordinary women.[76]

The hostility socialist women felt towards mainstream feminism was more than reciprocated. In France, bourgeois feminists were reluctant to lose the support of liberal men by siding with their less than respectable socialist counterparts.[77] In Britain working-class women were perturbed at the militant tactics of the largely middle-class-led Women's Social and Political Union (WSPU).[78] The WSPU – arguably the most formidable feminist organization in Europe, certainly the best-known thanks to Christabel Pankhurst's outrageous tactics and her flair for publicity – had started out with the intention of persuading the new Labour Party to support universal suffrage. By 1907, however, the WSPU was toying with the idea of suffrage for women restricted by property qualifications on a par with manhood suffrage, something which would benefit the Conservative Party far more than either Liberals or socialists.[79] By 1912, under the impetus of Christabel Pankhurst, never tender with the Independent Labour Party, the WSPU ceased to consider the labour movement its principal interlocutor. Christabel's sister, Sylvia Pankhurst, a committed socialist, was expelled from the WSPU and, years later, became one of the founders of the British Communist Party. The WSPU behaved increasingly like an underground organization for which tactics became everything.[80] When the war broke out, the WSPU and the other main suffragettes' organization, Millicent Fawcett's less militant but larger National Union of Women's Suffrage Societies, joined in patriotic support for the war effort.[81]

This rapid overview of some aspects of first-wave feminism brings us to the question of its relationship with feminists of the second wave. It may seem that the latter simply exhumed the half-forgotten demands of the former. But they did so in very different circumstances: by the 1960s, the percentage of educated women had grown markedly; the strength of conventional morality had much diminished; recognition of the central importance of equal rights was accepted by a very wide spectrum of political opinion, including most conservatives. The so-called sexual revolution made the much-despised double standard politically indefensible. A new generation of women, decisively more confident of their rights, could continue a struggle which the first-wave feminists could only initiate. The personal and psychological costs of fighting difficult battles, only to find oneself isolated later on, should not be underestimated. In a few significant instances, feminist leaders ended up embracing eccentric causes: Christabel Pankhurst took up the cause of the Second Coming of Christ; her mother, Emmeline Pankhurst, turned to campaigning against venereal diseases and sexual freedom and joined the Conservative Party. Sylvia Pankhurst eventually went to Ethiopia, and became a supporter of pan-Africanism and of the Emperor Haile Selassie. Adela Pankhurst became a fascist. Christabel's main working-class supporter, Annie Kenney, became a theosophist.[82]

The obstacles confronted by first-wave feminism in its encounter with socialism can be subsumed under a single heading: the theoretical framework of socialism, Marxist and non-Marxist alike, could accommodate only aspects of the relations between the sexes which could be explained in socio-economic terms, and traced back to an inequality in the relations of production. Lenin spoke for the whole Left, and not just for the Bolsheviks, when, with characteristically complete if unfounded confidence, he affirmed that the abolition of private property 'alone opens up the way towards a complete and actual emancipation of woman'.[83] Even when the first socialists attacked specifically sexual forms of oppression, they never failed to trace these back to their socio-economic origins. For example, August Bebel did not shrink from castigating the sexual oppression of women by dissolute men, condemning the fact that the seduced woman had no claim to support from society, or from the man responsible for her condition, and might have to resort to a dangerous and illegal abortion or to child murder: 'The unscrupulous man, the moral author of the crime, in reality the true murderer, is unpunished ... probably soon after (he) becomes a ... much respected man.'[84] Nearly a hundred years previously, Mary Wollstonecraft had likewise pointed out that 'men ought to maintain the women whom they have seduced'.[85] Bebel would have agreed, and went even further, castigating 'bourgeois marriage' as 'worse than prostitution', adding: ' a wife is sold into the hands of her husband and must endure his embraces though she may have a hundred causes to hate and abominate him.'[86] However, the ultimate responsibility for this state of affairs was firmly attributed to capitalist relations of production, not patriarchy.[87]

Socialists could be united against patriarchy as long as it was viewed as an effect of class society. As Rosalind Coward has pointed out, 'Questions of sexual behaviour, masculine behaviour, questions of control and expression of sexuality, questions of female autonomy were all in contradiction with Marxism's hierarchy of analytic and political priorities given in the deterministic account of sexual and familial relations.'[88]

Socialist and social-democratic parties could accept that women workers were more exploited than men workers. They could not accept that the bourgeois woman and the working-class woman shared a common bond: male oppression. The Left's class analysis inevitably had the function of intellectually breaking this bond – hence the attack upon bourgeois feminism – thus rendering an authentic feminism, the independent organization of women by women, practically impossible. The real challenge feminism presented to the Left was not that it asked the Left to incorporate women's demands in its general programme; there had never been objections to this, at least in principle. Feminism's real challenge was that it invited the organized Left fundamentally to recast its own ideological framework, abandoning the unspoken axiom that the socialist movement was a movement of men which women could join on men's terms and, in exchange, receive men's support. This new movement of universal emancipation required a de-masculinized politics; a socialism for women and men. To this demand the resistance was, not surprisingly, formidable. A century-old movement of men could not simply shed its skin like a snake during a change of season.

It does not follow from this that women failed to make considerable progress under the direction of liberals and socialists. They did. Conversely, women as women lost many rights under the authoritarian and semi-authoritarian right-wing governments which established their dominion over most of Europe between the wars. However, by 1945, after the defeat of Nazism and fascism, the central demand of all feminists, universal suffrage, had been met in most of Europe. This cannot be correlated with the strength of feminism, or the support of socialist parties, or the level of economic and social development. In spite of lukewarm socialist support, universal suffrage was obtained in Holland in 1917 and in Austria in 1919. True equality in voting was obtained in Britain, the home of the strongest suffragette movement, only in 1928. In industrially backward Spain, women gained the vote in 1931, after the establishment of the Second Republic. Economically advanced Belgium gained universal suffrage only in 1948. In decentralized and 'democratic' Switzerland, women had to wait until the 1970s. French women, whose emancipation appeared so well-established – at least in foreign eyes – had to wait until the end of the Second World War to vote, just as in post-fascist Italy. The women of Finland had been enfranchised in 1906, when their country was a rural backwater of Northern Europe and still a dependency of the Tsar. The best explanation available is that the political progress of women was speeded up by the establishment of a new regime or a new overall political settlement after a major conflict – in Austria (the First Republic), Germany (Weimar), France (the Fourth Republic), Italy (the post-1946 republic), Spain (the Second Republic), Britain (end of the First World War).

The new post-1945 European constitutions conferred on women rights they did not have before. In the newly established socialist countries of Central and Eastern Europe, women obtained equality of rights – such as they were – with men. In terms of their access to paid employment, they made faster progress than in the West, but the double standard in the domestic division of labour persisted utterly unchanged under socialism – a comprehensive refutation of Lenin's naively optimistic assertion that capitalism was the sole obstacle in the way of the liberation of women.

Legislative advances for women could thus be achieved without a significant contribution from feminists. Patriarchal attitudes, together with the ideology of male superiority, were barely dented as a result. The renewal of democracy in post-war Europe had led to an overall extension of rights to women, but this made little difference to power relations between the sexes. The extension of the suffrage to women in all European countries after the war (except Switzerland) did not significantly change the relations between parties.

In Italy, Article Three of the new republican constitution of 1946 guaranteed the equal 'social dignity' of all citizens, 'irrespective of sex, race, language, religion, political opinions or social or personal status', and stated that all obstacles to such equal social dignity would be removed by the state. Thus, there was a constitutional basis for legislation removing all causes of inequality. If this was not achieved, it was largely because the DC consistently upheld the traditional Catholic view of the woman's role. Notable legislative change in favour of women did not occur until much later when both the Left and feminists were stronger. While the constitution provided equal rights, a woman's adultery remained a criminal offence until the 1970s, and women employees could be legally dismissed (and often were) when they married or became pregnant.

In France, the preamble to the constitution of the Fourth Republic (1946) stated: 'The laws shall guarantee to women, in every sphere, equal rights with men.'[89] As elsewhere, the parties of the Left, though not supported by the female electorate, had the largest representation of women in Parliament. Of the thirty-nine women elected to the French National Assembly in the second election of 1946, twenty-six were members of the French Communist Party, which had 166 deputies.[90] The representation of women in the French Parliament decreased steadily between 1946 and 1973.

In Federal Germany, as in Italy and France, the Basic Law of 1949 (Article Three) established that men and women have equal rights and that no one may be 'prejudiced or favoured' because of sex (or race, religion, etc.).[91] The previous constitution of 1919 also had a sexual equality clause, but that had been specifically restricted to political rights such as voting, and did not interfere with the Civil Code which established, for instance, that a woman could not work without her husband's permission. The new, wider, equality clause was due mainly to the efforts of the SPD and its leading woman representative, Elizabeth Selbert.[92] Yet, even Selbert, while advancing the cause of women, had to make it clear that 'Our demand for this type of equal rights does not originate in feminist tendencies. In the thirty years I have spent in politics, I have never been and never will be a feminist.'[93] This 'I am not a feminist, but ...' would increasingly sound like a compulsory preamble to feminist demands, as if women had to disavow the inspirational source in order to achieve the goal. Socialists found themselves in a similar position – that of denying who they really were – only in countries where socialism was illegal or deeply unpopular (for instance, the USA). Such were the obstacles to the development of a feminist discourse.

The undeniable fact that more women than men tended to vote for conservative parties did not dictate any obvious strategy for the Left. Some socialists feared that feminism would simply make it more difficult for traditional God-fearing women to vote for the Left. Others, with as much justification, pointed out that traditionalists took women seriously, assigning to them a role which, though subordinate, provided them with dignity (good mother, exemplary spouse) and prized the condition of being woman. Against the idea of a feminine specificity, the Left still subsumed gender difference into an ideology based on the centrality of workers, final repositories of the values of the future society. Left-wing attempts to attract the mythical 'ordinary woman', by mimicking women's magazines, were often pathetic in their clumsy innocence: a questionnaire devised for women by the daily paper of the PCF in 1946 to establish whether the reader was a good wife, included such questions as 'Do you talk to your husband when he reads the newspaper?' 'Do you tell him not to drop ash on the carpet?' 'Do you squeeze the toothpaste tube in the middle?'[94]

Perhaps because there was no female discourse in the parties of the Left, more women voted for conservatives and Christian democrats, who appealed to traditions and family values, than for socialists and communists. In Germany, for instance, until the end of the 1960s, the CDU/CSU won about 10 per cent more votes from women than from men. Until 1969, the majority of SPD voters were male. The gender gap, while remaining favourable to the CDU/CSU, narrowed from 25 per cent in 1957 to 11 per cent in 1969.[95] It may well be, though it is difficult to prove, that the attempts of the SPD to 'de-Marxify' itself, and to become a less class-based party, helped it to gain ground with women.

In France, in November 1946, the two parties of the Left obtained proportionately more votes from men than from the newly enfranchised women.[96] In 1967 all the parties of the Left obtained among men just over 50 per cent of the total, yet lost the overall election. In the presidential contest of 1965, the candidate of the Left, François Mitterrand, gained 52 per cent of the male vote and only 38 per cent of the female vote, while de Gaulle proceeded to win the election with 55 per cent overall.[97] In June 1968, according to surveys, only 40 per cent of PCF voters and 45 per cent of socialist voters were women, against 54 per cent of Gaullist voters.[98] The anti-clericalism of the SFIO, far more pronounced than that of the PCF, made it particularly unappealing to women. Virtually all family associations and similar organizations were controlled either by the church, the MRP (Christian Democrats), or the communists.[99]

In Britain, the European country in which women's conservative voting has perhaps been best researched, more women voted for the Conservative Party than for the Labour Party until 1979, when there was no marked gender gap.[100] The gap reappeared in the early 1990s (see chapter 22). By the early 1970s, a clear majority of the membership of the Conservative Party was female. The mainly middle-class Women's Institute, with over half a million members in 1972, was one of the largest British voluntary associations. Working-class women gradually became excluded from the House of Commons: only one was elected in 1970. Those trade unions with parliamentary seats virtually in their gift, such as the miners, the engineers and the transport workers, were entirely dominated by men.[101] Of course, by 1992, working-class representation in the House of Commons was much reduced regardless of sex.

While fighting against sexual discrimination, throughout Europe the Left prevented the emergence of a feminist discourse in its traditional organizations. This occurred even where women-only associations were established specifically to take up women's issues. For example, in Italy, the Unione Donne Italiane (Union of Italian Women – UDI), which reached a peak of one million members in 1950, had been formed towards the end of 1944 by women already active in the main political parties of the Left – the PCI, PSI and the Action Party. In reality, the UDI was dominated by communist women as part of the PCI's strategy of creating 'non-party' organizations to develop its support among wider sectors of the population.[102] This is not to say that the UDI did not defend working women. It involved itself in issues which should have been taken up by the trade unions, had these not continued to assume that 'real' workers were men.[103] Nevertheless, by 1950 the political views of UDI activists were identical to those of the PCI. This was so, as Judith Hellman convincingly shows, not because the PCI imposed a line on the women of the UDI but because 'the socialization of these women was so complete that they were hard pressed to elaborate an analysis on any problem that differed significantly' from that of the PCI.[104]

In terms of feminist politics, the PCI was, at least in the ideals it expressed, the most advanced political party in Europe. Palmiro Togliatti repeatedly asserted that the emancipation of women was 'one of the central issues in the renewal of the Italian state and of Italian society'.[105] He argued that the cause of the backward social conditions of Italian women was the back-

wardness of Italian society, not the religiosity of the women themselves –
pointing out that in the distant past only religious women, like Saint Catherine,
had been able to make their mark on Italian history.[106] The emancipation of
women could not be achieved by a single party or a single class. It was the
task of all women, for they all had common interests 'with the exception,
obviously, of tiny groups connected to the ruling class and its privileges'.[107]
Accordingly, the UDI was not and should not be a party instrument, but the
organization of all Italian women.[108]

Further citations illustrating Togliatti's commitment to a pro-feminist
position could easily be assembled, but they would do little to alter the fact
that a substantial problem existed. Where there was no truly autonomous
feminist movement, where active women had to look over their shoulders to
ascertain if they were following a 'correct' political position decided elsewhere,
even a party under a leadership genuinely committed to the emancipation of
women could not be a party where women were as comfortable as men. In
fairness, it should be added, as Judith Hellman points out, that many women
of working-class background felt equally ill at ease at Italian feminist meetings,
conducted in the convoluted, obfuscatory, absurdly intellectualized and, at
times, inanely pompous language so beloved of the Italian intelligentsia and
so little challenged by feminists.[109]

The failure of Italian feminism to establish a common language for all
women cannot disguise Togliatti's failure to establish the liberation of women
as a major issue for the PCI. This much is clear if one reads the interviews
with communist women conducted towards the end of the 1970s by two
well-known Italian communist and feminist journalists, Laura Lilli and Chiara
Valentini, published by the PCI.[110] While most of the women interviewed
accepted that the PCI was the most pro-women party available, the overall
verdict was not positive. One, a self-confessed non-feminist who emphasised
that she would rather be on the side of a wife-beating 'macho' engineering
worker than of Susanna Agnelli, member of the wealthiest Italian family and
a liberal feminist, lamented that women in the party have 'to speak like
men'.[111] Another said: 'The male rank-and-file activists hardly engage in debate
and are usually of the opinion that feminists are tarts or loonies.'[112] Similar
feelings emerge from Hellman's interviews with women in five Italian cities.[113]

Much of what has been narrated so far explains why the revival of
feminism could not be generated from within the organized Left, in spite of
the greater concern for the unequal and disadvantaged condition of women
expressed by socialist and communist parties. Only an independent feminist
movement standing in a critical, even confrontational relation to the Left,
could create the conditions for a novel form of 'feminized' socialism. The
evidence is substantial and compelling. All the main theoreticians of feminism
in the post-war period belonged to the Left, yet stood at a critical distance
from its established form.

The most important feminist text of the immediate post-war years was the work of Simone de Beauvoir, who did not proclaim herself a feminist, but considered herself to be a non-orthodox Marxist. She was committed to the class struggle, to the notion of the working class as the universal class and, until the late 1960s, believed that socialism would bring about the emancipation of women.[114] Only in 1968 did she formally begin to describe herself as a feminist.

What could not be spoken aloud in political debate could be written about only in more rarefied sphere of theory, though even here the language of feminism encountered ridicule and scandal. Simone de Beauvoir's *Le deuxième sexe*, published in 1949, was denounced by the French communists as the work of a *petite bourgeoise* devoid of any interest to working-class women. It was blacklisted by the Roman Catholic church. Albert Camus accused her of ridiculing the French male.[115] A sophisticated writer of the stature of François Mauriac, a Nobel prize-winner, was so outraged that, with un-characteristic vulgarity, he told a member of the board of editors of *Les Temps modernes*, 'Now I know everything about your boss's vagina!'[116]

De Beauvoir's seminal work recovered one of the central intuitions of Wollstonecraft and expressed it in the strongest terms: 'being a woman' is a condition which is socially constructed. 'One is not born a woman: one becomes one.'[117] The subordination of women is not to be traced back to an inevitable biological destiny. Their status is not 'natural'. Women, explained de Beauvoir, are constructed in terms of their differences from men. Man is the standard: 'He is the Subject, the Absolute: she is the Other.'[118] Equality must thus imply the reconstruction of women as Subjects. For this to occur, it is not sufficient to change laws, institutions and customs. It is essential that women should acquire 'a new skin'. This can occur only through a collective effort: while women suffer and loathe the oppression of men, it does not follow that 'her ovaries condemn her to be on her knees for eternity'.[119]

Ultimately, de Beauvoir's thesis resolved itself into an injunction to women to abandon their position of 'being-a-woman'. This has often been interpreted as a Professor Higgins-like exhortation to 'be more like a man'. It is a possible, though naive reading. De Beauvoir was building on Sartre's character-ization of freedom as a state in which a subject has transcended or escaped the condition of being objectivized or defined by the Other.[120] Freedom consists of being able to define oneself, instead of being defined by others: 'the Other's existence brings a factual limit to my freedom ... Here I am – Jew or Aryan, handsome or ugly, one-armed, etc. All this I am for the Other ... with no hope of changing it.'[121]

De Beauvoir introduced a major feminist variation upon Sartre's position: one sex, the male sex, does the defining, while women are those who are looked at, defined, alienated from their 'own', 'real' self. What is worse, women connive at being the objectified Other, at accepting their status as objects, at adapting themselves, wax-like, to the mould men have made. This is why the liberation of women requires the concurrent destruction of 'woman-as-defined-by-men' – what later came to be called 'consciousness-raising'. Thus, though de Beauvoir refused to call herself a feminist until the late 1960s, and though she was committed to class struggle, *The Second Sex* is a central text of modern feminism and a direct challenge to the traditional ideology of class-centred socialism. The inescapable conclusion of de Beauvoir's work is that the conflict between men and women cannot in any way be subsumed as a variant or an effect of the struggle between capitalists and workers. The two struggles unquestionably intersect, but retain a reciprocal autonomy.

This radical view is the ideological core of all second-wave feminism. It holds that the liberation of women is a process and not an act, and therefore that it cannot be reached merely by introducing a new legal framework. What is required is a revolution in consciousness and organizational forms separate and different from those that operate where men prevail. Indeed, there is no facet of human endeavour which does not require redefinition from a woman's point of view. Of course, a 'woman's point of view' is something which cannot be defined. Women, like men, have different views. No political stance could receive the approval of all women. No mechanism could ever be devised to sort out the 'genuinely' feminine (i.e. a female-defined feminine) from that femininity which is male-defined. These objections, valid in philosophy, are irrelevant in practical politics, where the aim is not to reach logical certainties, but to set the agenda and define the struggle. This ambivalence is not exclusive to feminism. Socialists have claimed to represent 'the point of view' of the working class; nationalists that of the nation. All ideologies make dogmatic and universalistic claims. They are a necessity of politics.

De Beauvoir opened a territory. Others stepped in and redrew the map of the knowable from a woman's point of view, although it took twenty more years and the maturation of the new post-war generation for this task to be undertaken.

When the new feminists resurfaced in the 1960s, the style and mode of presentation of these arguments changed radically, as feminism returned to its 'Anglo-Saxon' origins – that is, to Britain and the USA. The complex language of phenomenology gave way to the radical pamphlet, the two-volume academic treatise to the paperback, the discourse addressed to the academy of the few to the bracing airwaves of mass society. As early as the mid-1960s, the British painter Pauline Boty was already satirizing the double-standard characteristic of the prevailing, media-constructed images of men and women in her two canvases, *It's a Man's World I & II* (1965–66).

In Britain, the Australian author Germaine Greer's *The Female Eunuch* (1970) became one of the most successful feminist books of all time. Like de Beauvoir before her – but with a pride and joy in being a woman which de Beauvoir never exhibited – Greer traced the foundations of male supremacy in all the myths and minutiae of daily life which restricted the freedom of women. Her protest was not just against domination but – to borrow a phrase from Frigga Haug – 'against the normality of domination, as it had become a daily habit'.[122] The situations displayed ranged from the 'mystery' which shrouds women's sexual organs[123] to unequal pay,[124] from the education of little girls[125] to the eternal smile of women in advertisements[126] and the 'titillating mush of Barbara Cartland'.[127] The tract contained no meticulously argued thesis on the origin of male domination and provided no strategy for female emancipation. But it forcefully stated its goal:

> Womanpower means the self-determination of women, and that means that all the baggage of paternalist society will have to be thrown overboard. Woman must have room and scope to devise a morality which does not disqualify her from excellence, and a psychology which does not condemn her to the status of a spiritual cripple.[128]

Notwithstanding Greer's bestseller, it is generally accepted that the initial impetus behind the feminism of the second wave came from the USA. With hindsight an impressive list of causal factors may be assembled. The image of modernity and emancipation of the American woman was part of an American myth which turned out to be a self-fulfilling prophecy. By accelerating the dissolution of traditional values, modernity itself created the conditions for the liberation of women from their conventional roles. The USA, as the pioneer of mass higher education, produced a proportionately higher number of educated women than other countries. The struggle for racial equality, which prefigured the student movement of the late 1960s, had laid some of the foundations for a feminism dominated by the values of equal rights. No strong class-based party existed to monopolize these new struggles and anchor them to socialism. The non-structured, fragmentary and non-party based nature of American politics was better suited to the development of feminism than the system of parties which dominated European states.

The vivid style and succinct quality of American political writing – as opposed to the turgid idiom of its political science – was also infinitely more suited to an era of mass readership, and the requirement of a popular movement than the ponderous tomes of de Beauvoir's analyses, notwithstanding the elegance of its language. Betty Friedan's *The Feminine Mystique* (1963) became one of the key texts of American and, soon thereafter, European feminism. This was a devastating critique of the condition to which the American woman, especially the educated American woman, had been reduced: a profound dissatisfaction with her existence as 'she made the bed in the morning, shopped for groceries, ate peanut butter sandwiches with her children, chauffeured Cub Scouts and Brownies, lay beside her husband at night ... and was afraid to ask even of herself the silent question – "Is this all?"'[129] The problem with women was that they could not be women, but had

to be 'feminine'. Friedan called on women to take their deserved place in
society, to 'change the insidious unwritten rules which let them do the political
housework while the men make the decisions', to make 'life plans geared to
their real abilities' without having 'to sacrifice marriage and motherhood'.[130]

The radical pendant to Friedan was Shulamith Firestone's self-assured *The
Dialectic of Sex. The Case for a Feminist Revolution*. Dedicated to Simone de
Beauvoir, 'who endured', *The Dialectic of Sex* attacked the central tenets of
familial ideology: child-bearing and motherhood. If 'biology was destiny'
(Freud), in the sense that pregnancy and child-rearing, and the consequent
entrapment in the family, handicapped women in their struggle to achieve
equality with men, then, wrote Firestone, it was necessary to break down not
only the social distinctions between the sexes – something many first-wave
liberal feminists would have agreed with – but the biological distinctions as
well. Advanced forms of contraception were already enabling women to
achieve considerable control over their reproductive cycle, separating sexual
passion from the fear of pregnancy (as is the case with men). Test-tube
babies – said Firestone – would break the remaining special link between
women and children, opening up the path for final emancipation. Just as
Marxists advocated the class struggle to eliminate classes, Firestone advocated
a sex struggle of women against men to eliminate 'sex classes'. Love between
a man and a woman was inevitably 'complicated, corrupted, or obstructed by
an unequal balance of power'.[131] To redress the balance, a major revolution
was required:

> the end goal of feminist revolution must be, unlike that of the first feminist
> revolution, not just the elimination of male *privilege* but of the sex *distinction* itself:
> genital differences between human beings would no longer matter culturally ...
> The reproduction of the species by one sex for the benefit of both would be
> replaced by (at least the option) of artificial reproduction: children would be born
> to both sexes equally ... the dependence of the child on the mother (and vice
> versa) would give way to a greatly shortened dependence on a small group of
> others in general ... The tyranny of the biological family would be broken.[132]

That the domination of men (or patriarchy) was not an epiphenomenon of
socio-economic relationships but the real site of a battle yet to be waged
was the centrepiece of the other major transatlantic feminist text of the
time: Kate Millett's *Sexual Politics*. For Millett, the dominating system of power
is underpinned by three patriarchal institutions: the state, society and the
family.[133] Class affiliation plays a less important role than gender: 'women
tend to transcend the usual class stratifications in patriarchy, for whatever
the class of her birth and education, the female has fewer permanent class
associations than does the male.'[134] Rape is the most complete realization of
a violent form of patriarchal force.[135] It follows that rape is a political act.
Well-established male authors, celebrated as forceful non-conformists bravely
struggling against the stultifying customs of bourgeois morality, emerge from

Sexual Politics as the 'cultural agents' of patriarchy, 'counterrevolutionary sexual politicians' who have helped to erect 'the vast grey stockades of the sexual reaction'.[136] D. H. Lawrence, Henry Miller and Norman Mailer, whom critics of both sexes had praised as paragons of the free radical spirit, surface from Millett's alternative reading as the zealous patrolmen of threatened phallocracy.

The Dialectic of Sex and *Sexual Politics* were landmarks in the development of radical feminism, a current united by the precept that 'the fight for women's liberation was primarily against men', that this overrode all other struggles, and that all attempts to connect it to a wider political strategy would be futile.[137]

A similar, profoundly anti-patriarchical, radical-feminist problematic was being pursued in France as a development of de Beauvoir's ideas. The separatist group Féministes Révolutionnaires, whose main spokeswoman was Monique Wittig, was devoted to the total destruction of the patriarchical order.[138] Years later, in the 1980s, Wittig would still pursue the battle for the abolition of gender differences in favour of what she called a 'sexless society':

> This is our historical task ... to make evident that women are a class, which is to say that the category 'woman' as well as the category 'man' are political and economic categories not eternal ones. Our aim is to suppress men as a class, not through a genocidal, but a political struggle. Once the class 'men' disappears, 'women' as a class will disappear as well, for there are no slaves without masters.[139]

It is unlikely that such radical feminism could ever have become the dominant trend in Western Europe. Socialism was so clearly the leading progressive tradition that politically active women were usually socialist and, consequently, sought to integrate their feminism with their socialism. In so doing, regardless of their apparent moderation, socialist feminists represented a greater practical challenge to the established socialist parties. The vocation of radical feminists was that of remaining a permanent minority with, perhaps, a special appeal to women who found the domination of heterosexual ideology unbearable or who had been subjected to sexual violence. In Britain, the 'rad-fems' presented a paper published in November 1971 at a national women's liberation conference which stated: 'as long as we have our closest emotional/ sexual relationships with men, Women's Liberation can be no more than a hobby.'[140]

This language inevitably led to separatism and, consequently, to political isolation. But the iconoclastic charge of radical feminism should not be dismissed. It prodded socialist feminism into moving on, extending its boundaries. Nevertheless, there is little doubt that – at least in Western Europe – socialist feminism remained the dominant strand. This should not be interpreted as implying that there were two homogeneous and distinct feminist blocs. In political practice, the ideological contours between the two tendencies remained remarkably fluid.

Table 15.1 Women studying in universities, 1960–75 (as a percentage of total student population)

	1960	1975
Austria	31.8	34.4
Belgium	19.1	33.3
Denmark	32.0	39.0
Finland	52.8	49.0
France	38.2	n/a
Holland	18.2	26.3
Italy	38.0	46.2[a]
Norway	22.1[b]	41.2
Sweden	37.5[c]	44.2
UK[d]	23.9	32.8
Scotland	27.2	37.5
West Germany	27.4	32.1

Notes: [a] 1970; [b] 1955; [c] 1959; [d] England and Wales only; 1975 data for Finland exclude Provisional Teachers' Colleges.

Source: P. Flora et al., *State, Economy and Society in Western Europe 1815–1975. A Data Handbook*, Vol. 1.

But why did feminism revive at the end of the 1960s? This is still unexplained; some conjectures may nevertheless be advanced. Though structural factors tell only a small part of the story, data on the growth of women's participation in paid urban employment and the expansion of educational opportunities for women may be enlightening. Table 15.1 shows that, between 1960 and 1975, there was an increase in the percentage of women among university students. As there was a massive increase in the percentage of the twenty to twenty-four age group attending university (both sexes), it follows that university women also increased in numbers. The gender gap in higher education was narrowing all the time between 1960 and 1975 in virtually all countries. Finland exhibits a regression, but this statistical oddity is due to the fact that there was no longer any gender gap in 1960 and that the 1975 data exclude Teachers' Colleges.

More women were acquiring the level of education which only a tiny minority of them could have aspired to at the end of the previous century, when the first wave of feminism was under way. Furthermore, women's entry into higher education was concentrated in those disciplines, such as the humanities and the social sciences, which provided the intellectual tools with which to criticize the existing order. This is precisely what many women did. Moreover, their qualifications gave them the right to demand a place in a power structure which tried to exclude them. More women were also in paid employment.

Table 15.2 Women's employment 1960–81, selected countries

	Female population (% of total active population)			Female working class (% of industrial working class)		
	1960–61	1970–71	1981–82	1960–61	1970–71	1980–81
Austria	40.4	38.4	40.4	20.9	19.4	16.9
Belgium	26.5	29.6	36.4	15.7	16.1	13.7
Denmark	30.8	36.6	44.2	17.1	15.1	16.9
Finland	39.4	42.1	46.6	23.1	23.4	22.3
France	34.6	34.9	40.9	33.3	15.6	16.2
Greece	32.8	28.0	27.1	17.5	14.6	16.8
Holland	22.3	25.9	32.3	8.9	7.3	6.6
Italy	24.9	27.4	34.4	17.3	17.5	20.6
Norway	22.8	27.6	41.4	11.0	11.3	15.0
Portugal	17.7	25.2	35.3	17.6	23.1	22.7
Spain	18.2	19.6	24.8	n/a	13.3	11.8
Sweden	29.8	38.1	45.0	14.6	16.6	14.5
UK	32.4	36.5	38.9	18.2	18.4	16.1
West Germany	37.1	34.9	38.5	19.7	17.6	n/a

Notes: The figures for France are, respectively, for 1962, 1968 and are estimated for 1982; for Germany the figures in the 1980–81 columns are for 1982.

My definition of the 'working class' corresponds to ILO occupational groups 7, 8 and 9, and includes all production and related workers, transport equipment operators and labourers. It excludes all white-collar occupations, all service workers such as caretakers, cleaners and waiters, all agriculture, farming, and fishing, all the unemployed and self-employed.

Source: my elaboration on data in ILO, *Yearbook of Labour Statistics. Retrospective Edition on Population Census 1945–1989*, ILO, Geneva 1990.

Table 15.2 shows a significant increase in female employment throughout Europe, with the exception of Greece (where the unaccounted heavy female employment in the countryside makes the figures less comparable to those of other countries). The overall increase in women's employment did not occur in the traditional industrial working class. (I have attempted here to use a statistical definition of the 'working class' as close as possible to the traditional image of the 'working class' in socialist parties: the factory proletariat.) Thus, women did join, in increasing numbers, the *non-manufacturing* labour force where socialist ideology is least strong and trade unions least implanted. It was also the section of the labour force which would expand in the 1980s, unlike the traditional proletariat (see chapter 22).

Traditional socialists assumed that when women finally joined the workforce, they would begin to identify themselves as true workers. But women, at least in the West, joined a 'new' labour force, heavily concentrated in the service sector. This was the workforce of late capitalism. In some of the countries of the Third World, such as South Korea, Singapore, Hong Kong and Taiwan, female labour became increasingly dominant in manufacturing.[141] Although it added to the burden of work for women, greater participation in the labour force also increased their bargaining power within the home. Many women became less financially dependent on men than their mothers had been. They expected more and acted accordingly. Working women tend to hold far less traditional views than non-working women.[142]

Data such as these demonstrate that the economic conditions facing women were changing faster than those facing men. The same was true of social conditions. The development of mass consumer goods liberated ordinary women more than it liberated men: the washing machine, the vacuum cleaner, the supermarket gave women more time to think for themselves. The suffragettes of the first wave had domestic servants who did their washing while they demonstrated. By the 1960s, in the advanced West, most women had machines toiling for them. By comparison, men's *private* lives were less affected by the impact of modernity.

The birth of the so-called permissive society and the technology which made it possible, such as the invention of the contraceptive pill, had much more significance for women than for men. That men had strong sexual needs; that sexuality in men could have a positive connotation or, at any rate, that it was something that needed satisfying; that celibacy prior to marriage was not required – these ideas long predated the 'swinging sixties'. The real significance of the 'permissive' society was that it marked the beginning of the end for the sexual double standard. It was the general and public realization – and, later, an at least partial acceptance – that virginity in women was not a virtue, that female sexuality was a potent force, that sex was not something to be enjoyed by men and endured by women, which made possible in the 1960s the acceptance at a mass level of a life-style which, at the beginning of the century, had been the prerogative only of a few 'emancipated women'. There were, of course, objective reasons too. For men sexuality was divorced from reproduction, partly because they bore little of the social stigma of pregnancy and could often escape the material care of the unwanted offspring; partly because reasonably effective male contraceptives had been easily available for a long time. It was only in the 1960s that similar relatively safe methods – such as the pill and the cap – became available to unmarried women.

Alongside these socio-economic changes, there were also powerful ideological developments which were probably the decisive determinants of second-wave feminism. In Europe and North America, the post-war generation which was emerging was more affluent, better educated, less deferential, less committed to traditional values – in a word, more modern than all previous generations in history. The origin of the second wave of feminism can be firmly located in the new social movements of the 1960s: student politics, civil rights movements in the USA, the anti-Vietnam War campaigns – in other words, the so-called New Left. Universities were the 'forcing

house of most of the younger women's liberation groups'.[143] Women expected
to encounter fewer constraints in the new social movements than in the
older class-based organizations. After all, these new movements were far less
male-based than the established trade unions or the socialist and communist
parties; they were inspired by a libertarian ideology which prized non-
hierarchical structures, decentralized decision-making, and direct forms of
democratic participation (rather than representative ones).

However, such libertarian structures, in spite of their pretensions, never
failed to reproduce a hierarchy. In the absence of formal institutional rules,
charismatic leaders came to the fore. The importance of impressing an
audience is far greater when decisions are made by an assembly than in a
committee. Good speakers win debates. Forceful personalities who are instinctively able to think quickly on their feet, encapsulate complex thought
in appropriate 'sound-bites', rapidly became captured by the mass media and,
through them, are promptly transformed into the *de facto* mouthpieces of the
movement. The media-designated leaders of the student movements of the
1960s were all men: Rudi Dutschke in Germany, Mario Capanna in Italy,
Tariq Ali in Britain, Daniel Cohn-Bendit in France, Jerry Rubin and Abe
Hoffman in the USA. This preponderance of male charismatic figures was
reproduced at all levels. Rare were the meetings and assemblies of students
at which the voice of women could be heard. Within the student movement,
the traditional division of labour which assigned a subordinate position to
women appeared to survive unchanged. Within the movement, the women
found themselves in a position of inferiority in spite of their equal status
with the men. They went to the same universities, attended the same courses
and classes, originated from similar social backgrounds – yet they found
themselves relegated to their 'historic' secretarial and caring functions: typing
leaflets, photocopying, preparing food for demonstrations and sit-ins. The
first feminist tracts to appear throughout Europe were brimming with the
same uncontainable anger. At the September 1968 conference of the SDS
(the German social-democratic students' organization), Helke Sander, a leader
of the Action Committee for the Liberation of Women, founded in West
Berlin in January 1968, threw tomatoes at her male comrades in a celebrated
outburst of exasperation.[144] In France, a feminist pamphlet remonstrated:
'when they are involved in "serious men's talk", we really have to battle to
have a turn to speak, and then when we've finished, we might as well not
have bothered, they haven't even been listening.'[145] In Germany: 'We typed
their speeches, we tried to follow what they said at meetings, we made
ourselves look nice as we had always done, we swallowed the Pill every day
or put up with abortions. Our exploitation in the home, the satisfaction of
their sexual desires – all this was supposed to be just our private problem ...
We don't want to imitate them, we have different objectives.'[146]

Later, in 1973, Marguerite Duras would declare with characteristic ir-
reverence and more than a grain of truth: 'Men must learn to be silent. This

is probably very painful for them ... One has scarcely the time to experience an event as important as May '68 before men begin to speak out, to formulate theoretical epilogues, and to break the silence. Yes, these prating men were up to their old tricks during May '68.'[147]

The belligerence against 'chattering men' notwithstanding, new-wave feminism cannot be understood outside the context of the radicalism of the 1960s. Its commitment to a rediscovery of its own history, so important to all nascent political ideologies, was part and parcel of the new 'history from below'. Here one of the most influential texts was E. P. Thompson's trailblazing *The Making of the English Working Class* (1963), aimed at reclaiming the hidden history of the labouring poor and their resistance to oppression. It was this new kind of social history which provided the impetus for the new feminist historiography.

In the field of abstract thought too, feminism made use of the modern theories developed or reappraised in the 1960s. It eschewed the traditional brand of Marxism and the well-established functionalism of mainstream sociology, opting instead for a critical appraisal of the new social sciences of the era: structuralism, the Marxism of Antonio Gramsci or Louis Althusser, the Freud of Jacques Lacan, and, later, the works of Michel Foucault, Roland Barthes and Jacques Derrida (see chapter 14). The feminism of the first wave had shown less interest in reconstructing the history of women or advancing theoretical knowledge. The more numerous and highly educated women of the second wave radically changed the study of history and the uses of social theory.

The women's movement shared with the students' and civil rights' movements an understanding of the importance of the symbolic act. Its use would increase sensationally. This was inevitable in the age of mass communication, something which could not have been foreseen even by the suffragettes – the real pioneers of twentieth-century grand gestures. (Some may argue that nineteenth-century anarchism was the real antecedent: the trouble with history is that nothing is ever entirely new.) When the suffragette Emily Wilding Davison threw herself in front of the King's horse at the Derby in June 1913, in the grandest of all symbolic acts, that of self-immolation, she preceded by fifty years the Venerable Duc, a Buddhist monk who, at the age of seventy-seven, transformed himself into a living torch to protest against the injustices inflicted upon his co-religionists by the Diem regime in Vietnam. This example was followed six years later, on 16 January 1969, by a twenty-one-year-old Czech history student, Jan Palach, in protest against the Soviet occupation of his country.

In France, in August 1970, several women tried to place a wreath by the Tomb of the Unknown Soldier at the Arc de Triomphe, dedicating it to his even more Unknown Wife. In Germany women bricked up sex shops[148] and disrupted beauty contests, as they did in the UK. In the USA there was an even more marked preference for publicity-seeking 'outrageous' events, as when brassieres, girdles and similar female accoutrements were dumped in a 'freedom trash bucket' at the Miss America pageant in Atlantic City in 1968 – an event quickly transformed by the media into the First Burning of the Bra.[149] In France *Elle*'s launching of a questionnaire to establish an identikit of the French Woman was ironically challenged by an alternative one, substituting for the predictable 'Do you think women are more, equally or less able than men to drive cars?', the sarcastic 'In your opinion, do double XX chromosomes contain the genes of double declutching?'[150]

Once the barriers between the private world and the realm of politics had been torn down, everything could be turned into an issue: abortion, pregnancy, the myth of the vaginal orgasm, rape (including marital rape) and sexual violence in general, sexual harassment, unequal pay, unequal access to better jobs, hierarchical organizations, war, competitive society, the tyranny of dominant aesthetic norms, being overweight ('fat is a feminist issue'), natural childbirth, male authorship, pornography, child-care, health, parliamentary representation of women, language, history, and much more. From Norway to Sicily, from Portugal to Greece, these themes were politicized. This was a language socialism had never spoken. A new agenda was being born.

The initial reaction of the Left ranged from the hostile to the sceptical. There was an understandable fear that concessions to a feminist vanguard would cause a rift not only with the male electorate, but also with the majority of women, whose outlook did not correspond to that of the feminists. Socialist parties began to examine feminist demands in an effort to disentangle the more palatable, co-optable and acceptable from the apparently outrageous. As there never was a unified feminist movement to establish the 'correct line', many women who were members of socialist parties co-operated in the process of focusing on a few clear-cut issues, while conducting a wider struggle to make feminism acceptable to the majority of women.

The main campaigns conducted by feminists in most of Western Europe were over equal pay, abortion, child-care, equal job opportunities and political representation. Of these, the battle for abortion turned out to be the most important.

Per se, abortion is not a particularly 'feminist' issue. It is a medical intervention involving the body of a woman, aimed at resolving a problem for which, generally speaking, the responsibility of men is as great as that of women, though the consequences are always far greater for women. Abortion became a feminist issue because it was presented as one which would increase women's control over their own destiny and, literally, over their own bodies. The legal prohibition of abortion affected virtually all women of child-bearing age, even though there was a class dimension because middle-class women could often contrive to obtain safe abortions even when intervention was illegal.

In the 1960s the struggle for the legalization of abortion had not yet become a rallying point for women. In the Scandinavian countries, Britain and some states of the USA, abortion was made legal without strong feminist pressure. In Britain it was introduced in 1967 by a Liberal MP, David Steel, and passed thanks to what Roy Jenkins described as the 'benevolent neutrality' of the Labour government.[151] On the crucial vote to proceed to the third reading of the Bill, 234 Labour MPs voted in favour, with eight Liberals and twenty Conservatives. The resistance to legalization by the anti-abortionists had been tame. In fact, anti-abortion as a campaign did not yet exist and would be brought into being by its legalization. It became the task of feminists to oppose attempts to turn the clock back.

Abortion was legalized in most of Western Europe in the 1970s. In most instances, the feminist movement acted as the main pressure group in favour of legalization, demanding that, in the final analysis, the decision to interrupt a pregnancy should belong to the woman and not to the state or to a group of experts, such as doctors or social workers. On the whole, the parties of the Left were the least anti-abortionist, though the extent to which they were prepared to uphold the principle of a woman's right to choose often depended on other political factors, such as electoral considerations and the requirements of alliance-building and coalition-making.

Socialists had many reasons to be suspicious of feminism and to fear that an alliance with it would destroy a respectability and credibility achieved after many decades of struggle. While it was true that feminism in Europe and in North America was 'of' the Left, it was usually the case that it was of the *far* Left. This was in part due to its origin in the student movement and, in the USA, the civil rights movement. In part, it simply reflected the radicalism of feminism itself. Active feminists throughout Western Europe tended to be either critical of the Left as a whole, because it was male-dominated, or critical of the official Left for being far too conservative and timid. This added to feminism's aura of extremism. However, active feminists exert considerable pressure, directly and indirectly, on women already in the official organizations of the labour movement. Unlike their predecessors, the new feminists were helped by a combination of circumstances: their increased numbers; the wider support they had among women, including those who said 'I am not a feminist, but ...'; sympathy among many men of their generation; the greater strength of the socialist parties. The majority of feminists, however critical they were of the official Left, refrained from adopting a strategy of pure confrontation. They never organized themselves as a political party directly challenging the Left, and never advocated the boycott of the traditional institutions of the labour movement. On the contrary, in Italy, Germany and Britain, women made efforts to forge links with the trade unions. In Britain, 'this was a key strategy of the socialist-feminist element of the movement. The unions were seen as a central site of struggle – around employment, pay and conditions.'[152] Some women trade unionists had campaigned for equal pay in the 1950s, but it was not until the late sixties that there were strikes for equal pay such as that of the women sewing machinists at the Ford motor factory in Dagenham and at the Halewood plant in Liverpool.[153]

The abortion issue illustrates the relationship which developed between feminism and the socialist parties. The autonomy of the women's movement was an indispensable requirement for the projection into the political arena of issues which reflected a woman's point of view. This autonomy protected women from being forced to adjudicate on the relative importance of 'their' issues vis-à-vis other issues not specific to women, such as the national interest, the economy, the concerns of the socialists or of any other party. Their autonomy made them far more powerful with respect to their privileged interlocutor, the parties of the Left, than if they had been subsumed within them. It also increased the negotiating position of the women who were active in the socialist parties. Thus, the socialist parties were increasingly conditioned by a movement they could not hope to control, and which they could not afford to ignore, since so many of their own members were influenced by it.

The 'dual militancy' of socialist feminists heralded a development of great significance: increasingly, the socialist parties would come to be considered as one of the sites where campaigns devised elsewhere would be conducted. This evolution amounted to a major 'reform' of the socialist parties, a reform largely engineered from the outside. By the end of the 1960s, the wider socialist movement was – unknowingly – poised on the threshold of the most momentous transformation in its history.

It had started out as a machine for the self-emancipation of the working class and the generator of endless campaigns. It was now becoming an instrument which could be used by those who had found elsewhere, in the feminist, pacifist or ecological movements, a political home. The instrument which socialists had forged at the turn of the century for the improvement of the conditions of the working class, the capture of state power, and the eventual transformation of capitalism into a classless society – the political party – had become the battleground of various types of progressive causes seeking to use the party for their own ends.

Over the years, socialists had accommodated themselves to the capitalist state, injecting into it a democratic content it did not originally possess. Socialists had accommodated themselves to the nation, the invention of liberals later taken over by conservatives. Socialists had reformed capitalism and the nation-state. In the course of these struggles, they had created and developed a formidable political instrument: a mass political party which, from its inception, had to be sufficiently malleable to be the vehicle of all progressive demands expressed by civil society. Socialists themselves encouraged this process. The working class, after all, was the universal class. Its emancipation was a prelude to the emancipation of the whole of society.

This political party, much abused and criticized, remained the fundamental tool for changing political life. This was never questioned *in practice* (though constantly in theory), even by feminism and the other movements which emerged from the 1960s. Armed with their own priorities and different end-goals, and dissatisfied with socialist ideology, goals and priorities, feminists could not fail to recognize that the political party still constituted a machine which could be used to meet many of their demands, an instrument which would carry their objectives and aspirations into parliaments and governments.

The women who were feminists were never 'just' feminists. They re-examined all political issues from a feminist perspective and were often active in the new social movements. They shared the outlook of 1960s radicalism – united by a common antipathy to the prevailing international arrangements underpinned by the East–West and North–South divisions of the world. They sympathized with dissidents East and West, turned against a Eurocentric view of the world, were tendentially 'Third Worldist', basically anti-American 'imperialism', uninterested in the federalist dream of a united Europe, and filled with revulsion at nuclear weapons and militarism in all its forms. From the perspective of socialism, feminism presented a challenge and an opportunity: to break the dominance of conservative ideas among the majority of women.

Book Three
Crisis

PART SIX

The End of the Great Capitalist Boom 1973–89

CHAPTER SIXTEEN

The Crisis and the Left:
An Overview

The End of the Golden Age of Capitalism

IN THE early 1970s the unprecedented economic performance of the advanced capitalist economies came to an end. Contrary to what many socialists had expected for decades, this did not signal *the* crisis of capitalism, but only one of its crises. The distinction is easy to grasp. The idea of *the* – and not simply *a* – crisis implies a kind of finality, a catastrophe from which one may exit only by pursuing a non-capitalist road. Catastrophism in this sense is compatible with both traditional social democracy (Kautsky and his followers), and with the insurrectionary communism of the Leninist variety (by the 1970s this position was held by small and relatively insignificant groups). This catastrophic view of the future of capitalism was a cause for optimism on the part of socialists, who believed that the transition to socialism depended on the eventual 'bursting asunder' – as Marx put it – of the 'capitalist integument'. It would then be possible to announce: 'The knell of capitalist private property sounds. The expropriators are expropriated.'[1]

The 'crisis' of the 1970s was in fact nothing of the sort. It resembled Marx's own view of crises as 'always but momentary and forcible solutions of the existing contradictions. They are violent eruptions which for a time restore the disturbed equilibrium.'[2] It was a crisis of a particular *form* of capitalist growth, one in which new investments constantly absorbed new labour, reaching a plateau of full employment – the most important condition of the welfare state – in which labour productivity kept ahead of wages. This form of capitalism, which dominated the West so successfully during what Jean Fourastié called *les trentes glorieuses* (1945–75),[3] afforded social democracy a key role. Thanks to constant capitalist growth and full employment, the minimum social-democratic programme (the sort of demands prefigured in the Erfurt Programme – see chapter 1) had been accomplished during these thirty glorious years. A considerable proportion of the surplus produced was allocated by political means (i.e. not by the market) to education, transport, health care, 'high' culture, child-care, old-age protection and so on. These measures stabilized the capitalist system, enabling it to endure the regulations which legislation and trade union strength imposed on it: restriction on the length of the working day, paid holidays, health and safety standards, minimum wages.

Such remarkable social stability would never have been achieved had the anarchistic behaviour of competing capitalists been the only motor of distribution. The largely unregulated capitalism described by Marx and other nineteenth-century thinkers was an utter failure. It was marked by constant economic crises, with terrible political effects: global wars, authoritarian regimes and massive unemployment. The triumph of capitalism, *les trentes glorieuses*, was, in reality, the triumph of *regulated* capitalism: the countries under such a regime enjoyed democracy, peace and unparalleled prosperity.

When this model of capitalism entered into crisis, so did the concomitant model of social-democratic politics. A new political conflict ensued between social democrats and conservatives. The previous combat between the two – in the 1950s and 1960s – had centred round the distribution of the surplus. In the 1970s and 1980s, the new 'positional warfare' – to use Gramsci's expression – was over the role of the state in the reorganization of capitalist relations. The Left tried to expand the prevailing regulatory regime even further. The Right advocated a substantial retrenchment of the state and the liberalization of a market expanded by privatization.

By the early 1990s, the Left had been comprehensively defeated in the West, while in the East the smouldering ruins of the communist experiment marked the apparent global triumph of the system of private capitalist accumulation. The parallel decline of social democracy and regulated capitalism, and the intricate contest between Left and Right during the 1970s and 1980s, are the chief concerns of the rest of this book.

In this chapter I shall examine the causes of the end of the long capitalist boom and map out the economic performance of the West European economies in the period 1973–89. I shall then provide an overall view of the political progress of the Left in the period.

Between 1945 and 1970, labour productivity grew more than *three* times the average rate of the previous eighty years.[4] After 1970, GNP growth, employment and productivity decreased, while prices increased. This was the onset of the great worldwide stagflation, whose consequences are still deeply felt. Chapter 8 enumerated the principal causes of the great boom: cheap labour, cheap raw materials (including cheap food), cheap money, and constant technological transfer from the USA. By 1970 this process had come to an end. The abrupt nature of the productivity slowdown, its evenness and near-universal aspect, suggest profound and global macro-economic origins. To date, economic science has failed to produce a convincing explanation of the phenomenon, which constitutes the most significant watershed in the post-war history of the advanced industrialized world.[5] It also marked the most critical caesura in the history of the socialist movement of Western Europe.

By the early 1970s, the relative backwardness of the European economies compared with that of the USA had almost disappeared, though why there was ot a continuous growth of productivity in the lead country, the USA, is still an unresolved puzzle. Europe, however, having recovered and closed the gap with the USA, found that the scope for effortless growth, by replicating the technology of the lead country, was reduced.[6] Europe in turn was being 'caught up' by Japan and the 'Four Little Dragons' of Taiwan, South Korea, Hong Kong and Singapore. The post-war era had come to an end. Full employment and the consequent strength of the trade unions had terminated the phase of cheap labour. No further skilled labour from East Germany moved into the western part of the country to fuel its economy. The reservoir of rural workers which had existed in Italy and France in the 1950s had been severely depleted. In 1973 the influx of foreign workers into Germany and Austria was halted. In Britain new immigration laws controlled the entry of workers from the former colonies. In France net immigration, which had been of significant proportions in the 1960s, became negligible during the 1970s. Thus, no external or mobile 'industrial reserve army' was available to smooth structural change and keep wages down.[7] Employment opportunities for unskilled labour had narrowed, surviving mainly in the public sector, whose contribution to overall productivity, though doubtless of enormous import, cannot be calculated or quantified. In this sector there occurred a large influx of native female labour.

Raw materials imported from the Third World were becoming expensive. The OPEC countries raised the price of oil more than twelvefold in two stages, in 1973 and 1979. From the view point of the principles of economic liberalism, this was a rational response to favourable market conditions, but one which was perceived by Western public opinion and much of its media as a perfidious ploy by greedy Arabs (a generic term which subsumed Iranians, Venezuelans and Nigerians along with the genuine article) to impoverish the West.

In all countries this oil price increase, which was accompanied by similar rises in the price of primary products, slowed down growth because of the costs involved in cutting energy inputs and substituting different kinds of fuel.[8] It should be added that the OPEC challenge was substantially contained: by 1989 oil prices had fallen by half from their 1982 peak, and the advanced economies were caught up in the euphoria of short-term economic recovery. Well before the oil shock, however, rising wages had squeezed profits throughout the OECD countries and productivity had slowed down in key OECD countries such as Japan, the USA and Germany.[9]

Conservative thinkers began to argue that the main cause of Europe's poor economic performance was the excessive role of the state. The welfare state was accused of stifling initiative by subsidising inefficient firms, imposing minimum wages, diverting resources from productive investment, substituting itself for entrepreneurship, discouraging success by punitive marginal rates of taxation.[10] High unemployment benefits were said to discourage people from looking for work, while non-market allocation of resources (as in national health-care systems) led to rationing (i.e. queues) rather than marginal cost-pricing. These anti-welfare arguments had always existed and had been unsuccessfully peddled throughout the 1950s and 1960s. In 1959 Norman Mackenzie raged against the so-called theory of the English Disease: 'We are, so the argument runs, suffering from a national malaise, a form of political sclerosis ... we are taxed to death and molly-coddled into the grave; ... our workers have become clock-watchers ... the greed of the trade unions is the cause of inflation.'[11] When growth came to an end, the new political climate made these anti-welfare state views more popular. By the early 1990s, they were so dominant that they were openly advocated even within the socialist parties.

Unsustained growth was not the major problem. What growth there was after 1970 was achieved mainly through an increase in productivity, often achieved by shedding labour. Thus, the real cause for concern was the growth of unemployment. By 1986, among the European members of the OECD, it stood at over 11 per cent. At the time of writing (1995) it is still at this level.

The importance of unemployment cannot be overestimated. Only full employment, Thomas Balogh wrote, 'removes the need for servility, and thus alters the way of life, the relationship between the classes. It changes the balance of forces in the economy. This is its outstanding, indeed revolutionary consequence.'[12] Unemployment is the single most important factor in the decline in trade union strength. Social democracy is unsustainable in a situation of high unemployment. By 1992, when the Maastricht Treaty was signed, it had become generally accepted that the struggle against inflation was the fundamental task of governments, while that against unemployment was hopeless or secondary. This was the clearest indication of the ideological victory of the forces of conservatism.

Any increase in unemployment, particularly when coupled with a reduction of social protection, is tantamount to an effective decrease in personal freedom. The importance of having an occupation which provides a reasonable income is directly commensurate with the magnitude of private consumption. In a society of this kind – that is to say, in a capitalist society – effective freedom is, in the final analysis, largely the freedom of the individual consumer. Where the consumer is 'sovereign', those who have no gainful occupation and no personal fortune are *de facto* disenfranchised. Conversely, those who are rich are freer; they can do more. It is the possession of money which transforms many formal rights into real, effective rights. No amount of liberal rhetoric, no shrill protestation of concern for the rights of the individual, can possibly disguise the fact that where the market rules, those without money effectively lose their membership of the consumer society. As they sink into the demoralizing morass of poverty, they are not only disempowered from obtaining so-called luxuries (the term which designates the necessities of the rich), and those commodities which make life comfortable and pleasant, but they are also effectively denied 'access' goods, such as culture and education. Eventually, they are condemned to a life dominated by an obsessive preoccupation with the cash nexus, by the endless worry of making ends meet, by the anger of being unwanted, unemployable, unacceptable, by the frustration of having become a human surplus which cannot be absorbed – a human mass whose only economic *raison d'être* is to keep those who are in employment pliant and disciplined and their wages lower than they would otherwise be.

The purely legal or formal definition of 'rights' clearly belongs to the liberal tradition. The distinctive socialist contribution to the question of rights lies precisely in the recognition that the distribution of power in society reflects not only legal relationships, but also the uneven distribution of wealth. The great achievement of liberalism was the proposition that all are equal before the law. The great project of socialism was the construction of an economic system which made real equality possible. Without full employment, this project inevitably faced insurmountable obstacles.

This is why the end of the golden age of capitalism, far from making socialism more likely, paradoxically made it more problematic. It signalled the end not only of high growth rates, but also of the general consensus that full employment was one of society's central objectives: the implicit contract between socialists and conservatives.

The end of the golden age marked the opening stage of the renegotiation of this contract. Would the new phase of capitalism bear the imprint of socialist ideas to the same or even a greater extent than the previous one? Or would it make them increasingly marginal and irrelevant? The events which unfolded caught both sides, socialists and conservatives, without a clear strategy. The peculiarity of the new situation was that, contrary to what had been assumed by economic science, high rates of inflation could co-exist with high rates of unemployment and low rates of growth. Not all countries, however, suffered in the same way, at least in the 1970s.

Success in containing unemployment was directly related to the degree to which the economic authorities tolerated inflation. There is a partial correlation between the presence of the Left in government and the disregard for price stability, as in the case of social-democratic governments in Scandinavian countries. In Germany the weight of anti-inflationary traditions, given a kind of cult status by opinion-leaders who fostered them, meant that price stability was regarded as the fundamental aim of public policy. Holland had a deeply entrenched consensual system which resulted in moderate wage claims. Italy had a weak government and an increasingly confident union movement, backed by a strong opposition: the political establishment eschewed confrontation and preferred inflation, while protecting the electorate with a strong indexation system.[13]

Table 16.1 compares and contrasts the unemployment and inflation rates

Table 16.1 Unemployment and inflation in fourteen European countries, 1973–89 (%)

	Unemployment		Inflation	
	1974–79	1979–89	1973–79	1980–89
OECD-Europe	5.1	9.1	11.9	7.4
Austria	1.8	3.3	6.3	3.8
Belgium	5.7	11.1	8.4	4.8
Denmark	6.0	8.0	10.8	6.9
Finland	4.4	4.9	12.8	7.3
France	4.5	9.0	10.7	7.3
Greece	1.9	6.6	16.1	19.4
Holland	4.9	9.8	7.2	2.8
Italy	6.6	9.9	16.1	11.1
Norway	1.8	2.8	8.7	8.3
Portugal	6.0	7.3	23.7	17.5
Spain	5.3	17.5	18.3	10.2
Sweden	1.9	2.5	9.8	7.9
UK	4.2	9.5	15.6	7.4
West Germany	3.5	6.8	4.7	2.9

Sources: OECD, *Economic Outlook, Historical Statistics 1960–1989*, Paris 1991, p. 43. Holland: my calculation on OECD data. Inflation rates calculated on consumer price indices; Turkey and Iceland excluded from OECD-Europe inflation average. Data on unemployment for 1974–79 in Austria and Denmark calculated on the basis of figures in Angus Maddison, *Dynamic Forces in Capitalist Development: A Long-run Comparative View*, Oxford University Press, Oxford 1991, p. 263.

Table 16.2 GDP growth in fourteen European countries 1973–89 (average annual rate)

	1973–79	1979–89
OECD-Europe	2.6	2.3
Austria	2.9	2.0
Belgium	2.2	2.0
Denmark	1.9	1.8
Finland	2.3	3.7
France	2.8	2.1
Greece	3.7	1.8
Holland	2.7	1.5
Italy	3.7	2.5
Norway	4.9	2.8
Portugal	2.9	2.8
Spain	2.2	2.7
Sweden	1.8	2.0
UK	1.5	2.3
West Germany	2.3	1.8

Source: OECD, *Economic Outlook, Historical Statistics 1960–1989*.

in fourteen West European countries in the post-oil shock 1970s and in the 1980s. Table 16.2 provides the figures for the year-on-year rate of growth.

All fourteen countries exhibit an upward trend for unemployment. In a group of 'virtuous' countries, both unemployment and inflation were lower than the average for the entire post-oil price rise period: Austria, Denmark, France, Germany, Norway and Sweden. In Greece there was a marked trade-off between low unemployment and high inflation. Spain and Italy were the only countries with higher than average unemployment *and* inflation through-out the 1970s and 1980s. Germany had an inflation rate lower than half the OECD average. The overall success stories were Austria, Sweden and Norway, which maintained very low unemployment rates while holding inflation below the average.

Only three countries sustained higher than average growth throughout the period: Italy, Portugal and Norway. Thus, Norway was the only country which succeeded in performing the feat of having lower than average unemployment and inflation, combined with higher than average growth.

Institutional factors and specific features of these economies can be used to explain some of the divergences. In Italy, wage indexation made high inflation tolerable; the black economy made unemployment acceptable. Enormous oil revenues enabled Norway to have the best of both worlds: on the back of the OPEC price rise, the Norwegians enjoyed a sustained Keynesian reflation while other countries were beginning to deflate; they could increase government spending and, at the same time, cut taxes. The ensuing increase in labour costs would have crippled any normal economy and led to massive unemployment. Oil revenues enabled the government to contain labour costs by subsidizing 20 per cent of Norway's jobs.[14] In practice, this amounted to a general redistribution of the country's oil wealth. Con-servative governments in Norway (1981–86) were as reflationary as any socialist government would have been. Here the Left had set the agenda. The economics of all this may appear bizarre, but no more so than in the only other West European country to strike it rich by striking oil: the United Kingdom. British oil policy in the 1980s – when British oil came ashore in larger quantities – enabled the government to cut taxes, pay for unemployment benefits, and shield the balance of payments from the consequences of the continuing decline in industrial competitiveness.[15] The political beneficiaries of British oil were the Thatcher governments. Oil paid for the income tax cuts which ensured Conservative victories. For the unlucky 1974–79 Labour government, North Sea oil was, for much of the time, a drain on the balance of payments because of the large capital investment required, as Denis Healey bitterly complained.[16] The post-1979 Conservative governments used oil to manufacture a consumer boom which directly benefited British consumers, Japanese exporters, foreign wine interests and the Dordogne tourist industry. However, not even Norway escaped the consequences of its enlightened profligacy. When oil prices fell in the 1980s, the country was plunged into a serious economic crisis and the Conservative-led coalition of Kåre Willoch was forced to resign (spring 1986). It was replaced by a minority Labour government led by Gro Harlem Bruntland, who was forced to devalue the Norwegian krone by 12 per cent.[17] The era of indulgence appeared to have come to a close even for lucky Norway.

Norway's circumstances were almost unique. No one ever claimed that it could serve as a model of how to avoid the evils of stagflation. The search for the causes of this phenomenon, and for the causes of unemployment in particular, opened a debate in which the voice of neo-liberal economists, hitherto stifled by the dominance of Keynesianism, made itself felt. Following Milton Friedman, they assumed the existence of a unique or 'natural' rate of unemployment consistent with stable prices.[18] They argued that if demand were stimulated by Keynesian or other means, unemployment would fall below this rate, but that this would accelerate inflation. In other words, there is a trade-off between unemployment and inflation for the medium to long run – a conclusion first arrived at by A. W. Phillips.[19] It appears that in the short run anything is possible for these economists, including high inflation concurrent with high unemployment, as was the case in many European countries. According to this view, any attempt to return to the level of unemployment in the 1960s will cause inflation to rise well above the level reached then.[20] This means that in the 1960s, the 'natural' rate of unemployment compatible with stable prices – technically known as NAIRU, or non-accelerating inflation rate of unemployment – was much lower than in the 1970s and 1980s.[21] Patrick Minford estimated that in Britain the 'natural' rate of unemployment in 1980 was of the order of 13.5 per cent, or around 3.25 million; then a decrease in unionization and abolition of the national insurance surcharge (phenomena which are as 'natural' as a peach melba) caused the 'natural' rate to fall to 2 to 2.5 million.[22]

The idea that there is such a thing as a 'natural' rate·sounds metaphysical, particularly as this rate appears to 'hop around from one triennium to another under the influence of unspecified forces, including past unemployment rates'.[23] Moreover, why should NAIRU be so different from country to country? If it is argued that there are national factors influencing NAIRU, then attention should be directed to national factors as the crucial variables affecting unemployment. The use of the term 'natural' in this context is purely ideological. It is possible to abandon the idea of a 'natural' (in the sense of immutable) NAIRU, while accepting its underlining principle: 'whatever the NAIRU happens to be at any given time, it places an obstacle to any attempt to expand employment by increasing demand.'[24]

If the excessively high wages theory is right, and the evidence is strong but not overwhelming, no government, socialist or otherwise, can lower unemployment by traditional methods, unless it is willing to face an acceleration of inflation. Inflation appears to affect the entire electorate, though in reality those able to increase their earnings at the same rate as inflation would not suffer unduly, while unemployment affects only those who lose their jobs. Politically speaking, those who are likely to lose their jobs are more likely to vote for the Left, while those hurt by inflation are more likely to support conservative policies. The population affected by inflation, usually being far larger than that affected by unemployment, inevitably becomes the prime preoccupation of politicians of all sides. A separate study yet to be written might unveil one of the great mysteries of the 1970s and 1980s: the construction of the great anti-inflationary consensus, embodied in the European Community's Maastricht Treaty of 1992, which established that the struggle against inflation was the bedrock of sound government.

NAIRU theorists have tried to explain why it is that the unemployment rate compatible with stable prices turned out to be so much higher in the 1970s and 1980s than in the 1960s. The orthodox neo-classical answer is unequivocal: real wages are too high. This view became increasingly prevalent in the course of the 1980s. Keynesians instead held the view that unemployment in the mid-1970s was caused by a fall in aggregate demand, due to deflationary government policies aimed at containing inflation which was in turn caused by the rise in oil prices. There is no unanimity among economists, even though most agree that, while there are wide-ranging explanations for the rise in NAIRU, high wages are a major determinant of unemployment.[25] This is one way of saying that unemployment is a mechanism for the control of wages. Even the most sophisticated econometric studies available found it difficult to separate the unemployment caused by high wages from that caused by cyclical factors and low aggregate demand. An authoritative study settled for the view that some unemployment is cyclical and some due to excessive levels of real wages, and frankly admitted that:

> This conclusion is perhaps a let-down. But it is worth stressing that no evidence whatsoever has been offered to date for the claim that unemployment is due to high real wages only, as the argument of those favouring a *lohnpause* (wage-freeze) would imply ... We conclude then that any real wage cuts that are part of a stabilization programme are in themselves insufficient to guarantee recovery and stability. There needs to be a complementary expansion in demand.[26]

As is often the case, the experts do not speak with a single voice, economics being roughly at the stage medicine was a couple of centuries ago: it kills more patients than it cures. There was not then, and there is not now, a fully tested theory which explains the causes of unemployment – as economists themselves, in rare moments of humility, have acknowledged. Thus, Bernard Donoughue, adviser to Labour prime ministers between 1974 and 1979, recalled a seminar on the causes and cures of unemployment convened in 10 Downing Street, in order to explain to James Callaghan the latest refinements of the discipline. Seven wise men assembled, including Richard Layard, Amartya Sen and David Hendry. There was a long discussion. 'We covered the field, but somehow we did not get anywhere. We were all aware that there was a part of the unemployment problem which we did not understand – and the part which we did understand we could do little about.'[27]

In these circumstances politicians pick and choose technical explanations according to political convenience and are, anyway, more likely to be persuaded by influential journalists, who write succinctly and clearly, than by professional academic economists whose jargon is often impenetrable, and who are seldom certain about anything. As Maddison points out, a system shock, such as the end of fixed exchange rates or the oil crisis, will produce the need for new policy instruments, but these are not always selected on the most rational basis.[28] Most technical explanations, moreover, do not point towards an inescapable political conclusion. The high wages theory of unemployment is a case in point. When embraced by conservatives and neoliberals, it may lead to a demand for liberalizing the labour market, reducing protection and job security, and making life difficult for the trade unions. When adopted by socialists and social democrats, the political consequences deduced from the theory are that only a pro-labour government – that is, only a government trusted by the unions – can convince them to hold down real wages.

By and large, the leftist view prevailed during the 1970s – the high watermark of attempts to adopt an incomes policy throughout Europe. On the assumption that consensual policies could protect employment better than conflicting ones, many believed that a corporate structure for negotiations between government, employers and unions – so-called corporatist intermediation – needed to be established. The conditions for such developments did not exist in all countries – not all have the required mix of a centralized and ideologically united union movement and a strong employers' organization – but they could be encouraged. At first, this helped the socialists. Who better than they could negotiate with the unions and convince them that an ideologically friendly government would be an ideal partner? The question of trust between unions and governments is more central than is realized, the reason being that to negotiate in terms of real wages is, in reality, a chancy affair. Unions can only negotiate nominal wages and hope that prices will not increase excessively; prices, however, do not simply respond to nominal wages, but to a myriad of factors. The more fragmented the unions are in their negotiating, the less informed they can be about the demands and strategies of other unions. They are forced to negotiate from a position of ignorance on real wages and inflation, and in these circumstances rational trade unionists will try to get as much as they can. Governments must succeed in convincing them that their moderation will pay off in the end and they can only do so by co-ordinating as much of the economy as possible. This is why a voluntary incomes policy requires a carefully worked out, highly interventionist economic strategy. The lessons of the 1970s are that incomes policy are difficult to sustain without an adequate framework of corporatism.

Some countries ranked high on the corporatist scale: Sweden, Norway and Austria above all, followed by Denmark, Holland, Belgium and Germany. Because some of the countries which were able to avoid the worst features of the stagflation of the 1970s were in this group, it was believed that corporatism could resolve the problem of unemployment. A systematic comparison of corporatist strength and employment record does not bear this out.[29]

Corporatism implied the involvement of trade unions at the centre of political decision-making. Industrial democracy, a popular panacea advocated in the 1970s, required a similar involvement in the single firm. Schemes, projects and, in some instances, laws advanced ways of increasing workers' rights, whether by appointing or electing worker-directors, or by providing workers with access to information, or by establishing procedures for dealing with dismissals and working conditions. Some of these will be discussed in greater detail later on. Here it will be sufficient to mention the Italian Statuto dei Lavoratori of 1970 (see chapter 13), the German Co-Determination Law of 1976 (see chapter 18), the Bullock Report of January 1977 in Britain (chapter 18), the French Auroux Law of 1982 (chapter 19), the 'democratic factory councils' (*Bedriftsforsamlinger*) in Norway instituted in 1973 by an Act of the Storting, the 1976 Joint Consultation Act in Sweden, and the EEC Commission's Fifth Directive on Company Law, endorsing the German model of industrial democracy.

The corporatist solution was one possible answer to the problem of high real wages. Some economists, committed to the high wages theory of unemployment, argued that unions and governments created too many 'rigidities' in the labour market: fixed wage differentials across regions or occupations; restrictions on the hiring and firing of workers; high unemployment benefits; limits on working hours; health hazards and safety regulations; pension schemes; tight housing market; strong unions.[30] The political consequence of this view is diametrically opposed to the pro-corporatist position. Here the culprit is the 'social democratic state': its lavish unemployment benefits keep workers in depressed areas instead of forcing them actively to seek jobs in growth areas and to compete with employed workers; 'socialist' regulations making it difficult to hire and fire are an obstacle to adjustments; high social insurance charges increase labour costs (the 'real' wage paid out by the employer). Market forces are stifled. The solution, widely advocated in the 1980s, was to dismantle the welfare state, unleash market forces, sap the powers of the trade unions. The promise was that, after a painful but unavoidable period of 'adjustment' (i.e. mass unemployment), happy days of growth, stable prices and full employment would be with us again.

In the period 1985–90 output increased by 3 per cent a year, while unemployment decreased by 2.5 per cent, but liberalizing labour markets contributed little to this revival. The trigger for this growth was the sharp drop in oil prices and rising business expectations in anticipation of the

European Single Market, due to start in 1992. In Britain the 1985–88 growth was due to government-led expansionary policies, particularly tax cuts. This greatly helped Britain's foreign competitors: they owed their own improved performance to the taste of the now richer British taxpayers and consumers who spent their money on foreign goods (the volume of British imports rose by 30 per cent in these years).[31]

That the unleashing of market forces as a solution to mass unemployment could have been advocated by intelligent people, and implemented by politicians, should not be surprising. Desperate situations require desperate remedies. That such ideas could still prevail in the 1990s is a monument to human folly. By 1995, oil was cheaper than anyone could have wished during the previous twenty years; trade unions were a spent force throughout Europe; eighteen million unemployed kept the labour market loose and flexible beyond the hopes entertained by many conservatives in the 1970s; interest rates were at their lowest in years; strikes were rare, and virtually confined to the defence of jobs in the public sector, rather than to pushing wages up. And still, inexplicably, the advanced countries faced a future characterized by mass unemployment and low growth.

In the 1980s in Britain, Conservative economists such as Patrick Minford, an adviser to Margaret Thatcher, were among those who believed that unemployment failed to depress high wages because of market distortion, due to union power and the welfare state. Minford suggested that all legal immunities be removed from the trade unions, that anti-strike legislation be introduced, that small businesses be exempt from all employment protection laws, that health and safety rules should become advisory.[32] All employment protection laws, he wrote, should be abolished 'lock stock and barrel and let the worker protect himself against poor conditions by voting with his feet'. Consequently, the Employment Protection Act of 1978, the Equal Pay Act of 1970, and the Sex Discrimination Act of 1975 would have to be repealed. Under the banner of increasing 'people's economic freedom', Minford advocated abolishing the notion of 'unfair dismissal', redundancy payments, statutory notice for dismissal (or, indeed, any obligation to give reason for dismissal), maternity rights, time off for ante-natal care, maternity pay, the right to return to work after giving birth, and so on.[33] Minford stopped short of advocating the reintroduction of child labour, though, logically and consistently, there should be no reason to interfere with the freedom of a ten-year-old to go down a chimney or a coalmine, or that of parents to dispose of their children in the most commercially profitable manner.

Many of the new institutional arrangements recommended by Minford were implemented by the Thatcher administration in order to foster a resumption of growth. Of course, much protective legislation was left untouched, but the extent to which the proposals of Minford and other right-wing thinkers were adopted went beyond the wildest hopes of academic economists seeking to influence governments. Yet, from the economic point of view, this has not been a success story. By 1993, unemployment in the UK was, in real terms, at an all-time post-war high, while British manufacturing industry was in ruins. The anti-union policy pursued, and the demolition of workers' rights, did nothing to lower real wages, which in the Thatcher years 1979–89 rose by 2.6 per cent, nearly three times the rate of the Labour years of 1973–79 (0.9 per cent).[34] Countries with very rigid and highly regulated labour markets, such as Finland, Sweden and Norway, performed better than the UK over the long term. As Göran Therborn has shown, there is no direct correlation between unemployment levels and rates of taxation or levels of social expenditure.[35] The most obvious reason is that money saved by the state when withdrawing subsidies to industry is soon spent on unemployment support to workers sacked from these same industries.

Contrary to what economists have suggested, there is no correlation between the level of unemployment pay and willingness to work. There is, it is true, a diminution of that shame of being out of work, which, in the past, forced many to accept work at derisory wages or in appalling conditions. Countries with high unemployment compensation, such as Sweden, had low unemployment for years. In the UK the ratio of benefits to net income had not changed since 1966 and therefore could not account for the increase in unemployment in the late 1970s. Moreover, if people had become less willing to work there would have been a sharp increase in unemployment at any given level of job availability. This did occur in Belgium and the UK, but not in Germany.[36]

In spite of the lack of strong evidence, the neo-liberal idea that markets should be liberalized as much as possible, because they were the most efficient allocator of prices – including the price of labour – became the dominant ideology, accepted, in one form or another, in most of the world by virtually the entire spectrum of political opinion, including many on the Left.

The idea that institutional problems were an obstacle to the downward adjustment of high wages at a time of high unemployment was not the property of right-wing economists. Many on the Left now accepted that the tight labour markets established in the early 1960s in Europe, and later in the USA and Japan, strengthened the trade unions, and that a purely Keynesian explanation in terms of deficient aggregate demand was not totally convincing.[37] In complex societies wages are not set by mere supply and demand. If this were the case, we should expect that under less than full employment firms would simply force down wages by turning to unemployed workers, and/or that unemployed workers would turn out at the factory gates to sell their labour at less than the going rate. In real life firms face costs for hiring and firing; existing workers may refuse to co-operate with new entrants or even harass them; and there are other costs implicit in the adverse effects of labour turnover.[38] It is often the case that key groups of workers in important sectors of the economy in prosperous regions set a wage trend to which everyone conforms, irrespective of the requirements of the real economy.

This may be aggravated by the fact that jobless workers in high unemployment areas do not move to prosperous areas, driving down high wages. They stay put, anchored by housing policies and subsidized by unemployment benefits. The pool of unemployment which is thus formed does little to contain real wages.[39] According to this model, called the 'insider-outsider' model, the unemployment sector can be theoretically divided into two categories: the long-term unemployed or 'outsiders' who are, in effect, unemployable and therefore have no impact on wages; and the temporarily unemployed or 'insiders', who are still in the real job market and who thus help keep wages in check.[40] The 'outsiders' become an outcast group, consisting of the old, unwell and unskilled. It has been calculated that in Germany in 1977, 74.5 per cent of all long-term unemployed – that is, those out of work for more than a year – were over fifty-five and/or had impaired health and/or no vocational qualifications.[41]

This may explain why high unemployment may not bring about its only possible benefit – namely, lower inflation – and why an increase in demand may push wages up even in a situation of high unemployment. It does not explain why unemployment increased in the first place. Similarly, if the real culprit is the social-democratic welfare state, how is it possible that growth, full employment and low inflation co-existed happily in the 'social-democratic' 1950s and 1960s? The most obvious answer lies in the exogenous shocks suffered by the West European economies in the 1970s – first, the fluctuation in exchange rates that resulted from the abandonment of fixed parities, and then the increase in oil prices by the OPEC countries.

The end of the fixed exchange rates system came about because confidence in the dollar was rapidly eroding. This reflected the deterioration in the global power of the USA, its excessive spending on the Vietnam War, its first trading deficit (1971) since 1893, differential inflationary rates between the USA and its international competitors, and the growing economic and political strength of Europe and Japan. Repeated deficits in the US balance of payments had flooded the world with dollars. The rapidly developing eurodollar markets caused excess liquidity, a major cause of the rising inflationary pressures. The American solution was to suspend the convertibility of the dollar into gold (15 August 1971). In December of that year, the dollar was devalued under the Smithsonian Institute Agreement. In response to the West Germans, no longer willing to support the dollar, on 19 March 1973 it was decided to let exchange rates float, effectively terminating the Bretton Woods system. The new system of floating rates was formalized at a meeting of the Group of Ten, the leading IMF members, in Jamaica in 1976.[42]

As the hegemonic role of the dollar was coming to a close, another pillar of the long boom – cheap oil – was collapsing. As we have seen, inflationary pressures had started before the oil shock. Nevertheless, the rise in oil prices was so drastic, so dramatic (it coincided with the Yom Kippur War between

Egypt and Israel) that in the popular imagination the great inflationary spiral of the 1970s was the direct consequence of the OPEC decision to raise the price of oil.[43] There is little doubt that an external shock, in the shape of an unprecedented rise in oil prices, initiated the slide into stagflation; but it was not its only cause.[44] The length of the recession suggests that, at most, the OPEC crisis was the trigger or catalyst which shifted the rate of unemployment compatible with stable prices.[45] By the late 1980s, oil and raw material prices had become cheap again, with little accompanying economic growth.

It may be thought that, in circumstances in which oil had become more expensive, a modicum of inflation would have been preferable to high unemployment. It is true that inflation affects more people than unemployment, but if earnings were to keep pace with inflation those in employment would not suffer particularly. Indexation of benefits would ensure that pensioners and the unemployed would also not be worse off. The real problem was that the West European economies were very active in international trade; consequently, any change in relative prices – that is, any difference in their respective rates of inflation – would inevitably affect international competitiveness, economic performance, growth and employment. It was because capitalism had become a truly international system that nationally based social democracies were subjected – like all national forces – to balance of payment constraints. The problem of adjustment would have been more serious in a system of fixed exchange rates, but after 1971 international trade was based on fluctuating rates and adjustments were simpler. Some countries – Sweden and Italy, for instance – resorted to regular devaluation of their currency to maintain international competitiveness.

Expansionary policies pursued in one country, but not in others, would cause that country's inflation to increase faster than elsewhere, by sucking in cheaper imports and harming competitiveness. The hope that some countries – the USA, Germany or Japan – would perform the role of 'locomotive', pulling others along, proved illusory. Co-ordinated expansion would appear to be the obvious answer. To expand demand when others are contracting is counter-productive. To contract when others are expanding is absurd. In the absence of co-ordination in the 1970s, all economies contracted when greater benefits might have been achieved by co-ordinated expansion. Yet the continuing strength of the nation-state, and the short-term nature of much contemporary politicking, has made it impossible for effective supranational co-ordination to occur. The Left, the force best suited for implementing a Europe-wide Keynesian co-ordinated reflation, was, during the 1970s, still unwilling to confront the erosion of national economic sovereignty. We should note here two mild exceptions to this residual left-wing faith in the nation: the first was Helmut Schmidt's decision to reflate unilaterally (following pressure at the Bonn economic summit of July 1978), thus making the German economy the putative 'locomotive' of Western recovery.[46] This attempt failed, as a result of the Iranian Revolution and the subsequent second oil shock. It was later much regretted by Schmidt. The second was François Mitterrand's total commitment to European unity in the mid-1980s, due to the failure of the go-it-alone French reflation of 1981–83.

These (failed) attempts excepted, the strategy of co-ordination of national economies remained adrift in the high seas of pious wishes, in spite of all the words and work spent on discussing international and European integration, in spite of the fact that the negative lessons of the protectionist 1930s had been regularly taught in schools and universities, in spite of the endless charade of expensive summits where politicians, goaded by the mass media, paraded with characteristic pomposity, masquerading as world statesmen while at the mercy of forces they were unable to understand.

The collapse of the Bretton Woods system of fixed exchange rates made co-ordination difficult to achieve. Flexible exchange rates increased the operational range of decision-makers, freeing them from an externally imposed discipline and enabling them to pursue their own macro-economic targets. This turned out to be a poisoned chalice, since 'policy coordination is almost always desirable and may be particularly important after a supply shock'.[47]

Throughout the 1970s, and 1980s, macro-economic policy remained a national affair. Though buffeted by international currents and increasingly interdependent, the national European economies pursued their own policies. As we have noted, they all had to conform to a general trend, but they did not do so in the same way. Unemployment and inflation increased everywhere, but not by the same amount. Growth was sluggish, but not uniformly so. Exogenous shocks, such as oil price increases, may explain what sparked the crisis, but they do not explain national differences. Trans-national macro-economic modelling may be fun and attract lavish funding, yet it is seldom true, as wise economists know only too well: 'More often than not we fail to take institutional differences seriously. One model is supposed to apply everywhere and always.'[48]

The key factor in institutional differences lies in politics. Therborn's and Fritz Scharpf's working hypothesis is that the decisive factor in determining unemployment levels is the degree of commitment to fighting unemployment.[49] This does not mean that a high level of employment can be obtained simply by pursuing the 'right' policies. It is clear that there must also be specific national and international conditions which enable social democrats to behave like social democrats. It is the interconnection between strategic choice and favourable conditions which, in the final analysis, determines a specific policy outcome. One should extend to all European states the hypothesis advanced by Peter Katzenstein regarding small states: 'the small European states frame political choices in a distinctive way. Their choices are conditioned by two sets of forces: historically shaped domestic structures and the pressures of the world economy. These two forces interact.'[50]

The assumption that socialist governments have defended full employment more consistently than conservative ones is almost impossible to prove empirically. One can readily demonstrate that the British Labour government gave priority to the defence of sterling in 1964–67 and, more importantly, the containment of inflation in 1976–79 over unemployment; but how can one demonstrate that the Conservative Party would have accepted an even higher level of unemployment in the same period? The Swedish social democrats successfully upheld the cherished principle of full employment in the 1970s, but the 'bourgeois' coalition which held power in Sweden in 1976–82 fought just as hard on behalf of the same principle. In the 1980s socialist governments in Spain and France abandoned any pretence to sustain jobs and were prepared to tolerate very high levels of unemployment. Would conservative governments have fared much worse in the defence of jobs?

Therborn's insistence that, in the final analysis, it is the depth of a society's commitment to full employment (as opposed to a political party's) which explains 'why some people are more unemployed than others', is plausible, but it can account only for prolonged resistance to joblessness, not for everlasting full employment.

By 1994, the view that left-wing governments provided a better defence of employment could no longer be sustained. Within the European Community the worst level of unemployment – 23.4 per cent, more than twice the EC average (10.9 per cent) – was recorded in Spain, governed since 1981 by the socialists; Germany and Portugal, ruled by conservatives since 1982 and 1985, respectively, were doing far better, with 8.3 and 5.9 per cent. Socialist-led Greece more than matched this performance, with 4.6 per cent. Tiny Luxemburg, governed by conservatives, was doing best of all, with 2.2 per cent.[51]

Eventually, in spite of its commitment to full employment, even Sweden had to accept rising unemployment. And why did such a commitment exist in the first place? Is it because of the strength of social-democratic traditions? Why, then, was unemployment lower in Norway and Sweden than in Denmark? Why was unemployment so low in Switzerland and Japan, where there are no social-democratic traditions at all? Why did Britain 'give up' on full employment under a Labour government in 1976–79, even though the consensus in favour of it was reputed to have been exceptionally high? Were the differences in unemployment levels between countries due to the fact that it was easier to defend employment in some than in others? A closer look at how the Left faced the end of the golden age of capitalism may bring these questions more sharply into focus.

The Vicissitudes of the Left

The closing of the golden age coincided with an apparent revitalization of the Left. In Germany the SPD obtained its best post-war results in 1972. In Britain the Conservative government of Edward Heath was decisively challenged and defeated by the coalminers in two lengthy strikes. In France the defeat and resignation of de Gaulle in 1969 was followed by the reorganization of the Socialist Party, and the beginning of the construction of socialist–communist unity – the necessary precondition for the victory of the Left in 1981. In Spain, Portugal and Greece, authoritarian governments had run their course; before the end of the 1970s, democracy had been successfully established in all three countries. The argument that the social-democratic parties of Northern Europe were successful in the 1970s while those in Southern Europe achieved their main triumphs in the 1980s is valid up to a point.[52] The political victories of socialists in Southern Europe had been prepared by a generalized shift to the left in the 1970s: the end of authoritarian rule in Spain, Portugal, Greece and the advance of the Communist Party in Italy.

Some of the surviving Western communist parties improved their prospects – particularly the Italians, who accelerated the process of renewal and distancing from the USSR, leading to the short-lived 'Eurocommunist' phase. In most European countries, the protagonists of the turbulent 1960s – radical youth, feminists and pacifists – joined with ecologists in popularizing new forms of politics. This apparent evolution in favour of the Left did not translate into electoral success. Table 16.3 indicates the percentage gained by the main parties of the Left in this period.

In Belgium, Finland and Sweden the main parties of the Left remained stable. In Austria, what was, in percentage terms, the strongest party of the Left in Europe – the SPÖ – declined in the course of the 1980s, but retained a strong following. In Germany, the SPD followed a similar trend of slow, but apparently inexorable decline. In the United Kingdom, the Labour Party lost votes systematically, particularly in the 1980s when it obtained the worst results in its history. In Italy, the PCI achieved its best ever results in 1976, whereupon decline set in, though the smaller, rival Italian Socialist Party advanced throughout the 1980s. The vote of the Danish and Norwegian socialists fluctuated remarkably, though the Danish results in the 1980s were well below their previous average. In Portugal, in a complex situation of transition to democracy, the Socialist Party at first emerged as a force to be reckoned with, but turned out, by the end of the period, to be one of the weakest socialist parties in Europe. In Greece, PASOK, having emerged as one of the strongest Left parties in Europe in 1981 and 1985, was, by 1989, in the midst of an apparent terminal crisis, though it revived sufficiently in 1993 to return to power. In Spain and France, the 1980s were periods of great success and electoral victories. By 1993, the French socialists suffered a catastrophic defeat, while the Spanish socialists lost their overall majority. In 1994, the Italian socialists collapsed in the most serious wave of financial scandals to have rocked any West European country since 1945.

Thus, the raw statistics we have tell a story of electoral uncertainty for the main parties of the Left. Two factors need to be examined, however, before concluding that the frequently written obituary of social democracy can be

Table 16.3 Share of the vote of the main party of the Left in fourteen countries, 1970–89

	1970	1971	1972	1973	1974	1975	1976	1977	1978	1979	1980	1981	1982	1983	1984	1985	1986	1987	1988	1989
Austria	48.4	50.0	–	–	–	50.4	–	–	–	51.0	–	–	–	47.6	–	–	41.3	–	–	–
Belgium	27.2	37.3	25.6	–	26.6	–	–	26.5	25.4	–	–	25.1	–	–	–	28.3	–	30.6	–	–
Denmark	–	–	–	–	–	29.9	–	37.0	–	38.3	–	32.9	–	–	31.6	–	–	29.3	29.9	–
Finland	23.4	25.8	–	–	–	24.9	–	–	–	23.9	–	–	–	26.7	–	–	–	24.1	–	–
France	–	–	–	19.2	–	–	–	–	25.0	–	–	37.8	–	–	–	–	32.8	–	37.5	–
Greece	–	–	–	–	13.6	–	–	25.3	–	–	–	48.1	–	–	–	45.8	–	–	–	40.7[a]
Holland	–	24.6	27.3	–	–	–	–	33.8	–	–	–	28.3	30.4	–	–	–	33.3	–	–	–
Italy	–	–	27.2	–	–	–	34.4	–	–	30.4	–	–	–	29.9	–	–	–	26.6	–	–
Norway	–	–	–	35.3	–	–	–	42.3	–	–	–	37.1	–	–	–	41.2	–	–	–	–
Portugal	–	–	–	–	–	40.7	36.7	–	–	28.9	28.7	–	–	36.1	–	20.7	–	22.7	–	–
Spain	–	–	–	–	–	–	–	30.3	–	30.5	–	–	46.5	–	–	–	44.1	–	–	–
Sweden	45.3	–	–	43.6	–	–	42.7	–	–	43.2	–	–	45.6	–	–	45.1	–	–	43.7	–
UK	43.1	–	–	–	39.2[a]	–	–	–	–	37.0	–	–	–	27.6	–	–	–	30.8	–	–
W. Germany	–	–	45.8	–	–	–	42.6	–	–	–	42.9	–	–	38.2	–	–	–	37.0	–	–

Notes: [a] UK 1974 and Greece 1989: second election result shown (respectively October 1974 and November 1989). The Labour Party obtained 37.2 in February 1974. PASOK obtained 39.1 in June 1989.

Main party of the left: the Socialist Party in Austria, Spain, Portugal and France; the Labour Party in Norway, United Kingdom and Holland; the Social Democratic Party in Finland, Germany, Sweden and Denmark; the Communist Party in Italy; the figure for Belgium represents the sum of the Walloon and Flemish socialist parties.

substantiated. In the first place, the votes 'lost' by the main parties of the Left may have been gained by other 'left' parties, such as ecologists or smaller, more militant socialist formations. This resulted in an increased fragmentation of the Left. Secondly, electoral results are not the only index of political strength. The capacity to remain in power through alliances with other parties may be of equal or greater importance.

AUSTRIA: 1986 represented a serious setback for the dominant SPÖ. Its share of the vote dropped from 47.6 per cent in 1983 to 41.3 per cent in 1986. Its Conservative opponents stood still and the apparent beneficiaries were the right-wing Freedom Party and the new green formation, made up of various ecological groups presenting a single list. The latter obtained 4.8 per cent, roughly the same percentage lost by the SPÖ. Though the greens cannot be automatically considered a left formation, it should be noted that seven of the eight green MPs later declared themselves to be part of the main green party, the GA (Grüne Alternativen), which opposed the 'conservative' greens.

BELGIUM: While the Belgian socialists remained relatively stable throughout the period, towards the end of the 1980s an ecological party emerged and secured between 6 and 7 per cent of the suffrage.

FINLAND: Here too the social democrats were relatively stable. However, the badly split Communist Party, which in some ways represented the hard core of Finnish radicalism, decreased in strength – even if we add together all the communist groups – throughout the 1980s, from 17.9 per cent in 1979 to 10.1 per cent in 1991. The Finnish greens gained 4 per cent in 1987 and 6.8 per cent in 1991.

GERMANY: In 1983 and 1987, the Green Party was able to obtain more than the 5 per cent required to gain representation in Parliament. In certain *Länder*, for instance in the Saarland, they enabled a 'red–green' coalition to emerge. The 'left' credentials of the German greens are not in dispute: not only were there no instances of a coalition with the CDU, but such a coalition was almost unthinkable. In 1990, in the first elections of reunited Germany, the greens lost their representation, but the Democratic Party of the Left (the former East German communists) was able to obtain a handful of seats.

FRANCE: The 1980s saw neither the increased fragmentation of the Left, nor the emergence of significant green parties. Prior to the Socialist rout of 1993, the decline of the Left vote was entirely attributable to the decline of the PCF.

GREECE: The growth of PASOK is attributable to its ability to attract the centrist votes which used to converge towards the Union of the Centre (which disappeared from political life during the 1980s). The Greek Communist Party held on to its one-tenth of the vote until 1990.

PORTUGAL: The two parties of the Left, socialist (PS) and communist (PCP), declined together. In the first free elections, the PCP obtained 17.9 per cent (less than half the vote of the PS); in 1987 the PCP had 12 per cent against 22 per cent for the PSP. The ratio had not altered significantly, though the total Left vote had, temporarily, almost halved.

SPAIN: Here the tendency does not closely match the overall European trend. The PSOE decreased from 46.5 per cent in 1982 to 38.7 per cent in 1993, though the party was able to remain in power throughout. The Spanish Communist Party (PCE) declined from a peak of 10.8 per cent in 1979 to 4.6 per cent in 1986, but, under various United Left umbrellas, it improved its prospects later (9.1 in 1989 and 9.6 in 1993).

SWEDEN: The rise of the Green Party (5.5 per cent in 1988) did not erode any of the support of the established Left, whose percentage remained substantially unaltered: the social democrats stood at around 43–45 per cent and the Communist Party at around 4–5 per cent. The Swedish Left expanded, but became more fragmented.

HOLLAND: the Labour Party's share, about 30 per cent of the suffrage, was not affected by the growing fragmentation of the overall political system.

NORWAY: The apparent collapse of the Det Norske Arbeiderparti vote in 1973 (down to 35.3 per cent) can be attributed to the rise of the leftist Socialist People's Party (11.2 per cent), which became in 1975 the Socialistisk Venstreparti (Socialist Left Party – SV).

DENMARK: The situation in Denmark was similar to that of Norway (and France, Portugal and Greece), in that there was a sizeable Left alternative to the main socialist party. In this instance, as in Norway, this was the radical Socialist People's Party (Socialistisk Folkeparti). By 1988, it had 13 per cent of the vote against 29.9 per cent for the mainstream social democrats.

UNITED KINGDOM: Here the electoral system was virtually impermeable to any new formation. Thus, the pronounced decline of the Labour Party is not paralleled by the emergence of a green or radical party. However, in 1981 the Labour Party split; the resulting centrist Social Democratic Party formed an alliance with the Liberal Party (1983) and eventually merged with it. This centrist formation came close to unseating the Labour Party as the main opposition in 1983. Here there occurred a greater fragmentation of the opposition in the sense that, in electoral terms at least, it became more equally divided between the Labour Party and the centre (the Liberal Democratic Party).

ITALY: Here the main party of the Left was the PCI. It reached its peak in 1976; thereafter, decline set in. The PSI, by contrast, appeared about to close the gap with the communists: in 1976 the PCI had nearly four times the electoral strength of the PSI; by 1987 it had just over twice the percentage. The background of this was the continuing fragmentation of the Italian political system: on the Left there was the small Radical Party, a leftist party (the PDUP) and, eventually, the greens. In 1987, even though the PCI appeared destined to inexorable decline, the sum total of the Left parties (PCI, PSI, radicals, far Left and green) stood at 47 per cent of the national vote – the highest percentage ever reached by the Italian Left. By 1992, a populist party, the Northern League, became the dominant force in much of northern Italy, while an anti-mafia party – La Rete – joined the increasingly complex spread of political parties. After 1992, the Italian political system was completely modified leading to the disappearance of the PSI and the PCI became the Partito Democratico della Sinistra (Democratic Party of the Left – PDS).

The electoral fortunes of the main parties of the Left in the 1970s and the 1980s can be tabulated in the following way:

Table 16.4 The changing political fortunes of the Left: the 1970s and 1980s compared

Significant gain	France (Socialist)
	Greece (PASOK)
	Holland (Labour Party)
	Italy (Socialist)
	Spain (Socialist)
Significant decline	Austria (Socialist)
	Denmark (Social Democrats)
	Germany (Social Democrats)
	Italy (Communist)
	Portugal (Communist and Socialist)
	United Kingdom (Labour Party)
	France (Communist)
No significant change	Belgium (Socialist)
	Finland (Social Democrat)
	Norway (Labour Party)
	Sweden (Social Democrat)

Table 16.4 tells only part of the story. The Austrian SPÖ, the British Labour Party and the French PCF all 'decline' – but not in the same way. The 'decline' of the Austrian socialists may have been numerically significant, but they remained the main Austrian party and stayed in power throughout the 1980s. By contrast, the decline of the Labour Party – the most pronounced of its history – was interpreted by many as a terminal illness. A similar prediction was made of the French Communist Party. All in all, no clear general trend emerged.

We are left with the task of examining actual success in achieving governmental power. We look only at governments constituted entirely by left-wing parties (such as the socialist–communist coalition established in France in 1981–84), or dominated by the main party of the Left (such as the Austrian governments of the late 1980s or the SPD–FDP coalition in Germany in the 1970s). In Table 16.5 the asterisk indicates any year in which such a 'Left' government held power.

No broad generalizations emerge. The Left dominated governments throughout the period in Austria; through most of the period in Sweden; in

Table 16.5 Left governments in fourteen European countries, 1970–89

	Aus	Bel	Dnk	Fra	Fin	Ger	Gre	Hol	Ita	Nor	Por	Spa	Swe	UK
1970	*					*							*	
1971	*		*			*							*	
1972	*		*			*							*	
1973	*					*				*			*	
1974	*					*				*			*	*
1975	*		*			*				*			*	*
1976	*		*			*				*	*			*
1977	*		*			*				*	*			*
1978	*		*			*				*				*
1979	*		*			*				*				
1980	*		*			*				*				
1981	*			*		*	*			*				
1982	*			*		*	*					*	*	
1983	*			*			*					*	*	
1984	*			*			*					*	*	
1985	*			*			*					*	*	
1986	*						*			*		*	*	
1987	*						*			*		*	*	
1988	*			*			*			*		*	*	
1989	*			*			*			*		*	*	

the 1970s more than the 1980s in Norway and Denmark; in the 1970s only in Germany; in the 1980s only in France and Spain. In Belgium, Finland, Portugal, Holland and Italy, the majority parties of the Left had little or no say in government. In the United Kingdom, the Labour Party was in power for only a few years (and with a tiny majority of seats) in the 1970s. The defeat of the British and German Left throughout the 1980s, and the inability of the Italian Left to patch up its differences and obtain power (the only country in Europe where the Left had never been the dominant force in government), are important signposts of the crisis of socialism. This, however, must be set against the revival of the Left in Spain, Portugal and Greece following the demise of authoritarian governments, and the major experiment constituted by the first post-war socialist government in France. The share of the popular vote, the number of seats obtained in Parliament, the degree of influence achieved in government are of great importance in establishing the effectiveness of the socialist tradition in the last decades of the century, but the picture remains indistinct. Reconnoitring the itinerary of the Left after the golden age requires a deeper historico-political analysis.

CHAPTER SEVENTEEN

Social Democracy in Small Countries: Austria, Sweden, Holland and Belgium

THE ECONOMIC data for the 1970s and 1980s examined in chapter 16 highlighted the outstanding performance of Austria, Sweden and Norway in maintaining full employment. For most of the 1970–90 period, all three had a socialist government. On both employment and price stability, Switzerland, run by a virtually permanent coalition government of national unity which included the socialists, performed as well as the other three. The Swiss commitment to full employment and price stability – the main economic foundations of social peace throughout this linguistically divided confederation – was upheld even at the cost of near-negative growth. This achievement must be put in perspective: unemployment in Switzerland was low mainly because the majority of workers who lost their jobs were foreigners on temporary permits who were forced to leave the country once they became unemployed.[1] In effect, Switzerland exported its unemployment. Foreign workers were thus the chief victims of the harsh deflation which allowed Switzerland to weather the oil shock. Other countries too, for example Austria and Germany, resorted to immigration restriction and repatriation, though not to the same extent as Switzerland. Such a policy appeared to cause very little uproar among socialists and, at least in Austria, was actively supported by the trade unions. In Britain, too, immigration was increasingly restricted by both Conservative and Labour governments, but in this case many social-ists reacted with dismay. Repatriation was never seriously considered as a feasible or desirable option (most migrant workers already were, or could easily become, British nationals – an option not available in other countries); it was advocated only by the far Right and by nationalist and racist person-alities in or out of the Conservative Party, such as Enoch Powell.

In this chapter I concentrate on two of what are generally taken to be the success stories of West European social democracy in the 1970s and 1980s – Austria and Sweden – contrasting them with Holland and Belgium, where the Left is weak, and which are comparable in terms of population and social stability.

Austria

Sweden has usually been presented as the most convincing showcase for West European social democracy. Yet Austria offers another powerful instance of social-democratic success. While the Swedish social democrats (SAP) faced their first post-1945 defeat in 1976, and were out of office until 1982, the Austrian Socialist Party (SPÖ) remained in power throughout the 1970s and 1980s, either on its own (1970–83), or in coalition with the liberal FPÖ (1983–86) or the conservative People's Party, the ÖVP (after 1986). In 1971 the SPÖ obtained an absolute majority of the popular vote, a rare accomplishment in Western Europe. Even more significant than these impressive political results have been economic successes: throughout the period, Austria achieved the unusual feat of maintaining a very high level of employment while holding inflation down. If we take into consideration the entire post-war period, however, the Austrian record in growth rate appears much less spectacular: the high growth rate of the 1950s was followed, in the 1960s, by one in line with the OECD average (3.9 per cent). The real achievement occurred in the 1970s, when Austria bucked the recessionary trend. This coincided with the rule of the SPÖ and the so-called 'Kreisky era'.[2]

Good economic management was the basis for the string of electoral victories by the SPÖ throughout these two decades. Other factors, however, were equally crucial in enabling the party to secure a majority of the popular vote. In the first place, the neutrality of the country was widely accepted and had been part of a deal with the USSR in exchange for the peace treaty of 1955. There was no pressure to shift from this position. Neutrality was popular and generally held to coincide with the national interest. In other countries, the parties of the Left were perceived as less reliable than their right-wing opponents in the conflict between West and East. In Austria (and Sweden), the socialists did not face such problems. The Austrian Chancellor Bruno Kreisky developed a high profile in international affairs (as did Olof Palme in Sweden and Willy Brandt in Germany), working tirelessly in favour of East–West dialogue, the United Nations (Austrian soldiers regularly served in peace-keeping missions in the Middle East and Cyprus), and a better deal for the Third World. Kreisky distinguished himself particularly with his outspoken commitment to the recognition of the Palestine Liberation Organization as the authentic representative of the Palestinian people. Perhaps only an independent-minded Jewish intellectual, leader of a neutral country, could have dared to welcome Yasser Arafat with the honours due to a head of state in 1979, when the Palestinian leader was still described by the Western media as little more than an international terrorist.

It may be argued that Kreisky's efforts, like those of Palme or even those of Brandt when he was leader of the Socialist International, were irrelevant, since control of international relations was solidly in the hands of the superpowers and could not be affected by small, peripheral countries or ineffective international organizations. This, however, misses the point. To use neutrality to a particular end, such as mediation between East and West or keeping open doors which others decide to close, is not inconsequential. Cold War politics required a special kind of negative posturing: not talking to some, not recognizing others. This situation, if it were not to deteriorate further, also required the existence of politicians and parties who would keep options open and talk to those boycotted by others. The function of small neutral countries was to try to escape from the politics of confrontation and maintain informal channels of communication. This flexible outlook turned out to be of help to the superpowers. Kreisky exploited all this with great cunning, obtaining considerable support at home. It is always a matter of great pride to the citizens of a small country to realize that their nation is able to play an international role and is not simply someone else's vassal or pawn. Thus, the foreign policy of the SPÖ fulfilled the double task of a socialist foreign policy: it contributed to détente *and* reinforced the popular acceptability of the socialists.

An 'exploitable' international position was the first of the many assets available to Austrian socialism. A second was that the long cohabitation in government with the ÖVP (1945–66) had fully legitimized the party. No one could seriously argue that the SPÖ could not run the economy, or that the country would have to face some dangerous experiment in social or economic engineering should the SPÖ govern alone. Furthermore, the system of *proporz*, whereby jobs in the public sector were divided up between the parties, had ensured that the SPÖ did not face a powerful establishment which was either 'above parties', yet conservative (as in the UK), or under the control of their opponents (as in France or Italy). Thanks to *proporz*, members or supporters of the SPÖ became part of the financial and economic establishment. Thus, the SPÖ had at its command a wealth of talents and expertise developed in the administration of the public sector. It never had to use experts whose values it did not share, or rely on 'neutral' civil servants, or appoint former opponents (as the British Labour Party often did in the nationalized industries). The *proporz* principle also applied to the large nationalized sector. This meant that the conservative opposition (the ÖVP) had a powerful party interest in preserving the state sector (as did the Christian Democratic Party in Italy). This, to some extent, impeded the development of Thatcher-style neo-liberalism in Austria.

Thirdly, the SPÖ was an extremely large and well-organized socialist party, with an exceptionally strong though declining mass membership (it fell from 703,000 in 1971 to 617,000 in 1989).[3] This made the Austrian socialists, proportionately speaking, the largest party in Western Europe, with a membership equal to one-third of its total vote and 9.6 per cent of the total population.[4] Like the Scandinavian and German social democrats and the Italian communists, the SPÖ also enjoyed the support of a large number of auxiliary associations. Some of these were closely linked to it, such as the

League of Socialist Freedom Fighters and Victims of Fascism (1,982 members in 1990), and the Workers' Association for Sport and Body Culture (ASKÖ – Arbeiterbund für Sport und Köperkultur in Österreich), with 1,080,000 members in 1990. Some had only loose ties to the Socialist Party, such as – and this is not a joke – the Central Association of Austrian Small Gardeners, Homecrofters and Pet Breeders, or the First Austrian Association of Workers' Stamp-collectors.[5] One in ten of SPÖ members were *Vertrauenspersonen*, trained activists who were expected to visit each member regularly and listen to their problems.[6]

The fourth asset of the SPÖ was represented by the considerable size of the Austrian public sector or, as the Austrians prefer to call it, the *Gemeinwirtschaft* ('economic community'). As was pointed out in chapter 5, the origin of this was the nationalization of German assets following the Second World War. This state takeover had been sanctioned by the ÖVP, as well as by the Western Allies then occupying parts of Austria. Thus, the public sector had not been the product of socialist 'dogma' bent on elimination of the free market, but the result of an overall national consensus. The Austrian state was in control of most mining, chemical and engineering industry – accounting for 20 per cent of the working population – as well as of the three leading banks which, in turn, were shareholders in a number of industries.[7] Political pressure was exerted on the nationalized banks to lend to industry in the name of social responsibility. However, ignoring commercial logic had negative consequences: by 1981, an accumulation of bad debts almost proved the undoing of Austria's second largest bank, the Österreichische Länderbank, and a massive infusion of capital from the government became necessary.[8]

Unlike the British public sector, which lacked central co-ordination and was (apart from steel and coal) prevalently a public utilities system, the Austrian stateholding system resembled the Italian: state property was controlled by a public holding company, the ÖIAG (Österreichische Industrieverwaltung AG), which supervised over two hundred nationalized enterprises. With this instrument at its disposal, the governing party could exercise considerable authority over both manufacturing and banking. Since the state had a direct say on wages in manufacturing, agreements with the trade unions on an incomes policy were more credible. Furthermore, the expansion of the public sector could be manipulated in order to maintain a high level of employment. Thus, between 1973 and 1983, redundancies in the state sector were half those in the private sector.[9] As we shall see later, a similar policy was adopted in Sweden and Italy. It is a common misconception to view an overmanned public sector as necessarily a Bad Thing. In real life, and this does occasionally include economics, it is wise not to reason so presumptively. For instance, during the recovery of 1966 and 1967, the labour-bloated Austrian public sector had a distinct advantage over its German private sector rivals, in that it could expand production on the basis of the existing workforce, thus rapidly exploiting new market opportunities. Comparable German

firms, which had slimmed down thanks to expensive and laborious redundancies, were less able and more reluctant to do the same.[10]

Another political asset of the SPÖ was that it could rely on a firm
understanding with the trade unions. Incomes policy never appeared, as in
Britain and some other countries, as an emergency measure aimed at blocking
wage increases; it was a central feature of the *Sozialpartnerschaft* (social
partnership) which has characterized the management of the economy since
1945. It had thus become part and parcel of political life, to be used
continuously, whether during the period of post-war reconstruction, the
subsequent capitalist boom, or the ensuing worldwide recession. It could not
be seen as a political device to force workers to pay for the consequences
of the recession. Austria's incomes policy required a highly centralized trade
union movement (the ÖGB), a feature of trade unionism also characteristic
of Sweden and Norway and, to a lesser extent, Germany, but which was
quite absent in France, Britain and Italy. Until the early 1980s, the key
economic parameters were set by the so-called Parity Commission, which
included members of the government, of the trade unions and the employers'
associations.

Like trade unions everywhere except Britain, the ÖGB remained formally
separate from the SPÖ, though the social democrats within it, organized as
a faction, were the dominant force. Around one-fifth of the Kreisky cabinet,
and one-third of socialist MPs, were trade unionists. The ÖGB was far more
than a federation of trade unions, unlike the British TUC. Members paid
their dues directly to the ÖGB, which then proceeded to fund the various
unions. The ÖGB held the strike funds and decided which strikes to support,
thus retaining control over industrial conflicts. Unlike in Sweden, the ÖGB
included both white-collar and blue-collar workers. The strength and centralization of the ÖGB enabled an effective incomes policy to be delivered, in
the belief that the government would compensate the unions by strengthening
their overall negotiating position. Austria was spared the sharp division
between public and private sector unions which considerably weakened
socialist parties elsewhere in the 1980s.

A further distinct advantage enjoyed by the SPÖ was that a number of
factors made the Austrian economy less susceptible to crisis. In the first
place, both the restrictive wages policy adopted in the mid-1960s and the
government's concurrent promotion of industrial investment had considerably
improved Austria's international competitiveness, well ahead of the oil shock.
Secondly, although the Austrian economy, like all small-scale economies, was
dependent on those of larger neighbouring countries, Austria was lucky in
having a successful neighbour, Germany, on whom it could depend – though
in the 1930s many would not have called it good luck. Furthermore, one-
fifth of its exports was directed towards the COMECON countries and
Yugoslavia, then an oasis of economic and political stability.[11] Thirdly, the
Austrian service industries (tourism, retail trade and the public sector) had

many unfilled vacancies, because it could not compete with wages paid in the manufacturing sector during the boom of the late 1960s. This later turned to Austria's advantage since, when the recession occurred, it had a major sector of the economy able to provide employment. Finally, the oil shock itself had led to a worldwide primary products boom which directly benefited the Austrian (and Swedish) raw materials industry, most of which was in state hands.[12]

The 'modernization' of Austrian socialism was achieved without excessive bloodletting. For the SPÖ, as for many other socialist parties, 'modernization' essentially meant the abandonment or toning down of the importance of the industrial working class and the class struggle between capital and labour. To some extent, this reflected the de-proletarianization of the party (a Europe-wide trend among parties of the Left): between 1970 and 1978, the percentage of working-class party members dropped from 38.3 per cent to 29.9 per cent.[13]

By 1975, a policy review process was under way. Working groups were formed to deal with internal party democracy, women, youth, leisure, and so on. Documents were produced, Catholics and liberals wooed, ideology de-emphasized.[14] Egon Matzner, who had frequently complained that the distribution of income had been left untouched,[15] produced, as head of the 1978 Programme Commission, a list of problems not yet solved by the socialists: the *Problemkatalog*.[16] The final document, 'Freedom, Equality, Justice and Solidarity', was adopted unanimously in 1978 as the new fundamental programme of the party. However, the ideological glue which held it together (the equivalent of Clause Four in the Labour Party or 'the dictatorship of the proletariat' in the PCF) – namely, the commitment to Marxism and the goal of a 'classless society' – was not modified.[17] There is substantial evidence to suggest that this policy review was meant to co-opt the left-wing factions within the party, while the government proceeded in its pragmatic manner.[18] However, it is unlikely that this kind of left-wing Bad Godesberg had any electoral effect. A poll showed that though 64 per cent of the population had heard that there was a new programme, it had only a vague idea of its contents; everyone assumed that the main pledge was to guarantee jobs and maintain full employment.[19]

To achieve modernization while maintaining a reasonable degree of party unity must rank as a success. Kreisky never used his pragmatism to eliminate long-term goals from the party's platform or to eliminate the 'new left'.[20] On the contrary, in a major speech of 12 March 1976, *Aufbruch in die 8oer Jahre* ('Towards the 1980s'), Kreisky pointed to the long-term task facing the Austrian socialists: to go beyond the *Wohlfahrtsstaat*, the welfare state.[21] Influenced by Swedish socialism, he adopted the view that the mission of social democracy had to be accomplished in three stages: first, political democracy (the suffrage); next, the welfare state; and finally, the full demo-cratization of all areas of society.[22] This commitment to long-term goals enabled the leader of the party's left faction, Josef Hindels, who regularly attacked *Sozialpartnerschaft* as another form of class collaboration, to approve heartily of Kreisky's modernization at the 1974 Party Congress, while lamenting the fact that 'this modern Austria remains a capitalist Austria'.[23] Kreisky continued to enjoy the support of the Left: at the 1979 Party Conference he paid homage to the teachings of Otto Bauer and was saluted by Hindels as a genuine Austro-Marxist.[24]

Last, but not least, the tasks of the SPÖ were facilitated by the positive political profile and personal credibility of Bruno Kreisky; the election slogan in 1975 was 'Kreisky – who else?', and in 1979 'Austria needs Kreisky'. An added bonus was the ineffectiveness of the ÖVP opposition, whose leaders were a succession of generally colourless politicians. The ÖVP shared too many of the principles of *Sozialpartnerschaft* to attack the SPÖ for excessive *étatisme*. Between 1971 and 1975, the ÖVP supported 88 per cent of all SPÖ legislation.[25] This included most of the social reforms promulgated by the SPÖ, such as the increase in statutory paid holidays from four weeks a year to five, and sexual equality legislation.[26] Between 1970 and 1975, the legal working week was gradually shortened: two hours were dropped in 1970, one in 1973, and two more in 1975. This increased total employment by 1.5 per cent.[27] Between 1972 and 1975, the government introduced free travel to school and free books for pupils. Pensions and family allowances were increased; a cash grant was given to the newly married and the newly born; and free medical examinations became available for all.[28] The 1979 SPÖ electoral manifesto emphasized that Austrians had never had it so good, were richer than ever before, were better clothed and better fed.[29]

Taken together, all these factors contributed to the overall success of Austrian socialism in the 1970s. Inflation was contained thanks to moderate unions and a strong schilling (tied to the Deutschmark after the devaluation of 1969). Growth was maintained thanks to the modernization of the private sector in co-operation with government. Full employment was preserved because the SPÖ had consistently privileged job creation programmes over budgetary deficits. It is not surprising, therefore, if Austro-Keynesianism, as this policy mix was baptized, was widely held up as a 'model' and favourably contrasted with the right-wing orthodoxy of monetarist financial rectitude prevailing elsewhere, especially in the United Kingdom.[30]

This miracle of social democracy relied on an explicitly pro-capitalist policy of promoting investment, though we must bear in mind that much of this 'capitalism' was in state hands. This does not mean that there was a rational industrial policy, except in the sense that Austria's goal was full employment.[31] There was instead a highly effective policy of short-term crisis management. As problems appeared, plenty of money was thrown at them and, for a while, the problems went away. Investment promotion was achieved with a battery of initiatives. The most important were indirect tax-based incentives – such as a system of depreciation allowances which made it virtually uneconomic for firms *not* to increase their capital stock – and a massive and expensive programme of interest rate subsidization. The financial inducements offered to individual industrialists in Austria were among the highest in the world and, of the OECD countries, only Japan and Norway (thanks to the oil boom) allocated a higher proportion of GNP to investment.[32]

High growth, low inflation, high employment – these were the gains achieved by Austria under the socialists. What were the losses? The neo-liberals had a perfectly valid case when they argued that subsidization inhibits innovation: Austrian firms in the public sector failed to modernize as much as private companies. Traditional trade union socialists have an equally valid case when they complain that capitalists gained more than workers: throughout the 1980s real wages in Austria grew at a lower rate than in most other countries.[33] Most Austrian trade unionists, however, had a definite empathy with enterprises (the state owned so many of them). They were used to negotiation rather than confrontation, were keen to obtain growth rather than distribution. It is possible that the substantial size of the state sector helped to influence the 'pro-capitalist' perspective of the trade unions – not a traditional objective of advocates of nationalization. Be that as it may, it is clear that the fate of this model of social democracy was closely related to, and contingent on, the fate of its national capitalism and this, in turn, was dependent on the fate of the international economy. This led Austrian socialists to adopt a conciliatory attitude towards the opposition though, thanks to their parliamentary majority, they could have ridden roughshod over their opponents. This points to a provisional conclusion: the Austrian model – like the better-known Swedish one – is not a model at all. It cannot be imitated or imported; it rests on an historically determined set of circumstances and institutional developments, many of which, from an externally imposed neutrality to the specific features of the Austrian economy, were not the result of the volition of socialists, or of their programmes, or even of their ability. The conservative opposition contributed to socialist achievement nearly as much as the socialists themselves. This story is thus replete with paradoxes: to the extent that the SPÖ was successful, it was because it was 'pro-capitalist' and its opponents were not anti-working class.

Nor is this a story of wondrous achievements unperturbed by setbacks. In 1983 the SPÖ lost its overall parliamentary majority. The revered Bruno Kreisky resigned (in part for health reasons) and the less charismatic Fred Sinowatz became Chancellor. There was a 'hung' Parliament. The capacity of the two main parties to control their respective sub-cultures was waning. This was a European-wide phenomenon, known as 'de-pillarization' in Holland and Belgium and 'de-alignment' in Britain. It is at this point that it becomes possible to argue that 'The SPÖ's hegemonic position within the Austrian party system ended'.[34] Sinowatz negotiated a coalition with the FPÖ or Freiheitliche Partei Österreichs (literally, 'Party for Freedom in Austria') which, in spite of its name, had long been a political home for nationalists and even pro-Nazi elements.

In 1986 there were further problems for the SPÖ: the former secretary-general of the UN, Kurt Waldheim, a conservative widely suspected of a pro-Nazi past, was elected president of the republic in spite of staunch opposition from the SPÖ. All previous federal presidents had been socialists, or, as had been the case with Rudolf Kirchschläger (elected in 1974 and 1980), SPÖ-sponsored. An extreme right-wing nationalist – Jörg Haider – took over the FPÖ. A SPÖ–FPÖ coalition was now politically impossible, and the SPÖ was forced to form a new grand coalition with the ÖVP in January 1987.

The second oil shock of 1979 made it difficult to sustain the remarkable growth rates of the 1970s. The worldwide recovery of the mid-1980s was not strong enough to absorb all of the labour force which had been sheltered by the strategy of subsidization. This, in turn, proved too expensive to sustain. But the most damaging effect of the international transformation of capital in the 1980s was the rapid loss of productivity and efficiency of Austrian firms in those traditional industries which had been the backbone of the economy: engineering and steel. The problem was no longer how to protect existing capitalism, but how to reduce the labour force in the traditional sectors and how to guide the restructuring of the industrial sector towards new products which might have a better chance of competing with the rest of the world. As unemployment rose, the Austrians were forced to step up subsidies to the public sector and to promote early retirement. Full employment remained the top priority, as the ÖVP maintained its firm commitment to it and, not willing to distance itself from the SPÖ on this issue, refrained from adopting the outright deregulation stance being canvassed throughout Europe.[35] What the Austrian socialists needed were new institutional mechanisms to achieve a regulated transition to post-golden age capitalism. This they could not do. Instead, they resorted to a partial and piecemeal dismantling of the existing system.

The new grand coalition of 1986 was at least in part motivated by a common recognition that it was necessary to cut public spending, reform the fiscal system and privatize (i.e. sell stocks and shares in the state-owned banks and national airline), in order to replenish the state coffers.[36] This followed the established rules of the *Sozialpartnerschaft*. At every stage the consent of the unions was sought; at every stage they delivered it, albeit grudgingly; and at every stage the SPÖ and the ÖVP negotiated the changes and reached agreement. Thus, the principle of consensus was maintained even though the reduction of the public sector was unlikely to bring comfort to socialist hearts.

The impetus for this scaling down was derived from the exceptionally high losses made in 1985 and 1986 by the state-owned VOEST-Alpine group, created by the government in 1973 from the merger of Alpine (in Donawitz) and VOEST (in Linz). This combine, one of the largest steel groups in the world, had not only been a casualty of the international steel crisis, but had also lost money in oil speculation, in the construction of industries in other countries, and in the attempt to diversify into new industrial sectors. All this had sapped public confidence in the state sector as a whole. In addition, many citizens had developed an increasing animosity towards these large state enterprises. They considered them to be over-protective towards their workers, granting them better job security and extra welfare benefits. Public sector firms, being in the traditional manufacturing sector, also tended to be the biggest polluters at a time when there was growing concern about the environment. After the fiasco of VOEST, privatisation was no longer a taboo subject even within the SPÖ.[37]

By 1988, Austria appeared to have recovered, though this was due as much or more to the boom in Germany than to the government's austerity measures. In any case, under pressure from the ÖVP (which was losing votes to the FPÖ) and from the Left, austerity was abandoned.[38] Little actual deregulation – the official policy of the coalition – had taken place.[39] The threat of privatization and a massive reduction of the workforce had helped the revitalization of the public sector. The political price to be paid was substantial: it was widely assumed that Austria had recovered because 'established' social-democratic policies had been abandoned. The SPÖ's traditional constituencies – such as the working class employed in the public sector – were in decline. The trade unions, widely admired for their moderation and regarded as the backbone of national stability, were now seen as less 'patriotic' because they opposed the restructuring of the public sector.[40] The importance of the Parity Commission declined. The entire system of patronage was in danger as the state was seen to be abandoning its central role in the economy. In effect, a friendly divorce between unions and SPÖ was under way. The vast restructuring of the state holding company, the breaking-up of the large conglomerates, and the consequent job losses considerably reduced the unions' political clout.[41]

The recession of the early 1990s finished off Austria's traditional industrial policy. In 1993 the integrated aluminium public sector group, Austria Metall (AMAG), collapsed, signalling the end of a state-led industrial policy. Not only the ÖVP but also the SPÖ decided to accelerate privatization. Austria's large public sector now became like an albatross round the neck of the socialists.

The political shift to the right which took place in the second half of the 1980s also affected Austrian foreign affairs. The firmly neutral bridge-building policy with the East developed by Kreisky, his Third-Worldism, his rapprochement with the Arabs: all were steadily toned down. Foreign policy turned increasingly towards the West and the European Community. Austria applied to join the EEC (acceding to it in 1995 with Sweden and Finland). At the same time, however, there was a new pull towards Eastern Europe as a consequence of the collapse of communism and the emerging market economy in Hungary, the Czech Republic and Slovakia. Austrian companies began to invest abroad, attracted by the pronounced differences in labour costs: the cost of twenty-five workers in an Austrian workshop could pay for two hundred in a factory in Slovakia.[42] By now, the SPÖ was unavoidably linked to its ÖVP partner (in spite of the latter's dismal electoral performance in 1990, down from 41 per cent in 1986 to 32). The Kreisky era was symbolically buried when, in June 1991, the SPÖ decided to change its name from 'Socialist' to 'Social Democratic'.

The achievements of the SPÖ were considerable, but must be viewed in perspective. The Austrian socialists demonstrated both a capacity to resist the trend of mounting unemployment and a determination to dominate a rapidly changing situation. Even though unemployment was at an all-time high in 1993 (7 per cent), it was still low by European standards. The Austrian socialists were not swept aside. There is no denying that they exhibited remarkable political intelligence (the rarest of commodities), but they also enjoyed the favourable circumstances and institutional advantages discussed above. The problems they faced in the late 1980s were due to objective constraints, not to an outdated devotion to an unchanging ideology, or to an incapacity to understand the modern world. In politics, as in real life, there is such a thing as a brick wall. If one cannot pull it down or walk round it, one must live with it as best one can, taking care not to collide with it. This brick wall is international interdependence; it cannot spare a small country in the heart of Europe.

Sweden

Sweden makes for an intriguing comparison with Austria. The two countries' achievements in fighting unemployment can be explained partly in terms of what they had in common. Yet each also took advantage of its distinctive features. What they shared is known: social-democratic victories, a small population, a well-established neutrality, a highly skilled workforce, strong and centralized trade unions, and non-membership of the European Community.

The divergences are no less significant: the Swedish industrial public sector was one of the smallest in Europe, the Austrian one of the largest; the Swedish krona was regularly devalued, the Austrian schilling remained an immovable vessel solidly anchored to the Deutschmark. Swedish social democracy was truly hegemonic, a virtual state ideology facing a timorous, ineffective and sharply divided opposition. Austrian socialism remained deeply committed to the *proporz* system and the consequent requirement of systematic negotiation. The SPÖ, unlike the Swedish SAP, always faced a single rival (in opposition or in coalition), ready at any moment to become an alternative government. The SAP, in spite of its political strength, was out of power from 1976 to 1982, while the SPÖ was in power (usually in coalition) throughout the 1970s and 1980s. While the SPÖ never seriously attempted to reform the Austrian state, the SAP was one of the few socialist parties in Europe which did so. The constitutional reforms that occurred between 1970 and 1974 did not always favour the Swedish social democrats: a new electoral system eliminated the Rikstag's First Chamber (indirectly elected by the regional assemblies) where the SAP was virtually assured of a majority; the term of office for the Second Chamber was reduced to three years; and a more proportional electoral system was installed, with a lower threshold for entry to Parliament.[43] Unicameralism, however, did not shift the political balance to the right but to the left, because it made the social democrats dependent on the support of the small Communist Party which, thanks to the lower threshold, became integral to the 'socialist bloc' and less prone, consequently, to the temptation of using its weight in an anti-social-democratic direction.[44]

The two countries had different class structures. Sweden was well on the way towards 'post-industrialism', while Austria in 1970–89 had an agricultural sector larger than all other central and northern West European countries, including France but excepting Finland. Austria's industrial sector, though slowly declining as elsewhere in Western Europe, remained after 1974 the second largest in the world after Germany.[45] Sweden's economy, unlike Austria's, was dominated by a few export-oriented industries such as shipbuilding and motor vehicles. Austria had a large proportion of small businesses and virtually no international companies: its largest corporation ranked 173rd among the world's top 300. Austria's industrial policy was designed to support domestic firms catering for the home market.[46] This meant that Sweden was more exposed than Austria to the vagaries of the international market.

In chapter 8 I examined the Swedish Rehn–Meidner model and its two pillars: a solidaristic and egalitarian wages policy and an active labour market policy. Though devised in the early 1950s, the model was fully operational and accepted by the main protagonists – the government and both sides of industry – only towards the beginning of the 1960s. By the early 1970s the model had proved its effectiveness, especially with regard to the labour market: it had ensured full employment, low inflation, a high degree of cyclical stability, no balance of payments troubles, no visible structural imbalances, and a satisfactory rate of growth.[47] Particularly significant for social democrats was the fact that these achievements occurred against a background of unparalleled income equality: the wage differentials among skilled workers ranked among the lowest in the world, and managers did not earn significantly larger sums than their workforce[48] – evidence, perhaps, that large salaries are a form of plunder by executives, not a precondition of economic success. The fundamental basis and the strength of the Swedish welfare state was its generous universalism: as Esping-Andersen put it, the old idea of minimalist equality was surrendered in favour of equalization at the top.[49] Thus, the Swedish welfare state attracted considerable middle-class support which benefited the SAP throughout the 1960s. The Achilles' heel of this system, however, is that it always requires heavy public expenditure.[50]

In common with others in Europe, the Swedish trade unions moved towards advocating some direct influence in the decision-making process within firms. This led to the Joint Consultation Act of 1976 (Medbestam-mandelagen, or MBL). Some regarded it as a comprehensive reform limiting managerial prerogative, though, in the end, it did not constitute a 'break-through for democracy in working life'.[51] It had been the product of trade union attempts to revitalize the movement following the jolt of wildcat strikes in the late 1960s. This rethinking produced a report on industrial democracy (see chapter 16), adopted at the 1971 Congress of the LO.[52] It failed to provoke any significant enthusiasm among workers, while arousing the hostility of employers.[53] The electoral defeat of 1976 delayed the adoption of further co-determination legislation. When the SAP returned to power in 1982, the LO was ready to implement its radical 1975 plan for controlling capitalist enterprises: the Meidner Plan on wage-earners funds (to be ex-amined in chapter 23).

Until around 1970, blue-collar wages set the pace for all other wages: the white-collar and public sector unions, whether grouped under the banner of the TCO federation or the mainstream LO, followed wages in manufacturing. In the early 1970s this pattern began to break down as wage competition reasserted itself. To prevent what could have become a wages spiral, the employers' association proposed that wages should be based on 'objective' criteria. The Swedish trade unions insisted that these could not be imposed unilaterally by the government. So opposed were they to any form of government intervention in the determination of income that they were prepared to accept any other mechanism – even one outside their direct control.

Eventually (1970), it was decided that the general level of wages would reflect that in the sector of the Swedish economy most exposed to inter-national competition – that of export, which represented one-third of the economy. Wages in the 'sheltered' sector – mainly building, retail trade, services and public administration – would follow the lead sector. This model of wage determination, known as the EFO model after the economists responsible for devising it (Gösta Edgren, Karl-Olof Faxén and Clas-Erik Odhner), clearly departed from the Rehn–Meidner model. Wages were no longer the product of negotiation, but were determined exogenously by the world market.[54] In this way Swedish wages would reflect the 'real' economy and not the strength of workers in the protected areas.[55] The effect of this move was to tie the fate of social-democratic management of the Swedish economy more tightly than ever before to the world market.

Initially, the first oil shock (1973) did not seem to affect Sweden. There was – as in Austria – a raw material export boom. At first, inflation remained within bounds. The rate of growth dropped without becoming negative.

Profits increased sharply. Real wages increased by 7.4 per cent in 1975, markedly above the EFO norms.[56] This, and the parallel increase in the employers' contribution to pension insurance, led to inflation and a rapid decline in Sweden's competitive position. The worst-hit sector of the economy was the shipbuilding industry, the third largest in the world, since the most immediate consequence of the first oil crisis was the collapse of the super-tanker market. When this recovered, it was dominated by South Korea and other newly industrialized countries.

The economic and industrial crisis coincided with a major political controversy, which brought about the first electoral defeat of the SAP since the 1930s. The Centre Party, formerly the Agrarian Party representing the farming community, had embraced, on ecological grounds, the anti-nuclear energy cause. This became the salient issue in the 1976 election campaign, which resulted in the first non-socialist government in forty-four years. It was a three-party alliance: the Conservatives (now the Moderates or Moderata samlingspartiet), the Liberals of the Folkpartiet (People's Party) and the Centre Party (Centerpartiet). The victorious bourgeois coalition was highly conscious that its victory was not due to dissatisfaction with the social-democratic model. It had spent much energy during the electoral campaign denying that they intended to put the clock back, destroy the welfare state and discontinue the policy of full employment.

While, in 1976, the British Labour government abandoned full employment (and hence social democracy), and was about to cut public spending severely, in Sweden a non-socialist centrist coalition government was determined to show that it could uphold the social-democratic agenda as well as the social democrats themselves.

The paradox did not end there. In order to defend full employment, the centrist coalition had to abandon some of the financial rectitude which had been embraced by its socialist predecessors. The krona was devalued in 1976, 1977 and again in 1981, thus eliminating the main external discipline on wage increases and restoring the international competitiveness of Swedish industrial exports such as pulp paper, iron ore and steel. The price paid was higher inflation. By the early 1980s, Swedish exporters looked to regular government devaluations rather than to union wage restraint as the source of profits. (A similar attitude prevailed in Italy where, as we shall see, an ever-devaluing lira enabled employers to maintain the international competitiveness they were losing by granting excessive wage rises.)

The so-called bourgeois government passed the first test of socialist economic management with flying colours: unlike the German and British socialist governments, they opted for full employment over inflation. The policy of job subsidization and active labour market intervention was expanded.[57] The shipyards became heavily subsidized, continuing to maintain employment but producing ships they could not sell. The ships were scrapped and the government bought the scrap metal.[58] When this policy could no longer be sustained, the coalition extended the policy initiated by the SAP in 1975 by completing the nationalization of the shipyards in 1979.[59] It did the same for the steel and raw material industries. The active labour market policy, the backbone of the Swedish model, had become very expensive: total spending on it doubled between 1975 and 1977. Without it, according to Scharpf, unemployment would have been 6.1 instead of 2.2 per cent.

The Swedish model of social democracy was not yet under threat. Full employment remained unassailable as one of the entrenched values of the system. The country seemed to be moving to the left. The bourgeois coalition was defeated in three successive elections, 1982, 1985 and 1988. In the last of these, for the first time since 1970 the SAP gained more seats than the combined total of the three bourgeois parties (156 against 152). The communists achieved their best results in twenty years (5.9 per cent). The new Green Party obtained 5.5 per cent of the vote and gained twenty members in Parliament.[60] The green issue of nuclear power was deftly defused by the SAP, helped by the enthusiasm of the Conservative Party (one of the centre's allies) for nuclear power. Popular belief in the superior economic competence of the social democrats remained undented until the end of the 1980s. In spite of the increasingly negative image of the idea of 'socialism', the electorate remained favourably disposed towards the social security system.[61] Finally, the SAP caught up with the changing *Zeitgeist*, began to backtrack on its longstanding commitment to a centralist state. In the course of the 1980s, administrative responsibilities were increasingly devolved to local authorities, while maintaining central financial control as Thatcher was doing in Britain.[62]

However, the social democrats were perfectly aware, when they returned to power in 1982, that unless they could orchestrate an economic recovery they would not be able to maintain popular support. As Arne Ruth remarked, 'Nothing fails like success. The Swedish model could not survive without the momentum of repeated accomplishment ... the promise of the future had to be constantly renewed.'[63]

The period of bourgeois government was not a parenthesis which could be ignored. The social-democratic monopoly of power had been broken without any noticeable disaster. Voters had acquired a taste for electoral mobility. The unions themselves had developed a habit of independence from government while the bourgeois parties were in power. This would not be promptly discarded.[64] Opposition had radicalized the SAP into adopting the so-called Meidner Plan, aimed at establishing some form of collective control over private capital. In the short term, the most pressing issue facing the new social-democratic administration was that they could not restore the economy, disrupted by the second oil crisis, with massive subsidies, as they had done previously. They opted for a rapid export-led growth by devaluing the krona by a hefty 16 per cent. This seemed to work and was helped by a fall in oil prices which facilitated the international recovery of the late 1980s. The budget deficit decreased and turned into a surplus. Sweden's

international competitiveness further increased between 1986 and 1988, thanks
to the weakness of the dollar, which the krona had shadowed. This economic
buoyancy did not last long. By 1989 the Swedish social democrats were
facing a serious decline in popularity due to the deteriorating economic
situation. Their worst electoral defeat followed in 1991 when their share of
the vote plummeted to below 40 per cent for the first time since the 1930s.
Yet they returned to power, once again, in 1994.

As in Austria, the public sector became the main instrument for absorbing
labour. But, unlike in Austria, the Swedish economy did not have a large
state-owned manufacturing branch, so public services took on the role of
job creation agency. Government employment rose by a third between 1973
and 1985.[65] Much of this was achieved through a massive expansion of female
labour, further facilitated by a change in tax assessment legislation which
favoured two-earner households. Thus, there was a significant shift in the
composition of the Swedish working class: manufacturing industry began to
lose its dominant position; there were more female wage-earners; the weight
of the state sector increased; and there was a growth in part-time labour.
Much of the increase in women's employment was associated with an expansion of the welfare state. The most significant development was the growth
of child-care arrangements. This offered more women the possibility of
entering the workforce, while at the same time providing more jobs for
women as carers in kindergartens. The outstanding mobilization of women
in the workforce became one of the central features of the Swedish model.
The labour force participation of women rose from 50 per cent in 1960 to
75 per cent in 1980, the highest within the OECD, where the overall average
in 1980 was 50 per cent.[66] In so doing, Sweden came closer than any other
country to producing a new concept of full employment: the full employment
of all those who wanted to work, and not just of the male labour force. As
if to emphasize this conceptual shift, the 1975 programme of the SAP did
not use the term 'full employment', but the term 'work for all' – meaning a
long-term employment policy aimed at achieving a steady rise in the number
of job opportunities.[67]

The price paid for this was an increased differential between wages in the
public and private sectors, which effectively marked the end of the 'solidaristic'
wages policy even in its reformed EFO version. EFO was now a dead letter.
The wage drift (i.e. locally agreed rates) in the private sector had accelerated,
responding to the fact that national negotiations between employers and
unions had resulted in blue-collar industrial workers receiving less than public
sector workers. The latter had become wage leaders.[68] With wage drift becoming widespread, the centralized bargaining system was no longer *the*
foremost mechanism for fixing wages. By the late 1980s, 60 per cent of the
income of blue-collar workers in private industry was attributable to wage
drift.[69] Between 1983 and 1988, the centralized bargaining system disintegrated
as the large white-collar industrial unions and Metall, the metalworkers' union,

Table 17.1 Government employment as a percentage of total employment

	1974	1980	1990
Denmark	22.2	28.3	30.5
Finland	13.8	17.8	22.4
France	n/a	20.0	22.6
Italy	13.4	14.5	15.5
Japan	6.3	6.7	6.0
Norway	19.0	23.2	27.7[a]
Sweden	24.8	30.3	31.7
UK	19.6	21.1	19.2
USA	16.1	15.4	14.4
West Germany	13.0	14.6	15.1

Note: [a] 1989 figure.
Source: OECD, Financial Times, 15 March 1993.

negotiated separately.[70] In April 1988 the unions accepted a deal which provided a major role for local bargaining based on individual merit and labour market conditions, thus establishing an important break in the forty-year-old centralized bargaining system.[71]

It was inevitable that the government would try to intervene directly in wages. The recalcitrant unions agreed to enter into a kind of social contract, the so-called Rosenbad meetings of 1984–85, to contain their wage demands within stated limits. This proved particularly difficult to enforce in the state sector: in 1986 one and a half million public sector workers took part in one of Sweden's worst labour disputes.[72] High public sector employment had been one of the unintended results of the Swedish model and proved to be one of the causes of its downfall. Sweden's post-industrial, public sector middle class was beholden to the social democrats, but had none of the traditional political attachments of the working class.

The growth in part-time work affected many other countries, especially in the 1980s. In the UK and the USA, this occurred mainly in the private sector; in Italy, in the private black economy; in Sweden and the other Scandinavian countries (including Finland), it was achieved by public sector expansion as the figures in Table 17.1 demonstrate.

This has more than merely technical significance. Part-time employment in the private sector is far less remunerative than the equivalent in the public sector. In the part-time private sector, employers are strong, unions weak, regulations more difficult to enforce; in the public sector, unions are relatively strong, the employer is the state and therefore more responsive to public pressures and more insulated from competition. In practice, part-time workers in the British, Italian and American private sectors help to subsidize, through their dismal wages, that part of the economy protected by unions and regulation. In the Scandinavian countries, the growth in part-time employment was financed by taxpayers. It was not cheap: by the mid-1980s, the marginal rate of income tax for the average Swedish worker was 64 per cent.[73]

Thus, the pursuit of full employment was doubly constrained: by the ability of Scandinavian capitalism to compete in the international economy to achieve rates of growth compatible with a high level of public expenditure; *and* by the willingness of taxpayers to tolerate a high tax burden. It was not accidental that the first significant anti-tax, populist parties to appear in Europe were in Scandinavian countries such as Mogens Glistrup's Fremskridtspartiet (Progress Party), which became the second largest party in Denmark in 1973 (having failed to obtain any seats in 1971).

A wider problem was presented by the difficulty of measuring productivity in public services. This sector coincides, approximately, with a type of economic activity which William Baumol, in a celebrated article, identified as 'the non-progressive sector'. He distinguished between a sector in which productivity increased cumulatively as technology developed, thus compensating for rising wages, and a non-progressive sector, in which this offset would be much smaller. New and better machinery would increase the productivity of bottled drink manufacturers, but the productivity of a barber would not increase so rapidly over the years.[74] If a high level of employment is secured by expanding the public sector, it follows that an increasing proportion of GNP is produced by a sector of activity which is not responsive to market stimuli and where productivity changes are slow or cannot be measured.[75]

Sweden's dependency on the vicissitudes of the international economy increased remarkably throughout the 1980s as the social democrats – like neo-liberals everywhere – dismantled the system of foreign exchange controls, in place since the Second World War, which restricted capital transactions with other countries. In so doing, the SAP acknowledged that controls had become far less effective in a world dominated by multinational firms and international capital markets.[76] By the mid-1980s, another of the central strategic conditions for the old Swedish model had disappeared: the international space for political autonomy. Sweden was forced to conform to the restrictive policies of leading countries.[77] By 1991, social democrats had reformed the tax system and applied to join the European Community. By 1993, in the second year of a 'bourgeois' government, Sweden had become the home of a battered model of social democracy. The paragon of full employment by now had an unemployment rate of 13 per cent of the workforce.[78] Rapidly deteriorating public finances led to cuts in unemployment benefits (though they remained a generous 80 per cent of salary), higher health care charges, and much stricter sick leave rules. A major shift occurred in the organization of the national health service, away from the centralized rational planning model, towards an internal market which would boost the power of doctors.[79] In the autumn of 1991, the SAP dropped its opposition to private child-care and accepted the principle of private, profit-oriented social services under the guise of recognizing the need for greater 'individual opportunity'.[80] By 1993, in preparation for the following year's election, the social democrats had given up the possibility of a return to full employment unless Sweden became a member of the European Union and there was a co-ordinated reflation.[81] Nevertheless, Sweden was still leading Europe in welfare provision – for instance, by retaining a universally available child day-care provision and generous maternity and paternity leave.[82]

The presence of multinational companies impinged on socialists in different ways in different countries. In the 1950s and 1960s domestic mass consumption had helped the establishment of a strong home-based manufacturing industry. By 1990, the home market had become too small and many Swedish firms became multinational.[83] Swedish socialists were now facing a less 'national' capitalism, though many were still Swedish-based in terms of the workforce employed. Volvo's export drive was substantial, but most of its workers were in Sweden. By 1993, however, the internationalization of Volvo was complete, even though its institutional shareholders opposed a merger with Renault (whose impending privatization heralded the beginning of the end for a 'national' French car manufacturing sector).

Holland

Belgium and Holland, like Austria and Sweden, conducted their political affairs on the basis of a considerable consensus, a system political scientists call consociationalism. The Dutch Social and Economic Council (Sociaal-Economische Raad or SER), consisting of representatives from government, trade unions and employers, as well as government-appointed experts, was the counterpart of the Austrian Parity Commission and of the Belgian Central Economic Council (CEC). In spite of these institutions, the Belgian and Dutch employment records do not match those of Austria or Sweden. Thus, there is little evidence that an understanding between political parties, or the 'two sides of industry', or the 'social partners' somehow ensures a proper balance between anti-inflationary and pro-employment policies.

In both Holland and Belgium (as in Austria and Sweden and, indeed, almost everywhere else) consensus prevailed in the 1970s, but declined throughout the 1980s, as did trade union strength and influence.

In Holland, as in the rest of Europe with the exception of France, the situation in the 1970s appeared favourable to the Left – if obtaining office at the end of the golden age of capitalism can be said to be a good thing (socialists have never expected, wrongly, to be saved by capitalist success). The PvdA (the Dutch Labour Party) had returned to power in 1973, after fifteen years of opposition briefly interrupted in the mid-1960s. A PvdA prime minister, Joop den Uyl, headed a broad coalition which included the Christian democrats. The cultural changes of the late 1960s induced in

Holland a process of deconfessionalization or *ontkerkelijking*. Religious parties lost ground. The aggregate vote of the three Christian parties decreased from 50 per cent in 1959 to 31 per cent in 1972.[84] Between 1961 and 1975, the proportion of Catholics attending Sunday mass declined from 71 to 33 per cent.[85] Various national censuses indicated that the percentage of those stating no religious preference increased by 5 per cent between 1960 and 1971.[86]

The decrease in the importance of religion in politics had an effect on the trade union movement. The Catholic trade union federation NKV – but not the Protestant Christian Trade Union – merged with the socialist federation in 1976, forming the Netherlands Trade Union Federation. By 1980, the Catholic Party and the two larger Protestant parties had decided to bury their differences and merge, forming the Christen Democratisch Appèl. The collapse of confessional dominance was 'the most dramatic event in modern Dutch politics'.[87] The distinctive 'pillarization' or segmentation of Dutch society was breaking down.

The Dutch welfare state was one of the world's most advanced, rivalling the Swedish in the breadth of its coverage.[88] The Dutch system was a product not of a hegemonic social democracy, but of the dominance of Christian parties prepared to develop generous welfare systems in times of prosperity, though not necessarily in periods of recession.[89]

In the coalition system which prevailed in Dutch politics, electoral success was far less important than the ability to forge alliances. The PvdA's share of the vote in the 1970s and 1980s was low by European standards, but slightly better than in the previous two decades. In the 1950s and 1960s the PvdA had oscillated between a high of 32.7 in 1956 and a low point of 23.6 per cent in 1967. It then climbed steadily to 24.6 per cent in 1971, to 27.3 in 1972, 33.8 in 1977, dipped to 28.3 in 1981, to climb up again to 30.4 in 1982 and 33.3 per cent in 1986.

Two major problems faced the 1973–77 PvdA-led government. In the first place it was forced to share power with the main Catholic Party. This party had in the past pursued pro-welfare state policies, but was not wholeheartedly committed to full employment. Its welfarism was permeated by a paternalistic outlook which expressed itself in a deeply conservative attitude towards women's employment. Holland's female labour force participation rate was one of the lowest in Europe.[90] The second problem facing Joop den Uyl's administration was that the Dutch economy was heavily exposed to international competition, while the public enterprise sector was too small to serve (as in Austria) as an instrument of macro-economic strategy (for instance, to combat unemployment).[91] Holland was the home of some of the largest multinationals in the world, but much of its workforce was elsewhere: a 1990 UNCTAD report ranked the Anglo-Dutch transnational corporations Royal Dutch Shell, Philips Electronics and Unilever first, ninth and eleventh in the world, respectively, in terms of foreign assets.[92] Foreign companies seeking access to the wider European Community often invested in Holland and Belgium, while those investing in Sweden and Austria did so because they were interested in the Austrian and Swedish markets.[93] The Dutch could not use the Swedish and Italian ploy of competitive devaluation, since theirs was fundamentally a 'transit' economy, importing half-finished goods which it then re-exported. This meant that instead of devaluing the currency, the Dutch government had to do the opposite. To reassure the private sector, it anchored the guilder to the Deutschmark and followed its upward path.

In this situation the incoming PvdA-led coalition government, to contain costs and restore profitability, resorted to an incomes policy. The Special Powers Act of January 1974 gave the government authority to regulate prices, wages, dividends, redundancies, working hours and foreign labour contracts.[94] In practice this was a temporary device to control wages. However, no agreement was reached with the unions the following year. When it came to the crunch, corporatism did not work in spite of the government's conspicuous attempt to have a social policy: it extended social welfare, introducing new supplementary measures, and expanded disability payments. Wage-related social benefits were indexed to the average wage and no longer to the minimum wage. The trade unions proposed to deal with unemployment by reducing working hours, introducing job-sharing schemes, and creating new part-time jobs in the public sector. The employers, supported by the Christian parties, wanted to eliminate labour market rigidities, not increase them. The PvdA, under pressure from the strong young leftist group Nieuw Links (the New Left) to democratize the party, completed the passage of long delayed proposals for changes in land-ownership, and introduced co-determination, profit-sharing and investment controls in industry.[95] As a result, the PvdA-led coalition broke down in 1977, though, in practice, the turn to the right had started after 1975–76 when inflation reached double figures and unemployment doubled. The end of full employment in Holland marked a real watershed in post-war economic policy – as it did in Britain. Afterwards, the priority of successive governments was to contain inflation and expand the private sector, while restricting public sector growth.[96]

In the elections of 1977 the PvdA gained ten seats, but was unable to reconstruct a coalition with the Christian parties, which formed a government led by the Catholic A. A. M. van Agt with the Liberals. The PvdA did succeed in re-entering the ruling coalition in 1981, but this was short-lived: Labour could not stomach either the planned austerity measures or the proposed installation of Cruise missiles on Dutch soil. The economic situation had deteriorated sharply, with growth rates in 1981 at an all-time low (minus 1.4 per cent) when a growth rate of 4.5 per cent would have been necessary to pay for the increasing demands which the unemployed were making on the welfare support system.[97] There was a massive loss in terms of trade, a decline in profitability, and the greatest downturn in real capital investment of the OECD.[98] Without the petro-guilders gained from the country's massive, but declining gas reserves, the situation would have been even worse. In the 1980s, when energy prices were low again, the state treasury lost a major source of revenue.[99]

The road was now open for a final rupture with the consensus of the post-war years. A new conservative government, led by the Christian democrat Ruud Lubbers in alliance with the increasingly neo-liberal Liberal Party (VVD), swept into power in 1982. It was endorsed by the voters for a second term in 1986, when Liberal electoral losses were compensated by Christian democrat gains. The latter became the largest party in Parliament, supplanting the PvdA in spite of the latter's gain of five seats. The Lubbers government reduced the level of social benefits and the minimum wage, though unemployment benefits remained the highest in Europe (three times those of the UK in 1986).[100] It de-indexed wages (as in Italy) and disposed of hallowed notions of consensual politics by cutting public sector wages by 3 per cent without consulting either unions or employers. This was the only Western government able and willing to take such action. Its task was facilitated by one of the lowest levels of trade unionization in Europe, just over a quarter of the workforce, and by the continuing decline of union membership.[101] These policies constituted a partial retrenchment of the welfare state.[102] Lubbers cut public sector pay and freed the private sector unions from the indexation mechanism. Workers in this sector were now free to achieve higher wages than their equivalents in the public sector.[103] The free-for-all wage bargaining system being to their decisive advantage, private sector workers became de facto supporters of the turn to the right – like their counterparts in Britain. The government explicitly expressed its willingness to tolerate high unemployment levels, which remained at around 14 per cent throughout the 1980s.[104] While in Sweden and Austria the public sector was used as a container for surplus labour (thus keeping unemployment figures down), the Dutch 'technique' was similar to that used, consciously or unconsciously, in Italy: a massive growth in the 'disabled' population. In the ten years prior to 1973 the number of registered disabled had increased by two-thirds; between 1973 and 1982, it doubled again. By January 1987, it appeared that 13.2 per cent of the population was in fact 'disabled' – and this in a country with one of the best welfare systems in the world.[105] Those rendered disabled through work – there were nearly a million people in this category in Holland – could obtain 75 per cent of their salary until their retirement. In spite of the efforts of the Lubbers governments of the 1980s, the turn to the right in Holland had little impact on the size of state spending on welfare. The social security system remained, as before, one of the most generous in Europe. Drastically cutting welfare spending became an uphill task, in part because the increase in unemployment pushed spending up, but mainly because of extensive popular support for welfare support directly related to its universalistic provisions. One in six workers was employed by the government, while 55 per cent of the population lived in rented houses and benefited from the widespread system of rent controls.[106] An inherently unstable coalition government, in which the main party was inspired by Christian principles, found further drastic welfare cuts politically impossible. By 1989 the PvdA, led by Wim Kok, had managed to return to power but, by then, it had been forced on to the defensive. Nevertheless, the OECD was still urging the recalcitrant Dutch to cut taxes and curb generous income transfer payments, imposing tighter criteria for claiming jobless benefits.[107] Even Holland was not left unscathed by the prevailing mood for the market-ization of everything. Following the suggestions of the Dekker Committee, market forces were to be introduced into the health service (as in the UK); private health insurers were to be invited to compete with public health insurance funds for the favour of the public.[108] In 1994 the issue of state benefits was nowhere nearing its solution. An electoral earthquake (May 1994) brought about the first government in the history of modern Holland without the Christian democrats; its longest-serving prime minister, Ruud Lubbers, had already announced his resignation. Led by the Labour leader Wim Kok, it included the conservative-liberals of the Volkspartij voor Vrijheid en Democratie (VVD, the People's Party for Freedom and Democracy) and the left-liberals of Democraten '66, originally a radical-democratic party campaign-ing for parliamentary reforms. The aim of the government, according to its published programme, was a thorough 'market-led' reform of the social security system in order to create employment, on the assumption that the generous benefit system constituted a major disincentive to work.[109] As if to underline the continuing importance of social security as an issue, two new parties repres-enting the pensioners gained seven seats out of 150.

Belgium

In percentage terms the Belgian socialists, since 1978 organizationally divided between the Flemish Belgische Socialistische Partij (BSP) and the Franco-phone Parti Socialiste Belge (PSB), were as weak as the Dutch, but had been in office more frequently as members of a succession of coalition govern-ments. In 1981 the PSB had become the first party in French-speaking Wallonia. In 1987 the combined vote of the Flemish and Walloon socialist parties was 30.6 per cent, larger than that of the Social Christians (27.5 per cent) who had been the majority party since the war and had dominated Belgian politics after 1958.

Otherwise, the vicissitudes of the Left in Belgium were comparable to those of the Dutch socialists: a political advance in the 1970s followed by a series of defeats in the 1980s, as the whole political system swayed to the right.

During the 1970s, it proved impossible to contain labour costs adequately. The most visible consequence of the oil shock was a cost-push inflation facilitated by a system of wage indexation. Between 1971 and 1980, real wages in Belgium increased at a higher rate than anywhere else in the OECD, an average of 4.6 per cent a year against 4.2 per cent in Japan, 3.2 per cent on average in the rest of the EC, 2.3 per cent in UK, and 1 per cent in USA.[110] The Belgian manufacturing sector faced growing labour costs and a consequent loss of international competitiveness. These high labour costs squeezed profits; workers were laid off, while depressed demand at a world level prevented Belgian exporters from passing on wage costs by increasing prices. Market shares were lost.[111]

As the budget deficit grew disproportionately, a new Social Christian-led coalition was formed in 1977, which included the PSB/BSP led by Guy Spitaels (in opposition since 1974). Unemployment was still seen as the major issue, however, and a number of special programmes were developed, from early retirement schemes to apprenticeships for the young and the fully subsidized hiring of unemployed persons. It has been calculated that without these programmes, the unemployment rate – over 10 per cent throughout the 1980s – would have been five percentage points higher, as in Sweden.[112] To contain labour costs the centre-left government imposed a wage freeze in 1980, justified by Spitaels on the grounds that it was temporary and did not apply to low wage-earners.[113]

Until then consensualism had prevailed in Belgian politics, even though the linguistic conflict between Flemish speakers and Francophones had grown to an intensity without parallel in Western Europe, quite incomprehensibly to outsiders. Along with most of the other Belgian parties, the socialists had split in 1978 along ethno-linguistic lines. But they faced specific problems. Their working-class base was in Wallonia, home of the first industrial revolution in continental Europe and of some of the traditional industries – above all, steel – which suffered severely in the recession of the 1970s. Flanders, traditionally more agricultural, grew much more in the post-1945 period and – in the 1960s and 1970s – became the centre of post-industrial growth and new technologies. There, the average rate of growth was 5.3 per cent in 1966–75 and 2.7 per cent in the period 1975–84, while the corresponding rates for Wallonia were 3.9 and 1.6 per cent.[114] Consequently, unemployment grew faster in Wallonia than in Flanders. Flemish taxpayers, few of whom inclined towards socialism, took exception to the growing public expenditure on unemployment benefits which appeared to favour the French-speakers. Flemish politicians, including the socialist leader Karel van Miert, resented the massive subsidies paid to the large, mainly state-owned steel industry, the giant Cockerill Sambre. They campaigned against the system of central financing which had hitherto prevailed and lobbied for direct control over resources. Once the concept of devolving state aid to the three regions of Flanders, Wallonia and Brussels had won the day, the socialist leader Guy Spitaels, who had at first opposed devolution and left the government (1980–81), performed a U-turn and espoused economic federalism: each linguistic group had to be in charge of its own economic future.[115] The recriminations between the two socialist parties multiplied. Spitaels became stridently pro-Walloon and absorbed the predominantly separatist left-wing Rassemblement Wallon. In 1987 he triumphantly obtained 44 per cent of the vote in Wallonia, one of the best results for any socialist party during the 1980s.[116] In this climate of bitter division between French and Flemish speakers, the regions were given increasingly wide powers: planning, housing, the environment, economic policy and culture. In 1987, when Brussels was established as the third self-governing region, education was transferred to the language communities. In 1993 major constitutional changes were approved, which transformed the country into a real federal state with separate, directly elected parliaments for Flanders and Wallonia (as had been the case for Brussels since 1987).[117]

That economic considerations were never detached from the irresistible impetus of linguistic nationalism is demonstrated by developments in the largely state-owned steel industry. In the early 1980s, Cockerill Sambre was thoroughly restructured by plant closures and new investment. By 1985 its workforce was less than one-third the 1974 level, although it was still no nearer to profitability. This Flemish-inspired move backfired. Steel was not the only troubled industry. The remaining so-called national industrial sectors – shipbuilding, glass and textiles, and, above all, coal – were similarly affected; these were mainly in Flanders. The coalmines in Limbourg in eastern Flanders, the large Kempense Steekolenmijnen complex, absorbed increasingly large subsidies.[118] It was the turn of Flemish politicians to seek, in vain, to bring back some form of national financing. The Flemish mines were 'rationalized' and 10,000 workers accepted redundancy payments. The end of consensus politics thus had profound implications, signalling not only the deepening linguistic division of the country, but also the virtual impossibility of adopting a national industrial strategy to confront the depression. The linguistic divide was no help to the cause of Belgian socialism.

The turning-point was the 1981 general election, which saw the effective victory of the Liberal Party and their newly adopted ideas of market de-regulation. The Liberals advanced from 15.5 per cent in 1978 to 21.5 per cent in 1981, while the Social Christians dropped from 36.1 per cent to 26.4 per cent. A new Christian–liberal alliance emerged and consensus politics now appeared discredited.

The new centre-right government led by the Christian democrat Wilfried Martens turned to the right just as its counterpart in Holland had done. Legislation approved on 2 February 1982 granted the government special powers until the end of the year to limit public spending, cut back on social security, and decrease labour costs by blocking the indexation of wages for a limited period. The Martens government did not hesitate to engage in a confrontation with the public sector unions.[119] The real wages of the average worker decreased by 3 per cent.

The 1980s proved to be a bitter experience for Belgian socialists. Even though their share of the poll improved, they were systematically squeezed out of all positions of power by the entente between Liberals and Christian democrats. Even though they were by far the largest party in Wallonia, they were ejected from that region's government as well as from the Flanders regional government, and even from the executive council of the small German-speaking autonomous area in eastern Belgium.[120] Only in 1988, after they had moved considerably towards the so-called 'new realism', did the two socialist parties once again join a coalition government with the Christian democratic parties and the Flemish nationalist Volksunie. In Belgium, 'new realism' was the term coined to indicate that the socialists had come to accept that the interdependency of the Belgian economy seriously constrained their policies. It is not clear why this realism should have occurred so late in the day. Since 1958 there had been massive foreign investment in Belgium; in 1971 foreign capital provided nearly 80 per cent of new investment. By 1990, sixty-two of the top one hundred firms were foreign owned, including 71 per cent of the chemical industry and 72 per cent of engineering firms.[121] De facto control of Belgian manufacturing industry had been transferred abroad well before the 'new realism'.[122] What 'new realism' meant was that the socialists had accepted the neo-liberal economic analysis of what interdependence required.

By 1988, trade unions, too, were demonstrating 'realism' by accepting laws on flexible working time described by the Financial Times as the 'most attractive in Europe' – presumably to employers.[123] Their initially strong opposition to the austerity measures of the Martens governments in the mid-1980s had failed because they were too weak in Flanders and had to struggle in an unfavourable political climate. Once again an exacerbated linguistic conflict damaged the socialists. Trade unions were weak because they reflected the divisions in Belgian society: there was a socialist union, the Fédération Générale du Travail de Belgique (or FTGB), which saw itself in opposition like 'its' party; a Catholic union, the Confédération des Syndicats Chrétiens (or CSC), de facto in government; and there was even a liberal union, the CGSLB. While the FTGB was strong in Wallonia, the larger CSC dominated in Flanders, until even the unions split along linguistic lines. This confirmed the tendency towards the formation of a 'two-speed' Belgium. Flanders, with its higher growth and productivity, fewer strikes and lower unemployment, was able to contribute 70 per cent of the country's exports,[124] and to attract direct foreign investment.

The Belgian conservatives, however, were never strong enough to eliminate the 'socialist' constraints upon them. In 1992 the socialists re-entered the coalition. The social security system was still regarded as far too generous, since it contributed decisively to the country's national budget deficit (7 per cent of gross domestic product).[125] The wage indexation system, in spite of the numerous attacks upon it, still subsisted, the last European survivor of the post-war mood of conciliation between labour and capital. Its abolition or modification was unlikely to occur without a similar consensus-seeking framework. The Right too faces powerful constraints.

The devaluation of the currency went some way towards re-establishing profitability and reducing the balance of payment deficits (more because imports were contained than because exports were enhanced). However, none of these measures reduced either unemployment or the larger than ever budget deficit.[126] No industrial policy was introduced. The three years of high productivity growth and low inflation enjoyed by the country in 1988–91 did little to contain the expense of a huge government debt equivalent to about 125 per cent of its national output. Growth was largely externally induced. The country's exports were equivalent to two-thirds of its GDP. Nearly two-thirds of them went to neighbouring Germany, Holland and France.[127] When these countries moved into recession, so did Belgium. The general assumption, in Belgium as in Holland, in Sweden as in Austria, was that all governments could do was to create conditions believed to be favourable for private manufacturing. One could bring water to the horses, but not force them to drink.

During the period of rapid growth, governments in these small countries, especially left-wing ones, expanded the public sector. When growth came to an end, the public sector was further expanded in the hope that it would stabilize the system until a recovery ensued. When the recovery failed to materialize, the governments of Belgium and Holland (and Britain) used their role as employer to contain public spending, confront the public sector unions and increase wage differentials to the advantage of the private sector. The Swedes and Austrians acted differently, using their public sector to maintain employment. In Sweden and Austria the socialists controlled the state; in Belgium and Holland they did not. Herein lies the difference. Where socialists were in power and had sufficient political strength to control the state machinery they could use it, at least temporarily, to achieve some of their objectives. Moreover, the ÖVP in Austria and the 'bourgeois' parties in Sweden shared many of the goals of the social democrats. The same was true of Belgium and Holland, but only in the 1970s.

The events of the 1980s showed that the achievement of limited social-democratic goals (high welfare benefits, full employment) depended not only on social-democratic hegemony, but also on the way in which national capital is interconnected with the wider global economy. The absence of multinationals in Austria, and the strong national basis of those in Sweden, constrained what was possible at the national level. In Belgium, the use of regional policy to prevent the collapse of employment in the mining districts of the centre of the country (in effect, the faultline between the two linguistic communities) was implemented by relying on foreign capital. As Katzenstein explained: 'Even if the Belgian government had wished to lower unemployment drastically … the option was foreclosed in a regional policy that predominantly relied on foreign and private rather than domestic and public funds.'[128]

The document *Rénover et Agir*, which Guy Spitaels introduced at the 1982 Congress of the Belgian socialists, underlined this theme: the Belgian economy was very small, it was a transit economy, its public debt was so large that no industrial policy was possible.[129] A similar analysis could have been made of Holland. Socialists in small, open economies facing the growing globalization of the world system increasingly accepted that they had to operate within powerful constraints. But was this a peculiarity of size and openness? In the age of interdependence, all Western European economies were open; none was large enough to rely on its own domestic market; all were forced to export.

All West European socialists were always dependent on the strength and structure of their own capitalist state. As capital became less anchored to specific nation-states, socialists found themselves in difficulty. When in power, they faced constraints which forced them to moderate their ambitions. When in opposition, they lost credibility or had to adopt pro-market ideas to return to office. This predicament will become more evident as I turn to examine the situation in the larger European countries, looking, first of all, at the parallel histories of the Left in Britain and West Germany: the events leading to the historic defeat of the Labour Party in the 1970s and the rise and fall of the *Modell Deutschland* of the SPD.

CHAPTER EIGHTEEN

Germany and Britain: SPD and Labour in Power

THE PRECEDING chapter illustrated the contrast between the 1970s and 1980s in four small countries. At the risk of being over-schematic, this was the discernible trend: during the 1970s, there was a 'social-democratic' attempt to return to high productivity and maintain full employment through co-operation with the trade unions and the utilization of the public sector to absorb labour; the underlying ideological assumption was that market failures had to be treated with a strong dose of political intervention. In the 1980s politics moved in the opposite direction. Deregulation, privatization, the containment of public spending became the passwords. The overarching goal was the containment of inflation, with little regard for employment. This swing of the pendulum correlated loosely with an effective shift in political power from left to right, except in Southern Europe (to be dealt with later). Thus, the Austrian socialists ruled on their own in the 1970s, but were forced into coalition in the 1980s. The Belgian and Dutch socialists were in power for some of the crucial years in the 1970s, but were out of office for most of the 1980s. In Sweden there appears to be a mismatch: the SAP was in opposition between 1976 and 1982, but the bourgeois coalition upheld the basic principles of the Swedish model; while the SAP, back in office after 1982, was forced on to the defensive. A similar shift took place in Britain and Germany.

In 1972 the SPD–FDP coalition government led by Willy Brandt was re-elected. The SPD increased its share of the vote and, for the only time in post-war history, overtook the CDU. In Britain the Labour Party was losing working-class votes, but the SPD was making inroads into the Catholic working-class vote, particularly in North–Rhine–Westphalia, the largest *Land*.[1]

In Britain it looked at first as if the Conservative government led by Edward Heath, elected in 1970, was set to break with the post-war consensus by adopting an anti-interventionist policy. The country, declared John Davies, the secretary of state for trade, in a famous speech, needed to gear its policies to 'the great majority of people who are not lame ducks, who are quite capable of looking after their own interests', and who did not live 'in a soft sodden morass of subsidized incompetence'.[2] Between June 1970 (when the Conservatives took over) and February 1972 – that is, well before the oil crisis for which Arabs and other foreigners could be blamed – unemployment had increased from 600,000 to one million. The cause of this rise was probably the delayed effect of the deflationary policies of Roy Jenkins, the previous Labour chancellor of the exchequer, rather than the reduction in government aid to 'lame ducks'. Nevertheless, Edward Heath reacted in a way which later became unfashionable in Conservative circles: he became, in the words of an adviser, 'emotionally concerned with unemployment'.[3] As a result, the government threw public money at the ailing Upper Clyde Shipbuilders, took over Rolls-Royce, marshalled an interventionist Industry Act through Parliament (1972), and created the Manpower Services Commission, a tripartite body, under the 1973 Education and Training Act. This last measure should be seen – in retrospect – as one of the last 'socialist' acts passed by the House of Commons. To this I would add the egalitarian effects, in terms of earnings differentials, of Stages 2 and 3 of Heath's incomes policy. It looked as if the post-war consensus was unassailable. The Conservatives appeared to be unwilling to become the first government to renounce full employment.

Understandably, they took interventionism seriously and believed that it had to be extended to the trade unions. These too would have to submit to regulation and accept wage restraint. The subsequent confrontation with the unions, especially with the National Union of Mineworkers, led to the downfall of the government. At the time, this was seen as a major victory for the Left and for the unions in particular. The Conservatives had fought the general election asking, 'Who runs the country, the unions or the government?' They were defeated by a narrow margin. Some have claimed that Heath's defeat at the polls 'represented the most spectacular single victory of labour over capital since the beginnings of working-class organization in Britain ... the only time in modern European history that an economic strike has precipitated the political collapse of a government'.[4]

Yet the defeat of the Conservatives did not mark a significant Labour advance. Though the Tories polled a dismal 37.9 per cent in the first election of 1974, they still remained ahead of Labour by 0.7 per cent; only the vagaries of the British electoral system gave Wilson a plurality of seats and enabled him to form a minority government. Wilson had been helped by the uncalled for, but unrejected, support of the anti-European nationalist Tory, Enoch Powell, who urged like-minded people to vote for Labour on anti-EEC grounds, rather than for the Europhile Heath. Later that year, in the October election, Labour moved ahead of the Conservatives (39.2 to 35.8 per cent – the Tories' worst result up to that time), but was condemned to run the country with a tiny majority of seats rapidly reduced to naught by a string of by-election defeats. In March 1976, Harold Wilson, weary of power, resigned. For reasons not related to Wilson's resignation, there was a run on the pound. The Parliamentary Labour Party was faced with the task of selecting the new prime minister. Jim Callaghan, a shrewd but visionless product of conservative Labourism, prevailed over the ineffectual Michael

Foot, still the darling of the Left and the antithesis of Callaghan (plenty of vision and no cunning). Over the succeeding months, the new prime minister tackled, not unsuccessfully, difficult negotiations with the International Monetary Fund (IMF), whose politics was not favourable to the Labour Party. However, it was in the battle against its putative allies, the trade unions, that Callaghan and his government met their nemesis.

Only much later did it become apparent that in vanquishing Heath and his followers, and then irreversibly damaging the Labour government of Callaghan, the unions had been instrumental in promoting the ascendancy of a new breed of Conservatives. The chief lesson the new Thatcher government drew from all this was that a successful anti-inflation policy could not rely on co-operation with the unions.

The incoming Labour administration of 1974–79 continued the employment policies of its Conservative predecessor. It expanded job creation schemes, rescued ailing firms, extended training programmes. These policies, however, were implemented in conjunction with a pro-cyclical strategy of cuts in public spending.

There is a substantial similarity in the manner in which these contradictory policies – creating jobs and training for jobs, while deflating the economy to contain inflation – were pursued in Britain and Germany. Economists had hitherto assumed that inflation and unemployment could not simultaneously increase. Politicians faced with both maladies used traditional remedies for both, having wrongly assumed that stagflation was impossible. Strategic coherence was never achieved: industrial policies aimed at training people co-existed with budgetary policies which eliminated jobs.

In Britain, Labour hoped that the unions would follow the example of their German counterparts and exercise restraint in wage negotiations. This 'social contract', as it was called, was reasonably successful at first. In 1976 a run on the pound triggered by balance of payments problems and the perception of an excessively large budget deficit led to massive cuts in public spending and the abandonment of full employment. The social contract was in tatters by the time the 1978–79 strikes paved the way for the victory of Margaret Thatcher's New Model Conservative Party and the radical neo-liberal experiment of the 1980s.

The acknowledged turning-point in Labour's economic policy occurred in 1976 when a run on sterling led to heavy borrowing from the IMF. The loans required the government to cut public spending. In a situation of mounting unemployment, Labour ministers had to explain that deflation was the way forward. Keynesian orthodoxy, still Labour's main economic doctrine, dictated the opposite remedy, but only on the assumption that the principal enemy was unemployment and not inflation, and that the effects of reflation would not be excessively deleterious to the balance of payments. This doctrine had increasingly come under fire after it became evident that it was unable to cure stagflation. Monetarism was becoming fashionable. It was easy to grasp, did not involve a confrontation with the unions, put the blame on something impersonal and 'commonsensical' ('there is too much money around, that's why there is inflation'). Journalists, rather than academics (who are hardly ever read by busy politicians), were the main proponents of the new gospel: the most influential were Peter Jay of *The Times* and Samuel Brittan of the *Financial Times*.[5]

Keynesianism was formally abandoned by Labour's prime minister, Callaghan, when, in a famous (or infamous) speech, he told the Labour Party Conference gathered at Blackpool on the morning of 28 September 1976:

> The cosy world we were told would go on for ever, where full employment would
> be guaranteed by a stroke of the Chancellor's pen, cutting taxes, deficit spending
> – that cosy world is gone ... what is the cause of unemployment? Quite simply
> and unequivocally it is caused by paying ourselves more than the value of what
> we produce. There are no scapegoats ... We used to think that you could spend
> your way out of a recession and increase employment by cutting taxes and boost-
> ing Government spending. I tell you in all candour that that option no longer
> exists.[6]

Callaghan may have made this speech with the intention of establishing his credentials of financial rectitude with foreign bankers and the Americans, rather than to signify a major departure from long-standing policies.[7] Nevertheless, in the words of one of his closest advisers, Bernard Donoughue, 'The broad policies which are now characterized as "Thatcherism", together with the now familiar language, were in fact launched in primitive form at Mr. Callaghan in 1976 from the Treasury, from the Bank, and, above all from the IMF and sections of the US Treasury.'[8] There was one fundamental difference between Thatcherism and Callaghan's policies: the latter, while cutting public spending and creating more unemployment, was still pursuing the (Keynesian) policy of containing wages through a compact with the unions.

Callaghan's speech had been written by his son-in-law, the economic journalist Peter Jay, who in the columns of *The Times* and elsewhere had been one of the most vociferous exponents of the new 'monetarist' doctrine.[9] The voice of the Left, led by Michael Foot and Tony Benn, and hence of that of the New Cambridge School and radical economists like Stuart Holland, was heard less and less. The fundamental reason why this happened is that the left-wingers had little support in the country at large, in the trade union movement, among Labour MPs, or in the media. They were substantially defeated when they fought a rearguard action against membership of the European Economic Community, even after Wilson had renegotiated the terms of entry. This useless battle, which ended in a rout for the Labour Left when a convincing majority of the electorate backed membership in a referendum, engaged much of their time and emotions. From 1975 (the EEC referendum) through to April 1976 (Callaghan's election in place of Wilson) and the end of 1976 (the negotiations with the IMF), the Labour Left lost all the battles they fought. For the remainder of the life of the government, they remained a marginal force.

In March 1977 the government lost its majority and was forced to make a tactical pact with the Liberals. The Labour cabinet had to listen to the views of Liberal MPs to ensure that they would not bring the government down. They did not need to do the same with the more numerous left-wing Labour MPs who were, in practice, unable to use their strength to blackmail the government. As for the Labour Party, its Conference and its National Executive Committee, they were ignored by the government for the entire period. In 1976, the NEC published a Labour Party programme quite at odds with the government. The nefarious words 'incomes policy' (or their equivalent) never appeared, even though controlling incomes was the keystone of the government's strategy.[10] This extraordinary split between party and government, quite unparalleled anywhere else in Europe, would be at the root of much of the internal strife within the Labour Party when it returned to opposition.

For years the Labour Left had been discontented with Keynesianism, correctly considered to be the ideology of right-wing social democrats such as Crosland.[11] But when the tocsin of Keynesianism rang throughout Europe, it was to herald the advent of so-called monetarism, not the surge of a new radical economics. Though Keynesianism was still upheld in Britain by distinguished economists who had been advising Labour for years, such as Nicholas Kaldor and members of the New Cambridge School (Wynne Godley, Francis Cripps and others), and by a majority of academics, in the higher reaches of government it had fewer adherents than in the past. Bernard Donoughue, head of the Policy Unit at 10 Downing Street, who advised Harold Wilson and James Callaghan, had reached the conclusion that Keynesianism was irrelevant to the modern world.[12] Denis Healey, chancellor of the exchequer from 1974, had stopped considering himself a Keynesian as early as 1975.[13]

No similar U-turn occurred in Germany. Historically, Keynesian fine-tuning had had few proponents apart from Karl Schiller in 1966–67. The German 'doctrine' equivalent to Britain's Keynesianism was the so-called social market principle, which was never a technique of economic management, but rather a statement of principles to which everyone subscribed. The main obstacle to strict Keynesianism was the independence of the Bundesbank and its statutory commitment to an anti-inflationary strategy. This independence from the national government grew in parallel with global interdependence: after the end of the fixed exchange rate regime (the Bretton Woods system), the growing importance of the Deutschmark as the pivot of Europe's currencies entailed a much increased role for the bank.

Germany's powerful economic machine enabled its decision-makers to withstand some of the negative effects of its own dependence on the global economy. The British government was not in this privileged situation. It was hemmed in by circumstances it could not control. Its export record was deteriorating. Foreigners still held large sterling balances, and were ready to shift them at short notice and subject the country to unpredictable and often not very rational exchange rate pressures. Internally, the government had to settle the miners' dispute largely on the expensive terms dictated by the NUM. It had to face the build-up of union wage claims which had accumulated under Heath's pay policies. Finally, as inflation marched on, it had to meet the larger bills caused by the triggering of the inflation-related threshold agreements made by the previous administration. Threshold agreements had been devised by the Conservatives before the oil crisis made inflation a virtual certainty. These agreements, automatically triggered as inflation increased, more than cushioned workers against price rises. They were the principal reason why Britain's inflation was markedly higher than that of its competitors in Europe and elsewhere.[14] Unions did not moderate their wage demands while inflation escalated into double figures. Labour leaders accused the unions of not keeping their side of the social contract.[15] The defeat of Heath by the NUM had so marked British politics that Wilson was determined to avoid anything remotely resembling a statutory incomes policy.[16] Yet 'the markets', the equivalent of the capricious and unpredictable Homeric Gods in Labour Party folklore, had been taught (by Labour leaders as much as anyone else) that an incomes policy was necessary to resolve the problems of the British economy. As Wilson wrote of the situation in July 1975: 'The Treasury ... was utterly depressed, and when depressed it tends to go fetishist. Their fetish on this occasion ... reflected international market demands for statutory controls over pay.'[17]

The event that highlighted the extent of Britain's dependency on the global economy, however, was the so-called IMF crisis of 1976. This started in March 1976 with a run on the pound, precipitated by the perception of the markets that the government itself thought the currency was overvalued. Healey blamed the Bank of England.[18] Some commentators, who agree that there were no real economic reasons for the major speculative attacks on sterling in 1976, blamed the government for not having a coherent policy towards the exchange rate, thus forcing the markets to second-guess it.[19]

Britain's massive inflation had contributed to a marked international lack of confidence in Labour's conduct of the British economy. Respected financial journals such as the *Wall Street Journal* and *The Economist* published leading articles in which the country was described as condemned to economic degeneration and heading towards a regime which would confiscate all wealth.[20] By July, sterling had depreciated by 12 per cent. An international rescue package, backed by Germany and the USA, was put together. Exacting conditions were attached to this short-term credit, designed to give the government a breathing space. The government was to cut public spending to reduce its inflationary deficit. Should it be unable to repay the loan by

December 1976, it would have to go to the IMF for further assistance. In practice, Britain had accepted that its economic policy would have to be approved by the IMF.

The painful debates which divided the Labour cabinet, and which figure prominently in the memoirs of the participants, concentrated on a key issue: whether or not the government should cut public spending to meet the conditions demanded by foreign lenders in order to placate the foreign exchange markets.[21] Whether or not public expenditure cuts were necessary to resolve the problems of the 'real' economy, was, in these circumstances, of secondary importance if one held the view that the markets had to be satisfied. According to this logic, the main reason for deflating was to obtain the approval of the IMF, which in turn was required in order to convince 'the markets' that the British economy was sound. This was the basis of Denis Healey's position.

The extent of the cuts inevitably depended on the Treasury's forecast of the size of the public sector borrowing requirement (the PSBR). This was grossly exaggerated. Britain did not need to borrow as much as was thought. Later, in his memoirs, having noted that the PSBR forecast is always wrong,[22] Healey wrote:

> The whole affair was unnecessary. The Treasury had grossly overestimated the PSBR, which would have fallen within the IMF's limits without any of the measures they prescribed. Later figures showed that we also managed to eliminate our current account deficit in 1977, before the IMF package had had time to influence it.[23]

Within the cabinet the old Keynesian social democrats, for whom public spending was the essence of Labourism, were the most outspoken against the cuts. They were led by Crosland, initially supported by Harold Lever, Shirley Williams and, later, Roy Hattersley. Crosland, who had written in *The Future of Socialism* that the problem of unemployment had been solved,[24] argued, quite justifiably, that to deflate in a situation of mounting unemployment was unnecessary. Ten years previously, virtually to the day, Richard Crossman had backed Crosland on a similar point of policy, stating: 'We came into office as socialists and the essence of socialist policy is a shift from private to public expenditure.'[25] Crosland accepted that the IMF loans were needed to satisfy the markets, but he suggested that if the IMF persisted in demanding onerous conditions, Britain could threaten to recall troops from Germany or Cyprus, introduce a siege economy, and withdraw from the EEC. Alternatively, he added, the government could satisfy the requirement to lop one billion pounds off the PSBR by selling the government's Burmah Oil shares and imposing import deposits.[26] As Tony Benn recollected, Crosland considered the proposed deflation 'wrong economically and socially, destructive of what he had believed in all his life'.[27]

Thus there was the basis for an alliance between the old 'revisionist'

Right, the Left of Tony Benn and Michael Foot, and the 'little Englander' Peter Shore, an advocate of import controls. Benn's position was well-known to the cabinet. Like Crosland, he was against deflation. For months he had been advocating the imposition of import controls, now part and parcel of that 'Alternative Economic Strategy' which would give a policy platform to the Labour Left in opposition.[28] Reflation, not deflation, was the answer, but it would have to be protected by import controls and backed by an industrial policy. The entente with the unions was the only guarantee against large pay claims.[29] Like Crosland, Benn was not above blackmailing the IMF: if you try to force us to deflate, we shall have to take protectionist measures which are anathema to Washington. Those who argued against these views stressed how weak the British economy was, how dependent on the goodwill of others, how reliant on trade, how constrained by a multiplicity of international agreements such as GATT and the EEC. After a lengthy discussion, minutely recounted in Benn's diaries, Callaghan threw his weight behind Healey. This move was decisive.[30] Had he been outvoted, he would have resigned. As Tony Crosland said, 'If it became known ... that Jim had been defeated by Cabinet, it would be murder. He is our strongest card ... we cannot afford not to support the Prime Minister.'[31] There would have been an election which Labour was bound to lose. An incoming Conservative government would have wielded the deflationary axe with far greater energy than Labour. The decision to deflate in order to satisfy the conditions of the IMF was accepted by a majority of ministers. Healey's crucial argument was that, although Crosland was right to hold the view that the situation was already under control and the loans were not necessary, 'the markets would not believe it'.[32]

This epic saga – later ensconced in Labour Party mythology as the day international capitalism destroyed the Labour government – developed because of the overwhelming importance of satisfying 'the markets'. Healey also blamed the Treasury's substandard economic forecasting:

> In practice ... we could have done without the IMF loan only if we – and the world – had known the real facts at the time. But in 1976 our forecasts were far too pessimistic, and we were still describing our public expenditure in a way which was immensely damaging to our standing in the financial markets.[33]

He also further pointed the finger at the young men (as they overwhelmingly were) who sold sterling short because they were influenced by young 'scribblers' – i.e. financial journalists writing in the sort of internal bulletins which circulate in the City – who had come to rely on two or three principles of monetarist economics as if they were the ten commandments: deficits cause inflation; hence, the minute you saw one, you sold sterling.[34] In the good old days of Bretton Woods, this could not have occurred so easily.

For the Labour Left the chief bugbear was the IMF itself, an impersonal bureaucracy staffed by enemies of the people who had already imposed

swingeing and disastrous deflationary policies on many Third World countries
such as Chile. It was in part because strict conditions had been imposed
upon countries poorer than Britain that IMF functionaries were reluctant to
be lenient. The IMF, in any case, had no funds of its own. Its function was
to arrange multilateral loans. The actual money came from the central banks
of the so-called Group of Ten, though in practice the cash was mainly
German and American.

Was the Labour government a victim of the anti-socialist reaction of
antipathetic foreign governments? In the USA there was a Republican
administration, but President Ford was James Callaghan's great friend –
according to Callaghan. Nevertheless, Ford was unable (or unwilling) to get
the US Treasury to consent to a rescue plan prior to completion of the
negotiations with the IMF. He would have had to face the opposition of the
three men in charge of the American side of the loan: the Secretary of the
Treasury, William Simon, a former bond dealer; his number two, Stephen
Yeo, a former Pittsburg banker; and Arthur Burns, chairman of the Federal
Reserve Bank and a self-confessed 'neanderthal conservative'. When Callaghan
and Healey met Simon and Yeo, they found them unbelievably right-wing,
'ready to fall off the edge'.[35] On the German side, Helmut Schmidt was, of
course, a social democrat generally sympathetic to Callaghan's conservative
brand of socialism, but his hands were tied by his government and, even
more, by the Bundesbank.[36]

The most conventional socialist interpretation of the crisis turned out to
be close to the truth: 'international capitalism will always work against the
best interests of socialist governments.' The Labour government was constrained by capitalism, that is, by market forces. This had always been true
domestically. But in the 1960s, and even more so in the 1970s, after the end
of fixed exchange rates, this had become true of the international markets as
well. This dependency affected Britain more than other European countries
because of the existence of large sterling balances which Labour tried,
unsuccessfully, to eliminate. Nevertheless, the fundamentals of the situation
were similar for most countries. There were three possible strategies. The
first consisted in putting up the shutters, withdrawing into a siege economy
and constructing socialism in one country, withstanding the inevitable retaliation of other countries against British goods, explaining to the electorate
that the consequent massive reduction in their standard of living and the
range of the goods at their disposal might last for a decade or two, and ...
winning the next election. The second consisted in declaring that national
sovereignty had ceased to exist, that economically domestic politics were an
irrelevancy, and that only transnational political organizations – the EEC, the
UN, or whatever – would be able to control the international markets. The
third option was to muddle through pragmatically – an option which had
served Labour reasonably well in the past and which, it was hoped, would
continue to serve it in the future.

This pessimism would have appeared unfounded to the German social democrats. They did not doubt that they were in charge of their economy. While Britain and other countries were suffering under the impact of the first oil shock, Germany seemed to have weathered the storm remarkably well. In alliance with the Liberal FDP, the SPD was in charge of a government which appeared to succeed in out-performing its main competitors in terms of inflation rates and balance of payments. Understandably, the SPD claimed that it had discovered the secret of economic management. Its national solution to national problems could be used by other countries. Miracles could be exported. The slogan of *Modell Deutschland* was born.

The contrast with Britain could not be more profound. While between 1973 and 1979 German inflation averaged 4.7 per cent, less than half the OECD European average (11.9 per cent), that of Britain hovered at a spectacular 15.6 per cent. The difference in inflation was eventually seen to matter more than anything else. *Modell Deutschland* turned out to be about keeping inflation down.

It was generally held that Britain was in the throes of a long-term, quasi-terminal decline, compounded by intractable industrial conflicts. The term 'the British disease' became widely used in Northern Europe. It usually meant that British trade unions were too militant. British strike rates, it is true, were higher than those of Germany, Sweden and Austria, but were comparable or inferior to those of Italy, the USA and Canada. A modified version of this diagnosis identified the source of infection not in unions alone, but in restrictive policies imposed by powerful producer groups, including the unions. Whatever the real causes, in Britain it was generally accepted that the economy was unhealthy and that the infection had to be isolated and eliminated. The enduring conflict between Keynesian and monetarist economists tends to obscure the near-universal consensus which united the leadership of all three parties: British wages were held to be too high. As they were, in fact, much lower than those in the USA, Canada, Sweden and Germany (1975), the problem was more likely to be one of productivity or bad management, or both. Moreover, the obvious area in which Britain was spendthrift was on defence, where it outspent not only the 'losers' of the Second World War, Japan and Germany, but also the French.[37]

This assumption of high wages was not new in British politics, and was not caused by the oil shock or the end of fixed exchange rates. As chapter 13 has shown, the Labour governments of 1964–70 also believed that wages were too high and that the unions would have to be cajoled or convinced, or perhaps even forced, to do something about it. The subsequent wave of ferocious anti-trade union legislation, unparalleled in Europe, which the Thatcher governments introduced, thus have an origin and justification in the consensus of the 1960s and 1970s. The distinguishing feature of the Thatcherite solution, not a trivial one, was that unions need not be convinced or cajoled. They could be legislated into subjection.

The evolution of Labour's pay policy was mainly reactive. The party had won the elections in 1974 on the basis that it would be able to deal with the trade unions. The 1973 programme carefully refrained from making any reference at all to wage restraint, while promising to control prices.[38] But no one could be in any doubt: the Social Contract would create the 'right' climate of opinion – that is, one in which unions would consider the wider political and economic implications of their pay claims. Labour would fulfil its manifesto pledges, especially those concerning the removal of the anti-trade union legislation of the Heath government. In exchange, the unions would moderate their wage demands.

Moderation was never numerically defined. Nevertheless, the pace of wage negotiation in 1974–75 – especially when added to the cumulative effects of threshold agreements – was unmistakably inflationary. The unions had not kept their side of the contract, while the Labour government was busy fulfilling its pledges. This led to the delineation of a much clearer incomes policy, although the term, so distasteful to unions, was not used at first.

This pay policy was articulated in four stages, each devised towards the end of the preceding one. In other words, the policy was totally unplanned. The first three stages were largely successful, in the sense that, by and large, wages followed the stipulated limits. Whether they were the most important cause of the reduction of inflation from 26 to 8 per cent, between 1975 and 1979, depends on one's theory of the causes of inflation. The policy was certainly successful in containing pay in the public sector. Unemployment, which grew apace with the various stages of the incomes policy, was probably at the root of wage containment in the private sector.[39] It is symptomatic of the extent of the perceived failure of the fourth and last stage of the policy, which led to the infamous 'winter of discontent' (1978–79), that the general view was that Labour could not control the unions, and the entire strategy had been an unmitigated disaster. A brief look at the evidence disproves this negative opinion, which has been reinforced not only by subsequent Conservative propaganda – as was only to be expected, given that a disregard for evidence is common practice in politics – but also by the reluctance of successive Labour Party and trade union leaders to put the record straight.

Stage 1 of the policy (July 1975–July 1976) set the permitted increase at the flat rate of £6 a week for all those earning under £8,500. This was the brainchild of Jack Jones, the TGWU general secretary and one of the outstanding British trade unionists of the post-war period. His role in ensuring acceptance of this redistributive policy can hardly be overestimated.[40] A flat-rate increase completely contravened the practice of British trade unionists, with their longstanding commitment to collective bargaining and pay differentials. This explains why there was no enthusiasm for it in TUC circles,[41] and why it encountered the outspoken opposition of the Labour Left as well as of the Communist Party which, for all its dedication to the idea of planning, was deeply *laissez-faire* when it came to industrial relations. Bert Ramelson, who as national industrial organizer of the Communist Party carried influence with trade unionists, criticized the policy because it was bound 'to lead to a distortion of accepted differentials ... It is a policy of redistribution not between the workers and the bosses, but within the working class, the better-off workers, instead of the bosses, paying for improving the lot of the worse off.'[42] Even Alan Fisher, leader of the public employees, one of the groups of workers which would benefit the most from the flat-rate policy, at first opposed it.

Eventually, the unions bought the policy, partly because they genuinely wanted to help the Labour government, partly because it was supposed to be a temporary measure, and partly because it was not statutory. Stage 2 of the policy (August 1976–July 1977) involved a milder form of redistribution: a general 5 per cent increase up to a maximum of £4 a week, except for the lower paid, who obtained a flat £2.50 per week. This stage too was strictly observed by the unions. The TUC officially rejected Stage 3, set at 10 per cent, with the ambiguous formula 'we are not party to it', pointing out that large catching-up increases would be 'self-defeating'.[43] In practice, most workers settled within the guidelines. By then, inflation had fallen to 8 per cent. Healey later claimed that 'this achievement was due above all to our pay policy', as if inflation were not also abating throughout Europe.[44]

Stage 4 (July 1978) set a target of 5 per cent. This was unrealistic, because the economy was recovering and the sense of urgency which had inspired the unions to do what the government wanted was no longer there. Unwilling to impose sanctions on trade unionists, the government thought it could impose them on those employers who breached the guidelines, by blacklisting them and denying them public contracts or subsidies. In November 1978, after a long strike, the engineering unions obtained 16.5 per cent from Ford. The government blacklisted the company in what proved to be a test case.[45] In the Commons Labour left-wingers joined the Conservatives to defeat the government. It was this, rather than the far better known and more widely remembered public sector strikes of that winter, which effectively destroyed the Social Contract and, with it, the government's credibility. According to Healey:

> The Winter of Discontent was not caused by the frustration of ordinary workers after a long period of wage restraint. It was caused by institutional pressures from local trade union activists who had found their roles severely limited by three years of incomes policies agreed by their national leaders.[46]

A series of politically explosive, but economically insignificant, strikes ensued in the public service sector – fewer days were lost in strikes in the year of the 'winter of discontent' than the average under the previous Conservative government.[47] The government resisted with an intransigence which it later came to regret. It caved in only to the BBC, whose differentials with the private sector had become excessive.[48] The government could risk everything except depriving the British public of their Christmas television.

As uncollected refuse accumulated in London parks and appeared on television screens, or as, in one instance, grave-diggers refused to bury the dead – one of the most offensive strikes in trade union history – a widely shared sense of outrage against the unions pervaded the electorate. In March 1979, having lost a vote of confidence in the Commons, Labour was forced to call an election. The Conservative Party was returned with a massive majority. The Thatcher era had begun.

The unions had resisted a permanent pay policy while accepting, in practice, the end of full employment. They had failed to recognize that unemployment is the strongest instrument for the containment of wages. As Thomas Balogh explained, full employment causes a continuous rise in prices which causes discontent and leads everyone to increase the price of their labour: 'It is this conflict of everyone against all whose growing bitterness undermines the social basis of any full employment policy that is not buttressed by an incomes policy.'[49]

The assumptions on which the Social Contract was based belonged to the golden age of capitalism, to the era of full employment and regular growth. Those on the Left who wanted to defend 'free' collective bargaining (in the trade union sense of bargaining unrestricted by regulation), and full employment (even in the narrow sense of the full employment of trade union members), lived in a world which no longer existed. This is why they failed. Thatcher regulated industrial relations to the advantage of employers and reinstituted, in this context, 'free' collective bargaining, in the shadow of millions of unemployed. The government used its powers as an employer to control wage increases in the public sector.

As the 1980s proceeded incomes policy became a near-irrelevancy. In continental Europe, it became less important because unions lost power as unemployment grew. That was true in Britain too. In addition, wage restraint was rejected by the Conservatives because it was too interventionist, by the unions because it broke with free collective bargaining, and by the Labour Party because it had failed.

The unemployment-induced weakness of the unions, especially the British unions, was further compounded by the industrial relations effect of the technological revolution, based on electronics and the 'microchip'. One of the chief characteristics of British unionism was the enduring strength of its craft-based ethos and the insistence on clear demarcation lines between jobs and their pay differentials. This went against the grain of the microchip technological revolution, which constantly reclassified skills, eliminating demarcation and jobs, particularly in electronically based sectors such as the new printing industry. Unions found themselves in an impossible situation. If they resisted change, they forced firms out of business. If they accepted flexibility, they also had to accept the consequent replacement of labour with capital. The highly skilled workers remaining in employment would derive considerable benefits, but those made redundant would become unemployable. All European unions suffered, but the British more than most, partly because of their structure and partly because of the low priority they gave to negotiating issues other than wages.[50] The Social Contract contributed power-fully to reinforcing the idea that industrial relations and trade unions were essentially about wages.

In the 1980s one of the criticisms levelled at the Social Contract was that it was yet another instance of the corporatist mentality of the times. Yet the opposite was the case. A true corporatist contract would have involved the CBI at all levels, but the CBI was hardly ever included in negotiations and had even less power to deliver the employers' side of the bargain than the trade unions had to deliver theirs. A stronger CBI, more closely integrated into decision-making, might have increased its prestige among employers and induced among them a more consensual mood than the rapid anti-trade unionism and the unreconstructed economic liberalism which prevailed. ·

A form of corporatism closer to real tripartism had been operating in Germany. By the time the second oil shock made itself felt (1981–82), there was substantial agreement in the political establishment on the chief economic problems facing the country: energy had become too costly, therefore energy-saving measures should be urgently promoted; wages were too high and should be contained; public spending was excessive and should be curbed.[51] Germany was falling into line with the rest of Europe.

Until then, however, the German model was seen as successful and eminently exportable. *Modell Deutschland* appeared to be the invention and the result of social democracy in power, and was heralded as such by Helmut Schmidt himself. The idea of a model is, after all, part and parcel of the vocabulary of the Left. Socialists and communists always maintained that national capitalisms were sufficiently similar to each other, socialist goals so convergent, principles so alike, that a relatively uniform model of political management was both thinkable and achievable. Furthermore, the differences between Britain and Germany, though not inconsequential (see, in particular, the institutional and constitutional differences examined in chapter 11), could not overwhelm the considerable similarities: both countries had large, well-established socialist parties, and were comparable in size, population and economic structure.

What was *Modell Deutschland*? Was it successful? Could socialists in Britain or in any other country adopt or adapt it? The existing literature suggests that the model possessed three distinguishing features: an *industrial policy* aimed at managing the decline of old industries and the promotion of new, high technology, knowledge-based industries; a *social policy* aimed at ensuring that this transition would not have negative social effects; and a *corporatist policy* aimed at achieving a consensual outlook between employers and trade unions.[52] Some authors also add to the list of constituent features of the

German model the federal system and constitution, the independent central bank, the system of industrial democracy.[53] These additions, however, mean that the model is equated with the entire political and economic system of the country.

The most significant innovation introduced by the SPD was the industrial policy. The social and corporatist policies were already in existence. There was an industrial policy prior to 1970, but it involved the banking system rather than the government. While British banks neither encouraged nor participated in industrial restructuring, in Germany banks were well represented on the boards of export companies, which tended to be the most powerful German firms. There was substantial interlocking between firms operating in the export sectors, their suppliers and their banks. Traditionally, British banks provided finance to industry against existing assets, German banks against future prospects. In fairness, it should be said that British banks have often insisted that the differences with Germany are not very significant.[54] Nevertheless, there is little doubt that German banks had a greater stake in the direction of the economy as a whole than their British counterparts (who were more involved abroad). Thus, in Germany there was substantial 'planning' or concerted action, but it was achieved by the commercial banks in conjunction with private manufacturers.[55] The state and hence the government hovered in the background.

The co-ordination achieved in Germany between the financial and the manufacturing sectors produced an organizational framework in which the Bundesbank, the trade unions and the government could participate. Everyone had a role. Economic losers and winners were identified. Banks lent money. Trade unions moderated wage claims. The Bundesbank kept the Deutschmark both stable and undervalued, thus helping exports. The government played its part by holding high the free trade banner in all international institutions. The German chancellor kept in touch with industrialists and trade unionists, bankers and research institutes. Priorities were established, announced openly, and specific policies formulated and implemented to deal with them, whether through tax concessions or by favouring mergers. This was 'organized capitalism' at its best.

The widespread consensus should not disguise the fact that the ruling coalition was divided. The FDP insisted that industrial investment, in the final analysis, should be left to the market, and that the supportive role of the state would have to take the form of tax reductions and hence of cuts in the growth rate of public expenditure. The SPD believed that investments were too important to be left entirely to the capitalists. They envisaged that the state would play a broadly supportive role by using public spending, developing its industrial policy, overseeing training programmes, targeting, through the Research and Technology Ministry, the development of key export sectors such as microelectronics, telecommunications and energy technology.[56]

The SPD embraced what one may call a 'state-modernization' strategy. In this context modernization has two meanings. First it can mean 'catching up' with 'more advanced countries'. This involves some clear assumptions: strategies may vary, but the goal is the same – namely, to achieve the 'correct' (i.e. 'modern') mix between the three basic sectors of the economy (extractive/ primary, manufacturing and service). Countries pursuing this pattern of modernization in reality treat the more advanced countries teleologically, as a model, the representation of their own future. The 'advanced countries', in turn, possess de facto hegemony: by being recognized as 'modern', they set the agenda for the development of others.

The second meaning of modernization, the one applicable to the German (and the Swedish) experience, involves adapting the existing set-up to the predicted one. Industries which are no longer competitive must be thoroughly reshaped or, more commonly, allowed to decline according to a plan. Winners must be identified and supported as and where appropriate. Modernization can occur 'spontaneously', in the sense that it is not the result of a specific policy of modernization, but rather the outcome of capitalist development itself – for instance, when low-productivity firms close down, markets collapse and new firms emerge, or are reorganized to respond to technological developments and the advent of new markets.

A 'state-modernization' strategy occurs when the political authorities estimate that it is not sufficient to create the conditions for economic restructuring through macro-economic intervention (aggregate demand, interest rates, budgetary policies), but believe that the state must take an active role in the promotion of high-flying sectors and the 'soft-landing' of declining ones. Gentle euthanasia for old industries and active midwifery for new ones are the twin pillars of the social-democratic strategy of state modernization. Was this the strategy of the SPD in power? To answer this, it is opportune to distinguish between the government's role vis-à-vis ailing industries – which was considerable – and its contribution to the development of new sectors, which was less prominent.

The steel industry can be used as an example of a declining sector, both because the structural crisis which struck it was particularly serious and because it affected all European countries.[57] In Germany this industry was concentrated in two regions: the Ruhr and the Saar. The crisis in the Saar was worse: by 1977 the two main producers, Roechling Burbach and Neunkircher Eisenwerke, faced bankruptcy. None of the main political or economic protagonists of German society could remain indifferent: it involved the government, and hence the social democrats and the Liberals, the largest trade union, IG Metall, the CDU which controlled the government of the Saar, and the banks implicated in the two stricken companies and represented on their supervisory boards. It was this interlocking of interests – rather than a social-democratic policy – which made possible the 'crisis cartel' to engineer the takeover of the Saar steel firms by the Luxemburg steel firm Arbed. The two firms were temporarily saved. The unions obtained federal government guarantees that a core of employed workers would be protected, and that adequate redundancy payments would be paid to the unemployed workers. Arbed obtained massive federal aid. The Saar was granted special regional aid.

These efforts were not entirely successful. In 1982 the newly established Saar steel firm, Arbed Saarstahl, was again on the verge of bankruptcy. This time the CDU was the main partner in the federal coalition. A second crisis cartel was set up and more aid directed to the Saar. The restructuring of the German steel industry was achieved at the cost of massive unemployment: 12 per cent in the Saar alone. Nevertheless, in comparative perspective, this is far from being a story of abject failure. The crisis of the European steel industry did not spare any country and Germany came out of it better than most. The Saar had been treated as a special case by an incoming centre-right administration committed to a reduction in state intervention in the economy. A line of continuity had emerged with the previous government. All political parties were committed to prolonging the life of *Modell Deutschland* for as long as possible.

This system of crisis management was made possible by the way German capitalism itself was organized. The federal government itself has a modest involvement in industrial policy; its principal role, at both central and local level, apart from subsidizing ailing sectors, 'has been in factor creation, especially in education and science and technology'.[58] This suggests that the state-modernization strategy was not an option that any socialist government could adopt whenever it chose (by 'importing' it as a model). It could be employed only within a specific political and economic context. It was not a strategy any incoming Labour government could activate upon entering 10 Downing Street, unless specific institutional reforms were first implemented.

In an effort to devise a new industrial strategy, these themes were explored between 1970 and 1974 by the Labour Party, then in opposition. Work in sub-committees proceeded speedily, but usually without much input from the senior leaders of the party, Harold Wilson, Jim Callaghan, Roy Jenkins and Tony Crosland. Neither the experience nor the co-operation of the leading trade unionists of the 1970s, Hugh Scanlon and Jack Jones, had been sought.[59] The divorce between the policy-making machine of the party and the Parliamentary Labour Party and the trade unions was far more pronounced than was the case in other social-democratic parties. In practice, Labour's working parties and committees and sub-committees – intellectually dominated by academics such as Stuart Holland – proceeded as if they were mere pressure groups. Their efforts were regarded by the leadership with a mixture of anxiety (should the policy proposals turn out to be unpopular) and contempt. The main theorist of the new industrial policy, Stuart Holland, was the butt of much of this derision.[60]

Two features were central to the new industrial strategy: the creation of the National Enterprise Board (NEB) and what were called planning agreements. The NEB would be a state holding company modelled after others on the Continent, above all Italy's IRI, but also on other, less significant companies such as France's IDI, Sweden's Sattsföretag and Germany's VIAG – a rare instance of the Labour Party learning from continental experience. According to the sub-committee's report (adopted by the National Executive Committee of the Labour Party), one of its main objectives was the creation of employment in the regions.[61] This would be achieved by the NEB undertaking joint ventures with national and multinational public or private companies, setting up its own companies, and acquiring a substantial base in the private sector. It was this last idea which would prove to be the most controversial, because it amounted to a strategy for a considerable extension of the nationalized sector:

> The NEB should, at the end of a five-year term, exert a controlling interest over a large slice of the economy. The top hundred manufacturers account for about half our net manufacturing output. About one-third of the turnover of the top one hundred manufacturers, two-fifths of their profit and about half of their employment should be vested in the NEB.

This meant between twenty and twenty-five companies.[62] A moderate version of this plan was eventually implemented. The NEB was not a success story but, in the short time-span allowed by the vagaries of British politics (it was wound down by the Conservatives), it managed to take the first faltering steps towards an industrial strategy.[63]

The pledge to introduce planning agreements and the NEB was inserted in the 1973 Labour Party programme, produced by the National Executive Committee and approved by the annual conference. The programme specified that the NEB would always have a controlling interest in its participating firms, and that it would take over 'some twenty-five of our largest manufacturers ... very early in the life of the Board'.[64]

The programme firmly stated that 'all the major companies in this country ... certainly the largest 100 or so manufacturing firms' would come under the planning agreement system.[65] What would these companies do? They would provide the government with information concerning the activities included in their future plans. This would help the government to set objectives. The firms would have to agree to meet these objectives – such as providing a certain number of new jobs in a designated area – though they would be free, the programme magnanimously added, to decide how.[66] In turn, these firms would receive government assistance. Whether or not firms would be forced to sign planning agreements is not clear from the text of this rather poorly drafted document. The manifesto for the 1974 election promised to create a powerful NEB along the lines of the programme,[67] and mentioned planning agreements, but avoided any reference to compulsion and the number of firms involved. The only nationalizations it promised were mineral rights, shipbuilding, ports and aircraft manufacturing. It is easy to understand Wilson's initial enthusiasm for the NEB and planning agreements. They would help the party to move away from what he called the 'outlandish proposal to commit the party to nationalize 25 of the 100 biggest companies'.[68] In fact, there was considerable hostility towards planning in the Labour cabinet. Roy Jenkins never even mentions the agreements or the NEB in his memoirs, even though in the early 1970s he had welcomed the new approach.[69] It was invoked at Labour Party conferences to rally the faithful and the trade unions – witness Wilson at the November 1974 Conference: 'the National Enterprise Board is the biggest leap forward in economic thinking as well as in economic policy since the war.'[70] In reality, he had become doubtful of the entire exercise.[71] The government White Paper of 1974 clearly specified that planning agreements were to be voluntary, based on consultation between the government and the company concerned.[72] In other words, if the company agreed to agree and the government agreed, they would agree to co-operate. No wonder the Left was outraged. Labour thus remained without an industrial strategy. As Healey explained: 'for most of the time my only tool for securing better industrial performance was public spending, which proved to be a very blunt instrument indeed.'[73]

The Industry Act 1975 still assumed that one of the functions of the NEB would be to extend public ownership into profitable areas of manufacturing industry. By March 1976, this assumption had disappeared. The NEB became a hospital for sick companies.[74] The only planning agreement was with Chrysler, owned by General Motors, in March 1977. The main purpose behind GM's move was to lay its hands on some ready public cash. The government was eminently blackmailable: it was pushing its Scottish Devolution Bill and was unlikely to allow the firm's Scottish plant at Lynwood to close.[75] When, in July 1978, it became convenient for GM to sell Chrysler UK to French Peugeot, it did so without even informing the government, making a mockery of the celebrated clause which had established the principle of reciprocal consultation.[76] Dell had written, sarcastically, that no one in March 1974 had the least idea what should constitute a planning agreement.[77] Clearly, even four years later, the mystery persisted.

Nationalizations did occur and all could be justified on various grounds. Labour nationalized shipbuilding, then in crisis, in 1977 and British Aerospace, a company which was so utterly dependent on state business that only its diminishing profits could be said to be private. Only the nationalization of the British National Oil Company (BNOC) responded to a wider strategic design: to procure a significant influence on the offshore oil industry. This objective was achieved.[78]

The principal aim of economic policy soon became the overwhelming need to combat inflation. The cause of this is not hard to ascertain. Though prices rose throughout Europe, British inflation was, as we have seen, exceptionally high. This, to some extent, explains why the Bank of England had become determined to defeat inflation regardless of the cost in unemployment.[79] The government had become similarly obsessed. As Denis Healey himself admits, the government had lost its sense of proportion in its fight against inflation, insisting on an inflexible 5 per cent pay norm in 1978–79.[80]

In Germany the obsession with inflation was – allegedly – part of the national psyche. The government was further constrained in economic policy by the Bundesbank's statutory obligation to contain inflation. In a situation of stagflation, the Bundesbank had no option but to defend monetary stability by a policy of high interest rates (1973–74). These restrictive policies nipped in the bud the inflationary pressures set in motion by the oil shock. The unions moderated their wage demands as employers realized that the Bundesbank would not automatically finance any wage increases they granted.[81] This was more effective than the Labour government's attempt to impose sanctions on employers who broke its pay guidelines. The credit squeeze forced all public spending authorities to contain expenditure and prevented the government, had it wanted to, from opting for a policy of counter-cyclical reflation.[82]

Whether the comparatively positive health of the German economy in 1976 was due to the strict monetarism of the Bundesbank, or to other factors such as the half a million foreign workers who had to leave the country (no increase in unemployment expenditure was needed to cope with this), is debatable. Had the foreign workers stayed and registered as unemployed, the level of unemployment in West Germany would have been higher than in Britain.[83] As was to be expected, both the Bundesbank and the government claimed credit for saving the country from the British disease.[84] Both economies, however, succumbed to similar pressures. Full employment, a policy to which both the SPD and the Labour Party were profoundly committed, was discarded while both parties were in power.

In any case, policies do not exist in a vacuum. The high profile role of the West German economy, and the chorus of demands suggesting that it should become the 'locomotive' of Western recovery (1978–79), depended as much on its sheer economic size as on its success. Irrespective of the particular policies implemented by the SPD–Liberal coalition, West Germany had the largest GNP in the European Community, was the largest trading partner of most European countries, and Europe's largest importer of services. No wonder its economy, in the age of integration, was crucial to Europe. Its particular performance has, however, been unexceptional: between 1960 and 1975, its growth rate was in line with EEC average, its increase in productivity per worker below that of France.[85] *Modell Deutschland* was loudly proclaimed in the 1976–80 period when German GNP and productivity growth exceeded the French and EC average, and Germany had become the bulwark of price stability in Europe.[86] Nevertheless, there was no real effort to return to full employment. Attempts by SPD ministers to introduce substantial job creation programmes were watered down.[87] The coalition government went along with the Bundesbank's restrictive policies. It upheld the primacy of the anti-inflationary strategy which it had adopted well ahead of other countries, thus contributing to, rather than following, the recessionary cycle of the 1970s.

Germany had been strong enough to withstand the first oil shock, but not the second. It was this which put paid to the aspirations of *Modell Deutschland*. In 1981–82 GNP fell. The balance of payments deficit turned from harmless to intolerable. This meant that monetary policy became even more dependent on US interest rates. The German rate had to be kept even higher to prevent an outflow of capital and attract funds.[88] Germany was as dependent on externalities as everyone else. Helmut Schmidt recognized this when he pinned the blame for worldwide unemployment on US interest rates, which were then so high that they mopped up investment that might have gone into fixed capital formation.[89] Germany's large balance of payment surplus had helped the country to weather the first oil shock. Since this surplus no longer existed, by 1979 it could not be used to face the second oil shock. Furthermore, between 1970 and 1980, the international competitiveness of German industry had deteriorated.[90]

Where the celebrated German model failed completely was on the issue of unemployment. The first crisis of 1973–74 destroyed one million jobs. The post-1980 recession destroyed another million.[91] By the time Schmidt left office, there were two million unemployed in Germany. The German SPD, like the Labour Party in Britain, had to oversee the end of full employment. Both parties were soon out of office and had to endure the chill climate of opposition for years to come.

Full employment had been achieved thanks to the long capitalist boom. It had not simply been the result of policy decisions. Nevertheless, it had become a socialist axiom that full employment was a political goal. Socialists could hardly return to the view, held by most conservatives, that it was beyond the control of politics.

The SPD-led government fought against unemployment by adopting a range of measures: labour market policies involving retraining and work creation schemes; public sector expansion programmes; and the expulsion of foreign workers. But labour market policies remained subordinated to a budgetary policy which was restrictive and which therefore worked against anti-unemployment measures. The spending cuts of 1981 sharply reduced the work creation schemes. The recession of 1981–82 did not lead to a massive exodus of foreign workers, because those without permanent work permits had already left after the 1973–74 recession.[92] As the economic crisis worsened and unemployment increased, the tripartite body in charge of labour market policy – the Bundesansalt für Arbeit, whose main obligation is the payment of unemployment benefits – found itself less able to finance labour market policies precisely because unemployment was rising.[93]

Why did the SPD–FDP coalition not pursue vigorous active labour market policies when, thanks to its excellent track record as the major exporting manufacturing economy in Europe, West Germany had greater scope to do so?[94] The generally accepted answer is that the SPD's coalition partners, the FDP, were increasingly moving towards an anti-interventionist position and brought pressure to bear on Helmut Schmidt to submit to the winds of change of the 1980s, the revolution in economic thinking represented by Margaret Thatcher and Ronald Reagan. Eventually, the SPD, as a party, could no longer support its hapless chancellor. This was the signal which allowed the FDP to switch to the CDU. The Liberals themselves had been emboldened by the unpredicted positive results they had obtained at the 1980 election. While the SPD had advanced by a puny 0.3 per cent to 42.9, and the CDU-CSU suffered a retreat from 48.6 to 44.5 per cent, the FDP had been the only winners: up to 10.6 from 7.9 per cent.

Thus began in Germany the shift to the right that would be characteristic of the 1980s. Curiously, the problems identified by the political establishment as in need of a solution were very similar to those singled out by their counterparts in Britain when explaining why the UK was less competitive than Germany. The following litany of complaints composed by a former president of the Bundesbank could have been produced in any central bank or employers' association. Predictably, he declared that all would be well without 'the corrupting effect of over-rapidly growing affluence', 'a welfare state run riot', 'a tendency for people to think in terms of ever-increasing "entitlements"', a reduced willingness among the young to do a hard day's work, a large public sector, an excessively high public sector borrowing requirement, and a shortage of skilled labour alongside a high level of unemployment, probably welfare-induced.

The right-wing offensive and the deteriorating economic conditions of 1981 – Germany had entered its worst recession since the war – exacerbated the dispute within the government between those social democrats trying to change economic policy in a more pro-industrial direction, and the liberals, who supported a deregulatory approach. The Bundesbank, supported by the Council of Economic Experts, persisted in its restrictive monetarist line. Keynesian demands for expansion were supported by the trade unions and sectors of the SPD, but to no avail.[95] The FDP, in the forefront of the anti-inflationary forces, opted for a different coalition partner. The *Wende*, the turnaround, produced the centre-right coalition led by Helmut Kohl (1982). This new alliance won decisively in the election of 1983, while the SPD, defeated, once again returned to a lengthy period in opposition.

The Kohl government was lucky. In spite of the rhetoric, there was no major change in economic policy. The economy recovered. From 1982 there was a balance of payments surplus reaching record levels in 1985 when inflation fell to 1.6 per cent. Economic growth, however, remained below the OECD average throughout most of the 1980s. By 1987, unemployment was eight times higher than at the onset of the first oil shock of 1973 – the worst performance after Spain and Britain.[96] Profits rose, but not real wages.[97]

It was now Kohl's turn to be congratulated for his perspicacity. German social democrats were held to possess a high level of economic competence. In the heyday of *Modell Deutschland*, in the mid-1970s, Helmut Schmidt, who behaved with the confidence of an intellectual heavyweight, had been acclaimed by entrepreneurs and bankers as the best chancellor big business could have. While Harold Wilson had boasted never to have read Karl Marx,[98] Schmidt never wore his knowledge lightly. In his address to a congress on philosophy and politics organized by the Friedrich Ebert Foundation in Bonn in March 1979, 'Kant in Our Time', he declared that 'Kant was important to me ... but so too were Karl Marx, Max Weber, and Marcus Aurelius', and peppered his speech with references to these thinkers and to Hegel and Lessing.[99] Public esteem for the SPD faded during the 1980s. According to an opinion poll conducted in May 1988 by the social democratic weekly *Vorwärts*, 56 per cent of the German public believed that the CDU was better able than the SPD to bring about economic growth, while only 20 per cent held the reverse position.[100]

In the 1980s the new CDU–FDP administration did not follow a policy of radical deregulation analogous to that of the British Conservatives. The German economy, unlike the British, was sufficiently strong to overcome even the crisis of the second oil shock without jeopardizing the consensual system of political and industrial relations which had existed for so long. Furthermore, the institutional constraints which inhibited any radical aspirations the social democrats might have nurtured, also operated in the opposite direction. It was difficult for the CDU to follow in the footsteps of the Thatcher government. The CDU had authority at the centre, but faced powerful regional authorities under the control of the social-democratic opposition. It was difficult to cut public spending drastically when so much of it was influenced by the *Länder*. An overt attack on the German unions would not have been approved by the public, who were aware of their longstanding habit of co-operating with the authorities. The unions, paradoxically, flexed their muscles far more in the 1980s than they had in the 1970s. Their advocacy of a shorter working day was generally popular and was seen, rightly or wrongly, as an anti-unemployment measure. Outside Germany, even the Swedish trade unions, usually in the vanguard of new ideas, remained sceptical about the benefits or the possibility of reducing the working day significantly, although the Swedish (and Austrian) working week in engineering was effectively shorter than in Germany.[101]

Thus, in 1984, the German trade unions, facing a conservative government, called for the introduction of the thirty-five-hour week and backed their demand with a lengthy strike led by the largest union, IG Metall. Although the full claim was not met, they obtained a reduction of the working week to thirty-eight and a half hours (IG Metall had been committed to the thirty-five-hour week without loss of earnings since its 1977 Congress).[102] At the same time, in Britain, a prolonged miners' strike, called to defend employment in the industry, ended in total defeat for the miners and with the Labour

Party in disarray. In 1986 the Kohl government passed measures aimed at restricting the ability of striking workers to draw welfare benefits. The unsuccessful struggle to block the law united the DGB (German Trade Union Federation – Deutscher Gewerkschaftsbund) as never before, and enabled it to report a strong rise in membership in the first half of 1986 – while British unions were losing members – and to obtain wage rises for metal workers of 4.4 per cent, four times the inflation rate.[103] Unions in Germany remained important because their co-operation on the firms' supervisory boards was still required to facilitate the constant process of industrial restructuring. In Britain it became increasingly common to reorganize a plant's production without consulting the unions. In the 'war' against organized labour, as in any war, the old Machiavellian principle must still prevail: strike your enemies when they are down, not when they are strong. When it came to industrial relations, the British Conservatives could take on the unions in a way which was not open to the CDU.

These considerations tell only half the story. In reality, if the CDU did not behave like the British Thatcherite Conservatives, it was also because they were not willing to do so. Though fundamentally a conservative party, the CDU was also a populist and Christian party. It could not simply sacrifice on the altar of the deregulated market its tradition of being a *Volkspartei*, and its ethic of Christian social responsibility and solidarity.[104] Kohl had to continue to appease the vast array of organized interest groups, of the Left as well of the Right (there are 200,000 clubs and federations, ranging in size from the fifteen-million-strong German Sport Federation to the Scent Makers' Association with three members). Hence the complaint that 'The CDU wants to be the best SPD of all time.'[105] This mirrors a frequent leftist criticism of Schmidt, namely that he was behaving like a CDU chancellor. All this reflects the lack of sharp political distinctions in German politics; after all, in the legislative period 1976–80, 90 per cent of legislation passed the Bundestag unanimously.[106] Nor was this an exceptional period of consensus.

In domestic affairs, the true German homologue of the Thatcherite deregulators was the Liberals, the junior party of the coalition. Their room for manoeuvre was circumscribed: having ditched the SPD in 1982, they were scarcely in a position to impose a full-blooded Thatcherite policy on the CDU, let alone threaten them with yet another coalition reversal.

Thus the CDU simply continued the policy mix which was peculiar to Germany: a 'conservative' policy aimed at keeping inflation as low as possible, promoting growth if viable, and economic efficiency if feasible, while trying to defend social welfare. This 'policy of the middle way' resulted in a share of social expenditure as a percentage of GDP among the highest in the OECD countries.[107] The lack of progress in the deregulation of the economy brought forth a barrage of complaints from the supporters of a robust neo-liberal approach to economic management, such as Herbert Giersch, president of the free market Kiel economic research institute, and Wilfried Guth, supervisory board chairman of Deutsche Bank ('this government has not shown enough courage').[108]

Within the SPD, the electoral defeat of 1983 opened an era of recrimination and frustration. Schmidt's pragmatic realism, once respected, was now scorned and singled out as one of the causes of the débâcle. Schmidt was accused of having given excessive priority to economic recovery and stability, while social and economic reforms, such as a comprehensive vocational training programme, a radical extension of co-determination legislation, a wage-earning shareholding scheme and radical pension reforms, were shelved or weakened.[109] Schmidt's economic policy had been more monetarist than Keynesian. Of course, there had been achievements: flexible age limits for retirement, guaranteed superannuation schemes, old-age pensions for the self-employed, pro-disabled policies, some extension of co-determination, new matrimonial and family law. All this, however, fell well short of the expectations harboured by many SPD activists and supporters.[110]

The party, claimed some, had lost its soul and become unable to generate enthusiasm. It may have been popular for a while with bankers and industrialists, but it had not been able to absorb and channel the new radical energies which the 1960s had generated. Germany's reputation for efficiency disguised the existence of corruption and bribery in public life, the widespread practice of tax evasion, and the laundering of corporate donations to party funds.[111] In the field of civil liberties, the record of the SPD was far from unblemished. In 1972, a decree concerning employment, the notorious *Berufsverbot*, allowed the government to ban people who held views 'hostile to the Constitution' (*Verfassungsfeindlichkeit*) from jobs in the public service (this would include postmen and schoolteachers).[112] This was so clearly a repressive measure, and embarrassing for the image of the SPD, that in 1978 the social democrats decided not to apply the rule in *Länder* where they were in power.[113] Later, in 1981, Helmut Schmidt agreed that the government 'overdid things', and that 'we would be deceiving ourselves if we felt that we could lastingly preserve the stability of our society by forcing large groups of young people onto the fringes of society.'[114] Willy Brandt, who had been responsible for the original decree, provides an unconvincing and muddled self-defence in his memoirs.[115]

In Britain the negative experiences of the Wilson governments of 1964–70 and the period in opposition (1970–74) had forced a process of rethinking and the first formulation of an alternative economic strategy. In the SPD the push for a reaffirmation of the longer-term aims of the party occurred while it was still in power. The impetus came from its rebellious youth wing, the Jusos, which was closest to the new, 'post-materialist' forces – the pacifists, ecologists and feminists who had emerged from the radical politics of the late 1960s. The Jusos found unexpected allies in the moderate wing of the party, such as the mayor of Munich, Hans-Jochen Vogel (later minister of justice), and Richard Löwenthal, one of its leading intellectuals, who also

wanted a general restatement of principles and aims.[116] Between the Jusos
and the Vogel–Löwenthal right stood a third tendency, which saw itself as
the heir of Bernstein. What characterized those who belonged to it was a
refusal to discard Marxism *en bloc* (Bernstein himself had never done so), and
an insistence that socialism remained the goal of the party, though whether
it was an end-state or a process (which would have been Bernstein's position)
was not always clear. These neo-Bernsteinian revisionists, including Willy
Brandt himself, Erhard Eppler and Peter Glotz, tried to walk a tightrope
between remaining a major credible political force able to represent the
aspirations of millions, and succeeding in developing some of the new ideas
of the alternativist Left.[117]

The SPD reacted to these ideological divisions – which had little impact
on government policies – in its traditional way: it appointed a commission
to prepare a programme. The commission initially produced a draft report
(1973), mobilized academics, created specialist committees, absorbed the
energies of hundreds of study groups at local and sub-district level, including
non-party members.[118] The outcome of this effort was a typically German
document, 100 pages long, with a title no public relations firm would have
devised: *Ökonomisch-politischer Orientierungsrahmen für die Jahre 1975–1985* ('Framework of Economic and Political Orientation of the SPD for the years 1975–
1985', commonly referred to as *OR'85*). It was duly presented and approved
at the Mannheim Party Conference of November 1975.

The original draft, submitted by a committee under Schmidt in 1972,
reflected his pragmatism and the optimism of the pre-oil crisis era.[119] The
final draft of *OR'85* was radically different. It was imbued with a profound
pessimism about the possibility of achieving major changes in Germany in
an increasingly interdependent environment. It reaffirmed, as all social-
democratic programmes did, the longer-term aims of the movement, its
fundamental values (freedom, justice and solidarity),[120] its rejection of liberalism, conservatism, communism, fascism, what it termed 'anti-authoritarian
romanticism', and even the tendency of market economies to produce for
profit and not in order to satisfy human needs.[121] However, the unquestioned
leitmotif of *OR'85* was the limit facing a national movement. Given the high
incidence of international interdependence, particularly in Europe, *OR'85*
urged social democrats to take a 'realistic' view of what could be achieved
in the long term in all matters concerning energy, raw materials, currency
fluctuations and the control of multinationals. It was no longer possible to
run the economy on purely national lines.[122] Governments could only partly
control factors contributing to economic growth.[123] Sluggish growth would
restrict the margins for social reforms.[124] Germany would be dependent on
the reform of the international monetary system and the economic policy of
its main trading partners, whose balance of payments deficits and the restrictive policies they consequently pursued were, in turn, caused by German
balance of payments surpluses.[125] This insistence on policy constraints in a

long-term programme is doubly unusual. In the first place, constraints are invoked by governments as a justification for being unable to achieve certain goals, rather than by political parties whose appeal must be that they *can* do things. Secondly, a programme like *OR'85* did not need to be so cautious, because it was not a detailed description of what the SPD-led government would do, but only an indication of what the SPD thought should be done, eventually. Schmidt had repeatedly made clear that it was unrealistic to commit future governments to specific actions.[126]

The principal reason why interdependence and constraints were so prominent in *OR'85* was that the SPD did not have to wait for the oil crisis to discover them. Living as they did in a country divided by the Cold War, the Germans had learnt the hard way the limitations on national sovereignty. Nations, Willy Brandt had declared in 1966, will last a long time, but nation-states were no longer able, on their own, to guarantee the existence and security of a people.[127] The British were still able to take refuge in the illusion of national sovereignty. The remains of imperial ascendancy insulated them from the realism which the Germans had acquired at enormous cost to themselves and to others.

This explains why the British Labour Party's parallel rethinking in the years 1970–74 was so different from that of the SPD, though it cannot account for all the differences. *OR'85* was the product of an extensive involvement of party activists. Its main 'internal' purpose was to reconcile the young activists who advocated the so-called 'dual strategy': the involvement of the membership not only in the traditional activities of the SPD and the unions, but also through the mobilization of community groups.[128] This kind of involvement was not open to the Labour Party. Labour had never been able or willing to mobilize its members in any significant way, except during elections as canvassers. In size of individual membership, the Labour Party was, with the French socialists, one of the smallest mainstream social-democratic parties in Europe. The party itself did not at the time have an accurate record of how many members it had, though some have calculated that, at the end of the 1970s, it had fewer than 250,000 members.[129] Contrast this with the SPD's comparatively thriving membership (albeit, proportionately speaking, still far below that of the Austrian SPÖ and the Swedish SAP), which increased throughout the 1960s, reaching in 1976 a peak of just over one million.[130]

Labour Party activists tended to behave like an internal pressure group, aimed at ensuring that the leaders adopted their preferred policies. Accordingly, much time was spent passing resolutions which might be adopted at the annual party conference, might form part of the next election manifesto, and might be implemented by an eventual Labour government if conditions allowed. Consequently, Labour activists were often in a semi-permanent 'oppositional' mood. Not expecting their resolutions to be accepted *in toto*, they raised the stakes by insisting on policies more radical than they themselves expected, in the hope of being met half-way by the leadership. In the SPD, the lengthy internal discussions led to a systematic watering down of demands, with the result that the programme tended to unify the party rather than divide it.

The other basis for the differences between the two parties in the programmatic renewal of the 1970s is much simpler: between 1970 and 1974, the Labour Party was in opposition, while the SPD was in power. The mood within Labour was one of recrimination, mainly from the Left. In the previous period of opposition, the 1950s, it was the Right which sought to revise the party's commitment to traditional socialism. In the 1970s, the situation was very different. A new generation of activists, radicalized by the 1960s, was well aware that the Labour Left had been kept out of power during the governments of 1964–70. Those of the Left who had been in positions of authority, such as Crossman and Castle, had been forced to compromise. While in the 1950s it was possible for Labour Party activists to look back on the Attlee period as one of radical reform, no such consolation was possible in the early 1970s: what was there to look back to? What achievements could be set against the craven submission to American policies over Vietnam, or the failure to bring about new social reforms? By the mid-1960s, the British welfare state had ceased to be an example to the world. Sweden had a superior pension scheme, while Holland and Germany had more generous unemployment insurance. In retrospect, the failure of the Wilson governments of 1964–70 to introduce a comprehensive review of supplementary earnings-based pensions and, more generally, its failure to expand the universalist approach to welfare prevented the development of popular solidarity towards the welfare state.[131]

Labour activists thus had many reasons to be dissatisfied with leaders who appeared to have been so hapless when in power and who went on to lose the next general election. Consequently, their rethinking went much further than that of the German social democrats. In the SPD, even those who felt Helmut Schmidt and his colleagues had been too cautious did not wish to rock a boat which appeared to be successfully afloat and which was guided by so strong, self-assured and respected a pilot as Schmidt himself.

Much of the disappointment caused by the Labour government of 1974–79 was due to the excessive expectation of radicalism generated in 1970–74, when the Left had become dominant in the trade unions and on the National Executive Committee (NEC), and a new generation of union leaders had come to the fore, close to the traditional Left.[132]

A large part of the strategic rethinking of the years 1970–74 produced policies which, though in a more moderate form, found their way into the 1974 election manifesto: the NEB, planning agreements, the nationalization of the docks and shipbuilding, industrial democracy. All this constituted the platform of the Labour Left and the core of the 'alternative economic strategy' (the AES), which would be further developed by the Bennite Left in the early 1980s (see chapter 23). During the period of the Labour government, this strategy was abandoned or watered down amid the pressures of inflation, unemployment, deflationary policies, IMF conditions, incomes policies. The supporters of the AES in the cabinet were outnumbered, as they were in the Parliamentary Labour Party, the trade unions (whose loyalty to a Labour government prevailed over their leftist inclination), the press, and the country at large. Only among party members did they have some strong backing.

Unlike *OR'85*, the AES was therefore always the expression of a minority of the movement – at least when Labour was in power. However, the AES shared some significant features with *OR'85*. The first of these was the acceptance of the mixed economy. The second was the recognition of the awesome importance of international constraints. These two features have not always been obvious, because many on the Left often obscured the strategy and dressed up the AES with unwarranted anti-capitalist bluster. They were helped in this by the alarming propaganda produced by the industrialists and their supporters in the press, who depicted the AES as an attempt to sovietize the British economy. Nevertheless, it should be obvious to anyone willing to brush aside the fog of rhetoric that an industrial policy which is based on planning agreements and a stateholding company is, in fact, a policy of *co-existence and partnership* with the private sector, aimed at improving the latter's performance. The AES should be taken to represent one of the very few attempts by British socialism to develop an industrial policy aimed at making capitalism more profitable. That it should have been supported by the Labour Left, and not by the Labour Right, is a demonstration of the extent to which the political reform of capitalism, and not its abolition, had become part of socialist thinking.

The second feature – the recognition of international constraints – was dealt with by resisting, rather than submitting, to them. The purported dangers of powerful transnational corporations were at the core of much of Holland's *The Socialist Challenge*. He wrote:

> In effect, national capitalist planning has had only a short lifetime. It is now being smothered in adolescence by the accelerating trend to monopoly and multinational domination ... In international policy, the State will increasingly see its sovereignty undermined by multinational capital rather than reinforced by international agencies.[133]

Yet, a staunch defence of the nation-state as the best instrument for the development of 'socialist' planning was part and parcel of the AES. In less sophisticated sectors of the Left, multinational companies had become as Satan to Christian fundamentalism. In their insistence on import controls, and their opposition to Britain's integration into Europe, proponents of the AES were backed by a well-established core of distinguished academics grouped round the New Cambridge School of Nicholas Kaldor and Wynne Godley. Though Keynesians, they did not accept that in the existing climate one 'could spend one's way out of recession' – as Crosland might (still) have put it. Reflation would simply suck in imports and lead to a balance of payments crisis. This is why one needed some form of protectionism or, at least, selective import controls, as Kaldor had consistently advocated for a number of years.

The problem with the AES was that it was essentially a strategy for the medium to long term. Labour had no policy for the short term, except the Social Contract. In order to develop its industrial strategy, it had to succeed in establishing an understanding with the trade unions similar to that in Germany. After the sad experience of *In Place of Strife*, the Labour leadership was reluctant to put forward any legislative proposals which could be interpreted as restricting the freedom of the unions. The issue had become even more sensitive because the Conservative government had introduced a statutory wage freeze (November 1972), and legislation (the Industrial Relations Act 1971) to regulate industrial disputes and codify the obligations of trade unions. Thus, the understanding Labour reached with the unions – the 'social contract' – remained vague. Ill-defined union co-operation was exchanged for the Labour Party's promise to repeal all Conservative anti-union legislation. The main innovation British trade unions wanted and obtained was that the state should enshrine in legislation many of the gains they had made during the 1950s and 1960s. Until then, one of the features which most distinguished British unions from their continental counterparts was their commitment to achieving gains directly through collective bargaining. The prevailing ethos was a kind of legal abstentionism. The British labour movement was marked by 'a traditional lack of central authority and obdurate resistance to rationalization of the factors of production, unlike its Nordic equivalents'.[134] Shorter hours, longer holidays and other benefits were obtained through union power and not via the state. Those without a powerful union obtained less and, consequently, had a powerful incentive to join one. In the 1970s this pattern was modified. The Labour government introduced rules in a situation hitherto defined by private bargaining. The four major statutes promulgated in 1974 and 1975 – the Trade Union and Labour Relations Act, the Health and Safety at Work Act, the Sex Discrimination Act, and the Employment Protection Act – as well as the coming into effect of the 1970 Equal Pay Act, universalized gains which only the lucky few had achieved. Labour also continued the Conservative policy of special programmes for the unemployed and the not-yet-employed, not only by developing the Manpower Services Commission (a tripartite body similar to the German Bundesanstalt für Arbeit), but also by instituting – alongside a new spate of acronyms – the Temporary Employment Scheme (TES), the Work Experience Programme (WEP), the Job Creation Programme (JCP), the Recruitment Subsidy for School-Leavers (RSSL), the Youth Employment Subsidy (YES), the Adult Employment Subsidy (AES), and the Youth Opportunities Programme (YOP), and many others.

The one piece of legislation which fulfilled the aims of universality and redistribution of classical welfare social democracy was the Child Benefit Act – an achievement all the more remarkable as it was introduced at a time of great financial stringency. By replacing child tax allowances, which were of greatest value to those families with the highest income and of little or less value to those with incomes below or close to the income tax threshold, child benefits achieved a powerful measure of redistribution.[135] This measure had been specifically promised in Labour's election manifesto, which mentioned 'a new scheme of child credits payable to the mother'.[136] It had been tenaciously fought for by Barbara Castle, when secretary of state for social services. James Callaghan had tried to delay it, and there was growing support among the Treasury team for the then still unfashionable view (in Labour circles) that universal benefits were a luxury which could not be afforded.[137] According to Healey, Callaghan's opposition to a measure which had figured for so long in Labour Party programmes was based on the realization that it 'might cost us male votes because it would mean a switch from the wallet to the handbag: it would be paid to the wife at the cost of withdrawing a tax allowance from the husband.'[138] The TUC, run by males for males in spite of the steady growth of female employment, was equally unenthusiastic for similar reasons.[139] There was also concern about the possible consequences for income policies of a reduction of take-home pay by removing the child tax allowance.[140] As a result, the legislation was unreasonably delayed and was finally introduced in 1978, bringing about a real increase in the value of child support relative to average earnings.

Further redistribution of economic power between men and women was achieved not only as a result of the implementation of the Equal Pay Act, but also by the adoption in July 1975 of a flat-rate incomes policy which increased wages by £6 a week. Because this increased the pay of the low-wage groups (where women were present in relatively greater numbers) proportionately more than that of high income earners, there was a reduction in pay inequality, including the distribution of earnings between men and women.[141]

These measures marked the high point of Labour's achievements in the period 1974–79. Paradoxically, they also signified a recognition that union power was no longer sufficient for achieving a less unequal distribution of power between employees and employers: more than ever, unions needed the state.

While legislation had been used to strengthen the position of trade unions and workers in factories, comparatively little was achieved to enable them to participate in the management of enterprises. British trade unions seldom advanced plans which would result in greater state involvement in industrial relations. The sacred cow of collective bargaining stood in the way. The unions expected more freedom, not more regulation, from a Labour government. German trade unions traditionally advocated some form of planning mechanism through which they would have unspecified, but considerable input into economic policy.[142] In the early 1970s, many German unions advocated some participation in the investment decisions of individual firms. Industrial democracy had for years been one of the main planks of the trade union movement. There was thus a considerable background to what would prove to be the most contentious issue in the field of industrial relations in Germany in the 1970s: the system of *Mitbestimmung* (co-determination).[143]

Much of the support the SPD government obtained from the trade unions was predicated on a general extension of the co-determination principle, which had existed since the early 1950s in the coal and steel industries. Nothing concrete happened until the 1970s. When the SPD–FDP coalition was formed in 1969, it was agreed, under FDP pressure, that the issue of co-determination would not be raised. After the remarkable victory of the SPD in the 1972 elections, the FDP relented, but it was not until 1976 that new legislation was passed.[144]

The principle of *Mitbestimmung* was accepted by all German political parties and they all proposed various schemes. The most controversial issue regarded the composition of the supervisory boards. The CDU wanted a board with a preponderance of shareholders' representatives. The SPD and the DGB wanted equal representation for employees and owners. The FDP wanted senior management to have independent representation – in effect, to have the casting vote between owners and workers. The law which was eventually passed provided for equality of representation between owners and workers on all supervisory boards, but with the proviso that there would be representatives of the senior management in proportion to their presence in the firm. This would have the effect of tilting the balance against the employees (and hence their unions), because it was widely assumed that management would favour the shareholders.[145]

As is usually the case with compromises, the 1976 law managed to dissatisfy everyone. The unions were disappointed because they did not get full parity. Some employers were so alarmed that they tried, unsuccessfully, to have the law declared unconstitutional.[146] The SPD did not disguise its disappointment. In a speech in Hannover on 14 March 1976, Helmut Schmidt, while praising the law as 'an epochal achievement ... without parallel anywhere in the world, west or east', frankly admitted that 'The present co-determination bill does not ... fully accord with my own objectives ... Full parity in co-determination is not achievable under the present political circumstances'.[147] A few days later, the SPD Labour minister, Walter Arendt, introducing the final stages of the co-determination bill in the Bundestag, echoed Schmidt's remarks.[148]

Did this law give more powers to the trade unions? In some trade union and social-democratic circles, it was held that workers' influence was increased more by the Work Promotion Law of June 1969, the *Arbeitsföderungsgesetz*, than by the adoption of *Mitbestimmung*. The 1969 legislation, passed when the SPD was still only the junior partner in the Grosse Koalition, established preventive measures to anticipate problems relating to unemployment, providing for generous re-education and retraining schemes. It was thanks to this law that the unions succeeded in getting the state to adopt something approximating to an active labour market policy.[149] Further gains for factory workers were achieved in 1972 when the Works Constitution Act (*Betriebsverfassungsgesetz*) was amended. In Germany the system of Works Councils (*Betriebsräte*) had existed since the early 1920s, when German workers acquired the legal right to be represented by councils elected by all the firm's employees, regardless of whether they were union members. The 1972 amendment considerably improved the position of workers in matters concerning dismissals, by establishing that the Works Council had to be consulted before any employee could be dismissed.[150] The Works Councils also dealt with new pay methods, overtime, piecework and bonus rates.[151] In theory, these councils could have become 'house unions' separate from, and in constant battle with, the official unions for the support of workers in factories. In practice, this was seldom the case, since in almost all industries the DGB candidates gained the overwhelming majority of the available *Betriebsräte* seats.[152] This led some – for example, Wolfgang Streeck – to suggest that the 1972 amendment 'amounted to a massive organizational support by the state for the unions in adapting their basic structures to new conditions and requirements without endangering the stability of trade unionism'.[153] Later, Streeck modified this view.[154] He pointed out that as central collective bargaining declined, the Works Councils became the main voice of those employed in a particular factory. These workers perceived their interests to be identical to those of their firm, and in contrast to those of the wider labour movement and the unemployed. Had one to design an institutional structure ideally suited to a crisis economy, added Streeck, one would produce something similar to the German Works Councils, at whose heart is a sort of *Betriebsegoismus* – i.e. the 'selfish' protection of one's job and one's firm.[155] This gradual 'Japanization' constituted a serious organizational challenge to German trade unions.

In Britain most trade unions were singularly unattracted by the prospects of enhanced industrial democracy, even when this was promoted throughout Europe by a wide spectrum of opinion, which ranged from those who believed that it would be a step towards socialism, to those who thought that it was a necessary price to pay to obtain moderation in wage negotiation. In 1975 the EEC had published a Green Paper entitled *Employee Participation and Company Structure*, on the basis of a 1972 Fifth Directive harmonizing company law. The EEC commissioner in charge, Finn Gunderlach, envisaged that when the Fifth Directive came into force, it would require member states to provide for workers' participation on the boards of companies. The Labour Party programme of 1973 had stated, rather tentatively, that it was 'considering' the 'provision of some kind of *direct* representation for workers ... based firmly upon trade union channels'.[156] Clearly, the idea was that unless the TUC backed the scheme, it would be dropped. The Labour election manifesto of February 1974 promised an Industrial Democracy Act, aimed at developing 'joint control' by management and workers'.[157] Once re-elected, the Labour government, unsure of the extent of TUC support and never having given the matter serious consideration, appointed a committee of inquiry under Lord Bullock. As is often the case with such committees, its composition was 'loaded' to ensure the desired result – in this instance, one favourable to the TUC, since industrial democracy was seen as one of the requirements of the Social Contract. Predictably, the committee split between a minority, made up of bankers and industrialists, who produced their own report, and a majority which included three academics sympathetic to Labour and two powerful trade unionists, Clive Jenkins of the white-collar ASTMS and Jack Jones, leader of the largest union, the Transport and General Workers' Union (TGWU). The resulting majority report proposed that companies employing over two thousand workers (as in Germany), after obtaining the consent of their employees, should have a board with equal representation from shareholders and employees, along with a small number of independent directors. In contrast to Germany, all worker-directors had to be members of a trade union.[158] The employers' association campaigned vigorously against the Bullock Report, as their counterparts in Germany had done. Their campaign stressed the importance of managerial prerogatives and of flexibility in decision-making.

The TUC had succeeded in convincing the unions to present a united front. After the report was produced, it became clear that the unanimity had been fictitious. Even Clive Jenkins, co-signatory of the report, found that his own union, ASTMS, rejected it.[159] Opposition to Bullock came from the Left (the Miners' Union and the Engineering Union) the centre (the Municipal Workers' Union), and the Right (e.g. the electricians).[160] The British Communist Party, small in votes but influential in trade union circles, stuck to the view that industrial democracy must be advanced exclusively via collective bargaining. The accepted view of the Left, including Hugh Scanlon, was that industrial democracy under capitalism was impossible – the age-old socialist argument against socialist reform. The left- and right-wing opposition to Bullock converged on one crucial aspect: the presence of trade unionists among the directors of a company would inhibit the development of effective, i.e. conflictual and adversarial, collective bargaining. As an academic champion of this confrontational spirit put it (though not very clearly): 'Today the industrial-democracy lobby wish to extend the methods of elitist representative democracy into the workplace which will involve undermining the existing participatory democracy entailed in unilateral shopfloor control.'[161] Some mavericks on the right of the political spectrum concurred: the Bullock Report, they claimed, was not about industrial democracy, but about making workers more malleable: 'That this aim should be disguised under the title of industrial democracy is so much claptrap, expressly intended to mislead the workers into supposing that they are being offered more freedom rather than less ... Under the present system trade union power is genuinely, if disastrously, libertarian on the shop floor.'[162] Among the workers themselves, indifference and ignorance over the issue reigned supreme – not surprisingly, as the idea of worker-directors had very weak roots in the British labour movement. Surveys indicated that most people were in favour of a voluntary system – another way of saying that there should be no legislation.[163] The Labour cabinet was itself divided over the issue and produced a White Paper (1978) which watered down the substance of the Bullock Report, and set out a very long timetable for its implementation. The relevant cabinet minister, Edmund Dell, was opposed, while Callaghan, the then prime minister (who makes only a passing reference to the report in his memoirs), worried mainly about antagonizing the CBI.[164] Denis Healey, who believed that the government had spent an 'inordinate' amount of time on the issue and 'unfortunately to no effect', thought that the proposals were vitiated by the unions' insistence that they should be in charge of appointing the worker-directors, while the CBI was short-sighted to oppose it because industrial democracy would have undermined the power of the unions at a national level.[165] The final TUC position on Bullock was a composite resolution passed at its Congress in 1977, which made it clear that statutory backing for industrial democracy would require union approval (and not employee backing, as Bullock had suggested). For the unions, industrial democracy meant trade union power.[166] In a situation such as this, with industrial democracy opposed by 'both sides of industry', it was hardly surprising if the matter was quietly dropped in spite of the TUC's crocodile tears. As Jack Jones bitterly noted, 'what was left of Bullock sank in the disaster of the winter of discontent.'[167]

Union prerogatives and workers' rights relied on the four major statutes of 1974–75 mentioned above, which strengthened procedural rights in matters of health, pay, dismissal and discrimination. Rather than grant democracy to individual workers, the Labour government preferred to shift power towards the trade unions. This was, after all, why the unions had created the Labour Party in the first place. The mantle of 'industrial' democracy was snatched from Labour by successive Conservative governments under Margaret Thatcher. Under her administrations, workers obtained the right to elect their union officials, the right to vote whether or not to go on strike, and, with the abolition of the closed shop, the right not to join a trade union.

In the meantime, the unions obtained considerable advantages. The 1974 Trade Union and Labour Relations Act repealed the hated Industrial Relations Act of 1971 and, with the help of a further amendment in 1976, restored immunities from civil and criminal action, including inducement of breaches of commercial contract. It meant that workers on strike against a firm could extend their action to that firm's customers or suppliers. The Employment Protection Act of 1975 further limited managerial prerogatives by strengthening *individual* employment rights, the most significant of which was the

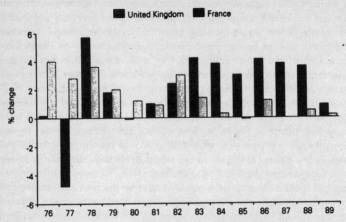

Figure 18.1 Real hourly wage rates in manufacturing in France and the UK, 1976–89
Source: OECD, *Economic Outlook, Historical Statistics 1960–1989*.

right not to be dismissed because of pregnancy and to be reinstated after maternity.[168] The Health and Safety Act (1974) continued the tradition of the first Factory Acts.[169] This legislation was used as evidence by opponents of trade unions to argue that their power had become intolerable.

This was an exaggeration. The legislation of 1974–76 increased the power of trade unions mainly by restoring in statutes rights they had enjoyed in practice before 1970. The rights of individual workers increased because they were better protected against unfair dismissal; health and safety procedures were better controlled; and gender-based inequalities were made illegal. This, of course, regulated the labour market more than ever before and entrepreneurs understandably objected on the grounds that labour costs were increased.

But average labour costs were never a real problem. Average real wages went up throughout the Conservative 1980s, something which had not occurred under Labour. Particularly illuminating here is the comparison with France which, politically speaking, was the mirror-image of Britain: conservative governments in the 1970s and prevalently socialist governments in the 1980s. Figure 18.1 suggests that real wages increased far more when conservatives were in power. On this basis workers in manufacturing who vote according to rational choice theory would have to desert socialist parties. This is precisely what many did.

What happened under the Thatcher administration was that 'inefficient' firms in the private sector – i.e. those with a pronounced gap between productivity and wages – went bankrupt and their former workers, now unemployed, were kept at the expense of taxpayers, rather than of share-holders. Thus, the high labour costs of inefficient firms were 'socialized'. Meanwhile, the close link between wages in the private and public sectors was severed. Private sector wages went up much faster than those in the public sector, whose potentially profitable branches, such as monopolistic utilities, were privatized and made profitable by further redundancies. In the remaining, as yet unsaleable, part of the public sector, such as the armed forces and the universities, a stringent system of 'cash limits' – inherited from Labour – was put into operation: a *de facto* incomes policy. Electorally, the strategy paid off: skilled workers in the private sector joined the ranks of Conservative supporters, clutching their higher pay, while Labour increasingly became the party of the poor, of those still working in the least efficient remains of manufacturing industry, and of public sector workers.

The working class had thus been further divided. The original post-war deal between labour and capital or, rather, between social democrats and conservatives, a deal which underpinned West European capitalism, was at an end. Subsequent developments indicate that in Britain this demise occurred in its purest – Marx would have said 'classic' – form. After Keynesianism, 'Thatcherism' became the only 'ism' this supposedly so un-ideological country had offered the world in its entire history.

CHAPTER NINETEEN

The French Experiment

THE TRIUMPH of the Parti Socialiste (PS) at the presidential election of 1981 and at the general election immediately afterwards marked a real turning-point in the complex history of the French Left. The French socialists, having established themselves as the main force on the Left, won an absolute majority of seats in the National Assembly for the first time. The Fifth Republic had acquired its first socialist head of state.

From the wider perspective of the West European Left, a socialist victory in a country as important as France, just as the economic tide was turning everywhere in favour of neo-liberal conservatism, constituted a momentous event. In Northern Europe, the Swedish SAP was still in opposition, the German SPD was approaching the end of its period in office, the British Labour Party, out of power since 1979, appeared increasingly unelectable. These once powerful battalions of social democracy looked to Mitterrand's striking victory with curiosity and anticipation. In Southern Europe, the French success appeared as a harbinger which would shift the epicentre of socialism from the North to the South of the continent. In Madrid, Felipe González's PSOE, and in Athens, Andreas Papandreou's PASOK were on the point of gaining power with massive majorities, while in Rome, Bettino Craxi, soon to become prime minister, entertained a credible hope that his PSI would supplant the PCI as the leader of the Italian Left. In Paris itself, Mitterrand's victory was celebrated with revolutionary gaiety, dancing in the streets and all-night parties which nostalgically recalled the radiant days of the Popular Front and the Liberation, the days of *les lendemains qui chantent*.

As is often the case, a spectacular defeat underlay this stunning victory. The humiliation suffered by the Left in the general election of 1968, and in the presidential election of 1969, had concentrated the minds of socialists and communists. To be divided would consign them to permanent opposition. To be united was the royal road to power. The old SFIO had been routed. Its seemingly eternal leader, Guy Mollet, had finally retired in 1969, thus concluding with yet another defeat his long career at the head of one of Europe's least successful socialist parties, a party without trade unions and without workers, full of schoolteachers and minor civil servants.

The ensuing reconstruction of the French Left took a course remarkably different from the socialist revisionism which prevailed in other countries.

Elsewhere, modernization, rethinking, revision, adaptation – be it in the SPD, the PCI or the Labour Party – always meant a shift away from the traditional values of the socialist movement, away from state ownership and the working class. The French socialists adapted by shifting to the left and embracing a distinctly socialist profile. This 'turn to the left', far from indicating any desire to retreat into socialist purity, was marked by a positive craving for political power. No longer was there a perceived contradiction between the idea of gaining power and a distinctive socialist profile.

This is all the more surprising as French socialism had been a veritable ideological circus since the days of its inception. When, in June 1971, the Parti socialiste was created, it was the culmination of a process of renewal which had begun in 1969, following the defeat at the presidential election. Between 1969 and 1971, 70 per cent of the secretaries of departmental federations of the old SFIO had been replaced and the average age of the holders of these key party posts had fallen dramatically.[1] In terms of membership, the party kept one of the distinguishing features of the old SFIO: it was a small party with few members. It would never aspire to the mass membership of the German SPD, the Swedish SAP, the Austrian SPÖ, or the Italian PCI. Nor did it succeed in abolishing the various factions and chiefdoms which had always marked the contours of the non-communist Left. Surviving in rivalry and united by the overwhelming desire to run the country were: Gaston Defferre's 'municipal' socialist Bouches-du-Rhône federation; its closest ally, Pierre Mauroy's traditional working-class bastion in the Nord Federation (Lille); the Left faction of Jean Poperen; and the marxisant CERES (Paris), led by Didier Motchane and Jean-Pierre Chevènement. Towering above them in national renown was François Mitterrand, whose diaphanous socialist credentials (he had never been a member of the SFIO) were amply compensated by an uncommon political intelligence. In fact, the new party became above all a machine to ensure the victory of Mitterrand at the presidential elections. This marked a final acceptance of the institutions of the Fifth Republic, which the socialists had opposed for nearly twenty years. De Gaulle's commitment to presidential politics over party politics had finally triumphed even in the PS. All faction leaders – Chevènement, Rocard, Mauroy, Defferre – now had to have 'presidential' qualities.[2] Once again, a socialist party modelled itself on the state it yearned to possess and modify.

All these factions, including what was left of the Radical Party and the power-hungry notables of provincial France, combined around a strategy of dialogue with the communists – all equally convinced that this was the only road to power.[3] The congress of Epinay in 1971 brought Mitterrand's Convention des Institutions Républicaines into the new united Parti Socialiste. The key motion affirmed that the new party was no longer equidistant from the Gaullists and the PCF, as the SFIO had claimed. It called for a dialogue with the PCF on the 'concrete problems of a government aiming to achieve the socialist transformation of society'.[4] The ensuing internal debate over the programme (*Changer la vie*) was a device to enable the various factions to establish their respective positions. As usual, it was the minority Left factions (CERES and Jean Poperen) which made most of the running, and the resulting document had a distinctive left-wing flavour: it was suspicious of European integration and of NATO; it wanted nationalizations and was vociferous in its support for *autogestion*. The programme was forgotten as soon as it had been agreed. Its purpose was simply to set out a position for negotiations with the PCF.[5] The *Programme commun* which emerged involved also the Left-Radicals. Thus, it became the charter of the Union of the Left. This paved the way for consolidating all the anti-Gaullist votes around a single candidate in the second round of the presidential and general elections.

The *Programme commun* was signed in July 1972 by François Mitterrand, Georges Marchais (for the PCF), and Robert Fabre (for the Left-Radicals). This document was widely seen as a compromise whereby the PCF officially accepted the principle of the alternance of political parties and political pluralism, while the PS subscribed to a substantially communist economic programme aimed at a massive expansion of the nationalized sector.[6] Thanks to this compromise, the PS established its credentials on the Left. It appeared as a truly reforming party and no longer as an ill-specified centre party in a polarized political system. Yet the alliance with the PCF was riven by profound conflicts: the expansion of the left electorate, necessary for victory, was more likely to benefit the socialists than the communists. The PS could establish a rapport with the more moderate sections of the electorate who wanted a new government, but remained suspicious of the communists.

The PS entered the alliance as the weaker partner. Fewer than six years later, it was stronger than the PCF. The stronger it became, the more credible the Union of the Left became for the non-communist electorate. There was no real chance for a communist party to join the government of a major West European country as its dominant force, politically and electorally. Communism could be tolerated by private industry, international economic operators and the USA, only if it was clear that it would remain subordinate to other, less threatening political parties.

The more Mitterrand talked about the need to 're-equilibrate' the Left, the more the PCF accused him of disloyalty. The more the conflict escalated, the more the PS could be distinguished from the PCF and the more electable it became.

Initially, the PCF concentrated on ensuring that the *Programme commun* reflected its own ideas, assuming that its hegemony could better be safeguarded through the adoption of a communist programme. In spite of its rhetoric, the PCF was, in fact, a much more 'French' party than the PS in its inordinate regard for texts, declarations, proclamations and written documents. The *Programme commun* quickly became a sacred text of the PCF. Its chief features were the following (I have kept the order of presentation in the document):[7]

1. Demand-led growth through a 'substantial increase in wages'.[8]
2. Extension of social protection, particularly health care; massive housing programme.[9]
3. Strengthening non-religious public education. Construction of a network of one thousand crèches to enable all children between the ages of two and six to attend.[10]
4. All discrimination against women to be abolished.[11]
5. Strengthening the rights of individual workers against unfair dismissal. Expansion of the rights to information; industrial democracy.[12]
6. Nationalization of the entire financial sector (all banks, including merchant banks and insurance companies); of all mining, armaments, aeronautics, pharmaceutics, space and nuclear industries. This includes some of the giants of French industry: Dassault, Rhône-Poulenc, Honeywell-Bull, Compagnie Générale d'Electricité.[13]
7. Increases in the marginal rates of income tax and corporation.[14]
8. Extension of civil liberties, abolition of existing laws restricting freedom of assembly (the law of 8 June 1970); abolition of the death penalty.[15]
9. A profound reform of the existing presidential system: abolition of Article 16 of the constitution (whereby the president can assume emergency powers), limitation of the president's term of office (from seven to five years), strengthening of the powers of Parliament.[16]

This programme could be called 'communist' only in the sense that it contained policies advocated by the French Communist Party in the previous decade. To insist that the PCF got everything it wanted with the *Programme commun* is misleading, for there was nothing in it which could not have been wholeheartedly embraced by a classical socialist party: higher wages, extension of the public sector, expansion of the welfare state, democratization of the institutions of the Fifth Republic. The proposed nationalizations, which aroused so much anxiety and controversy, would not have made the French public sector any larger than that of Austria or Italy (which never had a Left government).

The concessions made by the PCF, though implicit, were far more substantial than those which the PS appeared to make. For the first time the PCF acknowledged that the socialists represented an important section of the Left, without renouncing the idea of remaining the dominant party of the working class. It also accepted that the presidential candidate who would best represent the Left would be Mitterrand (whose commitment to socialism was recent), and refrained from demanding the post of prime minister. In fact, the PCF did not seriously insist – though the matter was raised – on having specific positions in an eventual government. Marchais behaved throughout the first phase of the PCF–PS alliance (1972–76) as someone who understood perfectly well that France could not have a communist as president, prime minister, foreign secretary or minister of the interior.

The PCF sealed the alliance by taking on board many of the changes which the Italian Communist Party had initiated. It espoused 'Eurocommunism'. It dropped the concept of the dictatorship of the proletariat. It supported the right of the dissident writer Alexander Solzhenitsyn to be allowed to speak freely. It criticized the attitude of the USSR towards religious freedom. It distanced itself from Soviet foreign policy by adopting a strong position on national autonomy.[17] Real efforts were made to adapt. For instance, the PCF candidate in the legislative elections in Tours in 1976 gave up the traditional hammer and sickle emblem in favour of the ecologists' green circle.[18] The manner in which these changes were achieved bore the mark of an authoritarian party. The dropping of the hallowed concept of the dictatorship of the proletariat occurred after a brief debate in the party press, prior to Marchais' brutal announcement at the 1976 Party Congress. The endorsement of French nuclear weapons in 1977 was similarly abrupt.

Nevertheless, the PCF gained that most elusive of political commodities: recognition as a legitimate party of government. Thanks to the *Programme commun*, the PCF, for the first time since the outbreak of the Cold War, emerged from the political ghetto.

The PS appeared to grant all the programmatic demands of the PCF. However, political parties of the Left usually require some fundamental ideas which set them apart from their rivals. The problem with French socialism was that it was singularly devoid of distinctive ideas. The old SFIO was constantly swaying between opportunism and revolutionary rhetoric. The new PS avoided this predicament by adopting the idea of self-management or *autogestion*, which had become increasingly fashionable in intellectual and trade union circles.

As we pointed out in chapter 13, the idea of *autogestion*, whose vagueness was its strength, had become one of the 'big ideas' of the non-communist Left. Although its origins can be traced to nineteenth-century anti-state socialism, the concept, in its modern construction, had reappeared in French political discourse in the mid-1960s when it was used to describe the Yugoslav system of industrial democracy and a decentralized economy.[19] The May events had reinforced the popularity of the concept by making it into a political rallying point for the non-communist Left, underlining their refusal to accept the Soviet model of central planning.[20] In 1970, *autogestion* became the *cheval de bataille* of the trade union federation CFDT, whose general secretary, Edmond Maire, became its chief advocate.[21] The CFDT favoured trade union action to bring about a *société autogestionnaire*, but had no strategy for establishing it.[22]

The other main proponent of *autogestion* as a distinctively French model of socialism was Michel Rocard and his PSU. At first, Rocard had refused to join the newly formed PS at the Epinay Congress, or sign the *Programme commun*, because of its emphasis on nationalization and *étatisme*. He agreed to join the new party only in 1974, when *autogestion* became a major theme in the PS (and when Mitterrand needed Rocard to contain the expansion of the CERES).[23] *Autogestion* was officially adopted by the National Convention of the PS in June 1975, in the form of *Quinze thèses sur l'autogestion*.[24]

Autogestion co-existed uneasily with the state-centred *Programme commun*, just as Rocard and the CFDT co-existed uneasily with traditional socialists such as the old SFIO activists led by Pierre Mauroy, whose Jacobinism and *étatisme* were similar to those of the PCF. Mitterrand never strongly supported the *autogestionnaires:* the Jacobinism of the *Programme commun* was essential to the alliance with the PCF and appealed to his political realism. His main ideological characteristic was a profound disdain for ideologies. He much preferred to remain committed to a general set of republican values which would enable him to preserve a free hand in the choice of actual policies.

What did *autogestion* mean? It would be easy to dismiss it as a purely ideological construct aimed at promoting the image of the PS as a party distinct from the old SFIO and the PCF. Its proponents believed passionately in it and they responded to a real problem in modern liberal democracy: the formal rules of political participation (voting, representation, civil liberties) were far too narrow to promote anything resembling genuine popular control.

The term *autogestion* conveyed a variety of sentiments: a form of resistance to modernization; an ideology of modernization; an alternative to capitalism; an alternative to 'state' socialism; an anti-hierarchical principle; another form of liberalism; an anti-productivist doctrine.[25] The 1976 *Quinze thèses sur l'autogestion* envisaged the creation of an administrative council for each nationalized enterprise, with representatives elected by workers, the state and some categories of consumers; a management council wholly elected by the workers – along the lines of certain co-operatives; the co-existence of a management council elected by the workers and a control board consisting of representatives of the state and consumers.[26]

Pierre Ronsanvallon, editor of the journal *CFDT aujourd'hui* (1973–77), and one of the main theorists of the *autogestionnaires*, saw the model as yet another instance of the long-sought third way between a social-democratic compromise with capitalism and the soviet model.[27] He recognized the existence of diverse definitions and approaches – technocratic, libertarian, soviet (in the original sense of decentralization by hierarchically organized workers' councils). Denying that *autogestion* was a complete model or blueprint, he stressed that it was as much a strategy as a goal, and that it was not limited to the traditional question of who owns the means of production, but was concerned with how political power is to be exercised.[28] What mattered to the workers was not nationalization, but the possibility of influencing the conditions of work, the command system in the enterprise, the norms of payments, and so on.[29] *Autogestion* was seen as the self-government of the masses, while nationalizations were simply about a transfer of property from shareholders to the state.[30] What should matter to socialists was how decision-making powers were distributed throughout society.[31]

Such ideas were compelling and it is easy to understand their appeal for socialists. Yet none of the theorists was able to delineate the practical steps required to pursue the proposed goal. They claimed, not unreasonably, that it would be contradictory to construct a strategy from on high. However, to set in motion a mass movement requires some concrete goals and concrete issues. For instance, the feminist movement, which likewise had vague and ill-specified strategies and generic goals, always targeted clearly defined issues which had a profound appeal: the suffrage, abortion, child-care, pornography, discrimination at work, etc. *Autogestion* remained vague and ill-defined in all its aspects. As one commentator suggested, it simply served as a recruiting theme for *soixante-huitards*.[32] In 1972 Michel Rocard, in his preface to the manifesto of his party (then the PSU), accepted that the concept was ambiguous, adding: 'The political value of a word must be measured not in terms of its linguistic coherence but in the way people use it.'[33] The problem with the term *autogestion* was that people never used it. *Autogestion* remained a weapon in an ideological battle within the Left. It never became a banner with which to rally ordinary people.

Once the PS obtained political power, it made no serious attempt to implement the concept. The Auroux laws – the French equivalent of German co-determination – were a mild and ineffective step towards *autogestion*, which remained inoperative.[34] Workers continued to prefer cash to *autogestion* and never fought for it; nor did the trade unions. It was never more than a polemical theme directed against traditional socialism.[35]

What eventually split the French Left again, however, was not ideology, but the realization that the socialists were gaining votes at the expense of the communists. The united Left advanced in the polls, but it did so unevenly, with the PS benefiting more than the PCF. That this should have surprised anyone is surprising. It was unlikely that first-time Left voters would bypass the more moderate PS to vote directly for the PCF – as even the PCF realized. What increasingly became a source of worry for the PCF was the fact that the PS deliberately appealed to the anti-communist Left, and openly insisted that it was necessary to 're-equilibrate the Left', meaning that the PS should overtake the PCF in terms of votes.[36] Mitterrand had never disguised that his long-term project was to end the supremacy of the PCF on the Left. In 1978 this project appeared less utopian than in 1969, when the goal had been openly announced.[37]

In 1974 Valéry Giscard d'Estaing narrowly defeated Mitterrand – sole candidate of the united Left – but the socialists emerged as the largest party of the Left in the local elections. This was the beginning of a trend which soon became firmly established.

At the parliamentary elections of March 1978, the Left was defeated once again, but for the first time since the 1930s the socialists obtained more votes than the communists. The 'popular front' of the 1970s, unlike that of the 1930s in which the communists benefited more than the socialists, signalled the beginning of the end for French communism.

This situation was intolerable for the PCF. It could accept being deprived of the most important positions of power (president, prime minister), but only because it assumed that it would be able to control the government effectively, thanks to its electoral superiority and its hegemony in the organized working class. Otherwise, it was preferable to be a strong force in opposition, rather than a marginal one in power. The future of the party, the communists believed, was more important than a Pyrrhic victory. Success for the Union of the Left in which the PCF lost ground would not be – in their view – a victory for socialism. It was time to rebuild the identity of the party.[38] The communists decided that a rapid retreat from the pact with the socialists was indicated. The final outcome of this strategy was that, instead of being junior partners, they became a marginal force.

The PCF had grossly miscalculated. The PS had obtained from the Union what it had long sought: to become credible as a true left-wing reformist party. By standing firm on its generally pro-Western outlook (pro-EEC and pro-NATO), it provided guarantees to France's foreign partners and to all French voters worried about a government of the Left. Paradoxically, by breaking with the PS, the PCF had also increased the electoral appeal of the socialists: it was now clear to even the most sceptical observer that Mitterrand's PS was not a stalking horse for the communists.

Could the PCF have behaved differently? As some of its supporters had always insisted, the party could have followed a strategy parallel to that of the PCI. It could have distanced itself more firmly from the USSR and encouraged internal debates. In so doing, it would certainly have angered many of its traditional activists, but this would not have presented major problems, since they had nowhere else to go. Moreover, precisely because they were traditional communists they would have obeyed all directives from above, just as the sudden dropping of the 'dictatorship of the proletariat' in 1976 did not really cause any substantial internal problems. If anything, the return to sectarianism was a source of greater internal dissent. Those who objected to Marchais' return to tradition quit the PCF to join the PS. The communist break with Mitterrand caused great dismay among PCF supporters, who had been looking forward to a Left victory.

It is difficult to find a convincing rational explanation for Marchais' decision. Was it just a case of a sclerotic party unable to understand that the world was changing, and ready to die rather than accept the need for some serious rethinking? Rhetoric notwithstanding, the PCF had often changed line in the past and had demonstrated that it could always find reasons to justify alliances with other forces. Had it not fought in the Resistance under the banner of de Gaulle? Had it not, later, supported a staunch anti-communist like Guy Mollet?

French communists, like most communists, assumed that any genuine advance towards socialism could not occur without the leading role of the Communist Party. This was understandable. The socialists' position was similar: they too assumed that the Union of the Left would be successful only if French socialists held all key positions of power.

Whatever their reasons, it is now clear that Georges Marchais and his colleagues miscalculated. In the fifteen years between 1978 and 1993, the electoral support of the PCF collapsed. Its fortunes became detached from those of the PS in the sense that, irrespective of the socialists' results, the PCF lost votes. Marchais obtained only 15.3 per cent at the presidential election of April–May 1981, while the previous PCF candidate, Jacques Duclos, had achieved a respectable 21.5 per cent in 1969. The party obtained 16.1 per cent at the subsequent general election (June 1981), while the PS surged to 37 per cent; for the first time since the end of the war, the PCF registered a significant decline in working-class support in its heartland, the red belt of Paris.[39] In 1984 the PCF failed to benefit from the difficulties of the PS, and obtained 11.2 per cent at the European election of 1984 and 9.8 at the general election of 1986. Having sunk to a dismal 6.7 per cent at the presidential election of 1988, with their candidate André Lajoinie, the communists recovered slightly to 11.3 per cent at the general election of 1988, (marked by the return to power of the socialists), and 9.2 per cent at that of 1993, with only twenty-three deputies elected (when the socialists were soundly defeated). In the twenty years between 1973 and 1993, the PCF's membership halved to around 300,000. As communism disappeared as a world force, the PCF, its name unchanged, appeared content to remain the expression of a radical working-class politics without a future. One of the many unforeseen consequences of the great 1981 victory of the French Left was that what, at the end of the Second World War, had been the strongest communist party in Western Europe, had, within the space of a few years, lost over half of its national electorate and seen the end of its ideological influence.[40]

Even after the 1978 break with the socialists, the PCF could not escape the constraints of the French electoral system. It was impossible for them not to support socialist candidates in the second round of elections. Mitterrand knew this perfectly well and made sure, against the advice of many in his own party, to adopt a platform which the PCF could not avoid supporting – for example, by making the minimum wage of 2,400 francs the basis of his 1978 campaign.[41] In the 1981 second round of the presidential election, Marchais had to instruct his supporters to vote for Mitterrand.

Cunningly, Mitterrand exploited Rocard's attempt to become the socialist presidential candidate in 1981 by allowing the former 'revolutionary' leader of the PSU, now the darling of moderate social democracy and the media, to occupy the space of the never triumphant anti-communist Left, formerly occupied by Mollet and Defferre. The PCF, like the CERES, had no choice. It had to support Mitterrand and the *Programme commun* against Rocard.

Deprived of a credible strategy, the PCF was trapped in a complex political web beyond its control.

The votes of the PCF were crucial to the victory of the socialists; but since the latter had a majority of the seats, its parliamentary support was unnecessary. With an eye to the future, Mitterrand conceded the PCF four ministerial posts – of the forty-four available – in the 1981 government: transport, public administration, health and training. In historical perspective this was no mean achievement. With the exception of Portugal in the throes of the anti-fascist revolution of 1974–75, and peripheral Finland and Iceland, it was the first time that communists had occupied ministerial seats in Western Europe since the beginning of the Cold War. It was the PCF's third experience of power. During the Popular Front of 1936–38 – when they did not occupy ministerial positions – and the period 1944–47, the PCF was in the ascendant, having increased its electoral support. In 1981, however, it had declined to the percentage of the vote obtained in 1936.[42]

The four communist ministers participated loyally and efficiently in the tasks of government – particularly in the first two years – while being completely marginalized by the socialists. They enjoyed only the nominal support of their party, which refused to develop a strategy for government. The four ministers sat there, in the cabinet room, as tolerated outsiders, the ears and eyes of a party which had no trust in the government.

The PCF kept its distance from the government, hoping to condition its activities from outside, from the streets and the factories, by mobilizing the masses. But the masses no longer followed them. The PCF, which prided itself – like the PCI – on being a party of struggle and of government, was neither. Finally, in 1984, having lost considerable support at the European elections, it refused to back the new government of Laurent Fabius, and ordered its reluctant ministers to leave the government, thus liberating the socialists from an alliance which was becoming useless and embarrassing.

Not without relish, the PCF resumed its traditional wait-and-see attitude (the position of classical social democracy in the era of the Second International). The explanatory scheme underlying it was the belief that the economic crisis which was overtaking France and Europe would create the conditions for the reawakening of the ideas of socialism. Seldom has a political force been so extraordinarily blind to everything that happened. Seldom has the refusal to think become so distinguishing a characteristic of a political party.

Many inside the party, who had hoped that the PCF would be able to contribute to the expansion of the Left in France, saw the withdrawal as a defeat. It was the final straw and they decided to leave what had become an increasingly unpopular party.[43] An exodus of great and small intellectuals and political activists – already alienated by the PCF's support for the military takeover in Poland – left Marchais and his praetorian guards proudly at the helm of a foundering ship, without the intellectual cohorts which usually imparted a certain *éclat* to the PCF.[44] The communist *renovateurs* had failed miserably. They had not succeeded in influencing the PCF when they were in it, and did not succeed in replacing it after they left it. Solidly in control of his dwindling party, Marchais had as his remaining priority electoral survival – not an easy task, since participation in government had done nothing to stop the haemorrhage of votes.[45] Despite its revolutionary rhetoric, the PCF was as obsessed with its electoral standing as the most 'reformist' of political parties.

As the 1981 elections approached, the Left offered a strange spectacle. Though no longer united, both sides, communists and socialists, purported to stand squarely on the *Programme commun*; yet each accused the other of having abandoned it. Those socialists who wished to discard it – for instance, Michel Rocard – had been marginalized. The 'Italianization' of the PCF, seen by many as a precondition for its entry into a future left-wing government, had been brutally interrupted. Unlike his Italian counterpart Enrico Berlinguer, Marchais had supported the largely pro-Soviet Portuguese Communist Party, approved of the Soviet invasion of Afghanistan, and refused to condemn the *coup d'état* of General Wojciech Jaruzelski in Poland. Yet Mitterrand declined to move to the right. The *Projet Socialiste pour la France des années 80*, drafted by the CERES, was an advanced *marxisant* document, overtly competing with the communists even on terrain long vacated by the majority of the West European Left.[46]

Projet Socialiste was probably the longest document produced in those years by a party of the Left – or, indeed, by any party. In 371 pages it depicted the context facing the socialists: the great crises of contemporary society – the crises of values, of capitalism, of bureaucratic societies, of Giscard's France. It sought to conflate many of the analyses of left-wing intellectuals fashionable at the time with an absorption of the mood of May 1968.[47] Authority in all its forms – not just capitalist authority – was being challenged.[48] The old SFIO 'third force' motif of equidistance between communism and capitalism, though openly denounced, re-entered through the back door in the guise of a struggle against all bureaucratic societies.[49] Yet the main enemy, in practical terms, was US capitalism and not the USSR, whose tanks were unlikely – the document pointed out – to advance on Paris as they had on Prague.[50] What is perhaps the most striking element of the *Projet* was the pervasive mood of optimism. It wore its radicalism with great panache, like someone who is certain that their hour has finally come. All the problems and issues of the contemporary world were listed with the assurance that they could be resolved: inequality, working conditions, the emancipation of women, the plight of the Third World, technological progress, alienation, bureaucracy, the over-centralization of the French state and so on. The division into three parts, with their bold characterization, *Comprendre–Vouloir–Agir*, perfectly illustrates the rationalist schema presented (the English translation – to understand, to will, to act – fails to convey the self-assurance of the original). This faith, this trust in the capacity to change things, this optimism was what united all the factions of the Left, and distinguished the banners of the socialists before and during the 1981 campaign. This was what inspired the dancing in the streets in May 1981. Mitterrand's polished rhetoric captured the mood as he entered the Elysée Palace:

> To have great designs is the privilege of great nations. In today's world there can be no greater exigency for our country than to forge a new alliance between socialism and freedom and no greater ambition than to be able to offer it to tomorrow's world ... May 10, 1981 has seen only one victor, Hope.[51]

As a party programme the *Projet Socialiste*, because of its sheer length and complexity, was a failure – the sort of document which loyal socialists would buy, but not read. Its main function was internal: it symbolized the determination of the PS to maintain a high left-wing profile and to isolate Rocard and his followers. It announced loudly that the aim of the Socialist Party was the transformation of the structures of society, 'to liberate Man and Woman'.[52] Its task was not to improve the capitalist system, but to create a new one.[53] The party openly appealed to

> simple but strong sentiments: resistance against injustice, human dignity and human solidarity, love of truth, faith in humanity and its potential, the taste for great enterprises and, above all, for the greatest of them all: to free the workers from age-old oppression and to provide all those who are exploited, men and women, with the instruments for their own self-emancipation.[54]

But that was like a flaming torch with no path to shine on. Once the *Projet* had been approved, it was quickly forgotten. Mitterrand did not use it in his 1981 presidential campaign, preferring his own more moderate and much shorter *110 Propositions*.[55]

Thus the French socialists entered the electoral fray with an unusually large set of programmatic documents: the *Programme commun*, the *Quinze thèses sur l'autogestion*, the *Projet Socialiste* and Mitterrand's *110 Propositions*. This was capped by a particularly enticing slogan: *Vivre mieux, changer la vie* (loosely translatable as 'Let's live better, let's change our lives'). This surfeit of promises and analyses consolidated the image of the Socialist Party as a modernizing force which had well understood the dire economic situation (*comprendre*) and was willing and ready to act accordingly (*vouloir* and *agir*). Its greatest ally was the recession facing the country and the rest of Europe in 1981. This recession, which had militated against the chances of victory for the German SPD in 1982 and for the British Labour Party in 1979, worked, this time, in favour of the Left. An added bonus was the division of the Right between the old Gaullists, led by Jacques Chirac, and the president, Giscard d'Estaing, who was deeply unpopular, having failed – like so many others – to deliver low inflation or to contain unemployment. Giscard d'Estaing's personal

arrogance was not justified, as Schmidt's might have been, by any personal
success in achieving anything of note. His promises of greater participation
and greater modernization floated on the waves of political logorrhea.

In his campaign Mitterrand stressed the most popular of the Left's demands: longer holidays, earlier retirement, shorter working week, an increase
in the minimum wage.[56] But more important than these promises was the
fact that a sufficient number of French voters believed that the election of
a socialist president would not destabilize the country. A new government
was both credible and possible. In the first round Giscard obtained 28.3 per
cent, Mitterrand 25.8 per cent, Chirac 18 per cent, and Marchais 15.3 per
cent. In the second round Mitterrand inherited most of Marchais' votes and
a sizeable proportion of the Gaullists', to beat Giscard by 51.75 per cent to
48.24. He quickly capitalized on his victory by appointing a new government,
dissolving Parliament and calling for new elections.

The parliamentary landslide which resulted – the PS secured 70 per cent
of the seats (that is, 269 against the PCF's 44 and the 144 of the combined
Right) – provided the French socialists with the most unassailable parliamentary majority any Left party had obtained anywhere in Europe since
1945. They were helped in this achievement by the lack of proportionality in
the second round of.the French electoral system. In the first round, when
voters cast their ballot for the party they really support, before picking the
one they dislike the least in the second, the PS obtained 37.5 per cent – still
one of the lowest scores reached by any socialist party in Western Europe.
The PS had won, but as Pierre Mauroy, prime minister between 1981 and
1984, admitted with hindsight: this was more a defeat of the Right than a
victory of the Left.[57]

France had once again, as so often in the course of its history, become
the testing ground for a major political experiment. What was at stake was
an attempt to repeat the Attlee experience in far less conducive economic
and political circumstances. What was being tested was the celebrated doctrine
of national sovereignty, which so many socialists throughout Europe had
espoused since the end of the Second World War: those who had captured
state power, and hence sovereignty, had all the instruments at their disposal
for the radical transformation of the country. Here we had a political party,
the Parti socialiste, in charge of one of the most powerful and richest
countries in Europe, its parliamentary majority overwhelming, and further
buttressed by the partial support of forty-four communists who would be
unable to vote against any recognizably left-wing measure. As if this was not
enough, it disposed, in the person of the president, of the most powerful
instruments of individual power in any democratic country outside of the
USA. The French president, elected by the people for seven years, could not
be ousted by anyone. The constitution, created by de Gaulle, had been devised
to concentrate power in the presidency, not to restrain presidential power as
in the USA. Unlike the Federal Republic of Germany or the USA, France

was a centralist country. What Paris decided would be transmitted and enforced throughout the departments by its centrally appointed prefects.

The socialists also inherited a strong state machine, well-oiled by excellent civil servants desirous of continuing in the Colbertian tradition of state interventionism, and an ideology of planning more favourable to socialist ideas than the *laissez-faire* obsessions prevailing in Britain. Most civil servants had been appointed by previous governments, but French political leaders enjoy a spoils system not unlike that of the USA, with various mechanisms for replacing untrustworthy characters with friends and comrades. There were limits, of course, in that some degree of competence is usually desirable. Given that as many leading socialist (and some communist) supporters held positions of prestige in the humanities and social sciences, and many others were school-teachers or magistrates, while left-wing generals and businessmen were comparatively rare, the Defence Ministry was left virtually unchanged, while the ministries of Justice, Education and Culture acquired a distinct red tint.[58]

The weakness of trade unions in France, where the degree of unionization was one of the lowest in Europe, was not a handicap for the Left. The last thing a socialist government needed was a strong organized labour movement it could not control. Of course, one could argue that the unions could have powerfully sustained the government, as they had done in 1936 and in 1945. But since the strongest union, the CGT, was communist-controlled, it was unlikely to be an uncritical supporter of the socialist government.

Furthermore, the socialists inherited from their predecessors a radio and television system which had none of the political independence enjoyed by its British counterpart. De Gaulle, unable to gag the printed press, had made sure that only those willing and able to toe the line would be in charge of broadcasting. This habit was enthusiastically adopted by all his successors. The socialists had simply to pension off handsomely those journalists, producers and functionaries closely connected to the previous administration, and appoint those expected to be loyal to their new masters.[59] Thus, the socialists could enjoy the advantage of a favourable broadcasting system, until their deregulation policies allowed commercial interests to acquire their own radio and television networks.

Finally, the new socialist government, unlike that in Britain, was not bound by any special relationship to the USA. It did not have the disadvantage of a subservient role in international affairs, unlike the Italians; or suffer from a historical necessity to prove its reliability, unlike the Germans. Once again, the Gaullists had created a situation in which French external policy was dictated by perceived national interests. The Americans were worried by the presence of four communist ministers, but there was little they could do.[60] They realized that, in terms of the zero-sum game of bipolar international diplomacy, they were unlikely to lose anything: after all, France was not even in the military structure of NATO. De Gaulle and his successors had been no great friends of theirs. Mitterrand could hardly be more anti-American than the French Foreign Ministry had been for years. They could even hope that, to distance himself from the communists, Mitterrand might consider a rapprochement with the USA. These hopes were not unfounded. President Mitterrand turned out to be more anti-Soviet and more pro-American than his predecessors, supporting Reagan's foreign policy in Europe and adding to the pressure on the German government to accept the installation of Cruise missiles, even though the SPD, once in opposition, had turned against this security policy.[61] At no stage was Mitterrand constrained by the PCF in assuming an anti-Soviet stance, unlike Léon Blum in 1936 and Guy Mollet in 1945–47.[62] The first authentically socialist government of France since the 1930s thus appeared all-powerful. It controlled all the institutions of state. It had no external enemies. It enjoyed great popular support. What did it do?

When asked this question – and they were incessantly – socialist ministers answered: an increase in the purchasing power of the poorer strata; lowering of the retirement age; reduction in the working week; the development of workers' rights; decentralization; abolition of the death penalty. However, modern governments are judged, and ask to be judged, by their economic performance. The French socialists had acquired power in the aftermath of the second oil shock. They faced a long-term challenge – the economic modernization of France – and a short-term one – the reorganization of production after the crises of the 1970s.

Both these challenges could be redefined in a single question, asked everywhere in Western Europe: what policies were required to return to full employment, growth and low inflation?

The paradox is evident: what was expected of the first left-wing government since the Popular Front was a return to the benefits brought by the golden age of capitalism. The horizon of the thinkable had shrunk to a restoration of the past. To be sure, those who surrounded the socialist president in the feverish days of June 1981 were determined to show that, in order for prosperity to return, it was necessary to change the management of the economy. The decentralized nature of capitalist decision-making had to be replaced by a far more overt mechanism of political intervention. That was the distinctive alternative offered by socialists.

The problem was that the Left had not devised a novel strategy for economic rejuvenation. It had one substantial economic theory, Keynesianism, and one substantial instrument, the state. Consequently, it is not surprising that the first measures of the new government consisted of a massive boost to demand through an increase in wages, pensions and other household incomes, with the aim of creating a demand-led boom, coupled with nationalization of the 'commanding heights' of the economy (banks and large firms), to create a sustained investment boom. Keynesian reflation and public ownership were thus the twin pillars of Mitterrand's strategy.

These measures were not dictated solely by economic necessity. They responded to political expectations largely generated by the promises contained in the *Programme commun* and the various manifestos underwritten by the Left. Many socialist ministers genuinely wanted to break with capitalism. Many felt that it was necessary to proceed speedily, and achieve much in the first hundred days in office, or at most in the first six months.[63] Mitterrand, it was generally accepted – nor did he ever deny it – had only the haziest notion of economic policy. But he knew he had been elected on a platform of radical change. He knew that he had to offer the electorate a distinct programme. Electoral promises, at least initially, are a powerful constraint. A newly elected government feels it must fulfil its pledges and maintain the momentum. A more prudent, if cynical, approach would suggest the opposite: ignore all promises at first in order to create an economic framework which will make the fulfilment of promises possible. In other words, do your dirty work as early and as quickly as possible: 'If it were done when 'tis done then 'twere well it were done quickly.' Thus, it would have been preferable to start off the socialist term with a massive devaluation of the franc (instead of being forced to do so in three painful instalments between the end of 1981 and the first quarter of 1983 – see below), particularly since international speculation against the franc had started even before Pierre Mauroy was installed as prime minister in the Hôtel Matignon.[64] However, such early devaluation appeared to the government to be incompatible with the demand-led growth promised during the electoral campaign – a promise made by all candidates for the presidency irrespective of parties.[65] The socialists, like Harold Wilson in the 1960s, allowed themselves to become mesmerized by the need to keep a 'strong' currency, an apparent symbol of financial rectitude. They also believed themselves to be constrained by France's membership of the European Monetary System. It was important that the crucial aspect of French foreign policy – the Paris–Bonn axis – be preserved; consequently, it was important not to allow the Germans to remain the only supporters of the system. Attali's diaries inform us that when Helmut Schmidt (who would have preferred Giscard to win) met Mitterrand on 24 May 1981, it was to convince him that Franco-German relations required monetary solidarity as well as French support for the installation of Pershing missiles in Germany. It was clear that French exchange rate policy was always carefully co-ordinated and negotiated with the Germans.[66] Mauroy wrote with Gallic bravado: 'one does not salute the victory of the Left with a devaluation', adding that France had to respect its international commitments: 'Unlike our predecessors I shall defend the franc.'[67] The archaic notion of equating a strong currency with a strong economy was particularly pronounced among the rural petty bourgeoisie of France and had contaminated the middle classes. The socialists' gravest mistake was to allow themselves to be restrained by this financial absurdity, whose origin can be traced to the backward and anti-capitalist habits of French peasants stuffing their mattresses with gold coins. In this instance, Marx had not been entirely wrong when he lambasted the 'idiocy of rural life'.

Others learned from the socialists' errors. As we have seen, the Swedish social democrats launched into a competitive devaluation of the krona as soon as they returned to power in 1982 under Olof Palme. In Spain, one of the first acts of the socialists led by Felipe González was to devalue the peseta by 8 per cent. Both accompanied these measures with an austerity programme.

In France no one would have understood the need for this. Socialists and communists were united by a common desire to combat unemployment, public enemy number one. Accordingly, the government initiated one of the most vigorous anti-unemployment packages in Western Europe – even though unemployment in France was less serious than in Britain, Belgium, Italy and Holland. The training system, early retirement schemes, and encouragement to hire young workers and women, all initiated under the previous government, were extended and reinforced by the Mauroy administration.[68] Public sector employment was expanded. The working day was cut on the assumption that this was an effective way of reducing unemployment. In fact, the effect on unemployment was minimal: there was an increase in productivity and no loss of production.[69] The initial goal of the government, in accordance with its commitments, was the reduction of the working week to thirty-five hours by 1985. After a few weeks in power, Mauroy linked this to gains in productivity. By September 1981, while insisting that a reduction in working hours was the best way of creating new jobs, he explained that it had to be accompanied by a 'sharing of income', meaning that a corresponding cut in salary had to be expected. As the communists protested, the government by-passed a parliamentary debate by using the procedure of ordinances and, on 16 January 1982, the legal working week was reduced to thirty-nine hours. Employers responded by reducing salaries by 2.5 per cent.[70] For a work-sharing policy to be successful, it is necessary to accompany the reduction in working time with a flexible working week and a clearly growth-oriented policy. Simply to cut hours and leave the rest to the market will have little effect on unemployment.[71]

All these measures ensured that French unemployment increased at a lower rate than it did in many other West European countries, such as Germany and the United Kingdom. They did not achieve what the socialists wanted and people expected – namely, an absolute diminution in the numbers of people out of work. In May 1981, there were 1,794,000 unemployed in France; in October, there were 1,818,000. By May 1982 the numbers had risen to 2,005,000.[72]

Socialist reflation in the years 1981 and 1982 took the following form: the minimum wage (SMIC or *Salaire Minimum Interindustriel de Croissance*) was raised by 10.6 per cent, increasing in real terms between June 1981 and March 1983 (the beginning of austerity) by 38 per cent, with some spill-over effects on all other wages; the basic housing subsidy and family allowances were increased by around 50 per cent; the minimum old-age pension was raised by 40 per cent in real terms.[73] Paid vacations were increased from four to five weeks, the age of retirement lowered to sixty (April 1983), and early retirement schemes introduced.[74]

In France social security is not funded by direct and indirect taxes, but by a special levy paid by employers and employees. To increase this special budget (4.5 per cent of GNP), the government increased more than proportionately the levy paid by large firms.[75] This constituted an obvious threat to employment and investment, so the government followed the Swedish and Austrian model of increasing public sector employment. In its first eighteen months in power, the government created between 105,000 and 110,000 jobs in the public sector.[76] The creation of employment by this route, which neo-liberals find so distasteful, is the cheapest and surest way of fighting unemployment. It has been calculated that the cost of this is four times lower than job creation in the private sector by budgetary expansion.[77]

In February 1982 the government nationalized thirty-nine banks, two finance houses and five large industrial corporations, ranging from engineering, electronics and pharmaceuticals to glass, computers and chemicals. This had been repeatedly promised and had long been an article of faith among communists and traditional socialists. They were, unavoidably, included in the first package of measures. This symbolized the left-wing commitment of the government, and kept the Left, whether the CERES faction or the PCF, loyal to it. Mitterrand, personally indifferent to nationalization, fought against those like Jacques Delors (who was then the finance minister), Michel Rocard and Claude Cheysson, who tried to backtrack or water down the proposals. He could not have done otherwise. He was the guarantor of the *Programme commun* and of the unity of the Socialist Party. No one was in any doubt that the expansion of the public sector was determined more by these political requirements than by any coherent economic strategy. The nationalization of the banking sector might have paved the way for a more rational credit system. This had been the main intention of the socialists.[78] However, the thirty-nine newly nationalized banks were simply annexed to an already existing state banking sector (60 per cent of the total), which had always behaved as if it were private. This enlarged public sector was not provided with a new mode of regulation.[79] The state had spent a considerable amount of money, but it did not appear to know what to do with this new instrument. It merely satisfied the left-wing desire to get hold of the entire financial sector. Nevertheless, opportunistic politics was not the only motivation behind nationalization. Although, originally, nationalizations had been planned in order to 'break with capitalism', Pierre Mauroy emphasized other priorities: to give a greater impetus to industrial growth; to achieve a sorely needed restructuring of the economy; to create jobs; to stimulate investment; and to advance towards economic democracy. There is no doubt that there were some sound economic motives behind the extension of the public sector. Corporations such as Rhône-Poulenc (chemicals and pharmaceuticals), and Péchiney-Ugine-Kuhlman (chemicals, pharmaceuticals, copper and aluminium), simply did not have the necessary finance with which to restructure themselves. In other cases, single ownership permitted a more rational division of the available market (the Compagnie Générale d'Electricité and Thomson in electronics).[80]

But what was also at stake was a socialist version of economic nationalism and of the national interest. To allow large companies to remain in private hands is to accept that they might be bought by foreigners. Nationalization is the surest way to prevent this from happening. The transformation of a publicly quoted company into a national asset stops outsiders from acquiring control.[81] To have saved large French enterprises from a foreign takeover was described by Laurent Fabius, speaking in 1984, as one of the great achievements of nationalization.[82]

The national road to socialism pursued by the PS rested on a definite sense that the internationalization of the economy had to be prevented. It also closely corresponded to a public anxiety far more prevalent in France than elsewhere: the fear that France, its culture, its industries, its way of life would increasingly be shaped by the globalization of the world and, in particular, by the Americans (or, as the French prefer to put it, *les anglo-saxons*). Such foreboding did not affect other European nations to the same extent. Most were too small to have any illusions. Italy's inferiority complex made it welcome a greater homogeneity with the advanced world, even at the cost of an identity crisis. Germany's need to forget its past made any kind of nationalism, even a cultural one, an international issue. Britain's national anxiety centred on denying its European identity; internationalization was seen as preferable, particularly if under the tolerable hegemony of its uncouth, but English-speaking, trans-Atlantic cousins. France alone stubbornly defended its national culture and its national industry – both increasingly unable to compete internationally. French socialism, unlike that of Britain or Germany, can legitimately claim to be the inheritor of a *national* revolutionary tradition.

Economic and cultural policies were intimately linked, to an extent unimaginable in other countries. This explains the exceptionally high cultural profile of the first socialist government. Mitterrand himself never disguised his intellect, his passion for books. His official photograph, destined to be hung, as tradition demands, in all the town halls of France, showed the president reading, a book-lined wall behind him. Half of his ministers had written books. Most of them had been teachers.[83] Jack Lang, the minister of culture, was a prominent – some would even say the most prominent – member of the government, certainly the most flamboyant. His ministry was promptly colonized by the intellectuals of the Left, many of whom had been conspicuous during the May 1968 events, or such international celebrities of the Left as Régis Debray, who had been at Che Guevara's side in Bolivia.[84] Mitterrand's closest adviser was not an *éminence grise* spinning webs in the corridors of the Elysée, but the colourful and highly visible Jacques Attali, economist, philosopher, novelist, *maître à penser* for some, mountebank on the make for others. Cultural policy was not merely a question of slashing the art budget, as in Britain, or deciding which clientele to subsidize – as in Italy – but a defence and extension of national culture. Leaving this to the private sector, it was feared, would transform France into a dependency of the USA: more stylish and polished than its trans-Atlantic paragon, perhaps, but a dependency nevertheless. Having doubled the cultural budget in 1982, the socialists built on the achievements of their predecessors, who had erected the Centre Pompidou, the Beaubourg (conceived by world-famous British architects, whose own plans received little public or royal support in Britain – French cultural nationalism was not always chauvinist). Mitterrand, whose cultural mandate had a Renaissance outlook, established the Musée d'Orsay, built a new opera house at the Bastille, expanded the Louvre, adorning its courtyard with a glass pyramid of stunning beauty, developed the vast rect-angular Arche de la Défense, and laid the foundations of a new national library, promptly baptized *La Très Grande Bibliothèque*. The problem with the cultural policy of the socialists was that it was always an 'arts policy', destined to make more high culture available to those who already had access to it.[85] By deregulating television without a corresponding policy for the production of good quality popular culture, the socialists opened the door to a massive import of foreign – generally American – works of fiction of inferior quality, cheap home-made chat-shows and games programmes, and the erection of Disneyland in the outskirts of Paris (a commercial failure, eloquent testimony that not all cultural garbage is profitable).

Nevertheless, at least in the first phase (1981–82), there was no divide between the 'national-cultural' policy and the nationalization of the leading banks and industries, just as the enthusiastic development of technological gadgetry happily co-existed with the strength of the lobbies defending France's cultural products. The *Programme commun* and the *Projet Socialiste* displayed an obsessive insistence on the need to defend national independence, as if France stood alone and pristine, surrounded by multinational barbaric hordes poised to destroy the uniqueness of its industries and its culture. The further one travelled to the left in the Parti socialiste, the more one encountered a peculiar brand of left-wing nationalistic socialism which, elsewhere in Europe, could only be found in the British Labour Party, and then in a more restrained form. Jean-Pierre Chevènement, the most articulate representative of this tendency, exclaimed in 1983:

I may be labelled a nationalist but I think that France and the French must rely more on themselves and less on the unlikely good will of Mr. Reagan or Mr. Kohl. We must return to the French the pride of being French! ... the nation is the only possible framework for democracy. The Republic was born under the rallying cry of *Vive la nation* ... either French socialism follows the traditions of the Republic or it will perish.[86]

In presenting nationalization as a 'national' policy, the socialists were trying, not unsuccessfully, to drape their economic policy with the tricolour, in the hope of uniting not only socialists and communists, but also conservatives. The real aim of the nationalizations of 1981–82 was not so much to pave the way for the transition to socialism as to save and modernize French capitalism.[87] If this had been made explicit, instead of being described as the last act of folly of moribund West European socialism, the 1982 nationalizations would have been hailed as a pro-capitalist strategy. Sober analysis convincingly points to the success of this policy in bringing about a beneficial restructuring of much of the French manufacturing sector.[88]

One of the central aims of the government was that the increase in investment in the expanded public sector should induce a similar expansion in the private sector. The 'problem' with capitalism is that entrepreneurs insist on achieving some return on their investments – something socialists were apt to forget. The government only partially succeeded in creating an environment in which adequate profits could be obtained. Many of its measures resulted in higher labour costs and a profit squeeze, though purchasing power and consumer demand were, of course, increased. Increasing consumer demand was a popular move, and it was only to be expected that a socialist government would seek to improve the incomes of the poorer sections of society. Nevertheless, this would not necessarily increase the demand for consumer goods made by French industry. Only *indirectly*, and in the *longer term*, would this policy affect the demand for capital goods, and then only provided the consumer goods industry had not exhausted its stocks.[89] Moreover, French firms, already uncompetitive because of high labour costs, were heavily in debt.[90] To expand they needed to borrow, which was expensive, since interest rates had to be kept high in response to high US interest rates. Thus, French firms were not in a position to take advantage of the government-sponsored reflation. In spite of a brief recovery in 1980, the level of industrial investment inherited from Giscard d'Estaing was 9 per cent below that of 1974.[91] Plant and machinery were old. French firms had to absorb the two oil shocks with very little help from the governments of the Right. As France had become increasingly exposed to foreign trade during the thirty glorious years, its industries had become less competitive and the domestic market was succumbing to foreign imports.[92] France was far more constrained by international factors than Germany, let alone Japan.[93] To put it another way: Mitterrand's predecessors had left French capitalism in a poor state; the socialists had found themselves in charge of a highly inefficient and remarkably uncompetitive private sector. The much criticized reflation stopped the French economy from going into recession in 1981–82. If it had, it would probably have lost some 320,000 more jobs than it did lose and suffered an even worse trade balance in 1982 and 1983.[94] Had the French elected a *laissez-faire* neo-liberal government, as the British did in 1979, its manufacturing sector would have collapsed for ever, as the British has done. Once again, the salvation of capitalism was in socialist hands.

Some socialists, notably Jacques Delors, had been quite aware that French firms, unlike German ones, were reluctant to invest during the second half of the 1970s.[95] This would have required an industrial policy that was more, rather than less, interventionist. However, as is often the case, most socialists had an exaggerated opinion of the strength of capitalism. Finally, the purchasing power of private consumers – which had grown more than production – was mainly spent on imports, such as cars and electrical goods. French socialist reflation was of greater benefit to the Germans and the Japanese than to French industrialists. As a consequence, the trade deficit spiralled upwards from 60 billion francs in 1981 to 92.7 billion in 1982.[96]

One of the problems with socialist reflation was that it relied excessively on the individual decisions of consumers and private capitalists. A tougher, more state-centred economic policy, aimed at containing individual consumption in favour of extensive spending on infrastructure, would have had a greater effect, though it would not have been popular. Furthermore, an investment-oriented policy required the co-operation of the private sector. Yet the international situation was extremely unfavourable to new investment, due to the enormous increase in the price of raw materials (not only oil), ceaseless fluctuation in currencies, and contracting demand. The French assumed that they could, if they so wished, achieve a rate of growth much higher than that of their trading partners, even though this meant French imports rising faster than exports. The gamble did not pay off.[97] The USA and the UK had been in the throes of deflation since at least 1979, and were joined by West Germany in 1980. France was the exception, not only because it reflated when others deflated, but also because its reflation was determined by the political will of its leaders, rather than by the industrial possibilities of the country.[98] This had precipitated inflation which, by 1982, was twice that of France's main competitor, Germany. French inflation had been largely French-induced. The international recession contributed to the difficulties facing the French socialists. It did not create them.

Before 1979 the USA had facilitated worldwide expansionary strategies through a cheap money policy. After the second oil shock, in October 1979, the USA abandoned any attempt to control interest rates in favour of fiscal expansion and a tight money policy. This brought about an unprecedented increase in interest rates. The dollar appreciated in value and, because of its importance in international trade, most other West European countries had to follow suit and return to very high interest rates. France at first refrained, but was soon compelled to conform so as to avoid massive outflows of capital and a devaluation that threatened to be even more dramatic than the ones which did occur.[99]

Could socialists have gone against the grain? Mitterrand has sometimes been referred to as 'the Florentine' for his Machiavellian cunning in the art of politics. Yet it appears that he did not heed Machiavelli's advice: 'I believe that success arises to a Prince whose policies fit the nature of the times, and conversely failure will befall those who are out of step with the times.' Would the policies of the socialists have been successful had the international situation been more favourable? Most commentators take it for granted that the answer would be yes. Yet one should pause for reflection. A major international recovery would work to the advantage of everyone involved in international trade, but not in the same way. The more internationally competitive firms would do better than the rest. If it is true that French firms were not very competitive – with the honourable exception of those operating in luxury goods, in low technology kitchen equipment (Moulinex), and in 'yuppy' goods (Perrier) – then even the 'favourable' international scenario would not benefit French capitalism.[100] The trade gap with the Germans and the Japanese would grow even further. Thus, it is not possible for socialists to disregard the key question: how can socialists make their own capitalism more viable?

Why did the socialists embark upon reflation in such an unpromising situation? Clearly, not enough attention was paid to the dismal state of the French economy even though, throughout the electoral campaign of 1981, the socialists accused their opponents of economic ineptitude. The Barre government had already dropped its austerity policy and initiated a reflation, offering the electorate considerable bribes in the form of increased pensions, social benefits and cash relief to farmers. Thus, when the socialists came to power, the French economy was already being stimulated. In the spring of 1981, there was considerable agreement among economic experts – including the OECD, the EEC and the leading French forecasting institutes – that Europe was poised for a substantial recovery.[101] The OECD, in particular, forecast a 2 per cent growth in GNP, sufficient to cover France's trade deficit.[102] But all these forecasts turned out to be totally wrong: far from expanding, the world economy contracted in 1982 when, instead of the expected 4–6 per cent expansion, world trade remained stationary. This only confirms the view that the main difference between modern economic forecasting and reading the entrails of slaughtered goats is that the former is more expensive (though kinder to goats). To argue that the French socialist government should have refrained from expanding is to be wise after the event. A newly elected government, victorious after decades in opposition or at the margins of power, sustained by the hopes and expectations not only of its supporters but of a wide segment of the electorate, backed by the forecasts of the most prestigious economists, could hardly have done the opposite of what it was elected to do, on the morrow of its victory. Some – like Michel Rocard – had presciently warned their socialist comrades that reflation on its own was not enough. He argued that the productive system, public and private, had to be able to respond to the increase in demand, and that you could not be a Keynesian in an economy which was no longer Keynesian.[103] Lionel Jospin, close supporter of Mitterrand and no friend of Rocard, later admitted that Rocard had been right all along, but argued that Rocard's strategy would not have united the Left in 1981 and would not have won the elections.[104] Jacques Julliard, a Rocard supporter, concurred: the 'archaic' Common Programme was necessary to obtain the support of the PCF and win the elections.[105] But Rocard's unheeded advice reflected not so much a superior understanding of economic realities as a profound disagreement with the idea, then dominant in the PS, that it was possible to 'break with capitalism'. It is because Rocard had a more realistic (and pessimistic) *political* appraisal of the chances of socialism's success that he opted for what turned out to be the more accurate *economic* forecast.

For this reflation to work, it would have been necessary either to insulate the French economy from the international economic system, or to achieve a simultaneous reflation in the other advanced countries. The first condition was absurd, although some of Mitterrand's advisers, as well as powerful ministers such as Jean-Pierre Chevènement and Pierre Bérégovoy and the PCF, suggested a disengagement from European integration by abandoning the exchange rate mechanism.[106] The second never materialized. A coordinated reflation might have done the trick, but Mitterrand's plea at the Versailles summit of the Group of Seven countries in June 1982 was ignored.[107] On the contrary, 1982 witnessed a particularly severe international recession and a marked increase in American interest rates, which inflated the value of the dollar. French exports became even less competitive and the franc was consequently devalued three times (October 1981, June 1982 and March 1983) – on the last occasion as part of an overall realignment of the currencies belonging to the European Monetary System. This was not enough to contain the deficit and, as the French government had no means with which to compel the US to lower interest rates, it was forced to perform a U-turn in economic policy in order to arrest the reflation. 'Socialist' deflation followed socialist reflation. France was squeezed between a *dirigiste* domestic economic strategy and a *neo-liberal* foreign economic policy, the latter rapidly overwhelming the former and dictating the realignment of the country – and particularly its rate of inflation – with the requirements of the international economic system.

In June 1982 *la rupture* with previous policies began. The struggle against inflation, not unemployment, became the priority. Wages and prices were frozen, in spite of vociferous communist resistance. Public spending was cut. Workers' social security contributions were increased. Benefits were cut in real terms. It was the beginning of a break – as elsewhere in Europe – with the tradition of universal social protection by the state. Hospitals began to impose 'hotel' charges. Some medicines were no longer free. Elements of national insurance were transferred to non-state agencies.[108] As these measures were insufficient, further deflationary cuts followed in the spring of 1983, leading to austerity measures reversing many of the policies of the 1981–82 phase. The re-equilibrium of the balance of payments joined inflation as a government priority. The prime minister, Pierre Mauroy, declared: 'If the French resign themselves to living with an inflation of twelve per cent, then they should know that because of our economic interdependence with Germany, we will be led into a situation of imbalance.'[109]

Devaluation, containment of wages and a more favourable international situation (a fall in interest rates) provided some of the supply-side conditions for investment. Exports improved in 1983–85, but the austerity policy had dampened domestic demand, discouraging investment.

The unions, divided and weak, were in no position to oppose the turn to the right of the government. Inside the government, the Left appeared soundly defeated. The left-wing minister for health Nicole Questiaux resigned, rather than be demoted. Jean-Pierre Chevènement, leader of the CERES, who had been minister of research and technology (1981–82) and then of Industry (1982–83), resigned in 1983 – though he returned to the cabinet in 1984 as education minister. In July 1984 Pierre Mauroy, the foremost representative of socialist tradition, was replaced by Laurent Fabius, a young Mitterrand protégé. As a result, the four communist ministers were withdrawn by the PCF, in the erroneous belief that the despondency on the Left would work to its advantage. There was nothing traumatic or unexpected about this divorce. By 1984, communists and socialists at all levels had reverted to holding highly negative views of each other.[110] A year later, at the Central Committee of his party (June 1985), Georges Marchais relapsed into his old sectarian act: 'What Capital wants ... is what this Socialist government does.'[111]

There was more than a grain of truth in this ancient gibe. Socialists did all they could to demonstrate to financial circles that they were pursuing economic policies not substantially different from those of the Right. Their U-turn was widely welcomed as a return to 'realism' by the increasingly numerous intellectuals who wanted a Left without socialism: 'The Left', wrote a journalist in one of the many instant books of the time,

> has finally become realistic once again. The Left has definitively chosen to manage capitalism and must draw the intellectual and cultural consequences ... If one agrees with this, the historical task of the Left must be redefined thus: it is the modernization of French society which is the order of the day, not its radical transformation.[112]

The Parti Socialiste hardly needed such prompting. Relatively free from communist pressure, it was able to insist more openly on what had been its underlying ideology all along: modernization – including 'Euro-modernization' as an alternative to autarchic, PCF-style modernization – and the need to regulate the mixed economy. To give up the ambition of abolishing capitalism, however, is not much of a strategy. Modernization as a slogan sounds appealing, but it has done so for over a hundred years. No party of the Left in post-war Europe (and hardly any party of the Right) has ever been against modernization. One suspects that the watchword, devoid as it is of any practical content, is used purely symbolically: to be for modernization means to be for progress without abolishing capitalism. In this instance, it signalled the end of ambition, the termination of passion, the beginning of routine. The PS became 'a grey party looking for colour' – to paraphrase the comment of a Labour MP on his own party.

At the Toulouse Congress of April 1985, Mauroy admitted that the social-ists had been wrongly reluctant to engage with 'the management of a market economy, a capitalist economy', and added, for good measure: 'The market has clearly demonstrated that it is one of the roads to freedom ... It is not for the State to produce. This is the task of enterprises.'[113] Upon returning to the fold, Chevènement proclaimed: 'France has understood, thanks to the crisis, the reality of economic struggle ... The private sector is recognized as the creator of social wealth.'[114] 'We have learnt much,' declared Michel Rocard, with more than a hint of 'I told you so':

> Why not admit it? ... Then [1981] the main question was how to break with capitalism ... Today everybody talks of modernization ... Facts have resolved our ancient quarrels. They now appear distant and insignificant. We have changed because we have learnt. If so, we were right to change.[115]

How had the socialists changed? On succeeding Mauroy, Laurent Fabius declared to the National Assembly that the priorities of the government were 'to modernize' and 'to unite'.[116] Modernization was necessary in order to combat unemployment. However, this combat would be 'long and difficult' and, in the meantime, 'one must have the courage to say it ... modernization would cost more jobs than it would create.'[117]

This was on 24 July 1984. By then it had become commonplace to point out that new investment no longer inevitably produced more jobs. The priorities of the new government only paid lip-service to the need to combat unemployment. The French socialists, like their comrades elsewhere in Europe, had accepted that full employment was no longer an option for the present. The idea that a necessary condition for a just society was that it should provide a job for all those willing and able to work was relegated to utopia – so slight had become the distance between the inconceivable and the inevitable. On the lips of Laurent Fabius, modernization consisted in scientific research, investment and training. This he explained was, 'the basic triangle of modernization'.[118] And from the Left, Chevènement, back in the cabinet as education minister, discovered that 'to defend the national interest is the best way, perhaps the only way, to be on the Left. And the national interest, today, is modernization.'[119]

With bitter sarcasm, Alain Touraine has written: 'the type of human being praised everywhere is now that of the young entrepreneur. If you hear an inflated tribute to profits, enterprise, competition, you can be sure you are listening to a socialist minister. We are witnessing the triumph of hedonism ... which transforms any social question, be it the media or education, into a question of consumption ... In a word, France has become Reaganite.'[120]

Modernization was only one ideological aspect of the new Socialist Party. Modern parties, if they aspire to success, need to keep one foot – but only one – solidly planted in the past. French traditions provided the socialists with a solid anchorage: 'republican values'.[121] Only in France could an appeal to combat the conservative Right be expressed in the euphemism 'republican values', constantly repackaged to encompass virtually anything the Socialist Party wanted to embrace. The term provided the CERES faction with the necessary nationalist ballast after it had recognized that 'socialism is no longer on the agenda'.[122] It provided Mitterrand with a radical flourish with which to cover the abandonment of his socialist ambition to 'break with capitalism'. It provided defenders of the welfare state with a positive attribute of the state itself: after all, it was, *l'état républicain* which was to be defended, not any old bureaucratic and centralist state. It provided those who wanted to pursue an alliance with the centre with a common ideological platform.[123] No wonder the historians who, in the run-up to the celebrations of the bicentenary of 1789, questioned the importance or necessity of the Revolution were acclaimed by the Right and, in 1988, even by Michel Rocard himself, when he was prime minister.[124]

Whether or not helped by such judicious ideological repackaging, the U-turn in economic and social policies 'worked'. By 1986, inflation had been reduced to 2.7 per cent, GDP growth was 2.1 per cent against 0.7 in 1983; the balance of trade was no longer in deficit.[125] Unemployment was over 10 per cent, but it was still just below the average for OECD–Europe, and one of the lowest in the European Community.

As elections approached, the government generated a small reflation which improved the overall situation, though it was not enough to ensure electoral victory. In March 1986 the socialists lost their majority. They obtained 32.8 per cent (down from 37.5 in 1981) and 211 seats; the communists sunk to 9.8 per cent and thirty-two seats; while the coalition of the Right (Giscard's Union pour la Démocratie Française and Chirac's Rassemblement pour la République) swept to power with 42 per cent and 265 seats. These elections had been fought under a new system of proportional representation, which had long been advocated by the PCF and which had been included in the *Programme commun*.[126] This provided the socialists with some clear advantages: it made a pact with the PCF no longer necessary and enabled far Right voters to converge on the National Front, led by Jean-Marie Le Pen, thus depriving the 'respectable' Right of precious votes.[127] The introduction of proportional representation also provided Rocard with a widely disbelieved excuse to resign from the government and abandon the agriculture portfolio to which he had been relegated.[128] A period of 'cohabitation' ensued, in which France had a socialist president overseeing a conservative government led by Jacques Chirac.

Peter Hall's lucid .comments on the lessons of Mitterrand's economic policies are worth reporting here: the socialist government had ignored supply-side conditions which, in 1981, were particularly adverse; they had mistakenly assumed that the nationalized sector could become the real motor of the economy:

> The turn toward austerity itself might have been less abrupt if the Socialists had developed a more complete appreciation of the degree to which their policies would have to mesh with the existing institutional structures of a mixed domestic economy and an increasingly interdependent world economy.[129]

Could not the socialists have used the planning system and the newly expanded nationalized sector? The problem with planning is that if it works at all, it is in the medium to long term. As such, it may be a suitable instrument if one expects to be in power for a reasonably long time – not a safe assumption for socialists in the 1980s and 1990s. In spite of much socialist rhetoric, planning was not a priority. The Ministry for Planning had originally been entrusted to Michel Rocard, Mitterrand's least favourite minister, mainly to immobilize him. Rocard's isolation at the time paralleled that of Tony Benn in the Labour government of 1974–79. Rocard from the right, Benn from the left, submitted plans and proposals at frequent cabinet meetings, only to see them rejected – though Rocard, unlike Benn, became prime minister in 1988 and in 1993, after the defeat of the PS, briefly leader of his party. By the time Rocard's Ninth Plan for 1984–88 was ready (1983), it was too late. In any case, the plan had been shaped by the growing recognition that inflation and the balance of payments deficit had to be reduced. It added nothing to government policy, which was increasingly developing on an *ad hoc* basis.[130]

The year 1983, when *la rupture* occurred, signalled a turning-point as important as that of 1976 for the Labour government, when Keynesianism was officially dropped. Until 1983, the French socialists had set the criteria for the success of their policies: a reduction in the level of unemployment, a reduction of social and economic inequalities, economic growth and an increase in the purchasing power of wage-earners. After 1983, the goals became monetary stabilization, the diminution of the budget deficit, and productivity growth rather than wage rises. On the basis of this second set of criteria, the socialist government of 1983–86 was successful. The problem, however, was whether adopting these targets was tantamount to accepting that there cannot be a distinctive socialist economic policy.[131]

The French socialist government had foundered on the question of socialist management of the capitalist economy. This, however, is not the only criterion of success. In 1981, Mitterrand's ambitious plans encompassed not only economic regeneration and modernization, but also the decentralization of the state, reform of education and the introduction of industrial democracy (the celebrated *autogestion*). Unlike economic policy, these reforms were not dependent on the international economic conjuncture. How did the socialists fare?

Decentralization is always, as Catherine Grémion so aptly put it, 'a passion of those in opposition'.[132] To those in power – that is, to those who have been able to seize control of the central apparatus of the state – decentralization is the equivalent of abandoning a powerful and useful instrument which one has just acquired with great effort.

Like *autogestion*, decentralization had become a slogan of the Left via that great maelstrom of ideas which goes under the name of May '68. As Mitterrand had suggestively put it to the electorate in May 1974: 'The only thought of the Right is to remain in power, my first aim is to restore power to you.' This 'restoration' of power would occur through the decentralization of the state and the introduction of industrial democracy.

The PS's commitment to decentralization had been greatly strengthened by the positive results of the local government elections of 1977 and 1978. By 1981, the socialists controlled more than half the regional councils. Nevertheless, the minister in charge of regional reform, Gaston Defferre, himself mayor of Marseille and an old supporter of local government, had an uphill struggle against his colleagues. The opposition itself was divided. The *giscardiens* were in favour of devolution; the Gaullists were more reluctant.[133] Defferre's draft legislation on decentralization eventually passed all the parliamentary hurdles without major modification, and became law in July 1983. The right of the state-appointed prefect (now known as Commissaire de la République) to veto decisions of local authorities was abolished; executive power with the regions and the departments was given to an elected president. Regions acquired new powers over the small and less effective departments. Regional councils were elected for the first time in 1986.

The consensus is that the socialist decentralization law was 'one of the most far-reaching administrative reforms that France had seen since World War II'.[134] Some add, for good measure, that 'it represented the most important reform in the area of decentralisation since the Acts of 1871 and 1884.'[135] 'The Socialist decentralisation reform was among the most substantial attempts in recent French history to revitalize sub-national government.'[136] 'It was certainly a *la grande affaire du septennat*.'[137] 'A revolutionary reform,' claimed Vivien A. Schmidt: 'the Socialists did in fact succeed where others had failed, breaking a long-standing pattern of much talk about decentralization and little action.'[138] Even a left-wing critic of the socialist government, Daniel Singer, while maintaining that the measures 'involved no upheaval, no major change in the way France is governed,' acknowledged that 'the Socialists did stop and even slightly reversed a secular trend, and that is not negligible.'[139]

The reforms appeared substantial only because France had for so long been one of the most centralized states in Europe. In some instances, the socialists simply sanctioned an existing practice; for example, even before 1981, the prefects had increasingly been appointed after consultation with the local authorities, and were well aware that they could not ride roughshod over elected mayors.[140] Local government remained substantially dependent on the centre for its financial needs. There was no real reform of local finances. There is no evidence that the reforms increased efficiency in the delivery of services – as local bureaucracies proliferated – or that it brought local communities closer to those who governed them.[141] The new *président du conseil général*, though elected, seemed no less remote than the prefect had been. On the other hand, one may cynically remark that local government is about the transfer of power from national political bosses to local political bosses. What decentralization probably contributed to was the politicization of the periphery, not its democratization.[142] The main beneficiaries of the reforms were the local holders of office.[143] France's 36,000 mayors became more powerful and many used this power to build robust political machines for themselves. As local politics developed, so did the opportunities for strengthening party finances through local corruption. By 1989, the police had uncovered a massive network of corruption set up to bolster party finances and implicated hundreds of local politicians, including many socialists.[144]

None of this constitutes a strong argument against decentralization, whose true advantage is this: as cultural and technological developments increasingly concentrate powers in the hands of the executive at the centre of the political life of the country, it is important to have a source of power, however minimal, able to exercise some restraint at the periphery. Because national and local elections seldom occur at the same time, and because, on the whole, voters use all elections to express their satisfaction or dissatisfaction with national leaders, it is often the case that the majority in local governments is different from the parliamentary majority. This balance enables even the least successful opposition to learn the difficult art of government (as was the case with the communists in Italy), and provides them with a role in public life.

Closely connected to decentralization were the four legislative measures, known as the Auroux laws (named after the socialist minister of labour, Jean Auroux), whose aim was the strengthening of the trade unions. Employers were required to enter into collective bargaining with the unions over wages, hours and working conditions at plant level. Workers could elect works committees with new consultative rights over closures, health and safety, and technological change, and they were allowed to meet periodically during working time to propose improvements in working conditions.[145] Predictably, the employers fought against the new legislation, thought not as hard as it may have appeared from the rhetoric of their spokesmen. The major unions, the CGT and the CFDT, had reservations too, but mainly because the legislation did not go far enough.[146]

Did the laws make any difference to workers? Even senior government ministers admitted that, if asked, most workers would say that little if anything had changed.[147] But what really mattered was how these new rights were used. Laws, by themselves, can at best create a framework and new opportunities. In the case of industrial democracy, activists (trade unionists) are given the chance to participate in the management of plants. Whether or not they are effective and whether or not 'things really change' for the majority of workers will depend on economic and political circumstances. Opponents will warn that any interference with management's right to manage will cause intolerable damage to the economic fabric of the enterprise; supporters will raise romantic expectations of workers 'running their own lives'. But whether laws on industrial democracy and other forms of direct participation have opened up new opportunities, and whether these are really taken up, can be judged only with hindsight.

The other issue to examine is whether trade unions were really strengthened by the Auroux laws.[148] In the 1980s, because of increasing unemployment, trade unions lost power and members throughout Europe. France conformed to this trend. The index of trade unionism, which had hovered around 25 per cent in the 1960s and 1970s, had dropped to under 20 per cent in May 1985, while in the same year the index of industrial conflicts was the lowest in twenty years.[149] This percentage continued to decline to such an extent that, by 1991, France's degree of unionization was estimated by the OECD to be at 12 per cent, below that of Turkey or the USA.[150] The fact was that the unions, which had been united in the other great moments of the Left in French history – 1936 and 1944 – were substantially divided in 1981, and largely unprepared for the task ahead. The socialist-leaning CFDT was uncertain on how critical it should be of 'its' government, while the communist CGT, having strongly supported the government during the reflationary phase of 1981–82, proceeded to denounce it after 1984.[151] The Auroux laws had been inspired by the CFDT. Most of Auroux's own advisers came from CFDT circles, as did other important government figures such as Jacques Delors and Michel Rocard – all representatives of what came to be known as the 'second left'.[152] It was the CFDT, once the trade union of Catholic workers and the main advocate of *autogestion*, which was also the champion of the modernizing 'second left', which surged in French socialism after the failures of 1981–82. The mere existence of a socialist government had given the unions some confidence and greater access to ministers, but the CFDT and the larger CGT were unable to present a united front on any of the major issues of the day, from economic policy to industrial reform.

In the wider context of the 1980s, the Auroux laws were a solitary instance of a strengthening of workers' rights and union power: everywhere else, and above all in Great Britain, unions lost power. Nevertheless, even the Auroux laws illustrate the weakness of trade unionism in the period: it was necessary for the state to intervene directly in industrial relations to grant the unions powers which they were too weak to obtain through collective bargaining.

It was in the field of civil liberties, the political issue furthest removed from international constraints, that the achievements of the socialist government loom largest. The socialists abolished the death penalty (October 1981) and the special military tribunals (June 1982); ratified Article 25 of the European Convention on Human Rights, which allows individual access to the European Court; repealed the *loi anticasseurs*, which made all participants in a demonstration liable for any damage caused; repealed anti-homosexual legislation; gave more rights to defendants; abolished all remaining legal distinctions between 'legitimate' children and those born out of wedlock.[153] They also initiated a new draft of the old *Code Napoléon*, emphasizing the protection of the individual rather than of private property.[154] The socialists, so often unjustly accused of restricting freedom by their conservative opponents, had thus, in a few years, abolished many antiquated and anti-libertarian aspects of French legislation, just as the British Labour Party had done, or allowed to occur, during its period in government in the 1960s. None of these measures, however, with the possible exception of the death penalty, became a matter of national debate or received widespread press coverage. Politics had increasingly become a matter of 'getting the economy right'.

The non-economic issue which caused the most popular interest was the attempt to reform education. This provoked the largest anti-government demonstrations of the 1980s and forced the socialists to backtrack. In France education has always had great political importance. It had been the foundation of modern republican France since 1870. At the turn of the century, when republicanism had not yet become an unquestioned national ideology, its chief weapon was a centralized education system. Since the middle of the nineteenth century, anti-republican governments had sought to help or subsidize private (mainly Catholic) schools, or to introduce religious education in state schools, as in the Falloux law of 1851 and the Vichy legislation during the Second World War. Republicans reversed the trend in the late nineteenth century and in 1945. The Gaullists tried to compromise (Michel Debré's 1959 law), by associating the private sector with the public education system through subsidies, while allowing considerable autonomy to the former. Many socialists regarded this independence as unwarranted, since the private religious schools were highly dependent on state support.

Mitterrand had promised a 'great and unified public education system' (Proposition 90 of his election manifesto). His party was solidly behind him. Forty-eight per cent of socialists elected to the National Assembly in 1981 had been school-teachers in state schools. Most of the teachers' unions were close supporters of the Left; most teachers voted for it.[155] The French socialists' education plans, drafted by Louis Mexandeau, the party's education spokesman, were devised so as not to offend any of the trade union and socialist lobbies in education.[156] However, the education minister, Alain Savary, to obtain a wider consensus, initiated widespread consultations. Eventually, he drafted a less anti-clerical plan than Mexandeau's, which retained subsidies but integrated the Catholic schools more closely into the state system. However, the compromise was intolerable to the anti-clerical socialist lobby and the Savary plan was redrafted.

Public support for private schools was, in fact, much more extensive than was realized. On 24 June 1984 there were massive demonstrations in Paris – estimates vary between one and one and a half million people. Mitterrand was frightened by their magnitude, withdrew the Savary Bill (12 July), accepted Savary's resignation, and took advantage of the crisis to sack his prime minister, Pierre Mauroy. Savary's successor, Jean-Pierre Chevènement, reinstated the original compromise. The socialists had learnt their lesson. Chevènement mounted a robust defence of traditional (i.e. republican) values: 'the values of the school system must be simple and strong in the eyes of teachers, parents and pupils';[157] the duty of teachers was to teach and that of students to learn. The crisis had been averted. 'National education,' Chevènement declared, 'must be the spearhead of modernization.'[158]

> We are facing the rise of a Japanese–American technological condominium. Those who are unable to use the new technologies in order to achieve productivity gains will be forced into backwardness and decadence. If we become dependent on foreigners our democracy will be in danger! The Republic will be a mere word![159]

Religious education ceased to be a national issue of major electoral relevance.[160] The religious conflict which had divided France for nearly two centuries finally appeared concluded in 1992, when Jack Lang, the new minister of education, accorded religious schools equal dignity with those of the state and recognized their contribution.[161] The main victim of the affair was the Fédération de l'Education Nationale (FEN), the education union. In 1981 it had been the largest union in the country, and the backbone of the Left with 550,000 members.[162] By 1992 it had lost 40 per cent of its membership. In 1993, as rival unions were formed, the FEN had become a shadow of its former self.

The French socialists had assumed that what concerned their immediate supporters was also of national concern. In fact, the old clerical versus secular debate had become almost irrelevant to France in the 1980s. Those who sent their children to private religious schools were not much more or less Catholic than the rest of the population. French private schools were not a bastion of the middle classes, as in Britain; nor did they provide a particularly large proportion of those destined for the Grandes Ecoles. Some of the prestigious lycées of Paris were (and are) far more elitist than the majority of private schools. Parents sent their children to religious schools for diverse reasons: because the teaching was more traditional; because their children had to repeat a year; or because the local state school had a bad reputation. Being subsidized, the private schools drew their pupils from a wide social group:

one-third of pupils in private elementary schools in 1978–79 were the children of manual workers.[163] What the Socialists had failed to understand was that parents were behaving like consumers of educational services, not clerical ideologues. Parents wanted to choose and perceived the Savary Bill as an attack on the freedom to send their children to the school of their choice. It was easy for the Right, for whom freedom of choice had become a major slogan (as elsewhere in Europe), to depict the government as a prisoner of ideologues who prized their obsession more than the education of children.[164] The socialists had lost the opportunity to rethink the education system as a whole. The government of decentralization and democracy once again appeared as the government of moribund Jacobinism in the era of neo-liberal revival.

Post-mortems are difficult for political parties, unless they are decisively and repeatedly beaten. In 1986, the French socialists were down but not out. Mitterrand was still in the Elysée Palace, using his consummate political skills to cause as much disarray as possible in the right-wing coalition led by Jacques Chirac, making it clear that he disagreed with the conservatives on privatization, the abolition of the wealth tax (a largely symbolic measure with little effect on redistribution), the easing of redundancy procedures. At the same time, Chirac, with a parliamentary majority of three, had to face 200 socialist deputies who did not hesitate to use parliamentary procedure to obstruct legislation.[165] The Chirac government tried to appear more right-wing than it really was, presumably influenced by the success of the Thatcher governments across the Channel. In reality, it was barely distinguishable from its predecessors. Consensus had been forced on the French political system by a combination of institutional and economic constraints. As some commentators have written, exaggerating only a little, '"Socialism" had given way to "Liberalism", but that was about the only difference immediately obvious to the man on the number 32 bus.'[166] The Gaullist–UDF coalition began to privatize some of what had been nationalized, without encountering much opposition from the Left. The share issues were oversubscribed – paradoxically, a sign of how efficient the newly privatized firms had become during their period of public ownership and how cheaply they were sold. Chirac also questioned the concept of universal social protection, but could not do so effectively given that poll after poll revealed how unpopular any move to end it would be with the French electorate.

Now in opposition, the Parti socialiste avoided the masochistic exercise of internecine warfare which plagued the British Labour Party between 1979 and 1987. Having fought the elections of 1986 on the record of its years in power, the PS prepared for the 1988 presidential elections on the understanding that, should Mitterrand stand and win again, there would be a new general election. Thus, at the Lille Congress of April 1987, in a superb display of public relations, the PS appeared singularly united. It declared that there could be no return to a formal alliance with the PCF, but it defended its traditional values, sang the Internationale once again, denounced the Right and neo-liberalism, insisted that it espoused modernity, justified its policies of 1981–83 as well as those of 1983–86, and contained the ritual struggle between Chevènement and his main opponents, Rocard and Delors.[167]

By then, the death of socialism as a serious political force was being regularly predicted and analysed, well before the collapse of the USSR added substance to the prediction. Alain Touraine had written as early as 1985 that France had acquired a socialist government just when the era of post-socialism had begun.[168] What could the Socialist Party offer France? Was it more than a machine to elect (or re-elect) a president – as the Gaullist party had been envisaged by de Gaulle? On the morrow of the defeat of 1986, Jacques Julliard described it as composed of a lobby of functionaries, fragments of social democracy (in the north), areas of clientelism (the south), assorted new dealers and modernizers (Rocard), and 'yuppies' disenchanted with traditional politics, but craving influence in public life.[169]

By 1988, François Mitterrand had acquired the presidential qualities he had lacked in 1981. He was now regarded as one of Europe's most creative politicians. Paradoxically for a man who had fought Gaullism all his life, Mitterrand had become a personality who, like de Gaulle, was somewhat above squabbling parties and wrangling politicians. He now represented the whole country, not a mere section of it. De Gaulle had been satirized in *Le canard enchaîné* as Louis XIV, the Sun-King. Mitterrand, more simply, was caricatured in TV satires as 'God'.

Instead of putting forward a left-wing programme along the lines of his *110 Propositions* of 1981, he opted instead for a *Lettre à tous les Français*, a document of fifty-nine typewritten pages which he had personally composed and which was printed in twenty-three provincial papers and two national dailies. It is widely assumed that very few people read it in its entirety, but no one could have missed the symbolism. The president of the republic had become a father figure, detached from political parties, addressing himself directly to the people of France, explaining his values – justice, solidarity, Europeanism – and his priorities – education and redistribution. The old controversy of nationalization versus privatization should be disregarded: 'let us leave these arguments aside.'[170] A majority of the 'left' electorate confirmed that the personality of the presidential candidate mattered more than his policies, indicating an overall shift to the right.[171] In the first round of the election Mitterrand emerged a clear winner with 34.1 per cent; the Gaullist candidate Chirac obtained 19.9 per cent, Raymond Barre 16.5. On the far Right, Jean-Marie Le Pen scored an impressive 14.4 per cent. The official communist candidate, André Lajoinie, obtained 6.76 per cent (the lowest score hitherto recorded by a PCF candidate). If we added to Mitterrand's score the percentages obtained by the PCF, the 'dissident' communist Pierre Juquin (2.1 per cent), the ecologist Antoine Waechter (3.78), the far left Arlette Laguiller (1.99), and the Trotskyist Pierre Boussel (0.38), we would obtain a grand left total of 49.1 per cent, just short of a majority. Yet in the second round against Chirac, Mitterrand won clearly with 54 per cent. The votes of some of those who had not opted for any of the left candidates were decisive for the second seven-year stint of François Mitterrand.

By re-electing a socialist government a few weeks later, albeit with a much smaller majority than in 1981, the electorate signalled its dissatisfaction with the Chirac administration, rather than that positive desire for major change which had been so palpable in 1981. In terms of issues, the difference between Right and Left had virtually disappeared: both sides supported a wider single European market, both were committed to monetary stability; both advocated a European central bank; both wished to improve the French economy through competition, education and training; both were in favour of a guaranteed minimum income. Such differences as still existed could be found at the level of values, symbols and language. The socialists followed Mitterrand by talking of republican values, social justice, tolerance towards immigrants and political refugees, solidarity and equality. By voting for the socialists, one could vote for progress and social justice in principle, and for orthodox fiscal and monetary policies in practice. One could be virtuous and selfish at the same time. It was thus demonstrated that in electoral politics one could have one's cake and eat it.

This new mood was well understood by Mitterrand, the most professional political fox in the increasingly impoverished menagerie of West European politics. He appointed his erstwhile enemy, Michel Rocard, the politician he had so often marginalized, prime minister. Rocard had advocated the formation of a new majority, not dependent on the PCF, in the name of a new policy of *ouverture* – a vague and ill-defined term, suggesting that one should eschew traditional and obsolete Left–Right issues such as anti-clericalism or the role of the market.[172] As the socialists no longer had an absolute majority in the National Assembly (they had 276 seats and needed 288), they required the support of other forces anyway. This they obtained by forming *ad hoc* majorities. Some laws and measures were passed by all parties; some only with the support of the UDF; others with the help of the Gaullists; others again with the PCF. Parliament acquired power it had not been able to use when the government was able to rely on a solid majority. The Rocard government (1988–91), and those of the two socialist prime ministers who succeeded him, Edith Cresson (1991–92) and Pierre Bérégovoy (1992–93) all followed a similar path. Fiscal prudence – shifting the burden of taxation from direct to indirect taxes – was combined with a rigid anti-inflationary policy, based on the *franc fort* policies once upheld by Raymond Barre. Unemployment grew continuously. Between 1982 and 1988, average wage-earners lost 2 per cent of their purchasing power. During Mitterrand's second term, the rich got richer and the poor poorer.[173] Real hourly wages in manufacturing increased at a much lower percentage rate than they did in Thatcher's Britain or Kohl's Germany (where the higher purchasing power of blue-collar workers was achieved at the expense of employment and public sector incomes).[174]

References to socialism disappeared from socialist documents, except to stress how far the government had strayed from it. Thus, when the new National Plan was presented in 1989, the minister in charge, Lionel Stoleru, declared: 'Undoubtedly, there is a certain ideological discrepancy between the Socialist Plan and that part of the Plan which accepts the case for reducing the level of taxation on capital. But there you are: this is a courageous programme by a Government conscious of its European commitments.'[175] The socialists had learnted the lessons of interdependence the hard way. European integration and France's role in it now dominated their policies. They had become arch-federalists, as had been, self-confessedly, Michel Rocard.

In 1991, at the end of Rocard's period in office, the French economy had become one of the healthiest in Europe, the franc one of the world's strongest currencies. The budget deficit and inflation were under control; the interest rate gap with Germany was narrowing; and the country had received a high approval rating from the OECD.[176] All this was to no avail. The government appeared increasingly exhausted, aimless and tainted by the occasional financial scandal. Its anti-inflationary zeal had reached such proportions that it persisted in upholding the franc through a high interest rate policy, in spite of the negative effect on jobs. After the dissolution of the USSR, socialism seemed to have become yesterday's pious hope. In 1993 the socialists were swept aside. Their percentage dropped from 37.5 in 1988 to 17.6. In 1988 they had 276 seats; now they had only 54 and faced a government coalition with a combined 39.5 per cent of the vote and 460 seats. Michel Rocard, who had lost his seat, became the new party leader. A year later, having lost the European election, he resigned. European socialism had lost another battle, or perhaps, as some pessimists concluded, the entire war. The new centre-right government surrendered to international speculation, and effectively devalued the franc in the summer of 1993 by obtaining a widening of the fluctuation bands of the European exchange rate mechanism.

The shift to the right in France during the 1980s was reflected in the rest of Europe. We saw this in our analysis of Holland and Belgium, Sweden and Austria, Britain and Germany. What distinguished the French shift was that the accompanying intellectual change was more profound than elsewhere. In retrospect, Sartre's funeral in 1980 could be seen as the last act of a drama in which the Parisian intelligentsia celebrated its greatest representative. In the years to follow, many French intellectuals, particularly those with access to the media (once the prerogative of Sartre and his followers), mapped out a new field of neo-liberal anti-statism. Much of the groundwork had been laid beforehand, for instance by Raymond Aron. The new liberals were former left-wing intellectuals who had turned against the French socialists as if Mitterrand's aim was to establish a new totalitarianism in France. A few years previously, this intelligentsia had taken the battle to Italy, descending on communist-run Bologna, the most civilized administration in Italy, as if the city had been managed by a clique of unreconstructed Stalinists. Now they exhumed Friedrich von Hayek to declare that social democracy was the road to serfdom, that unions were a threat to liberty, that détente was a conspiracy to enable the USSR to maintain a Gulag system of repression, that unemployment was caused by social regulation.[177]

When the socialists were defeated in 1993, they bequeathed an economy which was far stronger and sounder than it had been when they first began to manage it in 1981 – something for which they have not been given much credit. But the France they left behind was a less tolerant place: it now had a racist party with over 10 per cent of the population behind it, and an anti-immigration lobby openly supported by some conservative ministers; there were daily attacks on immigrants and a growing xenophobia. This, of course, was not an exclusively French phenomenon, but ten years of nearly continuous socialist government had not shielded France from an escalation of racism. At the end of the Mitterrand experiment, the French Left appeared more devoid of ideas, hopes and support than it had been in its entire history.

CHAPTER TWENTY

The Failure of Italian Communism

IT IS customary to compare the Italian and the French Left. Unlike other West European countries, both had powerful communist parties. In neither – from the beginning of the Cold War (1947) to Mitterrand's 1981 victory – had both parties of the Left succeeded in achieving power together. In both, a centrist coalition (Gaullist-led in France after 1958, Christian democrat-led in Italy after 1947) seemed destined to remain in power.

The differences, however, are equally significant. In France the Gaullist coalition had effectively created the conditions for an understanding between the two left parties. This was achieved by keeping the entire Left, socialists as well as communists, out of power and by adopting a two-round electoral system which virtually compelled political parties of the same 'family' to come to some sort of agreement in the second round, in order to maximize their gains. In Italy the Christian democrats had managed to split the Left in the early 1960s (precisely when the French socialists had rejoined the opposition), by enabling the PSI to enter the centre–left coalition. The division within the Italian Left was further exacerbated by its proportional electoral system. This forced each party, during elections, to maximize its own votes and emphasize its differences with all other parties. Socialists and communists, whose programmes were often very similar, co-operated least during elections.

As we saw in chapter 13, the DC–PSI coalition had emerged bruised from the trade union assault of the 'hot autumn' of 1969. Socialist leaders had become pessimistic about their chances of compelling the centre-left coalition to adopt more radical measures. It was increasingly evident to them that they were seen as the supporters of a government unable to resolve any of what were widely considered to be the main problems facing the country. These were a fall in international competitiveness caused by the large wage rises achieved by the unions in 1969–70; an increasingly inefficient state machine and public administration apparatus; and the widening of the social and economic gap between north and south.

This overall crisis, the new political weight achieved by the labour movement, and the dissatisfaction of the Socialist Party with the Christian democrats forced the communists to specify more clearly the strategy required to achieve power.

In Britain, the maximization of votes and seats is the only requirement for achieving office. In the rest of Europe, political parties must not only gain as many votes as possible but – and this is the crucial precondition – they must be able to achieve an alliance with other political parties. These two conditions – votes and friends – equally applied to the PCI. But its problems were more complex. To increase votes under a proportional representation system where many parties compete is far more difficult than in a two-party system. Dissatisfied electors have a wider choice. The PCI had started out in 1946 with slightly less than 20 per cent of the vote. By 1972 it had reached 27.2 per cent. To assume that the PCI would eventually be able to obtain an absolute majority on its own was totally unrealistic. Was a French Union de la Gauche strategy – i.e. an alliance between the PCI and the PSI – possible? The sum of the vote of the two parties had barely altered since 1946: 39.7 per cent in 1946, 31 in 1953, 35.3 in 1958 and 39.1 in 1963. In 1968, the socialist and the staunchly anti-communist social democrats had fought the election together, obtaining 14.5 per cent; dissident socialists obtained 4.5 and the PCI 27 per cent. Adding these figures together, such an improbable coalition would gain only 46 per cent; and in any case, the united Socialist Party broke up again so that, in 1972, the sum of communists and socialists was only 36.8 per cent – even less than in 1946.

It could be argued that these electoral calculations do not take into account the possibility that new generations of voters might be persuaded to vote for a credible Left coalition, just as significant sections of the French electorate eventually deserted the centrist parties to support the Union de la Gauche. However, for this strategy to work it, would have been necessary for the socialists to abandon their long-term alliance with the Christian democrats and join the communists in opposition. This would have compelled the DC to rely exclusively on the support of the three remaining 'constitutional parties' of the centre – the Republicans, the Liberals and the Social Democrats – at least as long as the far-right Movimento Sociale Italiano (Italian Social Movement – MSI) remained beyond the pale of respectable politics. Such a centrist coalition would have been shaky even by Italian standards: in 1972, it would have had a majority of only eighteen in the Chamber of Deputies. Given the lack of stringent party discipline, this majority would not be sufficient to govern Italy effectively.

Thus, the socialists were the linchpin of any serious coalition. They could choose whether to support a DC 'centre–left' coalition, or work towards building a united front with the PCI. The latter, their original post-war strategy, had been abandoned in the late 1950s (see chapter 10). By 1970, even the centre-left option appeared exhausted. The DC–PSI axis of the 1960s had achieved very little. None of the reforms advocated by the PSI, with the exception of comprehensive education and the extension of the school-leaving age, had materialized. The reforms which did eventually occur were a frightened response to the student unrest of 1968 and the working-class militancy of the 'hot autumn' of 1969. These had spurred the Christian

Democrats into making major concessions, such as the regional system and the Statuto dei Lavoratori (see chapter 13). In 1970 a bill legalizing divorce introduced by a Socialist, Loris Fortuna, and a liberal, Antonio Baslini, was approved by Parliament. This was the first important piece of legislation passed since the war in the teeth of Christian-democratic opposition.

Though, by 1970, the PSI no longer thought that a centre-left government could be an agent of social transformation, it still refrained from abandoning the DC in favour of the PCI. There were many reasons for this. Parties in office are reluctant to give up power. New attachments are created, new expectations produced. During its years in power, the PSI had also established its own network of clienteles and provided jobs for its supporters. There was thus considerable pressure to stay in power. Although the years in office had failed to swing votes away from the PCI (or any other party) towards the PSI, the socialists were reluctant to burn all bridges with the DC. This would have looked like openly admitting that they had been wrong to join the centre-left in the first place and that the dissident left-wing socialists, the so-called 'tankists' (because they had supported the Russian tanks in the streets of Budapest in 1956), had been right to leave the party.

Nevertheless, the PSI refrained from entering the government in 1972 and 1973, and reconsidered its position. It eventually rejoined the DC in government partly for the reasons listed above, but also because of encouragement from an unexpected quarter: the PCI.

Enrico Berlinguer, the communist leader, set out his position on the PSI in an article in *Rinascita* on 27 October 1972. The Socialist Party, he wrote, had characteristics which made it substantially different from the Communist Party. It had its own distinctiveness. This should be respected: 'Sister parties, if different, are a useful thing; twin parties, fundamentally identical, even if possible, would be superfluous.'[1] It was not in the interests of the PSI or the PCI, he wrote, either to interrupt their reciprocal co-operation in the trade unions or local government, or to try to erase their distinctive characteristics.[2] The Italian political system, unlike the British, was not a two-party system, and it should not attempt to become one. A polarization of the country between two opposing blocs was not in the interests of the Left. In Italy there were not two but three components of the 'popular movement': the communist, the socialist and the Catholic.[3] The task of the Left was to prepare the grounds for an *incontro* (agreement) between these three forces; and the task of the PSI would be to facilitate such an entente.[4] Co-operation between the PCI and the PSI was possible even if the PSI was in government with the DC and the PCI remained in opposition. They could still have a 'common general strategy'. Berlinguer added: 'it follows that we are not opposed in principle to the entry of the PSI into the government.' This would be a transitional phase, preparing a 'democratic alternative'.[5]

Even allowing for the peculiar obscurity of Italian political language, the message was reasonably clear, at least to the initiated. The aim of the PCI was not a united front of the Left (the French model). As Berlinguer had declared at the Thirteenth Congress of the PCI (March 1972), the unity of the Left was a necessary, but insufficient, condition to break the mould of Italian politics: it was necessary to involve the Catholics too.[6] In the meantime, it was better if the PSI was in government, as long as its objectives were no longer those of the past – the ambition to reform Italian society, while leaving the PCI in a permanent oppositional ghetto: 'we reject the idea that the PSI's role is to be in government and the PCI's to be in opposition.'[7] In practice, Berlinguer was asking the PSI to become the PCI's Trojan horse.

It could be argued that Berlinguer was simply accepting the inevitable. He assumed the PSI would re-enter the coalition anyway. The PCI might as well put on a brave face and refrain from further damaging its relations with the socialists. The communist thesis that Italy could change only through co-operation between 'the three great popular traditions: Communist, Socialist and Catholic', had been formally approved at the Thirteenth Congress.[8] This reflected the view, first propounded by Togliatti, that it would be dangerous to exclude the 'Catholic masses' from power. This strategy, launched during the Resistance, was advocated until the beginning of the Cold War (see chapter 5). It was never entirely abandoned: in the early 1960s, when the PSI joined forces with the DC, Togliatti took a soft line, condemning the attempt to isolate the communists, rather than the principle of an alliance with the DC. He thus avoided a complete rupture between socialists and communists, who continued to co-operate within the CGIL union federation and in local government. Thus, Berlinguer's article must be read in the context of a well-established strategy.

All this became clearer when Berlinguer himself, a year later, labelled the strategy 'a new, great, *compromesso storico*', or 'historic compromise'. In a rare reference to Lenin (such an apparent return to tradition is always a tell-tale sign of political innovation), he pointed out that Lenin himself had not been averse to serious compromises, first with imperial Germany over the peace of Brest–Litovsk, and then with the market economy when he introduced the New Economic Policy. The historic compromise rapidly became the most discussed political initiative of the 1970s. Berlinguer had first propounded it in three articles in September and October 1973 in the party weekly *Rinascita*. The occasion for this was the *coup d'état* which ousted the Chilean Unidad Popular government of socialists and communists, led by Salvador Allende. The three articles on Chile constitute the most representative expression of Berlinguer's strategic flair, while revealing, at the same time, the central flaws of the political approach of the Italian communists. The purpose of the articles was to explain why, in Italy, it would be 'illusory to assume that, should the parties of the Left succeed in obtaining fifty-one per cent of the vote and of the parliamentary seats ... this would be sufficient to guarantee the survival of a government which represented this fifty-one per cent.'[9] The Italian communists, Berlinguer explained, always understood that they had to accept as a 'fundamental' fact that Italy belonged to a politico-military bloc dominated by the USA, and that this constrained all their activities.[10] Those who, like the Greek communists in 1945, did not understand this, paid heavily: they were defeated and forced underground.[11] Berlinguer proceeded, rather pedagogically, to explain that a 'reform strategy' needed to be sustained by a social 'bloc' encompassing more than just the working classes and involving the largest possible proportion of the population.[12] A coalition limited to the parties of the Left would encourage the formation of a centre-right bloc, possibly in alliance with the far Right. By involving the DC in a progressive coalition, the *compromesso storico* would prevent it from shifting to the right. Italian Christian democracy, explained Berlinguer, was not purely the party of the bourgeoisie; it was also the party of the middle and lower-middle classes, and had the support of many workers and peasants, women and young people.[13] The DC, he added, could not try another alliance with the far Right, as it had done in 1960 – the short-lived Tambroni government, which collapsed because of widespread popular hostility. The centre-left government with the socialists had failed. The centrist government of 1972–73 had much too narrow a majority to govern the country.[14] Thus, the DC was at a dead end, and was more amenable to compromise with the PCI than at any other time since what might be termed the first 'historic compromise' of 1944–47.

Optimism and comfort could be derived from the increasing evidence that the Catholic world was in political turmoil. The CISL, the trade union confederation of Catholic workers, had emerged from the experience of the 'hot autumn' more independent of the DC and keen to work closely with the other two trade union confederations, the socialist–communist CGIL and the social-democratic UIL. The Associazioni Cristiane Lavoratori Italiani (ACLI), the most powerful working-class Catholic association, for years at the service of the electoral interests of the DC, shifted to the left. At its Twelfth Congress, in April 1972, the ACLI, while affirming its political independence from all political parties, announced that it had adopted an anti-capitalist and socialist 'class position' – a language which even the communists were beginning to eschew.[15]

In the wider Catholic world, the doctrine of 'Liberation theology', with its emphasis on the need to fight alongside the poor against the great injustices which plague the world, was in the ascendant. In Italy, left-wing priests supported by members of the church hierarchy were abandoning the intransigent anti-communism of yesteryear, and embraced the ethos of the 1960s. Inside the DC, Aldo Moro, a master-tactician who had once been one of the architects of the centre-left coalition, kept up an intense dialogue with the PCI, which he came to regard as one of the guarantors of the Italian constitution against the 'fascist menace'.[16]

The situation thus seemed to indicate that Italy was ready for a change. A communist party in the ascendant, yet cautious and keen to be flexible, could become a possible partner for a DC which had run out of steam. Berlinguer's analysis, depicting a communist party not sufficiently strong to rule without the centre, and Christian democrats no longer able to rule in the old way, was reminiscent of Otto Bauer's own investigation into the causes of fascism, which suggested (see chapter 3) that a precarious balance of forces between the two main parties, each unable to establish full control on its own, may create the conditions for the emergence of an authoritarian party on a law-and-order platform. It was in the interests of the two blocs to prevent this possibility, by coalescing in defence of democracy.

The continued support enjoyed by the DC rested not merely on religious beliefs, or on American support, but on much more material – if not necessarily more solid – grounds: namely, the fabulous increase in prosperity which had transformed Italy under Christian democracy from a relatively poor country to one of the richest in the world. Those who had been unable or unwilling to be absorbed in the constantly expanding private sector had found jobs in an even faster swelling state sector – grossly overmanned, perhaps, but none the less a beneficent dispenser of regular pay and secure jobs. There was much cause to be grateful to Christian democracy, and gratitude in democratic politics is repaid in votes. But what would happen if capitalism, the goose which lays the golden egg, stopped growing? Would the citizens, hitherto judiciously bribed by an uninhibited attitude towards state budgeting, still vote for the DC and its allies? The rapidly developing economic crisis triggered by the oil crisis seemed to lend weight to Berlinguer's strategy. Just as the DC had brought the PSI into government in order not to face the end of the 1958–63 boom alone, would it now be forced to come to terms with the PCI as the golden age of capitalism came to a close? Or would the economic crisis induce a turn to the right? Was the rise of a proto-fascist regime possible in the 1970s?

Those without the benefit of hindsight could be forgiven for thinking so. The threat of fascism appeared real in the 1970s. In 1970 Prince Valerio Borghese, a former blackshirt, attempted a farcical coup – called off because it was raining. In 1971 Giovanni Leone, a right-wing Christian democrat from Naples, was elected president of the republic with the decisive support of the neo-fascist MSI. In 1972 the MSI obtained 8.7 per cent, its best results up to then. After 1969, a campaign of terror was launched by right-wing extremists, with the alleged connivance of the Italian secret services.[17] There was ample circumstantial evidence to link right-wing terrorists to the most devastating acts of bloodshed in post-war Italian history: seventeen people were the victims of bombs at the Bank of Agriculture in Milan in December 1969; eight at an anti-fascist demonstration in Piazza della Loggia in Brescia on 28 May 1974; twelve died on the Florence–Bologna train on 4 August 1974; and eighty-five at the Bologna railway station on 2 August 1980. The full truth about these massacres has not yet emerged.

Anti-fascism had once again become a symbol of national unity. This helped the communist strategy and enabled even the power-corrupted DC to reclaim some semblance of political rectitude – with the encouragement of the PCI, for which a DC purged of its right-wing tendency was the ideal partner for the historic compromise. Berlinguer's scenario was an attempt to revisit the crucial years of the immediate aftermath of the Second World War, when the PCI was in a government of national unity and when anti-fascism was the ideological cement which bound together the parties which had fought together in the Resistance.

Though in difficulties, the DC was still the strongest party in the country and still appeared to be the immovable centre of the Italian political system. Although handicapped by its link with the USSR and years of anti-communism, the PCI could use, albeit with caution, the new opportunities brought about by the social changes experienced by the Italians. Student unrest and the 'hot autumn' had certainly sapped the stability of the Christian-democratic regime. It was unlikely, however, that the anarchistic impetus of students or the (predominantly northern) workers' movement would provide the PCI with social movements that could be galvanized in a consciously democratic and necessarily gradual bid for power. Many student activists had, by 1973, regrouped themselves into hard Leninist or anarchist organiza-tions, some ready to degenerate into terrorism and inspired by a profound hatred of the PCI (as the supreme betrayer of the revolution), others – totally blind to sixty years of European history – were still seeking the chimera of the revolutionary hour, a repeat performance of October 1917. The workers' unrest had been innovative and radical but, stripped of rhetoric, their demands were either traditional trade union ones – working hours, working conditions, pay – or traditional social-democratic ones – better housing, better schools, better health care. These the PCI could advance in opposition or, if resources allowed, governments could deliver.

Berlinguer's analysis was sober and realistic. It is rare for an opposition leader to face up to the constraints on his party, openly examine before the entire nation the available options, and explain the necessity for compromise, while refraining from arousing his followers with optimistic rallying cries.

Nevertheless the strategy of the historic compromise, as revealed in the Chile articles and pursued in practice, involved two fundamental tactical mistakes which eventually precipitated its failure. The first consisted in taking the Socialist Party for granted – an attitude unwittingly encouraged by the pro-PCI posture of the then leader of the PSI, Francesco De Martino. The communists somehow assumed that the PSI had little choice but to support their grand strategic plan. Though always denying it, the communists often behaved, in the final analysis, as if they were coterminous with the entire Left. The ritualistic inclusion of the 'socialists', whenever communist leaders mentioned the 'three great Italian political traditions', was always seen by the socialists for what it really was: tokenism. At the local level communists repeatedly by-passed the socialists and focused their attention on the Christian democrats, as if it were not apparent that a DC–PCI entente would leave the PSI without a meaningful function. Only later – too late – did senior communists admit that the frustration of the socialists had not been taken seriously.[18]

It is understandable that, as the junior party of the Left, the PSI was primarily concerned with itself and its own role. It had a vested interest in the PCI remaining in opposition. Only this would secure the PSI's position at the centre of the political arena, allowing it to remain the maker and unmaker of governments, and the object of the solicitous consideration of the DC. As long as the PCI remained in opposition, the PSI could be the main interlocutor of the DC in government, and yet be in power with the PCI in all cities and regions where a left majority existed. Elsewhere, it could form an administration with the DC. With around 10 per cent of the vote, the PSI could be in power everywhere. For this privileged political position to persist, things had to proceed as before: the DC in power, the PCI in opposition. Thus the PSI, which looked only to its own party interests, had no alternative but to remain in practice a profoundly conservative force. All the claims of modernity which the PSI would make throughout the 1980s, and its disparagement of the DC and the PCI as the representatives of the old order, cannot disguise this simple fact.

The second and more serious tactical mistake of the communists was that there was never any serious discussion of what the eventual alliance between the DC and the PCI needed to achieve. The PCI constantly referred to the necessity for 'deep' and 'radical' social reforms, but it was not clear what they wanted concretely. This vagueness could be overlooked in the initial stages of the construction of an alliance. It became a major error of judgement, however, when the DC and the PCI were actively discussing a programme of government. A vague intention to effect a fiscal reform or a health reform is not the same as a commitment to a practical set of policies. Vagueness allows all parties to pay lip-service to policies, while taking evasive action.

Much has been written on the historic compromise and its subsequent failure. I have discussed, here and elsewhere, its theoretical and historical antecedents.[19] What needs to be further elucidated is the political context of the strategy. Berlinguer had a profoundly pessimistic view of the chances of the survival of democracy in Italy in the absence of an alliance with 'progressive Catholicism', whose potential he overestimated. Reinforcing this pessimism were the widespread belief that the Italian secret services were pursuing a policy of destabilization known, tolerated, perhaps even encouraged by the USA, and the absence – among Western leaders – of any sympathy for, or understanding of, the Italian communists' distinctive position of independence from the USSR. Most leading European social democrats refused to support Berlinguer privately, let alone publicly. From Harold Wilson and James Callaghan to Helmut Schmidt (in spite of the PCI's contribution to the development of Ostpolitik), there was a consistent refusal to facilitate the incorporation of the PCI into the mainstream (social-democratic) fold of the European Left. On 27 June 1976, at the Puerto Rico summit of the leaders of the most advanced industrial countries, not only conservatives, such as the US and the French presidents, Gerald Ford and Giscard d'Estaing, but also Helmut Schmidt and James Callaghan met secretly, having excluded Aldo Moro, then Italian prime minister, to consider the 'problems' posed by the advance of the PCI at the 20 June election in Italy.[20] The official view was that the Italian communists' claim to be democratic was another trick with which to dupe 'useful idiots'. This knee-jerk reaction was based on profound political ignorance of Italian politics. Virtually the entire corpus of scholarship on Italian communism, though divided in its assessment of the PCI, at least agreed on one point: the Italian communists were genuinely independent of the USSR and were as committed to parliamentary democracy as the overwhelming majority of West European parties. The main division among scholars, many of whom were critical of the PCI, was whether the party could still be considered a radical force for social change, or whether it was simply a social-democratic organization, albeit one still encrusted with the symbolism and rhetoric of the communist movement.[21] All subsequent developments completely vindicated this scholarship.

To add to the international isolation of the PCI was the fact that most of Southern Europe itself was, in 1973, the last remaining enclave of right-wing dictatorship. Authoritarian regimes of the Right in Spain and Portugal were joined in 1967 by Greece, under the rule of the Colonels – all enjoying firm direct or indirect NATO support. Berlinguer was regularly warned by the USSR, and even by some Christian democrats, that a fascist coup was a real possibility in Italy.[22] All this contributed to the PCI's impression of being under siege. A Left government which excluded the DC (in 1976, electorally impossible) would thus find itself in an extremely precarious international position.

This problem pales into insignificance when account is taken of the likely domestic opposition. By 1973, the DC had ruled Italy for thirty years, systematically colonizing the civil service, the security services, the armed forces, the public sector (including most of the banking system, and the radio and television network). Hardly a single public service appointment had been made without the consent of the DC or one of its allies. To achieve a position of power or prestige in the state sector or even, at times, a humble job in the post office or in public transport, it was necessary to seek the favour of Christian democrats. The DC controlled also the Casse di risparmio, where the vast savings of the Italians were deposited, and which constituted the main source of investment funds. How could one hope to govern the country against a party which exercised such extensive control? The experience of the PSI in government was particularly illuminating, for the socialists had naively assumed that they could run the country once inside the *stanza dei bottoni* (the central control room). But in modern societies power is diffused. There is no control room which, once stormed, grants the occupier more than the illusion of power. In the course of its years in office, the PSI came to realize how difficult it was to secure the effective implementation of agreed legislation against the obstruction, sabotage and delaying tactics of public administration personnel. In these circumstances, the idea that a united left government, on the basis of a slim parliamentary majority, would be able to reform Italy and change the system against the opposition of the DC and its liberal, social-democratic and republican allies, belongs to fairy tales. The parties thus excluded from power would inevitably lurch further to the right, would enjoy international (especially American) support, would be able to activate the loyalty of millions of minor civil servants, municipal employees, police officers, journalists, television producers, post office workers, and others who owed their jobs to the DC. Last, but not least, the DC, by rapidly returning to a defence of old-fashioned morality, would enjoy the still powerful help of the church, while receiving massive financial and practical help from the entire entrepreneurial class and the newspapers it controlled.

So much for the background to the historic compromise. Nevertheless, events in the three years following Berlinguer's proposals facilitated the ascendancy of Italian communism. One after the other, the three remaining authoritarian regimes of Southern Europe – the Portuguese, the Spanish and the Greek – came tumbling down. In all three instances, the communist parties were legalized and immediately gained in prestige. Of these, however, only the Spanish Communist Party modelled its strategy on that of the Italian. In Greece and Portugal, as we shall see in greater detail in the next chapter, the communists remained attached to the traditional 'hard' workerist position which had triumphed in Central and Eastern Europe after the war. In France the pact of unity between socialists and communists, though representing the 'popular front' strategy quite explicitly rejected by Berlinguer, still held good. Berlinguer distanced himself from the Portuguese communists – still harking back to the vision of a revolutionary takeover – and forged alliances with the French and the Spanish.[23] It was the birth of 'Eurocommunism', an attempt to map out a new path for European communism based on a firm commitment to the values of parliamentary democracy. Eurocommunism would not survive the increasingly erratic behaviour of the French, and the eccentricities of the then Spanish leader, Santiago Carrillo. But for a time, it provided Western communism, and particularly the PCI, with a platform from which it could speak to the entire European Left.

Inside Italy, a Christian democrat backlash against the historic compromise led by Amintore Fanfani, the DC leader, met its Waterloo. Fanfani directed a Catholic attempt to abrogate the divorce legislation through a popular referendum which was held in 1974. A clear majority of the electorate sanctioned divorce. Fanfani was ousted and a new team, led by Benigno

Zaccagnini and Aldo Moro, took over Christian democracy. The unambiguous anti-communism of Fanfani and his supporters was temporarily defeated.

On 15 June 1975 regional and local elections were held. The results were generally regarded as a triumph for the PCI, which obtained its best results so far – 33.4 per cent (up from 25.8 per cent in the same elections of 1970) – and nearly closed the gap with the DC (down to 35.3 per cent).[24] The PSI had moved forward too, reaching 11.7 per cent. The Left had never been stronger in relation to the DC. After the election, PCI–PSI coalitions took over the government of six regions (previously they ruled in only three), thirty provinces and twenty-nine main cities. Communist or communist-supported mayors were now in power in Naples, Rome, Turin, Florence and Bologna. Nearly half the population lived in areas ruled by a coalition which included the PCI.

These successes boosted Berlinguer's strategy and enabled him to consolidate his hold over a remarkably united party. The ambiguity surrounding the historic compromise helped in this, for each communist could read into it what he or she wanted. The rank and file, though always suspicious of the DC, wearied of being eternally in opposition and were willing to embrace any strategy which would take the PCI into government. From this favourable position, Berlinguer sought to reassure the 'West'. No anti-NATO, left-wing party had ever entered the government of a NATO country in 'normal' political conditions. The Italian socialists themselves had accepted Atlanticism before joining the DC in the centre-left government of 1963. The German SPD had dropped its opposition to NATO in 1960, six years before forming the coalition with the CDU. The price of power was acceptance of Italy's membership of the international alliance system of the West. On 15 June 1976, a few days before the general election, the *Corriere della Sera*, Italy's most influential paper, published an interview with Berlinguer in which the communist leader explained that he no longer questioned Italy's membership of NATO. Asked whether he felt that NATO could be a useful shield in order to build socialism in freedom, Berlinguer replied:[25]

> I don't want Italy to withdraw from the Atlantic Pact 'also' for this reason, and not only because our withdrawal would upset the international equilibrium. I feel safer over here ...

He then added:

> Over there, in the East, they would perhaps like to see us build socialism as they like it. But over here, in the West, some people don't even want to let us start building it, even if we do so respecting freedom. I realize that it is a little risky on our part to pursue a road that is not always appreciated either over here or over there.

This reassurance was only half-believed. The difference between the PCI, on the one hand, and parties such as the SPD or the PSI, on the other, was that the PCI was, after all, a *communist* party with particular links with the USSR. However strongly the PCI distanced itself from Soviet foreign policy; however often it reiterated its disagreement with the political forms under which socialism had been constructed in the East; however frequently it reminded its listeners that the PCI was committed to democracy, Parliament and all the basic freedoms of 'bourgeois' society – it remained a party which was on the wrong side of the Cold War divide, and hence a party whose loyalty to the West was in doubt. The others, as long as they were not communists, were 'reliable' – however corrupt (Italian Christian democracy); however illiberal or fascistic (the Greek Colonels, Portugal's António Salazar, Spain's Francisco Franco); however murderous (Chile's Augusto Pinochet or Indonesia's General Suharto). The consequences of considering the communists 'unreliable' from the Western democratic point of view were formidable: the struggle against them need not remain confined within the formal rules of liberal democracy, for, to defend freedom, it was argued, it may be necessary to use any weapons, including detestable ones (murder, terrorism, deceit, external interference, bribery). It was as if, alongside Italy's democratic constitution, there was another unwritten, but widely recognized, set of rules which decreed that the communists were to be excluded from political power, irrespective of the wishes of the electorate: the *conventio ad escludendum* (agreement to exclude).[26] A similar phenomenon, known as *parasyntagma* (parallel constitution), occurred in Greece. Cold War politics made full democracy difficult, because the decision of electorates would always have to be judged and validated in terms of their international consequences. Though national sovereignty in the West was never as severely limited as it was in the Soviet sphere, few believed that people could choose any government they wanted and not suffer possible destabilization. The popular success of conspiracy theories in the 1970s and 1980s would not have been possible had not the Italian situation provided a context in which everything seemed possible and credible. At one time or another, it was suggested in books, films or newspaper articles that the CIA had killed Aldo Moro, that the KGB had tried to assassinate Pope John Paul II, that the church hierarchy had killed his predecessor (who died of a heart attack), that the Red Brigades were Italian secret servicemen in disguise, and that Giulio Andreotti was the boss of the Italian mafia. Of course, all this had been amply prepared by the mystery surrounding Kennedy's assassination: once it was mooted that the president of the USA had been murdered by the CIA, anything seemed possible.

Conspiracy theories always generate a climate of fear and suspicion which affects politicians more than ordinary people, to whom much of everyday politics does in fact look like a conspiracy. The leaders of the PCI were not indifferent to this predicament, and behaved accordingly – that is, with an excess of prudence and caution – particularly after their success in the general election of June 1976.

In this elections the PCI continued to gain votes, reaching the zenith of its post-war growth: 34.4 per cent. The PSI vote fell to below 10 per cent. The DC recouped some of the ground lost in 1975, and achieved a respectable 38.7 per cent. From the point of view of the historic compromise, this was a creditable result. The fact that the PCI had not been the sole winner enabled Berlinguer to argue, quite legitimately, that those who had assumed that the DC would simply fade away were wrong, and that while it was becoming apparent that one could not rule the country against the PCI (as communist banners incessantly proclaimed), the same could be said of the DC. What was negative about the overall result, from the PCI's point of view, was that the PSI had lost. At the time, the communists, blinded by their hour of triumph, had not realized how much the hurt pride of the socialists aggravated their fear of being squeezed out of power. Francesco De Martino resigned soon after, in the summer of 1976, and Bettino Craxi, a staunch anti-communist determined to renew the socialist party, became leader.

After the election Parliament was effectively deadlocked. For the first time since the war, the 'centrist' coalition – that is, the DC and the three small parties of the centre – did not have a majority. The DC could not renew the centre-left government, because the PSI was no longer willing to co-operate without the PCI. Nor could the DC let the PCI enter the government, without risking an internal split. The Left (PCI plus PSI) did not attempt to build a majority with the small republican, social-democratic, radical and proletarian unity parties. This was understandable: no coherent set of policies could possibly have held together such a heterogeneous conglomeration of parties on the basis of a tiny parliamentary majority. The PCI could have insisted that it would not support a government of which it was not part. The byzantine solution eventually agreed was that the DC would form a government on its own – led by Giulio Andreotti (once the man of the right wing of the DC and a close ally of the USA) – and would ask the other parties, specifically, the PCI, the PSI, and the small social-democratic and republican parties, to abstain.[27]

This was widely seen as a move towards the full legitimation of the PCI. Though still kept out of the executive, the communists strengthened their influence in Parliament when they obtained the chairmanships of a number of powerful committees, and when the veteran leader of the PCI Left, Pietro Ingrao, became the first communist president of the Chamber of Deputies. These were, the PCI believed, the first steps towards government. Italian industrialists, the conservative electorate and the rest of the world (especially the USA) would gradually but surely discover that one could, after all, trust the Italian communists.

A year later (June 1977), the DC negotiated a government programme with all the parties, including the PCI. Was this another small step towards full PCI participation? It appeared to be so when, another year later (March 1978), a new DC-only government, again led by Andreotti, was launched. The negotiations surrounding it had been long and difficult, but the PCI felt it had obtained sufficiently strong guarantees to vote in favour, instead of abstaining. On 16 March this new government received the support of Parliament. The political situation, however, had changed dramatically. That morning, a group of left-wing terrorists, the Red Brigades, kidnapped Moro, killing his five bodyguards. Moro was kept hidden for fifty-five days, while the terrorists attempted to obtain some official recognition from the Italian government, such as the release of some of their comrades from jail. The government held firm, supported by a Communist Party determined to be totally unwavering in its rejection of negotiations. There were large anti-terrorist demonstrations, mainly communist-sponsored, and widespread dis-taste for the Red Brigades. Some prestigious intellectuals, however, such as the poet Eugenio Montale (a Nobel prize-winner), and Leonardo Sciascia, irresponsibly declared that the Italian state was not worth dying for – as if the five young policemen brutally murdered by the terrorists had not done just that. The PCI had become the party of law and order, the bulwark of democratic legality, the shield of the constitution. The PSI decided to adopt a less intransigent position.[28] The aim was to distance itself from both the PCI and the DC, presenting a 'human' face against the 'ideologies' of Catholicism and communism. This stance – an easy one to take, for it was never pushed far enough to have any practical consequences for Moro – attracted much praise.[29] At the time, Craxi's socialists regularly attacked the communists as if they controlled the Italian state and its establishment, criticizing, for instance, the leading Milanese bourgeois paper, the *Corriere della Sera*, for its alleged pro-Communist views.[30] Craxi thus set a new course towards the conquest of the PSI's 'rightful' share of power. Henceforth, the PSI's own interest as a party became the sole beacon guiding its course towards the systematic plunder of the country's wealth in competition with the DC. Meanwhile, the PCI, in the name of the *national* interest, remained the pathetic defender of the tattered Italian state from whose leadership it had always been excluded.

Unable to achieve their goal, the Red Brigades killed Moro and abandoned his body in a car near the headquarters of the PCI and the DC. By the end of 1978, the attempt to achieve a historic compromise had failed. The PCI – still out of power – had been defeated. It never recovered. From 1979 its history was one of electoral decline, dwindling membership and political marginalization.

On 27 November 1980 an earthquake devastated the already impoverished hills of the Irpinia in southern Italy. In the ensuing confusion – rescue teams arriving too late, wild rumours suggesting that the disaster could have been foreseen, a pervasive feeling that the Italian state was hopelessly ill-prepared for any emergency – Berlinguer announced that the strategy of the historic compromise was to be abandoned in favour of the so-called 'democratic alternative'. The only thing that was clear about this U-turn was that the PCI no longer sought a partnership with the DC. The party began to pursue an alliance with the PSI instead. Seldom was so half-hearted a suitor so regularly rejected. Between 1976 and 1979, the PSI had been totally ignored by the PCI, whose main interlocutor was the DC. What socialist MPs did or thought or said had become irrelevant. The socialists were only too conscious of this, and no longer bothered to propose legislation, or even to state their position. Out of 666 Bills passed by Parliament between 1976 and 1979, communists and Christian democrats expressed their position in over 90 per cent of instances, the PSI in fewer than 50 per cent.[31] Once the PCI had returned to opposition, the PSI abundantly repaid the humiliations suffered. In the following decade, the DC and the PSI embarked on a major division of the spoils. With the audacity and arrogance of racketeers convinced that they could not be caught, they extorted a crescendo of pay-offs from the private sector, in exchange for contracts, while carving up the entire public sector between themselves.

By the time the Berlin Wall collapsed in November 1989, the PCI had become a party without a future. A change of name caused a serious split and a prolonged period of introspection in search of a new identity. Its fortunes revived only when the financial scandals of 1992–93 destroyed the credibility of the government parties. But these events belong to the history of post-communism.

Why in 1976 did the PCI agree to support a government which refused it a place – in retrospect, a major tactical blunder? The idea of the historic compromise was predicated on the need to eliminate, once and for all, the *conventio ad escludendum*. By supporting a DC-only government, and accepting exclusion from the cabinet, the PCI implicitly sanctioned its own illegitimacy, allowing the DC (and the USA) to dictate the terms, modality and timing of any eventual communist entry. Gerardo Chiaromonte, one of the communist leaders most closely involved in the decision, later explained that they thought this was the inevitable first step towards full participation in government.[32] Berlinguer stressed the need to show everyone that the PCI could not simply 'sit out' the crisis which was engulfing the country. It had to show a sense of duty. We had, wrote Chiaromonte, 'a high sense of national responsibility'.[33] Had the PCI refused to support the government, had it imposed a trial by strength, there would have been new elections with, presumably, similar results (or with an increase in communist and DC votes). With Parliament dead-locked once again, a solution would have been as remote as ever. What also worried the PCI was that the PSI under Craxi would be tempted to break with the communists once more and – if the political price was right – agree to revive its alliance with the DC.[34] Does all this sufficiently explain why, if Chiaromonte's account is to be believed (and no one has contradicted it), the entire party secretariat was solidly behind the decision to support the government? Whatever the answer, there is little doubt that once this initial decision had been taken, the PCI felt trapped in a mechanism from which it could not extricate itself.[35]

What was the actual situation which had entrapped the PCI? In the first place, Italy was in the midst of a wave of terrorism unparalleled in Europe – far wider, deeper and with greater popular support (particularly among young people and disaffected intellectuals) than in Germany (the Baader-Meinhoff gang remained a relatively minor episode in the history of the Federal Republic), or in Britain (where the IRA never questioned the legitimacy of the British state – only its presence in Northern Ireland). Coinciding with the rise of the PCI as a credible government force was the advent of left-wing terrorism alongside right-wing terror. Peaking in the 1976–80 period, between 1969 and 1980, there were 7,866 acts of violence, leading to 172 people being severely wounded and 362 deaths, including those of 65 policemen, nine magistrates and three politicians, primarily at the hands of left-wing terrorists.[36] While the terrorism of the Right tended to be indiscriminate (the bombs in public places in Brescia and Bologna reported above), the terrorism of the Left was clearly targeted: journalists, intellectuals and magistrates (nearly all of progressive inclination). Because so much of this left-wing terrorism was conducted in the name of 'socialism', it was inevitable that the opponents of the Italian communists would draw a parallel between the behaviour of the terrorists and the ideology of communism (totalitarian, pro-violence, anti-democratic, anti-human) and, by implication, that of the PCI. The PCI reacted by becoming the party of law and order and the chief defender of the Italian state. This identification with the Italian state reveals the extent to which the PCI had abandoned its communist integument and acquired that of social democracy. As we have seen in the course of this narrative, left-wing parties of government, potential or actual, intensely identify themselves with 'their' state. In the course of their political evolution, they have shaped this state, given it substance, influenced its legal system, obtained the support of myriads of voters, established themselves in the nooks and crannies of its civil society, contributed to its ethos, made use of its system of rights. This state was no longer just the state of the capitalists, an alien, external force, threatening and authoritarian, a state to be taken over and destroyed, to be replaced by something else yet to be defined. The Italian communists had shed their blood during the Resistance on behalf of the new post-war Italian Republic, had participated in the drafting of its constitution, defended its Parliament. None of this impressed Italy's international 'allies'. The USA openly militated for a return to the centre-left government, manifesting its displeasure at the growth of communist influence in government. On 12 January 1978, the State Department declared: 'we do not favour (Communist) participation and would like to see Communist influence in any Western European country reduced.'[37] The PCI's anti-terrorist policies cut no ice in Washington.

But Italy did not just need to be defended from terrorism. The economic crisis which was engulfing Europe affected Italy more significantly than other nations. In the 1970s Italian unemployment (see Table 16.1 in chapter 16) was the highest in OECD–Europe. As for inflation rates, Italy was second only to Portugal, which was undergoing a complex transition crisis. Between 1973 and 1977, the Italian lira depreciated continuously. This further increased the cost of imports already augmented by rising oil prices, resulting in an expanding balance of payments deficit. At the beginning of 1974, to contain inflation, a harsh credit squeeze was imposed by the Bank of Italy. This aggravated the recession and brought about a further fall in investments. Italy began to borrow heavily from the IMF (1974 and 1976) and the EEC (1976).[38] Italy's dependency on international borrowing was explicitly recognized in the *Accordo programmatico* (Agreement Programme) of June 1977, signed by the DC, the PCI, the PSI and two minor parties of the centre. The agreement stated that, to comply with the conditions set out in the 'Letter of Intent' to the IMF, it would be necessary to cut public spending, switch resources away from consumption towards investment, reduce production costs (a euphemism for wages), and bring inflation into line with the rest of the European Community.[39] How the cuts in public spending were to be achieved is described in the Agreement in the most general terms, as if the most important thing for the communists was to be part of the entente. One of the signal failures of the PCI was not clearly to have specified the concrete economic and social policies which would have been acceptable. This enabled the DC to enter into a generic agreement which would leave the foundations of its power unchanged – as Giorgio Napolitano self-critically pointed out.[40]

The main problem facing the PCI was similar to that confronting all other forces of the Left in Europe at the time: the oil-shock-induced recession had increased costs and squeezed profits. In the medium term the return to growth would require an increase in investments; but in the short term – the time-span which matters in electoral politics – there appeared to be little alternative but to contain labour costs. In the 1970s, most West European governments, assuming that the weakening of trade union power was either undesirable or unfeasible, tried to involve the unions in political bargaining. Could this be done in Italy? On the surface it appeared possible. Because it needed the support of the PCI, the Andreotti government was the most 'left-dependent' government Italy was likely to have, given its peculiar situation. The three trade union federations had 'their' parties (DC, PCI, PSI, etc.) in government, or supporting it. By 1976, Italian labour costs had increased at a faster rate than in most of Western Europe. The recognized culprit was the so called *scala mobile*. This was a flat-rate wage indexing system agreed in 1975, according to which wages would increase by a definite amount (not a percentage) for each percentage point of inflation. Two effects of this rather complex mechanism should be highlighted here. In the first place, it led to a reduction of differentials because, as inflation grows, the proportional increase for those on lower incomes is greater than it is for the better-off (this was similar to Stage 1 of the British Labour government's incomes policy of July 1975 – see chapter 18). Secondly, by 1976, this mechanism had displaced the unions as the chief instrument for increases in wages.[41] The labour market became relatively inflexible and wages were automatically dependent on inflation. Those on lower incomes had a built-in interest in inflation. The level of inflation-proof protection would depend on the construction of the basket of goods which defined the index; on the degree of uniformity of inflation across all goods; and on the time-lag between the calculation of the inflation level and the moment at which wages were increased. These variables became the basis for negotiations between trade unions and governments.

Like all West European parties of the Left, the PCI was committed to full employment. To maintain employment, it was necessary to achieve a high level of exports and a low level of imports. To obtain a high level of exports, it was necessary to remain competitive. This required the containment of wage inflation, and yet wage inflation was built into the situation through the *scala mobile*. To achieve a lower level of imports, one would have had to reduce the private consumption of imported goods – given that many imports (e.g. oil) were necessary for the manufacture of exports. To persuade consumers not to spend their money on some imported goods, one would have had to increase the price of these goods (tariffs or devaluation), thus adding to inflation, and hence to wages, and so on. Thus, the PCI was squeezed between two unappealing policies: to tamper with the *scala mobile*, thereby lowering the real wages of those employed; or to accept a higher level of unemployment. There were, of course, other alternatives, such as some form of protectionism, autarchy, etc., which the PCI had always rejected.

The response of the communists was to underline the gravity of the crisis. It was, they stressed, a crisis of capitalism which had so dramatically changed the relation of forces between social classes that it had become impossible for the ruling class to force the workers to accept sacrifices. Now sacrifices were to be 'negotiated'. Their object would be to reinvigorate the economy, bring about a recovery, and increase employment.[42] This was the socio-economic counterpart of the historic compromise. As in other West European countries, moderation on the part of workers was supposed to be exchanged for ill-specified social and industrial policies. The crisis provided an opportunity which should not be allowed to slip away, declared Berlinguer in January 1977. He did so in the course of two notable speeches on the theme of 'austerity', one in Rome to a conference on culture which gathered together the cream of the progressive intelligentsia, and the other in Milan to the national assembly of communist factory workers. The PCI, he said, could not simply stand by while the system collapsed around it. Austerity should not mean an economic policy which was supposed to shore up the existing regime. Austerity meant rigour, efficiency and social justice.[43] Economic development based on a constant and artificial expansion of consumption, declared Berlinguer to the left-wing intellectuals assembled in Rome (most of whom appeared never to have neglected an opportunity to consume), was in direct conflict with the needs and exigencies of the Third World.[44] Sacrifices and austerity were necessary and were acceptable, as long as they were directed against the waste, injustice, privilege and the excesses of private consumption.

Some of these themes – especially the question of the waste occasioned by consumption – were developed by the Green movement in the 1980s, the decade when the consumer society, occasionally criticized in the past, re-asserted itself with a vengeance barely dampened by the crocodile tears of the well-heeled. Berlinguer's suggestion that there should be some sort of solidarity pact between the better-off (including the better-off workers), and those who had been particularly affected by the crisis, provoked an outcry.

Rereading Berlinguer's speeches, nearly twenty years later, I wonder whether this diffident Sardinian *haut bourgeois*, whose integrity was doubted only by those who had none, was hopelessly out of touch with the vulgar and coarse society surrounding him, or whether he was simply too much in advance of his age.

Luciano Lama, the communist trade union leader of the CGIL, supported the austerity line in a speech at the EUR in February 1978. The workers would moderate their wage demands, accept mobility, and increase productivity in exchange for more jobs and more investment for the south.[45] This line was never popular with his members. The non-communist unions, the CISL and the UIL, and even the socialists inside the CGIL adopted a more pronounced anti-government attitude than communist trade unionists. Within the PCI itself there was much dissent.[46] Many on the Left denounced Berlinguer for accepting, in practice, the DC's definition of austerity. Others, including the renowned philosopher Norberto Bobbio, succumbed to an easy populism, pointing out that austerity is what the bosses wanted.[47] Soon the PCI became the main target of the amorphous youth movement, the so-called *autonomi*. These groups, a fertile recruiting ground for left-wing terrorists, constituted an indistinct coagulation of colourful anarchists, temporary libertarians and unemployed petty-bourgeois, whose magazines and broadcasts from 'pirate' radios have been aptly described as 'a mishmash of American Underground drugs and "peace and love" thinking, Reichian notions of sexual liberation, manifestos and communiqués from the Weathermen and Red Brigades, and Communist visions of cultural revolution'.[48] Had the disenchantment with the PCI been limited to these groups, Berlinguer's project would probably have survived. But disappointment spread to ordinary voters and many communist supporters. The special characteristics of 'communist' austerity, which were supposed to distinguish it from that of the ruling classes, never emerged. Ordinary citizens could note only that the government's imposition of new taxes on tobacco, petrol, telephones, stamps and rail fares, and its partial reform of the *scala mobile*, had all received the support of the PCI.

In the collective memory of the country, as represented in the outpourings of columnists and publicists, the period of the governments of so-called 'national solidarity' became a time best forgotten, or to be remembered as a brief era when 'normal' politics – the PCI in opposition and everyone else in power – was suspended. The communists too contributed to this amnesia. They supinely accepted the verdict of the victors. It had been a Big Mistake. Some of the protagonists tried to remind their audience of the achievements of the period: the strengthening of the powers of the regions; fairer controls on rented housing; a public housing plan; the legalization of abortion; resistance to terrorism; the abolition of forced detention for those affected by mental illness; the reform of public health; and so on. In vain. Because they were seen by the DC as a concession with which to buy time, and because they were half-heartedly implemented by an administrative machine not controlled by those intending to make them effective, most of these reforms were resounding failures. As Berlinguer himself later admitted, the law on youth employment failed. The tax reform did not go far enough, because all parties were afraid of antagonizing those middle and lower-middle class groups among whom tax evasion and avoidance were widespread.[49] The *Unità Sanitaria Locali* (local health units), far from bringing community health under democratic control, became another arena for patronage: jobs for the boys and the very occasional girl. The reform of local government failed to give the regions the necessary degree of financial autonomy. The mentally ill were 'liberated' from the mental hospitals on to the streets or, if they were lucky, into the care of their ill-prepared families, without the support of an adequate system of community care. Fair rent legislation, the so-called *equo canone*, enhanced the development of a black market in rented property. The counterpart of austerity was a new industrial policy. Its main plank was Law 675 of 1977 which created CIPI, the committee for the co-ordination of industrial policy, with the task of establishing priorities among sectors and areas and a planning framework for state intervention. On balance, Law 675 was a failure: its plans were too numerous, too generic, too late; it was operationally inefficient and too slow; and it ended up simply throwing money at problems in the worst traditions of Italian state intervention. It was hampered by excessive subservience to Parliament (in other words, to the political parties). It lacked qualified personnel.[50]

The PCI belatedly discovered that to be a 'party of government' it was necessary (if not sufficient) to be in government. The communists had responsibility without power, and were blamed accordingly. They subsequently complained that the DC had been 'disloyal', while they had behaved with impeccable commitment to the spirit of 'national solidarity'. This terminology makes little sense. The PCI's avowed goal was the introduction of elements of socialism into the Italian system. The DC was unavoidably committed to restoring its position, which had been damaged by the recession. Political struggle – not loyalty – was the name of the game.[51]

Leaving aside tactical blunders, the PCI had also committed two major strategic errors. First, between 1976 and 1979, it behaved as if the Italian state was a normally efficient state, as if all that was required were 'good' laws. Had Italy had an honest and efficient civil service, able to enforce the will of Parliament, 'good' laws might have improved the situation facing the country.[52] But Italy's public administration was mainly a machine to mop up unemployment, protect established privileges, and deliver votes to the DC. Most of its employees had little civic sense and little pride in their jobs. Furthermore, a segment of this state machine – the police, the secret services, the armed forces, the diplomatic corps – considered the communists as the enemy to be subdued. None of this was a secret. The communists themselves had never ceased to criticize this deplorable situation. But what could be done? To reform the state, it was necessary to clash with the DC which controlled it, and from which it thereby derived strength and votes. Yet, in order to share power, it was necessary to be acceptable to the DC. The question of the state was thus quietly 'forgotten' – an astonishing feat for the PCI, whose antecedent Leninist ideology had theorized the view that socialists could not simply get hold of the bourgeois state and use it for their own purpose. There are times, and this was one of them, when some of the 'dogmas' of the past contain more truth than the sophisms of the present.

The other major strategic mistake of the PCI was that it had not been able to break completely with the communist and (ancient) socialist tradition, which assumed that capitalism would encounter catastrophic crises. As early as 1974, Berlinguer had insisted that 'We are not facing just one of the frequent "cyclical crises" of capitalism. The present crisis involves all sectors: the economy, politics, culture, the internal life of each country and the ensemble of international relations.'[53] As I pointed out at the beginning of chapter 16, this idea – part of the lore of the socialist tradition – fails to recognize that crises are mechanisms which enable capitalism to restructure itself. As became apparent in the 1990s, the crisis of the 1970s was a clear example of this. Inflation and the battle against it provided an opportunity to abandon the constraint of full employment, and hence break down the trade unions and the system of national social and economic regulation which had characterized the development of capitalism. The strategy of the PCI, not unlike that of the SPD, the French Parti Socialiste, the Swedish SAP and the British Labour Party, was profoundly and unavoidably a *national* strategy: 'reformism in a single country.'[54] Like their counterparts elsewhere, the Italian communists saw the crisis as the symptom of a decaying national capitalism unable to face the challenges of the future. For the long term the PCI was committed to growth and to an expansion of the productive basis of society. In the short term, it opted for a policy of 'austerity' understood as deflation – a policy which contradicted its long-term aim. Keynesianism was dismissed as incompatible with worldwide stagflation – as Giorgio Napolitano later explained, thus echoing Callaghan's celebrated 'you can't spend your way out of recession'.[55]

The PCI experienced the 'crisis of capitalism' as an impending catastrophe to be prevented. Italian capitalism needed to be rescued, if only to be reconstructed in a manner which would favour the working classes – that is, by strengthening the non-market allocation of resources. To hold this position required the politics of the 'historic compromise' or the 'social contract' or, as some would say, neo-corporatist intermediation. To 'capitalism' in danger (to use a terminology which erroneously takes capitalism to be a thinking, undivided subject), the Left in each West European state proposed a pact, a political exchange, in which the workers would make 'sacrifices' and obtain in return a say in its reconstruction. What happened, instead, was that the 1970s was the decade in which key sectors of capitalism – those able to reorganize production by the intensive use of new technologies and information systems backed by adequate finance – advanced at the expense of the traditional sectors, i.e. those dominated by the traditional working class, and classical 'fordist' production and trade unionism.

In the course of the 1980s, the Italian economy temporarily recovered, as did the other economies of Western Europe. The unions, much weakened, were unable to defend the *scala mobile*. The ideology of the market triumphed while, in practice, the state was used to buttress the reorganization of Italian capitalism, though the capitalists themselves had to bribe the politicians to do so. With uncanny ability, Giulio Andreotti recycled himself yet again as one of the guarantors of a new centre-left coalition aimed at keeping the communists out of power. Craxi declared that the communists had still some way to go: they had to furnish further proof of their revisionism and their independence from the USSR.[56] As for the DC, the PSI was ready to co-operate with it provided it renounced all hegemonic pretensions.[57] Bettino Craxi, eventually the longest continuously serving prime minister in Italy since Mussolini, took corruption to heights unattained by previous Italian politicians, an awesome achievement. The Italian intelligentsia, the journalists, university professors, TV gurus – with the usual rare exceptions – participated with relish and at the expense of the taxpayers in an orgy of mutual self-congratulation. Italian GNP, inflated by the largest black economy in Europe, had overtaken the declining remnants of the British economy. Defeated and marginalized, the PCI witnessed the spectacle, resenting its own impotence and not realizing that what was being celebrated were the last years of Italy's 'First' republic.

CHAPTER TWENTY-ONE

The End of Authoritarian Regimes in Western Europe: Portugal, Spain and Greece

Economic Preconditions

COMPARATIVE history is sometimes a disheartening craft. Its apparent object is to identify and explain divergences and correspondences. The almost simultaneous fall of the authoritarian regimes of Greece, Spain and Portugal between 1974 and 1976 would appear to provide strikingly fertile ground for an exercise of this kind. Unfortunately, while the parallelism is impressive, there is no apparent explanation of why these three regimes collapsed at the same time.

Two general international developments, however, explain why the situation in each of the three countries was particularly favourable to a change of regime. The first was the end of the golden age of capitalism, triggered off by the marked increase in oil prices – a commodity on which Greece, Portugal and Spain were signally dependent. The three countries were particularly exposed to the oil shock, because they already had a large public sector deficit, with rising nominal wages and domestic demand; much of their 'reserve army' of labour, which could have contained wage rises, had emigrated.

The other paramount international development was the temporary waning of American power. This was manifested in the most conspicuous manner by the evacuation of US troops from the whole of Indo-China in 1973, which was followed by the military and political collapse of US allies in the area, and the seizure of power by the Khmer Rouge in Cambodia, the North Vietnamese in South Vietnam and the Pathet Lao in Laos. Meanwhile, the USA sacrificed its oldest ally in South East Asia, the nationalist regime in Taiwan, on the altar of a new China policy, whose principal initiators had been not the Americans, but Mao Zedong and Zhou Enlai. Finally, in August 1974, the Watergate scandal forced the resignation of Richard Nixon. Although Henry Kissinger, confirmed as secretary of state, ensured a degree of continuity, the new – and unelected – president of the USA was now Gerald Ford, a modest and hapless politician with no grasp of international affairs.

In the three countries in question, those entrenched in positions of power – Marcello Caetano, the heir to the regime founded by António O. Salazar, in Lisbon, Franco in Madrid, and the Greek Colonels in Athens – must have observed these developments with increasing concern. The world they had known, and which had protected them for so long, was rapidly changing. They were under increasing pressure to adapt, modernize, reform and liberalize in order to avoid a major crisis. To advance reforms from a position of strength, undercutting the opposition's demands before they were even made, would have been the correct tactic. To 'change everything so that everything stays the same' – as young Tancredi tells the Prince of Salina in Tomasi di Lampedusa's novel *Il Gattopardo* – is usually the prerogative of those in charge; but they cannot always choose when to do so. By the mid-1970s the time for reforms which would leave everything unchanged had come and gone, and the rulers knew it.

The three authoritarian regimes had been profoundly debilitated by the social and economic changes of the preceding decade. How else can one explain the minimal resistance offered by them? Once the dictatorships fell, all the ensuing fierce political struggles focused on the form and direction of the transition *away* from the previous order. No one of any significance tried to turn back the clock. The nearest the old guard ever came to restoring the old order was in Spain on 23 February 1981. On that day Lieutenant-Colonel Antonio Tejero occupied by force the Spanish Cortes (Parliament), while Lieutenant-General Milans del Bosch brought his troops on to the streets of Valencia. The hopes of the conspirators lasted less than eighteen hours. King Juan Carlos de Borbón's broadcast defending democracy was sufficient to demonstrate how out of touch with political realities the old guard had become.[1]

In none of the three countries were the parties of the Left, socialist or communist, instrumental in directly bringing about the end of the regime. In Spain the catalyst was the death of the dictator Francisco Franco, and the decision of his designated successor, King Juan Carlos, to become the guarantor and promoter of a peaceful transition to some form of democratic rule. In Portugal the end of the regime was achieved thanks to a coup led by left-wing officers radicalized, at least initially, by professional grievances and by a lengthy and unwinnable war in the country's African colonies.[2] In Greece a failed foreign adventure, the Cyprus affair of the summer of 1974, precipitated the fall of the Colonels.

In all three instances a mediating political figure belonging to the old order appeared to guarantee a relatively painless changeover: General António Spínola in Portugal; King Juan Carlos and his prime minister, Adolfo Suárez in Spain; and Kostantinos Karamanlis in Greece. This parallelism should not be pursued too far. Spínola, a Kerensky-like figure, was removed a few months after the coup, in September 1974, when the younger officers decided to do away with unreliable figureheads. In Greece and Spain the politicians of the transition lasted long enough to pave the way for a consolidated democracy. Karamanlis, the foremost representative of the old political class, but a firm opponent of the Greek junta from his Paris exile, remained in charge as prime minister from 1974 to 1980. Suárez, who had been a prominent Francoist, remained in office until 1981.

Socialists – unlike the communists – had played only a minor role in the clandestine struggle against dictatorship in Portugal and in Spain (after the civil war). They had been virtually non-existent in Greece before the military takeover. Yet the Greek PASOK (Panellinio Sosialistiko Kinima or Pan-Hellenic Socialist Movement), the Spanish PSOE (Partido Socialista Obrero Español), and the Portuguese PS (Partido Socialista) all eventually emerged as the dominant national political force. The three politicians associated with this unquestionable success – Mário Soares in Portugal, Andreas Papandreou in Greece and Felipe González in Spain – were either the founders of their parties (Papandreou and Soares), or had taken it over shortly before the end of the regime (González). They were all 'new' men.

As can be seen in Table 21.1, the progression of the three socialist parties was astonishingly rapid. The socialists were the great victors of the transition, the representatives of a new brand of Mediterranean socialism which emerged just as the well-established British and German parties were about to enter a long period of electoral decline.

When in opposition, the PSOE, the PS and PASOK embraced a some-what Marxist anti-capitalist rhetoric, distancing themselves from conventional social-democratic parties.

While PASOK became a mass party very quickly, recruiting members who had never been involved in politics before, the PSOE and the PS shared with their French and Italian counterparts a low level of membership. This permitted them a much greater doctrinal flexibility than their communist rivals. A small organization, rapidly growing, can react in a less inhibited manner to a fast moving situation. Redundant ideological baggage can be unloaded in a relatively painless way.

Neither the Portuguese nor the Spanish socialists used nationalism as a rallying cry. On the contrary, their modernity was based on a commitment to 'Europe' and, in particular, to European integration. In Portugal, national-ism could not be appropriated by the Left because it was indissolubly connected to its colonial past. In Spain, nationalism was seen as a centralizing ideology which conflicted directly with the regional nationalisms so strong in Catalonia and Euzkadi (the Basque country). Only in Greece could national-ism be identified with the Left. PASOK's discourse suggested that for Greece to become a truly modern country, it had to rid itself of its subordination to the West and, above all, to the USA. PASOK insisted that it stood in open opposition not only to the military junta, but also to the corrupt party system which existed before. In fact, it was not a party at all, but a 'movement' – hence its name and slogan: *PASOK: Kinima Laou* (PASOK is a People's Movement).

From the moment it was created (1974), PASOK distanced itself from the

Table 21.1 Percentage share of the vote of the main political parties in the period of transition to democracy in Spain, Portugal and Greece

Spain	1977	1979	1982
PSOE	29.3	30.5	48.4
PCE	9.4	10.8	4.1
UCD	34.4	35.0	6.7
AP	8.3	6.0	26.5
Portugal	1975	1976	1979
PS	40.7	36.7	28.9
PCP	17.9	15.3	19.5
PPD/PSD	28.3	25.2	46.3
CDS	8.2	16.7	
Greece	1974	1977	1981
PASOK	13.6	25.3	48.1
KKE	9.5	9.4	10.9
ND	54.3	41.8	35.9
UC	20.4	12.0	0.4

Notes: Socialists: PSOE, PS and PASOK. *Communists:* PCE, PCP and KKE (the latter – in coalition with other smaller parties – fought the 1974 election under the name of Enomeni Aristera (United Left). *Conservatives and centrist parties:* Spain: UCD (Unión Centro Democrático), AP (Alianza Popular), Portugal: PSD (Partido Social Democrata, formerly PPD or Partido Popular Democrata) which in 1979 presented a joint list with the more conservative Centro Democrático Social (CDS). Greece: ND (Nea Dimokratia, New Democracy – conservative), UC (Enosis Kentrou, Union of the Centre).

other social-democratic parties of Europe. This was partly due to the fact that, when the military took over in 1967, socialists were in power in a number of European countries (for instance, West Germany, Britain, Sweden and Italy), and yet no major sanctions were imposed on Greece, though a number of EEC agreements were suspended.[3] West European socialists supported the 'struggle of the Greek people' against the dictatorship with characteristic verbiage and trifling deeds. The British Labour Party passed the appropriate resolution at its Annual Conference in 1967, and proceeded to offer £100 to the Panellinio Apeleftherotiko Kinima (PAK – the Panhellenic Liberation Movement, led by Andreas Papandreou, which would become PASOK in 1974) – an insulting sum even in 1967.

By contrast, both Spanish and Portuguese socialists were virtually sponsored by their respected and powerful Western counterparts. The driving force was Willy Brandt, President of the Socialist International, supported by the Swedish, Austrian and German socialists and social democrats. The resources of the International were devoted first to sustaining and developing the socialist parties of Spain and Portugal while they were illegal, and later to boosting their standing and prestige when they were competing for votes with the other national parties.[4] The intention was to ensure that the communists, who had been the main force in clandestinity, would not emerge as the principal party of the Left after the end of authoritarianism. The Portuguese PS, which lacked organization and grassroots support, was virtually created in Germany under the sponsorship and – as Soares himself admitted – with the money of the SPD.[5] Thanks to this international help, by the summer of 1975 the PS quickly became a cohesive and effective organization.[6] In the spring of 1976, Soares held an electoral rally in Oporto, described by his biographer as a 'Hollywood spectacular', attended by most of the big names of European socialism including Brandt, Palme and Kreisky.[7] This international support had been decisive for Soares' career. In 1974, shortly after the successful coup, Soares was chosen by General Spínola to be foreign minister precisely because of his international contacts.[8] Finally, Soares obtained the all-important support of the USA when the US ambassador in Lisbon, Frank Carlucci, convinced the initially reluctant Kissinger that the USA had no alternative but to support the socialists.

Endorsement by the Socialist International was also vital to the fortunes of the Spanish socialists who, between 1946 and 1974, never had more than 2,000 activists.[9] Until the late 1960s, the party was inefficiently run by leaders in exile who had lost touch with the country. As a consequence, rival organizations sprung up everywhere.[10] By 1972, two tendencies competed for control within the PSOE: the old guard, or the *históricos*, under Rodolfo Llopis, and the younger *renovadores* led by activists within the country. The main difference between them, apart from generational and personality clashes, was the willingness of the *renovadores* to recognize the communists' prominence in the struggle against Franco and the refusal to define the PSOE in purely anti-communist terms.[11]

The *renovadores* were the realists in the sense that, by 1970, they recognized that Spain had changed and modernized, and that the regime was not about to collapse. Strictly speaking, they were, of course, only half-right. The regime *was* about to collapse, but this was precisely because Spain had changed. The *renovadores* won the day because they were more in tune with the new Spain which was emerging from under the stifling mantle of the dictatorship. They did not simply wait for it to collapse. Thanks to his organizational skills, and his frenetic travels throughout Franco's Spain, Felipe González, supported by the Andalusian and Basque federations, emerged in 1974 as the paramount leader, just as the fall of the regime was in sight.

The victory of the *renovadores* was sealed by the Socialist International's decision to recognize them, and not the followers of Llopis, as the true leaders of the PSOE. The last congress in exile of the PSOE was held at Suresnes, on the outskirts of Paris, in 1974.

Communists could never hope to obtain international support on this scale. They were situated in the 'wrong' sphere of influence, where Soviet support was more of a liability than an asset (except, presumably, for finances).

Santiago Carrillo, the leader of the Partido Comunista de España (PCE), sought to buttress his international position through the development of 'Eurocommunism' and a close relationship with the Italian PCI. This was no match for González's reliance on socialist parties in power. The attendance of Willy Brandt, Olof Palme, Michael Foot, Pietro Nenni and François Mitterrand at the Twenty-seventh Congress of the PSOE in December 1976 – when the party was still officially banned – enhanced the prestige of the socialists.[12] Conversely, in Portugal, Alvaro Cunhal, leader of the Partido Comunista Português (PCP), soon lost the support of the PCI, which was embarrassed by the PCP's disregard for pluralist democracy. Though Cunhal – a manifestly unreconstructed Stalinist – followed Berlinguer in accepting Portugal's membership of NATO, and stopped using the expression 'the dictatorship of the proletariat' at the PCP's first legal congress (20 October 1974), he was soon left with no powerful friends in the West.[13] Cunhal's conscious decision to support the Soviet Union in all matters helped Soares to emerge as the West's best bet.[14] Soares' criticism of Cunhal, based on considerable international experience, was well-founded: Cunhal, explained Soares in 1976, believed that it was possible to make a 'socialist revolution in the far corner of the old continent with no regard for the international situation, neglecting the constraints of European politics and forgetting the immediate vicinity of Spain'.[15]

International prestige in the countries of Southern Europe is an important political currency. The craving to be assimilated into the efficient, civilized, prosperous and, above all, modern world of Northern Europe, the fear of backwardness and underdevelopment, the memories of dependency – all this created, particularly among the urban classes, an attitude of deferential respect towards anyone supported by rich and modern foreigners.

The overt support of the Socialist International helped the Portuguese and Spanish socialists to receive the endorsement of entrepreneurs who could no longer countenance being excluded from the European Community and its markets. Repression and dictatorship had helped Iberian capitalism by protecting it from unruly trade unions and foreign competition. But the situation was rapidly changing. Capitalists, who, unlike socialists, are quick to get rid of unprofitable ideas, were busy becoming tomorrow's democrats.

Crises of transition from one regime to another share a fundamental trait: no single political force is able to dominate events and plan the whole process. The name of the game is short-term responsiveness, not long-term planning. Each initiative changes the overall relation of forces. Each of the contending parties must continuously reassess its position. The outcome is uncertain. In transitional crises of the kind we are examining, the old opponents are quickly defeated. The subsequent struggle takes place among yesterday's allies.

Just as, in wartime Europe, communists had dominated the Resistance against fascism and Nazism (see chapter 4), so they had been also the only serious opposition under the dictatorship. In Spain, the PCE, an insignificant force before 1936, banned between the end of the Spanish Civil War (1939) and April 1977, had become by the time of Franco's death the largest party in Spain in terms of membership.[16] The PCE's illegal trade union organization, Comisiones Obreras (CC.OO.), had been the main source of strength for the defence of workers' rights under Franco.

In Portugal, the PCP, virtually the sole significant opposition, had never been able to achieve any notable political mobilization until the coup of 1974.[17] Nevertheless, through long and patient clandestine work, it had managed to secure a foothold in the state-controlled trade unions.[18]

In Greece the Kommounistiko Komma Ellados (KKE) was banned between 1947 and 1974. Nevertheless, it was able to fight elections under the banner of the United Democratic Left (Eniaia Dimokratiki Aristera – EDA). Thus Greece, until the advent of the military junta in 1967, had some of the genuine ingredients – as well as the façade – of a liberal democracy.

As had happened elsewhere, the ideology of the communists, their organization, commitment and selfless dedication stood them in good stead when fighting an oppressive regime. When this started to crumble, and democracy was restored, the communist parties – whether 'Eurocommunist' like the PCE, or traditionalist like the PCP and the KKE – were unable to remain the leading party of the Left as the PCI and the PCF had done after 1945.

Until the early 1960s, the PCE assumed that well-organized general strikes could bring down the regime. The failure of the strike waves of the late 1950s proved this to be illusory. During the 1960s, under the leadership of Carrillo, the PCE adopted more flexible policies, shedding some of its traditional anti-clericalism and its rigid adherence to Soviet-style Marxism–Leninism. In so doing, it differed from the 'unreconstructed' communist parties of Greece and Portugal, though even they were not averse to some drastic modernization when required. The PCE's revisionism commenced in 1956 when it called for 'National Reconciliation' in its *Declaración del PCE por la Reconciliación Nacional*. The date is significant, for in 1956 Stalin was openly denounced in Moscow and the strategy of 'national roads to socialism' was given the green light by the CPSU. It was also the twentieth anniversary of the beginning of the Spanish Civil War. The PCE's call was meant to reassure the Spanish people that it had no intention of reopening the wounds of the civil war.[19] The PCE feared that its association with the civil war and with Soviet communism would prevent it from being accepted as a normal party in post-Franco Spain.

This was not a problem the PSOE suffered from. As long as it kept its distance from any form of Soviet communism, and appeared to be a Western democratic party, the Socialist Party could assume that it would have a major role to play in an eventual democratic Spain. Consequently, the socialists had much greater freedom of manoeuvre than the communists, whose search for legitimacy shaped their every action.

Perhaps mesmerized by the Italian model provided by the PCI, the PCE overestimated the importance of the Roman Catholic church in Spain. No progress, the communists assumed, could be made against the wishes of Catholics. Although the church had provided the crucial ideological cover for Franco, thanks to the *aggiornamento* of the Vatican Council and the growing grassroots unrest among priests working in the community, it was no longer the monolithic reactionary force it had once been. By 1970, even formerly conservative bishops were condemning police brutality and supporting strikers.[20] The PCE reasoned that, as in post-fascist Italy, post-Franco Spain would witness the emergence of a large and powerful Christian Democratic Party, which would become the main source of political legitimacy. Accordingly, the PCE would have to cultivate all potential and actual Christian democrats, just as Togliatti had co-operated with the DC between 1944 and 1947 (see chapter 5), and Berlinguer had called for a historic compromise with the DC in 1973 (chapter 20). Thus, the PCE's 'Spanish road to socialism' was all too often an Italian version in Spanish clothes.

Throughout the 1960s and 1970s, the PCE performed a complex balancing act. It sought to reassure its erstwhile 'enemies' – the church, the middle classes, the entrepreneurs and the liberals – by insisting that Spanish communists would behave just like any other party in a democratic Spain. Along with the Italian and the French, the Spanish communists condemned the Soviet invasion of Czechoslovakia and were active participants in the development of Eurocommunism. Santagio Carrillo's own *'Eurocomunismo' y Estado* (1977) was sternly and, one should add, helpfully attacked by the Soviet journal *New Times* in June 1977.[21]

This distancing from the Soviet model of communism was well received by the new, better educated recruits to the party, but not by the older militants who had valiantly fought during the civil war and had remained active during the harshest years of the regime. They had come to disbelieve everything the 'bourgeois' world and the Franco regime said and wrote on the USSR. They remained committed to the idea that a swift transition to socialism could begin as soon as the regime had disappeared.[22] Thus, the PCE – which had fought against the dictatorship with greater consistency than anyone else – was constantly forced to defend its democratic intentions, while resisting accusations of duplicity. Its critical accomplishment was to contribute to the establishment of democracy in Spain by organizing demonstrations and strikes, by being the main focus of opposition to Franco, and by accepting rather than sabotaging the process of democratic transition.

In all three countries socialists thus dominated the post-transition period, while the communists had been the main opposition force in the pre-transition period.

In Greece and Spain the transition was directed by moderate forces. Whether they went further than they had thought feasible or desirable is arguable. Nevertheless, they established the building blocks for a transition which was surprisingly painless and peaceful. In Portugal, by contrast, the process was longer and more open-ended: between 1974 and 1976, it was not clear whether the country would become a Western liberal democracy, or whether it would turn out to be, as the communists hoped, a 'progressive' people's democracy. However, by the late 1970s, all three countries had converged with the rest of Western Europe. None of them exhibited an important anti-systemic, far Right party harking back to authoritarianism. All of them produced a fairly 'normal' left–right bipolarization between a Left dominated by socialist or social-democratic parties, and a Right made up of moderate conservative parties favouring a market economy and traditional values. In all three there was a communist party able and willing to play a role in parliamentary politics, like those in Finland, France and Sweden. Contrary to expectations, in none of the three countries did there emerge strong parties closely allied to the church. Neither the Roman Catholic church in Spain and Portugal nor the Orthodox church in Greece intervened strongly in the politics of the post-transition period.[23] Italy thus remained a special case on two counts: it had both a Left where the Communist Party was the main force and a hegemonic Catholic party.

In Spain and Portugal capitalist development itself was the harbinger of change. Until the late 1950s, the economic development of Spain and Portugal was based on autarchic policies. The idea that capitalism should be allowed to develop according to liberal principles of non-state intervention, free trade and deregulation never held sway in Franco's Spain or in Salazar's Portugal.

Portugal's large state sector was in part the result of the dominant political philosophy of the regime: an authoritarian corporatist New State (*Estado Novo*), based on the Roman Catholic concept of social harmony among all groups in society, and traditional religious and family values (*Deus, pátria e família*).[24] In this corporate state employers accepted significant state control in return for various privileges, including protectionism and other restrictions on competition.[25] The hallmark of the *Estado Novo* was not, however, its corporate structure, but what Opello has called an 'overinstitutionalized' administrative apparatus, dominated by technocrats in effective charge of policy.[26]

The policy of autarchy followed by the Salazar regime prevented the country from benefiting from the European economic expansion of the 1950s. In 1960 Portugal was still the poorest country in Europe. It decided to change course radically. Portugal joined EFTA, GATT, the World Bank and the International Monetary Fund.[27] The country became more dependent on Europe, as exports and imports grew more rapidly than GNP.[28] After 1960, the importance of Europe as a market for Portugal increased steadily, while that of the African colonies declined correspondingly.[29] The reorientation of Portuguese trade towards Europe coincided with the growth of anti-colonial armed struggle in its African colonies, beginning in 1961 in Angola, in 1963 in Guinea Bissau, and in 1964 in Mozambique. There was thus a major conflict of interest between maintaining an empire by force and Portugal's integration into the international economy. The abandonment of the empire was becoming an economic necessity.

As these processes developed, industry replaced agriculture as the main contributor to economic growth.[30] Portugal became an importer of food, especially of meat.[31] There was a massive exodus from the countryside and a shortage of labour, aggravated by constant emigration. Portugal and Spain were becoming increasingly dependent on foreign trade and on remittances from workers who had emigrated. Emigration was a substantial contributor to the regular balance of payments surpluses achieved by both countries, while GNP increase averaged over 6 per cent throughout most of the 1960s.[32] Emigration was such a significant factor in the Portuguese economy that the working population of the country actually shrank between 1960 and 1963. By 1973, 14 per cent of the workforce was abroad.[33] By the time of the military coup, Paris had become the second Portuguese city in population – not surprisingly, as the minimum wage in France was more than could be obtained by almost any worker in Portugal.[34] Emigration meant that domestic unemployment had been virtually eliminated.[35]

A modernizing tendency emerged at the heart of the Portuguese establishment. Its organizing network was the Opus Dei, a lay order of Catholic intellectuals founded in 1928 by José Maria de Balaguer. By 1950, this kind of 'holy mafia' was exceptionally strong among the academic élites in both Portugal and Spain. Politically, its main aim was the incorporation of the Iberian economies into the framework of the West European capitalist system. In Portugal the Opus Dei technocrats, who had become junior ministers in the Caetano government of the late 1960s, had come to view the colonial wars as a major obstacle to modernization.

Economic developments in Spain resembled those in Portugal. Until the late 1950s, the Spanish economy, like the Portuguese, had been driven by state interventionism, protectionism in the form of quantitative restriction on imports, severe exchange controls and an overvalued currency.[36] It suffered social unrest and discontent, inflation, a balance of payments deficit, flight of capital and low productivity.[37] In 1957 Alberto Ullastres Calvo and Mariano Navarro Rubio, both leading members of Opus Dei, entered the government in positions of far greater importance than their Portuguese counterparts. They rationalized economic management by creating the Office of Economic Co-ordination and Planning, with the intention of integrating Spain into 'the booming world of advanced Western capitalism'.[38] By 1958 Spain had joined the World Bank, the IMF and OEEC (later OECD). Yet in January 1959 the economy was approaching catastrophe. This considerably strengthened the hands of the Opus Dei reformers. In July 1959, under pressure from the IMF and the OECD, whose May 1959 report criticized the gross overvaluation of the peseta, Spain broke decisively with its protectionist past. The currency was devalued by a sweeping 42.9 per cent, establishing a fixed gold parity. A few months later, the Stabilization Plan was launched, international trade was liberalized, tourism promoted, foreign credits obtained.[39] Spain failed in its attempt, post-1962, to gain full membership of the EEC, because of the undemocratic nature of its regime. However, a preferential trade agreement was signed between Spain and the European Community in 1970.

The Stabilization Plan was essentially a symbolic gesture. Spain's indicative planning system, which the Opus Dei technocrats had set up, had the central aim of protecting a selected élite of business groups from the impact of change.[40] Planning requires flexibility and Spain's planners were severely constrained; they lacked reliable statistics and proper funding.[41] What made Spain grow was foreign trade not Francoist *dirigisme*. Spain's GNP grew in the 1960s at an average annual rate of 7 per cent – higher than Portugal, though lower than Greece. Productivity in industry increased at a yearly rate of 6.8 per cent in the period 1960–72.[42] This was one of the highest rates in Europe though, of course, Spanish productivity remained very low in absolute terms.

The share of the labour force in agriculture and fisheries shrank from 42 per cent in 1960 to 23 per cent in 1974. There was a considerable increase in the manufacturing sector which, by 1973, accounted for 67 per cent of exports.[43] Between 1960 and 1974 exports nearly doubled.[44] Growth followed a pattern similar to the earlier Italian 'miracle' of 1958–63: a consumer boom based on spending on cars and consumer durables; real estate speculation; a massive expansion of the building industry; and the irrevocable destruction of the beauty of the Costa del Sol. As in Italy, this growth was grossly unbalanced and increased regional disparities; for instance, in 1970, 70 per cent of Madrid homes had a television against only 11 per cent in the province of Soria.[45]

Portugal and Spain became heavily reliant on trade. Portugal was particularly dependent on trade with Britain, a fellow member of EFTA. When Britain joined the EEC in 1973, Portugal had no choice but to seek to do the same. An agreement was reached in 1973 between the EEC and Portugal. However, no further steps could be taken because the Community, following the Birkelbach Report of 1962, had adopted political conditions for admission which prevented the acceptance of undemocratic regimes. It was simply unthinkable that a future democratically elected European Parliament (as it was after 1979) should have members selected through a rigged or distorted electoral mechanism. Thus, there was a serious and growing contradiction between the economic interests of the business community and the ruling political establishment.

During the last ten to fifteen years of dictatorships, the Portuguese and Spanish economies restructured themselves along similar lines – though Spain was always much richer. Per capita income increased steadily, helped by a spectacular increase in productivity. The growth of capitalism created the conditions which made the authoritarian regimes obsolete and social democracy possible. As Baklanoff so aptly put it:

the dynamic expansion of the world economy from around 1960 to 1973 was a necessary condition for the realization of accelerated growth in the Iberian peninsula. For it was the international economy, and most especially the industrialized countries of Western Europe, that presented Spain and Portugal with surging markets for their products, sent them free-spending tourists by the millions, invested in their factories and real estate, and employed a goodly share of their 'surplus' manpower.[46]

Emigration and economic growth brought about an 'induced' full employment resulting in upward pressure on real wages. Even though workers could not strike freely and were deprived of independent trade unions, the movement of their wages reflected conditions in other advanced economies. Interdependence is blind to political ideologies: it constrains everyone – fascists and social democrats, liberals and right-wing dictators.

In both Portugal and Spain the early 1970s were characterized by rising expectations. Although only state-sanctioned trade unions were allowed to function, wages increased steadily. Spain, in particular, had a consistently high level of industrial unrest, with frequent and bitter strikes in the Asturias and Catalonia. The communists' decision to work within the official unions reduced the ability of the Franco regime to control the working class. By the end of the 1960s, many industrialists had been forced to negotiate with the communist-led CC.OO.[47] By the time Franco died, the Spanish working class had accumulated more than ten years' experience of strike action and trade union negotiations.[48] The period of maximum pressure on wages (1972–74) occurred at the worst possible time (from the point of view of the dictatorships in all three countries), because it coincided with the oil shock. The negative effect of this was felt directly and indirectly: directly, because the shock increased the oil import bill – with particular severity in Portugal, which relied on imports for all its oil supplies;[49] indirectly, because the recession had hit other countries, so that the vital remittances of Portuguese and Spanish emigrants from abroad was reduced. Portugal's balance of payments, in surplus thanks to these remittances, moved into deficit after 1974.[50]

The relative absence of social conflict in Portugal (as compared to Spain) had the effect of containing the internal pressure for reform. The Portuguese diehards hampered Caetano's timid reformist initiatives.[51] In Spain, however, social unrest was one of the determinants of the transition to democracy. Attempts to buy it off through increases in wages aggravated the plight of an economy badly hit by the oil price rise. In Portugal social unrest occurred only after the military takeover, and helped to push the revolution forwards. In Greece the transition was far more restricted to the élites than in the other two countries.

Economic prosperity is a great engine for change. Democracies are much better at adapting to modernization than other systems. In Italy, for instance, one might have expected that the consumer boom of the late 1950s would have destabilized a traditional party like the DC. But the DC was forced by electoral politics to find new ways of keeping in touch with the changing aspirations of the population. It played the cards of tradition *and* modernization, both in politics *and* in economics. The Franco and Salazar regimes could accept the modernization of the economy, but not of the political system. When the 'economic miracle' had nearly run its course, the Italian DC could renew the political system by bringing in new blood, in the shape of the Italian Socialist Party. Franco and Salazar could bring in, at best, enlightened technocrats, at worst obtuse bureaucrats.

Mass consumption is a revolutionary force. It cannot be used to pacify the workers without inducing political changes. High consumption requires high wages. But what is the point of an authoritarian regime if it cannot contain wages? As the consumer society expanded in Spain and, to a lesser extent, in Portugal, it made these two countries more similar to the rest of Western Europe. Psychologically, this meant that the Spanish middle classes were readier to experiment with democracy which, as France, Britain and West Germany testified, co-existed quite happily with consumer capitalism. The young executives recruited by foreign firms picked up the habits and culture of the international business class (including sharp clothes, airport novels and bad manners), and passed them on to their counterparts in Spanish-owned firms.[52] Traditional Catholic values, the life-support system of the regime, could not co-exist, unsullied, with the alleged delights of the consumer society: easier sex, pornography, topless bathing, hedonism, the pursuit of wealth. The tourism boom was particularly pronounced in the poorest part of Spain. Local farmers' sons were transformed into waiters overnight. In John Hooper's perceptive words: 'Accustomed to measuring the time in hours, they were all of a sudden expected to think in minutes.'[53] As a result, according to a study carried out in 1971, 90 per cent of all non-chronic mental illness in rural Málaga was among young males who had gone to work on the coast.[54]

The economic successes of the two Iberian dictatorships had catapulted their societies into the modern world. But this, far from solidifying their regimes, made them appear redundant, technically obsolete, and anachronistic.[55] This had become so evident that many supporters of the two regimes began to advocate change. In Spain, Manuel Fraga Iribarne, later leader of the conservative Alianza Popular, published *El desarrollo político* (Political Development) in 1971, in which he argued that Spain required modern political institutions since it had now become an industrial society.[56] In Portugal a senior general, António Spínola, had written a book, *Portugal e o futuro* (Portugal and the Future), which appeared in 1974, a few weeks before the military takeover, in which he provided a plan for extricating Portugal from its unwinnable colonial wars.

The *Revolução* in Portugal

The transition to democracy was far more dramatic in Portugal than in the other two countries. The bloodless military takeover of April 1974 was followed by twenty-seven months of political crisis and six provisional governments, before the establishment of the first constitutional government on 22 July 1976. It became clear, soon after the coup, that the Socialist Party (PS) was, electorally speaking, the dominant force. Consequently, the sooner a Western-type liberal democracy was established, the sooner political power would shift away from the military and their supporters, the communists. In Greece and Spain it was always clear that the only credible alternative to the old regime was a parliamentary democracy.

From its inception the Portuguese Revolution – as the military takeover was called, with some justification – was strongly reminiscent of the fervour and hopes of May 1968 in Paris: the same belief that everything was possible; a similar feeling that 'normality' was suspended; the same intoxicating excitement. The way it was launched was emblematic. On the night of 24–25 April 1974, a DJ working at Radio Clube Portuguesa selected a song the regime had banned, *Grandola vila morena* – a ballad about a village in the Alentejo. This was the agreed signal for military units to converge on Lisbon to take power. It was the first revolution launched by a DJ.

That the regime was tottering was obvious to many. That it would be brought down by an internal military coup led by young officers was not. The socialist leader, Mário Soares, for instance, in a book which first appeared in France in 1972 (publication in Portugal was then impossible), referred to possible sources of opposition to the regime in the church and business circles, but not in the military.[57]

The officers now in charge appointed as provisional president General Spínola, the best-known advocate of reform under the old regime, and constituted themselves as the Movimento das Forças Armadas or MFA (the Armed Forces Movement). They declared their objective to be the establishment of a democratic regime and legalized all political parties. Less than a month after their takeover, in May 1974, the MFA proceeded to constitute a largely civilian government, including four socialists and two communists. The contradiction between a democratic party system and a special role for the military (presumably unsanctioned by election) was glossed over by all concerned, because it was felt that the army was the only force which could prevent the return of the old regime. This had become obvious on 11 March 1975, when plans for a coup led by General Spínola – who, worried by the strength of the Left, had resigned on 30 September 1974 – were thwarted by the MFA. This signalled a further radicalization of the revolution and confirmed the general belief that it was not possible to govern the country without granting considerable powers of veto to the MFA. This assumption was shared by all the parties, though only the communists accepted it wholeheartedly.

Though the paths of the PS and of the PCP soon diverged, in the early days after the coup the main preoccupation of the whole Left was a speedy establishment of democracy. That this was the objective of the socialists was never in doubt; but even the PCP was, in this initial phase, in favour of fully-fledged civilian government. This was made clear by the PCP leader himself, Alvaro Cunhal, after he landed at Lisbon airport on 30 April. His hero, Lenin, on arriving in similar circumstances (i.e. following the outbreak of a revolution he had not initiated) at Petrograd's Finland Station, had changed the party line and urged the Bolsheviks to withdraw their support from the provisional government. Cunhal did nothing of the sort. He declared that the immediate demands of the PCP were the consolidation of the revolution by re-establishing all democratic freedoms, legalizing all political parties, ending the colonial war, increasing wages, and electing a Constituent Assembly.[58] Socialism as an immediate objective was not mentioned. Notwithstanding its pro-Soviet rhetoric and its espousal of the idea of a democracy 'supervised' by a progressive military, the PCP was then as moderate in its demands as any Eurocommunist party might have been.

Co-operation between the newly-formed political parties, especially those of the Left, and the military thus seemed at first to be based on mutual interest. The military needed the civilians to demonstrate that the revolution had been democratic. The Left parties needed the military to defend the revolution. Problems arose when it became apparent that a significant faction of the MFA intended to go beyond the mere establishment of democracy, towards the institution of socialism. Having legalized strikes in August 1974, the MFA indicated how close it had come to acknowledging the PCP as the true representative of the working class by recognizing the communist-dominated trade union, Intersindical, as the sole workers' organization in Portugal.[59]

After the abortive right-wing coup of 11 March 1975, the *Revolução* turned further to the Left. The government nationalized banks and insurance companies. As a result, the state found itself in partial or complete control of over one thousand enterprises in which the banks had a controlling share.[60] Though the government wisely refrained from nationalizing foreign-owned concerns,[61] the takeovers appeared to suggest that the objective was the rapid construction of a planned economy. That there were radicals in the MFA committed to this policy, was not in dispute. This, however, does not explain why the nationalizations occurred.

As General Vasco Gonçalves, prime minister at the time, explained, many of the nationalizations, which occurred after March 1975, were occasioned by necessity. Some firms (for instance in the cement industry) had been taken over at the request of their workforce, in order to defend jobs since the owners had fled abroad; or because only a government takeover would enable them to obtain the necessary funds to keep production going.[62]

Even after these nationalizations, the Portuguese public sector accounted for only a quarter of GDP – a modest proportion at the time in Western Europe.[63] Nevertheless, the impression at home and abroad was that Portugal could be 'lost' to the West. This impression was constantly reinforced by communist activists – whom the leadership could not always fully control – who deployed a comprehensive arsenal of revolutionary rhetoric, culled from the history of the communist movement and liberation struggles. Collective farms adopted names like Red Star Collective, while people found themselves being addressed as *camarada* (comrade) by total strangers.

Between 1974 and 1975, a key difference had emerged between communists and socialists. The communists recognized that the military were the best guarantors of the success of the revolution, and feared that a return to parliamentary democracy would bring about their own marginalization. Accordingly, they refused to challenge the military publicly. Equally coherently, the PS, having surfaced as the leading Portuguese political party in the elections to the Constituent Assembly of 25 April 1975, became the leading proponent of parliamentary democracy and, consequently, the rallying point, nationally and internationally, for all those opposing the radicalization of the Portuguese Revolution.

The elections to the Constituent Assembly – the first ever free elections in the history of the country – demonstrated that the PCP had no hope of achieving power by electoral means. The results speak for themselves: the socialists, with 37.9 per cent, obtained 116 seats; the centrist Partido Popular Democrata (PPD), led by Francisco Sá Carneiro, a former liberal critic of Caetano, obtained eighty-one seats; with 26.4 per cent and the conservatives of the CDS, with 7.6 per cent, obtained sixteen seats. The PCP and its allies obtained a disappointing 17.9 per cent and thirty-five seats.

The elections also revealed that the PS was an authentically national party; it did well in all urban areas, north and south, and in southern rural areas.[64] The moderate parties, the PPD and the CDS, did well only in the north. The communist vote remained heavily concentrated in the south. In the north, they were the target of widespread violence.[65] Though on the whole the church kept a low profile, the Archbishop of Braga called for an anti-communist crusade. Two hundred PCP offices were burned in rural violence co-ordinated by right-wing underground movements.[66]

Even before the 1975 elections, Cunhal had become convinced that to call for a return of the military to their barracks after the elections to the Constituent Assembly was tantamount to calling for the liquidation of the revolution. He became the principal civilian exponent of the 'institutionalization' of the MFA.[67]

After the 1975 elections, Soares prudently opted for the continuation of a government of national unity, hoping to contain the growing influence of the PCP and of the armed forces, and to avoid splitting the country into two hostile blocs.[68] Soares was well aware that even though, electorally, his party was much stronger than the PCP, in reality, the superior organization of the communists, and their close ties to a section of the military, made them stronger should a revolutionary situation develop further.[69]

However, a growing section of the military was reluctant to pursue the cause of militancy. The time was propitious for a socialist disengagement from the government. The socialists used the excuse of the 'takeover' by leftist supporters of the hitherto pro-socialist daily *República* to withdraw from the coalition (10 July 1975). This was the signal for the final parting of the ways between socialists and communists. Cunhal denounced the 'hysterical anti-communism' of the socialists,[70] and accused Soares of being a 'reactionary'.[71] Cunhal moved towards an increasingly military solution: 'Our party', he proclaimed, 'considers that the MFA, a revolutionary progressive movement, is the best armed guarantor of the Revolution and of its continuation in alliance with the popular forces.' [72]

The backlash was almost inevitable. The move towards a further radicalization of the revolution would have required either nationwide popular backing, or the near-unanimous support of the military. Neither condition existed. Internationally, the revolution was isolated. The power vacuum caused by the temporary difficulties of the USA had been sufficient to allow the revolution to take place in the first instance, but to not let it develop into a Cuban-type fortress regime at the westernmost extremity of Western Europe.

Soares' longer-term aim was the elimination of the military from politics, but to reach this goal he needed allies within the military. Only the armed forces could send the armed forces back to their barracks. Having rejoined the government in September 1975, the socialists cultivated close relations with the so-called Group of Nine, which included important military officers led by Lieutenant-Colonel Melo Antunes. On 25 November, the Group moved swiftly to prevent an alleged attempted left-wing coup, led by Otelo de Carvalho and his internal security force, COPCON. Carvalho always denied the allegation.[73] Whether the Group of Nine intervention was a move by moderate officers to prevent a revolutionary coup, or, as Otelo claimed, a plot of the 'Right' to stop the revolution, is immaterial. The truth is probably that each group had a plan of defence against a suspected coup from the other side.[74] The 'moderates' were better prepared and better organized than the 'revolutionaries', and had the majority of the population on their side (as expressed in the elections earlier that year).

The strategy of the PCP had failed. The communists had been dragged by the radicals in the military further to the left than they had ever intended. They had been trapped. Had they shadowed Soares, they would have obtained the praise of the *bien-pensant* middle classes, but not their votes. Now defeated, they lived on as they had always done, in the antechamber of History, waiting, once again, for the hour of the revolution.

After that, in practice, 'the party was over.' The sixth provisional government under Admiral Pinheiro de Azevedo explained that the country's economy now depended on the discipline of the workers and the unions.[75] This led to the first austerity budget in January 1976.

It has generally been assumed that the revolution's utter disregard for the laws of economics were the main cause of the painful financial rectitude which was to follow the festive spirit of 1974–76.[76] A more sober analysis shows that the deterioration in economic conditions was attributable to the 'normal' effects of the oil-triggered recession in the West, rather than to the excesses of leftist officers. Had a group of inter-galactic economists been provided with all the relevant economic data, but kept ignorant of the political turmoil of 1974–76, they would have come to the conclusion that the Portuguese economy, in spite of a revolution and six provisional revolutionary governments in two years, behaved in much the same way as all the others.[77] The outstanding economic consequence of the revolution was a massive increase in the incomes of industrial and rural workers. Between 1973 and 1975, the share of wages in national income rose from 52 per cent to 69 per cent.[78] There was thus a significant shift in the proportion of the national wealth going to the working class, accompanied by a sharp increase in personal consumption and a narrowing of differentials, thanks to the introduction of the minimum wage in June 1974.[79]

The very high inflation of those years (over 30 per cent) was often blamed on this movement of wages. But prices had begun to surge before April 1974, under the impetus of high military spending and rising oil prices.[80] In addition to the problems connected with the worldwide recession, Portugal was also faced by economic difficulties caused by the fall of its empire in Africa.

Even before the successful completion of the negotiations aimed at granting independence to the three Portuguese colonies (January 1975), nearly one hundred thousand settlers had returned from Africa – the so-called *retornados*. They were followed by a further 339,000 in 1975.[81] This was a very high number – the entire population of Portugal was then 8.6 million. The *retornados* were nearly as numerous as the French settlers who returned to the mother country after Algerian independence; but the population of France was five times that of Portugal and France, of course, was a far richer country.[82] Portugal not only had to absorb these refugees, who obviously had little sympathy for the revolution, but also had to cope with the demobilization of many of the troops who had been deployed against the guerrillas: military manpower was halved between 1975 and 1978, while unemployment increased fourfold, from 2.2 per cent in 1974 to 8.4 per cent in 1978. Finally, one should not discount the loss of privileged markets in colonies. Following a trend established in the 1960s, exports to the former empire declined, while exports to Europe continued to rise.[83]

This economically negative trend coincided with the European recession, and the consequent balance of payments deficit. Portugal now faced a new problem: 'managing economic growth with a balance of payments constraint.'[84]

The austerity which was imposed at the beginning of 1976 must be seen in this perspective. To avoid austerity, it would have been necessary to insulate Portugal from the rest of the world behind a brick wall or an iron curtain of protectionism (these metaphors suggest themselves). Rationing would have followed. The pain and misery would have been more equally shared, but no democratically elected government would have survived the inevitable unpopularity. In other words, the stark choice facing Portugal was some form of capitalist austerity or some kind of Soviet-style protectionism. Wisely, in July 1976, a majority of the Portuguese electorate opted for the Socialist Party, a party which would continue the policy of 'capitalist' austerity as a painful necessity, rather than – as the conservatives would have seen it – as a joyful return to reason and realism.

At the July election, the PS had lost some ground (from 40.7 per cent to 36.7 per cent), but remained the largest party. Soares became the prime minister of a minority socialist government which, unable and unwilling to reach an agreement with the communists, who had decided to remain 'the party of the revolution', had to rely on the two conservative parties to continue with austerity policies. The predicament of the Portuguese Left was that it was divided between two parties, neither of which had a distinctive strategy for the governance of capitalism. The communists did not believe that 'managing capitalism' was their responsibility; it was something best left to the bourgeoisie. Their own task was to make the revolution. If the conditions for it had evaporated, then it was preferable to wait for better times. Underneath their old Leninist rhetoric, Portuguese communists exhibited a deep passivity reminiscent of the Kautskyist 'wait-and-see' tradition which they themselves affected to despise. In this, they were no different from the French Communist Party. The socialists were left to run Portuguese capitalism as best they could – that is, as a minority government – under the full impact of constraints stemming from the country's historically weak position and its recent upheaval. As they had no ideas of their own as to what to do, they had to accept those prevailing at the time, while trying to protect their electorate from the worst effects of austerity policies.

Austerity was dictated only in part by the requirements of the domestic economy. It was also necessary to pay back some of the heavy borrowing obtained from foreign banks and institutions. Taxes were raised. Public sector prices were increased. A tight monetary policy was established. Wage restraint was imposed. Firms were again enabled to dismiss workers.

The Soares government also compensated those who lost land or other assets during the revolution. In the autumn of 1976, the government moved troops to evict some of the peasants who had illegally seized estates in the Alentejo, even though the farms were small and the soil was poor.[85] The evictions were designed to demonstrate that the revolutionary period was over by moving against the poor farmers of the Alentejo, which had been one of the centres of communist support.

The agrarian reform had been the most important measure implemented by the previous revolutionary governments. It surpassed in social and economic amplitude, and in its redistributive impact, any other progressive measure taken by any of the transitional governments of the three countries we are examining. It had been openly and consistently advocated by the landless labourers of the south, where agriculture was based on large estates or *latifundia*. Those southern rural workers who had left the land found employment in Portuguese cities (unlike northerners who emigrated). This had led to a close connection between the industrial working class and the rural proletariat of the south. Southern industrial plants were larger than in the north; the concentration of workers facilitated the development of radical trade unionism. Thus, southerners tended to be more radical than northerners. The party which best represented this revolutionary potential was the PCP.[86] In the north things were different. The farmers owned small farms, or *minifundia*, and were opposed to agrarian reform and the distribution of land. They were conservatives, deeply religious and ferociously anti-communist.

Though all parties – not only the communists – had initially agreed that an agrarian reform was necessary, nothing of significance occurred until, in the early months of 1975, many southern farmers occupied the land, initiating their own 'agrarian reform'. In July 1975, the government reacted by establishing guidelines, but these always fell short of what the 'spontaneous' occupation of the land had achieved. The result was that 1,300 landowners were expropriated *de facto*, if not *de jure*, and, as a consequence, one million hectares passed under the control of collective units.[87] The PCP had consistently backed the peasants. Illegal seizure of the land was often condoned in the hectic tumult of constant revolutionary change. It was only in 1976, when the socialists were in control and the communists had been defeated, that the government proceeded to take back some of the occupied land. The peasants were forced to give up part of the land they had acquired by the same armed forces who had let them seize it in the first place.[88]

Nothing better illustrates the complexity of the Portuguese transition than the fact that the country was entering its post-revolutionary phase with a 'revolutionary' constitution. This became operational on the second anniversary of the military coup, 25 April 1976. Its first two articles committed Portugal to a classless society and to the 'transition to socialism by creating the conditions for the democratic exercise of power by the working classes'.[89] It provided for a single chamber, a directly elected president with considerable powers of veto over legislation, and a 'Council of the Revolution' in which the military, still held to be the guardians of the revolution, would have a significant presence. But revolutionary constitutions are worth little without revolutionary will. In 1982 the constitution was amended, the powers of the president restricted, and the Council of Revolution abolished.[90]

The re-establishment of 'normal' economic management was more painful. The reasoning behind the austerity policies described above was that they were necessary in order to return to economic growth. Thus, in the spring of 1976, the authorities tried to reflate while keeping incomes and prices under control. The reflation sucked in imports, while failing to generate export growth.[91] In February 1977 the escudo was devalued by 15 per cent, but as this was not enough it was set on a crawling-peg mechanism against a basket of currencies, and depreciated at a monthly rate of 1 per cent.[92] The minority PS government tried to borrow from a consortium of fourteen countries led by the USA. After complex negotiations, the consortium agreed, in June 1977, to lend $750 million in medium-term balance of payments support, on condition that Portugal obtained $50 million stand-by credit from the IMF.[93] The rationale was to ensure that, in return for this comparatively small sum, the IMF would impose conditions which, for political reasons, the USA and the other Western countries were reluctant to inflict.

Had anyone still been in doubt, this signalled that the revolutionary period was truly over. The Portuguese Revolution destroyed an authoritarian regime, not capitalism.

The conditions stipulated by the IMF were the standard package: devaluation, tax increases, public spending cuts. In the context of existing austerity policies, they were politically almost unacceptable and would have destabilized even Soares' socialist government. Portugal had also formally applied to join the EEC, and was required to bridge the gap with the rest of the Community. To do so, it would need higher than average growth. This meant reflating, while others were deflating – which had proved impossible for wealthy France (see chapter 19). For Portugal, so much poorer and in a difficult situation, the added burden of IMF deflationary conditions would be intolerable. The IMF appeared to have overplayed its hand. Even Schmidt and Callaghan protested.[94]

In an attempt to obtain better terms, while still negotiating with the IMF, Soares introduced a new economic package which contained some of the IMF recommendations. The package was turned down in Parliament by communists and conservatives.

The patient Soares realized that he had to bring another party into a formal coalition government to ensure a relatively stable majority. The new partner was the CDS, the conservative party farthest to the right, whose leader Freitas do Amaral had originally been close to Spínola. Negotiations with the IMF were resumed, while Soares tried to mobilize as much international support as possible. It was explained to Portugal's Western allies that excessively onerous conditions would destabilize not only the Socialist Party, but all the other anti-communist parties. Interdependence always works both ways. The borrower has some influence on the lender. By then, even the most suspicious foreigners could not fail to be convinced that Portugal was back in the Western fold; that communism had been defeated; and that whatever ambition the Socialist Party might have had to strike a special economic path had been consigned to the dustbin of revolutionary rhetoric.

Everything would be contained within the bounds of parliamentary democracy and the market economy. Soares obtained some improvements on the conditions originally imposed, as the 1978 'Letter of Intent' to the IMF indicated. However, he was now required to reduce further the government spending which had been expanded in 1975 and 1976 to meet the social goals of the Portuguese Revolution. Inflation and wage control ensured the return to a more 'balanced' – that is, smaller – share of working-class earnings: real wages fell by 9.4 per cent in 1977, by another 5.6 per cent in 1978, and by a further 3.1 per cent in 1979.[95]

In July 1978 the PS–CDS coalition collapsed, because the CDS claimed that the PS had become too cautious in dealing with the rebellious rural workers of the Alentejo. The PS remained out of power, although the coalition between the CDS and the PSD (the new name of the PPD since October 1976) did not have a majority. There were further consultations with the IMF, more loans, more austerity, and more government instability. In preparation for the election of 1979, the PS declared that the time for austerity was over and promised that it would pursue a policy of economic growth.[96] The PSD and the CDS responded by forming Aliança Democrática (Democratic Alliance – AD), under the leadership of Francisco Sá Carneiro (who died in an air disaster in December 1980). AD obtained a stunning victory with 45 per cent of the vote. The PS suffered a serious defeat (down to 27 per cent), while the PCP, under the banner of the APU (United Popular Alliance), mustered 19 per cent. Both parties of the Left were now out of power, a mere four years after the revolution had swept away the Caetano regime. Portugal disappeared once again from the front pages of the international press. Everything was back to normal. Although the socialists returned to power in 1983 to implement a savagely deflationary economic programme, they were ousted again in 1985, when they gained only 20.8 per cent. Soares was narrowly elected president of the republic in 1986 (thanks to communist support). After his victory, he renounced his membership of the PS to be able to be 'above parties', while his former party lost the election again in 1987, with 22.3 per cent. The PS remained out of office until 1995.

Once the transition was over, the PS revealed itself to be little more than an old-fashioned Iberian radical party, riven by factionalism, and not the modern social-democratic party it had claimed to be.[97] Thus, the 'rediscovery' of the market, which became a trademark of modernity among socialist parties in the late 1980s, never presented a particularly difficult problem for the PS.

Portugal enjoyed a significant economic expansion during 1985–93, but the main beneficiaries of this growth were the middle classes. The agricultural sector remained backward and uncompetitive. Twenty years after the *Revolução*, shanty towns still surround Lisbon, where thousands live in abject poverty. Average wages are lower than in developing countries such as Singapore, Thailand and Taiwan. The banks and insurance companies nationalized after the revolution have been privatized.[98] The strategies propounded by the two strands of the Portuguese Left – the social revolution of the PCP and the welfare society of the PS – led nowhere.

The *Ruptura Negociada* in Spain

The Portuguese Revolution could not have been predicted. In Spain, the end of Francoism had been widely anticipated, especially after Franco's designated successor, Luis Carrero Blanco, was blown up in his car by the Basque separatist terrorist organization ETA (Euskadi Ta Askatasuna), as he was returning home after mass on 20 December 1973. Well before this, however, the opposition had been positioning itself in the expectation that the dictator's death would signal the long-awaited *ruptura democrática*. When, finally, the life-support machine which had kept Franco technically alive for the final months of his life was switched off in November 1975, there were few tears: 'Madrid and Barcelona were quietly drunk dry of champagne.'[99]

In June 1974, the PCE (Partido Comunista de España) announced that it had formed a Junta Democrática in alliance with Tierno Galván's Partido Socialista Popular (PSP), various small liberal and leftist parties, Prince Carlos Hugo's Carlist Party, 'a Carlist princess and a handful of political adventurers'.[100] Its programme was characteristically moderate. It demanded political and trade union freedoms, autonomy for Euzkadi, Galicia and Catalonia, and the separation of shurch and state. It accepted the continuation of the treaty allowing the USA to maintain military bases in Spain, and promised to seek membership of the EEC. The heterogeneity of the Junta Democrática, and the inconsequential size of the allies of the PCE, doomed it to failure. The socialists refused to join it, alleging that it was a communist front – which it was. They proceeded to establish their own front, the rival Plataforma de Convergencia Democrática, with Christian democrats, social democrats and some inconsequential leftist groups. What all this showed was how far the Spanish Left was from uniting. In this first phase (1974–76), the main preoccupation of the PSOE was to distance itself from the communists.

The assumption that there would be a rupture, rather than a smooth transition, was made by most opposition forces even after the death of Franco, because King Juan Carlos had reappointed Franco's Prime Minister, Carlos Arias Navarro, thus suggesting that nothing was going to change.[101] This led directly to the ephemeral, but symbolically significant, unification of the Junta and the Plataforma into the so-called Coordinación Democrática (26 March 1976), soon nicknamed the Platajunta.

Massive industrial and social unrest, and not this fragile unification of the Left, led Juan Carlos and his advisers to recognize that partial liberalization was no longer sufficient to stem the tide of change. Student unrest had reached unprecedented levels – in 1973 every university in Spain went on strike.[102] The church could no longer be relied upon to sustain the regime and Pope Paul VI increasingly sided with liberal prelates. Not only had Basque and Catalonian nationalism become a major force, but, more significantly, in 1975–76 the number of strikes had doubled and the numbers of workers involved had increased sevenfold (to two and a half million workers).[103] Many of the strikes were politically motivated, often led by the communists, though in most cases the trigger was the oil-induced inflation and wage restraints imposed by the government. In Euzkadi strikes reached a characteristically high intensity.[104] With a severe profit squeeze under way, it was impossible to cajole the workers back to work through wage increases. Thus, there could be no half-way house: the alternatives were a rapid retreat towards brutal repression, or the acceleration of the reform programme with the legalization of the parties which represented the workers.[105] The failure of the government to stop the strikes convinced an increasing section of the Francoist establishment, including entrepreneurs, that the time had come for a less timid break with the past.[106]

The consequence of this was the replacement, in July 1976, of Arias Navarro with Adolfo Suárez. Between July 1976 and June 1977, the new prime minister amended the constitution, held a popular referendum on the reform programme; legalized most political parties (February 1977); abolished the Francoist trade unions; offered an amnesty to all political prisoners (March 1977); legalized the PCE (April 1977); dismantled the Francoist National Movement (May 1977); and held free and democratic elections (June 1977). Only when it had become clear that the transition would be relatively smooth – that is, in 1976–77 – did the PCE accept that Suárez's reform agenda was being seriously implemented, abandoning its assumption that there would a *ruptura*, a clean break between Francoism and post-Francoism.[107] The PCE, which had aspired to the leading role during and after this transition, was now simply asking to participate in the construction of democratic Spain along lines largely sketched by King Juan Carlos and Suárez.

The strength of the communists had been overestimated thanks to the presentational skills and high profile of Santiago Carrillo, the Franco regime's insistence on the communist threat, and their own role before 1976. Many of those who supported the PCE before 1975 had done so because it was the best opponent of Franco; once the regime capitulated, its appeal faded.[108] In practice, none of this made much difference to the strategy of the PCE. Whether or not the *ruptura* was going to be negotiated, a broad united front policy was the only realistic path.[109]

Like the PCE, the PSOE had assumed that there would be a *ruptura*. Consequently, it had sought to retain much of its traditional radicalism. [110] While the PCE, at pains to show its moderation, refrained from mentioning nationalization,[111] the PSOE continued to define itself as a 'Marxist and democratic' class party, which rejected any accommodation with capitalism, and which was determined to nationalize the ten largest banks and fifty of the two hundred largest companies.[112] Events soon forced the PSOE to modify its views. Once it had realized that a clean break was no longer

necessary, it announced that the transition toward a 'state of formal democracy' would occur through a *ruptura negociada*.[113]

By 1977, it was clear to virtually everyone on the Left that there was no
alternative to this 'soft' transition. Though a majority of the PCE-led unions,
the *Comisiones obreras*, believed in 1981 that an historical opportunity to
establish a more advanced form of democracy had been missed,[114] at the
time the negotiated transition pleased all the main protagonists, who knew
that none of them was strong enough on their own to lead (or oppose) the
transition. The Left, in particular, had little cause for dissatisfaction. Its
strength and the social unrest in the country had led to a transition to a real
parliamentary democracy, in which all parties – including the PCE, the object
of incessant and brutal persecution since the end of the civil war – had
become legal. All the institutions of Western-oriented parliamentary democracy were in place less than three years after the death of Franco. The
country was poised to close the chasm which separated civil liberties in
Spain from those enjoyed on the other side of the Pyrenees.

The PSOE offered a radical reading of the *ruptura negociada*. This would be
only the first step towards the final aim, what the PSOE called *socialismo
autogestionario* which, in any case, was 'possible only on a world scale'. The
second step would establish a state under the hegemony of the working
classes. The third and final phase would be a classless society, where self-
management would replace the machinery of the state.[115] The idea of clearly
demarcated stages enabled the party to be as moderate as necessary in the
first phase, on the grounds that it was, after all, only a beginning. Eventually,
the full range of socialist policies would be displayed. Although this modest
formula, whose simplicity probably gratified some party militants, was eventually abandoned, the notion of stages was maintained as a handy device with
which to justify existing policies.

Throughout 1976 the two parties of the Left kept their mutual dislike for
each other under reasonable control. The PSOE, overestimating the threat
from the PCE, was keen to demonstrate that it was well to the left of the
traditional social-democratic parties of Northern Europe. González insisted
that there was no rationale for a rightist 'social-democratic' formation.[116]
Alfonso Guerra, the number two in the socialist hierarchy, explained that,
while in Northern Europe superior economic growth could satisfy basic
working-class demands, in Southern Europe a rapacious capitalism sought
simply to maximize profits at the expense of long-term national prosperity.
This is why Mediterranean countries had produced a radicalized working
class, strong socialist and communist parties, and a progressive brand of
Catholicism.[117] Guerra's purpose was to tone down the polemic against the
Eurocommunist PCE, whose co-operation was still required, assuming that
neither the PCE nor the PSOE could achieve power on its own. Communists and socialists, he continued, had to be aware of their common aims,
exchange experience and co-ordinate trade union struggles. The true model

for Guerra was not Italy, where the socialists were in a minority, or Portugal, where the communists were not 'Euro', but France, where the PS–PCF alliance – he thought – was poised to win the 1978 elections. Victory in France and Spain, in conjunction with the continuation of socialist governments in Britain and Germany, might help shift the whole of Western Europe towards socialism.[118]

There is no reason to suppose that this optimistic scenario was dictated solely by electoral considerations. Nevertheless, shifting the hegemonic axis of an entire continent would have required not just the piecemeal concurrence of national victories by the parties of the Left, as envisaged by Guerra, but also the co-ordination of policies and favourable circumstances for economic development. None of these conditions obtained. Parties and nations (and their electorates) went their separate ways, responding to local requirements and impulses. The various capitalisms, meanwhile, continued their anarchic development, restructuring themselves to the advantage of some and the detriment of others, unstoppable in their blind pursuit, like water seeking the lowest level, demanding the termination of the constraints and regulations which the nation-state had erected in the course of the century.

In the face of this sea-change all politicians, including the socialists, succumbed to the short-term tactical necessities imposed by the structure of democratic politics: electioneering, image-making, the need to maintain a façade of internal unity, establishing a share of the electoral market.

As they approached the general election to be held on 15 June 1977 – the first free elections in Spain since the 1930s – all parties began to shed their ideological past with a remarkable lack of inhibition. André Malraux would have found his old aphorism particularly appropriate to Spain: 'The historians who will judge our era will say: what a strange era where the left was not on the left, the right was not on the right and the centre was not in the middle.'

The communists emphasized their moderation, their respect for the church, their European credentials and never mentioned nationalization. The socialists too dropped all references to state ownership and the other radical resolutions passed at their Congress held the previous year.[119] Suárez's Unión Centro Democrático (UCD) campaigned as if it had never anything to do with Franco. Only Alianza Popular (AP), ably led by Manuel Fraga Iribarne, showed its true colours by deliberately appealing to the nostalgic vote.[120] It was recompensed with a mere 8.3 per cent of the vote. The far Right did much worse: it obtained less than one per cent. The *bunker*, as the ultra-Francoists were dubbed, was defeated. Less than two years after the dictator's death, his regime was laid to rest.[121]

The UCD, with 34.4 per cent of the vote, was the largest single party. Though it was hailed as the winner of the 1977 elections, this was a pyrrhic victory, not large enough to enable the main architect of the transition, Adolfo Suárez, to establish his party's hegemony. The pattern established in Italy – the domination of the Christian democrats for nearly fifty years –

would not be repeated in Spain. Like Karamanlis in Greece, Suárez, triumphant in the period of the transition, was routed in the period of consolidation.
His party had not obtained an absolute majority and he had not stopped the
socialists' bandwagon. This was not for want of trying. Suárez had hoped
that the Left would emerge heavily fragmented. As only the PSOE could
hope to unite it, all the PSOE's rivals were Suárez's friends. Suárez's attempt
to boost other, smaller socialist parties, such as Enrique Tierno Galván's
PSP, failed.[122] By 1978 they were all absorbed by the PSOE – now the only
credible Socialist Party left.[123] With 29.3 per cent of the vote in 1977, Felipe
González could look to the future with considerable optimism.

Suárez's strategy of fragmenting the Left suffered a further blow when it
became clear that, with only 9.4 per cent of the 1977 vote, the Communist
Party would not be able to contain the PSOE. Suárez had been, *de facto*,
Carrillo's senior ally, the dominant partner in an informal coalition. This
view was widely held by the socialists.[124] Suárez, like Carrillo, had been hoping
for an 'Italian' development. Both men needed to contain the PSOE. But
Suárez's best scenario was a 'blocked' democracy – that is, a permanently
divided opposition, an unelectable Communist Party and a centrist party, his
own, invariably in power. Carrillo's aim was, understandably, quite different.
He realized – like Berlinguer – that his internationally unacceptable party
could share power only under the cover of a broadly based coalition government. For this to occur, it was necessary that the situation of emergency
continued. The communists could thrive only as long as Spain's young
democracy appeared to be in danger. It was they, and not their socialist
rivals, who time and again warned the public of the fragility of democratic
institutions and preached consensus.[125] The ease with which the attempted
coup of 1981 was put down demonstrated, albeit with hindsight, that there
was little to worry about. Spanish democracy had become consolidated. The
PCE could, of course, like the Greek and Portuguese parties, be content to
remain a party of radical working-class protest, remonstrating from the
sidelines while the main show proceeded without them. Indeed, when the
Eurocommunist experiment was over, this became Carrillo's new strategy.

In 1977, however, Carrillo still hoped that an 'Italian' strategy could be
pursued, in spite of the disastrous electoral results. But he was in a trap. The
PCE's aim was the unity of the Left. To succeed, it needed to convince the
reluctant PSOE to abandon its rightward path. It would do so only by losing
votes to the PCE. Consequently, in order to unite with the socialists, the
PCE had to teach them a lesson. Accordingly, in the 1979 elections, the PCE
conducted an aggressively anti-socialist campaign.[126] But the results – 10.8
per cent – were very similar to those of 1977: a disappointment for the
communists.

The real winner of the 1977 election was the PSOE. It emerged as a truly
national party, scoring clear victories in Madrid, Barcelona, Valencia and
Seville. Felipe González had fought a highly professional, American-style

campaign and had become the most popular politician in the country. He thus joined the pantheon of Southern European socialist leaders, along with Soares, Craxi and Papandreou. Like Papandreou in Greece, he was the only politician referred to by his Christian name.[127]

The PSOE's strategy was largely dictated by circumstances, although it is the merit of its leadership to have recognized what these circumstances were. Elections had forced the PSOE and the PCE to fight against each other even before the process of consolidation had been completed. The two parties were vying for a similar political space. The PSOE 'had' to move to the right by appealing to the centre. Had it stayed on the left, its economic programme would have been indistinguishable from that of the PCE. Yet the PSOE had to remain a 'left' party – that is, the repository of the vote of those who wanted Spain to change. Accordingly, it had to ensure that it did not have a serious enemy on the Left. The only way to pacify the PCE was to give in to their offer and form a common front with them. But this would have been incompatible with the PSOE's march towards the centre. Consequently the PSOE had to fight the PCE. In the absence of an electoral system which, like the French one, would have forced co-operation, there was no other way. When it was electorally convenient for the Left to unite, it did so – as in April 1979, when an agreement between the PCE and the PSOE led to the election of left-wing mayors in most large cities. What really mattered, however, were the national elections. Like most of Spain's politicians, González too had the 'Italian model' in mind, though for him it was a model to avoid. At the 1946 election, the first after fascism, the Italian socialists (PSI) had pushed the PCI into third place; but in just over ten years, the PSI, still closely allied to the PCI, had tumbled to a 14.3 per cent vote; while the PCI was nearly twice as strong.[128] No wonder the Spanish socialists saw only negative lessons in the so-called Italian scenario.

Soon after the 1977 election, the problem of the economy, which had been conveniently forgotten in the first phase of the transition, reasserted itself. The Suárez government, which had not dared to face up to the economic situation, now did not dare to implement austerity policies and continued to increase public sector spending.[129] It soon had to face the fact that the austerity measures recommended by the IMF could not be delayed. The peseta was devalued by 19.7 per cent against the dollar. This, however, was not enough to deal with an economy on the verge of collapse, an inflation rate of 24.5 per cent, falling rates of productivity growth, and a balance on current account showing a deficit of $250 million.[130]

To implement the required austerity programme, and to tackle ETA terrorism, the government needed the co-operation of the Left. In October 1977, all political parties were invited to the presidential palace, the Moncloa, to establish common policies on the economy and terrorism. The ensuing pact, known as the Pacto de la Moncloa, was signed by the political parties. The agreements largely reflected the proposals drafted by the government's

leading economic expert, Enrique Fuentes Quintana, and continued the
dirigiste neo-Keynesian economic policy characteristic of the last years of the
Franco regime.[131] The Left obtained the promise of higher pensions and
unemployment benefits, and a progressive tax on wealth – a measure advocated by the French *Programme Commun* and which, in Britain, only the
Labour Left recommended. The counterpart of taxing the rich was the
imposition of an incomes policy. Prices would increase by no more than 22
per cent, lower than the rate of inflation.[132] The incomes policy was immediately imposed; the taxes which were supposed to hit the rich never
materialized.[133]

The supreme advocate of the Pacto de la Moncloa was Santiago Carrillo,
still hoping to be able to remain a major player. Though a long way from the
government of 'democratic concentration' he advocated, the pact would give
the PCE a respectability and credibility denied by the elections. Here we
should note a significant parallel between Carrillo's reliance on the pact and
Cunhal's reliance on the military. Both communist politicians were trying to
recoup by other means what electoral politics had denied them. González
responded like Soares. The socialists could obtain all they wanted through
the ballot box; why; then; sustain governments and parties whose days were
numbered? They accepted the pact with great reluctance. Unlike the communists, they refused to consider it as anything more than a short-term
necessity to be abandoned as soon as possible. The reluctance of the PSOE
had little to do with the content of the pact which, in the words of a leading
socialist supporter, 'incorporated large parts of the economic programme of
the Socialist Party'.[134] The growing authority of the PSOE meant that the
party had little to gain by submerging its identity in a vague multi-party pact.
The rivalry between the PSOE and the PCE was reflected in the divergent
behaviour of the respective trade unions. The pro-socialist Unión General de
Trabajadores (UGT), unlike the pro-Communist Comisiones obreras, refused
to support formally the Pacto de la Moncloa.[135]

On balance, the pact or, at any rate, a generalized truce on key issues
between all the main parties, was a necessary stage in the consolidation of
Spanish democracy, even though it did not achieve an immediate demobilization of labour conflicts.[136] The value of the pact was largely symbolic. But
symbols are what matter in the politics of transition. If the democratic game
is to be played properly, it is indispensable that the new rules be established
among all the players. Implicit in the austerity agreements was the recognition
by all parties that Spain would remain a mixed economy, in which the workers
would be somewhat protected. It was also agreed that Spain would become
a modern European country, not one in which traditional morality would be
defended by the might of the state. Thus, the libertarian demands advanced
by the parties of the Left were given ample satisfaction. Spain rapidly caught
up with the rest of Europe: the sale of contraceptives was allowed; adultery
by women was no longer a crime (that of men had never been considered

criminal); the police forces were reorganized.[137] The socialists were more identified with this new 'permissive' legislation than any other party. This laid the ground for an alliance between the PSOE and the new young middle classes, who could no longer stomach the traditional Catholic values and the repressive sexual ethics upheld by the regime and its cronies.[138] The alliance would be finally sealed after 1982 when the PSOE in power would become an instrument for the personal advancement of its middle-class members.[139]

The most important by-product of the truce between the political parties was the new constitution. González's success at the election of 1977 enabled him to become the principal interlocutor of the centrist party, Suárez's UCD, in determining the shape of the constitution.[140] Although the final draft of the constitution represented a genuine consensus among all democratic parties, including the PCE, the most important sections of it were agreed by González's and Suárez's negotiators during sessions of hard bargaining at the restaurant José Luis in Madrid. González accepted that Spain would remain a monarchy, though a constitutional one. The communists agreed. It was important to ensure that the monarchy would not become a rallying force for the conservative middle classes and the armed forces, by reassuring them that the outcome of the civil war was not being totally reversed. In exchange the final document abolished the death penalty and did not preclude national-ization, divorce and abortion.[141] It gave equal rights to children born out of wedlock. The constitution made illegal all forms of sex discrimination, thus reinstating in Spanish law a principle which had been enshrined in the republican constitution of 1931.[142] In December 1978 the constitution was overwhelmingly approved by a popular referendum. Spain had become a democracy.

The PSOE emerged triumphantly from the *ruptura negociada*. González's achievement was to have realized sooner than anyone else that to win the transition it was necessary to prepare for the post-transition. He adopted a strategy which was the reverse of that of the communists – they were still raising the issue of the perils threatening democracy – and attacked the Suárez government decisively and mercilessly as soon as the 1979 electoral campaign was over – partly in retaliation for Suárez's attacks.[143] The general election held on 1 March 1979 confirmed the PSOE as the second party, with 30.5 per cent, after the UCD with 35 per cent, but well ahead of the PCE (10.8 per cent). All three parties had slightly improved their position compared to the results of 1977. The communists and Suárez were pleased, mistakenly believing that the socialist advance had been stopped.

González realized that the PSOE had come of age and could reasonably expect to gain a majority at the next elections. To enhance its chances, it was necessary to accelerate the 'modernization' of the party – that is, the abandon-ment of its traditional ideological baggage. This was not achieved without a fight. At the Twenty-eighth Congress (May 1979), the left wing of the party, the so-called *críticos*, who advocated a closer relationship with the PCE, lost the motion on organizational reform. They had sought more proportionality in the allocation of party posts, hoping to decrease the power of the Seville-based majority group of González and Guerra. However, they succeeded in defeating González's proposal to delete all references to Marxism from the party programme.

Deprived of his own Spanish Bad Godesberg, González counter-attacked by refusing to stand for the party leadership again. This astute move revealed what everyone knew: the *críticos* had no one to take his place.[144] The reality of modern electoral politics means that a party needs to be led by a well-known personality, able to withstand incessant exposure to the media. Left-wing activists throughout Europe were discovering that they could acquire considerable formal powers, but that these counted for little against a leader with easy access to the media, able and often forced to make policy on the spot. For the ordinary Spaniard, González *was* the PSOE. The *críticos* were painfully aware of this.

To resolve the crisis, an Extraordinary Congress was called for September 1979. By then, González's supporters, the *Felipistas*, had a clear majority of the delegates. They controlled the debates. The Left was marginalized. The new executive was completely *Felipista*.[145] The PSOE no longer called itself a Marxist party. González was firmly in charge. This sharply contrasted with the 'federated and decentralized party within a federated and decentralized state' which had been his avowed aim less than three years before.[146] Control over the party machine, and not questions of Marxist theory, had been the main issue all along. In any case, it was clear to all except the very naive that voters neither knew nor cared whether the PSOE called itself Marxist.[147] In common with all previous 'revisionist' debates on the West European Left since 1945 – Bad Godesberg, Clause Four, etc. – what was at stake was a factional fight between Left and Right.[148] The position of the traditional Left – in all these instances – was that public opinion had to be rallied round the party programme, while the modernizers sought to adapt programme and image to public opinion.

In Spain this kind of revisionism had been initiated by the communists. At the Ninth Congress of the PCE (April 1978), the term Leninism was formally dropped after an open and wide-ranging debate.[149] The PCE now declared itself to be just non-dogmatically 'Marxist', though the Partit Social-ista Unificat de Catalunya (PSUC), the Catalan branch of the party, kept 'Leninism' for a while longer.[150]

None of this mattered. The national elections of 1982 delivered the *coup de grâce* to both Suárez and the PCE. In January 1981 Suárez had resigned from the post of prime minister; he had come under constant attack from within his own party, still little more than an agglomeration of sects. Having forced the resignation of their only popular leader, the barons of the UCD cancelled each other out in the struggle for the succession. The least despised candidate, Leopoldo Calvo Sotelo, became prime minister. These events led to the complete humiliation of the UCD at the polls. It achieved a miserable 6.7 per cent of the vote. Suárez's small splinter group, the Centro Democrático y Social, did even worse, obtaining only 3 per cent. Alianza Popular, the party of 'reformed' Francoists, emerged as the leading conservative party with 26.5 per cent, but was in no position to form a government. The communists received only 3.8 per cent of the vote and four out of 350 seats in the Congress of Deputies. The failure of the attempted coup by Tejero Molina and Milans del Bosch the previous year had demonstrated that the pro-Franco 'bunker' was not only unelectable, but also powerless. The far-right party, Fuerza Nueva, whose leader Blas Piñar had been his party's only elected deputy in 1979, lost the seat and dissolved itself. It had also become clear that, however important the national regional parties may have appeared, there was never any serious risk of the country breaking up. The leading parties, especially the PSOE after the decomposition of the UCD, were authentic national parties. The only area where nationalism was far more important than class-based politics was Euzkadi, the most industrialized region of Spain and home to a large working class. There the PSOE and the PCE fared very poorly. Terrorism remained a serious threat, but no democratic country has yet been seriously destabilized by terrorists.

Not only had the PCE been less successful than its Italian model, the PCI, but it never did as well, electorally, as its semi-Stalinist counterparts in Greece and Portugal. Moderation is not necessarily the key to electoral victory. The principal cause of the setbacks of the PCE was the way the transition to democracy took place in Spain. From the beginning it was directed from above by an élite which held the initiative throughout until the transition was completed. There was never an abrupt transition, a clear-cut *ruptura*, as in Greece and Portugal.

Outside Euzkadi, the Spanish communists had been the backbone – as someone remarked, at times the only bone – of the most determined opposition to the regime.[151] Their activists had suffered years in jail or in exile. As Paul Preston has pointed out, the combination of mass strength and moderation exhibited by the PCE during the early part of the transition (1976–77) was essential for the establishment of the democratic system in Spain.[152] For this – as if to prove that historical justice is a fantasy – the PCE obtained neither votes nor gratitude and after 1977 it even began to lose members.[153]

His strategy in shreds, Carrillo lost the trust of his party. Even before the 1982 elections he had been attacked by the pro-Soviet wing for having pushed through the abandonment of Leninism and for his repeated censure of the Soviet intervention in Afghanistan. He was also attacked by the 'Euro-communist' wing for his increasing authoritarianism, and for not dealing firmly with the pro-Soviet wing of the Communist Party in Catalonia, the PSUC.[154] At the Tenth Congress of the PCE (July 1981), Carrillo – in a belligerent mood – used his majority to deal a heavy blow to his erstwhile

Eurocommunist supporters, known as the *renovadores*, and expelled a number of them, including Manuel Azcárate, the party's 'foreign minister' and a highly respected veteran communist.[155] After the electoral disaster of 1982, Carrillo could not escape being blamed for the defeat. He engineered his replacement by a much younger man, Gerardo Iglesias, in the hope of being able to control him and to continue to rule indirectly. This backfired. Iglesias and his followers quickly embraced the programme of the *renovadores*. In a leading article in the party's theoretical journal, *Nuestra Bandera*, Iglesias called for open debate, less centralization, the thorough renewal of the party so that its organisation reflected its Eurocommunist strategy and Spain's new democratic structures, and advocated an alliance with the so-called new social movements of pacifists, ecologists and feminists.[156] In 1985 Carrillo found himself isolated, and was expelled from the executive of the party he had led for twenty-two years (1960–82). With a loyal band of supporters, he followed a politically erratic course, veering from pro-Sovietism to social democracy until, in February 1991, he rejoined the PSOE he had left in the 1930s. Meanwhile, the 'renewed' PCE sought to mend fences with the PSOE. By 1984 accommodation had become difficult. The González government was following an increasingly neo-liberal policy of holding down wages, fighting inflation by reducing public sector spending, allowing unemployment to increase, and reviving private investment.

Throughout the 1980s, the PCE was unable, even under a more modern post-Carrillo leadership and, from 1986, a new electoral name, Izquierda Unida (United Left), to play a significant role in Spanish politics. The PCE had paid a heavy price for its moderation and for the sacrifice of its ideological identity. However, a hard-line Communist Party might have had more votes in the new Spain, but not much more influence than the rump which survived into the 1980s.

The unquestionable winner of the 1982 election was the PSOE. With 48.4 per cent of the vote, and an absolute majority in Parliament, it had obtained one of the best electoral results gained by a socialist party anywhere in Europe. Felipe González became prime minister and remained in power longer than any other socialist leader in Europe, except for Sweden's Tage Erlander. The PSOE had successfully humbled the communists and routed Suárez. It had campaigned on the values which best represented what so many Spaniards wanted above all: modernity, progress, hope in the future, realism. Other parties could not compete with this. Fraga's AP represented the old Spain of Franco without the dictatorship. The UCD was hopelessly divided and, without Suárez, had lost the little identity it ever had. The PCE, partly because it had had such a high profile during the struggle against Franco, also appeared as the party of the past, still led by veterans of a civil war so many wanted to forget. Alone of all the parties, the PSOE had caught the mood of the public. It was now ready to inaugurate the González era in Spanish politics.

As recently as 1974, the PSOE had been a party of radical firebrands.

Now it had become a moderate party of government. By the mid-1980s, as it pursued impeccable liberal policies of deregulation, its name – with its emphasis on 'socialist' and 'workers party' – had become anachronistic. It is easy to berate this kind of transformation. Yet by moving to the right, the PSOE not only prevented a polarization of party politics which would have produced a staunchly right-wing alternative, but also guaranteed that the complex consolidation of democracy would be entrusted to a socialist party (however moderate), rather than to a conservative party with populist leanings, as had occurred in Germany and Italy after 1945.

The victory of the PSOE had occurred within the context of an acute economic crisis. Spain had the highest unemployment, the highest inflation and the largest foreign debt in Western Europe.[157] The PSOE was clearly perceived as a force which would modernize the country, solve the economic problems and establish a welfare state – not the easiest of tasks in the climate of the early 1980s. Its economic programme, published in 1980, *Estrategia economica del PSOE*, contained a spirited defence of the role of the public sector, which, once 'modernized', would be an indispensable instrument for economic recovery and the satisfaction of collective needs.[158] Nevertheless, belying the self-confident tones characteristic of the manifestos of political parties, the socialists realized the intensity of the worldwide crisis. Though full employment remained on the agenda, the PSOE was also aware that the massive restructuring required to enable Spain to compete with the rest of the European Community would require a job shake-out.[159] The outcome was that, for well over ten years, Spain topped the European league of unemployment. By 1987, Spain was also the fastest growing economy in Western Europe: Spanish cities were the scene of a consumption boom without 'precedent in the country's history'.[160] González's success in 'modernizing' the Spanish economy was impressive, if by 'modernization' we mean economic restructuring, GNP growth, and a more flexible labour market. The context of the achievement, however, was massive unemployment, a large public sector deficit, growing corruption, and frequent devaluation of the peseta. By 1995, as the González government appeared to be in its death throes, Spain had not 'caught up' with Europe: none of the five convergence criteria agreed at Maastricht by the European Community had been met.

The Greek *Allaghi*

Greece shared with the two Iberian countries a level of economic development markedly inferior to that of their West European neighbours. All three were latecomers to industrialization and, consequently, had a large peasant population. In Greece, however, the peasantry had been free of the oppression of landlords for much longer than in Spain or Portugal. Small peasant property has prevailed in Greece since the nineteenth century – as in Denmark and France.[161] Latifundia appeared only when Greece annexed Thessaly in

1881 and lasted only until the agrarian reforms of 1917.[162] As a result, Greece was the only Balkan country without a peasant movement or peasant party. At a time when Alexander Stamboliski's Agrarian Party was taking power in Bulgaria on an anti-oligarchic and populist programme of social reform (1919–23),[163] the Greek peasants were drawn by their local notables and politicians into a conflict largely irrelevant to their needs: the *dichasmos* between the monarchy and the liberal urban classes (a conflict which would be settled only in the 1970s).[164] The Greek Civil War (1944–49) had little in common with that of Spain, whose origin lay in a belated attempt at agrarian reform and not, like the Greek, in an international conflict.[165] The Greeks, being members of the Orthodox church, did not share the Catholic beliefs and the consequently pro-Western orientation of their south-west European neighbours. Unlike Portugal and Spain, modern Greece possessed no empire. On the contrary, until the nineteenth century it was a possession of the Ottomans. Turkish rule was relatively tolerant in that it did not seek to impose a given set of religious or political beliefs on its Greek subjects. All the Turkish authorities wanted was obedience, taxes and the performance of military service. This was sufficient to generate a widespread suspicion of political authority, which led the Greek peasants and artisans to seek the protection of politicians and bureaucrats – all those with privileged access to political power and resources. This private link between strongly family-oriented subordinate groups and Greek-born political intermediaries was further developed after Greece became an independent state in 1830. Political life became characterized by strongly personalized links between patron–politician and client–voter, and by the exchange of *rousfeti* (political favours).[166] Politics was a necessary evil, a self-defence mechanism used to uphold a traditional way of life, not an instrument of emancipation.[167] Clientelist and patronage relations became commonplace. No serious socialist party emerged. Between the wars the main political divide in Greece was between the monarchist forces and the followers of Eleutherios Venizelos, the Cretan-born liberal statesman who dominated Greek politics from 1910, when he became prime minister, until his death in 1936.

The elections of 1936 produced a deadlock between monarchists and the Venizelists. King George II asked a military strongman, Joannis Metaxas, to intervene. It was a classic case of 'royal bureaucratic dictatorship', far closer to that of the Balkan states of Bulgaria, Yugoslavia and Romania than to the authoritarian regimes of Spain and Portugal.[168]

The Second World War and the civil war brought about significant foreign involvement and tied Greece firmly to the West. As a result, Greece did not adopt the protectionist policies, tariffs and overvalued currency of Portugal and Spain.[169]

Throughout the 1950s productivity in agriculture remained low. The service sector was large and overmanned, the industrial sector unable to absorb excess rural labour. Peasants emigrated, while capital sought refuge from taxation by investing in shipping and other economic activity which the state could not control.[170] Ninety per cent of the country's large savings were concentrated in the two principal banks (one of which, the National Bank of Greece, was owned by the state). The banks preferred to invest in the commercial and housing sector (where profits were higher than in manufacturing), rather than in industry.[171] Only in the 1960s did foreign firms start investing in Greece to any sustainable degree.[172] By 1962, the manufacturing sector contributed more to GNP than agriculture, thanks to foreign capital. Thus, Greece acquired a manufacturing sector which was technologically advanced and foreign-controlled, especially the metal and chemical industries. Throughout the 1960s, the share of foreign capital in GNP increased. Average growth was well above OECD average.[173] However, as in developing countries, rapid growth secured beneficial effects for the centre, not the periphery. This caused a massive movement of people from the countryside to Athens and Thessaloniki. Little trickled down to the agricultural and artisan sectors; the gains were transferred abroad.[174]

Dependence on external capitalism was thus a fundamental trait of Greek development. Until 1957 US aid covered more than three-quarters of the budget deficit.[175] Nevertheless, Greece did share with Portugal and Spain two economic characteristics which benefited the balance of payments: remittances from nationals working abroad and revenues from tourism.[176]

The main peculiarity of the Greek economy was that its main 'capitalist' sector was maritime transport. This was located outside the national territory. It brought little wealth to the country, though a great deal to the shipowners themselves. Its power was politically reflected in the strength of Greek lobbies in the USA and Australia.

The country was politically dependent on the USA to an extent unparalleled in Western Europe. Throughout the 1950s American intervention in the internal affairs of Greece was so blatant as to interfere openly in the debate on electoral reform, successfully threatening the suspension of aid if the Greeks did not comply with US requests.[177] The outcome was that EDA, the left-wing umbrella used by the banned KKE to compete in elections, had no seat in Parliament in 1952, though it had obtained 9.6 per cent of the vote. That Greece was an American client during the 1950s and 1960s was not seriously in dispute. Even the US ambassador-designate Robert Keeley, at his confirmation hearing in July 1985, admitted that US–Greek relations had been those of patron to client from the end of the Second World War to the mid-1960s.[178]

In the 1950s Greek politics was dominated by a right-wing conservative party, the ERE (Elliniki Rizospastiki Enosis – Radical Union of Greece). Only in the early 1960s was this hegemony challenged. The contestant was not the left-wing EDA, but EK (Enosis Kentrou – Centre Union) led by the charismatic Georgios Papandreou, the victor of the 1964 elections. Georgios' son, the even more charismatic Andreas, was then the leader of the Centre

Union's left-wing faction, which had a Trotskyist leaning. A distinguished economist, educated in the USA, Andreas Papandreou had already developed an egalitarian and strongly pro-growth ideology – though he began to call himself a socialist only after the Colonels' coup in 1967. In 1962 he advocated radical economic reforms to enable Greece to achieve self-sustained growth in ten years while avoiding a serious labour shortage.[179]

Papandreou's Centre Union Party had won the February 1964 elections in a landslide facilitated by the fact that the EDA stood down in twenty constituencies. The slogan of the Centre Union Party, which particularly infuriated the army, had been 'The Army Belongs to the Nation', the subtext of which was that it should be controlled by Parliament and not by the monarchy.[180] The ensuing post-1964 clash between the moderately modernizing party of Georgios Papandreou and a conservative establishment protected by the army and the monarchy was strikingly similar to the great conflict between Venizelists and the monarchist oligarchy during the 1930s.[181] In both instances the outcome was a dictatorship.

The military coup of 1967 was not launched to stop an agrarian reform (as in Spain in 1936), or to block communism, or even social democracy. To the outside world, the colonels explained that they wanted to save Greece from totalitarian communism – the standard justification for right-wing military intervention. In reality, they wanted to stop the imposition of parliamentary control over the Ministry of Defence. Between 1964 and 1967, the monarchic establishment had tried to block Georgios Papandreou, using all means short of dismantling the representative system. The colonels had become impatient with such scruples and decided to intervene directly. Thus, the Greek coup was a form of corporate self-defence whereby a threatened interest group resorted to force in order to stop its modernization by a reform-minded 'bourgeois' party. In other words, the junta, broadly speaking, aimed at blocking demands for democratizing the institutional framework advanced by Georgios Papandreou's Centre Party. As Nicos Mouzelis wrote: 'the Greek colonels intervened strictly "from above", not to defend their country from Marxism but to defend their role within the State.'[182] Middle- and upper-class interests were not in danger (as they appeared to be in Spain during the days of the Republic). There was no stalemate between conservatives and socialists as in Italy in 1922, or Germany and Austria in the 1930s. The colonels never enjoyed the kind of popular support which Franco and Salazar had for a time.

The leaders of the Greek military government were second-level officers: Colonel Nikolaos Makarezos, Brigadier Stylianos Patakos and Colonel George Papadopoulos. Papadopoulos, the strongman of the regime, had been removed from key positions by Papandreou in the 1960s. The junta claimed that the purpose of the 'Revolution' of 21 April 1967 was to create a New Democracy of New Men and New Ideas, imbued with the Helleno-Christian ideals of *Patris–Thriskeia–Ikogenia* (Fatherland, Religion and Family).[183] They thus used the established language of the conservatives. Even Kostantinos Karamanlis, in January 1981, *after* the return to democracy, speaking to the Greek community in Australia, felt the need to reiterate the traditional message: 'The nation (*ethnos*) and Orthodoxy ... have become in the Greek conscience virtually synonymous concepts, which together constitute our Helleno-Christian civilization.'[184] Needless to say, the identification of a particular religion with the nation contradicts modern democratic principles, because it automatically disbars from full membership of the national community all religious minorities.

The colonels' popular support was non-existent. They had not developed the personal ties which bound most Greeks to their politicians and local notables. They were not supported by any of the parties in Parliament, or the traditionalist right, or the King.[185] Their obtuse manners were offensive to the sophisticated middle classes of Athens. Their regime was widely believed to have been imposed on Greece by the CIA and the Pentagon or, at least, to be controlled by the USA. This view was not confined to the Left. It was widely held even in the conservative Greek bureaucracy.[186] The colonels were supported only by some specific vested interests – such as the Association of Greek Shipowners – and mainly for reasons of short-term opportunism.

Nevertheless, there was little organized opposition to the regime. The Communist Party (KKE) was divided between 'Eurocommunist' forerunners and orthodox traditionalists. The KKE eventually split in August 1968 over the Soviet invasion of Czechoslovakia, when Secretary-General Kostas Koliyannis and the external office of the party (located in Bucharest) expelled the reformers, who were in the majority in the clandestine Central Committee in Athens. Those expelled formed the Communist Party of Greece-Interior (Kommounistiko Komma Ellados-esoterikou or KKE-es). In the same year Andreas Papandreou formed PAK, never a real threat to the regime. There were times when the unpopularity of the military became evident, as at the funeral of Georgios Papandreou, which became an opportunity for half a million mourners to manifest their dissent. The colonels were the object of numerous ineffectual challenges. They foiled an alleged plot by King Constantine which led to the king's exile. They ruthlessly crushed frequent student protests, leading to the brutal repression of the occupation of the Polytechnic of Athens on the night of 16–17 November 1973, which ended with over thirty people killed and many more wounded.

The colonels pursued an economic policy markedly similar to that of their predecessors.[187] However, by making strikes illegal, they ensured that real wages would be severely contained. Agriculture suffered, as the EEC withdrew from a number of agreements with Greece, thereby guaranteeing the unpopularity of the regime with many workers and peasants.[188]

Though the economic growth of the 1960s was sufficiently strong to enable the colonels to claim some success, they had no political resources to survive the end of the long boom. The oil shock hit Greece proportionately harder than most other European countries. Before 1973, inflation in Greece was lower than the OECD average. Its acceleration in 1973 was mainly due to the rise in oil prices.[189]

The difficulties encountered by the regime had already become manifest in July 1973 (before any impact of the oil price increase), when Papadopoulos, having abolished the monarchy and elbowed his two colleagues out of power, had himself elected president. A few months later, in November 1973, he was in turn overthrown by another member of the original military junta, Lieutenant-Colonel Dimitrios Ioannidis. The position of the junta was further weakened when Richard Nixon and Spiro Agnew (the Greek-American vice-president of the USA) found themselves in difficulties of their own. Agnew was forced to resign in 1973, after revelations concerning income tax evasion, corruption and extortion, while Nixon was compelled to defend himself from charges of a cover-up in the wake of the Watergate affair.

A desperate attempt was made to obtain a major foreign policy success. In 1974 the military regime tried to force through a union (*enosis*) between Cyprus and Greece, installing an extreme nationalist and possible psychopath, Nikos Sampson, as head of the island. In the words of Rauf Denktash, this was as unacceptable to the Turkish-Cypriot minority as it would have been for the Israelis to find that Adolf Hitler had been made president of Israel. In July 1974, Turkey, unrestrained by the USA (still entangled in Vietnam), invaded the island and established a military base in north-western Cyprus.[190]

The failure of the Cyprus adventure demolished what little credibility the regime still had. Now a key section of the military decided that they had no alternative but to ask Kostantinos Karamanlis to return to Greece from his Paris exile, and to lead the country back to democracy in an orderly manner. They hoped to re-establish the quasi-democratic regime which had prevailed before 1967.

Karamanlis returned, but there could be no simple going back to the pre-1967 situation. The time had come for *Allaghi* – the Change. A genuine democracy was established. The Communist Party was legalized, and communists were no longer persecuted. The monarchy – from which most anti-democratic activity had originated in the course of the century – was abolished after a referendum.[191] It was the first such change in Western Europe since Italy became a republic in 1946.

In Portugal, the transitional government had contained all democratic forces. In Spain, the government had sought to reach an understanding with the Left. In Greece, however, Karamanlis sought to monopolize the transition. He saw Papandreou's PASOK as the main threat and probably legalized the KKE in order to divide the opposition (just as, in Spain, Suárez tried to boost the PCE). He was careful to exclude representatives of the Left from his 'government of national unity', which was mainly composed of conservative and liberal opponents of the military junta.[192] Elections were held only four months after his return, in an effort to prevent the opposition parties from organizing in time. Karamanlis had wisely reconstructed his old conservative party with the new name of Nea Dimokratia (New Democracy – ND). Because in Greek *Dimokratia* means both 'democracy' and 'republic', the new name marked a significant break with Karamanlis' monarchist past. The term 'Nea Dimokratia' had been used by the KKE in its 1935 programme to describe the 'popular front' stage of the revolution. By adopting it Karamanlis precluded its use by the legalized KKE: another case of political clothes-stealing. On 8 December 1974, a popular referendum confirmed the abolition of the monarchy by a majority of 69 per cent. Karamanlis then drafted the Greek constitution of 1975, which maintained a powerful executive by establishing a strong president (an office Karamanlis coveted). This was done without the participation of PASOK and the KKE (unlike in Spain and Portugal, where the Left was involved in constitution-making). The constitution was revised later, in 1986, by Papandreou, but to give more power to the prime minister (i.e. himself), in line with the tradition of strong executive power.[193]

The 1974 elections were fought under a system of 'reinforced' proportional representation, which granted parties with more than 17 per cent of the vote a disproportionate number of seats. Thus, Karamanlis' ND, with 54.4 per cent, had nearly three-quarters of the seats (219 out of 300). The old Centre Party or Enosis Kentrou, once led by Georgios Papandreou and now by the colourless Georgios Mavros, merged with a smaller grouping, Nees Dynamies (New Forces), and won 20 per cent of the vote, but 30 per cent of seats (sixty). Papandreou's PASOK could claim only 13.6 per cent and thirteen seats, while Enomeni Aristera (United Left), which regrouped the KKE and the smaller KKE-es as well as other Left fragments, won only 9.5 per cent and eight seats (see Table 21.1 on page 597 for details).

In spite of its dismal results, the KKE was not entirely dissatisfied. It did not aspire to power. Its immediate objective was to consolidate itself as the one and only Communist Party by deflecting the challenge from the KKE-es. This was achieved in 1977, when the two parties fought separately and the KKE-es lost. Unlike the PCP and the PCE, whose ambition was their permanent insertion in a governing coalition, the KKE's general aim was to consolidate itself as the representative of the radical Left. It was an opposition party through and through. Its attempt to reach an understanding with PASOK was propagandist. Superficially, the KKE and PASOK had much in common: like PASOK, the KKE was against NATO, bitterly opposed to the EEC, and profoundly anti-American.[194] Both wanted a comprehensive welfare state and the nationalization of the commanding heights of the economy. True co-operation, however, was never on the cards. The KKE had no wish to yoke itself to PASOK. Its longer-term ambition was to appropriate most of PASOK's electorate, on the assumption that such a new and unpredictable, charismatically led party would not have the staying power of the KKE which, after all, had survived a civil war, years of discrimination, repression and dictatorship.

Papandreou, similarly, had no interest in attaching his rising fortunes to an organization which was unlikely ever to get out of its ghetto. His greatest asset was that he was a 'new' man, leading a new party. He was not burdened by the weight of history and the memories of the civil war. Here Papandreou stood close to Felipe González. Neither of the two Socialist leaders intended to reopen the barely healed wounds of the civil wars.

In many other respects, PASOK was very different from its counterparts in Portugal and Spain. It called itself a 'movement' (*Kinima*), rather than a party (*Komma*). It was a new product and not the mere reconstruction of an older socialist party, which – in any case – had never really existed in Greece. Its chief trait was a blend of nationalism and socialism. It considered Greece to be a part of the Third World, fighting for national liberation from imperialism. Consequently, it advocated the total withdrawal of the country from NATO and a loose agreement with the EEC, instead of the full membership negotiated by the Karamanlis government. It vowed to eliminate the condition of subordination and dependency to which the country had been reduced by the activities of US multinational companies. The theoretical underpinning of this ideology was provided by 'dependency' and neo-Marxist theorists, often based in American universities and influential mainly among the intelligentsia.

Papandreou's book, *Paternalistic Capitalism*, displayed a familiarity with the central concepts of the New Left of the 1960s. No other European socialist leader had ventured so openly into this domain. The book points to a world system of 'paternalistic capitalism', efficient in a technocratic manner, with, at its centre, the 'American metropolitan establishment' and its military–industrial complex. Economic growth on the periphery, where we find Greece, 'is channelled in paths which reflect the requirements of the metropolis rather than its own requirements'.[195] 'Thus,' wrote Papandreou, 'revolution calls for a confrontation with the Establishment, which is metropolis-dominated. It identifies itself with national liberation. It places the political act ahead of the economic act.'[196]

In the 1950s Papandreou had been a professor of economics at Berkeley in the USA. He had returned to Greece in 1961 at the behest of Karamanlis, his future opponent, who had asked him to set up a research centre in Athens. Papandreou returned to the USA in 1968, after his release from prison, where he had been confined after the coup. Thus, his 'socialism' was formed outside the influence of the dominant European tradition. It would be difficult to find in any sectors of the mainstream European Left – even in Southern Europe, even among communists – such overwhelming insistence on national sovereignty and liberation, such bitter anti-Americanism, such a single-minded indictment of multinational companies.[197]

However, while the claim that 'PASOK equals Papandreou' is largely correct,[198] PASOK's peculiarity was not due exclusively (or even mainly) to the distinctive political biography of its supreme leader. Papandreou's rise to power continued the Greek tradition of parties being led by an established charismatic personality, a member of a politically well-connected family. Leaders may make parties, but they cannot make large and electorally successful parties out of thin air. It is the particular structure of the country, including its fragile civil society and weak trade union movement, and its interconnection with the wider world, which provide the most plausible explanation for PASOK's policies. PASOK's call for national independence, its lambasting of the condition of dependency of the country, its anti-Americanism, its populist call to struggle against the multinationals – these reflected a *real* position of subjugation or, at least, one widely felt and widely shared by Greeks to an extent unknown among the Spanish or the Portuguese. Even Karamanlis responded to this national consciousness and this pervasive anti-Americanism by withdrawing from the military structure of NATO, while presenting himself as the 'Europeanizer' of Greece.[199]

In all other European countries, the issue of NATO was always closely related to the Cold War and the attitude to be taken towards the USSR and the question of détente. This was not so in Greece, where NATO was seen as a defence mechanism against the 'real' enemy: Turkey (also a member of NATO). When Turkey invaded Cyprus in July 1974, many Greeks had expected the USA, through NATO, to exercise considerable pressure on Turkey to withdraw, and thus to work in a pro-Greek direction. This did not occur. NATO had failed to protect Greece and the Greeks from their ancient enemy.

The role of the so-called 'foreign factor' and concern about foreign interference were profoundly rooted in Greek history. From the beginning of the nineteenth century to the civil war, all Greek political parties sought relations with a great power, be it Russia, Britain or France (the three powers which had decided that the first king of modern Greece would be Otto of Bavaria, a German) – in all instances with the same hope, namely to be protected against Turkey.[200]

Papandreou's demand that Greece should adopt a policy of non-alignment was not new either. It was reminiscent of that adopted by Venizelos after 1922.[201] In fact, much of PASOK's political personnel and electoral support came from a liberal-national tradition which can be traced back, through Papandreou's own father Georgios, to Venizelos.[202] The ideology of non-alignment, however, owes far more to the incorporation of the left-wing (i.e. communist) tradition of the Greek Resistance into PASOK.

The emphasis on independence from 'the West' was pursued even by the military junta, widely viewed, especially by the Greeks, as a simple emanation of the Pentagon. The colonels had distanced themselves from mainstream Western attitudes by adopting a far more pro-Arab attitude than any other Western government (with the possible and significant exception of Franco's Spain). As a consequence, Greece never suffered an oil embargo by the

Arabs after the Yom Kippur War of 1973, though the much hoped for Arab investment never materialized and it had to pay regular OPEC prices.[203]

After the fall of the colonels, PASOK kept the Cyprus issue alive and, in the run-up to the elections of 1981, Papandreou pledged his support to the 'struggle' of the Cypriot people to eliminate foreign troops and bases.[204]

Papandreou's anti-Americanism originated more from a national-populist reaction to the US complicity with, or toleration of, the military coup and to an older state of dependency on foreign capital, than from socialist antagonism towards the world's leading capitalist country. His insistence that Greek dependency was similar to that of a Third World country was thus far from being purely ideological. The social geography of Greece resembled that of many Latin American countries, with its sharp contrast between a metropolitan centre, Athens, where half the population lived, and a periphery where rural relations prevailed. PASOK was similarly coming to resemble more and more the populist parties of Latin America, especially the Peronist movement of Argentina, which likewise blended a strident anti-USA appeal with a commitment to modernization and anti-capitalism.[205]

PASOK thus fused a socialist with a nationalist strategy. At the source of this fusion was the Greek Civil War, a long and bloody struggle waged first against the Italian and German fascists, and then against the monarchy seen as the puppet of British and American interests. Such nationalist and socialist discourse had no parallel in either Spain or Portugal. Its nearest equivalent – in Western Europe – was the socialism 'in the colours of France' advocated by the PCF.

But the parallel stops here, because Papandreou clearly displayed his lack of sympathy for the Soviet model, which he called 'a paternalistic socialism ... hardly a genuine alternative', while he was generous in his praise for Mao's Cultural Revolution and its voluntarism on the grounds that it attempted (as it appeared at the time) to reverse the centralization of society.[206]

The nationalist-socialist discourse was enshrined in the 'Proclamation of Fundamental Principles and Objectives' of 3 September 1974.[207] According to the proclamation, the origin of the disaster which befell Greece in 1967 was 'the dependent situation of our Motherland'; the dictatorship was merely 'an especially harsh expression of the dependence of Greece on the imperialistic establishment of the USA and of NATO'; the Greek economy had been plundered by the multinationals.[208] PASOK appealed to peasants, workers, artisans, white-collar employees, and 'our bold and enlightened youth' to help create a political system free of foreign control by withdrawing from NATO. Its objectives were the 'national rebirth' and 'a socialist and democratic Greece'.[209] This meant an independent foreign policy, the denuclearization of the Mediterranean and of the Balkan region, the nationalization of the entire financial system and the 'basic units of production', and a welfare state centred on a national health service.[210]

PASOK attempted to combine two distinct strands: a traditional social-democratic position (economic growth, full employment and a welfare state) with non-alignment. Even though it claimed to be seeking a 'third way' between Soviet communism and capitalism, and refused to join the Socialist International (denounced as an instrument of US-oriented German social democracy),[211] it is clear, both from the declaration of 1974 and from Papandreou's *Paternalistic Capitalism*, that neutral and social-democratic Sweden was the closest paradigm.

PASOK's social-democratic strand has tended to be overlooked by the majority of commentators, who deny that the party is socialist and prefer to describe it as 'populist' – a category even vaguer than that of socialism.[212] Most of the proponents of the 'populism' of PASOK have an ideal type of a socialist or social-democratic party in mind and PASOK, understandably enough, falls somewhat short of it – like most socialist parties. What is called the populism of PASOK is a form of politics which any newly emergent Greek socialist party would have had to adopt, given the national background. Setting the issue in the proper comparative framework, the concrete aims and proposals of PASOK can be seen as conventionally social-democratic. While its rhetoric was that of Third World and national liberation movement populism, it had a mass organization akin to that of the SPD and the PCI. PASOK's uninhibited use of the state machine was typical of Greek ruling parties and, more generally, of Southern European clientele politics. Even the highly personalized nature of the movement, though unique in its intensity, reflects the growing personalization of leading political figures in the age of television.

In Portugal, the initially leftist rhetoric of the PS was dictated by the general radicalization of Portuguese society. In Spain, this rhetoric was part of the tradition of the PSOE itself. In Greece, the radical jargon of the declaration and the 1975 electoral campaign responded to three distinct pressures. There was, in the first place, a need to capitalize on the general revulsion against the regime of the colonels and the system of bastardized democracy which had prevailed before it. In the second place, PASOK needed to tap the radical tradition of the Greek Resistance and the civil war to prevent it from being hegemonized by its natural heir, the KKE. Finally, PASOK's radicalism was also a reflection of the desires and expectations of its more active cadres – that is the various leftist sects and student organizations which had joined it.[213]

By 1975, Papandreou had defeated his leftist wing. Nevertheless, PASOK fought the 1977 elections on a programme fundamentally similar to that of 1975, although it no longer insisted that it was a Marxist party, emphasizing instead that socialism, although not on the immediate agenda, remained its distant aim.[214] The results of the 1977 elections reinforced the ascendancy of PASOK as the main opposition party: it doubled its percentage and obtained ninety-three parliamentary seats. It had become a national party, strong not only in traditionally radical areas, such as Achaia and Crete, but throughout the country.[215] The collapse of Mavros' Enosis Kentrou opened the possibility for a systematic absorption of the Centre Party by PASOK. The patent inability of the KKE to reach beyond its traditional electorate ensured that PASOK was unlikely to lose votes to its left.

It was evident that Greece, like Spain and Portugal at a similar stage of the transition, was shifting towards the Left. Karamanlis tried to follow the trend by nationalizing some parts of the financial sector and, acknowledging the desire for civic modernization, by allowing civil divorce in February 1979.[216] His identity established, Papandreou shifted towards the centre.

The de-radicalization of PASOK paralleled that of the PSOE in Spain, with the significant difference that PASOK had become a true mass party with branches and activists in hundreds of villages and towns.[217] By the early 1980s, PASOK claimed 200,000 members. If this claim is accurate, it was a significant achievement in a country of ten million people – in contrast to Spain, where popular involvement in party politics has remained low.[218] Electoral success was the foundation of this surge in political participation. A direct charismatic appeal of leaders to voters was replacing the former radical ideological message; yet the anti-imperialist rhetoric, though more muted than previously, remained a distinguishing feature of PASOK.

In May 1980, Karamanlis resigned from his position as prime minister and became president of Greece. The new prime minister, Georgios Rallis, did not have the statesmanlike stature of his predecessor. The Centre Party was disintegrating; its principal cadres, including the leader Georgios Mavros, were moving lock, stock and barrel into Papandreou's camp. Young technocrats followed this trend, reinforcing PASOK's centrist appeal, in a movement similar to that of Spain around the PSOE.[219] The economic situation had profoundly deteriorated, with inflation running at 25 per cent and real wages dropping by 5.5 per cent in 1979–81.[220] At the same time, the personality cult around Papandreou had reached Maoist proportions: he was described in the party weekly, *Exormissi*, as 'the great leader of the Greek people who designed the great spiral march of the popular forces'.[221] Much of this cult was facilitated by the fact that seventy-three PASOK deputies of the ninety-three elected in 1977 were new to parliamentary life.[222]

Elections were held in October 1981. PASOK openly campaigned for socialism as a means of overcoming capitalism (the same slogan used by the French Socialist Party), in a country which never had a socialist party.[223] PASOK's triumph was unquestionable. It led to the first left-wing government in Greek history. With over 48 per cent of the popular vote and 172 seats, PASOK had an unassailable majority. This was all the more remarkable as the KKE managed to improve slightly on its previous results. The KKE-es obtained only 1.35 per cent and no parliamentary representation. The overall tally for the Left – that is, PASOK, the KKE and the KKE-es – was 60.36 per cent – a percentage hitherto unparalleled in the electoral history of the West European Left.

PASOK's 1981 election manifesto, the *Declaration of Government Policy. A Contract with the People*, while remaining highly critical of NATO, had toned down its Third World rhetoric without abandoning it. The party now simply promised a gradual removal of American military bases, rather than the immediate evacuation demanded in 1974. In September 1983, an agreement was reached between Greece and the USA, and the Americans were allowed to retain their bases until 1988. By 1987, Papandreou made it clear that the bases would remain in the country even after the deadline. PASOK no longer declared that it would withdraw from NATO. Attacks on the EEC were curtailed (in January 1981 Greece had joined the Community). Some mellowing towards the EEC had started even when PASOK was in opposition. Its 1977 election manifesto had called for a referendum, and implicitly recognized the need for some links with the Community.[224] The referendum was not held, on the grounds that the constitution required the president's authorization and Karamanlis was unlikely to agree to this. By 1982, Papandreou had renegotiated the terms of entry (as Harold Wilson had done in 1975 for similar reasons) and accepted the Community as a counter-weight to the two superpowers. By 1984, he was openly admitting that withdrawal would damage the country.[225]

Nevertheless, Greece continued to be NATO's 'awkward member'. Its independence was marked by vetoing a European Community statement condemning the USSR for shooting down the Korean civilian aircraft KAL-007 in 1983; by not imposing sanctions on Jaruzelski after his clampdown on Solidarity; by supporting the Sandinistas in Nicaragua (like the French government); by welcoming Arafat in 1982 (as Kreisky had done in Austria); by refusing the deployment of Cruise and Pershing missiles. Many of these largely symbolic actions were either in continuity with those of PASOK's predecessors, or were similar to those taken by some of its West European counterparts.[226] By 1994, however, anti-Americanism had become, at most, a cultural attitude, rather than an official policy. PASOK no longer supported anti-Western regimes such as Iraq and Libya. What remained a constant was the nationalist card. This was deployed – when required – with considerable domestic success (and to complete incomprehension outside Greece), when Greece refused to recognize Macedonia until the new country (one of the products of the fragmentation of Yugoslavia) abandoned its name and symbol, which suggested (to the Greeks) irredentist designs on Greek Macedonia.

The social and economic programme of PASOK was characteristically social-democratic; it sought growth and redistribution: 'Our fundamental goal is self-sufficient economic and social development, the development of all productive forces in combination with a more just distribution of income and wealth among the various groups in the population and among the regions.'[227] The most important promises concerned the reform of the health system, the democratization of the civil service, and a reduction in the severe environmental damage in Athens.[228]

Before October 1981, Papandreou had declared that he intended to break with capitalism.[229] Similar declarations had been made by Soares before 1976, González before 1979, and Mitterrand before 1981. Their common crucial assumption was that capitalism was in crisis. The assumption was correct. Its corollary – namely, that the crisis would provide a way out of capitalism itself – was not.

The crisis in the economy had reached dangerous proportions; nevertheless, against the entire European trend, PASOK preferred, in the years immediately after its 1981 victory, to protect employment, rather than price stability. Wages were increased. Public sector borrowing rose from 12.5 per cent of GDP in 1983 to 17.5 in 1985, mainly in order to contain unemployment.[230] As a result, Greece was the only country in Europe where inflation in the 1980s (whose main cause was the devaluation of the drachma)[231] was higher than in the 1970s, while unemployment was well below the OECD average for the decade (see Table 16.1 on page 450).

In terms of civil liberties, PASOK continued the work of its conservative predecessor far more decisively. It legalized civil marriage, confronted the Greek Orthodox church over its landholding, abolished the institution of the dowry, established equal rights for children born out of wedlock, further liberalized divorce, decriminalized adultery, abolished selectivity in secondary education, instituted pensions for female peasants, introduced sex equality legislation.[232] Under the impetus of Margaret Papandreou (Andreas' first wife) and her Union of Greek Women, the government created a Council for Sex Equality and a network of Equality Bureaux in every prefecture of the country. Paternal leave was instituted along with maternal leave. Hundreds of new day-care centres were created. PASOK thus implemented many of the reforms advocated by Greek feminists.[233]

A National Health Service Bill was introduced on 10 August 1983. It declared that health care was a social right and, consequently, that it should not be subject to profit-making.[234] The creation of rural health centres, one of the most important state measures of health promotion ever adopted in Greece, was a key component of the new health service. All this led to a significant increase in social expenditure.

Public spending increased during the 1982–88 period by 40 per cent (against a 28 per cent increase in the 1975–81 period), while the public debt skyrocketed.[235] Electoral expediency prevailed over economic considerations. Thus, the stabilization plan of 1985 was discontinued in 1988, in view of the impending elections.[236] For as long as possible PASOK avoided following in the footsteps of Soares in Portugal, where the brakes were applied to the expansion of real wages and public spending as soon as the socialists gained power.[237] The left-leaning trajectory of PASOK in power continued, uninterruptedly, for the first four years of its term of office, until the 1985 elections. Between 1985 and 1987, a stabilization programme (from which Papandreou cannily distanced himself), proposed by the then finance minister,

Kostas Simitis (a modernizer and future prime minister), and involving limitation of the right to strike, anti-inflationary measures and devaluation, was largely unsuccessful. Thereafter, the weight of scandals and corruption and, above all, the disillusionment resulting from the failure of the government to live up to its programme led to Papandreou's defeat in 1989.

What had happened between 1985 and 1989 was that PASOK realized it could no longer keep the outside world at bay. Financial scandals and state corruption become election losers only when they are coupled with a contraction of public spending – that is, when corruption benefits the few, instead of the many. 'Democratic' corruption takes the form of wide access to public employment jobs and to the source of public expenditure. State-sponsored, get-rich-quick schemes, such as public building contracts, can be tolerated as long as the benefits are widely spread. They become dysfunctional only to the extent that they represent a mopping-up operation of scarce resources by a few powerful people. Thus, 'democratic' corruption succeeds under the same conditions as the welfare state: regular and constant economic growth. When growth rates deteriorate, as they did in the 1980s, both the welfare state and widespread corruption enter into crisis.

Papandreou ignored the warning signs and continued the tradition of an overmanned state sector, state-dependent economic development, a rigidly regulated labour market, an extensive black economy, and a restrictive, guild-like trade union mentality.[238] PASOK had become the 'champion of the state as a mechanism for the protection of specific interests and the allocation of favours and spoils to politically loyal groups'.[239] This enabled Papandreou to maintain widespread support against all odds. It took three elections (June 1989, November 1989, April 1990) to prise him from office.

The short-lived government coalition (June–October 1989), led by Tzannis Tzannetakis, between the conservative ND and Synaspismos, the communist-led Coalition of the Forces of the Left and Progress, was the oddest in recent European history, because it brought together the bitter opponents of the civil war and symbolically ended it. The coalition programme, known as *Katharsis*, was to ensure that Papandreou would be put on trial to face charges arising from the financial scandal involving his protégé George Koskotas and the Bank of Crete, and to purge the civil service of corruption. Papandreou was acquitted. The elections of November 1989 were a blow for Synaspismos. Its electorate had obviously been alienated by the prospect of a continuing coalition with the conservatives. Thus, the Greek-style 'historic compromise' between communists and ND gave way to another provisional 'historic compromise' (November 1989 to February 1990), which included all three parties – ND, the KKE and PASOK – led by Xenophon Zolotas, the eighty-five-year-old former governor of the Bank of Greece, with the largest parliamentary majority in post-war European history: 298 seats out of 300.[240]

The stalemate was resolved with the election of April 1990 and the victory of ND. The KKE had lost its chance to make its mark on Greek politics.

In 1989 Papandreou, needing the support of the communists, had offered them a place in government in return for changing the electoral system, which had hitherto severely penalized them. Had the KKE accepted the offer, the chances of a lengthy period of PASOK–KKE government would have been excellent.[241] The KKE preferred the path of political rectitude (the *Katharsis* government). In so doing, it lost the battle and the war. PASOK and Papandreou swept back to power in 1993, and the KKE was more marginalized than ever. For all its hardline Sovietism, the KKE had behaved commendably from the point of view of the ethical values of liberal democracy, by putting principles ('clean government') before political power. It thereby once again manifested its alienation from mainstream Greek political life.

The KKE were not the only communists to discover that they had no serious future. The crumbling of the Berlin Wall in 1989 and of the USSR in 1991 simply confirmed that, for communism, history had come to an end.

What did the Left contribute to the transition to, and consolidation of, democracy in the countries of Southern Europe? This survey has established that no single force was directly responsible for the termination of the authoritarian regimes. All momentous historical events are part of a complex structural process of change and adaptation. The paradox with which socialists had to grapple was that one of the most significant ideological dimensions of the story of late capitalism was the close relationship between liberal democracy and capitalist development, and that this relationship had been established largely through their efforts. For democracy is not intrinsic to capitalist development as such; it is impossible to deduce a particular political regime from the requirements of capitalist accumulation.

Nevertheless, the Southern European authoritarian states appeared to have been inexorably pushed towards the regulated welfare-state capitalism of Western Europe. Attempts to hold back the process (protectionism, military intervention) were successful only as a delaying tactic. In the end, the regimes could not even rely on the support of the middle classes, who had realized that they had nothing to fear from democracy because it was perfectly compatible with capitalism.

The account of the three transitions highlights the activities and roles of various forces and personalities and the outcomes of a complex political chess-game. What emerges quite clearly is that the political situation determined the strategy of 'the Left', more than the converse. The Left usually reacted, seldom initiated. Before the transition, during the dictatorships, the main combatants for the establishment of a democratic order were the three communist parties, whether 'Eurocommunists' or 'unreconstructed dogmatists'. During the transition, the communists always trailed after other forces: the PCP after the MFA, the PCE after Suárez and the UCD, while, in Greece, the KKE was never a major player.

The 'liberal-conservatives', whose record during the dictatorship was usually less than glorious, came into their own during the actual transition, and guaranteed the relative smoothness of the process. The greater their importance (as in Greece and Spain), the smoother the transition. Socialists emerged only during the third phase, that of consolidation. They had to abandon their traditional aim, to overcome capitalism, as most of their counterparts in Western Europe already had. It was the socialists who 'modernized' their societies by fighting for, and promulgating, the great 'liberal' civil liberties reforms for which liberals so often failed to fight. In all three countries, the Left appeared as the most articulate proponent of a complete return to democracy. None of the communist or socialist parties involved would have settled for anything less than the kind of civil liberties which existed in the rest of Western Europe. This was true even of those organisations of the Left, such as the Greek and Portuguese communist parties, which had connived at the infringement of these same liberties in the 'socialist' countries of Eastern Europe.

The débâcle of the three southern communist parties confirms the hypothesis suggested in chapter 4, namely that the Leninist organization of the party was suited to conditions which best approximated to those of the Bolsheviks under Tsarism: a state of repression, necessitating a quasi-militarist organization of the party coupled with a single-mindedness which would make it the natural home for all those determined to fight the existing order. This form of organization was unsuited to democratic systems wherein the other party of the Left, be it socialist or socialist-populist, could provide a better alternative. Only two communist parties were able to effect the transition from clandestine work under dictatorship or occupation to open political activity in a democracy, while maintaining a hegemonic role as a rallying point of the Left: the PCF and the PCI. In the long run, even the PCF failed the decisive test; as soon as French socialism abandoned its centrist position, and defined itself as a party of social reform and not simply an anti-communist organization, the PCF began to decline. Togliatti's genius was to have realized at the moment of the transition to democracy – that is, in 1945–46 – that the military-type party, which had conducted the struggle in clandestinity, had to be ditched in favour of a broader and looser mass organization, with far less ideological control. This is what for so long saved the PCI from the ghettoization which befell its counterparts. Eventually, in order to survive, the PCI had to abandon communism altogether and embrace social democracy unambiguously, by transforming itself into the Democratic Party of the Left (see chapter 24). The enormous price the Italian Left paid for this peculiarity was that it was condemned never to reach office – the only Western European country never to have had the Left in power.

These are things which – it must be admitted – no historical reconstruction will ever demonstrate to everyone's complete satisfaction. In theory, it would be possible to imagine a transition from authoritarian rule to democracy in Spain, Portugal and Greece without the actions and sacrifices of trade unions, communist and socialist parties. Yet it is only 'in theory' that democratic transitions occur without the Left. In real history, the relatively civilized and regulated capitalism that was eventually established in Southern Europe would be unthinkable without the decisive intervention of sizeable parties of the Left.

With the arrival of democracy in Spain, Portugal and Greece, the long and difficult establishment of formal democratic rules in the advanced capitalist countries of Western Europe was complete. Most of the political and economic demands of the Erfurt Programme of 1891 (see chapter 1) had been fulfilled. Yet, as we have seen, capitalism was bursting out of its national integument, establishing itself as a world system of accumulation. In so doing, capitalism increasingly emancipated itself from the narrow bounds of the national regulatory framework, the nation-state, which had cocooned it throughout its first phase of growth and accumulation. Therewith it significantly altered the social structures confronting socialists. It is to these changes, and the wider crisis of socialism, that I shall devote the final part of this work.

PART SEVEN

The Great Crisis of Socialism

CHAPTER TWENTY-TWO

Workers, Women and Greens

Only the Workers?

'LE SOCIALISME est mort' – 'Socialism is dead' – announced Alain Touraine in 1980, on the opening page of his *L'après socialisme*.[1] Following the revolutions of 1989, Ralf Dahrendorf reiterated: 'the point has to be made unequivocally that socialism is dead, and that none of its variants can be revived for a world awakening from the double nightmare of Stalinism and Brezhnevism.'[2] Writing in 1994, Anthony Giddens was more circumspect, but still had little comfort to offer socialists: 'perhaps', he wrote, the idea of 'burying socialism' has become a reality.[3] Few socialists would have claimed the movement was healthy. As the survivors of the collapsed Soviet empire were busy rebuilding stock exchanges and pulling down statues of Lenin, only the most naïve or stout-hearted left-wing optimists could continue to say, with the once prevalent self-confidence in the movement, 'the future belongs to socialism'.

Yet in the mid-1970s much of this gloom would have appeared rather odd. At that time, the unfolding crisis seemed to be that of capitalism, not of socialism. The USA, beaten militarily by Vietnamese peasants, had devalued the dollar, pillar of the international economy and of the Bretton Woods system. Third World countries, pillaged for decades by Western imperialism, demanded and obtained the market price for their raw materials. The era of cheap primary products appeared to be over. Growth rates tumbled through-out the West, while unemployment soared, demonstrating – or so it was thought – that capitalist prosperity was ephemeral, as socialists had often predicted. Only a few years earlier, rebellious students – from Tokyo to California via Berlin, Paris and Rome – and militant workers had challenged the prevailing ideological and social consensus. Feminists were contesting ancient and hallowed norms of behaviour. In Southern Europe, right-wing regimes were toppled, while social-democratic governments dominated in the North. In the years 1974–75 there were social-democratic premiers in Austria, Belgium, Denmark, Finland, Germany, Great Britain, Holland and Sweden.[4] Socialists could legitimately look towards the future with confidence. By the 1980s, it had become apparent that this optimism was misplaced. Perhaps the economic crisis of the early 1970s, the end of the 'golden age', instead of making socialism possible, had simply been the beginning of a new phase of capitalist accumulation in which socialism would be regarded as irrelevant.

A decade later, it had become commonplace to hold that socialism – West European socialism, not the defunct Eastern variety – was in crisis. This was not a rumour put about by liberals and conservatives. It was the object of agonizing discussions and analyses by socialism's most fervent supporters. Were there objective forces or tendencies operative against the traditional agencies of socialism – political parties, their strategies and values? What was the nature of this crisis? Had the male industrial working class, the bastion of socialist parties, become a thing of the past? Had socialist and social-democratic parties, deserted by voters, ceased to win elections and form governments?

To take the last question first, there is no overwhelming evidence to suggest that socialist parties were deserted by their voters. During the 1980s, the so-called 'yuppy' decade of Margaret Thatcher and Ronald Reagan, the Left suffered serious and repeated electoral defeats only in Germany and Great Britain. Elsewhere, the verdict was not so gloomy. The advance of the Italian communists was halted after 1979, but their socialist rivals were on the move: their forceful leader, Bettino Craxi, was prime minister for five continuous years (1983–87) – quite an achievement by Italian standards. As we noted in chapter 17, socialists were returned to government in Sweden and Norway, and repeatedly confirmed in office in Austria. They dominated Spanish and Greek politics. In France, in 1981, they achieved a parliamentary majority for the first time in their history and, although they lost in 1986, they were back in power in 1988. A socialist president, François Mitterrand, became the longest ruling French head of state since Napoleon III. If elections and gaining office are the criteria for political success, then socialists in the 1980s were not unsuccessful. They performed far better than in the 1950s, when they were consistently in power only in the Scandinavian countries and Austria. Wolfgang Merkel has highlighted the exceptional stability of the vote of socialist, social-democratic and labour parties between 1945 and 1990. Their average share of the vote in this period was 31.2 per cent. During the 'golden age' (1945–73), it was 31.7 per cent. In 1974–90 this 'dropped' to 31.5 per cent:[5] not enough to warrant characterizing the 'crisis of socialism' as a crisis of electoral consent.

However, West European socialism, evolutionary 'welfare' socialism, pioneered by Bernstein, developed in Britain, Germany and Sweden, based on strong unions, state intervention and a growing public sector was, by the 1980s, unmistakably in crisis. By the 1990s, it even proved difficult to defend the gains thus far achieved: the welfare state, full employment and trade union rights; the first was in danger, the second had become a thing of the past, and the third were severely curtailed.

In the field of ideas the crisis of socialism was even more obvious. The view that the capitalist market was a highly wasteful mechanism for allocating resources, and that collective means of providing services were better than private, became unfashionable – even on the Left. The Left lost ground to those they derided in the past as the apologists of capitalism, the worshippers of the market, the high priests of the Invisible Hand. Old ideas were resurrected: serving one's own interests somehow helped everyone to prosper. The state should let people get on with their lives, limiting its role to the provision of a few ground rules – as Hayek had suggested thirty years previously. Socialists looked like an army which, though once powerful, was now everywhere in retreat, demoralized, anxious to regroup around a few ideas which it sought, unconvincingly, to defend, while accepting that much of what it had supported in the past should be discarded. As for the few remaining revolutionaries of the 1960s, they had become – to use Arthur Miller's characterization of the American communists – little more than inconsequential loiterers on the platform, waiting for the redemption train to arrive.

Socialists had run out of ideas. In the 1960s they had abandoned the aim of abolishing capitalism; in the 1970s and 1980s they proclaimed that they were the ideal managers of it. By 1989, when the Berlin Wall collapsed, the conventional reformist idea that it was necessary to possess a large public sector to countervail the negative tendencies of the private sector had evaporated from the programmes of *all* socialist parties. The privatization of the public sector, previously unthinkable even among most conservatives, came to be accepted by many socialists. The world of socialists had irrevocably changed. It no longer rested on a manufacturing society of male industrial workers. The entry of women into the workforce had feminized an already fragmenting working class. Economic growth had become problematic. The notion of class politics was being challenged. The only way forward, some claimed, was pragmatic coalition-building to maximize electoral support, by offering different things to different groups on an *ad hoc* basis in the knowledge that each group was ephemerally constructed through discourse. It was not accidental that the USA was often regarded as the model for this approach. Deprived of European-style 'class' parties and of a socialist tradition, the USA, with its multi-ethnic population, its fragmentation into a myriad of religious groupings, its highly localized interest groups, apparently showed Europe the shape of its own future – as so many writers from de Tocqueville onward have suggested.

It is, of course, true that the working class could be considered simply as a class 'out there', produced by capitalism and somehow endowed with consciousness and an implicit project (see chapter 1). The class itself, as a social group united by a common consciousness, was constructed by socialists through political struggle, though there really were industrial workers sharing similar social and economic conditions. Nevertheless, people never have a single identity and much of the struggle of politics consists in attempts to privilege a particular identity at the expense of others. When Marx and Engels concluded their famous *Manifesto* with the rousing call, 'Workers of all countries unite!' they expressed a statement of aims, not a statement of fact. A far less exciting, but more analytically correct formulation might have been: 'All wage-workers in capitalist production *should* regard their socio-economic condition as being of greater political importance than any ties they might have to a particular religion, ethnic group or nation.' They should, perhaps, but they often don't, because – as John Dunn wrote – 'There are no human beings whose sense of social identity is fully and exclusively given for themselves by the membership of the working (or any other) class.'[6] The issue of identity is far more complex than that of class. With amazing ease we slip in and out of identities. In the course of a single day, we can be a parent, a consumer, a teacher, a citizen, a transport user, a patient, a Jew, a gourmand, a taxpayer, and so on, without any consequence save the usual mildly neurotic symptoms common to late twentieth-century humans in complex 'post-industrial' societies.

For a long time, the claim of socialists (and communists) to represent a common identity was not unsuccessful. By and large, the socialist movement, at least in Europe, had obtained the allegiance of the majority of the industrial working class, though it often had to accept, recognize and at times even uphold the national or religious feelings of the workers. Although socialists never lost sight of the working class, this did not prevent them from agitating on behalf of other groups. They fought, not always consistently, for peace, for women, for minorities; above all, they fought for universal democratic and social rights. It is simply not true that socialists and communists always addressed themselves exclusively to the working class. Nor, in their everyday *practice*, did socialists ever assume that the working class was monolithic. At the end of the last century, socialist militants were well aware of the diversity in working-class experience, of the differences in skills or regional traditions, or wage levels. That such differences caused problems was recognized and constantly debated.

For all their indisputable class-centredness, parties of the Left usually realized that they needed to obtain support from other classes. As early as 1869 the leaders of the newly founded Social Democratic Workers' Party of Germany, Wilhelm Liebknecht and August Bebel, 'wanted to win over the working class without losing the democratic lower middle class groups they had organised'.[7] The universalist demands of the Erfurt Programme – a free health service, a national insurance system, the right to vote – were framed so as to include everyone. Allies in other classes were always sought. Lenin led the October Revolution on the basis of general demands: peace, bread and land. When the British Labour Party became socialist, in 1918, it opened its ranks to 'workers by brain', as its first socialist programme made clear. Italian communists after 1945 consistently courted small entrepreneurs. In 1959, at Bad Godesberg, the SPD sought to diminish its reliance on the working class and become a *Volkspartei*, a people's party. These 'revisionists' were taking stock not only of structural and economic changes, but also of the fact that democratic politics compelled socialist parties to appeal to the entire electorate.

Thus, the new 'revisionists' of the 1980s – or 'modernizers', as they preferred to be called – were not the first to attribute the difficulties facing socialists to the excessive importance they had assigned to the working class. However, unlike the revisionism of the late 1950s, which tended to be on the right of the socialist spectrum, the neo-revisionists cannot be so identified *en bloc*. Some of them, of course, belonged to the old revisionist right, but they co-existed with a new generation of activists who had discovered socialism through their experiences in the student movement, single-issue campaigns, anti-war activities and the new feminist and ecological movements.

Fewer Workers

The modernizers accepted that the industrial working class was diminishing and that a working-class identity was no longer central to many 'workers'. The question of size is relatively straightforward. Once a class is defined, all that one needs to do is count its members. In 1900 most socialists believed that, eventually, nearly everyone would be a worker. In 1990 few socialists were so disdainful of the reality before their eyes as to hold this point of view. But was the working class, however defined, actually disappearing? Had the predictions made in the course of past decades by social theorists such as André Gorz in his *Farewell to the Working Class*, or Serge Mallet in his *The New Working Class*, come true?[8] Of course, if the term 'worker' is used in the classical Marxist sense (all those who exchange their labour-power for wages), then the 'working class' would include the overwhelming majority of society – and in this sense Karl Marx and the 'vulgar' Marxists of the Second International, though computerless, were exceptionally accurate in their long-range social science forecasts: nearly everyone had become a wage-earner, there were far fewer shopkeepers and artisans, and hardly any peasants. But to hold that miners, hospital cleaners, computer operators, senior civil servants, university professors, footballers, night club bouncers and other 'wage-earners' all have an affinal class position – and *hence* the same identity and interests – is rather implausible.

If we narrow the definition and define the working class simply as all those involved in manufacturing, then the evidence presented in Tables 22.1 and 22.2 substantiates many of the empirical claims of the modernizers, though not necessarily the political implications they draw from them. Greece, Portugal and Spain, the latecomers in the race towards industrialization, were the most obvious exceptions to the general trend away from employment in manufacturing. Spain, the most advanced of the three, was already becoming 'post-industrial' in the 1980s, having peaked around 1970. Greece showed signs of having reached its peak around 1990. In Germany, Austria and Finland the manufacturing sector had resisted longer than elsewhere. In other countries the declining share of employment of manufacturing was indisputable, particularly in Scandinavia and Great Britain.

Table 22.1 Percentage of economically active population in manufacturing and social services

	Manufacturing				Community, social and personal services			
	1960–61	1970–71	1980–81	1992–93	1960–61	1970–71	1980–81	1992–93
Austria	29.8	31.5	30.4	26.6	14.1	16.0	19.6	23.4
Belgium	34.6	32.1	21.9	17.7	21.4	20.6	26.4	32.9
Denmark	28.5	25.9	17.2	19.9	22.2	24.2	32.0	35.0
Finland	21.5	24.7	24.8	18.8	14.8	18.1	24.7	31.8
France	27.0	25.8	22.3	18.9	20.1	20.1	25.4	27.8
Germany	36.5	37.6	32.7	28.2	18.8	19.0	n/a	26.5
Greece	13.4	17.2	18.7	18.8	12.1	10.8	15.0	18.9
Holland	29.9	24.0	18.8	16.6	23.5	21.1	28.6	32.7
Italy	26.6	31.1	22.3	19.8	13.5	17.4	19.3	24.9
Norway	25.5	26.7	20.2	14.3	18.4	20.2	30.4	37.2
Portugal	23.3	21.7	24.1	23.7	14.6	14.3	19.2	24.1
Spain	17.7	25.4	24.4	19.0	14.1	15.7	16.0	20.0
Sweden	34.2	28.3	24.0	16.8	19.9	26.1	34.0	37.1
UK	34.8	32.4	20.6	18.9	24.3	27.3	23.7	25.5

Notes: Column 1960–61: Spain 1950, France 1962; *Column 1970–71:* France 1968; *Column 1980–81:* France 1982; *Column 1990–91:* France 1989, Denmark and Italy 1990; figure for Germany refers to West Germany. *Community, social and personal services* corresponds to Division 9 of the Service sector. It includes domestic services, public administration, social and health services, education, entertainment and excludes all financial and business services.

Sources: ILO, *Yearbook of Labour Statistics 1945–89. Retrospective Edition on Population Censuses;* ILO, *Yearbook of Labour Statistics 1991, 1992,* and *1994.* For the 1980–81 figure for Germany, see OECD *Economic Outlook, 1960–1989 Historical Statistics.*

The 'services' columns include a range of services which are mostly associated with the public administration of 'caring' services, that is, with the welfare state (though it includes private domestic services and entertainment). Here too the trend is unmistakable: expansion in terms of employment is general, with the remarkable exception of Britain (community, social and personal services had even suffered a contraction, against a Europe-wide trend during the 1970s, which includes a period of Labour administration). By the 1990s, a greater proportion of the population was employed in the 'community' services than in manufacturing everywhere except Germany; the gap between the two was less pronounced in Austria, as well as in the 'latecomer' countries of Greece, Portugal and Spain. In all the Nordic countries, Belgium and Holland, the 'community' sector was, by far, a greater provider of employment than manufacturing. The 'post-industrial' society, at least in the advanced countries, had come of age. A considerable proportion of this 'post-industrial' sector was the direct result of the development of the welfare state. The state had thus become a major actor in the structuring of

Table 22.2 Economically active population in manufacturing and social services

	Manufacturing				Community, social and personal services			
	1960–61	1970–71	1980–81	1992–93	1960–61	1970–71	1980–81	1992–93
Austria	100	105.7	102.0	89.3	100	113.5	139.0	166.0
Belgium	100	92.8	63.3	51.2	100	96.3	123.4	153.7
Denmark	100	90.9	60.3	69.8	100	109.0	144.1	157.66
Finland	100	114.9	115.3	87.4	100	122.3	166.9	214.9
France	100	95.6	82.6	70.0	100	100.0	126.8	138.3
Germany	100	103.0	89.6	77.3	100	101.1	n/a	141.0
Greece	100	128.4	139.5	140.3	100	89.3	124.0	156.2
Holland	100	80.3	62.9	55.5	100	89.8	121.7	139.1
Italy	100	116.9	83.8	74.4	100	128.9	143.0	184.4
Norway	100	104.7	79.2	56.1	100	109.78	165.2	202.2
Portugal	100	93.1	103.4	101.7	100	97.9	131.5	165.1
Spain	100	143.5	137.8	107.3	100	111.3	113.5	141.8
Sweden	100	82.7	70.2	49.1	100	131.2	170.8	186.4
UK	100	93.1	59.2	54.3	100	112.35	97.5	104.9

Source: Table constructed on the same statistical basis as Table 22.1.

social classes. A new, wider public sector now had a stake in the expansion of the state and shared in the ethos of non-market-based public service. Significantly, this sector employed more women than men everywhere, except Spain and Greece.

The remarkable shrinking of the traditional working class is further substantiated by examining employment in the iron and steel industry, the backbone of the industrial world. In Germany there were nearly 170,000 steel-workers in 1954. Their number increased steadily, until they reached a peak in 1961 (212,000); then decline set in. By 1991, there were only 83,000. In the same period France had lost nearly 80,000 steel-workers, Belgium over

Table 22.3 Workers in the iron and steel industry, 1973–90

	1973	1990	% change
Belgium	52,512	20,019	-61.88
France	107,872	24,678	-77.12
Italy	72,795	42,359	-41.81
UK	139,601	32,799	-76.51
West Germany	171,688	86,688	-49.51

Source: Table constructed on the basis of figures in Eurostat, *Iron and Steel. Yearly Statistics 1992*, Luxemburg 1992, pp. 6 and 12.

30,000, and Britain more than 110,000. The numbers of those employed would have been even lower had not the state intervened with subsidies. Statistics on employment in other key manufacturing sectors would tell the same story. But can this numbers game explain the 'crisis' of socialism? In 1961, the 'peak' year for German steel-workers, the SPD was in opposition. Ten years later, there were 40,000 fewer steel-workers (and the country was de-industrializing), and the SPD was in power. The industrial proletariat was shrinking, but this did not correlate with the electoral history of the Left, as the electoral results in Table 16.3 show (see p. 463).[9] As Kirschelt put it: 'the varying electoral fortunes of socialist parties are all but unrelated to cross-national differences in the size of the working class or working class decline over time.'[10] The Labour Party lost four elections in a row not only because there were fewer workers, but because many workers deserted Labour. In 1979, at the general election which inaugurated the longest period of Conservative rule in Britain in the twentieth century, there was a swing away from the Labour Party of between 10 and 11 per cent among skilled workers, and as high as 16 per cent among younger working-class men.[11]

If the main problem for the Left was that it was losing the allegiance of workers, and not just that there were fewer of them, then the problem should be one of class identity, not of size. But not all 'workers' are in manufacturing industries. Too many 'proletarians', such as hospital cleaners, garbage collectors, coalminers, truck drivers, are excluded from the 'manufacturing' sector, while too many computer operators and accountants are included in it. Furthermore, the term 'post-industrial', often used in these discussions, lacks theoretical precision. Following Daniel Bell, who popularized the concept, I have used it here as shorthand for a society in which the tertiary sector has become dominant.[12] The problem is that it entirely depends on the statistical definition of the service sector. This lumps together such disparate social figures – making bus drivers 'post-industrial', along with strip-tease artistes, schoolteachers and stockbrokers – as to make sociological generalizations implausible. Finally, the pace of change has been so rapid in recent history that many of the categories used to describe the 'new' labour force correspond less and less to the reality of the labour market in the 1990s. Within the same industries one is faced with dualist labour markets: part-time against full-time, core versus periphery, Fordist production against post-Fordist, temporary against permanent employment, in-house versus contracted-out workforce, and so on. The labour market tends to a point where no single form of work is dominant.[13]

Even within the more traditional sectors of the working class, differences are so pronounced that it has become increasingly difficult for trade unions, especially centralized trade union confederations, as in Italy, Germany and Sweden, to mediate between different categories purely on the basis of wage demands.[14] Trade unions themselves ceased to be the powerful organizations they were in the 1970s. Between 1970 and 1990, union density (trade union

Table 22.4 Trade union density rates in Western Europe, 1970–90

	1970	1980	1990
Austria	62.2	56.2	46.2
Belgium	45.5	55.9	51.2
Denmark	60.0	76.0	71.4
Finland	51.4	69.8	72.0
France	22.3	17.5	9.8
Greece	35.8	36.7	34.1
Italy	36.3	49.3	38.8
Holland	38.0	35.3	25.5
Norway	51.4	56.9	56.0
Portugal	60.8	60.7	31.8
Spain	27.4	25.0	11.0
Sweden	67.7	79.7	82.5
UK	44.8	50.4	39.1
West Germany	33.0	35.6	32.9

Notes: Data for Portugal and Greece not corrected for possibly retired, unemployed and self-employed members. Data for Greece (1970, 1980), Norway (1970), Portugal (1970, 1980), Spain (1970) not exactly comparable.

Source: OECD, *Employment Outlook*, July 1994, p. 184.

membership as a percentage of wage- and salary-earners) declined through-out Western Europe, as Table 22.4 shows.

Changes in social structures and trade union density do not automatically modify political alignments. Union membership collapsed in France and Spain during long periods of socialist government, and was relatively stable in Germany while the CDU was in power. Parties well entrenched in particular regions may have established long lasting loyalties which enable them to survive these changes. In most instances such adaptation is their main guarantee of survival. For instance, in Italy the PCI – the dominant party in the Emilia-Romagna region – has remained strong (as has the PDS), even though the number of workers has decreased and the social structure has changed considerably.[15]

Rough predictions along the lines of 'the fewer workers, the fewer socialist voters' may be difficult to sustain. Nevertheless, the idea that major economic changes would have no effect on the fortunes of socialist parties is equally unsustainable. The collapse of manufacturing in much of Western Europe and North America was part of a new phase of capitalism, one in which a large factory-based working class was no longer necessary. The 'Fordist worker', whose prominence in Europe was taken for granted by the socialist tradition, had become less central to capitalism. In Europe, capitalism required a smaller, highly paid and highly flexible, skilled working class. These skilled workers were now a relatively prosperous group, a real 'aristocracy' of the proletariat', fairly well-integrated into the market economy, partaking of the abundance of consumer capitalism, requiring, if at all, the protection of organizations more similar to the craft unions of the last century than the politicized mass unions of later years.

The outcome of these processes was not only a smaller working class, but also a more fragmented one. The change in size and composition of the European (and North American) working class was a major feature of the end of the 'Fordist' phase of modern capitalism, that of the mass production of standardized commodities. The socialist movement, forced as usual to follow the development of capitalism, thus needed to develop new forms of political intervention suited to the post-Fordist age. On their own, changes do not necessarily militate against the fortunes of the Left. The key variable is the ability of the Left to exploit them. The fragmentation of the working class, mass unemployment, the decrease in manufacturing, the expansion of female labour – these could equally well have proved favourable to the Left.[16] Socialist parties themselves became increasingly dominated by middle-class activists and, as a paradoxical result, came to reflect more accurately the class basis of post-industrial society. In some cases, new anomalies appeared. For instance, the typical member of the British Labour Party – one of the most class-bound parties of Europe, in terms of image and rhetoric – was, by 1989, middle-class, middle-aged and male.[17] Only one in four members was a manual worker.[18] Among the individual members of the Labour Party, more belong to the white-collar public sector union NALGO – not affiliated to the party – than to any other union; more are members of the Association of University Teachers than of the National Union of Mineworkers.[19] The average Labour Party member was considerably richer than the average voter: in 1989 30 per cent of members belonged to households earning more than £20,000 a year, while only 6 per cent of voters were so fortunate.[20]

Some social scientists argued that classes were still a major factor of self-identification and that the parties of the Left would gain little by abandoning class appeal. Their task is to mobilize as many members of 'their' class, without losing support in other classes.[21] Other analysts propounded a 'dealignment' theory (a variant of the idea of multiple identities), suggesting that being a worker was no longer electorally significant: social complexity had increased, while modern communications and social and geographical mobility had changed the way individuals related to each other.[22] Dealignment theorists pointed out that the British Labour Party's share of the working-class vote fell from 62 per cent to 42 per cent between 1945 and 1983.[23] Nor was this an exclusively British phenomenon. In the 1980s many European workers were beginning to desert their traditional parties. In Germany, for instance, over one million blue-collar workers in the Rhine–Ruhr region turned away from the social democrats to support the CDU.[24] In Italy the PCI began to lose workers in the industrial belts around Milan and Turin, while in France the PCF could no longer count on the loyal support of the workers in the *banlieue* of Paris.[25]

Table 22.5 How Britain voted in 1992: percentage of voters

	Results	Women	Men	AB	C1	C2	DE
Electorate		52	48	19	24	27	30
Conservative	43	44	41	56	52	39	31
Labour	35	34	37	19	25	40	49

Source: Adapted from MORI table in David Butler and Dennis Kavanagh, *The British General Election of 1992*, Macmillan, London 1992, p. 277.

What was really in dispute was the electoral behaviour of the skilled working class, once a bastion of the Left and now electorally volatile. Other groups were more predictable. Taking as an example the 1992 British election results, it is clear from Table 22.5 that – to use simple language – the more money one has, the more likely one is to vote for the Conservative Party.

The top two census groups, the managerial and professional middle classes (A and B), and the skilled non-manual workers (C1) voted disproportionately for the Conservatives. The Labour Party did very well in the bottom two groups (D and E), the semi-skilled and unskilled. The skilled manual workers (the C2 group), however, were almost equally divided between Labour and Conservative. If dealignment occurred anywhere, it was in this group. In the UK no other social cleavage, be it age, gender or occupation, appeared to be a better predictor of voting than class cleavage, although, at least since 1987, there was significant subdivision within the middle class: those working within the public sector were far less pro-Conservative than those in the private sector – though, of course, the Tories had a majority in both sub-groups.[26]

The problem with social classes is that they do not stand still.

Working Women

I turn now to an examination of the growing feminization of the labour force and the growth, in many countries, of part-time work. Drawing a precise picture of these changes is an intricate task. All the following section aims to do is to provide an impression of the growing social complexity of the world of labour, the intersection between class segmentation and political action faced by socialists as they approached the end of the century.

We can start, conventionally, by noting that technology accelerates the process of change, affecting the boundaries between skills and creating new jobs. A typical example was the rapid disappearance, throughout most of Europe, of the category of print workers, who were overwhelmingly male and well-paid. Thanks to the development of computer-related technology (photosetting), the print workers were eliminated. In many instances, this led to the employment of women workers (who had typing skills) and the enhancement of home working, piece rates, jobs without security. These jobs were considered to be less skilled than those of printers and paid accordingly.[27]

Changes in the composition of the working class were indissolubly linked to its feminization. This was brought about by the increase in female employment in the 1970s as full male employment began to collapse. This, however, was not a universal phenomenon even in the advanced countries. Germany, which in 1960 had a considerable proportion of working women, in the 1980s had a relatively low female participation rate (this is obtained by dividing the total female labour force by the potential female labour force, i.e. women between the school-leaving age and the retirement age). This was due to the fact that, in the 1980s, German economic restructuring was led by the manufacturing sector and not – as in Sweden or Britain – by a rapidly expanding service sector. Moreover, the celebrated German apprenticeship system, which provided access to the best jobs in manufacturing, was dominated by boys, while girls preferred to stay on in education.[28] A pronounced feminization of the labour force occurred in Britain and Holland in the 1980s in the form of an expansion of part-time labour, while in Italy, where, officially, only 10 per cent of women workers were part-timers, the same process was a direct result of the growth of the informal economy. In the American electronics industry, the prevalence of women workers had been well-established for a while: in Santa Clara County, California, women working in this industry outnumbered men by two to one in the semi-skilled and unskilled categories as early as 1970.[29]

It was becoming increasingly difficult to describe the 'typical' worker as a man employed for over forty hours a week in heavy industry. Classes were not disappearing; they were changing. The massive increase in female workforce participation which occurred in Britain was a recent phenomenon. As Catherine Hakim has shown, there was no substantial change in workforce participation between 1851 and the late 1980s: 'adult women's economic activity rates were no higher in the period 1951–1971 than they had been a century earlier in 1851–1871, standing at 42–44 per cent in both periods.'[30] What happened was that there were fewer full-time and more part-time male workers in Britain. The number of full-time male workers dropped from just over 15.2 million men in 1951 to 12.8 million in 1991. In 1951 there were hardly any part-time male workers, while in 1991 there were one and a half million – that is, 11 per cent of the male workforce. A similar trend was taking place in the Nordic countries.[31] As for female full-time employment, this was, between 1951 and 1991, remarkably stable in Britain, at around the six million mark. The real increase was in female part-timer workers. In 1951 there were only 784,000, in 1991 5.1 million, or 45 per cent of the total number of women employed.[32] In other words, the general trend is that, while overall employment was falling, there was a substantial increase in part-time work, much of which was accounted for by female labour, as Table 22.6 indicates.

Table 22.6 Women and part-time work, 1992–93

	A: Part-time employment as a proportion of total employment	B: Women's share in part-time employment	C: % of women employed in part-time work in the European Community, 1993.
Austria	9.1	89.1	25.0
Belgium	12.4	89.7	25.0
Denmark	22.5	75.8	40.1
Finland	7.9	64.3	
France	12.7	83.7	23.8
Germany	14.1	91.0	30.7
Greece	4.8	61.3	8.0
Holland	32.8	75.0	60.1
Ireland	n/a	n/a	16.5
Italy	5.9	68.5	10.9
Luxemburg	6.9	88.5	16.4
Norway	26.9	80.1	
Portugal	7.2	67.4	10.0
Spain	6.5	76.8	11.9
Sweden	24.3	82.3	
UK	23.5	85.2	43.6

Sources A and B: Department of Employment cited in the *Financial Times*, 29 September 1994, p. 8; 1992 figures. C: Eurostat, *Unemployed Women in the EC. Statistical Facts*, Brussels and Luxembourg 1995, pp. 18–19.

Not only was the British working class being feminized, but it was increasingly a dualistic class, made up of a stagnant or declining sector of full-time employees (two-thirds men) and an expanding and mainly female sector of part-timers.[33] Until the late 1980s, 'The much trumpeted rise in women's employment in Britain consisted entirely of the *substitution of part-time for full-time jobs* from 1951 to the late 1980s.'[34] After 1988, a new trend, as yet unexplained, emerged: a sharp rise in *full-time* female employment. In Germany, part-time employment was the fastest growing sector of the labour market, with an expansion rate of over 40 per cent. Though this increase slowed down in the 1980s to about 13 per cent, there were three times more part-time workers, overwhelmingly women, at the end of the 1980s than during the 1960s.[35] Table 22.6 shows the significant difference in part-time female employment in Western Europe.

There are many obvious differences between a working class made up of (mainly female) part-timers and one made up of (still mainly male) full-timers. The most significant is that work, for part-timers, was unlikely to be the defining activity of their lives. Most part-timer female workers positively want a part-time job and have different work priorities from traditional male workers – which is why they are typically restricted to low-skill jobs with low earnings.[36] Part-timers have low status, little influence, little incentive to change their work. In Britain they tend not to be unionized. They are less protected even in the Nordic countries. In Sweden, for instance, part-time workers are excluded from unemployment compensation if they work fewer then seventeen hours a week (twenty in Denmark and Finland).[37] Part-time jobs were paid less per hour than the equivalent full-time job.[38]

In Britain, women 'working part-time or not at all hold the most traditional sex-role attitudes and are married to men with even more extreme views of women's roles'.[39] The conservatism of part-time female workers lies in their attitude to gender roles, rather than in their voting preferences, because there are no significant electoral differences between housewives and women in paid employment.[40] Studies of marital power found that male dominance was greater when the wife was a home-maker, or a part-time worker, than when she had a full-time occupation.[41] Research into the division of household chores has shown that housework is far more likely to be shared equally when the woman has a full-time job. Women working part-time carried virtually the same responsibility for house and family as women who were not employed.[42] The women who provided feminism with its core of activists and supporters were those employed full-time (preponderantly the educated). They were unlikely to be supported by women in part-time occupations. Here, at least, the traditional socialist view, which assumed that participation in paid work would be a radicalizing experience, found some empirical verification. It also meant, however, that the exacerbation of the division of the working class into part-time and full-time threatened both the traditional labour movement and the feminist movement. It does not follow that the only alternatives facing socialist feminists were either an unrealistic rearguard action aimed at restoring the status quo ante, or a supine acceptance of the increasing dualism of the labour force. What did follow was that the length of the working day, the issue over which the labour movement fought one of its first battles, was likely to re-emerge as a crucial question for the twenty-first century. The abolition of dualism could occur by drastically redefining full-time work through a significant reduction of the length of the working day, in order to 'put an end to the present distinction between "part-time" and "full-time" workers, which acts so much to women's disadvantage'.[43] Alternatively, part-time work could cease to be a lifelong condition in which an overwhelmingly female, low-skilled and low-paid workforce is for ever enclosed, becoming, instead, a temporary phase in everyone's life.[44] Either way – and the two are not mutually exclusive – the socialist movement and the trade unions in particular would be compelled to re-examine their traditional antagonism to labour market flexibility – the battle-cry of the Right in the 1980s and 1990s.

Gender differences underlay even the diversity of unemployment experience. Female unemployment was the result of the fact that the employment opportunities available for women did not keep pace with the increase in the number of women in the labour force. Women were 'ahead' of economic development. Male unemployment was a consequence of the decline in industrial employment and the low growth rate of male employment in the service sector.[45] In other words, it was a reflection of the de-industrialization of the advanced economies after 1973. The increase in female unemployment was due to the growing tendency of women to stay in the labour force (often as part-timers) even after they had married and had children, and thus to a change in attitude, mentality and expectation.

The occupation gap between women and men narrowed everywhere, but not at the same rate. By the mid-1980s it was still fairly high in Holland and Italy, was closing rapidly in Austria, Germany, the UK and Belgium, and had virtually disappeared in Sweden and Finland.[46] In Norway the participation rate of women – not particularly high in the 1960s – almost doubled in the 1970s, while that of men continued to decline.[47] The 'quality' gap between the sexes – i.e. the fact that men were still massively over-represented in the better paid and more responsible jobs – was still very wide.

The new, post-golden age capitalism marked the beginning of the end of the separation of women from paid employment in productive life, a separation which had started with the early, skills-based phase of industrial capitalism. This, at least in the advanced countries, signalled the end of the dominant Fordist system of production based on the male industrial worker, in which 'his' job description and 'his' wages … were at the centre of the bargaining process between employers and unions and … provided the focus of state policies.[48]

The labour movement was ill-equipped to deal with the new inequalities arising, almost inevitably, from the less secure, part-time and low-paid nature of women's occupations. Though these inequalities appeared to grow out of the productive process, they reverberated through the rest of society. Women were caught in a classic vicious circle. Because of their family commitments, women 'preferred' part-time work.[49] Because they worked part-time, there were fewer incentives for women living with full-time working partners to redress the unequal division of unpaid work in the home. For other women, who found themselves raising a family on their own – a result of the growth in divorce and separations – the volume of unaided 'caring' work made career-oriented full-time employment more difficult – particularly if child-care arrangements were not satisfactory. To equalize responsibilities between men and women would require a long-term perspective and involve a profound change in values beyond the scope of governments – although they could of course significantly contribute to it.

Like all complex structural changes, these issues presented specific problems to the parties of the Left. They discovered that most policies, like most things in life, were not gender-neutral. For instance, many anti-unemployment policies aimed at job preservation and protection – such as keeping 'uneconomic' coalmines working – usually favoured male employment.

Conversely, attempts to bolster occupations in the service sector were likely to lead to a greater proportion of female employment. This is what happened in the 1970s, when an increase in public sector jobs led to more female employment.[50] Tables 22.1 and 22.2 revealed the spectacular growth of 'caring' services in most countries. This explains why Sweden, where the housewife, as a social category, had been virtually eliminated, had one of the most severely segregated labour markets in the West.[51] In effect, women's traditional role was socialized. The extensive Swedish child-care programme expanded employment opportunities for married women, while providing them with additional jobs in child-care centres. What women had always done, unpaid, in the home, was now done outside it, paid by the state. In this way Sweden's model of development, aimed at reinforcing 'class' solidarity, also reinforced separate spheres for men and women in production and social policy.[52] In general, as the OECD noted in 1980, the higher the female participation rate, the higher the level of job segregation.[53] This is less true where female participation is full-time. For instance, in Britain the substantial increase in *full-time* female employment in the late 1980s led to a decrease in occupational segregation.[54]

To combat job segregation, the socialist parties would have needed to combat the division between part-time and full-time work and labour market dualism. This was politically difficult. When in power, under the pressure of rising unemployment, socialist parties defended traditional male jobs through subsidies, and expanded female employment by increasing welfare spending and public sector employment. This dual action was a consequence of the dual role of socialist parties: as trade-union-based 'industrial' parties, they defend traditional male employment; as welfare parties, they tried to expand public services, thus contributing to the growth of female employment. But through the deregulation of the labour market, conservatives too helped to provide more jobs for women. The leaner, smaller and more flexible industrial sector and the expanding private service sector attracted low-paid and part-time female labour. Thus, the contrasting policies of both Left and Right effectively promoted the expansion of female employment.

More women at work does not render them more equal with men. Providing women with more part-time jobs helps them and their households financially, but has little to do with equality. A fairer distribution of hours between women and men would be an advance, assuming that this would provide conditions for a fairer division of domestic labour as well. A full-time job in addition to all the ordinary household chores is hardly a liberation – as Soviet women discovered to their cost. Nevertheless, full-time employment for women is a better road towards equality than part-time. But under which conditions would an expansion of full-time employment for women occur?

The conditions are institutional, cultural and political. They are not generated by 'spontaneous' capitalist development. The differences between

France and Britain illustrate this point. By 1989, the female participation rate was exactly the same in both countries.[55] The difference was in part-time work, which was far more prevalent in Britain than in France: 45 per cent in Britain and 23 per cent in France.[56]

Surveys in France, including data from the 1982 census, showed that, before the 1980s, female participation (which was mainly full-time) decreased after the birth of the first child and increased again when the children were grown-up. In the course of the 1980s, this 'dip' disappeared, but female employment remained substantially full-time and increased in jobs requiring a professional qualification. Thus, in France, the feminization of employment became particularly strong in jobs with executive functions – what the French call the *cadres*.[57]

How did French women manage to hold down skilled full-time jobs even with small children? French men had little to do with it. French employers had fewer incentives to employ part-timers than their British counterparts. France – like all European countries, except Britain, Italy and Ireland – gave part-time workers the same legal rights as full-timers, with regard to job protection, notice periods and redundancy pay.[58] An important reason for the greater proportion of mothers in full-time employment in France was that child-care was more widely available in France than in Britain.[59] In Britain, to be the mother of a child of pre-school age was a real obstacle to full-time employment: in the European Union, only Holland has a worse full-time participation rate for mothers of young children.[60] Even though the rate of employment of mothers with children under five increased in Britain between 1983 and 1989, it remained well below that of other mothers.[61] Britain – where the market was left to determine the pattern of child-care arrangements – had the worst child-care provisions for children under school age in the European Community;[62] it was the only EC country not to offer all employed pregnant women maternity leave and to have no statutory parental leave (with Ireland and Luxembourg).[63] In France, by contrast, the employment rate among women with very young children (under five) was similar to that of women with children between the ages of five and nine. A French mother could count on an extensive network of scholastic and para-scholastic arrangements to take charge of her child throughout the day without interruption.[64] This could not be attributed either to the strength of the Left in France (in opposition until 1981) or to French trade unions (the weakest in Europe) or to French feminism (an intellectual élite) but to decades of French pro-natalist policies. The aim of such policies was not to liberate women, or enable them to pursue successful careers, but to make sure that they would go on having children.

In Sweden, in contrast to both France and Britain, the Left was instrumental in bringing about a state-sponsored and heavily subsidized child-care system to enable more women to work full-time. This public day-care programme was the most radical item in the 1982 manifesto of the social democrats.[65] Feminists, of course, had no reason to idealize the Swedish system: in spite of its advanced nature, most Swedish women were still economically dependent on men's income.[66]

In some circumstances, tax policies were highly effective in expanding female participation. For instance, in 1971, tax reform in Sweden established the principle of separate assessment. In a regime of high marginal tax rates, this favoured female employment, since joint assessment would result in the woman's initial earnings (assuming the male partner was already employed) being immediately taxed at the high marginal rate.[67] The tax reform also contributed to a decrease in part-time work.[68] In Germany, until 1982, the tax regime discouraged female employment, because couples where only one person was gainfully employed benefited more than two-income families.[69] However, if the aim was to encourage women to work outside the home, it was necessary to provide the jobs as well. Here Sweden did far more than Germany. Work opportunities for women were promoted through an unprecedented increase in employment in health, education and welfare.[70] A strong, independent feminist movement was not a major factor in this; in Sweden, as in other Nordic countries, women rarely organized separately from the established political parties.[71]

In France, the employment policies of the Mitterrand presidency, which aimed at increasing jobs in general, benefited women disproportionately, with 70 per cent of the 167,000 public sector jobs created in the first year going to women.[72] The socialist government also established a Ministry of the Rights of Women. The Loi Roudy of 13 July 1983, named after the minister, Yvette Roudy, made discrimination on grounds of sex illegal.[73] The law of 10 July 1982 gave juridical status (pensions and benefits) to the spouses of merchants and artisans (300,000 women), who were in effect working as partners or employees, but without rights.[74]

In Italy, the development of the informal or 'black' economy achieved what public sector expansion had done elsewhere: it became the major source of female labour. This was an unintended result of trade union strength after 1969, which had produced a rigidly regulated labour market. Overtime had been reduced and equal pay for equal work introduced, thus eliminating the cost competitiveness of female labour. The Statuto dei Lavoratori made redundancies difficult, especially in large firms where enforcement of the law could not be avoided. This favoured the development of the new Italian 'model', based on highly flexible small firms operating in the informal economy. After 1973, these firms reversed the trend of the 1960s and absorbed female labour in increasing quantities. Of the one and a half million people newly employed between 1972 and 1980, only 253,000 were men, while 1,247,000 were women. This was also a major factor behind the rapid decline in childbirth.[75] As Daniela Del Boca pointed out, 'All the usual characteristics of women's labor force participation – high turnover, willingness to work fewer hours, a discontinuous work life – which made women less sought after in the larger industrial sector, turned out to be advantageous for the small firm sector.[76] Employers now had an incentive to hire women. Since these firms had to respond rapidly to changes in demand, and since female turnover was high, employers could avoid costly lay-offs. Moreover, in firms with fewer than fifteen employees, little or no unionization combined with ineffective law enforcement to enable employers to dismiss workers at will, avoid social security payments, and maintain a high gender-based wage differential.[77] A paradoxical conclusion must be drawn. Thanks to the vigorous action of the Italian trade unions, a vast protective system had been erected. It sheltered a large proportion of employed men, but at the expense of young recruits seeking 'real jobs' in the 'official' sector. Most of the new jobs available were in the informal sector. They were highly precarious, poorly paid and badly protected. As there were no unemployment benefits, the new entrants, mainly women and the young, could not afford to be choosers.[78]

Sex Equality

Various factors contributed to increased female participation in the labour market: new 'post-Fordist' capitalist development; 'post-industrial' expansion; growth in employment in the social and welfare services; the availability of child-care; and fiscal incentives. Left or left-inspired policies played a sub-sidiary role. Many of the jobs women acquired had been created by the expansion of the 'socialist' public sector. Many, however, were also the result of the 'spontaneous' workings of the 'free market'. The increased productivity of domestic labour had been considerably enhanced by consumer goods, such as washing machines and convenience foods, which enabled women to seek paid employment. Capitalism appeared to 'liberate' women from domestic drudgery — without inconveniencing the men. Feminists pointed out that liberation was hardly an appropriate description for those relegated to the lowest grades, denied equality at home, and dignity and self-esteem in civil society.

The wider equality women wanted was a distant and imprecise goal, which political parties were unable to define in legislative terms. Equality at work was more easily pinpointed. Equal pay had been accepted as a principle long before the 1970s, but gender discrimination produced either outright under-payment of women, or the downgrading of jobs mainly performed by women. By the early 1970s, most socialist parties had eagerly embraced the concept of equal pay. The new climate created by feminist activists had put pressure on socialists and trade unionists to 'do something about women'. Equal pay was a 'woman' issue which could easily be absorbed in the traditional frame-work of socialist policies: it had to do with wages, working women and, therefore, class.

The 'normal' European pattern was for the principle of non-discrimination to be enshrined in the constitution – for instance, the German Basic Law (Article Three, paragraph 3); the general principles of the constitutions of the French Fourth and Fifth Republics; Article Three of the Italian constitution; the Treaty of Rome – as well as in ordinary legislation, such as the Equal Pay Act of 1970 in Britain or the 1972 Works Constitution Act in Germany. Legal rights, however, often needed to be fought for. In Germany, works councils made inadequate use of the rights available to them to enforce anti-discriminatory legislation. In Britain, the law contained many loopholes and allowed employers to leave women in lower-paid grades.[79]

This legislative road was one of two strategies available to resolve wage inequality. The other was collective bargaining. Which of the two would prevail depended on the institutional political framework. The Swedish SAP and the trade unions refused to treat women as a special case, preferring to use the solidaristic wages policy to reduce the differentials between low and high wages. This was a non-gender specific-policy, which helped women more than men because they constituted the majority of the low paid.[80] By the early 1980s, the hourly rate of Swedish women in manufacturing was 90 per cent of that of men – the narrowest gap in Europe. Clearly, Swedish women had gained more from collective bargaining than women elsewhere had achieved through equal pay legislation.[81] In Sweden it had been the Folkpartiet (Liberal Party), rather than the SAP, which had campaigned on this issue and which, as a member of the 'bourgeois' government, introduced the Act of Equality Between Men and Women (1980), outlawing discrimination and establishing an equality ombudsman and a commission, as had Britain. (The concept of ombudsman, however, came from Norway, *ombud* meaning commissioner.)[82]

Swedish social democrats, trade unionists as well as employers, however, stuck to the view that work equality issues were best dealt with by collective bargaining.[83] To some extent, they were right: in Sweden and Norway (where it was the Labour Party which had passed the Equal Status Act), anti-discrimination legislation achieved little.[84] The best available systematic comparison of Sweden and Britain showed that non-gender-specific Swedish policies proved more effective than British legislation.[85] The combination of centralized collective bargaining with high public sector employment and expenditure and an active labour market policy contributed more to bridging the pay gap than a 'liberal' approach relying mainly on legislation.[86]

In Britain, in the 1970s, the fragmented trade union movement was ill-equipped for an egalitarian incomes policy, while public spending cuts prevented a Swedish-style expansion of the public sector. An efficient way to bridge the wage gap among low-income groups would have been non-gender-specific legislation such as a minimum wage, but it was feared that this would increase wage costs excessively. Because women earners were at the bottom of the pay league, any measure – such as a legally enforceable minimum wage or a flat-rate incomes policy which raises low incomes –

would have had an effect disproportionately favourable to women. Thus, the considerable improvement in the relative earnings of low-paid women which occurred in 1976–77 is probably to be attributed to the flat-rate incomes policy, possibly combined with the effect of employers having to meet the deadline for the implementation of the Equal Pay Act in 1975.[87]

The British Labour Party's policy towards women remained based on the less efficient, but cheaper, legislative road, largely unopposed by the Conservatives.[88] British unions, stimulated by the growth of female membership and feminism, achieved notable legislative gains for their women members on equal pay, sex discrimination and maternity leave.[89] Nevertheless, given the unions' decreasing strength in the 1980s, the lack of commitment of many local union officials, for whom equal pay was a minor issue, and women's failure to put pressure on management and unions for equal pay, the legislation failed to achieve even its own limited objectives.[90] Equal pay and anti-discriminatory legislation did little to reduce job segregation and income inequality. This is not to say that such legislation was useless. The effectiveness of laws cannot always be judged in terms of their overt intention or immediate political effects. Laws are often made to express collective ethical principles, to establish a climate of opinion and the state's disapproval of certain discriminatory practices. It compels those who wish to discriminate to do so by subterfuge, through technicalities or in defiance of the law. Like all the great constitutional principles – liberty, equality, solidarity – anti-discrimination legislation anticipates a future, desirable state of affairs. National legislation was usually less effective than the subsequent equal pay directives of the European Commission. On the basis of Article 119 of the Treaty of Rome, the European Community adopted binding directives which forced all member states to change their national equality statutes.[91] Women's rights were further extended by a number of Court of Justice rulings and by the EEC Charter on Basic Social Rights of October 1989 – opposed only by the Thatcher administration.[92] The result of all this is that women's rights had been enhanced and better protected by a supra-national body (originally disdained by most parties of the Left), rather than through nationally elected assemblies.

Equal pay was never a straightforward matter of differences at the workplace. It could help, in some instances, to bridge an overtly wide wage gap between men and women doing the same job, but it could not modify the overall gap between the earnings of men and women resulting from the differences in work experience (men's being more continuous than that of women), and from the kind of education received.[93] Women's position in the labour market was far more affected by their domestic responsibilities, and the conditions under which they entered the labour market, than by direct sexual discrimination.[94] In most instances, cultural factors were the main obstacles to parity.

The gender conflict was part of a relatively peaceful, but nevertheless momentous, social upheaval, a true revolution which forced everyone – not only socialists – to adjust. Conservatives faced a particular predicament: the traditional family they defended was being eroded by the capitalist system they staunchly upheld. The parties of the Left, traditionally committed to the emancipation of women and their integration into the labour market, were faced with a paradox of a different nature. Women were becoming 'productive' workers in unprecedented numbers According to socialist ideology, this would make them more susceptible to left-wing values. However, women were not, on the whole, joining a skilled and highly unionized proletariat, but a de-regulated labour market of the kind socialists had fought against for over a hundred years.

The feminization of the working class, which socialists had always believed would shift women's consciousness towards socialism, was thus an ambivalent phenomenon. Socialists believed that it was necessary to fight alongside women workers against discrimination, not only as a matter of principle, but also to avoid the formation of a parallel workforce able to undercut male employment. The problem, if it was a problem, was that the 'new' lean and agile capitalism favoured women workers because they were more flexible, less unionized, could be paid less, and were allegedly more docile.[95] Socialists opposed deregulation and fought for equal rights in the work-place, while recognizing that the full realization of such goals would en-danger the competitive advantage of female labour. They were finally taking women's demands seriously, but the time was not propitious. In the 1980s, even modest objectives were more difficult to achieve, because they required an expansion in the funding of the welfare state or a stronger regulation of the labour market. A growing consensus, supported by the Right, was clamouring for state expenditure to be reduced and labour market flexibility to be restored.

In any case, the minimalist reforms advocated by socialists to make it easier for mothers to find jobs seemed based on the assumption that the problem was to enable women to be in the workplace like men, while little else needed to change. Yet, it was becoming clear that the old model of welfare capitalism in a regulated full employment labour market was no longer valid. The model had been devised when the system of production was industrial, the workers were mainly men, families were relatively stable, and women stayed at home as carers or worked intermittently. The situation established at the end of the nineteenth century had changed. What had occurred then was the rupture of the link between women and paid work. This link had existed in rural society and in the first, 'primitive' phase of capitalist accumulation, when women went down the mines and worked with their children in factories. A new form of family – modelled on that of the relatively prosperous middle class – had become the central cultural model. Its foundations were a male producer, separated from his children, and transformed into a provider of cash (in exchange for various services), and

a female consumer involved in the production of 'unpaid' family services –
in reality, non-tradable services 'paid' by the sustenance brought home by the
man. To a large extent, modern notions of masculinity and femininity were
defined by these distinctions and intertwined with more ancient ones. The
blurring of separate roles and boundaries produced the contemporary period
of gender conflict. Women (re)entered the world of production, to find it
had become a male world. At first, working women were compelled to adapt
to an alienating environment. As their numbers expanded, the workplace
altered until all participants, not only the women, faced a problem of
adaptation. At the same time, men too, albeit with fewer problems, began to
enter a hitherto unfamiliar world, that of supermarkets and consumption.[96]
Men, however, were less familiar than women with the complex and bewilder-
ing maze of contradictory injunctions which is part of the modern condition.
In the 1950s, women's magazines urged their readers to be good full-time
wives *and* to take advantage of the new consumer goods, which would be
available to them only if they also worked.[97] By the 1980s, new magazines
urged them to have a successful career, master the intricacies of *nouvelle
cuisine*, excel in love-making, look glamorous and be good mothers. Men were
still expected to be just men.

This 'male' model of production was a historically determined construct
characteristic of Europe, Japan and North America. Even in Britain, where
industrialism began, there was at first a preponderance of female and child
labour, at least among the unskilled.[98] Until the first half of the nineteenth
century, only a minority of men supported, on their own, their entire family.
The historical life-span of the 'male model of production' has thus coincided
with that of the traditional organized labour movement. It can be roughly
calculated as enduring, from country to country, for between seventy-five
and one hundred and fifty years.

The preponderance of male labour is not an iron law of industrialization;
nor is it a universal stage through which all countries have to progress. It has
not been a feature of the newly industrialized countries, such as South Korea
and the Philippines, Singapore and Taiwan, where women are a majority of
the industrial labour force. China, the likely dominant producer of the twenty-
first century, will probably follow this 'Asian' pattern too.

The feminization of the working class is a worldwide phenomenon, part
of what Alain Lipietz has called 'primitive Taylorization'. Specific segments
of production are transferred from the centre (the old industrialized countries)
to states where the rate of exploitation is high, wages low, and the working
day long. Products are then re-exported to the centre. This process occurs
principally in textiles and electronics, both ideally suited to Taylorist production: they are labour-intensive; jobs are fragmented and repetitive; there
is no assembly line; and they require light equipment for a single operator
– a sewing machine in clothing, and tweezers and a microscope in electronics.[99] This labour is overwhelmingly performed by women. For instance,

in Malaysia, women carry out 70 per cent of all unskilled work in textiles and 80 per cent in electronics – the industries which provide the country with most of its export earnings.[100] Moreover, in Asia women also do most of the traditional plantation work: tea, rubber, cocoa and coffee. The men remain on the farms, engaging in pre-capitalist work for the home market, or move to city slums, and join the unemployed and the new lumpenproletariat.

Even educational opportunities in many of the newly industrializing countries do not replicate the gender pattern of the West. For example, Western engineering faculties are still totally dominated by men, even though half of those in higher education are women; while in Singapore, 23.8 per cent of female students are studying engineering.[101]

Thus, there is no necessary connection between patriarchy, a near-universal phenomenon, and the specific modern sexual division of labour in the West. Was the malaise of late twentieth-century socialism due, at least in part, to its being a Western system so wedded to a specifically Western 'male' production model as to be unable to extract itself from it? As a male-dominated movement, committed to 'the working class' in the traditional sense, was socialism doomed to follow the decline of this model and disappear with it? Would this new 'feminized' working class force traditional class issues into the background? Have non-class identities overwhelmed older proletarian ones? Should socialist parties pay heed to new non-class identities, new issues and new politics? These are not questions which can be answered with any confidence in what are the early stages of a momentous transformation. There are times when it is more important to ask the questions than to provide the answers.

The 'New Politics'?

There are those who claim that class has become a less important factor in determining identity, and hence voting choices. Consequently, they say, issues have become more relevant to the formation of identities[102] and socialist parties should dispose of 'classes' and adopt 'issues'. It does not follow, however, that issues should be contrasted with class, unless by 'class' one means a group of people welded together by an invariant set of interests. Socialist parties (and many non-socialist ones) have often linked issues to classes. For instance, in Wilhelmine Germany, the SPD – followed by most of the parties of the Second International – turned anti-militarism, which has no fixed class 'sign', into a class issue by claiming that war was the inevitable outcome of capitalist competition. Such examples are common.

In the 1970s and 1980s, it was not just class which was being challenged, but the idea that all political differences could be located on a Right–Left spectrum. The time for such dichotomies – it was claimed – was over. New issues, beyond both Left and Right, were advanced by young 'post-materialist' cohorts, who took it for granted that Western societies had achieved material wealth and well-being.[103] A new individualism, or new 'subjectivity', was said to challenge the 'old' parties across the board: representative democracy, patriarchy, Adamticism and commitment to growth. The point, however, is that 'Left' and 'Right' are always being redefined, often in response to social and political change.

As new issues arise, they are taken up by political parties and inserted into their existing discourse. Under certain circumstances, being against nuclear power or being a pacifist becomes a part of Left identity. How this occurs is not always clear. An issue may be generated by a combination of actual events, the activities of pressure groups, the influence of the media, the disposition of active party supporters, the inclination of the leaders, the strength of public opinion. An issue becomes part of the world-view of a party only through a complex and continuing political struggle. This is how parties commit themselves, perhaps temporarily, to positions which can be described as pro-European, anti-war, pro-feminist or pro-Third World. Because parties are already located on a Left–Right continuum, new issues are taken on board as further signifiers of leftism or rightism (or centrism). Issues, however, are seldom 'innocent' or 'above' politics. Some are more compatible than others with existing political discourses. For instance, it may be argued that pacifism, in the abstract, has no definite Left–Right connotation, whereas in the specific conditions of the 1970s and 1980s it entailed embracing a 'left' view of international affairs. Not many socialist parties, especially those in power, accepted such pacifism. Nevertheless, most pacifists were on the Left while trying, in order to widen their appeal, to appear as 'non-party' as possible. Had nuclear weapons been aimed at right-wing regimes, we might have expected to see a different Right–Left alignment. Feminism, a 'new politics' issue *par excellence*, is far more likely to be embraced by socialists (and socialism by feminism) than by conservatives.[104]

In the 1970s and 1980s, supporters of pacifism, feminism and ecology were mainly on the left of the political spectrum, though that never stopped them from challenging socialist and communist parties over ideology, basic aims, style, image and organization. They were innovative at a time when established left-wing parties appeared to have run out of ideas. The emergence of these movements coincided with the transformation of the working class sketched above. They appeared to be both the bearers and the symptoms of the transition to a 'post-industrial' society. Consequently, many argued that socialist parties would do well to widen their appeal to the predominantly middle-class supporters of the new social movements, so as to compensate for their increasing difficulty in mobilizing a rapidly changing working class. In politics nothing is quite as simple as this. New issues did not always appeal to existing working-class supporters of socialist and communist parties; nor did they attract significant middle-class support. While a movement like that of the greens may have drawn its support overwhelmingly from the middle class, its supporters represented a very specific sector of that class –

one which regarded monetary rewards as inadequate recompense for the deterioration of the environment. Lower-income groups could not make a similar computation: they had just achieved some material well-being and had little to give up. As for the majority of the middle classes, they remained trapped in a mentality which held that greater personal prosperity was the overarching goal.

For the parties of the Left a complicated balancing act between these groups was inevitable. Accounting for votes lost and gained became commonplace. For instance, promoting homosexual rights might gain support from 'post-materialist' activists, but would lose votes elsewhere: as a British Labour Party adviser pointed out in the 1980s in a memorandum: 'The gays and lesbians issue is costing us dear among the pensioners.'[105]

The parties of the Left also had to face the fact that there were 'new' social movements of the Right – though these tend to be ignored by those writing on post-materialism. Many of these 'right' social movements were a response to the activities of those on the Left. Anti-abortion groups, for instance, were a reaction to successful pro-abortion campaigns. Religious fundamentalist groups may have been against modernity, but they used mass rallies, demonstrations, hunger strikes (whose pioneers were the suffragettes and Gandhian non-violent anti-imperialists), fax machines and computerized direct mailing. These were groups which had been mobilized using all the techniques of the modern age in order to defend tradition. On the whole, however, most supporters of the social movements of the Right who agitated against further immigration, or on behalf of law and order, or against sex education in schools, or for capital punishment remained relatively isolated and passive individuals, whose ideas were expressed mainly through public opinion polls and whose thoughts were directly articulated by the right-wing popular press or politicians.

The asymmetry is evident. On the one hand, we have socialist parties apparently besieged by articulate middle-class campaigners putting forward novel ideas which challenge existing conceptions of common sense. On the other, we have established political parties of the Right (or politicians within them), supported by large sections of the mass media, articulating the ideas and fears of 'ordinary' men and women (i.e. not middle-class intellectuals). In some cases these fears amounted to a well-constructed moral panic. Conjured-up images struck a chord: here were honest citizens, many of them the self-same workers of socialist lore, entrenched in the privacy of their own homes, unable to walk the streets for fear of young hoodlums, the protégés of left-wing sociologists, threatened by sexually intimidating feminists, imperilled by pacifists willing to let Russian communists overrun Western civilization, taxed to death by an exacting and remote state to subsidize the lazy and the incompetent. As so often, the caricature reveals the contours of a discernible reality. There was always at least a grain of truth in even the most extreme and abusive of the new social movements of the Right. Like those of the Left, they often articulated ideas which were by and large outside the agreed consensus.

It was because the parties of the Left were entrenched in society and to some extent aware of, and responsive to, common fears and prejudices, that they could not rapidly and wholeheartedly adopt the programmes of the new ('left') social movements. After all, 'nothing unites them except their organizational separation from the labour movement'.[106] It was only by selecting some of the acceptable ideological strands, recruiting some of the activists, and discarding the more unconventional 'alternative lifestyle' elements from the packaging, that the issues raised by the new social movements were injected into the mainstream discourse of the socialist parties.

A process of this kind was unavoidable. New issues (or, to be precise, newly revived issues, for ecologism and feminism predated the 1970s) could be pushed forward by forceful and determined activists, not 'ordinary' people. Nothing new ever comes to the fore unless launched in an intransigent manner. Unconventional demands cannot be advanced in conventional terms. But these demands, unless co-opted, translated, adapted and transformed, would remain marginal. Though often abused, and deemed to be terminally ill, political parties have thus far remained the only political instrument able to transform generic demands for change into legislation. Hence the fraught division of labour between new social movements and parties of the Left: the former provide new ideas; the latter provide an organization which can put the ideas into practice.

The new social movements of the Left were the product of the maelstrom of the 1960s. This is why they are often lumped together. Nevertheless, distinctions need to be made. Ecology and feminism – the two most important – are loosely structured movements seeking to redefine mentalities. Alongside and sometimes related to them is a plethora of organizations and campaigns. Many aspire to the establishment of rights – for instance, for homosexuals, disabled people or ethnic minorities. Others demand specific legislative changes – for instance, the abolition of vivisection or the elimination of lead from petrol. Then there are self-help groups founded on the idea that those who experience a problem (drug abuse, disablement, discrimination) can organize effectively on their own behalf. Finally, there are single-goal campaigns seeking, for instance, the maintainance of a service or the blocking of a scheme, such as a road project, or the obtaining of justice for wrongly convicted criminals.

On the whole, these activities have not been initiated or even supported by established political parties; hence the widely held view that parties were dying. In reality, what was moribund was the old socialist idea of parties as agenda-setting vanguards. Parties continued to exist, but they responded to demands arising elsewhere and became increasingly unwilling (and unable) to initiate campaigns themselves. This is politically quite rational. It is preferable to respond to pressure groups once it has become evident that the campaign has political potential and support. Problems arise only when pressure groups seek to become parties themselves.

The Greens

Of all the new social movements only the greens pursued this path. By the late 1980s, nearly all West European countries had green parties, but none had made a substantial electoral impact. Between 1980 and 1988, the best 'green' result in Austria was 4.4 per cent of the vote (1986); in Belgium it was 7.1 per cent (1987) – shared, of course, between the Flemish-speaking Agalev and the Walloon Ecolo. In Holland the parties of the Green Progressive Accord obtained 5.7 per cent in 1982. In Sweden the Environment Party reached 5 per cent in 1988. The strongest greens were in Germany, where they peaked in 1987 with 8.3 per cent.[107]

Whatever the ambition of their supporters, green parties were unlikely ever to become hegemonic government parties displacing the main parties of the Left or the Right. The best they could hope for was either to be strong enough to enter a coalition government, and ensure its adherence to ecological principles (thus becoming a sort of pressure group within), or to become such an electoral threat as to compel existing parties to become more environmentally aware. The second strategy was more successful than the first. Even as late as 1995, no green party had yet managed to become a fully-fledged member of a coalition government in Western Europe.

The dilemma facing green parties was that if 'their' issues were to become an accepted part of the mainstream political agenda, the original reason for their advent might evaporate. Integration would become a sign of success, not of failure.[108] Thus, even though, as most observers agree, by the middle of the 1980s the wave of political mobilization of the new movements had ebbed, their themes – environmental protection, equality for women, self-help, decentralization – had won a fairly secure slot on the political agenda.[109] Many of the values of the new social movements could easily be co-opted by most parties, not just those of the Left. By the end of the twentieth century, no conservative or liberal party would oppose the idea that women and men should have equal rights, or that the environment should be protected, or that minorities should be safeguarded. Conservative voters in rural or suburban districts frequently oppose the construction of an airport or a motorway by using the themes, and even the methods, of green activists. Under the leadership of Margaret Thatcher, the most radical conservative government in Europe, unafraid to battle against the trade unions, felt it necessary to pay lip-service to environmentalism and did nothing to repeal the Equal Pay Act or the Race Relations Act. The principle of equality before the law was too well entrenched to be disregarded. Differences between the Left and their conservative opponents emerged either over specific legislation (for instance, abortion), or over the emphasis to be given to specific real inequalities inherited from the past.

The rise of the greens largely coincided with the development of nuclear power. Until their advent, nuclear power was not a contentious issue among political parties. Socialist parties and the trade unions especially were, on the whole, committed to it, particularly in Sweden, Austria, Germany and Britain, which had socialist governments in the 1970s. In Sweden the social democrats had become so identified as the party of nuclear power that it lost the 1976 and 1979 elections largely on this issue. The Swedish Centre Party, formerly the Agrarian Party, had taken the lead in the campaign against nuclear power. This was sufficient to tip the scales in favour of the 'bourgeois' coalition, even though the other parties were pro-nuclear (opportunistically, they kept a low profile on the issue). To avoid the fate of his Swedish counterparts, Austrian Chancellor Bruno Kreisky held a referendum in November 1978, which was narrowly won by the ecologists.[110] The idea of letting the people decide on this issue was adopted in Sweden by the SAP. It skilfully readjusted its strategy, campaigned in favour of the gradual phasing out of nuclear power, and was thus successful in the referendum of March 1980. Thereafter, the issue disappeared from the agenda. The greens did not. Calling themselves the Environment Party, they entered Parliament for the first time in 1988.[111]

The initial ambivalence of the parties of the Left towards nuclear power was not surprising. The oil crisis had renewed interest in it as a new source of energy cheaper and cleaner than most (as long as reactors did not explode). Cheap energy was necessary for economic growth. Economic growth was essential to end mass unemployment and preserve the welfare state. This commitment to growth had provided the *trait d'union* with pro-capitalist parties and a basis for the great post-war consensus. The commitment of working-class parties to the industrial society, without which they and the working class would not exist, may suggest that there was a massive ideological Chinese Wall dividing ecologists from socialists. In reality, the two also had much in common. The Left was never committed to growth for growth's sake. Had that been the case, it would never have fought – almost regardless of productivity – for a shorter working day, a regulated labour market and higher wages.

The essence of the 'green' idea was that it was necessary to regulate and constrain capitalist firms in order to impose some general – hence 'collectivist' – goals, such as a better environment. Ideologically, this was far more acceptable to the Left than to the Right. The real supporters of unhindered quantitative growth in Western Europe were the partisans of the free market, the champions of the 'new' ideology of the 1980s, who held that market efficiency could be obtained by using nature's products as if they were inexhaustible.[112]

In 'socialist' Eastern and Central Europe, ruled by communists until 1989–

91, environmental destruction was far more pronounced than in the capitalist West. In their determination to 'catch up', they had pursued growth, un-trammelled by democratic or popular control. Capitalism as a world system established a pattern of growth which other countries were forced to follow. What made a difference, in ecological terms, and protected the West better than the East (and the Third World, where the West dumped some of its own environmental problems), was not capitalism as such, but the regulatory system imposed on it. This system, like the laws protecting labour, was not the result of the 'spontaneous' workings of capitalism (whatever these may be), but of the political struggle between Right and Left. Traditionally, the Left favoured ecological issues when a clear class element was involved. Thus, for instance, socialists took an environmental stance in the long struggle for improving working conditions in factories and in specific campaigns such as the 1932 mass trespasses on the Duke of Devonshire's grouse moors, which led to the establishment – by a Labour government – of national parks in England and Wales in 1949.[113]

In practice, however, socialists appeared more interested in quantitative than in qualitative growth. The greens were more in tune with the rapidly developing post-Fordist *Zeitgeist* than the traditional parties of Left or Right. Such a *Zeitgeist*, however, was still that of an élite of 'post-modern' intellectuals, who scoffed at the conception of progress as a remnant of eighteenth-century rationalist thought. Most ordinary people expected things to get better, as they had done for most of their lives. They were prepared to acknowledge the importance of the environment to any pollster, but failed to exhibit diminishing enthusiasm for the artefacts of the consumer society. At most, by 1980, they might take their empty bottles and old newspapers to their local recycling centres in their Volvos or Fiats. This understandable equivocation was echoed by parties of Left and Right – all promising a growing economy with no adverse environmental effects.

The oil shock had helped the ecological movement. The crisis created a public awareness of the finite state of world energy reserves and the im-portance of conservation. However, the idea of zero growth – launched by conservative associations such as the Club of Rome – appeared even more 'reactionary' during the recession of the 1970s, when growth rates tumbled and unemployment increased. Thus, there was nothing surprising in the position adopted by the PCF at its Twenty-second Congress in 1976 which explicitly rejected the idea of *croissance zéro*, seen as preparing for a future of penury and restrictions.[114] Georges Marchais' claim that 'growth is necessary to meet the requirements of social and national progress' was not some communist idiosyncrasy, but an idea firmly held by most social democrats. In 1971 Anthony Crosland had branded ecologists as middle-class élitists who were indifferent to the needs of ordinary people, and who preferred to defend rural peace rather than do something about urban decay.[115] Four years later, in the middle of the energy crisis, he was unrepentant.[116] In conversation with Brandt and Kreisky, Olof Palme quite candidly declared that rescuing 'industrial society' was the proper task of socialists.[117]

The initial vacillation of the Left over ecological issues reflected the political ambivalence of the green movement itself. As Anna Bramwell has shown, the ideological underpinning of the ecological movement has shifted through-out its multifaceted hundred-year history. In the intellectual ancestry of modern greens, we find co-existing the themes of reverence for rural life, respect for nature, pre-industrialist values, mysticism, anti-urbanism, holistic culture, Romanticism, anti-rationalism, as well as social Darwinism, vitalist philosophy, eugenics, Kropotkinite anarchism and technophilism.[118] Pro-ecologists like David Pepper concurred, detecting at the roots of English environmentalism a complex web of contradictory elements, including the mythopoeia of William Blake, the reactionary Romanticism of Thomas Carlyle, and the scientific approach of Malthus and Darwin.[119]

Environmentalism had also been a distinctive ideological trait in German National Socialism. Some of its leaders even shared some of the values of contemporary proponents of alternative lifestyles: Adolf Hitler and Heinrich Himmler were vegetarians; Rudolf Hess was a homeopath and a naturist; Walther Darré, the minister of agriculture (1933–42), devoted his last two years in office to campaigning for organic farming. The regime passed anti-vivisection laws, supported rural conservation, and was the first country in Europe to institute nature reserves.[120] Being fundamentally anti-capitalist, the greens could turn to either the socialist Left to redefine 'progress', or the reactionary Right to defend pre-capitalist traditions.

Even the present-day German green movement – the most influential in Europe – was conservative in its early stages. One of the first green groups in Germany was the Grüne Aktion Zukunft (GAZ), led by a former CDU politician Herbert Gruhl, author of A Planet is Plundered, a bestseller in 1975.[121] Only when the greens formed themselves into a party to fight the 1979 European elections did the former activists of the student movement join in sufficient numbers to push the organization well to the left.[122]

As soon as they had become a party, the greens found themselves divided into two factions, the intransigent Fundis, or fundamentalists – who refused to enter into an alliance with the SPD – and the more accommodating Realos, or realists. The Greens thus replicated the great debate on participation in bourgeois governments which perturbed the social-democratic movement at the turn of the century. Fundis such as Rudolf Bahro, a former East German dissident expelled from the DDR in the 1970s, declared that 'the working class forms a second industrial class alongside the bourgeoisie', that the trade unions 'belong to the most conservative forces in society', and that the Greens should look forward to the disintegration of working-class organizations.[123] Another leading Fundi, the charismatic Petra Kelly, announced with glee that the SPD was 'fully washed-out'.[124] A ferocious internecine struggle ensued, resulting in the rout of the Fundis.[125] The Realos set up coalitions with the SPD, notably in the social democratic stronghold of Hessen where the leader of the *Realos*, Joschka Fischer, became minister of the environment (1985–87). Eventually, the Greens, like others presuming to break the mould of the political system, became more obsessed with electoral politics than their better established rivals. This is hardly surprising; the 5 per cent of the vote required to obtain representation in the Bundestag was bound to prey on the mind of a party perpetually on the verge of extinction.

The German Greens were in fact more red than green: the themes of participatory democracy, anti-hierarchical values, egalitarianism, women's rights, ending unemployment, a social wage, nationalization of steel, anti-NATO and anti-Americanism loomed larger than specifically ecological campaigns.[126] They fought more against nuclear missiles than against nuclear reactors. This is why post-materialist claims that 'the ideological composition of the Green Party's programme cannot easily be placed on a left–right continuum', are puzzling and unconvincing.[127] Ecologists in Germany and elsewhere were often the New Left of the 1960s in green clothes.

It took electoral defeat to propel the SPD toward embracing an ecological strategy (see chapter 23). Traditionalists within the SPD thought that ecological politics would alienate a considerable segment of the workers, without making compensating inroads into the middle classes. The 'modernizers' assumed that by embracing ecology the SPD would establish a more positive image with younger generations, without losing touch with their traditional supporters. Yet it became apparent that any 'flirtation' with left-libertarian causes reduced socialist electoral support.[128]

The German Greens broke the monopoly of the three main parties (CDU–CSU, SPD and FDP) in the Federal Republic, winning seats in all *Länder* but two by 1992. However, they were never able to be more than an effective protest party.[129] The red–green coalition in Hesse was voted out of office in 1987, after only fourteen months in power.[130] In the Saar and in North Rhine–Westphalia, the Greens were soundly defeated in 1985. In 1989 Otto Schily, one of the ablest Green parliamentary leaders, who had played a prominent part in revealing the shady financial side of the Flick affair, defected to the SPD.[131] After German unification, the Greens suffered a real setback in the western part of the country where they failed to reach the 5 per cent barrier in the 1990 election. They did not collapse and recouped most of their losses in October 1994. After 1990, with the *Fundis* utterly routed, moreover, red–green coalitions became acceptable, as in the Rhineland-Palatinate. In Bremen and Brandenburg even the FDP joined in a coalition with the Greens and the SDP. The Greens had thus become fairly well integrated into the mainstream of the German political system.[132]

The green cause was not tied to the fate of the Green Party. The SPD, spurred by the Chernobyl disaster, by its failure to regain office after 1982, by pressures from its own activists, and by a shift in public opinion, adopted a policy aimed at the gradual winding down of nuclear power (Nuremberg

Congress in August 1986). As we have seen with the Swedes and the Austrians, this 'greening' of socialist parties occurred elsewhere. Other parties, notably the PCI and the British Labour Party, followed the same trajectory. The ecological question represented a major challenge to industrial society and hence to both Left and Right. The problem was truly global; it could not be resolved by the simple expedient of exporting it to the Third World. A dense network of Indian or Chinese nuclear reactors would stimulate the economic development of these countries, but would present a potential threat to the entire planet. Once the question had emerged as a serious one, no party could afford to ignore it. The issue was eminently co-optable. Free marketeers could use the market mechanism, by asking that the polluters be made to pay ecological taxes – a seductive proposal endorsed by many on the Left. Firms competed to produce 'green' and recycled products. The Achilles' heel of the movement, however, was that the greatest polluters were the people themselves: their plastic bags, their battery-powered gadgets and, above all, their cars.

The political challenge of the greens was never sufficiently strong to cause a real crisis in West European socialism. At most, they were only one of the challenges social democrats faced in the 1970s and 1980s.[133] Where the greens did not present a major electoral challenge, as in Britain or France (except at the odd European election), all socialists needed to do was to adopt more overt environmental policies than their conservative counterparts. Outside Sweden in 1976 and 1979, no electoral contest was ever fought on ecology. Elsewhere, after the nuclear power issue had been defused, the advance of the greens represented a net loss of electoral support for the socialist parties – as in Germany or Sweden – precisely because the greens were a left-wing party. Socialists (or, in Italy, communists) faced a dilemma. Should they absorb green demands in order to eliminate the greens as a party and inherit their electorate? Or should the Green Party be accepted as a potential ally and coalition partner? The first route was obviously the most profitable, because it did not pre-empt the second and could even be a precondition for it. Socialists were then, almost inevitably, forced into the business of co-opting green demands originating elsewhere. It is not because of electoral losses or the collapse of the industrial working class that one can talk of a 'crisis' of socialism. It is because the socialist movement was forced to renew itself by going outside its own traditions and re-examining its own basic values.

The Presence of Women

This process of renewal was – at least in part – visible in its riposte to feminism. Socialists, the inheritors of a certain liberal-democratic and – except in Britain – anti-clerical tradition, may have had fewer inhibitions about policies concerned with sexual freedom than their conservative counterparts who, at least in continental Europe, were often Christian democrats. Nevertheless, the need to be genuinely popular parties stopped them from enthusi-astically embracing any form of sexual radicalism such as easy divorce, free and legal abortion, sex education, equal treatment for homosexuals, or birth control. One of the effects of the 1960s generation and the advance of feminism was to push socialists (and not only socialists) towards a fuller acceptance of the new sexual politics.[134] That the main terrain on which this shift took place should have been the issue of abortion was mainly due to the feminists themselves who, in the 1970s, made it the 'indispensable plank of contemporary feminism'.[135]

This suggests that the agenda of the left-wing parties on women's issues was often determined by the pressure of active feminists, rather than by a mass feminist movement. In Spain, for instance, there was no mass movement at all, and the political and cultural gap between feminists and 'ordinary' women was wider than usual.[136] Yet these Spanish feminists so obviously represented what the new Spain aspired to – namely, 'modernization' and 'catching up with Europe' – that the PSOE strengthened its image by adopting many of their demands. Once in power, the PSOE eliminated discriminatory practices in the labour market, introduced maternal and parental leave, equal opportunities, child-care arrangements, sex education in schools, new laws on the family, illegitimacy and divorce. Spain was effectively catching up – as were Portugal and Greece.[137] A similar development was occurring in Greece, where PASOK took up feminist demands even though there was no sizeable feminist movement. With the exception of Ireland – where neither of the main parties was socialist – a legal termination of pregnancy was available to women, usually free of charge, though the terms of legislation varied from country to country.

The response of the parties of the Left throughout Europe was always more sympathetic than that of the Right. The chief constraints were electoral, namely the fear that voters would find the legalization of abortion so dis-tasteful that they would swing behind the conservative parties. The evidence that abortion was a 'Left' issue was overwhelming.

In Germany the SPD–FDP coalition government passed a law in 1974 making abortion legal virtually on request. A year later, on an appeal initiated by the CDU–CSU, the law was declared unconstitutional by the Constitutional Court. The SPD and its Liberal allies responded by passing a more restrictive law (1976) making abortion legal up to the twelfth week of pregnancy for specified social and medical reasons. In practice this meant that a woman wishing to obtain an abortion had to find sympathetic counsellors or doctors and, generally speaking, these were more readily available in areas under left-wing influence, such as Frankfurt, than in those dominated by the Christian democrats, such as Bavaria.

In Holland, abortion became available virtually on demand after 1973, with the remaining restrictions being repealed in 1981. In Spain and Greece, the PSOE and PASOK were directly responsible for introducing abortion reform.[138]

In Austria, Article 144 of the penal code, which criminalized abortion, was abrogated in 1972 by the SPÖ government and a new law passed in 1973 – the only piece of legislation sufficiently controversial to break the traditional political consensus between the two largest parties.[139] In Britain, the TUC organized an official demonstration against a Conservative attempt to restrict abortion rights. It was 'the largest union demonstration that had yet been held for a cause which lay beyond the traditional scope of collective bargaining'.[140]

In Italy, abortion was legalized in June 1978 after a lengthy parliamentary battle principally conducted by the PSI and the PCI against Christian democrats. The pursuit of a 'historic compromise' with the DC had not deflected the communists, though they hesitated before throwing their full weight behind the abortion campaign (as they had done during the previous divorce campaign). They had seriously overestimated the traditionalism of Italian women and the power of the church. Even though Berlinguer, in 1972, had declared that 'the woman question has become one of the central questions of the nation', he was genuinely worried at the prospect of antagonizing the Catholics and was convinced that the Left would lose the abortion referendum.[141] In fact, the pro-abortionists won with a handsome majority: 68 per cent. Later, Berlinguer admitted that he had 'underestimated women'. We won thanks to them. We have to realize that today they have become a leading force'.[142] The resulting legislation – on paper at least – was one of the most progressive in Europe in terms of the principle of the woman's right to choose.[143]

Abortion had been constructed as a specifically feminist issue, even though it also enabled men to evade their responsibilities and did little to modify the imbalance of power between the sexes. Its legalization was of benefit to women, who were no longer forced to resort to illegal and dangerous interventions. By asserting the rights of women over their own bodies, and stressing the central importance of individual choice over social or collective responsibility, abortion reform was perfectly compatible with the spirit of the 1980s and in harmony with the ideology of individualism, which was at the root of the rediscovery of the market. Of course, it does not follow that socialist parties should have opposed abortion reform: upholding individual rights has never been the prerogative of liberals. Abortion reform may not have been a specifically 'class' issue, but socialist parties, as we have seen, had always fought for universal and civil rights. The hesitation of the parties of the Left was due to electoral calculation, not ideology. The issue did not involve the jettisoning of any particular socialist idea, outdated or otherwise. Socialist parties could be as anchored in the past as they wished, while fighting vigorously for abortion. Moreover, most civil rights legislation – abortion reform, divorce, abolition of capital punishment, homosexual rights, etc. – did not cost very much. The effect of these reforms was to 'clean out' from present-day society some of the remnants of the old order, the no

Table 22.7 The representation of women in politics, 1975–92

	% of women elected in lower chamber, 1975	Percentage of women elected as deputies			
		Year	In lower chamber	In main party of the Left	In main party of the Right
Austria	7.6	1990	21.9	SPÖ 26.3	ÖVP 11.7
Belgium	6.6	1990	9.0	Soc 10.0	CVP 14.0
Denmark	15.6	1990	33.0	Soc Dem 34.8	Cons 23.3
Finland	23.0	1991	38.5		
France	1.6	1988	5.7	PS 6.3	RPR 6.9
Greece	2.0	1990	5.3	PASOK 4.8	ND 5.3
Holland	9.3	1989	27.3	PvdA 32.7	CD 18.5
Italy	3.8	1992	8.0	PDS 20.6	DC 4.8
Norway	15.5	1989	36.0	Labour 50.8	Cons 29.7
Portugal	8.0	1991	7.6		
Spain	n/a	1989	13.4	PSOE 18.3	PP 9.3
Sweden	21.4	1988	38.1	Soc Dem 40.0	Mod 27.0
UK	4.2	1991	6.8	Labour 10.4	Cons 4.6
W. Germany	5.6	1990	20.5	SPD 27.2	CDU 13.8

Source: Table constructed on the basis of data in Paula Snyder, *The European Women's Almanac*, Scarlet Press, London 1992, and in Joni Lovenduski and Pippa Norris (eds), *Gender and Party Politics*, Sage, London 1993, pp. 94 and 191. The 1975 data are based on Aglaia Paoletti, 'La presenza femminile nelle assemblee parlamentari', *Il Politico*, Vol. 56, no. 1, 1991, pp. 85–8.

longer relevant encrustations of the world of yesterday. Much of this was part of the indispensable task of modernization, but it was largely irrelevant from the point of view of capitalist accumulation.

Once this campaign was over, no other general feminist issue of wide public impact took its place. Feminists had come to accept that their goals could only be realized if women were present in adequate numbers in all the institutions of society. The issue of representation came to the fore largely because of the objective fact that an increasing number of women qualified to fill positions of power and influence were denied access to them, either as a result of direct and indirect discrimination, or through the unconscious reluctance of women themselves to seek power with the single-mindedness exhibited by men.

The substantive difference between a campaign for abortion reform and one for increased representation was that the goal of the former was an end in itself, while the goal of the latter was a means to achieve an end. The former addressed itself to all women, the second only to those willing and qualified to obtain positions of power and influence.

This was not the issue facing most ordinary women, who had relatively

recently entered the labour force or were working in the home with no
prospects. An increasing number of women faced a situation in which the
disintegration of the traditional family, far from offering liberation, forced
many of them into the exhausting double task of raising children and earning
a living. For these women, the issue of a more equal balance between men
and women in government, Parliament, company boards, the press and
universities could not have the compelling and justifiable force it had for
their more privileged counterparts. As some women acquired advantages
hitherto confined to men, new differences emerged within the 'class' of
women. Feminists had constructed the category of women, as socialists had
constructed that of workers: as an undifferentiated social category. Now they
had to take into account the fact that different women faced different forms
of oppression and were affected differently.

Institutions were bound to be modified by the greater presence of women.
But the impact would be reciprocal. Whether feminists or not, as they entered
these male preserves, women would accept, at least in part, their ethos and
practices. All 'professionals' are to some extent gatekeepers in charge of
institutions. Their task is to ensure that only those who are similar to
themselves are let in – hence the overarching continuity of organizations and
the immense task confronting all those who wish to change them by taking
them over.

The argument for fairer representation for women was none the less exceptionally strong, though not an entirely novel idea. In 1920 Lenin urged the
Bolsheviks to 'elect more women to the Soviet, both Communist women and
non-party women ... The Proletariat cannot achieve complete liberty until it
has won complete liberty for women.'[114] Seventy years later, there was still a
considerable way to go, and not just in the Soviet Union – by then nearing
its end. Table 22.7 shows how serious was the imbalance in political representation, but also demonstrates how much better women fared in the parties of
the Left (except in France, Belgium and Greece). At first sight these data
confirm familiar stereotypes. Women do better in Protestant Europe, where
social democracy is well entrenched, than in Southern Europe. However, they
do better in Italy than in Belgium, and worst of all in France and Britain.
Nordic countries do not only have a history of social progress on their side,
but also elections based on party lists and proportional representation.

Electoral systems are, in fact, a key determinant of the size of female
representation, as the example of Italy illustrates. In 1987, eighty women
were elected to the 630 members of the Italian Chamber of Deputies,
including forty-four who had been on the PCI's electoral list (the party had
urged its disciplined supporters to vote for them, thus contributing decisively
to this advance).[115] In 1992, only fifty-two women were elected to Chamber (including twenty-
two for the Democratic Party of the Left, the former Communist Party).
This drop was due to a modification in the electoral system, which had had

In 1994, ninety-six women were elected, more than ever before, and half of them under the banner of the Left. What determined this massive increase (over 1992)? The elections had been fought under a new system in which one-quarter of all deputies (155) would be elected by proportional representation of party lists, and the remaining 475 on the basis of a plurality in individual constituencies. In the constituencies women obtained only 10 per cent of the available seats (i.e. forty-four seats), but they did extremely well in the much smaller party list section, where fifty-two women (nearly one-third of the total) were elected. Why? Because the new legislation established that each party list had to alternate men and women.[147]

Thus, electoral systems, parties and a favourable climate of opinion determined the electoral success of women where there was no strong independent women's movement.[148] The greatest progress achieved in this area was in Norway after Gro Harlem Brundtland, the leader of the social-democratic DNA, became prime minister in 1986. She proceeded to appoint a cabinet in which nearly half the ministers were women. This established a pattern: the two governments (one non-socialist) which succeeded that of Brundtland after 1989 had a similarly high proportion of women cabinet ministers.[149] Other Norwegian parties followed in the DNA's footsteps, when Anne Enger Lahnstein became leader of the anti-EEC Centre Party in 1991 and another woman, Kaci Kullmann-Five, took charge of the Conservative Party. There is no simple explanation for the prominence of women in Norwegian politics. They were not particularly prominent in other spheres: women had only 24 per cent of the seats of the General Council of the Confederation of Trade Unions, 10.9 per cent of the senior posts of the civil service, 7.2 per cent of academic chairs, and 3.3 per cent of senior positions in business.[150]

There is no solid evidence linking a strongly feminist climate of opinion to parliamentary representation. A study comparing Germany, where women were relatively well represented, and the UK shows that virtually no one in Great Britain and West Germany approves of women working full-time when there is a pre-school child in the family.[151] A study based on a 1983 Eurobarometer survey concluded that between 25 and 50 per cent of West European women could be termed 'feminist'. In Italy, France and Belgium, where women were poorly represented, women came out on top of this feminist league, with British women at the bottom, well behind Ireland.[152] 'Climate of opinion on matters like sexism are difficult to assess seriously. Gisela Kaplan cites the 1983 *Men and Women of Europe* EEC survey, where Greece scores very high marks on feminism because – contrary to anecdotal evidence and common stereotypes – 50 per cent of Greek women and *men* declared that the best division of roles within the family was equal-gender sharing.[153] Yet Greek women are less well represented in Parliament than in any other country else in the EC.

There is also no clear positive correlation between the number of women in Parliament and the extent of legislation favouring women. In Greece, for instance, the pitifully small number of women in Parliament contrasts sharply with the remarkably progressive legislation which characterized the PASOK government throughout the 1980s.[154] The legislation defending the rights of women in France or Britain is no worse and in many respects better than that of other European countries, even though there are relatively few women in the Assemblée nationale or the House of Commons.

As Gisela Kaplan has observed, the relative wealth of countries is a not insignificant factor in the progress of women: 'social engineering takes money.'[155] Northern Europe is richer than Southern Europe. Civil rights may be cheap, but domestic appliances, health care and child-care, good schools and universities are not. Wealth may not necessarily be the decisive element in the progress of women, but it does create the conditions for further emancipation and equality. Once again, socialist determination without a solid economy cannot deliver the goods.

To satisfy the growing demand for parity from politically active women, short-cuts had to be found. The usual route was to institute quota systems. This left unanswered the issue of whether the women so selected or elected actually 'represented' women.[156] In the 1980s and 1990s, political parties became virtually the only institutions willing to establish compulsory quotas for women. The British Labour Party for many years had a 'women's section' in the National Executive Committee, consisting of five seats (less than one-sixth of the total). Further quotas were later established, including one for the shadow cabinet.[157] In 1988, at its Münster Congress, the SPD – competing with the Greens for the votes of younger women – approved a *Frauenquote* plan to bring the representation of women to 40 per cent at all levels of the party organization and in Parliament by 1994. Quotas were intended to apply for a twenty-five-year period, on the assumption that positive discrimination would then no longer be required.[158]

By 1993, the overwhelming majority of the parties of the Socialist International, and quite a few non-socialist parties, had established a minimum quota for women – usually 30 or 40 per cent – either in the party organization or in the candidates' lists.[159] The prominence of the issue of quotas in the 1980s coincided with a phase in which support for the women's movement had abated. The great civil rights campaigns, legislation on equal pay and anti-discrimination, abortion, divorce and family law – these had been won virtually everywhere. Other struggles, ultimately of even greater importance, such as that over child-care or over the redefinition of work, entailed costly reforms at a time when public expenditure was being cut. Quotas were cheap and satisfied the advanced battalions of modern feminism. It was a dangerous strategy, reminiscent of traditional social-democratic gradualism:

'first we must get into power, then we must play by the rules, then we must prove ourselves, then, eventually, trust us, we'll get true socialism.' Parties adept at establishing electoral clienteles for themselves can find that the incorporation of feminists is not necessarily an expensive operation. In 1983 the PSOE established the Istituto de la Mujer (the Women's Institute), whose task was to invigilate equality policies, run training programmes for women, and fund women's organizations. This was part of the creation of a steady flow of jobs for women resulting in what is arguably the largest women's bureaucracy in Europe (228 staff in 1992), and a budget which trebled between 1984 and 1990. Yet, in comparison with authentic clienteles (such as farming communities), both the budget and personnel involved are puny (though there are far more women than farmers).[160] Nevertheless, the incorporation of feminism into party politics discloses a real problem. Noting the 'drying up' of the women's movement, Frigga Haug attributed it to 'the nationalisation (*Verstaatlichung*) of the woman question – a typical result of social-democratic reformist politics', and warned that 'It is a political trap to allow one woman to rise and enjoy the fruits of the struggle of many ... The state, and a certain form of politics from above, take control of the women's movement by bribing individual members.'[161] The fear expressed by Haug was that the incorporation of women's demands into the manifestos of socialist parties was a concession, often made under external pressure, to win votes or members. It did not entail any rethinking of strategy. Because the approach was piecemeal, it could be discarded at will and at any time without jettisoning the rest of the manifesto.[162]

It is not even certain that the adoption of many of the demands of the new social movements was of electoral benefit to the Left. In some instances, pro-women policies were overwhelmed by the party's traditional image. For example, the French Communist Party always had a higher profile on women's issues than any of the other parties, yet in 1981 it obtained the lowest percentage of women voters of any major French party.[163] The French socialists did far better. This could be attributed to Mitterrand's pronounced sympathy towards feminist issues, or to the party manifesto on the rights of women (1979).[164] On the other hand, the SFIO (the old pre-Mitterrand socialist party), even though it had never exhibited the slightest concern for women's rights, always did better than the communists with women voters – though never as well as de Gaulle who, in 1965, obtained the votes of 61 per cent of women and 41 per cent of men.[165] However, by 1988 Mitterrand had effectively closed the electoral gender gap, though his party – unlike most other Left parties – elected proportionately fewer women than its conservative opponents (see Table 22.7).

In Germany, until the late 1960s, the CDU–CSU obtained, on average, 10 per cent more votes from women than from men. In the 1970s and 1980s the gap narrowed. In spite of their high profile on feminist issues, the Greens did better among men than among women in 1983 and 1987.[166] In Sweden the gender gap, which had evaporated in the 1970s, reappeared in the 1980s; proportionately more women supported the Liberals (who campaigned strongly on women's issues); in 1991 older women favoured the small Christian Democratic Party, while younger ones preferred the Green Party,[167] Nevertheless, the SAP, because it was the party of the highly feminized public sector, had proportionately more women voters in 1985 than the conservative and pro-capitalist Moderate Party.[168]

In Britain, 'the voting behaviour of women was virtually identical to that of men', with 44 per cent of men and women voting the Conservative Party to victory in 1987.[169] This, of course, meant that the Labour Party had closed the gender gap and was now less unpopular with women voters than it used to be.[170] It could thus be assumed that there would be a natural generational change. As the older, more traditional women passed away, the new cohorts would vote for pro-feminist parties. Thus, in the 1987 British elections, young women went against the otherwise pro-Conservative trend of the rest of the electorate. Labour had a lead over the Conservatives of thirty points among working-class women between the ages of eighteen and twenty-four. This group, however, constituted only 7 per cent of the population, while the Conservatives had a twenty-one point lead among young middle-class women and a massive one among older middle-class women.[171] Accordingly, the claim that 'women are Labour's natural constituency', was premature.[172] Labour Party feminists persevered: the 'policy review' documents published in 1989 were unusually innovative in their approach to gender issues, prompting two feminist writers to remark that the review policies 'seemed to exhibit a genuine commitment to the particular needs of women. They were dealt with explicitly, not in a brief addendum, as had been the practice, but as an integral – even prominent – part of the main text.'[173] These efforts were not rewarded with votes. In 1992 the gender gap had reopened and the Tory lead over Labour among women was 8 per cent higher than among men.[174] Women over the age of thirty-five shifted away from Labour, even though the party had specifically promised to increase the number of women in Parliament and more women were in the shadow cabinet – as recommended by Labour feminists.[175]

This new 'conservative' tendency among women was far from irrational. After 1988, while the recession was sweeping Britain, there was a considerable increase in the number of women working full-time, while male unemployment continued to rise. The Conservatives may not have been enthusiastic supporters of equal opportunities legislation, but did not oppose it and, in any case, as we have seen, such legislation did not change the lives of most women. On the other hand, the party had been a consistent advocate of the deregulation of the labour market. These policies expanded job opportunities for women and were therefore 'arguably advantageous for working women, even if they were disastrous for working men'.[176]

In addition, conservatives, in Britain and elsewhere, have usually been able to present themselves as the party of the family and therefore of women.177 Their appeal was not only of a traditionalist nature. Many conservative and Christian parties, precisely because they enjoy the support of many women, have been more sensitive to women's issues than is generally acknowledged. For instance, the Italian Christian Democratic Party, traditionalist on matters of sexual behaviour, family life, abortion and divorce, passed a law in 1950 giving protection to working mothers, prescribing compulsory and paid leave for pregnant women two months before and three months after birth, and ratifying the 1954 ILO Convention on Equal Pay earlier than any other European government.178 The British Conservative Party paid attention to women's issues as soon as universal suffrage had been achieved. By 1929 the Tories had taken care to arm themselves 'with a catalogue of reforms for women.'179 Other conservative parties reacted to feminism by moving with the times. For instance, in Germany the CDU–CSU developed a new policy towards 'modern' women.180 It no longer propagandized a conservative model of women, offering instead a dynamically remodelled hybrid: the caring housewife and mother with part-time work. The policy, 'ingratiatingly worded in feminist language', was greeted by some feminists as 'exceptionally progressive'.181 In Britain, in the autumn of 1991, John Major declared his support for Operation 2000, a programme aimed at placing more women in top jobs.182

It is not evident that the adoption of feminist (or ecological) positions benefited the parties of the Left electorally, though it is unlikely to have damaged any of them. Women, like men, have multiple identities and are not necessarily swayed by feminist arguments. In most countries, class, education, religion and regions are better predictors of voting behaviour than sex.183 The idea that the mere adoption of a set of demands would automatically detach a definite portion of the electorate was a fantasy, held only by those who could not tell the difference between a market of commodities and the political market. Inserting demands in a manifesto few people read does not automatically convert the voters. Gender would make a real difference in voting behaviour only if gender issues became dominant during an electoral campaign. But if a party were to adopt a feminist agenda, would many male voters (and traditional women) desert it? In a situation in which elections could be won or lost by a few percentage points, it would not be surprising if caution prevailed. Thus in Britain, as in many other countries, political parties fought elections on conventional issues such as inflation and taxation.184 Out of 1,031 television appearances by politicians in the 1992 British general election only thirty-three were by women, even though, in 'phone-in' programmes, 'women' issues such as child-care allowances and nursery education were often raised.185

Feminism and ecology became typical lip-service issues. Politicians picked them up and mentioned them, as if to show goodwill and concern; then they were returned to the bottom of the list and attention refocused on 'real' politics. For instance, Bryan Gould, who, in the late 1980s, was regarded as one of the Labour Party's leading modernizers, lamented the party's neglect of women in his ambitiously titled *A Future for Socialism*, and added that socialists had to recognize that the feminist agenda 'illuminates the whole range of political and social issues, whether directly or exclusively affecting women'.[186] This was the *only* mention of women or feminism or gender in the entire book.

A less striking but parallel ambivalence characterized the 1987 electoral campaign of the Italian Communist Party. As Marc Lazar noted, communist posters throughout the campaign carried slogans such as 'I vote communist in order to elect a woman' and 'Vote for women, vote communist'; yet the banner headline of *L'Unità* reporting the final appeal of the party leader Alessandro Natta was 'The workers, before all else'.[187]

A similarly equivocal approach was generally taken towards environmental issues. After the success of the British Greens in the 1989 election to the European Parliament (15 per cent of the vote, but no seats), the two main British parties put ecology higher up their agenda. Three years later, during the campaign leading to the 1992 election, ecology reverted to its former status as a minor issue.[188]

The two key issues of the new politics – ecology and feminism – do not target a small group of easily identifiable enemies like the capitalists. The targets are broad. Which political party could expect wide popularity in singling out 'consumers' or 'men' as the opponent to beat? Green politics involves a society with different priorities where, for instance, private motoring – by far the most formidable source of pollution – would have to be severely restricted. This is likely to be resisted not only by those workers and employers involved in production of motor cars, but also by millions of ordinary car drivers – often the first generation in history with access to private trans-portation. This is not a constituency any party is likely to antagonize.

As for feminism, the 'enemy' can only be men or, rather, the way men of flesh and blood come to become 'men'. The real, long-term purpose of feminism is not to ensure women's access to the world of men, but to change this world by changing men and women. This was clearly felt and recognized as early as 1979 even by Helmut Schmidt – hardly an uncritical supporter of the 'new politics' – when he told the Bundestag that 'The emancipation of women will only be successful if the traditional world of men also changes.'[189] It was not a situation which could afford great solace to many men. A survey conducted in Britain indicates that 'a substantial proportion of men with partners who work full-time … seem to be somewhat uncomfortable about it'.[190] Many women too felt threatened by feminism. The redefinition of masculinity, an inescapable component of the gender revolution, meant redefining femininity. Feminism challenged women as well as men – as all great feminist theorists of the past, from Wollstonecraft to de Beauvoir, have pointed out. The oppression of women by men throughout the whole of recorded history could never have taken place without the collusion of women.

It is abundantly clear from the considerable body of work now available that the fundamental obstacle to real equality between men and women lay in the persistence of women's conflicting roles as carers and producers. This was pointed out more than forty years ago by Alva Myrdal and Viola Klein.[191] In the short term, even the provision of extensive child-care would not resolve the problems. The strength of guilt-inducing cultural patterns, the children's own induced expectation that their mothers were the only person they could truly rely on, the established pattern of work which prized long hours and dedication to the job, all worked against the inclusion of women – on equal terms with men – in a productive system largely determined by an established division of labour.[192] For instance, between 1974 and 1979, Sweden introduced an advanced system of parental leave, the first in the world to allow either parent or both to care for the newborn or for a sick child, and a statutory right to reduced working hours.[193] Yet it was over-whelmingly women who took advantage of this 'gender-neutral' parental leave system.[194] Only by changing the meaning of fatherhood, and hence of a conception of masculinity more ancient than capitalism itself, can some progress be made on the road towards true sexual equality. Effecting such a cultural revolution was quite beyond the scope of political parties. They played only a marginal role in the democratization of the sphere of intimacy.[195] It is unrealistic to expect these enfeebled organizations to change attitudes rooted in the experience of centuries, when they are no longer able to provoke any widespread enthusiasm or even to think beyond the next election.

What socialist parties could legitimately be expected to do, however, was to create some of the conditions for the development of genuine equality between the sexes. As the old ideal of the full employment of males crumbled, perhaps it would be possible to reconstruct the welfare state as 'a welfare society' in which women, no longer 'involuntary social exiles' bereft of the resources for social participation, could enjoy full social membership on the same terms as men.[196] This minimalist assumption, if valid, would redefine the tasks of socialists as 'enablers'. Socialists liberate no one; at best, they create the possibility of liberation.

At its origins the socialist movement had the ambition of leading the workers towards self-emancipation; one hundred years later, the goals were more modest and not centred on workers. The emancipation of the working class was no longer seen as a necessary condition for human emancipation. The new social movements may not have brought many votes to socialist parties; but they brought new ideas. In the long term, ideas are always more important than votes. Yet by the end of the 1980s, the gloomy prediction that socialism had fallen into a deep coma seemed to have been confirmed. The last attempts to inject some further life into the traditional socialist agenda ended in failure. These I shall examine in the next chapter.

CHAPTER TWENTY-THREE

The 1980s: Radicalism in
its Last Redoubt

POWER, IT is said, concentrates the mind wonderfully. In government political parties perceive the limits of their power. They discover that alternatives they previously regarded as available have in fact been foreclosed. The unintended results of previous policy decisions compel them to take actions they had not planned. To be realistic or pragmatic is no longer an injunction one can choose to disregard. It is imposed and structured by the constraints within which one operates. This reflection is as old as politics itself, but it acquired greater significance in the modern age, as that great master of politics, Otto von Bismarck, reminds us:

The pathway a Prussian ministry is able to take is never very wide; the man from the far Left, when he becomes a minister, will have to move to his right, and the man from the far Right, when he becomes a minister, will have to move to his Left, and there is no room in this narrow trail that the government of a large country is able to tread for the kind of sweeping divagations of doctrine that a man may unfold as an orator or a member of parliament.

Life in opposition is even more frustrating, but those without political power at least have the freedom to dream. This may not be much of a consolation, however, but in opposition the goal is single, simple and overarching; the conquest of power. Policies are not tested for what they actually achieve, but in terms of how the electorate or one's own supporters are likely to respond. A prolonged period in opposition reduces this freedom of manoeuvre. Policies which repeatedly fail the test of electoral acceptability have to be discarded. The social and economic environment and the policies of opponents in government render previous plans inadequate or obsolete, forcing an overall reassessment.

For instance, the widespread privatizations which took place in Europe, and particularly in Britain, during the course of the 1980s made the Left's classic programme of nationalization, and its corresponding model of interventionist economic management, highly implausible. It could be exhumed only on the assumption that the entire economic system was about to collapse. But no party could present a programme predicated on unforeseeable catastrophic events. Renationalization remained an expensive option which would merely amount to a return to the *status quo ante*. Similarly, it was one thing to defend full employment when it existed; another to advocate it when there was massive unemployment.

We saw in the preceding sections how in Holland and Belgium, Sweden and Italy, Britain and Austria, France and Germany, socialists and social democrats, when in power, had to adapt themselves to the new era of world stagflation, interdependence, low growth. By the end of the 1980s, all parties of the Left – there were hardly any exceptions – went through the most dramatic programmatic reappraisal in the entire history of the movement.

To illustrate this, I shall examine the plans for radical renewal of some socialist parties while in opposition. First, I shall analyse the policies of the Labour Party in the period 1979–83. This was a phase when the party was still reacting to the failures of its policies in government (1974–79), by seeking to reform its constitution and ensure that its alternative economic strategy would be pursued by a future Labour government. Next, I shall examine the ambitious Meidner Plan adopted by the Swedish social democrats – the first post-war socialist programme aimed at eliminating private control over the principal means of production. Finally, I shall consider the German SPD's attempt to graft a 'new politics' dimension on to its new 'fundamental programme'. Each plan was abandoned either because those who supported it were defeated (the Labour Left), or because the opposition to it was too massive (Sweden), or because of the unforeseen change to the map of Europe and Germany brought about by the Gorbachevite revolution in the USSR.

In the final chapter, I shall examine the establishment of the new ideological consensus of European social democracy: the neo-revisionism of the late 1980s which marks the second historical reconciliation between socialism and capitalism. The first, on social-democratic terms, took place after 1945. The second represented a compromise on the terms set by neo-liberalism. Whether this signals the *de facto* demise of the socialist movement, or simply the end of its pre-history, is something I shall happily leave to futurologists. With history, as historians know only too well, you can never tell.

Rise and Fall of the Labour Party Left

In May 1979, when Margaret Thatcher entered Downing Street, most Conservatives were as unaware as the rest of the population that she was to preside over the most radical administration in twentieth-century Britain. Most governments water down their ideology as they accede to power. The new Conservative administration, though it quickly abandoned its original strict monetarism, fortified its own wine as it went along. In the course of the succeeding ten years, it made the unions weaker and local government ineffectual; it deregulated the labour market; reduced income tax to levels unimaginable in the 1970s; sold most of the state sector to private owners; and introduced a semblance of market criteria into the allocation of resources within the as yet unsaleable public sector, including education and health. The result was a net distribution of resources from the poorest to the richest, achieved with minimal social strife.[2] Much of this, of course, could not have happened without favourable circumstances. For instance, British trade unions were weakened by the growth in unemployment, not by Conservative laws; but had they not become weaker, it would have been harder to pass anti-union legislation.

Had the Labour Party been in possession of the proverbial crystal ball in May 1979, it might have hesitated before conceding to so right-wing a government so much of the centre ground by moving rapidly to the left. Some left-wing intellectuals sounded an early warning: the government led by Mrs Thatcher would, they wrote, shift the ideological climate to the right, irrespective of its actual achievements. As Stuart Hall pointed out in a pioneering and much quoted article published in December 1978, six months before the Tories' historic victory, the strength of Thatcher's political inter-vention was 'partly in the radicalism of its commitment to break the mould and not simply to rework the elements of the prevailing "philosophies"'.[3] This analysis was further developed in the pages of the 'Eurocommunist' journal *Marxism Today*, the most influential left-wing publication of the 1980s.[4] The Labour Party itself conducted no analyses of Thatcherism; as Michael Rustin, a critic of the journal, recognized, 'Such is the thinness of the Labour Party's political culture that *Marxism Today* has ... become more or less the theoretical organ of Labour revisionism too.'[5]

The Labour Left, emboldened by the disarray of its internal right-wing opponents, agreed with *Marxism Today* in identifying Mrs Thatcher as a dangerous opponent whose aim was to bury, once and for all, the cosy post-war social-democratic consensus between 'one-world' Tories and right-wing Labour. It saw no reason for shedding tears. The old consensus was, after all, that of capitalism. If Margaret Thatcher was going to radicalize politics, the Labour Left would respond with its own brand of radicalism. The class struggle, so it was thought, would finally become visible. However, the Labour Left did not heed the prognosis of *Marxism Today*. It refused to accept that a new hegemony could not be built on the radical policies of yesteryear. New policies were required to cope with the 'New Times' of globalism and post-Fordism.

The iconoclasm of *Marxism Today* was indispensable, but once the ground was cleared of old-fashioned leftism, the journal and its followers remained unable to go beyond it. They were left trying to unpick from Thatcherite discourse the radical bits they admired and hailing them as the harbingers of modernity.[6] In the manner of modern gurus they noted a trend (post-Fordism, flexible specialization, or charity events for Third World countries), called it 'progress', and projected it into the future. By the time the journal folded in the 1990s, it had nothing left to say.

As far as the Labour Left was concerned, 'its' programme had never been given a chance by Wilson and Callaghan. Responsibility for the failures of the 1974–79 government belonged to those Labour right-wingers who had cut public expenditure, permitted unemployment to rise to unprecedented levels, and imposed unacceptable pay restraint upon Labour's core supporters. This analysis, though crude, was not entirely vacuous. Few could claim that the Callaghan government had been an impressive success. The Labour Left acquired unprecedented strength as a direct consequence of the failure of the policies pursued by Callaghan and Healey and the electoral defeat of 1979. Michael Foot, the Left's erstwhile guide, succeeded James Callaghan as leader of the Labour Party in 1980. He had lost some of his aura as a 'pure' champion of the Left because of his loyalty to the Wilson and Callaghan governments. Nevertheless, his election represented a departure from the Callaghan years and a victory for the Left.

Labour Party activists, overwhelmingly left-wing, became more influential than ever, holding the balance of power within the party thanks to a profound right–left split within the trade unions. The Transport and General Workers' Union, the largest organization affiliated to the Labour Party, was a staunch supporter of the Left and played a decisive role in counter-balancing the power of right-wing trade union leaders.[7] In the 1950s and 1960s, the trade unions' block vote could be wheeled out at annual party conferences to back the moderate leadership against the Left. By the early 1980s, many of the unions had grown resentful of the Callaghan–Healey pay policy and refused to help the Right. Hence the growing demands by some on the right of the party for abolition of the block vote, not so much because it was un-democratic, which it patently was, but because it was unreliable.

As the remaining source of power still in the hands of the party, Labour-controlled local government became a significant force, especially when run by the Labour Left – notably the Greater London Council under Ken Livingstone, Sheffield under David Blunkett, and Liverpool, where the Labour Party was dominated by the Trotskyist Militant Tendency.

How did the Left utilize this renewed strength? At the national level, it did not advance any new ideas, but preferred to dig up the old Alternative Economic Strategy (AES), developed in the 1970s (see chapter 18). Because it had remained untested, it had preserved all its allure.[8] This 'alternative' strategy, in spite of the bloodcurdling claims made for and against it, consisted in a policy for the expansion of *both* the public and private sectors through selective nationalizations, planning agreements and the regulation of the pricing policies of large firms. Import controls – it was thought – would allow economic growth to take place without a drastically deteriorating balance of payments.[9] The AES was conspicuously silent on wages – the rock on which the Callaghan government foundered – except in its advocacy of a 'national economic assessment' – a euphemism for an incomes policy negoti-ated with the unions. This vagueness was repeatedly criticized even by supporters of the policy.[10]

Unlike the Swedish employee investment funds, and the SPD's revision of the Bad Godesberg Programme (the Berlin Programme of 1989), the AES was never widely discussed among trade unionists and party members, in spite of the efforts of organizations such as the Labour Co-ordinating Committee and the Institute for Workers' Control. Like the Swedish and German plans, the AES, though briefly the official policy of the party, was never enthusiastically endorsed by the parliamentary leadership.[11]

The Left's analysis was quite simple. The AES would arrest Britain's historical economic decline and open the way for socialism. The main political problem was not what to do – the AES was the answer to that – but how to eliminate the obstacles to its implementation. These were of two kinds. The first was that the Labour leadership was unlikely to adopt it when in power. It was therefore necessary to devise new internal rules to ensure that the leadership and the parliamentary party would accept and implement the party programme. The second obstacle was the web of international de-pendence that would constrain a future Labour government – namely, the European Economic Community and the US-dominated Atlantic alliance. Withdrawal from the EEC and disregard for NATO were the solution. The AES was to be the last attempt by the Labour Party to develop a socialist strategy which required insulating the country from the constraints of the international economy.[12]

The decision to install Cruise and Pershing missiles in Europe (including some on British soil) and to 'modernize' the British nuclear force was opposed by successive Labour Party conferences after 1980. This coincided with a dramatic revival of the activities of the Campaign for Nuclear Disarmament, which had been dormant since the 1960s. The 1983 manifesto promised that a future Labour government would include Polaris missiles in any nuclear disarmament negotiations. The 1987 manifesto promised that Polaris would be decommissioned. In fact, Labour's defence policy was in a mess. It moved from the 'pure' unilateralism of 1983 to the 'fudged' unilateralism of 1987.[13] In order to please everyone, the 1983 manifesto was simultaneously in favour of unilateral and multilateral disarmament. Michael Foot and Denis Healey (his deputy leader) offered contradictory explanations.[14]

Ever suspicious that on this and other issues the leadership would not comply with the rank and file, the Left proposed that the leader of the Labour Party be no longer elected by the parliamentary group, but by an electoral college in which the decisive weight would be held by individual members and trade unions. It further proposed that the election manifesto of the party should be drafted by the National Executive Committee (NEC) – where the Left had gained a majority – and not jointly with the shadow cabinet – as had been established practice. Finally, it suggested that existing MPs would have to go through a new process of reselection by their local parties before every general election. The Left hoped that moderate MPs, as well as the lazy and the incompetent, would gradually be eliminated in favour of left-wing ones.

The logic behind these proposals was easily understood. The democrat-ization of the party – in effect, a shift of power to the membership – would bring about the election of a left-wing leader; the AES, overwhelmingly approved, as it usually was, at conference, would be incorporated by the Left-dominated NEC into the election manifesto. Members of Parliament reluctant to accept this state of affairs would be deselected. This entire operation rested on two assumptions: that the trade union movement, whose votes determined the politics of Labour Party conferences, would remain paralysed between Left and Right; and that the rank and file would always support the Left. It had not yet become apparent that though activists cannot ensure electoral victory, they can contribute decisively to defeat.[15]

The full story of these plans need not detain us here. They are abundantly documented elsewhere.[16] Mandatory reselection was achieved in 1979. This was the most immediate cause behind the creation of the Social Democratic Party (SDP). The leaders of the Labour Right who spearheaded the SDP – the so-called 'gang of four': Roy Jenkins, David Owen, Shirley Williams and William Rodgers – would have been content for things to remain as they were, as long as the parliamentary leadership could continue to ignore Labour conference decisions.[17] But right-wing dissatisfaction with the state of the party preceded mandatory deselection. In his 1979 Dimbleby Lecture, 'Home Thoughts from Abroad', delivered when he was still president of the Commission of the EC, Roy Jenkins sounded the original clarion call for a party of the centre.[18] Wider dissatisfaction with the existing state of affairs had been expressed by social-democratic intellectuals. For instance, David Marquand complained of the growing 'proletarianist' style of the Labour Party, 'increasingly at odds with society' and aimed at making middle-class recruits uncomfortable, and went on to suggest that the 'social democrats' no longer had any business being part of the same movement as the 'socialists' – a position many on the 'socialist' wing shared.[19]

A special conference held at Wembley in 1981 took away from MPs their exclusive power to elect the party leader. The drafting of the manifesto remained in the hands of the leadership. By the end of the year, Tony Benn, the acknowledged leader of the Left, came within a few votes of becoming deputy leader of the Labour Party: 49,574 per cent to Denis Healey's 50,426. Benn had obtained 83 per cent of the constituency vote (whose weight in the electoral college was 30 per cent), but he lost in both the trade union and parliamentary party sections. The Left's analysis of where its strength lay was thus confirmed: it had won the overwhelming support of the rank and file and the hostility of most MPs.

To those outside the Labour Party (and even to some inside it), the whole affair appeared remote and Byzantine. The unions' consultative machinery, the way they cast their votes, the language they spoke appeared to confirm Conservative propaganda: these organizations were run by an incompetent and ill-organized oligarchy who, far from representing 'ordinary people' – as they constantly claimed – behaved in a strange and alienating way. The rank and file had an even worse image. To working-class supporters it appeared as if the party of Attlee and Bevin had fallen into the hands of ineffectual, college-educated militants, commanding an incomprehensible jargon borrowed from the communist tradition, pandering to a intimidating lobby of neurotic lesbians, holier-than-thou ecologists, puritanical vegetarians and loud-mouthed black power activists. To the vast middle classes it looked as if Labour had been commandeered by disrespectful proletarians, or, as the *Guardian's* colum- nist Peter Jenkins insultingly put it, the 'lumpen-polytechnic'. These arrogant and truculent activists, instead of listening deferentially to their relatively reasonable leaders – as they had previously done – demanded, at a time of economic difficulty, massive tax increases to fund a deteriorating welfare state, while giving the unions the run of the kingdom. These ludicrous images, beneath which lurked the proverbial grain of truth, were reinforced by the media, where the Labour Left had hardly any friends. All daily papers supported either the Conservatives or the Labour Right. Television was more balanced in its approach, but, as 'balance' meant to be neither left nor right, the values it held were those of the centre of the political spectrum – precisely the place occupied by the Labour Left's most dangerous opponents: the Labour Right and the SDP.[20] A particularly venomous campaign was waged against Tony Benn – one of the most interesting Labour politicians of the post-war period and, for a while, the 'red bogeyman' of the tabloid press – though he did not easily fit any of the available stereotypes used to caricature the 'hard' Left. Nevertheless, there were repeated attempts to represent him as an appropriately maniacal leader of the 'loony' left. Tony Benn was, in fact, with the historian E. P. Thompson, one of the last representatives of a distinguished, if somewhat insular, English radical tradition doomed to dis- appear.[21]

Benn's genuine preoccupation with the democratization of the Labour Party and British society in general, his remarkable performances in Parliament and on television, his polished skills as a public debater and his sense of humour, were more than counter-balanced by poor political judgement and frequent inconsistencies.[22] This, in turn, was caused by an over-optimistic, romantic and quite unwarranted assessment of the desire for socialism of the British people, and of the strength and maturity of the labour movement. The image of the Labour Party had become so negative and so patently an electoral handicap that for years afterwards image-making became a distinctive obsession of the party, spreading from the leadership to the entire trade union movement and, eventually, to the rank and file.[23] Well before that, however, the tide had begun to turn against the Labour Left.

What I have so far described as the Left should now be reclassified, following then current journalistic usage, as the 'hard Left', to distinguish it from the 'soft Left'. Initially, the difference between the two was one of personalities and styles; the 'soft Left' emerged only when Neil Kinnock and others refused to support Tony Benn for the deputy leadership at the party's Brighton Conference in 1981. As the soft Left moved to the right, the differences became more clearly-policy oriented. In 1981, however, both 'hard' and 'soft' Left agreed on the AES, on nuclear disarmament, on withdrawal from the EC, on mandatory reselection of MPs, and so on. What distinguished the two was that the soft Left was increasingly alarmed at the methods and tactics used by the radicals, and particularly at the growing strength of the Militant Tendency. This Trotskyist group, well aware that its rhetoric and agenda made it totally unelectable on its own, had successfully followed the tactics of 'entryism'. It had discovered that it was possible to take over the Labour Party more or less by stealth, simply by turning up at local party meetings, passing resolutions and accumulating offices. Eventually, through mandatory reselection, the Parliamentary Labour Party – so they believed – would be overwhelmed by MPs loyal to the Militant Tendency. This absurd strategy had well-established credentials in the Trotskyist movement and was well known to the Labour Party. In 1975, the party's national agent, Reg Underhill, had prepared a report warning of the threat to it. Nothing was done because the Labour Left, with some justification, saw it as a ploy to marginalize the entire Left.[4]

Besides the soft and hard Lefts, two further groups need to be identified: the social democrats, whose alienation from the party climaxed in the formation of the Social Democratic Party in 1981; and the traditional Labour Right. There were hardly any differences between the two on policy. Both were in favour of European integration and NATO, both opposed unilateral disarmament and all the organizational reforms proposed by the Left. The difference was that the social democrats were convinced that nothing could be done to stop the Left taking over the Labour Party. History proved them wrong. During the course of the 1980s, the soft Left recaptured the party, developed its own agenda, isolated the hard Left, made peace with the traditional Labour Right, and adopted positions increasingly similar to those originally propounded by the SDP. By then, the SDP, whose leadership, much praised by the press, proved itself to be politically incompetent, had been taken over by its ally, the Liberal Party, now rechristened the Liberal Democratic Party. As for the Labour Party, after its fourth consecutive defeat (1992), it became a relatively united force with a coherent ideology, a much improved public image, and a campaigning style far superior to that of the Conservatives.

The year 1981 marked the beginning of the end for the hard Left. Having contributed to the secession of the SDP, and alienated those subsequently labelled the 'soft Left', it had even failed to rally those sections of the 'New Left' which had abandoned the rhetoric of the 1960s and grown closer to the Labour Party. Feminists, ecologists, libertarians and the 'Eurocommunist' faction of the CPGB were less than enthusiastic about the AES, which was seen simply as a return to the *étatique* tradition of labourism. Ecology and feminism were still being ignored by much of the hard Left.[25] Nuclear pacifism, which was not ignored, predated the 1960s and belonged to Labour's radical tradition.

Criticism of the hard Left had poured in from quarters quite distant from the political centre even before the second electoral defeat in 1983. In 1981, the historian Eric Hobsbawm, a communist for more than half a century who could hardly be suspected of pandering to social-democratic revisionism, warned against the excessive idealization of rank-and-file activities. He argued against the belief that the Labour Party could be captured by 'a smallish minority' without reference to the masses outside it. He warned against the illusion that 'organization can replace politics', the expectation that the 'old calls for socialism' would have 'the same resonance as in the past', the idea that 'all that stands between us and the next Labour government is a good Left-wing programme'. Further, he deplored the secession of the SDP, because it represented 'the loss of a significant section of the Left-of-centre middle class, which had long looked to Labour, and in many cases actively worked for Labour ... it potentially represents a significant electoral weakening of the Labour Party – how much is still unclear'.[26] It became clear in 1983, when Labour obtained its worst results since 1923 – a disaster of such proportions that it had not been anticipated even 'by the gloomiest among us'.[27]

Feminists too were less than supportive of the hard Left and the AES. They were not simply objecting to the 'macho' style and language of many hard Left supporters. They were also critical of the traditionalism embedded in the 'patriarchal' productivism of the AES. Anna Coote remarked that the AES had not only failed to take into account changes in the world of work, and primarily the increasing role of women in it, but had also overlooked the work women did at home and their economic dependency on men. It assumed that returning to the full employment of the 1950s – when virtually all men and only a minority of women went out to work – was both desirable and possible, while it was in fact unacceptable and unrealistic. 'Our starting point for an alternative strategy', she wrote, 'might begin with a different kind of question, such as "how shall we care for and support our children?" ... in the sense not of private domestic choices, but of our collective responsibility towards the next generation.'[28] It would take more than ten years for this kind of thinking to become part of Labour's general agenda.

By the end of 1982, even the influential rank-and-file group, the Labour Co-ordinating Committee (LCC), an organization which had spearheaded the constitutional changes within the party, which had supported the AES and approved of unilateralism, was distancing itself from the hard Left. An LCC pamphlet berated the naive 'parliamentarist' belief that all that was required was for the leadership to be made accountable to the base in order to avoid betrayals.[29] It castigated the intolerant view which saw the labour movement, narrowly defined as the party and the unions, as the only agent of socialist change – thus disregarding the new social movements. Finally, it pointed out that though the hard Left appeared obsessed with inner-party democracy, it had no ideas on how to democratize schools or the health service or local governments.[30] The LCC pamphlet objected to party meetings being domin-ated 'by this endless cycle of resolutions passing upwards and reports trickling down'. It is a process striking for its entirely *internal* character.[31]

Thus, the hard Left had not succeeded in establishing support even within the wider Labour Left, let alone the party as whole – not to speak of the electorate. Margaret Thatcher's successful handling of the Falklands dispute with Argentina accelerated the crisis of the hard Left. The majority of the population shared the nationalist fervour which pervaded the country during the war. Thatcher interpreted this mood as few other politicians could have done. The leadership of the Labour Party around Michael Foot simply followed, looking indecisive. The Bennite Left was isolated.

The Falklands War marked a turning-point in the fortunes of the Con-servative government. Before the war, it was unpopular. After it, Thatcher acquired the self-confidence and the international authority she had hitherto lacked. Thatcherism, a notion popularized by the Left, had now become a successful phenomenon which even a united Labour Party might not have been able to stop. For a divided party, it proved impossible. The spectacular defeat of the Labour Party at the 1983 general election – one of the most severe setbacks ever experienced by a socialist party in Western Europe – was simply the *coup de grâce*. The scale of the reverse was openly acknowledged by Michael Foot: 'We won fewer seats than at any election since 1935. We found ourselves with no MPs in the seventy-seven constituencies in the southern region. We lost a record number of deposits and came third, or worse, in 292 constituencies.[32]

Labour's campaign had been exceptionally amateurish. Professionalization of electoral campaigning and greatly improved presentation in the 1987 and 1992 elections, however, did not lead to victory. Labour's problems were too deep to be resolved merely by better management of its image, as Denis Healey explained to the NEC during the 1983 election post-mortem: 'The election was not lost in the three weeks of the campaign but in the three years which preceded it ... In that period the Party itself acquired a highly unfavourable public image, based on disunity, extremism, crankiness and general unfitness to govern.[33]

Aspects of this unfavourable image were deserved, but even at its imagin-ative finest Labour was never truly popular. The best example of radicalism at work in this period was the Greater London Council, which had been taken over by the Left in 1981. It tried to apply in an ingenious way the AES to London's problems, though it never possessed the institutional means with which to implement it. The GLC produced an industrial strategy for the capital, a 620-page volume which identified, sector by sector, from the furniture industry to Heathrow airport, the various ways in which the de-industrialization of the capital might be reversed.[34] It instituted a London version of the National Enterprise Board, the Greater London Enterprise Board (GLEB). It attempted to develop an integrated London transport strategy by lowering, in the first instance, transport fares. It developed an imaginative cultural policy, which pleased the wider Left intelligentsia. It took feminism seriously by developing a research programme into anti-discrimina- tory policy and set up a project for a wider network of child-care. Nevertheless, only the lower fares policy, understandably enough, was really popular. In the minds of many Londoners, the GLC evoked the negative image constructed by the tabloid newspapers: a scheme to subsidize, at the taxpayer's expense, the antics of gays and lesbians. No mass protest followed the Thatcher government's decision to abolish it in 1986, along with other metropolitan authorities, thus reducing London to the status of being the only European capital without an administration, and making Britain one of the most centralized countries in Europe. The GLC had even failed to obtain the support of the Labour leadership because its leaders had been unwilling to side with Foot's successor, Neil Kinnock, in his battle against the hard Left.

This battle had become the paramount preoccupation of the new leader- ship. The story of the party from 1983 until 1987 and beyond was essentially the story of the successful campaign against the hard Left conducted by Neil Kinnock. It was symptomatic of the profound crisis of the Labour Party that so much time and effort had to be expended by a major party of the European Left to get rid of a rather unsophisticated Trotskyist sect, able to count on no more than a few thousand members. It is equally symptomatic that Kinnock's major achievement, 'the bravest and most perceptive act of his leadership', was his successful attack on the Militant Tendency at the party's Annual Conference at Bournemouth in 1985.[35] Kinnock had two purposes: to reassert the authority of the leadership, which had been in- creasingly challenged by the rank and file; and 'to reassure frightened electors by refurbishing Labour's image as a respectable and pragmatic party'.[36] Paradoxically, Kinnock was helped in his task by Arthur Scargill, the leader of the National Union of Mineworkers, who led his union in the most disastrous strike in post-war British history (1984–85). Kinnock could not possibly have distanced himself from the strikers, whose attempt to stop mining pits (and villages) from being closed down evoked deep sympathy in the broad labour movement. He refused, however, to identify himself closely with Scargill.[37] But the failure of the NUM brought home to Labour sup- porters how dangerous it was for any political party to entrust its destiny and its wider electoral goals to particular interests under a leadership it could not control. The defeat of the miners signalled the defeat of the 'hard' trade unionism which had prevailed hitherto. It was the signal for Kinnock's counter-attack.

Between 1983 and 1987, Tony Benn and his followers were ousted from all positions of power; some, however, joined the soft Left, as did most of the left-wing Tribune group of MPs and the LCC. After 1987, all the distinctive policies which had been adopted between 1979 and 1983 were eventually abandoned: anti-Europeanism, state ownership, high levels of income tax, and the Alternative Economic Strategy. The NEC finally dropped unilateralism on 9 May 1989. Eight of its members voted against this decision, including Tom Sawyer (one of the architects of the review process), David Blunkett and Margaret Beckett – all protagonists of the 'new look' Labour Party of the early 1990s.[38] Underpinning this 'review' process, as it was called, was the growing expansion, not just in Britain but throughout Europe and the rest of the world, of a new market ideology.

The defeat of the Labour Left had been inevitable. It was not due to its excessive radicalism, but to its profound conservatism. Its strategy was predicated on a concept of national sovereignty which was no longer relevant. This strategy assumed that a majority in the House of Commons led by a trustworthy leadership (one which would not 'betray' the movement) was all that was required to implement a left-wing programme. Much followed from this assumption. In the first place, the existing electoral system had to be preserved at all costs, for it was ideally suited to award a majority of seats to a party with 40 per cent or so of the electorate. Secondly, no constitution or bill of rights would be necessary. This would simply strengthen the power of judges and further limit a Labour government. An absolute Labour parliamentary majority would be a better protector than the judiciary of individual and collective rights. This attitude, far from being peculiar to the Labour Left, was characteristic of the entire party, having been endorsed by Anthony Crosland and, later, Roy Hattersley.[39] Tony Benn, on the other hand, while defending the existing electoral system on pragmatic rather than principled grounds, was a consistent proponent of a wider democratization of the British state and a written constitution.[40] Thirdly, as British sovereignty in all its aspects had to be preserved, the transfer of powers to the European Community had to be blocked and the process of British integration had to be reversed. In this way Britain would 'plan its trade' (how is unclear, as it takes at least two to trade) and, if necessary, impose import controls. The rest of the world would presumably just submit meekly, as when Britain ruled the waves. Finally, by disarming unilaterally, the country would provide the two superpowers with a stunning moral example and shame them into following the British lead. The fact that whatever was decided in the UK about nuclear policy would not have the slightest effect on détente between the two superpowers was never mentioned by senior Labour or Tory politicians. All kept up the pretence that Britain still had a major role to play in international affairs. Thus a sovereign House of Commons, unfettered by constitutions and unrestrained by international institutions, would be in charge of its destiny. A new Labour government would be fully controlled by Labour MPs in turn accountable to local parties.

To call this strategy 'conservative' is therefore not a polemical exaggeration. It was the consequence of a profound identification between labourism and the British state. It is therefore not surprising that it had many features in common with a major strand in British conservatism: confidence in the country's world importance and in the superiority of its political institutions; distrust of European integration and fear that crucial aspects of its economic sovereignty would be subsumed in a wider Europe – in short, 'the acceptance of the national-imperial mould as the optimal foundation for the New Jerusalem'.[41]

Even those who realized that economic interdependence posed a serious problem for the AES pretended that somehow it could be waved away. An example of this was Stuart Holland, a major AES theorist of the Labour Left, who favoured simultaneously a 'European' strategy and an anti-EC one. In his writings, full of warnings against multinational companies, he was supremely aware of globalism and interdependence, and frequently argued for a European co-ordinated reflation. Yet he could countenance Britain 'going it alone' by reflating unilaterally, and dismissed the EC because it would not be able to 'cope with the scale of spending, planning and international cooperation necessary to transform the crisis' or make multinationals more accountable.[42]

In a more substantial work, Holland warned against European monetary union because it would occur in a monetarist (i.e. deflationary) context and would 'deprive individual member countries and societies of the chance readily to change their model of development'.[43] A similarly pessimistic reading of the potential of the European Community was characteristic of the soft Left. Thus Neil Kinnock in 1984: 'Confined by out-of-date treaties, the Community is in a political cul-de-sac. It can develop a new deal neither for Europe nor for the rest of the world.'[44]

The main alternative to the hard Left, the social-democrat secessionists, were equally conservative. Presenting themselves as the arch-modernizers, they coined a slogan which soon became a cliché, claiming that it was necessary to 'break the mould' of British politics. This whiff of radicalism disguised a rather conventional approach. The 1982 economic package of the SDP consisted of a limited expansion of the economy through a mix of devaluation and fiscal and monetary relaxation. The approach was thus conventionally Keynesian.[45] Inflation would be contained by holding wages below the growth of demand. This revamped incomes policy would not be operated through a social contract with the unions – an option the SDP did not have – but through taxing wage increases above the established norm, thus nullifying any incentive to break government pay guidelines.[46] This last proposal, the so-called counter-inflation tax, had originally been advanced by the Liberal Party in the early 1970s. On constitutional matters too the SDP simply adopted existing Liberal policies in advocating electoral reform, a Freedom of Information Act, a Bill of Rights, devolution of power and a local income tax.[47]

The SDP, like the hard Left, refrained from engaging with 'new politics'

– here too the Liberals were more radical. The SDP was committed to growth, had a low profile on green issues, was not hostile to nuclear power, and showed little interest in feminism in spite of having noted feminists in its ranks such as Polly Toynbee and Sue Slipman. Shirley Williams, the one woman of the 'gang of four', in her wide-ranging though insubstantial book *Politics is for People*, devoted only one page (out of 230) to women – and then only to explain that more women than ever were in paid employment.[48]

The ephemeral rise of the SDP should be seen in the context of the growing disenchantment with established politics which characterized the European party systems after the end of the golden age. This disenchantment took the form of the creation of new parties which, somehow, appeared to be 'different', unconventional, less 'political' – that is, less *conventionally* political. Examples include the Greens, the left-libertarian socialist people's parties of Denmark and Norway, the Christian democrats in Sweden, the far right Freedom Party in Austria, the anti-tax Progress Party in Denmark and, in Italy, the Radical Party and later the Northern League. However, these parties, unlike the British SDP, often had something genuinely new to say. The SDP said what the Labour Party used to say before its shift to the left. It was the only British party still firmly anchored to the social-democratic consensus of yesteryear. It did not become a rallying point for new forces – indeed, it was hostile to them. It did, however, attract people who had never been involved in politics before. Nevertheless, it turned out to be no more than a 'flash-party' – as political scientists, with the benefit of hindsight, call these ephemeral formations.[49]

Pressure groups emerging from the 'new politics' of the 1960s were forced to work within the Labour Party and to try to graft on to it their own particular programmes. Their primary loyalty was not to the party, but to the agenda of their own group. The 'entryism' of the Militant Tendency should be seen in this context. The problem was, as Bernard Crick pointed out, that all these minorities could never add up to a majority.[50]

In the early 1980s, this collection of minorities, each unpopular with the wider majority, had become Labour's main problem. To put it at its simplest: the majority of Labour voters did not share the values of Labour members. Many Labour voters were in favour of further restrictions on immigration, tougher law-and-order policies, controlling union power, reintroducing capital punishment, dealing harshly with welfare 'scroungers'.[51] Most voters, including most Labour voters, grossly overestimating the nation's status in the world, thought that Britain should retain its own nuclear weapons.[52] Labour's defence specialist Mike Gapes complained that 'as long as British people see nuclear weapons as a kind of national status symbol then it will be extremely difficult to introduce a coherent and rational defence policy in this country.'[53] These Labour-voting 'conservatives', overwhelmingly working class, could easily transfer their allegiance to Thatcher's Conservatives. Indeed, many did just that, particularly when tax cuts were dangled before them. Could this defection be compensated by increased support from the so-called public sector 'salariat', who tended to be liberal-minded on civil rights issues and interested in protecting the public sector? Possibly, but many of these middle-class voters had little sympathy with Labour's traditional programme of unalloyed defence of trade union power, nationalization and state intervention. Thus, Labour was exposed on two fronts: it was losing the more prosperous sections of the working class to the Conservatives, while the liberal salariat defected to the SDP. Labour gained nothing by becoming a party of the hard Left.

The main consequence of the formation of the SDP was that it facilitated the victory of the soft Left within the Labour Party and hence Labour's electoral survival. The SDP and its Liberal allies provided Labour with some of the key words it would use in the 1990s: 'community', the 'enabling society', 'individual responsibility'. These words of David Owen's, the SDP leader, could be recited, with no modification, by any senior Labour figure after 1992:

> An 'enabling society' is one where individuals have declared rights and can achieve their full potential, where a sense of community thrives in the open acceptance of duties, obligations and responsibility for others, and where effort is respected no less than altruism is encouraged.[54]

That Labour would be able to reappropriate some of this language, just over a decade after the SDP split, was far from apparent in the early 1980s. The majority of commentators believed that the destiny of the anti-Conservative cause was in the hands of the SDP, and particularly of David Owen, arguably the most overrated British politician of the post-war period.[55]

To be successful, the SDP and its Liberal partners required something beyond their control: the continuing strength of the hard Left inside the Labour Party. Once the unusual set of circumstances – radicalized activists and disaffected union leaders – which had favoured the Left evaporated, the road was open for a Labour revival. This was not strong enough to ensure outright electoral victory, but was sufficient to ensure Labour's political survival as the only serious opposition to the Conservatives.

The Labour Party was a slow learner. It took the astounding defeat of 1983 to eliminate the power of the hard Left. There followed an attempt to change the image of the party without substantially changing its policies. This led to the more professional electoral campaign of 1987,[56] whose success was rather limited: Labour's vote went up by only 3.5 per cent and Thatcher's majority was barely dented. Clearly, a better media image was not necessarily a major factor in deciding elections.[57]

Labour fought the 1987 election with a programme which was still substantially left-wing: unilateralist on defence, distrustful of Europe, taxing the rich, a publicly funded programme of industrial regeneration. But the agenda of British politics had shifted to the right. The Conservatives' radical programme appeared irreversible: council houses had been sold, education and health reformed, labour markets deregulated, the public sector privatized,

exchange controls abolished, and a single European market established. Even
the original programme of the centrist SDP/Liberal Alliance began to appear
too 'left-wing'. The bitterness of the clash between the Labour Party and the
Alliance, and the polarizing requirements of electoral politics, disguised the
fact that there was considerable agreement on economic policy.[58] In 1981,
Roy Jenkins, the most centrist of the original 'gang of four', presented a
programme advocating a substantial increase in state intervention in the
economy. In his speech to the Institute of Fiscal Studies on 23 February
1981, he called for a North Sea Oil Revenue Investment Fund to be used for
productive public sector investment, such as the expansion of British Tele-
com.[59] His call for a co-ordinated strategy of expansion of the world economy
paralleled similar solicitations from more left-wing voices, such as Stuart
Holland's.[60] The SDP had been formed as a reaction against the hard Left,
not against traditional social democracy. It shared with Labour the radical
interventionism of national Keynesianism. In his diaries Tony Benn reported
that in October 1976, David Owen, then a junior minister, had told him that
he too was 'one hundred per cent' in favour of planning agreements, the
National Entreprise Board and industrial democracy.[61] This was no aberration.
Six years later, Owen was still praising Labour for the NEB (eventually
wound up by the Conservatives) and the British National Oil Corporation
(later privatized).[62]

In effect, classical social democracy in all its facets, from Anthony Crosland
to the traditional socialism of the Labour Left, was moribund, perhaps dead.
The Labour Party recognized this gradually and hesitantly. No party dumps
its past lightly. Between 1987 and 1992, Labour did not simply refurbish its
image, as it had done before 1987, but accepted much of the agenda
propounded by the Conservatives. In so doing, it joined the other parties of
the West European Left on the road towards a new revisionist synthesis,
preparing, or so they hoped, a socialism for the twenty-first century.

The Swedish Wage-earners Funds

Electoral defeat in 1979 had propelled the Labour Party to the left. Further
defeats propelled it back to the right. In Sweden it was victory and political
self-confidence which led to the first formulation of the employee or wage-
earners investment funds (literal translation of the Swedish *löntagarfonder*).
They were the centrepiece of a 'reform offensive' launched by the Swedish
labour movement in the early 1970s.[63] This offensive was – as we have seen
– part and parcel of a Europe-wide phenomenon of increasing control over
the labour market. This included the British legislation of 1974–76 (the Trade
Union and Labour Relations Act, the Health and Safety at Work Act, the Sex
Discrimination Act, and the Employment Protection Act); the German 1972
Works Constitution Act and 1976 Co-determination Act; and the Italian 1970
Statuto dei lavoratori. In Sweden the same offensive had seen the Security

of Employment Act of 1974, protecting employees against unfair dismissals, the 1974 Promotion of Employment Act, requiring employers to notify the labour market authorities of planned cutbacks and negotiate accordingly, and the 1976 Act on the Joint Regulation of Working Life, subjecting a number of managerial prerogatives to negotiations with the unions.

The idea that after the establishment of political democracy (universal suffrage), and social democracy (the welfare state), there should be a third stage, economic democracy, paving the way to socialism, had been part of the credo of the Swedish Social Democratic Party (SAP) for a considerable period of time.[64] In 1971 many felt the time had come for a decisive advance towards the third phase. As this advance ultimately turned into a retreat, it is important to bear in mind the momentous international changes which occurred between the period when the original employee investment funds plan was drafted (1971–76), when it was debated, modified and passed into legislation (1976–83), and when it was implemented (1983–91). During the first period, the anti-capitalist aspirations of Swedish social democracy (and, more specifically, of the trade unions) were at their peak. By 1983, this radicalism had been thwarted. By the end of the decade, the market had triumphed and the Swedish model had collapsed.

What came to be known as the Meidner Plan (after its author) was more a result of the radicalization of the LO (Landorganisationen), the Swedish confederation of blue-collar trade unions, than of changes in the SAP. It was the outcome of the influence on the union movement exercised by the rank-and-file militancy of the late 1960s, the student movement, the New Left, and the wildcat strikes of 1969 spearheaded by the Gothenburg dockers and the far north iron ore miners. The end of the golden age had led unions to become less optimistic about the ability of capitalism to deliver full employment. The plan was thus discussed in the context of a new union ideology, which 'dissociated itself clearly from the market-oriented philosophy of the "golden age"'.[65] The initial impetus came, as so often in Swedish social democracy, from the trade unions. At the 1971 Congress of the LO it was noted that one of the effects of the 'solidaristic wages policy' was to create excess profits, since the wages of workers in the more profitable industries were kept lower than they would otherwise be, in deference to the principle of relating pay to the work performed and not to the employer's ability to pay. This led to wider questions: should unions be involved in capital formation, profits and ownership?

Rudolf Meidner, co-author with Gösta Rehn of the 1951 wages/labour market model (see chapter 8), was asked to head a working party which included Anna Hedborg and Gunnar Fond, and report back to the LO. Thus, the long and complex saga of the employee investment funds began in the style characteristic of Swedish social democracy: a few general principles followed by a concrete, highly detailed and frequently revised plan.

The plan devised by Meidner was different from all other attempts to establish some form of industrial democracy, such as the German *Mitbestimmung*. Its essential trait was the gradual transfer of the assets of enterprises from private shareholders to the employees.[66] It had three aims: to complement the solidaristic wages policy; to counteract the concentration of wealth; and to increase the influence of employees over the economy.[67] The last of these aims was the most controversial, because it amounted to the abolition of private ownership and control by the capitalists themselves, in a country where most industry was still in private hands after fifty years of social-democratic government.

The plan was never a 'pure' anti-capitalist plan. It sought to control or dispose of 'excess' profits not only for ideological reasons, but in order to convince workers in highly profitable firms to contain their wages. It would give workers 'something essential in return for their restraint and sacrifices – influence over the large private companies'.[68]

Capital formation would be enhanced by the compulsory reinvestment of at least 20 per cent of pre-tax profits. More naively, it was believed that workers would contain their wage demands because higher wages would eat into 'their' profits too. The phenomenon of wage drift at the enterprise level (see chapter 17), particularly pronounced in highly profitable enterprises, meant that the central trade union had to devise an institutional mechanism to block inflationary wages. Thus the Meidner Plan was, at least in part, the result of the increasing difficulty facing the famous Rehn–Meidner model, and an alternative to controlling wages through unemployment – the solution adopted by the Right throughout Europe.[69] In other words, excess profits threatened the solidaristic wage policy, the principle that market forces should not be the major determinant of wages.[70] This policy, the centrepiece of Swedish social democracy, had narrowed wage differentials. As Meidner wrote, it 'has been a welfare gain of decisive significance, and it must not be lost'.[71] The wider aim of the funds was that they would provide

> a new opportunity for also making more democratic those decisions which are arrived at within enterprises but which affect a firm's relations with the community as a whole, with consumers, local authorities, the total environment, and so forth. In short, the funds would make it possible to arrive in a democratic manner at those investment decisions which affect what is to be produced and where. Thus it can be argued that the funds would involve a new stratum of democracy in industry, lying somewhere between the two levels that have been attempted so far, government industrial policy on the one hand and ... co-determination within enterprises on the other.[72]

Placing some of these profits in a fund subject to collective control would be better than abolishing them because, in a capitalist economy, high profits were desirable, indeed necessary. They make possible reinvestment, productivity growth and full employment. Thus, paradoxically, the funds would make high profits popular with the workers.[73] To some extent, the Meidner

Plan resembled the profit-sharing schemes which had been widely discussed elsewhere, especially in Germany, Holland, Denmark and France.[74] But the differences were of greater significance because the Swedish scheme would transfer not just profits but – eventually – control to the workers.

To ensure capital formation, it was essential that the employees should not have the right to dispose of 'their' shares, but that the assets accruing to the funds would remain as working capital within the enterprise.[75] Meidner had originally proposed that 20 per cent of the profits of firms of a given size (the minimum to be set between fifty and one hundred employees) would be issued in the form of shares to the fund.[76] Gradually, the funds would increase their shareholding, since they would receive new shares every year. The larger the profits, the faster the funds would build up. If the profits were of the order of 20 per cent a year, the fund would acquire over half of the shares in twenty years; but if profits were only 5 per cent a year, it would take seventy-five years.[77] In practice, the fund-holders would obtain control much earlier because, generally speaking, it was often sufficient to have 10 per cent or less of the shares of a company to control it.

Once a company was under the control of the funds, it would be 'easier to bring a firm's decisions into harmony with social objectives without the community having therefore to step in and control the various decisions in detail'.[78] This implied the adoption of policies which enterprises might not otherwise have pursued. In this case the funds represented a new constraint on capital accumulation. The funds could nevertheless co-exist with capitalism. After all, a substantial body of legislation in capitalist states – for instance, industrial health and safety laws – constrained and shaped capitalist development. However, such legislation sets known parameters within which enterprises have to operate. What would happen when a sizeable body of 'shareholders' wished to pursue ill-defined 'social' objectives? It was this element of unpredictability that caused consternation among the leading representatives of Swedish management. They were no longer sure whether capitalism had a future in a social-democratic Sweden.[79] These fears were compounded by the radical 'we shall take over' rhetoric of trade unionists, while successive opinion polls revealed a lack of popular enthusiasm for the funds and encouraged opposition to them.[80]

The original Meidner Plan had been accepted in principle in 1976 but, as the SAP lost that year's election, much of the subsequent discussion on it occurred while the social democrats were in opposition. The 1976 version was watered down in 1978: only firms with over five hundred workers – of which there were about two hundred in the country – would be compelled to participate in the fund and workers were to contribute to it through a 1 per cent levy on payrolls (to be increased later).[81] This meant that workers were in fact asked to exercise two kinds of restraint: 'normal' wage restraint plus a 1 per cent wage cut to build up the funds.[82] No wonder they were less than enthusiastic.

In the early 1970s, there seemed to be some chance that an amended version of the plan would be acceptable even to the 'bourgeois' parties. Indeed, the liberal and centre parties had themselves advanced various capital fund schemes.[83] However, as the post-golden age crisis swiftly internationalized the economy, many employers no longer believed that the abandonment of managerial prerogatives was a price worth paying for the restoration of competitiveness. The growing internationalization of firms also increased their bargaining power *vis-à-vis* their workforce. Capital, unlike labour, can easily relocate and is all the more likely to do so when social costs are higher than elsewhere.[84] Swedish employers came to the conclusion that union or any other form of collective control over enterprises would make them less internationally competitive. Thus, the employers' association and the 'bourgeois' parties turned sharply against all proposals to establish employees' funds, in spite of the social democrats' growing caution. Further modifications introduced by the SAP in 1981 made the funding mechanism dependent on 20 per cent of 'real' profits – i.e. excess profit calculated on the basis of interest and inflation rates – and not simply pre-tax profit as before. Furthermore, instead of a single fund, there would be twenty-four regional funds.[85] Meidner had originally envisaged that local and national unions would eventually appoint the number of company board members to which they were entitled by the shareholding owned by the fund.[86] Now it was proposed that the boards of the twenty-four funds would be elected by all those who had worked sufficiently to qualify for some pension rights. This took into account the criticism that the original version had been too centralist and would have given excessive powers to the trade unions. In practice, this meant enfranchising everyone except students, housewives and disabled people.

None of this satisfied the opposition. In 1977 the employers made it clear that they believed the Meidner Plan 'would have fateful economic and political consequences for Swedish society'.[87] Assar Lindbeck, a prominent economist, resigned from the SAP and became one of the main ideological opponents of the plan.[88] There were serious fears that during the period of phasing in of the funds, there would be a stock exchange crisis and a flight of capital abroad.[89]

In the weeks leading up to the 1982 elections, the Meidner Plan had become a central plank of the SAP's programme. Though the social democrats won the elections, it is generally accepted that this was achieved in spite of the plan, rather than thanks to it.[90] Only union activists and left-wing intellectuals wholeheartedly supported the employee investment funds. The much-repeated fact that 80 per cent of the adult population were members of trade unions did not mean that they wished the unions to have a greater weight in the management of the economy.

The new SAP government sought a compromise, but the bourgeois parties and the employers backing them remained inflexible. Antagonism to the funds became the one attitude uniting Sweden's fragmented bourgeois opposition. A protest march sponsored by the employers' association brought 75,000 people out onto the streets of Stockholm.[91] In spite of this, in 1983 the SAP, with the help of the communists, passed the legislation. It was assumed that the bourgeois parties would eventually accept the inevitable.[92] In the past they had forcefully opposed major social-democratic legislation, such as the 1959 pension reform, arguing that it was the slippery slope to an authoritarian planned economy. Later they accepted it and did not question it when in power between 1976 and 1982.

The 1983 law watered down the already amended plan even further. The fund system was to be set up 'experimentally' for seven years in the first instance. In effect, it would never be renewed – as Olof Palme and his finance minister made clear.[93] Later, in 1987, Palme declared that the funds were not devised to bring about a new society, but to help Sweden out of the crisis.[94] The ambitions and hopes aroused in the mid-1970s were quietly forgotten. Five regional funds were established, modelled on a pension fund created in 1973 to invest in the stock market (the so-called Fourth AP fund).[95] There was a new, more restrictive definition of profits, which meant that only a few thousand companies (out of 100,000) would be affected. By 1990, the total value of the assets of the five funds, plus the 1973 Fourth AP fund, plus a Fifth AP fund created in 1988, was only 7 per cent of the value of all the assets listed on the stock exchange.[96]

In March 1991, the SAP government proposed a further comprehensive reorganization: all existing pension and employee funds would be merged into five funds with powers to invest 60 per cent of their assets in any way they liked. This regularized *de facto* arrangements: most of the employee investment funds behaved like ordinary pension funds; they accepted prevailing market constraints, did not invest heavily in manufacturing, and did not have a long-term view. The ethos of capitalism prevailed once again, confounding the fears of all critics and, obviously, displeasing those radicals who had believed that they would bring about a gradual transition to socialism. The 1991 move was clearly aimed at providing Swedish firms with a source of local investment capital to protect them from foreign takeovers. Existing laws designed for this purpose were incompatible with membership of the European Community, which the SAP government had decided to seek.[97]

The original project devised by Meidner and his colleagues had generated considerable expectations on the Swedish and European Left; for some it represented the most promising development of collective control over investment and capitalism. The failure of the experiment cannot be traced to a single cause.[98] Like the AES, the Meidner Plan had no widespread popular support. The SAP was not wholeheartedly behind it; nor were the trade unions (the white-collar union confederation had remained neutral). The employers were so strongly opposed that they had mobilized *en masse*, spending more on their media campaign than all the political parties spent on the

1982 election.[99] The workers were less than enthusiastic. The notion of ownership envisaged by the proponents of the funds was abstract, too distant from everyday concepts of private property as something one has the right to dispose of as one sees fit.

The funds had originally been devised in order to support an egalitarian wages policy. The defeat of the proposal was accompanied by a general retreat of the SAP, the LO and the TCO on the question of wage equalization. The strikes of the 1980s were mainly about differentials, especially between the public and the private sectors, pitting (largely female) public employees (leaning increasingly towards the social democrats) against male private sector white-collar workers.[100]

In spite of its 'modern' form and presentation, the ideology behind the funds was that of traditional social democracy. It appealed to the workers and producers as such, identifying them as the class which, by virtue of its position in the production process, was endowed with uniform interests. In this sense the strategy was fundamentally 'workerist' and never freed itself of this original sin, even though it had been so amply reformulated.[101] Housewives, students, disabled people, most pensioners and those working in the public sector, many of whom were women, would have had only an indirect connection with the funds; 'it will be the trade unions and not the people that control the economy,' warned a critic.[102] Had the original plans been implemented, two forms of participation would have co-existed in Swedish society: that of all the citizens, through the normal democratic process; and that of the wage-earners; who would have a restricted franchise in the management of the economy. As Walter Korpi, a supporter of the concept of the funds, pointed out, this was unacceptable from a democratic point of view.[103] His suggestion to extend this 'economic franchise' to all citizens, through an additional ballot in the general election, was never taken up.[104]

The most formidable obstacle to the implementation of the Meidner proposals, however, was the internationalization of the Swedish economy. Strictly speaking, of course, the Swedish economy had been 'opened up' for a long time; being in charge of its exchange rate, however, it could export its own inflationary problems through devaluation. Its wages were high by international but not by Swedish standards – hence the large profits of the 1960s. Until the 1970s, Swedish companies were authentic national enterprises competing among themselves for an expanding share of foreign markets. They confronted similar constraints and the same internal regulatory agency, the Swedish social-democratic state. Had this situation continued, they might have been able to face the new constraints represented by the employee investment funds, particularly as these would also have delivered wage restraint and increased capital. In an internationalized setting any new constraint, 'social' or otherwise, set by the funds might make Swedish firms less competitive than their foreign rivals. The most obvious constraint the funds would certainly have established was to make it more difficult for firms to shed labour – just as in nationalized industry. Thus, Swedish firms would have been at a disadvantage relative to foreign competitors in the all-important restructuring of the European labour market towards greater flexibility.

By the late 1980s, unable to control wage inflation, the SAP adopted policies which had long prevailed elsewhere. It deregulated financial markets and dismantled foreign exchange controls. The exchange rate was pegged to the European Monetary System. An external discipline was imposed to contain wages. Growth and employment were sacrificed at the altar of price stability.[105]

By the 1990s the Meidner Plan and the funds had been forgotten. They had become so peripheral to the problems of Sweden that they were virtually ignored in a collection of essays by leading sociologists and political scientists dedicated to 'Scandinavia in a New Europe'.[106] The idea that it was possible to establish some form of national collective control over investment was abandoned. The great reform offensive was over. The key question now was whether it was possible to preserve key elements of the Swedish welfare state in the new interdependent European and world economy.

The New Politics of the SPD

The SPD's fifteen years of government came to an end in 1982, when it was defeated in a 'constructive vote of no-confidence' in the Bundestag. The SPD's erstwhile ally, the FDP, had switched sides and joined a CDU-led coalition with Helmut Kohl as chancellor. The subsequent election in 1983 turned out to be a disaster for the SPD. At just over 38 per cent, it had the lowest share of the vote since 1961. The SPD was reduced to its core working-class support.[107] A new era of conservative hegemony was beginning in Germany. Having triumphed in 1983, Helmut Kohl went on to win three consecutive elections in January 1987, December 1990 and October 1994.

During the 1980s, the SPD faced two contrasting strategies: to reconstitute an alliance with the FDP; or to move to the left and seek a 'red–green' coalition. But the FDP coalition with the CDU appeared to be too stable, while a formal 'red–green' coalition would have cost the SPD some of its traditional support.[108] A return to a 'Grand Coalition' with the CDU, advocated by some influential SPD politicians, was unlikely. In practice, the social democrats had to try to maximize their share of the vote, hoping that the CDU–FDP coalition would eventually lose its majority. Unencumbered by immediate coalition-building considerations, the party had to decide to what extent it should distance itself from the Schmidt era by embracing the new 'alternative' politics, and how it should reconcile the traditional working class (unionized but contracting) and the service sector (less unionized but expanding).[109]

Initially, the SPD moved to the left, an event lauded by Günter Grass: 'The SPD has once again found peace of mind and the self-esteem gained in the days of August Bebel. It seemed for a long time in danger of adopting mere pragmatism as a substitute ideology, of yielding to force of circumstance.'[110] However, more than peace of mind and self-esteem were required. The general secretary of the SPD, Peter Glotz (1980–87), warned against simply chasing after the centre or the new social movements. What should be done was to formulate 'a project which will counter the right's current programme of undermining the bonds of solidarity within West German society'. He isolated six problem areas: structural unemployment, funding the welfare state, patriarchy, the plundering of the environment, armaments, anti-statism.[111] It was necessary, he added, to find a way of reconciling industrialism and ecology, to avoid 'a hysterical confrontation between new social movements and the production-oriented sectors of society'.[112]

In the period leading up to the 1987 election, the SPD tried to resolve this dilemma through a compromise between old and new politics. It adopted a traditional candidate in the Schmidt mould – namely, Johannes Rau, minister-president of the largest and most industrialized *Land*, North Rhine–Westphalia – and decided to prepare a new 'fundamental programme' to replace that of Bad Godesberg. Rau would provide continuity; the new programme would be a way of acknowledging that the world had changed considerably since 1959. The old programme had little to say about women or the Third World or the European Community.[113] The assumptions that growth could be unlimited and that redistribution was the main political problem had become unrealistic at a time of rising unemployment and environmental concerns.

Johannes Rau loyally embraced much of the new politics. In a speech accepting his party's nomination for the Chancellorship on 16 December 1986, he appealed to the pacifists by asking for the new European-based missiles to be removed.[114] He then appealed to the Greens and stressed that 'work and the environment should not be played off against each other', that the SPD would tax energy in order to finance investment in the reduction of energy consumption.[115] To the feminists, he admitted that:

> Our society has the stamp of 'paid work' all over it ... I will not accept anybody's claim that they are striving for equal rights for women when they refuse to agree to a radical redistribution of work – both gainful employment and unpaid work. Put into concrete terms: anyone who wants equality for women must campaign for shorter working hours in all forms. The reduction of working hours is a decisive means of creating a sufficient number of jobs.[116]

Electorally speaking, all these efforts were in vain. Rau was defeated by Kohl in 1987.

After Rau's defeat, the SPD moved further towards the new politics by adopting Oskar Lafontaine, minister-president of the Saarland and once an advocate of a red–green coalition, as chancellor-candidate. An unexpected political event – the collapse of the Berlin Wall and the subsequent reunification of Germany – intervened to dash any chances Lafontaine might have had.

What distinguished the SPD from some of the other parties of the West European Left was that the 'traditionalist' position – which was supported in the main by blue-collar workers and union activists – was held by the 'right wing' and was particularly strong in the parliamentary party, the *Bundestagsfraktion*. While this tendency was resolutely opposed to any attempt to introduce labour market flexibility (as the revisionists of the Left around Lafontaine tried to do), it was equally opposed to modifying the Bad Godesberg principle of 'planning only when necessary'. In the SPD the Left was anti-workerist, the Right traditionalist. In Germany, to be a left-wing social democrat meant to be generally associated with post-materialist values. This Left was green, pacifist, tendentially feminist, anti-authoritarian, more middle-class and better-educated. It was not, as in Britain or France, in favour of nationalization or against European integration.

The post-Bad Godesberg SPD had ceased to be the old working-class party of Weimar days. While it had not achieved its declared aim of becoming a real *Volkspartei*, it had expanded into the ranks of the intelligentsia and the middle classes.[117] These social groups no longer felt excluded from the party, while the working class in the period of rapid economic growth no longer felt marginal to the rest of society.

By the 1980s, the situation had changed again – as it had throughout much of the West European Left. The 'traditionalist' wing was still determined to pursue a strategy based on the principle of industrial growth, while the 'ecological' wing had taken on board many of the new 'post-materialist' values. The SPD had moved beyond the ideological clash which still divided the British Labour Party, where a frankly socialist ideology, inspired by an ethos of working-class solidarity, was determined to fight bourgeois economic development, while 'modern' revisionism viewed the class struggle as a thing of the past. Outside the tiny German Communist Party and the green *Fundis* there was no 'hard' Left in Germany.

However, on at least one 'post-materialist' issue the left of the SPD and that of the Labour Party were in general agreement: the campaign against nuclear weapons. This was nothing new: in the 1950s there were important anti-nuclear campaigns in both Germany and Britain (see chapter 9). In both parties the traditional right had been strongly Atlanticist. Schmidt, in particular, had been the great strategist behind the rethinking of NATO's defence policy in December 1979. According to this strategy, USSR–USA negotiations on the reduction of intermediate-range nuclear forces (INF) should take place in the context of the deployment of a new generation of European-based missiles, Cruise and Pershing-2 – hence the name 'twin-track' strategy.[118] These missiles were to be stationed in West Germany, Britain, Holland, Belgium and Italy.

The SPD, which had gone along with Schmidt only out of loyalty to its chancellor, reversed its position at its conference on peace and security held in Cologne on 18–19 November 1983. It announced that 'the double-track decision has failed to reach its goal of stopping the arms build-up and of promoting détente', and rejected the deployment of new American intermediate-range systems on national territory.[119] The resolution, proposed by the party's executive, was opposed by only thirteen delegates, including Schmidt and four former cabinet ministers.[120] By then, of course, the SPD was out of power and Helmut Schmidt was no longer its leader. In the Labour Party, the pacifist option was more complex because it was made up of two strands: unilateralism and the campaign against the euromissiles. Protests against foreign (i.e. US) missiles under NATO command being stationed on British soil could have a patriotic dimension, while the campaign against an 'independent' British nuclear deterrent would not appeal to British patriots still proud of a nuclear weapon flying the Union Jack. The anti-Cruise and Pershing campaign had an internationalist dimension, because the movement could link arms with protestors in Germany, Belgium, Holland and Italy; the unilateralist campaign could only be British based. In Germany, however, the idea of unilateralism was anathema, not for the obvious reason that Germany did not have its own nuclear weapons, but because unilateral acts in foreign policy were bound to be associated with a German 'go-it-alone' policy and hence with a revival of the nationalist idea of a German role in the world, unconstrained by the European Community or NATO links. This kind of German 'Gaullism' belonged to the Right.

In Germany the pacifist movement was broader than in Britain. Opinion surveys in 1983–84 showed that as many as 86 per cent of Germans were opposed to the deployment of the missiles. In 1983, 300,000 pacifists paraded in Bonn and a 'human chain' was formed by protesters joining hands along the fifty-five mile stretch from Stuttgart to the US base at Ulm.[121] The strength of this protest was almost certainly due to the fact that no one could claim that Germany might survive the circumstances in which the new weapons would be used, i.e. in retaliation against a Soviet nuclear or conventional attack.[122]

The new anti-twin-track policy of the SPD brought the party into the same camp as the Greens, the most overtly pacifist (and anti-American) party in Germany. Pacifism, though, was not the only reason behind the relative popularity of the anti-euromissile campaign. Uncertainty and fear played a major role. Locating Pershing-2 missiles in the middle of one of the most densely populated *Länder*, Baden-Württemberg, made many Germans feel they were being used by the Americans as hostages.[123] Germans could view total dependence on US nuclear weapons with equanimity as long as American superiority created an impression of complete security. In the course of the 1980s, this feeling of security was replaced by the growing fear of a nuclear holocaust.[124] This was caused in part by the pessimistic message of the peace movement itself, and in part by the rhetoric of President Reagan, whose image in Europe was that of an unreliable warmonger with a finger on the nuclear button. Reagan thus became, quite unwittingly, one of the peace movement's most active recruiting agents. This kind of fear, amounting almost to national panic, did not affect the British or the French. Evidently, the terrible fate that had befallen the German people during two world wars had created a 'gut-pacifism' that was more deeply rooted than in Britain and France, while it did not exist at all in the USA which, on the whole, did rather well out of the two world wars. Schmidt himself had to explain these simple facts to his American audience in the course of his 1985 Stimson lectures:

> Think of Oregon or of Colorado with six non-American forces, under a foreign high command, on their soil, and think also of the foreign high commander having some 5,000 nuclear weapons within his command and not under the host nation's control. Perhaps, if you reflect on that situation, you will understand why some young people in Germany, as well as older people and professors and bishops, protest our joint military posture ... There is no other country in the world that has such concentration of military weapons and military power from seven nations on its soil – and all of it under someone else's command.[125]

What also alarmed all Germans (and confirmed French suspicions that the Americans were unreliable) was that the negotiations between the two superpowers were normally conducted with an unequivocal disregard of other Western allies. They had no input into the famous compromise on the INF negotiations in Geneva achieved by the US chief negotiator Paul Nitze and Yuli Kvitinsky, his Soviet counterpart, during their 'walk in the woods' in Geneva in the summer of 1982; nor in the subsequent rejection of this compromise by Moscow and Washington. Helmut Schmidt, who often boasted of his ability to influence Germany's allies, was deeply resentful.[126] Later he wrote: 'No matter who occupies the presidency, Washington tends to unilateralism. As long as Western Europe cannot work its way to a joint design for overall strategy ... the West will always be confronted with American solo adventures.'[127] As many on the SPD left pointed out, the USA was in charge of the negotiation 'track' of the famous strategy, while Germany had to deploy on its own territory the nuclear weapons of the 'second' track.

The SPD had been pushed towards a pacifist position by a growing Europe-wide peace campaign, led in Germany by the Greens. But this campaign was not the only element in the SPD shift. There was a *raison d'état* which did not exist in Britain. The SPD felt that the installation of the new missiles was bound to jeopardize the relationship with East Germany which had been carefully nurtured by the SPD. This constituted the foundation of Ostpolitik, the greatest achievement of the SPD since the war, the basis of German foreign policy. This pessimism turned out to be unwarranted. Relations with the DDR improved throughout the 1980s. Hans-Dietrich Genscher, leader of the FDP and Germany's foreign minister (1974–92), never ceased cultivating links with the USSR and turned out to be the Western leader most supportive of the revolution initiated by Gorbachev.

An Eastern-oriented and détente-based policy was unavoidable for any German leader, provided it was set in a West European context. For all Schmidt's ambition to tie the USA to Europe, there was simply no mechanism, political or otherwise, which would force the USA, in all circumstances, to put the security of Europe on the same footing as its own. It had become obvious to the SPD that 'the security interests of Western Europe, in view of the geopolitical situation, cannot be identical with those of our transatlantic partners'.[128]

Clearly, the SPD needed a new security policy which would unite the party and achieve popularity, while maintaining an open door towards the peace campaign. A working group chaired by Egon Bahr, the architect of Ostpolitik, produced the framework for a new policy in June 1983. Traditional deterrence theory called for building up armaments in order to dissuade an enemy. It thus created a climate of fear and reciprocal suspicion. The new doctrine, called 'common security', applied the concept of interdependence to the field of security. Its aim was to involve the 'enemy' in a common search for an environment which would lead to a relaxation of tension. The concept had been expressed in 1982 in the report of the Independent Commission on Disarmament and Security Issues, chaired by Olof Palme – to which the ubiquitous Egon Bahr had contributed. 'Common security' differed from the concept of 'partnership in security', used in the late 1970s by the SPD, which asserted that European security could be obtained only through a USA–West European partnership. In 'common security', the 'partnership' which could ensure 'security' was a 'partnership with the adversary'. It was a recognition that, in the nuclear age, security was a situation to be reached *with* – not *against* – one's opponent. The adversary would become a partner because both sides faced the threat of nuclear catastrophe and recognized that they could not defeat the other through the use of force. In the words of the SPD parliamentary leader Hans-Jochen Vogel: 'Security can no longer be attained by arming ourselves against a potential enemy, rather security is attainable only with his co-operation.'[129]

The leadership of the SPD subsequently attempted to blur the differences between the old 'partnership in security' and the new 'common security'. The last major document on security produced before the collapse of the Berlin Wall mentions neither.[130] The two positions, however, were mutually exclusive. To adopt 'common security' entailed giving up the strategy of deterrence, limiting armaments, and refusing to establish first-strike capacity. It also meant opposing Reagan's Strategic Defense Initiative (SDI), or 'Star Wars', which would have given the West such a capability. In the long term, the object of the 'common security' doctrine was the dissolution of the blocs.[131] The Berlin Programme adopted on 20 December 1989, a few weeks after the collapse of the Berlin Wall, stated boldly:

No country in Europe can enjoy more security today than any potential adversary can. So each country must, even if only in its own interest, assume responsibility for the security of others. That is the principle of common security. It requires that each side grants the other side its right to exist and its ability to live in peace. Common security effects detente and requires detente. Common security aims to eliminate anxieties caused by constant threat, and to overcome the confrontation of the blocs.[132]

From an internationalist point of view, 'common security' appeared the most fruitful position to hold. It reflected growing interdependence, was resolutely non-nationalist, was consistent with détente and, consequently, contributed to strengthening the reformist wing of Soviet communism. German membership of NATO was never seriously in question. Yet the SPD received mixed support from its counterparts in the rest of Europe.

The British Labour Party had, until the late 1980s, adopted a pacifist position close to that of the Germans, but too unilateralist to be of real help to the SPD – though Denis Healey tried to get the party to shift towards 'common security'.[133] Besides, the Labour Party was in opposition, as was the Dutch Labour Party (after 1981), a consistent opponent of the missiles.

In Holland and Belgium, the peace campaign was exceptionally strong and popular even among older people (elsewhere an overwhelming majority of peace protestors was young). The movements against the missiles in these two countries were also genuinely cross-party, mainly because of the decisive role played by the Protestant churches.[134]

The Swedish social democrats were very supportive, but this was of symbolic significance only. Being neutral, Sweden had no influence in the debates concerning 'euromissiles'. Norway and Denmark were both in NATO, but the missiles were never meant to be stationed there in the first place. In Southern Europe the Italian communists were the most enthusiastic supporters of the SPD; coming from communists, however, such support was of little political benefit to the SPD. Craxi's PSI, in government with the Christian democrats, accepted the installation of the missiles in Italy. Craxi himself had become prime minister by the time the missiles were installed in Sicily. In Spain González was busy convincing his supporters to back Spanish entry into NATO.

The lack of support from the French socialists was particularly marked. From the beginning Mitterrand had been an enthusiastic proponent of the missiles – not one of which, incidentally, was to be based in France. Following de Gaulle's precepts, Mitterrand had consistently refused to include French nuclear weapons in the INF negotiations – many of them were aimed at German territory to stop an anticipated Soviet advance. The position of the French socialists was seen by all shades of SPD opinion as favouring the ruling CDU–FDP coalition.[135] No support came – not that it would have been welcomed – from the PCF or the left-wing CERES faction of the Parti Socialiste. Both were committed to traditional concepts of deterrence; both seemed to want to construct socialism under the (French) nuclear umbrella. In France there was no peace movement worthy of the name. Meanwhile,

the French intelligentsia had relinquished, virtually *en masse*, its historic
commitment to leftist neutralism in favour of a frenetic anti-Sovietism
unparalleled in Western Europe, while insisting, for inexplicable reasons unless
it was nostalgia, that it was still *de gauche*.

As it turned out, the events of 1989 leading to the collapse of communism
in Europe made the concept of 'common security' obsolete – at least as
originally conceived. The SPD never expected that the long-hoped-for dissolution of the blocs would take the form of a collapse of the Eastern one.
In fact, the premise of the SPD (and of the Italian communists, whose own
foreign policy was virtually indistinguishable from that of the SPD) was that
the blocs would last a long time and dissolve on the basis of reciprocity and
mutual negotiation. Their overall assumption was that Western Europe and
the Soviet bloc would eventually converge upon some version of social
democracy, not that the East would seek to adopt a market economy.

As the direct continuation of Ostpolitik, 'common security' could be
interpreted as a neutralist policy. It was difficult for those who adopted it to
occupy the high ground of the crusade against totalitarian communism. Their
attitude implied that they supported the existing regimes of Eastern and
Central Europe in practice. The SPD's frequent contacts with the communist
parties of the Warsaw Pact countries tainted German social democrats. This
led some to claim that the West German Left perceived the DDR as morally
superior to the capitalist world, thus becoming 'perhaps the most solid
Western supporter of the status quo in Eastern Europe and the Soviet Union
throughout the 1970s and 1980s'.[136] Garton Ash points out that 'West
Germany was constrained from being an outspoken advocate of freedom
and respect for human rights in Eastern Europe by its geopolitical position,'
but argues that a 'somewhat more outspoken policy would have been possible,
even within these constraints'.[137] 'Common security' facilitated the task of
communist reformists in the USSR. It was thus a successful policy. It assumed,
however, that communism could gradually be reformed. It was thus also a
failure.[138]

'Common security' achieved a 'domestic' aim: it enabled the SPD to go
beyond Ostpolitik, defined as a purely German foreign policy. 'Common
security' was a policy for the whole of Europe. This completed the 'Europeanization' of the SPD. It now became the pro-European party *par excellence* in
Germany. Both in the so-called Irsee draft of its programme (June 1986),
and in the final document (1989), the commitment to European unity became
more pronounced than ever before. The SPD now aimed at nothing less
than 'The United States of Europe'.[139] The EC was seen as a 'building block
for a regionally structured world community'.[140] This would require 'full rights
for a European Parliament, a capable government which would be answerable
to Parliament ... We want a social order throughout Europe.'[141] The programme also called for a common economic policy, monetary union, a
common currency, and more power for the European Parliament. The Euro-

pean single market, welcomed by most European conservatives, including Mrs Thatcher, was seen by SPD leaders not only as the opportunity to expand intra-European trade, but also as a stepping-stone towards a 'social Europe'. The SPD was looking forward to Europe-wide co-determination in industry, an action programme for jobs, and the establishment of minimum standards of welfare.[142]

The call for a 'social Europe', which, following the Maastricht Treaty of February 1992, united most of the West European Left, aimed at harmonizing aspects of the welfare state throughout the European Community. This would eliminate the economic disadvantage of higher welfare costs in the more socially advanced countries. Or, to put it differently, it would ensure that the least socially advanced countries would not enjoy an 'unfair' advantage. Thus, the German Left sought to turn to its own benefit one of the claims of the Right – namely, that the welfare state made their own economy less competitive. The demand that welfare should be standardized was aimed at preventing so-called 'social dumping', whereby the countries of Southern Europe, Ireland and even Britain would be able to benefit from lower pay and poorer working conditions. By supporting the concept of 'social Europe', the SPD was defending the German welfare state and the gains achieved by the German working class.

The second dimension of the Europeanism of the SPD was that it consolidated the division of Europe. Unavoidably, the more EC member countries developed their own supra-national institutions, the greater the gulf with the 'backward' post-communist countries, and the greater the obstacle to their inclusion into the European Union would be.

Thus, 'federal' Europe, like 'common security', assumed the continuation of different economic regimes on the continent of Europe. However, unlike the concept of 'common security', the project of a federal Europe, far from being abandoned after the collapse of communism, was enhanced despite the growth of nationalism in the West. Those previously unenthusiastic about 'Europe' now knocked at the door. By 1995, of the countries of Western Europe, only Norway, Switzerland and Iceland remained outside the union.

In Germany, the CDU followed the same European path as the SPD. This corresponded to the wider interests of German capitalism, while at the same time preserving the social consensus which was recognized as the basis of German economic success. German capitalism might be made more competitive, in a narrow economic sense, by a Thatcher-like attack on social consensus but, at least until the mid-1990s, this was not an option the CDU was prepared to adopt. Better to tolerate some loss of competitiveness than to jeopardize a consensus which had served German industry so well for so long. Europe – unlike security policy – was not to be a matter of dispute between Left and Right in Germany.

Where the SPD clearly differentiated itself from the CDU (and from the old Bad Godesberg programme) was on the two most salient issues of the 'new politics': ecology and feminism. The SPD turned its back on the idea of unlimited growth in favour of 'qualitative' and ecologically aware growth. This was a genuine political shift.[143] In the post-war period the SPD had acquired legitimacy by accepting fundamental assumptions of liberal capitalism – namely, that the gradual deployment of technical progress would bring about a continuous increase in the welfare of society – that modern societies faced an infinite trend towards growth and technological progress. It further assumed that this would go hand in hand with the gradual development of socialism. This was not a peculiarity of German socialists. The entire socialist movement, including communists, accepted this teleological view, present, in one form or another, throughout Marx's own writings and shared by all liberals since the days of the Enlightenment. 'History is on our side' is, perhaps inevitably, the battle-cry of all progressive forces. The real line of demarcation between liberals and socialists was that the latter believed that 'progress', if abandoned to the market, would generate major social problems. During the golden age of capitalism, this line had become blurred. Now socialists, because of the Green movement and the end of the golden age, had regained their suspicion of capitalist development. They realized that the untrammelled development of the productive forces led to the destruction of the environment. A mechanism had to be found to ensure qualitative rather than quantitative growth. As Willy Brandt put it, we did not need more but better medicines, not more cars but safer and cleaner ones.[144] Qualitative growth accepted that nature's productivity was not infinite, that there was not an endless supply of lakes and rivers to pollute, and that water and air were not 'free' goods. This green politics, claimed the SPD, did not have be pursued at the expense of employment – as many Greens asserted. Investment in the environment could be job-intensive. The so-called limits to growth were limits to a kind of development which disregarded environmental constraints.

How to achieve ecologically responsible growth? The SPD was careful to avoid any suggestion that the best way was through centrally administered control or by increasing public investment. The way forward was a combination of elements: the democratization of the economy; the consolidation of co-determination; strong trade unions; and state action.[145] This was not an anti-capitalist position. The Berlin Programme maintained that 'capital must serve humanity, not humanity capital'.[146] The possibility that humanity would be better served by abolishing capitalism was pointedly avoided. The 'mixed economy in which competition and government measures complement each other ... has proved itself to be exceedingly productive and superior to all forms of centralised economic government.'[147]

Though aware that environmental control in a single country, especially after Chernobyl, was limited in scope, the SPD believed that the power of the Federal Republic was such that it offered considerable scope for state action: 'Those who only wait for European or global regulations will not get them in the end.'[148] The appropriate mechanisms were taxes and financial incentives: 'Anything that is ecologically harmful must become more expensive, anything that is right for the environment must become economically more advantageous.'[149] What this amounted to, in the end, was the market principle that the polluters should pay.

The principle was legitimate, although of limited efficacy. It would not stop pollution. It would only make it more expensive and thus dependent on opportunity costs. Further taxes on cars or petrol might lead to a reduction in car ownership or use by the less well-off members of the community, but would not stop the prosperous middle classes who would benefit from lower traffic density. Some environmentally expensive goods would no longer be worth producing in Germany, if costs were too high. They would then be imported from countries where environmental controls were less stringent. German firms would shift production to countries willing to tolerate environmental damage in order to attract investment. Making the polluters pay 'in a single country', while eliminating barriers to trade and capital movement, would thus be of limited value.

The reaction of trade unions was mixed. The rather rough sketch I have drawn above in which right-wing social-democratic trade unions always confronted middle-class green activists, ignores the complexities of real politics. The largest German trade union, IG-Metall, was not averse to ecological themes, and had strongly supported the programme 'Work and Environment' adopted by Lafontaine in the Saar election of March 1985 – a prototype for the Irsee draft. IG-Chemie was at first on the opposing side, but was gradually won over. The main reason was the realization that environmental protection, if taken seriously, could turn out to be a vast job creation scheme. Already in 1985 some two hundred thousand workers were directly employed in the environment industry.[150]

Energy-saving had the potential to become a growth industry. The whole paraphernalia of emission control, recycling, renewable energy, natural resources preservation, the replacement of environmentally harmful products, waste management, reconditioning waste and so on could be seen as a business like any other, and one in which Germany had a lead. By 1985, Volkswagen was already producing more ecologically sound – or, rather, less environmentally destructive – cars than its rivals in France and Italy. Germany could export pollution-reducing material to countries which would need them if they wanted to export finished goods to Germany which met the exacting domestic standards. An environmentally regulated Europe might cause European firms to lose some competitiveness with other countries, but not necessarily within the largest single market in the world.

Those who saw the endless search for increased safety and environmental protection simply as an added cost to business, and tried to limit it, did not understand that the effects of new regulations were difficult to anticipate. Sweden, for instance, was one of the first countries in the world to have compulsory seat belts. When these became adopted in other countries, Sweden became one of the world's leading suppliers. Its lead in products for disabled people was similarly recompensed. Conversely, the Swedes' initial suspicions about possible radiation dangers from microwave ovens meant they lost their chance to have a foothold in that particular market.[151]

Nevertheless, as German unemployment grew, it became increasingly difficult to 'sell' the principle of ecologically regulated growth to the electorate. Although, in the late 1980s, the SPD did reasonably well in some of the old industrial *Länder* such as North Rhine–Westphalia, Lower Saxony and the Saarland, it went on losing votes in those *Länder* where restructuring successfully developed the new science-based industries, such as Bavaria and Baden-Württemberg.[152] Nor was any success achieved by calling for a reduction in working hours, a policy which might have appealed to workers as well as to 'post-materialists'. A shorter working day had been one of the oldest demands of the working-class movement. The six-hour day in a thirty-hour working week was now proposed to facilitate the division of housework between partners, to enable men and women to devote themselves to their children, or to engage in training or further education. The demand, however, was advanced in a framework which would further regulate the already rigid labour market: 'Saturday must not become a regular working day. Sunday work should be allowed only in compelling exceptions. We want to restrict night work to exceptional situations.'[153] The Irsee draft had not mentioned this clause; it was inserted in the full programme to placate the unions.[154]

The attempt to compromise between the new and old politics was at its most evident in the sections dealing with the environment. Where gender was concerned, the tone was less compromising and unmistakably feminist:

> We want a society which is no longer divided into people with either supposedly feminine or masculine ways of thinking and acting; in which highly-valued paid work is no longer assigned to men, leaving undervalued house and family responsibilities to women; in which one half of the population is no longer brought up to dominate the other half, with that other half brought up to subordinate itself. ...
>
> Women's consciousness is changing rapidly. They realise more acutely than most men do that both women and men are constantly suppressing some of their wishes, possibilities and abilities ... Both men and women suffer from the division between a masculine and a feminine world. It deforms both genders, alienating them from each other ... we must also transform the working world, so that women and men can take on responsibility in the family, for each other and for their children.[155]

This was a long way from the class struggle. The SPD now claimed to be fighting for 'a child-orientated society',[156] while at the Munster Congress of the SPD (31 August 1988) Oskar Lafontaine declared that the party's policy was not just to return to 'classical' full employment, but to create jobs for women.[157] The SPD general secretary, Peter Glotz, announced dramatically that the slogan to adopt had to be 'patriarchy must die'.[158]

The concluding paragraphs of the Berlin Programme exhibited the characteristic balancing-act of so many party documents. It compensated for its feminism and ecologism, first by proposing a 'reform alliance composed of social movements old and new', and then by restraining it, abandoning symmetry in favour of tradition: 'The core of this alliance continues to be our .cooperation with the trade unions.'[159] This balancing-act, though ambiguous and contradictory, was not surprising: real modernizers must never lose sight of the past. The drafters of the new programme turned out to be more conscious of, and truer to, their history than the revisionists of Bad Godesberg. In 1959 German socialism had been described as being rooted in Christianity, classical philosophy and humanism. No mention was made of Marx. In 1989, as street after street dedicated to Marx and Engels were about to be renamed throughout much of Eastern and Central Europe, the SPD included 'Marx's historical and sociological doctrine' among the spiritual roots of democratic socialism.[160]

The end of the Cold War, the reunification of Germany and the collapse of communism had made the international section of the programme obsolete. Throughout the world foreign policy makers were reviewing the foundations of their policies in the light of the extraordinary changes that had taken place. Other sections of the Berlin Programme were not directly affected. In fact, the plans for environmental protection would have been particularly suitable for dealing with the vast ecological problems of the former DDR.[161] Nevertheless, the reunification of Germany – apart from becoming the dominant issue of the 1990 election – dealt a treble blow to the SPD.

In the first place, it wiped out at a stroke most of the political gains achieved by Ostpolitik. The entente with the old East German regime of the DDR had not induced a slow and gradual reform, paving the way for an even more gradual unification. The regime had collapsed like a pack of cards once it had become apparent that its citizens were ready to desert the country *en masse* and seek entry into West Germany via Hungary, and once Gorbachev had made it clear that the Red Army would not intervene to save it. That the end of the DDR should have damaged the SPD was undeserved; not only because *all* German parties had become supporters of Ostpolitik, and détente had forced the Honecker regime to grant concessions on human rights, thus contributing to the emergence of public dissent in the DDR, but also because détente and Ostpolitik had made possible the advent of a reformer like Gorbachev.[162]

In the second place, the collapse of the centrally planned-economies, and the advocacy of market reforms in the USSR and the other 'post-communist' countries, helped to strengthen the prestige and triumph of pro-market ideologies over the social-democratic tradition of the West. This damaged even social-democratic parties such as the SPD, which had never advocated central planning. For nearly forty years, its main principle had been 'as much competition as possible, as much planning as necessary' – not the other way round.

In the third place, the all-German 1990 election delivered a powerful advantage to the CDU, which was seen as the main architect of unification – though all it had done was to seize the opportunity. The CDU triumphed overwhelmingly throughout the new East German *Länder*, SPD strongholds in the days of Weimar. Only East Berlin voted for the Left: 34 per cent of votes going to the SPD and 30 per cent to the former communist party, the PDS (Partei des Demokratischen Sozialismus – Democratic Socialist Party). The party of the former dissidents, Bündis 90, obtained less than 6 per cent. Gains in East Germany made good the losses Kohl suffered in the western regions. The SPD secured 35.9 per cent in the West, but only 23.6 per cent in the East, where it was seen as contaminated by its association with socialism. This was quite unwarranted: social democrats had been banned in the former DDR, but not Christian democrats and liberals, who had been encouraged to form their own parties and who had participated in the government as Erich Honecker's junior and loyal allies. They now joined their Western counterparts without the slightest public embarrassment.

It proved impossible for the SPD to campaign in 1990 around the Berlin Programme, which had been devised with such a different situation in mind. Inevitably, the unification of Germany was the issue of 1990. Ecology and feminism, which probably would not have figured so prominently during an electoral campaign at the best of times, were barely mentioned. Determined campaigners would have pointed out that a strict environmental policy was necessary to bring the former DDR up to the level of West Germany, or that East German women had achieved more rights in the fields of abortion, equality at work and child-care than their Western counterparts. But this strategy could have backfired. The environmental problems of the DDR were used to show that, after all, West Germany had been an ecological paragon all along. The capitalist Federal Republic had an environmental record far superior to that of 'real socialism'. The issue of women's rights also presented problems. The DDR had a more liberal abortion policy than the Federal Republic and a more comprehensive child-care system. But to suggest, in the immediate post-reunification climate, that there was anything at all to learn from the DDR would not have gained the SPD many votes in the eastern *Länder*, and would have lost quite a few in the western ones.

The SPD could not have done well electorally in the former DDR. In spite of Helmut Schmidt's and Willy Brandt's eventual enthusiasm for unification, Oskar Lafontaine, correctly interpreting the feelings of his rank and file, was, from the very beginning, opposed to rapid unification and refused to sign a common declaration with the government, calling Kohl's ten-point plan 'a collection of banalities'.[163] The SPD deputy chairman, Horst Ehmke, had previously attacked the government for having encouraged the mass exodus from the East (through Hungary), which led to the pulling down of the wall.[164] The greens were even less eager than the SPD to see rapid unification. Lafontaine opposed the one-for-one conversion of the two currencies, claiming that it would have catastrophic consequences for the East German economy, would cause inflation and a massive increase in public spending in the West, and would lead to higher taxes. Though he turned out to be right on the cost of unification, it is unrealistic to assume that a two-state situation without a policed border would have been viable: East Germany would have collapsed. Nevertheless, Lafontaine's warnings, and the pessimism they signalled, clashed with the general euphoria in the East as in the West. It looked as if the SPD was against German unity. In reality, it had refused to pander to nationalism. This may not pay electorally, but it showed a sense of history. As Stefan Berger wrote: 'As a German, to be cautious about stirrings of nationalism is not ahistorical. On the contrary it means drawing the lessons of twentieth-century German history.'[165]

Soon after the election, the brief love affair between Westerners and Easterners was over. Lafontaine may not have been far wrong in advocating gradual unification, but in politics what matters is to be right at the right time.[166]

While Lafontaine was thinking of the costs of unity, Kohl seized the opportunity history had given him and ran with it. Wearing the mantle of *Kanzler für Deutschland*, he negotiated with Mikhail Gorbachev from a position of strength and dealt swiftly with all those Western countries (especially Britain) which expressed anxiety at the rise of a powerful and united Germany. 'Germany is our Motherland, Europe our future,' he announced.[167] The 'new' Germany would not go it alone and would remain a loyal member of NATO. This satisfied the Western nations – somewhat less than delighted at the prospect of a reunited Germany. They had no choice. They could hardly try to slow down the tempo of unification. Poland was reassured: its western borders – the Oder–Neisse line – were declared *unverletzlich*, inviolable.

Reunification was in fact a takeover. East Germany was completely absorbed into West Germany. The Basic Law and all other Western institutions were extended to the East with only minor modifications. The DDR simply disappeared. The party of Adenauer, which for so long had looked only to the West and ignored Eastern Germany, had become the party of German unity. The SPD, which under Schumacher had been the party most committed to German unification, had become thoroughly 'westernized'. It had profoundly identified itself with the institutions and structures of the Federal Republic, a political edifice it had long considered purely temporary. When the crunch came, the SPD was reluctant to accept the end of West Germany. The new citizens being absorbed would turn out to be either vociferously anti-socialist, or nostalgic for the old certainties. Either way, they would be rather distant from the new emancipatory politics which had become so important to the SPD.

A greater Germany would have a greater international weight, be subject to the temptations of the past, and be less concerned with maintaining its links with the European Community – or so the social-democratic leaders implied. Like most West Germans, the SPD had become comfortable in the Federal Republic, with its wealth, its strong unions, its system of co-determination and the entire apparatus of diffuse democracy – division of powers and federal constitution – which enabled social democrats to rule something, somewhere, even when they were in opposition. The German social democrats were no longer German 'nationalists', as they had been in 1914 or, with Schumacher, in 1945; but they had become 'patriotic' about the Federal Republic. On the back of West German prosperity, the SPD had adopted some of the mentality, as well as some of the ideas, of 'post-materialism'. The citizens of former communist lands, about to be absorbed, had missed out on the materialism of the consumer society. They wanted the same wealth and prosperity their Western counterparts had enjoyed for so many years. They wanted freedom, yes, but also BMWs and compact disc players. They wanted capitalism. The 'revolution', as it was called, was celebrated by a frenetic spending spree in the streets of West Berlin – a telling illustration of the victorious appeal of capitalism. Those in East Germany who thought that they would lose out in this fast annexation turned not to the SPD, but to the former communists of the PDS. It was this party, and not the SPD, which became the repository of the hopes (and votes) of those who had been negatively affected by massive unemployment (absent under the old regime), the disintegration of the traditional industrial structures, and the waning of the certitudes of communism.

Thus, the SPD, in spite of its Europeanism and internationalism, had remained a 'national' party (not the same as a nationalist party). The nation which had become the centre of its concern was West Germany. Reunification had been for long a distant prospect. Willy Brandt, in 1989 so enthusiastic about the fall of the wall, had declared only the previous year that the belief in reunification was a sham.[168] Other SPD leaders, well before Lafontaine, had systematically downplayed it, often on grounds of strict *Realpolitik*. Schmidt, for example, in his state of the nation address in 1979, reminded his audience that the division of Germany 'is today part of the European balance of power that secures peace in Europe ... we Germans cannot allow ourselves a political schizophrenia, which on the one hand pursues a realistic policy of peace and at the same time carries on an illusionary debate about reunification.'[169] Helmut Schmidt, the supreme realist, the last great pragmatic *Kanzler* of the SPD, later discovered what he already knew: that what was illusory one day could become reality the next.

The defeats suffered by the Swedish, German and British socialists predated the collapse of the USSR and Soviet communism. They created a climate in which those holding out against market forces appeared to be swimming against the tide of history. When communism itself collapsed, this tide became unstoppable. Socialism became the most unfashionable word in the political dictionary. However, socialists did not disappear. Their parties, tossed and battered, survived. They were still the only serious opponents of conservatives. But they could no longer maintain the policies of the past. They could no longer advocate the uninhibited use of state planning to rectify the dysfunctions of capitalism. They could no longer promise to tax and spend. They had to reinvent themselves. Where social democracy was still strong and had authentic roots, as in Sweden and Norway, social democrats did not engage in as profound a revision as in France or Britain. Yet all parties eventually realized that they could no longer carry on in the old manner, even if they were not certain what should follow or what else to do. Cutting loose from their moorings was only the first part of an operation which, as I write, is far from over. Whether the boat thus freed will drift aimlessly into the fog of history or find a new course will remain an open question for years to come. All we can do in the remaining pages of this book is to give a brief account of the development of the new revisionism which has swept the West European Left since the mid-1980s.

CHAPTER TWENTY-FOUR

The New Revisionism

ONE HUNDRED years after the founding of the Second International, Soviet communism collapsed. This marked the termination of the first experiment in 'actually existing socialism'. Though the fall of the Berlin Wall in November 1989 surprised everyone, the signs of the impending demise of communism had been in the air for some time. Poland and Hungary were already on the way towards a post-communist system. Slovenia was disengaging from the Yugoslav Federation. In the Soviet Union Mikhail Gorbachev had started his ultimately unsuccessful attempt to reform communism in March 1985, when he became the last of Lenin's successors. By 1989, he had intimated that the communist rulers of Central and Eastern Europe could not expect the Soviet Union to intervene on their behalf. In September of that year, the reformist communist leadership in Hungary opened the border with Austria and, through this first chink in what was still called the iron curtain, thousands of East Germans fled to West Germany. The Berlin Wall had lost its purpose. Its destruction hastened the end of communism. By and large, this process had been the task of the communists themselves. A dismayed ruling class had lost the will to rule. By the end of 1989, East Germany was swiftly moving towards reunification with the Federal Republic. In Czechoslovakia, the dissident writer Václav Havel was elected president. On Christmas Day 1989, the communist regime in Romania crumbled, and Nicolae and Elena Ceausescu were shot. Bulgaria and, later, Albania moved rapidly towards a multi-party system. By the end of 1991, the USSR had been dismembered, while fragments of the Yugoslav Federation lapsed into civil war. Communism in Europe was no longer a reality. Outside Europe, its days also appeared numbered. China and Vietnam, nominally under the direction of a communist party, were briskly developing a market economy. At the time of writing, centrally planned economies are extant only in North Korea and Cuba. Should communism survive in these peripheral formations, an unlikely though not impossible prospect, it will not provide the stage for the rebirth of a great historical gamble whose failures outweigh its successes. There will be no return match. Perceptive communists realized this ten years before the end of the Soviet Union: 'we must accept that the phase of socialist development which began with the October Revolution has exhausted its driving force' – so declared Enrico Berlinguer in December 1979.[1]

The socialist and social-democratic parties of Western Europe observed the enactment of this tumultuous change with a quiet detachment – as if it were not part of their own history. Some practical factors were at work. In Britain and Germany the Left was out of power and quite unable to influence the West's response. In France, whose foreign policy had been based on an entente with Bonn for decades, the creation of a powerful united Germany was seen as of greater importance than the disappearance of the USSR. The Italian, Belgian, Dutch and other socialist parties could never hope to be involved in global politics. These practicalities aside, what remains perplexing is the absence throughout of a strong response. The Left observed the unfolding of *glasnost* and *perestroika* at first with scepticism, then with sympathy, as did public opinion, but went no further. The West as a whole, Left and Right, offered little practical succour to Gorbachev, preferring instead to squeeze out of the situation all possible political advantage so that, should he fail, some Cold War gains would have been made. Socialists and social democrats behaved as if the path they had followed in the West had so diverged from that pursued by the USSR, following Lenin's extraordinary experiment, that they could look upon its termination with the same apparent equanimity as the other parties of Western Europe. Of course, socialists and social democrats had long made their opposition to the regimes of Soviet Europe absolutely clear. The 'socialism' which was being constructed there, they had argued for years – indeed, from its very inception – was not socialism at all. The regimes were only socialist in that 'someone in Moscow pinned on them the label of "real existing socialism"'.[2] Social democrats had little in common with Stalin and his epigones. Communism – so far as they were concerned – belonged to a different planet.

Reality was not so simple. Liberals, Christian democrats and conservatives lived the collapse of communism with the exhilarating satisfaction of those who had unexpectedly turned out to be on the right side of History. They had denounced communism not as the wrong application of a just principle – socialism – but as the inevitable consequence of a deleterious ideology carried to its logical conclusion. Without the market, they claimed, there could be no freedom. No conscious mechanism for the allocation of resources could provide greater happiness than the innumerable decisions of millions of individual consumers.

Neither such principled hostility to Soviet communism nor such open exultation at its downfall could be voiced by socialists and social democrats. However arbitrary the exercise of power, gruesome the repression, inefficient the economy and stultifying the bureaucracy, there was no denying that the USSR had achieved at least one of the conditions defining a socialist society: the absence of capitalism. The collapse of the system had not only removed the 'deformations' of socialism, but even this one defining feature. Nor could social democrats rejoice at the collapse of the centrally planned economy, because it did not usher in a social-democratic alternative. On the contrary, the 'market' turned out to be more uncritically worshipped in what was once 'the Motherland of Socialism' than it had ever been in the West. Disappointingly for those who had lived under the Soviet system, the immediate outcome of post-communism was not the anticipated consumer society, but a bazaar capitalism of unusual proportions, sustained by the relics of unaccountable state companies run as individual fiefdoms by managers on the loose, amid the surviving debris of a clumsy and lethargic bureaucracy. The whole catastrophic mixture turned out to be the ideal breeding ground for the blossoming, if this is the word, of mafia-like criminal organizations. The West, Left and Right, while celebrating the development of its own 'European Union', could find no contradiction between its pursuit of supra-nationalism and its support for the economically damaging splintering of the Soviet Union into rival nationalisms.

In this turmoil, the solution offered by the Right, encapsulated in the victorious concept of 'the market', was, unquestionably, the one initially preferred by a majority in all former communist countries. Was there a social-democratic alternative? Could not socialists have pointed out that the capitalism which had prevailed in Western Europe, so much closer to the cultural context of Eastern and Central Europe than to American or Japanese capitalism, bore little relationship to the 'free market' so admired in post-Soviet Russia? West European capitalism developed and prospered under the aegis of an ever-vigilant state, and had been 'hounded', throughout its existence, by a powerful labour movement. Without such 'hounding', the various capitalisms of Western Europe would have been politically weak, for they enjoyed none of the particular advantages of the USA, with its wide open frontier, its large single market, the constant arrival of immigrants eager to work, its lack of feudal residues. Nor did European society possess the distinctive features of Japan, with its strong ethos of co-operation, its cohesion and political continuity.

Why were the socialists and social democrats so reluctant or so unable to trumpet their achievements and provide a perspective for post-communism? There are two answers. The first is speculative: they had in a way been pre-empted by Gorbachev, who turned out to be 'standing in' for social democracy. His original intention may have been to make the communist economy more efficient, but he soon found himself ineluctably pushed towards attempting a 'social-democratic' restructuring of the USSR: introducing market reforms gradually, while maintaining a sturdy welfare state which would preserve the two single 'social-democratic' features of the Soviet economy: full employment and the welfare state.[3] However, as he moved towards this, his popularity plummeted and he was assailed from all sides, for moving either too fast or not fast enough. His great historical merit, well recognized in the West but utterly ignored in his homeland, was that he never looked back. If the category 'man of destiny' can be used at all, it can be used of Gorbachev. The events of 1989 'would not have happened then and in the particular way in which they occurred had it not been for the President of the Soviet Union and his remarkable approach'.[4] Accusations of indecisiveness, so frequently made against Gorbachev in the USSR and echoed in the West, did not take into account the uncharted nature of the territory into which he ventured. He was more solitary than any modern statesman has ever been, supported neither by a discontented intelligentsia, nor by a demoralized and apathetic populace.[5] This was yet another repeat of the interminable Russian drama, in which 'the political class generally fails while the intelligentsia is anguished and creative'.[6] Gorbachev's failure to transform Soviet communism into a social democracy suggested that there were no social-democratic solutions to the conundrum of post-communist Russia – at least in the short term. This 'extraordinary historical figure',[7] this master tactician, was the arch-modernizer of our times. But history is not always on the side of modernity. The failure of Gorbachev's project foreclosed the possibility of a major social-democratic revival and sanctioned the uncontested, worldwide supremacy of the ideology of the free market.

The second factor behind the silence of West European socialism was that its own model was already in crisis *before* the collapse of communism. Social democrats, by and large, had lost faith in traditional social democracy. They were not optimistic about their own future. They had doubts about themselves. They mentioned socialism less and less. In 1973 the Labour Party could still state in its programme that 'Only a socialist strategy now makes any sense at all.'[8] Twenty years later, such a statement – if made – would astonish almost all observers. In the opposing camp the situation was quite different. Modern conservatives were full of faith and confidence in their own ideas. This conviction and determination was promulgated with the self-assurance of those who had won all their national battles: Margaret Thatcher in Britain (1979, 1983, 1987); Ronald Reagan (1980, 1984) and George Bush (1988) in the USA; Helmut Kohl in Germany (1983, 1987, 1990, 1994). The socialists who had been electorally successful in the 1980s – González in Spain, Papandreou in Greece, Craxi in Italy and Mitterrand in France – could only boast that they had rediscovered the market. Their vaunted 'realism' was a sign that they had the resolve to accept the inevitable, namely the superiority of capitalism. They paraded their 'modernity' as evidence that they understood the obsolescence of traditional socialism. Elsewhere, as we have seen in the previous chapter, defeat piled upon defeat.

The 'new' realists – the *renovadores* in Spain, the *riformisti* in Italy, the *modernizers* in Britain, *les nouveaux réalistes* in Belgium – built on the revisionist tradition initiated by Eduard Bernstein and continued in the late 1950s by Anthony Crosland and the drafters of Bad Godesberg. The neo-revisionism of the 1980s and 1990s shared with that of the past the idea that capitalism would not be destroyed by a self-generated crisis, or by a revolution, or by the steady expansion of public property.

When the Socialist International was founded in 1951, its *Declaration of*

Aims, for all its Cold War rhetoric and anti-communism, did not hold back
from declaring that the aim of socialists was the abolition of capitalism. The
1989 Stockholm Declaration of the Socialist International claimed freedom,
solidarity and social justice to be the aims of the movement. The abolition
of capitalism was not mentioned.[9] The long-term aim had to be discarded
altogether. The loss of an historical dimension effectively delivered socialists
from a utopian albatross. Capitalism was not a particular transitory phase in
the historical development of humanity, but a mode of production which
was subject to political (i.e. non-market) regulation. The task of socialists was
to devise a regulatory framework which would enable the advancement of
certain values, such as justice and equality, while ensuring that the viability
of capitalism was not seriously impaired.

In practice, this is exactly what West European socialism had always done.
While its rhetoric looked forward to a non-capitalist society, the way in
which it exercised power, when it had it, assumed that the system would
grow and enable capitalists to accumulate further capital; meanwhile, socialists
would protect workers, extend welfare, redistribute access to education,
expand health care. What then, if anything, distinguished the great 'neo-
revisionist' challenge of the 1980s and 1990s from the mainstream tradition
of socialism? Did the new revisionism amount to no more than the dumping
of traditionalist symbols and images, the discarding of the utopian vision of
a socialist society? The evidence is strong: the Italian Communist Party
discarded its name, the hammer and the sickle, and adopted an oak tree as
its new symbol; the Italian socialists chose a carnation as their symbol in
1978, while the French socialists and, later, the Labour Party, opted for the
rose. The implication of the questions, however, is that visions, images and
symbols are trivial concerns and all that really matters are policies and issues.
In the world of ordinary women and men, this is far from being the case.
Would a papal decision to drop the Holy Cross in favour of – say – the
'Holy Triangle' be regarded as 'just' a change of logo? Symbols and images
define and sustain all great social and political movements. They communicate
a meaning. To modify or dispose of them is the most effective indication of
change. To say of any church, sect or party that they have 'merely' dropped
their image and symbols is an oxymoron. Neo-revisionists did not seek to
change an image in order to remain where they were. It does not follow that
they knew where to go.

Neo-revisionism is not a finite doctrinal corpus which can be easily
analysed. It implies that markets should be regulated by legislation and not
through state ownership. It means accepting that the object of socialism is
not the abolition of capitalism, but its co-existence with social justice; that
regulation of the market will increasingly be a goal achieved by supra-national
means; that national – and hence parliamentary – sovereignty is a limited
concept; that the concept of national roads to socialism should be abandoned.
It means that the historic link with the working class, however defined, is no

longer of primary importance, and that the trade unions are to be regarded as representing workers' interests with no *a priori* claim to have a greater say in politics than other interest groups. It means giving a far greater priority than in the past to the concern of consumers. Neo-revisionism entails accepting important aspects of the conservative critique of socialism – including the association between collective provision and bureaucratic inertia.

Socialist parties in power tended to proceed towards 'neo-revisionism' more rapidly than those in opposition, because they felt the real constraints of economic management more acutely. By the mid-1990s, however, the differences had become far less prominent. More generally, neo-revisionism meant accepting that socialist parties did not have a plausible response to the question: what is to be done about capitalism? Planning used to be the stock response but, in the climate of the 1980s and in the context of globalization, it looked increasingly outdated. One of the most lucid German Social Democrats, Peter Glotz, bluntly asked: 'what kind of economic future does the Left want?' His answer, vague as it was, could have come from any part of the political spectrum:

> the Left must shelve its centralist megalomania and drop the obsessive conviction that the State can effectively manage the whole economy ... As part of its plans for exerting control over the market economy, the Left must stand up for consumer rights, free investment decisions, the free disposal of assets and a decentralised decision making process.[10]

To know that it is necessary to innovate, without knowing how to do it or in which direction to proceed, is not necessarily an intellectually vacuous position to hold. Neo-revisionists may not know where to go, but they must know what precisely needs revising. Otherwise the operation really is purely cosmetic. Not all self-styled modernizers are necessarily neo-revisionists: for instance, Bryan Gould, widely regarded as one of the more prominent Labour Party modernizers in the 1980s, was not a revisionist when it came to policies. In his book *A Future for Socialism*, consciously alluding to Crosland's *The Future of Socialism*, he acknowledged that 'the option of simply reverting to the doctrines and policies of the 1960s and 1970s is no longer open to the Left.'[11] However, he then proceeded to defend the Labour Party's organizational link with the trade unions,[12] Clause Four,[13] the existing electoral system, and argued against a Bill of Rights.[14] He further suggested that the Labour Party could and should 'resist' the internationalization of capital, while never mentioning the European Community.[15] What this position exemplified was a desire to renew the image of socialism, while defending its traditional agenda. By the late 1980s, this operation had lost all credibility. Not surprisingly, Gould, defeated in the election to the leadership of the Labour Party in 1992, withdrew from political life.

This example indicates that neo-revisionism needs to be defined in terms of its content, and not only in terms of presentation. This is far from simple because, as I write, the reappraisal of socialism has just begun. Its future is uncertain. How it will evolve is a question to which no clear answer can be provided. One should bear in mind, however, that neo-revisionism cannot be viewed simply as a right-wing, social-democratic takeover of 'genuine' socialist parties, as traditionalists have all too often lamented. Right-wing social democrats were pragmatic, trade-union oriented, statist and gradualist social-ists. They had little time for feminism or ecology, which they regarded as middle-class fads. In contrast, neo-revisionists often originated from the first 'New Left', and had been deeply influenced by the new individualist politics of the 1960s and 1970s.

These new 'liberal' socialist ideas did not simply crop up in one or two countries as a national response to specific problems, such as repeated electoral defeats. They developed throughout the socialist parties of Western Europe and even in Australia and New Zealand, where, perhaps, they acquired their most extreme form.[16]

In Norway, the DNA (Labour Party), out of power between 1981 and 1986, sought to reappropriate the concept of freedom from the bourgeois parties. Its 1969 programme had stated that its goal was 'a socialist society'; by 1981 this had been replaced by generic values such as freedom, democracy and equality.[17] By 1989, during the electoral campaign, the DNA emphasized individualism and individual freedom, accepted that the state had become too burdensome, the public sector too large, and that the state regulation of markets should be in the interests of consumers, and not only of producers. In the rhetoric of most renewed socialist parties this 'anti-statism' became prevalent. There were exceptions, however: the new 1989 draft programme of the Austrian socialists had no compunction about declaring that they did not wish to reduce government influence: 'What we want is a better quality of government and a higher degree of efficiency. Only those who are eco-nomically strong can afford a weak government.'[18]

In the countries of Northern Europe, 'modernity' meant the modernization of socialist ideas – in essence, a partial conversion to the ethos of the market. Elsewhere, to embrace modernity meant that the priority was the modern-ization of the country itself, not just the ideas of socialists. This was obviously of significant appeal in countries for ever seeking to 'catch up' with Europe – Spain, Portugal, Greece, Italy – but also in a former 'leading' country, such as Britain, now struggling to catch up with its more successful rivals on the Continent.

This shift in agenda can be better grasped by examining one of the central 'modernizing' documents of the British Labour Party, *Looking to the Future*, adopted in 1990.[19] This document systematically contrasted other 'advanced' countries to Britain. A rather gloomy image of the country under Conservative rule emerged. Britain was a country, the document claimed, where managers and workforce were not supported by the government,[20] where production was of low quality and value, and for which there was little demand.[21] It was a country whose exchange and interest rates were less stable than elsewhere,[22] whose tax system was less fair,[23] and whose competitors were more advanced in training, education, science and technology, transport and telecommunications, environmental modernization, industrial investment, support for small firms, regional policy and export promotion.[24] 'Far-sighted countries', the document continued, such as Germany, Sweden and Denmark, encouraged their companies to invest in cleaner and safer products, while Britain's great cities were 'grubby and grimy, especially when compared with other European cities'.[25] Britain invested less in the arts than almost any other European Community country; life expectancy for the middle-aged was one of the worst in Europe; and it had one of the highest death rates from lung cancer in the world.[26] Britain had fewer nursery places than Italy, France and Belgium,[27] and sent more people to prison than any other EC country.[28] In comparison with other EC countries, British workers were disadvantaged when it came to individual and collective rights, and had no legally enforceable minimum wage.[29]

The purpose of this long list is not to show that the Labour Party believed that Britain under the Conservatives was a bleak place to live in, but to make two points. The first is that this document, which had the status of a programme rather than of an electoral manifesto, made it clear that Britain's deficiencies were not the inevitable result of capitalist rule (if that were the case, then only socialism could put these right), but of Conservative mismanagement. The second, which followed from the first, is that the document accepted that, in so far as the economy was concerned, what distinguished the Labour Party from its Conservative opponents was a strategy to make the British economy more competitive. Far from being against capitalism, the Labour Party sought to improve it: 'The difference between ourselves and the Conservatives is not that they accept the market and we do not, but that we recognise the limits of the market and they do not.'[30]

By itself this was not particularly new. In the early 1960s Harold Wilson, speaking, as did Kinnock after 1987, with three consecutive election defeats behind his party, pointed to 'the white heat of the technological revolution' as the strategic road for closing the gap between Britain's growth performance and that of its overseas competitors. This was the essence of the document *Signposts for the 1960s*, adopted in 1961. Like *Looking to the Future* it was a plan for economic growth in partnership with private industry to obtain adequate investment and modernize backward industries. The documents may appear similar, but the political and economic contexts of the 1960s and the 1980s were strikingly different. In the 1960s there was considerable trust in the ability of the state to create the economic instruments for modernization. By the 1980s, this trust had evaporated. There was little talk of new instruments of intervention in *Looking to the Future*. The document does not even attempt to graft an ecological dimension onto a policy for growth, as the SPD had tried to do in its Berlin Programme (see chapter 23).[31] After the defeat of

1992, anything that smacked of corporatism and intervention from the top sounded too reminiscent of the old days, not 'modern'. The review process conducted by the party was about dropping policies which, it was felt, would make Labour unelectable. By the end of 1989, Labour had reversed most of the policies which had been prominent in 1983 and 1987.[32]

Parties in the midst of a major process of revision need to reassert their traditional values. The means may change, the image alter, but the ethics stay the same. The Labour Party document *Democratic Socialist Aims and Values*, prepared for the 1988 conference, opened with the statement that 'The true purpose of democratic socialism and, therefore, the true aim of the Labour Party, is the creation of a genuinely free society, in which the fundamental objective of government is the protection and extension of individual liberty.'[33] It proceeded to define freedom in terms of the 'material ability' to make choices. The role of the state is to ensure that everyone possesses such material ability. The rest of the document is a vigorous defence of the need for state intervention, action and supervision.[34] Some interpreted the document as marking a retreat from the principles of social equality via state redistribution *à la* Crosland.[35] It was probably only the first step. *Aims and Values* sought to recast traditional principles in the more fashionable language of the 1980s: social ownership, community, individualism. Socialists, even modern socialists, cannot change their ethical principles when they discuss ethics. Principles can, of course, be forgotten, or left unmentioned or disregarded, while other contradictory policies are pursued. When asked what values they have, socialists cannot but reply that they seek to use non-market means in order to achieve a desirable state of affairs: namely, a more equitable distribution of power. Neo-revisionism involves rejecting old policies, not old ethical principles, old ways of achieving desirable ends, not the ends. This is why the attempts to update values were unsuccessful. Efforts to involve members and ordinary citizens in the review process were even less successful than similar exercises elsewhere. The debate at the 1988 Labour Party Conference on *Aims and Values* was ill-attended and poorly conducted[36] – as were most of the 'Labour Listen' meetings called while the review process was under way. The disaffection of the grassroots reflected a Europe-wide phenomenon: even in Norway few turned up to debate the Labour Party's so-called 'Freedom Campaign' of 1989. It is not surprising that *Aims and Values* was forgotten as soon as it was published.

Its contents, however, survived. Shorn of their positive emphasis on the role of the state, they were recast in a manner fitting to Labour's tradition: a constitutional change – a sure way of generating debate and concentrating attention. The distilled essence of *Aims and Values* found its way into a new Clause Four, adopted by the Labour Party at the end of April 1995, with the overwhelming support of the constituencies, at a time of increased membership and renewed optimism about eventual electoral victory. By then, however, the defence of traditional ethical values had turned into a generic defence of social justice. The Commission on Social Justice – set up at the behest of the Labour Party – produced four principles of social justice: 'the equal worth of all citizens', the satisfaction of basic needs, equal opportunities, and the reduction 'where possible' of 'unjust' inequalities.[37] It is difficult to disagree with these principles. Not many people appear to advocate – although most are quite prepared to tolerate – a society where some people are worth less than others, where basic needs are not met, where opportunities are not equal, and where unjust inequalities are upheld.[38]

Where the strategic outlook of the Labour Party particularly differed from its previously held views, and those of many of its opponents, was that it was now wholeheartedly committed to European integration. The party which had campaigned for withdrawal in 1983, then wavered in 1987, finally adopted a pro-EC position for the 1989 election to the European Parliament. With *Looking to the Future* the Labour Party endorsed the European Social Charter, advocated a European Environmental Charter and British membership of the exchange rate mechanism. By the time the Maastricht Treaty was drafted (1992), Labour accepted what it was still rejecting in 1988 – namely, the creation of a European Central Bank and a common European currency. In so doing, Labour's ancient enmity towards European integration was renounced. After the single market came into force (1992), the old Alternative Economic Strategy, buried since the middle of the 1980s, could not be exhumed while the country remained in the European Union. The new rules would make it impossible to re-establish import controls, indirect subsidies and a 'national' regional policy. The Maastricht Treaty had decreed that inflation, and not unemployment, was the main enemy. This was now fully accepted by the Labour Party and by all other European socialist parties. A national road to social democracy – or even modernization – was no longer possible. Here lies the authentic neo-revisionism of the 1990s.

After its fourth consecutive defeat in 1992, the Labour Party moved even more resolutely towards neo-revisionism. The long period in opposition had united the party round a single objective: to regain power at virtually any cost. The remaining internal divisions reflected either jockeying for party posts, or divergence on the speed of change, which proceeded briskly. In 1993 there was relatively little opposition to the significant reform of the trade union block vote. In April 1995, Tony Blair achieved what Gaitskell had sought in vain: amid thunderous applause and a few tears of nostalgia, Clause Four, Labour's chief sacred cow, was replaced. Like virtually all the other socialist parties, the Labour Party too no longer aspired to the common ownership of the means of production, distribution and exchange. In the new statement of principles replacing Clause Four, the Labour Party committed itself to constructing a community in which 'power, wealth and opportunity' would be 'in the hands of many not the few'. To achieve these ends, what was required was a 'dynamic economy', with 'a thriving private sector' and 'high quality public services', a 'just society', an 'open democracy' and 'a healthy environment' – noble aspirations with which few would argue.

In the new economic climate, the parties of the Left throughout Europe accepted two fundamental constraints: the electoral undesirability of increasing taxes and the primacy of anti-inflationary policies. According to the opinion polls, low taxes and low inflation were precisely what people wanted. Socialists, of course, knew that opinion polls usually revealed that people had contradictory desires: they want lower taxes *and* more spending on education and health; they want low inflation *and* higher wages. However, it was generally felt that the crucial segment of the electorate, the floating voters of the centre, were more disturbed by higher taxes than by anything else. Those in employment had seen a sharp increase in their standard of living. This contented majority effectively silenced the growing underclass, while rich and poor had few expectations of improvements resulting from government policies.[39] By fighting in 1993–94 against unpopular VAT increases, Labour reinforced the popular consensus against *all* taxes. Anti-inflationary policies imposed a substantial restriction on public expenditure, but massive unemployment exercised a constant pressure to expand it. In addition to having to provide for welfare and unemployment benefits, governments were faced with the huge costs associated with joblessness: poor health, family breakdown, criminality.

The kind of acceptable economic growth needed to generate full employment (however redefined) was now beyond the capabilities of the European nation-states. Could the European Community provide the supra-national instruments necessary to accomplish what the nation-state could no longer achieve? The answer could only be 'no' or 'not yet'. Without a new supranational regulatory regime, the only mechanism which could ensure a move towards full employment was the market (i.e. the world economy). Only neoliberals could hold these beliefs. It should be added that the chances that full employment would be achieved in harmony with the market, as occurred in the 1950s and 1960s, were remote in the 1990s, when the markets were alarmed whenever unemployment decreased.[40]

The dilemma of the Labour Party – whether to pursue unpopular high taxation policies, or turn its back on redistribution – was thus a genuine, historically determined one. It was not the result of mistakes or betrayal by leaders. Above all, it was not unique. A glance at the other parties of the West European Left shows how widespread were the pressures towards tax reduction.

In Germany, for instance, the SPD which, like the Labour Party, had faced a series of consecutive defeats, was gradually forced to demand lower taxes and relinquish some of the policies which appealed to the supporters of the 'new politics'. It did not use its majority in the Bundesrat to force the coalition government to abandon new VAT increases.[41] In May 1994 the new SPD leader, Rudolf Scharping, launched the party's new tax plan, proposing tax cuts for the lower paid and limiting the tax surcharge imposed to pay for unification to the higher-income earners. However, a large number of middle-income earners were caught on the wrong side of the threshold.[42] Middle-class resistance to taxation probably made a difference to the election results, which saw a narrow victory for Helmut Kohl, his fourth.

In Holland, the PvdA had fought the 1986 election defending the welfare state and opposing the deployment of cruise missiles. Although it won more votes and seats than in 1982, it was unable to avoid being excluded from the government – a coalition of Christian Democrats and Liberals under the CD leader Ruud Lubbers (see chapter 17).[43] Its exclusion was due, in essence, to its defence policy, which was opposed by its potential coalition partners. This led, however, to a wide-ranging reappraisal of the party's ideology not confined to defence issues.

In 1988, one of the party neo-revisionists and director of its research department, Paul Kalma, wrote *Het socialisme op sterk water* ('Socialism in formaldehyde'), which quickly became the *de facto* manifesto of the modernizers. The party was warned not to respond to the offensive of those who asserted the superiority of the market by retreating into the traditional socialist position, which equated the market with exploitation. What it should do was to accept that 'when the market actually works', it is 'better able than any other mechanism to chart reliably the economic performances of companies and cater for the preferences of consumers'; that capitalism was a condition of democracy; and that the welfare state had to be reformed in order to strike a new balance between efficiency and justice.[44] Successive party reports suggested organizational changes aimed at making it more open to outside debates. In 1987, a party commission chaired by a former minister, Jan Pronk, produced a long document called *Schuivende panelen* ('Shifting Panels') and subtitled 'Continuity and renewal in social democracy'. It suggested the party should drop the goal of the shorter working week, but advocated a basic income for the unemployed, suggested more co-operation with NATO, and less opposition to nuclear defence.[45] The report pointed out that the room for manoeuvre open to any Dutch government would be limited not only by the internationalization of the economy, but also by the increasingly strong position of 'market partners' such as banks, public sector interest groups, and the like.[46]

The new conciliatory attitude towards potential coalition partners paid off. In 1989 the PvdA returned to government in a CD-led coalition. The new PvdA parliamentary leader, Wim Kok, became finance minister. Government responsibility did not stop the proliferation of party documents and programmes. Much of Dutch socialist revisionism addressed questions of organization and membership. This reflected the disintegration of the stable dividing lines in Dutch society, the *verzuiling* system of sub-cultures such as socialist, Protestant, Catholic and liberal (see chapter 11), and the necessity of accepting that old loyalties were breaking down (what was called in Britain dealignment – see chapter 22). But the 1991 report, *Een partij om te kiezen* ('A

Party to Choose' – adopted in March 1992), also dealt with ideology. It proposed de-emphasizing the working class, stressed social justice and the fight against poverty, and accepted the market as the best mechanism for increasing wealth – in short, all the central tenets of neo-revisionism.[47] Given that the PvdA was able in 1994 to lead the first government in modern Dutch history without the Christian democrats, the supporters of neo-revisionism could use the Dutch case as a model (though they would have to explain the defeats of the Left in Britain in 1992, France in 1993 and Italy in 1994). It is, of course, impossible to establish a clear connection between electoral performance and programmatic renewal. What the Dutch case and others like it illustrate was that a majority of socialists now assumed that much of what they had hitherto considered as the basis of their ideas and principles had become an obstacle to political advance.

Not many, though, went as far as the leader of the Finnish Social Democratic Party, Paavo Lipponen, who, having lost the general election in 1991, embraced market reforms with such alacrity as to declare – admittedly to the *Financial Times* – 'I am a liberal in the sense that I believe people have really suffered because of lack of competition. We need a real paradigm change ... We have to get more flexibility and reduce labour costs and social security costs.'[48] In 1995 he had become prime minister.

Socialists in small countries realized that the constraints upon state action would grow and that their scope would be increasingly limited. The socialist leaders of Austria, Sweden, Norway and Finland discarded their long-standing opposition to membership of the European Union. By 1994, popular referenda in three of these countries backed entry – Norway remained the exception, as had been the case in 1972. The trend toward interdependence was regarded by all as irreversible. The Austrian socialists' 'Proposals for Discussion on the Future of Austria' (October 1989) declared that:

> By the turn of the century, the interdependence of states and nations will have grown ever stronger and manifested itself in areas even more varied than it does today. Consequently, the scope for action of a small state like Austria will be influenced increasingly by external factors.[49]

Throughout this document the Austrian socialists referred to themselves as 'social democrats'. The draft contained endless positive references to the market, each tempered by a limiting clause reminiscent of the famous Bad Godesberg passage 'the market when possible, planning when necessary'. For instance, it stated that:

> Social-democratic economic policies draw on the dynamism of a competitive economy and make use of market mechanisms. But in contrast to conservative concepts, it is not limited to these two factors. It seeks to build into the system a network of social safeguards against threats to one's livelihood. It combines the achievement principle with the principle of solidarity.[50]

This principle of solidarity, however, was being considerably modified by the suggestion that 'tomorrow's welfare state' should be based on the principle of 'who really needs help?' – an obvious reference to the need to abandon the principle of universal benefits.[51] As the draft was being printed, the Berlin Wall collapsed. This accelerated the 'modernization' of the party. In June 1991 it changed its name (but not its initials) to the 'Austrian Social Democratic Party'.

The Swedish SAP, often seen as the moderate alternative to the radicalism of Southern socialist and communist parties, at first proved resistant to neo-revisionism, even though, as we saw in chapters 17 and 23, its staunchest supporters had to take stock of certain hard facts. The celebrated active labour market policy could not create employment. It was a policy which was admirably well suited to preserving full employment, when it ensured labour mobility. Swedish full employment had been created by the expansion in international demand in the 1950s; once the golden age had come to a close, it had been sustained by a policy of devaluation and expansion of public sector employment.[52] Government economists and social democrats alike agreed that neither instrument could be resorted to indefinitely.

Supporters of the 'bourgeois' parties suggested that the krona should eventually enter a fixed exchange rate system, such as the European ERM, that the public debt should be stabilized, and that the central bank should be made independent of government.[53] They advocated the extensive deregulation of what had been one of the most regulated labour markets in the world, an increase in competition for services produced by the public sector, and the decentralization of public sector wage bargaining.[54] In his 1993 Tinbergen lecture Assar Lindbeck, a relatively recent recruit to the ranks of neo-conservatism, dealt with the problems of an over-extended welfare state (i.e. one which absorbs too high a percentage of public expenditure), and suggested a shift from welfare to 'workfare' – a system increasingly used in the USA, where welfare payments are made on condition that recipients accept work offered or participation in training programmes.[55] The idea behind this and similar schemes was a tightening of the criteria for receiving benefits in order to maximize the disincentive to staying unemployed.[56] It should be noted, however, that a kind of 'workfare' system already existed in Sweden, but in the context of an effective labour market policy: the Swedish employment service, whose task it is to find jobs for those out of work, employed twenty times more people than its British equivalent.[57]

Thus, even in Sweden the intellectual climate had shifted somewhat towards neo-liberal positions, at least among the supporters of the 'bourgeois' government of 1991–94. In this way, one of the central conditions for the growth of neo-revisionism on the Left was fulfilled: the breaking down of a long-standing national social-democratic consensus. In late twentieth-century Western European political systems, a sharp polarization between Left and Right was unusual. In the period of social-democratic hegemony (1945–75), the 'Right' had adopted many of the positions of the Left. By the 1990s, the position had been reversed: a new right-of-centre consensus emerged. Left-wing shifts to the right necessarily had to be preceded or accompanied by the rightward movement of conservative parties. Sweden was no exception to this general rule. Between 1976 and 1982, Swedish bourgeois governments behaved like social democrats. After 1991 and the defeat of the Meidner Plan, the Right had a stock of ideas (deregulation, entrepreneurship etc.), which they could use against the social democrats. Inside the SAP, well before 1991, modernizers had established a bridgehead.

The proletarian tradition and rhetoric of the Swedish labour movement had come under fire ever since the early 1980s. There was a decidedly 'unmodern' air about Swedish social democracy. There still existed remnants of a working-class consciousness which could be dated back to the 1920s and 1930s. The old idea of constructing the *folkhem* or 'people's home' – the Swedish idea of a true social-democratic welfare state – had a certain ring of puritanism and austerity. Its institutions – the 'Young Eagles' as the 'left' alternative to the Scouts, other youth organizations, the co-operative movement, the sports clubs, the housing co-operatives, the workers' press, the workers' educational association, the tenants union, the pensioners' organizations – appeared to belong to a different era.[58] Neo-revisionists were growing intolerant not simply of the old imagery, but of the centrepiece of the SAP economic management of the economy – namely, its 'rigid' labour market. One of the leading Swedish neo-revisionists, Berndt Ahlqvist warned social democrats in a controversial book that in the new interdependent world they would have to give up many of their hallowed notions.[59]

Many of these views were developed by Kjell-Olof Feldt, the SAP minister of finance (1982–90). He and his principal adviser, Klas Eklund, had long criticized the debilitating effects of the Swedish tax system (a traditional position of the Right).[60] They spoke on behalf of an articulate group of 'liberal' socialists who advocated greater reliance on market forces, less regulation, a smaller public sector share, lower rates of tax even if this implied high profits, more 'yuppie' millionaires, and lower real wages.[61] They were warmly applauded, to their embarrassment, by the Conservative Party. In 1989 Feldt argued in the theoretical journal of the SAP that the movement should accept the fact that the market economy had won the contest against the only known alternative – the command economy – and had done more to abolish poverty than any government.[62] In 1989–90, with the help of the Liberal Party, Feldt pushed through a tax reform which reduced the marginal rate for most employees – to OECD acclaim.[63] Until that time, the tax policies of the social democrats had been a key instrument of redistribution. The net effect of the reform, however, was to finance the large shortfall in revenues caused by the decrease in direct taxation mainly through an extension of VAT.[64] Earlier, in 1985–6, the financial markets had been deregulated and exchange controls abolished. On the back of the international recovery,

Sweden recovered a sound growth rate and a balance of payments surplus. The budget deficit had been eliminated without cutting welfare spending. Unemployment, already exceptionally low by OECD standards, fell from 3.5 per cent in 1983 to 2 per cent in 1988. However, Sweden's high inflation rate (6.6 per cent in 1989, against an OECD average of 4.5 per cent) was threatening to bring about a new balance of payments deficit.[65] Feldt's reaction was to propose, in February 1990, an economic package whose main feature was a strict wage freeze and a ban on strikes for two years. It had come less than a year after the unions had forced him to abandon another deflationary package.[66] These new proposals were initially accepted by the LO leadership, but caused rank-and-file uproar which forced the government to retreat and Feldt to resign.[67]

Swedish social democracy had proved more resistant to outright neo-revisionism than its weaker counterparts in Britain and Germany, but this resistance had limits. As Pontusson has indicated, Feldt went but his ideas survived. Public opinion had shifted to the right.[68] The SAP government was forced to defer the three promises they had made in 1988: the introduction of a sixth week of paid holidays; the extension of parental leave; and the expansion of the public day-care programme.[69]

The austerity measures which the SAP implemented contributed to the rise of unemployment. As a result, the SAP was out of office for three years (1991–94). Its membership had begun to decline rapidly in 1977,[70] as had that of the Norwegian Labour Party.[71] The industrial unions lost power and prestige. The employers' association withdrew from centralized bargaining. Decentralization – often a banner under which public expenditure is cut – became the catchword of the late 1980s in Sweden too.[72] The Metalworkers' Union (by far the strongest union in the manufacturing sector, with 470,000 members) had adopted a 'modernizing' document in 1985, 'Rewarding Work', which became the official policy of the entire LO in 1991. This aimed at reforming the workplace by integrating fragmented production jobs and transferring administrative decision-making to the shop floor.[73] Some of these principles were at work in the highly publicized experiment at the Volvo assembly plant in Uddevalla which started in 1989. This, however, remained a show case for radical work reform largely because it was not integrated with the rest of the company.[74] At best, this experiment could be seen as an attempt by the labour movement to embrace the concept of labour flexibility; it was not a response to the internationalization of Swedish industry. The crucial variable remained productivity. Under a regime of relatively high wages, Swedish firms were compelled to increase productivity as fast as their immediate competitors or to relocate an increasing proportion of their production abroad.[75]

When capitalism changes, so must socialism. As Pontusson has pointed out, the ascendancy of Swedish social democracy in the 1930s coincided with a decline in the country's dependence on foreign trade.[76] It is thus not surprising if the ideological weakness of the SAP coincided with the growth

of interdependence (as illustrated in chapter 17). This development was at
the heart of the SAP volte-face of 1990 when it decided to apply to join the
EC. The decision was backed by the electorate in a referendum held in
November 1994, two months after the SAP had been returned to government.
Swedish social democracy had survived, but its agenda had to conform to a
situation quite different from that which had forged the Swedish model: it
now faced mass unemployment, pressures to contain inflation, the end of
centralized bargaining, a flexible labour market, the collapse of the manufacturing sector, the loss of national control over the economy – all obstacles
to the expansion of the welfare state.

The Swedish model may be dead in the sense that the conditions which
made it possible have been irreversibly modified. Nevertheless, its resistance
has been remarkable. In 1993, the Swedish economy had been shrinking for
three years in a row; the krona had been devalued again the previous year
(to prepare for entry to the EC); and labour costs had fallen to seventh place
in Europe. But the tax burden was still 60 per cent of GNP (against a 40
per cent EC average); employers' contributions still represented 31 per cent
of salary; wage differentials were still lower than elsewhere in Europe; and
maternity and paternity leave were still very generous.[77]

In terms of programmes, the SAP remained to the left of most other
social-democratic parties. The political platform agreed between the SAP
and the LO (24 January 1991) highlighted a set of traditional guidelines: the
maintenance of full employment (which disappeared soon after) and a universal (not means-tested) welfare state.[78] In the 1950s and 1960s the SAP had
been stigmatized for its moderation and its reluctance to extend the public
sector. In the 1980s and 1990s, as the market was being celebrated as the
best mechanism for the distribution of resources by socialists (and former
communists) in much of Europe, the SAP was still talking of transforming

> society in such a way that the right of determination over production and its
> distribution is placed in the hands of the entire nation and that the members of
> society are emancipated from dependence on power groupings of any kind beyond
> their control and a social order based on classes is superseded by a community of
> people in partnership on a basis of liberty and equality.[79]

The difference from the previous programme was that the SAP was now
fully conscious that:

> The ongoing internationalisation of the economy is confronting the labour move-
> ment in Sweden, as in other countries, with new problems ... The international-
> isation of capital is making it more difficult for trade union organisations to
> safeguard workers' interests. It is limiting the ability of the Government, the Bank
> of Sweden and the Swedish Riksdag to accomplish the national objectives defined
> by the democratic process.[80]

This alone explains the Swedish decision to join the European Union.

Socialism had no other recourse than to follow capitalism. As Olof Palme had said as far back as 1975: 'We socialists live to some extent in symbiosis with capitalism. The labour movement was a reaction to capitalism.'[81]

Countries with a strong and successful social-democratic tradition, such as Austria, Sweden and Norway, offered greater resistance to neo-revisionist tendencies. In Sweden the 1995 package to cut public spending – including unemployment, sickness and parental leave benefits – was partly moderated by proposals to increase taxes.[82] In Austria, the SPÖ-led coalition fought hard to avoid reducing welfare entitlements.[83]

Where the social-democratic tradition was weaker, as in Germany and Britain (where the parties were in opposition), or non-existent, as in France and most of the rest of Southern Europe (where they were still in power), there was less opposition. But there were also 'local' factors at work.

The Spanish Socialist Party, the PSOE, embarked on the path of pro-grammatic renewal in the mid-1980s, not in order to become more acceptable to an electorate afraid of left-wing radicalism – as in Britain – but because it self-confidently assumed that it would govern Spain for a long time: hence the title *Programa 2000*.[84] Commentators have suggested various motives behind this vast effort: to consolidate the influence of the socialists in Spanish society; to make González's neo-liberal economic policies and pro-Atlantic stance more acceptable to traditional socialists and left-wing intellectuals perturbed by the short-termism of their government, or, more simply, to promote the rise of Alfonso Guerra and his friends (the main force behind *Programa 2000*) within the party.[85]

The 1990 draft of the PSOE manifesto opened with the central theme of Southern European neo-revisionism: modernization.[86] The PSOE – unlike the British Labour Party which saw transnational economic integration as a reality it had to accept – welcomed the increased internationalization of the economy, the emergence of a world system and a politically united Europe.[87] This was accompanied by an unequivocally pro-market assertion: 'the market is *the most efficient* known means for the allocation of resources ... socialists reaffirm the necessity for a mixed and shared economy ... In the economic arena, the State must act as a strategic agent guiding the economic growth which is created by private initiative.'[88] The idea that the state can exercise its strategic role only by being the direct owner of a strategic sector of the economy was thus abandoned in Spain, as it was in Italy by both the PSI and the PCI (after it changed its name), and in Britain by the Labour Party.

Where traditional rhetoric survived, it was for the purpose of internal factional struggle. Thus the 'Declaration of Principles' of the French Parti socialiste (March 1990) had a decidedly 'left' tone. It claimed that the PS 'puts reformism at the service of revolutionary hopes, thus continuing the historical tradition of democratic socialism'.[89] Its main objective, however, was to isolate Michel Rocard. Similarly, *Programa 2000* was used by Guerra to strengthen his own hold over the PSOE.

The PSOE's modernization drive failed to do much for those without jobs. Spain's unemployment remained the highest in Europe even at the height of the boom of the late 1980s.[90] Instead of creating employment, the PSOE government initially destroyed 500,000 jobs, privatizing large sectors of industry, increasing taxation, and pushing up interest rates to deflate the economy.[91] It then proceeded to expand the public sector bureaucracy. González justified his policies by indicating the difficulty of creating a welfare state at a time of crisis.[92] Nevertheless, prodded by the trade unions, the PSOE expanded health and pensions and doubled spending on education. As Patrick Camiller has pointed out, González had not been pursuing a Spanish equivalent of Thatcherism.[93]

The PSOE was also successful in reducing inflation and – between 1987 and 1990 – achieving the highest growth rates in the OECD, winning four elections in a row. Towards the end of the González era, however, the party was engulfed by mounting accusations of corruption, of using the security services against political opponents, of over-extending patronage, and of excessive concentration of power in the hands of the leader.

Protests at the high level of unemployment were muted. When pensions had come under attack in 1988, by contrast, the response had not been feeble. The rival UGT and CC.OO. unions united to paralyse the country by 'the most effective strike action in Western Europe in the 1980s'.[94] The PSOE gave in and granted considerable increases in spending on health, pensions and unemployment compensation. In practice, the socialist government of Spain had pursued economic policies indistinguishable from those that enlightened Spanish conservatives – had they existed – would have pursued.[95]

Like Craxi's PSI in Italy, the PSOE had become 'the vehicle for the coming to power of a new class of upwardly mobile professionals'.[96] There is little doubt that the PSOE, the PSI and, to a lesser extent, the French PS attracted in the 1980s a considerable share of what might be regarded as 'yuppie socialists'. This, however, was not the hallmark of Southern European neo-revisionism, only one of its less pleasant by-products. The attempted renewal of the parties of the Left cannot be reduced to the simplistic notion that they were taken over by careerists. Organizations are always eventually taken over by professionals. These are like pilots on a ship in a stormy sea: they may be able to keep the vessel afloat, but changing course is beyond most of them. Towards the end of the twentieth century, the organizations of European socialism had a simple choice: either self-isolation in the hope of better days – the option followed by the French, Portuguese and Greek communist parties; or adjustment to the new course taken by capitalism. How they should adjust was far from clear. But not all revisionism had to pursue identical paths. Countries and parties are different. They might be shaped by the same global environment, but they retain distinctive traits.

In Italy, for instance, it is necessary to distinguish between the neo-revisionism of the PSI, a party which was in government throughout the 1980s, and that of the PCI. The neo-revisionism of the PSI was adopted not only to meet a new situation, but to demarcate itself as clearly as possible from the PCI. This was not always easy, because the neo-revisionism of the PCI was directed towards minimizing its ideological differences with the PSI. The image all this conjured up was of a communist party in hot pursuit of the socialists. Every revision made by the PCI was supposed to demonstrate that it had finally abandoned its communist past and embraced 'European' social democracy. Yet every time it emphasized the decisive nature of its last step, the PCI implicitly admitted that its critics had been right all along: until this final move, it had still been tainted by some of the sins of communism. The PCI found itself constantly on the defensive, as if on trial: whenever it accepted a charge made by the prosecution and pronounced a *mea culpa*, a new indictment would spring up. The great paradox was that while the PCI was asked again and again to prove its commitment to Western democratic values, the two dominant Italian parties, the PSI and the DC, systematically ransacked the public purse.

The neo-revisionism of the PSI consisted in occupying – at least in rhetoric – the political space which no other Italian party could inhabit, that of a modernizing neo-liberal party. Both the DC and the PCI were parties committed to public spending and social protection. The PSI appeared less encumbered. It could cultivate the rising entrepreneurial middle classes of Milan and the rest of Lombardy, while continuing to appeal to a (diminishing) proportion of skilled workers. By the end of 1989, its purported economic policies of fiscal rigour, public sector efficiency and privatization were virtually indistinguishable from those of neo-liberals.[97] In the south, however, the practice of the PSI was frankly clientelist and hence in direct competition with the DC, which is why, in 1990, it reaffirmed its traditional belief that the public sector would be determinant in ending the backwardness of the *Mezzogiorno*.[98] There was thus a profound contradiction between an interventionist strategy in the south and a neo-liberal one in the north. In 'image' terms the neo-liberal strategy prevailed: in the 1980s the PSI sought to decrease inflation and the budget deficit, deregulate the financial and labour markets and reform the welfare system. In reality, the PSI had become an alter ego of the DC: by 1992, it had become a thoroughly clientelist party, particularly strong in the south. Bribery had become a common mechanism for replenishing the coffers of the party and enriching some of its leading members.[99] When the corruption scandals demolished Italy's 'first republic' (1992–94), a section of the DC survived, but the PSI, which had just celebrated its centenary, was utterly destroyed. It was dissolved on 12 November 1994 – an ignominious end for Italy's oldest party. Many of its leaders were investigated or indicted for bribery. Craxi fled the country and took refuge in his Tunisian villa to avoid possible imprisonment. The champion of modernity had become the supreme example of everything that was old and corrupt in Italy.[100]

It should not be thought that neo-revisionism was simply the adoption of neo-liberalism by socialist parties. All socialists tried to maintain and defend the welfare state. Where this had taken the form of clientelism, the socialists defended and expanded it, as Craxi had done in southern Italy and González in Andalusia and Extremadura, where he enjoyed growing political support.[101] The French socialists, while remaining committed to a strong franc and wage control, did not stop protecting the welfare state. All this exemplified the predicament of late twentieth-century socialists. They were forced to turn away from Keynesian state interventionism, but could not and would not become anti-welfare parties. Yet all parties had to offer obeisance to the principle of the fight against inflation. More than by any direct act of governments, the welfare state was damaged by anti-inflationary policies, which led to greater unemployment. This, in turn, damaged the welfare state, unable to cope with such high levels of joblessness. Unemployment turned out to be the fundamental anti-inflationary mechanism of the 1980s. In this situation the crisis of socialist ideas was not a surprising state of affairs, since there is no widespread agreement among economists about what kind of policies, if any, would accomplish the goal of a non-inflationary return to higher levels of employment.[102] A consensus emerged whereby governments were expected to follow an anti-inflationary path, more or less regardless of the employment consequences. In some countries, this was supposed to mean keeping a tight control over interest rates; in others, on public spending and hence public sector pay.

Once committed to anti-inflationary policies, socialists inevitably confronted the unions. Where modernizers were in charge, this confrontation was conducted with the rationale of going beyond the old class politics or in the name of efficiency. Thus, when Craxi became prime minister (1983), he introduced a minor modification of indexation by decree (February 1984), which the majority of the trade unions, demoralized and divided (the modification affected only a minority of workers), accepted. The communist-led CGIL federation fought back, but lost the referendum it had launched (June 1985). The decree made relatively little difference to wage levels, but it signalled the end of an era of trade union power.[103]

The PSI's confrontation with the unions was not unique to Italy. In Greece, Papandreou sought to subject the unions to control via legislation.[104] In France, the socialists had de-indexed wages, something which the Right would have found difficult to do.[105] In Northern Europe, the unions – still relatively powerful – were treated with greater respect.

Another common feature of Southern European modernizers was the emphasis on leadership. The PSI, in particular, sought to establish what was commonly referred to as a 'decisionist' style, a 'resolute' approach to politics (a similar style was cultivated by the Thatcher leadership in Britain). Here a major role was played by Craxi himself, whose political profile stood out in the otherwise relatively grey world of Italian politics – as was true of González in Spain and Papandreou in Greece. By 1981, Craxi had established an unparalleled degree of personal power inside the PSI.[106] For all the criticism levelled at the cult of personality, no Italian communist leader, not even Palmiro Togliatti, ever enjoyed during his lifetime the sycophantic praise Craxi received from so many of his supporters.[107] Craxi's leadership style paved the way for Silvio Berlusconi. Indeed, once he became prime minister Craxi developed a close friendship with Berlusconi, who was beginning to build up his own private media empire. This was mutually beneficial. Berlusconi, unhindered by any regulatory or anti-trust legislation, established a private television monopoly which regularly supported Craxi.[108]

Craxi, who defined his brand of socialism as 'liberal socialism', had become obsessed with the theme of 'governability', and sought to strengthen the executive pending a thorough reform of the Italian polity and its transformation into a presidential republic.[109] Nevertheless, the official documentation of the PSI, including its manifestos and programmes, tended to be couched in a generic and vague language (like that of most other Italian political parties), which refrained from making definite political commitments.[110] This is one of the reasons why the famed 'modernization' of the PSI was always nebulous. In Italy, as in other Southern European countries, modernity means adopting a foreign model. In the first phase of Craxi's reconstruction of the PSI, the goal seemed to be that of building an Italian-style Labour Party. It soon became apparent that the majority of the working class would remain loyal to the PCI. Then Craxi turned for inspiration to Mitterrand's Parti Socialiste – particularly enticing as the PS had just supplanted the PCF as the largest party of the French Left. The idea was to adopt the French model of a federation of 'clubs'. What actually developed was an Italian replica of the old and discredited SFIO of the Mollet years: a set of federations controlled by local bosses, usually loyal to Craxi, who took all the decisions.[111]

Craxi's neo-revisionism must be understood with reference to the peculiar circumstance of the PSI as a minority partner in a coalition government (few other socialist parties have been in this position), and the exceptional position of being still the junior party of the Left. As a governing party, the PSI distinguished itself from the PCI by becoming vociferously anti-Soviet, accepting, more or less unquestioningly, the siting of Cruise missiles in Italy (against the strong opposition of the PCI and many Catholic and pacifist groups). In so doing, it paralleled the policies of some of the other governing socialist parties, such as the Parti socialiste in France – which supported the installation of the Euromissiles – and the PSOE, which led Spain into NATO.[112] Nevertheless, no systematic project characterized the revisionism of the PSI. It had many and hence it had none. Projects, schemes, plans, manifestos, slogans, self-definitions were produced for specific purposes and then disposed of, once consumed. How better to discomfit the enemy than to shift constantly? Now a Europeanist, now a nationalist, now pro-Arab, now pro-Israeli, now reformist, now moderate, now populist, now technocratic,

Craxi kept his followers loyal by having no fixed rules, no certain principles and no directions.[113] The PSI was, so to speak, the first 'post-modern' political party and as ephemeral as its ideology.

Faced with the hostility of the PSI (whose commitment to continuing the alliance with the DC was unwavering, in spite of occasional intimations to the contrary) and of the DC, the PCI found itself forced into a defensive position. To some extent, this predicament was similar to that of most social-democratic parties. Like all social democrats, the communists had to prove that they were no longer a tax-and-spend party, in the pockets of the trade unions, soft on crime and welfare scroungers, the sworn enemies of the market and the entrepreneurial spirit. The PCI had a further handicap: it was a *communist* party. Unlike 'true' social-democratic parties, the PCI could not assume a detached attitude towards the fall of the Berlin Wall. The party leader, Achille Occhetto, who had rejected the notion of changing the name of the party at its Eighteenth Congress (18 March 1989), announced to a group of Resistance veterans on 12 November 1989 (three days after the fall of the Wall) that it was necessary to open a process for a new 'formation of the Left'. Because of the coded language in which all these pronouncements were made, it was not immediately clear that Occhetto was proposing to change the PCI's name. A new name, he felt, should not simply reflect the *de facto* social-democratization of the PCI. It should signal a 'refounding' of the party and the beginning of a process of realignment of the entire Italian Left.[114] Occhetto wrongly believed that there existed a vast sector of public opinion open to the ideas of the Left, but reluctant to commit itself to a communist party and vote accordingly. By changing the name, he felt he had undertaken the final step towards the elimination of Italy's major post-war peculiarity: the lack of a united reformist party able to form a government of the Left.

To all intents and purposes, the PCI had become a mainstream social-democratic party before the collapse of the Berlin Wall. The profile of its activists had changed considerably since the 1950s and 1960s. A survey of the one thousand or so delegates at its congress of March 1989 revealed that over one-third had university degrees. Women were one-third of all delegates and 70 per cent of those under the age of thirty. Thirty per cent of all delegates no longer believed that the working class was 'central'. Sexual equality was regarded as the most important goal by 97.7 per cent. Only one in four believed in the desirability or possibility of a classless society, and a mere one in ten believed that it was necessary to abolish the private ownership of the means of production. Only 3 per cent still retained a belief in the inevitability of the withering away of the state.[115]

After a year and a half of internecine disputes, the PCI was finally dissolved in February 1991 at the Rimini Congress into a new party, the Partito Democratico della Sinistra (Democratic Party of the Left – PDS), with a sturdy oak as its new symbol. A coalition of traditionalists (Armando

Cossutta) and supporters of the old 'New Left' within the party (Lucio Magri and Luciana Castellina) split and formed Rifondazione Comunista. The PDS was accepted as a member of the Socialist International. West European communism had effectively lost its most prominent voice. All that was left of any significance were the French, Greek and Portuguese communist parties. In 1990 the Swedish communists had become the Left Party or Vänsterpartietwere – in effect, a 'New Left' formation. A similar course had been followed by the Spanish communists since 1986, when they had formed an electoral front, Izquierda Unida. The Finnish communists, once one of the largest communist parties in Western Europe, had dropped the concept of the dictatorship of the proletariat as early as September 1966,[116] and had renamed themselves Vasemmistö Liitto (United Left) in 1990, when Clees Andusson (who had never been a member of the Communist Party) was elected leader. Elsewhere in Western Europe, communism had long ceased to be of any political relevance.[117]

After the collapse of the PSI in 1993, the PDS in effect remained the only significant force of the Left in Italy. It was the principal motor of an electoral cartel, the 'Progressive Coalition', which unsuccessfully fought the 1994 election, the first to be held under a new electoral system where 75 per cent of the seats were allocated by the first-past-the-post method. The Italian 'peculiarity' had resisted even the collapse of the First Republic. A conservative alliance had emerged once again to deny power to the Left. It was made up of the Lega Nord (Northern League), an anti-southern populist party, Alleanza nazionale (a right-wing group which included the former neo-fascists), and a new party, Forza Italia!, formed by the media tycoon Silvio Berlusconi, who became prime minister in 1994. At the time of writing the Italian political system is still in a state of unprecedented turmoil. The survivors of the old Italian Left – the foundation for a future one – are the successors of the old PCI (the PDS and Rifondazione comunista); the rest are minor fragments.

The PDS fought the 1994 electoral campaign on the basis of a strict adherence to all the tenets of neo-revisionism: a state which 'would do less but enable more', which 'would step back from directly managing economic activities and develop instead a role in regulating the market';[118] the principle that 'in the present historical circumstances there are no alternatives to the market economy';[119] the recognition that it is not possible to return to 'traditional recipes of sustaining employment through global demand management';[120] the acceptance that privatization 'can provide the opportunity to restructure the national economy on a more modern foundation'.[121] Some of these pronouncements preceded the end of the PCI and the collapse of the Wall: on 18 March 1989, at the Eighteenth Congress, Occhetto had already acknowledged that 'the market is the irreplaceable motor of the entire economic system and provides a way for measuring its efficiency.'[122] Not much was left of the patrimony of Gramsci and his notion that a party had to develop its own view of the world, its hegemony, and struggle to ensure that this view became the 'common sense' of the whole of society. By the time the PCI, in the guise of the PDS, had finally become part of West European social democracy, as its opponents and many of its supporters had urged it to do, it had gone a long way towards accepting the 'new' orthodoxy of market economics. The party which had so frequently proclaimed itself a force antagonistic to capitalism, had made its peace with its enemy.

In Eastern and Central Europe, the former communist parties, having reconstructed themselves as social-democratic formations, survived. They too had accepted that nothing could replace the market, but they stood out in various ways as the parties best equipped to resist it. They appeared to have retained the acceptable traits of their former despotic personae: a commitment to social protection and a suspicion of market forces. This rebirth, especially pronounced in Hungary, Poland and the former DDR, appeared to signal a further feature of post-Cold War Europe: the end of the great schism which had been inaugurated by the guns of the *Aurora* in October 1917. Symbolically, in November 1994 the Socialist International met in Budapest. None of this in any way betokened a revival of traditional socialism on either side of the continent of Europe. Neo-revisionism encountered little resistance.

Neo-revisionists had followed in the footsteps of their predecessors. They explained and justified their reform of socialist doctrine by using the guiding criterion of all socialists: the transformation of capitalism. This is what Bernstein had proposed in the 1890s: an evolutionary socialism to match an evolutionary capitalism. This is what characterized Lenin, a revisionist *malgré lui*, when he 'explained' the possibility of a revolution in 'backward' Russia in terms of its being the weakest link of the new worldwide chain of capitalist power. The revisionists of the late 1950s in Germany, Britain, Italy and elsewhere had to take stock of the extraordinary, unprecedented growth of post-war capitalism. By the 1990s, socialist and social democrats throughout Europe were converging upon neo-revisionist positions. The division between 'traditional' social-democratic parties in Northern Europe, strongly rooted in the working class, and those in the South, where capitalist modernization was still on the agenda, had become tenuous.

As the twentieth century was coming to a close, socialists could not but re-examine, yet again, the framework of their doctrine. They did so as they had always done: in a confused and unco-ordinated manner, propelled by the contingency of everyday politics and the pressure of electoral considerations. They could not do otherwise. Moving forward is no guarantee of success. Standing still offers the certainty of defeat.

Epilogue

IN CONTEMPORARY history, it has been said, there are no conclusions, only postponements. Nevertheless, as the century draws to a close, it is difficult to avoid casting a backward glance and, more reluctantly, gazing into the future. This is where even the questionable certitude derived from writing a narrative based on known facts must be abandoned. This work, after all, can have different endings, none of them definitive. Meanwhile, history will continue, and will continue to take us by surprise.

The arrow of creation may have a downward trajectory, but there is no way of knowing when or where – or if – its final target will be reached. Historians know better than to declare that history has come to an end. They should not behave – to borrow an Althusserian metaphor – like the omniscient traveller who, upon embarking on a train journey, knows all the stations on the way, as well as the train's final destination.[1] In the study of history the correct attitude is to jump on a moving train not knowing where it comes from or where it is going, walk up and down the cars, examine the furnishings, talk to the passengers, find out how they have interacted, what their aspirations and hopes have been. The historian can look at the landscape and note how it changes. By leaning out of the window – a risky enterprise – it may even be possible to observe which way the train will veer, whether a mountain is approaching or a river is to be crossed, but no more than that. Although anything can happen within the train, much of it unpredictable, there is one thing the historian must not forget: trains can go faster or slower, they can come to a stop, they can explode; but they are constrained by their tracks. History is about what people do within the limits of their landscape, their needs and their past.

Shortly after the Bolsheviks took power, Gramsci wrote a short article in celebration of revolutionary voluntarism. The Russian Revolution, he proclaimed, had been a revolution *against* Karl Marx's *Capital*:

> In Russia, Marx's *Capital* was more a book of the bourgeoisie than of the proletariat. It stood as the critical demonstration of how events should follow a predetermined course: how in Russia a bourgeoisie had to develop, and a capitalist era had to open, with the setting-up of a Western-type civilization, before the proletariat could even think in terms of its own revolt, its own class demands, its own revolution.[2]

The communist revolutionaries ruled Russia and its dominions for nearly three-quarters of a century. Their revolution was neither a voluntarist act against the laws of History (as Gramsci had implied, while approving of it), nor the clear-sighted and premeditated climax of a long-planned process. A unique historical conjuncture provided the Bolsheviks with the opportunity of seizing power. They won the civil war, repelled foreign intervention, were repelled in turn at the gates of Warsaw, and saw the prospect of world revolution quickly evaporate. They turned inward and faced the task inherited from their Tsarist predecessors: the modernization of the country. They continued to struggle against 'capital' – both Karl Marx's and the real capitalism which surrounded them. They built a powerful industrial machine, vanquished Nazi Germany, conquered half of Europe, extended their influence throughout the globe. Under their banner, wars of national liberation were fought, crimes were perpetrated, hopes were raised, and grandiose and often ill-conceived schemes were devised to improve the conditions of the people. The history of the twentieth century is indissolubly linked to this epic struggle against capitalism. The Bolsheviks tried to reach the sun; or, as Lenin exclaimed, 'we are out to rebuild the world'.[3] But no soaring phoenix can aspire to such heights when its wings are burdened with so much blood and human suffering. We are now certain, to the extent that such presumption is admissible in the study of history, that that revolution – the revolution against capital – failed.

So severe a verdict is not invalidated by the recognition that many socialist societies were able to improve the material conditions of life of the majority of their population far more than many comparable non-socialist ones. For instance, in 1955, Cuba had a life expectancy of 59.5 years, shorter than Paraguay, Argentina and Uruguay; and infant mortality was higher than in these three countries. In 1985, the average Cuban could expect to live until the age of seventy-five, longer than anyone else in Latin America and just short of the average American (75.9 years). Infant mortality in Cuba, thirty years after its socialist revolution, was the lowest in Latin America. Cuba's children were the best fed and the level of literacy was the highest.[4] In the 1950s, life expectancy in China was shorter than that of India and infant mortality higher. By the late 1980s, China had made more progress in these respects than India.[5] Even within India, the state of Kerala, run by communists for most of the years after 1957, outperformed in literacy and health indicators all other Indian states.[6] Taking the same standards of measurement, the Central Asian republics of the USSR – at least until 1975 – did better than neighbouring Iran, Afghanistan and even Turkey.[7] However, estimates of the post-1975 period in the USSR show an unprecedented deterioration of all health indicators, including infant mortality.[8]

It is when we compare the socialist states of Central and Eastern Europe – including the USSR – with their capitalist neighbours in Western Europe, that the failure of central planning in advanced societies becomes manifest – though not from the outset, and not in the 1950s and 1960s. Communism had failed to adapt to the challenges of the 1970s and 1980s. Capitalism – as we saw – also faced 'its' crisis, but survived it with enhanced strength: 'the West ... opted for the discipline of the world market. The East ... retreated from economic reforms it had begun to institute.'[9] The ambition of communists (including Lenin) was to manage a society of abundance – not scarcity – and to challenge capitalism at its highest levels, where it was most developed. In these aims communism failed miserably. In developing countries still dominated by pre-capitalist forms of production and property, the inadequacy of communist planning has been less evident. Communism as an instrument of modernization was not a failure. Communism as an instrument for the emancipation of human beings from the servitude of necessity was a catastrophe.

In Western Europe, the Bolshevik Revolution had ceased to be regarded, even by communists, as a model for the seizure of power long before the end of the USSR (see chapter 4). Some political sects, of course, went on dreaming of insurrection in Western Europe, though this was even less likely to occur after 1945 than at any time in the preceding one hundred years. Such groups were, at most, able to mount a terrorist campaign (as the Red Brigades had in Italy), or to inspire, for a brief period, the young and not so young – as various Maoist, Guevarist, Trotskyist and anarcho-libertarian organizations did, intermittently, in the late 1960s and 1970s. Riots and other forms of political violence may still occur here and there but – unlike the women of Petrograd, whose demonstration on International Women's Day in March 1917 sounded the tocsin for Tsardom – any future outburst is likely to amount to little more than a cry of anguish, rather than a political programme.

Marx, of course, never seriously examined how a society could overcome capitalism and establish socialism. He had defined socialism in the most generic terms of distributive justice – 'to each according to the work performed' – to be followed by 'to each according to needs'.[10] He never developed a theory of socialism, or considered how socialism should be planned, or what forms of communal property should exist within it. He never produced a grand theory explaining how the conditions of capitalist production are themselves produced and reproduced. These conditions are the non-market means whereby market relations are maintained: ideology, culture, politics, the state, the family. There is nothing of any importance in Marx on nationalization, the public sector, or economic planning. Marx was a theorist of capitalism, who sought to discover how the system worked. He was not a theorist of socialism and was contemptuous of those who wrote utopian blueprints. He was convinced that capitalism would not last for ever, but he never explained how it could be abolished or how it would end. Marx had no doubt that capitalism was the most dynamic system ever to appear on the surface of the earth. It was an unsettled, innovating and expansive system, which would revolutionize the world and draw it together in a tightly-knit mesh: the world market. He accurately predicted that the centralization of capital would develop 'on an ever-extending scale', entangling 'all peoples in the net of the world-market', giving capitalism 'an international character'.[11] As for the political shell which would contain this worldwide formation, Marx and his followers remained silent.

As I write, all advanced capitalist countries are governed according to the principles and rules of liberal democracy. The market for consumer goods appears to be the economic counterpart of politics: individuals exercise their consumer sovereignty by walking up and down the aisles of supermarkets, opting for Daz over Persil, before casting, as sovereign citizens, their ballot for the Left or the Right. Yet, as Terry Eagleton has written:

> The logic of the market-place is one of pleasure and plurality, of the ephemeral and the discontinuous, of a great decentred network of desires of which individual consumers are the passing functions. Yet to hold all this anarchy in place requires a political, ethical and ideological order which is a good deal less laid-back and dishevelled ... What goes on in the supermarket is nothing at all like what happens in the chapel or the crèche.[12]

I would add that what goes on in the supermarket is nothing at all like what happens at work, the place where consumers, metamorphosed into producers, earn the money which empowers them to be consumers. In the world of production, authority, hierarchy and discipline prevail. We vote for whomever we like, we buy whatever we can afford, but at work we do as we are told. Socialists have traditionally tried to intervene in the world of work and, after one hundred years of struggle, producers – in Europe at least – work a little less, and in far more salubrious circumstances, than they did a century ago, and perhaps with greater dignity. But they have not increased their control over their conditions of work at a pace remotely comparable to the expansion of political democracy, the increase in material prosperity, the extension in social welfare, or the advance in science and technology. Controlling capitalism has proved far more difficult than controlling anything else, because capitalism is a system based on the control of the many by the few – the reverse of the conventional definition of political democracy. Such control, of course, is also difficult to institute in all known technologically complex societies, including the centrally planned economies. It may well be that the only way back to the Garden of Eden, towards freedom and individual autonomy, would be to eliminate work or, at least, to work as little as possible.[13] That hierarchies may never be eliminated does not make them any less un-democratic or unpleasant. Rape may always have existed and may never disappear; yet we continue to view it as an act of outrageous brutality.

Capitalist expansion may, in hindsight, appear inevitable. Yet it encountered resistance from a multiplicity of sources. Three, in particular, stand out analytically (in practice, the distinctions are not so clear-cut). The first was the resistance by tradition, embodied in those social, economic and cultural structures which had developed before the advent of capitalism and continued to survive alongside it. The second was constituted by 'the socialist camp' – that is to say, those countries which, after the Bolshevik Revolution and the Second World War, pursued a policy of centrally planned modernization and industrial development antagonistic to capitalism and the world market. The third source of resistance is the object of this study: the socialist and communist parties of Western Europe, which restrained capitalism through regulation, while dreaming of its eradication.

The terminology I have just used requires some clarification. Two of the concepts are especially problematic: 'resistance to capitalism' and 'regulation'.

The word 'resistance' may imply that capital has its own logic, its own preordained fate like a ship whose destination is known. Tempests and storms may hamper its voyage and temporarily send it astray, but soon it gets itself back on course, recovered from the gales of the previous day. This teleological view has supporters on the Left and Right, who argue that capitalism has an end or purpose – though they differ on what this might be. On the Left, European socialists (including socialist ecologists) have argued that 'untrammelled capitalism' would inevitably have led to mass unemployment, poverty, wars, the despoliation of the planet, unbearable inequality, even barbarism. They maintain that anarchic capitalist development, unchecked by the conscious regulating activities of human beings, would be disastrous for humanity. Having acknowledged the gravity of the environmental crisis, they now point out that capitalism has no spontaneous mechanism for preventing major ecological crises. On the Right, Hayek, the most articulate and consistent theoretical opponent of socialism in this century, has argued that capitalism naturally and spontaneously tends towards the best society, or, at least, the best of all *possible* societies. *The Fatal Conceit* – Hayek's *envoi* against socialism – reiterates the central point of much of his thought.[14] It argues that capitalism requires no more than a few 'abstract rules' to prevent any one from invading the free sphere of others. This doctrine, recently reinvigorated by neo-liberals as if it were the last word in post-socialist economics, reminds me of an anecdote attributed to François Quesnay (1694–1774), founder of the Physiocratic school, proponent of *laissez-faire* and archenemy of Colbertian state interventionism. One day, Quesnay was asked by Louis XV (whose physician he was) what would he do if he were King. 'Simple, Sire, I would do nothing at all.' 'Who would be sovereign, then?', asked Louis. 'The Law,' replied Quesnay.[15] Needless to say, this advice was not heeded. Yet, for Hayek, to strive to do more than Quesnay suggested has been the 'fatal conceit' of those who believe that 'man is able to shape the world around him according to his wishes'.[16] Hayek added that socialists and all those who seek to make society adopt some 'common concrete ends' create a situation which can only lead to 'slavery'.[17] It is plain, however, that even Hayek cannot escape a fatal conceit: his 'abstract rules' – when he spells them out – would require both an implausible return to the moral values of the past, and a major and even more unlikely constitutional revolution which, among other absurdities, would require people to vote only once in their lives, at forty-five, and only for people older than themselves![18]

I agree with Hayek, however, when he refuses to ascribe to capitalism, or any other mode of production, any preordained inner direction. 'Modern capitalism,' wrote Joan Robinson, 'has no purpose except to keep the show going.'[19] If capitalism has no aim, then it can provide no criterion for its own success except one: its own survival, which in turn depends on its expansion. As Hayek asserts: 'Life has no purpose but itself ... Life exists only so long as it provides for its own continuance.'[20] If these are values, cancer cells have them. Hayek was echoing Marx, for whom the 'self-expansion' of capital is the only purpose of capitalist production.[21] Marx added later: 'Capital produces essentially capital'.[22] Capitalism is not an ideology, or a philosophy or a set of beliefs. It is a mode of production, an abstract model of how human beings have been organized to produce tradable commodities – as Marx and Weber explained. However, it can exist in a determinate historical context only if it is structured, regulated, organized, shaped, justified, legitimized, and hence restrained by the interplay of different ideologies. To be in favour of capitalism has little meaning, unless one is prepared to favour whatever political organization of society is required in any given situation to ensure the reproduction of the conditions of capitalist accumulation. But this would be abdicating from politics in favour of technique. Some real-life capitalists may do so and support any system which happens to suit capitalism at a given conjuncture: American liberal democracy, Nazi Germany, social-democratic Sweden or, perhaps soon, even 'communist' China. But they would do so on the basis of pragmatic expediency, not of moral and political principles. Hayek's assertion that capitalism grows best where there is maximum economic freedom has often been invalidated by events. His belief in the possibilities of a 'natural' and unrestrained capitalism has no historical foundation.

The three obstacles or 'resistances' I have referred to should not, therefore, be taken to mean features which interrupt, slow down or redirect capitalism from a non-existent 'natural' course. These obstacles belong to the same history as capitalism itself. Capitalism is like a powerful river which must flow somewhere. Nature, luck and the conscious activities of human beings may force it hither and thither. The river may run dry and leave the soil parched. Or, if untamed, it may run wild and destroy all before it. But it has no inner logic, no preordained progression.

To understand precisely how European capitalism would have fared without the existence of socialist parties or trade unions would require a level of counter-factual reasoning beyond our analytical powers, for it would involve 'rewriting' not one or two episodes, but the history of the last hundred years. The partisan historiography of the socialist and labour movement has been excessively concerned with 'missed opportunities'; based on the mystical claim that 'if only' its leaders had been wiser, or more principled, or more trusting of the masses, or less treacherous, then defeats would have been averted. Whenever possible, one should avoid constructing a whole scenario which is dependent on certain people acting differently. Moreover, an act which might damage a group of capitalists may turn out to be beneficial for others. For instance, forcing wages up by legislation or trade union action could be seen as 'anti-capitalist', because it may decrease the profitability of entrepreneurs. But would this necessarily damage capitalism as a whole? Inefficient firms kept afloat by the low wages they paid their workers might go out of business, releasing resources for new investments. Higher wages may expand demand and provide a wider market. There is simply no way of knowing in advance how certain struggles affect the composition of the system of production and exchange we call capitalism in the long or even medium run. Hayek argued that this should counsel prudence before we attempt to tinker with the world. Logically, however, if the future is unknowable, there is no more reason to stand still than to move. Besides, standing still is the one option which has never been embraced by humanity. If we never had any reason to move beyond the horizon of the present, we would have stayed where we were, and so never have given the future a chance to exist. Humanity would have declared with Doctor Pangloss, 'all is for the best in the best of all possible worlds'. It would have been the end of history and, therefore, of civilization.

As the heir to the Enlightenment and its rationalist tradition, the Left inescapably deploys optimism of the will. To remain a significant political force, it must assume that 'things can get better', that the future is on its side. Historians and logicians, for once in accord, will point out that there is no more reason to be optimistic than to be pessimistic. Yet one must ask what the world would be like without political movements committed to a belief in progress, to the assumption that it is possible to move from a less to a more desirable state of affairs, to the idea that human distress can be alleviated, perhaps removed? It is not necessary that this belief be 'true'; it may be necessary that it should be held.

Thus, the resistances I have mentioned must not be understood as interruptions on the road to an inevitable destiny, but as elements framing alternative paths of development. Abandoning temporarily the Eurocentric perspective adopted in this study, we can distinguish three models of capitalism: the Japanese, where capitalist development has been shaped by an exceptionally strong traditional society, while lacking a socialist movement of any significance; the American, distinguished by the relative absence of both feudal residues and a socialist movement; and the European, where both traditionalism and socialism are present. Thus, of the three, the American model is the one which most approximates to the Hayekian vision of a capitalism which encounters no resistance. This distinction is, of course, conceptual. No capitalism – not even the American one – is 'pure'.

Which of three models has been the most successful is a matter of constant debate. In the 1950s and 1960s, a majority of commentators would have opted for the American. In the 1980s and 1990s, the relative success of Japan, and the fear inspired by its manufacturing capabilities dominated decision-makers in the European Union and the United States. European capitalism is not a model anyone pursues (though the social-democratic transformation of the former communist parties of Eastern and Central Europe suggests that this may not be the case in the future). The restraints imposed on West European development by one hundred years of socialism are alleged by conservatives to be the chief cause of its lack of competitiveness and high unemployment rates. Whether European capitalism would have been more 'successful' without socialist parties is a question historians cannot answer, especially as it is not clear what 'success' entails here: full employment? More goods produced? A better environment? Higher productivity? More rapid growth? A healthier population? More equality? This enumeration is sufficient evidence that the definition of success belongs to the domain of value-judgements and not of statistics. Yet value-judgements do provide us with perfectly valid criteria of comparison. Relativists are right to warn comparativists: what is 'good' in Zimbabwe may not be considered 'good' in Lisbon or Copenhagen. Nevertheless, cultural differences between the main centres of capitalist developments are not so significant as to impede minimalist notions of what a good society is. High infant mortality, high levels of criminality, widespread ignorance, drug addiction, urban squalor, lack of opportunities, social disintegration and family breakdown are considered to be social evils in Tokyo, New York and Paris (and also in Capetown, Rio de Janeiro and Cairo, but we will keep to our three models). On these indicators, the USA scores worse than either Japan or Western Europe.

The USA, the only society to be born both 'modern' and 'democratic', throughout this century has represented capitalism *par excellence*. Modernity, rapid change, technological progress, mass communication, the consumer society, have all been so closely associated with the United States that the twentieth century can be characterized as the 'American century'. No socialist party 'plagued' American capitalism. No strong and powerful welfare state shaped its growth. The dead hand of tradition, deference and obedience did not obstruct its rapid expansion. American liberalism did not have to destroy feudalism.[23] Existing pre-capitalist cultures, such as those of the native Americans, were easily wiped out in a series of genocidal wars of astounding ferocity, later celebrated in endless films to the delight of children throughout the world. Social theorists, from de Tocqueville through to Weber and onward, portrayed the optimistic and individualistic ethos which underpinned American development as one of the main cultural preconditions for the rise of the entrepreneurial spirit (although – as the ever-perceptive de Tocqueville noticed so many years ago – America also provided ample evidence of monumental conformism). For many in Europe, in Japan, in countries at an 'earlier' stage of development, America was the future.

Yet the evidence accumulated by Americans themselves reveals another picture. The relatively unrestrained capitalism which has characterized the United States has been accompanied by social problems of an intensity unmatched anywhere in Western Europe, and virtually unobservable in Japan.

Measuring poverty may be hard and transnational comparisons are unreliable, but the American evidence cannot be belittled. A review of the enormous literature on poverty concludes that – at a rough estimate – the so-called 'underclass' is made up of eight million members or 3.5 per cent of the total population. This constitutes a separate culture within society, deprived of social citizenship. These eight million people are about half of the number of the 'persistently poor', in turn half of the total poor population of thirty-two million people.[24] Of the developed countries, the United States has the highest percentage of poor people (persons in families with adjusted incomes less than half the median): 16.6 per cent, more than three times the percentage of Germany (4.9), Sweden (5.0) and Norway (4.8), and more than twice that of Holland (7.5). The USA is followed at some distance by other 'Anglo-Saxon' capitalist countries: Canada (12.3 per cent), the UK (11.7), and Australia (11.4).[25] More than half of the American poor are lone parents with children. This is not so in Germany, Sweden and Norway, where only 10 per cent of the poor are single parents. Most of the destitute American lone parents are women, many black. No political party is ready to champion their cause. The racial divide has traditionally been one of the main reasons why class politics – and hence the Left – have been weak.[26] In turn, the weakness of the Left may have reinforced this divide. The increased power and politicization of American women has not reduced the growing proportion of poor women – what has been called the 'feminization' of poverty.[27] Weak trade unions can at best defend only those already employed. Anti-discrimination programmes disproportionately help the less unfortunate members of groups which are discriminated against.

The American Right has declared this underclass to be the product of a culture of dependency created by the welfare state and – when operating in its socio-sadistic mode – has urged a drastic reduction in welfare spending. But even though the welfare state is less developed in the USA than in most West European countries, the underclass is much larger. The welfare state in the USA, moreover, protects the middle-income groups even more than its European counterpart. Americans spend far less on welfare than Europeans, unless one takes into account 'indirect welfare' in the form of tax allowances and benefits. Even in doing so, 'one crucial fact remains: the middle and upper income classes are the main beneficiaries of the hidden welfare state'.[28]

The US poverty rate for female householders decreased between 1960 and 1970, when the country embarked on its 'war on poverty' (in other words, when it expanded welfare), and continued to drop throughout the

1970.[29] It may be true that 'poverty has been alleviated not mainly by redistribution from the more affluent to the poor but because of overall increases in wealth which moved everyone up.'[30] But this trickle-down effect has limits. It is not always the case that overall increases in wealth move everyone up. There can be situations in which the 'rich' get richer, the middle class stands still, and the poor get relatively poorer, as in the USA and the UK in the 1980s. Nor can it be the case that unemployment *per se* is a major cause of the formation of an underclass; otherwise, the European underclass (which *does* exist, as the colonies of homeless young mendicants sleeping rough in Europe's main cities indicate) would by now be at least as large as the American, since European unemployment rates have been higher than those in the USA for most of the 1980s and 1990s.[31]

Unmitigated by traditional values or social democracy, capitalism has spawned among the ethnic minorities of Chicago, Los Angeles and New York what Galbraith has called 'centers of terror and despair'.[32] These have become 'Hobbesian jungles', where 'wild, adolescent males, now increasingly armed' cause a 'universal fear'.[33] In the USA as a whole, pregnancy rates for teenage women are twice those in Sweden or France.[34] The consequences are worse in the USA than elsewhere. While the fundamentalist Right extols the importance of family values, the poverty rate of young families with children in the United States in the mid-1980s was 39.5 per cent, compared with 23.2 per cent in the UK, 18.8 in Germany, 9.1 in France and 5.3 in Sweden.[35] In the black community *half the children* under six live below the poverty line. In 1989, 375,000 American babies were born already addicted to cocaine or heroin. The US has the worst child mortality rate and life expectancy of the major industrialized countries. All health indicators for black women and even more for black men have deteriorated in the last twenty years. The USA consumes half the world output of cocaine. This contributes to the highest level of criminality in the world and, correspondingly, the largest prison population – proportionally, 60 per cent higher than that of the former Soviet Union and ten times that of Holland. More people are murdered in New York than in Calcutta's slums. While the USA spends less on primary and secondary schools than most advanced countries, it devotes 40 per cent of its education spending to colleges and universities. The result is that the country produces more Nobel prize-winners than all other countries put together, but millions of Americans are illiterate. A study suggests that 22 per cent of adults cannot address a letter correctly, and nearly as many cannot read the instructions on a bottle of medicine.[36] In the midst of all this, American capitalism, unfettered, pursues its upward and asymmetric course, giving more to the rich and less to the poor. Between 1980 and 1993, the income of the richest 5 per cent rose by 34 per cent in real terms; the income of the poorest 20 per cent fell by 2 per cent. All human beings may be created equal but, in the USA, they end up more unequal than anywhere else in the developed world.[37] Such gross inequalities are not just morally repugnant; they are in many instances a matter of life and death. In the developed world, income inequality *within the country* is the most important determinant of health standards and life expectancy.[38]

Of the three resistances mentioned, that exerted by tradition was unavoidable, at least for the first capitalist societies. The second, the Bolshevik Revolution and the state system which eventually ensued, was in no sense inevitable. From the point of view of the history of capitalism, communism was a visible threat to its expansion because it offered an alternative, while withdrawing potential markets from capital's ambit. However, with some hindsight, communism appears *also* to have been an element of stabilization. It held together the territory of the old Tsarist Empire which, without a strong centralist force, might have imploded during the inter-war years into a myriad of rival nationalisms which would have offered no resistance at all to the Nazi onslaught. It would have taken longer for the Western liberal democracies to defeat Hitler, and longer for them to recover afterwards. Or they would have been vanquished. And history would have 'ended' differently. Bolshevik resistance to capitalism might turn out to have been one of the contributory factors in the 'success' of the liberal-democratic form of capitalism. Not quite what was intended when the guns of the *Aurora* gave the signal for the seizure of the Winter Palace . . .

Even the Cold War, by inducing a high level of military spending, may be viewed as contributing to the sustenance of international capitalist recovery. In the 1970s and 1980s the American economy became more dependent on world trade than it had ever been. American imports from the other OECD countries vastly increased, helped by the strong dollar policy which effectively devalued US imports (i.e. made them less expensive). The growth in domestic demand in the US led to the recovery of the OECD as a whole in the 1980s. But a considerable proportion of this increased domestic demand was based on the increase in US military spending, aimed at countering the so-called Soviet threat. Thus, the capitalist economies were rescued – at least temporarily – by the increase in military spending that precipitated the Soviet crisis.[39] Again, not quite what Khrushchev meant when he said: 'We shall bury you.'

The third source of resistance, the European socialist parties, is the only one to have developed within the body of capitalism. Of course, originally, both socialists and Bolsheviks shared the same aim: the abolition of capitalism itself. We have traced the way in which, as they developed, European socialist parties were forced, by sheer necessity, to co-exist with capitalism and abandon what Willy Brandt called 'the theology of the final goal'.[40] From the very beginning, as they assembled in rue Rochechouart in July 1889, or two years later, when the SPD drafted the Erfurt Programme, the socialist parties named their terms for such co-existence: universal suffrage and civil rights, or political democracy; a state-wide system of social protection for the old, the sick and the unemployed (pensions and social insurance), or the modern welfare state; the eight-hour day, or what we now call the regulation of the labour market. The history of the Left in Western Europe has been the history of this co-existence. Regulated under the pressure of socialist parties, capitalism was rendered less hierarchical than in Japan and more humane than in the USA. This is no mean accomplishment, as David Marquand has contended:

> The capitalist free market is a marvellous servant but a disastrous master. In one of the greatest achievements of the second half of this century, a few favoured societies learned to convert it from master to servant. The danger now is that a smug and vainglorious capitalism will not remember the lesson. [41]

Here we must turn to our second 'problematic' concept, that of regulation. Strictly speaking, an unregulated capitalism is impossible. The very act of exchange, the necessary condition for the existence of market relations, requires – as an absolute minimum – a system of enforceable rules. In the real world of advanced capitalism, regulation has proceeded well beyond the minimal boundaries, the 'abstract rules' proposed by Hayek. At the end of this century, the fundamental difference between socialists and their opponents is often represented as a mere struggle between regulators and deregulators. Once socialists were more ambitious. They wanted to abolish capitalism. Later, when they first acquired power, their goal became the management of national capitalism by the acquisition or control of the commanding heights of the economy. Now, the goal is the 'regulation' of national capitalism. But to what purpose? And how can it be achieved when capitalism has become increasingly globalized?

Habermas has explained that capitalists themselves cannot reproduce, on their own, the conditions which make capitalism itself possible. Marx had perceived this when he implied that it is not in the interest of capitalists that they should themselves be the rulers: 'the bourgeoisie confesses that its own interests dictate that it should be delivered from the danger of its own rule; ... that in order to preserve its social power intact, its political power must be broken; ... that in order to save its purse, it must forfeit the crown.'[42] Capitalism, Habermas added, requires the existence of a state that confronts individual capitalists as a 'non-capitalist', in order to carry out their 'collective will'.[43] This is a conception of capitalists as Hobbesian atomized units, locked in perpetual mortal struggle. Only the intervention of a Leviathan-state can preserve them from self-destruction. This function of the state as a night-watchman approximates Hayek's 'abstract rules'. This may have been sufficient in the early period of capitalist accumulation. Since the end of the nineteenth century, and particularly after the inter-war crisis, the state in capitalist societies has had to intervene massively, not only to establish the basic rules of the game, but to ensure the reproduction of the system: by adapting laws to new forms of capitalist enterprise, by stabilizing the currency, by providing constantly expanding health care, education, transport and communications systems. Furthermore, the state has also had to take charge of the negative

– and politically intolerable – consequences of capitalist accumulation: uneven development, regional imbalances, unemployment, closure or decline of sectors such as mining, shipbuilding or agriculture.[44] In Europe, far more than elsewhere, the parties of the Left, acting as the political expression of the labour movement, have in fact reformed capitalism, making it politically tolerable by separating the distribution of welfare services from market relations. Not only is this a far more equitable system of providing for unemployment protection, health care and old age, but it is also far more efficient than any known market system (as the predicament of the USA in the sphere of health care abundantly demonstrates). Thus, social democracy has been an important stage in capitalist development.[45] The equity crash of 1987 did not drag down the European economies as the 1929 crash had done, largely because of structural differences between 1929 and 1987. Of these, two stand out: in 1930, the tertiary sector represented one-third of the total workforce; in 1987, the share was two-thirds – nearly half being made up of public employees. As employment in the state sector is more stable than in manufacturing, this stabilized the employment situation in the European economies and helped prevent an unemployment crisis of the proportion of the 1930s. The second structural difference is that transfer incomes (mainly welfare benefits) represented in 1930 less than 4 per cent of GNP, but in 1987 this share was nearly 30 per cent.[46] These benefits economically and socially buttressed the negative consequences of 'Black Monday' 1987, in a way which had not been possible in 1930. Had the state really been 'rolled back' to the frontiers it possessed in the 1920s, European capitalism in the 1990s would probably have been in a far worse shape than it appears to be. The welfare state may well have saved European capitalism in the 1980s.[47]

In Western Europe, the main achievement of socialism in the last hundred years has been the civilizing of capitalism. Other political traditions have also played a part in this mission. On the Continent, one should single out the social Christian tradition; in Great Britain, the reforming activities of liberal administrations at the beginning of the century; in the USA, the New Deal in the 1930s and the 'Great Society' legislation of the 1960s. Nevertheless, as a critic of socialism, Leszek Kolakowski, wrote:

> Whatever has been done in western Europe to bring about more justice, more security, more educational opportunities, more welfare and more state responsibility for the poor and helpless, could never have been achieved without the pressure of socialist ideologies and socialist movements, for all their naivities and illusions.[48]

In Western Europe, this has been true not only of socialists but, as much or even more, of the large communist parties, like the Italian, and even their less imaginative French counterparts. It is probably with this in mind that in August 1991, shortly after the failed coup which signalled the beginning of the end of the Soviet Union, Jean-Denis Bredin, of the Académie Française, invited the respectable citizens of *la France moyenne*, as they returned, well-rested and well-fed, from their summer vacations, to reflect that they perhaps owed some of their freedoms and rights to the communists of France:

> Am I allowed to suggest that we owe much to these stubborn and sectarian people, these indefatigable strikers who take over our factories and bring disorder to our streets, these obstinate creatures who ceaselessly fought for reforms while fantasising of the Revolution, these Marxists who, marching against the current of History, disturbed the complacent sleep of capitalism? ... Communism is dead. Let us rejoice. Am I allowed, however, thinking of the French communists, those who died so that we can be free, those who fought on behalf of the destitute among us, am I allowed to say that, quite often, they have been more disinterested, more passionate and more just, in other words, better, than most of us?[49]

Socialists not only played a crucial role in the establishment of the welfare system, but were the true heirs of the European Enlightenment, the champions of civil rights and democracy. They fought for the expansion of the suffrage when it was restricted. They fought for the rights of women more consistently and earlier than other parties. They fought for the abolition of the entrenched rights and privileges of the old regime. They supported, often decisively, all the struggles against racial discrimination. They played a significant – and sometimes the major – role in the abolition of capital punishment, the legalization of homosexuality and the decriminalization of abortion.

Notwithstanding these successes, socialists neither abolished capitalism, nor directed it through economic planning. This failure is inherent in the nature of the relationship between politics and modern capitalism. As Charles Lindblom has argued, individual capitalists are in charge of a wide range of decisions which, because of their consequences for the general welfare of society, are in fact public policy decisions taken by private individuals: allocation of resources, allocation of labour, location of plants, utilization of technologies, quality of goods and services.[50] This does not mean that capitalist power is unlimited; only that the overarching imperative of keeping capitalism on the road limits everyone else's power. There are times when consumers appear to wield a kind of veto, but in reality they mainly react to the initiative of private corporate decision-making. Besides, consumers may exercise 'sovereignty' when they choose between commodities; but many of the conditions making this choice meaningful are established elsewhere. It is only when consumers organize themselves through lobbies, parties and campaigns or, more frequently, when someone does it on their behalf, that firms are forced to provide the necessary information which might enable consumers to exercise some discretion over what they buy. This is a long and tortuous process, which always lags behind capitalist development. In the end governments must serve capitalism by establishing and maintaining a framework which enables capitalism to develop. It can induce it to grow, but cannot command it to do so.[51] However great the authority exercised by a government over the activities of capitalists, it is restrained by the fear that this exercise of power will have adverse effects on capitalism, resulting in unemployment and low growth. Current political language substantiates Lindblom's insight: 'How will the markets react?', ask socialists and conservatives alike, whenever they are in charge of the economy. The difference is that conservatives are ideologically committed to capitalism, and do not object to being guided by market signals, while socialists have had to accept, often unwillingly, that capitalist prosperity is an indispensable condition for social welfare and working-class well-being.

Over a century ago, West European socialist parties sought to regulate capitalism within two distinct sets of constraints. The first was the requirements of capitalism itself, which prevented the parties of the Left from deploying anti-capitalist policies – that is, policies which, if implemented, would result in the collapse of the system. The second constraint was the nation-state. This provided the legal boundaries to any regulatory framework. Capitalists could elude such boundaries by escaping from the nation-state. But only the strongest among them could do so, and even then they were forced by circumstances to maintain a strong commitment to their 'home' base. Capitalism's forays into the four corners of the globe could not have occurred without the backing of strong nation-states building empires and establishing colonies. The rise of the European nation-states was one of the conditions for development and economic growth, for the spread of technologies and trade and, as E. L. Jones has suggested, 'in several countries for the actual founding of manufactories where there had only been handicrafts'.[52] Many multinational companies would not exist unless they had first been able to operate in a national market protected by the state and, as often as not, by the social-democratic state.[53]

The nation-state has provided the essential framework for the activities of capital. Yet capital has never been circumscribed by state boundaries. European capitalism, in particular, has been forced to break out of these national borders far more than its Japanese and American 'rivals'. European national states are small, their domestic markets restricted. Interdependence may affect all capitalisms, but none more so than those of Europe.[54] These may merge into a global capitalism, but national regulations still exist and are doubtless destined to survive for the foreseeable future, albeit with reduced efficacy. Before imposing or maintaining any regulations, politicians have to take into account the relative position of 'their' capitalists (i.e. those operating within the nation-state) vis-à-vis their competitors outside. The welfare of their electorates depends on capitalism. The reverse is not always the case. Capital can relocate elsewhere; electorates cannot.

Socialists have responded to this by attempting to recreate a new regulatory framework at the European level. Their initially hostile attitude towards European integration has been discarded. Jacques Delors, the long-sighted exponent of the historical vision of 'post-national' socialism throughout the

1980s and early 1990s, indicated a way forward when he explained in 1989 that the key issue of the contemporary age was the reality of a world economy without a pilot. A new political division of labour would have to be established. In the old continent, 'the European road must not empty of substance the powers of the nation-states, but must recreate a margin of autonomy which would enable them to perform their essential tasks. Macro-economic policy would have to be recast at the European community level.'[55] In the same year in France, under Michel Rocard, once an arch-anti-marketeer, now an enthusiastic federalist, the socialist government promulgated a national plan which, for the first time in the history of French planning, took Monnet's lesson on board by describing France's future in terms of its European destiny: the title of the plan was *La France, L'Europe: Le Plan 1989–1992.*[56] Previously reluctant Europeans – socialists in Finland, Sweden, Austria and, unsuccessfully, in Norway – backed their country's adhesion to the European Union in 1994. In 1993, John Smith, leader of what was once the least pro-European of European socialist parties, declared:

> Whether we like it or not interdependence is the reality of the modern world. Matters of vital importance to our lives such as our economic prosperity and the protection of our environment all depend on international collaboration. These days no country can go it alone.[57]

In Greece, Papandreou, once a bitter opponent of the EC, whose five-year plan for 1983–88 contained virtually no reference to Europe, declared in his party's 1988 manifesto: 'Europe encapsulates our national prospects.'[58] He was succeeded by Kostas Simitis, a staunch Europeanist. Europe was now seen as the terrain where politics could reacquire the power lost at the national level.

This project, whose basic contours we can only dimly perceive at this stage, is fraught with difficulties. To begin with, socialist parties have had to accept that European regulation of capitalism must take place through the institutions of the European Union. This presents many problems. One of them is that the Union has no democratic legitimacy – this is what is meant by the expression 'the democratic deficit' – because national politicians do not wish it to be democratic. As a result, the European Union conjures up in the minds of Europeans a powerful technocratic image.[59] Another problem is that the European Community was originally devised as a free-trade area, as a 'capitalist club', to use the jargon of traditional left-wing anti-Europeans. It is far more difficult to reform and redirect an existing state of affairs than to create one *ab initio*. Moreover, the decisive pressure towards the formation of a single market – however moderated by Delors' initiatives – came from a powerful neo-liberal culture aiming at the removal of national barriers to trade.[60] To create European institutions and norms, replacing those of each nation-state, will be a momentous enterprise whose outcome is uncertain.

In modern-day Europe there are few, if any, of the preconditions which existed in the nineteenth century for the building of nations: there is no

European consciousness, not even among the intellectual élites; no central authority, and hence no army or police force, established by conquest, revolution or tradition to carry out the task of 'making the Europeans'; no feeling of community or solidarity; no real or imagined outside threat to (Western) Europe as a whole. Furthermore, the European Union is the creation of nation-states pursuing what they conceived as their national interests. As Loukas Tsoukalis has written: 'The political game remains predominantly national. It is usually played as if national units were more independent economically than they actually are.'[61]

For better or for worse, the nation-state is an enduring reality. The main reason is that it is the first ever political construct with some form of democratic legitimacy. Though nation-building has always been initiated by an élite, nations have eventually secured a massive popular endorsement. Nations thus provide the necessary political framework for both capitalist development and democracy. It is therefore almost inevitable that the pre-rogatives of nations, whether real or imaginary, will be defended by national electorates understandably anxious to avoid any erosion of democratic control. They will be supported by their own national governments – even by those enthusiastic about economic and political integration – which would not wish to relinquish power to a larger state.

After all, the European nation-states joined forces in order to obtain through European co-operation what they were unable to secure at the national level. As Milward has explained, 'whenever the Community member-states have had to implement their surrenders of sovereignty they have produced an arrangement which left almost all political power with the nation-state.'[62] Though they used the dreams and aspirations of European federalists, their intention was never that of abolishing the nation. Much of the con-struction of the European union occurred through rounds of negotiation between national governments. Sovereignty has, of course, been ceded. This is hardly new. Absolute sovereignty exists only in the imagination of some nationalists. What was crucial in the construction of the European entity was that control of this pooled sovereignty remained in the hands of the executives of the nation-state. It was never ceded to a faceless civil service (as anti-European propagandists repeat *ad nauseam*), or to a democratically elected and publicly accountable parliament. Socialist parties are unlikely to work hard at eroding national prerogatives. They too derive their legitimacy from nationally based electorates. When in opposition, lack of power may lead them to support an extension of the powers of the European Parliament. But in office, the pressures may work the other way, towards preserving the prerogatives of their own nation-state. The close collaboration between the modern democratic nation-state and the parties of the Left has profoundly marked the experience of the last hundred years. These habits will not be easily discarded. Socialists, unavoidably, became 'nationalist'. They responded to the aspirations of their 'national' constituents.

Capital is not so constrained. Marx described it as the 'historical means of developing the material forces of production and creating an appropriate world-market'.[63] It can fly around the world. From its inception (whether we wish to date it from the sixteenth century or later), capitalism as an economic system operated within a territory larger than any state could control.[64] It was, however, dependent on the support of national states and globalization has never been a continuous trend: it stopped advancing in 1914 and regressed in the inter-war years.[65] What is now occurring is that capitalism has entered a transitional phase, from an international economy, where nation-states are still the chief regulatory agents and in which multinational companies have an important home base, to a truly 'global' economy, free of its various national integuments. Of course it is not inevitable that such a transition will be realized. To a large extent, the contemporary crisis of socialism is a by-product of the globalization of capitalism.[66]

That the 'nation-state is just about through as an economic unit' was perceived by lucid economists such as C. P. Kindleberger as early as 1969, though he promptly added: 'the nation-state ... will survive and flourish.'[67] However, if we can talk about a crisis of the nation-state at all, it is in terms of its capacity to meet the expectations of its population, notwithstanding the fact that the powers of national governments have grown immensely even in the weakest of contemporary states, such as some states in West Africa.[68]

Unlike real neo-liberals, socialists will find it difficult to establish a level of political struggle appropriate to this new phase. They will have to distinguish between reforms which will be dependent on international accords, and those domestic reforms which affect public spending or employers' costs. International and European-based social policy will seek to establish a basic framework, such as minimal norms of welfare and working conditions. Regulators of this kind can afford to ignore the costs implied in their policies, since these are borne by employers. This is the direction taken by members of the European Community (now the European Union), when it adopted its Social Charter at Maastricht in 1992.[69] As long as regulations are imposed on a supra-national basis, the effects on competition will be to the benefit of the best organized firms – just as, in the old Rehn–Meidner Swedish model, the establishment of the 'fair wage' worked to the advantage of efficient firms. Socialists in charge of thriving capitalist economies will be able to demand more progressive forms of international regulation than socialists in less advanced countries. The EU is a good example of this type of regulator. Its social policy is cheaper to administer than the more traditional socialist welfare system (which socialized welfare costs), because it does not involve further public expenditure (except for public employers). The main problem with such public policy is that it will be directed merely towards the protection of those who are employed and do little to provide the unemployed with jobs. Yet unemployment will be the most important challenge facing socialists in the next decades. This problem cannot be underestimated: in Western Europe in 1992, unemployment stood at 18,455,700, more than the total population of Denmark, Norway and Sweden combined. Today, as yesterday – as Keynes stated in his 'Concluding Notes' to the *General Theory* – 'The outstanding faults of the economic society in which we live are its failure to provide for full employment and its arbitrary and inequitable distribution of wealth and incomes.'[70]

Of all fields of state economic activity, monetary policy is where governments have lost the most autonomy. But many of the other traditional 'core' functions of European nation-states have been, at least in part, 'Europeanized': border controls, commerce and trade, economic management, industrial policy, immigration, equality at work, foreign policy, taxation. Welfare has remained largely in the hands of national governments.[71] In regulating their own capitalism in the interests of social justice, socialists or their inheritors will have to look – more than in the past – not only to production, but also to reproduction, culture, communications, gender relations and the quality of life. Much of this remains within the reach of nationally based politics. Meaningful domestic reforms will deal mainly with issues such as the organization (rather than the funding) of the public sector, particularly education (including child-care) and health care. These are least subject to the governance of the interdependent world and, at least in the short run, the organization of education and health care (as distinct from their costs) does not affect the competitiveness of capitalist firms. In the long run, of course, education is of decisive importance to economic growth.

Much of this book has been concerned with highlighting the effect that interdependence has had on socialist politics. That what happens in one part of the world may affect what happens in other parts is not new. Some of the more perceptive minds of the Left, such as the Italian communist leader, Palmiro Togliatti, had indicated in the late 1950s that this would require a change in socialist politics.[72] What is new, especially since the 1980s, is that interdependence has reached such an intensity that it has thrown into crisis traditional concepts of national politics and all political parties and ideologies. Socialists have been more affected than conservatives, because of their essential conviction that politics can govern the economy. In a global economy, national politics can survive only at a less ambitious level, although this will not necessarily lead to the end of major differences in economic policy between Left and Right.[73]

How does interdependence manifest itself? In the first place, in the spectacular growth of international trade, which more than twice outstrips the growth of world output.[74] Secondly, in the development of an international money market ten times larger than that required by trade. This largely speculative market in essentially footloose money responds to the widespread uncertainty surrounding future price movements.[75] This uncertainty is the other side of the unregulated nature of the markets. It forces the operators into a series of very short-term reactions to minor fluctuations. The origin of much of this has been national decisions – or the lack of them.[76] For instance, in October 1979 the British government abolished exchange controls. In so doing, it created an irreversible situation: controls could not be restored without provoking a disastrous run on the currency.[77]

By detaching itself from the secure moorings of the nation-state, capitalism has lost its principal regulatory framework. In the absence of a world regulator – which is what the Pax Americana had been for nearly fifty years – will the system collapse in anarchy? The omens do not favour the optimists. As long as the debt burden on Third World countries remains, it will be impossible for them to aspire to any kind of prosperity. Any trade surplus they achieve quickly evaporates in debt repayment: during the UN 'decade of development', the poorer Third World countries transferred over 236 billion dollars to the advanced world – a kind of 'development aid in reverse'.[78]

It is not only capitalism which has been 'globalized'. National politicians (including socialists) have also had to face the international effects of this globalization. Virtually all environmental problems have now become international problems, and nearly all of these are connected to economic development: car exhaust fumes, acid rain, river and sea pollution, oil spillages, nuclear power and global warming. It has become impossible to visualize self-contained 'national' problems which will not, sooner rather than later, affect other countries. In the era of mass communications, everything travels: Islamic fundamentalism as well as models of sexual behaviour, CNN news as well as pop music. The problems of the so-called Third World are not confined to the Third World. Drug addiction and terrorism have been an issue at least since the nineteenth century, but they have become a major problem of public policy requiring international co-ordination only since the 1970s.

The response has been the multiplication of international agencies aimed at dealing with cross-border problems and the growth of international regional co-operation – in fact, trading blocs – all based on nation-states. On 1 January 1995, the European Union included all Western European countries except Switzerland, Norway and Iceland – thus constituting the largest single market in the world. Before then, the USA, Canada and Mexico had established the North Atlantic Free Trade Area; the countries of the Organization of African Unity had formed the African Economic Community (1991); Algeria, Libya, Morocco, Mauritania and Tunisia had created the Union du Maghreb Arabe (1989); in December 1991, Bolivia, Venezuela, Ecuador, Peru and Colombia had reactivated the Pacto Andino aimed at abolishing all custom duties by 1996; while Brazil, Argentina, Uruguay and Paraguay had established the Mercado Común del Sur (MERCOSUR, or 'Common Market of the South'); soon after acquiring independence, Estonia, Latvia and Lithuania formed a Baltic common market; while ASEAN, the Association of South East Asian Nations, comprising Thailand, Singapore, the Philippines,

Malaysia, Indonesia and Brunei, was reactivated.[79] At the international level, the General Agreement on Tariffs and Trade (GATT) negotiations were completed, leading to the formation of the World Trade Organization. All these are associations of 'sovereign' nation-states. Thus, the response to the *de facto* weakening of national powers has been to consolidate national governments as the best negotiators on behalf of the nation as a whole. Internal politics will increasingly become a contest between parties over who can best defend the 'national interest'. The new global stage of capitalism will constrain socialists far more than conservatives. Conservatives will use their nationalist credibility to negotiate better terms in the international arena on behalf of their own nation-state. At the same time, in the name of the international requirements of modern capitalism, they will accept the abandonment of internal – that is national – regulation. Old Marxists will be left to smile wryly at this conservative embrace of terms once so central to socialism: internationalism and the 'withering away of the state'.

Any political discourse which can conjoin both untrammelled global capitalism *and* nationalism will provide conservatism with an enormous political advantage. While capital (and its accompanying problems) is further internationalized, politics is further 'nationalized'. While nationalism is the growing force in the former communist camp, in Western Europe it is acquiring a new lease of life. In 1994, the enthusiastically pro-European French Socialist Party was destroyed at the election by a Right signalling its coolness towards Europe. In Britain, the Conservative Party was 'defending British interests' (i.e. those of inefficient British entrepreneurs able to compete in Europe only by denying their workforce rights obtained elsewhere), by opting out of the European regulation of the labour market. In Italy, a new force emerged in 1994 to snatch from the Left the victory it had sought for so long. Significantly enough, it was called Forza Italia! – the roar one hears in the stadium from football nationalists. Its principal ally was Alleanza nazionale, heir to Mussolini, now fully legitimized.

Elsewhere, nationalism co-exists with the trend towards integration, as in Greece, where PASOK waves the flag to prevent Macedonia using the same name as a Greek province, while its own economic recovery is utterly dependent on EU funds amounting to 5 per cent of GDP.[80] Even in so small a country as Norway, alone in voting against EU membership in 1994, some figment of national sovereignty is touchingly preserved, even though the reality is that Norway, outside a political and economic community which includes nearly the whole of Western Europe, will simply be forced to comply with rules established elsewhere and upon which it will have no say.[81]

National executives increase their powers at the expense of national parliaments – whose remaining function is to provide governments with democratic legitimacy. Issues will become of less relevance because, in a climate of ceaseless negotiations whose outcome can never be ensured in advance (nor, therefore, guaranteed in a pre-electoral manifesto), what will become ever more important is the notion of *fides implicita* between electorates and politicians – that is, the delegation of decisions to someone not on the basis of what they promise, or what they stand for, but in the belief that they can be 'trusted'.[82] If policies are not clear, and we do not know what anyone will do, the question of the personality of politicians (already thrown into high relief by television) will assume ever greater significance. In principle, this should not *a priori* favour Left or Right. What it does, however, is to reproduce a conception of politics in which electorates – once they have chosen their rulers – remain passive spectators of a game played at some distance, although none of this prevents the increasingly frequent outbursts of campaigning on specific issues. Is it surprising, then, that under these conditions electorates wish to retain for themselves the only power which may matter – purchasing power – by electing tax-cutting governments? Impoverished nation-states, now simple actors in a complex international arena, governed by ephemeral personalities elected for their looks, their acceptable private moral habits, or their ability to face questions on television, are not likely to provide socialists with the best framework for moulding the future. Socialist activists will be tempted – and many have already succumbed – to dump their values in the turmoil of renewal, forgetting Machiavelli's lesson that the true innovators are those who change their strategy and adapt it to the new terrain, not those who have lost their compass, the values which impart direction to their politics. The ideology of the 'end-of-ideology' is not that of socialists, while those who claim that the division between Left and Right has lost all meaning may do well to remember Alain's famous aphorism of 1930: 'When I am asked whether the division between Left and Right still has any meaning, the first thought which comes to my mind is that the person who asks the question is not on the Left.'[83]

The pressures on all parties, especially those of the Left, to remain enclosed in national shells are compelling. How they will respond to this, and how national politics will develop in the course of the next century, is impossible to predict, though for the Left to remain national, while capitalism is international, would be like becoming a shadow that has lost its body. But parties can continue to exist well after the conditions which brought them into being have disappeared.

The story I have traced indicates that the fate and probably the future of West European socialism cannot be separated from that of European capitalism. The crisis of the socialist and social-democratic tradition in Western Europe is not the crisis of an ideology defeated by the superior political and organizational strength of its opponents – as communism has been. It is an integral component of a *fin-de-siècle* turmoil reshaping the planet at momentous speed.

The socialist design, however defined, may fade away while socialist parties survive. I do not know whether the idea of socialism will weather the great chaos of the end of this millennium and the beginning of the next. Those who have had sympathy for the socialist project, shared its hopes and its values, and have been impatient with the endless prevarications, the unending compromises, the stultifying hesitations of its organized parties, may well be reminded that, when all is said and done, these parties are the only Left that is left.

Notes

Introduction

1. For a discussion of the interpretations of the centenary by the French socialists, see Marc Angenot, *1889. Un état du discours social*, Editions du Préambule, Québec 1989, pp. 697–703.

2. For a reflection on the first centenary of 1789, see Eric J. Hobsbawm, *Echoes of the Marseillaise. Two Centuries Look Back on the French Revolution*, Verso, London 1990, chapter 3. On the decision leading to the adoption of 14 July, see Charles Rearick, 'Festivals in Modern France: The Experience of the Third Republic', *Journal of Contemporary History*, Vol. 12, no. 3, July 1977, pp. 443–5.

3. Editorial in *Le cri du peuple*, edited by the Blanquist Edouard Vaillant, Friday, 4 January 1889.

4. Marc Angenot, *Le centenaire de la révolution 1889*, La documentation française, Paris 1989, p. 12.

5. Patrick Garcia, 'L'Etat républicain face au centenaire: raisons d'Etat et universalisme dans la commémoration de la Révolution française', in Jacques Bariety (ed.), *1889: Centenaire de la Révolution Française*, Peter Lang, Berne 1992, pp. 145–6.

6. Cited in Jean Garrigues, 'Le Boulangisme et la Révolution française', in Bariety (ed.), op. cit., p. 171.

7. *Histoire de la IIᵉ Internationale. Congrès International Ouvrier Socialiste*, Paris 14–22 July 1889, Vols 6–7, Minkoff Reprint, Geneva 1976, pp. 19–20.

8. Patricia van der Esch, *La deuxième internationale 1889–1923*, Librairie Marcel Rivière, Paris 1957, p. 22.

9. Ibid., p. 37.

10. Ibid., p. 40.

11. Ibid., p. 41; see pp. 187–279 for the resolutions of the *possibilistes*.

12. The working classes were absent. It is this 'fourth estate' which is depicted on the jacket of this book.

13. See, for instance, Jerzy Topolski, 'Continuity and Discontinuity in the Development of the Feudal System in Eastern Europe (Xth to XVIIth Centuries)', *Journal of European Economic History*, Vol. 10, no. 2, Fall 1981.

14. Fernand Braudel, *A History of Civilizations*, trans. Richard Mayne, Allen Lane/Penguin, London 1994, pp. 316–17, reminds us that 'all liberties ... threaten each other; one limits another, and later succumbs to a further rival'.

15. E. L. Jones, *The European Miracle. Environments, Economies and Geopolitics in the History of Europe and Asia*, Cambridge University Press, Cambridge 1987, pp. 45, 57.

1. The Establishment of Socialism Before 1914

1. See Otto Bauer, 'Die Geschichte eines Buches', *Neue Zeit*, 1908 (written in 1907 on the fortieth anniversary of the publication of the first volume of *Das Kapital*), cited in

Günther Roth, *The Social Democrats in Imperial Germany. A Study in Working-Class Isolation and National Integration*, Bedminster Press, Towota NJ 1963, p. 200.

2. See Eric J. Hobsbawm, 'The Fortunes of Marx's and Engels' Writings', in E. J. Hobsbawm (ed.), *The History of Marxism*, Vol. I: *Marxism in Marx's Day*, Harvester Press, Brighton 1982, p. 331.

3. See Bauer's own list of the principal components of vulgar Marxism cited in Roth, op. cit., p. 201.

4. See the text and the accompanying article in Simonetta Soldani, 'Un primo maggio piccolo piccolo', *Italia Contemporanea*, no. 190, March 1993, pp. 37–64.

5. Eric J. Hobsbawm, *The Age of Empire 1875–1914*, Weidenfeld and Nicolson, London 1987, pp. 118–21.

6. How trade union values were constructed through discourse by activists among British workers has been ably explained by Patrick Joyce in his *Visions of the People. Industrial England and the Question of Class 1848–1914*, Cambridge University Press, Cambridge 1991, especially chapters 4 and 5.

7. Cited in Stanley Pierson, *Marxist Intellectuals and the Working Class Mentality in Germany 1887–1912*, Harvard University Press, Cambridge MA 1993, p. 64.

8. Carl E. Schorske, *German Social Democracy 1905–1917. The Development of the Great Schism*, John Wiley and Sons, New York 1965 (1st edn 1955), p. 3.

9. Friedrich Engels, Introduction to Karl Marx, *Class Struggles in France 1848–1850*, International Publishers, New York 1964, pp. 19, 20 and 27.

10. Peter Nettl, 'The German Social Democratic Party 1890–1914 as a Political Model', *Past and Present*, no. 30, April 1965, p. 65. Socialists and Catholics in pre-fascist Italy suffered a similar fate.

11. David Blackbourn, *Class, Religion and Local Politics in Wilhelmine Germany. The Centre Party in Württemberg before 1914*, Yale University Press, New Haven CT 1980, p. 26. This book provides a detailed analysis of the construction of the Centre Party as a modern mass political party.

12. Franco Andreucci, 'La diffusione e la volgarizzazione del marxismo', in *Storia del Marxismo*. Vol. 2: *Il Marxismo nell'età della Seconda Internazionale*, Einaudi Editore, Turin 1979, pp. 16–17 and pp. 25–7.

13. Pierson, op. cit., p. 61.

14. Georges Haupt, *Aspects of International Socialism 1871–1914*, Cambridge University Press, Cambridge 1986, p. 70.

15. See *La Charte de Quaregnon, déclaration de principes du Parti Socialiste Belge*, Fondation Louis de Brouckère, Brussels 1980, pp. 146–7.

16. E. H. Krossman, *The Low Countries 1780–1940*, Clarendon Press, Oxford 1978, pp. 341, 344.

17. David Kirby, 'The Finnish Social Democratic Party and the Bolsheviks', *Journal of Contemporary History*, Vol. 11, nos 2–3, July 1976, pp. 100, 109–10.

18. Haupt, op. cit., pp. 49, 59.

19. See James Joll, *The Second International 1889–1914*, Routledge and Kegan Paul, London 1974, pp. 13–16.

20. Hugues Portelli, *Le socialisme français tel qu'il est*, Presses Universitaires de France, Paris 1980, pp. 13–14.

21. A useful description of the principal tendencies can be found in Roger Magraw, *A History of the French Working Class*. Vol. 2: *Workers and the Bourgeois Republic*, Blackwell, Oxford 1992, pp. 82–3.

22. Jean-Marie Mayeur and Madeleine Rebérioux, *The Third Republic from Its Origins to the Great War 1871–1914*, Cambridge University Press, Cambridge 1984, pp. 137–8. The name

was changed from *Parti ouvrier* (PO) to *Parti ouvrier français* (POF) out of patriotism: see Portelli, op. cit., p. 21.

23. Ibid., p. 141 and Magraw, op. cit., p. 86.

24. Portelli, op. cit., p. 15.

25. Madeleine Rebérioux, 'Il dibattito sulla guerra', in *Storia del Marxismo*, Vol. 2: *Il marxismo nell'età della Seconda Internazionale*, p. 918.

26. Mayeur and Rebérioux, op. cit., p. 302. See also Jean Touchard, *La gauche en France depuis 1900*, Editions du Seuil, Paris 1977, pp. 37–9.

27. Haupt, op. cit., pp. 60–1.

28. Magraw, op. cit., p. 82.

29. Tony Judt in his *Marxism and the French Left*, Clarendon Press, Oxford 1986, p. 16.

30. Portelli, op. cit., p. 31.

31. Richard Gillespie, *The Spanish Socialist Party*, Clarendon Press, Oxford 1989, pp. 9, 15.

32. Gaetano Arfè, *Storia del socialismo italiano 1892–1926*, Einaudi Editore, Turin 1965, p. 29.

33. *Il Partito Socialista Italiano nei suoi Congressi*, Vol. II, Edizioni *Avanti!*, Milan 1961, p. 35.

34. Ernesto Ragionieri, *Il marxismo e l'Internazionale*, Editori Riuniti, Rome 1972, p. 184.

35. Ernesto Ragionieri, *Storia d'Italia. Dall'Unità a oggi*, Vol. 4, Tome 3, Einaudi Editore, Turin 1976, p. 1910.

36. Ibid., pp. 1905–7.

37. The literature on this is vast. For a fine introductory article focusing on Germany and England, see Christiane Eisenberg, 'The Comparative View in Labour History. Old and New Interpretations of the English and the German Labour Movement before 1914', *International Journal of Social History*, Vol. 34, 1989, pp. 403–32.

38. David Kirby, 'The Labour Movement' in Max Engman and David Kirby (eds), *Finland. Peopie, Nation and State*, C. Hurst and Co., London 1989, p. 206.

39. Risto Alapuro, *State and Revolution in Finland*, University of California Press, Berkeley 1988, pp. 109–10, 117. See also D. G. Kirby, *Finland in the Twentieth Century*, C. Hurst and Co., London 1979, pp. 32–3.

40. Carl F. Brand, *The British Labour Party*, Hoover Institution Press, Standford 1974, pp. 4–12.

41. Eric J. Hobsbawm, *Labouring Men. Studies in the History of Labour*, Weidenfeld and Nicolson, London 1972, p. 234.

42. Ibid., p. 232.

43. See the extracts from this Fabian Report in Eric J. Hobsbawm (ed.), *Labour's Turning Point 1880–1900*, Harvester Press, Brighton 1974, pp. 57, 58.

44. Brand, op. cit., p. 12.

45. Gregory Elliott, *Labourism and the English Genius. The Strange Death of Labour England?*, Verso, London 1993, p. 3.

46. Iring Fetscher, 'Bernstein e la sfida all'ortodossia', in *Storia del Marxismo*. Vol. 2: *Il marxismo nell'età della Seconda Internazionale*, pp. 244–5.

47. Eduard Bernstein, *Evolutionary Socialism*, Schocken Books, New York 1963, pp. 54–73. For a more recent translation, see Eduard Bernstein, *The Preconditions of Socialism*, edited and translated by Henry Tudor, Cambridge University Press, Cambridge 1994. Here I have used the older edition.

48. Ibid., p. 79.

49. Ibid., p. 80.

50. Eduard Bernstein, 'The Struggle of Social Democracy and the Social Revolution: 2. The Theory of Collapse and Colonial Policy', originally in *Neue Zeit*, 19 January 1898; English translation in H. Tudor and J. M. Tudor (eds) *Marxism and Social Democracy. The Revisionist Debate 1896–1898*, Cambridge University Press, Cambridge 1988, pp. 168–9.

51. Nettl, op. cit., p. 68.

52. Roth, op. cit., p. 161.

53. See Herbert Tingsten, *The Swedish Social Democrats*, Bedminster Press, Totowa NJ 1973, (originally published in 1941), pp. 118–28, 139.

54. Robert Wohl, *French Communism in the Making 1914–1924*, Stanford University Press, Stanford CA 1966, pp. 8–9.

55. *Il Partito Socialista Italiano nei suoi Congressi*, p. 30.

56. Arfè, op. cit., pp. 149–51.

57. Marek Waldeberg 'La strategia politica della socialdemocrazia tedesca', in *Storia del Marxismo*, Vol. 2: *Il Marxismo nell'età della Seconda Internazionale*, op. cit., p. 211.

58. Cited in Vernon L. Lidtke, *The Outlawed Party: Social Democracy in Germany 1878–1890*, Princeton Univeristy Press, Princeton NJ 1966, p. 328.

59. Judt, op. cit., p. 116.

60. Cited in Pierre Bezbakh, *Histoire et figures du socialisme français*, Bordas, Paris 1994, p. 135.

61. Krossman, op. cit., p. 341.

62. Douglas V. Verney, *Parliamentary Reform in Sweden 1866–1921*, Clarendon Press, Oxford 1957, pp. 196–8.

63. Neil Harding, *Lenin's Political Thought*, Macmillan, London 1983, Vol. 1, pp. 197–9.

64. For Kautsky, see Massimo Salvadori, *Kautsky e la rivoluzione socialista 1880/1938*, Feltrinelli, Milan 1976, p. 141.

65. Haupt, op. cit., p. 139.

66. Ibid., chapter 5.

67. See Perry Anderson, 'The Antinomies of Antonio Gramsci', in *New Left Review*, no. 100, November 1976–January 1977, pp. 64–5; see also Oskar Negt, 'Rosa Luxemburg e il rinnovamento del marxismo', in *Storia del Marxismo*. Vol. 2: *Il marxismo nell'età della Seconda Internazionale*, op. cit., p. 318. See also Peter Nettl, *Rosa Luxemburg*, Oxford University Press, abridged edn, 1969, pp. 283–4.

68. Nettl, 'The German Social Democratic Party 1890–1914 …', p. 73.

69. Dieter K. Buse, 'Party Leadership and Mechanism of Unity: The Crisis of German Social Democracy Reconsidered, 1910–1914', *Journal of Modern History*, Vol. 62, no. 3, September 1990, p. 490.

70. George Lichtheim, *A Short History of Socialism*, Weidenfeld and Nicolson, London 1970, p. 221.

71. Barrington Moore, Jr, *Injustice. The Social Bases of Obedience and Revolt*, Macmillan, London 1978, p. 219.

72. Dick Geary, *Karl Kautsky*, Manchester University Press, Manchester 1987, pp. 62–3.

73. His pamphlet on the political mass strike was published in 1905; see Massimo L. Salvadori, 'La socialdemocrazia tedesca e la rivoluzione russa del 1905', in *Storia del marxismo*. Vol. 2: *Il marxismo nell'età della Seconda Internazionale*, op. cit., p. 591.

74. Janet Polasky, 'A Revolution for Socialist Reforms: The Belgian General Strike for Universal Suffrage', *Journal of Contemporary History*, Vol. 27, no. 3, July 1992. See also Robert Gildea, *Barricades and Borders. Europe 1800–1914*, Oxford University Press, Oxford 1987, p. 315.

75. Kirby, op. cit., pp. 30–1.

76. Wolfgang Abendroth, *A Short History of the European Working Class*, New Left Books, London 1972, p. 44.

77. Berndt Schiller, 'Years of Crisis, 1906–1914', in Steven Koblik (ed.), *Sweden's Development from Poverty to Affluence*, University of Minnesota Press, Minneapolis 1975, p. 202.

78. See Harding, op. cit., chapter 7.

79　Merle Fainsod, *International Socialism and the World War*, Octagon Books, New York 1973 (first published in 1935), p. 10.

80. Cited in Joll, op. cit., pp. 94–5.

81. Cited in Nettl, *Rosa Luxemburg*, p. 132.

82. For Luxemburg's position, see ibid., p. 133.

83. The text used here can be found in Susanne Miller and Heinrich Potthoff, *A History of German Social Democracy. From 1848 to the Present.* Berg, Leamington Spa 1986, pp. 240–2.

84. Schorske, op. cit., p. 6.

85. W. O. Henderson, *The Life of Friedrich Engels*, Frank Cass, London 1976, Vol. 2, p. 665.

86. Geary, op. cit., p. 40.

87. Ibid., p. 65.

88. Schorske, op. cit., p. 19.

2. From War to War (1914–40)

1. G. D. H. Cole, *A History of Socialist Thought*. Vol. V: *Socialism and Fascism 1931–1939*, Macmillan, London 1960, p. 61.

2. See Raimund Loew, 'The Politics of Austro-Marxism', in *New Left Review*, no. 118, November–December 1979, pp. 23–4. For a fuller account of the attitude of the Left to the First World War, see Merle Fainsod, *International Socialism and the World War*.

3. Quoted in Joll, *The Second International 1889–1914*, p. 168.

4. Polasky, 'A Revolution for Socialist Reforms ...', p. 450.

5. Fainsod, op. cit., p. 36.

6. Barrington Moore, Jr, *Injustice*, p. 226.

7. Haupt, *Socialism and the Great War. The Collapse of the Second International*, Clarendon Press, Oxford 1972, p. 220.

8. Ibid., p. 219.

9. Nettl, 'The German Social Democratic Party 1890–1914 ...', p. 81.

10. See Fainsod's perceptive words in op. cit., p. 41.

11. Nettl, op. cit., pp. 83–4.

12. Miller and Potthoff, *A History of German Social Democracy*, p. 48.

13. Richard J. Evans, *Death in Hamburg. Society and Politics in the Cholera Years 1830–1910*, Penguin, Harmondsworth 1990, pp. 553–4.

14. Hobsbawm, *Labouring Men*, p. 324.

15. Gareth Stedman Jones, *Languages of Class*, Cambridge University Press, Cambridge 1983, p. 237.

16. See Bob Holton, *British Syndicalism 1900–1914. Myth and Realities*, Pluto Press, London 1976, especially the conclusions.

17. Daniel Ligou, *Histoire du socialisme en France 1871–1961*, Presses Universitaires de France, Paris 1962, p. 242.

18. Fainsod, op. cit., pp. 42–3,59.

19. Charles S. Maier, *Recasting Bourgeois Europe. Stabilization in France, Germany, and Italy in the Decade after World War I*, Princeton University Press, Princeton NJ 1975, p. 192.

20. Eric J. Hobsbawm, *Age of Extremes. The Short Twentieth Century 1914–1991*, Michael Joseph, London 1994, p. 69.

21. On the importance of the Polish campaign, see Aldo Agosti, *La Terza Internazionale. Storia Documentaria*, Vol. 1, Editori Riuniti, Rome 1974, p. 196.

22. V. I. Lenin, '"Left-Wing Communism" – An Infantile Disorder' (April–May 1920) in *Collected Works*, Vol. 31, Progress Publishers, Moscow 1965–74, p. 97.

23. Fritz Hodne, *The Norwegian Economy 1920–1980*, Croom Helm, London 1983, p. 19.

24. Erik Hansen, 'Crisis in the Party: *De Tribune* Faction and the Origins of the Dutch Communist Party 1907–9', *Journal of Contemporary History*, Vol. 11, nos 2–3, July 1976, pp. 43–64.

25. Judt, *Marxism and the French Left*, p. 122.

26. For the Italian cases, see Tommaso Detti, *Serrati e la formazione del Partito comunista italiano*, Editori Riuniti, Rome 1972, especially chapter 3. For the Spanish see Gillespie, *The Spanish Socialist Party*, p. 36.

27. The original Nineteen Conditions are in V. I. Lenin, 'Terms of admission into the Communist International', *Collected Works*, Vol. 31, pp. 206–11. The Twenty-one Conditions can be found in Agosti, op. cit., pp. 285–91.

28. See Paolo Spriano, *Stalin and the European Communists*, Verso, London 1985, pp. 9–10.

29. Eberhard Kolb, *The Weimar Republic*, Unwin and Hyman, London 1988, p. 35.

30. Eric D. Weitz, 'State Power, Class Fragmentation, and the Shaping of German Communist Politics, 1890–1933', *Journal of Modern History*, Vol. 62, no. 2, June 1990, p. 254.

31. Kolb, op. cit., p. 45.

32. David Abraham, *The Collapse of the Weimar Republic. Political Economy and Crisis*, Princeton University Press, Princeton NJ 1981, p. 266.

33. See the accounts in Ben Fowkes, *Communism in Germany under the Weimar Republic*, Macmillan, London 1984, pp. 85–6, 91–109, and in Rosa Leviné-Meyer's memoirs, *Inside German Communism. Memoirs of Party Life in the Weimar Republic*, Pluto Press, London 1977, pp. 50–6.

34. Figures in Fowkes, op. cit., pp. 204–5. The 1921 figures are almost certainly an overestimate.

35. Weitz, op. cit., pp. 285, 292.

36. Philippe Bernard and Henri Dubief, *The Decline of the Third Republic 1914–1938*, Cambridge University Press, Cambridge 1988, p. 301.

37. Touchard, *La gauche en France depuis 1900*, p. 198. See also Alberto Castoldi, *Intellettuali e Fronte popolare in Francia*, De Donato, Bari 1978, pp. 46–150.

38. Hobsbawm, *Echoes of the Marseillaise*, p. 50; the entire second chapter is devoted to this issue.

39. Daniel R. Brower, *The New Jacobins. The French Communist Party and the Popular Front*, Cornell University Press, Ithaca NY 1968, pp. 246–7.

40. Maurice Thorez, *France Today and the People's Front*, Victor Gollancz, London 1936, p. 178.

41. Touchard, op. cit., p. 203.

42. Data in Touchard, op. cit., p. 205 and Ronald Tiersky, *French Communism 1920–1972*, Columbia University Press, New York and London 1974, p. 58.

43. Maurice Adereth, *The French Communist Party. A Critical History (1920–84): From Comintern to 'he colours of France'*, Manchester University Press, Manchester 1984, p. 72.

44. Ibid., p. 78.

45. Tiersky, op. cit., p. 72.

46. Touchard, op. cit., p. 277.

47. For Britain the best treatment of this is Nina Fishman's *The British Communist Party and the Trade Unions, 1933–45*, Scolar Press, Aldershot 1995.

48. See the introduction to William E. Paterson and Alastair H. Thomas (eds), *The Future of Social Democracy*, Clarendon Press, Oxford 1986, p. 2.

49. Article in the SAP journal *Tiden*, quoted in Herbert Tingsten, *The Swedish Social Democrats*, p. 425.

50. Christine Buci-Glucksmann and Göran Therborn, *Le défi social-démocrate*, Maspero, Paris 1981, pp. 187, 206.

51. Tingsten, op. cit., p. 201.

52. Ibid., pp. 251, 262–3.

53. Ibid., p. 228.

54. Richard Scase, *Social Democracy in Capitalist Society: Working Class Politics in Britain and Sweden*, Croom Helm, London 1977, pp. 29, 39, 22.

55. Walter Korpi, *The Democratic Class Struggle*, Routledge and Kegan Paul, London 1983, p. 47.

56. Mario Telò, *La Socialdemocrazia europea nella crisi degli anni trenta*, Franco Angeli, Milan 1985, pp. 264, 301–2.

57. This is ably explained by Sven Anders Söderplan in 'The Crisis Agreement and the Social Democratic Road to Power', in Steven Koblic (ed.), *Sweden's Development from Poverty to Affluence 1750–1970*, trans. Joanne Johnson, University of Minnesota Press, Minneapolis 1975, pp. 258–78.

58. Buci-Glucksmann and Therborn, op. cit., pp. 203–5.

59. Hodne, op. cit., p. 96.

60. Sven E. Olsson, *Social Policy and Welfare State in Sweden*, Arkiv förlag, Lund 1990, p. 110.

61. Carl Landauer, *European Socialism. A History of Ideas and Movements*, Vol. II, University of California Press, Berkeley and Los Angeles 1959, p. 1542.

62. Ibid., p. 1551.

63. H. Arndt, *The Economic Lessons of the Nineteen-Thirties*, Oxford University Press, London 1944, pp. 214–18.

64. Landauer, op. cit., p. 1541.

65. Tingsten, op. cit., p. 707.

66. W. Glyn Jones, *Denmark. A Modern History*, Croom Helm, London 1986, pp. 135–48.

67. Landauer, op. cit., pp. 1556–9.

68. Paul Preston, *The Coming of the Spanish Civil War*, Methuen, London 1983, pp. 6–10.

69. Ibid., pp. 13–15, 84.

70. See Helen Graham, *Socialism and War. The Spanish Socialist Party in Power and Crisis 1936–1939*, Cambridge University Press, Cambridge 1991.

71. Helen Graham, 'The Spanish Popular Front and the Civil War', in H. Graham and Paul Preston (eds), *The Popular Front in Europe*, Macmillan, London 1987.

72. Preston, op. cit.; see also his 'The Agrarian War in the South', in Preston (ed.), *Revolution and War in Spain 1931–1939*, Methuen, London 1984.

73. This is the only conclusion possible on the basis of the research available so far. See Kolb, op. cit., p. 142.

74. W. L. Guttsman, *The German Social Democratic Party 1875–1933*, Allen and Unwin, London 1981, p. 311.

75. Miller and Potthoff, op. cit., p. 77.

76. See text of the Görlitz Programme in Miller and Potthoff, op. cit., pp. 253–5; the sentence quoted is on p. 254.

77. Ibid., p. 255.

78. Ibid., p. 254; emphasis in the original.

79. Guttsman, op. cit., p. 315.

80. Charles S. Maier, *In Search of Stability. Explorations in Political Economy*, Cambridge University Press, Cambridge 1987, p. 205.

81. Ibid., p. 204.

82. Abraham, op. cit., pp. 249–51 and Gian Enrico Rusconi, *La crisi di Weimar. Crisi di sistema e sconfitta operaia*, Einaudi Editore, Turin 1977, pp. 46–56.

83. Text in Miller and Potthoff, op. cit., pp. 258–64. The passage quoted is on p. 259.

84. Ibid., p. 258.

85. On Hilferding, see Rusconi, op. cit., pp. 177–230.

86. Rudolf Hilferding, speech to the SPD Conference 1927; extracts in David Beetham (ed.), *Marxism in the Face of Fascism*, Manchester University Press, Manchester 1983 (citation on pp. 251–2; my emphasis).

87. David Abraham, 'Labor's Way: On the Successes and Limits of Socialist Parties in Interwar and Post-World War II Germany', *International Labor and Working Class History*, no. 28, Fall 1985, p. 7.

88. Donna Harsh, *German Social Democracy and the Rise of Nazism*, University of North Carolina Press, Chapel Hill 1993, p. 156, see also p. 163.

89. Knut Borchardt, *Perspectives on Modern German Economic History*, trans. Peter Lambert, Cambridge University Press, Cambridge 1991, pp. 182–3.

90. G. Feldman, 'German Interest Group Alliances in War and Inflation, 1914–1923' in Suzanne D. Berger (ed.), *Organizing Interests in Western Europe*, Cambridge University Press, Cambridge 1983, p. 172.

91. Magraw, *A History of the French Working Class*, Vol. 2, p. 227.

92. Touchard, op. cit., pp. 141–51 and Magraw, op. cit., p. 242.

93. Judt, op. cit., pp. 136–41.

94. Touchard, op. cit., pp. 163–5.

95. He developed these ideas in a series of articles in *Le Populaire*, between July and December 1922: see *L'Oeuvre de Léon Blum*, Vol. III-1 (1914–28), Albin Michel, Paris 1972, pp. 245–52. He later revived this distinction in a speech at the Ecole Normale Supérieure; see *L'Oeuvre de Léon Blum*, Vol. VI-1 (1945–47), pp. 427–37. This selection of Blum's writings, published in nine volumes, rather surprisingly leaves out his major speech at the special congress in the Salle Bellevilloise, 10–11 January 1926, as well as seminal articles in *Le Populaire*, from 27 November to 26 December 1929, in which he further develops his key concepts.

96. Gilbert Ziebura, 'Léon Blum à la veille de l'exercice du pouvoir', in *Léon Blum chef du gouvernement 1936–37*, Cahiers de la Fondation Nationale des Sciences Politiques, Colin, Paris 1967, pp. 29–31.

97. Cited in Michael Newman, *John Strachey*, Manchester University Press, Manchester 1989, p. 23.

98. Ziebura, op. cit., p. 35.

99. Julian Jackson, *The Popular Front in France. Defending Democracy, 1934–38*, Cambridge University Press, Cambridge 1988, pp.66–70, where it is pointed out that there is insufficient evidence for a definite answer on the question of communist non-participation in the Popular Front government.

100. The full text of the Popular Front programme can be found in ibid., pp. 299–302.

101. Etienne Gout, Pierre Juvigny and Michel Moussel, 'La politique sociale du front populaire', in *Léon Blum chef du gouvernement 1936–37*, pp. 245–7.

102. Gary Cross, *A Quest for Time. The Reduction of Work in Britain and France, 1840–1940*, University of California Press, Berkeley 1989, p. 226.

103. See Parti Communiste Français, *Histoire du Parti communiste français*, Editions Sociales, Paris 1964, p. 318. This is a book written by a committee of 'historians' appointed by the Central Committee of the PCF.

104. See the detailed discussion of the strikes in Magraw, op. cit., pp. 262–88 and in Jackson, op. cit., pp. 85–112.

105. Francis Horden, 'Genèse et vote de la loi du 20 juin 1936 sur les congés payés', *Le Mouvement social*, no. 150, January–March 1990, p. 20.

106. Allan Bullock, *The Life and Times of Ernest Bevin*. Vol. 1: *Trade Union Leader 1881–1940*, Heinemann, London 1960, p. 601.

107. Ibid., p. 575.

108. Cross, op. cit., pp. 131–5. See also Lex Heerman Van Voss, 'The International Federation of Trade Unions and the Attempt to Maintain the Eight-hour Working Day (1919–1929)', in Fritz Van Holtoon and Marcel van der Linden (eds), *Internationalism and the Labour Movement 1830–1940*, Vol. II, E. J. Brill, Leiden 1988, p. 519.

109. Jackson, op. cit., p. 171.

110. Ibid., p. 167.

111. Ibid., p. 169.

112. Ibid., p. 271. The historiography on this issue is discussed on pp. 272–7.

113. Joel Colton, *Léon Blum. Humanist in Politics*, Alfred A. Knopf, New York 1966, pp. 274–5. Jackson points out that Blum's hands were tied by the radicals; see op. cit., p. 277.

114. James Joll, *Intellectuals in Politics*, Weidenfeld and Nicolson, London 1960, pp. 46–7.

115. Tiersky, op. cit., p. 61.

116. See, for instance, Fernando Claudín, *The Communist Movement. From Comintern to Cominform*, Penguin, Harmondsworth 1975, pp. 204–7 and Daniel Guérin, *Front populaire, révolution manquée*, Paris 1963.

117. Brand, *The British Labour Party*, p. 95.

118. Ibid., p. 115.

119. See Robert Skidelsky, *Politicians and the Slump. The Labour Government of 1929–1931*, Macmillan, London 1967, pp. 170–82. A detailed analysis of the Mosley memorandum can be found in Skidelsky's *Oswald Mosley*, Macmillan, London 1981, pp. 199–220.

120. Ben Pimlott, *Labour and the Left in the 1930s*, Cambridge University Press, Cambridge 1977, pp. 10–11.

121. Skidelsky, *Politicians and the Slump*, p. 43.

122. Ibid., p. xii.

123. Ross McKibbin, 'The Economic Policy of the Second Labour Government 1929–1931', *Past and Present*, no. 68, August 1975, pp. 96–102.

124. Ibid., p. 105.

125. Ibid., p. 108.

126. Robert W. D. Boyce, *British Capitalism at the Crossroads 1919–32. A Study in Politics, Economics and International Relations*, Cambridge University Press, Cambridge 1987, p. 197.

127. Skidelsky, *Politicians and the Slump*, p. 395.

128. C. R. Attlee, *The Labour Party in Perspective*, Left Book Club edn, Victor Gollancz, London 1937, p. 156.

129. Ibid., pp. 169–75.

3. Thwarted Alternatives

1. Telò, *La socialdemocrazia europea nella crisi degli anni trenta*, p. 23.

2. C. Maier, '"Fictitious bonds … of wealth and law": On the Theory and Practice of Interest Representation', in Suzanne D. Berger (ed.), *Organizing Interests in Western Europe*, Cambridge University Press, Cambridge 1983, p. 47.

3. Bullock, *The Life and Times of Ernest Bevin*, Vol. 1, pp. 601 ff. See also Keith Middlemas' history of the transformation of trade unions into 'an estate of the realm': *Politics in Industrial Society. The Experience of the British System since 1911*, André Deutsch, London 1979.

4. Harsh, *German Social Democracy and the Rise of Nazism*, p. 162. Chapter 6 of Harsh's book lucidly examines this and similar proposals.

5. Ibid., pp. 166–8.

6. John A. Garraty, *Unemployment in History. Economic Thought and Public Policy*, Harper, New York 1979, p. 194.

7. Harsh, op. cit., p. 190.

8. Maier, *In Search of Stability*, pp. 39–41 and G. Feldman's essay in Berger (ed.), op. cit.

9. Skidelsky, *Oswald Mosley*, pp. 179–220.

10. Newman, *John Strachey*, p. 58.

11. Ibid., pp. 87–97, 135.

12. Pimlott, *Labour and the Left in the 1930s*, pp. 39–40.

13. See *For Socialism and Peace. The Labour Party's Programme of Action*, London 1934, p. 14.

14. Ibid., p. 15.

15. Ibid., pp. 28–30.

16. Pimlott, op. cit., p. 202.

17. A. W. Wright, *G. D. H. Cole and Socialist Democracy*, Clarendon Press, Oxford 1979, pp. 170–73. See also L. P. Carpenter, *G. D. H. Cole. An Intellectual Biography*, Cambridge University Press, Cambridge 1973, pp. 151–2.

18. See Bullock, op. cit., p. 530 and Kenneth Harris, *Attlee*, Weidenfeld and Nicolson, London 1982, pp. 108–9.

19. They added to their 1937 edition, 'What we have learnt of the developments during 1936–1937 has persuaded us to withdraw the interrogation mark.' See Sidney and Beatrice Webb, *Soviet Communism: A New Civilization*, Longmans, Green and Co., London 1944, p. 971.

20. Elizabeth Durbin, *New Jerusalems. The Labour Party and the Economics of Democratic Socialism*, Routledge and Kegan Paul, London 1985, pp. 173–5.

21. See Carpenter, op. cit., chapters 2 and 5.

22. See Sidney and Beatrice Webb, *A Constitution for the Socialist Commonwealth of Great Britain*. For Karl Renner's comments on the Webbs and Cole, see his 1921 essay 'Democracy and the Council System', now in Tom Bottomore and Patrick Goode (eds), *Austro-Marxism*, Clarendon Press, Oxford 1978, pp. 189–93.

23. Durbin, op. cit., p. 179.

24. Richard K. Kuisel, *Capitalism and the State in Modern France. Renovation and Economic Management in the Twentieth Century*, Cambridge University Press, Cambridge 1981, pp. 60–1.

25. Telò, op. cit., p. 27.

26. Kuisel, op. cit., p. 101.

27. Ibid., p. 112.

28. Touchard, *La gauche en France depuis 1900*, p. 180 and Alain Bergourioux, 'Le néo-socialisme. Marcel Déat: réformisme traditionnel ou esprit des années trentes', *Revue Historique*, Vol. 102, no. 528, October–December 1978, p. 394.

29. Kuisel, op. cit., p. 113.

30. See Touchard, op. cit., pp. 180–1, 188 and Bergourioux, op. cit., pp. 396–7.

31. Bernard and Dubief, *The Decline of the Third Republic 1914–1938*, p. 204 and Donald N. Baker, 'Two Paths to Socialism: Marcel Déat and Marceau Pivert', in *Journal of Contemporary History*, Vol. 11, no. 1, 1976, p. 115.

32. Touchard, op. cit., p. 187.

33. See text of the programme in Jackson, *The Popular Front in France*, pp. 299–302.

34. Thorez, *France Today and the People's Front*, pp. 228, 237–48.

35. Ligou, *Histoire du socialisme en france 1871–1961*, p. 392; see also the account in Bergourioux, op. cit., pp. 400–12. For an extensive account of the neo-socialists and the passage of some of them to Nazism and fascism see Dan S. White, *Lost Comrades. Socialists of the Front Generation 1918–1945*, Harvard University Press, Cambridge MA 1992, esp. pp. 117–39, 157–74.

36. Philippe Burrin, *La Dérive fasciste. Doriot, Déat, Bergery 1933–1954*, Editions du Seuil, Paris 1986, p. 415.

37. For instance, James A. Gregor, *Young Mussolini and the Intellectual Origins of Fascism*, University of California Press, Berkeley 1979.

38. Burrin, op. cit., p. 13.

39. Dick Pels, 'The Dark Side of Socialism: Hendrik de Man and the Fascist Temptation', *History of Human Sciences*, Vol. 6, no. 2, 1993, p. 76. Much light has been thrown by Burrin, op. cit.

40. Maier, *In Search of Stability*, p. 58.

41. See Kuisel, op. cit., pp. 108–12, Touchard, op. cit., pp. 179–82 and Burrin, op. cit., pp. 152–3.

42. The text of the plan is in Hendrik de Man, *A Documentary Study of Hendrik de Man, Socialist Critic of Marxism,* compiled, edited and translated by Peter Dodge, Princeton University Press, Princeton NJ 1979, pp. 290–9, see especially p. 292.

43. This summary of de Man's ideas, including the following citation, can be found in Kuisel op. cit., p. 108. The citation comes from the *Thèses de Pontigny* originally published in 1935; see de Man, op. cit., p. 303.

44. De Man, op. cit., p. 159; his emphasis.

45. Ibid., p. 173.

46. Telò, op. cit., p. 203.

47. Erik Hansen, 'Hendrik de Man and the Theoretical Foundations of Economic Planning: The Belgian Experience, 1933–1940', *European Studies Review*, Vol. 8, no. 2, April 1978, pp. 247–9.

48. Erik Hansen, 'Depression Decade Crisis: Social Democracy and Planisme in Belgium and the Netherlands 1929–39', *Journal of Contemporary History*, Vol. 16, no. 2, April 1981, p. 304.

49. White, op. cit., pp. 128, 137.

50. Hansen, 'Depression Decade Crisis …', pp. 305–7. See also Erik Hansen and Peter A. Prosper, 'Political Economy and Political Action: The Programmatic Response of Dutch Social Democracy to the Depression Crisis', *Journal of Contemporary History*, Vol. 29, no. 1, January 1994, pp. 129–54.

51. Hansen, 'Depression Decade crisis …', pp. 315–16.

52. Hansen, 'Hendrik de Man …', p. 236.

53. Ibid., pp. 243–4.

54. Dodge, Introduction to De Man, op. cit., p. 15.

55. Hansen, 'Hendrik de Man …', pp. 245, 252.

56. Pels, op. cit., p. 90.

57. Dodge, Introduction to De Man, op. cit., p. 16.

58. Otto Bauer, 'What Is Austro-Marxism?', in *Arbeiter-Zeitung*, 3 November 1927; now in Bottomore and Goode, *Austro-Marxism*, p. 47.

59. In Bottomore and Goode, op. cit., p. 150.

60. From *The Austrian Revolution* (1924), extract in Bottomore and Goode, op. cit., p. 164.

61. Ibid., p. 162.

62. Ibid., pp. 162–3.

63. Cited in Enzo Collotti, Introduction to Otto Bauer, *Tra due guerre mondiali?* (the Italian translation of *Zwischen zwei Weltkriegen?*), Einaudi Editore, Turin 1979, pp. xxvi–xxvii.

64. Ibid., p. xxvii.

65. Barbara Jelavich, *Modern Austria. Empire and Republic 1815–1986*, Cambridge University Press, Cambridge 1987, pp. 198–202.

66. Otto Bauer, *Austrian Democracy under Fire*, London 1934; extracts in Beetham (ed.), *Marxists in Face of Fascism*, pp. 284–94 (passage cited on p. 292). The most important text for Bauer's analysis of the defeat of Austrian socialism and his 'class equilibrium' analysis

of fascism is *Zwischen zwei Weltkriegen?* (1936). I have consulted the Italian translation cited above but, whenever possible, I have quoted from the Beetham anthology. Readers who know Italian will learn much from Giacomo Marramao's lengthy Introduction to his anthology, *Austromarxismo e socialismo di sinistra fra le due guerre*, La Pietra, Milan 1975, especially pp. 105–15.

67. Beetham (ed.), op. cit., p. 293.

68. Originally in *Zwischen zwei Weltkriegen?* (1936); citation in Beetham (ed.), op. cit., p. 296. Bauer was not the only Austro-Marxist who used the category of class equilibrium (inspired by Marx's analysis of Bonapartism in *The Eighteenth of Brumaire of Louis Bonaparte*): for Max Adler's and Karl Renner's views, see Gerhard Botz, 'Austro-Marxist Interpretation of Fascism', in *Journal of Contemporary History*, Vol. 11, no. 4, 1976, pp. 129–56. Leon Trotsky and August Thalheimer, a leading member of the KPD until his expulsion in 1928, used a class equilibrium analysis; see 'Bonapartism and Fascism', in *Writings of Leon Trotsky, 1934–35*, New York 1971, pp. 51–7 and Thalheimer's 1928 article 'On Fascism', in Beetham (ed.), op. cit., pp. 187–95.

69. Helmut Gruber, *Red Vienna: Experiment in Working Class Culture, 1919–1934*, Oxford University Press, Oxford 1991.

70. Jill Lewis, 'Red Vienna: Socialism in One City, 1918–1927', in *European Studies Review*, Vol. 13, no. 3, 1983, pp. 335, 352. See also her *Fascism and the Working Class in Austria 1918–1934. The Failure of Labour in the First Republic*, Berg, New York 1991, chapter 5. I should point out that, in her book, Lewis emphatically rejects Bauer's theory of a balance of class forces as 'completely inappropriate': pp. 56–7, 204.

71. Cited in Beetham (ed.), op. cit., p. 300.

72. In *Zwischen zwei Weltkriegen?* (Italian translation, p. 197). For de Man's similar views, see Telò, op. cit., p. 212.

73. Bauer, *Tra due guerre mondiali?*, p. 324.

74. Arfè, *Storia del socialismo italiano (1892–1926)*, p. 259.

75. Ibid., pp. 261–9.

76. Franco De Felice, *Serrati, Bordiga, Gramsci e il problema della rivoluzione in Italia 1919–1920*, De Donato, Bari 1974, p. 120.

77. Ibid., pp. 121–2.

78. Giuseppe Berti makes the analogy with Carlo Pisacane in the Introduction to his edition of the documents from the Tasca archives: *I primi dieci anni di vita del PCI. Documenti inediti dell'archivio Angelo Tasca*, Feltrinelli, Milan 1967, pp. 22–3.

79. See V. I. Lenin, 'Left-wing Communism – an Infantile Disorder', in *Collected Works*, Vol. 31, pp. 65 n., 113; see also the remarks on parliamentarism (speech to the Second Congress of the Communist International of 2 August 1920), ibid., p. 253.

80. See the pro-Bordiga reconstruction of events in Andreina De Clementi, *Amadeo Bordiga*, Einaudi Editore, Turin 1971, pp. 150–75.

81. Antonio Gramsci, *Selections from Political Writings 1921–1926*, trans. and ed. Quintin Hoare, Lawrence and Wishart, London 1978 (henceforward referred to as SPW), see especially pp. 207–309 and 'Some Aspects of the Southern Question', pp. 441–62.

82. The text of the Lyons Theses is in SPW, pp. 340–75, the historical and theoretical sections are to be found on pp. 340–54.

83. Ibid., p. 357.

84. Ibid., p. 358.

85. Ibid., p. 359.

86. Ibid., pp. 373–5.

87. On Gramsci's 'Bukharinism', see Leonardo Paggi, *Le strategie del potere in Gramsci*, Editori Riuniti, Rome 1984, p. 354.

88. Palmiro Togliatti, *Opere*, Vol. 2, Editori Riuniti, Rome 1972, p. 794.

89. Togliatti, op. cit., Vol. IV, i, p. 152. I examine these issues in greater detail in 'Italian Communism and the Popular Front', in Graham with Preston (eds), *The Popular Front in Europe*.

90. See his Political Report to the Central Committee in *Collected Works*, Vol. 27, pp. 98–9; cited by Christine Buci-Glucksmann in her *Gramsci and the State*, Lawrence and Wishart, London 1980, p. 193.

91. Antonio Gramsci, *Selections from the Prison Notebooks*, ed. and trans. Quintin Hoare and Geoffrey Nowell Smith, Lawrence and Wishart, London 1971, p. 235.

92. Ibid., p. 238.

93. Ibid., p. 233.

94. Ibid., p. 239.

95. Ibid., pp. 238–9.

96. Ibid., pp. 57–8.

97. Ibid., p. 234.

98. Ibid., p. 239.

99. Ibid., p. 109.

100. Ibid., p. 108.

101. This analysis was evident in the Lyons Theses of 1926; see SPW, especially p. 350.

102. Gramsci, *Prison Notebooks*, p. 279.

103. Ibid., p. 281.

104. Ibid., p. 285.

105. Ibid., p. 312.

106. For a fuller description of the various uses of the concept of party, see Anne Showstack Sassoon, *Gramsci's Politics*, Hutchinson, London 1987, p. 154.

107. See Stephen J. Lee, *The European Dictatorships 1918–1945*, Routledge, London 1987, pp. 251–92; for a wider discussion of authoritarian movements and regimes, see Martin Blinkhorn (ed.), *Fascists and Conservatives. The Radical Right and the Establishment in Twentieth-Century Europe*, Unwin Hyman, London 1990.

108. John H. Hodgson, *Communism in Finland. A History and Interpretation*, Princeton University Press, Princeton NJ 1967, p. 140 n; why such information should be relegated to a footnote in a book on Finnish communism is not clear.

4. The War, Resistance and Its Aftermath

1. Soviet fears had been further heightened by the fact that both Latvia and Estonia had concluded a non-aggression pact with Germany on 7 June; see David Kirby, 'The Baltic States 1940–50', in Martin McCauley (ed.), *Communist Power in Europe 1944–1949*, Macmillan, London 1977, p. 23. That Stalin's action was entirely comprehensible, if not justifiable from the point of view of Soviet national interests, had been the view of many politicians at the time – for instance, Attlee and Eden; see Harris, *Attlee*, pp. 161, 167 and see *The Eden Memoirs. The Reckoning*, Cassell, London 1965, pp. 55–6. A staunch anti-Stalinist writer like Fernando Claudin criticized the way the pact was used, not the pact itself: see *The Communist Movement*, p. 297. Less partisan writers find the pact unsurprising on *realpolitik* grounds; see Geoffrey Roberts, *The Unholy Alliance. Stalin's Pact with Hitler*, I.B. Tauris, London 1989, where the main causes of the pact are traced to the failure of the collective security programme and of the negotiations between the USSR, Britain and France. Subsequent post-*glasnost* archival work appear to confirm this; see Geoffrey Roberts, 'The Soviet Decision for a Pact with Nazi Germany', *Soviet Studies*, Vol. 44, no. 1, 1992, pp. 57–78.

2. Agosti, *La Terza internazionale. Storia documentaria*, Vol. 3, p. 1163.

3. Gerhard Hirschfeld, *Nazi Rule and Dutch Collaboration. The Netherlands under German Occupation 1940–1945*, Berg, Oxford 1988, p. 110.

4. Edward Mortimer, *The Rise of the French Communist Party 1920–1947*, Faber and Faber, London 1984, pp. 283–4.

5. H. R. Kedward, 'Behind the Polemics: French Communists and the Resistance 1939–41', in Stephen Hawes and Ralph White (eds), *Resistance in Europe: 1939–45*, Pelican, Harmondsworth 1976, p. 99. This essay convincingly demolishes the established view that one cannot speak of French communist resistance before the invasion of the Soviet Union. For further evidence, see John F. Sweets, *Choices in Vichy France*, Oxford University Press, New York 1986, pp. 204–6 and Lynne Taylor, 'The Parti communiste français and the French Resistance in the Second World War', in Tony Judt (ed.) *Resistance and Revolution in Mediterranean Europe 1939–1948*, Routledge, London and New York 1989, pp. 53–71.

6. The minutes of the Central Committee meetings of the CPGB of 25 September and 2–3 October 1939 have been published in Francis King and George Matthews (eds), *About Turn. The British Communist Party and the Second World War* Lawrence and Wishart, London 1990. They demonstrated that loyalty to Moscow was not an automatic response, but something that prevailed after painful discussions. See the account in Noreen Branson, *History of the Communist Party of Great Britain 1927–1941*, Lawrence and Wishart, London 1985, pp. 266–7, written before the Soviet authorities had released the minutes, and Nina Fishman, *The British Communist Party and the Trade Unions, 1933–45*, pp. 252–56 (published afterwards), who also shows (pp. 257 ff.) that the attitude of rank-and-file communists changed very little: they never ceased to consider Nazi Germany the main enemy.

7. The secret protocols themselves established spheres of influence; they were not an agreement to partition Poland militarily. See Roberts, 'The Soviet Decision ...', pp. 73–4.

8. Eric. J. Hobsbawm, *Revolutionaries*, Quartet Books, London 1977, pp. 5–6.

9. Agosti, op. cit., pp. 1166–72.

10. Paolo Spriano, *Storia del Partito comunista italiano*. Vol. III: *I fronti popolari, Stalin, la guerra*, Einaudi Editore, Turin 1970, p. 332.

11. The commonly held view that it suppressed strikes energetically is dispelled by Fishman, op. cit., pp. 277–8, 315–18.

12. Agosti, op. cit., p. 1181.

13. Text in Jane Degras (ed.), *The Communist International 1919–1943. Documents*, Vol. III, Frank Cass, London 1971, pp. 476–81.

14. Stig Ekman, 'The Research Project Sweden During the Second World War', Report to the XIth IALHI Conference, 2–4 September 1980, Stockholm, in *Meddelande Fran Arbetarrörelsens Arkiv Och Bibliotek*, no. 16, 1980, p. 21.

15. Henri Michel, *The Second World War*, André Deutsch, London 1975, pp. 291–2. See also Maria-Pia Boëthius's *Heder och Samvete* (Honour and Conscience), Norsteds Förlag, Stockholm 1991 – a controversial book intended to castigate the Swedes for failing to come to terms with their role in the war. For the strategic importance to Germany of Swedish supplies, see Alan S. Milward, *War, Economy and Society 1939–1945*, Penguin, Harmondsworth 1987, pp. 308–13.

16. Michel, op. cit., p. 73.

17. Susan Seymour, *Anglo-Danish Relations and Germany 1933–1945*, Odense University Press, 1982, pp. 168–9.

18. Jørgen Haestrup, *Europe Ablaze. An Analysis of the History of the European Resistance Movements 1939–45*, Odense University Press, 1978, p. 53.

19. This episode is reconstructed in Leo Goldberger (ed.), *The Rescue of the Danish Jews: Moral Courage under Stress*, New York University Press, New York 1987.

20. Hirschfeld, op. cit., pp. 94–100.

21. Michel, op. cit., pp. 78, 297.

22. Radomir V. Luza, *The Resistance in Austria 1938–1945*, University of Minnesota Press, Minneapolis 1984, pp. 12, 21, 83.

23. Haestrup, op. cit., pp. 282–5.

24. Hodgson, *Communism in Finland*, p. 195.

25. Kirby, *Finland in the Twentieth Century*, p. 152.

26. Francesca Taddei, *Il socialismo italiano del dopoguerra: correnti ideologiche e scelte politiche (1943–1947)*, Franco Angeli, Milan 1984, p. 35.

27. Document in Pietro Secchia (ed.), *Il PCI e la guerra di liberazione 1943–45*, Feltrinelli, Milan 1973, p. 509.

28. See Partito Socialista Italiano (PSI), *Il Partito socialista italiano nei suoi congressi*. Vol. V: *1942–1955: Il socialismo italiano di questo dopoguerra*, ed. Franco Pedone, Edizioni del Gallo, Milan 1968, p. 25. Note, however, that the final resolution did not mention a socialist republic.

29. Cited in David Ellwood, *Italy 1943–1945*, Leicester University Press, Leicester 1985, p. 107.

30. For evidence of US interference in the internal affairs of the Socialist Party see Ronald L. Filipelli, *American Labor and Postwar Italy, 1943–1953. A Study of Cold War Politics*, Stanford University Press, Stanford CA, 1989, pp. 51–68.

31. Marc Sadoun, *Les socialistes sous l'occupation. Résistance et collaboration*, Presses de la Fondation Nationale des Sciences Politiques, Paris 1982, p. 35.

32. Ibid., pp. 50–3.

33. Ibid., p. 194.

34. See text in Léon Blum, *L'Oeuvre de Léon Blum (1940–1945)*, Editions Albin Michel, Paris 1955, p. 383. See also Touchard, *La gauche en France depuis 1900*, p. 251.

35. Michel, op. cit., p. 505.

36. John F. Sweets, *The Politics of Resistance in France 1940–1944*, Northern Illinois University Press, DeKalb IL. 1976, pp. 160–1.

37. For the renewal plans, see Andrew Shennan, *Rethinking France. Plans for Renewal 1940–1946*, Clarendon Press, Oxford 1989 and Henri Michel, *Les courants de pensée de la Résistance*, Presses Universitaires de France, Paris 1962.

38. Cited in Michel, *Les courants* ..., p. 524.

39. Ibid., p. 527.

40. Shennan, op. cit., p. 35.

41. Michel, *Les courants* ..., p. 226.

42. See Charles de Gaulle, *Mémoires de Guerre. L'Unité 1942–1944*, Librairie Plon, Paris 1956, p. 492.

43. Adereth, *The French Communist Party*, p. 122.

44. Stéphane Courtois, *Le PCF dans la guerre. De Gaulle, La Résistance, Staline* ... , Editions Ramsay, Paris 1980, chapter 15.

45. See Blum, op. cit., pp. 457, 402.

46. Courtois, op. cit., p. 416.

47. M. D. R. Foot, *Resistance. An Analysis of European Resistance to Nazism 1940–1945*, Eyre Methuen, London 1976, p. 86. This tribute is significant: the author has no sympathy for communism.

48. See Hans-Joachim Reichhardt's essay, 'Resistance in the Labour Movement', in Hermann Graml et al., *The German Resistance to Hitler*, B.T. Batsford, London 1970 and F. L.Carsten's introduction, esp. p. x; see also Anthony Williams, 'Resistance and Opposition among Germans', in Hawes and White (eds), op. cit., p. 154.

49. Alan Milward, 'The Economic and Strategic Effectiveness of the Resistance', in Hawes and White (eds), op. cit., p. 200. For some of the reasons why this might be the case, see T.

Gjelsvik, *Norwegian Resistance 1940–1945*, C. Hurst and Co., London 1979, especially p. ix.

50. Reported in M. D. R. Foot, 'What Good Did Resistance Do?', in Hawes and White (eds), op. cit., p. 211. This is entirely believable, as anyone who has experienced French (or British) non-co-operation could testify.

51. Haris Vlavianos 'The Greek Communist Party: In Search of Revolution', in Judt (ed.), op. cit., p. 169.

52. Ibid., p. 191.

53. Ibid., p. 195.

54. Giuliano Procacci (ed.), *The Cominform. Minutes of the Three Conferences 1947/1948/1949*, *Annali 1994*, Feltrinelli, Milan 1994, p. 301.

55. Cited in Michael Dockrill, *The Cold War 1945–1963*, Macmillan, London 1988, p. 40.

56. Peter Calvocoressi and Guy Wint, *Total War*, Penguin, Harmondsworth 1972, p. 487.

57. Ibid., pp. 551–2.

58. These two seats were lost in the 1950 elections, in which there were less than 92,000 communist voters; see Kenneth O. Morgan, *Labour in Power 1945–1951*, Clarendon Press, Oxford 1984, p. 295.

59. Palmiro Togliatti, *On Gramsci and Other Writings*, ed. Donald Sassoon, Lawrence and Wishart, London 1979, pp. 91–2.

60. For the French communists' lack of insurrectionary intentions, see Irwin Wall, *French Communism in the Era of Stalin. The Quest for Unity and Integration, 1945–1962*, Greenwood Press, Westport CT and London 1983, p. 29 and Jean-Jacques Becker, *Le parti communiste veut-il prendre le pouvoir? La stratégie du PCF de 1930 à nos jours*, Editions du Seuil, Paris 1981, pp. 152–65; for the Italian PCI see Donald Sassoon, *The Strategy of the Italian Communist Party. From the Resistance to the Historic Compromise*, Frances Pinter, London 1981, pp. 31–3.

61. The KKE leader Nikos Zachariades maintained that he had been promised all-out help from the Yugoslavs; see D. George Kousoulas, *Revolution and Defeat. The Story of the Greek Communist Party*, Oxford University Press, London 1965, p. 237.

62. Cited in Mortimer, op. cit., p. 332. Note that the SFIO had taken the initiative for a merger; see Becker, op. cit., p. 183.

63. 'The Tasks of the Party in the Current Situation', in Togliatti, *Communist Power in Europe 1944–1949*, pp. 84.

64. Vladimir V. Kusin, 'Czechoslovakia', in Martin McCauley (ed.), *Communist Power in Europe 1944–1948*, Macmillan, London 1977, pp. 78–9.

65. Procacci (ed), op. cit., pp. 195, 253–63, 275–9, 293, 297. On these points the minutes confirm the account provided by Eugenio Reale, *Nascita del Cominform*, Mondadori, Milan 1958, pp. 17, 118–19, 123. On the particular dispute between the PCI and the USSR, see Silvio Pons, 'Le politica estera dell'URSS, il Cominform e il PCI (1947–1948)', *Studi Storici*, Vol. 35, no. 4, October–December 1995, pp. 1123–47.

66. Procacci (ed.), op. cit., p. 195.

67. Ibid., p. 297.

68. Ibid., p. 263.

69. Ibid., p. 281.

70. See Jon Bloomfield, *Passive Revolution. Politics and the Czechoslovak Working Class 1945–1948*, St Martin's Press, New York 1979, pp. 216–17.

71. Becker, op. cit., p. 174

72. See Adereth, op. cit., p. 141 and Becker, op. cit., p. 161.

73. Mortimer, op. cit., p. 347.

74. The text of the Waziers speech is in Maurice Thorez, *Oeuvres*, Vol. 5, Part 21 (June 1945–March 1946), Editions Sociales, Paris 1963; the references to working conditions and higher wages are on pp. 158 and 160, to women on p. 159, to discipline, holidays, absenteeism and laziness on pp. 163–8.

75. The text of the *Programme* is in Maurice Thorez, *Oeuvres*, Vol. 5, Part 23 (November 1946–June 1947), Editions Sociales, Paris 1963, pp. 152ff.

76. Wall, op. cit., pp. 35–3.

77. Palmiro Togliatti, *Opere*. Vol. 5: *1944–1955*, Editori Riuniti, Rome 1984, pp. 165–7, 171–2.

78. Palmiro Togliatti, *Discorsi Parlamentari*, Vol. 1, Ufficio Stampa e Pubblicazioni della Camera dei Deputati, Rome 1984, p. 46.

79. Palmiro Togliatti, 'The Tasks of the Party in the Current Situation', in *Discorsi Parlamentari*, p. 84.

80. Mortimer, op. cit., p. 350.

81. Adereth, op. cit., p. 139.

82. See the chapter on the constitution in my *Contemporary Italy*, Longman, London 1986, pp. 195–209.

83. For a detailed analysis, see my 'The Role of the Italian Communist Party in the Consolidation of Parliamentary Democracy in Italy', in Geoffrey Pridham (ed.), *Securing Democracy: Political Parties and Democratic Consolidation in Southern Europe*, Routledge, London and New York 1990.

84. See, for example, the positive portrait of Bologna by three Swiss journalists: Max Jäggi, Roger Müller and Sil Schmid, *Red Bologna*, Writers and Readers, London 1977.

85. Hodgson, op. cit., p. 221.

86. See David G. Kirby, 'New Wine in Old Vessels? The Finnish Socialist Workers' Party, 1919–1923', *Slavonic and East European Review*, Vol. 66, no. 3, July 1988, p. 443.

87. Anthony Upton, 'Finland', in McCauley (ed.), op. cit., p. 134.

88. Hodgson, op. cit, pp. 206–7.

89. Ibid., pp. 212–13, 230.

90. Upton, op. cit., p. 136.

91. Kirby, *Finland in the Twentieth Century*, p. 194.

92. In this case too, as in many similar ones, there is no evidence at all to substantiate the view – propounded, for instance, by Pekka Haapakoski, 'Brezhnevism in Finland', *New Left Review*, no. 86, July–August 1974, p. 34 – that communist moderation in government in 1945–48 eroded its credibility among the working class and led to its defeat. Workers defecting from the SKP ranks shifted their allegiance to the more moderate social democrats, as evidenced by elections in the trade unions.

93. Some historians settle for stating the obvious; see, for instance, the not very helpful remark of L. A. Puntila in *The Political History of Finland 1809–1966*, Heinemann, London 1975, p. 205: 'The experience gained in establishing people's democracies in the occupied countries of Eastern Europe was apparently not applicable to Finland.'

94. Z. A. B. Zeman, *The Making and Breaking of Communist Europe*, Blackwell, Oxford 1991, pp. 241–2.

95. See Bloomfield, op. cit., pp. 199–200, 225–6.

96. This last point is made by Pertti Hyhynen in his 'The Popular Front in Finland', *New Left Review*, no. 57, September–October 1969, pp. 8–9.

97. For the persecution of Dutch communists see J. van Lingen and N. Slooff, *Van Verzetsstrijder tot Staatsgevaarlijk Berger*, Anthos, Baarn 1987, discussed by Bob Moore in 'Occupation, Collaboration and Resistance', *European Historical Quarterly*, Vol. 21, no. 1, January 1991, p. 116. The post-war repression of communist partisans in Belgium is documented in Hans Depraetere and Jenny Dierickx, *La guerre froide en Belgique. La répression envers le PCB et le FI*, Editions EPO, Brussels 1986, esp. pp. 211–18.

98. Mortimer, op. cit., p. 145 and Becker, op. cit., p. 193.

99. Becker, op. cit., p. 197.

5. The Socialists After 1945

1. Karl Marx, *Capital*, trans. Moore-Aveling, Vol. 1, Progress Publishers, Moscow 1965, p. 302.

2. Ibid., Vol. 3, Progress Publishers, Moscow 1971, p. 820.

3. Melanie Ann Sully 'Austrian Social Democracy' in Paterson and Thomas (eds), *The Future of Social Democracy*, p. 154.

4. Ernst Christiansen, 'The Ideological Development of Democratic Socialism in Denmark', *Socialist International Information*, Vol. 18, no. 1, 4 January 1958, p. 15.

5. Lewis J. Edinger, *Kurt Schumacher*, Stanford University Press, Stanford CA, 1965, pp. 78–9.

6. Ibid., pp. 106–8.

7. Richard Evans, *Rethinking German History. Nineteenth Century Germany and the Origins of the Third Reich*, Unwin Hyman, London 1987, p. 196; see also Miller and Potthoff, *A History of German Social Democracy*, p. 176.

8. See comments on such erosion in Britain in Raphael Samuel, 'The Lost World of British Communism', *New Left Review*, no. 154, November–December 1985, pp. 10–11. There is little comparative research in this area.

9. Edinger, op. cit., pp. 99–103.

10. Henry Ashby Turner, Jr, *The Two Germanies since 1945*, Yale University Press, New Haven CT, 1987, p. 19.

11. Perry Anderson, 'The Figures of Descent', *New Left Review*, no. 161, January–February 1987, p. 54.

12. Roger Eatwell, *The 1945–1951 Labour Governments*, Batsford Academic, London 1979, p. 43.

13. Jelavich, *Modern Austria*, p. 253.

14. Ibid., pp. 273–4.

15. Luza, *The Resistance in Austria 1938–1945*, p. 284.

16. For a critical view of Togliatti see Paul Ginsborg, *A History of Contemporary Italy. Society and Politics 1943–1988*, Penguin, Harmondsworth 1990, p. 92.

17. Peter Gowan, 'The Origins of the Administrative Elite', *New Left Review*, no. 162, March–April 1987, especially pp. 18–19.

18. Morgan, *Labour in Power*, pp. 85–6.

19. See Frank Honigsbaum, *Health, Happiness and Security: The Creation of the National Health Service*, Routledge, London 1989 and Paul Lodge and Tessa Blackstone, *Educational Policy and Educational Inequality*, Martin Robertson, London 1982.

20. Morgan, op. cit., p. 81.

21. Correlli Barnett, *The Audit of War. The Illusion and Reality of Britain as a Great Nation*, Macmillan, London 1986, pp. 291–2.

22. Betty D. Vernon, *Ellen Wilkinson 1891–1947*, Croom Helm, London 1982, p. 209.

23. Ibid., p. 217.

24. Ibid., p. 208.

25. See resolutions on education in F. W. S. Craig (ed.), *Conservative and Labour Party Conference Decisions 1945–1981*, Parliamentary Research Services, Chichester 1982, pp. 41, 184–7.

26. Alec Cairncross, 'The United Kingdom', in Andrew Graham and Anthony Seldon (eds), *Government and Economies in the Postwar World. Economic Policies and Comparative Performance 1945–85*, Routledge, London 1990, p. 33

27. Tim Tilton, *The Political Theory of Swedish Social Democracy. Through Welfare State to Socialism*, Clarendon Press, Oxford 1990, p. 179.

28. Kurt L. Shell, *The Transformation of Austrian Socialism*, State University of New York Press, New York 1962, pp. 186–7.

29. Michel, *Les courants de pensée de la Résistance*, pp. 511–18.

30. Shell, op. cit., p. 30.

31. See the accounts in John Fitzmaurice, *The Politics of Belgium. Crisis and Compromise in a Plural Society*, C. Hurst and Co., London 1988, pp. 46–7 and in Xavier Mabille, *Histoire politique de la Belgique*, CRISP, Brussels 1986, pp. 310–11.

32. Quoted by the liberal-radical jurist Pietro Calamandrei in 1947 in agreeing with Togliatti's position; cited in Ragionieri, *Storia d'Italia. Dall'Unità a oggi*, Vol. 4, Book 3, p. 2476.

33. Gordon Smith, *Democracy in Western Germany. Parties and Politics in the Federal Republic*, 3rd edn, Gower, Aldershot 1986, pp. 44–5.

34. Miller and Potthoff, op. cit., p. 163.

35. Ibid., p. 164.

36. Smith, op. cit., p. 46.

37. Tilton, op. cit., p. 151. The original sources are Alva and Gunnar Myrdal, *Kris i befolkningsfragan*, Bonniers, Stockholm 1935 and G. Myrdal, 'Kosta sociala reformer pengar?', *Arkitektur och samhälle*, 1/1 (1932b), pp. 33–44. For a critical treatment of the Myrdals' natalist views in the 1930s, see Allan Carlson, *The Swedish Experiment in Family Politics: The Myrdals and the Interwar Population Crisis*, Transaction Books, New Brunswick 1990.

38. SAP, *The Postwar Programme of Swedish Labour. Summary in 27 Points and Comments*, Stockholm 1948 (English translation of the Swedish edition published in 1944), p. 27.

39. Ibid., p. 91.

40. See Orvar Löfgren, 'Consuming Interests', in the Danish journal *Culture and Society*, no. 7, 1990, p. 23.

41. Tilton, op. cit., p. 143.

42. See François Lafon, 'Structures idéologiques et nécessités pratiques au congrès de la SFIO en 1946', *Revue d'histoire moderne et contemporaine*, Vol. XXXVI, 1989, pp. 675–9, 688.

43. Sadoun, *Les socialistes sous l'occupation*, pp. 240–1.

44. Touchard, *La gauche en France depuis 1900*, pp. 295–6.

45. Hughes Portelli, *Le socialisme français tel qu'il est*, Presses Universitaires de France, Paris 1980, pp. 67–73.

46. See, for instance, the emphasis on the party's Marxist heritage in the 1945 Programme of the Danish Social Democrats in Gøsta Esping-Andersen, *Politics against Markets. The Social Democratic Road to Power*, Princeton University Press, Princeton NJ 1985, pp. 90–1.

47. Cited in Werner Abelshauser, 'Les nationalisations n'auront pas lieu. La controverse sur l'instauration d'un nouvel ordre économique et social dans les zones occidentales de l'Allemagne de 1945 à 1949', in *Le mouvement social*, no. 134, January–March 1986, p. 89; original text in V. Agartz, *Sozialistische Wirtschaftspolitik Rede gehatten auf dem Parteitag der SPD in Hannover* (May 1946), Karlshruhe 1946, p. 8.

48. Shell, op. cit., p. 141.

49. Jelavich, op. cit., p. 247.

50. Shell, op. cit., p. 127.

51. Ibid., p. 142.

52. Ibid., p. 164.

53. This is the motion of the 'Base' group, which obtained 46.1 per cent; see PSI, *Il Partito socialista italiano nei suoi congressi*. Vol. V, p. 85.

54. Non-specialists can learn by reading Francesca Taddei, *Il socialismo italiano del dopoguerra: correnti ideologiche e scelte politiche (1943–1947)*, especially pp. 268–78.

55. Paola Caridi, *La scissione di Palazzo Barberini*, Edizioni Scientifiche Italiane, Naples 1991, pp. 253–8.

6. Building Social Capitalism 1945–50

1. Olsson, *Social Policy and Welfare State in Sweden*, pp. 95, 147–9, 216–17.

2. Massimo Paci, 'Long Waves in the Development of Welfare Systems', in Charles S. Maier (ed.), *Changing Boundaries of the Political*, Cambridge University Press, Cambridge 1987, pp. 192–3.

3. See, in particular, Walter Korpi, 'Power, Politics, and State Autonomy in the Development of Social Citizenship: Social Rights During Sickness in Eighteen OECD Countries Since 1930', *American Sociological Review*, Vol. 54, no. 3, June 1989.

4. Harold L. Wilensky, 'Leftism, Catholicism, and Democratic Corporatism: The Role of Political Parties in Recent Welfare State Development', in Peter Flora and Arnold J. Heidenheimer (eds), *The Development of Welfare States in Europe and America*, Transaction Books, New Brunswick and London 1981, p. 355. The argument had been developed in his *The Welfare State and Equality*, University of California Press, Berkeley 1975.

5. See Peter Flora and Jens Alber, 'Modernization, Democratization and the Development of Welfare States in Western Europe', in Flora and Heidenheimer (eds), op. cit.; see also the review of the literature in Joan Higgins, *States of Welfare*, Basil Blackwell and Martin Robertson, Oxford 1981.

6. Gøsta Esping-Andersen, *The Three Worlds of Welfare Capitalism*, Polity Press, Cambridge 1990, p. 118.

7. See these positions explained and discussed in James O'Connor, *The Fiscal Crisis of the State*, St Martin's Press, New York 1973; Ian Gough, *The Political Economy of the Welfare State*, Macmillan, London 1979; Claus Offe, *The Contradictions of the Welfare State*, Hutchinson, London 1984, chapter 3; and Ramesh Mishra, *The Welfare State in Crisis*, Harvester Wheatsheaf, New York and London 1984. See also the review article by Theda Skocpol and Edwin Amenta, 'States and Social Policies', *Annual Review of Sociology*, Vol. 12, 1986, pp. 131–57.

8. Paul Addison, *The Road to 1945*, Quartet Books, London 1977, pp. 227–8.

9. See Kevin Jefferys, *The Churchill Coalition and Wartime Politics, 1940–1945*, Manchester University Press, Manchester 1991, pp. 112–33.

10. See F. W. S. Craig's compilation of conference resolutions, *Conservative and Labour Party Conference Decisions 1945–1981*, pp. 49, 60.

11. T. K. Derry, *A History of Modern Norway 1814–1972*, Oxford University Press, Oxford 1973, p. 409.

12. Esping-Andersen, *Politics against Markets*, p. 101.

13. Dorothy Wilson, *The Welfare State in Sweden. A Study in Comparative Social Administration*, Heinemann, London 1979, p. 9. Sven E. Olsson argues convincingly that it is excessive to present the 1946 pension reform as a specifically conservative effort: op. cit., pp. 90–107. Olsson's target is Peter Baldwin, 'The Scandinavian Origins of the Social Interpretation of the Welfare State', *Comparative Studies in Society and History*, Vol. 13, no. 1, 1989, pp. 3–24; see Baldwin's reply; 'Class, Interest and the Welfare State. A Reply to Sven E. Olsson', in *International Review of Social History*, Vol. 34, 1989, pp. 471–84.

14. Jose Harris, 'War and Social History: Britain and the Home Front during the Second World War', *Contemporary European History*, Vol. 1, Part 1, March 1992, p. 26–7.

15. See Eatwell, *The 1945–1951 Labour Governments*, p. 41.

16. See text in A. Lepre (ed.), *Dal crollo del fascismo all'egemonia moderata*, Guida Editori, Naples 1973, pp. 75–81.

17. David Curtis, 'Marx against the Marxists: Catholic Uses of the Young Marx in the *Front populaire* period (1934–1938)', *French Cultural Studies*, Vol. 2, Part 2, no. 5, June 1991, pp. 165–81.

18. See Michael Balfour, *West Germany. A Contemporary History*, Croom Helm, London 1982, p. 156 and Jeremy Leaman, *The Political Economy of West Germany, 1945–1985*, Macmillan, London 1988, p. 51.

19. Text in Maria Grazia Maiorini, *Il Mouvement republicain populaire partito della IV Repubblica*, Giuffrè Editore, Milan 1983, pp. 47–9.

20. See Morgan, *Labour in Power*, p. 20 and Elizabeth Durbin, *New Jerusalems. The Labour Party and the Economics of Democratic Socialism*, especially pp. 262–3.

21. John Ramsden, 'From Churchill to Heath', in Lord Butler (ed.), *The Conservatives. A History from the Origins to 1965*, Allen and Unwin, London 1977, p. 423.

22. Esping-Andersen, *The Three Worlds of Welfare Capitalism*, p. 27.

23. Esping-Andersen, *Politics against Markets*, p. 157. One should note that Beveridge's own conception of a universal subsistence minimum was more restrictive that it might have appeared at first, according to an unpublished paper by John Veit-Wilson cited by J. Harris in op. cit., p. 31.

24. D. Wilson, op. cit., p. 10 and Olsson, op. cit., pp. 96, 312.

25. Tilton, *The Political Theory of Swedish Social Democracy*, p. 181.

26. See Olsson, op. cit., p. 117 and his table of Swedish welfare reforms 1945–82 on p. 114.

27. Esping-Andersen, *Politics against Markets*, p. 91.

28. Ibid., p. 158.

29. Leif Lewin, *Ideology and Strategy. A Century of Swedish Politics*, Cambridge University Press, Cambridge 1988, pp. 162–73.

30. See Susan Pedersen's remarkable *Family, Dependence and the Origins of the Welfare State. Britain and France 1914–1945*, Cambridge University Press, Cambridge 1993, pp. 413–15.

31. Shennan, *Rethinking France*, p. 213.

32. Jean-Pierre Rioux, *La France de la Quatrième République*. Vol. 1: *L'ardeur et la nécessité 1944–1952*, Editions du Seuil, Paris 1980, p. 119.

33. Ibid., p. 120.

34. Shennan, op. cit., pp. 222–3. See also Henry C. Galant, *Histoire politique de la sécurité sociale française, 1945–1952*, Colin, Paris 1955 and Pierre Laroque, *Succès et faiblesses de l'effort social français*, Colin, Paris 1961.

35. See G. Esping-Andersen and W. Korpi, 'Social Policy as Class Politics in Post-war Capitalism: Scandinavia, Austria, and Germany', in John H. Goldthorpe (ed.), *Order and Conflict in Contemporary Capitalism*, Clarendon Press, Oxford 1984, pp. 190–2 and Shell, *The Transformation of Austrian Socialism*, p. 233.

36. Anthony Upton, 'Finland' in McCauley (ed.), *Communist Power in Europe 1944–1949*, pp. 139–40.

37. Maurizio Ferrera, *Il Welfare State in Italia*, Il Mulino, Bologna 1984, p. 36.

38. Pier Paolo Donati, 'Social Welfare and Social Services in Italy since 1950', in R. Girod, P. de Laubier and A. Gladstone (eds), *Social Policy in Western Europe and the USA, 1950–85*, Macmillan, London 1985, p. 101.

39. Ginsborg, *A History of Contemporary Italy*, p. 151.

40. See Marina Bonaccorsi, 'Gli enti pubblici del settore della sicurezza sociale', in Franco Cazzola (ed.), *Anatomia del potere DC. Enti pubblici e "centralità democristiana"*, De Donato, Bari 1979, especially pp. 104ff.

41. See Camillo Daneo, *La politica economica della ricostruzione 1945–1949*, Einaudi Editore, Turin 1974, pp. 297–300.

42. The defeat of the DC left, and of its leader Giuseppe Dossetti, is chronicled in Gianni Baget-Bozzo, *Il Partito cristiano al potere. La DC di De Gasperi e di Dossetti 1945/1954*, Vallecchi, Florence 1974.

43. See Ginsborg, op. cit., p. 187 and Carlo Pinzani, 'L'Italia repubblicana', in Ragionieri, *Storia d'Italia. Dall'Unità a oggi*, pp. 2520–1.

44. Paragraph 309 of the Act, cited in Howard Glennerster, 'Social Policy since the Second World War', in John Hills (ed.), *The State of Welfare. The Welfare State in Britain since 1974*, Clarendon Press, Oxford 1990, p. 13.

45. Morgan, op. cit., p. 172 and Paci, op. cit., p. 193.

46. Esping-Andersen, *The Three Worlds of Welfare Capitalism*, p. 21.

47. T. H. Marshall, *Citizenship and Social Class and Other Essays*, Cambridge University Press, Cambridge 1950, p. 8.

48. Ibid., p. 44.

49. Karl Marx and Friedrich Engels, *The German Ideology*, International Publishers, New York 1968, p. 26.

50. V. I. Lenin, 'A Great Beginning' (July 1919), *Collected Works*, Vol. 29, Progress Publishers, Moscow 1974, p. 429 (his emphasis). Quite erroneously, Lenin believed that, under capitalism, these 'shoots' would remain a rarity, confined to charities or profit-making bodies.

51. See A. B. Atkinson, 'Poverty and Income Inequality in Britain' and W. G. Runciman, 'Occupational Class and the Assessment of Economic Inequality in Britain', in Dorothy Wedderburn (ed.), *Poverty, Inequality and Class Structure*, Cambridge University Press, Cambridge 1974, pp. 43–70, 93–106.

52. See W. D. Rubinstein, *Wealth and Inequality in Britain*, Faber and Faber, London 1986, pp. 78–9 and the authorities cited therein.

53. Henry Pelling, *The Labour Governments 1945–51*, Macmillan, London 1984, p. 77.

54. See Eatwell, op. cit., p. 56.

55. Peter Hennessy, *Never Again. Britain 1945–1951*, Jonathan Cape, London 1992, p. 198.

56. Morgan, op. cit., p. 98.

57. Ibid., p. 99. Ben Pimlott argues that Dalton had hoped that the Bank could be turned into 'the dynamo of a socialist plan', in *Hugh Dalton*, Macmillan, London 1985, p. 458.

58. Pelling, op. cit., p. 77.

59. Ibid., pp. 79–80.

60. Malcom B. Hamilton, *Democratic Socialism in Britain and in Sweden*, Macmillan, London 1989, p. 88.

61. Morgan, op. cit., p. 103.

62. Alec Cairncross, *Years of Recovery. British Economic Policy 1945–51*, Methuen, London and New York 1985, p. 464. The compensation paid was 'inconceivably generous' according to Morgan, op. cit., p. 109.

63. See Addison, op. cit., pp. 273–4 and Morgan, op. cit., p. 130

64. C. Barnett, *The Audit of War*, p. 265.

65. See the account of this débâcle in Martin Chick, 'Private Industrial Investment', in Helen Mercer, Neil Rollings and Jim Tomlinson (eds), *Labour Governments and Private Industry. The Experience of 1945–51*, Edinburgh University Press, Edinburgh 1992, pp. 74–90.

66. The best attempt to refute this prevailing view is Jim Tomlinson's *Mr. Attlee's Supply-Side Socialism: Survey and Speculations*, Discussion Papers in Economics no. 9101, Brunel University, London (no date but 1991).

67. Jean Monnet, *Memoirs*, trans. Richard Maine, Collins, London 1978, pp. 279–80.

68. Cairncross, op. cit., pp. 304, 329.

69. Morgan, op. cit., p. 364.

70. Cairncross, op. cit., p. 501.

71. Norman Chester, *The Nationalisation of British Industry 1945–51*, HMSO, London 1975, p. 1025.

72. This question is raised by Morgan, among others, op. cit., especially pp. 130–6.

73. Those fascinated by these questions can turn to Hamilton, op. cit., pp. 87–92, who takes up the old challenge thrown down by Ralph Miliband in his *Parliamentary Socialism*, Allen and Unwin, London 1961, p. 288.

74. Hodne, *The Norwegian Economy 1920–1980*, pp. 148–9.

75. Derry, op. cit., p. 426.

76. *1944 SAP Postwar Programme*, pp. 11, 15.

77. Ibid., p. 23.

78. Lewin, op. cit., pp. 170–2 and Hamilton, op. cit., p. 180.

79. Milward, *War, Economy and Society 1939–1945*, p. 328.

80. Sven E. Olsson, 'Swedish Communism Poised between Old Reds and New Greens', in *Journal of Communist Studies*, Vol. 2, no. 4, December 1986, p. 362.

81. See *1944 SAP Postwar Programme*, p. 34.

82. Lewin, op. cit., p. 185.

83. *1944 SAP Postwar Programme*, p. 42.

84. See G.-M. Nederhorst, 'Les nationalisations aux Pays-Bas confronteés à l'expérience britannique', *La revue socialiste*, no. 30, October 1949, pp. 219–20.

85. Steven B. Wolinetz, 'Socio-economic Bargaining in the Netherlands: Redefining the Post-war Policy Coalition', *West European Politics*, Vol. 12, no. 1, January 1989, pp. 81–2.

86. Miller and Potthoff, *A History of German Social Democracy*, pp. 155–6.

87. Abelshauser, 'Les nationalisations n'auront pas lieu', pp. 86–90.

88. Ibid., p. 90–4.

89. Leaman, op. cit., pp. 36–7.

90. Philip Armstrong, Andrew Glyn and John Harrison, *Capitalism since World War II. The Making and Breakup of the Great Boom*, Fontana, London 1984, chapter 3; the point about Japan is on p. 55.

91. Volker R. Berghahn, *The Americanisation of West German Industry 1945–1973*, Berg, Leamington and New York 1986, p. 96.

92. Hans Kernbauer, Eduard März, Siegfried Mattl, Robert Schediwy and Fritz Weber, 'Les nationalisations en Autriche', *Le mouvement social*, no. 134, January–March 1986, p. 56.

93. Shell, op. cit., pp. 201–207.

94. Ibid., pp. 211–13.

95. Kernbauer et al., op. cit., p. 68.

96. Ibid., p. 60.

97. The development of this 'technocratic corporatism' was examined by Bernd Marin in his *Die paritätische Kommission. Aufgeklärter Techno-korporatismus in Österreich*, Internationale Publikationen, Vienna 1982.

98. Shell, op. cit., pp. 215–20.

99. Kuisel, *Capitalism and the State in Modern France*, p. 202.

100. André Malraux, *Les chênes qu'on abat …* , Gallimard, Paris 1971, p. 29.

101. Some have argued that in the years 1944–48 French policies were 'to the left' of those implemented in Austria, Germany, Italy and Britain. This may be so only if one discounts welfare reforms which were far more extensive in Britain; see Claire Andrieu, 'La France à gauche de l'Europe', *Le mouvement social*, no. 134, January–March 1986.

102. See Jean-Charles Asselain, *Histoire économique de la France*. Vol. 2: *De 1919 à la fin des années 1970*, Editions du Seuil, Paris 1984, pp. 110–11.

103. Kuisel, op. cit., p. 208.

104. See Jean-Jacques Becker, 'Le PCF', p. 163 and Serge Berstein, 'La SFIO', pp. 179–81 in Claire Andrieu, Lucette Le Van and Antoine Prost (eds) *Les nationalisations de la Libération*, Presses de la Fondation Nationale des Sciences Politiques, Paris 1987; see also Kuisel, op. cit., pp. 202–4.

105. Berstein, op. cit., p. 181.

106. Maiorini, op. cit., pp. 44–9.

107. Cited in Mario Einaudi, Maurice Byé and Ernesto Rossi, *Nationalization in France and Italy*, Cornell University Press, Ithaca NY 1955, p. 80.

108. Monnet, op. cit., p. 238.

109. Kuisel, op. cit., p. 222.

110. Monnet, op. cit., pp. 268–70.

111. Kuisel, op. cit., p. 271.

112. Peter A. Hall, 'Economic Planning and the State: The Evolution of Economic Challenge and Political Response in France', in G. Esping-Andersen and R. Friedland (eds), *Political Power and Social Theory*, Vol. 3, JAI Press, Greenwich CT and London 1982, pp. 179ff.

113. Sima Lieberman, 'The Ideological Foundations of Western European Planning', *Journal of European Economic History*, Vol. 10, no. 2, Fall 1981, p. 348.

7. External Constraints: A Socialist Foreign Policy?

1. Francis Castles, *The Social Democratic Image of Society: A Study of the Achievements and Origins of Scandinavian Social Democracy in Comparative Perspective*, Routledge and Kegan Paul, London 1978, p. 37.

2. Derry, *A History of Modern Norway 1814–1972*, p. 409

3. Helge Pharo, 'Bridgebuilding and Reconstruction. Norway faces the Marshall Plan', *Scandinavian Journal of History*, Vol. 1, 1976, p. 176; Nikolai Petersen, 'The Cold War and Denmark', *Scandinavian Journal of History*, Vol. 10, 1985, p. 194.

4. This has been demonstrated by G. Lundestad, *America, Scandinavia and the Cold War 1945–1949*, Oslo 1980.

5. See Helge Pharo, 'The Cold War in Norwegian and International Historical Research', *Scandinavian Journal of History*, Vol. 10, 1985, especially pp. 166–70, 175.

6. Jonathan Schneer, *Labour's Conscience. The Labour Left 1945–51*, Unwin and Hyman, Boston 1988, p. 28.

7. Schneer identifies a group of fewer than ten pro-Soviet MPs, led by Konni Zilliacus, in op. cit., chapter 5.

8. Leslie J. Solley, 'Europe Today', *Labour Monthly*, March 1947, p. 74.

9. Schneer, op. cit., p. 31.

10. Mario Telò and Sven Schwersensky, 'L'unità tedesca e l'Europa. Difficoltà di ieri e di oggi della sinistra', in *Politica Europa Annali 1990–1991*, edited by the Sezione Politica e Istituzioni in Europa del Centro per La Riforma dello Stato, Franco Angeli, Milan 1991, p. 100.

11. Ossip K. Flechtheim, 'The German Left and the World Crisis', in Bernard Brown (ed.), *Eurocommunism and Eurosocialism: The Left Confronts Modernity*, Cyrco Press, New York and London 1979, p. 293.

12. Miller and Potthoff, *A History of German Social Democracy*, p. 157 and Gordon A. Craig, *Germany 1866–1945*, Oxford University Press, Oxford 1981, pp. 418–19.

13. From Schumacher's Kiel speech of 27 October 1945; extracts in Miller and Potthoff, op. cit., p. 270.

14. This sceptical view is abundantly documented by Alan S. Milward in his *The European Rescue of the Nation-State* (with the assistance of George Brennan and Federico Romero), Routledge, London 1992; see, in particular, the chapter entitled 'The Lives and Teachings of the European Saints'.

15. Cited in Alan Bullock, *Ernest Bevin Foreign Secretary 1945–1951*, Oxford University Press, Oxford 1985, pp. 64–5.

16. Peter Weiler, *British Labour and the Cold War*, Stanford University Press, Stanford CA 1988, pp. 131–3.

17. Margaret Gowing, 'Britain, America and the Bomb', in David Dilks (ed.), *Retreat from Power. Studies in Britain's Foreign Relations in the Twentieth Century*. Vol. 2: *After 1939*, Macmillan, London 1981, p. 130–5.

18. Morgan, *Labour in Power*, pp. 282–4.

19. Gowing, op. cit., p. 130.

20. Kenneth Harris writes that on all broad issues Attlee and Bevin agreed; see his *Attlee*, p. 294; R. Smith and J. Zametica disagree with this in 'The Cold Warrior: Clement Attlee Reconsidered 1945–47', *International Affairs*, Vol. 61, no. 2, 1985.

21. Hobsbawm, *Age of Extremes*, p. 51.

22. Ellwood, *Italy 1943–1945*, pp. 32–5.

23. Vera Zamagni, 'The Marshall Plan: An Overview of its Impact on National Economies', in Antonio Varsori (ed.), *Europe 1945–1990s. The End of an Era?*, Macmillan, London 1995, p. 86.

24. Michael Newman, *Socialism and European Unity. The Dilemma of the Left in Britain and France*, Junction Books, London 1983, pp. 17, 20.

25. Pharo, 'Bridgebuilding and Reconstruction', pp. 134–5.

26. Tapani Paavonen, 'Neutrality, Protectionism and the International Community. Finnish Foreign Economic Policy in the Period of Reconstruction of the International Economy, 1945–1950', *Scandinavian Economic History Review*, Vol. XXXVII, no. 1, 1989, p. 31.

27. Procacci (ed.), *The Cominform*, p. 195.

28. In Finland all political parties except the communist SKDL were in favour of accepting the plan. But the government recognized that to accept Marshall Aid would alienate the USSR; see Roy Allison, *Finland's Relations with the Soviet Union, 1944–84*, Macmillan, London 1985, p. 119.

29. Daniel Yergin, *Shattered Peace. The Origins of the Cold War and the National Security State*, Penguin, Harmondsworth 1977, p. 309.

30. Alan S. Milward, *The Reconstruction of Western Europe 1945–51*, Methuen, London 1984, pp. 97–8, 125.

31. Charles S. Maier, 'The Two Postwar Eras and the Conditions for Stability in Twentieth-Century Western Europe', *American Historical Review*, Vol. 86, no. 2, 1981, p. 341.

32. David Ellwood, *Rebuilding Europe. Western Europe, America and Postwar Reconstruction*, Longman, London 1992, p. 94.

33. Maier, *In Search of Stability*, chapter 3.

34. See the deftly drawn portrait of Bevin's character in Bullock, op. cit., pp. 81–96.

35. See Raymond Smith, 'Ernest Bevin, British Officials and British Soviet Policy, 1945–47' and Anne Deighton, 'Towards a "Western Strategy": The Making of British Policy Towards Germany, 1945–46', in Anne Deighton (ed.), *Britain and the Second World War*, Macmillan, London 1990.

36. See Pimlott, *Hugh Dalton*, p. 390. Bevin recognized early on that there could never be peace in Palestine without taking into account Arab as well as Zionist claims; see Bullock, op. cit., p. 841.

37. Cited in Weiler, op. cit., p. 194.

38. John Kent questions Bevin's commitment to a special relationship with the USA in 'Bevin's Imperialism and the Idea of Euro-Africa, 1945–49', in Michael Dockrill and John W. Young (eds), *British Foreign Policy 1945–56*, Macmillan, London 1989, p. 47.

39. Newman, op. cit., pp. 138–47.

40. See the *New Statesman* of 10 June 1950, cited in Morgan, op. cit., p. 393.

41. Morgan, op. cit., pp. 423, 434.

42. Philip M. Williams, *Hugh Gaitskell*, Oxford University Press, Oxford 1982, p. 169.

43. Eatwell, *The 1945–1951 Labour Governments*, p. 140.

44. Cited in Bullock, op. cit., p. 126.

45. C. Barnett, *The Audit of War*, p. 304

46. H. W. Brands, 'India and Pakistan in American Strategic Planning, 1947–54: Commonwealth as Collaborator', *Journal of Imperial and Commonwealth History*, Vol. XV, no. 1, October 1986, p. 51.

47. Cited with corroborative evidence in E. H. Carr, *The Bolshevik Revolution 1917–1923*, Vol. 3, Penguin, Harmondsworth 1971, p. 28.

48. Cairncross, *Years of Recovery*, p. 8.

49. Sir Richard W. B. Clarke, *Anglo-American Economic Collaboration in War and in Peace 1942–1949*, ed. Sir Alec Cairncross, Clarendon Press, Oxford 1982, p. 70.

50. Ibid., p. 152.

51. D. C. Watt makes a similar point in his 'American Aid to Britain and the Problem of Socialism, 1945–51', in his *Personalities and Politics*, University of Notre Dame Press, South Bend, IN 1965, p. 66.

52. For a succinct and lucid account see Pimlott, op. cit., pp. 429–41.

53. Monnet, *Memoirs*, p. 250.

54. Annie Lacroix-Ritz, 'Négociation et signature des accords Blum-Byrnes (Octobre 1945–Mai 1946). D'après les archives du Ministère des Affaires Etrangères', *Revue d'histoire moderne et contemporaine*, Vol. XXXI July–September 1984, pp. 442–6.

55. Shennan, *Rethinking France*, p. 144.

56. D. K. Fieldhouse, 'The Labour Governments and the Empire-Commonwealth, 1945–51', in Ritchie Ovendale (ed.), *The Foreign Policy of the British Labour Governments, 1945–1951*, Leicester University Press, Leicester 1984, pp. 82–4.

57. Ibid., p. 85.

58. Ibid., pp. 95–7.

59. Ibid., p. 98.

60. Thomas Balogh, 'Britain and the Dependent Commonwealth, in A. Creech Jones (ed.), *New Fabian Colonial Essays*, Hogarth Press, London 1959, p. 106.

61. Allister E. Hinds, 'Sterling and Imperial Policy, 1945–1951', *Journal of Imperial and Commonwealth History*, Vol. XV, no. 2, January 1987, pp. 148–69.

62. See the comments by his senior civil servants Sir Hilton Poynton, Sir Leslie Monson and his private secretary Sir Duncan Watson, in Nicholas Owen (ed.), 'Decolonisation and the Colonial Office' (Witness Seminar), *Contemporary Record*, Vol. 6, no. 3, Winter 1992, p. 502.

63. Arthur Creech Jones, 'The Labour Party and Colonial Policy 1945–51', in A. Creech Jones (ed.), *New Fabian Colonial Essays*, pp. 21, 23, 24, 25, 36–7. For the role of the Colonial Office, see L. J. Butler, *Economic Development and the 'Official Mind': The Colonial Office and Manufacturing in West Africa, 1939–1951*, unpublished doctoral dissertation, University of London 1991.

64. See Rita Hinden's article 'Imperialism Today' in the August 1945 issue of *Fabian Quarterly*, cited in Partha Sarathi Gupta, *Imperialism and the British Labour Movement 1914–1964*, Macmillan, London 1975, p. 283.

65. K. Harris, op. cit., pp. 362, 385–6; see also Nicholas Owen, '"More Than a Transfer of Power": Independence Day Ceremonies in India, 15 August 1947', *Contemporary Record*, Vol. 6, no. 3, Winter 1992, pp. 419–21.

66. Hennessy, *Never Again*, p. 234.

67. Shennan, op. cit., p. 152.

68. Ibid., p. 163.

69. Quoted in ibid., p. 159.

70. Daniel Le Couriard, 'Les socialistes et les débuts de la guerre d'Indochine (1946–1947)', *Revue d'histoire moderne et contemporaine*, Vol. XXXI, April–June 1984, p. 351.

71. R. F. Holland, *European Decolonization 1918–1981*, Macmillan, London 1985, p. 95.

72. Richard F. Kuisel, *Seducing the French. The Dilemma of Americanization*, University of California Press, Berkeley 1993, pp. 43ff.

73. Holland, op. cit., pp. 90–1.

74. Ibid., p. 93.

75. Kevin Featherstone, *Socialist Parties and European Integration*, Manchester University Press, Manchester 1988, pp. 264–5.

76. Wilfried Loth, 'Les projets de politique extérieure de la Résistance socialiste en France', *Revue d'histoire moderne et contemporaine*, Vol. XXIX, 1977, pp. 557–67.

77. Newman, op. cit., p. 5.

78. William James Adams, *Restructuring the French Economy. Government and the Rise of Market Competition since World War II*, Brookings Institution, Washington DC 1989, p. 122.

79. Frances M. B. Lynch, 'Resolving the Paradox of the Monnet Plan: National and International Planning in French Reconstruction', *Economic History Review*, Vol. XXXVII, no. 2, May 1984, p. 242.

80. Milward, *Reconstruction*, p. 475.

81. Ibid., see chapter IV, especially pp. 129 and 159. One of the most valuable analyses of French foreign policy in this period is by John W. Young, *France, the Cold War and the Western Alliance, 1944–49: French Foreign Policy and Post-War Europe*, Leicester University Press, Leicester and London 1990.

82. William D. Graf, *The German Left since 1945. Socialism and Social Democracy in the German Federal Republic*, Oleander Press, New York 1976, p. 69.

83. Newman, op. cit., pp. 131–3 and Henry Pelling, *Britain and the Marshall Plan*, Macmillan, London 1988, p. 100. On the same theme, see also Denis Healey's 1948 pamphlet, 'Feet on the Ground', reprinted in his *When Shrimps Learn to Whistle*, Penguin, Harmondsworth 1991, pp. 70–75.

84. See conference resolution in F. W. S. Craig (ed.), *Conservative and Labour Party Conference Decisions 1945–1972*, p. 234.

85. This was the basis of Stafford Cripps's statement to the OEEC Council meeting on 1 November 1949. See Geoffrey Warner, 'The Labour Government and the Unity of Western Europe', in Ovendale (ed.), op. cit., pp. 70–71.

86. US State Department Policy Planning Staff Memorandum of July 1947, cited in Weiler, op. cit., p. 281. See also Pelling, op. cit., pp. 94, 126.

87. Cited in Newman, op. cit., pp. 131–2; see also pp. 132ff.

88. The words are those of the pro-Communist Labour MP Konni Zilliacus, cited in Newman, op. cit., p. 145.

8. The Golden Age of Capitalism

1. Tiersky, *French Communism 1920–1972*, p. 210.

2. Philip M. Williams, *Crisis and Compromise. Politics in the Fourth Republic*, Longman, London 1972, p. 314.

3. Tiersky, op. cit., p. 189.

4. This is well documented in Joanne Barkan, *Visions of Emancipation. The Italian Workers' Movement since 1945*, Praeger, New York 1984, pp. 45–7.

5. Angus Maddison, *Phases of Capitalist Development*, Oxford University Press, Oxford 1982, p. 91; see also Stephen Marglin and Juliet Schor (eds), *The Golden Age of Capitalism. Reinterpreting the Postwar Experience*, Clarendon Press, Oxford 1990.

6. Maddison, op. cit., pp. 126–7.

7. The classic exposition of this view is in Charles P. Kindleberger, *Europe's Postwar Growth. The Role of Labor Supply*, Harvard University Press, Cambridge MA 1967.

8. For a thorough account of European labour migration, see Stephen Castles and Godula Kosack, *Immigrant Workers and Class Structure in Western Europe*, Oxford University Press, Oxford 1985.

9. A. G. Kenwood and A. L. Lougheed, *The Growth of the International Economy 1820–1980. An Introductory Text*, Allen and Unwin, London 1983, p. 266.

10. Data in Antonio Missiroli, *La questione tedesca. Le due Germanie dalla divisione all'unità 1945–1990*, Ponte Alle Grazie, Florence 1991, pp. 64–6.

11. William Beveridge, *Social Insurance and Allied Services*, Cmd. 6404, HMSO, London 1942, p. 155 and p. 51 respectively.

12. Beveridge, op. cit., p. 49; also cited in Laura Balbo, 'Family, Women, and the State', in Maier (ed.), *Changing Boundaries of the Political*, p. 209. Balbo points out that women were also hired in large numbers in the expanding public sector, thus providing cheap labour for welfare services.

13. Nicholas Kaldor, *Further Essays on Applied Economics*, Duckworth, London 1978, p. 170.

14. Frank B. Tipton and Robert Aldrich, *An Economic and Social History of Europe from 1939 to the Present*, Macmillan, London 1987, p. 113.

15. The CIA figures for the USSR are cited in Philip Hanson, 'The Soviet Union', in Graham with Seldon (eds), *Government and Economies in the Postwar World*, p. 207; those for the other countries are estimates by T. P. Alton, *National Product of the Planned Economies of Eastern Europe*, New York 1987, cited in Jaroslav Krejcí, 'Eastern Europe', in Graham with Seldon (eds), op. cit., p. 182.

16. Cited in Perry Anderson, 'Trotsky's Interpretation of Stalinism', in *New Left Review* no. 139, May–June 1983, p. 53.

17. Cited by Christopher Lasch, himself a left-wing critic of the consumer society, in his *The Minimal Self. Psychic Survival in Troubled Times*, Pan Books, London 1984, pp. 34–5.

18. Hannah Arendt, *The Human Condition. A Study of the Central Dilemmas Facing Modern Man*, Doubleday Anchor Books, New York 1959, p. 116.

19. Daniel Bell, *The End of Ideology. On the Exhaustion of Political Ideas in the Fifties*, Free Press, New York 1965 (1st edn 1960), pp. 312–13.

20. On the death of the avant-garde in the 1950s, see Hobsbawm, *Age of Extremes*, pp. 514ff.

21. Cited in Marc Lazar, *Maisons rouges. Les partis communistes français et italien de la Libération à nos jours*, Aubier, Paris 1992, p. 75.

22. Kuisel, *Seducing the French*, pp. 54–69. See also Pier Paolo D'Attorre, 'Sogno americano e mito sovietico nell'Italia contemporanea', in his (ed.), *Nemici per la pelle. Sogno americano e mito sovietico nell'Italia contemporanea*, Franco Angeli, Milan 1991, p. 31.

23. Karen Ruoff, '*Warenästhetik* in America, or Reflections on a Multi-National Concern', in W. F. Haug (ed.) *Warenästhetik. Beiträge zur Diskussion Weiterentwicklung und Vermittlung ihner Kritik*, Suhrkamp, Frankfurt 1975, p. 57.

24. David Childs, *Britain since 1945*, Methuen, London 1984, p. 74.

25. Jane Jenson and George Ross, 'The Tragedy of the French Left', *New Left Review*, no. 171, September–October 1988, p. 16; Marie-Françoise Mouriaux and René Mouriaux, 'Unemployment Policy in France, 1976–82', in J. Richardson and R. Henning (eds), *Un-*

employment: Policy Responses of Western Democracies, Sage, London 1984, p. 149; P. A. Hall, 'Economic Planning and the State', op. cit., p. 184.

26. M. Balfour, *West Germany*, p. 147.

27. Volker R. Berghahn, *Modern Germany*, Cambridge University Press, Cambridge 1982, p. 206 and Michael Schneider, *A Brief History of the German Trade Unions*, trans. B. Selman, Verlag J. H. W. Dietz Nachf, Bonn 1991, p. 251.

28. Leaman, *The Political Economy of West Germany, 1945–1985*, p. 154 and Schneider, op. cit., p. 251.

29. Schneider, op. cit., pp. 254–5.

30. The literature on corporatism is vast and tedious; those interested should start with Philippe C. Schmitter and Gerhard Lehmbruch (eds), *Trends towards Corporatist Intermediation*, Sage, Beverly Hills and London 1979.

31. See chart in Karl-Olof Faxén, 'Incomes Policy and Centralized Wage Formation', in A. Boltho (ed.), *The European Economy. Growth & Crisis*, Oxford University Press, Oxford 1982, p. 368 (the chart is derived from C. A. Blyth's paper in OECD, *Collective Bargaining and Government Policies*, Paris 1979).

32. John D. Stephens, *The Transition from Capitalism to Socialism*, Macmillan, London 1979, p. 115.

33. Stephen Bornstein, 'States and Unions: From Postwar Settlement to Contemporary Stalemate', in S. Bornstein, D. Held and J. Krieger, *The State in Capitalist Europe*, Allen and Unwin, London 1984, p. 62.

34. Shell, *The Transformation of Austrian Socialism*, pp. 226–8.

35. Faxén, op. cit., p. 370.

36. Wolinetz, 'Socio-economic Bargaining in the Netherlands, p. 82.

37. Willy Van Rijkeghem, 'Benelux', in Boltho (ed.), op. cit., p. 585.

38. Derry, *A History of Modern Norway 1814–1972*, pp. 413, 426.

39. Walter Korpi, *The Working Class in Welfare Capitalism. Work, Unions and Politics in Sweden*, Routledge and Kegan Paul, London 1978, p. 87.

40. For a succinct survey, see Berndt Öhman, *LO and Labour Market Policy since the Second World War*, Prisca, Stockholm 1974.

41. Tilton, *The Political Theory of Swedish Social Democracy*, p. 195.

42. Swedish Confederation of Trade Unions (LO), *Trade Unions and Full Employment*, (Rehn–Meidner Report), Report to the 1951 Congress, English trans., Stockholm 1953, p. 91.

43. Ibid., p. 89.

44. Ibid., p. 91.

45. Ibid., pp. 94–6.

46. Ibid., p. 93.

47. Jonas Pontusson, *Swedish Social Democracy and British Labour: Essays on the Nature and Condition of Social Democratic Hegemony*, Western Societies Program Occasional Paper no. 19, Center for International Studies, Cornell University, Ithaca NY 1988, pp. 38–9.

48. Ibid., p. 39.

49. Gösta Rehn, 'Swedish Active Labor Market Policy: Retrospect and Prospect', *Industrial Relations*, Vol. 24, no. 1, 1985 (SOFI Reprint Series no. 140), p. 69.

50. Rudolf Meidner, *Employee Investment Funds. An Approach to Collective Capital Formation*, Allen and Unwin, London 1978, pp. 13–14.

51. See Korpi, op. cit., p. 102.

52. Olsson, *Social Policy and Welfare State in Sweden*, pp. 219–21.

53. William (Lord) Beveridge, *Full Employment in a Free Society*, second edn with a new prologue, Allen and Unwin, London 1960, p. 199.

54. Ibid., p. 200.

55. Ibid., p. 11.

9. Between Neutralism and Atlanticism

1. Quoted in Geoffrey Foote, *The Labour Party's Political Thought. A History*, Croom Helm, London 1985, p. 203.

2. Oliver Rathkolb, 'Die SPÖ und der aussenpolitische Entscheidungsprozess 1945–1955. Mit einem Ausblick auf die Neutralitätspolitik bis 1965', in Wolfgang Maderthaner (ed.), *Auf dem Weg zur Macht. Integration in den Staat, Sozialpartnerschaft und Regierungspartei*, Loecker-Verlag, Vienna 1992, pp. 51–72.

3. Shell, *The Transformation of Austrian Socialism*, pp. 156–8.

4. Cited in Daniel Blume et al., *Histoire du réformisme en France depuis 1920*, Vol. 2, Editions Sociales, Paris 1976, p. 112.

5. R. H. S. Crossman, 'Towards a Philosophy of Socialism', in R. H. S. Crossman (ed.), *New Fabian Essays*, Turnstile Press, London 1952, p. 12.

6. Text in PSI, *Il Partito Socialista Italiano nei suoi Congressi*, Vol. V, pp. 302, 307 and 321.

7. The italics are mine; quoted in Parti communiste français, *Histoire du Parti communiste français*, p. 523.

8. Article by François Billoux in *Cahiers du communisme*, May 1952, cited in ibid., p. 538.

9. Danièle Joly, *The French Communist Party and the Algerian War*, Macmillan, London 1991, pp. 56–67.

10. Allison, *Finland's Relations with the Soviet Union, 1944–84*, pp. 136–8.

11. John H. Hodgson, 'The Finnish Communist Party and Neutrality', *Government and Opposition*, Vol. 2, no. 2, 1966–67, pp. 279–80.

12. Michael Balfour, *The Adversaries. America, Russia and the Open World 1941–62*, Routledge and Kegan Paul, London 1981, p. 120.

13. Some moderate or right-wing socialists were also against it out of deep distrust for all things German – for instance, Hugh Dalton. See Pimlott, *Hugh Dalton*, p. 608.

14. P. M. Williams, *Crisis and Compromise*, p. 46.

15. Touchard, *La gauche en France depuis 1900*, p. 299.

16. See text of treaty in Trevor N. Dupuy and Gay M. Hammerman (eds), *A Documentary History of Arms Control and Disarmament*, R. R. Bowker and T. N. Dupuy Associates, New York and Dunn Loring, VA 1973, p. 366.

17. William R. Keylor, *The Twentieth-Century World*, Oxford University Press, Oxford 1984, p. 290.

18. The text is available in the collection *The Essential Stalin*, ed. Bruce Franklin Croom Helm, London 1973, p. 472.

19. For the SPD position, see Point Thirteen of the *Sixteen Durkheim Points* approved by the leadership of the party on 29–30 August 1949, in SPD, *Jahrbuch der SPD 1948/1949*, p. 140.

20. See the account of the Soviet offer in Rolf Steininger, *The German Question. The Stalin Note of 1952 and the Problem of Reunification*, trans. Jane T. Hedges, Columbia University Press, New York 1990. This analysis supports Brandt's view: though sceptical of Stalin's good intentions, he thought the offer should be taken seriously; see his *My Life in Politics*, Penguin, Harmondsworth 1993, p. 148. For a different view, see Gerhard Wettig, 'Stalin and German Reunification: Archival Evidence on Soviet Foreign Policy in Spring 1952', *Historical Journal*, Vol. 37, no. 2, 1994, pp. 411–19.

21. Steininger, op. cit., p. 69.

22. Ibid., p. 97.

23. See the documents appended to ibid., pp. 125–58.

24. Sven Allard, *Russia and the Austrian State Treaty. A Case Study of Soviet Policy in Europe*, Pennsylvania State University Press, University Park, PA 1970, p. 117; on the reasons behind the Austrian adoption of the Swiss principle of 'perpetual neutrality', see pp. 224–9.

25. See the texts of the various proposals and counter-proposals in Dupuy and Hammerman (eds), op. cit., pp. 353–451.

26. M. Saeter, 'Nuclear Disengagement Efforts 1955–80: Politics of *Status Quo* or Political Change?', in Sverre Lodgaard and Marek Thee (eds), *Nuclear Disengagement in Europe*, SIPRI and Pugwash publication, Taylor and Francis, London and New York 1983, pp. 56–7.

27. Keylor, op. cit., p. 302.

28. See the text in Dupuy and Hammerman (eds), op. cit., pp. 436–8.

29. Saeter, op. cit., p. 59.

30. Guy Mollet, 'The Rapacki Plan and European Security', *Socialist International Information*, Vol. 8, no. 16, 19 April 1958, p. 237; originally in *Le Populaire*, 8 April 1958. For the Dutch position, see Editorial in *Het Vrije Volk*, 23 January 1958; translated and reprinted in *Socialist International Information*, Vol. 8, no. 5, 1 February 1958, pp. 70–1.

31. Joint statement of the NEC and the TUC of 23 April 1958, reprinted in *Socialist International Information*, Vol. 8, no. 18, 3 May 1958, p. 278.

32. Erich Ollenhauer, 'A New Chance for the Rapacki Plan', *Socialist International Information*, Vol. 8, no. 46, 15 November 1958, p. 695; originally in *Pressedienst*, 3 November 1958.

33. Dennis L. Bark and David R. Gress, *A History of West Germany*, Vol. 1: *From Shadow to Substance 1945–1963*, Basil Blackwell, Oxford 1989, p. 308.

34. M. Balfour, *West Germany*, pp. 170, 192.

35. PSD, *Aktions-Programm der SPD*, approved on 28 September 1952 at the Dortmund Party congress, published in Bonn, pp. 6–7; henceforth cited as *Aktions-Programm, Dortmund*.

36. Ibid., p. 11.

37. Miller and Potthoff, *A History of German Social Democracy*, p. 168.

38. *Aktions-Programm, Dortmund*, p. 12.

39. *Aktions-Programm der SPD*, approved in 1952, expanded at the Berlin party congress, 24 July 1954, p. 10.

40. Ibid., p. 13.

41. Ibid., pp. 14–17.

42. Schneider, *A Brief History of the German Trade Unions*, p. 280.

43. SPD, *Deutschlandplan*, Bonn, April 1959, pp. 6–7.

44. Ibid., pp. 8–11.

45. Ibid., p. 8.

46. Bark and Gress, op. cit., p. 380.

47. See the parliamentary record of the Bundestag: *Deutscher Bundestag*, 3. Wahlperiode, 122 Stzung, Bonn, Donnerstag, den 30 Juni 1960, p. 7055; henceforth: *Wehner/Bundestag*.

48. *Wehner/Bundestag*, p. 7058.

49. Beatrix W. Bouvier, *Zwischen Godesberg und Grosser Koalition: der Weg der SPD in die Regierungsverantwortung*, Dietz, Bonn 1990, pp. 65–6.

50. *Basic Programme of the Social Democratic Party of Germany*, adopted by an Extraordinary Conference held on 13–15 November 1959, at Bad Godesberg; English translation published by the SPD, Bonn, no date, p. 20 (henceforth cited as *Bad Godesberg Programme*).

51. Ibid., p. 9.

52. *Wehner/Bundestag*, p. 7057.

53. Bouvier, op. cit., p. 68.

54. *Wehner/Bundestag*, p. 7060.

55. Ibid., p. 7061.

56. See text in Dupuy and Hammerman (eds), op. cit., p. 350.

57. See the calculation in Olivier Le Cour Grandmaison, 'Le Mouvement de la paix pendant la guerre froide: le cas français (1948–1952)', *Communisme*, nos 18–19, 1988, p. 128.

58. Palmiro Togliatti, speech to the Chamber of Deputies, 17 June 1952, in his *Opere*, Vol. 5, pp. 698–9.

59. Ibid., p. 700.

60. 'Per un accordo tra comunisti e cattolici per salvare la civiltà umana', in Togliatti, op. cit., pp. 832–46.

61. James Hinton, *Protests and Visions. Peace Politics in 20th Century Britain*, Hutchinson Radius, London 1989, p. 157.

62. Ibid., p. 181.

63. Richard Taylor, *Against the Bomb. The British Peace Movement 1958–1965*, Clarendon Press, Oxford 1988, pp. 305–7.

64. Hinton, op. cit., pp. 158–9.

65. Taylor, op. cit., pp. 278–81.

66. Ibid., p. 280.

67. A. J. R. Groom, *British Thinking About Nuclear Weapons*, Frances Pinter, London 1974, pp. 314–17; see also Taylor, op. cit., pp. 290–1.

68. Taylor, op. cit., p. 295.

69. For an account – though overly commendatory – of Gaitskell's position, see P. M. Williams, *Hugh Gaitskell*, pp. 278–90.

70. See the text of the resolution in *Socialist International Information*, Vol. 6, no. 49, 8 December 1956, pp. 848–9. Later, the Jewish Bund rescinded the abstention of its delegate and accepted the entire resolution.

71. See his Lille speech of 10 May 1957 cited in Maurice Pivert, 'Le socialisme internationale et l'opération de Suez', *La revue socialiste*, no. 109, July 1957, p. 191. Many in the SFIO expressed serious doubts over the French intervention; see, for example, Roger Quillot, 'Les leçons de Suez', *La revue socialiste*, no. 103, January 1957 and the Pivert article cited above, which was published in the official review of the SFIO with an editorial comment underlining the fact that the article did not represent the position of the review or of the party.

72. On the pro-Sovietism of the PSI at the time, see Giovanni Sabbatucci, *Il riformismo impossibile. Storie del socialismo italiano*, Laterza, Rome-Bari 1991, pp. 96–8.

73. John Pinder, 'Positive Integration and Negative Integration: Some Problems of Economic Union in the EEC', in Michael Hodges (ed.), *European Integration*, Penguin, Harmondsworth 1972, p. 126.

74. Featherstone, *Socialist Parties and European Integration*, p. 25.

75. Ibid., p. 270.

76. The official history of the Belgian Socialist Party, written in the celebratory style of pre-*perestroika* Soviet historiography, contains not a single mention of the EEC; see Robert Abs, *Histoire du Parti socialiste Belge de 1885 à 1978*, Editions Fondation Louis de Brouckère, Brussels 1979.

77. For the Belgian socialists, see G. Marchal-Van Belle, *Les socialistes belges et l'intégration européenne*, Editions de l'Institut de Sociologie, ULB, Brussels 1968, particularly the remarks on p. 76.

78. Newman, *Socialism and European Unity*, p. 35.

79. André Philip, *Les socialistes*, Editions du Seuil, Paris 1967, p. 143.

80. See 'Marché commun et socialisme', signed 'Y', *La revue socialiste*, no. 105, March 1957, p. 282.

81. Newman, op. cit., pp. 42–3.

82. Georges Cogniot, 'Les nouveaux pièges "européens"', *Cahiers du communisme*, Vol. 33, no. 2, February 1957, pp. 179–81; see also Frédéric Bon, 'Structure de l'idéologie communiste', in *Le Communisme en France*, Cahiers de la Fondation Nationale des Sciences Politiques, Colin, Paris 1969, p. 118.

83. Newman, op. cit., pp. 49–50.

84. David Pace, 'Old Wine, New Bottles: Atomic Energy and the Ideology of Science in Postwar France', *French Historical Studies*, Vol. 17, no. 1, Spring 1991, pp. 38–61.

85. Cogniot, op. cit., pp. 186–7.

86. See text of the communiqué in L. Barca, F. Botta and A. Zevi (eds), *I comunisti e l'economia italiana 1944–1974*, De Donato, Bari 1975, pp. 237–41.

87. See, in particular, the communiqué of 8 January 1959 in Partito comunista italiano, *La politica economica italiana (1945–1974). Orientamenti e proposte dei comunisti*, ed. Sezione centrale scuole di partito, PCI, Rome n.d., pp. 174–80.

88. For a more detailed account of developments leading up to the 1970s see my 'The Italian Communist Party's European Strategy', *Political Quarterly*, no. 3, 1976.

89. F. Roy Willis, *Italy Chooses Europe*, Oxford University Press, Oxford 1971, p. 306.

90. Alberto Benzoni, 'I socialisti e la politica estera', in Massimo Bonanni (ed.), *La politica estera della Repubblica italiana*, I.A.I and Edizioni di Comunità, Milan 1967, pp. 943–4.

91. The book, published by the PSI, came out during the lifetime of Pietro Nenni, who had obviously given his imprimatur; see Pietro Nenni, *I nodi della politica estera italiana*, ed. Domenico Zucàro, SugarCo Edizioni, Milan 1974.

92. Klaus Misgeld, 'As the Iron Curtain Descended: the Co-ordinating Committee of the Nordic Labour Movement and the Socialist International between Potsdam and Geneva (1945–1955)', *Scandinavian Journal of History*, Vol. 13, no. 1, 1988, p. 61.

93. Newman, op. cit., p. 157.

94. Robert J. Lieber, *British Politics and European Unity*, University of California Press, Berkeley and London 1970, p. 143.

95. See text in *British General Election Manifestos 1900–1974*, compiled and edited by F. W. S. Craig, Macmillan, London 1975, p. 231.

96. Ibid., p. 220.

97. Lieber, op. cit., pp. 138–9.

98. All these figures are based on R. E. Rowthorne and J. R. Wells, *De-Industrialization and Foreign Trade*, Cambridge University Press, Cambridge 1987, p. 169.

99. Lieber, op. cit., pp. 147–9.

100. Cited in A. Philip, op. cit., p. 144.

101. Benzoni, op. cit., pp. 944–5.

102. William E. Paterson, *The SPD and European Integration*, Saxon House, Farnborough 1974, p. 125.

103. Crossman, op. cit., p. 30.

104. David Lipsey, 'Crosland's Socialism', in David Lipsey and Dick Leonard (eds), *The Socialist Agenda. Crosland's Legacy*, Jonathan Cape, London 1981, pp. 24–5.

105. Bark and Gress, op. cit., p. 381.

106. Ibid., pp. 384–5.

107. They have been well documented in Paterson, op. cit., especially pp. 115–27.

108. Flechtheim, 'The German Left and the World Crisis', in B. Brown (ed.), *Eurocommunism and Eurosocialism*, p. 295.

109. Leaman, *The Political Economy of West Germany, 1948–1985*, pp. 111–12.

110. Paterson, op. cit., p. 129.

111. Miller and Potthoff, op. cit., pp. 166–7.

10. The Foundations of Revisionism

1. SPD, *Bad Godesberg Programme*, p. 5.

2. C. A. R. Crosland, *The Future of Socialism*, Jonathan Cape, London 1956, pp. 81–7.

3. Ibid., p. 83.

4. *Aktions-Programm Berlin*, p. 10.

5. Cited in Shell, *The Transformation of Austrian Socialism*, p. 181.

6. Alfred Mozer, 'Socialist Victory in the Netherlands', *Socialist International Information*, Vol. 6, no. 26, 30 June 1956, pp. 442–3.

7. Léo Collard, then socialist minister of education, in his speech of 16 November 1958 to the Special Congress of the Belgian Socialist Party, *Socialist International Information*, Vol. 8, no. 48, 29 November 1958.

8. Pietro Amato, *Il PSI tra frontismo e autonomia (1948–1954)*, Cosenza 1978, p. 97.

9. Ibid., p. 295; see also Maurizio Degl'Innocenti, *Storia del PSI.* Vol. 3: *Dal Dopoguerra a Oggi*, Laterza, Rome-Bari 1993, pp. 193–4.

10. Amato, op. cit., p. 302.

11. Degl'Innocenti, op. cit., p. 196.

12. D. Sassoon, *The Strategy of the Italian Communist Party*, pp. 54–5.

13. Palmiro Togliatti, 'Per un accordo tra comunisti e cattolici per salvare la civiltà umana', in *Opere*, Vol. 5, p. 839.

14. Palmiro Togliatti, 'Rapporto all'VIII Congresso del Partito comunista italiano', in *Opere*, Vol. 6: *1956–1964*, Editori Riuniti, Rome 1984, p. 223.

15. Cited by Luciano Gruppi in his introduction to Palmiro Togliatti, *Comunisti socialisti cattolici*, Editori Riuniti, Rome 1974, pp. 21–2.

16. See Lipsey and Leonard (eds), *The Socialist Agenda. Crosland's Legacy*; the first comment is by David Lipsey (p. 9), the second by Anthony King (p. 22). One can readily agree, however, with Henry Drucker when he says that it was one of the few works of stature produced by a Labour politician; see '"All the King's horses and all the King's men": The Social Democratic Party in Britain', in Paterson and Thomas (eds), *The Future of Social Democracy*, p. 110.

17. See Foote, *The Labour Party's Political Thought*, pp. 206–34.

18. Ibid., p. 204.

19. See P. M. Williams, *Hugh Gaitskell*, pp. 129, 231.

20. Ibid., p. 245.

21. C. A. R. Crosland, *The Future of Socialism* (2nd edn), Jonathan Cape, London 1967.

22. Alec K. Cairncross, *Factors in Economic Development*, cited in Sidney Pollard, *The Idea of Progress*, C. A. Watts, London 1968, p. 185.

23. Crossman (ed.), *New Fabian Essays*, pp. 8–10.

24. Crosland, op. cit., p. 19; this and all subsequent citations are from the 1956 edition.

25. Ibid., p. 62.

26. Ibid., pp. 26–30.

27. Ibid., p. 68.

28. John M. Keynes, 'The End of Laissez-Faire', in *Essays in Persuasion, Collected Works*, Vol. IX, Macmillan, London 1972, p. 289.

29. James Burnham, *The Managerial Revolution*, Penguin, London 1945, p. 68.

30. Shell, op. cit., p. 145.

31. André Philip, *Le Socialisme trahi*, Plon, Paris 1957, pp. 33–4. This book cost the author his expulsion from the SFIO – not surprisingly, as it accused Mollet of abandoning republican values for reactionary nationalistic positions.

32. Jules Moch, *Confrontations*, Gallimard, Paris 1952, pp. 448–9.

33. Crosland, op. cit., p. 497.

34. Ibid., p. 115.

35. Ibid., p. 216.

36. Ibid., p. 218.

37. Ibid., pp. 232–7.

38. Ibid., pp. 282–3. Note the particular English obsession with the symbols of class distinctions, snobbery and class envy: Crosland assumed that once the mass of people have tinned asparagus, South African sherry and a mass-produced suit, it will not be important if others eat fresh asparagus, drink Spanish sherry and wear a tailor-made suit.

39. Ibid., pp. 295–301, 319–32.

40. Ibid., p. 378.

41. Ibid., p. 415.

42. Ibid., p. 418.

43. Ibid., p. 499.

44. Crossman, op. cit., p. 25.

45. Denis Healey, 'Power Politics and the Labour Party', in Crossman (ed.), op. cit., pp. 161–2.

46. Crosland, op. cit., p. 521.

47. Ibid., pp. 521–2.

48. Bark and Gress, *A History of West Germany*, p. 443.

49. John H. Herz, 'Social Democracy versus Democratic Socialism. An Analysis of SPD Attempts to Develop a Party Doctrine', in B. Brown (ed.), *Eurocommunism and Eurosocialism*, p. 248.

50. Miller and Potthoff, *A History of German Social Democracy*, p. 174.

51. *Bad Godesberg Programme*, p. 9.

52. See Mario Telò's introduction to his edited book, *Tradizione socialista e progetto europeo. Le idee della socialdemocrazia tedesca tra storia e prospettiva*, Editori Riuniti, Rome 1988, pp. 25ff. and the essay in the same collection by Thomas Meyer, 'Un mutamento di paradigma: il nuovo programma nella storia della SPD', pp. 110–12.

53. *Aktions-Programm Berlin*, p. 27.

54. *Bad Godesberg Programme*, p. 10.

55. *Aktions-Programm Dortmund*, p. 20.

56. *Aktions-Programm Berlin*, pp. 28–32.

57. *Bad Godesberg Programme*, p. 11.

58. For instance, Herz, op. cit., p. 250.

59. Miller and Potthoff, op. cit., pp. 166–7.

60. *Aktions-Programm Dortmund*, p. 19.

61. *Aktions-Programm Berlin*, p. 10

62. Silvano Presa, 'La socialdemocrazia austriaca', in Leonardo Paggi (ed.), *Americanismo e riformismo. La socialdemocrazia europea nell'economia mondiale aperta*, Einaudi Editore, Turin 1989, pp. 348–9; see also Jelavich, *Modern Austria*, p. 281.

63. Cited in de Man, *A Documentary Study of Hendrik de Man*, p. 220.

64. Otto Kirchheimer, 'The Transformation of the Western European Party Systems', in Joseph LaPalombara and Myrin Weiner (eds), *Political Parties and Political Development*, Princeton University Press, Princeton NJ 1966, p. 185.

65. Ibid., p. 186.

66. Bell, *The End of Ideology*, p. 404.

67. See Adam Przeworski and John Sprague, *Paper Stones. A History of Electoral Socialism*, University of Chicago Press, Chicago 1988, pp. 42–3. I find debatable the authors' assumption – made explicit on p. 45 – that a socialist working-class appeal gains working-class votes.

68. See also P. M. Williams, *Crisis and Compromise*, pp. 79–80, 86, 92–7.

69. P. Togliatti, 'Ceto medio e Emilia Rossa', in *Opere scelte*, Editori Riuniti, Rome 1974, p. 460.

70. Pietro Ingrao, 'Democrazia socialista e democrazia interna di partito', *Rinascita*, no. 17, 25 April 1964; now in *Masse e potere*, Editori Riuniti, Rome 1964, p. 183.

71. P. Togliatti, in *Opere*, Vol. 6, p. 212.

72. William E. Paterson, 'The German Social Democratic Party', in Paterson and Thomas (eds), op. cit., p. 128. These symbolic changes had been advocated since the early 1950s by reformers such as Carlo Schmidt; see Miller and Potthoff, op. cit., p. 173.

73. *Aktions-Programm Berlin*, p. 10.

74. Ibid., p. 9.

75. Miller and Potthoff, op. cit., pp. 175–6.

76. See the English-language translation of the *Programme of the Swedish Social Democratic Party* adopted in Stockholm in June 1960, *Socialdemokraterna*, Stockholm 1961, p. 9. The assertion, made by Christine Buci-Glucksmann and Göran Therborn, that this programme constituted the Bad Godesberg of the SAP, is not sustainable; see their *Le défi social-démocrate*, p. 190.

77. So wrote the party's international secretary, Alfred Mozer, in his 'Thoughts on the Seventy-fifth Anniversary of the Death of Karl Marx', in *Socialist International Information*, Vol. 8, no. 11, 15 March 1958, p. 175.

78. Val R. Lorwin, 'Labor Unions and Political Parties in Belgium', in *Industrial and Labor Relations Review*, Vol. 28, no. 2, January 1975, p. 253.

79. The socialists were not pleased with the law resulting from the *Pacte scolaire*, as is evident from Pierre Vanbergen, 'Pacte scolaire et projet de loi Moureaux', in *Socialisme*, Vol. 6, no. 33, May 1959, pp. 338–51.

80. Abs, *Histoire du Parti socialist belge de 1995 à 1978*, pp. 66–70.

81. Pierre Vermeylen, 'Vue cavalière des programmes socialistes', in *Socialisme*, Vol. 6, no. 35, September 1959, pp. 543–4.

82. Following the Party Congress of December 1958, a number of reports were commissioned. These citations come from a summary of the report on economic planning by René Evalenko; see his 'Planification et organisation de l'économie', in *Socialisme*, Vol. 6, no. 34, July 1959, pp. 427, 431–2.

83. Léon Collard, 'The Future of Socialism', *Le Peuple*, 21 September 1959; reprinted and translated in *Socialist International Information*, Vol. 9, no. 41, 10 October 1959, p. 612.

84. For instance, in the second half of 1957 alone, *La revue socialiste* published the following essays, all written from a Marxist position: Pierre Rimbert, 'Une vue d'ensemble sur Karl Marx', Nos 111 and 112, November and December 1957; G. Chappaz, 'Reflexion sur le matérialisme marxiste', no. 110, October 1957; P. Bonnel, 'Hegel et Marx', nos 110 and 111, October and November 1957; E. Antonelli, 'Pour penser le socialisme', nos 108 and 109, June and July 1957.

85. In spite of this decline, one of the SPÖ's more right-wing spokesmen, Benedikt Kautsky, argued that whereas in the 1920s the enemy had been the bourgeoisie, now it was the communists, who were 'traitors to the working class'; see his 'The Ideological Development of Democratic Socialism in Austria', *Socialist International Information*, Vol. 6, no. 16, 21 April 1956, p. 283.

86. 'Austrian Social Democracy', in Paterson and Thomas (eds), p. 157.

87. Cited in Shell, op. cit., pp. 139–41, which also contains the most thorough discussion in English of Austrian revisionism. For an example of the Left's criticism of the original draft, see Serban Voinea, 'Le projet de programme du parti socialiste autrichien', published in the SFIO's review, *La revue socialiste*, no. 116, April 1958, pp. 412–23 alongside the draft itself.

88. Oscar Pollack, 'The Programme Debate in Austria', *Socialist International Information*, Vol. 8, no. 8, 22 February 1958, pp. 124-5.

89. Alan Warde, *Consensus and Beyond. The Development of Labour Party Strategy since the Second World War*, Manchester University Press, Manchester 1992, pp. 58-9 and Stephen Haseler, *The Gaitskellites. Revisionism in the British Labour Party 1951-64*, Macmillan, London 1969, p. 143.

90. See the full text in F. W. S. Craig, *British General Election Manifestos 1900-1974*, the points highlighted here are to be found on pp. 223-31.

91. Warde, op. cit., p. 59.

92. Elliott, *Labourism and the English Genius*, pp. 17, 69.

93. Haseler, op. cit., p. 147.

94. P. M. Williams, op. cit., pp. 330-4.

95. Haseler, op. cit., p. 169.

96. Warde, op. cit., p. 63.

97. Cited in David Howell, *British Social Democracy. A Study in Development and Decay*, Croom Helm, London 1976, p. 229.

98. Ibid., p. 206.

99. Ibid., pp. 187-8 and Mark Jenkins, *Bevanism. Labour's High Tide: The Cold War and the Democratic Mass Movement*, Spokesman, Nottingham 1979, pp. 294-6.

100. For a fuller treatment see D. Sassoon, op. cit., Part II.

101. P. Togliatti, 'L'Intervista a *Nuovi argomenti*', originally in *Nuovi argomenti*, no. 20, May-June 1956; now reprinted in Togliatti, *On Gramsci and Other Writings*, p. 129.

102. Togliatti, *On Gramsci*, p. 121.

103. Togliatti, *Intervista*, p. 116; he reaffirmed this in his report to the Eighth Congress of the PCI at the end of 1956 – see his 'Rapporto all' VIII Congresso', reprinted in *Nella democrazia e nella pace verso il socialismo*, Editori Riuniti, Rome 1963, p. 32.

104. The entire debate has been reprinted in Giuseppe Vacca (ed.), *Gli intellettuali di sinistra e la crisi del 1956*, Editori Riuniti, Rome 1978. Calvino's words can be found on p. 28, Pizzorno's on p. 122.

105. Cited in D. Sassoon, op. cit., p. 106.

106. Denis Healey, 'Communism and Social Democracy', originally in *The New Leader*, 16 September 1957; now reprinted in Healey, *When Shrimps Learn to Whistle*, p. 67.

107. Fundamental to this development were the two papers Togliatti gave at the first major Gramsci conference, organized in 1958: 'Leninism in the Theory and Practice of Gramsci' and 'Gramsci and Leninism', in Togliatti, *On Gramsci*.

108. See Carl A. Linden, *Khrushchev and the Soviet Leadership 1957-1964*, Johns Hopkins Press, Baltimore MD 1966, pp. 109-11 and Zdeněk Mlynár, 'Khrushchev's Policies as a Forerunner of the Prague Spring', in R. F. Miller and F. Féhér (eds), *Khrushchev and the Communist World*, Croom Helm, London 1984.

109. N. S. Khrushchev, *Report to the 22nd Congress of the Communist Party of the Soviet Union*, Soviet Booklet no. 80, London 1961, p. 71.

110. Ibid., p. 69.

111. For Kuusinen's role, see Fedor Burlatsky, *Khrushchev and the First Russian Spring*, Weidenfeld and Nicolson, London 1991.

112. Cited in Linden, op. cit., pp. 106-7.

113. Roger Garaudy, 'A propos de la "voie italienne vers le socialisme"', *Cahiers du communisme*, Vol. 33, no. 1, January 1957.

114. Martelli, 'L'année 1956', in Bourderon et al., *Le PCF*, p. 416. This collection of articles is a rare attempt by French communist historians to write a reasonably objective and self-critical history of their own party.

115. Extracts from Duclos' speech can be found in Bourderon et al., op. cit., p. 436.

116. See comments in Jacques Fauvet, *Histoire du Parti communiste français*. Vol. II: *Vingt-cinq ans de drames 1939–1965*, Fayard, Paris 1965, pp. 283–90.

117. See the PCF journal *Cahiers du communisme* and, in particular, Paul Courtieu and Jean Houdremont, 'La paupérisation absolue de la classe ouvrière', Vol. 31, no. 4, April 1955, pp. 437–60; Maurice Thorez, 'Nouvelles données sur la paupérisation. Réponse à Mendès-France', Vol. 31, nos 7–8, July–August 1955, pp. 803–26; Henri Krasucki, 'Salaire réel et valeur de la force de travail' and Henri Chauveau, 'Le parti, la SFIO et la paupérisation', Vol. 33, no. 3, March 1957, pp. 352–68. See also Thorez's speech to the Fourteenth Congress of the PCF in July 1956, in *XIV Congrès du Parti communiste français, Numero special des 'Cahiers du Communisme'*, July–August 1956, where he designated pauperization 'the principal question examined by the Central Committee' (p. 54); and his 'Encore une fois la paupérisation!', *Cahiers du communisme*, Vol. 33, no. 5, May 1957, pp. 657–86.

118. Pierre Rimbert, in his 'Pourquoi le Parti communiste a-t-il lancé la campagne de la paupérisation?', in *La revue socialiste*, no. 95, March 1956, p. 297, believes that the variations in intensity were entirely due to tactical requirements; this may be so, but it does not follow that the entire campaign was engendered for purely tactical reasons.

119. Maurice Larkin, *France since the Popular Front. Government and People 1936–86*, Clarendon Press, Oxford 1988, p. 174.

120. The main SFIO writer on this issue was Pierre Rimbert, a Marxist socialist who, in his five-part essay 'Paupérisation et niveau de vie des travailleurs' (*La revue socialiste*, nos 89 to 94, 1955–56), concluded that 'the standard of living of the workers in spite of ups and downs, has without doubt improved in the last 150 years. This improvement is the result of the economic and political struggle of the working class' (no. 94, February 1956, p. 153).

121. Citation in Nicole Racine, 'Le parti communiste français devant les problème idéologiques et culturels', in *Le communisme en France*, Cahiers de la Fondation Nationale des Sciences Politiques, Colin, Paris 1969, pp. 173–4.

122. Claudio Di Toro and Augusto Illuminati, *Prima e dopo il centrosinistra*, Edizioni Ideologie, Rome 1970, p. 117.

123. See Antonio Giolitti, *Riforme e rivoluzione*, Einaudi Editore, Turin 1957 and 'Le basi scientifiche della politica economica', in *Passato e presente*, Vol. 1, no. 1, January–February 1957. For a critique from the left see Di Toro and Illuminati, op. cit., pp. 116–36.

124. Pietro Ingrao, 'Risposta a Lombardi', *Rinascita*, no. 21, 23 May 1964.

125. See the Resolution of the Central Committee of the PCI, Rome, 29 April 1961, in Barca, Botta and Zevi (eds), *I comunisti e l'economia italiana 1944–1974*, p. 233.

126. The answer will not be found in David Caute's *Communism and the French Intellectuals 1914–1960*, André Deutsch, London 1964, which relies more on tiresome moralism than on analysis. Tony Judt, in his *Past Imperfect. French Intellectuals, 1944–1956*, University of California Press, Berkeley 1992, writes much in the same vein, but with greater restraint and scholarship.

127. Judt, op. cit., p. 195.

128. Jean-Paul Sartre, *The Communists and Peace*, trans. I. Clephane, Hamish Hamilton, London 1969, p. 123

129. Larkin, op. cit., p. 244.

130. Tiersky, *French Communism 1920–1972*, p. 177.

131. Martelli, op. cit., pp. 409–10.

132. Joly, *The French Communist Party and the Algerian War*, pp. 47, 109, 112.

133. Ibid., p. 44.

134. This is the plausible opinion of both Touchard, *La gauche en France depuis 1900*,

pp. 331–2 and Joly, op. cit., p. 73, though neither author explains that the PCF supported the right of Algeria to self-determination.

135. Maurice Thorez, 'Rapport d'Activité du Comité Central', in *XIV Congrès du Parti communiste français*, p. 36; see also Laurent Casanova, 'A propos de la guerre d'Algérie: L'internationalisme prolétarien et l'intérêt national', *Cahiers du communisme*, Vol. 33, no. 4, April 1957, pp. 467–80.

136. Portelli, *Le socialisme français tel qu'il est*, pp. 77–8.

137. Larkin, op. cit., p. 159.

138. This opinion is upheld and substantiated by Ligou, *Histoire du socialisme en France 1871–1961*, p. 567.

139. Touchard, op. cit., p. 303.

140. Ibid., pp. 305–6.

141. See Jules Moch's announcement in *Le Populaire*, 9 March 1959; reprinted and translated as 'Socialist Re-Thinking in France', *Socialist International Information*, Vol. 9, nos 13–14, 28 March 1959, p. 201–2.

142. See Portelli's analysis in op. cit., pp. 78–82.

143. Albert Gazier, a member of the Mollet government, in 'French Socialist on Algeria', *Socialist International Information*, Vol. 6, no. 31, 4 August 1956, p. 538.

144. Philip, op. cit., p. 161. Similar electoral considerations must have occurred to the French communists.

145. R. W. Johnson, *The Long March of the French Left*, Macmillan, London 1981, pp. 141–2.

146. Roger Garaudy, 'De Gaulle et le fascisme', *Cahiers du communisme*, Vol. 34, no. 6, June 1958, p. 899; see also Léo Figueres, 'Non! au plébiscite', *Cahiers du communisme*, Vol. 34, no. 7, July 1958, pp. 990–1006.

147. Adereth, *The French Communist Party*, pp. 170–71.

148. See Roger Bourderon, 'PCF, pouvoir gaulliste, union, 1958–1964', in Bourderon et al., op. cit., p. 456.

11. The Return of the Left

1. See figures in Derek H. Aldcroft, *The European Economy 1914–1980*, Croom Helm, London 1980, p. 163.

2. Michael E. Porter, *The Competitive Advantages of Nations*, Free Press, New York 1990, p. 279.

3. On the crucial importance of the expansion in food production, see Thomas McKeown, *The Modern Rise of Population*, Edward Arnold, London 1976, p. 161.

4. Maier, *In Search of Stability*, Cambridge University Press, Cambridge 1987, p. 223.

5. Fritz W. Scharpf, *Crisis and Choice in European Social Democracy*, Cornell University Press, Ithaca NY and London 1991, p. 24

6. I have used Gordon Smith's figures: see his *Politics in Western Europe*, Heinemann, London 1972, p. 388.

7. Douglas A. Hibbs Jr, 'Political Parties and Macroeconomic Policy', *American Political Science Review*, Vol. 71, no. 4, December 1977, pp. 1467–987; the UK time series analyses can be found on pp. 1476–82.

8. David R. Cameron, 'The Expansion of the Public Economy: A Comparative Analysis', *American Political Science Review*, Vol. 72, no. 4, December 1978, pp. 1249–53.

9. Ibid., p. 1256.

10. Ibid., p. 1258.

11. An argument amply theorized by Mancur Olson Jr in his *The Logic of Collective Action: Public Goods and the Theory of Groups*, Harvard University Press, Cambridge MA 1965.

12. Korpi, 'Power, Politics, and State Autonomy in the Development of Social Citizenship.

13. Wilensky, 'Leftism, Catholicism, and Democratic Corporatism: The Role of Political Parties in Recent Welfare State Development', in Flora and Heidenheimer (eds), *The Development of Welfare States in Europe and America*, p. 355.

14. This proposition is advanced in Peter Baldwin's excellent analysis, *The Politics of Social Solidarity. Class Bases of the European Welfare State 1875–1975*, Cambridge University Press, Cambridge 1990.

15. Richard Rose, *Do Parties Make a Difference?*, 2nd edn, Macmillan, London 1984, p. xxxi.

16. Ibid., p. 147.

17. V. I. Lenin, *The State and Revolution* (1917), trans. Robert Service, Penguin Books, Harmondsworth 1992: 'A democratic republic is the best possible shell for capitalism' (p. 14) and 'the democratic republic is the shortest path to the dictatorship of the proletariat' (p. 64).

18. Alastair H. Thomas, 'Denmark: Coalitions and Minority Governments', in Eric C. Browne and John Dreijmanis (eds), *Government Coalitions in Western Democracies*, Longman, New York and London 1982, p. 109.

19. Marcel Liebman, 'The Crisis of Belgian Social Democracy', in Ralph Miliband and John Saville (eds), *The Socialist Register 1966*, Merlin Press, London 1966, pp. 55–8

20. The classical analysis of the Dutch system as an instance of a 'consociational' political system is Arend Lijpart's *The Politics of Accommodation. Pluralism and Democracy in the Netherlands*, University of California Press, Berkeley 1968. For a debate on this, see Ronald A. Kieve, 'Pillars of Sand: A Marxist Critique of Consociational Democracy in the Netherlands', *Comparative Politics*, Vol. 13, no. 3, April 1981, pp. 313–37 and Herman Bakvis, 'Towards a Political Economy of Consociationalism. A Commentary on Marxist Views of Pillarization in the Netherlands', *Contemporary Politics*, Vol. 16, no. 3, April 1984.

21. Rudy B. Andeweg, T. H. van der Tak and K. Dittrich, 'Government Formation in the Netherlands', in Richard T. Griffiths, *The Economy and Politics of the Netherlands since 1945*, Martinus Nijhoff, The Hague 1980, pp. 235–7; Ken Gladdish, *Governing from the Centre. Politics and Policy-Making in the Netherlands*, C. Hurst and Co., London 1991, pp. 51–2.

22. Gladdish, op. cit., p. 53.

23. Melanie Ann Sully, *Continuity and Change in Austrian Socialism. The Eternal Quest for the Third Way*, Columbia University Press, New York 1982, p. 183.

24. Jelavich, *Modern Austria*, pp. 285–6.

25. Alastair H. Thomas, 'Social Democracy in Denmark', in William E. Paterson and Alastair H. Thomas (eds), *Social Democratic Parties in Western Europe*, Croom Helm, London 1977, p. 245.

26. Franco Cazzola, 'Consenso e opposizione nel parlamento italiano. Il ruolo del PCI dalla I alla IV Legislatura', *Rivista Italiana di Scienza Politica*, January 1972, pp. 80–5.

27. Sully, op. cit., p. 191.

28. Ibid.

29. See the description of this process in ibid., pp. 195ff.

30. Jelavich, op. cit., p. 301.

31. Arend Lijphart, 'Typologies of Democratic Systems', originally in *Comparative Political Studies*, Vol. 1, pp. 3–44; later reprinted in Arend Lijphart (ed.), *Politics in Europe*, Prentice Hall, Englewood Cliffs NJ 1969, where the definition cited can be found on p. 63. In fairness, Lijphart admits that his model has limited predictive powers; see p. 64.

32. Maurice Parodi, *L'économie et la société française depuis 1945*, Colin, Paris 1981, pp. 58–61.

33. Andrew Shonfield, *Modern Capitalism. The Changing Balance of Public and Private Power*, Oxford University Press, Oxford 1965, pp. 130–1.

34. Ibid., pp. 132–3.

35. Pierre Birnbaum, 'The State in Contemporary France', in Richard Scase (ed.), *The State in Western Europe*, Croom Helm, London 1980 p. 109.

36. Peter Hennessy, *Whitehall*, Fontana, London 1990, p. 186.

37. For a more positive assessment of the success of MinTech in identifying the 'right' sectors to modernize (i.e. computers, electronics, machine tools and telecommunications), see Richard Coopey, 'The White Heat of Scientific Revolution', *Contemporary Record. The Journal of Contemporary British History*, Vol. 5, no. 1 Summer 1991, p. 119.

38. Cited in Frank L. Wilson, *The French Democratic Left 1963–1969. Towards a Modern Party System*, Stanford University Press, Stanford CA 1971, p. 66.

39. See *Cahiers du communisme*, Vol. 38, no. 12, December 1962, pp. 34–5.

40. Adereth, *The French Communist Party*, p. 174.

41. See text of resolution in *Cahiers du Communisme* Vol. 38, no. 12, December 1962, p. 363. see also Georges Lavau, 'The Effects of Twenty Years of Gaullism on the Parties of the Left', in William G. Andrews and Stanley Hoffmann (eds), *The Impact of the Fifth Republic on France*, State University of New York Press, Albany NY 1981, p. 96.

42. Ronald L. Meek, 'Marx's "Doctrine of Increasing Misery"', *Science and Society*, Vol. XXVI, no. 4, Autumn 1962, p. 440.

43. Touchard, *La gauche en France depuis 1900*, pp. 336–7.

44. See Thorez's remark and Roger Garaudy's main report in *Cahiers du Communisme*, Vol. 38, no. 7–8, July–August 1962.

45. Paul Boccara, *Etudes sur le capitalisme monopoliste d'Etat, sa crise et son issue*, Editions Sociales, Paris 1974, p. 50; this volume includes the author's introduction and the main paper to the conference of Choisy-le-Roi, published in June–July 1966 in the party journal *Economie et Politique*.

46. Boccara, op. cit., p. 32.

47. François Hincker, *Le parti communiste au carrefour. Essai sur quinze ans de son histoire 1965–1981*, Albin Michel, Paris 1981, pp. 60–1.

48. Jeannine Verdès-Leroux, *Le réveil des somnanbules. Le parti communiste, les intellectuels et la culture (1956–1985)*, Fayard/Editions de Minuit, Paris 1987, p. 269.

49. Louis Althusser, 'What Must Change in the Party', *New Left Review*, no. 109, May–June 1978, p. 36. This was originally published in four parts in *Le Monde* on 24, 25, 26 and 27 April 1978.

50. François Mitterrand, *Ma part de vérité. De la rupture à l'unité*, Fayard, Paris 1969, pp. 55–6.

51. See Waldeck Rochet's statement in *L'Humanité*, 8 March 1966, cited in Jean Poperen, *L'Unité de la Gauche 1965–1973*, Fayard, Paris 1975, p. 35.

52. Lavau, op. cit., pp. 110–11.

53. For a sympathetic account of Defferre's campaign, see F. L. Wilson, op. cit., pp. 109–34.

54. On the PSU and the clubs, see Touchard, op. cit., pp. 317–22.

55. Wilson, op. cit., pp. 142–4.

56. See Togliatti's speech to the Central Committee meeting of February 1962, in *Opere scelte*, p. 1048.

57. Giovanni XXIII (John XXIII), *Pacem in Terris*, Pontificia Editrice Arcivescovile Daverio, Milan 1963, pp. 54–5.

58. Togliatti, 'Il destino dell'uomo', in *Opere scelte*, pp. 1123–35.

59. Giorgio Amendola, 'Il socialismo in occidente', *Rinascita*, 7 November 1964 and 'Ipotesi sulla riunificazione', *Rinascita*, 28 November 1964.

60. Now in Ingrao, *Masse e potere*, p. 182.

61. The Ingrao–Amendola debate and its repercussions throughout the PCI are examined in Grant Amyot, *The Italian Communist Party. The Crisis of the Popular Front Strategy*, Croom Helm, London 1981.

62. Lewis Minkin, *The Labour Party Conference. A Study in the Politics of Intra-Party Democracy*, Allen Lane, London 1978, pp. 126, 52.

63. The passages removed from the final draft were leaked to *New Left Review*, which published them under the title 'Missing Signposts' in *New Left Review*, no. 12, November–December 1961, pp. 9–10.

64. P. M. Williams, *Hugh Gaitskell*, p. 383–4.

65. The Labour Party, *Signposts for the Sixties. A Statement of Labour's Home Policy Accepted by the 60th Annual Conference of the Labour Party at Blackpool*, 2–6 October 1961, p. 7.

66. Ibid., p. 8.

67. Ibid., p. 9.

68. The Labour Party could have also pointed out that in the Parliament elected in 1959 one in five of the 365 Conservative MPs had been educated at Eton, a concentration of the crop of a single school unparalleled in any legislature in Europe. See figures in R. W. Johnson, 'The British Political Elite, 1955–1972', *Archives européennes de sociologie*, Vol. XIV, no. 1, 1973, p. 46.

69. Labour Party, *Signposts*, p. 13

70. Ibid., p. 14.

71. Ibid., p. 15.

72. Extracts from a speech made at Birmingham, 19 January 1964, reprinted in Harold Wilson, *The New Britain*, Penguin, Harmondsworth 1964, pp. 9–10.

73. Ibid., p. 14.

74. See report in *Socialist International Information*, Vol. 11, no. 41, 14 October 1961.

75. See comments on Adenauer in William Carr, *A History of Germany 1815–1985*, Edward Arnold, London 1987, p. 376 and Gordon A. Craig, *The Germans*, Penguin, Harmondsworth 1984, p. 48.

76. Smith, *Democracy in Western Germany*, p. 115.

77. Data on strikes in Flora (ed.), *State, Economy and Society in Western Europe 1815–1975*, p. 715.

78. Leaman, *The Political Economy of West Germany, 1945–1985*, p. 173.

79. See M. Balfour, *West Germany*, p. 213.

80. Cited in Scharpf, op. cit., p. 206.

81. Balfour, op. cit., pp. 215–16.

82. Bark and Gress, *A History of West Germany*, Vol. 2, p. 127.

83. Smith, op. cit., p. 118.

84. Charles Feinstein, 'Benefits of Backwardness and Costs of Continuity', in Graham with Seldon (eds), *Government and Economics in the Postwar World*, p. 289. Such conclusions had been reached by Eric Hobsbawm in his classic *Industry and Empire*, Penguin, Harmondsworth 1969 (1st edn, 1968).

85. Robert J. Lieber, 'Labour in Power: Problems of Political Economy', in B. Brown (ed.), *Eurocommunism and Eurosocialism*, p. 188.

86. These costs are explained by Susan Strange in her *Sterling and British Policy. A Political Study of an International Currency in Decline*, Oxford University Press, Oxford 1971, pp. 237–43.

87. Andrew Graham and Wilfred Beckerman, 'Introduction: Economic Performance and the Foreign Balance', in Wilfred Beckerman (ed.), *The Labour Government's Economic Record 1964–1970*, Duckworth, London 1972, pp. 13–14.

88. Alec Cairncross and Barry Eichengreen, *Sterling in Decline*, Blackwell, Oxford 1983, p. 166.

89. Richard N. Cooper, 'The Balance of Payments', in Richard E. Caves (ed.), *Britain's Economic Prospects*, Brookings Institution and Allen and Unwin, Washington and London 1968, pp. 168–71.

90. Harold Wilson, *The Labour Government 1964–70. A Personal Record*, Weidenfeld and Nicolson and Michael Joseph, London 1971, p. xvii.

91. Stuart Holland, *The Global Economy: From Meso to Macroeconomics*, Weidenfeld and Nicolson, London 1987, p. 205.

92. Wilson, *The Labour Government*, p. 37.

93. W. Beckerman, 'Objectives and Performance: An Overall View' in Beckerman, op. cit., p. 62. The writer was an economic adviser to the government at the DEA from 1964–65 and the Board of Trade 1967–69.

94. Wilson, *The Labour Government*, p. 513.

95. Hennessy, op. cit., pp. 186–8.

96. Andrei S. Markovits, *The Politics of the West German Trade Unions. Strategies of Class and Interest Representation in Growth and Crisis*, Cambridge University Press, Cambridge 1986, p. 109 and Schneider, *A Brief History of the German Trade Unions*, p. 305.

97. Leaman, op. cit., pp. 176–7.

98. Cited in Jon Clark, 'Concerted Action in the Federal Republic of Germany', *British Journal of Industrial Relations*, Vol. 17, no. 2, July 1979, p. 242.

99. Michael Hudson, '"Concerted Action": Wages Policy in West Germany, 1967–1977', *Industrial Relations Journal*, Vol. 11, no. 4, September–October 1980, p. 13.

100. J. Clark, op. cit., p. 249.

101. Hudson, op. cit., p. 10.

102. Markovits, op. cit., p. 106.

103. Leaman, op. cit., pp. 194–5.

104. Scharpf, op. cit., pp. 123–6.

105. J. Clark, op. cit., p. 256.

106. Massimo D'Angelillo, 'Crisi economica e identità nazionale nella politica di governo della socialdemocrazia tedesca', in Paggi (ed.), *Americanismo e riformismo*, p. 232.

107. Missiroli, *La questione tedesca*, p. 110.

108. See Mary Nolan and Charles F. Sabel, 'The Social Democratic Reform Cycle in Germany', in Esping-Andersen and Friedland (eds), *Political Power and Social Theory*, Vol. 3, p. 165.

109. Gerard Braunthal, *The West German Social Democrats, 1969–1982. Profile of a Party in Power*, Westview Press, Boulder CO 1983, p. 243.

110. Bark and Gress, op. cit., p. 56

111. Miller and Potthoff, *A History of German Social Democracy*, p. 187.

112. Roy Jenkins, 'British Labour – Retrospect and Prospect', *Socialist Information International*, Vol. 20, no. 11, November 1970, p. 157.

113. Hyhynen, 'The Popular Front in Finland', p. 11.

114. Ibid., p. 13

115. Ibid., pp. 13–15.

116. I owe this information on the PCF's view of Sweden to notes provided to me by Jean Rony in May 1989.

117. Perry Anderson, 'Sweden: Mr. Crosland's Dreamland', *New Left Review*, no. 7, January–February 1961, p. 6.

118. Sully, op. cit., p. 202.

119. Jelavich, op. cit., pp. 302–3.

120. Sully, op. cit., p. 203.

12. The Establishment of a Foreign
Policy Consensus

1. Hanspeter Neuhold, 'Background Factors of Austria's Neutrality', in Karl E. Birnbaum and Hanspeter Neuhold (eds), *Neutrality and Non-alignment in Europe*, Wilhelm Braumüller, Vienna 1982, p. 58.

2. See Bruno Kreisky's speech at the Helsinki Conference of the Socialist International of 25–27 May 1971, text in *Socialist International Information*, Vol. 21, nos 5–6, May-June 1971, p. 101.

3. Cited in H. Wilson, *The Labour Government 1964–70*, pp. 404–5.

4. See extracts of his speech in *Socialist International Information*, Vol. 20, no. 1, January 1970, p. 7.

5. David Reynolds, *Britannia Overruled. British Policy and World Power in the 20th Century*, Longman, London 1991, p. 228.

6. Ibid., pp. 229–30.

7. Cited in C. F. Brand, *The British Labour Party*, p. 365.

8. Bouvier, *Zwischen Godesberg und Grosser Koalition*, p. 76.

9. Joel M. Fisher and Sven Groennings, 'German Electoral Politics in 1969', *Government and Opposition*, Vol. 5, no. 2, Spring 1970, p. 223.

10. Bouvier, op. cit., p. 214 and Paterson, *The SPD and European Integration*, pp. 142–4.

11. Stephen Padgett and William E. Paterson, *A History of Social Democracy in Postwar Europe*, Longman, London 1991, p. 237.

12. Michael Kreile, 'Ostpolitik Reconsidered', in Ekkehart Krippendorff and Volker Rittberger (eds), *The Foreign Policy of West Germany. Formation and Contents*, Sage, London and Beverly Hills 1980, p. 128.

13. Willy Brandt, *The State of the Nation*, speech at the SPD party conference at Dortmund, 1 June 1966, SPD, Bonn, n.d.; p. 6 in English-language text.

14. The documented evidence for this is in Klaus Gotto, 'Adenauers Deutschland und Ostpolitik 1954–1963', in Rudolf Morsey and Konrad Repgen (eds), *Adenauer-Studien Bd.III. Untersuchungen und Dokumente zur Ostpolitik und Biographie*, Mainz 1974, pp. 3–91.

15. Kreile, op. cit., p. 125.

16. Wolfram F. Hanrieder, *Germany, America, Europe. Forty Years of German Foreign Policy*, Yale University Press, New Haven CT 1989, p. 195; see also pp. 200, 355.

17. William E. Paterson, 'The Ostpolitik and Régime Stability in West Germany', in Roger Tilford (ed.), *The Ostpolitik and Political Change in Germany*, Saxon House, Farnborough 1975, p. 33.

18. Klaus von Beyme 'The Ostpolitik in the West German 1969 Elections', in *Government and Opposition*, Vol. 5, no. 2, Spring 1970, pp. 194–5.

19. See the analysis by Reinhold Roth, *Aussenpolitische Innovation und Politische Herrschaftssicherung*, Meisenheim 1976; summarized in Kreile, op. cit., p. 131.

20. Peter H. Merkl, 'The Role of Public Opinion in West German Foreign Policy', in Wolfram F. Hanrieder (ed.), *West German Foreign Policy: 1949–1979*, Westview Press, Boulder CO 1980, pp. 164–6.

21. Henry Kissinger, *White House Years*, Little, Brown, Boston 1979, pp. 529–30.

22. Willy Brandt, *A Peace Policy for Europe*, Weidenfeld and Nicolson, London 1969, p. 24.

23. Hanrieder, *Germany, America, Europe*, p. 203.

24. Kreile, op. cit., p. 124.

25. Roger Morgan, 'The *Ostpolitik* and West Germany's External Relations', in Tilford, op. cit., p. 96.

26. Brandt, op. cit., p. 45.

27. Richard Nixon, 'President's Message on Foreign Policy for the 1970s', *National Diplomacy 1965–1970, Congressional Quarterly*, May 1970, pp. 118–47.

28. Ibid., pp. 118–19.

29. See 'On the Differences between Comrade Togliatti and Us', *Peking Review*, 4 January 1963 and 'More on the Differences between Comrade Togliatti and Us', *Peking Review*, 15 March 1963.

30. Palmiro Togliatti, 'Per l'unità del movimento operaio e comunista internazionale', report to the Central Committee meeting of 21–23 April 1964, in Palmiro Togliatti, *Sul movimento operaio internazionale*, Editori Riuniti, Rome 1964, pp. 319, 353 and 355.

31. Palmiro Togliatti, 'Yalta Memorandum', in his *On Gramsci and Other Writings*, p. 295.

32. Ibid., p. 286.

33. I likewise excessively amplified and read too much into what were still tentative suggestions; see my *The Strategy of the Italian Communist Party*, pp. 115–16.

34. Joan Barth Urban, *Moscow and the Italian Communist Party. From Togliatti to Berlinguer*, I.B. Tauris, London 1986, pp. 254–5.

35. For instances of the PCI's increasingly independent line in cultural policy, see Donald L. M. Blackmer, *Unity in Diversity. Italian Communism and the Communist World*, MIT Press, Cambridge MA 1968, pp. 340–49.

36. Ibid., pp. 396–7; Urban, op. cit., p. 254.

37. See the reliable reconstruction of this side of Ostpolitik by a German social democratic foreign affairs adviser and specialist, Heinz Timmermann, *I comunisti italiani*, De Donato Editore, Bari 1974, pp. 23–52; originally in the journal *Osteuropa*, no. 6, 1971, pp. 388–99.

38. Giorgio Amendola, *Lotta di classe e sviluppo economico dopo la Liberazione*, Editori Riuniti, Rome 1962, p. 86.

39. For a wider treatment of this question, see my 'The Italian Communist Party's European Strategy' and *The Strategy of the Italian Communist Party*, p. 114.

40. Ugo Pecchioli, 'Le forze democratiche e l'Europa del Mec', *Critica Marxista*, Vol. 4, no. 3, May–June 1966, p. 13.

41. Giorgio Amendola, speech to the European Parliament, 12 March 1969, in *I comunisti italiani al parlamento europeo – Interventi dei parlamentari della delegazione PCI-PSIUP-Ind. Sinistra*, December 1972.

42. See Giorgio Amendola, *I comunisti e l'Europa*, Editori Riuniti, Rome 1971, p. 80.

43. Philippe Robrieux, *Histoire intérieure du parti communiste 1945–1972*, Vol. 2, Fayard, Paris 1981, p. 639.

44. Jacques Kahn, 'Monopoles, nations et Marché commun', *Cahiers du communisme*, Vol. 42, no. 4, April 1966, p. 19.

45. Fernand Clavau, 'La crise du Marché commun', *Cahiers du communisme*, Vol. 41, no. 6, September 1965, p. 116.

46. Charles Fiterman, 'Les communistes, l'Europe et la nation française', *Cahiers du communisme*, Vol. 42, no. 4, April 1966, p. 30.

47. Ibid., pp. 35–8.

48. Newman, *Socialism and European Unity*, pp. 66–8.

49. Jens-Otto Krag, 'Why Denmark Applied to Join the Common Market', *Socialist International Information*, Vol. 11, no. 35, 2 September 1961, pp. 533–4.

50. Featherstone, *Socialist Parties and European Integration*, p. 88.

51. A. H. Thomas, 'Social Democracy in Denmark', in Paterson and Thomas (eds), *Social Democratic Parties in Western Europe*, p. 252.

52. Data in Nils Örvik (ed.), *Fears and Expectations. Norwegian Attitudes Towards European Integration*, Universitetsforlaget, Oslo 1972, pp. 12–14.

53. On the Belgian and Dutch parties, see Featherstone, op. cit., pp. 28–9, 271–2.

54. Paterson, *The SPD and European Integration*, pp. 145–6, 151.

55. Bruno Kreisky, 'Social Democracy's Third Historical Phase', *Socialist International Information*, Vol. 20, no. 5, May 1970, pp. 65–7.

56. Jens-Otto Krag, 'The Danish View', *Socialist International Information*, Vol. 21, nos 5–6, May–June 1971, p. 104.

57. Willy Brandt 'The German View', *Socialist International Information*, Vol. 21, nos 5–6, May–June 1971, p. 100.

58. Trygve Bratteli, 'The Norwegian View' in *Socialist International Information*, Vol. 21, no. 5–6, May–June 1971, p. 104.

59. Ibid., p. 102.

60. Ibid.

61. P. M. Williams, *Hugh Gaitskell*, p. 394.

62. Newman, op. cit., p. 214.

63. P. M. Williams, op. cit., pp. 407–9.

64. Newman, op. cit., p. 216 and Lieber, *British Politics and European Unity*, p. 252.

65. The most devastating – if one-sided – indictment of the Left's attitude towards the EEC came from the ranks of the New Left: see Tom Nairn, 'The Left Against Europe?', special number of *New Left Review*, no. 75, September–October 1972.

66. Bulletin No. 4, Common Market Safeguard Campaign, March 1971, cited in Tom Nairn, 'British Nationalism and the EEC', *New Left Review*, no. 69, September–October 1971, p. 8.

67. Lieber, op. cit., pp. 245–6.

68. See extracts of his press conference of 27 November 1967 in Uwe Kitzinger, *The Second Try. Labour and the EEC*, Pergamon Press, Oxford 1968, pp. 311–17.

69. Pierre Viansson-Ponté, *Histoire de la République Gaullienne*. Vol. II: *Le temps des orphelins*, Fayard, Paris 1971, p. 325.

70. The gist of this was communicated to Wilson by de Gaulle himself; see H. Wilson, *The Labour Government 1964–70*, p. 409.

71. Ibid., pp. 340, 410–13; see also Ben Pimlott, *Harold Wilson*, HarperCollins, London 1992, pp. 439–40.

72. H. Wilson, op. cit., pp. 337, 443; see also Crossman, *The Diaries of a Cabinet Minister*, Vol. II, Hamish Hamilton and Jonathan Cape, London 1976, p. 532.

73. Cited in Crossman, op. cit., Vol. I, p. 574; see also Barbara Castle's diaries cited in Pimlott, op. cit., p. 433.

74. Newman, op. cit., pp. 204–6.

75. L. J. Robins, *The Reluctant Party: Labour and the EEC 1961–75*, Hesketh, Ormskirk 1979, p. 59.

76. See Gallup poll results in Kitzinger, op. cit., p. 172.

77. Lieber, op. cit., p. 251 and Robins, op. cit., p. 50.

78. This was Anthony Wedgwood Benn's perception at the time, when he was pro-European; see Pimlott, op. cit., p. 440.

79. Newman, op. cit., pp. 206–8; see also Lieber, op. cit., p. 264 and Robins, op. cit., p. 58.

80. Cited in Robins, op. cit., p. 58.

81. H. Wilson, op. cit. pp. 247–8.

82. Alfred Grosser, *The Western Alliance. European–American Relations since 1945*, Macmillan, London 1978, p. 238.

83. Brandt, *My Life in Politics*, p. 364.

84. In his White House memoirs, Kissinger represented himself as having realized that the US could not win in Vietnam after a short trip there in 1965: op. cit., p. 232.

85. Ibid., p. 424.

86. Ibid., p. 92.

87. Ibid., p. 1453.

88. This symbolism was pointed out to me for the first time, in these or similar words, by Alphonso Lingis in his open lecture, *The Will to Revolution*, on 22 May 1970, at the Pennsylvania State University.

89. For the effects on the British Labour Party, see Pimlott, op. cit., p. 393.

90. This is hinted in ibid., p. 387.

91. H. Wilson, op. cit., p. 404.

92. Malraux, *Les chênes qu'on abat* ... , p. 106.

93. Kissinger, op. cit., p. 91.

94. Samuel Brittan, 'Some Common Market Heresies', in *Journal of Common Market Studies*, Vol. 8, no. 4, June 1970, p. 294.

95. Kissinger, op. cit., p. 933.

96. Ibid., pp. 957-8.

97. See Pietro Nenni, 'La relazione di Pietro Nenni' in Partito socialista italiano, *35° Congresso Nazionale*, Rome, 25-29 October 1963, Edizioni *Avanti!*, Milan 1964, p. 55: Nenni's words found their way into the majority resolution; see p. 589.

98. Benzoni, 'I socialisti e la politica estera', in Bonanni (ed.), *La politica estera della Repubblica italiana*, p. 946.

99. 'Relazione di Francesco Di Martino', in Partito socialista italiano (PSI), *37° Congresso e l'unificazione socialista, Roma, ottobre 1966*, ed. Maurizio Punzo, Edizioni La Squilla, Bologna 1976, p. 34.

100. 'Il documento sul Vietnam presentato da Enriques Agnoletti', in PSI, *37° Congresso*, p. 135.

101. 'Carta dell'unificazione socialista', in ibid., p. 227.

102. *The Action Programme of the Czechoslovak Communist Party. Prague, April 1968*, Spokesman Pamphlet no. 8, Nottingham n.d. (1970), p. 22.

103. Urban, op. cit., pp. 255-7.

104. See, for instance, the lucid analyses of Zdeněk Mlynár, one of the foremost Czech reformers, expelled from the CP in 1969, *Praga questione aperta*, De Donato Editore, Bari 1976, p. 209.

105. Richard Löwenthal, 'Communism: Clear Position of German Social Democracy', *Socialist International Information*, Vol. 20, no. 12, 1970, pp. 171-3.

106. Hincker, *Le parti communiste au carrefour*, p. 81.

107. Hanrieder, op. cit., pp. 192-3; see also, on the same point, R. Morgan, op. cit., p. 99.

108. D. Reynolds, op. cit., p. 215.

109. Pimlott, op. cit., p. 383.

110. Michael M. Harrison, 'Consensus, Confusion and Confrontation in France: The Left in Search of a Defense Policy', in Andrews and Hoffmann (eds), *The Impact of the Fifth Republic on France*, p. 269.

111. Philip G. Cerny, *The Politics of Grandeur. Ideological Aspects of de Gaulle's Foreign Policy*, Cambridge University Press, Cambridge 1980, pp. 261, 265.

112. IFOP poll cited in Pierre Bourdieu, *Distinction. A Social Critique of the Judgement of Taste*, Routledge and Kegan Paul, London 1984, p. 427.

113. Pierre Villon, 'Les contradictions de la politique étrangère gaulliste', *Cahiers du communisme*, Vol 41, no. 1, January 1965, pp. 32-3.

114. Cerny, op. cit., p. 267.

13. The Revival of Working-class
Militancy 1960–73

1. Gérard Adam, 'Etude statistique des grèves de Mai–Juin 1968, *Revue française de science politique*, Vol. 20, no. 1, February 1970, p. 118.

2. J. Bergmann et al., *Gewerkschafen in der Bundesrepublik*, Frankfurt, EVA 1975; cited in Klaus von Beyme, *Challenge to Power. Trade Unions and Industrial Relations in Capitalist Countries*, Sage, London and Beverly Hills 1980, p. 156.

3. See David Soskice, 'Strike Waves and Wage Explosions, 1968–1970: An Economic Interpretation', in Colin Crouch and Alessandro Pizzorno (eds), *The Resurgence of Class Conflict in Western Europe since 1968*. Vol. 2: *Comparative Analyses*, Holmes and Meier, New York 1978, especially pp. 221–2, 232–4.

4. Ibid., pp. 223–4.

5. See Michael Shalev, 'The Problem of Strike Measurement', in Crouch and Pizzorno (eds), op. cit., Vol. 1, pp. 321–8 and Pierre Dubois, 'New Forms of Industrial Conflict' in ibid. Vol. 2, pp. 1–35.

6. Dubois, op. cit., p. 9

7. Soskice, op. cit., p. 237.

8. See Georges Marchais' article in *L'Humanité* of 3 May, analysed in Claude Journès, 'Les interprétations de Mai 68', in *Pouvoirs*, no. 39, 1986, p. 27.

9. See Edward Shorter and Charles Tilly, *Strikes in France 1830–1968*, Cambridge University Press, Cambridge 1974, p. 141.

10. Bruno Trentin, *Il Sindacato dei Consigli*, Editori Riuniti, Rome 1980, p. 14.

11. Ibid., p. 36.

12. Robert Lumley, *States of Emergency. Cultures of Revolt in Italy from 1968 to 1978*, Verso, London 1990, pp. 246–7.

13. Alessandro Pizzorno, *I soggetti del pluralismo. Classi Partiti Sindacati*, Il Mulino, Bologna 1980, p. 139.

14. See Luciano Lama, *Intervista sul sindacato*, Laterza, Rome-Bari 1976, p. 54, and *Il potere del sindacato*, Editori Riuniti, Rome 1978, p. 63.

15. Rainer Deppe, Richard Herding and Dietrich Hoss, 'The Relationship between Trade Union Action and Political Parties', in Crouch and Pizzorno (eds), op. cit., Vol. 2, p. 181.

16. Ibid., p. 184.

17. Lumley, op. cit., p. 251; Barkan, *Visions of Emancipation*, p. 89.

18. M. Donald Hancock, 'Sweden's Emerging Labor Socialism', in B. Brown (ed.), *Eurocommunism and Eurosocialism*, p. 326.

19. Tilton, *The Political Theory of Swedish Social Democracy*, p. 219.

20. The Norwegian book by Einar Thosrsud and F. E. Emery, *Industrielt Demokrati*, University of Oslo Press, Oslo 1964, was influential in Sweden. The two authors were members of a commission on industrial democracy appointed by the Norwegian Employers' Association and the Norwegian LO.

21. Tilton, op. cit., p. 226.

22. Richard B. Peterson, 'The Swedish Experience with Industrial Democracy', *British Journal of Industrial Relations*, Vol. 6, no. 2, July 1968, p. 201.

23. Lorwin, 'Labor Unions and Political Parties in Belgium', p. 252.

24. Ibid., pp. 250–1.

25. Ibid., p. 255.

26. Derek Robinson, 'Labour Market Policies', in Beckerman (ed.), *The Labour Government's Economic Record 1964–1970*, p. 308.

27. H. A. Turner, 'Collective Bargaining and the Eclipse of Incomes Policy: Retrospect,

Prospect and Possibilities', *British Journal of Industrial Relations*, Vol. 8, no. 2, July 1970, p. 201.

28. Ibid., p. 203.

29. See the summary of the report in the *British Journal of Industrial Relations*, Vol. 6, no.3, November 1968, pp. 275–86.

30. H. A. Turner, *Is Britain Really Strike Prone?: A Review of the Incidence, Character and Costs of Industrial Conflict*, Occasional Paper 20, Cambridge University Press, Cambridge, May 1969 argued against the popular orthodoxy, by suggesting that the evidence available precludes making international comparisons. *Contra* Turner and in defence of Donovan, see W. E. J. McCarthy, 'The Nature of Britain's Strike Problem', *British Journal of Industrial Relations*, Vol. 8, no. 2 July 1970, pp. 224–36. McCarthy was a member of the Donovan Commission.

31. Turner, 'Collective Bargaining and the Eclipse of Incomes Policy', p. 206.

32. Lewis Minkin, *The Contentious Alliance. Trade Unions and the Labour Party*, Edinburgh University Press, Edinburgh 1991, pp. 115–16.

33. Keith Middlemas, *Politics in Industrial Society. The Experience of the British System since 1911*, André Deutsch, London 1979, p. 440.

34. Susan Crosland, *Tony Crosland*, Jonathan Cape, London 1982, p. 202.

35. Middlemas, op. cit., p. 372.

36. Walther Müller-Jentsch, 'Strikes and Strike Trends in West Germany, 1950–1978', *Industrial Relations Journal* (UK), Vol. 12, no. 4, July–August 1981, pp. 36–7.

37. Fritz W. Scharpf, 'A Game-Theoretical Interpretation of Inflation and Unemployment in Western Europe', *Journal of Public Policy*, Vol. 7, no. 3, p. 172 and Müller-Jentsch, op. cit., p. 45.

38. See data in J. Clark, 'Concerted Action in the Federal Republic of Germany', p. 243.

39. Ibid.

40. Nolan and Sabel, 'The Social Democratic Reform Cycle in Germany', in Esping-Andersen and Friedland (eds), *Political Power and Social Theory*, p. 165.

41. Markovits, *The Politics of the West German Trade Unions*, pp. 203–5.

42. J. Clark, op. cit., p. 249.

43. R. J. Adams and C. H. Rummel, 'Workers' Participation in Management in West Germany: Impact on the Worker, the Enterprise and the Trade Union', *Industrial Relations Journal*, Vol. 8, no. 1, Spring 1977, p. 11.

44. Ibid., p. 14.

45. Jeff Bridgford, 'The Events of May. Consequences for Industrial Relations in France', in D. L. Hanley and A. P. Kerr (eds), *May '68: Coming of Age*, Macmillan, London 1989, p. 115.

46. Parodi, *L'économie et la société française depuis 1945*, pp. 210–11.

47. René Mouriaux, 'Trade Union Strategies After May 1968', in Hanley and Kerr (eds), op. cit., p. 121.

48. Ibid., p. 119.

49. Parodi, op. cit., pp. 215–16.

50. Touchard, *La gauche en France depuis 1900*, p. 352.

51. Markovits, op. cit., p. 124.

52. Jean-Daniel Reynaud, 'Trade Unions and Political Parties in France: Some Recent Trends', *Industrial and Labor Relations Review*, Vol. 28, no. 2, January 1975, p. 215.

53. R. W. Johnson, 'The British Political Elite, 1955–1972', p. 68.

54. Barry Hindess, *The Decline of Working Class Politics*, Paladin, London 1971, p. 9.

14. The Revival of Ideology and the Student Contestation

1. H. Wilson, *The Labour Government 1964-70*, p. 445.

2. Edward Short, 29 January 1969, *Parliamentary Debates (Hansard)*, Vol. 776, pp. 1371-2.

3. Bark and Gress, *A History of West Germany*, p. 126

4. Speech to the National Council of the Christian Democratic Party, 21 November 1968, in Aldo Moro, *L'intelligenza e gli avvenimenti. Testi 1959-1978*, Garzanti, Milan 1979, p. 223. Ten years later, Aldo Moro was kidnapped and murdered by young terrorists.

5. Richard Johnson, *The French Communist Party versus the Students*, Yale University Press, New Haven and London 1972, pp. 96-9.

6. For a provisional balance-sheet of Western Marxism as an intellectual tradition, see Perry Anderson, *Considerations on Western Marxism*, New Left Books, London 1976, especially chapter 3.

7. The words of Wolfdietrich Schnurre published in the journal *Ruf* in 1947 before it was prohibited by the Americans; cited in Heinz Ludwig Arnold, 'From Moral Affirmation to Subjective Pragmatism: The Transformation of German Literature since 1947', in Stanley Hoffmann and Paschalis Kitromilides (eds), *Culture and Society in Contemporary Europe*, Allen and Unwin, London 1981, p. 133.

8. Hans Magnus Enzensberger in *The Times Literary Review*, 1967, cited in Arnold, op. cit., p. 135.

9. Ronald Inglehart, *The Silent Revolution. Changing Values and Political Styles Among Western Publics*, Princeton University Press, Princeton NJ 1977, p. 265.

10. R. Roberts, *The Classic Slum*, Manchester 1971, cited in John Clarke et al., 'Subcultures, Cultures and Class', in Stuart Hall and Tony Jefferson, *Resistance through Rituals. Youth Subcultures in Post-war Britain*, Hutchinson, London 1977, p. 17.

11. Dora Russell, *The Tamarisk Tree. My Quest for Liberty and Love*, Virago, London 1977, p. 62.

12. Mary Quant, *Quant by Quant*, 1965, p. 74; cited in Tamar Horowitz, 'From Elite Fashion to Mass Fashion', *Archives européennes de sociologie*, Vol. XVI, no. 2, 1975, p. 284.

13. Sunil Khilnani, *Arguing Revolution. The Intellectual Left in Postwar France*, Yale University Press, New Haven CT and London 1993, p. 137.

14. Alain Touraine, *Le mouvement de Mai ou le communisme utopique*, Editions du Seuil, Paris 1968, pp. 9, 278.

15. Some sociologists directly involved in the protest perceived early on the novelty of the situation, without abandoning a critical perspective. For Italy, see Carlo Donolo's lucid 'La politica ridefinita. Note sul Movimento studentesco', in *Quaderni piacentini*, no. 35, July 1968. For later studies, see Sidney Tarrow, *Democracy and Disorder. Protest and Politics in Italy 1965-1975*, Clarendon Press, Oxford 1989, especially chapter 6, and Lumley, *States of Emergency*. There are no good comparative studies; David Caute's *Sixty-eight. The Year of the Barricades*, Hamish Hamilton, London 1988, lacks depth and analysis.

16. Giuseppe Chiarante, *La rivolta degli studenti*, Editori Riuniti, Roma 1968, p. 42.

17. John Vazey, *The Political Economy of Education*, Duckworth, London 1972, p. 85.

18. D. L. Hanley, A. P. Kerr and N. H. Waites, *Contemporary France. Politics and Society since 1945*, Routledge and Kegan Paul, London 1979, p. 261.

19. Vazey, op. cit., p. 87.

20. John Ardagh, *Germany and the Germans*, Penguin, Harmondsworth 1988, p. 205.

21. John Ardagh, *The New France. A Society in Transition 1945-1977*, Penguin, Harmondsworth 1977, p. 466.

22. Cited in Dorothy Pickles, *The Government and Politics of France*, Vol. 2, Methuen, London 1973, pp. 154-5.

23. Walter Laqueur, *Europe since Hitler. The Rebirth of Europe*, Penguin, Harmondsworth 1982, p. 294.

24. Pierre Bourdieu and Jean-Claude Passeron, *The Inheritors. French Students and Their Relation to Culture*, University of Chicago Press, Chicago and London 1979, p. 79.

25. Lasch, *The Minimal Self*, pp. 226–7.

26. See the remarks to this effect in Pascal Ory, 'The Concept of Generation as Exemplified by the Class of 68', in Hanley and Kerr, op. cit., p. 186.

27. Jürgen Habermas, *Towards a Rational Society*, trans. Jeremy J. Shapiro, Heinemann, London 1971, p. 42. This book first appeared in 1969.

28. Tarrow, op. cit., p. 147.

29. Bridgford, 'The Events of May', pp. 105–6.

30. Ernest Mandel, 'The Lessons of May 1968', *New Left Review*, no. 52, November–December 1968, p. 21.

31. Text of the interview in Jacques Sauvageot et al., *The Student Revolt. The Activists Speak*, Panther, London 1968, pp. 98–9.

32. Angelo Quattrocchi and Tom Nairn, *The Beginning of the End. France May 1968*, Panther, London 1968, pp. 7, 10.

33. From the bulletin of the Faculty of Medicine of Paris, 6 June 1968, in Centre de regroupement des informations universitaires, *Quelles université? Quelle société?*, Editions du Seuil, Paris 1968, p. 9.

34. Raymond Aron, *La révolution introuvable. Réflexions sur la Révolution de Mai*, Fayard, Paris 1968, p. 22.

35. Ibid., p. 31.

36. Ibid., p. 35.

37. Ibid., p. 54.

38. Mitterrand, *Ma part de vérité*, pp. 87–8.

39. Ibid., p. 90.

40. Philippe Bénéton and Jean Touchard, 'Les interpretations de la crise de mai–juin 1968', *Revue française de science politique*, Vol. 20, no. 3, June 1970, pp. 503–43.

41. Inglehart, op. cit., p. 273.

42. Adereth, *The French Communist Party*, p. 237.

43. Wilson, *The French Democratic Left 1963–1969*, pp. 186–7.

44. A. H. Thomas, 'Social Democracy in Denmark', pp. 251–2.

45. Knut Heidar, 'The Norwegian Labour Party: Social Democracy in a Periphery of Europe', in Paterson and Thomas (eds), op. cit., p. 298.

46. Inglehart, op. cit., p. 274.

47. Philip M. Williams and Martin Harrison, *Politics and Society in De Gaulle's Republic*, Longman, London 1971, p. 119.

48. Michel Rocard, *Le PSU et l'avenir socialiste de la France*, Editions du Seuil, Paris 1969, p. 52.

49. The theses are reproduced in Rocard, op. cit., pp. 124–82; the statement on the crisis of capitalism appears on p. 125

50. Ibid., p. 133.

51. Ibid., pp. 141–2.

52. Harvey G. Simmons, 'The French Socialist Opposition in 1969', *Government and Opposition*, Vol. 4, no. 3, 1969, p. 304.

53. Laurence Bell, 'May 68: Parenthesis or Staging Post in the Development of the Socialist Left?', in Hanley and Kerr, op. cit., p. 88.

54. Braunthal, *The West German Social Democrats, 1969–1982*, pp. 141ff.

55. Johnson, op. cit., pp. 48–55, and Hervé Hamon, ''68. The Rise and Fall of a Generation?', in Hanley and Kerr (eds), op. cit., p. 14.

56. See Lumley, op. cit., pp. 77–81.

57. Luigi Longo, 'Il movimento studentesco nella lotta anticapitalista', *Rinascita*, no. 8, 3 May 1968.

58. Giorgio Amendola, 'I comunisti e il movimento studentesco: necessità della lotta su due fronti', *Rinascita*, no. 23, 7 June 1968.

59. See Longo, op. cit. Longo's positions prevailed at the Congress of the PCI and its youth organization, the FGCI, held at Ariccia 29–30 November 1968; see the text of the main reports by Gian Franco Borghini and Achille Occhetto in a supplement to *Nuova Generazione*, no. 24, 1968, and the comments in Gianfranco Camboni and Danilo Samsa, *PCI e movimento degli studenti 1968–1973*, De Donato, Bari 1975, pp. 11–34.

60. Inglehart, op. cit., p. 263.

15. The Revival of Feminism

1. Raymond Williams (ed.), *May Day Manifesto 1968*, Penguin, Harmondsworth 1968; cf. the references to fatherless families on pp. 21–2.

2. Juliet Mitchell, 'Women: The Longest Revolution', *New Left Review*, no. 40, November–December 1966. This article can also be found reprinted in a book of the same title, *Women: The Longest Revolution*, Virago, London 1984.

3. Ibid., pp. 30–3.

4. Anna Coote and Beatrix Campbell, *Sweet Freedom*, 2nd edn, Basil Blackwell, Oxford 1987, p. 1. This rediscovery is also underlined by Renate Becker and Rob Burns, 'The Women's Movement in the Federal Republic of Germany', in *Contemporary German Studies*, *Occasional Papers no. 3*, Department of Modern Languages, Strathclyde 1987.

5. Olive Banks, *Becoming a Feminist. The Social Origins of 'First Wave' Feminism*, Wheatsheaf, Brighton 1986, p. 46.

6. Maïté Albistur and Daniel Armogathe, *Histoire du féminisme français*, Vol. 1, Edition des Femmes, Paris 1978, p. 333.

7. Cited in ibid., p. 331. See also an analysis of her demands in Joan Landes, *Women and the Public Sphere in the Age of the French Revolution*, Cornell University Press, Ithaca NY and London 1988, pp. 124–7 and Joan Wallach Scott, '"A Woman Who Has Only Paradoxes to Offer": Olympe de Gouges Claims Rights for Women', in Sara E. Melzer and Leslie W. Rabine (eds), *Rebel Daughters. Women and the French Revolution*, Oxford University Press, New York 1992, pp. 102–20.

8. Cited in Albistur and Armogathe, op. cit., Vol. 1, p. 333.

9. Mary Wollstonecraft, *The Rights of Woman*, Dent, Everyman's Library, London 1977, p. 209.

10. Ibid., pp. 214–15.

11. Landes, op. cit., p. 113.

12. Antoine de Condorcet, *Foundations of Social Choice and Political Theory*, trans. and ed. Iain McLean and Fiona Hewitt, Edward Elgar, Aldershot 1994, p. 335.

13. Cited in Ute Frevert, *Women in German History. From Bourgeois Emancipation to Sexual Liberation*, Berg, Oxford 1989, p. 11.

14. Irene Coltman Brown, 'Mary Wollstonecraft and the French Revolution or Feminism and the Rights of Men', in Siân Reynolds (ed.), *Women, State and Revolution*, Wheatsheaf, Brighton 1986, pp. 1–2.

15. On the diffusion of Mill's work, see the evidence in Richard J. Evans, *The Feminists*, Croom Helm, London 1977, pp. 18–19, 40.

16. John Stuart Mill, *The Subjection of Women*, Virago, London 1983, p. 1.

17. Ibid., p. 145

18. Alan Ryan, *J.S. Mill*, Routledge and Kegan Paul, London 1974.

19. See Wollstonecraft, op. cit., especially her criticisms of Rousseau on pp. 17–19, 30–1 and 86–90.

20. See Galvano Della Volpe's interpretation in his *Rousseau e Marx*, Editori Riuniti, Rome 1971, esp. pp. 38–42. This redistributive Rousseauian principle contrasts with Rousseau's conventionally misogynist views in *Emile* and other writings; see Diana Coole, *Women in Political Theory*, Wheatsheaf, Brighton 1988, pp. 103–32 and Umberto Cerroni, *Il rapporto uomo-donna nella civiltà borghese*, Editori Riuniti, Rome 1975, pp. 37–9. Joan Landes is kinder towards Rousseau and declares him 'far from a pedestrian misogynist'. See op. cit., p. 67. The most complete, if controversial, treatment of this fascinating issue is Joel Schwartz, *The Sexual Politics of Jean-Jacques Rousseau*, University of Chicago Press, Chicago 1984.

21. See Mike Gane, *Harmless Lovers? Gender, Theory and Personal Relationships*, Routledge, London and New York 1993, pp. 59–82.

22. Barbara Taylor, 'Mary Wollstonecraft and the Wild Wish of Early Feminism', *History Workshop*, no.33, Spring 1992.

23. Wollstonecraft, op. cit., pp. 113–14.

24. Ryan, op. cit., pp. 154–5.

25. Karl Marx, *Economic and Philosophic Manuscripts of 1844*, in *Early Writings*, trans. and ed. Tom Bottomore, McGraw-Hill, New York 1964, pp. 153–5; my emphasis.

26. Friedrich Engels, *The Origin of the Family, Private Property and the State*, Progress Publishers, Moscow 1968, p. 74.

27. August Bebel, *Woman in the Past, Present and Future*, Zwan Publications, London 1988, p. 7; this was the new title given by Bebel on the publication of the second edition in 1883. On the popularity of this text, see Hobsbawm, *Age of Empire*, p. 209 and Barrington Moore, Jr, *Injustice*, p. 210.

28. Cited in Albistur and Armogathe, op. cit., Vol. 1, p. 411.

29. Letter of 12 December 1868, in Karl Marx and Friedrich Engels, *Selected Correspondence 1846–1895*, Martin Lawrence, London 1934, p. 255.

30. Richard Stites, *The Women's Liberation Movement in Russia. Feminism, Nihilism, and Bolshevism, 1860–1930*, Princeton University Press, Princeton NJ 1978, pp. 7–8, 87.

31. Ghulam Murshid, *Reluctant Debutante: Response of Bengali Women to Modernization, 1849–1905*, Sahitya Samsad, Rajshahi University, 1983, pp. 49–50.

32. Bebel, op. cit., p. 5.

33. Letter of 12 September 1894, in *The Selected Letters of Bertrand Russell*. Vol. 1: *The Private Years (1884–1914)*, ed. Nicholas Griffin, Allen Lane, Penguin, Harmondsworth 1992, p. 114. He added, rather touchingly: 'Of course I know so little about the subject as yet that I may be mistaken, but I should love to go into it thoroughly.'

34. Frevert, op. cit., p. 141.

35. Karen Hagemann, 'La "question des femmes" et les rapports masculin–féminin dans la social-démocratie allemande sous la République de Weimar', *Le Mouvement Social*, no. 163, April–June 1993, pp. 25–44.

36. Barbara Taylor, *Eve and the New Jerusalem. Socialism and Feminism in the Nineteenth Century*, Virago, London 1983, p. 276.

37. Olive Schreiner, *Woman and Labour*, Virago, London 1978, p. 68.

38. Stites, op. cit., p. 35.

39. Bebel, op. cit., p. 115.

40. Ibid., pp. 226–7.

41. Coole, op. cit., p. 211.

42. Marta Bizcarrondo, 'Los origenes del feminismo socialista en España', in *La mujer en la historia de España*, Actas de las II jornadas de investigacion interdisciplinaria, Universidad Autonoma de Madrid, Madrid 1984, p. 139.

43. Bebel, op. cit., p. 113.

44. Patricia Penn Hilden, *Women, Work, and Politics. Belgium, 1830–1914*, Clarendon Press, Oxford 1993, p. 238.

45. Landauer, *European Socialism,* Vol. II, p. 1561.

46. Stites, op. cit., p. 236

47. See his report, 'The International Socialist Congress in Stuttgart', in V. I. Lenin, *Collected Works*, Vol. 13, Progress Publishers, Moscow 1972, pp. 89–91.

48. Hilden, op. cit., p. 243.

49. Cited in R. Evans, op. cit., p. 161.

50. Stites, op. cit., p. 237.

51. Clara Zetkin, *Selected Writings*, Philip S. Foner (ed.), International Publishers, New York 1984, p. 101.

52. Ibid., p. 99.

53. Ibid., p. 105. On this and the wider question of female suffrage and socialism, see Ellen Carol DuBois, 'Woman Suffrage and the Left: An International Socialist-Feminist Perspective', *New Left Review*, no. 186, March–April 1991, pp. 20–45.

54. Charles Sowerwine, *Sisters or Citizens? Women and Socialism in France since 1876*, Cambridge University Press, Cambridge 1982, p. 118.

55. Harriet Anderson, *Utopian Feminism. Women's Movements in fin-de-siècle Vienna*, Yale University Press, New Haven and London 1992, p. 42.

56. Ibid., p. 86.

57. Ibid., p. 89.

58. Cited by Maria Casalini in her 'Femminismo e socialismo in Anna Kuliscioff. 1890–1907', *Italia Contemporanea*, no. 143, June 1981, A wider treatment of Anna Kuliscioff can be found in Casalini's *La Signora del socialismo italiano. Vita di Anna Kuliscioff*, Editori Riuniti, Rome 1987.

59. In 'Il femminismo', *Critica Sociale*, 16 June 1897; cited in Claire LaVigna, 'The Marxist Ambivalence Toward Women: Between Socialism and Feminism in the Italian Socialist Party', in Marilyn J. Boxer and Jean H. Quataert (eds), *Socialist Women. European Socialist Feminism in the Nineteenth and Early Twentieth Centuries*, Elsevier, New York 1978, pp. 148–9.

60. See paper given by Maria Casalini at the conference '1892–1992. Percorsi e contrasti della sinistra italiana', organized by the Gramsci Foundation, 25 June 1992.

61. LaVigna, op. cit., p. 159.

62. Sowerwine, op. cit., p. 114. On Pelletier, see also Christine Bard (ed.), *Madeleine Pelletier (1874–1939). Logique et infortunes d'un combat pour l'égalité*, Côté-femmes éditions, Paris 1992 and Claudine Mitchell, 'Madeleine Pelletier (1874–1939): The Politics of Sexual Oppression', *Feminist Review*, no. 33, Autumn 1989, pp. 72–92.

63. James E. McMillan, *Housewife or Harlot. The Place of Women in French Society 1870–1940*, Harvester, Brighton 1981, p. 91.

64. Sowerwine, op. cit., p. 118.

65. Cited in ibid., p. 24.

66. Ibid. See also Albistur and Armogathe, op. cit., Vol. 2, pp. 558–9.

67. Sowerwine, op. cit., p. 109

68. Magraw, *A History of the French Working Class*, Vol. 2, p. 95.

69. See McMillan, op. cit., p. 14.

70. Hilden, op. cit., p. 268.

71. Beryl Williams, 'Kollontai and After: Women in the Russian Revolution, in Siân Reynolds (ed.), *Women, State and Revolution*, Wheatsheaf, Brighton, 1986, pp. 65–6; see also Stites, op. cit., p. 213.

72. V. I. Lenin, 'International Working Women's Day', in *Collected Works*, Vol. 32, Progress Publishers, Moscow 1965, p. 161.

73. Editorial, *The Past Before Us. Twenty Years of Feminism*, special issue of *Feminist Review*, no. 31, Spring 1989, p. 3.

74. See the evidence in R. Evans, op. cit., pp. 31–2.

75. Beate Fieseler, 'The Making of Russian Female Social Democrats, 1890–1917', *International Review of Social History*, Vol. 34, 1989, p. 208.

76. See Sowerwine's perceptive comments in op. cit., pp. 184–7.

77. McMillan, op. cit., p. 87.

78. Sheila Rowbotham, *Hidden from History*, Pluto Press, London 1973, p. 80.

79. Olive Banks, *Faces of Feminism*, Martin Robertson, Oxford 1981, p. 126.

80. Jill Liddington and Jill Norris, *One Hand Tied Behind Us. The Rise of the Women's Suffrage Movement*, Virago, London 1978, p. 210.

81. The Pankhursts' WSPU has remained the best-known suffragette organization. Liddington and Norris, op. cit., convincingly present the story of Millicent Fawcett's National Union as an antidote to the over-emphasis on the Pankhursts' importance. Rowbotham's now classic *Hidden from History* makes no mention of Millicent Fawcett's organization; obviously some people are always more hidden than others.

82. Liddington and Norris, op. cit., p. 258.

83. Lenin, op. cit., p. 162.

84. Bebel, op. cit., p. 102.

85. Wollstonecraft, op. cit., p. 152.

86. Bebel, op. cit., pp. 55–6.

87. See Coole, op. cit., p. 209.

88. Rosalind Coward, *Patriarchal Precedents. Sexuality and Social Relations*, Routledge and Kegan Paul, London 1983, pp. 168–9.

89. See text of the preamble in S. E. Finer (ed.), *Five Constitutions*, Penguin, Harmondsworth 1979, p. 275.

90. Claire Laubier (ed.), *The Condition of Women in France 1945 to the Present*, Routledge, London and New York 1990, p. 1.

91. Finer, op. cit., p. 198.

92. Frevert, op. cit., p. 278.

93. Cited in Eva Kolinsky, *Women in West Germany*, Berg, Oxford 1989, p. 45.

94. Text of the questionnaire originally in *L'Humanité*, 27 July 1946; reprinted in Laubier (ed.), op. cit., p. 15.

95. Kolinsky, op. cit., pp. 200–1.

96. Gisèle Charzat, *Les Françaises sont-elles des citoyennes?*, Editions Denoël, Paris 1972, p. 25, citing the work of M. Dogan and J. Narbonne, 'Les Françaises face à la politique', *Cahiers de la Fondation Nationale des Sciences Politiques*, no. 72.

97. Charzat, op. cit., p. 28.

98. Ibid., p. 29.

99. P. M. Williams, *Crisis and Compromise*, pp. 95–6.

100. Joni Lovenduski, *Women and European Politics. Contemporary Feminism and Public Policy*, Wheatsheaf, Brighton 1986, p. 125.

101. R. W. Johnson, 'The British Political Elite, 1955–1972', pp. 55–6.

102. Miriam Mafai, *L'apprendistato della politica. Le donne italiane nel dopoguerra*, Editori Riuniti, Rome 1979, pp. 50–1.

103. Ibid., pp. 103–5.

104. Judith Hellman, *Journeys among Women. Feminism in Five Italian Cities*, Polity Press, Cambridge 1987, p. 36.

105. Palmiro Togliatti, 'Discorso alla conferenza delle donne comuniste', Rome 2–5 June 1945, in *Opere*, Vol. 5, p. 151.

106. Ibid., p. 153.

107. Ibid., p. 157.

108. Palmiro Togliatti, 'Discorso alle delegate comuniste alla Conferenza dell'UDI', 8 September 1946, Rome, in *L'emancipazione femminile*, Editori Riuniti, Rome 1973, p. 62.

109. J. Hellman, op. cit., pp. 199–200.

110. Laura Lilli and Chiara Valentini, *Care compagne. Il femminismo nel PCI e nelle organizzazioni di massa*, Editori Riuniti, Rome 1979.

111. Ibid., pp. 52–3.

112. Ibid., p. 65

113. Hellman, op. cit., especially pp. 97, 120, 134 and 171–2.

114. See her conversation with Jean-Paul Sartre in *l'Arc*, no. 61, 1975, cited in Albistur and Armogathe, op. cit., Vol. 2, p. 631.

115. Laubier (ed.), op. cit., p. 17.

116. Cited in Albistur and Armogathe, op. cit., Vol. 2, p. 632.

117. Simone de Beauvoir, *Le deuxième sexe*, Vol. 1, Gallimard, Paris 1968, p. 285.

118. Ibid., p. 16.

119. Ibid., Vol. 2, pp. 494–5, 498.

120. For a perceptive explanation of this connection, see Genevieve Lloyd, *The Man of Reason. 'Male' and 'Female' in Western Philosophy*, Methuen, London 1984, pp. 96–102; see the criticisms of de Beauvoir on pp. 100–1.

121. Jean-Paul Sartre, *Being and Nothingness*, trans. Hazel E. Barnes, Washington Square Press, New York 1966, p. 671; see also pp. 654–80.

122. Frigga Haug, 'Lessons from the Women's Movement in Europe, *Feminist Review*, no. 31, Spring 1989, p. 108.

123. Germaine Greer, *The Female Eunuch*, Paladin, London 1991, p. 44.

124. Ibid., pp. 132–40.

125. Ibid., pp. 90–2.

126. Ibid., pp. 68–9.

127. Ibid., p. 212.

128. Ibid., pp. 130–1.

129. Betty Friedan, *The Feminine Mystique*, W. W. Norton, New York 1963, p. 15.

130. Ibid., p. 375.

131. Shulamith Firestone, *The Dialectic of Sex. The Case for a Feminist Revolution*, Paladin, London 1971, p. 124.

132. Ibid., p. 19; emphasis in original.

133. Kate Millett, *Sexual Politics*, Doubleday, New York 1970, p. 33.

134. Ibid., p. 38.

135. Ibid., p. 44.

136. Ibid., p. 233.

137. Coote and Campbell, op. cit., p. 20.

138. Elaine Marks and Isabelle de Courtivron (eds), *New French Feminisms*, Harvester, Brighton 1981, p. 33.

139. Monique Wittig, *The Straight Mind and Other Essays*, Harvester Wheatsheaf, Hemel Hempstead 1992, pp. 15–16.

140. Cited in Coote and Campbell, op. cit., p. 242.

141. Swasti Mitter, *Common Fate, Common Bond. Women in the Global Economy*, Pluto Press, London 1986, p. 15.

142. For British data, see Catherine Hakim, 'Grateful Slaves and Self-Made Women: Fact and Fantasy in Women's Work Orientations', *European Sociological Review*, Vol. 7, no. 2, September 1991, p. 105; as well as her 'Segregated and Integrated Occupations: A New

Approach to Analysing Social Change', *European Sociological Review*, Vol. 9, no. 3 , December 1993, pp. 308, 310.

143. Greer, op. cit., p. 335; see also pp. 13–14.

144. Becker and Burns, op. cit., p. 6.

145. Cited in Claire Duchen, *Feminism in France. From May '68 to Mitterrand*, Routledge and Kegan Paul, London 1986, p. 7.

146. Cited in Frevert, op. cit., p. 293.

147. Extracts of interview in Marks and de Courtivron (eds), op. cit., p. 111.

148. Frevert, op. cit., p. 296.

149. Coote and Campbell, op. cit., p. 3.

150. Duchen, op. cit., p. 10.

151. Victoria Greenwood and Jock Young, *Abortion in Demand*, Pluto Press, London 1976, p. 26.

152. Coote and Campbell, op. cit., p. 153.

153. Ibid., p. 9.

16. The Crisis and the Left: An Overview

1. Marx, *Capital*, Vol.1, p. 763.

2. Ibid., *Capital*, Vol. 3, p. 249.

3. Jean Fourastié, *Les trentes glorieuses ou la révolution invisible de 1946 à 1975*, Fayard, Paris 1979.

4. Robert Z. Lawrence and Charles L. Schultze (eds), *Barriers to European Growth. A Transatlantic View*, Brookings Institution, Washington DC 1987, p. 1.

5. Gottfried Bombach, *Post-war Economic Growth Revisited*, Elsevier Science, Amsterdam 1985, p. 105.

6. Angus Maddison, *Dynamic Forces in Capitalist Development. A Long-Run Comparative View*, Oxford University Press, Oxford 1991, p. 131.

7. Herbert Giersch, Karl-Heinz Paqué and Holger Schmieding, *The Fading Miracle. Four Decades of Market Economy in Germany*, Cambridge University Press, Cambridge 1992, p. 218; Scharpf, *Crisis and Choice in European Social Democracy*, p. 50; Edmond Malinvaud, 'The Rise of Unemployment in France' *Economica*, Vol. 53, 1986, Supplement to no. 210, *Unemployment*, p. S198.

8. Maddison, op. cit., p. 155.

9. Stephen A. Marglin, 'Lessons of the Golden Age: An Overview', in Marglin and Schor (eds), *The Golden Age of Capitalism*, p. 19 and the essay by A. Glyn, A. Hughes, A. Lipietz and A. Singh, 'The Rise and Fall of the Golden Age', in ibid., p. 73. See also Edmond Malinvaud, 'Wages and the Unemployed', *Economic Journal*, Vol. 92, no. 365, March 1982, p. 1, and Michael Bruno and Jeffrey D. Sachs, *Economics of Worldwide Stagflation*, Basil Blackwell, Oxford 1985, p. 167.

10. Examples of such indictments can be found in Lawrence and Schultze (eds), op. cit., p. 7.

11. Norman Mackenzie (ed.), *Conviction*, MacGibbon and Kee, London 1959, p. 15.

12. Thomas Balogh, *The Irrelevance of Conventional Economics*, Weidenfeld and Nicolson, London 1982, p. 47.

13. Maddison, op. cit., p. 187.

14. Esping-Andersen, *The Three Worlds of Welfare Capitalism*, p. 182.

15. Jim Tomlinson, *Monetarism: Is There an Alternative?*, Basil Blackwell, Oxford 1986, p. 97.

16. Denis Healey, *The Time of My Life*, Michael Joseph, London 1989, p. 401.

17. Kevin Done, 'Windfall wilts away', Survey on Norway, *Financial Times*, 23 June 1986, p. i.

18. For Milton Friedman's influential redefinition of this relationship, see his 'The Role of Monetary Policy', *American Economic Review*, Vol. 58, 1968, pp. 1–17.

19. A. W. Phillips' classic statement on the unemployment/inflation relation (the Phillips curve) is 'The Relation between Unemployment and the Rate of Change of Money Wage Rates in the United Kingdom, 1861–1957', *Economica*, Vol. 25, 1958, pp. 283–99.

20. Paul R. Krugman, 'Slow Growth in Europe: Conceptual Issues', in Lawrence and Schultze (eds), op. cit., p. 58.

21. See the evidence in Robert J. Flanagan, 'Labor Market Behavior and European Economic Growth', in Lawrence and Schultze (eds), op. cit., p. 177.

22. Patrick Minford, *Unemployment: Cause and Cure*, Basil Blackwell, Oxford 1985, p. 34.

23. Robert M. Solow, 'Unemployment: Getting the Questions Right', in *Economica*, Vol. 53, 1986, Supplement to no. 210, *Unemployment*, p. S33.

24. Paul R. Krugman, *The Age of Diminished Expectations*, rev. edn, MIT Press, Cambridge MA 1994, p. 34.

25. See Charles L. Schultze, 'Real Wages, Real Wage Aspirations, and Unemployment in Europe', in Lawrence and Schultze (eds), op. cit., pp. 230–89 and the comments by Jacques R. Artus, pp. 292–5 and Charles R. Bean, pp. 295–9. See also C. R. Bean, R. Layard and S. J. Nickell, 'The Rise in Unemployment: A Multi-country Study', *Economica*, Vol. 53, 1986, Supplement to no. 210, *Unemployment*, pp. S1–S22, who argue that demand factors and wages cannot be separated (p. S19). In the same issue of *Economica*, however, R. Layard and S. J. Nickell argue that most of the unemployment after 1979 in the UK has been due to a fall in demand; see 'Unemployment in Britain', p. S146.

26. Rudiger Dornbusch, Giorgio Basevi, Olivier Blanchard, Willem Buiter and Richard Layard, 'Macroeconomic Prospects and Policies for the European Community', in Olivier Blanchard, Rudiger Dornbusch and Richard Layard (eds), *Restoring Europe's Prosperity: Macroeconomic Papers from the Centre for European Policy Studies*, MIT Press, Cambridge MA and London 1986, pp. 13–14.

27. Bernard Donoughue, *Prime Minister. The Conduct of Policy under Harold Wilson and James Callaghan*, Jonathan Cape, London 1987, p. 146.

28. Maddison, op. cit., p. 110.

29. See Göran Therborn, 'Does Corporatism Really Matter? The Economic Crisis and Issues of Political Theory', *Journal of Public Policy*, Vol. 7, Part 3, July–September 1987, pp. 259–84.

30. See Minford, op. cit.; Herbert Giersch, *Liberalisation for Faster Economic Growth*, Occasional Paper no. 74, Institute of Economic Affairs, London 1986, pp. 14–15.

31. Andrea Boltho, 'Western Europe's Economic Stagnation', in *New Left Review*, no. 201, September–October 1993, pp. 65–6.

32. Minford, op. cit., pp. 6–7.

33. Ibid., p. 128.

34. OECD, *Historical Statistics 1960–1989*, Paris 1991.

35. Göran Therborn, *Why Some People Are More Unemployed than Others*, Verso, London 1986, pp. 64–5.

36. Richard Layard, Giorgio Basevi, Olivier Blanchard, Willem Buiter and Rudiger Dornbusch, 'Europe: The Case for Unsustainable Growth', in Blanchard, Dornbusch and Layard (eds), op. cit., pp. 48–9.

37. See, for instance, Glyn et al., op. cit., p. 82.

38. Assar Lindbeck and Dennis J. Snower, 'Wage Setting, Unemployment and Insider–Outsider Relations' *American Economic Review*, Vol. 76, no. 2, May 1986, pp. 235–6.

39. Krugman, op. cit., p. 64.

40. See the contribution by R. Layard and S. J. Nickell, 'Performance of the British Labour Market', in Blanchard, Dornbusch and Layard (eds), and Lindbeck and Snower, op. cit., pp. 235–9.

41. Giersch, Paqué and Schmieding, op. cit., p. 200.

42. Robert Gilpin, *The Political Economy of International Relations*, Princeton University Press, Princeton NJ 1987, pp. 135–41. See also Strange, *Casino Capitalism*, pp. 6–8.

43. This view found its best-known adherent in the OECD McCracken Report: Paul McCracken et al., *Towards Full Employment and Price Stability: A Report to the OECD by a Group of Independent Experts*, OECD, Paris 1977.

44. Bruno and Sachs, op. cit., p. 7.

45. Scharpf, op. cit., p. 41; see also the introduction in Marglin and Schor (eds), op. cit.

46. Giersch Paqué and Schmieding, op. cit., pp. 189–90.

47. Bruno and Sachs, op. cit., p. 122.

48. Solow, op. cit., p. S23.

49. Therborn, *Why Some People* ... , p. 92 and Scharpf, op. cit.

50. Peter J. Katzenstein, *Small States in World Markets. Industrial Policy in Europe*, Cornell University Press, Ithaca NY and London 1985, p. 207.

51. Data (April 1994), reported in *The European*, 6–12 May 1994, p. 19. Source: Datastream.

52. Perry Anderson, Introduction to Perry Anderson and Patrick Camiller (eds), *Mapping the West European Left*, Verso, London 1994 and Herbert Kitschelt, *The Transformation of European Social Democracy*, Cambridge University Press, Cambridge 1994, p. 1.

17. Social Democracy in Small Countries

1. Bob Rowthorn and Andrew Glyn, 'The Diversity of Unemployment Experience since 1973', in Marglin and Schor (eds), *The Golden Age of Capitalism*, p. 245.

2. Antonio Missiroli, 'Tra Waldheim e la Cee: Democrazia consociativa e crisi economica in Austria', in *Annali Sinistra Europea 1988–1989*, Franco Angeli, Milan 1989, p. 307.

3. Richard S. Katz and Peter Mair (eds), *Party Organizations. A Data Handbook on Party Organizations in Western Democracies, 1960–1990*, Sage, London 1992, p. 41.

4. Sully, *Continuity and Change in Austrian Socialism*, p. 209.

5. See Kurt Richard Luther, 'Consociationalism, Parties and the Party System' *West European Politics*, Vol. 15, no. 1, January 1992, p. 54. Of course, the ÖVP was equipped with a similar range of associations.

6. Sully, 'Austrian Social Democracy', in Paterson and Thomas (eds), *The Future of Social Democracy*, 1986, p. 165.

7. Missiroli, op. cit., p. 305.

8. Katzenstein, *Small States in World Markets*, p. 77. The storing up of bad debts became quite common throughout the banking system of most advanced countries in the 1980s.

9. Paulette Kurzer, 'The Internationalization of Business and Domestic Class Compromises: A Four Country Study', *West European Politics*, Vol. 14, no. 4, October 1991, p. 11.

10. Scharpf, op. cit., p. 57.

11. Raimund Loew, 'The Politics of the Austrian "Miracle"', *New Left Review*, no. 123, September–October 1980, p. 75.

12. Scharpf, op. cit., pp. 56–8.

13. Sully, 'Austrian Social Democracy', p. 166.

14. Jelavich, *Modern Austria*, p. 305.

15. Sully, *Continuity and Change*, p. 208.

16. Ibid., p. 219.

17. Sully, 'Austrian Social Democracy', p. 157.

18. Wolfgang C. Müller, 'The Catch-all Party Thesis and the Austrian Social Democrats', *German Politics*, Vol. 1, no. 2, August 1992, p. 186.

19. Sully, *Continuity and Change*, p. 225.

20. See the reluctant praise lavished on Kreisky by one of his critics, Raimund Loew, in op. cit., p. 76.

21. Felix Kreissler, 'Le parti socialiste Autrichien entre le nouveau programme (Mai 1978) et les nouvelles elections générales (Mai 1979)' in *Austriaca*, Vol. 8, 1979, pp. 36–7.

22. Sully, *Continuity and Change*, p. 201.

23. Cited in Felix Kreissler, 'Un bilan de cinq années de gouvernement socialiste. Reformes et "Sozialpartnerschaft" (1970–1975)' in *Austriaca*, no. 1, 1975, p. 39. See also Sully, *Continuity and Change*, p. 204.

24. Sully, *Continuity and Change*, p. 232

25. Kreissler, 'Un bilan ... ', p. 50.

26. Jelavich, op. cit., pp. 305–7.

27. Scharpf, op. cit., p. 58.

28. Kreissler, 'Un bilan ... ' pp. 34–5.

29. Sully, *Continuity and Change*, pp. 206, 228.

30. See the praise for the Austrian model in Giles Radice and Lisanne Radice, *Socialists in the Recession. The Search for Solidarity*, Macmillan, London 1986, p. 97. Even Ian Birchall, author of a Trotskyist critique of social democracy, grudgingly accepts that 'there were real reforms' in Austria; see his *Bailing Out the System. Reformist Socialism in Western Europe 1944–1985*, Bookmarks, London 1986, p. 200.

31. Wolfgang C. Müller, 'Economic Success without an Industrial Strategy: Austria in the 1970s', *Journal of Public Policy*, Vol. 3, no. 1, February 1983, p. 123.

32. Katzenstein, op. cit., pp. 76–7.

33. Scharpf, op. cit., p. 67.

34. Fritz Plasser, Peter A. Ulram and Alfred Grausgruber, 'The Decline of "*Lager* mentality" and the New Model of Electoral Competition in Austria', *West European Politics*, Vol. 15, no. 1, January 1992, p. 29.

35. Volkmar Lauber 'Changing Priorities in Austrian Economic Policy', *West European Politics*, Vol. 15, no. 1, January 1992, p. 156.

36. Ibid., pp. 157–8.

37. Wolfgang C. Müller, 'Privatising in a Corporatist Economy: The Politics of Privatisation in Austria', *West European Politics*, Vol. 11, no. 4, October 1988, pp. 105, 109.

38. Lauber, op. cit., p. 159.

39. Peter Gerlich, 'Deregulation in Austria', in *European Journal of Political Research*, Vol. 17, no. 2, 1989, pp. 209–22.

40. Lauber, op. cit., p. 166.

41. Judy Dempsey, 'Austria's working class trade unionism coming to an end', *Financial Times*, 7 October 1987.

42. Patrick Blum, 'An attractive deal is needed', Survey on Austria, *Financial Times*, 10 November 1993, p. iii.

43. R. Kent Weaver, 'Political Foundations of Swedish Economic Policy', in Barry Bosworth and Alice M. Rivlin (eds), *The Swedish Economy*, Brookings Institution, Washington DC 1987, pp. 303–4.

44. Olsson, 'Swedish Communism Poised Between Old Reds and New Greens', p. 369.

45. OECD, *Economic Outlook, Historical Statistics 1960–1989*, p. 40.

46. Kurzer, op. cit., p. 12.

47. Erik Lundberg, 'The Rise and Fall of the Swedish Model', *Journal of Economic Literature*, Vol. 23, March 1985, p. 3.

48. Porter, *The Competitive Advantages of Nations*, p. 343.

49. Gøsta Esping-Andersen, 'The Making of a Social Democratic Welfare State', in Klaus Misgeld, Karl Molin and Klas Åmark (eds), *Creating Social Democracy. A Century of the Social Democratic Labor Party in Sweden*, Pennsylvania State University Press, University Park PA, 1992, p. 50.

50. Ibid., p. 54.

51. Korpi, *The Democratic Class Struggle*, pp. 210, 225.

52. Tilton, *The Political Theory of Swedish Social Democracy*, pp. 223–6.

53. Esping-Andersen, op. cit., p. 59.

54. Lundberg, op. cit., p. 21.

55. See Scharpf's lucid description of these developments in op. cit., pp. 94–7.

56. Scharpf, op. cit., pp. 97–8 and Lundberg, op. cit., p. 25.

57. Roger Henning, 'Industrial Policy or Employment Policy? Sweden's Response to Unemployment', in Richardson and Henning (eds), *Unemployment: Policy Responses of Western Democracies*, p. 197.

58. Scharpf, op. cit., pp. 99–100.

59. Kjell Lundmark, 'Welfare State and Employment Policy: Sweden', in Kenneth Dyson and Stephen Wilks (eds), *Industrial Crisis*, Blackwell, Oxford 1983, p. 232.

60. David Arter, 'A Tale of Two Carlssons: The Swedish General Elections of 1988', *Parliamentary Affairs*, Vol. 42, no. 1, January 1989, p. 94.

61. Hans Bergström, 'Sweden's Politics and Party System at the Crossroads', *West European Politics*, Vol. 14, no. 3, July 1991, pp. 11–12.

62. See Ingemar Elander and Stij Montin, 'Decentralization and Control: Central–Local Government Relations in Sweden', *Policy and Politics*, Vol. 18, no. 3, July 1990 and Buci-Glucksmann and Therborn, *Le défi social-democrate*, pp. 232–3.

63. Arne Ruth, 'The Second New Nation: The Mythology of Modern Sweden', *Daedalus*, Spring 1984, p. 90.

64. Lundberg, op. cit., p. 24.

65. Rowthorn and Glyn, op. cit., p. 252.

66. Lundberg, op. cit., p. 21.

67. See the *Programme of the Swedish Social Democratic Party adopted by the 1975 Party Conference*, Socialdemokraterna, Stockholm 1975, p. 17; English-language version.

68. Lundberg, op. cit., p. 25.

69. Kristina Ahlén, 'Swedish Collective Bargaining Under Pressure: Inter-union Rivalry and Incomes Policies', *British Journal of Industrial Relations*, Vol. 27, no. 3, November 1989, p. 337.

70. Ahlén, op. cit., p. 334.

71. Robert Taylor, 'Swedes' pay deal breaks old mould', *Financial Times*, 30 April 1988.

72. Ahlén, op. cit., pp. 340–1.

73. Gary Burtless, 'Taxes, Transfers and Swedish Labor Supply', in Bosworth and Rivlin (eds), op. cit., p. 189. Strictly speaking, Swedish part-time workers cannot be compared with those of other countries because the Swedish definition of part-time work includes all those who work fewer than thirty hours a week; elsewhere, the cut-off point is usually twenty hours.

74. William J. Baumol, 'Macroeconomics of Unbalanced Growth: The Anatomy of Urban Crisis', *American Economic Review*, Vol. 57, no. 3, June 1967, pp. 419–20.

75. Robert Bacon and Walter Eltis, *Britain's Economic Problem: Too Few Producers*, London, Macmillan 1978 – a work primarily concerned with the UK, where it provided a justification

for cuts in public spending. See the critique in *Economic Journal*, Vol. 89, June 1979: George Hadjimatheou and A. Skouras, 'Britain's Economic Problem: The Growth of the Non-Market Sector?', pp. 392–401 and Bacon and Eltis's reply, pp. 402–15.

76. Barry Bosworth and Robert Z. Lawrence, 'Economic Goals and the Policy Mix', in Bosworth and Rivlin (eds), op. cit., p. 105.

77. Lundberg, op. cit., p. 27.

78. This figure is reached by adding the 8.5 per cent of unemployed to the 5 per cent of the workforce on training schemes; see *Financial Times*, Survey on Sweden, 21 December 1993, p. ii.

79. Peter Garpenby, 'The Transformation of the Swedish Health Care System, or The Hasty Rejection of the Rational Planning Model', *Journal of European Social Policy*, Vol. 2, no. 1, 1992, pp. 17–31.

80. Jane Jenson and Rianne Mahon, 'Representing Solidarity: Class, Gender and the Crisis in Social-Democratic Sweden', *New Left Review*, no. 201, September–October 1993, p. 92.

81. See the interview with the SAP leader Ingvar Carlsson, Survey on Sweden, *Financial Times*, 21 December 1993, p. v.

82. Hugh Carnegy, 'Reluctant to walk the gangplank', *Financial Times*, 4 November 1993, p. 19, and 'Sweden shows effects of painful cure', *Financial Times*, 8 November 1993, p. 3.

83. Rudolf Meidner, 'Why Did the Swedish Model Fail?', in Ralph Miliband and Leo Panitch (eds), *Real Problems, False Solutions, Socialist Register, 1993*, London, Merlin Press, London 1993, pp. 225–6.

84. Dietmar Braun, 'Political Immobilism and Labour Market Performance: The Dutch Road to Mass Unemployment', *Journal of Public Policy*, Vol. 7, no. 3, July–September 1987, p. 319.

85. Göran Therborn, '"Pillarization" and "Popular Movements". Two Variants of Welfare State Capitalism: The Netherlands and Sweden', in Francis G. Castles (ed.) *The Comparative History of Public Policy*, Polity Press, Oxford 1989, p. 210.

86. G. A. Irwin, 'Patterns of Voting Behaviour in the Netherlands', in Richard T. Griffiths (ed.), *The Economics and Politics of the Netherlands since 1945*, Martinus Nijhoff, The Hague 1980, pp. 209–10.

87. Gladdish, *Governing from the Centre*, p. 47.

88. Ibid., p. 29, which cites as its source the OECD.

89. Braun, op. cit., p. 325.

90. Therborn, op. cit., p. 234.

91. Rudy B. Andeweg, 'Less Than Nothing? Hidden Privatisation of the Pseudo-Private Sector: The Dutch Case', *West European Politics*, Vol. 11, no. 4, October 1988, p. 122.

92. See table in *Financial Times*, 21 July 1993, p. 3; the ranking is for non-financial transnational corporations. The ranking had not significantly changed in 1994. The fourth UNCTAD World Investment Report ranks Shell first, Philips eleventh and Unilever twentieth; see *Financial Times*, 31 August 1994, p. 4.

93. Kurzer, op. cit., pp. 13–15.

94. Gladdish, op. cit., pp. 151–2.

95. Wolinetz, 'Socio-economic Bargaining in the Netherlands', pp. 85–9.

96. Gladdish, op. cit., p. 151.

97. Ibid., p. 153.

98. Braun, op. cit., p. 312.

99. Laura Raun, 'Forecast of meagre expansion', Survey on the Netherlands, *Financial Times*, 16 October 1986, p. 2 and 'Many losers, but some winners', Survey on the Netherlands, *Financial Times*, 23 November 1987, p. 5.

100. Gladdish, op. cit., p. 155.

101. Charles Batchelor, 'Concern at decline in membership', Survey on the Netherlands, *Financial Times*, 16 October 1986, p. 5.

102. See the description of the social security cuts in Ilja Scholten, 'Corporatism and the Neo-Liberal Backlash in the Netherlands', in Ilja Scholten (ed.), *Political Stability and Neo-corporatism*, Sage, London 1987, pp. 144–7.

103. Wolinetz, op. cit., p. 92.

104. Braun, op. cit., p. 309.

105. Therborn, op. cit., p. 232.

106. Laura Raun, 'Facing tough decisions', Survey on the Netherlands, *Financial Times*, 23 November 1987, p. 1.

107. Laura Raun, 'OECD prescribes more bitter medicine for Dutch economy', *Financial Times*, 7 June 1989, p. 3.

108. See P. M. M. W. van de Ven, 'From Regulated Cartel to Regulated Competition in the Dutch Health Care System' *European Economic Review*, Vol. 34, 1990, pp. 632–45.

109. Alain Franco, 'Le nouveau gouvernement donne la priorité à l'emploi', *Le Monde*, 16 August 1994, p. 4.

110. Henri R. Sneessens and Jacques H. Drèze, 'A Discussion of Belgian Unemployment, Combining Traditional Concepts and Disequilibrium Econometrics', *Economica*, Vol. 53, 1986 Supplement to no. 210, *Unemployment*, p. S93.

111. Ibid., p. S97.

112. Ibid., p. S95.

113. Claude Demelenne, *Le Socialisme du possible. Guy Spitaels: Changer la gauche?*, Editions Labor, Brussels 1985, p. 39.

114. Michel Mignolet, 'Les économies régionales', in Guy Quaden (ed.), *L'économie belge dans la crise*, Editions Labor, Brussels 1987, p. 320. The reader should be aware that in Belgium the statistics on relative growth rates between Flanders and Wallonia are disputed with great political vigour.

115. Demelenne, op. cit., p. 48.

116. Dick Leonard, 'Mr. Wallonia pulls the strings', *Financial Times*, 12 July 1993, p. 11.

117. Dick Leonard, 'Fashioning federalism', *Financial Times*, 12 July 1993, p. 10.

118. Paul Cheeseright, 'Cry for help in mining crisis', Survey on Belgium, *Financial Times*, 13 June 1986, p. 3.

119. Mabille, *Histoire politique de la Belgique*, p. 365; Georges Vandermissen, 'La crisi delle relazioni industriali in Belgio', in Paolo Perulli and Bruno Trentin (eds), *Il sindacato nella recessione*, De Donato, Bari 1983, p. 167; and Katzenstein, op. cit., p. 197.

120. Dick Leonard, 'Eye on coalition chances', Survey on Belgium, *Financial Times*, 19 June 1987, p. 4.

121. Herman Daems and Peter Van de Weyer, *L'économie belge sous influence*, Academia/Fondation Roi Baudouin, Brussels 1993, p. 39.

122. Michel Monitor, 'Social Conflicts in Belgium', in Crouch and Pizzorno (eds), *The Resurgence of Class Conflict in Western Europe since 1968*. Vol. 1: *National Studies*, p. 21.

123. Tim Dickson, 'Flexible times', Survey on Belgium, *Financial Times*, 16 June 1988, p. 3.

124. Tim Dickson, 'High cost of cultural divide', Survey on Belgium, *Financial Times*, 13 June 1986, p. 4.

125. Andrew Hill, 'Franc fears for Belgian social pact talks', *Financial Times*, 7 October 1993, p. 3.

126. Quaden (ed.), op. cit., p. 16.

127. David Gardner, 'Export fall fuels recession', *Financial Times*, 12 July 1993, p. 10.

128. Katzenstein, op. cit., p. 119.

129. Demelenne, op. cit., p. 79.

18. Germany and Britain: SPD and Labour in Power

1. William Carr, 'German Social Democracy since 1945', in Roger Fletcher (ed.), *Bernstein to Brandt. A Short History of German Social Democracy*, Edward Arnold, London 1987, p. 199.

2. Cited in Jeremy Moon, 'The Responses of British Governments to Unemployment', in Richardson and Henning (eds), *Unemployment*, p. 24.

3. Cited in Martin Holmes, *Political Pressure and Economic Policy: British Government 1970–1974*, Butterworth, London 1982, p. 46; on p. 47 Holmes himself shows no such emotional concern.

4. Anderson, 'The Figures of Descent', p. 64.

5. Kathleen Burk and Alec Cairncross, *'Goodbye, Great Britain'. The 1976 IMF Crisis*, Yale University Press, New Haven and London 1992, p. 145 and the whole of chapter 5,'The Movement of Opinion'. This book is the key text on the IMF crisis.

6. James Callaghan, *Time and Chance*, Collins, London 1987, p. 426.

7. Burk and Cairncross, op. cit., p. 160.

8. Donoughue, *Prime Minister*, p. 94.

9. On Peter Jay's authorship, see Healey, *The Time of My Life*, p. 443; Donoughue, op. cit., p. 82; and Callaghan's hint in his own memoirs, op. cit., p. 425. The British public's apparently insatiable appetite for the memoirs of politicians has led to a constant spate of such publications to an extent unequalled in the rest of Europe. Though all are self-serving, it is possible, by judicious cross-referencing, to obtain an impression of perceived constraints.

10. See Labour Party, *Labour's Programme 1976*, May 1976.

11. Holland pointed out that Keynes's macro-economic focus left no room for policies aimed at the level of the large firms, the 'meso-economic sector': *The Socialist Challenge*, Quartet Books, London 1976, p. 28.

12. Donoughue, op. cit., pp. 82–4.

13. Healey, op. cit., p. 379.

14. Michael Artis and David Cobham (eds), *Labour's Economic Policies 1974–1979*, Manchester University Press, Manchester 1991, p. 21.

15. Healey, op. cit., p. 394.

16. Ibid., pp. 394–5 and Edmund Dell, *A Hard Pounding. Politics and Economic Crisis 1974–1976*, Oxford University Press, Oxford 1991, pp. 163–4.

17. Harold Wilson, *Final Term. The Labour Government 1974–1976*, Weidenfeld and Nicolson and Michael Joseph, London 1979, p. 115.

18. Healey, op. cit., p. 426.

19. Christopher Allsopp, 'Macroeconomic Policy: Design and Performance', in Artis and Cobham (eds), op. cit., pp. 31–4.

20. Burk and Cairncross, op. cit., p. xiv.

21. Callaghan, op. cit., p. 436.

22. Healey, op. cit., pp. 380–1.

23. Ibid., p. 432.

24. Crosland, op. cit., pp. 289–90.

25. Crossman, *The Diaries of a Cabinet Minister*, Vol. 1, entry for 12 July 1966, p. 568.

26. Crosland, *Tony Crosland*, pp. 377–8; corroborated in Tony Benn, *Against the Tide. Diaries 1973–76*, Hutchinson, London 1989, p. 667.

27. Benn, op. cit., p. 674.

28. The outline of this strategy – coded Strategy B – is reproduced in Appendix IV of Benn, op. cit., pp. 725–7.

29. Ibid., p. 664.

30. Donoughue, op. cit., p. 90; Dell, op. cit., p. 226; Callaghan, op. cit., pp. 436–8.

31. S. Crosland, op. cit., p. 381.

32. Healey, op. cit., p. 431.

33. Ibid., p. 433.

34. Ibid., p. 434.

35. Burk and Cairncross, op. cit., pp. 37, 46.

36. Callaghan, op. cit., pp. 431–2; Healey, op. cit., p. 430.

37. Lieber, 'Labour in Power: Problems of Political Economy', pp. 197, 202.

38. Labour Party, *Labour Programme 1973*, London 1973, pp. 22–5.

39. Paul Ormerod, 'Incomes Policy', in Artis and Cobham (eds), op. cit., p. 62.

40. This recognition comes from one of the Labour ministers least sympathetic to the unions, Edmund Dell (see his op. cit., p. 159), and is confirmed by all those involved; see also Jack Jones's own recollections in his *Union Man. An Autobiography*, Collins, London 1986, pp. 296–302.

41. See the TUC pamphlet *The Development of the Social Contract*, London, July 1975.

42. Bert Ramelson, *Social Contract: Cure-all or Con-trick?*, Communist Party pamphlet, London n.d. (1974), p. 21.

43. See TUC, *TUC Economic Review 1978*, London 1978, pp. 40–1.

44. Healey, op. cit., p. 398.

45. Artis and Cobham (eds), op. cit., p. 15.

46. Healey, op. cit., p. 467.

47. William Brown, 'Industrial Relations', in Artis and Cobham (eds), op. cit., p. 215.

48. Joel Barnett, *Inside the Treasury*, André Deutsch, London 1982, pp. 166–8.

49. Balogh, *The Irrelevance of Conventional Economics*, p. 47.

50. On this and the general theme of the new technologies and their impact on labour, see Ian Benson and John Lloyd, *New Technology and Industrial Change*, Kogan Page, London 1983, especially chapters 3 and 8.

51. Leaman, *The Political Economy of West Germany, 1945–1985*, p. 241.

52. Josef Esser and Wolfgang Fach, '"Social Market" and Modernization Policy: West Germany', in Dyson and Wilks (eds), *Industrial Crisis*, p. 103.

53. Graham Hallett, 'West Germany', in Graham with Seldon (eds), *Government and Economies in the Postwar World*, pp. 80–1.

54. See the Clearing Banks' 1982 report, cited in Wyn Grant and Stephen Wilks, 'British Industrial Policy: Structural Change, Policy Inertia', *Journal of Public Policy*, Vol. 3, no. 1, February 1983, p. 19.

55. Esser and Fach, op. cit., p. 105.

56. Ibid., p. 109.

57. The following paragraphs on the restructuring of the steel industry are based on Esser and Fach, op. cit., pp. 111–14 and Kenneth Dyson, 'The Politics of Corporate Crises in West Germany', *West European Politics*, Vol. 7, no. 1, January 1984, pp. 34–6.

58. Porter, *The Competitive Advantages of Nations*, p. 378.

59. Minkin, *The Contentious Alliance*, p. 173.

60. See, for instance, Edmund Dell, later Treasury minister and trade secretary, who, in his memoirs, mused that Holland could produce a lengthy policy paper at the drop of a hat: Dell, op. cit., p. 90.

61. Labour Party, *The National Enterprise Board. Labour's State Holding Company, An Opposition Green Paper*, London, n.d. (1973), p. 14.

62. Ibid., p. 21.

63. This is ackowledged by S. A. Walkland, a critic of Stuart Holland's and the Labour

Left's proposals, in Andrew Gamble and S. A. Walkland, *The British Party System and Economic Policy 1945–1983*, Clarendon Press, Oxford 1984, pp. 133–40.

64. Labour Party, *Labour's Programme 1973*, p. 34.

65. Ibid., p. 17.

66. Ibid., p. 18.

67. F. W. S. Craig (ed.), *British General Election Manifestos 1900–1974*, p. 403.

68. Wilson, op. cit., p. 30.

69. Tom Forester, 'Neutralising the Industrial Strategy', in Ken Coates (ed.), *What Went Wrong*, Spokesman, Nottingham 1979, p. 77 and Roy Jenkins, *A Life at the Centre*, Macmillan, London 1991.

70. Wilson, op. cit., p. 125.

71. Ibid., p. 141.

72. Malcom Sawyer, 'Industrial Policy', in Artis and Cobham (eds), op. cit., p. 160.

73. Healey, op. cit., p. 407.

74. Sawyer, op. cit., p. 162; Forester, op. cit., p. 86.

75. Stephen Wilks, 'Liberal State and Party Competition: Britain', in Dyson and Wilks (eds), op. cit., p. 145.

76. The episode is examined in David Coates, *Labour in Power? A Study of the Labour Government 1974–1979*, Longman 1980, pp. 102–6.

77. Dell, op. cit., p. 90.

78. Sawyer, op. cit., p. 166.

79. Donoughue, op. cit., p. 83, who points out that unemployment was a fate unlikely to befall any of the employees of this august institution.

80. Healey, op. cit., p. 398.

81. Klaus Hinrich Hennings, 'West Germany', in Boltho (ed.), *The European Economy*, p. 496.

82. Leaman, op. cit., pp. 217–18.

83. Douglas Webber, 'Social Democracy and the Re-emergence of Mass Unemployment in Western Europe', in Paterson and Thomas (eds), *The Future of Social Democracy*, 1986, p. 53n.

84. Leaman, op. cit., p. 218.

85. See the analysis of a former president of the Bundesbank, Otmar Emminger, in 'West Germany: Europe's Driving Force?', in Ralf Dahrendorf (ed.), *Europe's Economy in Crisis*, Weidenfeld and Nicolson, London 1981, p. 23.

86. Ibid., p. 24.

87. Leaman, op. cit., p. 226.

88. Emminger, op. cit., p. 31.

89. Helmut Schmidt, *The World Crisis: Between Recession and Hope*, Foundation for International Relations, n.p. 1984, pp. 18–19; this is the text of a lecture given in Lisbon on 4 November 1983.

90. Hennings, 'West Germany', p. 497.

91. Douglas Webber and Gabriele Nass, 'Employment Policy in West Germany', in Richardson and Henning (eds), op. cit., pp. 166–7.

92. Ibid., pp. 169–79.

93. Günther Schmid, 'Labour Market Policy under the Social–Liberal Coalition', in Klaus von Beyme and Manfred G. Schmidt (eds), *Policy and Politics in the Federal Republic of Germany*, Gower, Aldershot 1985, p. 126.

94. Webber and Nass, op. cit., p. 183.

95. Giersch, Paqué and Schmieding, *The Fading Miracle*, p. 193.

96. David Marsh, 'Wunder turns to whimper', *Financial Times*, 4 November 1987, p. 26.

97. Hallett, op. cit., pp. 94–5.

98. Pimlott, *Harold Wilson*, p. 150.

99. The text of this address is in Helmut Schmidt, *Perspectives on Politics*, Westview Press, Boulder CO 1982; the citation is on p. 194.

100. Cited in Horst Heimann, 'Fine del movimento operaio?', in Antonio Missiroli (ed.), *Modernizzazione e sistema politico. Italia e Germania federale a confronto*, Supplement to *Democrazia e diritto*, no. 1–2, January–April 1989; the survey was published in no. 21 of *Vorwärts*, 21 May 1988.

101. Webber, 'Social Democracy and the Re-emergence of Mass Unemployment in Western Europe', pp. 23, 27.

102. Volker R. Berghahn and Detlev Karsten, *Industrial Relations in West Germany*, Berg, Oxford 1987, p. 246.

103. Peter Bruce, 'West German unions set might against "demon Kohl"', *Financial Times*, 3 June 1986.

104. Ute Schmidt, 'La Cdu e le difficoltà della "svolta"', in Missiroli (ed.), op. cit., p. 131.

105. Ronaldo Schmidtz, finance director of BASF, the chemicals company, quoted in David Marsh, 'In the clutch of corporatism', *Financial Times*, 5 November 1987, p. 27.

106. Kenneth Dyson, 'The Problem of Morality and Power in the Politics of West Germany', *Government and Opposition*, Vol. 16, no. 2, Spring 1981, p. 131.

107. See Manfred G. Schmidt, 'Learning from Catastrophes: West Germany's Public Policy', in Francis G. Castles (ed.), *The Comparative History of Public Policy*, Polity Press, Oxford 1989, pp. 56–61. Schmidt points out that in the 1950s Germany's share of social expenditure was higher than in other OECD countries.

108. Marsh, op. cit., p. 26.

109. Padgett and Paterson, *A History of Social Democracy in Postwar Europe*, pp. 149–50.

110. Miller and Potthoff, *A History of German Social Democracy*, pp. 198–9.

111. Ardagh, *Germany and the Germans*, pp. 406–7.

112. Sebastian Cobler, *Law, Order and Politics in West Germany*, trans. Francis McDonagh, Penguin, Harmondsworth, 1978, pp. 33–4.

113. Victorial Isenberg, 'Le SPD et l'Etat', *Nouvelle Revue Socialiste*, April–May 1983, pp. 83–4.

114. Schmidt, *Perspectives on Politics*, pp. 187–8.

115. Brandt, *My Life in Politics*, pp. 275–6.

116. Enzo Collotti, *Esempio Germania. Socialdemocrazia tedesca e coalizione social-liberale 1969–1976*, Feltrinelli, Milan 1977, p. 97.

117. Braunthal, *The West German Social Democrats 1969–1982*, pp. 144–5.

118. Miller and Potthoff, op. cit., pp. 192–3.

119. John H. Herz, 'Social Democracy versus Democratic Socialism', p. 255.

120. SPD, *Ökonomisch-politischer Orientierungsrahmen für die Jahre 1975–1985*, published by the Press and Information of the SPD, p. 8.

121. Ibid., p. 11.

122. Ibid., p. 30.

123. Ibid., p. 38.

124. Ibid., p. 39.

125. Ibid.

126. Braunthal, op. cit., p. 151.

127. Brandt, *The State of the Nation*, p. 11 in English-language text.

128. Herz, op. cit., pp. 265–6.

129. See Paul Whiteley, 'The Decline of Labour's Local Party Membership and Electoral Base 1945–79', in Dennis Kavanagh (ed.), *The Politics of the Labour Party*, Allen and Unwin, London 1982, p. 113.

130 Katz and Mair (eds), *Party Organizations*, p. 332.

131. Pontusson, *Swedish Social Democracy and British Labour*, p. 25. The connection between social-democratic hegemony and a universalist welfare system is at the centre of Gøsta Esping-Andersen, *Politics against Markets*; see especially pp. 245–6 and see also the same author's *The Three Worlds of Welfare Capitalism*, pp. 26–33.

132. Minkin, op. cit., pp. 115–16; Leo Panitch, *Social Democracy and Industrial Militancy. The Labour Party, the Trade Unions and Incomes Policy 1945–1974*, Cambridge University Press, Cambridge 1976, p. 228.

133. S. Holland, op. cit., pp. 139–40.

134. Colin Leys, *Politics in Britain*, Heinemann, London 1983 p. 75.

135. Child benefits also replaced family allowances payable to the mother, but only for the second and subsequent children, and worth much less than the child benefits; see Nicholas Barr and Fiona Coulter, 'Social Security: Solution or Problem?' in Hills (ed.), *The State of Welfare*, pp. 279–80.

136. *Labour Manifesto 1974*, in F. W. S. Craig (ed.), op. cit., p. 459.

137. Barbara Castle, *The Castle Diaries 1974–76*, Weidenfeld and Nicolson, London 1980, p. 708.

138. Healey, op. cit., pp. 448–9.

139. Barnett, op. cit., pp. 54–5.

140. Allan Gillie, 'Redistribution', in Artis and Cobham (eds), op. cit., p. 232.

141. See figures in William Brown and Keith Sisson, *A Positive Incomes Policy*, Fabian Tract no. 442, May 1976, p. 6.

142. Markovits, *The Politics of the West German Trade Unions*, p. 108.

143. Ibid., pp. 117–20.

144. Berghahn and Karsten, op. cit., p. 204.

145. Ibid., pp. 120–2.

146. Ibid., p. 124.

147. Helmut Schmidt, 'The Role of the Trade Unions in the Federal Republic', 14 March 1976, Hannover, in *The Bulletin of the Press and Information Office of the Government of the FRG*, Vol. 3, no. 3, 6 April 1976, Bonn, p. 2; henceforth: *Press Bulletin, FRG*.

148. Walter Arendt, 'Speech at the Second and Third Reading of the Co-Determination Bill', 18 March 1976, in *Press Bulletin, FRG*, 6 April 1976, p. 4.

149. Markovits, op. cit., p. 112.

150. Doug Miller, 'Social Partnership and the Determinants of Workplace Independence in West Germany', in *British Journal of Industrial Relations*, Vol. 20, no. 1, March 1982, pp. 52–3.

151. Walther Müller-Jentsch and Hans-Joachim Sperling, 'Economic Development, Labour Conflicts and the Industrial Relations System in West Germany', in Crouch and Pizzorno (eds), *The Resurgence of Class Conflict in Western Europe since 1968*, Vol. 1, pp. 288–90.

152. Wolfgang Streeck, 'Organizational Consequences of Neo-Corporatist Co-operation in West German Labour Unions', in Gerhard Lehmbruch and Philippe C. Schmitter (eds), *Patterns of Corporatist Policy-Making*, Sage, Beverly Hills 1982, pp. 35–6.

153. Ibid., p. 51.

154. Wolfgang Streeck, 'Neo-Corporatist Industrial Relations and the Economic Crisis in West Germany', in John H. Goldthorpe (ed.), *Order and Conflict in Contemporary Capitalism*, Clarendon Press, Oxford 1984, pp. 291–314.

155. Ibid., p. 307.

156. Labour Party, *Labour Programme 1973*, p. 27.

157. *Labour Manifesto 1974*, in F. W. S. Craig, op. cit., pp. 403, 458.

158. The standard account of the road to the Bullock Report is John Elliott, *Conflict or*

Cooperation? The Growth of Industrial Democracy, Kogan Page, London 1978; the analysis of the actual report is on pp. 234–40.

159. Ibid., p. 245.

160. Coates, op. cit., p. 139; Colin Crouch, *The Politics of Industrial Relations*, Fontana/Collins, Glasgow 1979, p. 109.

161. Tom Clarke, 'Industrial Democracy: The Institutionalized Suppression of Industrial Conflict?', in Tom Clarke and Laurie Clements (eds), *Trade Unions Under Capitalism*, Fontana, n.p. 1977, p. 357.

162. Peregrine Worsthorne, 'Beefing up the bosses', *Sunday Telegraph*, 30 January 1977, p. 18.

163. Rhys David, 'Employee polls back worker directors', *Financial Times*, 26 January 1977, p. 1.

164. J. Elliott, op. cit., pp. 243–4; see also Benn, op. cit., p. 690.

165. Healey, op. cit., p. 459.

166. See the resolution in *TUC Report 1978*, pp. 561–2 and the speech by Lord Allen of the shopworkers' union, USDAW, who moved the resolution, p. 562.

167. J. Jones, op. cit., p. 316.

168. W. Brown, 'Industrial Relations', p. 219.

169. Kevin Hawkins, *Trade Unions*, Hutchinson, London 1981, pp. 61–4.

19. The French Experiment

1. Vincent Wright and Howard Machin, 'The French Socialist Party in 1973: Performance and Prospects', in *Government and Opposition*, Vol. 9, no. 2, 1974, pp. 127–8.

2. Hugues Portelli, 'L'intégration du Parti socialiste a la Cinquième République', *Revue française de science politique*, Vol. 34, no. 4–5, August–October 1984, p. 821.

3. Jenson and Ross, 'The Tragedy of the French Left', p. 27.

4. Cited in *Socialist International Information*, no. 5–6, May–June 1971.

5. D. S. Bell and Byron Criddle, *The French Socialist Party*, Clarendon Press, Oxford 1988, p. 70.

6. An example of this view is in Lazar, *Maisons rouges*, p. 136.

7. I have used the text in the volume published by the PCF – the most easily available – with an introduction by Georges Marchais: *Programme commun de gouvernement*, Editions Sociales, Paris 1972.

8. Ibid., p. 53.

9. Ibid., pp. 61–4, 68.

10. Ibid., pp. 75, 97.

11. Ibid., pp. 95–6.

12. Ibid., pp. 105–12, 117.

13. Ibid., pp. 115–16.

14. Ibid., p. 131.

15. Ibid., pp. 143–9.

16. Ibid., pp. 150–4.

17. See Portelli, 'La voie nationale des PC français et italien', pp. 659–72.

18. Jean-Pierre Cot, 'Autogestion and Modernity in France', in B. Brown (ed.), *Eurocommunism and Eurosocialism*, p. 82.

19. Ibid., p. 71.

20. Ibid., p. 83.

21. See E. Maire, A. Detraz and F. Krumnov, *La CFDT et l'Autogestion*, Editions de

Cerf, Paris 1973 and E. Maire and J. Julliard, *La CFDT d'aujourd'hui*, Editions du Seuil, Paris 1975.

22. George Ross, 'French Trade Unions Face the 1980s: The CGT and the CFDT in the Strategic Conflicts and Economic Crisis of Contemporary France', in Esping-Andersen and Friedland, *Political Power and Social Theory*, Vol. 3, p. 59.

23. Bell and Criddle, op. cit., p. 88.

24. Cot, op. cit., p. 74, Jenson and Ross, op. cit., p. 30.

25. Cot, op. cit., pp. 77–8.

26. Hugues Portelli, 'La voie nationale ... ', pp. 659–72; see also a succinct summary of *le socialisme autogestionnaire* in D. L. Hanley, A. P. Kerr and N. H. Waites, *Contemporary France. Politics and Society since 1945*, Routledge and Kegan Paul, London 1979, p. 156.

27. Pierre Rosanvallon, *L'âge de l'autogestion*, Editions du Seuil, Paris 1976, p. 8.

28. Ibid., pp. 16–17.

29. Ibid., p. 117.

30. Ibid., p. 119.

31. Ibid., p. 120.

32. Byron Criddle, 'The French Socialist Party', in Paterson and Thomas (eds), *The Future of Social Democracy*, p. 227.

33. Extracts in Michel Rocard, *Parler Vrai. Textes politiques*, Editions du Seuil, Paris 1979, p. 102.

34. W. Rand Smith, 'Towards *Autogestion* in Socialist France? The Impact of Industrial Relations Reform', *West European Politics*, Vol. 10, no. 1, January 1987, pp. 57–8.

35. Jacques Julliard, 'Epinay-sur-Seine et retour ou la fin d'un cycle', *Intervention*, no. 13, July–September 1985, p. 6.

36. Lazar, op. cit., p. 136.

37. Mitterrand, *Ma part de vérité*, p. 120 and his *Politique. Textes et discours 1938–1981*, Fayard, Paris 1984, p. 333.

38. Lazar, op. cit., p. 138

39. See the analysis in Jean Ranger, 'Le déclin du Parti communiste français', *Revue française de science politique*, Vol. 36, no. 1, February 1986, especially pp. 46–53.

40. Jenson and Ross, op. cit., p. 13.

41. Bell and Criddle, op. cit., p. 99.

42. François Platone, 'Les communistes au gouvernement: une expérience "complexe" et contradictoire', *Revue politique et parlementaire*, Vol. 87, no. 914, January–February 1985, p. 31.

43. For the constant deterioration of the image of the PCF in French public opinion, see Ranger, op. cit., pp. 53–5.

44. For an examination of the role of communist intellectuals in the 1970s and 1980s, see Sudhir Hazareesingh, *Intellectuals and the French Communist Party. Disillusion and Decline*, Clarendon Press, Oxford 1991.

45. Platone, op. cit., p. 42.

46. Parti socialiste, *Projet socialiste. Pour la France des années 80*, Club Socialiste du Livre, Paris 1980; henceforth cited as *Projet socialiste*.

47. Among those cited we find: Edgar Morin, Theodor Adorno, David Riesman, Noam Chomsky, Régis Debray, Antonio Gramsci, Dominique Lecourt.

48. *Project socialiste*, p. 43.

49. Ibid., pp. 64ff.

50. Ibid., p. 78.

51. Speech of 21 May 1981, in Mitterrand, *Politique*, p. 415.

52. *Project socialiste*, p. 33.

53. Ibid., p. 32.

54. Ibid., p. 33.

55. Bell and Criddle, op. cit., p. 252.

56. Ibid., p. 111.

57. Pierre Mauroy, 'La gauche au pouvoir', *Revue politique et parlementaire*, Vol. 87, no. 916, May–June 1985, p. 6.

58. José Frèches, 'L' Etat socialiste', in Michel Massenet et al., *La France socialiste. Un premier bilan*, Hachette, Paris 1983, pp. 401–12, 386–91 and Anne Stevens, '"L'Alternance" and the Higher Civil Service', in Philip G. Cerny and Martin A. Schain (eds), *Socialism, the State and Public Policy in France*, Frances Pinter, London 1985, p. 157.

59. On the problems of replacing one set of grovellers with another, see the inside view of Thierry Pfister, *La vie quotidienne à Matignon au temps de l'union de la gauche*, Hachette, Paris 1985, p. 138; for an implied promise that non-interference in the media was the hallmark of the true democrat, see François Mitterrand, *L'Abeille et l'architecte*, Flammarion, Paris 1978, p. 26.

60. Pfister, op. cit., p. 103 and Pierre Favier and Michel Martin-Roland, *La Décennie Mitterrand*. Vol. 1: *Les ruptures*, Editions du Seuil, Paris 1990, pp. 90–3.

61. Jenson and Ross, op. cit., p. 12.

62. Dominique Reynié, 'La question russe', *Intervention*, no. 13, July–September 1985, pp. 80–1.

63. Lionel Jospin, *L'invention du possible*, Flammarion, Paris 1991, p. 98.

64. Pfister, op. cit., p. 244.

65. Ibid., pp. 248–9. Pfister denies that Rocard had suggested an early devaluation, but this is supported neither by Pierre Mauroy (see his *C'est ici le chemin*, Flammarion, Paris 1982, p. 19), nor by Jacques Attali (*Verbatim, I 1981–1986*, Fayard, Paris 1993, p. 22).

66. Attali, op. cit., pp. 24–5, 408, 411–12 and *passim*. Schmidt later lamented that the close co-operation between France and Germany withered away after the departure of Giscard d'Estaing; see Helmut Schmidt, *A Grand Strategy for the West. The Anachronism of National Strategies in an Interdependent World*, Yale University Press, New Haven CT 1985, p. 15.

67. Mauroy, op. cit., pp. 19, 24.

68. M.-F. and R. Mouriaux, 'Unemployment Policy in France 1976–82', p. 160.

69. Pierre-Alain Muet and Alain Fonteneau, *Reflation and Austerity. Economic Policy under Mitterrand*, trans. Malcom Slater, Berg, Oxford 1990, pp. 198–204.

70. M.-F. and R. Mouriaux, op. cit., pp. 162–3.

71. Muet and Fonteneau, op. cit., p. 308.

72.   Favier and Martin-Roland, op. cit., Vol. 1, p. 114.

73. Muet and Fonteneau, op. cit., pp. 75, 79; Beatrice Bazil, 'L'irrésistible logique de la socialisation', in Massenet et al., op. cit., pp. 312–13; and André Helder, 'Les trois phases de la politique économique', *Revue politique et parlementaire*, Vol. 87, no. 916, May–June 1985, p. 118.

74. Muet and Fonteneau, op. cit., p. 239.

75. Bell and Criddle, op. cit., pp. 155–6.

76. M.-F. and R. Mouriaux, op. cit., p. 162; Muet and Fonteneau, op. cit., p. 83.

77. Muet and Fonteneau, op. cit., pp. 84–5.

78. See Rose Solfeco, 'Nationalisation des banques et nouvelle politique du crédit', *Nouvelle revue socialiste*, September–October 1982, p. 28 ('Rose Solfeco' is the collective pseudonym of the economic commission of the Socialist Party). See also Alain Redslob, 'Un système bancaire socialisé', in Massenet et al., pp. 143–5 and Richard Holton, 'Industrial Politics in France: Nationalisation under Mitterrand', *West European Politics*, Vol. 9, no. 1, January 1986, p. 70.

79. See, in Howard Machin and Vincent Wright (eds), *Economic Policy and Policy-Making Under the Mitterrand Presidency 1981–1984*, Frances Pinter, London 1985, the analysis of Paul Fabra, 'Banking Policy under the Socialists', pp. 173–83; and the comments by Alan Butt Philip, pp. 183–6.

80. Claude Walon, 'L'économie: la rupture avec l'ancien socialisme', *Intervention*, no. 13, July–September 1985, pp. 58–9.

81. Philip G. Cerny, 'State Capitalism in France and Britain and the International Economic Order', in Cerny and Schain (eds), op. cit., p. 213.

82. Laurent Fabius, *Le coeur du futur*, Calmann-Lévy, Paris 1985, p. 207.

83. Serge July, *Les années Mitterrand*, Bernard Grasset, Paris 1986, p. 49.

84. See the critical comments on this 'cultural Colbertism' in Frèches, op. cit., pp. 432–41.

85. Jill Forbes, 'Cultural Policy: The Soul of Man under Socialism', in Sonia Mazey and Michael Newman (eds), *Mitterrand's France*, Croom Helm, London 1987, p. 155.

86. Jean-Pierre Chevènement, interview in *Intervention*, nos 5–6, August–October 1983, pp. 97–8.

87. This is lucidly described in Cerny op. cit., pp. 213ff.

88. Christian Stoffaës, 'The Nationalizations: An Initial Assessment, 1981–1984', in Machin and Wright (eds), op. cit., pp. 144–69.

89. Roland Granier, 'Expérience socialiste, emploi, chômage', in Massenet et al., op. cit., p. 287.

90. Ibid., p. 288 and Peter A. Hall, 'The Evolution of Economic Policy under Mitterrand', in George Ross, Stanley Hoffmann and Sylvia Malzacher (eds), *The Mitterrand Experiment*, Polity Press, Oxford 1987, p. 68.

91. Helder, op. cit., p. 114.

92. W. Rand Smith, '"We can make the Ariane, but we can't make washing machines": The State and Industrial Performance in Post-War France', in Jolyon Howorth and George Ross (eds), *Contemporary France*, Vol. 3, Frances Pinter, London 1989, p. 180.

93. Pierre Biacabe, 'Les mésaventures du franc', in Massenet et al., op. cit., pp. 125–6.

94. Muet and Fonteneau, op. cit., pp. 100–1.

95. See Jacques Delors, 'France: Between Reform and Counter-Reform', in Dahrendorf (ed.), *Europe's Economy in Crisis*, p. 65.

96. Claude Jessua, 'La rupture des grands équilibres', in Massenet et al., op. cit., p. 103.

97. See the data in Biacabe, op. cit., pp. 119–20.

98. Jospin, op. cit., p. 250.

99. Scharpf, 'A Game-Theoretical Interpretation of Inflation and Unemployment in Western Europe', pp. 253–4.

100. This point is made by some critics of the socialist government; see, for instance, Jean Féricelli, 'Les logiques de l'Etat socialiste', in Massenet et al., op. cit., pp. 69–71.

101. Muet and Fonteneau, op. cit., p. 73.

102. Favier and Martin-Roland, op. cit., Vol. 1, p. 111.

103. Rocard, op. cit., p. 74, this is the text of an article which appeared in *Le Monde*, 11–12 September 1977.

104. Jospin, op. cit., p. 101.

105. Jacques Julliard, 'Réflexions d'après le prochain congrès', *Intervention*, no. 5–6, August–October 1983, p. 7.

106. July, op. cit., pp. 96–100 and Pfister, op. cit., pp. 263–4.

107. Pfister, op. cit., p. 255.

108. Walon, op. cit., p. 57 and Muet and Fonteneau, op. cit., pp. 154–8.

109. Cited in P. A. Hall, 'Evolution … ', p. 57.

110. See the surveys examined by Florence Haegel in her 'Le dernier acte de l'Union de la gauche', *Intervention*, no. 13, July–September 1985, p. 35–6.

111. Cited in ibid., p. 37.

112. Laurent Joffrin, *La Gauche en voie de disparition. Comment changer sans trahir?*, Editions du Seuil, Paris 1984, p. 77.

113. Cited in Gérard Grunberg, 'Le cycle d'Epinay', *Intervention*, no. 13, July–September 1985, p. 83.

114. Jean-Pierre Chevènement, *Le pari sur l'intelligence* (interview with Hervé Hamon and Patrick Rotman), Flammarion, Paris 1985, p. 38.

115. Michel Rocard, *A l'épreuve des faits. Textes politiques 1979–1985*, Editions du Seuil, Paris 1986, pp. 41–3.

116. Fabius, op. cit., p. 49

117. Ibid., p. 51.

118. Ibid., pp. 52–4.

119. Chevènement, *Le pari sur l'intelligence*, p. 267.

120. Alain Touraine, 'Fin de Partie', *Intervention*, no. 13, July–September 1985, p. 17; see on the same theme Machin and Wright, 'Introduction' to their collection *Economic Policy and Policy-Making Under the Mitterrand Presidency 1981–1984*, p. 3.

121. See Lionel Jospin's considerations on the subject when he was First Secretary of the Socialist Party, 'Le socialisme français, défenseur et garant de la République', *Revue politique et parlementaire*, Vol. 87, no. 915, March–April 1985, pp. 33–9.

122. Cited in Grunberg, op. cit., p. 84.

123. All these points are made by Diana Pinto in her perceptive 'Vive la République!', *Intervention*, no. 10, August–December 1984, pp. 89–90. See also her 'The Atlantic Influence and the mMellowing of French Identity', in Howorth and Ross (eds), Vol. 2, especially pp. 122–4.

124. See the quotation by Rocard in Hobsbawm, *Echoes of the Marseillaise*, pp. ix–x. This book is a rebuttal of the new revisionism of the French Revolution; for the revisionist historiography, see in particular François Furet, *Penser la révolution française*, Gallimard, Paris 1978; in Britain students of the French Revolution who had read Alfred Cobban's *The Myth of the French Revolution* (1955) were already familiar with these arguments.

125. W. Rand Smith, '"We can make the Ariane … ', p. 193.

126. See *Programme commun*, p. 150.

127. See Jenson and Ross, op. cit., pp. 10–11.

128. Rocard gave his reasons in 'Les raisons d'un départ', *Le Monde*, 6 April 1985; reprinted in his *A l'épreuve des faits*, pp. 160–4.

129. P. A. Hall, 'Evolution … ', p. 70.

130. Peter Holmes, 'Broken Dreams: Economic Policy in Mitterrand's France', in Mazey and Newman (eds), op. cit., p. 45.

131. Lionel Jospin, First Secretary of the PS between 1981 and 1988, later a cabinet minister, and, in 1995, the Socialist presidential candidate, lucidly explained this dilemma in the terms I have set out; see his *L'invention du possible*, pp. 252–3.

132. Catherine Grémion, 'Decentralisation in France. A Historical Perspective', in Ross, Hoffmann and Malzacher (eds), op. cit., p. 237.

133. Ibid., p. 245.

134. Ibid., p. 246.

135. Yves Mény, 'The Socialist Decentralisation', in Ross, Hoffmann and Malzacher (eds), op. cit., p. 249.

136. Mark Kesselman, 'The Demise of French Socialism', *New Politics*, Vol. 1, no. 1, Summer 1986, p. 142.

137. Sonia Mazey, 'Decentralisation: La grande affaire du septennat?', in Mazey and Newman (eds), op. cit., p. 124.

138. Vivien A. Schmidt, 'Decentralization: A Revolutionary Reform', in Patrick McCarthy, *The French Socialists in Power 1981–1986*, Greenwood Press, New York 1987, p. 83.

139. Daniel Singer, *Is Socialism Doomed? The Meaning of Mitterrand*, Oxford University Press, New York 1988, p. 110.

140. Mény, op. cit., p. 250; Mark Kesselman, 'The Tranquil Revolution at Clochemerle: Socialist Decentralisation in France', in Cerny and Schain, op. cit., pp. 169, 175.

141. Mény, op. cit., p. 261.

142. This is the view of V. A. Schmidt, op. cit., p. 102.

143. Kesselman, 'The Tranquil Revolution ...', p. 181 and Mazey, op. cit., p. 125.

144. Ian Davidson, 'French Socialists under siege', *Financial Times*, 31 May 1990, p. 22.

145. Kesselman, 'The Demise ...', p. 144.

146. Duncan Gallie, 'Les lois Auroux: The Reform of French Industrial Relations?' in Machin and Wright (eds), pp. 211, 214.

147. Fabius, op. cit., p. 213.

148. See, for instance, Hubert Landier, 'Vers un renforcement du corporatisme syndical', in Massenet et al., op. cit., p. 361. Rand Smith too thinks that the laws mainly strengthened the unions; see his 'Towards *Autogestion* in Socialist France?', p. 56. This article also contains a succinct summary of the legislation; see pp. 49–50.

149. Alain Bergounioux, 'Sur la crise du syndicalisme', *Intervention*, no. 13, July–September 1985, p. 50.

150. David Buchan, 'France's grassroots shake the union tree', *Financial Times*, 28 October 1993, p. 2.

151. Bergounioux, op. cit., p. 53.

152. Hervé Hamon and Patrick Rotman, *La deuxième gauche. Histoire intellectuelle et politique de la CFDT*, Editions du Seuil, Paris 1984 (1st edn, 1982), pp. 344–5 – a book whose enthusiasm for the CFDT and its leader, Edmond Maire, is close to idolatry.

153. Hélène Gras, 'Justice: la fin des archaïsmes', *Revue politique et parlementaire*, Vol. 87, no. 916, May–June 1985, pp. 26–7.

154. Ian Davidson, 'France's penal Code Napoléon meets its Waterloo at last', *Financial Times*, 11 May 1989.

155. John S. Ambler, 'Educational Pluralism in the French Fifth Republic', in James F. Hollifield and George Ross (eds), *Searching for the New France*, Routledge, London and New York 1991, p. 198.

156. Jean-Paul Martin and Jol Roman, 'Le socialisme en proie à l'école', *Intervention*, no. 13, July–September 1985, p. 35.

157. Chevènement, *Le pari sur l'intelligence*, p. 140.

158. Jean-Pierre Chevènement, *Apprendre pour entreprendre*, Livre de Poche, Paris 1985, p. 28.

159. Ibid., p. 8.

160. Ambler, op. cit., p. 200.

161. Gérard Courtois, '1981–1993: l'érosion des ambitions', *Le Monde*, 18 March 1993, p. 13.

162. Data in Gérard Courtois, 'La FEN en miettes', *Le Monde*, 18 March 1993, p. 15.

163. Ambler, op. cit., p. 202, see also Antoine Prost, 'The Educational Maelstrom', in Ross, Hoffmann and Malzacher (eds), op. cit., p. 231–3.

164. Michalina Vaughan, 'Education: Cultural Persistence and Institutional Change', in P. McCarthy (ed.), op. cit., p. 74.

165. David Housego, 'Chirac beset by handicaps', Survey on France, *Financial Times*, 16 June 1986, p. iii.

166. Jolyon Howorth and George Ross, 'Introduction: In Search of New Parameters For National Identity?', in their *Contemporary France*, Vol. 2, p. 1.

167. See the analysis of the Lille Congress in Sandro Guerrieri, 'Il Congresso di Lilla del Partito socialista francese', in *Sinistra Europea 1987*, supplement to *Democrazia e diritto*, nos 4–5, July–October 1987, pp. 117–33.

168. Touraine, op. cit., p. 16.

169. Jacques Julliard, 'Comment la gauche peut revenir', *Intervention*, no. 16, April–June 1986, p. 5.

170. See extracts of the letter in *Le Monde, L'élection présidentielle, supplément aux dossiers et documents du Monde*, May 1988, pp. 20–1.

171. Steven C. Lewis and Serenella Sferza, 'The Second Mitterrand Experiment: Charisma and the Possibilities of Partisan Renewal', in Howorth and Ross (eds), op. cit., Vol. 3, p. 38.

172. See his interview in *Le Monde*, 3 June 1988, reprinted in *Le Monde, L'élection législative, supplément aux dossiers et documents du Monde*, June 1988, p. 27.

173. See the summary of the survey of the Centre d'Etude des Revenus, *Les Français et leurs Revenus*, in Ian Davidson, 'Inequality grows in "socialist" France', *Financial Times*, 24 November 1989.

174. See OECD, *Economic Outlook, Historical Statistics 1960–1989*, p. 95.

175. Cited in Ian Davidson, 'France charts a new course for the economy', *Financial Times*, 21 February 1989, p. 2.

176. Ian Davidson, 'Prudent policies beginning to bear fruit', in Survey on France, *Financial Times*, 17 June 1991, p. ii.

177. Suzanne Berger, 'Liberalism Reborn: The New Liberal Synthesis in France', in Howorth and Ross (eds), op. cit., Vol. 1. The itinerary of French intellectuals from Marxism to anti-collectivist liberalism is ably mapped out by George Ross in his 'Where Have All the Sartres Gone? The French Intelligentsia Born Again', in Hollifield and Ross (eds), op. cit., pp. 221–49. For a more sympathetic account, see Khilnani, *Arguing Revolution*, pp. 121–54. *Contra* Khilnani read Gregory Elliott, 'Contentious Commitments: French Intellectuals and Politics', *New Left Review*, no. 206, July–August 1994, pp. 110–24.

20. The Failure of Italian Communism

1. Enrico Berlinguer, 'La peculiarità socialista', reprinted in E. Berlinguer, *La 'Questione Comunista'*, Vol. 1, Editori Riuniti, Rome 1975, p. 508.

2. Ibid., p. 505.

3. Ibid., p. 506.

4. Ibid., p. 508.

5. Ibid., pp. 510–11.

6. See Enrico Berlinguer, speech to the Thirteenth Congress, in *La 'Questione Comunista'*, Vol. 1, p. 415.

7. Berlinguer, 'La peculiarità socialista', p. 510.

8. See text in Berlinguer, *La 'Questione Comunista'*, Vol. 1; the words cited are on p. 415.

9. I use here the text published in Berlinguer, *La "Questione Comunista"*, Vol. 2, p. 633. Berlinguer's original articles in *Rinascita* were 'Imperialismo e coesistenza alla luce dei fatti cileni', 28 September 1973; 'Via democratica e violenza reazionaria', 5 October 1973; and 'Alleanze sociali e schieramenti politici', 12 October 1973.

10. Ibid., p. 616.

11. Ibid., p. 619. Referring to Greece, Berlinguer clearly alluded to Chile.

12. Ibid., p. 631.

13. Ibid., p. 636.

14. Ibid., pp. 636–8.

15. See text of declaration in Domenico Rosati, *La questione politica delle ACLI*, Edizioni Dehoniane, Naples 1975, pp. 254–61.

16. Aniello Coppola, *Moro*, Feltrinelli, Milan 1976, p. 136.

17. G. De Lutiis, *Storia dei servizi segreti in Italia*, Editori Riuniti, Rome 1985 (especially the conclusion); G. Flamini, *Il partito del golpe*, 3 vols, Bovolenta, Ferrara 1981–83; R. Chiarini and Paolo Corsini, *Da Salò a piazza della Loggia. Blocco d'ordine, neofascismo, radicalismo di destra a Brescia (1945–1974)*, Franco Angeli, Milan 1983; Paolo Corsini and Laura Novati (eds), *L'eversione nera. Cronache di un decennio 1974–1984*, Franco Angeli, Milan 1985.

18. See Gerardo Chiaromonte, *Le scelte della solidarietà democratica. Cronache, ricordi e riflessioni sul triennio 1976–1979*, Editori Riuniti, Rome 1986, pp. 30, 163; Giorgio Napolitano, *In mezzo al guado*, Editori Riuniti, Rome 1979, p. xix; and Fernando Di Giulio, *Un ministro ombra si confessa* (with Emmanuele Rocco), Rizzoli, Milan 1979, p. 28. Berlinguer, however, at the Fifteenth Congress of the PCI in April 1979, denied the existence of a special relationship between the PCI and the DC; see his *Per il socialismo nella pace e nella democrazia in Italia e in Europa*, Editori Riuniti, Rome 1979, p. 109.

19. See my *The Strategy of the Italian Communist Party*, chapter 3, and 'The Role of the Italian Communist Party in the Consolidation of Parliamentary Democracy in Italy', in Pridham (ed.), *Securing Democracy*.

20. Giacomo Luciani, *Il PCI e il capitalismo occidentale*, Longanesi, Milan 1977, p. 11; and Giulio Andreotti, *Visti da vicino. Il meglio delle tre serie*, Rizzoli, Milan 1986, pp. 226–7.

21. To mention just some non-Italian scholars who are reasonably distant from the daily vicissitudes of Italian politics: D. L. M. Blackmer and Sidney Tarrow (eds), *Communism in Italy and France*, Princeton University Press, Princeton NJ 1975; Ginsborg, *A History of Contemporary Italy*; Urban, *Moscow and the Italian Communist Party*; Sidney Tarrow, *Peasant Communism in Southern Italy*, Yale University Press, New Haven CT 1967; D. L. M. Blackmer, *Unity in Diversity*; Amyot, *The Italian Communist Party*; James Ruscoe, *The Italian Communist Party 1976–81. On the Threshold of Government*, Macmillan, London 1982; Lumley, *States of Emergency*; Stephen Hellman, *Italian Communism in Transition: The Rise and Fall of the Historic Compromise in Turin 1975–80*, Oxford University Press, New York 1988; Chris Shore, *Italian Communism: The Escape from Leninism*, Pluto Press, London 1990; Lazar, *Maisons rouges*; Timmermann, *I comunisti italiani*. See also the numerous references to the Italian Communist Party in the works of Joseph La Palombara, Percy Allum, Peter Lange, Robert Leonardi and many others; the work of younger scholars suggests that the overwhelming consensus on the democratic reliability of the PCI in the 1970s and 1980s is unlikely to be challenged.

22. Chiara Valentini, *Berlinguer Il Segretario*, Mondadori, Milan 1987, pp. 32–3.

23. See Berlinguer's criticisms of the Portuguese communists in his concluding remarks to the Fourteenth Congress of the PCI (23 March 1975), in Enrico Berlinguer, *La politica internazionale dei comunisti italiani*, Editori Riuniti, Rome 1976, p. 29.

24. Celso Ghini, *Il terremoto del 15 giugno*, Feltrinelli, Milan 1976, p. 162.

25. The quoted passages of this interview can be found in Donald Sassoon (ed.), *The Italian Communists Speak for Themselves*, Spokesman, Nottingham 1978, pp. 73–4.

26. See Franco De Felice's perceptive essay 'Doppia lealtà e doppio stato', *Studi Storici*, no. 3, 1989, pp. 516ff.

27. Andreotti was asked by Moro to become the next prime minister because he could reassure both the DC right and the USA; see Giulio Andreotti, *Diari 1976–1979. Gli anni della solidarietà*, Rizzoli, Milan 1981, p. 19.

28. The position of the PSI was explained and defended by Bettino Craxi in his report to the Central Committee in May 1978; see his *Prove marzo 1978 gennaio 1980*, Sugarco Edizione, Milan 1980, especially p. 31.

29. See Adriano Sofri's accolade for Craxi's alleged libertarian vocation and his respect for the individual, in *L'ombra di Moro*, Sellerio, Palermo 1991, p. 153. Sofri had been the leader of *Lotta continua*, a revolutionary organization active in the 1970s.

30. See Giampaolo Pansa, *Comprati e venduti. I giornali e il potere negli anni '70*, Bompiani, Milan 1977, p. 271.

31. Franco Cazzola, 'La solidarietà nazionale dalla parte del Parlamento', *Laboratorio politico*, nos 2–3, March–June 1982, pp. 188–9.

32. Chiaromonte, op. cit., p. 34.

33. Ibid., p. 36.

34. Valentini, op. cit., p. 119.

35. Chiaromonte, op. cit., p. 160.

36. Data in Mauro Galleni, *Rapporto sul terrorismo. Le stragi, gli agguati, i sequestri, le sigle 1969–1980*, Rizzoli, Milan 1981, pp. 49–63.

37. Cited in Zbigniew Brzezinski, *Power and Principle: Memoirs of the National Security Advisor 1977–1981*, Weidenfeld and Nicolson, London 1983, p. 312. Brzezinski, who recognized that Italians were becoming increasingly alienated from the DC by political scandals, thought, with simplistic smugness, that this 'firm stand' was vindicated by the failure of the communists. Andreotti found this useless, inopportune, 'inelegant' and an interference in Italian affairs; see *Diari*, p. 173.

38. Vittorio Valli, *L'economia e la politica economica italiana 1945–1979*, Etas Libri, Milan 1979, pp. 133–6.

39. I use the text of the *Accordo Programmatico* published in Gerardo Chiaromonte, *L'accordo programmatico e l'azione dei comunisti*, Editori Riuniti, Rome 1977, pp. 53–116; the passage on the Letter of Intent is on pp. 69–70.

40. Napolitano, op. cit., pp. xviii–xix.

41. Renato Filosa and Ignazio Visco, 'Costo del lavoro, indicizzazione e perequazione delle retribuzioni negli anni '70', in Giangiacomo Nardozzi (ed.), *I Difficili anni '70. I problemi della politica economica italiana 1973/1979*, Etas Libri, Milan 1980, pp. 111ff.

42. Enrico Berlinguer, *Austerità occasione per trasformare l'Italia*, Editori Riuniti, Rome 1977, pp. 52–3; this volume includes the text of both speeches. The theme of austerity had earlier been presented to the Central Committee meeting of October 1976.

43. Ibid., p. 13.

44. Ibid., p. 18.

45. Ginsborg, op. cit., p. 389.

46. For evidence of local communist resistance to Lama's EUR line, see Miriam Golden, *Labor Divided. Austerity and Working Class Politics in Contemporary Italy*, Cornell University Press, Ithaca NY and London 1988, pp. 150–51.

47. See the various citations in Valentini, op. cit., pp. 140–1.

48. Lumley, op. cit., p. 297.

49. Enrico Berlinguer, *La nostra lotta dall'opposizione verso il governo*, Editori Riuniti, Rome 1979, pp. 47–50.

50. Maurizio Ferrera, 'Politics, Institutional Features, and the Government of Industry', in Peter Lange and Marino Regini (eds), *State, Market, and Social Regulation*, Cambridge University Press, Cambridge 1989, pp. 121–3. Ferrera also provides an impressive bibliography mapping out the disaster which was Law 675.

51. For a critique of the notion of 'loyalty', see Giuseppe Vacca's critique of his party's policy in the 1970s: *Tra compromesso e solidarietà. La politica del Pci negli anni '70*, Editori Riuniti, Rome 1987 especially p. 117.

52. Fernando Di Giulio, 'Lotta politica e riforme istituzionali', *Democrazia e diritto*, no. 5, pp. 6–7.

53. Enrico Berlinguer, report to the Central Committee (10 December 1974), published as *La proposta comunista*, Einaudi Editore, Turin 1975, p. 5.

54. Vacca, op. cit., p. 189.

55. Napolitano, op. cit., pp. lix–lx.

56. Craxi, op. cit., pp. 112, 230.

57. See Craxi's 1979 speeches in ibid., especially pp. 111, 164 and 232.

21. The End of Authoritarian Regimes in Western Europe

1. On the events surrounding the attempted coup, see Paul Preston, *The Triumph of Democracy in Spain*, Methuen, London 1987, especially pp. 195–206.

2. Walter C. Opello Jr, 'Portugal: A Case Study of International Determinats of Regime Transition', in Geoffrey Pridham (ed.), *Encouraging Democracy. The International Context of Regime Transition in Southern Europe*, Leicester University Press, Leicester and London 1991, p. 85.

3. Susannah Verney and Panos Tsakaloyannis, 'Linkage Politics: The Role of the European Community in Greek Politics in 1973', *Byzantine and Modern Greek Studies*, Vol. 10, 1986, pp. 184–9.

4. Willy Brandt admitted in 1980 that the SPD was bankrolling the PSOE; see Richard Gunther, Giacomo Sani and Goldie Shabad, *Spain After Franco. The Making of a Competitive Party System*, University of California Press, Berkeley 1985, pp. 75, 460n.

5. Mário Soares, *Portugal: Quelle révolution?*, Calmann-Lévy, Paris 1976, p. 93.

6. Thomas C. Bruneau, 'The Left and the Emergence of Portuguese Liberal Democracy', in B. Brown (ed.), *Eurocommunism and Eurosocialism*, p. 167.

7. See Hans Janitschek, *Mário Soares. Portrait of a Hero*, Weidenfeld and Nicolson, London 1985, p. 33; Janitschek, a former general secretary of the Socialist International, provides a sycophantic portrait of Soares in the personality cult school of historiography.

8. Soares, op. cit., p. 26.

9. Gillespie, *The Spanish Socialist Party*, p. 137.

10. José María Maravall, 'The Socialist Alternative: The Policies and the Electorate of the PSOE', in Howard Penniman and Eusebio M. Mujal-León (eds), *Spain at the Polls 1977, 1979, and 1982. A Study of National Elections*, American Enterprise Institute and Duke University Press, n. p. 1985, p. 132.

11. Gillespie, op. cit., pp. 276–7 and Maravall, op. cit., p. 134.

12. Donald Share, *Dilemmas of Social Democracy. The Spanish Socialist Workers Party in the 1980s*, Greenwood Press, Westport CT 1989, p. 40.

13. On NATO, see *Programa e Estatutos do PCP aprovado No VII Congresso (Extraordinário) em 20/10/74*, 2nd edn, Edições *Avante!*, Lisbon 1975, pp. 60–1.

14. For an examination of the PCP's pro-Sovietism, see Alex Macleod, 'Portrait of a Model Ally: The Portuguese Communist Party and the International Communist Movement, 1968–1983', *Studies in Comparative Communism*, Vol. XVII, no. 1, Spring 1984.

15. Soares, op. cit., p. 62.

16. Gunther, Sani and Shabad, op. cit., p. 67.

17. Ken Gladdish, 'Portugal: An Open Verdict', in Geoffrey Pridham (ed), *Securing Democracy: Political Parties and Democratic Consolidation in Southern Europe*, Routledge, London 1990, p. 104.

18. Diamantino P. Machado, *The Structure of Portuguese Society. The Failure of Fascism*, Praeger, New York 1991, p. 125.

19. Eusebio Mujal-León, *Communism and Political Change in Spain*, Indiana University Press, Bloomington 1983, p. 22.

20. Preston, op. cit., pp. 25–6.

21. Mujal-León, op. cit., p. 129.

22. Victor Alba, *The Communist Party in Spain*, Transaction Books, New Brunswick 1983, p. 387.

23. Gianfranco Pasquino, 'Party Elites and Democratic Consolidation: Cross-national Comparison of Southern European Experience', in Pridham (ed.), *Securing Democracy*, p. 49.

24. Machado, op. cit., pp. 52–3, 83.

25. Eric N. Baklanoff, *The Economic Transformation of Spain and Portugal*, Praeger, New York 1978, p. 104.

26. Walter C. Opello Jr, 'The Continuing Impact of the Old Regime on Portuguese Political Culture', in Lawrence S. Graham and Douglas L. Wheeler (eds), *In Search of Modern Portugal. The Revolution and Its Consequences*, University of Wisconsin Press, Madison 1983, pp. 207–8.

27. Machado, op. cit., pp. 15–16.

28. Mário Murteira, 'The Present Economic Situation: Its Origins and Prospects', in Lawrence S. Graham and Harry M. Makler (eds), *Contemporary Portugal. The Revolution and its Antecedents*, University of Texas Press, Austin 1979, p. 333.

29. Baklanoff, op. cit., p. 132.

30. Machado, op. cit., p. 24 and Murteira, op. cit., p. 333.

31. Murteira, op. cit., p. 334.

32. Rodney J. Morrison, *Portugal: Revolutionary Change in an Open Economy*, Auburn House, Boston 1981, p. 5 and Joan Esteban, 'The Economic Policy of Francoism: An Interpretation', in Paul Preston (ed.), *Spain in Crisis. The Evolution and Decline of the Franco Régime*, Harvester Press, Hassocks, Sussex 1976, pp. 99–100.

33. Hans O. Schmitt, *Economic Stabilization and Growth in Portugal*, Occasional Paper no. 2, International Monetary Fund, Washington DC April 1981, p. 2.

34. Tom Gallagher, *Portugal. A Twentieth-century Interpretation*, Manchester University Press, Manchester 1983, pp. 157, 163n.

35. Baklanoff, op. cit., p. 130.

36. Ibid., p. 21.

37. Sima Lieberman, *The Contemporary Spanish Economy: A Historical Perspective*, Allen and Unwin, London 1982, p. 193.

38. Raymond Carr and Juan Pablo Fusi, *Spain: Dictatorship to Democracy*, Allen and Unwin, London 1979, p. 54.

39. Lieberman, op. cit., pp. 201–3.

40. Ibid., p. 223.

41. Ramón Tamames, *¿Adónde vas, España?*, Editorial Planeta, Barcelona 1976, pp. 192–3.

42. Lieberman, op. cit., p. 234.

43. Baklanoff, op. cit., p. 68 and Lieberman, op. cit., p. 212.

44. Lieberman, op. cit., p. 214.

45. Carr and Fusi, op. cit., p. 59.

46. Baklanoff, op. cit., p. 175.

47. Lieberman, op. cit., p. 238.

48. Víctor M. Pérez-Díaz, *The Return of Civil Society. The Emergence of Democratic Spain*, Harvard University Press, Cambridge MA 1993, p. 14.

49. Morrison, op. cit., p. 13.

50. Schmitt, op. cit., p. 2, and Rudiger Dornbusch, Richard S. Eckaus and Lance Taylor,

'Analysis and Projection of Macroeconomic Conditions in Portugal', in Graham and Makler (eds), op. cit., p. 299.

51. Gallagher, op. cit., p. 169.

52. John Hooper, *The Spaniards*, Penguin, Harmondsworth 1986, p. 28.

53. Ibid., p. 28.

54. Ibid., p. 29.

55. Tamames, op. cit., pp. 54, 62–4.

56. Cited in Carr and Fusi, op. cit., p. 192.

57. Mário Soares, *Le Portugal bâillonné. Un témoignage*, Calmann-Lévy, Paris 1972. The book was published in English in 1975 unaltered, except for a new preface, see *Portugal's Struggle for Liberty*, Allen and Unwin, London 1975.

58. Alvaro Cunhal, *Discursos políticos (Abril/Julho de 1974)*, Vol. 1, Edições *Avante!*, Lisbon 1975, pp. 11–12 and PCP, op. cit., pp. 12ff.

59. Morrison, op. cit., p. 23.

60. Ibid., p. 47.

61. Lawrence S. Graham, 'The Military in Politics: The Politicization of the Portuguese Armed Forces', in Graham and Makler (eds), op. cit., p. 243.

62. See interview with Vasco Gonçalves in Hugo Gil Ferreira and Michael W. Marshall, *Portugal's Revolution: Ten Years On*, Cambridge University Press, Cambridge 1986, p. 92. Confirmation of this account can be found in OECD, *Economic Survey, Portugal*, November 1976. p. 7; see also Gallagher, op. cit., p. 210.

63. Morrison, op. cit., p. 48.

64. John L. Hammond, 'Electoral Behavior and Political Militancy', in Graham and Makler (eds), op. cit., pp. 262–3.

65. Ibid., p. 273.

66. Tom Gallagher, 'From Hegemony to Opposition: The Ultra Right before and after 1974', in Graham and Wheeler (eds), op. cit., p. 92.

67. See Alvaro Cunhal's speech of 16 March 1975, in *Discursos políticos, Dezembro 1974/Março 1975*, Vol. 3, Edições *Avante!*, Lisbon 1975, p. 161.

68. Soares, *Portugal: Quelle révolution?*, p. 117.

69. Ibid., p. 118.

70. Speech to the Central Committee of 10 August 1975, in Alvaro Cunhal, *A crise político-militar. Discursos políticos, Maio/Novembro 1975*, Vol. 5, Edições *Avante!*, Lisbon 1975, p. 132.

71. Ibid., p. 145.

72. Ibid., pp. 131, 136.

73. See his interview in Ferreira and Marshall, op. cit., p. 119.

74. Martin Kayman, *Revolution and Counter-revolution in Portugal*, Merlin Press, London 1987, pp. 168–9.

75. Morrison, op. cit., p. 60.

76. Baklanoff, op. cit., p. 140.

77. Dornbusch, Eckaus and Taylor, op. cit., pp. 300–1.

78. Schmitt, op. cit., p. 3.

79. OECD, *Economic Survey, Portugal*, 1976, pp. 16–17.

80. Morrison, op. cit., p. 13.

81. Figures provided by the Portuguese authorities and cited in Schmitt, op. cit., p. 17.

82. OECD, *Economic Survey, Portugal*, p. 9.

83. Ibid., p. 24.

84. Dornbusch, Eckaus and Taylor, op. cit., pp. 299–300.

85. Morrison, op. cit., p. 68.

86. On the characteristics of the southern rural proletariat, see Caroline B. Brettell,

'Emigration and Its Implications for the Revolution in Northern Portugal', in Graham and Makler (eds), op. cit., p. 285. See also Hammond, op. cit., p. 259.

87. Murteira, op. cit., p. 337.

88. Morrison, op. cit., p. 45.

89. Gladdish, op. cit., p. 109.

90. Ibid., pp. 107–8. See also Tom Gallagher, 'The Portuguese Socialist Party: The Pitfalls of Being First', in Tom Gallagher and Allan M. Williams (eds), *Southern European Socialism. Parties, Elections and the Challenge of Government*, Manchester University Press, Manchester 1988, p. 14.

91. Schmitt, op. cit., p. 4.

92. Morrison, op. cit., p. 74.

93. See Schmitt, op. cit., p. 4. The full story is succinctly described in Morrison, op. cit., pp. 75–87.

94. Donoughue, *Prime Minister*, p. 95.

95. Official figures cited in Schmitt, op. cit., p. 17.

96. Morrison, op. cit., p. 107.

97. Gallagher, 'The Portuguese Socialist Party ...', p. 27.

98. Peter Wise, 'A time for celebration and reflection', *Financial Times*, 22 February 1994, p. 11.

99. Preston, *The Triumph of Democracy in Spain*, p. 76.

100. Alba, op. cit., p. 406.

101. Carr and Fusi, op. cit., pp. 208–9.

102. Ibid., pp. 148–9.

103. Baklanoff, op. cit., p. 91 and Share, op. cit., p. 37.

104. Preston, *The Triumph of Democracy in Spain*, p. 81.

105. Maravall, op. cit., p. 135.

106. Sebastian Balfour, *Dictatorship, Workers, and the City. Labour in Greater Barcelona Since 1939*, Clarendon Press, Oxford 1989, pp. 219–20.

107. Mujal-León, op. cit., pp. 159–60.

108. Paul Heywood, 'Mirror-images: The PCE and PSOE in the Transition to Democracy in Spain', *West European Politics*, Vol. 10, no. 2, April 1987, p. 195.

109. Eusebio Mujal-León, 'Decline and Fall of Spanish Communism', *Problems of Communism*, Vol. XXXV, no. 2 March–April 1986, p. 3.

110. Share, op. cit., p. 40.

111. Mujal-León, *Communism and Political Change in Spain*, p. 158.

112. Maravall, op. cit., p. 136.

113. PSOE, *XXVII Congreso. Memoria de gestión de la Comisión Ejecutiva. Informe de la Comisión Ejecutiva al Congreso*, n.p. and n.d, pp. 13, 29, and 101.

114. Robert M. Fishman, *Working-Class Organization and the Return to Democracy in Spain*, Cornell University Press, Ithaca NY and London 1990, p. 145. Fishman reads far too much into his survey which, at most, establishes that communist trade unionists were dissatisfied with how things had turned out for them and their party.

115. See the Transitional Programme presented by the National Committee of the PSOE in PSOE, *XXVII Congreso*, pp. 112–13.

116. Felipe González, 'La unidad de los socialistas', *Sistema*, no. 15, October 1976, pp. 46–7.

117. Alfonso Guerra, 'Los partidos socialistas del sur de Europa y las relaciones socialistas-comunistas', *Sistema*, no. 15, October 1976, pp. 54–5.

118. Ibid., pp. 59–60.

119. Share, op. cit., pp. 41–3.

120. David Gilmour, *The Transformation of Spain*, Quartet Books, London 1985, p. 182.

121. Preston, *The Triumph of Democracy in Spain*, p. 119.

122. Share, op. cit., p. 42.

123. Gunther, Sani and Shabad, op. cit., pp. 160–1.

124. Mujal-León, *Communism and Political Change in Spain*, p. 178; on the close relationship between the two leaders, see also the testimony of Manuel Azcárate, *Crisis del Eurocomunismo*, Editorial Argos Vergara, Barcelona 1982, p. 98.

125. Richard Gunther, 'Democratization and Party Building: The Role of Party Elites in the Spanish Transition', in Robert P. Clark and Michael H. Haltzel (eds), *Spain in the 1980s. The Democratic Transition and a New International Role*, Ballinger, Cambridge MA 1987, p. 59.

126. Mujal-León, *Communism and Political Change in Spain*, pp. 181–2.

127. Gillespie, op. cit., p. 326 and Richard Clogg, *Parties and Elections in Greece. The Search for Legitimacy*, C. Hurst and Co., London 1987, pp. 90, 143.

128. This point is made in José Maravall, *The Transition to Democracy in Spain*, Croom Helm, London 1982, pp. 158–9, where, however, the figures and years are wrong.

129. Baklanoff, op. cit., pp. 90–4 and Carr and Fusi, op. cit., p. 219.

130. Lieberman, op. cit., p. 276.

131. Gilmour, op. cit., p. 190 and Lieberman, op. cit., pp. 276–7.

132. R. M. Fishman, op. cit., p. 217.

133. Preston, *The Triumph of Democracy in Spain*, p. 137.

134. Maravall, op. cit., p. 138.

135. Fishman, op. cit., pp. 219–20.

136. Ibid., p. 216. The author points out that strike statistics for this period are not very reliable.

137. Carr and Fusi, op. cit., pp. 234–5.

138. Ibid., pp. 95–103.

139. Heywood, op. cit., p. 201.

140. On the making of the Spanish constitution, see Andrea R. Bonime, 'The Spanish State Structure: Constitution Making and the Creation of the New State', in Thomas D. Lancaster and Gary Prevost (eds), *Politics and Change in Spain*, Praeger, New York 1985, pp. 10–34.

141. Share, op. cit., p. 49, though note that the Constitution established the right to life, an ambiguous concept which could have been used by the courts to block pro-abortion legislation. See Monica Threlfall, 'Social Policy Towards Women in Spain, Greece and Portugal', in Tom Gallagher and Allan M. Williams (eds), *Southern European Socialism. Parties, Elections and the Challenge of Government*, Manchester University Press, Manchester 1989, pp. 219, 235.

142. Monica Threlfall, 'The Women's Movement in Spain', *New Left Review*, no. 151, May–June 1985, p. 49.

143. Share, op. cit., pp. 58–9.

144. On the complete ineffectiveness of the PSOE Left, see Gillespie, op. cit., pp. 348–54.

145. Share, op. cit., pp. 54–7 and Heywood, op. cit., p. 206.

146. González, op. cit., pp. 50–51.

147. Gillespie, op. cit., pp. 340–1.

148. Ibid., pp. 337–8.

149. Mujal-León, *Communism and Political Change in Spain*, pp. 174–6.

150. Gunther, Sani and Shabad, op. cit., p. 153.

151. Patrick Camiller, 'The Eclipse of Spanish Communism', *New Left Review*, no. 147, September–October 1984, p. 122.

152. Paul Preston, 'The PCE in the Struggle for Democracy in Spain', in Howard Machin (ed.), *National Communism in Western Europe. A Third Way for Socialism?*, Methuen, London 1983, p. 158.

153. Mujal-León, 'Decline and Fall of Spanish Communism', p. 7.

154. Azcárate, op. cit., pp. 21ff.

155. See Pedro Vega and Peru Erroteta, *Los herejes del PCE*, Editorial Planeta, Barcelona 1982, especially pp. 207–31.

156. Gerardo Iglesias, 'Adecuar el partido a la estrategia', *Nuestra Bandera*, Nos 118–19, 1983 pp. 6–11.

157. Benny Pollack, 'The 1982 Spanish General Election and Beyond', in *Parliamentary Affairs*, Vol. 36, no. 2, Spring 1983, p. 205.

158. PSOE, *Estrategia economica del PSOE*, Editorial Pablo Iglesias, Madrid 1980, p. 19.

159. Ibid., p. 49.

160. Camiller, op. cit., p. 255.

161. Georges B. Dertilis, 'Terre, paysans et pouvoir politique (Grèce, XVIIIe–XXe siècle)', *Annales*, Vol. 48, no. 1, January–February 1993, p. 85.

162. Nicos P. Mouzelis, 'Capitalism and Dictatorship in Post-war Greece', *New Left Review*, no. 96, March–April 1976, p. 61. A thorough analysis of Greek government land policies to 1881 is contained in William W. McGrew, *Land and Revolution in Modern Greece, 1800–1881: The Transition in the Tenure and Exploitation of Land from Ottoman Rule to Independence*, Kent State University Press, Kent OH 1985, especially Part II.

163. See John D. Bell, *Peasants in Power. Alexander Stamboliski and the Bulgarian Agrarian National Union, 1899–1923*, Princeton University Press, Princeton NJ 1977.

164. Nicos Mouzelis, 'On the Greek Elections', *New Left Review*, no. 108, March–April 1978, p. 73.

165. On the agrarian causes of the Spanish Civil War, see Preston, *The Coming of the Spanish Civil War*.

166. On the historical roots of modern personalistic and clientelistic politics in Greece, see George Th. Mavrogordatos, *Stillborn Republic: Social Conditions and Party Strategies in Greece 1922–1936*, University of California Press, Berkeley 1983.

167. P. Nikiforos Diamandouros, 'Greek Political Culture in Transition: Historical Origins, Evolution, Current Trends', in Richard Clogg (ed.), *Greece in the 1980s*, Macmillan, London 1983, pp. 44–5.

168. David Close, 'Conservatism, Authoritarianism and Fascism in Greece, 1915–45', in Blinkhorn (ed.), *Fascists and Conservatives*, p. 205.

169. A. F. Freris, *The Greek Economy in the Twentieth Century*, Croom Helm, London and Sydney 1986, p. 151.

170. Nicos P. Mouzelis, *Modern Greece. Facets of Underdevelopment*, Holmes and Meier Publs., New York 1978, pp. 27, 118–19.

171. Mouzelis, *Modern Greece*, p. 25 and Freris, op. cit., pp. 168–76.

172. Mouzelis, *Modern Greece*, p. 37.

173. Freris, op. cit., p. 156.

174. Mouzelis, *Modern Greece*, pp. 28–9.

175. Freris, op. cit., pp. 144–9.

176. Ibid., p. 187.

177. Clogg, *Parties and Elections in Greece*, p. 29.

178. Cited in John O. Iatrides, 'Beneath the Sound and the Fury: US Relations with the PASOK Government', in Richard Clogg (ed.), *Greece, 1981–89. The Populist Decade*, St Martin's Press, New York 1993, p. 166.

179. Andreas G. Papandreou, *A Strategy for Greek Economic Development*, Center of Economic Research, Contos Press, Athens 1962, p. 96.

180. Robert McDonald, 'The Colonels' Dictatorship 1967–1974', in Marion Sarafis and Martin Eve (eds), *Background to Contemporary Greece*, Vol. II, Merlin Press, London 1990, p. 258.

181. Jon V. Kofas, *Authoritarianism in Greece: The Metaxas Regime*, Columbia University Press, New York 1983.

182. Mouzelis, *Modern Greece*, p. 128.

183. Constantine P. Danopoulos, 'Military Professionalism and Regime Legitimacy in Greece, 1967–1974', *Political Science Quarterly*, Vol. 98, no. 3, Fall 1983, p. 491; and McDonald, op. cit., p. 270.

184. Kallistos Ware, 'The Church: A Time of Transition', in Clogg (ed.), *Greece in the 1980s*, p. 208.

185. S. Victor Papacosma, 'The Historical Context', in Clogg (ed.), *Greece in the 1980s*, p. 37.

186. Danopoulos, op. cit., p. 493.

187. Freris, op. cit., p. 162.

188. Danopoulos, op. cit., p. 497.

189. George S. Alogoskoufis, 'On the Determinants of Consumer Price Inflation in Greece', *Greek Economic Review*, Vol. 8, no. 2, December 1986, p. 251.

190. William S. Shepard, 'The Cyprus Issue: Waiting for Sadat', in Nikolaos A. Stavrou (ed.), *Greece under Socialism. A NATO Ally Adrift*, Orpheus Publishing, New Rochelle NY 1988, p. 381.

191. See Yannis Papadopoulos, 'Parties, the State and Society in Greece: Continuity within Change', *West European Politics*, Vol. 12, no. 2, April 1989.

192. Clogg, *Parties and Elections in Greece*, p. 59.

193. Geoffrey Pridham and Susannah Verney, 'The Coalitions of 1989–90 in Greece: Interparty Relations and Democratic Consolidation', *West European Politics*, Vol. 14, no. 4, October 1991, p. 47.

194. Clogg, *Parties and Elections in Greece*, p. 78.

195. Andreas G. Papandreou, *Paternalistic Capitalism*, Minneapolis University Press, Minneapolis 1972, p. 160.

196. Ibid., p. 161.

197. On the anti-Americanism of the Greeks, see Ioannis Papadopoulos, *Dynamique du discours politique et conquête du pouvoir. Le cas du PASOK: 1974–1981*, Peter Lang, Berne 1989 (University of Geneva doctoral dissertation no. 321), citing Eurobarometers surveys showing that in 1980 there was more distrust of the USA in Greece than in any of the other ten EEC countries: pp. 234–5.

198. Michalis Spourdalakis, *The Rise of the Greek Socialist Party*, Routledge, London and New York 1988, p. 5.

199. C. M. Woodhouse, *Karamanlis. The Restorer of Greek Democracy*, Clarendon Press, Oxford 1982 pp. 216–18, 236–7.

200. Panayote E. Dimitras, 'La Grèce en quête d'une politique indépendante', *Revue française de science politique*, Vol. 33, no. 1, February 1983, pp. 110–12.

201. Ibid., p. 115.

202. This view is developed in George Mavrogordatos, *The Rise of the Greek Sun: The Greek Elections of 1981*, King's College London, Centre for Contemporary Greek Studies, Occasional Paper no. 1, 1983; see also Spourdalakis, op. cit., p. 23.

203. Dimitras, op. cit., pp. 125–6.

204. Shepard, op. cit., p. 382.

205. See Nicos Mouzelis, 'On the Demise of Oligarchic Parliamentarism in the Semi-Periphery: A Balkan-Latin American Comparison', *Sociology*, Vol. 17, no. 1, February 1983, pp. 28–43.

206. Papandreou, *Paternalistic Capitalism*, pp. 168–9.

207. This text can be found in Clogg, *Parties and Elections in Greece*, pp. 217–22 and in Spourdalakis, op. cit., pp. 288–95.

208. Clogg, *Parties and Elections in Greece*, pp. 217–18.

209. Ibid., p. 220.

210. Ibid., pp. 222–1.

211. Angelos Elephantis, 'PASOK and the Elections of 1977: The Rise of the Populist Movement', in Howard R. Penniman (ed.), *Greece at the Polls. The National Elections of 1974 and 1977*, American Enterprise Institute for Public Policy Research, Washington and London 1981, p. 113.

212. See, among many others, Spourdalakis, op. cit.; see also Vassilus Fouskas, *Populism and Modernization, the Exhaustion of the Third Hellenic Republic, 1974–94*, Athens 1995 (in Greek). Fouskas acknowledges the 'positive' aspects of PASOK's populism, especially its welfare policies in 1981–85. Elephantis, op. cit., p. 119 should be read as an instance of exaggerated anti-PASOK *parti pris* by a KKE-es activist.

213. Spourdalakis, op. cit., chapter 3, gives a detailed first-hand account of this inner-party strife, somewhat exaggerating its importance.

214. Clogg, *Parties and Elections in Greece*, p. 84.

215. Spourdalakis, op. cit., p. 166 and Clogg, *Parties and Elections in Greece*, p. 92.

216. Ware, op. cit., p. 226.

217. Nicos P. Mouzelis, 'Continuities and Discontinuities in Greek Politics: From Elefterios Venizelos to Andreas Papandreou', in Kevin Featherstone and Dimitrios K. Katsoudas (eds), *Political Change in Greece. Before and after the Colonels*, Croom Helm, London 1987, pp. 275–6.

218. Richard Gillespie, 'Regime Consolidation in Spain: Party, State, and Society', in Pridham (ed.), *Securing Democracy*, p. 140.

219. Spourdalakis, op. cit., p. 187.

220. Ibid., p. 212.

221. Cited in ibid., p. 195.

222. Mouzelis, 'On the Greek Elections', p. 66.

223. Stylianos Hadjiyannis, 'Democratization and the Greek State', in Ronald H. Chilcote et al., *Transitions from Dictatorship to Democracy. Comparative Studies of Spain, Portugal and Greece*, Crane Russak, New York 1990, p. 143.

224. On this and the gradual Europeanization of PASOK, see Susannah Verney, 'Greece and the European Community', in Featherstone and Katsoudas (eds), op. cit., pp. 264ff.

225. Clogg, *Parties and Elections in Greece*, pp. 97, 133 and 141.

226. See Theodore A. Couloumbis, 'PASOK's Foreign Policies, 1981–89: Continuity or Change?', in Clogg (ed.), *Greece, 1981–89*, pp. 120–1 and Iatrides, op. cit., p. 155.

227. Cited in Spourdalakis, op. cit., p. 202.

228. Ibid., p. 203.

229. See the string of quotations cited by Matthew Nimetz in his introduction to Stavrou (ed.), op. cit., pp. 1–3.

230. James Petras, 'The Contradictions of Greek Socialism', *New Left Review*, no. 163, May–June 1987, p. 13.

231. Alogoskoufis, op. cit., p. 256.

232. Efthalia Kalogeropoulou, 'Election Promises and Government Performance in Greece: PASOK's Fulfilment of its 1981 Election Pledges', *European Journal of Political Research*, Vol. 17, no. 3, 1989, p. 291.

233. See Eleni Stamiris, 'The Women's Movement in Greece', *New Left Review*, no. 158, July–August 1986, pp. 109–10. See also Gisela Kaplan, *Contemporary Western European Feminism*, Allen and Unwin, Sydney 1992, pp. 223–7.

234. George Tsalikis, 'Evaluation of the Social Health Policy in Greece', *International Journal of Health Services*, Vol. 18, no. 4, 1988, p. 554.

235. Christos Lyrintzis, 'PASOK in Power: From "Change" to Disenchantment', in Clogg (ed.), *Greece, 1981–89*, p. 27.

236. Athanasios P. Papadopoulos, 'The Effects of Monetary, Fiscal and Exchange-rate Policies on Output, Prices and the Balance of Payments in the Open Economy of Greece, 1955–90', *Applied Economics*, Vol. 25, no. 7, July 1993, p. 879.

237. For a comparison of public spending in Greece and Portugal, see Anthony S. Courakis, Fatima Mouraroque and George Tridimas, 'Public-expenditure Growth in Greece and Portugal, the Wagner Law and Beyond', *Applied Economics*, Vol. 25, no. 1, January 1993, pp. 125–34.

238. An analysis of this 'underdog' culture is provided by P. Nikiforos Diamandouros' essay 'Politics and Culture in Greece, 1974–91: An Interpretation', in Clogg (ed.), *Greece, 1981–89*, pp. 1–25.

239. Lyrintzis, op. cit., p. 36.

240. For a clear account of these complex events, see Pridham and Verney, and, in Greek, Fouskas, op. cit.

241. Pridham and Verney, op. cit., pp. 55–6.

22. Workers, Women and Greens

1. Alain Touraine, *L'après socialisme*, 2nd edn, Grasset, Paris 1983, p. 19.

2. Ralf Dahrendorf, *Reflections on the Revolution in Europe*, Chatto and Windus, London 1990, p. 38.

3. Anthony Giddens, *Beyond Left and Right. The Future of Radical Politics*, Polity Press, Cambridge 1994, p. 52.

4. Perry Anderson, Introduction to Perry Anderson and Patrick Camiller (eds), *Mapping the West European Left*, Verso, London 1994, p. 2.

5. Wolfgang Merkel, 'After the Golden Age. Is Social Democracy Doomed to Decline?', in Christiane Lemke and Gary Marks (eds), *The Crisis of Socialism in Europe*, Duke University Press, Durham and London 1992, p. 140. On the stability of West European electorates, see also Peter Mair and Stefano Bartolini, *Identity, Competition and Electoral Availability. The Stabilization of European Electorates 1885–1985*, Cambridge University Press, Cambridge 1990.

6. John Dunn, *The Politics of Socialism*, Cambridge University Press, Cambridge 1984, p. 25.

7. Roth, *The Social Democrats in Imperial Germany*, p. 52.

8. Gorz's much-acclaimed theoretical framework is criticized in Anthony Giddens, 'The Perils of Punditry: Gorz and the End of the Working Class', in his *Social Theory and Modern Sociology*, Polity Press, Cambridge 1987, pp. 275–96.

9. See also a similar statistically backed point in Wolfgang Merkel, 'Between Class and Catch-all: Is There an Electoral Dilemma for Social Democratic Parties in Western Europe?', in Institut de Ciències Polítiques i Socials (ICPS), *Socialist Parties in Europe II: of Class, Populars, Catch-all?*, Barcelona 1992, p. 29.

10. Kitschelt, *The Transformation of European Social Democracy*, p. 41.

11. Ivor Crewe, 'The Labour Party and the Electorate', in Dennis Kavanagh (ed.), *The Politics of the Labour Party*, Allen and Unwin, London 1982, pp. 10–11.

12. Daniel Bell, *The Coming of Post-Industrial Society*, Heinemann, London 1974.

13. For an analysis of this in the Nordic countries, see Thomas P. Boje and Lise Drewes Nielsen, 'Flexible Production, Employment and Gender', in Thomas P. Boje and Sven E. Olsson Hort (eds), *Scandinavia in a New Europe*, Scandinavia University Press, Oslo 1993.

14. Mimmo Carrieri, 'Superare il "modello proletario" di azione sindacale', *Democrazia e diritto*, nos 1–2, January–February 1989, pp. 58–9.

15. Mario Caciagli, 'Apogeo e declino delle due grandi subculture politiche territoriali', paper presented to the Third Conference of the SISE, *Italia 1948–1988: Quarant'anni di dinamiche elettorali e istituzionali*, Naples, 6–8 October 1988.

16. See Ivor Crewe, 'Labor Force Changes, Working Class Decline and the Labour Vote: Social and Electoral Trends in Postwar Britain', in Frances Fox Piven (ed.), *Labor Parties in Postindustrial Societies*, Polity Press, Cambridge 1991, pp. 25–9, where it is pointed out that in the 1983 British general election there was a 4.5 per cent swing to Labour among unemployed manual workers – against the national trend.

17. Patrick Seyd and Paul Whiteley, *Labour's Grass Roots. The Politics of Party Membership*, Clarendon Press, Oxford 1992, pp. 28, 34.

18. Ibid., p. 34.

19. Ibid., p. 35. NUM members do not need to join as individuals because their union is affiliated; nevertheless; this gives an indication of the class basis of the Labour Party's grassroots.

20. Ibid.; see table on p. 39.

21. In their study of British voting patterns, *How Britain Votes*, Pergamon Press, Oxford 1985, Anthony Heath, Roger Jowell and John Curtice show that 'Labour remained a class party in 1983; it was simply a less successful class party than before', p. 29; see also chapter 3.

22. See Ivor Crewe and David Denver, *Electoral Change in Western Democracies: Patterns and Sources of Electoral Volatility*, Croom Helm, London 1985; Russell J. Dalton, Scott C. Flanagan and Paul Allen Beck (eds), *Electoral Change in Advanced Industrial Democracies: Realignment or Dealignment?*, Princeton University Press, Princeton NJ 1984; Paul Whiteley, *The Labour Party in Crisis*, Methuen, London and New York 1983, pp. 81–107; and Mark Franklin, *The Decline of Class Voting in Britain. Changes in the Basis of Electoral Choice 1964–1983*, Clarendon Press, Oxford 1985.

23. Ivor Crewe, 'On the Death and Resurrection of Class Voting: Some Comments on *How Britain Votes*', *Political Studies*, Vol. 34, no. 4, December 1986, p. 620; see the rejoinder by Anthony Heath, Roger Howell and John Curtice, 'Trendless Fluctuation: A Reply to Crewe', *Political Studies*, Vol. 35, no. 2, June 1987, pp. 256–77.

24. Andrei S. Markovits and Philip S. Gorski, *The German Left. Red, Green and Beyond*, Polity Press, Cambridge 1993, p. 267.

25. On the PCF, see Lazar, *Maisons rouges*, pp. 212–15; on the PCI, see Donald Sassoon, 'The 1987 Elections and the PCI', in Robert Leonardi and Piergiorgio Corbetta (eds), *Italian Politics. A Review*, Vol. 3, Pinter Publishers, New York and London 1989, p. 130.

26. David Butler and Dennis Kavanagh, *The British General Election of 1987*, Macmillan, London 1988, p. 275.

27. Frigga Haug, *Beyond Female Masochism*, Verso, London and New York 1992, p. 176.

28. Gisela Erler, 'The German Paradox; Non-feminization of the Labor Force and Post-industrial Social Policies', in Jane Jenson, Elisabeth Hangen and Ceallaigh Reddy (eds), *Feminization of the Labour Force. Paradoxes and Promises*, Polity Press, Cambridge 1988, pp. 232–4.

29. John F. Keller, 'The Division of Labour in Electronics', in June Nash and María Patricia Fernández-Kelly (eds), *Women, Men, and the International Division of Labor*, SUNY Press, Albany NY 1983, p. 354.

30. Catherine Hakim, 'The Myth of Rising Female Employment', *Work, Employment and Society*, Vol. 7, no. 1, 1993, pp. 97–100.

31. Jouko Nätti, 'Atypical Employment in the Nordic Countries: Towards Marginalisation or Normalisation?', in Boje and Olsson Hort (eds), op. cit., p. 180.

32. See calculation in Hakim, 'The Myth ...', p. 103.

33. See table in ibid., p. 103.

34. Ibid., p. 102; her emphasis.

35. Eva Kolinsky, *Women in Contemporary Germany. Life, Work and Politics*, Berg, Providence and Oxford 1993, pp. 174–5.

36. Norman Bonney and Elizabeth Reinach, 'Housework Reconsidered: The Oakley Thesis Twenty Years Later', *Work, Employment and Society*, Vol. 7, no. 4, December 1993, pp. 615–27. See also Catherine Hakim, 'Five Feminist Myths about Women's Employment', *British Journal of Sociology*, Vol. 46, no. 3, pp. 429–55, September 1995.

37. Kristin Tornes, 'The Timing of Women's Commodification – How Part-time Solutions Became Part-time Traps', in Boje and Olsson Hort (eds), op. cit., pp. 298ff, where other exclusions of benefits are listed.

38. John F. Ermisch and Robert E. Wright, 'Differential Returns to Human Capital in Full-time and Part-time Employment', in Nancy Folbre, Barbara Bergmann, Bina Agarwal and Maria Floro (eds), *Women's Work in the World Economy*, Macmillan, London 1993, p. 196. This situation may be rectified after 1995 when the directives of the European Commission will be implemented.

39. Hakim, 'The Myth ...', pp. 104–6, substantiates this by citing an extensive literature; see also her 'Grateful Slaves and Self-Made Women: Fact and Fantasy in Women's Work Orientations', p. 109.

40. Richard Rose and Ian McAllister, *The Loyalties of Voters*, Sage, London 1990, p. 51.

41. See Hakim, 'Grateful Slaves ...', p. 109.

42. Patricia Hewitt, *About Time. The Revolution in Work and Family Life*, IPPR/Rivers Oram Press, London 1993, pp. 53–4.

43. Anna Coote, 'The AES: A New Starting Point', *New Socialist*, November–December 1981, p. 5; this was reprinted in James Curran (ed.), *The Future of the Left*, Polity Press, Cambridge 1984.

44. A proposal for regulating working time, to achieve 'different working hours for different people at different stages of their lives', is contained in Hewitt, op. cit.; the citation is on p. 172. A reduction in working hours occurred in France and Holland between 1973 and 1987 through job-sharing schemes to reduce unemployment; see Maddison, *Dynamic Forces in Capitalist Development*, pp. 137–8.

45. Bob Rowthorn and Andrew Glyn, 'The Diversity of Unemployment Experience since 1973', in Marglin and Schor (eds), *The Golden Age of Capitalism*, pp. 220–3.

46. Therborn, *Why Some People Are More Unemployed Than Others*, pp. 72–3.

47. Harriet Holter and Bjørg Aase Sørensen, 'Norway', in Alice H. Cook, Val R. Lorwin and Arlene Kaplan Daniels (eds), *Women and Trade Unions in Eleven Industrialized Countries*, Temple University Press, Philadelphia 1983, p. 244.

48. Jane Jenson and Elisabeth Hangen 'Paradoxes and Promises. Work and Politics in the Postwar Years', in Jenson, Hangen and Reddy (eds), op. cit., p. 9; authors' emphasis.

49. Most surveys confirm such 'preference'; see Hakim, 'Five Feminist Myths'. The really important question is how this 'preference' is socially constructed.

50. Mary Ruggie, *The State and Working Women. A Comparative Study of Britain and Sweden*, Princeton University Press, Princeton NJ 1984, p. 85.

51. Mary Ruggie 'Gender, Work, and Social Progress. Some Consequences of Interest Aggregation in Sweden', in Jenson, Hangen and Reddy (eds), op. cit., p. 181; and Christina Jonung, 'Patterns of Occupational Segregation by Sex in the Labor Market', in Günther Schmidt and Renate Weitzel (eds), *Sex Discrimination and Equal Opportunity. The Labour Market and Employment Policy*, Gower, Aldershot 1984, p. 55.

52. See Tornes, op. cit., p. 292; see also Jenson and Mahon, 'Representing Solidarity:

Class, Gender and the Crisis in Social-Democratic Sweden', p. 84, who, however, suggest that the separateness involves social policy only.

53. Alice H. Cook, 'Introduction' in Cook, Lorwin and Daniels (eds), op. cit., p. 5.

54. Catherine Hakim, 'Explaining Trends in Occupational Segregation: The Measurement, Causes, and Consequences of the Sexual Division of Labour', *European Sociological Review*, Vol. 8, no. 2, September 1992, pp. 127–52; see also Kathleen Kiernan, 'Men and Women at Work and at Home', in Roger Jowell et al. (eds), *British Social Attitudes. The 9th Report*, SCPR/Dartmouth, Aldershot 1992, p. 95, who shows that part-time women workers are far more segregated than full-timers.

55. OECD, *Economic Outlook, Historical Statistics 1960–1989*, p. 37.

56. Marie-Gabrielle David and Christophe Starzec, 'Women and Part-time work: France and Great Britain compared', in Folbre, et al. (eds), op. cit., pp. 180–1.

57. Dominique Gambier and Michel Vernières, *L'emploi en France*, Editions La Découverte, Paris 1988, pp. 22–4.

58. Marianne Sundström, 'Part-time Work in Sweden and Its Implications for Gender Equality', in Folbre, et al. (eds), op. cit., p. 217. The definition of part-time may change from country to country; in Sweden part-time work is define as working fewer than thirty hours a week; in Britain the cut-off point is twenty hours. This inconsistency causes endless statistical misunderstanding.

59. Hakim calls this a 'myth', though the evidence she cites (European Commission, Employment in Europe 1993, COM(93), p. 314) suggests that child-care is an important factor. Portugal, Hakim points out, has a high full-time work rate for women, but 'non-existent child care services' – although, presumably, this is amply compensated by a vast informal family network; see Hakim, 'Five Feminist Myths'. Some empirical studies have shown that government subsidization of child-care costs helps mothers in low income families to enter the labour force; see David M. Blau and Philip K. Robins, 'Child-care Costs and Family Labor Supply', *Review of Economics and Statistics*, Vol. 70, no. 3, August 1988, pp. 374–81.

60. Bronwen Cohen and Neil Fraser, *Childcare in a Modern Welfare System. Towards a New National System*, IPPR, London 1991; see table on p. 48.

61. Joni Lovenduski and Vicky Randall, *Contemporary Feminist Politics. Women and Power in Britain*, Oxford University Press, Oxford 1993, p. 29.

62. Ruggie, *The State and Working Women*, pp. 248, 285, 297.

63. Cohen and Fraser, op. cit., pp. 44–7.

64. David and Starzec, op. cit., p. 190.

65. Olsson, *Social Policy and Welfare State in Sweden*, p. 283.

66. Chris Meyer, 'Nordic State Feminism in the 1990s: Whose Ally?', in Boje and Olsson Hort (eds), op. cit., p. 277.

67. Burtless, 'Taxes, Transfers, and Swedish Labor Supply', p. 190 and Siv Gustafsson, 'Equal Opportunity Policies in Sweden', in Schmidt and Weitzel (eds), op. cit., p. 139.

68. Sundström, op. cit., p. 213.

69. Heide M. Pfarr and Ludwig Eitel, 'Equal Opportunity Policies for Women in the Federal Republic of Germany', in Schmidt and Weitzel (eds), op. cit., pp. 168–9.

70. Jonung, 'Patterns of Occupational Segregation by Sex in the Labor Market', p. 48.

71. Joyce Gelb, 'Feminism and Political Action', in Russell J. Dalton and Manfred Kuechler (eds), *Challenging the Political Order. New Social and Political Movements in Western Democracies*, Polity Press, Cambridge 1990, p. 148; Maud L. Eduards, 'The Swedish Gender Model: Productivity, Pragmatism and Paternalism' *West European Politics*, Vol. 14, no. 3, July 1991, p. 176; and Kaplan, *Contemporary Western European Feminism*, p. 28.

72. Jane Jenson, 'The Limits of "and the" Discourse. French Women as Marginal Workers', in Jenson, Hangen and Reddy (eds), op. cit., p. 165.

73. Wayne Northcutt and Jeffra Flaitz, 'Women, Politics and the French Socialist Government', *West European Politics*, Vol. 8, no. 4, October 1985, p. 58.

74. Jenson 'The Limits of "and the" Discourse', pp. 161–2.

75. Daniela Del Boca, 'Women in a Changing Workplace. The Case of Italy', in Jenson, Hangen and Reddy (eds), op. cit., pp. 121–3.

76. Ibid., p. 125.

77. Ibid., p. 127.

78. In 1993 in Italy, while overall unemployment was 11 per cent, it climbed to 38 per cent for those under nineteen years of age. In Spain the gap was similar. See ILO, *World Labour Report 1993*, Geneva 1993, p. 19.

79. On Germany, see Pfarr and Eitel, op. cit., p. 159; on Britain see Coote and Campbell, *Sweet Freedom*, pp. 116–18.

80. Robert J. Flanagan, 'Efficiency and Equality in Swedish Labor Markets', in Bosworth and Rivlin (eds), *The Swedish Economy*, pp. 143ff.

81. Ruggie, *The State and Working Women*, p. 71; Korpi, *The Working Class in Welfare Capitalism*, p. 103.

82. Ruggie, 'Gender, Work, and Social Progress' pp. 176, 180 and Gustafsson, op. cit., p. 132.

83. Gustafsson, op. cit., p. 144; see also Eduards, p. 172; Maud Eduards, Beatrice Halsaa and Hege Skjeie, 'Equality: How Equal?', in Elina Haavio-Mannila et al. (eds), *Unfinished Democracy. Women in Nordic Politics*, trans. Christine Badcock, Pergamon Press, Oxford 1985. German unions shared the views of those in Sweden; see Alice H. Cook, 'Federal Republic of Germany', in Cook, Lorwin and Daniels (eds), op. cit., p. 83.

84. Jenson and Mahon, op. cit., p. 90; for Norway, see Hege Skjeie, 'The Uneven Advance of Norwegian Women', *New Left Review*, no. 187, May–June 1991, p. 87.

85. Ruggie, *The State and Working Women*, pp. 7, 71.

86. Gillian Whitehouse, 'Legislation and Labour Market Gender Inequality: An Analysis of OECD Countries', *Work, Employment and Society*, Vol. 6, no. 1, March 1992, pp. 65–86.

87. Pauline Glucklicht, 'The Effects of Statutory Employment Policies on Women in the United Kingdom Labour Market', in Schmidt and Weitzel (eds), op. cit., pp. 119–20; Coote and Campbell, op. cit., p. 160 and table on p. 81.

88. On the Conservative Party's willingness to go along with this legislation see Vicky Randall, *Women and Politics*, Macmillan, London 1987, p. 287.

89. Coote and Campbell, op. cit., p. 155.

90. Glucklicht, op. cit., pp. 114–15; this essay is based on findings included in M. W. Snell, P. Glucklicht and M. Povall, *Equal Pay and Opportunities*, Research Paper no. 20, Department of Employment, London 1981. On the failure of legislation, see also Christine Jackson, 'Policies and Implementation of Anti-Discrimination Strategies', in Schmidt and Weitzel (eds), op. cit., p. 194.

91. These are 75/117/EEC (1975) on equal pay, 76/207/EEC (1976) on equal treatment, and 79/7/EEC (1979) on social security.

92. Susan Cunningham, 'The Development of Equal Opportunities. Theory and Practice in the European Community', *Policy and Politics*, Vol. 20, no. 3, 1992, pp. 177–89.

93. June O'Neill, 'Earnings Differentials: Empirical Evidence and Causes', in Schmidt and Weitzel (eds), op. cit., pp. 82–5.

94. See Ben Fine's review of the literature in his *Women's Employment and the Capitalist Family*, Routledge, London 1992, pp. 163–5.

95. Jenson and Hangen, 'Paradoxes and Promises', p. 10; see also on female wages Isabella Bakker, 'Women's Employment in Comparative Perspective', in Jenson, Hargen and Reddy, op. cit., p. 26.

96. On gender and production-consumption, see Nancy Fraser, *Unruly Practices. Power, Discourse and Gender in Contemporary Social Theory*, Polity Press, Cambridge 1989, pp. 124–5.

97. Martin Pugh, *Women and the Women's Movement in Britain 1914–1959*, Macmillan, London 1992, p. 291.

98. Hobsbawm, *Industry and Empire*, pp. 65–9.

99. Alain Lipietz, *Mirages and Miracles. The Crisis of Global Fordism*, Verso, London 1977, pp. 75–7.

100. Joan Smith, 'Women's Unwaged Labour and the Formation of the World Labour Force', in Erik Aerts, Paul M. M. Klep, Jürgen Kocka and Marina Thorborg (eds), *Women in the Labour Force: Comparative Studies on Labour Market and Organization of Work since the 18th Century*, Leuven University Press, Louvain 1990, p. 13.

101. Singapore Department of Statistics, *Yearbook of Statistics*, Singapore 1990, pp. 298–9.

102. Franklin, op. cit., p. 150.

103. See the works of Ronald Inglehart, especially *The Silent Revolution*; 'The Changing Structure of Political Cleavages in Western Society', in Dalton, Flanagan and Beck (eds), op. cit; and 'Values, Ideology, and Cognitive Mobilization in New Social Movements', in Dalton and Kuechler (eds), op. cit.

104. Another instance where common perceptions are substantiated by empirical research such as that of Geoffrey Evans, 'Is Gender on the "New Agenda"?', *European Journal of Political Research*, Vol. 24, 1993, pp. 135–58.

105. Memorandum from Patricia Hewitt to Neil Kinnock, promptly leaked to the media and cited in Colin Hughes and Patrick Wintour, *Labour Rebuilt. The New Model Party*, Fourth Estate, London 1990, p. 19.

106. Francis Mulhern, 'Towards 2000, or News From You-Know-Where', *New Left Review*, no. 148, November–December 1984, p. 20.

107. See table in Herbert Kitschelt, 'New Social Movements and the Decline of Party Organization', in Dalton and Kuechler (eds), op. cit., p. 183.

108. Alan Scott, *Ideology and the New Social Movements*, Unwin Hyman, London 1990, pp. 10–11.

109. Karl-Werner Brand, 'Cyclical Aspects of New Social Movements: Waves of Cultural Criticism and Mobilization Cycles of New Middle-class Radicalism', in Dalton and Kuechler (eds), op. cit., pp. 23, 32.

110. Sully, *Continuity and Change in Austrian Socialism*, p. 231 and Jelavich, *Modern Austria*, pp. 306–7.

111. Göran Therborn, 'Swedish Social Democracy and the Transition from Industrial to Postindustrial Politics', in Fox Piven (ed.), op. cit., pp. 114–18.

112. Elmar Altvater, *The Future of the Market. An Essay on the Regulation of Money and Nature after the Collapse of 'Actually Existing Socialism'*, trans. Patrick Camiller, Verso, London 1993, p. 183.

113. The trespasses were organized by the (Labour and communist) British Workers' Sports Federation and the Ramblers' Rights Movement; for a brief account, see Howard Newby, *The Countryside in Question*, Hutchinson, London 1988, p. 117.

114. Jean-Pierre Cot, 'Autogestion and Modernity in France', p. 84.

115. See Anthony Crosland's 1971 Fabian Tract, *A New Social Democratic Britain*, cited in Neil Carter, 'The "Greening" of Labour', in Martin J. Smith and Joanna Spear (eds), *The Changing Labour Party*, Routledge, London 1992, p. 120.

116. Anthony Crosland, *Social Democracy in Europe*, Fabian Tract no. 438, December 1975, pp. 9–10.

117. The text of the conversation, held in Vienna on 25 May 1975, was published in Willy Brandt, Bruno Kreisky and Olof Palme, *La Social-démocratie et l'avenir*, Gallimard, Paris 1976. The original German-language edition was *Briefe und Gespräche* (1975).

118. Anna Bramwell, *Ecology in the 20th Century. A History*, Yale University Press, New Haven and London 1989, pp. 7–8. This book, written from an anti-Green and anti-collectivist perspective, is a good antidote to the rest of the literature on the subject, most of which is pro-ecologist.

119. David Pepper, *The Roots of Modern Environmentalism*, Routledge, London 1984, pp. 68–84, 91–103.

120. Bramwell, op. cit., pp. 197–203. To avoid tedious misunderstandings, I hereby declare that I am *not* suggesting that vegetarians and animal lovers are incipient Nazis.

121. Original title: *Ein Planet wird geplündert. Die Schreckensbilanz unserer Politik*. See the rather anti-Gruhl account, from a Left–Green perspective, in Werner Hülsberg's *The German Greens. A Social and Political Profile*, trans. Gus Fagan, Verso, London 1988, pp. 87–9.

122. A. Scott, op. cit., pp. 84–5.

123. Rudolf Bahro, *From Red to Green. Interviews with New Left Review*, Verso, London 1984, pp. 133, 185–6.

124. A. Scott, op. cit., p. 89.

125. The infighting was acted out with the bitterness of conflicts within the far Left; see E. Gene Frankland and Donald Schoonmaker, *Between Protest and Power. The Green Party in Germany*, Westview Press, Boulder CO 1992, p. 113; see also Markovits and Gorski, op. cit., whose marked enthusiasm for the Green cause does not blind them to what they call the 'zealotry and intolerance (of the Greens) *vis-à-vis* each other ... reminiscent of a Leninist-style party' (p. 274).

126. Bramwell, op. cit., pp. 221–3.

127. The claim is made by Ferdinand Müller-Rommel in 'The German Greens in the 1980s: Short-term Cyclical Protest or Indicator of Transformation', *Political Studies*, Vol. 37, no. 1, March 1989, p. 115.

128. Kitschelt, 'New Social Movements', p. 202.

129. See tables in Frankland and Schoonmaker, op. cit., pp. 70–1.

130. On the demise of the red–green coalition in Hessen and Hamburg see Diane L. Parness, *The SPD and the Challenge of Mass Politics*, Westview Press, Boulder CO 1991, pp. 135–67; see also Markovits and Gorski, op. cit., pp. 221–5.

131. Frankland and Schoonmaker, op. cit., pp. 160–2.

132. Klaus von Beyme, 'A United Germany Preparing for the 1994 Elections', *Government and Opposition*, Vol. 29, no. 4, Autumn 1994, pp. 459–60.

133. As Herbert Kitschelt recognized in his Introduction to *The Transformation of European Social Democracy*, p. xiii.

134. For the contribution of the generation of 1968 to the decline in anti-feminist sentiments in the 1970s and 1980s, see April Morgan and Clyde Wilcox, 'Anti-feminism in Western Europe 1975–1987', *West European Politics*, Vol. 15, no. 4, October 1992, p. 154.

135. Lesley Caldwell, *Italian Family Matters. Women, Politics and Legal Reform*, Macmillan, London 1991, p. 87.

136. Monica Threlfall, 'The Women's Movement in Spain', pp. 56–7.

137. Threlfall, 'Social Policy Towards Women in Spain, Greece and Portugal', in Gallagher and Williams (eds), *Southern European Socialism*; on Greece in particular, see Stamiris, 'The Women's Movement in Greece', and chapter 21 above.

138. Stamiris, op. cit., pp. 234–7.

139. Jelavich, op. cit., p. 302.

140. Coote and Campbell, op. cit., p. 157.

141. Enrico Berlinguer, *La 'Questione Comunista'*, Vol. 1, p. 410.

142. See Valentini, *Berlinguer Il Segretario*, pp. 54–5, 80, 83.

143. See Bianca Beccalli, 'The Modern Women's Movement in Italy', *New Left Review*, no. 204, March–April 1994, pp. 98–100. An extensive treatment of the roles of the parties in

this issue can be found in Caldwell, op. cit., pp. 87–101; see also, on the role of the PCI, Hellman, *Journeys among Women*, p. 36.

144. Lenin, 'To the Working Women', in *Collected Works*, Vol. 30, p. 372.

145. Marila Guadagnini, 'A "Partitocrazia" Without Women: The Case of the Italian Party System', in Joni Lovenduski and Pippa Norris (eds), *Gender and Party Politics*, Sage, London 1993, p. 190.

146. For a fuller analysis see Guadagnini, op. cit., pp. 186–8.

147. The lists are regionally based ones, so small parties gaining only one seat in each 'region' will usually return the male candidate who tops the list. This explains why women did not gain half the list seats.

148. Pippa Norris, 'Women's Legislative Participation in Western Europe', *West European Politics*, Vol. 8, no. 4, October 1985, pp. 94–9 and, along similar lines, her 'Conclusions: Comparing Legislative Recruitment', in Lovenduski and Norris, op. cit., pp. 312–15. On the advantage to women of party list systems, see Pippa Norris, *Politics and Sexual Equality. The Comparative Position of Women in Western Democracies*, Wheatsheaf, Brighton 1987, pp. 129–30. On how the preference voting system worked to the advantage of women in Finland, see Torild Skard and Elina Haavio-Mannila, 'Women in Parliament', in Haavio-Mannila et al. (eds), op. cit., p. 58.

149. Skjeie, op. cit., pp. 79, 84.

150. Ibid., p. 80.

151. Duane F. Alwin, Michael Braun and Jacqueline Scott, 'The Separation of Work and Family: Attitudes Towards Women's Labour-Force Participation in Germany, Great Britain and the United States', *European Sociological Review*, Vol. 8, no. 1, May 1992, p. 18–19.

152. Clyde Wilcox, 'The Causes and Consequences of Feminist Consciousness among West European Women', *Comparative Political Studies*, Vol. 23, no. 4, January 1991; see table on p. 529. On p. 521 a 'feminist' was defined as someone agreeing with at least three of the following: against anti-women prejudice, for equality at work, for equality in politics, and ensuring that either parent could stay at home with a sick child. This survey may have some comparative value; other similar surveys rank Britain low – for instance, the EEC *Women and Men of Europe 1983* survey cited in Kaplan, op. cit., pp. 17, 266. It should not be taken as evidence of the intensity of anti-egalitarian beliefs in Britain; other surveys conducted at the same time tell a different story – see Sharon Witherspoon, 'Sex Roles and Gender Issues', in Roger Jowell and Sharon Witherspoon (eds), *British Social Attitudes. The 1985 Report*, Gower, Aldershot 1985, pp. 55–94.

153. Kaplan, op. cit., p. 223. Assuming that mendacity distorted the results, why would so many Greeks wish to appear so enlightened on women's issues?

154. Ibid., pp. 224–9.

155. Ibid., p. 265.

156. Anne Phillips, 'Democracy and Difference: Some Problems for Feminist Theory', *Political Quarterly*, Vol. 63, no. 1, January–March 1992, p. 89.

157. A thorough account of the evolution of British Labour Party attitudes towards women is provided by Valerie Atkinson and Joanna Spear in 'The Labour Party and Women: Policies and Practices', in Smith and Spear (eds), op. cit., pp. 151–67.

158. Eva Kolinsky, 'Party Change and Women's Representation in Unified Germany', in Lovenduski and Norris (eds), op. cit., pp. 130ff.

159. See the *Report on Quota in SI Member Parties* presented at the Bureau meeting of the Socialist International Women of 3–4 October 1993, Lisbon, mimeo.

160. Monica Threlfall, 'Feminism and Social Change in Spain', in M. Threlfall (ed.), *Mapping the Women's Movements*, Verso, London 1996.

161. Frigga Haug, 'Lessons from the Women's Movement in Europe', pp. 111–12.

162. Haug, *Beyond Female Masochism*, p. 163.

163. Judt, *Marxism and the French Left*, p. 278.

164. Robert Ladrech, 'Social Movements and Party Systems: The French Socialist Party and New Social Movements', *West European Politics*, Vol. 12, no. 3, July 1989, p. 270.

165. On the SFIO, see Judt, op. cit., p. 278; on de Gaulle, see Andrew Appleton and Amy G. Mazur, 'Transformation or Modernization: The Rhetoric and Reality of Gender and Party Politics in France', in Lovenduski and Norris (eds), op. cit., p. 99.

166. See Kolinsky, *Women in Contemporary Germany*, p. 204 and the table on p. 201.

167. Jenson and Mahon, op. cit., p. 95.

168. Therborn, 'Swedish Social Democracy', p. 122.

169. Rose and McAllister, op. cit., p. 50.

170. Lovenduski and Randall, op. cit., p. 160; see MORI poll in Butler and Kavanagh, op. cit., p. 275.

171. Patricia Hewitt and Deborah Mattinson, *Women's Votes: The Key to Winning*, Fabian Research Series no. 353, June 1989, pp. 4–5, using MORI polls as their source.

172. Ibid., p. 1.

173. Anna Coote and Polly Pattullo, *Power and Prejudice. Women and Politics*, Weidenfeld and Nicolson, London 1990, p. 186.

174. David Butler and Dennis Kavanagh, *The British General Election of 1992*, Macmillan, London 1992, p. 279.

175. See, for instance, the Fabian pamphlet by Hewitt and Mattinson, op. cit.

176. Catherine Hakim, 'Explaining Trends in Occupational Segregation', pp. 129–30.

177. Beatrix Campbell, *Iron Ladies. Why Do Women Vote Tory?*, Virago Press, London 1987, p. 151.

178. Beccalli, op. cit., p. 91.

179. Pugh, op. cit., p. 128, and pp. 124–9 for an analysis of the Conservatives' approach to women in the inter-war period.

180. Kolinsky, *Women in Contemporary Germany*, p. 241.

181. Haug, *Beyond Female Masochism*, pp. 213–14.

182. Lovenduski and Randall, op. cit., p. 164.

183. For an examination of female voting behaviour in Holland, Italy and Germany, see Lawrence C. Mayer and Roland E. Smith, 'Feminism and Religiosity: Female Electoral Behaviour in Western Europe', *West European Politics*, Vol. 8, no. 4, October 1985, pp. 38–49.

184. Rose and McAllister, op. cit., p. 52.

185. Butler and Kavanagh, *The British General Elections of 1992*, p. 165.

186. Bryan Gould, *A Future for Socialism*, Jonathan Cape, London 1989, p. 53.

187. Marc Lazar, 'Le parti communiste italien et le défi des années quatre-vingt', *Commentaire*, no. 44, Winter 1988–89, p. 939.

188. Sharon Witherspoon and Jean Martin, 'What do we Mean by Green?', in Jowell et al. (eds), op. cit., p. 22.

189. Helmut Schmidt's address to the Bundestag, 17 May 1979, in *Perspectives on Politics*, p. 138.

190. Kiernan, op. cit., pp. 97–9.

191. Alva Myrdal and Viola Klein, *Women's Two Roles. Home and Work*, Routledge and Kegan Paul, London 1956; the authors, however, did not assume that a change in the role of men would be part of the solution: 'There is no doubt that society can be organized in such a way as to give practical scope for both feminine roles.' See pp. xii–xiii.

192. For an exploration of women's guilt about their dual role and their ambivalent attitude to work and career, see Rosalind Coward, *Our Treacherous Hearts*, Faber and Faber, London 1992, pp. 28ff.

193. Gustafsson, op. cit., p. 136 and Sundström, op. cit., p. 219. Much of this legislation was the work of the 'bourgeois' coalition and specifically of the Liberal Party.

194. Sundström, op. cit., p. 220; Jenson and Mahon, op. cit., p. 90.

195. Significantly, but quite understandably, political parties do not rate a single mention in Anthony Giddens' *The Transformation of Intimacy*, Polity Press, Cambridge 1992.

196. Carole Pateman, *The Disorder of Women*, Stanford University Press, Stanford CA 1989, p. 204.

23. The 1980s: Radicalism in its Last Redoubt

1. Speech of 29 January 1863, cited in Lothar Gall, *Bismarck, The White Revolutionary*. Vol.1: *1815–1871*, trans. J. A. Underwood, Unwin Hyman, London 1986, p. 226.

2. Figures showing the widening gap between rich and poor since 1979 were provided in the official publication of the Department of Social Security, *Households Below Average Income*, HMSO, July 1994.

3. See his 'The Great Moving Right Show', originally in *Marxism Today*, December 1978; now in Stuart Hall, *The Hard Road to Renewal*, Verso, London 1988, p. 44.

4. See the collection of the magazine's most significant articles in Stuart Hall and Martin Jacques (eds), *New Times. The Changing Face of Politics in the 1990s*, Lawrence and Wishart, London 1989.

5. Michael Rustin, 'The Politics of Post-Fordism: or, The Trouble with "New Times"', *New Left Review*, no. 175, May–June 1989, p. 56.

6. See Gregory Elliott's criticisms of *New Times*, in *Labourism and the English Genius*, pp. 148–51.

7. On this, and more generally on the role played by the unions in the internal struggle of the Labour Party in this period, see Lewis Minkin, *The Contentious Alliance*, especially pp. 301–5.

8. See the first formulations of the AES in the early 1970s – for instance, Stuart Holland, *The Socialist Challenge*; John Eaton, Michael Barratt Brown and Ken Coates, *An Alternative Economic Strategy for the Labour Movement*, Spokesman Pamphlet no. 47, Nottingham 1975.

9. A good summary can be found in the Conference of Socialist Economists London Working Group, *The Alternative Economic Strategy*, LCC/CSE, London 1980; a detailed account of Labour's proposals is in *Labour's Programme 1982*, published by the Labour Party, London 1982, especially pp. 15–25.

10. For instance, by David Currie in his critique of the SDP's economic proposals; 'SDP: A Prop For Profits', *New Socialist*, March–April 1982, p. 11.

11. See comments about the AES and the rank and file in Patrick Seyd, *The Rise and Fall of the Labour Left*, Macmillan, London 1987, p. 94.

12. Andrew Gamble, 'The Labour Party and Economic Management', in Smith and Spear (eds), *The Changing Labour Party*, p. 62.

13. Bruce George, *The British Labour Party and Defense*, Praeger, New York 1991, p. 70.

14. Ibid., pp. 40ff.

15. See Paul Whiteley, who wrote of the 'negative power' of the activists in *The Labour Party in Crisis*, p. 9.

16. For an incisive SDP-leaning journalistic account, see David Kogan and Maurice Kogan, *The Battle for the Labour Party*, Fontana, n.p. 1982.

17. See Noel Tracy, *The Origins of the Social Democratic Party*, Croom Helm, London and Canberra 1983, pp. 37–8.

18. Reprinted in Roy Jenkins, *Partnership of Principle*, Secker and Warburg, London 1985; see especially pp. 16, 20. Of course, similar calls had been made in the past – for instance by Woodrow Wyatt and, later, by Dick Taverne – but never by anyone of the political stature of Jenkins.

19. David Marquand, 'Inquest on a Movement. Labour's Defeat and Its Consequences', *Encounter*, Vol. 53, no. 1, July 1979, pp. 14, 17.

20. Colin Seymour-Ure, 'The SDP and the Media', *Political Quarterly*, Vol. 53, no. 4, October–December 1982, pp. 433–42.

21. A sympathetic but not apologetic biography, written by a Conservative merchant banker, narrates Benn's political itinerary up to the late 1970s: see Robert Jenkins, *Tony Benn: A Political Biography*, Writers and Readers, London 1980.

22. Some of these are well brought out by the interviewers confronting Benn in Tony Benn, *Parliament, People and Power*, Verso, London 1982. See, for instance, pp. 39–40 (on Britain's unique system of rights and the undemocratic nature of the British state); p. 69 (on popular democracy and parliamentary sovereignty); p. 95 (on the EEC); p. 107 (on Britain's international role).

23. The adoption by Labour of modern advertising and communication techniques is described in fascinating detail in Colin Hughes and Patrick Wintour, *Labour Rebuilt. The New Model Party*, Fourth Estate, London 1990, esp. pp. 22–35.

24. On the Underhill Report, see Michael Crick, *The March of Militant*, Faber and Faber, London 1986, p. 103; see also Seyd, op. cit., pp. 161–6 on the saga of the Militant Tendency.

25. On the lack of a green dimension, see Neil Carter, 'The "Greening" of Labour', p. 120.

26. 'Observations on the Debate' in Eric Hobsbawm et al., *The Forward March of Labour Halted?*, Verso, London 1981; the cited passages are on pp. 170, 173, 177 and 180.

27. Eric Hobsbawm, 'Labour's Lost Millions', *Marxism Today*, October 1983, p. 7, where he warns that to return to power Labour will either have to make a deal with the centre parties or regain the voters lost by adopting frankly reformist policies.

28. Coote, 'The AES: A New Starting Point', p. 7, now in Curran (ed.), *The Future of the Left*.

29. Charles Clarke and David Griffiths, *Labour and Mass Politics. Rethinking our Strategy*, Labour Co-ordinating Committee, November 1982, p. 3.

30. Ibid., p. 5.

31. Ibid., p. 29; emphasis in the original.

32. Michael Foot, *Another Heart and Other Pulses*, Collins, London 1984, p. 157.

33. Cited in ibid., pp. 157–8.

34. See Greater London Council, *The London Industrial Strategy*, London 1985 and the 158-page *The London Financial Strategy*, London 1986.

35. The appreciation is that of David Blunkett, a reformed hard leftist, cited in Hughes and Wintour, op. cit., p. 11.

36. Eric Shaw, 'The Labour Party and the Militant Tendency', *Parliamentary Affairs*, Vol. 42, no. 2, April 1989, p. 189. For a wider treatment of Labour's internal problems, see the same author's *Discipline and Discord in the Labour Party 1951–87*, Manchester University Press, Manchester 1988.

37. Seyd, op. cit., p. 167.

38. George, op. cit., p. 84.

39. David Marquand, 'Half-way to Citizenship? The Labour Party and Constitutional Reform', in Smith and Spear (eds), op. cit., pp. 47, 55.

40. See Benn, *Parliament, People and Power*, pp. 39–70 and the collection of his speeches and writings on democratic reform *Arguments for Democracy*, Penguin, Harmondsworth 1982.

41. G. Elliott, op. cit., p. 199.

42. Stuart Holland, 'New Strategy for Europe', *New Socialist*, November–December 1982, pp. 12–13; reprinted in Curran (ed.), op. cit.

43. Stuart Holland, *UnCommon Market. Capital, Class and Power in the European Community*, Macmillan, London 1980, p. 82.

44. Neil Kinnock, 'New Deal for Europe', in Curran (ed.), op. cit., p. 236. This article, because it did not explicitly advocate withdrawal, was a sign that the party was preparing to change its European policies. It was reprinted in the journal of the Socialist International, *Socialist Affairs*, no. 1, 1984, pp. 13–17.

45. Tomlinson, *Monetarism*, p. 31.

46. See Roy Jenkins' speech of 23 February 1981, now in *Partnership of Principle*, p. 76.

47. See the joint statement by Shirley Williams (President of the SDP) and Des Wilson (President of the Liberal Party), *People in Power. Why Constitutional Reform Matters to Everyone in Britain*, SDP–Liberal Alliance, Autumn 1986, especially pp. 3, 10. See also Wilson Finnie, 'The SDP's Plans for Britain's Constitution', *Political Quarterly*, Vol. 54, no. 1, January–March 1983, pp. 32–42.

48. Shirley Williams, *Politics is for People*, Penguin, Harmondsworth 1981, pp. 63–4.

49. For a definition of the SDP as a 'typical flash party', see David Denver and Hugh Bochel, 'Merger or Bust: Whatever Happened to Members of the SDP?', *British Journal of Political Science*, Vol. 24, Part 3, July 1994, p. 403.

50. Bernard Crick, 'The Future of the Labour Party, *Political Quarterly*, Vol. 54, no. 4, October–December 1983, p. 348.

51. See Martin Harrop, 'The Changing British Electorate', *Political Quarterly*, Vol. 53, no. 4 October–December 1982, pp. 395–6.

52. George, op. cit., pp. 60–1 and Hughes and Wintour, op. cit., p. 109.

53. Cited in Hughes and Wintour, op. cit., pp. 105–6.

54. David Owen, 'The Enabling Society', in Wayland Kennet (ed.), *The Rebirth of Britain*, Weidenfeld and Nicolson, London 1982, p. 236.

55. Among countless examples of such overestimation, see Ian Bradley's *Breaking the Mould? The Birth and Prospects of the Social Democratic Party*, Martin Robertson, Oxford 1981, especially the comments on p. 160; and Geoffrey Lee Williams and Alan Lee Williams, *Labour Decline and the Social Democrats' Fall*, Macmillan, London 1989, p. 173.

56. Hughes and Wintour, op. cit., pp. 48–63.

57. Seyd and Whiteley, *Labour's Grass Roots*, p. 207.

58. See the systematic comparison in Tomlinson, op. cit., especially pp. 158ff.

59. Roy Jenkins, op. cit., p. 76.

60. Ibid., p. 100; see also Holland's 1982 *New Socialist* article cited above.

61. Tony Benn, *Against the Tide. Diaries 1973–76*, p. 631.

62. D. Owen, 'The Enabling Society', p. 238.

63. The most systematic treatment of this issue is in Jonas Pontusson, *The Limits of Social Democracy. Investment Politics in Sweden*, Cornell University Press, Ithaca NY and London 1992; an earlier essay on the same theme was published as 'Radicalization and Retreat in Swedish Social Democracy', *New Left Review*, no. 165, September–October 1987.

64. Its origin can be traced back to the 1930s and 1940s, particularly to the writings of Ernst Wigforss, one of the major theoreticians of Swedish social democracy and a former Finance Minister; see the discussion in Tilton, *The Political Theory of Swedish Social Democracy*, pp. 39–69.

65. Rudolf Meidner, 'Swedish Union Strategies Towards Structural Change', *Nordisk Tidskrift för Politisk Economi*, no. 20, 1987, p. 34.

66. Meidner, *Employee Investment Funds*, p. 51; this is the English translation of the 1976 version of the Meidner Plan.

67. Ibid., p. 15.

68. Korpi, *The Democratic Class Struggle*, p. 235.

69. Gösta Rehn, 'The Debate on Employees' Capital Funds in Sweden', *Report to the Commission of the European Communities*, August 1983, mimeo text, p. 30.

70. Esping-Andersen and Korpi, 'Social Policy as Class Politics in Post-War Capitalism', p. 189.

71. Meidner, *Employee Investment Funds*, p. 94.

72. Ibid., p. 77.

73. Lundberg, 'The Rise and Fall of the Swedish Model', p. 30.

74. Tilton, op. cit., p. 230.

75. Meidner, *Employee Investment Funds*, p. 45.

76. Ibid., pp. 47, 74.

77. Ibid., p. 59.

78. Ibid., p. 82.

79. Erik Lundberg and Olle Lindgren, 'Uncertainty about Employee Investment Funds – Economic Effects', *Skandinaviska Enskilda Banken Quarterly Review*, no. 2, 1982, pp. 22–5; see also the objections raised in Ulf Himmelstrand, Göran Ahrne, Leif Lundberg and Lars Lundberg, *Beyond Welfare Capitalism. Issues, Actors and Forces in Societal Change*, Heinemann, London 1981, p. 274.

80. Pontusson, op. cit., p. 196; Tilton, op. cit., p. 231; and Rehn, op. cit., p. 28.

81. Rehn, op. cit., p. 10; Pontusson, op. cit., p. 194; Himmelstrand et al., op. cit., pp. 264–5.

82. Erland Waldenström, 'The Investment Fund Debate in the Shadow of the General Election', *Skandinaviska Enskilda Banken Quarterly Review*, no. 2, 1982, p. 27.

83. Rehn, op. cit., p. 18.

84. See data in Pekka Kosonen, 'The Scandinavian Welfare Model in the New Europe', in Boje and Olsson Hort (eds), *Scandinavia in a New Europe*, pp. 63–5.

85. Rehn, op. cit., p. 11; Himmelstrand et al., op. cit., p. 272. The shifting definition of profits is analysed by Sven-Erik Johansonn in 'Profit-sharing. Excess Profits. Wage Solidarity', *Skandinaviska Enskilda Banken Quarterly Review*, no. 2, 1982, p. 34.

86. Meidner, *Employee Investment Funds*, p. 103.

87. Cited in Rehn, op. cit., p. 22.

88. Assar Lindbeck's critique of the funds was published in 1982 with the title *Makt och ekonomi* (Power and Economy).

89. Himmelstrand et al., op. cit., p. 276.

90. Pontusson, op. cit., p. 15; Rehn, op. cit., p. 29.

91. Ruth, 'The Second New Nation, p. 57.

92. Himmelstrand et al., op. cit., p. 277.

93. Pontusson, op. cit., p. 198.

94. Tilton, op. cit., p. 234.

95. Pontusson, op. cit., p. 187.

96. Ibid., p. 187.

97. Ibid., p. 201.

98. See ibid., pp. 225ff.

99. Sven Ove Hansson, *SAF i politiken*, 1984, cited in Pontusson, op. cit., p. 230.

100. Gøsta Esping-Andersen, 'Postindustrial Cleavage Structures: A Comparison of Evolving Patterns of Social Stratification in Germany, Sweden, and the United States', in Fox Piven (ed.), *Labour Parties in Postindustrial Society*, p. 166.

101. Pontusson, op. cit., p. 231, rightly points out that the plan would not have empowered only industrial workers; however, this is not how it was perceived.

102. Nils Elvander, 'Interest Organisations and Democracy', in *Skandinaviska Enskilda Banken Quarterly Review*, no. 2, 1982, p. 46.

103. Korpi, *The Democratic Class Struggle*, pp. 234–5.

104. Korpi, *The Working Class in Welfare Capitalism*, p. 333; this was elaborated in his *Fonder för ekonomisk democrati*, Sveriges Kommunaltjänstemannaförbund, Stockholm 1980.

105. Ton Notermans, 'The Abdication from National Autonomy: Why the Macroeconomic Policy Regime Has Become So Unfavorable to Labor', *Politics and Society*, Vol. 21, no. 2, June 1993, pp. 140, 147–53.

106. The cited collection edited by Boje and Olsson Hort.

107. Paterson, 'The German Social Democratic Party', pp. 147–8.

108. Gordon Smith, 'The "New" Party System', in Gordon Smith, William E. Paterson, Peter H. Merkl and Stephen Padgett (eds), *Developments in German Politics*, Macmillan, London 1992, p. 96.

109. Peter Glotz, 'German Futures', *Socialist Affairs*, no. 4, 1984, p. 36.

110. Günter Grass, 'Dear Willy' (on Willy Brandt's seventieth birthday), *Socialist Affairs*, no. 1, 1984, p. 4, originally published in *Sozialdemokrat magazin*.

111. Peter Glotz, 'Let's Stop Waiting for the Right to Fail', *Socialist Affairs*, no. 1, 1985, pp. 28–30.

112. Ibid., p. 32.

113. Peter Glotz, 'Otto tesi per una nuova Bad Godesberg', *Mondoperaio*, Vol. 39, no. 3, March 1986, pp. 85–6. For a thorough account of the drafting of the new programme, see Stephen Padgett, 'The German Social Democrats: A Redefinition of Social Democracy or Bad Godesberg Mark II?', *West European Politics*, Vol. 16, no.1, January 1993, pp. 20–37.

114. Johannes Rau, 'The Right Divides, We Unite', *Socialist Affairs*, no. 2, 1986, p. 31.

115. Ibid., pp. 31–2.

116. Ibid., p. 32.

117. Stephen Padgett and William Paterson, 'The Rise and Fall of the German Left', *New Left Review*, no. 186, March–April 1991, p. 49.

118. The origin of this policy is usually traced back to the NATO report drafted by the Belgian Foreign Minister Pierre Harmel in 1967.

119. SPD, *Resolution Adopted by the SPD Party Conference on Peace and Security*, Cologne, 19 November 1983; unofficial translation, typescript, pp. 5,6.

120. Diana Johnstone, *The Politics of Euromissiles. Europe's Role in America's World*, Verso, London 1984, p. 68.

121. Ardagh, *Germany and the Germans*, p. 450.

122. See the discussion of the German peace movement in Markovits and Gorski, *The German Left*, pp. 106–12.

123. Johnstone, op. cit., p. 49.

124. Richard Löwenthal, 'Letter from Berlin: Neutralism and Nationalism', *Partisan Review*, no. 2, 1984, p. 186.

125. H. Schmidt, *A Grand Strategy for the West*, p. 20.

126. Ibid., p. 60.

127. Helmut Schmidt, *Men and Powers. A Political Retrospective*, trans. Ruth Hein, Jonathan Cape, London 1990, pp. 279–80. These memoirs are replete with often justifiable resentment against US foreign policy makers.

128. See resolution at the Munich Party Conference in April 1982, SPD, *Preventing War in the Atomic Age. Towards a New Strategy for NATO*, mimeo text, English trans., p. 2.

129. Hans-Jochen Vogel, *NATO in the year 1983. The Testing of a Partnership*, speech at the Friedrich-Ebert-Stiftung, 23 June 1983, mimeo text, English trans., p. 5.

130. See SPD, *European Security 2000 – A Comprehensive Concept for European Security from a*

Social-Democratic Point of View, English trans. by SPD Press office, mimeo text, Bonn, 6 July 1989.

131. Dieter S. Lutz, 'La difficile strada verso una nuova concezione della sicurezza', in Mario Telò (ed.), *Tradizione socialista e progetto europeo*, pp. 175–81.

132. SPD, *Basic Programme and Berlin Declaration of the Social Democratic Party of Germany*, adopted by the Programme Conference at Berlin, 20 December 1989, Friedrich-Ebert-Stiftung, Bonn 1990, p. 12; henceforth cited as *Berlin Programme*.

133. See Denis Healey's Fabian Autumn lecture of 26 November 1985, published as Fabian Tract no. 510, *Beyond Nuclear Deterrence*, especially p. 9.

134. April Carter, *Peace Movements. International Protest and World Politics since 1945*, Longman, London 1992, p. 260 and Thomas R. Rochon, 'The West European Peace Movement and the Theory of New Social Movements' in Dalton and Kuechler (eds), *Challenging the Political Order*, p. 113.

135. Johnstone, op. cit., pp. 81–7.

136. Andrei S. Markovits, 'The West German Left in a Changing Europe', in Lemke and Marks (eds), *The Crisis of Socialism in Europe*, pp. 176–78. Note, however, that Markovits' definition of this 'Left' is impressionistic, since it involves not only 'a good part of the SPD and the unions', but also all communists, fundamentalist greens, feminists and pacifists.

137. Timothy Garton Ash, *In Europe's Name. Germany and the Divided Continent*, Jonathan Cape, London 1993, p. 373.

138. I thus accept Garton Ash's judgement, in ibid., pp. 118ff.

139. SPD, *Irsee Draft for a new Manifesto of the Social Democratic Party of Germany*, June 1986, mimeo text, English trans., p. 22 (henceforth cited as *Irsee Draft*); and *Berlin Programme*, p. 13.

140. *Berlin Programme*, p. 13.

141. Ibid., pp. 13–14.

142. Hans-Jochen Vogel, 'La dimensione politica del Mercato unico europeo', *Nuova Rivista Internazionale*, no. 5–6, May–June 1989, pp. 6–8.

143. T. Meyer, 'Un mutamento di paradigma', pp. 109–10.

144. Willy Brandt, 'No Limits to Qualitative Growth', *Socialist International Information*, no. 4, 1982, p. 162.

145. *Berlin Programme*, p. 30.

146. Ibid.

147. Ibid.

148. Ibid., pp. 32–3.

149. Ibid., p. 34.

150. Volker Hauff, 'Lavoro e ambiente. Tesi per una riforma ecologica', in Telò (ed.), op. cit., p. 225.

151. Porter, *The Competitive Advantages of Nations*, p. 346.

152. Padgett and Paterson, op. cit., pp. 56–7.

153. *Berlin Programme*, pp. 22–3.

154. See the paragraph 'Working hours' in *Irsee Draft*, pp. 68–9.

155. *Berlin Programme*, pp. 16–18.

156. Ibid., p. 18.

157. Oskar Lafontaine, 'Progresso e solidarietà', *Democrazia e diritto*, nos 1–2, January–February 1989, pp. 211–12 (Italian trans. of Munster Congress Report).

158. Peter Glotz, *La socialdemocrazia tedesca a una svolta*, Editori Riuniti, Rome 1985, p. 32 (Italian trans. of *Die Arbeit der Zuspitzung. Über die Organisation einer regierungsfähigen Linken*, Berlin 1984).

159. *Berlin Programme*, p. 45.

160. Ibid., p. 8.

161. Padgett and Paterson, op. cit., pp. 76–7.

162. On human rights in the DDR, see Missiroli, op. cit., pp. 143–4.

163. Peter H. Merkl, *German Unification in the European Context*, Penn State University Press, University Park PA, 1993, pp. 126–7; note the dissenting voices of Johannes Rau and Hans-Jochen Vogel. See also Konrad H. Jarqusch, *The Rush to German Unity*, Oxford University Press, New York and Oxford 1994, p. 68 and Stephen Padgett, 'The German Social Democratic Party: Between Old and New Left', in David S. Bell and Eric Shaw (eds), *Conflict and Cohesion in Western European Social Democratic Parties*, Pinter Publishers, London 1994, p. 25. *The* book on German unification is that of Garton Ash, op. cit.

164. Jarqusch, op. cit., p. 28.

165. Stefan Berger, 'Nationalism and the Left in Germany', *New Left Review*, no. 206, July–August 1994, p. 68.

166. On the SPD's ambivalence over national unity, see Melanie Drane, 'A Divided Left Faces German Unity: A Response to Andrei Markovits', *German Politics*, Vol. 1, no. 2, August 1992, pp. 279–80.

167. Cited in Missiroli, op. cit., p. 173.

168. Berger, op. cit., p. 63.

169. Cited in G. A. Craig, *The Germans*, p. 309.

24. The New Revisionism

1. This statement also formed part of the resolution on Poland of the PCI, 29 December 1979, in Enrico Berlinguer, *After Poland*, ed. and trans. Antonio Bronda and Stephen Bodington, Spokesman, Nottingham 1982, p. 16.

2. Willy Brandt, 'Social Democracy After the Communist Collapse', *Socialist Affairs*, no. 3, 1991, p. 4.

3. See, for instance, Gorbachev's comments on social policy and workers' protection under socialism in *Perestroika. New Thinking for Our Country and the World*, Fontana, London 1988, pp. 98–102, 113–14.

4. Dahrendorf, *Reflections on the Revolution in Europe*, p. 13.

5. On the ambivalent attitude of the Russian intelligentsia to Gorbachev, see Giulietto Chiesa, *Da Mosca. Alle origini di un colpo di stato annunciato*, Laterza, Rome-Bari 1993.

6. Ernest Gellner, 'The Struggle to Catch Up', *Times Literary Supplement*, 9 December 1994, p. 14.

7. This accolade is from Robert V. Daniels in *The End of the Communist Revolution*, Routledge, London 1993, p. 27 – an exceptionally lucid and readable account.

8. Labour Party, *Labour's Programme 1973*, London 1973, p. 14.

9. Guillaume Devin, *L'internationale socialiste: Histoire et sociologie du socialisme international (1945–1990)*, Presses de la Fondation nationale des sciences politiques, Paris 1993, reports in appendices the two declarations; see especially pp. 366 and 381.

10. Peter Glotz, 'What Is To Be Done?', *Socialist Affairs*, Nos 1–2, 1988, pp. 25–6.

11. Gould, *A Future for Socialism*, p. xiii.

12. Ibid., p. 90.

13. Ibid., p. 120.

14. Ibid., pp. 177, 179–80.

15. Ibid., p. 35.

16. See Ian McAllister and Jack Vowles, 'The Rise of New Politics and Market Liberalism in Australia and New Zealand', *British Journal of Political Science*, Vol. 24, part 3, July 1994.

17. Knut Heidar, 'The Norwegian Labour Party: "En Attendant l'Europe"', *West European Politics*, Vol. 16, no. 1, January 1993, p. 64.

18. SPÖ, *Sozial Demokratie 2000. Vorschläge zur Diskussion über Österreichs Zukunft*, Vienna 1989, p. 19.

19. This is the updated version of *Meet the Challenge, Make the Change. A New Agenda for Britain, Final Report of Labour's Policy Review for the 1990s*, Labour Party, London 1989. I have given a more detailed treatment of this in my 'Reflections on the Labour Party's Programme for the 1990s', *Political Quarterly*, Vol. 62, no. 3, July–September 1991, pp. 365–76.

20. Labour Party, *Looking to the Future*, London 1990, p. 5.

21. Ibid., p. 6.

22. Ibid., p. 7.

23. Ibid., p. 9.

24. Ibid., p. 11; see also more detailed references on pp. 12, 13, 14, 15, 17, 22, 29, 30.

25. Ibid., pp. 21–2.

26. Ibid., p. 27.

27. Ibid., p. 32.

28. Ibid., p. 37.

29. Ibid., p. 34.

30. Ibid., p. 6. See also Neil Kinnock's speech in Nottingham, in March 1989, reprinted in the *Guardian* with the title 'A Hand on the Tiller – and the Till', 10 April 1989, p. 38.

31. N. Carter, 'The "Greening" of Labour', p. 127.

32. See the comparison in Crewe, 'Labor Force Changes, table 2.3.

33 Labour Party, *Democratic Socialist Aims and Values*, London, n.d. (1988), endorsed by the NEC on 23 March 1988, mimeo, p. 3; this statement was purportedly drafted by Neil Kinnock and Roy Hattersley.

34. Ibid.; see especially p. 11.

35. Gregory Elliott, op. cit., pp. 17ff.

36. Hugues and Wintour, *Labour Rebuilt*, p. 75.

37. Commission on Social Justice, *Social Justice. Strategies for National Renewal*, Vintage, London 1994, pp. 17–18.

38. For a philosopher's response to the Report, see G. A. Cohen, 'Back to Socialist Basics', *New Left Review*, no. 207, September–October 1994, pp. 3–16.

39. For a commentary on this state of affairs, see two key texts by a superior breed of modern gurus: John Kenneth Galbraith, *The Culture of Contentment*, Penguin, Harmondsworth 1992 and Krugman, *The Age of Diminished Expectations*.

40. For a characteristic headline of the 1990s, see the *Financial Times* of 3–4 February 1995 (weekend edition): 'US markets surge on jobless data', capped by 'Investors see less risk of early rate increase as unemployment rise hints at slowing recovery'.

41. Padgett, 'The German Social Democratic Party', p. 26.

42. Quentin Peel and Judy Dempsey, 'Firmly footed for the final hurdle', *Financial Times*, 10 September 1994, p. 6.

43. Steven B. Wolinetz, 'Reconstructing Dutch Social Democracy', *West European Politics*, Vol. 16, no. 1, January 1993, p. 101.

44. Paul Kalma, 'Towards a New Class Compromise', *Socialist Affairs*, no. 1, 1986, pp. 33–5.

45. Laura Raun, 'Viewpoints are converging', Survey on the Netherlands, *Financial Times*, 23 November 1987, p. ii.

46. Wolinetz, op. cit., p. 103, who also analyses the other main PvdA reports of 1986–9. See also Gerrit Voerman, 'De la confiance à la crise. La gauche aux Pays-Bas depuis les années soixante-dix', in Pascal Delwit and Jean-Michel De Waele (eds), *La gauche face aux mutations en Europe*, Editions de l'Université de Bruxelles, Brussels 1993, pp. 75–6.

47. Wolinetz, op. cit., pp. 107–8.

48. Hugh Carnegy, 'Liberal who may be the next prime minister', Survey on Finland, *Financial Times*, 9 November 1994, p. iv.

49. SPÖ, *Sozial Demokratie 2000*, p. 5.

50. Ibid., p. 49.

51. Ibid., p. 65.

52. These views had become widely accepted and were reiterated in a report of a government commission (when the SAP was out of office) chaired by one of the main opponents of the Meidner funds, Assar Lindbeck. See the summary of the report in Assar Lindbeck et al., *Options for Economic and Political Reform in Sweden*, Seminar Paper no. 540, Institute for International Economic Studies, Stockholm University, Stockholm 1993, p. 9.

53. Ibid., p. 10.

54. Ibid., pp. 19, 24, 37.

55. Assar Lindbeck, *Overshooting, Reform and Retreat of the Welfare State*, Seminar Paper no. 552, Institute for International Economic Studies, Stockholm University, Stockholm 1993, p. 13.

56. Ibid., pp. 17–18.

57. Richard O'Brien, 'Swedes show how to save money by spending it', *Financial Times*, 4 May 1988, p. 23.

58. Tilton, *The Political Theory of Swedish Social Democracy*, p. 3. Similar problems faced other left parties with similar organizations – for instance, the Austrian socialists, the German social democrats and the Italian communists.

59. Berndt Ahlqvist, *I bräcklig farkost* ('In a fragile craft'), published in 1983; cited in Tilton, op. cit., p. 238.

60. Tilton, op. cit., p. 261.

61. Lundberg, 'The Rise and Fall of the Swedish Model', p. 32.

62. Robert Taylor, 'Minister champions market socialism for Sweden', *Financial Times*, 21 February 1989.

63. Robert Taylor, 'Swedish tax reforms endorsed by OECD', *Financial Times*, 7 April 1989, p. 2.

64. Diane Sainsbury, 'Swedish Social Democracy in Transition: The Party's Record in the 1980s and the Challenge of the 1990s', *West European Politics*, Vol. 14, no. 3, July 1991, pp. 36–7.

65. Jonas Pontusson, 'Sweden: After the Golden Age', in Anderson and Camiller (eds), *Mapping the West European Left*, p. 36.

66. Robert Taylor, 'Swedish parties agree on economic package', *Financial Times*, 24 May 1989, p. 2.

67. Therborn, 'Swedish Social Democracy, p. 120.

68. Sainsbury, op. cit., p. 49.

69. Pontusson, op. cit., p. 37.

70. Therborn, op. cit., p. 105.

71. Heidar, op. cit., pp. 73–4.

72. Sainsbury, op. cit., p. 35.

73. Christian Berggren, 'Work Reforms in Sweden 1970–1990: From Labour Market Pressures to Corporate Strategies', in Boje and Olsson Hort (eds), *Scandinavia in a New Europe*, pp. 222–3, and his *The Volvo Experience. Alternatives to Lean Production in the Swedish Auto Industry*, Macmillan, London 1993, p. 81.

74. Berggren, *The Volvo Experience*, p. 81.

75. Hugh Carnegy, 'Swedish companies look overseas for salvation', *Financial Times*, 22 July 1993 p. 2.

76. Pontusson, op. cit., p. 40.

77. Hugh Carnegy, 'Swedes go to ground while summer days are long', *Financial Times*, 7–8 August 1993, p. 2.

78. SAP, *Political Platform Adopted by the Party Executive and the National Executive of the Swedish Confederation of Trade Unions*, 24 January 1991; mimeo.

79. SAP, *Draft New Party Programme*, Socialdemokraterna, Stockholm 1989, mimeo, English trans. p. 2; the draft was approved in September 1990.

80. Ibid., p. 11. A 1990 government publication makes exactly the same point; see Sweden, Ministry for Foreign Affairs, *Sweden and West European Integration*, Stockholm 1990, p. 11.

81. Brandt, Kreisky and Palme, *La Social-démocratie et l'avenir*, p. 224.

82. Christopher Brown-Humes, 'Swedish package lifts taxes and cuts spending', *Financial Times*, 26 April 1995, p. 2.

83. Ian Rogers, 'Austria's old parties feel winds of change', *Financial Times*, 26 April 1995, p. 3.

84. I have used the official English-language translation: PSOE, *Manifesto of Programme. Draft for Discussion (Programma 2000)*, January 1990, Editorial Pablo Iglesias, n.p., mimeo.

85. See Richard Gillespie, '"Programa 2000": The Appearance and Reality of Socialist Renewal in Spain', *West European Politics*, Vol. 16, no. 1, January 1993, pp. 82–4. See also Paul Heywood, 'Rethinking Socialism in Spain: *Programa 2000* and the Social State', *Coexistence*, Vol. 30, 1993, pp. 167–85, who is less critical of the PSOE than Gillespie, while providing a detailed analysis of central features of the programme.

86. PSOE, *Manifesto of Programme*, p. 9.

87. Ibid., p. 17.

88. Ibid., pp. 25–6; my emphasis.

89. See the text of the declaration in *Vendredi, L'hebdomadaire des socialistes*, no. 53, 16 March 1990, and the text in the appendix to Centro per La Riforma dello Stato (ed.), *Politica Europa Annali 1990–1991*, Franco Angeli, Milan 1991, pp. 345–6. See also the comments in the same volume by Sandro Guerrieri, 'Regime presidenziale e forma-partito: il Ps nel sistema politico della quinta repubblica', especially pp. 248–51.

90. John Hooper, 'Catching the Spanish drift', *Guardian*, 13 April 1989, p. 23.

91. Patrick Camiller, 'Spain: The Survival of Socialism?', in Anderson and Camiller (eds), op. cit., p. 250.

92. Felipe González, 'Taking on the Challenge of Modernisation', *Socialist Affairs*, no. 3, 1987, pp. 24–5.

93. Camiller, op. cit., p. 261.

94. Ibid., p. 256.

95. I share Camiller's doubts about the enlightenment of Spanish conservatives; see ibid., p. 262.

96. James Petras, 'Spanish Socialism: The Politics of Neoliberalism', in James Kurth and James Petras (eds), *Mediterranean Paradoxes. The Politics and Social Structure of Southern Europe*, Berg, Providence and Oxford 1993, p. 95.

97. Martin Rhodes, 'Craxi and the Lay-Socialist Area: Third Force of Three Forces?', in Robert Leonardi and Piergiorgio Corbetta (eds), *Italian Politics: A Review*, Vol. 3, Pinter Publishers, London and New York 1989, p. 116.

98. Partito Socialista Italiano (PSI), *Un riformismo moderno. Un socialismo liberale. Tesi Programmatiche*, Conferenza programmatica di Rimini, 22–23 March 1990, pp. 94–5.

99. On the corruption scandals, see Donatella Della Porta, 'La capitale immorale: le tangenti di Milano', in S. Hellman and G. Pasquino (eds), *Politica in Italia 1993*, Il Mulino, Bologna 1993. On the financial extent of the scandals, see Andrea Pamparana, *Il processo*

Cusani. Politici e faccendieri della Prima Repubblica, Mondadori, Milan 1994 and Marcella Andreoli, *Processo all'Italia. Il Belpaese alla sbarra: storie di delitti ordinari e di castighi eccellenti*, Sperling and Kupfer Editori, Milan 1994. For a wider analysis, see Giulio Sapelli, *Cleptocrazia*, Feltrinelli, Milan 1994.

100. Degl'Innocenti, *Storia del PSI*. Vol. 3, p. 472.

101. Pérez-Díaz, *The Return of Civil Society*, p. 49.

102. Krugman, op. cit., p. 37.

103. Peter Lange, 'The End of an Era: The Wage Indexation Referendum of 1985', in *Italian Politics: A Review*, Vol. 1, Pinter Publishers, London and New York 1986, pp. 42–3. Degl'Innocenti concurred; see his op. cit., p. 455.

104. Kevin Featherstone, 'Political Parties and Democratic Consolidation in Greece', in Pridham (ed.), *Securing Democracy*, pp. 193–4.

105. George Ross, 'The Changing Face of Popular Power in France', in Fox Piven (ed.), *Labor Parties in Postindustrial Societies*, p. 92.

106. How this was achieved is clearly explained in Degl'Innocenti, op. cit., especially pp. 430ff.

107. For a particularly grovelling instance, see Virgilio Dagnino's Introduction to Bettino Craxi, *L'Italia liberata*, Sugarco Edizioni, Milan 1984.

108. I examined some of these issues in 'Political and Market Forces in Italian Broadcasting', *West European Politics*, Vol. 8, no. 2, April 1985.

109. See PSI, *Un riformismo moderno*, pp. 113–14.

110. See, for instance, Partito Socialista Italiana (PSI), *Governare il cambiamento. Conferenza programmatica del PSI*, Rimini, 31 March–4 April 1982, pp. 107, 264.

111. See the perceptive analysis of Gianfranco Pasquino, in his 'Modernity and Reforms: The PSI between Political Entrepreneurs and Gamblers', *West European Politics*, Vol. 9, no. 1, January 1986, pp. 123–4.

112. See Paul Preston and Denis Smyth, *Spain, the EEC and NATO*, Chatham House Papers 22, RIIA/RKP, London 1984, pp. 72–8.

113. For a wider treatment of this theme, see Giorgio Ruffolo, 'La grande inflazione craxiana', *Micromega*, no. 3, June–August 1993, especially pp. 120–1.

114. The key texts are Occhetto's report to the Executive Committee of the PCI (the Direzione) of 14 November 1989, now in Achille Occhetto, *Il sentimento e la ragione*, Rizzoli, Milan 1994, pp. 181–9 (especially pp. 185–6); and his *Relazione al Comitato centrale*, 20 November 1989, *L'Unità*, 21 November 1989.

115. See *Politica e economia*, supplement to no. 6, June 1989, 'Il nuovo PCI: due congressi a confronto'.

116. Hodgson, 'The Finnish Communist Party and Neutrality', p. 286.

117. See the surveys in Martin Bull and Paul Heywood (eds), *West European Communist Parties after the Revolutions of 1989*, St Martin's Press, New York 1994 and D. S. Bell (ed.), *Western European Communists and the Collapse of Communism*, Berg, Oxford and Providence 1993.

118. PDS, *Programma di Governo del PDS. Elezioni politiche 27–28 marzo 1994*, Rome, February 1994, pp. 13, 15, 21.

119. Ibid., p. 15.

120. Ibid., p. 17.

121. Ibid., p. 22.

122. Achille Occhetto, *Relazione al 180 Congresso, Il nuovo Pci in Italia e in Europa*, *L'Unità*, 19 March 1989. This was reiterated at the Central Committee meeting of 20 November 1989.

Epilogue

1. In his original metaphor Louis Althusser contrasts the 'idealist' philosopher, who knows the origin and end of everything, to the 'materialist' philosopher; see Louis Althusser, 'Philosophie et marxisme. Entretiens avec Fernanda Navarro (1984–87)', in *Sur la philosophie*, Gallimard, Paris 1994, pp. 64–5 and his *Ecrits philosophiques et politiques*, Vol. 1, Stock/IMEC, Paris 1994, pp. 581–2.

2. 'The Revolution against "Capital"', in Antonio Gramsci, *Selections from Political Writings 1910–1920*, Quintin Hoare (ed.), trans. John Mathews, Lawrence and Wishart, London 1988, p. 34.

3. V. I. Lenin, 'The Tasks of the Proletariat in Our Revolution', in *Collected Works*, Vol. 24, Progress Publishers, Moscow 1974, p. 88.

4. Vicente Navarro, 'Has Socialism Failed? An Analysis of Health Indicators under Socialism', *International Journal of Health Services*, Vol. 22, no. 4, 1992, pp. 586–7.

5. Ibid., pp. 588–9.

6. Ibid., p. 591.

7. Ibid., p. 592.

8. See data in Paul Kennedy, *The Rise and Fall of the Great Powers*, Fontana, London 1989, p. 641. See also Murray Feshbach and Alfred Friendly Jr, *Ecocide in the USSR: Health and Nature Under Siege*, Basic Books, New York 1992.

9. Charles S. Maier, 'The Collapse of Communism: Approaches for a Future History', *History Workshop*, no. 31, Spring 1991, p. 39. This essay contains the most insightful considerations on the end of communism I have come across.

10. Karl Marx, *Critique of the Gotha Programme*, International Publishers, New York 1970, p. 10.

11. Marx, *Capital*, Vol. 1, p. 763.

12. Terry Eagleton, 'Discourse and discos', *Times Literary Supplement*, 15 July 1994, p. 4.

13. A view amply promoted by André Gorz, *Les chemins du paradis*, Editions Galilée, Paris 1983, especially pp. 85–6; but see also Marx, *Capital*, Vol. 3, p. 820.

14. See, for instance, Hayek's *The Constitution of Liberty*, Routledge and Kegan Paul, London 1960, whose prescriptions – see especially chapter 18 on the trade unions – twenty years later strengthened the anti-trade union resolve of the Right in the USA and the UK.

15. A version of this story can be found in Pierre Rosanvallon, *Le libéralisme économique*, Editions du Seuil, Paris 1989, p. 82. The first writer to use the expression *laissez-faire* in economic theory was the Marquis d'Argenson, a contemporary of Quesnay's.

16. Friedrich A. Hayek, *The Fatal Conceit. The Errors of Socialism*, Vol. 1 of the *Collected Works*, ed. W. W. Bartley, Routledge, London 1988, p. 27.

17. Ibid., p. 63.

18. This gem can be found on p. 113 of Friedrich A. Hayek, *Law, Legislation and Liberty*. Vol. 3: *The Political Order of a Free People*, Routledge, London 1993, where more details of platonesque social engineering penned by this libertarian can be discovered (including, on p. 117, the suggestion that younger people thus disenfranchised should be encouraged to join 'clubs of contemporaries' made more attractive by having the women two years younger than the men). I was made aware of this text by David Marquand in his *The Unprincipled Society. New Demands and Old Politics*, Fontana, London 1988, pp. 81–3.

19. Joan Robinson, *Economic Heresies. Some Old-fashioned Questions in Economic Theory*, Macmillan, London 1972, p. 143.

20. Ibid., p. 133.

21. Marx, *Capital*, Vol. 3, p. 240.

22. Ibid., p. 880.

23. The unsurpassed statement of this position is that of Louis Hartz in his classic *The Liberal Tradition in America*, Harcourt, Brace and World, New York 1955.

24. Patricia Ruggles, 'Short- and Long-Term Poverty in the United States: Measuring the American "Underclass"', in Lars Osberg (ed.), *Economic Inequality and Poverty. International Perspectives*, M.E. Sharpe, Armonk NY 1991, p. 186.

25. See Albert Berry, François Bourguignon and Christian Morrison, 'Global Economic Inequality and Its Trends since 1950', in Osberg (ed.), op. cit., p. 48.

26. This is the central point of Jill Quadagno's important book, *The Color of Welfare. How Racism Undermined the War on Poverty*, Oxford University Press, New York and Oxford 1994, pp. 191–2.

27. Gertrude Schaffner Goldberg, 'The United States: Feminization of Poverty amidst Plenty', in Gertrude Schaffner Goldberg and Eleanor Kremen (eds), *The Feminization of Poverty: Only in America?*, Praeger, New York 1990, pp. 45–6.

28. Christopher Howard, 'The Hidden Side of the American Welfare State', *Political Science Quarterly*, Vol. 108, no. 3, 1993, p. 416.

29. Goldberg, op. cit., p. 42 and Ruggles, op. cit., p. 162.

30. Giddens, *Beyond Left and Right*, p. 149

31. In 1993 unemployment in OECD-Europe was 10.7 per cent, in the USA 6.8 per cent, and in Japan only 2.5 per cent. See OECD, *Employment Outlook*, Paris, July 1994, p. 6.

32. Galbraith, *The Culture of Contentment*, p. 39.

33. Hobsbawm, *Age of Extremes*, p. 341.

34. Goldberg, op. cit., p. 41.

35. Quadagno, op. cit., p. 183.

36. All of the above information comes from Paul Kennedy's dazzling *Preparing for the Twenty-First Century*, Fontana, London 1994, pp. 304–7.

37. Source: US Bureau of the Census in Michael Prowse, 'Clinton budget a manifesto to middle classes', *Financial Times*, 7 February 1995, p. 6.

38. Richard Wilkinson, 'Health, Redistribution and Growth', in Andrew Glyn and David Miliband (eds), *Paying for Inequality. The Economic Cost of Social Injustice*, IPPR/Rivers Oram Press, London 1994, pp. 24–43, especially pp. 27–30.

39. The point that military spending is not necessarily a burden on growth is aptly made by Massimo Pivetti in 'Military Spending as a Burden on Growth: An "Underconsumption" Critique', *Cambridge Journal of Economics*, Vol. 16, no. 4, December 1992.

40. Brandt, 'Social Democracy After the Communist Collapse', p. 7.

41. David Marquand, 'After Socialism', *Political Studies*, Vol. 41, Special Issue 1993, p. 51.

42. Karl Marx, *The Eighteenth Brumaire of Louis Bonaparte*, Progress Publishers, Moscow 1967, p. 55.

43. Jürgen Habermas, *Legitimation Crisis*, trans. Thomas McCarthy, Heinemann, London 1976, pp. 50–1.

44. Ibid., pp. 53–4.

45. Alan Wolfe, 'Has Social Democracy a Future?', *Comparative Politics*, Vol. 11, no. 1, October 1978, p. 103.

46. Paul Bairoch, *Economics and World History. Myths and Paradoxes*, Harvester Wheatsheaf, Hemel Hempstead 1993, p. 174.

47. Hobsbawm, op. cit., pp. 95–6.

48. See his introductory remarks at a conference held in April 1973 with the original title of *What Is Wrong with the Socialist Idea?* The proceedings were published with the more neutral title of *The Socialist Idea. A Reappraisal*, Leszek Kolakowski and Stuart Hampshire (eds), Weidenfeld and Nicolson, London 1974; the remark cited is on p. 16.

49. Jean-Denis Bredin, 'Est-il permis?', *Le Monde*, 31 August 1991.

50. Charles Lindblom, *Politics and Markets. The World's Political-Economic Systems*, Basic Books, New York 1977, p. 171.

51. Ibid., p. 173.

52. E. L. Jones, *The European Miracle*, pp. 149 and 124.

53. For instance, in Sweden, the furniture chain IKEA developed by equipping the millions of apartments built as part of the SAP's social housing policy in the 1950s and 1960s; see Meidner, 'Why Did the Swedish Model Fail?' p. 226.

54. Krugman, *The Age of Diminished Expectations*, p. 197.

55. Jacques Delors, 'Une nouvelle frontière pour la social-démocratie: l'Europe?' in Piet Dankert and Ad Kooyman (eds), *Europe sans frontières. Les socialistes et l'avenir de la CEE*, EPO, Antwerp 1989, p. 9.

56. Davidson, 'France charts a new course, p. 2.

57. John Smith, 'No One Can Go It Alone', *Socialist Affairs*, no. 1, 1993, p. 4.

58. Susannah Verney, 'From the "Special Relationship" to Europeanism: PASOK and the European Community, 1981–89', in Clogg (ed.), *Greece 1981–89*, pp. 140, 148.

59. As discussed by Jean-Louis Quermonne in his 'Le spectre de la technocratie et le retour de la politique', *Pouvoir*, no. 69, 1994, p. 11.

60. See John Grahl and Paul Teague, *1992 – The Big Market. The Future of the European Community*, Lawrence and Wishart, London 1990, especially chapter 1.

61. Loukas Tsoukalis, *The New European Economy. The Politics and Economics of European Integration*, Oxford University Press, Oxford 1991, p. 305.

62. Milward with the assistance of Brennan and Romero, *The European Rescue of the Nation-State*, p. 446.

63. Marx, *Capital*, Vol. 3, p. 250.

64. Immanuel Wallerstein, *The Modern World-System I. Capitalist Agriculture and the Origins of the European World-Economy in the Sixteenth Century*, Academic Press, San Diego 1974, p. 348.

65. Hobsbawm, op. cit., p. 88.

66. The literature, particularly the left-wing literature, on this is vast. I should single out, among the modern pioneers, Robin Murray, 'The Internationalization of Capital and the Nation State', *New Left Review*, no. 61, May–June 1971 and Wallerstein, op. cit., and his *The Politics of the World-Economy*, Cambridge University Press, Cambridge 1984. See also: David M. Gordon, 'The Global Economy: New Edifice or Crumbling Foundations?', *New Left Review*, no. 168, March–April 1988; Anderson, 'The Figures of Descent'; Holland, *The Global Economy*; Robert Cox, *Production, Power and World Order*, Columbia University Press, New York 1987; Leo Panitch, 'Globalization and the State', in Ralph Miliband and Leo Panitch (eds), *Between Globalism and Nationalism, Socialist Register 1994*, Merlin Press, London 1994 – which also contains useful contributions by Manfred Bienefeld and Arthur McEwan. Paul Hirst and Grahame Thompson warn that globalization is still a distant possibility in 'The Problem of "Globalization": International Economic Relations, National Economic Management and the Formation of Trading Blocs', *Economy and Society*, Vol. 21, no. 4, November 1992.

67. Charles P. Kindleberger, *American Business Abroad. Six Lectures on Direct Investment*, Yale University Press, New Haven and London 1969, pp. 207–8.

68. A point made by John Dunn in his 'Introduction: Crisis of the Nation State', *Political Studies*, Vol. 42, Special issue 1994: *Contemporary Crisis of the Nation State?*, ed. John Dunn, p. 7.

69. This point is made by Laura Cram, 'Calling the Tune without Paying the Piper? Social Policy Regulation: The Role of the Commission in European Community Social Policy', *Policy and Politics*, Vol. 21. no. 2, 1993, p. 141.

70. John Maynard Keynes, *The General Theory of Employment, Interest and Money*, in *Collected Writings*, Vol. VII, Macmillan, London 1972, p. 372; see also his 'The End of Laissez-Faire', in *Essays in Persuasion*, Vol. IX, pp. 291–2.

71. William Wallace, 'Rescue or Retreat? The Nation State in Western Europe, 1945–93', *Political Studies*, Vol. 42, Special issue 1994, pp. 65–6.

72. See Palmiro Togliatti, 'Alcuni problemi della storia dell'Internazionale comunista' (1959), in *Opere*, Vol. 6, p. 380. Togliatti, of course, wrongly believed that interdependence was leading towards a socialist world order.

73. As Geoffrey Garrett and Peter Lange suggest in 'Political Responses to Interdependence: What's "Left" for the Left?', *International Organization*, Vol. 45, no. 4, Autumn 1991, pp. 539–64, and in the same issue and along the same lines, Jeffrey A. Frieden, 'Invested Interests: The Politics of National Economic Policies in a World of Global Finance', pp. 425–51.

74. Michael Stewart, *The Age of Interdependence*, MIT Press, Cambridge MA 1984, p. 20.

75. Strange, *Casino Capitalism*, p. 111.

76. On the power of 'non-decisions', see the brilliant analysis in Strange, op. cit., pp. 26–46.

77. Stewart, op. cit., p. 85.

78. Altvater, *The Future of the Market*, pp. 162–5.

79. On the emergence of these regional organizations, see Henri Bourguinat, 'L'émergence contemporaine des zones et blocs régionaux', in Louis Mucchielli and Fred Célimène (eds), *Mondialisation et régionalisation*, Economica, Paris 1993, especially the table on p. 6.

80. Kerin Hope, 'European prosperity proves elusive', Survey on Greece, *Financial Times*, 14 November 1994, p. i.

81. See comments in Inger-Lise Ostrem, 'La Norvège et la communauté européenne: d'une appartenance de fait à une appartenance de droit?', *Revue du Marché commun et de l'Union européenne*, no. 364, January 1993, pp. 8–23.

82. On the notion of *fides implicita*, see Pierre Bourdieu, *Questions de sociologie*, Editions de Minuit, Paris 1981, pp. 245–8.

83. Alain, *Propos*, ed. Maurice Savin, Gallimard/Bibliothèque la Pléiade, Paris 1956, p. 983. Alain was the pseudonym of Emile Chartier.

Bibliography

Abelshauser, Werner, 'Les nationalisations n'auront pas lieu. La controverse sur l'instauration d'un nouvel ordre économique et social dans les zones occidentales de l'Allemagne de 1945 à 1949', *Le mouvement social*, no. 134, January–March 1986.

Abendroth, Wolfgang, *A Short History of the European Working Class*, New Left Books, London 1972.

Abraham, David, *The Collapse of the Weimar Republic. Political Economy and Crisis*, Princeton University Press, Princeton NJ 1981.

— 'Labor's Way: On the Successes and Limits of Socialist Parties in Interwar and Post-World War II Germany', *International Labor and Working Class History*, no. 28, Fall 1985.

Abs, Robert, *Histoire du Parti socialiste Belge de 1885 à 1978*, Editions Fondation Louis de Brouckère, Brussels 1979.

Adam, Gérard, 'Etude statistique des grèves de Mai–Juin 1968', *Revue française de science politique*, Vol. 20, no. 1, February 1970.

Adams, R. J. and C. H. Rummel, 'Workers' Participation in Management in West Germany: Impact on the Worker, the Enterprise and the Trade Union', *Industrial Relations Journal*, Vol. 8, no. 1, Spring 1977.

Adams, William James, *Restructuring the French Economy. Government and the Rise of Market Competition since World War II*, Brookings Institution, Washington DC 1989.

Addison, Paul, *The Road to 1945*, Quartet Books, London 1977.

Adereth, Maurice, *The French Communist Party. A Critical History (1920–84): From Comintern to 'The Colours of France'*, Manchester University Press, Manchester 1984.

Agosti, Aldo, *La Terza Internazionale. Storia documentaria*, 3 vols, Editori Riuniti, Rome 1974–79.

Ahlén, Kristina, 'Swedish Collective Bargaining Under Pressure: Inter-union Rivalry and Incomes Policies', *British Journal of Industrial Relations*, Vol. 27, no. 3, November 1989.

Alain, *Propos*, ed. Maurice Savin, Gallimard/Bibliothèque la Pléiade, Paris 1956.

Alba, Victor, *The Communist Party in Spain*, Transaction Books, New Brunswick 1983.

Albistur, Maïté and Daniel Armogathe, *Histoire du féminisme français*, Vol. 1, Edition des Femmes, Paris 1978.

Aldcroft, Derek H., *The European Economy 1914–1980*, Croom Helm, London 1980.

Allard, Sven, *Russia and the Austrian State Treaty. A Case Study of Soviet Policy in Europe*, Pennsylvania State University Press, University Park, PA 1970.

Allison, Roy, *Finland's Relations with the Soviet Union, 1944–84*, Macmillan, London 1985.

Allsopp, Christopher, 'Macroeconomic Policy: Design and Performance', in Artis and Cobham (eds), op. cit.

Alogoskoufis, George S., 'On the Determinants of Consumer Price Inflation in Greece', *Greek Economic Review*, Vol. 8, no. 2, December 1986.

Althusser, Louis, 'What Must Change in the Party', *New Left Review*, no. 109, May–June 1978.

— 'Philosophie et marxisme. Entretiens avec Fernanda Navarro (1984–87)', in *Sur la philosophie*, Gallimard, Paris 1994.

— *Ecrits philosophiques et politiques*, Vol. 1, Stock/IMEC, Paris 1994.

Altvater, Elmar, *The Future of the Market. An Essay on the Regulation of Money and Nature after the Collapse of 'Actually Existing Socialism'*, trans. Patrick Camiller, Verso, London 1993.

Alwin, Duane F., Michael Braun and Jacqueline Scott, 'The Separation of Work and Family: Attitudes Towards Women's Labour-force Participation in Germany, Great Britain and the United States', *European Sociological Review*, Vol. 8, no. 1, May 1992.

Amato, Pietro, *Il PSI tra frontismo e autonomia (1948–1954)*, Cosenza 1978.

Ambler, John S., 'Educational Pluralism in the French Fifth Republic', in Hollifield and Ross (eds), op. cit.

Amendola, Giorgio, *Lotta di classe e sviluppo economico dopo la Liberazione*, Editori Riuniti, Rome 1962.

— 'Il socialismo in occidente', *Rinascita*, 7 November 1964.

— 'Ipotesi sulla riunificazione', *Rinascita*, 28 November 1964.

— 'I comunisti e il movimento studentesco: necessità della lotta su due fronti', *Rinascita*, 7 June 1968.

— Speech to the European Parliament, 12 March 1969, in *I comunisti italiani al parlamento europeo – Interventi dei parlamentari della delegazione PCI-PSIUP-Ind. Sinistra*, December 1969.

— *I comunisti e l'Europa*, Editori Riuniti, Rome 1971.

Amyot, Grant, *The Italian Communist Party. The Crisis of the Popular Front Strategy*, Croom Helm, London 1981.

Anderson, Harriet, *Utopian Feminism. Women's Movements in fin-de-siècle Vienna*, Yale University Press, New Haven and London 1992.

Anderson, Perry, 'Sweden: Mr. Crosland's Dreamland', *New Left Review*, no. 7, January–February 1961.

— *Considerations on Western Marxism*, New Left Books, London 1976.

— 'The Antinomies of Antonio Gramsci', *New Left Review*, no. 100, November 1976–January 1977.

— 'Trotsky's Interpretation of Stalinism', *New Left Review*, no. 139, May–June 1983.

— 'The Figures of Descent', *New Left Review*, no. 161, January–February 1987.

— and Patrick Camiller (eds), *Mapping the West European Left*, Verso, London 1994.

Andeweg, Rudy B., 'Less Than Nothing? Hidden Privatisation of the Pseudo-Private Sector: The Dutch Case', *West European Politics*, Vol. 11, no. 4, October 1988.

— T. H. van der Tak and K. Dittrich, 'Government Formation in the Netherlands', in Richard T. Griffiths, *The Economy and Politics of the Netherlands since 1945*, Martinus Nijhoff, The Hague 1980.

Andreoli, Marcella, *Processo all'Italia. Il Belpaese alla sbarra: storie di delitti ordinari e di castighi eccellenti*, Sperling and Kupfer Editori, Milan 1994.

Andreotti, Giulio, *Diari 1976–1979. Gli anni della solidarietà*, Rizzoli, Milan 1981.

— *Visti da vicino. Il meglio delle tre serie*, Rizzoli, Milan 1986.

Andreucci, Franco, 'La diffusione e la volgarizzazione del marxismo', in *Storia del Marxismo*. Vol. 2: *Il marxismo nell'età della Seconda Internazionale*, Einaudi Editore, Turin 1979.

Andrews, William G. and Stanley Hoffmann (eds), *The Impact of the Fifth Republic on France*, State University of New York Press, Albany 1981.

Andrieu, Claire, 'La France à gauche de l'Europe', *Le mouvement social*, no. 134, January–March 1986.

— Lucette Le Van and Antoine Prost (eds), *Les nationalisations de la Libération*, Presses de la Fondation Nationale des Sciences Politiques, Paris 1987.

Angenot, Marc, *Le centenaire de la révolution 1889*, La documentation française, Paris 1989.

— *1889. Un état du discours social*, Editions du Préambule, Québec 1989.

Antonelli, E. 'Pour penser le socialisme', *La revue socialiste*, nos 108–109, June and July 1957.

Appleton, Andrew and Amy G. Mazur, 'Transformation or Modernization: The Rhetoric and Reality of Gender and Party Politics in France', in Lovenduski and Norris (eds), op. cit.

Ardagh, John, *The New France. A Society in Transition 1945–1977*, Penguin, Harmondsworth 1977.

— *Germany and the Germans*, Penguin, Harmondsworth 1988.

Arendt, Hannah, *The Human Condition. A Study of the Central Dilemmas Facing Modern Man*, Doubleday Anchor Books, New York 1959.

Arendt, Walter, 'Speech at the Second and Third Reading of the Co-Determination Bill', 18 March 1976, *Press Bulletin, FRG*, 6 April 1976.

Arfè, Gaetano, *Storia del socialismo italiano 1892–1926*, Einaudi Editore, Turin 1965.

Armstrong, Philip, Andrew Glyn and John Harrison, *Capitalism since World War II. The Making and Breakup of the Great Boom*, Fontana, London 1984.

Arndt, H., *The Economic Lessons of the Nineteen-Thirties*, Oxford University Press, London 1944.

Arnold, Heinz Ludwig, 'From Moral Affirmation to Subjective Pragmatism: The Transformation of German Literature since 1947', in Stanley Hoffmann and Paschalis Kitromilides (eds), *Culture and Society in Contemporary Europe*, Allen and Unwin, London 1981.

Aron, Raymond, *La révolution introuvable. Réflexions sur la Révolution de Mai*, Fayard, Paris 1968.

Arter, David, 'A Tale of Two Carlssons: The Swedish General Elections of 1988', *Parliamentary Affairs*, Vol. 42, no. 1, January 1989.

Artis, Michael and David Cobham (eds), *Labour's Economic Policies 1974–1979*, Manchester University Press, Manchester 1991.

Asselain, Jean-Charles, *Histoire économique de la France.* Vol. 2: *De 1919 à la fin des années 1970*, Editions du Seuil, Paris 1984.

Atkinson, A. B., 'Poverty and Income Inequality in Britain' in Wedderburn (ed.), op. cit.

Atkinson, Valerie and Joanna Spear, 'The Labour Party and Women: Policies and Practices', in Smith and Spear (eds), op. cit.

Attali, Jacques, *Verbatim, I 1981–1986*, Fayard, Paris 1993.

Attlee, C. R., *The Labour Party in Perspective*, Left Book Club edn, Victor Gollancz, London 1937.

Avon (Lord), *The Eden Memoirs. The Reckoning*, Cassel, London 1965.

Azcárate, Manuel, *Crisis del Eurocomunismo*, Editorial Argos Vergara, Barcelona 1982.

Bacon, Robert and Walter Eltis, *Britain's Economic Problem: Too Few Producers*, London, Macmillan 1978.

— 'Reply to Hadjimatheou and Skouras', *Economic Journal*, Vol. 89, June 1979.

Baget-Bozzo, Gianni, *Il Partito cristiano al potere. La DC di De Gasperi e di Dossetti 1945/1954*, Vallecchi, Florence 1974.

Bahro, Rudolf, *From Red to Green. Interviews with New Left Review*, Verso, London 1984.

Bairoch, Paul, *Economics and World History. Myths and Paradoxes*, Harvester Wheatsheaf, Hemel Hempstead 1993.

Baker, Donald N., 'Two Paths to Socialism: Marcel Déat and Marceau Pivert', *Journal of Contemporary History*, Vol. 11, no. 1, 1976.

Bakker, Isabella, 'Women's Employment in Comparative Perspective', in Jenson, Hangen and Reddy (eds), op. cit.

Baklanoff, Eric N., *The Economic Transformation of Spain and Portugal*, Praeger, New York 1978.

Bakvis, Herman, 'Towards a Political Economy of Consociationalism. A Commentary on Marxist Views of Pillarization in the Netherlands', *Contemporary Politics*, Vol. 16, no. 3, April 1984.

Balbo, Laura, 'Family, Women, and the State', in Maier (ed.), op. cit.

Baldwin, Peter, 'Class, Interest and the Welfare State. A Reply to Sven E. Olsson', *International Review of Social History*, Vol. 34, 1989.

— 'The Scandinavian Origins of the Social Interpretation of the Welfare State', *Comparative Studies in Society and History*, Vol. 13, no. 1, 1989.

— *The Politics of Social Solidarity. Class Bases of the European Welfare State 1875–1975*, Cambridge University Press, Cambridge 1990.

Balfour, Michael, *The Adversaries. America, Russia and the Open World 1941–62*, Routledge and Kegan Paul, London 1981.

— *West Germany. A Contemporary History*, Croom Helm, London and Canberra 1982.

Balfour, Sebastian, *Dictatorship, Workers, and the City. Labour in Greater Barcelona since 1939*, Clarendon Press, Oxford 1989.

Balogh, Thomas, 'Britain and the Dependent Commonwealth, in A. Creech Jones (ed.), *New Fabian Colonial Essays*, Hogarth Press, London 1959.

— *The Irrelevance of Conventional Economics*, Weidenfeld and Nicolson, London 1982.

Banks, Olive, *Faces of Feminism*, Martin Robertson, Oxford 1981.

— *Becoming a Feminist. The Social Origins of 'First Wave' Feminism*, Wheatsheaf, Brighton 1986.

Barca L., F. Botta, and A. Zevi (eds), *I comunisti e l'economia italiana 1944–1974*, De Donato, Bari 1975.

Bard, Christine (ed.), *Madeleine Pelletier (1874–1939). Logique et infortunes d'un combat pour l'égalité*, Côté-femmes éditions, Paris 1992.

Bariety, Jacques (ed.), *1889: Centenaire de la Révolution Française*, Peter Lang, Berne 1992.

Bark, Dennis L. and David R. Gress, *A History of West Germany*, 2 vols, Basil Blackwell, Oxford 1989.

Barkan, Joanne, *Visions of Emancipation. The Italian Workers' Movement since 1945*, Praeger, New York 1984.

Barnett, Correlli, *The Audit of War. The Illusion and Reality of Britain as a Great Nation*, Macmillan, London 1986.

Barnett, Joel, *Inside the Treasury*, André Deutsch, London 1982.

Barr, Nicholas and Fiona Coulter, 'Social Security: Solution or Problem?', in Hills (ed.), op. cit.

Bartolini, Stefano, 'I primi movimenti socialisti in Europa. Consolidamento organizzativo e mobilitazione politica', *Rivista italiana di scienza politica*, Vol. 23, no. 2, August 1993.

Batchelor, Charles, 'Concern at decline in membership', Survey on the Netherlands, *Financial Times*, 16 October 1986.

Bauer, Otto, 'What Is Austro-Marxism?' *Arbeiter-Zeitung*, 3 November 1927, in Tom Bottomore and Patrick Goode, *Austro-Marxism*, Clarendon Press, Oxford 1978.

— *Austrian Democracy under Fire*, London 1934, in Beetham (ed.), op. cit.

— *Tra due guerre mondiali?*, (Italian trans. of *Zwischen zwei Weltkriegen?*), Einaudi Editore, Turin 1979.

Baumol, William J., 'Macroeconomics of Unbalanced Growth: The Anatomy of Urban Crisis', *American Economic Review*, Vol. 57, no. 3, June 1967.

Bazil, Béatrice, 'L'irrésistible logique de la socialisation', in Massenet et al., op. cit.

Bean, C. R., R. Layard and S. J. Nickell, 'The Rise in Unemployment: A Multi-country Study', *Economica*, Vol. 53, 1986, Supplement to no. 210, *Unemployment*.

Bebel, August, *Woman in the Past, Present and Future*, Zwan Publications, London 1988.

Beccalli, Bianca, 'The Modern Women's Movement in Italy', *New Left Review*, no. 204, March–April 1994.

Becker, Jean-Jacques, *Le parti communiste veut-il prendre le pouvoir? La stratégie du PCF de 1930 à nos jours*, Editions du Seuil, Paris 1981.

— 'Le PCF', in Andrieu, Le Van and Prost (eds), op. cit.

Becker, Renate and Rob Burns, 'The Women's Movement in the Federal Republic of Germany', *Contemporary German Studies, Occasional Papers,* no. 3, Department of Modern Languages, Strathclyde 1987.

Beckerman, Wilfred (ed.), *The Labour Government's Economic Record 1964–1970,* Duckworth, London 1972.

Beetham, David (ed.), *Marxism in the Face of Fascism,* Manchester University Press, Manchester 1983.

Bell, Daniel, *The End of Ideology. On the Exhaustion of Political Ideas in the Fifties,* Free Press, New York 1965 (1st edn 1960).

— *The Coming of Post-Industrial Society,* Heinemann, London 1974.

Bell, D. S. (ed.), *Western European Communists and the Collapse of Communism,* Berg, Oxford and Providence 1993.

— and Byron Criddle, *The French Socialist Party,* Clarendon Press, Oxford 1988.

Bell, John D., *Peasants in Power. Alexander Stamboliski and the Bulgarian Agrarian National Union, 1899–1923,* Princeton University Press, Princeton NJ 1977.

Bell, Laurence, 'May 68: Parenthesis or Staging Post in the Development of the Socialist Left?', in Hanley and Waiter (eds), 1989.

Bénéton, Philippe and Jean Touchard, 'Les interprétations de la crise de mai–juin 1968', *Revue française de science politique,* Vol. 20, no. 3, June 1970.

Benn, Tony, *Arguments for Democracy,* Penguin, Harmondsworth 1982.

— *Parliament, People and Power,* Verso, London 1982.

— *Against the Tide. Diaries 1973–76,* Hutchinson, London 1989.

Benson, Ian and John Lloyd, *New Technology and Industrial Change,* Kogan Page, London 1983.

Benzoni, Alberto, 'I socialisti e la politica estera', in Massimo Bonanni (ed.), *La politica estera della Repubblica italiana,* I.A.I and Edizioni di Comunità, Milan 1967.

Berger, Stefan, 'Nationalism and the Left in Germany', *New Left Review,* no. 206, July–August 1994.

Berger, Suzanne, 'Liberalism Reborn: The New Liberal Synthesis in France', in Howorth and Ross (eds), op. cit., Vol. 1.

Berggren, Christian, 'Work Reforms in Sweden 1970–1990: From Labour Market Pressures to Corporate Strategies', in Boje and Olsson Hort (eds), op. cit.

— *The Volvo Experience. Alternatives to Lean Production in the Swedish Auto Industry,* Macmillan, London 1993.

Berghahn, Volker R., *The Americanisation of West German Industry 1945–1973,* Berg, Leamington and New York 1986.

— *Modern Germany,* Cambridge University Press, Cambridge 1982.

— and Detlev Karsten, *Industrial Relations in West Germany,* Berg, Oxford 1987.

Bergounioux, Alain, 'Sur la crise du syndicalisme', *Intervention,* no. 13, July–September 1985.

— 'Le néosocialisme. Marcel Déat: réformisme traditionnel ou esprit des années trentes', *Revue Historique,* Vol. 102, no. 528, October–December 1978.

Bergström, Hans, 'Sweden's Politics and Party System at the Crossroads', *West European Politics,* Vol. 14, no. 3, July 1991.

Berlinguer, Enrico, *La proposta comunista,* Einaudi Editore, Turin 1975.

— *La 'Questione Comunista',* 2 vols, Editori Riuniti, Rome 1975.

— *La politica internazionale dei comunisti italiani,* Editori Riuniti, Rome 1976.

— *Austerità occasione per trasformare l'Italia,* Editori Riuniti, Rome 1977.

— *La nostra lotta dall'opposizione verso il governo,* Editori Riuniti, Rome 1979.

— *Per il socialismo nella pace e nella democrazia in Italia e in Europa,* Editori Riuniti, Rome 1979.

— *After Poland,* ed. and trans. Antonio Bronda and Stephen Bodington, Spokesman, Nottingham 1982.

Bernard, Philippe and Dubief, Henri, *The Decline of the Third Republic 1914–1938*, Cambridge University Press, Cambridge 1988.

Bernstein, Eduard, *Evolutionary Socialism*, Schocken Books, New York 1963.

— 'The Struggle of Social Democracy and the Social Revolution: 2. The Theory of Collapse and Colonial Policy', originally in *Neue Zeit*, 19 January 1898; English trans. in H. Tudor and J. M. Tudor (eds), *Marxism and Social Democracy. The Revisionist Debate 1896–1898*, Cambridge University Press, Cambridge 1988.

— *The Preconditions of Socialism*, ed. and trans. Henry Tudor, Cambridge University Press, Cambridge 1994.

Berry, Albert, François Bourguignon and Christian Morrison, 'Global Economic Inequality and its Trends since 1950', in Osberg (ed.), op. cit.

Berstein, Serge, 'La SFIO', in Andrieu, Le Van and Prost (eds), op. cit.

Berti, Giuseppe (ed.), *I primi dieci anni di vita del PCI. Documenti inediti dell'archivio Angelo Tasca*, Feltrinelli, Milan 1967.

Beveridge, William, *Social Insurance and Allied Services*, Cmd. 6404, HMSO, London 1942.

— *Full Employment in a Free Society*, 2nd edn with a new prologue, Allen and Unwin, London 1960.

Beyme, Klaus von, 'The Ostpolitik in the West German 1969 Elections', *Government and Opposition*, Vol. 5, no. 2, Spring 1970.

— *Challenge to Power. Trade Unions and Industrial Relations in Capitalist Countries*, Sage, London and Beverly Hills 1980.

— 'A United Germany Preparing for the 1994 Elections', *Government and Opposition*, Vol. 29, no. 4, Autumn 1994.

Bezbakh, Pierre, *Histoire et figures du socialisme français*, Bordas, Paris 1994.

Biacabe, Pierre, 'Les mésaventures du franc', in Massenet et al., op. cit.

Birchall, Ian, *Bailing Out the System. Reformist Socialism in Western Europe 1944–1985*, Bookmarks, London 1986.

Birnbaum, Pierre, 'The State in Contemporary France', in Richard Scase (ed.), *The State in Western Europe*, Croom Helm, London 1980.

Bizcarrondo, Marta, 'Los origenes del feminismo socialista en España', in *La mujer en la historia de España*, Actas de las II jornadas de investigación interdisciplinaria, Universidad Autonoma de Madrid, Madrid 1984.

Blackbourn, David, *Class, Religion and Local Politics in Wilhelmine Germany. The Centre Party in Württemberg before 1914*, Yale University Press, New Haven 1980.

Blackmer, D. L. M., *Unity in Diversity. Italian Communism and the Communist World*, MIT Press, Cambridge MA 1968.

— and Sidney Tarrow (eds), *Communism in Italy and France*, Princeton University Press, Princeton NJ 1975.

Blanchard, Olivier, Rudiger Dornbusch and Richard Layard (eds), *Restoring Europe's Prosperity: Macro-economic Papers from the Centre for European Policy Studies*, MIT Press, Cambridge MA and London 1986.

Blau, David M. and Philip K. Robins, 'Child-care Costs and Family Labor Supply', *Review of Economics and Statistics*, Vol. 70, no. 3, August 1988.

Blinkhorn, Martin (ed.), *Fascists and Conservatives. The Radical Right and the Establishment in Twentieth-Century Europe*, Unwin Hyman, London 1990.

Bloomfield, Jon, *Passive Revolution. Politics and the Czechoslovak Working Class 1945–1948*, St Martin's Press, New York 1979.

Blum, Léon, *L'Oeuvre de Léon Blum (1940–1945)*, Albin Michel, Paris 1955.

— *L'Oeuvre de Blum*, Vol. III-1 (1914–1928), Vol. VI-1 (1945–1947), Albin Michel, Paris 1972.

Blume, Daniel et al., *Histoire du réformisme en France depuis 1920*, Vol. 2, Editions Sociales, Paris 1976.

Blum, Patrick, 'An attractive deal is needed', Survey on Austria, *Financial Times*, 10 November 1993.

Boccara, Paul, *Etudes sur le capitalisme monopoliste d'Etat, sa crise et son issue*, Editions Sociales, Paris 1974.

Boje, Thomas P. and Lise Drewes Nielsen, 'Flexible Production, Employment and Gender', in Boje and Olsson Hort (eds), op. cit.

Boje, Thomas P. and Sven E. Olsson Hort (eds), *Scandinavia in a New Europe*, Scandinavia University Press, Oslo 1993.

Boltho, Andrea 'Western Europe's Economic Stagnation', *New Left Review*, no. 201, September–October 1993.

— (ed.), *The European Economy. Growth & Crisis*, Oxford University Press, Oxford 1982.

Bombach, Gottfried, *Post-war Economic Growth Revisited*, Elsevier Science, Amsterdam 1985.

Bon, Frédéric, 'Structure de l'idéologie communiste', in *Le Communisme en France*, Cahiers de la Fondation Nationale des Sciences Politiques, Colin, Paris 1969.

Bonaccorsi, Marina, 'Gli enti pubblici del settore della sicurezza sociale', in Franco Cazzola (ed.), *Anatomia del potere DC. Enti pubblici e "centralità democristiana"*, De Donato, Bari 1979.

Bonime, Andrea R., 'The Spanish State Structure: Constitution Making and the Creation of the New State', in Lancaster and Prevost (eds), op. cit.

Bonnel, P., 'Hegel et Marx', *La revue socialiste*, nos 110 and 111, October and November 1957.

Bonney, Norman and Elizabeth Reinach, 'Housework Reconsidered: The Oakley Thesis Twenty Years Later', *Work, Employment and Society*, Vol. 7, no. 4, December 1993.

Borchardt, Knut, *Perspectives on Modern German Economic History*, trans. Peter Lambert, Cambridge University Press, Cambridge 1991.

Borghini, Gian Franco and Achille Occhetto, text of reports to the Congress of the FGCI held at Ariccia 29–30 November 1968, in supplement to *Nuova Generazione*, no. 24, 1968.

Bornstein, Stephen, 'States and Unions: From Postwar Settlement to Contemporary Stalemate', in S. Bornstein, D. Held and J. Krieger, *The State in Capitalist Europe*, Allen and Unwin, London 1984.

Bosworth, Barry and Robert Z. Lawrence, 'Economic Goals and the Policy Mix', in Bosworth and Rivlin (eds), op. cit.

Bosworth, Barry and Alice M. Rivlin (eds), *The Swedish Economy*, Brookings Institution, Washington DC 1987.

Botz, Gerhard, 'Austro-Marxist Interpretation of Fascism', *Journal of Contemporary History*, Vol. 11, no. 4, 1976.

Bourderon, Roger et al., *Le PCF: étapes et problèmes*, Editions Sociales, Paris 1981.

Bourdieu, Pierre, *Questions de sociologie*, Editions de Minuit, Paris 1981.

— *Distinction. A Social Critique of the Judgement of Taste*, Routledge and Kegan Paul, London 1984.

— and Jean-Claude Passeron, *The Inheritors. French Students and Their Relation to Culture*, University of Chicago Press, Chicago and London 1979.

Bourguinat, Henri, 'L'émergence contemporaine des zones et blocs régionaux', in Louis Mucchielli and Fred Célimène (eds), *Mondialisation et régionalisation*, Economica, Paris 1993.

Bouvier, Beatrix W., *Zwischen Godesberg und Grosser Koalition: der Weg der SPD in die Regierungsverantwortung*, Dietz, Bonn 1990.

Boyce, Robert W. D., *British Capitalism at the Crossroads 1919–32. A Study in Politics, Economics and International Relations*, Cambridge University Press, Cambridge 1987.

Bradley, Ian, *Breaking the Mould? The Birth and Prospects of the Social Democratic Party*, Martin Robertson, Oxford 1981.

Bramwell, Anna, *Ecology in the 20th Century. A History*, Yale University Press, New Haven and London 1989.

Brand, Carl F., *The British Labour Party*, Hoover Institution Press, Standford 1974.

Brand, Karl-Werner, 'Cyclical Aspects of New Social Movements: Waves of Cultural Criticism and Mobilization Cycles of New Middle-class Radicalism', in Dalton and Kuechler (eds), op. cit.

Brands, H. W., 'India and Pakistan in American Strategic Planning, 1947–54: Commonwealth as Collaborator', *Journal of Imperial and Commonwealth History*, Vol. 15, no. 1, October 1986.

Brandt, Willy, *The State of the Nation*, speech at the SPD Party Conference at Dortmund, 1 June 1966, SPD, Bonn n.d., English language text.

— *A Peace Policy for Europe*, Weidenfeld and Nicolson, London 1969.

— 'The German View', *Socialist International Information*, Vol. 21, no. 5–6, May–June 1971.

— 'No Limits to Qualitative Growth', *Socialist International Information*, no. 4, 1982.

— 'Social Democracy after the Communist Collapse', *Socialist Affairs*, no. 3, 1991.

— *My Life in Politics*, Penguin, Harmondsworth 1993.

— Bruno Kreisky and Olof Palme, *La Social-démocratie et l'avenir*, Gallimard, Paris 1976.

Branson, Noreen, *History of the Communist Party of Great Britain 1927–1941*, Lawrence and Wishart, London 1985.

Bratteli, Trygve, 'The Norwegian View', *Socialist International Information*, Vol. 21, nos 5–6, May–June 1971.

Braudel, Fernand, *A History of Civilizations*, trans. Richard Mayne, Allen Lane/Penguin, London 1994.

Braun, Dietmar, 'Political Immobilism and Labour Market Performance: The Dutch Road to Mass Unemployment', *Journal of Public Policy*, Vol. 7, no. 3, July–September 1987.

Braunthal, Gerard, *The West German Social Democrats, 1969–1982. Profile of a Party in Power*, Westview Press, Boulder, CO 1983.

Bredin, Jean-Denis, 'Est-il permis?', *Le Monde*, 31 August 1991.

Brettell, Caroline B., 'Emigration and Its Implications for the Revolution in Northern Portugal', in Graham and Makler (eds), op. cit.

Bridgford, Jeff, 'The Events of May. Consequences for Industrial Relations in France', in Hanley, Kerr and Waites (eds), op. cit.

Brittan, Samuel, 'Some Common Market Heresies', *Journal of Common Market Studies*, Vol. 8, no. 4, June 1970.

Brower, Daniel R. *The New Jacobins. The French Communist Party and the Popular Front*, Cornell University Press, Ithaca, NY 1968.

Brown, Bernard (ed.), *Eurocommunism and Eurosocialism: The Left Confronts Modernity*, Cyrco Press, New York and London 1979.

Brown, Irene Coltman, 'Mary Wollstonecraft and the French Revolution or Feminism and the Rights of Men', in Siân Reynolds (ed.), *Women, State and Revolution*, Wheatsheaf, Brighton 1986.

Brown, William, 'Industrial Relations', in Artis and Cobham (eds), op. cit.

— and Keith Sisson, *A Positive Incomes Policy*, Fabian Tract, no. 442, May 1976.

Brown-Humes, Christopher, 'Swedish package lifts taxes and cuts spending', *Financial Times*, 26 April 1995.

Bruce, Peter, 'West German unions set might against "demon Kohl"', *Financial Times*, 3 June 1986.

Bruneau, Thomas C., 'The Left and the Emergence of Portuguese Liberal Democracy', in B. Brown (ed.), op. cit.

Bruno, Michael and Jeffrey D. Sachs, *Economics of Worldwide Stagflation*, Basil Blackwell, Oxford 1985.

Brzezinski, Zbigniew, *Power and Principle: Memoirs of the National Security Advisor 1977–1981*, Weidenfeld and Nicolson, London 1983.

Buchan, David, 'France's grassroots shake the union tree', *Financial Times*, 28 October 1993.

Buci-Glucksmann, Christine, *Gramsci and the State*, Lawrence and Wishart, London 1980.

— and Göran Therborn, *Le défi social-democrate*, Maspero, Paris 1981.

Bull, Martin and Paul Heywood (eds), *West European Communist Parties after the Revolutions of 1989*, St Martin's Press, New York 1994.

Bullock, Alan, *The Life and Times of Ernest Bevin*. Vol. 1: *Trade Union Leader 1881–1940*, Heinemann, London 1960.

— *Ernest Bevin Foreign Secretary 1945–1951*, Oxford University Press, Oxford 1985.

Burk, Kathleen and Alec Cairncross, *'Goodbye, Great Britain'. The 1976 IMF Crisis*, Yale University Press, New Haven and London 1992.

Burlatsky, Fedor, *Khrushchev and the First Russian Spring*, Weidenfeld and Nicolson, London 1991.

Burnham, James, *The Managerial Revolution*, Penguin, London 1945.

Burrin, Philippe, *La Dérive fasciste. Doriot, Déat, Bergery 1933–1954*, Editions du Seuil, Paris 1986.

Burtless, Gary, 'Taxes, Transfers, and Swedish Labor Supply', in Bosworth and Rivlin (eds), op. cit.

Buse, Dieter K., 'Party Leadership and Mechanism of Unity: The Crisis of German Social Democracy Reconsidered, 1910–1914', *Journal of Modern History*, Vol. 62, no. 3, September 1990.

Butler, David and Dennis Kavanagh, *The British General Election of 1987*, Macmillan, London 1988.

— *The British General Election of 1992*, Macmillan, London 1992.

Butler, L. J., *Economic Development and the 'Official Mind': The Colonial Office and Manufacturing in West Africa, 1939–1951*, Unpublished doctoral dissertation, University of London 1991.

Caciagli, Mario, 'Apogeo e declino delle due grandi subculture politiche territoriali', paper presented to the Third Conference of the SISE, *Italia 1948–1988: Quarant'anni di dinamiche elettorali e istituzionali*, Naples 6–8 October 1988.

Cairncross, Alec, *Years of Recovery. British Economic Policy 1945–51*, Methuen, London and New York 1985.

— 'The United Kingdom', in Graham with Seldon (eds), op. cit..

— and Barry Eichengreen, *Sterling in Decline*, Blackwell, Oxford 1983.

Caldwell, Lesley, *Italian Family Matters. Women, Politics and Legal Reform*, Macmillan, London 1991.

Callaghan, James, *Time and Chance*, Collins, London 1987.

Calvocoressi, Peter and Guy Wint, *Total War*, Penguin, Harmondsworth 1972.

Camboni, Gianfranco and Danilo Samsa, *PCI e movimento degli studenti 1968–1973*, De Donato, Bari 1975.

Cameron, David R., 'The Expansion of the Public Economy: A Comparative Analysis', *American Political Science Review*, Vol. 72, no. 4, December 1978.

Camiller, Patrick, 'The Eclipse of Spanish Communism', *New Left Review*, no. 147, September–October 1984.

— 'Spain: The Survival of Socialism?', in Anderson and Camiller (eds), op. cit.

Campbell, Beatrix, *Iron Ladies. Why Do Women Vote Tory?*, Virago Press, London 1987.

Caridi, Paola, *La scissione di Palazzo Barberini*, Edizioni Scientifiche Italiane, Naples 1991.

Carlson, Allan, *The Swedish Experiment in Family Politics: The Myrdals and the Interwar Population Crisis*, Transaction, New Brunswick 1990.

Carlsson, Ingvar, 'Interview', Survey on Sweden, *Financial Times*, 21 December 1993.

Carnegy, Hugh, 'Swedish companies look overseas for salvation', *Financial Times*, 22 July 1993.

— 'Swedes go to ground while summer days are long', *Financial Times*, 7–8 August 1993.

— 'Reluctant to walk the gangplank', *Financial Times*, 4 November 1993.

— 'Sweden shows effects of painful cure', *Financial Times*, 8 November 1993.

— 'Liberal who may be the next prime minister', Survey on Finland, *Financial Times*, 9 November 1994.

Carpenter, L. P., *G. D. H. Cole. An Intellectual Biography*, Cambridge University Press, Cambridge 1973.

Carr, E. H., *The Bolshevik Revolution 1917–1923*, Vol. 3, Penguin, Harmondsworth 1971.

Carr, Raymond and Juan Pablo Fusi, *Spain: Dictatorship to Democracy*, Allen and Unwin, London 1979.

Carr, William, *A History of Germany 1815–1985*, Edward Arnold, London 1987.

— 'German Social Democracy since 1945', in Roger Fletcher (ed.), *Bernstein to Brandt. A Short History of German Social Democracy*, Edward Arnold, London 1987.

Carrieri, Mimmo, 'Superare il "modello proletario" di azione sindacale', *Democrazia e diritto*, nos 1–2, January–February 1989.

Carter, April, *Peace Movements. International Protest and World Politics since 1945*, Longman, London 1992.

Carter, Neil, 'The "Greening" of Labour', in Smith and Spear (eds), op. cit.

Casalini, Maria, 'Femminismo e socialismo in Anna Kuliscioff. 1890–1907', *Italia Contemporanea*, no. 143, June 1981.

— *La Signora del socialismo italiano. Vita di Anna Kuliscioff*, Editori Riuniti, Rome 1987.

Casanova, Laurent, 'A propos de la guerre d'Algérie: L'internationalisme prolétarien et l'intérêt national', *Cahiers du communisme*, Vol. 33, no. 4, April 1957.

Castle, Barbara, *The Castle Diaries 1974–76*, Weidenfeld and Nicolson, London 1980.

Castles, Francis, *The Social Democratic Image of Society: A Study of the Achievements and Origins of Scandinavian Social Democracy in Comparative Perspective*, Routledge and Kegan Paul, London 1978.

Castles, Stephen and Godula Kosack, *Immigrant Workers and Class Structure in Western Europe*, Oxford University Press, Oxford 1985.

Castoldi, Alberto, *Intellettuali e Fronte popolare in Francia*, De Donato, Bari 1978.

Caute, David, *Communism and the French Intellectuals 1914–1960*, André Deutsch, London 1964.

— *Sixty-eight. The Year of the Barricades*, Hamish Hamilton, London 1988.

Cazzola, Franco, 'Consenso e opposizione nel parlamento italiano. Il ruolo del PCI dalla I alla IV Legislatura', *Rivista Italiana di Scienza Politica*, January 1972.

— 'La solidarietà nazionale dalla parte del Parlamento', *Laboratorio politico*, no. 2–3, March–June 1982.

Centre de regroupement des informations universitaires, *Quelles université? Quelle société?*, Editions du Seuil, Paris 1968.

Centro per La Riforma dello Stato (ed.), *Politica Europa Annali 1990–1991*, Franco Angeli, Milan 1991.

Cerny, Philip G., *The Politics of Grandeur. Ideological Aspects of de Gaulle's Foreign Policy*, Cambridge University Press, Cambridge 1980.

— 'State Capitalism in France and Britain and the International Economic Order', in Cerny and Schain (eds), op. cit.

— and Martin A. Schain (eds), *Socialism, the State and Public Policy in France*, Frances Pinter, London 1985.

Cerroni, Umberto, *Il rapporto uomo-donna nella civiltà borghese*, Editori Riuniti, Rome 1975.

Chappaz, G., 'Réflexion sur le matérialisme marxiste', *La revue socialiste*, no. 110, October 1957.

Charzat, Gisèle, *Les Françaises sont-elles des citoyennes?*, Editions Denoël, Paris 1972.

Chaveau, Henri, 'Le parti, la SFIO et la paupérisation', *Cahiers du communisme*, Vol. 33, no. 3, March 1957.

Cheeseright, Paul, 'Cry for Help in Mining Crisis', Survey on Belgium, *Financial Times*, 13 June 1986.

Chester, Norman, *The Nationalisation of British Industry 1945–51*, HMSO, London 1975.

Chevènement, Jean-Pierre, 'Interview' in *Intervention*, no. 5–6, August–October 1983.

— *Apprendre pour entreprendre*, Livre de Poche, Paris 1985.

— *Le pari sur l'intelligence* (with Hervé Hamon and Patrick Rotman), Flammarion, Paris 1985.

Chiarante, Giuseppe, *La rivolta degli studenti*, Editori Riuniti, Rome 1968.

Chiarini R. and Paolo Corsini, *Da Salò a piazza della Loggia. Blocco d'ordine, neofascismo, radicalismo di destra a Brescia (1945–1974)*, Franco Angeli, Milan 1983.

Chiaromonte, Gerardo, *L'accordo programmatico e l'azione dei comunisti*, Editori Riuniti, Rome 1977.

— *Le scelte della solidarietà democratica. Cronache, ricordi e riflessioni sul triennio 1976–1979*, Editori Riuniti, Rome 1986.

Chick, Martin, 'Private Industrial Investment', in Helen Mercer, Neil Rollings and Jim Tomlinson (eds), *Labour Governments and Private Industry. The Experience of 1945–51*, Edinburgh University Press, Edinburgh 1992.

Chiesa, Giulietto, *Da Mosca. Alle origini di un colpo di stato annunciato*, Laterza, Rome-Bari 1993.

Childs, David, *Britain since 1945*, Methuen, London 1984.

Chinese Communist Party, 'On the Differences between Comrade Togliatti and Us', *Peking Review*, 4 January 1963.

— 'More on the Differences between Comrade Togliatti and Us', *Peking Review*, 15 March 1963.

Christiansen, Ernst, 'The Ideological Development of Democratic Socialism in Denmark', *Socialist International Information*, Vol. 18, no. 1, 4 January 1958.

Clark, Jon, 'Concerted Action in the Federal Republic of Germany', *British Journal of Industrial Relations*, Vol. 17, no. 2, July 1979.

Clark, Robert P. and Michael H. Haltzel (eds), *Spain in the 1980s. The Democratic Transition and a New International Role*, Ballinger, Cambridge MA 1987.

Clarke, Charles and David Griffiths, *Labour and Mass Politics. Rethinking our Strategy*, Labour Co-ordinating Committee, November 1982.

Clarke, John et al., 'Subcultures, Cultures and Class', in Stuart Hall and Tony Jefferson (eds), *Resistance through Rituals. Youth Subcultures in Post-war Britain*, Hutchinson, London 1977.

Clarke, Sir Richard W. B., *Anglo-American Economic Collaboration in War and in Peace 1942–1949*, ed. Sir Alec Cairncross, Clarendon Press, Oxford 1982.

Clarke, Tom, 'Industrial Democracy: The Institutionalized Suppression of Industrial Conflict?', in Tom Clarke and Laurie Clements (eds), *Trade Unions Under Capitalism*, Fontana, n.p. 1977.

Claudin, Fernando, *The Communist Movement. From Comintern to Cominform*, Penguin, Harmondsworth 1975.

Clavau, Fernand, 'La crise du Marché commun', *Cahiers du communisme*, Vol. 41, no. 6, September 1965.

Clogg, Richard, *Parties and Elections in Greece. The Search for Legitimacy*, C. Hurst and Co., London 1987.

— (ed.), *Greece in the 1980s*, Macmillan, London 1983.

— (ed.), *Greece, 1981–89. The Populist Decade*, St Martin's Press, New York 1993.

Close, David, 'Conservatism, Authoritarianism and Fascism in Greece, 1915–45', in Blinkhorn (ed.), op. cit.

Coates, David, *Labour in Power? A Study of the Labour Government 1974–1979*, Longman, London 1980.

Cobler, Sebastian, *Law, Order and Politics in West Germany*, trans. Francis McDonagh, Penguin, Harmondsworth 1978.

Cogniot, Georges, 'Les nouveaux pièges "européens"', *Cahiers du communisme*, Vol. 33, no. 2, February 1957.

Cohen, Bronwen and Neil Fraser, *Childcare in a Modern Welfare System. Towards a New National System*, IPPR, London 1991.

Cohen, G. A., 'Back to Socialist Basics', *New Left Review*, no. 207, September–October 1994.

Cole, G. D. H., *A History of Socialist Thought*. Vol. 5: *Socialism and Fascism 1931–1939*, Macmillan, London 1960.

Collard, Léon, speech of 16 November 1958 to the special Congress of the Belgian Socialist Party, *Socialist International Information*, Vol. 8, no. 48, 29 November 1958.

— 'The Future of Socialism', *Le Peuple*, 21 September 1959; reprinted and trans. in *Socialist International Information*, Vol. 9, no. 41, 10 October 1959.

Collotti, Enzo, *Esempio Germania. Socialdemocrazia tedesca e coalizione social-liberale 1969–1976*, Feltrinelli, Milan 1977.

Colton, Joel, *Léon Blum. Humanist in Politics*, Alfred A. Knopf, New York 1966.

Commission on Social Justice, *Social Justice. Strategies for National Renewal*, Vintage, London 1994.

Condorcet, Antoine de, *Foundations of Social Choice and Political Theory*, trans. and ed. Iain McLean and Fiona Hewitt, Edward Elgar, Aldershot 1994.

Conference of Socialist Economists London Working Group, *The Alternative Economic Strategy*, LCC/CSE, London 1980.

Cook, Alice H., 'Federal Republic of Germany', in Cook, Lorwin and Daniels (eds), op. cit.

Cook, Alice H., Val R. Lorwin and Arlene Kaplan Daniels (eds), *Women and Trade Unions in Eleven Industrialized Countries*, Temple University Press, Philadelphia 1983.

Coole, Diana, *Women in Political Theory*, Wheatsheaf, Brighton 1988.

Cooper, Richard N., 'The Balance of Payments', in Richard E. Caves (ed.), *Britain's Economic Prospects*, Brookings Institution and Allen and Unwin, Washington and London 1968.

Coopey, Richard, 'The White Heat of Scientific Revolution', *Contemporary Record. The Journal of Contemporary British History*, Vol. 5, no. 1 Summer 1991.

Coote, Anna, 'The AES: A New Starting Point', *New Socialist*, November–December 1981.

— and Beatrix Campbell, *Sweet Freedom*, 2nd edn, Basil Blackwell, Oxford 1987.

— and Polly Pattullo, *Power and Prejudice. Women and Politics*, Weidenfeld and Nicolson, London 1990.

Coppola, Aniello, *Moro*, Feltrinelli, Milan 1976.

Corsini, Paolo and Laura Novati (eds), *L'eversione nera. Cronache di un decennio 1974–1984*, Franco Angeli, Milan 1985.

Cot, Jean-Pierre, 'Autogestion and Modernity in France', in B. Brown (ed.), op. cit.

Couloumbis, Theodore A., 'PASOK's Foreign Policies, 1981–89: Continuity or Change?', in Clogg (ed.) op. cit., 1993.

Courakis, Anthony S., Fatima Mouraroque and George Tridimas, 'Public-expenditure Growth in Greece and Portugal, the Wagner Law and Beyond', *Applied Economics*, Vol. 25, no. 1, January 1993.

Courtieu, Paul and Jean Houdremont, 'La paupérisation absolue de la classe ouvrière', *Cahiers du communisme*, Vol. 31, no. 4, April 1955.

Courtois, Gérard, '1981–1993: l'érosion des ambitions', *Le Monde*, 18 March 1993.

— 'La FEN en miettes', *Le Monde*, 18 March 1993.

Courtois, Stéphane, *Le PCF dans la guerre. De Gaulle, La Résistance, Staline ...*, Editions Ramsay, Paris 1980.

Coward, Rosalind, *Patriarchal Precedents. Sexuality and Social Relations*, Routledge and Kegan Paul, London 1983.

— *Our Treacherous Hearts*, Faber and Faber, London 1992.

Cox, Robert, *Production, Power and World Order*, Columbia University Press, New York 1987.

Craig, F. W. S. (ed.), *British General Election Manifestos 1900–1974*, Macmillan, London 1975.

— (ed.), *Conservative and Labour Party Conference Decisions 1945–1981*, Parliamentary Research Services, Chichester 1982.

Craig, Gordon A., *Germany 1866–1945*, Oxford University Press, Oxford 1981.

— *The Germans*, Penguin, Harmondsworth 1984.

Cram, Laura, 'Calling the Tune without Paying the Piper? Social Policy Regulation: The Role of the Commission in European Community Social Policy', *Policy and Politics*, Vol. 21, no. 2, 1993.

Craxi, Bettino, *Prove marzo 1978 gennaio 1980*, Sugarco Edizioni, Milan 1980.

— *L'Italia liberata*, Sugarco Edizioni, Milan 1984.

Creech Jones, Arthur, 'The Labour Party and Colonial Policy 1945–51', in A. Creech Jones (ed.), *New Fabian Colonial Essays*, Hogarth Press, London 1959.

Crewe, Ivor, 'The Labour Party and the Electorate', in Dennis Kavanagh (ed.), *The Politics of the Labour Party*, Allen and Unwin, London 1982.

— 'On the Death and Resurrection of Class Voting: Some Comments on *How Britain Votes*', *Political Studies*, Vol. 34, no. 4, December 1986.

— 'Labor Force Changes, Working Class Decline and the Labour Vote: Social and Electoral Trends in Postwar Britain', in Fox Piven (ed.), op. cit.

— and David Denver, *Electoral Change in Western Democracies: Patterns and Sources of Electoral Volatility*, Croom Helm, London 1985.

Crick, Bernard, 'The Future of the Labour Party, *Political Quarterly*, Vol. 54, no. 4, October–December 1983.

Crick, Michael, *The March of Militant*, Faber and Faber, London 1986.

Criddle, Byron, 'The French Socialist Party' in Paterson and Thomas (eds), op. cit., 1986.

Crosland, Anthony, *The Future of Socialism*, Jonathan Cape, London 1956 (2nd edn 1967).

— *Social Democracy in Europe*, Fabian Tract no. 438, December 1975.

Crosland, Susan, *Tony Crosland*, Jonathan Cape, London 1982.

Cross, Gary, *A Quest for Time. The Reduction of Work in Britain and France, 1840–1940*, University of California Press, Berkeley 1989.

Crossman, R. H. S., *The Diaries of a Cabinet Minister*, Vols 1 and 2, Hamish Hamilton and Jonathan Cape, London 1976.

— (ed.), *New Fabian Essays*, Turnstile Press, London 1952.

Crouch, Colin, *The Politics of Industrial Relations*, Fontana/Collins, Glasgow 1979.

— and Alessandro Pizzorno (eds), *The Resurgence of Class Conflict in Western Europe since 1968*. Vol. 1: *National Studies*, Macmillan, London 1978; Vol. 2: *Comparative Analyses*, Holmes and Meier, New York 1978.

Cunhal, Alvaro, *Discursos políticos (Abril/Julho de 1974)*, Vol. 1, Edições *Avante!*, Lisbon 1975.

— *Discursos políticos, Dezembro 1974/ Março 1975*, Vol. 3, Edições *Avante!*, Lisbon 1975.

— *A crise politico-militar. Discursos políticos, Maio/Novembro 1975*, Vol. 5, Edições *Avante!*, Lisbon 1975.

Cunningham, Susan, 'The Development of Equal Opportunities. Theory and Practice in the European Community', *Policy and Politics*, Vol. 20, no. 3, 1992.

Curran, James (ed.), *The Future of the Left*, Polity Press, Cambridge 1984.

Currie, David, 'SDP: A Prop For Profits', *New Socialist*, March–April 1982.

Curtis, David, 'Marx against the Marxists: Catholic Uses of the Young Marx in the *Front populaire* period (1934–1938)', *French Cultural Studies*, Vol. 2, part 2, no. 5, June 1991.

Czechoslovak Communist Party, *The Action Programme of the Czechoslovak Communist Party. Prague, April 1968*, Spokesman Pamphlet no. 8, Nottingham n.d. (1970).

Daems, Herman and Peter Van de Weyer, *L'économie belge sous influence*, Academia/Fondation Roi Baudouin, Brussels 1993.

Dahrendorf, Ralf (ed.), *Europe's Economy in Crisis*, Weidenfeld and Nicolson, London 1981.
— *Reflections on the Revolution in Europe*, Chatto and Windus, London 1990.

Dalton, Russell J., Scott C. Flanagan and Paul Allen Beck (eds), *Electoral Change in Advanced Industrial Democracies: Realignment or Dealignment?*, Princeton University Press, Princeton NJ 1984.

Dalton, Russell J. and Manfred Kuechler (eds), *Challenging the Political Order. New Social and Political Movements in Western Democracies*, Polity Press, Cambridge 1990.

Daneo, Camillo, *La politica economica della ricostruzione 1945–1949*, Einaudi Editore, Turin 1974.

D'Angelillo, Massimo, 'Crisi economica e identità nazionale nella politica di governo della socialdemocrazia tedesca', in Paggi (ed.), op. cit.

Daniels, Robert V., *The End of the Communist Revolution*, Routledge, London 1993.

Danopoulos, Constantine P., 'Military Professionalism and Regime Legitimacy in Greece, 1967–1974', *Political Science Quarterly*, Vol. 98, no. 3, Fall 1983.

D'Attorre, Pier Paolo, 'Sogno americano e mito sovietico nell'Italia contemporanea', in Pier Paolo D'Attorre (ed.), *Nemici per la pelle. Sogno americano e mito sovietico nell'Italia contemporanea*, Franco Angeli, Milan 1991.

David, Marie-Gabrielle and Christophe Starzec, 'Women and Part-time Work: France and Great Britain Compared', in Folbre et al. (eds), op. cit.

David, Rhys, 'Employee polls back worker directors', *Financial Times*, 26 January 1977.

Davidson, Ian, 'France charts a new course for the economy', *Financial Times*, 21 February 1989.
— 'France's penal Code Napoléon meets its Waterloo at last', *Financial Times*, 11 May 1989.
— 'Inequality grows in "socialist" France', *Financial Times*, 24 November 1989.
— 'French Socialists under siege', *Financial Times*, 31 May 1990.
— 'Prudent policies beginning to bear fruit', Survey on France, *Financial Times*, 17 June 1991.

De Beauvoir, Simone, *Le deuxième sexe*, Gallimard, Paris 1968.

De Clementi, Andreina, *Amadeo Bordiga*, Einaudi Editore, Turin 1971.

De Felice, Franco, *Serrati, Bordiga, Gramsci e il problema della rivoluzione in Italia 1919–1920*, De Donato, Bari 1974.
— 'Doppia lealtà e doppio stato', *Studi Storici*, no. 3, 1989.

De Gaulle, Charles, *Mémoires de Guerre. L'Unité 1942–1944*, Librairie Plon, Paris 1956.

Degl'Innocenti, Maurizio *Storia del PSI*. Vol. 3: *Dal Dopoguerra a Oggi*, Laterza, Roma-Bari 1993.

Degras, Jane (ed.), *The Communist International 1919–1943. Documents*, Vol. 3, Frank Cass, London 1971.

Deighton, Anne (ed.), *Britain and the Second World War*, Macmillan, London 1990.
— 'Towards a "Western Strategy": The Making of British Policy Towards Germany, 1945–46', in Deighton (ed.), op cit.

Del Boca, Daniela, 'Women in a Changing Workplace. The Case of Italy', in Jenson, Hangen and Reddy (eds), op. cit.

Dell, Edmund, *A Hard Pounding. Politics and Economic Crisis 1974–1976*, Oxford University Press, Oxford 1991.

Della Porta, Donatella, 'La capitale immorale: le tangenti di Milano', in Hellman and Pasquino (eds), *Politica in Italia 1993*, Il Mulino, Bologna 1993.

Della Volpe, Galvano, *Rousseau e Marx*, Editori Riuniti, Rome 1971.

Delors, Jacques, 'France: Between Reform and Counter-Reform', in Dahrendorf (ed.), op. cit.

— 'Une nouvelle frontière pour la social-démocratie: l'Europe?', in Piet Dankert and Ad Kooyman (eds), *Europe sans frontières. Les socialistes et l'avenir de la CEE*, EPO, Antwerp 1989.

De Lutiis, G., *Storia dei servizi segreti in Italia*, Editori Riuniti, Rome 1985.

De Man, Hendrik, *A Documentary Study of Hendrik de Man, Socialist Critic of Marxism*, compiled, ed. and trans. Peter Dodge, Princeton University Press, Princeton NJ 1979.

Demelenne, Claude, *Le Socialisme du possible. Guy Spitaels: Changer la gauche?*, Editions Labor, Brussels 1985.

Dempsey, Judy, 'Austria's working class trade unionism coming to an end', *Financial Times*, 7 October 1987.

Denver, David and Hugh Bochel, 'Merger or Bust: Whatever Happened to Members of the SDP?', *British Journal of Political Science*, Vol. 24, part 3, July 1994.

Deppe, Rainer, Richard Herding and Dietrich Hoss, 'The Relationship between Trade Union Action and Political Parties', in Crouch and Pizzorno (eds), op. cit., Vol. 2.

Depraetere, Hans and Jenny Dierickx, *La guerre froide en Belgique. La répression envers le PCB et le FI*, Editions EPO, Brussels 1986.

Derry, T. K., *A History of Modern Norway 1814–1972*, Oxford University Press, Oxford 1973.

Dertilis, Georges B., 'Terre, paysans et pouvoir politique (Grèce, XVIIIᵉ-XXᵉ siècle)', *Annales*, Vol. 48, no. 1, January–February 1993.

Detti, Tommaso, *Serrati e la formazione del Partito comunista italiano*, Editori Riuniti, Rome 1972.

Devin, Guillaume, *L'internationale socialiste: Histoire et sociologie du socialisme international (1945–1990)*, Presses de la Fondation Nationale des Sciences Politiques, Paris 1993.

Diamandouros, P. Nikiforos, 'Greek Political Culture in Transition: Historical Origins, Evolution, Current Trends', in Clogg (ed.), op. cit., 1983.

— 'Politics and Culture in Greece, 1974–91: An Interpretation', in Clogg (ed.) op. cit., 1993.

Dickson, Tim, 'High cost of cultural divide', Survey on Belgium, *Financial Times*, 13 June 1986.

— 'Flexible times', Survey on Belgium, *Financial Times*, 16 June 1988.

Di Giulio, Fernando, 'Lotta politica e riforme istituzionali', *Democrazia e diritto*, no. 5.

— *Un ministro ombra si confessa* (with Emmanuele Rocco), Rizzoli, Milan 1979.

Dimitras, Panayote E., 'La Grèce en quête d'une politique indépendante', *Revue française de science politique*, Vol. 33, no. 1, February 1983.

Di Toro, Claudio and Augusto Illuminati, *Prima e dopo il centrosinistra*, Edizioni Ideologie, Rome 1970.

Dockrill, Michael, *The Cold War 1945–1963*, Macmillan, London 1988.

Donati, Pier Paolo, 'Social Welfare and Social Services in Italy since 1950', in R. Girod, P. de Laubier and A. Gladstone (eds), *Social Policy in Western Europe and the USA, 1950–85*, Macmillan, London 1985.

Done, Kevin, 'Windfall Wilts Away', Survey on Norway, *Financial Times*, 23 June 1986.

Donolo, Carlo, 'La politica ridefinita. Note sul Movimento studentesco', *Quaderni piacentini*, no. 35, July 1968.

Donoughue, Bernard, *Prime Minister. The Conduct of Policy under Harold Wilson and James Callaghan*, Jonathan Cape, London 1987.

Dornbusch, Rudiger, Richard S. Eckaus and Lance Taylor, 'Analysis and Projection of Macroeconomic Conditions in Portugal', in Graham and Makler (eds), op. cit.

Dornbusch, Rudiger, Giorgio Basevi, Olivier Blanchard, Willem Buiter and Richard Layard, 'Macroeconomic Prospects and Policies for the European Community', in Olivier Blanchard, Rudiger Dornbusch and Richard Layard (eds), *Restoring Europe's Prosperity: Macroeconomic Papers from the Centre for European Policy Studies*, MIT Press, Cambridge MA and London 1986.

Drane, Melanie, 'A Divided Left Faces German Unity: A Response to Andrei Markovits', *German Politics*, Vol. 1, no. 2, August 1992.

DuBois, Ellen Carol, 'Woman Suffrage and the Left: An International Socialist-Feminist Perspective', *New Left Review*, no. 186, March–April 1991.

Dubois, Pierre, 'New Forms of Industrial Conflict', in Crouch and Pizzorno (eds), op. cit., Vol. 2.

Duchen, Claire, *Feminism in France. From May '68 to Mitterrand*, Routledge and Kegan Paul, London 1986.

Dunn, John, *The Politics of Socialism*, Cambridge University Press, Cambridge 1984.

— 'Introduction: Crisis of the Nation State', *Political Studies*, Vol. 42, Special issue 1994: *Contemporary Crisis of the Nation State?*, ed. John Dunn.

Dupuy, Trevor N. and Gay M. Hammerman, *A Documentary History of Arms Control and Disarmament*, R. R. Bowker and T. N. Dupuy Associates, New York and Dunn Loring VA 1973.

Dyson, Kenneth, 'The Problem of Morality and Power in the Politics of West Germany', *Government and Opposition*, Vol. 16, no. 2, Spring 1981.

— 'The Politics of Corporate Crises in West Germany', *West European Politics*, Vol. 7, no. 1, January 1984.

— and Stephen Wilks (eds), *Industrial Crisis*, Blackwell, Oxford 1983.

Eagleton, Terry, 'Discourse and discos', *The Times Literary Supplement*, 15 July 1994.

Eaton, John, Michael Barratt Brown and Ken Coates, *An Alternative Economic Strategy for the Labour Movement*, Spokesman Pamphlet no. 47, Nottingham 1975.

Eatwell, Roger, *The 1945–1951 Labour Governments*, Batsford Academic, London 1979.

Edinger, Lewis J., *Kurt Schumacher*, Stanford University Press, Stanford CA 1965.

Eduards, Maud, 'The Swedish Gender Model: Productivity, Pragmatism and Paternalism', *West European Politics*, Vol. 14, no. 3, July 1991.

— Beatrice Halsaa and Hege Skjeie, 'Equality: How Equal?', in Haavio-Mannila et al. (eds), op. cit.

Einaudi, Mario, Maurice Byé and Ernesto Rossi, *Nationalization in France and Italy*, Cornell University Press, Ithaca NY 1955.

Eisenberg, Christiane, 'The Comparative View in Labour History. Old and New Interpretations of the English and the German Labour Movement before 1914', *International Journal of Social History*, Vol. 34, 1989.

Ekman Stig, 'The Research Project Sweden During the Second World War', Report to the XIth IALHI Conference, 2–4 September 1980, Stockholm, in *Meddelande Fran Arbetarrörelsens Arkiv Och Bibliotek*, no. 16, 1980.

Elander, Ingemar and Stij Montin, 'Decentralization and Control: Central–Local Government Relations in Sweden', *Policy and Politics*, Vol. 18, no. 3, July 1990.

Elephantis, Angelos, 'PASOK and the Elections of 1977: The Rise of the Populist Movement', in Howard R. Penniman (ed.), *Greece at the Polls. The National Elections of 1974 and 1977*, American Enterprise Institute for Public Policy Research, Washington and London 1981.

Elliott, Gregory, *Labourism and the English Genius. The Strange Death of Labour England?*, Verso, London 1993.

— 'Contentious Commitments: French Intellectuals and Politics', *New Left Review*, no. 206, July–August 1994.

Elliott, John, *Conflict or Cooperation? The Growth of Industrial Democracy*, Kogan Page, London 1978.

Ellwood, David, *Italy 1943–1945*, Leicester University Press, Leicester 1985.

— *Rebuilding Europe. Western Europe, America and Postwar Reconstruction*, Longman, London 1992.

Elvander, Nils, 'Interest Organisations and Democracy', *Skandinaviska Enskilda Banken Quarterly Review*, no. 2, 1982.

Emminger, Otmar, 'West Germany: Europe's Driving Force?', in Dahrendorf (ed.), op. cit.

Engels, Friedrich, 'Introduction' to Karl Marx, *Class Struggles in France 1848–1850*, International Publishers, New York 1964.

— *The Origin of the Family, Private Property and the State*, Progress Publishers, Moscow 1968.

Erler, Gisela, 'The German Paradox: Non-feminization of the Labor Force and Post-industrial Social Policies', in Jenson, Hangen and Reddy (eds), op. cit.

Ermisch, John F. and Robert E. Wright, 'Differential Returns to Human Capital in Full-time and Part-time Employment', in Folbre et al. (eds), op. cit.

Esping-Andersen, Gøsta, *Politics against Markets. The Social Democratic Road to Power*, Princeton University Press, Princeton NJ 1985.

— *The Three Worlds of Welfare Capitalism*, Polity Press, Cambridge 1990.

— 'Postindustrial Cleavage Structures: A Comparison of Evolving Patterns of Social Stratification in Germany, Sweden, and the United States', in Fox Piven (ed.), op. cit., p. 166.

— 'The Making of a Social Democratic Welfare State', in Klaus Misgeld, Karl Molin and Klas Åmark (eds), *Creating Social Democracy. A Century of the Social Democratic Labor Party in Sweden*, Pennsylvania State University Press, University Park PA, 1992.

— and R. Friedland (eds), *Political Power and Social Theory*, Vol. 3, JAI Press, Greenwich CT and London 1982.

— and Walter Korpi, 'Social Policy as Class Politics in Post-war Capitalism: Scandinavia, Austria, and Germany', in John H. Goldthorpe (ed.), *Order and Conflict in Contemporary Capitalism*, Clarendon Press, Oxford 1984.

Esser, Josef, and Wolfgang Fach, ' "Social Market" and Modernization Policy: West Germany', in Dyson and Wilks (eds), op. cit.

Esteban, Joan, 'The Economic Policy of Francoism: An Interpretation', in Preston (ed.), op. cit.

Eurostat, *Iron and Steel. Yearly Statistics 1992*, Luxemburg 1992.

Evalenko, René, 'Planification et organisation de l'économie', *Socialisme*, Vol. 6, no. 34, July 1959.

Evans, Geoffrey, 'Is Gender on the "New Agenda"?', *European Journal of Political Research*, Vol. 24, 1993.

Evans, Richard J., *The Feminists*, Croom Helm, London 1977.

— *Rethinking German History. Nineteenth Century Germany and the Origins of the Third Reich*, Unwin Hyman, London 1987.

— *Death in Hamburg. Society and Politics in the Cholera Years 1830–1910*, Penguin, Harmondsworth 1990.

Fabius, Laurent, *Le coeur du futur*, Calmann-Lévy, Paris 1985.

Fabra, Paul, 'Banking Policy under the Socialists', in Machin and Wright (eds), op. cit.

Fainsod, Merle, *International Socialism and the World War*, Octagon Books, New York 1973 (first published in 1935).

Fauvet, Jacques, *Histoire du Parti communiste français*. Vol. 2: *Vingt-cinq ans de drames 1939–1965*, Fayard, Paris 1965.

Favier, Pierre and Michel Martin-Roland, *La Décennie Mitterrand*. Vol. 1: *Les ruptures*, Editions du Seuil, Paris 1990.

Faxén, Karl-Olof, 'Incomes Policy and Centralized Wage Formation', in Boltho (ed.), op. cit.

Featherstone, Kevin, *Socialist Parties and European Integration*, Manchester University Press, Manchester 1988.

— 'Political Parties and Democratic Consolidation in Greece', in Pridham (ed.), op. cit., 1990.

Feinstein, Charles, 'Benefits of Backwardness and Costs of Continuity', in Graham with Seldon (eds), op. cit.

Feldman, G., 'German Interest Group Alliances in War and Inflation, 1914–1923', in Suzanne D. Berger (ed.), *Organizing Interests in Western Europe*, Cambridge University Press, Cambridge 1983.

Feminist Review, Editorial, *The Past Before Us. Twenty Years of Feminism*, no. 31, Spring 1989.

Féricelli, Jean, 'Les logiques de l'Etat socialiste', in Massenet et al., op. cit.

Ferreira, Hugo Gil and Michael W. Marshall, *Portugal's Revolution: Ten Years On*, Cambridge University Press, Cambridge 1986.

Ferrera, Maurizio, *Il Welfare State in Italia*, Il Mulino, Bologna 1984.

— 'Politics, Institutional Features, and the Government of Industry', in Peter Lange and Marino Regini (eds), *State, Market, and Social Regulation*, Cambridge University Press, Cambridge 1989.

Feshbach, Murray and Alfred Friendly Jr, *Ecocide in the USSR: Health and Nature Under Siege*, Basic Books, New York 1992.

Fetscher, Iring, 'Bernstein e la sfida all'ortodossia', in *Storia del Marxismo*. Vol. 2: *Il marxismo nell'età della Seconda Internazionale*, Einaudi Editore, Turin 1979.

Fieldhouse, D. K., 'The Labour Governments and the Empire-Commonwealth, 1945–51', in Ovendale (ed.), op. cit.

Fieseler, Beate, 'The Making of Russian Female Social Democrats, 1890–1917', *International Review of Social History*, Vol. 34, 1989.

Figueres, Léo, 'Non! au plébiscite', *Cahiers du communisme*, Vol. 34, no. 7, July 1958.

Filipelli, Ronald L., *American Labor and Postwar Italy, 1943–1953. A Study of Cold War Politics*, Stanford University Press, Stanford CA, 1989.

Filosa, Renato and Ignazio Visco, 'Costo del lavoro, indicizzazione e perequazione delle retribuzioni negli anni '70, in Giangiacomo Nardozzi (ed.), *I Difficili anni '70. I problemi della politica economica italiana 1973/1979*, Etas Libri, Milan 1980.

Fine, Ben, *Women's Employment and the Capitalist Family*, Routledge, London 1992.

Finer, S. E. (ed.), *Five Constitutions*, Penguin, Harmondsworth 1979.

Finnie, Wilson, 'The SDP's Plans for Britain's Constitution', *Political Quarterly*, Vol. 54, no. 1, January–March 1983.

Firestone, Shulamith, *The Dialectic of Sex. The Case for a Feminist Revolution*, Paladin, London 1971.

Fisher, Joel M. and Sven Groennings, 'German Electoral Politics in 1969', *Government and Opposition*, Vol. 5, no. 2, Spring 1970.

Fishman, Nina, *The British Communist Party and the Trade Unions, 1933–45*, Scolar Press, Aldershot 1995.

Fishman, Robert M., *Working-Class Organization and the Return to Democracy in Spain*, Cornell University Press, Ithaca NY and London 1990.

Fiterman, Charles, 'Les communistes, l'Europe et la nation française', *Cahiers du communisme*, Vol. 42, no. 4, April 1966.

Fitzmaurice, John, *The Politics of Belgium. Crisis and Compromise in a Plural Society*, C. Hurst and Co., London 1988.

Flamini, G., *Il partito del golpe*, 3 vols, Bovolenta, Ferrara 1981–83.

Flanagan, Robert J., 'Efficiency and Equality in Swedish Labor Markets', in Bosworth and Rivlin (eds), op. cit.

— 'Labor Market Behavior and European Economic Growth', in Lawrence and Schultze (eds), op. cit.

Flechtheim, Ossip K., 'The German Left and the World Crisis', in B. Brown (ed.), op. cit.

Flora, Peter and Heidenheimer, Arnold J. (eds), *The Development of Welfare States in Europe and North America*, Transaction Books, New Brunswick and London 1981.

— et al., *State, Economy and Society in Western Europe 1815–1975. A Data Handbook*, 2 vols, Campus Verlag, Macmillan Press and St James Press, Frankfurt, London and Chicago 1983 and 1987.

Folbre, Nancy, Barbara Bergmann, Bina Agarwal and Maria Floro (eds), *Women's Work in the World Economy*, Macmillan, London 1993.

Foot, M. D. R., *Resistance. An Analysis of European Resistance to Nazism 1940–1945*, Eyre Methuen, London 1976.

— 'What Good Did Resistance Do?', in Hawes and White (eds), op. cit.

Foot, Michael, *Another Heart and Other Pulses*, Collins, London 1984.

Foote, Geoffrey, *The Labour Party's Political Thought. A History*, Croom Helm, London 1985.

Forbes, Jill, 'Cultural Policy: The Soul of Man under Socialism', in Mazey and Newman (eds), op. cit.

Forester, Tom, 'Neutralising the Industrial Strategy', in Ken Coates (ed.), *What Went Wrong*, Spokesman, Nottingham 1979.

Fourastié, Jean, *Les trentes glorieuses ou la révolution invisible de 1946 à 1975*, Fayard, Paris 1979.

Fouskas, Vassilis, *Populism and Modernization, the Exhaustion of the Third Hellenic Republic, 1974–1994*, Ideokinissi, Athens 1995.

Fowkes, Ben, *Communism in Germany under the Weimar Republic*, Macmillan, London 1984.

Fox Piven, Frances (ed.), *Labor Parties in Postindustrial Societies*, Polity Press, Cambridge 1991.

Franco, Alain, 'Le nouveau gouvernement donne la priorité à l'emploi', *Le Monde*, 16 August 1994.

Frankland, E. Gene and Donald Schoonmaker, *Between Protest and Power. The Green Party in Germany*, Westview Press, Boulder CO 1992.

Franklin, Mark, *The Decline of Class Voting in Britain. Changes in the Basis of Electoral Choice 1964–1983*, Clarendon Press, Oxford 1985.

Fraser, Nancy, *Unruly Practices. Power, Discourse and Gender in Contemporary Social Theory*, Polity Press, Cambridge 1989.

Frèches, José, 'L'Etat socialiste', in Massenet et al., op. cit.

Freris, A. F., *The Greek Economy in the Twentieth Century*, Croom Helm, London and Sydney 1986.

Frevert, Ute, *Women in German History. From Bourgeois Emancipation to Sexual Liberation*, Berg, Oxford 1989.

Friedan, Betty, *The Feminine Mystique*, W. W. Norton, New York 1963.

Frieden, Jeffrey A., 'Invested Interests: The Politics of National Economic Policies in a World of Global Finance', *International Organization*, Vol. 45, no. 4, Autumn 1991.

Friedman, Milton, 'The Role of Monetary Policy', *American Economic Review*, Vol. 58, 1968, pp. 1–17.

Furet, François, *Penser la révolution française*, Gallimard, Paris 1978.

Galant, Henry C., *Histoire politique de la sécurité sociale française, 1945–1952*, Colin, Paris 1955.

Galbraith, John Kenneth, *The Culture of Contentment*, Penguin, Harmondsworth 1992.

Gall, Lothar, *Bismarck, The White Revolutionary*. Vol. 1: *1815–1871*, trans. J. A. Underwood, Unwin Hyman, London 1986.

Gallagher, Tom, 'From Hegemony to Opposition: The Ultra Right before and after 1974', in Graham and Wheeler (eds), op. cit.

— *Portugal. A Twentieth-century Interpretation*, Manchester University Press, Manchester 1983.

— 'The Portuguese Socialist Party: The Pitfalls of Being First', in Gallagher and Williams (eds), op. cit.

— and Allan M. Williams (eds), *Southern European Socialism. Parties, Elections and the Challenge of Government*, Manchester University Press, Manchester 1988.

Galleni, Mauro, *Rapporto sul terrorismo. Le stragi, gli agguati, i sequestri, le sigle 1969–1980*, Rizzoli, Milan 1981.

Gallie, Duncan, 'Les lois Auroux: The Reform of French Industrial Relations?', in Machin and Wright (eds), op. cit.

Gambier, Dominique and Michel Vernières, *L'emploi en France*, Editions La Découverte, Paris 1988.

Gamble, Andrew, 'The Labour Party and Economic Management', in Smith and Spear (eds), op. cit.

— and S. A. Walkland, *The British Party System and Economic Policy 1945–1983*, Clarendon Press, Oxford 1984.

Gane, Mike, *Harmless Lovers? Gender, Theory and Personal Relationships*, Routledge, London and New York 1993.

Garaudy, Roger, 'A propos de la "voie italienne vers le socialisme"', *Cahiers du communisme*, Vol. 33, no. 1, January 1957.

— 'De Gaulle et le fascisme', *Cahiers du communisme*, Vol. 34, no. 6, June 1958.

Garcia, Patrick, 'L'Etat républicain face au centenaire: raisons d'Etat et universalisme dans la commémoration de la Révolution française', in Bariety (ed.), op. cit.

Gardner, David, 'Export fall fuels recession', *Financial Times*, 12 July 1993.

Garpenby, Peter, 'The Transformation of the Swedish Health Care System, or The Hasty Rejection of the Rational Planning Model', *Journal of European Social Policy*, Vol. 2, no. 1, 1992.

Garraty, John A., *Unemployment in History. Economic Thought and Public Policy*, Harper, New York 1979.

Garrett, Geoffrey and Peter Lange, 'Political Responses to Interdependence: What's "Left" for the Left?', *International Organization*, Vol. 45, no. 4, Autumn 1991.

Garrigues, Jean, 'Le Boulangisme et la Révolution française', in Bariety (ed.), op. cit.

Garton Ash, Timothy, *In Europe's Name. Germany and the Divided Continent*, Jonathan Cape, London 1993.

Gazier, Albert, 'French Socialist on Algeria', *Socialist International Information*, Vol. 6, no. 31, 4 August 1956.

Geary, Dick, *Karl Kautsky*, Manchester University Press, Manchester 1987.

Gelb, Joyce, 'Feminism and Political Action', in Dalton and Kuechler (eds), op. cit.

Gellner, Ernest, 'The Struggle to Catch Up', *Times Literary Supplement*, 9 December 1994.

George, Bruce, *The British Labour Party and Defense*, Praeger, New York 1991.

Gerlich, Peter, 'Deregulation in Austria', *European Journal of Political Research*, Vol. 17, no. 2, 1989.

Ghini, Celso, *Il terremoto del 15 giugno*, Feltrinelli, Milan 1976.

Giddens, Anthony, *Social Theory and Modern Sociology*, Polity Press, Cambridge 1987.

— *The Transformation of Intimacy*, Polity Press, Cambridge 1992.

— *Beyond Left and Right. The Future of Radical Politics*, Polity Press, Cambridge 1994.

Giersch, Herbert, *Liberalisation for Faster Economic Growth*, Occasional Paper no. 74, Institute of Economic Affairs, London 1986.

— Karl-Heinz Paqué and Holger Schmieding, *The Fading Miracle. Four Decades of Market Economy in Germany*, Cambridge University Press, Cambridge 1992.

Gildea, Robert, *Barricades and Borders. Europe 1800–1914*, Oxford University Press, Oxford 1987.

Gillespie, Richard, *The Spanish Socialist Party: A History of Factionalism*, Clarendon Press, Oxford 1989.

— 'Regime consolidation in Spain: Party, State, and Society', in Pridham (ed.), op. cit., 1990.

— ' "Programa 2000": The Appearance and Reality of Socialist Renewal in Spain', *West European Politics*, Vol. 16, no. 1, January 1993.

Gillie, Allan, 'Redistribution', in Artis and Cobham (eds), op. cit.

Gilmour, David, *The Transformation of Spain*, Quartet Books, London 1985.

Gilpin, Robert, *The Political Economy of International Relations*, Princeton University Press, Princeton NJ 1987.

Ginsborg, Paul, *A History of Contemporary Italy. Society and Politics 1943–1988*, Penguin, Harmondsworth 1990.

Giolitti, Antonio, *Riforme e rivoluzione*, Einaudi Editore, Turin 1957.

— 'Le basi scientifiche della politica economica', *Passato e presente*, Vol. 1, no. 1, January–February 1957.

Giovanni XXIII (John XXIII), *Pacem in Terris*, Pontificia Editrice Arcivescovile Daverio, Milan 1963.

Gjelsvik, T., *Norwegian Resistance 1940–1945*, C. Hurst and Co., London 1979.

Gladdish, Ken, 'Portugal: An Open Verdict', in Pridham (ed.), op. cit., 1990.

— *Governing from the Centre. Politics and Policy-Making in the Netherlands*, C. Hurst and Co., London 1991.

Glennerster, Howard, 'Social Policy since the Second World War', in Hills (ed.), op. cit.

Glotz, Peter, 'German futures', *Socialist Affairs*, no. 4, 1984.

— *La socialdemocrazia tedesca a una svolta*, Editori Riuniti, Rome 1985 (Italian trans. of *Die Arbeit der Zuspitzung. Über die Organisation einer regierungsfähigen Linken*, Berlin 1984).

— 'Let's Stop Waiting for the Right to Fail', *Socialist Affairs*, no. 1, 1985.

— 'Otto tesi per una nuova Bad Godesberg', *Mondoperaio*, Vol. 39, no. 3, March 1986.

— 'What Is To Be Done?', *Socialist Affairs*, no. 1–2, 1988.

Glucklicht, Pauline, 'The Effects of Statutory Employment Policies on Women in the United Kingdom Labour Market', in Schmidt and Weitzel (eds), op. cit.

Glyn, Andrew, A. Hughes, A. Lipietz and A. Singh, 'The Rise and Fall of the Golden Age', in Marglin and Schor (eds), op. cit.

Goldberg, Gertrude Schaffner, 'The United States: Feminization of Poverty amidst Plenty', in Gertrude Schaffner Goldberg and Eleanor Kremen (eds), *The Feminization of Poverty: Only in America?*, Praeger, New York 1990.

Goldberger, Leo (ed.), *The Rescue of the Danish Jews: Moral Courage under Stress*, New York University Press, New York 1987.

Golden, Miriam, *Labor Divided. Austerity and Working Class Politics in Contemporary Italy*, Cornell University Press, Ithaca NY and London 1988.

González, Felipe, 'La unidad de los socialistas', *Sistema*, no. 15, October 1976.

— 'Taking on the Challenge of Modernisation', *Socialist Affairs*, no. 3, 1987.

Gorbachev, Mikhail, *Perestroika. New Thinking for Our Country and the World*, Fontana, London 1988.

Gordon, David M., 'The Global Economy: New Edifice or Crumbling Foundations?', *New Left Review*, no. 168, March–April 1988.

Gorz, André, *Les chemins du paradis*, Editions Galilée, Paris 1983.

Gotto, Klaus, 'Adenauers Deutschland und *Ostpolitik* 1954–1963', in Rudolf Morsey and Konrad Repgen (eds), *Adenauer-Studien Bd.III. Untersuchungen und Dokumente zur Ostpolitik und Biographie*, Mainz 1974.

Gough, Ian, *The Political Economy of the Welfare State*, Macmillan, London 1979.

Gould, Bryan, *A Future for Socialism*, Jonathan Cape, London 1989.

Gout, Etienne, Pierre Juvigny and Michel Moussel, 'La politique sociale du front populaire', in *Léon Blum chef du gouvernment 1936–37*, Cahiers de la Fondation Nationale des Sciences Politiques, Colin, Paris 1967.

Gowan, Peter, 'The Origins of the Administrative Elite', *New Left Review*, no. 162, March–April 1987.

Gowing, Margaret, 'Britain, America and the Bomb', in David Dilks (ed.), *Retreat from Power. Studies in Britain's Foreign Relations in the Twentieth Century*. Vol. 2: *After 1939*, Macmillan, London 1981.

Graf, William D., *The German Left since 1945. Socialism and Social Democracy in the German Federal Republic*, Oleander Press, New York 1976.

Graham, Andrew and Wilfred Beckerman, 'Introduction: Economic Performance and the Foreign Balance', in Beckerman (ed.), op. cit.

Graham, Andrew with Anthony Seldon (eds), *Government and Economies in the Postwar World. Economic Policies and Comparative Performance 1945–85*, Routledge, London 1990.

Graham, Helen, 'The Spanish Popular Front and the Civil War', in Helen Graham and Paul Preston (eds), *The Popular Front in Europe*, Macmillan, London 1987.

— *Socialism and War. The Spanish Socialist Party in Power and Crisis 1936–1939*, Cambridge University Press, Cambridge 1991.

Graham, Lawrence S., 'The Military in Politics: The Politicization of the Portuguese Armed Forces', in Graham and Makler (eds), op. cit.

— and Harry M. Makler (eds), *Contemporary Portugal. The Revolution and its Antecedents*, University of Texas Press, Austin TX 1979.

Graham, Lawrence S. and Douglas L. Wheeler (eds), *In Search of Modern Portugal. The Revolution and Its Consequences*, University of Wisconsin Press, Madison 1983.

Grahl, John and Paul Teague, *1992 – The Big Market. The Future of the European Community*, Lawrence and Wishart, London 1990.

Graml, Hermann et al., *The German Resistance to Hitler*, Batsford, London 1970.

Gramsci, Antonio, *Selections from the Prison Notebooks*, ed. and trans. Quintin Hoare and Geoffrey Nowell Smith, Lawrence and Wishart, London 1971.

— *Selections from Political Writings 1921–1926*, trans. and ed. Quintin Hoare, Lawrence and Wishart, London 1978.

— *Selections from Political Writings 1910–1920*, ed. Quintin Hoare, trans. John Mathews, Lawrence and Wishart, London 1988.

Granier, Roland, 'Expérience socialiste, emploi, chômage', in Massenet et al., op. cit.

Grant, Wyn and Stephen Wilks, 'British Industrial Policy: Structural Change, Policy Inertia', *Journal of Public Policy*, Vol. 3, no. 1, February 1983.

Gras, Hélène, 'Justice: la fin des archaïsmes', *Revue politique et parlementaire*, Vol. 87, no. 916, May–June 1985.

Grass, Günter, 'Dear Willy' (on Willy Brandt's seventieth birthday), *Socialist Affairs*, no. 1, 1984; originally published in *Sozialdemokrat magazin*.

Greater London Council, *The London Industrial Strategy*, London 1985.

— *The London Financial Strategy*, London 1986.

Greenwood, Victoria and Jock Young, *Abortion in Demand*, Pluto Press, London 1976.

Greer, Germaine, *The Female Eunuch*, Paladin, London 1991.

Gregor, James A., *Young Mussolini and the Intellectual Origins of Fascism*, University of California Press, Berkeley CA 1979.

Grémion, Catherine, 'Decentralisation in France. A Historical Perspective', in Ross, Hoffmann and Malzacher (eds), op. cit.

Groom, A. J. R., *British Thinking About Nuclear Weapons*, Frances Pinter, London 1974.

Grosser, Alfred, *The Western Alliance. European–American Relations since 1945*, Macmillan, London 1978.

Gruber, Helmut, *Red Vienna: Experiment in Working Class Culture, 1919–1934*, Oxford University Press, Oxford 1991.

Grunberg, Gérard, 'Le cycle d'Epinay', *Intervention*, no. 13, July–September 1985.

Guadagnini, Marila, 'A "Partitocrazia" Without Women: The Case of the Italian Party System', in Lovenduski and Norris (eds), op. cit.

Guerra, Alfonso, 'Los partidos socialistas del sur de Europa y las relaciones socialistas-comunistas', *Sistema*, no. 15, October 1976.

Guerrieri, Sandro, 'Il Congresso di Lilla del Partito socialista francese', *Sinistra Europea 1987*, supplement to *Democrazia e diritto*, no. 4–5, July–October 1987.

— 'Regime presidenziale e forma-partito: il Ps nel sistema politico della quinta repubblica', in Centro per La Riforma dello Stato (ed.), op. cit.

Gunther, Richard, 'Democratization and Party Building: The Role of Party Elites in the Spanish Transition', in Clark and Haltzel (eds), op. cit.

— Giacomo Sani and Goldie Shabad, *Spain After Franco. The Making of a Competitive Party System*, University of California Press, Berkeley 1985.

Gupta, Partha Sarathi, *Imperialism and the British Labour Movement 1914–1964*, Macmillan, London 1975.

Gustafsson, Siv, 'Equal Opportunity Policies in Sweden', in Schmidt and Weitzel (eds), op. cit.

Guttsman, W. L., *The German Social Democratic Party 1875–1933*, Allen and Unwin, London 1981.

Haapakoski, Pekka, 'Brezhnevism in Finland', *New Left Review*, no. 86, July–August 1974.

Haavio-Mannila, Elina et al. (eds), *Unfinished Democracy. Women in Nordic Politics*, trans. Christine Badcock, Pergamon Press, Oxford 1985.

Habermas, Jürgen, *Towards a Rational Society*, trans. Jeremy J. Shapiro, Heinemann, London 1971.

— *Legitimation Crisis*, trans. Thomas McCarthy, Heinemann, London 1976.

Hadjimatheou, George and A. Skouras, 'Britain's Economic Problem: The Growth of the Non-Market Sector?', *Economic Journal*, Vol. 89, June 1979, pp. 392–401.

Hadjiyannis, Stylianos, 'Democratization and the Greek State', in Ronald H. Chilcote et al., *Transitions from Dictatorship to Democracy. Comparative Studies of Spain, Portugal and Greece*, Crane Russak, New York 1990.

Haegel, Florence, 'Le dernier acte de l'Union de la gauche', *Intervention*, no. 13, July–September 1985.

Haestrup, Jørgen, *Europe Ablaze. An Analysis of the History of the European Resistance Movements 1939–45*, Odense University Press 1978.

Hagemann, Karen, 'La "question des femmes" et les rapports masculin–féminin dans la social-démocratie allemande sous la République de Weimar', *Le Mouvement Social*, no. 163, April–June 1993.

Hakim, Catherine, 'Grateful Slaves and Self-Made Women: Fact and Fantasy in Women's Work Orientations', *European Sociological Review*, Vol. 7, no. 2, September 1991.

— 'Explaining Trends in Occupational Segregation: The Measurement, Causes, and Consequences of the Sexual Division of Labour', *European Sociological Review*, Vol. 8, no. 2, September 1992.

— 'The Myth of Rising Female Employment', *Work, Employment and Society*, Vol. 7, no. 1, 1993, pp. 97–100.

— 'Segregated and Integrated Occupations: A New Approach to Analysing Social Change', *European Sociological Review*, Vol. 9, no. 3, December 1993.

— 'Five Feminist Myths about Women's Employment', *British Journal of Sociology*, Vol. 46, no. 3, September 1995, pp. 429–55.

Hall, Peter A., 'Economic Planning and the State: The Evolution of Economic Challenge and Political Response in France', in Esping-Andersen and Friedland (eds), op. cit.

— 'The Evolution of Economic Policy under Mitterrand', in Ross, Hoffmann and Malzacher (eds), op. cit.

Hall, Stuart, The Great Moving Right Show', Marxism Today, December 1978.

— The Hard Road to Renewal, Verso, London 1988.

— and Martin Jacques (eds), New Times. The Changing Face of Politics in the 1990s, Lawrence and Wishart, London 1989.

Hallett, Graham, 'West Germany', in Graham with Seldon (eds), op. cit.

Hamilton, Malcom B., Democratic Socialism in Britain and in Sweden, Macmillan, London 1989.

Hammond, John L., 'Electoral Behavior and Political Militancy', in Graham and Makler (eds), op. cit.

Hamon, Hervé, '68. The Rise and Fall of a Generation?', in Hanley and Kerr (eds), op. cit.

— and Patrick Rotman, La deuxième gauche. Histoire intellectuelle et politique de la CFDT, Editions du Seuil, Paris 1984 (1st edn 1982).

Hancock, M. Donald, 'Sweden's Emerging Labor Socialism', in B. Brown (ed.), op. cit.

Hanley, D. L. and A. P. Kerr (eds), May '68: Coming of Age, Macmillan, London 1989.

Hanley, D. L., A. P. Kerr and N. H. Waites, Contemporary France. Politics and Society since 1945, Routledge and Kegan Paul, London 1979.

Hanrieder, Wolfram F., Germany, America, Europe. Forty Years of German Foreign Policy, Yale University Press, New Haven CT 1989.

Hansen, Erik, 'Crisis in the Party: De Tribune Faction and the Origins of the Dutch Communist Party 1907–9', Journal of Contemporary History, Vol. 11, nos 2–3, July 1976.

— 'Hendrik de Man and the Theoretical Foundations of Economic Planning: the Belgian Experience, 1933–1940', European Studies Review, Vol. 8, no. 2, April 1978.

— 'Depression Decade Crisis: Social Democracy and Planisme in Belgium and the Netherlands 1929–39', Journal of Contemporary History, Vol. 16, no. 2, April 1981.

— and Peter A. Prosper, 'Political Economy and Political Action: The Programmatic Response of Dutch Social Democracy to the Depression Crisis', Journal of Contemporary History, Vol. 29, no. 1, January 1994.

Hanson, Philip, 'The Soviet Union', in Graham with Seldon, (eds), op. cit.

Harding, Neil, Lenin's Political Thought, Macmillan, London 1983.

Harris, Jose, 'War and Social History: Britain and the Home Front during the Second World War', Contemporary European History, Vol. 1, part 1, March 1992.

Harris, Kenneth, Attlee, Weidenfeld and Nicolson, London 1984.

Harrison, Michael M., 'Consensus, Confusion and Confrontation in France: The Left in Search of a Defense Policy', in Andrews and Hoffmann (eds), op. cit.

Harrop, Martin, 'The Changing British Electorate' Political Quarterly, Vol. 53, no. 4, October–December 1982.

Harsh, Donna, German Social Democracy and the Rise of Nazism, University of North Carolina Press, Chapel Hill 1993.

Hartz, Louis, The Liberal Tradition in America, Harcourt, Brace and World, New York 1955.

Haseler, Stephen, The Gaitskellites. Revisionism in the British Labour Party 1951–64, Macmillan, London 1969.

Hauff, Volker, 'Lavoro e ambiente. Tesi per una riforma ecologica', in Telò (ed.), op. cit.

Haug, Frigga, 'Lessons from the Women's Movement in Europe', Feminist Review, no. 31, Spring 1989.

— Beyond Female Masochism, Verso, London and New York 1992.

Haupt, Georges, Socialism and the Great War. The Collapse of the Second International, Clarendon Press, Oxford 1972.

— Aspects of International Socialism 1871–1914, Cambridge University Press, Cambridge 1986.

Hawes, Stephen and Ralph White (eds), Resistance in Europe: 1939–45, Pelican, Harmondsworth 1976.

Hawkins, Kevin, *Trade Unions*, Hutchinson, London 1981.

Hayek, Friedrich A., *The Constitution of Liberty*, Routledge and Kegan Paul, London 1960.

— *The Fatal Conceit. The Errors of Socialism*, Vol. 1 of the *Collected Works*, ed W. W. Bartley, Routledge, London 1988.

— *Law, Legislation and Liberty.* Vol. 3: *The Political Order of a Free People*, Routledge, London 1993.

Hazareesingh, Sudhir, *Intellectuals and the French Communist Party. Disillusion and Decline*, Clarendon Press, Oxford 1991.

Healey, Denis, 'Power Politics and the Labour Party', in Crossman (ed.), op. cit.

— *Beyond Nuclear Deterrence*, Fabian Tract no. 510.

— *The Time of My Life*, Michael Joseph, London 1989.

— *When Shrimps Learn to Whistle*, Penguin, Harmondsworth 1991.

Heath, Anthony, Roger Jowell and John Curtice, *How Britain Votes*, Pergamon Press, Oxford 1985.

— 'Trendless Fluctuation: A Reply to Crewe', *Political Studies*, Vol. 35, no. 2, June 1987.

Heidar, Knut, 'The Norwegian Labour Party: Social Democracy in a Periphery of Europe', in Paterson and Thomas (eds) 1986, op. cit.

— 'The Norwegian Labour Party: "En Attendant l'Europe"', *West European Politics*, Vol. 16, no. 1, January 1993.

Heimann, Horst, 'Fine del movimento operaio?', in Missiroli (ed.), op. cit.

Helder, André, 'Les trois phases de la politique économique', *Revue politique et parlementaire*, Vol. 87, no. 916, May–June 1985.

Hellman, Judith, *Journeys among Women. Feminism in Five Italian Cities*, Polity Press, Cambridge 1987.

Hellman, Stephen, *Italian Communism in Transition: The Rise and Fall of the Historic Compromise in Turin 1975–80*, Oxford University Press, New York 1988.

Henderson, W. O., *The Life of Friedrich Engels*, Vol. 2, Frank Cass, London 1976.

Hennessy, Peter, *Whitehall*, Fontana, London 1990.

— *Never Again. Britain 1945–1951*, Jonathan Cape, London 1992.

Henning, Roger, 'Industrial Policy or Employment Policy? Sweden's Response to Unemployment', in Richardson and Henning (eds), op. cit.

Hennings, Klaus Hinrich, 'West Germany', in Boltho (ed.), op. cit.

Herz, John H., 'Social Democracy versus Democratic Socialism. An Analysis of SPD Attempts to Develop a Party Doctrine', in B. Brown (ed.), op. cit.

Hewitt, Patricia, *About Time. The Revolution in Work and Family Life*, IPPR/Rivers Oram Press, London 1993.

— and Deborah Mattinson, *Women's Votes: The Key To Winning*, Fabian Research Series no. 353, June 1989.

Heywood, Paul, 'Mirror-images: The PCE and PSOE in the Transition to Democracy in Spain', *West European Politics*, Vol. 10, no. 2, April 1987.

— 'Rethinking Socialism in Spain: *Programa 2000* and the Social State', *Coexistence*, Vol. 30, 1993.

Hibbs, Douglas A. Jr., 'Political Parties and Macroeconomic Policy', *American Political Science Review*, Vol. 71, no. 4, December 1977.

Higgins, Joan, *States of Welfare*, Basil Blackwell and Martin Robertson, Oxford 1981.

Hill, Andrew, 'Franc fears for Belgian social pact talks', *Financial Times*, 7 October 1993.

Hills, John (ed.), *The State of Welfare. The Welfare State in Britain since 1974*, Clarendon Press, Oxford 1990.

Himmelstrand, Ulf, Göran Ahrne, Leif Lundberg and Lars Lundberg, *Beyond Welfare Capitalism. Issues, Actors and Forces in Societal Change*, Heinemann, London 1981.

Hincker, François, *Le parti communiste au carrefour. Essai sur quinze ans de son histoire 1965–1981*, Albin Michel, Paris 1981.

Hindess, Barry, *The Decline of Working Class Politics*, Paladin, London 1971.

Hinds, Allister E., 'Sterling and Imperial Policy, 1945–1951', *Journal of Imperial and Commonwealth History*, Vol. 15, no. 2, January 1987.

Hinton, James, *Protests and Visions. Peace Politics in 20th Century Britain*, Hutchinson Radius, London 1989.

Hirschfeld, Gerhard, *Nazi Rule and Dutch Collaboration. The Netherlands under German Occupation 1940–1945*, Berg, Oxford 1988.

Hirst, Paul and Grahame Thompson, 'The Problem of "Globalization": International Economic Relations, National Economic Management and the Formation of Trading Blocs', *Economy and Society*, Vol. 21, no. 4, November 1992.

Histoire de la IIe Internationale. Congrès International Ouvrier Socialiste, Paris 14–22 July 1889, Vols 6–7, Minkoff Reprint, Geneva 1976.

Hobsbawm, Eric J., *Industry and Empire*, Penguin, Harmondsworth 1969.

— *Labouring Men. Studies in the History of Labour*, Weidenfeld and Nicolson, London 1972.

— *Revolutionaries*, Quartet Books, London 1977.

— 'The Fortunes of Marx's and Engels' Writings', in E. J. Hobsbawm (ed.), *The History of Marxism*. Vol. 1: *Marxism in Marx's Day*, Harvester, Brighton 1982.

— 'Labour's Lost Millions', *Marxism Today*, October 1983.

— *The Age of Empire 1875–1914*, Weidenfeld and Nicolson, London 1987.

— *Echoes of the Marseillaise. Two Centuries Look Back on the French Revolution*, Verso, London 1990.

— *Age of Extremes. The Short Twentieth Century 1914–1991*, Michael Joseph, London 1994.

— et al., *The Forward March of Labour Halted?*, Verso, London 1981.

— (ed.), *Labour's Turning Point 1880–1900*, Harvester, Brighton 1974.

Hodgson, John H., 'The Finnish Communist Party and Neutrality', *Government and Opposition*, Vol. 2, no. 2, 1966–67.

— *Communism in Finland. A History and Interpretation*, Princeton University Press, Princeton NJ 1967.

Hodne, Fritz, *The Norwegian Economy 1920–1980*, Croom Helm, London 1983.

Holland, R. F., *European Decolonization 1918–1981*, Macmillan, London 1985.

Holland, Stuart, *The Socialist Challenge*, Quartet Books, London 1976.

— *UnCommon Market. Capital, Class and Power in the European Community*, Macmillan, London 1980.

— 'New Strategy for Europe', *New Socialist*, November–December 1982.

— *The Global Economy: From Meso to Macroeconomics*, Weidenfeld and Nicolson, London 1987.

Hollifield, James F. and George Ross (eds), *Searching for the New France*, Routledge, London and New York 1991.

Holmes, Martin, *Political Pressure and Economic Policy: British Government 1970–1974*, Butterworth, London 1982.

Holmes, Peter, 'Broken Dreams: Economic Policy in Mitterrand's France', in Mazey and Newman (eds), op. cit.

Holter, Harriet and Bjørg Aase Sørensen, 'Norway', in Cook, Lorwin and Kaplan Daniels (eds), op. cit.

Holton, Bob, *British Syndicalism 1900–1914. Myth and Realities*, Pluto Press, London 1976.

Holton, Richard, 'Industrial Politics in France: Nationalisation under Mitterrand', *West European Politics*, Vol. 9, no. 1, January 1986.

Honigsbaum, Frank, *Health, Happiness and Security: The Creation of the National Health Service*, Routledge, London 1989.

Hooper, John, *The Spaniards*, Penguin, Harmondsworth 1986.
— 'Catching the Spanish drift', *Guardian*, 13 April 1989.
Hope, Kerin, 'European prosperity proves elusive', Survey on Greece, *Financial Times*, 14 November 1994.
Horden, Francis, 'Genèse et vote de la loi du 20 juin 1936 sur les congés payés', *Le Mouvement social*, no. 150, January–March 1990.
Horowitz, Tamar, 'From Elite Fashion to Mass Fashion', *Archives européennes de sociologie*, Vol. 16, no. 2, 1975.
Housego, David, 'Chirac beset by handicaps', Survey on France, *Financial Times*, 16 June 1986.
Howard, Christopher, 'The Hidden Side of the American Welfare State', *Political Science Quarterly*, Vol. 108, no. 3, 1993.
Howell, David, *British Social Democracy. A Study in Development and Decay*, Croom Helm, London 1976.
Howorth, Jolyon and George Ross (eds), *Contemporary France*, Vols 1–3, Frances Pinter, London 1987–89.
Hudson, Michael, ' "Concerted Action": Wages Policy in West Germany, 1967–1977', *Industrial Relations Journal*, Vol. 11, no. 4, September–October 1980.
Hughes, Colin and Patrick Wintour, *Labour Rebuilt. The New Model Party*, Fourth Estate, London 1990.
Hülsberg, Werner, *The German Greens. A Social and Political Profile*, trans. Gus Fagan, Verso, London 1988.
Hyhynen, Pertti, 'The Popular Front in Finland', *New Left Review*, no. 57, September–October 1969.
Iatrides, John O., 'Beneath the Sound and the Fury: US Relations with the PASOK Government', in Clogg (ed.), op. cit., 1993.
Iglesias, Gerardo, 'Adecuar el partido a la estrategia', *Nuestra Bandera*, no. 118–19, 1983.
ILO, *Yearbook of Labour Statistics*, ILO, Geneva 1990, 1991, 1992 and 1994.
— *Yearbook of Labour Statistics. Retrospective Edition on Population Census 1945–1989*, ILO, Geneva 1990.
— *World Labour Report 1993*, Geneva 1993.
Inglehart, Ronald, *The Silent Revolution. Changing Values and Political Styles Among Western Publics*, Princeton University Press, Princeton NJ 1977.
— 'The Changing Structure of Political Cleavages in Western Society', in Dalton, Flanagan and Beck (eds), op. cit.
— 'Values, Ideology, and Cognitive Mobilization in New Social Movements', in Dalton and Kuechler (eds), op. cit.
Ingrao, Pietro, 'Risposta a Lombardi', *Rinascita*, no. 21, 23 May 1964.
— *Masse e potere*, Editori Riuniti, Rome 1964.
Irwin, G. A., 'Patterns of Voting Behaviour in the Netherlands', in Richard T. Griffiths (ed.), *The Economics and Politics of the Netherlands since 1945*, Martinus Nijhoff, The Hague 1980.
Jackson, Christine, 'Policies and Implementation of Anti-Discrimination Strategies', in Schmidt and Weitzel (eds), op. cit.
Jackson, Julian, *The Popular Front in France. Defending Democracy, 1934–38*, Cambridge University Press, Cambridge 1988.
Jäggi, Max, Roger Müller and Sil Schmid, *Red Bologna*, Writers and Readers, London 1977.
Janitschek, Hans, *Mário Soares. Portrait of a Hero*, Weidenfeld and Nicolson, London 1985.
Jarqusch, Konrad H., *The Rush to German Unity*, Oxford University Press, New York and Oxford 1994.

Jefferys, Kevin, *The Churchill Coalition and Wartime Politics, 1940–1945*, Manchester University Press, Manchester 1991.

Jelavich, Barbara, *Modern Austria. Empire and Republic 1815–1986*, Cambridge University Press, Cambridge 1986.

Jenkins, Mark, *Bevanism. Labour's High Tide: The Cold War and the Democratic Mass Movement*, Spokesman, Nottingham 1979.

Jenkins, Robert, *Tony Benn: A Political Biography*, Writers and Readers, London 1980.

Jenkins, Roy, 'British Labour – Retrospect and Prospect', *Socialist Information International*, Vol. 20, no. 11, November 1970.

— *Partnership of Principle*, Secker and Warburg, London 1985.

— *A Life at the Centre*, Macmillan, London 1991.

Jenson, Jane, 'The Limits of "and the" Discourse. French Women as Marginal Workers', in Jenson, Hangen and Reddy (eds), op. cit.

— and Elisabeth Hangen, 'Paradoxes and Promises. Work and Politics in the Postwar Years', in Jenson, Hangen and Reddy (eds), op. cit.

— and Rianne Mahon, 'Representing Solidarity: Class, Gender and the Crisis in Social-Democratic Sweden', *New Left Review*, no. 201, September–October 1993.

— and George Ross, 'The Tragedy of the French Left', *New Left Review*, no. 171, September–October 1988.

— Elisabeth Hangen and Ceallaigh Reddy (eds), *Feminization of the Labour Force. Paradoxes and Promises*, Polity Press, Cambridge 1988.

Jessua, Claude, 'La rupture des grands équilibres', in Massenet et al., op. cit.

Joffrin, Laurent, *La Gauche en voi de disparition. Comment changer sans trahir?*, Editions du Seuil, Paris 1984.

Johansonn, Sven-Erik, 'Profit-sharing. Excess Profits. Wage Solidarity', *Skandinaviska Enskilda Banken Quarterly Review*, no. 2, 1982.

Johnson, R., *The French Communist Party versus the Students*, Yale University Press, New Haven CT and London 1972.

— 'The British Political Elite, 1955–1972', *Archives européennes de sociologie*, Vol. 14, no. 1, 1973.

— *The Long March of the French Left*, Macmillan, London 1981.

Johnstone, Diana, *The Politics of Euromissiles. Europe's Role in America's World*, Verso, London 1984.

Joll, James, *Intellectuals in Politics*, Weidenfeld and Nicolson, London 1960.

— *The Second International 1889–1914*, Routledge and Kegan Paul, London 1974.

Joly, Danièle, *The French Communist Party and the Algerian War*, Macmillan, London 1991.

Jones, E. L., *The European Miracle. Environments, Economies and Geopolitics in the History of Europe and Asia*, Cambridge University Press, Cambridge 1987.

Jones, Jack, *Union Man. An Autobiography*, Collins, London 1986.

Jones, W. Glyn, *Denmark. A Modern History*, Croom Helm, London 1986.

Jonung, Christina, 'Patterns of Occupational Segregation by Sex in the Labor Market', in Schmidt and Weitzel (eds), op. cit.

Jospin Lionel, 'Le socialisme français, défenseur et garant de la République', *Revue politique et parlementaire*, Vol. 87, no. 915, March–April 1985.

— *L'invention du possible*, Flammarion, Paris 1991.

Journès, Claude, 'Les interprétations de Mai 68', *Pouvoirs*, no. 39, 1986.

Joyce, Patrick, *Visions of the People. Industrial England and the Question of Class 1848–1914*, Cambridge University Press, Cambridge 1991.

Judt, Tony, *Marxism and the French Left*, Clarendon Press, Oxford 1986.

— *Past Imperfect. French Intellectuals, 1944–1956*, University of California Press, Berkeley 1992.

— (ed.) *Resistance and Revolution in Mediterranean Europe 1939–1948*, Routledge, London and New York 1989.

Juillard, Jacques, 'Réflexions d'après le prochain congrès', *Intervention*, nos 5–6, August–September–October 1983.

— 'Epinay-sur-Seine et retour ou la fin d'un cycle', *Intervention*, no. 13, July–September 1985.

— 'Comment la gauche peut revenir', *Intervention*, no. 16, April–May–June 1986.

July, Serge, *Les années Mitterrand*, Bernard Grasset, Paris 1986.

Kahn, Jacques, 'Monopoles, nations et marché commun', *Cahiers du communisme*, Vol. 42, no. 4, April 1966.

Kaldor, Nicholas, *Further Essays on Applied Economics*, Duckworth, London 1978.

Kalma, Paul, 'Towards a New Class Compromise', *Socialist Affairs*, no. 1, 1986.

Kalogeropoulou, Efthalia, 'Election Promises and Government Performance in Greece: PASOK's Fulfilment of its 1981 Election Pledges', *European Journal of Political Research*, Vol. 17, no. 3, 1989.

Kaplan, Gisela, *Contemporary Western European Feminism*, Allen and Unwin, Sydney 1992.

Katz, Richard S. and Peter Mair (eds), *Party Organizations. A Data Handbook on Party Organizations in Western Democracies, 1960–1990*, Sage, London 1992.

Katzenstein, Peter J., *Small States in World Markets. Industrial Policy in Europe*, Cornell University Press, Ithaca NY and London 1985.

Kautsky, Benedikt, 'The Ideological Development of Democratic Socialism in Austria', *Socialist International Information*, Vol. 6, no. 16, 21 April 1956.

Kayman, Martin, *Revolution and Counter-revolution in Portugal*, Merlin Press, London 1987.

Kedward, H. R., 'Behind the Polemics: French Communists and the Resistance 1939–41', in Hawes and White (eds), op. cit.

Keller, John F., 'The Division of Labour in Electronics', in June Nash and María Patricia Fernández-Kelly (eds), *Women, Men, and the International Division of Labor*, SUNY Press, Albany NY 1983.

Kennedy, Paul, *The Rise and Fall of the Great Powers*, Fontana, London 1989.

— *Preparing for the Twenty-First Century*, Fontana, London 1994.

Kent, John, 'Bevin's Imperialism and the Idea of Euro-Africa, 1945–49', in Michael Dockrill and John W. Young (eds), *British Foreign Policy 1945–56*, Macmillan, London 1989.

Kenwood, A. G. and A. L. Lougheed, *The Growth of the International Economy 1820–1980. An Introductory Text*, Allen and Unwin, London 1983.

Kernbauer, Hans, Eduard März, Siegfried Mattl, Robert Schediwy and Fritz Weber, 'Les nationalisations en Autriche', *Le mouvement social*, no. 134, January–March 1986.

Kesselman, Mark, 'The Tranquil Revolution at Clochemerle: Socialist Decentralisation in France', in Cerny and Schain (eds), op. cit.

— 'The Demise of French Socialism', *New Politics*, Vol. 1, no. 1, Summer 1986.

Keylor, William R., *The Twentieth-Century World*, Oxford University Press, Oxford 1984.

Keynes, John Maynard, *The General Theory of Employment, Interest and Money*, in *Collected Writings*, Vol. 7, Macmillan, London 1972.

— 'The End of Laissez-Faire', in *Essays in Persuasion, Collected Writings*, Vol. 9, Macmillan, London 1973.

Khilnani, Sunil, *Arguing Revolution. The Intellectual Left in Postwar France*, Yale University Press, New Haven CT and London 1993.

Khrushchev, N. S., *Report to the 22nd Congress of the Communist Party of the Soviet Union*, Soviet Booklet no. 80, London 1961.

Kiernan, Kathleen, 'Men and Women at Work and at Home', in Roger Jowell et al. (eds), *British Social Attitudes. The 9th Report*, SCPR/Dartmouth, Aldershot 1992.

Kieve, Ronald A., 'Pillars of Sand: A Marxist Critique of Consociational Democracy in the Netherlands', *Comparative Politics*, Vol. 13, no. 3, April 1981.

Kindleberger, Charles P., *Europe's Postwar Growth. The Role of Labor Supply*, Harvard University Press, Cambridge MA 1967.

— *American Business Abroad. Six Lectures on Direct Investment*, Yale University Press, New Haven CT and London 1969.

King, Francis and George Matthews (eds), *About Turn. The British Communist Party and the Second World War*, Lawrence and Wishart, London 1990.

Kinnock, Neil, 'New Deal for Europe', *Socialist Affairs*, no. 1, 1984.

— 'A Hand on the Tiller – and the Till', *Guardian*, 10 April 1989.

Kirby, David, 'The Finnish Social Democratic Party and the Bolsheviks', *Journal of Contemporary History*, Vol. 11, no. 2–3, July 1976.

— 'The Baltic States 1940–50', in Martin McCauley (ed.), *Communist Power in Europe 1944–1949*, Macmillan, London 1977.

— *Finland in the Twentieth Century*, C. Hurst and Co., London 1979.

— 'New Wine in Old Vessels? The Finnish Socialist Workers' Party, 1919–1923', *Slavonic and East European Review*, Vol. 66, no. 3, July 1988.

— 'The Labour Movement', in Max Engman and David Kirby (eds), *Finland. People, Nation and State*, C. Hurst and Co., London 1989.

Kirchheimer, Otto, 'The Transformation of the Western European Party Systems', in Joseph LaPalombara and Myrin Weiner (eds), *Political Parties and Political Development*, Princeton University Press, Princeton NJ 1966.

Kissinger, Henry, *White House Years*, Little, Brown and Co., Boston 1979.

Kitschelt, Herbert, 'New Social Movements and the Decline of Party Organization', in Dalton and Kuechler (eds), op. cit.

— *The Transformation of European Social Democracy*, Cambridge University Press, Cambridge 1994.

Kitzinger, Uwe, *The Second Try. Labour and the EEC*, Pergamon Press, Oxford 1968.

Kofas, Jon V., *Authoritarianism in Greece: The Metaxas Regime*, Columbia University Press, New York 1983.

Kogan, David and Maurice Kogan, *The Battle for the Labour Party*, Fontana, n.p. 1982.

Kolakowski, Leszek and Stuart Hampshire (eds), *The Socialist Idea. A Reappraisal*, Weidenfeld and Nicolson, London 1974.

Kolb, Eberhard, *The Weimar Republic*, Unwin and Hyman, London 1988.

Kolinsky, Eva, *Women in West Germany*, Berg, Oxford 1989.

— *Woman in Contemporary Germany. Life, Work and Politics*, Berg, Providence and Oxford 1993.

— 'Party Change and Women's Representation in Unified Germany', in Lovenduski and Norris (eds), op. cit.

Korpi, Walter, *The Working Class in Welfare Capitalism. Work, Unions and Politics in Sweden*, Routledge and Kegan Paul, London 1978.

— *The Democratic Class Struggle*, Routledge and Kegan Paul, London 1983.

— 'Power, Politics, and State Autonomy in the Development of Social Citizenship: Social Rights During Sickness in Eighteen OECD Countries Since 1930', *American Sociological Review*, Vol. 54, no. 3, June 1989.

Kosonen, Pekka, 'The Scandinavian Welfare Model in the New Europe', in Boje and Olsson Hort (eds), op. cit.

Kousoulas, D. George, *Revolution and Defeat. The Story of the Greek Communist Party*, Oxford University Press, London 1965.

Krag, Jen Otto, 'Why Denmark Applied to Join the Common Market', *Socialist International Information*, Vol. 11, no. 35, 2 September 1961.

— 'The Danish View', *Socialist International Information*, Vol. 21, no. 5–6, May–June 1971.

Krasucki, Henri, 'Salaire réel et valeur de la force de travail', *Cahiers du communisme*, Vol. 33, no. 3, March 1957

Kreile, Michael, 'Ostpolitik Reconsidered', in Ekkehart Krippendorff and Volker Rittberger (eds), *The Foreign Policy of West Germany. Formation and Contents*, Sage, London and Beverly Hills 1980.

Kreisky, Bruno, 'Social Democracy's Third Historical Phase', *Socialist International Information*, Vol. 20, no. 5, May 1970.

— Speech at Helsinki Conference of the Socialist International of 25–27 May 1971, *Socialist International Information*, Vol. 21, nos 5–6, May–June 1971.

Kreissler, Felix, 'Un bilan de cinq années de gouvernement socialiste. Reformes et "Sozial-partnerschaft" (1970–1975)', *Austriaca*, Vol. 4, 1975.

— 'Le parti socialiste Autrichien entre le nouveau programme (Mai 1978) et les nouvelles elections générales (Mai 1979)', *Austriaca*, Vol. 8, 1979.

Krossman, E. H., *The Low Countries 1780–1940*, Clarendon Press, Oxford 1978.

Krugman, Paul R., 'Slow Growth in Europe: Conceptual Issues', in Lawrence and Schultze (eds), op. cit.

— *The Age of Diminished Expectations*, rev. edn, MIT Press, Cambridge MA 1994.

Kuisel, Richard F., *Seducing the French. The Dilemma of Americanization*, University of California Press, Berkeley 1993.

— *Capitalism and the State in Modern France. Renovation and Economic Management in the Twentieth Century*, Cambridge University Press, Cambridge 1981.

Kurzer, Paulette, 'The Internationalization of Business and Domestic Class Compromises: A Four Country Study', *West European Politics*, Vol. 14, no. 4, October 1991.

Labour Party, *For Socialism and Peace. The Labour Party's Programme of Action*, London 1934.

— *Signposts for the Sixties. A Statement of Labour's Home Policy Accepted by the 60th Annual Conference of the Labour Party at Blackpool*, 2–6 October 1961.

— draft of *Signposts for the Sixties*, published as 'Missing Signposts' in *New Left Review*, no. 12, November–December 1961.

— *Labour's Programme 1973*, London 1973.

— *The National Enterprise Board. Labour's State Holding Company, An Opposition Green Paper*, London, n. d. (1973).

— *Labour's Programme 1976*, London 1976.

— *Labour's Programme 1982*, London 1982.

— *Democratic Socialist Aims and Values*, London, n.d. (1988); mimeo.

— *Meet the Challenge, Make the Change. A New Agenda for Britain, Final Report of Labour's Policy Review for the 1990s*, London 1989.

— *Looking to the Future*, London 1990.

Lacroix-Ritz, Annie, 'Négociation et signature des accords Blum-Byrnes (Octobre 1945–Mai 1946). D'après les archives du Ministère des Affaires Etrangères', *Revue d'histoire moderne et contemporaine*, Vol. XXXI, July–September 1984.

Ladrech, Robert, 'Social Movements and Party Systems: The French Socialist Party and New Social Movements', *West European Politics*, Vol. 12, no. 3, July 1989.

Lafon, François, 'Structures idéologiques et nécessités pratiques au congrès de la SFIO en 1946', *Revue d'histoire moderne et contemporaine*, Vol. XXXVI, 1989.

Lafontaine, Oskar, 'Progresso e solidarietà', *Democrazia e diritto*, no. 1–2, January–February 1989 (Italian trans. of Munster Congress Report).

Lama, Luciano, *Intervista sul sindacato*, Laterza, Rome-Bari 1976.

— *Il potere del sindacato*, Editori Riuniti, Rome 1978.

Lancaster, Thomas D. and Gary Prevost (eds), *Politics and Change in Spain*, Praeger, New York 1985.

Landauer, Carl, *European Socialism. A History of Ideas and Movements*, Vol. II, University of California Press, Berkeley and Los Angeles 1959.

Landes, Joan, *Women and the Public Sphere in the Age of the French Revolution*, Cornell University Press, Ithaca NY and London 1988.

Landier, Hubert, 'Vers un renforcement du corporatisme syndical', in Massenet et al., op. cit.

Lange, Peter, 'The End of an Era: The Wage Indexation Referendum of 1985', in Robert Leonardi and Raffaella Y. Nanette, (eds), *Italian Politics: A Review*, Vol. 1, Pinter Publishers, London and New York 1986.

Laqueur, Walter, *Europe since Hitler. The Rebirth of Europe*, Penguin, Harmondsworth 1982.

Larkin, Maurice, *France since the Popular Front. Government and People 1936–86*, Clarendon Press, Oxford 1988.

Laroque, Pierre, *Succès et faiblesses de l'effort social français*, Colin, Paris 1961.

Lasch, Christopher, *The Minimal Self. Psychic Survival in Troubled Times*, Pan Books, London 1984.

Lauber, Volkmar, 'Changing Priorities in Austrian Economic Policy', *West European Politics*, Vol. 15, no. 1, January 1992.

Laubier, Claire (ed.), *The Condition of Women in France 1945 to the Present*, Routledge, London and New York 1990.

Lavau, Georges, 'The Effects of Twenty Years of Gaullism on the Parties of the Left', in Andrews and Hoffmann (eds), op. cit.

LaVigna, Claire, 'The Marxist Ambivalence Toward Women: Between Socialism and Feminism in the Italian Socialist Party', in Marilyn J. Boxer and Jean H. Quataert (eds), *Socialist Women. European Socialist Feminism in the Nineteenth and Early Twentieth Centuries*, Elsevier, New York 1978.

Lawrence, Robert Z. and Charles L. Schultze (eds), *Barriers to European Growth. A Transatlantic View*, Brookings Institution, Washington DC 1987.

Layard, R. and S. J. Nickell, 'Unemployment in Britain', *Economica*, Vol. 53, 1986, Supplement to no. 210, *Unemployment*.

— 'Performance of the British Labour Market', in Blanchard, Dornbusch and Layard (eds), op. cit.

Layard, Richard, Giorgio Basevi, Olivier Blanchard, Willem Buiter and Rudiger Dornbusch, 'Europe: The Case for Unsustainable Growth', in Blanchard, Dornbusch and Layard (eds), op. cit.

Lazar, Marc, 'Le parti communiste italien et le défi des années quatre-vingt', *Commentaire*, no. 44, Winter 1988–89.

— *Maisons rouges. Les partis communistes français et italien de la Libération à nos jours*, Aubier, Paris 1992.

Leaman, Jeremy, *The Political Economy of West Germany, 1945–1985*, Macmillan, London 1988.

Le Couriard, Daniel, 'Les socialistes et les débuts de la guerre d'Indochine (1946–1947)', *Revue d'histoire moderne et contemporaine*, Vol. XXXI, April–June 1984.

Le Cour Grandmaison, Olivier, 'Le Mouvement de la paix pendant la guerre froide: le cas français (1948–1952)', *Communisme*, no. 18–19, 1988.

Lee, Stephen J., *The European Dictatorships 1918–1945*, Routledge, London 1987.

Lemke Christiane and Gary Marks (eds), *The Crisis of Socialism in Europe*, Duke University Press, Durham and London 1992.

Lenin, V. I., *Collected Works*, Volumes 13, 27, 29, 30, 31 and 32, Progress Publishers, Moscow 1965–74.

— 'The Tasks of the Proletariat in Our Revolution', in *Collected Works*, Vol. 24, Progress Publishers, Moscow 1974.

— *The State and Revolution* (1917), trans. Robert Service, Penguin, Harmondsworth 1992.

Leonard, Dick, 'Eye on coalition chances', Survey on Belgium, *Financial Times*, 19 June 1987.

— 'Fashioning federalism', *Financial Times*, 12 July 1993.

— 'Mr. Wallonia pulls the strings', *Financial Times*, 12 July 1993.

Lepre, A. (ed.), *Dal crollo del fascismo all'egemonia moderata*, Guida Editore, Naples 1973.

Leviné-Meyer, Rosa, *Inside German Communism. Memoirs of Party Life in the Weimar Republic*, Pluto Press, London 1977.

Lewin, Leif, *Ideology and Strategy. A Century of Swedish Politics*, Cambridge University Press, Cambridge 1988.

Lewis, Jill, 'Red Vienna: Socialism in One City, 1918–1927', *European Studies Review*, Vol. 13, no. 3, 1983.

— *Fascism and the Working Class in Austria 1918–1934. The Failure of Labour in the First Republic*, Berg, New York 1991.

Lewis, Steven C. and Serenella Sferza, 'The Second Mitterrand Experiment: Charisma and the Possibilities of Partisan Renewal', in Howorth and Ross (eds), op. cit., Vol. 3.

Leys, Colin, *Politics in Britain*, Heinemann, London 1983.

Lichtheim, George, *A Short History of Socialism*, Weidenfeld and Nicolson, London 1970.

Liddington, Jill and Jill Norris, *One Hand Tied Behind Us. The Rise of the Women's Suffrage Movement*, Virago, London 1978.

Lidtke, Vernon L., *The Outlawed Party: Social Democracy in Germany 1878–1890*, Princeton University Press, Princeton NJ 1966.

Lieber, Robert J., *British Politics and European Unity*, University of California Press, Berkeley and London 1970.

— 'Labour in Power: Problems of Political Economy', in B. Brown (ed.), op. cit.

Lieberman, Sima, 'The Ideological Foundations of Western European Planning', *Journal of European Economic History*, Vol. 10, no. 2, Fall 1981.

— *The Contemporary Spanish Economy: A Historical Perspective*, Allen and Unwin, London 1982.

Liebman, Marcel, 'The Crisis of Belgian Social Democracy', in Ralph Miliband and John Saville (eds), *The Socialist Register 1966*, Merlin Press, London 1966.

Ligou, Daniel, *Histoire du socialisme en France 1871–1961*, Presses Universitaires de France, Paris 1962.

Lijpart, Arend, *The Politics of Accommodation. Pluralism and Democracy in the Netherlands*, University of California Press, Berkeley 1968.

— 'Typologies of Democratic Systems', in Arend Lijphart (ed.), *Politics in Europe*, Prentice Hall, Englewood Cliffs NJ 1969.

Lilli, Laura and Chiara Valentini, *Care compagne. Il femminismo nel PCI e nelle organizzazioni di massa*, Editori Riuniti, Rome 1979.

Lindbeck, Assar, *Overshooting, Reform and Retreat of the Welfare State*, Seminar Paper no. 552, Institute for International Economic Studies, Stockholm University, Stockholm 1993.

— et al., *Options for Economic and Political Reform in Sweden*, Seminar Paper no. 540, Institute for International Economic Studies, Stockholm University, Stockholm 1993.

— and Dennis J. Snower, 'Wage Setting, Unemployment and Insider–Outsider Relations', *American Economic Review*, Vol. 76, no. 2, May 1986.

Lindblom, Charles, *Politics and Markets. The World's Political-Economic Systems*, Basic Books, New York 1977.

Linden, Carl A., *Khrushchev and the Soviet Leadership 1957–1964*, Johns Hopkins Press, Baltimore MD 1966.

Lingis, Alphonso, *The Will to Revolution*, 22 May 1970 public lecture at Pennsylvania State University.

Lipietz, Alain, *Mirages and Miracles. The Crisis of Global Fordism*, Verso, London 1977.

Lipsey, David and Dick Leonard (eds), *The Socialist Agenda. Crosland's Legacy*, Jonathan Cape, London 1981.

Lloyd, Genevieve, *The Man of Reason. 'Male' and 'Female' in Western Philosophy*, Methuen, London 1984.

Lodge, Paul and Tessa Blackstone, *Educational Policy and Educational Inequality*, Martin Robertson, London 1982.

Loew, Raimund, 'The Politics of Austro-Marxism', *New Left Review*, no. 118, November–December 1979.

— 'The Politics of the Austrian "Miracle"', *New Left Review*, no. 123, September–October 1980.

Löfgren, Orvar, 'Consuming Interests', *Culture and Society* (Denmark), no. 7, 1990.

Longo, Luigi, 'Il movimento studentesco nella lotta anticapitalista', *Rinascita*, no. 8, 3 May 1968.

Lorwin, Val R., 'Labor Unions and Political Parties in Belgium', *Industrial and Labor Relations Review*, Vol. 28, no. 2, January 1975.

Loth, Wilfried, 'Les projets de politique extérieure de la Résistance socialiste en France', *Revue d'histoire moderne et contemporaine*, Vol. XXIX, 1977.

Lovenduski, Joni, *Women and European Politics. Contemporary Feminism and Public Policy*, Wheatsheaf, Brighton 1986.

— and Pippa Norris (eds), *Gender and Party Politics*, Sage, London 1993.

— and Vicky Randall, *Contemporary Feminist Politics. Women and Power in Britain*, Oxford University Press, Oxford 1993.

Löwenthal, Richard, 'Communism: Clear Position of German Social Democracy', *Socialist International Information*, Vol. 20, no. 12, 1970.

— 'Letter from Berlin: Neutralism and Nationalism', *Partisan Review*, no. 2, 1984.

Luciani, Giacomo, *Il PCI e il capitalismo occidentale*, Longanesi, Milan 1977.

Lumley, Robert, *States of Emergency. Cultures of Revolt in Italy from 1968 to 1978*, Verso, London 1990.

Lundberg, Erik, 'The Rise and Fall of the Swedish Model', *Journal of Economic Literature*, Vol. 23, March 1985.

— and Olle Lindgren, 'Uncertainty about Employee Investment Funds – Economic Effects', *Skandinaviska Enskilda Banken Quarterly Review*, no. 2, 1982.

Lundestad, G., *America, Scandinavia and the Cold War 1945–1949*, Oslo 1980.

Lundmark, Kjell, 'Welfare State and Employment Policy: Sweden', in Dyson and Wilks (eds), op. cit.

Luther, Kurt Richard, 'Consociationalism, Parties and the Party System', *West European Politics*, Vol. 15, no. 1, January 1992.

Lutz, Dieter S., 'La difficile strada verso una nuova concezione della sicurezza', in Telò (ed.), op. cit.

Luza, Radomir V., *The Resistance in Austria 1938–1945*, University of Minnesota Press, Minneapolis 1984.

Lynch, Frances M. B., 'Resolving the Paradox of the Monnet Plan: National and International Planning in French Reconstruction', *Economic History Review*, Vol. XXXVII, no. 2, May 1984.

Lyrintzis, Christos, 'PASOK in Power: From "Change" to Disenchantment', in Clogg (ed.) op. cit., 1993.

McAllister, Ian and Jack Vowles, 'The Rise of New Politics and Market Liberalism in Australia and New Zealand', *British Journal of Political Science*, Vol. 24, Part 3, July 1994.

McCarthy, Patrick, *The French Socialists in Power 1981–1986*, Greenwood Press, New York 1987.

McCarthy, W. E. J., 'The Nature of Britain's Strike Problem', *British Journal of Industrial Relations*, Vol. 8, no. 2, July 1970.

McCauley, Martin (ed.), *Communist Power in Europe 1944-1949*, Macmillan, London 1977.

McCracken, Paul, et al., *Towards Full Employment and Price Stability: A Report to the OECD by a Group of Independent Experts*, OECD, Paris 1977.

McDonald, Robert, 'The Colonels' Dictatorship 1967-1974', in Marion Sarafis and Martin Eve (eds), *Background to Contemporary Greece*, Vol. II, Merlin Press, London 1990.

McGrew, William W., *Land and Revolution in Modern Greece, 1800-1881: The Transition in the Tenure and Exploitation of Land from Ottoman Rule to Independence*, Kent State University Press, Kent OH 1985.

McKeown, Thomas, *The Modern Rise of Population*, Edward Arnold, London 1976.

Mackenzie, Norman (ed.), *Conviction*, MacGibbon and Kee, London 1959.

McKibbin, Ross, 'The Economic Policy of the Second Labour Government 1929-1931', *Past and Present*, no. 68, August 1975.

Mackie, Thomas T. and Richard, Rose, *The International Almanac of Electoral History*, Macmillan, London 1974.

Macleod, Alex, 'Portrait of a Model Ally: The Portuguese Communist Party and the International Communist Movement, 1968-1983', *Studies in Comparative Communism*, Vol. XVII, no. 1, Spring 1984.

McMillan, James E., *Housewife or Harlot. The Place of Women in French Society 1870-1940*, Harvester, Brighton 1981.

Mabille, Xavier, *Histoire politique de la Belgique*, CRISP, Brussels 1986.

Machado, Diamantino P., *The Structure of Portuguese Society. The Failure of Fascism*, Praeger, New York 1991.

Machin, Howard and Vincent Wright (eds), *Economic Policy and Policy-Making Under the Mitterrand Presidency 1981-1984*, Frances Pinter, London 1985.

Maddison, Angus, *Phases of Capitalist Development*, Oxford University Press, Oxford 1982.

— *Dynamic Forces in Capitalist Development. A Long-run Comparative View*, Oxford University Press, Oxford 1991.

Mafai, Miriam, *L'apprendistato della politica. Le donne italiane nel dopoguerra*, Editori Riuniti, Rome 1979.

Magraw, Roger, *A History of the French Working Class*. Vol. 2: *Workers and the Bourgeois Republic*, Blackwell, Oxford 1992.

Maier, Charles S. *Recasting Bourgeois Europe. Stabilization in France, Germany, and Italy in the Decade after World War I*, Princeton University Press, Princeton NJ 1975.

— 'The Two Postwar Eras and the Conditions for Stability in Twentieth-Century Western Europe', *American Historical Review*, Vol. 86, no. 2, 1981.

— '"Fictitious bonds ... of wealth and law": on the theory and practice of interest representation' in Suzanne D. Berger (ed.) *Organizing Interests in Western Europe*, Cambridge University Press 1983.

— *In Search of Stability. Explorations in Political Economy*, Cambridge University Press 1987.

— 'The Collapse of Communism: Approaches for a Future History', *History Workshop*, no. 31, Spring 1991.

— (ed.), *Changing Boundaries of the Political*, Cambridge University Press, Cambridge 1987.

Maiorini, Maria Grazia, *Il Mouvement republicain populaire partito della IV Repubblica*, Giuffrè Editore, Milan 1983.

Mair, Peter and Stefano Bartolini, *Identity, Competition and Electoral Availability. The Stabilization of European Electorates 1885-1985*, Cambridge University Press, Cambridge 1990.

Maire, E., A. Detraz and F. Krumnov, *La CFDT et l'Autogestion*, Editions de Cerf, Paris 1973.

— and J. Julliard, *La CFDT d'aujourd'hui*, Editions du Seuil, Paris 1975.

Malinvaud, Edmond, 'The Rise of Unemployment in France', *Economica*, Vol. 53, 1986, Supplement to no. 210, *Unemployment*.

— 'Wages and the Unemployed', *Economic Journal*, Vol. 92, no. 365, March 1982.

Malraux, André, *Les chênes qu'on abat ...*, Gallimard, Paris 1971.

Mandel, Ernest, 'The Lessons of May 1968', *New Left Review*, no. 52, November–December 1968.

Maravall, José María, *The Transition to Democracy in Spain*, Croom Helm, London 1982.

— 'The Socialist Alternative: The Policies and the Electorate of the PSOE', in Penniman and Mujal-León (eds), op. cit.

Marchal-Van Belle, Graziella, *Les socialistes belges et l'intégration européenne*, Editions de l'Institut de Sociologie, ULB, Brussels 1968.

Marglin, Stephen A. and Juliet Schor (eds), *The Golden Age of Capitalism. Reinterpreting the Postwar Experience*, Clarendon Press, Oxford 1990.

Markovits, Andrei S., *The Politics of the West German Trade Unions. Strategies of Class and Interest Representation in Growth and Crisis*, Cambridge University Press, Cambridge 1986.

— 'The West German Left in a Changing Europe', in Lemke and Marks (eds), op. cit.

— and Philip S. Gorski, *The German Left. Red, Green and Beyond*, Polity Press, Cambridge 1993.

Marks, Elaine and Isabelle de Courtivron (eds), *New French Feminisms*, Harvester, Brighton 1981.

Marquand, David, 'Inquest on a Movement. Labour's Defeat and Its Consequences', *Encounter*, Vol. 53, no. 1, July 1979.

— *The Unprincipled Society. New Demands and Old Politics*, Fontana, London 1988.

— 'Half-way to Citizenship? The Labour Party and Constitutional Reform', in Smith and Spear (eds), op. cit.

— 'After Socialism', *Political Studies*, Vol. 41, Special Issue 1993.

Marramao, Giacomo, *Austromarxismo e socialismo di sinistra fra le due guerre*, La Pietra, Milan 1975.

Marsh, David, 'Wunder turns to whimper', *Financial Times*, 4 November 1987.

— 'In the clutch of corporatism', *Financial Times*, 5 November 1987.

Marshall, T. H., *Citizenship and Social Class and Other Essays*, Cambridge University Press, Cambridge 1950.

Martelli, Roger, 'L'année 1956', in Bourderon et al., op. cit.

Martin, Jean-Paul and Jol Roman, 'Le socialisme en proie à l'école', *Intervention*, no. 13, July–September 1985.

Marx, Karl, *Critique of the Gotha Programme*, International Publishers, New York 1970.

— *Capital*, trans. Moore-Aveling, Progress Publishers, Moscow, Vol. 1, 1965; Vol. 3, 1971.

— *Economic and Philosophic Manuscripts of 1844*, in *Early Writings*, trans. and ed. Tom Bottomore, McGraw-Hill, New York 1964.

— *The Eighteenth Brumaire of Louis Bonaparte*, Progress Publishers, Moscow 1967.

— *The Communist Manifesto*, Penguin, Harmondsworth 1967.

Marx, Karl and Friedrich Engels, *The German Ideology*, International Publishers, New York 1968.

— *Selected Correspondence 1846–1895*, Martin Lawrence, London 1934.

Massenet, Michel et al., *La France socialiste. Un premier bilan*, Hachette, Paris 1983.

Mauroy, Pierre, *C'est ici le chemin*, Flammarion, Paris 1982.

— 'La gauche au pouvoir', *Revue politique et parlementaire*, Vol. 87, no. 916, May–June 1985.

Mavrogordatos, George, *The Rise of the Greek Sun: The Greek Elections of 1981*, King's College London, Centre for Contemporary Greek Studies, Occasional Paper no. 1, 1983.

— *Stillborn Republic: Social Conditions and Party Strategies in Greece 1922–1936*, University of California Press, Berkeley 1983.

Mayer, Lawrence C. and Roland E. Smith, 'Feminism and Religiosity: Female Electoral Behaviour in Western Europe', *West European Politics*, Vol. 8, no. 4, October 1985.

Mayeur, Jean-Marie and Madeleine Rebérioux, *The Third Republic from Its Origins to the Great War 1871–1914*, Cambridge University Press, Cambridge 1984.

Mazey, Sonia, 'Decentralisation: La grande affaire du septennat?', in Mazey and Newman (eds), op. cit.

— and Michael Newman (eds), *Mitterrand's France*, Croom Helm, London 1987.

Meek, Ronald L., 'Marx's "Doctrine of Increasing Misery"', *Science and Society*, Vol. 16, no. 4, Autumn 1962.

Meidner, Rudolf, *Employee Investment Funds. An Approach to Collective Capital Formation*, Allen and Unwin, London 1978.

— 'Swedish Union Strategies Towards Structural Change', *Nordisk Tidskrift för Politisk Economi*, no. 20, 1987.

— 'Why Did the Swedish Model Fail?', in Ralph Miliband and Leo Panitch (eds), *Real Problems, False Solutions, Socialist Register*, Merlin Press, London 1993.

Mény, Yves, 'The Socialist Decentralisation', in Ross, Hoffmann and Malzacher (eds), op. cit.

Merkel, Wolfgang, 'Between Class and Catch-All: Is There an Electoral Dilemma for Social Democratic Parties in Western Europe?', in Institut de Ciències Polítiques i Socials (ICPS), *Socialist Parties in Europe II: Class, Populars, Catch-all?*, Barcelona 1992.

— 'After the Golden Age. Is Social Democracy Doomed to Decline?', in Lemke and Marks (eds), op. cit.

Merkl, Peter H., 'The Role of Public Opinion in West German Foreign Policy', in Wolfram F. Hanrieder (ed.), *West German Foreign Policy: 1949–1979*, Westview Press, Boulder CO 1980.

— *German Unification in the European Context*, Penn State University Press, University Park, PA 1993.

Meyer, Chris, 'Nordic State Feminism in the 1990s: Whose Ally?', in Boje and Olsson Hort (eds), op. cit.

Meyer, Thomas, 'Un mutamento di paradigma: il nuovo programma nella storia della SPD', in Telò (ed.), op. cit.

Michel, Henri, *Les courants de pensée de la Résistance*, Presses Universitaires de France, Paris 1962.

— *The Second World War*, André Deutsch, London 1975.

Middlemas, Keith, *Politics in Industrial Society. The Experience of the British System since 1911*, André Deutsch, London 1979.

Mignolet, Michel, 'Les économies régionales', in Guy Quaden (ed.), *L'économie belge dans la crise*, Editions Labor, Brussels 1987.

Miliband, Ralph, *Parliamentary Socialism*, Allen and Unwin, London 1961.

Mill, John Stuart, *The Subjection of Women*, Virago, London 1983.

Miller, Doug, 'Social Partnership and the Determinants of Workplace Independence in West Germany', *British Journal of Industrial Relations*, Vol. 20, no. 1, March 1982.

Miller, Susanne and Heinrich Potthoff, *A History of German Social Democracy. From 1848 to the Present*, Berg, Leamington Spa 1986.

Millett, Kate, *Sexual Politics*, Doubleday, New York 1970.

Milward, Alan S., *The Reconstruction of Western Europe 1945–51*, Methuen, London 1984.

— *War, Economy and Society 1939–1945*, Pelican, Harmondsworth 1987.

— with the assistance of George Brennan and Federico Romero, *The European Rescue of the Nation-State*, Routledge, London 1992.

Minford, Patrick, *Unemployment: Cause and Cure*, Basil Blackwell, Oxford 1985.

Minkin, Lewis, *The Labour Party Conference. A Study in the Politics of Intra-Party Democracy*, Allen Lane, London 1978.

— *The Contentious Alliance. Trade Unions and the Labour Party*, Edinburgh University Press, Edinburgh 1991.

Misgeld, Klaus, 'As the Iron Curtain Descended: The Co-ordinating Committee of the Nordic Labour Movement and the Socialist International between Potsdam and Geneva (1945–1955)', *Scandinavian Journal of History*, Vol. 13, no. 1, 1988.

Mishra, Ramesh, *The Welfare State in Crisis*, Harvester Wheatsheaf, New York and London 1984.

Missiroli, Antonio, 'Tra Waldheim e la Cee: Democrazia consociativa e crisi economica in Austria', *Annali Sinistra Europea 1988–1989*, Franco Angeli, Milan 1989.

— *La questione tedesca. Le due Germanie dalla divisione all'unità 1945–1990*, Ponte Alle Grazie, Florence 1991.

— (ed.), *Modernizzazione e sistema politico. Italia e Germania federale a confronto*, Supplement to *Democrazia e diritto*, no. 1–2, January–April 1989.

Mitchell, B. R., 'Statistical Appendix, 1920–1970', in Carlo M. Cipolla (ed.), *The Fontana Economic History of Europe, Contemporary Economies*, Vol. 2, Collins/Fontana, Glasgow 1976.

Mitchell, Claudine, 'Madeleine Pelletier (1874–1939): The Politics of Sexual Oppression', *Feminist Review*, no. 33, Autumn 1989.

Mitchell, Juliet, 'Women: The Longest Revolution', *New Left Review*, no. 40, November–December 1966.

— *Women: The Longest Revolution*, Virago, London 1984.

Mitter, Swasti, *Common Fate, Common Bond. Women in the Global Economy*, Pluto Press, London 1986.

Mitterrand, François, *Ma part de vérité. De la rupture a l'unité*, Fayard, Paris 1969.

— *L'Abeille et l'architecte*, Flammarion, Paris 1978.

— *Politique. Textes et discours 1938–1981*, Fayard, Paris 1984.

Mlynár, Zdeněk, *Praga questione aperta*, De Donato Editore, Bari 1976.

— 'Khrushchev's Policies as a Forerunner of the Prague Spring', in R. F. Miller and F. Féhér (eds), *Khrushchev and the Communist World*, Croom Helm, London 1984.

Moch, Jules, *Confrontations*, Gallimard, Paris 1952.

— 'Socialist Re-Thinking in France', *Socialist International Information*, Vol. 9, no. 13–14, 28 March 1959.

Mollet, Guy, 'The Rapacki Plan and European Security', *Socialist International Information*, Vol. 8, no. 16, 19 April 1958.

— *L'élection présidentielle, supplément aux dossiers et documents du Monde*, May 1988.

Le Monde, *L'élection législative, supplément aux dossiers et documents du Monde*, June 1988.

Monitor, Michel, 'Social Conflicts in Belgium', in Crouch and Pizzorno (eds), op. cit., Vol. 1.

Monnet, Jean, *Memoirs*, trans. Richard Maine, Collins, London 1978.

Moon, Jeremy, 'The Responses of British Governments to Unemployment', in Richardson and Henning (eds), op. cit.

Moore, Barrington, Jr, *Injustice. The Social Bases of Obedience and Revolt*, Macmillan, London 1978.

Moore, Bob, 'Occupation, Collaboration and Resistance', *European Historical Quarterly*, Vol. 21, no. 1, January 1991.

Morgan, April and Clyde Wilcox, 'Anti-feminism in Western Europe 1975–1987', *West European Politics*, Vol. 15, no. 4, October 1992.

Morgan, Kenneth O., *Labour in Power*, Clarendon Press, Oxford 1984.

Morgan, Roger, 'The *Ostpolitik* and West Germany's External Relations', in Roger Tilford (ed.), *The Ostpolitik and Political Change in Germany*, Saxon House, Farnborough 1975.

Moro, Aldo, *L'intelligenza e gli avvenimenti. Testi 1959–1978*, Garzanti, Milan 1979.

Morrison, Rodney J., *Portugal: Revolutionary Change in an Open Economy*, Auburn House, Boston 1981.

Mortimer, Edward, *The Rise of the French Communist Party 1920–1947*, Faber and Faber, London 1984.

Mouriaux, Marie-Françoise and René, 'Unemployment Policy in France, 1976–82', in Richardson and Henning (eds), op. cit.

Mouriaux, René, 'Trade Union Strategies After May 1968', in Hanley, Kerr and Waites (eds), op. cit.

Mouzelis, Nicos P., 'Capitalism and Dictatorship in Post-war Greece', *New Left Review*, no. 96, March–April 1976.

— *Modern Greece. Facets of Underdevelopment*, Holmes and Meier, New York 1978.

— 'On the Greek Elections', *New Left Review*, no. 108, March–April 1978.

— 'On the Demise of Oligarchic Parliamentarism in the Semi-Periphery: A Balkan–Latin American Comparison', *Sociology*, Vol. 17, no. 1 February 1983.

— 'Continuities and Discontinuities in Greek Politics: From Elefterios Venizelos to Andreas Papandreou', in Kevin Featherstone and Dimitrios K. Katsoudas (eds), *Political Change in Greece. Before and after the Colonels*, Croom Helm, London 1987.

Mozer, Alfred, 'Socialist Victory in the Netherlands', *Socialist International Information*, Vol. 6, no. 26, 30 June 1956.

— 'Thoughts on the Seventy-fifth Anniversary of the Death of Karl Marx', *Socialist International Information*, Vol. 8, no. 11, 15 March 1958.

Muet, Pierre-Alain and Alain Fonteneau, *Reflation and Austerity. Economic Policy under Mitterrand*, trans. Malcom Slater, Berg, Oxford 1990.

Mujal-León, Eusebio, *Communism and Political Change in Spain*, Indiana University Press, Bloomington 1983.

— Decline and Fall of Spanish Communism', *Problems of Communism*, Vol. XXXV, no. 2 March–April 1986.

Mulhern, Francis, 'Towards 2000, or News From You-Know-Where', *New Left Review*, no. 148, November–December 1984.

Müller, Wolfgang C., 'Economic Success without an Industrial Strategy: Austria in the 1970s', *Journal of Public Policy*, Vol. 3, no. 1, February 1983.

— 'Privatising in a Corporatist Economy: The Politics of Privatisation in Austria', *West European Politics*, Vol. 11, no. 4, October 1988.

— 'The Catch-all Party Thesis and the Austrian Social Democrats', *German Politics*, Vol. 1, no. 2, August 1992.

Müller-Jentsch, Walther, 'Strikes and Strike Trends in West Germany, 1950–1978', *Industrial Relations Journal*, Vol. 12, no. 4, July–August 1981.

— and Hans-Joachim Sperling, 'Economic Development, Labour Conflicts and the Industrial Relations System in West Germany', in Crouch and Pizzorno (eds), op. cit., Vol. 1.

Müller-Rommel, Ferdinand, 'The German Greens in the 1980s: Short-term Cyclical Protest or Indicator of Transformation', *Political Studies*, Vol. 37, no. 1, March 1989.

Murray, Robin, 'The Internationalization of Capital and the Nation State', *New Left Review*, no. 61, May–June 1971.

Murshid, Ghulam, *Reluctant Debutante: Response of Bengali Women to Modernization, 1849–1905*, Sahitya Samsad, Rajshahi University, 1983.

Murteira, Mário, 'The Present Economic Situation: Its Origins and Prospects', in Graham and Makler (eds), op. cit.

Myrdal, Alva and Viola Klein, *Women's Two Roles. Home and Work*, Routledge and Kegan Paul, London 1956.

Nairn, Tom, 'British Nationalism and the EEC', *New Left Review*, no. 69, September–October 1971.

— 'The Left Against Europe?', special number of *New Left Review*, no. 75, September–October 1972.

Napolitano, Giorgio, *In mezzo al guado*, Editori Riuniti, Rome 1979.

Nätti, Jouko, 'Atypical Employment in the Nordic Countries: Towards Marginalisation or Normalisation?', in Boje and Olsson Hort (eds), op. cit.

Navarro, Vicente, 'Has Socialism Failed? An Analysis of Health Indicators under Socialism', *International Journal of Health Services*, Vol. 22, no. 4, 1992.

Nederhorst, G.-M., 'Les nationalisations aux Pays-Bas confronteés à l'expérience britannique', *La revue socialiste*, no. 30, October 1949.

Negt, Oscar, 'Rosa Luxemburg e il rinnovamento del marxismo', in *Storia del marxismo*. Vol. 2: *Il marxismo nell'età della Seconda Internazionale*, Einaudi, Turin 1979.

Nenni, Pietro, 'La relazione di Pietro Nenni', in Partito socialista italiano, *35° Congresso Nazionale*, Rome, 25–29 October 1963, Edizioni *Avanti!*, Milan 1964.

— *I nodi della politica estera italiana* (ed.), Domenico Zucàro, Sugarco Edizioni, Milan 1974.

Nettl, Peter, 'The German Social Democratic Party 1890–1914 as a Political Model', *Past and Present*, no. 30, April 1965.

— *Rosa Luxemburg*, Oxford University Press, Oxford 1969.

Neuhold, Hanspeter 'Background Factors of Austria's Neutrality', in Karl E. Birnbaum and Hanspeter Neuhold (eds), *Neutrality and Non-alignment in Europe*, Wilhelm Braumüller, Vienna 1982.

Newby, Howard, *The Countryside in Question*, Hutchinson, London 1988.

Newman, Michael, *Socialism and European Unity. The Dilemma of the Left in Britain and France*, Junction Books, London 1983.

— *John Strachey*, Manchester University Press, Manchester 1989.

Nimetz, Matthew, Introduction to Stavrou, op. cit.

Nixon, Richard, 'President's Message on Foreign Policy for the 1970s', *National Diplomacy 1965–1970, Congressional Quarterly*, May 1970.

Nolan, Mary and Charles F. Sabel, 'The Social Democratic Reform Cycle in Germany', in Esping-Andersen and Friedland (eds), op. cit.

Norris, Pippa, 'Women's Legislative Participation in Western Europe', *West European Politics*, Vol. 8, no. 4, October 1985.

— *Politics and Sexual Equality. The Comparative Position of Women in Western Democracies*, Wheatsheaf, Brighton 1987.

Northcutt, Wayne and Jeffra Flaitz, 'Women, Politics and the French Socialist Government', *West European Politics*, Vol. 8, no. 4, October 1985.

Notermans, Ton, 'The Abdication from National Autonomy: Why the Macroeconomic Policy Regime Has Become So Unfavorable to Labor', *Politics and Society*, Vol. 21, no. 2, June 1993.

O'Brien, Richard, 'Swedes show how to save money by spending it', *Financial Times*, 4 May 1988.

Occhetto, Achille, *Il sentimento e la ragione*, Rizzoli, Milan 1994.

— *Relazione al 18o Congresso, Il nuovo Pci in Italia e in Europa*, L'Unità, 19 March 1989.

— *Relazione al Comitato centrale*, 20 November 1989, *L'Unità*, 21 November 1989.

O'Connor, James, *The Fiscal Crisis of the State*, St Martin's Press, New York 1973.

OECD, *Economic Outlook, Historical Statistics 1960–1989*, Paris 1991.

— *Employment Outlook*, Paris, July 1994.

— *Economic Survey, Portugal,* November 1976.

Offe, Claus, *The Contradictions of the Welfare State,* Hutchinson, London 1984.

Öhman, Berndt, *LO and Labour Market Policy since the Second World War,* Prisca, Stockholm 1974.

Ollenhauer, Erich, 'A New Chance for the Rapacki Plan', *Socialist International Information,* Vol. 8, no. 46, 15 November 1958.

Olson Jr., Mancur, *The Logic of Collective Action: Public Goods and the Theory of Groups,* Harvard University Press, Cambridge MA 1965.

Olsson, Sven E., 'Swedish Communism Poised Between Old Reds and New Greens', *Journal of Communist Studies,* Vol. 2, no. 4, December 1986.

— *Social Policy and Welfare State in Sweden,* Arkiv förlag, Lund 1990.

O'Neill, June, 'Earnings Differentials: Empirical Evidence and Causes', in Schmidt and Weitzel (eds), op. cit.

Opello, Jr., Walter C., 'The Continuing Impact of the Old Regime on Portuguese Political Culture', in Graham and Wheeler (eds), op. cit.

— Portugal: A Case Study of International Determinants of Regime Transition', in Geoffrey Pridham (ed.), op. cit., 1991.

Ormerod, Paul, 'Incomes Policy', in Artis and Cobham (eds), op. cit.

Örvik, Nils (ed.), *Fears and Expectations. Norwegian Attitudes Towards European Integration,* Universitetsforlaget, Oslo 1972.

Ory, Pascal, 'The Concept of Generation as Exemplified by the Class of 68', in Hanley, Kerr and Waites, (eds) op. cit.

Osberg, Lars (ed.), *Economic Inequality and Poverty. International Perspectives,* M. E. Sharpe, Armonk NY 1991.

Ostrem, Inger-Lise, 'La Norvège et la communauté européenne: d'une appartenance de fait à une appartenance de droit?', *Revue du Marché commun et de l'Union européenne,* no. 364, January 1993.

Ovendale, Ritchie (ed.), *The Foreign Policy of the British Labour Governments, 1945–1951,* Leicester University Press, Leicester 1984.

Owen, David, 'The Enabling Society', in Wayland Kennet (ed.), *The Rebirth of Britain,* Weidenfeld and Nicolson, London 1982.

Owen, Nicholas, '"More Than a Transfer of Power": Independence Day Ceremonies in India, 15 August 1947', *Contemporary Record,* Vol. 6, no. 3, Winter 1992.

— (ed.), 'Decolonisation and the Colonial Office' (Witness Seminar), *Contemporary Record,* Vol. 6, no. 3, Winter 1992.

Paavonen, Tapani, 'Neutrality, Protectionism and the International Community. Finnish Foreign Economic Policy in the Period of Reconstruction of the International Economy, 1945–1950', *Scandinavian Economic History Review,* Vol. XXXVII, no. 1, 1989.

Pace, David, 'Old Wine, New Bottles: Atomic Energy and the Ideology of Science in Postwar France', *French Historical Studies,* Vol. 17, no. 1, Spring 1991.

Paci, Massimo, 'Long Waves in the Development of Welfare Systems, in Maier (ed.), op. cit.

Padgett, Stephen, 'The German Social Democrats: A Redefinition of Social Democracy or Bad Godesberg Mark II?', *West European Politics,* Vol. 16, no. 1, January 1993.

— 'The German Social Democratic Party: Between Old and New Left', in David S. Bell and Eric Shaw (eds), *Conflict and Cohesion in Western European Social Democratic Parties,* Pinter Publishers, London 1994.

— and William Paterson, 'The Rise and Fall of the West German Left', *New Left Review,* no. 186, March–April 1991.

Padgett, Stephen and William E. Paterson, *A History of Social Democracy in Postwar Europe,* Longman, London 1991.

Paggi, Leonardo, *Le strategie del potere in Gramsci*, Editori Riuniti, Rome 1984.

— (ed.), *Americanismo e riformismo. La socialdemocrazia europea nell'economia mondiale aperta*, Einaudi Editore, Turin 1989.

Pamparana, Andrea, *Il processo Cusani. Politici e faccendieri della Prima Repubblica*, Mondadori, Milan 1994.

Panitch, Leo, *Social Democracy and Industrial Militancy. The Labour Party, the Trade Unions and Incomes Policy 1945–1974*, Cambridge University Press, Cambridge 1976.

— 'Globalization and the State', in Ralph Miliband and Leo Panitch (eds), *Between Globalism and Nationalism, Socialist Register 1994*, Merlin Press, London 1994.

Pansa, Giampaolo, *Comprati e venduti. I giornali e il potere negli anni '70*, Bompiani, Milan 1977.

Papacosma, S. Victor, 'The Historical Context', in Clogg (ed.), op. cit., 1983.

Papadopoulos, Athanasios P., 'The Effects of Monetary, Fiscal and Exchange-Rate Policies on Output, Prices and the Balance of Payments in the Open Economy of Greece, 1955–90', *Applied Economics*, Vol. 25, no. 7, July 1993.

Papadopoulos, Ioannis, *Dynamique du discours politique et conquête du pouvoir. Le cas du PASOK: 1974–1981*, Peter Lang, Berne 1989 (University of Geneva doctoral dissertation no. 321).

Papadopoulos, Yannis, 'Parties, the State and Society in Greece: Continuity within Change', *West European Politics*, Vol. 12, no. 2, April 1989.

Papandreou, Andreas G., *A Strategy for Greek Economic Development*, Center of Economic Research, Contos Press, Athens 1962.

— *Paternalistic Capitalism*, Minneapolis University Press, Minneapolis 1972.

Parness, Diane L., *The SPD and the Challenge of Mass Politics*, Westview Press, Boulder CO 1991.

Parodi, Maurice, *L'économie et la société française depuis 1945*, Colin, Paris 1981.

Parti Communiste Français, *Histoire du Parti communiste français*, Editions Sociales, Paris 1964.

Parti Communiste Français–Parti Socialiste, *Programme commun de gouvernement*, Editions Sociales, Paris 1972.

Parti Socialiste, *Projet Socialiste. Pour la France des années 80*, Club Socialiste du Livre, Paris 1980.

Parti Socialiste Belge, *La Charte de Quaregnon, déclaration de principes du Parti Socialiste Belge*, Fondation Louis de Brouckère, Brussels 1980.

Partito Comunista Italiano, *La politica economica italiana (1945–1974). Orientamenti e proposte dei comunisti*, ed. Sezione centrale scuole di partito, PCI, Rome n.d.

Partito Socialista Italiano, *Il Partito Socialista Italiano nei suoi Congressi*, Vol. II, Edizioni *Avanti!*, Milan 1961.

— *Il Partito Socialista Italiano nei suoi Congressi*. Vol. V: *1942–1955. Il Socialismo italiano di questo dopoguerra*, ed. Franco Pedone, Edizione del Gallo, Milan 1968

— *37° Congresso e l'unificazione socialista, Roma, ottobre 1966*, ed. Maurizio Punzo, Edizioni La Squilla, Bologna 1976.

— *Governare il cambiamento. Conferenza programmatica del PSI*, Rimini, 31 March–4 April 1982.

— *Un riformismo moderno. Un socialismo liberale. Tesi Programmatiche*, Conferenza di Rimini, 22–23 March 1990.

Pasquino, Gianfranco, 'Modernity and Reforms: The PSI between Political Entrepreneurs and Gamblers', *West European Politics*, Vol. 9, no. 1, January 1986.

— 'Party Elites and Democratic Consolidation: Cross-national Comparison of Southern European Experience', in Pridham (ed.), op. cit. 1990.

Pateman, Carole, *The Disorder of Women*, Stanford University Press, Stanford CA 1989.

Paterson, William E. *The SPD and European Integration*, Saxon House, Farnborough 1974.

— 'The Ostpolitik and Régime Stability in West Germany', in Roger Tilford (ed.), *The Ostpolitik and Political Change in Germany*, Saxon House, Farnborough, 1975.

— 'The German Social Democratic Party', in Paterson and Thomas (eds), op. cit., 1986.
— and Alastair H. Thomas (eds), *Social Democratic Parties in Western Europe*, Croom Helm, London 1977.
— *The Future of Social Democracy*, Clarendon Press, Oxford 1986.
PCP, *Programa e Estatutos do PCP aprovado No VII Congresso (Extraordinário) em 20/10/74*, 2nd edn, Edições *Avante!*, Lisbon 1975.
PDS, *Programma di Governo del PDS. Elezioni politiche 27–28 marzo 1994*, Rome, February 1994.
Pecchioli, Ugo, 'Le forze democratiche e l'Europa del Mec', *Critica Marxista*, Vol. 4, no. 3, May–June 1966.
Pedersen, Susan, *Family, Dependence and the Origins of the Welfare State. Britain and France 1914–1945*, Cambridge University Press, Cambridge 1993.
Peel, Quentin and Judy Dempsey, 'Firmly footed for the final hurdle', *Financial Times*, 10 September 1994.
Pelling, Henry, *Britain and the Marshall Plan*, Macmillan, London 1988.
Pels, Dick, 'The Dark Side of Socialism: Hendrik de Man and the Fascist Temptation', *History of Human Sciences*, Vol. 6, no. 2, 1993.
Penniman, Howard and Eusebio M. Mujal-León (eds), *Spain at the Polls 1977, 1979, and 1982. A Study of National Elections*, American Enterprise Institute and Duke University Press, n.p. 1985.
Pepper, David, *The Roots of Modern Environmentalism*, Routledge, London 1984.
Pérez-Díaz, Víctor M., *The Return of Civil Society. The Emergence of Democratic Spain*, Harvard University Press, Cambridge MA 1993.
Petersen, Nikolai, 'The Cold War and Denmark', *Scandinavian Journal of History*, Vol. 10, 1985.
Peterson, Richard B., 'The Swedish Experience with Industrial Democracy', *British Journal of Industrial Relations*, Vol. 6, no. 2, July 1968.
Petras, James, 'The Contradictions of Greek Socialism', *New Left Review*, no. 163, May–June 1987.
— 'Spanish Socialism: The Politics of Neoliberalism', in James Kurth and James Petras (eds), *Mediterranean Paradoxes. The Politics and Social Structure of Southern Europe*, Berg, Providence and Oxford 1993.
Pfarr, Heide M. and Ludwig Eitel, 'Equal Opportunity Policies for Women in the Federal Republic of Germany', in Schmidt and Weitzel (eds), op. cit.
Pfister, Thierry, *La vie quotidienne à Matignon au temps de l'union de la gauche*, Hachette, Paris 1985.
Pharo, Helge, 'Bridgebuilding and Reconstruction. Norway Faces the Marshall Plan', *Scandinavian Journal of History*, Vol. 1, 1976.
— 'The Cold War in Norwegian and International Historical Research', *Scandinavian Journal of History*, Vol. 10, 1985.
Philip, André, *Le Socialisme trahi*, Plon, Paris 1957.
— *Les socialistes*, Editions du Seuil, Paris 1967.
Phillips, Anne, 'Democracy and Difference: Some Problems for Feminist Theory', *Political Quarterly*, Vol. 63, no. 1, January–March 1992.
Phillips, A. W., 'The Relation between Unemployment and the Rate of Change of Money Wage Rates in the United Kingdom, 1861–1957, *Economica*, Vol. 25, 1958.
Pickles, Dorothy, *The Government and Politics of France*, Vol. 2, Methuen, London 1973.
Pierson, Stanley, *Marxist Intellectuals and the Working Class Mentality in Germany 1887–1912*, Harvard University Press, Cambridge MA 1993.
Pimlott, Ben, *Labour and the Left in the 1930s*, Cambridge University Press, Cambridge 1977.
— *Hugh Dalton*, Macmillan, London 1985.

— *Harold Wilson*, HarperCollins, London 1992.

Pinder, John, 'Positive Integration and Negative Integration: Some Problems of Economic Union in the EEC', in Michael Hodges (ed.), *European Integration*, Penguin, Harmondsworth 1972.

Pinto, Diana, 'Vive la République!', *Intervention*, no. 10, August–December 1984.

— 'The Atlantic Influence and the Mellowing of French Identity', in Howorth and Ross (eds), *Contemporary France*, Vol. 2.

Pinzani, Carlo, 'L'Italia repubblicana', in Ragionieri, op. cit., 1976.

Pivert, Maurice, 'Le socialisme internationale et l'opération de Suez', *La revue socialiste*, no. 109, July 57.

Pivetti, Massimo, 'Military Spending as a Burden on Growth: An "Underconsumption" Critique', *Cambridge Journal of Economics*, Vol. 16, no. 4, December 1992.

Pizzorno, Alessandro, *I soggetti del pluralismo. Classi Partiti Sindacati*, Il Mulino, Bologna 1980.

Plasser, Fritz, Peter A. Ulram and Alfred Grausgruber, 'The Decline of *"Lager* Mentality" and the New Model of Electoral Competition in Austria', *West European Politics*, Vol. 15, no. 1, January 1992.

Platone, François, 'Les communistes au gouvernement: une expérience "complexe" et contradictoire', *Revue politique et parlementaire*, Vol. 87, no. 914, January–February 1985.

Polasky, Janet L., 'A Revolution for Socialist Reforms: The Belgian General Strike for Universal Suffrage', *Journal of Contemporary History*, Vol. 27, no. 3, July 1992.

Politica e economia, Supplement to no. 6, June 1989, 'Il nuovo PCI: due congressi a confronto'.

Pollack, Benny, 'The 1982 Spanish General Election and Beyond', *Parliamentary Affairs*, Vol. 36, no. 2, Spring 1983.

Pollack, Oscar, 'The Programme Debate in Austria', *Socialist International Information*, Vol. 8, no. 8, 22 February 1958.

Pollard, Sidney, *The Idea of Progress*, C. A. Watts, London 1968.

Pons, Silvio, 'Le politica estera dell'URSS, il Cominform e il PCI (1947–1948)', *Studi Storici*, Vol. 35, no. 4, October–December 1995,

Pontusson, Jonas, 'Radicalization and Retreat in Swedish Social Democracy', *New Left Review*, no. 165, September–October 1987.

— *Swedish Social Democracy and British Labour: Essays on the Nature and Condition of Social Democratic Hegemony*, Western Societies Program Occasional Paper no. 19, Center for International Studies, Cornell University, Ithaca NY 1988.

— *The Limits of Social Democracy. Investment Politics in Sweden*, Cornell University Press, Ithaca NY and London 1992.

— 'Sweden: After the Golden Age', in Anderson and Camiller (eds), op. cit.

Poperen, Jean, *L'Unité de la Gauche 1965–1973*, Fayard, Paris 1975.

Portelli, Hugues, 'La voie nationale des PC français et italien', *Projet*, June 1976.

— *Le socialisme français tel qu'il est*, Presses Universitaires de France, Paris 1980.

— L'Intégration du Parti socialiste a la Cinquième République', *Revue française de science politique*, Vol. 34, no. 4–5, August–October 1984.

Porter, Michael E., *The Competitive Advantages of Nations*, Free Press, New York 1990.

Presa, Silvano, 'La socialdemocrazia austriaca', in Paggi (ed.), op. cit.

Preston , Paul, *The Coming of the Spanish Civil War*, Methuen, London 1983.

— 'The PCE in the Struggle for Democracy in Spain', in Howard Machin (ed.), *National Communism in Western Europe. A Third Way for Socialism?*, Methuen, London 1983.

— 'The Agrarian War in the South', in Preston (ed.), *Revolution and War in Spain 1931–1939*, Methuen, London 1984.

— *The Triumph of Democracy in Spain*, Methuen, London 1987.

— (ed.), *Spain in Crisis. The Evolution and Decline of the Franco Régime*, Harvester Press, Hassocks Sussex 1976.

— and Denis Smyth, *Spain, the EEC and NATO*, Chatham House Papers 22, RIIA/RKP, London 1984.

Pridham, Geoffrey (ed.), *Securing Democracy: Political Parties and Democratic Consolidation in Southern Europe*, Routledge, London 1990.

— (ed.), *Encouraging Democracy. The International Context of Regime Transition in Southern Europe*, Leicester University Press, Leicester and London 1991.

— and Susannah Verney, 'The Coalitions of 1989–90 in Greece: Inter-party Relations and Democratic Consolidation', *West European Politics*, Vol. 14, no. 4, October 1991.

Procacci, Giuliano (ed.), *The Cominform. Minutes of the Three Conferences 1947/1948/1949*, Annali *1994*, Feltrinelli, Milan 1994.

Prost, Antoine, 'The Educational Maelstrom', in Ross, Hoffmann and Malzacher (eds), op. cit.

Prowse, Michael, 'Clinton budget a manifesto to middle classes', *Financial Times*, 7 February 1995.

Przeworski, Adam and John Sprague, *Paper Stones. A History of Electoral Socialism*, University of Chicago Press, Chicago 1988.

PSOE, *Estrategia economica del PSOE*, Editorial Pablo Iglesias, Madrid 1980.

— *Manifesto of Programme. Draft for Discussion (Programa 2000)*, January 1990, Editorial Pablo Iglesias, n.p., mimeograph.

— *XXVII Congreso. Memoria de gestión de la Comisión Ejecutiva. Informe de la Comisión Ejecutiva al Congreso*, n.p. and n.d.

Pugh, Martin, *Women and the Women's Movement in Britain 1914–1959*, Macmillan, London 1992.

Puntila, L. A., *The Political History of Finland 1809–1966*, Heinemann, London 1975.

Quadagno, Jill, *The Color of Welfare. How Racism Undermined the War on Poverty*, Oxford University Press, New York and Oxford 1994.

Quattrocchi, Angelo and Tom Nairn, *The Beginning of the End. France May 1968*, Panther, London 1968.

Quermonne, Jean-Louis, 'Le spectre de la technocratie et le retour de la politique', *Pouvoir*, no. 69, 1994.

Quillot, Roger, 'Les leçons de Suez', *La revue socialiste*, no. 103, January 1957.

Racine, Nicole, 'Le parti communiste français devant les problème idéologiques et culturels', *Le communisme en France*, Cahiers de la Fondation Nationale des Sciences Politiques, Colin, Paris 1969.

Radice, Giles and Lisanne Radice, *Socialists in the Recession. The Search for Solidarity*, Macmillan, London 1986

Ragionieri, Ernesto, *Il marxismo e l'Internazionale*, Editori Riuniti, Rome 1972.

— *Storia d'Italia. Dall'Unità a oggi*, Vol. 4, Tome 3, Einaudi Editore, Turin 1976.

Ramelson, Bert, *Social Contract: Cure-all or Con-trick?*, Communist Party pamphlet, London n.d. (1974).

Ramsden, John, 'From Churchill to Heath', in Lord Butler (ed.), *The Conservatives. A History from the Origins to 1965*, Allen and Unwin, London 1977.

Rand Smith, W., 'Towards *Autogestion* in Socialist France? The Impact of Industrial Relations Reform', *West European Politics*, Vol. 10, no. 1, January 1987.

— '"We can make the Ariane, but we can't make washing machines": The State and Industrial Performance in Post-war France', in Howorth and Ross (eds), op. cit., Vol. 3.

Randall, Vicky, *Women and Politics*, Macmillan, London 1987.

Ranger, Jean, 'Le déclin du Parti communiste français', *Revue française de science politique*, Vol. 36, no. 1, February 1986.

Rathkolb, Oliver, 'Die SPÖ und der aussenpolitische Entscheidungsprozess 1945–1955. Mit einem Ausblick auf die Neutralitätspolitik bis 1965', in Wolfgang Maderthaner (ed.),

Auf dem Weg zur Macht. Integration in den Staat, Sozialpartnerschaft und Regierungspartei, Loecker-Verlag, Vienna 1992.

Rau, Johannes, 'The Right Divides, We Unite', *Socialist Affairs,* no. 2, 1986.

Raun, Laura, 'Forecast of meagre expansion', Survey on the Netherlands, *Financial Times,* 16 October 1986.

— 'Viewpoints are converging', Survey on the Netherlands, *Financial Times,* 23 November 1987.

— 'Facing tough decisions', Survey on the Netherlands, *Financial Times,* 23 November 1987.

— 'Many losers, but some winners', Survey on the Netherlands, *Financial Times,* 23 November 1987.

— 'OECD prescribes more bitter medicine for Dutch economy', *Financial Times,* 7 June 1989.

Reale, Eugenio, *Nascita del Cominform,* Mondadori, Milan 1958.

Rearick, Charles, 'Festivals in Modern France: The Experience of the Third Republic', *Journal of Contemporary History,* Vol. 12, no. 3, July 1977.

Rebérioux, Madeleine, 'Il dibattito sulla guerra', *Storia del Marxismo.* Vol. 2: *Il marxismo nell'età della Seconda Internazionale,* Einaudi Editore, Turin 1979.

Redslob, Alain, 'Un système bancaire socialisé', in Massenet et al., op. cit.

Rehn, Gösta, 'The Debate on Employees' Capital Funds in Sweden', *Report to the Commission of the European Communities,* August 1983, mimeo.

— 'Swedish Active Labor Market Policy: Retrospect and Prospect', *Industrial Relations,* Vol. 24, no. 1, 1985 (SOFI Reprint Series no. 140).

Rehn–Meidner Report: see under Swedish Confederation of Trade Unions.

Reichhardt, Hans-Joachim, 'Resistance in the Labour Movement', in Graml et al., op. cit.

Renner, Karl, 'Democracy and the Council System', in Tom Bottomore and Patrick Goode (eds), *Austro-Marxism,* Clarendon Press, Oxford 1978.

Reynaud, Jean-Daniel, 'Trade Unions and Political Parties in France: Some Recent Trends', *Industrial and Labor Relations Review,* Vol. 28, no. 2, January 1975.

Reynié, Dominique, 'La question russe', *Intervention,* no. 13, July–September 1985.

Reynolds, David, *Britannia Overruled. British Policy and World Power in the 20th Century,* Longman, London 1991.

Reynolds, Siân (ed.), *Women, State and Revolution,* Wheatsheaf, Brighton 1986.

Rhodes, Martin, 'Craxi and the Lay-Socialist Area: Third Force of Three Forces?', in Robert Leonardi and Piergiorgio Corbetta (eds), *Italian Politics: A Review.* Vol. 3, Pinter Publishers, London and New York 1989.

Richardson, Jeremy and Roger Henning (eds), *Unemployment: Policy Responses of Western Democracies,* Sage, London 1984.

Rimbert, Pierre, 'Paupérisation et niveau de vie des travailleurs', *La revue socialiste,* nos 89–94, 1955–56.

— 'Pourquoi le Parti communiste a-t-il lancé la campagne de la paupérisation?', *La revue socialiste,* no. 95, March 1956.

— 'Une vue d'ensemble sur Karl Marx', *La revue socialiste,* nos 111 and 112, November and December 1957.

Rioux, Jean-Pierre, *La France de la Quatrième République.* Vol. 1: *L'ardeur et la nécessité 1944–1952,* Editions du Seuil, Paris 1980.

Roberts, Geoffrey, *The Unholy Alliance. Stalin's Pact with Hitler,* I.B. Tauris, London 1989.

— 'The Soviet Decision for a Pact with Nazi Germany', *Soviet Studies,* Vol. 44, no. 1, 1992.

Robins, L. J., *The Reluctant Party: Labour and the EEC 1961–75,* Hesketh, Ormskirk 1979.

Robinson, Derek, 'Labour Market Policies', in Beckerman (ed.), op. cit.

Robinson, Joan, *Economic Heresies. Some Old-fashioned Questions in Economic Theory,* Macmillan, London 1972.

Robrieu, Philippe, *Histoire intérieure du parti communiste 1945–1972*, Vol. 2, Fayard, Paris 1981.

Rocard, Michel, *Le PSU et l'avenir socialiste de la France*, Editions du Seuil, Paris 1969.

— *Parler vrai. Textes politiques*, Editions du Seuil, Paris 1979.

— *A l'épreuve des faits. Textes politiques 1979–1985*, Editions du Seuil, Paris 1986.

Rochon, Thomas R., 'The West European Peace Movement and the Theory of New Social Movements', in Dalton and Kuechler (eds), op. cit.

Rogers, Ian, 'Austria's old parties feel winds of change', *Financial Times*, 26 April 1995.

Rosanvallon, Pierre, *L'âge de l'autogestion*, Editions du Seuil, Paris 1976.

— *Le libéralisme économique*, Editions du Seuil, Paris 1989.

Rosati, Domenico, *La questione politica delle ACLI*, Edizioni Dehoniane, Naples 1975.

Rose, Richard, *Do Parties Make a Difference?*, 2nd edn, Macmillan, London 1984.

— and Ian McAllister, *The Loyalties of Voters*, Sage, London 1990.

Rose Solfeco (pseud.), 'Nationalisation des banques et nouvelle politique du crédit', *Nouvelle revue socialiste*, September–October 1982.

Ross, George, 'The Changing Face of Popular Power in France', in Fox Piven (ed.), op. cit.

— 'French Trade Unions Face the 1980s: The CGT and the CFDT in the Strategic Conflicts and Economic Crisis of Contemporary France', in Esping-Andersen and Friedland, op. cit.

— 'Where Have All the Sartres Gone? The French Intelligentsia Born Again', in Hollifield and Ross (eds), op. cit.

— Stanley Hoffmann and Sylvia Malzacher (eds), *The Mitterrand Experiment*, Polity Press, Oxford 1987.

Roth, Günther, *The Social Democrats in Imperial Germany. A Study in Working-Class Isolation and National Integration*, Bedminster Press, Towota NJ 1963.

Rowbotham, Sheila, *Hidden from History*, Pluto Press, London 1973.

Rowthorn, Bob and Andrew Glyn, 'The Diversity of Unemployment Experience since 1973', in Marglin and Schor (eds), op. cit.

Rubinstein, W. D., *Wealth and Inequality in Britain*, Faber and Faber, London 1986.

Ruffolo, Giorgio, 'La grande inflazione craxiana', *Micromega*, no. 3, June–August 1993.

Ruggie, Mary, 'Gender, Work, and Social Progress. Some Consequences of Interest Aggregation in Sweden', in Jenson, Hangen and Reddy (eds), op. cit.

— *The State and Working Women. A Comparative Study of Britain and Sweden*, Princeton University Press, Princeton NJ 1984.

Ruggles, Patricia, 'Short- and Long-Term Poverty in the United States: Measuring the American "Underclass"', in Osberg (ed.), op. cit.

Runciman, W. G., 'Occupational Class and the Assessment of Economic Inequality in Britain', in Wedderburn (ed.), op. cit.

Ruoff, Karen, '*Warenästhetik* in America, or Reflections on a Multi-National Concern', in W. F. Haug (ed.), *Warenästhetik. Beiträge zur Diskussion, Weiterentwicklung und Vermittlung ihrer Kritik*, Suhrkamp, Frankfurt 1975.

Ruscoe, James, *The Italian Communist Party 1976–81. On the Threshold of Government*, Macmillan, London 1982.

Russell, Bertrand, *The Selected Letters of Bertrand Russell*. Vol. 1: *The Private Years (1884–1914)*, ed. Nicholas Griffin, Allen Lane, Penguin, Harmondsworth 1992.

Russell, Dora, *The Tamarisk Tree. My Quest for Liberty and Love*, Virago, London 1977.

Rustin, Michael, 'The Politics of Post-Fordism: or, The Trouble with "New Times"', *New Left Review*, no. 175, May–June 1989.

Ruth, Arne, 'The Second New Nation: The Mythology of Modern Sweden', *Daedalus*, Spring 1984.

Ryan, Alan, *J. S. Mill*, Routledge and Kegan Paul, London 1974.

Sabbatucci, Giovanni, *Il riformismo impossibile. Storie del socialismo italiano*, Laterza, Rome-Bari 1991.

Sadoun, Marc, *Les socialistes sous l'occupation. Résistance et collaboration*, Presses de la Fondation Nationale des Sciences Politiques, Paris 1982.

Saeter, M., 'Nuclear Disengagement Efforts 1955–80: Politics of *Status Quo* or Political Change?', in Sverre Lodgaard and Marek Thee (eds), *Nuclear Disengagement in Europe*, SIPRI and Pugwash publication, Taylor and Francis, London and New York 1983.

Sainsbury, Diane, 'Swedish Social Democracy in Transition: The Party's Record in the 1980s and the Challenge of the 1990s', *West European Politics*, Vol. 14, no. 3, July 1991.

Salvadori, Massimo L., *Kautsky e la rivoluzione socialista 1880/1938*, Feltrinelli, Milan 1976.

— 'La socialdemocrazia tedesca e la rivoluzione russa del 1905', *Storia del marxismo*. Vol. 2: *Il marxismo nell'età della Seconda Internazionale*, Einaudi Editori, Turin 1979.

Samuel, Raphael, 'The Lost World of British Communism', *New Left Review*, no. 154, November–December 1985.

SAP, *The Postwar Programme of Swedish Labour. Summary in 27 Points and Comments*, Stockholm 1948, English trans. of the Swedish edition published in 1944.

— *Programme of the Swedish Social Democratic Party* (1960), Socialdemokraterna, Stockholm 1961.

— *Programme of the Swedish Social Democratic Party adopted by the 1975 Party Conference*, Social-demokraterna, Stockholm 1975 (in English).

— *Draft New Party Programme*, Socialdemokraterna, Stockholm 1989, mimeo, English trans.

— *Political platform adopted by the Party Executive and the National Executive of the Swedish Confederation of Trade Unions*, 24 January 1991, mimeo.

Sapelli, Giulio, *Cleptocrazia*, Feltrinelli, Milan 1994.

Sartre, Jean-Paul, *Being and Nothingness*, trans. Hazel E. Barnes, Washington Square Press, New York 1966.

— *The Communists and Peace*, trans. I. Clephane, Hamish Hamilton, London 1969.

Sassoon, Anne Showstack, *Gramsci's Politics*, Hutchinson, London 1987.

Sassoon, Donald, 'The Italian Communist Party's European Strategy', *Political Quarterly*, no. 3, 1976.

— *The Strategy of the Italian Communist Party. From the Resistance to the Historic Compromise*, Frances Pinter, London 1981.

— 'Political and Market Forces in Italian Broadcasting', *West European Politics*, Vol. 8, no. 2, April 1985.

— *Contemporary Italy*, Longman, London 1986.

— 'Italian Communism and the Popular Front', in Graham and Preston (eds), *The Popular Front in Europe*, Macmillan, London 1987.

— 'The 1987 Elections and the PCI', in Robert Leonardi and Piergiorgio Corbetta (eds), *Italian Politics: A Review*, Vol. 3, Pinter Publishers, New York and London 1989.

— 'The Role of the Italian Communist Party in the Consolidation of Parliamentary Democracy in Italy', in Pridham, op. cit.

— 'Reflections on the Labour Party's Programme for the 1990s', *Political Quarterly*, Vol. 62, no. 3, July–September 1991.

— (ed.), *The Italian Communists Speak for Themselves*, Spokesman Books, Nottingham 1978.

Sauvageot, Jacques et al., *The Student Revolt. The Activists Speak*, Panther, London 1968.

Sawyer, Malcom, 'Industrial Policy', in Artis and Cobham (eds), op. cit.

Scase, Richard, *Social Democracy in Capitalist Society: Working Class Politics in Britain and Sweden*, Croom Helm, London 1977.

Scharpf, Fritz W., 'A Game-Theoretical Interpretation of Inflation and Unemployment in Western Europe', *Journal of Public Policy*, Vol. 7, no. 3, July–September 1987.

— *Crisis and Choice in European Social Democracy*, Cornell University Press, Ithaca NY and London 1991.

Schiller, Berndt, 'Years of Crisis, 1906–1914', in Steven Koblik (ed.), *Sweden's Development from Poverty to Affluence*, University of Minnesota Press, Minneapolis 1975.

Schmidt, Günther, 'Labour Market Policy under the Social–Liberal Coalition', in Klaus von Beyme and Manfred G. Schmidt (eds), *Policy and Politics in the Federal Republic of Germany*, Gower, Aldershot 1985.

— and Renate Weitzel (eds), *Sex Discrimination and Equal Opportunity. The Labour Market and Employment Policy*, Gower, Aldershot 1984.

Schmidt, Helmut, 'The Role of the Trade Unions in the Federal Republic', 14 March 1976, *The Bulletin of the Press and Information Office of the Government of the FRG*, Vol. 3, no. 3, 6 April 1976, Bonn.

— *Perspectives on Politics*, Westview Press, Boulder CO 1982.

— *The World Crisis: Between Recession and Hope*, Foundation for International Relations, n.p. 1984.

— *A Grand Strategy for the West. The Anachronism of National Strategies in an Interdependent World*, Yale University Press, New Haven CT 1985.

— *Men and Powers. A Political Retrospective*, trans. Ruth Hein, Jonathan Cape, London 1990.

Schmidt, Manfred G., 'Learning from Catastrophes: West Germany's Public Policy', in Francis G. Castles (ed.), *The Comparative History of Public Policy*, Polity Press, Oxford 1989.

Schmidt, Ute, 'La Cdu e le difficoltà della "svolta"', in Missiroli (ed.), op. cit.

Schmidt, Vivien A., 'Decentralization: A Revolutionary Reform', in McCarthy, op. cit.

Schmitt, Hans O., *Economic Stabilization and Growth in Portugal*, Occasional Paper no. 2, International Monetary Fund, Washington DC April 1981.

Schmitter, Philippe C. and Gerhard Lehmbruch (eds), *Trends towards Corporatist Intermediation*, Sage, Beverly Hills and London 1979.

Schneer, Jonathan, *Labour's Conscience. The Labour Left 1945–51*, Unwin and Hyman, Boston 1988.

Schneider, Michael, *A Brief History of the German Trade Unions*, trans. B. Selman, Verlag J. H. W. Dietz Nachf, Bonn 1991.

Scholten, Ilja, 'Corporatism and the Neo-Liberal Backlash in the Netherlands', in Ilja Scholten (ed.), *Political Stability and Neo-corporatism*, Sage, London 1987.

Schorske, Carl E., *German Social Democracy 1905–1917. The Development of the Great Schism*, John Wiley and Sons, New York 1965.

Schreiner, Olive, *Woman and Labour*, Virago, London 1978.

Schultze, Charles L., 'Real Wages, Real Wage Aspirations, and Unemployment in Europe', in Lawrence and Schultze (eds), op. cit.

Schwartz, Joel, *The Sexual Politics of Jean-Jacques Rousseau*, University of Chicago Press, Chicago 1984.

Scott, Alan, *Ideology and the New Social Movements*, Unwin Hyman, London 1990.

Scott, Joan Wallach, '"A Woman Who Has Only Paradoxes to Offer": Olympe de Gouges Claims Rights for Women', in Sara E. Melzer and Leslie W. Rabine (eds), *Rebel Daughters. Women and the French Revolution*, Oxford University Press, New York 1992.

Secchia, Pietro, (ed.), *Il PCI e la guerra di liberazione 1943–45*, Feltrinelli, Milan 1973.

Seyd, Patrick, *The Rise and Fall of the Labour Left*, Macmillan, London 1987.

— and Paul Whiteley, *Labour's Grass Roots. The Politics of Party Membership*, Clarendon Press, Oxford 1992.

Seymour, Susan, *Anglo-Danish Relations and Germany 1933–1945*, Odense University Press, 1982.

Seymour-Ure, Colin, 'The SDP and the Media', *Political Quarterly*, Vol. 53, no. 4, October–December 1982.

Shalev, Michael, 'The Problem of Strike Measurement', in Crouch and Pizzorno (eds), op. cit., Vol. 1.

Share, Donald, *Dilemmas of Social Democracy. The Spanish Socialist Workers Party in the 1980s*, Greenwood Press, Westport CT 1989.

Shaw, Eric, *Discipline and Discord in the Labour Party 1951–87*, Manchester University Press, Manchester 1988.

— 'The Labour Party and the Militant Tendency', *Parliamentary Affairs*, Vol. 42, no. 2, April 1989.

Shell, Kurt L., *The Transformation of Austrian Socialism*, State University of New York Press, New York 1962.

Shennan, Andrew, *Rethinking France. Plans for Renewal 1940–1946*, Clarendon Press, Oxford 1989.

Shepard, William S., 'The Cyprus Issue: Waiting for Sadat', in Nikolaos A. Stavrou (ed.), *Greece under Socialism. A NATO Ally Adrift*, Orpheus Publishing, New Rochelle NY 1988.

Shonfield, Andrew, *Modern Capitalism. The Changing Balance of Public and Private Power*, Oxford University Press, Oxford 1965.

Shore, Chris, *Italian Communism: The Escape from Leninism*, Pluto Press, London 1990.

Short, Edward, speech, 29 January 1969, *Parliamentary Debates (Hansard)*, Vol. 776.

Shorter, Edward and Charles Tilly, *Strikes in France 1830–1968*, Cambridge University Press, Cambridge 1974.

Simmons, Harvey G., 'The French Socialist Opposition in 1969', *Government and Opposition*, Vol. 4, no. 3, 1969.

Singapore Department of Statistics, *Yearbook of Statistics*, Singapore 1990.

Singer, Daniel, *Is Socialism Doomed? The Meaning of Mitterrand*, Oxford University Press, New York 1988.

Skard, Torild and Elina Haavio-Mannila, 'Women in Parliament', in Haavio-Mannila et al. (eds), op. cit.

Skidelsky, Robert, *Politicians and the Slump. The Labour Government of 1929–1931*, Macmillan, London 1967.

— *Oswald Mosley*, Macmillan, London 1981.

Skjeie, Hege, 'The Uneven Advance of Norwegian Women', *New Left Review*, no. 187, May–June 1991.

Skocpol, Theda and Edwin Amenta, 'States and Social Policies', *Annual Review of Sociology*, Vol. 12, 1986.

Smith, Gordon, *Politics in Western Europe*, Heinemann, London 1972.

— *Democracy in Western Germany. Parties and Politics in the Federal Republic*, third edn, Gower, Aldershot 1986.

— 'The "New" Party System', in Gordon Smith, William E. Paterson, Peter H. Merkl and Stephen Padgett (eds), *Developments in German Politics*, Macmillan, London 1992.

Smith, Joan, 'Women's Unwaged Labour and the Formation of the World Labour Force', in Erik Aerts, Paul M. M. Klep, Jürgen Kocka and Marina Thorborg (eds), *Women in the Labour Force: Comparative Studies on Labour Market and Organization of Work since the 18th Century*, Leuven University Press, Louvain 1990.

Smith, John, 'No One Can Go It Alone', *Socialist Affairs*, no. 1, 1993.

Smith, Martin J. and Joanna Spear (eds), *The Changing Labour Party*, Routledge, London 1992.

Smith, R. and J. Zametica, J., 'The Cold Warrior: Clement Attlee Reconsidered 1945–47', *International Affairs*, Vol. 61, no. 2, 1985.

Smith, Raymond, 'Ernest Bevin, British Officials and British Soviet Policy, 1945–47', in Deighton (ed.), op. cit.

Sneessens, Henri R. and Jacques H. Drèze, 'A Discussion of Belgian Unemployment, Combining Traditional Concepts and Disequilibrium Econometrics', *Economica*, Vol. 53, 1986 Supplement to no. 210, *Unemployment*.

Snell, M. W., P. Glucklicht and M. Povall, *Equal Pay and Opportunities*, Research Paper no. 20, Department of Employment, London 1981.

Snyder, Paula, *The European Women's Almanac*, Scarlet Press, London 1992.

Soares, Mário, *Le Portugal bâillonné. Un témoignage*, Calmann-Lévy, Paris 1972.

— *Portugal's Struggle for Liberty*, Allen and Unwin, London 1975.

— *Portugal: Quelle révolution?*, Calmann-Lévy, Paris 1976.

Socialist International Women, *Report on Quota in SI Member Parties*, presented at the Bureau meeting of the Socialist International Women of 3–4 October 1993, Lisbon, mimeo.

Söderplan, Sven Anders, 'The Crisis Agreement and the Social Democratic Road to Power', in Steven Koblic (ed.), *Sweden's Development from Poverty to Affluence 1750–1970*, trans. Joanne Johnson, University of Minnesota Press, Minneapolis 1975.

Sofri, Adriano, *L'ombra di Moro*, Sellerio, Palermo 1991.

Soldani, Simonetta, 'Un primo maggio piccolo piccolo', *Italia Contemporanea*, no. 190, March 1993.

Solley, Leslie J., 'Europe Today', *Labour Monthly*, March 1947.

Solow, Robert M., 'Unemployment: Getting the Questions Right', *Economica*, Vol. 53, 1986, Supplement to no. 210, *Unemployment*.

Soskice, David, 'Strike Waves and Wage Explosions, 1968–1970: An Economic Interpretation', in Crouch and Pizzorno (eds), op. cit., Vol. 2.

Sowerwine, Charles, *Sisters or Citizens? Women and Socialism in France since 1876*, Cambridge University Press, Cambridge 1982.

SPD, *Ökonomisch-politischer Orientierungsrahmen für die Jahre 1975–1985*, n.p. n.d., published by the Press and Information of the SPD.

— *Sixteen Durkheim Points*, in *Jahrbuch der SPD 1948/1949*.

— *Aktions-Programm der SPD*, Bonn 1952.

— *Aktions-Programm der SPD*, Berlin 1954.

— *Basic Programme of the Social Democratic Party of Germany (Bad Godesberg Programme)* Bonn 1959.

— *Deutschlandplan*, Bonn, April 1959.

— *Resolution Adopted by the SPD Party Conference on Peace and Security*, Cologne, 19 November 1983; unofficial translation, typescript.

— *Irsee Draft for a new Manifesto of the Social Democratic Party of Germany*, June 1986, mimeo, English trans.

— *European Security 2000 – A Comprehensive Concept for European Security from a Social-Democratic Point of View*, English trans. by SPD Press office, mimeo, Bonn, 6 July 1989.

— *Basic Programme and Berlin Declaration of the Social Democratic Party of Germany*, adopted by the Programme Conference at Berlin, 20 December 1989, Friedrich-Ebert-Stiftung, Bonn 1990.

— *Preventing War in the Atomic Age. Towards a New Strategy for NATO*, mimeo, English trans.

— Text of programmes from Gotha to Bad Godesberg in appendix to Miller and Potthoff, op. cit.

SPÖ, *Sozial Demokratie 2000. Vorschläge zur Diskussion über Österreichs Zukunft*, Vienna 1989.

Spourdalakis, Michalis, *The Rise of the Greek Socialist Party*, Routledge, London and New York 1988.

Spriano, Paolo, *Storia del Partito comunista italiano*. Vol. III: *I fronti popolari, Stalin, la guerra*, Einaudi, Turin 1970.

— *Stalin and the European Communists*, Verso, London 1985.

Stalin, J. V., *The Essential Stalin*, ed. Bruce Franklin, Croom Helm, London 1973.

Stamiris, Eleni, 'The Women's Movement in Greece', *New Left Review*, no. 158, July–August 1986.

Stavrou, Nikolaus A. (ed.), *Greece Under Socialism. A NATO Ally Adrift*, Orpheus Publishing, New Rochelle NY 1988.

Stedman Jones, Gareth, *Languages of Class*, Cambridge University Press, Cambridge 1983.

Steininger, Rolf, *The German Question. The Stalin Note of 1952 and the Problem of Reunification*, trans. Jane T. Hedges, Columbia University Press, New York 1990.

Stephens, John D., *The Transition from Capitalism to Socialism*, Macmillan, London 1979.

Stevens, Anne, '"L'Alternance" and the Higher Civil Service', in Cerny and Schain (eds) op. cit.

Stewart, Michael, *The Age of Interdependence*, MIT Press, Cambridge MA 1984.

Stites, Richard, *The Women's Liberation Movement in Russia. Feminism, Nihilism, and Bolshevism, 1860–1930*, Princeton University Press, Princeton NJ 1978.

Stoffaës, Christian, 'The Nationalizations: An Initial Assessment, 1981–1984', in Machin and Wright (eds), op. cit.

Strange, Susan, *Sterling and British Policy. A Political Study of an International Currency in Decline*, Oxford University Press, Oxford 1971.

— *Casino Capitalism*, Blackwell, Oxford 1986.

Streeck, Wolfgang, 'Organizational Consequences of Neo-Corporatist Co-operation in West German Labour Unions', in Gerhard Lehmbruch and Philippe C. Schmitter (eds), *Patterns of Corporatist Policy-Making*, Sage, Beverly Hills 1982.

Streeck, Wolfgang, 'Neo-Corporatist Industrial Relations and the Economic Crisis in West Germany', in John H. Goldthorpe (ed.), *Order and Conflict in Contemporary Capitalism*, Clarendon Press, Oxford 1984.

Sully, Melanie Ann, *Continuity and Change in Austrian Socialism. The Eternal Quest for the Third Way*, Columbia University Press, New York 1982.

— 'Austrian Social Democracy', in Paterson and Thomas (eds), op. cit., 1986.

Sundström, Marianne, 'Part-time Work in Sweden and Its Implications for Gender Equality', in Folbre et al. (eds), op. cit.

Sweden, Ministry for Foreign Affairs, *Sweden and West European Integration*, Stockholm 1990.

Swedish Confederation of Trade Unions (LO), *Trade Unions and Full Employment*, (Rehn–Meidner Report), Report to the 1951 Congress, English trans., Stockholm 1953.

Sweets, J. F., *The Politics of Resistance in France 1940–1944*, Northern Illinois University Press, DeKalb IL 1976.

— *Choices in Vichy France*, Oxford University Press, 1986.

Taddei, Francesca, *Il socialismo italiano del dopoguerra: correnti ideologiche e scelte politiche (1943–1947)*, Franco Angeli, Milan 1984.

Tamames, Ramón, *¿Adónde vas, España?*, Editorial Planeta, Barcelona 1976.

Tarrow, Sidney, *Peasant Communism in Southern Italy*, Yale University Press, New Haven CT 1967.

— *Democracy and Disorder. Protest and Politics in Italy 1965–1975*, Clarendon Press, Oxford 1989.

Taylor, Barbara, *Eve and the New Jerusalem. Socialism and Feminism in the Nineteenth Century*, Virago, London 1983.

— 'Mary Wollstonecraft and the Wild Wish of Early Feminism', *History Workshop*, no. 33, Spring 1992.

Taylor, Lynne, 'The Parti communiste français and the French Resistance in the Second World War', in Judt (ed.), op. cit.

Taylor, Richard, *Against the Bomb. The British Peace Movement 1958–1965*, Clarendon Press, Oxford 1988.

Taylor, Robert, 'Swedes' pay deal breaks old mould', *Financial Times*, 30 April 1988.

— 'Minister champions market socialism for Sweden', *Financial Times*, 21 February 1989.

— 'Swedish tax reforms endorsed by OECD', *Financial Times*, 7 April 1989.

— 'Swedish parties agree on economic package', *Financial Times*, 24 May 1989.

Telò, Mario, *La Socialdemocrazia europea nella crisi degli anni trenta*, Franco Angeli, Milan 1985.

— (ed.), *Tradizione socialista e progetto europeo. Le idee della socialdemocrazia tedesca tra storia e prospettiva*, Editori Riuniti, Rome 1988.

— and Sven Schwersensky, 'L'unità tedesca e l'Europa. Difficoltà di ieri e di oggi della sinistra', in *Politica Europa Annali 1990–1991*, ed. Sezione Politica e Istituzioni in Europa del Centro per La Riforma dello Stato, Franco Angeli, Milan 1991.

Therborn, Göran, *Why Some People Are More Unemployed than Others*, Verso, London 1986.

— 'Does Corporatism Really Matter? The Economic Crisis and Issues of Political Theory', *Journal of Public Policy*, Vol. 7 Part 3, July–September 1987.

— '"Pillarization" and "Popular Movements". Two Variants of Welfare State Capitalism: The Netherlands and Sweden', in Francis G. Castles (ed.) *The Comparative History of Public Policy*, Polity Press, Cambridge 1989.

— 'Swedish Social Democracy and the Transition from Industrial to Post-industrial Politics', in Fox Piven (ed.), op. cit.

Thomas, Alastair H., 'Social Democracy in Denmark' in Paterson and Thomas (eds), op. cit., 1977.

— 'Denmark: Coalitions and Minority Governments', in Eric C. Browne and John Dreijmanis (eds), *Government Coalitions in Western Democracies*, Longman, New York and London 1982.

Thorez, Maurice, *France Today and the People's Front*, Left Book Club edn, Victor Gollancz, London 1936.

— 'Nouvelles données sur la paupérisation. Réponse à Mendès-France', *Cahiers du communisme*, Vol. 31, nos 7–8, July–August 1955

— Speech to the Fourteenth Congress of the PCF, July 1956 in *XIV Congrès du Parti communiste français, Numero special des 'Cahiers du Communisme'*, July–August 1956.

— 'Encore une fois la paupérisation!', *Cahiers du communisme*, Vol. 33, no. 5, May 1957.

— *Oeuvres*, Vol. 5, part 21 (June 1945–March 1946), and part 23 (November 1946–June 1947), Editions Sociales, Paris 1963.

Thosrsud, Einar and F. E. Emery, *Industrielt Demokrati*, University of Oslo Press, Oslo 1964.

Threlfall, Monica, 'The Women's Movement in Spain', *New Left Review*, no. 151, May–June 1985.

— 'Social Policy Towards Women in Spain, Greece and Portugal', in Gallagher and Williams (eds), op. cit.

— 'Feminism and Social Change in Spain', in M. Threlfall (ed.), *Mapping the Women's Movements*, Verso, London, 1996.

Tiersky, Ronald, *French Communism 1920–1972*, Columbia University Press, New York and London 1974.

Tilton, Tim, *The Political Theory of Swedish Social Democracy. Through Welfare State to Socialism*, Clarendon Press, Oxford 1990.

Timmermann, Heinz, *I comunisti italiani*, De Donato Editore, Bari 1974.

Tingsten, Herbert, *The Swedish Social Democrats*, Bedminster Press, Totowa NJ 1973.

Tipton, Frank B. and Robert, Aldrich, *An Economic and Social History of Europe from 1939 to the Present*, Macmillan, London 1987.

Togliatti, Palmiro, 'Rapporto all' VIII Congresso', in *Nella democrazia e nella pace verso il socialismo*, Editori Riuniti, Rome 1963.

— *L'emancipazione femminile*, Editori Riuniti, Rome 1973.

— *Sul movimento operaio internazionale*, Editori Riuniti, Rome 1964.

— *Opere scelte*, Editori Riuniti, Rome 1974.

— *On Gramsci and Other Writings*, ed. Donald Sassoon, Lawrence and Wishart, London 1979.

— 'Alcuni problemi della storia dell'Internazionale comunista' (1959), in *Opere*, Vol. 6, 1956–1964 Luciano Gruppi (ed.), Editore Riuniti, Rome 1984.

— *Discorsi Parlamentari*, Vol. 1, Ufficio Stampa e Pubblicazioni della Camera dei Deputati, Rome 1984.

— *Opere Vol. 5, 1944–1955*, Editori Riuniti, Rome 1984.

Tomlinson, Jim, *Monetarism: Is There an Alternative?*, Basil Blackwell, Oxford 1986.

— *Mr. Attlee's Supply-Side Socialism: Survey and Speculations*, Discussion Papers, in Economics no. 9101, Brunel University, London n.d. (1991).

Topolski, Jerzy, 'Continuity and Discontinuity in the Development of the Feudal System in Eastern Europe (Xth to XVIIth Centuries)', *Journal of European Economic History*, Vol. 10, no. 2, Fall 1981.

Tornes, Kristin, 'The Timing of Women's Commodification – How Part-time Solutions Became Part-time Traps', in Boje and Olsson Hort (eds), op. cit.

Touchard, Jean, *La gauche en France depuis 1900*, Editions du Seuil, Paris 1977.

Touraine, Alain, *Le mouvement de Mai ou le communisme utopique*, Editions du Seuil, Paris 1968.

— *L'après socialisme*, 2nd edn, Grasset, Paris 1983.

— 'Fin de Partie', *Intervention*, no. 13, July–September 1985.

Tracy, Noel, *The Origins of the Social Democratic Party*, Croom Helm, London and Canberra 1983.

Trentin, Bruno, *Il Sindacato dei Consigli*, Editori Riuniti, Rome 1980.

Trotsky, Leon, 'Bonapartism and Fascism', in *Writings of Leon Trotsky, 1934–35*, New York 1971.

Tsalikis, George, 'Evaluation of the Social Health Policy in Greece', *International Journal of Health Services*, Vol. 18, no. 4, 1988.

Tsoukalis, Loukas, *The New European Economy. The Politics and Economics of European Integration*, Oxford University Press, Oxford 1991.

TUC, *The Development of the Social Contract*, London, July 1975.

— *TUC Economic Review 1978*, London 1978.

— *TUC Report 1978*, London 1978.

Turner, H. A., 'Collective Bargaining and the Eclipse of Incomes Policy: Retrospect, Prospect and Possibilities', *British Journal of Industrial Relations*, Vol. VIII, no. 2, July 1970.

— *Is Britain Really Strike Prone?: A Review of the Incidence, Character and Costs of Industrial Conflict*, Occasional Paper 20, Cambridge University Press, Cambridge May 1969.

Turner, Jr, Henry Ashby, *The Two Germanies since 1945*, Yale University Press, New Haven CT 1987.

Upton, Anthony, 'Finland' in McCauley (ed.), op. cit.

Urban, Joan Barth, *Moscow and the Italian Communist Party. From Togliatti to Berlinguer*, I.B.Tauris, London 1986.

Vacca, Giuseppe (ed.), *Gli intellettuali di sinistra e la crisi del 1956*, Editori Riuniti, Rome 1978.

— *Tra compromesso e solidarietà. La politica del Pci negli anni '70*, Editori Riuniti, Rome 1987.

Valentini, Chiara, *Berlinguer Il Segretario*, Mondadori, Milan 1987.

Valli, Vittorio, *L'economia e la politica economica italiana 1945–1979*, Etas Libri, Milan 1979.

Vanbergen, Pierre, 'Pacte scolaire et projet de loi Moureaux' in *Socialisme*, Vol. 6, no. 33, May 1959.

van der Esch, Patricia, *La deuxième internationale 1889–1923*, Librairie Marcel Rivière, Paris 1957.

Vandermissen, Georges, 'La crisi delle relazioni industriali in Belgio', in Paolo Perulli and Bruno Trentin (eds), *Il sindacato nella recessione*, De Donato, Bari 1983.

Van de Ven, P. M. M. W., 'From Regulated Cartel to Regulated Competition in the Dutch Health Care System', *European Economic Review*, Vol. 34, 1990.

Van der Wee, Herman, *Prosperity and Upheaval. The World Economy 1945–1980*, Penguin, Harmondsworth 1987.

Van Lingen, J. and N. Slooff, *Van Verzetsstrijder tot Staatsgevaarlijk Berger*, Anthos, Baarn 1987.

Van Rijkeghem, Willy, 'Benelux', in Boltho (ed.), op. cit.

Van Voss, Lex Heerman, 'The International Federation of Trade Unions and the Attempt to Maintain the Eight-hour Working Day (1919–1929), in Fritz Van Holtoon and Marcel van der Linden (eds), *Internationalism and the Labour Movement 1830–1940*, Vol. II, E. J. Brill, Leiden 1988.

Vaughan, Michalina, 'Education: Cultural Persistence and Institutional Change', in P. McCarthy (ed.), op. cit.

Vazey, John, *The Political Economy of Education*, Duckworth, London 1972.

Vega, Pedro and Peru Erroteta, *Los herejes del PCE*, Editorial Planeta, Barcelona 1982.

Verdès-Leroux, Jeannine, *Le réveil des somnanbules. Le parti communiste, les intellectuels et la culture (1956–1985)*, Fayard/Editions de Minuit, Paris 1987.

Vermeylen, Pierre, 'Vue cavalière des programmes socialistes', *Socialisme*, Vol. 6, no. 35, September 1959.

Verney, Douglas V., *Parliamentary Reform in Sweden 1866–1921*, Clarendon Press, Oxford 1957.

Verney, Susannah, 'From the "Special Relationship" to Europeanism: PASOK and the European Community, 1981–89 in Clogg (ed.), op. cit., 1993.

— and Panos Tsakaloyannis, 'Linkage Politics: The Role of the European Community in Greek Politics in 1973', *Byzantine and Modern Greek Studies*, Vol. 10, 1986.

Vernon, Betty D., *Ellen Wilkinson 1891–1947*, Croom Helm, London 1982.

Viansson-Ponté, Pierre, *Histoire de la République Gaullienne*. Vol. II: *Le temps des orphelins*, Fayard, Paris 1971.

Villon, Pierre, 'Les contradictions de la politique étrangère gaulliste', *Cahiers du communisme*, Vol. 41, no 1, January 1965.

Vlavianos, Haris, 'The Greek Communist Party: In Search of Revolution', in Judt (ed.), op. cit.

Voerman, Gerrit, 'De la confiance à la crise. La gauche aux Pays-Bas depuis les années soixante-dix', in Pascal Delwit and Jean-Michel De Waele (eds), *La gauche face aux mutations en Europe*, Editions de l'Université de Bruxelles, Brussels 1993.

Vogel, Hans-Jochen, *NATO in the year 1983. The Testing of a Partnership*, speech at the Friedrich-Ebert-Stiftung, 23 June 1983, mimeo, English trans.

— 'La dimensione politica del Mercato unico europeo', *Nuova Rivista Internazionale*, no. 5–6, May–June 1989.

Voinea, Serban, 'Le projet de programme du parti socialiste autrichien', *La revue socialiste*, no. 116, April 1958.

Waldeberg, Marek, 'La strategia politica della socialdemocrazia tedesca', in *Storia del marxismo*, Vol. 2: *Il marxismo nell'età della Seconda Internazionale*, Einaudi Editore, Turin 1979.

Waldenström, Erland, 'The Investment Fund Debate in the Shadow of the General Election', *Skandinaviska Enskilda Banken Quarterly Review*, no. 2, 1982.

Wall, Irwin, *French Communism in the Era of Stalin. The Quest for Unity and Integration, 1945–1962*, Greenwood Press, Westport CT and London 1983.

Wallace, William, 'Rescue or Retreat? The Nation State in Western Europe, 1945–93', *Political Studies*, Vol. 42, Special issue 1994.

Wallerstein, Immanuel, *The Modern World-System I. Capitalist Agriculture and the Origins of the European World-Economy in the Sixteenth Century*, Academic Press, San Diego 1974.

— *The Politics of the World-Economy*, Cambridge University Press, Cambridge 1984.

Walon, Claude, 'L'économie: la rupture avec l'ancien socialisme', *Intervention*, no. 13, July–September 1985.

Warde, Alan, *Consensus and Beyond. The Development of Labour Party Strategy since the Second World War*, Manchester University Press, Manchester 1992.

Ware, Kallistos, 'The Church: A Time of Transition', in Clogg (ed.), op. cit., 1983.

Warner, Geoffrey, 'The Labour Government and the Unity of Western Europe', in Ovendale (ed.), op. cit., 1984.

Watt, D. C., *Personalities and Politics*, University of Notre Dame Press, South Bend, IN 1965.

Weaver, R. Kent, 'Political Foundations of Swedish Economic Policy', in Bosworth and Rivlin (eds), op. cit.

Webb, Sidney and Beatrice, *Soviet Communism: A New Civilization*, Longmans, Green and Co., London 1944.

Webber, Douglas, 'Social Democracy and the Re-emergence of Mass Unemployment in Western Europe', in Paterson and Thomas (eds), op. cit., 1986.

— and Gabriele Nass, 'Employment Policy in West Germany', in Richardson and Henning (eds), op. cit.

Wedderburn, Dorothy, (ed.), *Poverty Inequality and Class Structure*, Cambridge University Press, Cambridge 1974.

Weiler, Peter, *British Labour and the Cold War*, Stanford University Press, Stanford CA 1988.

Weitz, Eric D., 'State Power, Class Fragmentation, and the Shaping of German Communist Politics, 1890–1933', *Journal of Modern History*, Vol. 62, no. 2, June 1990.

Wettig, Gerhard, 'Stalin and German Reunification: Archival Evidence on Soviet Foreign Policy in Spring 1952', *Historical Journal*, Vol. 37, no. 2, 1994.

White, Dan S., *Lost Comrades. Socialists of the Front Generation 1918–1945*, Harvard University Press, Cambridge MA 1992.

Whitehouse, Gillian, 'Legislation and Labour Market Gender Inequality: An Analysis of OECD Countries', *Work, Employment and Society*, Vol. 6, no. 1, March 1992.

Whiteley, Paul, 'The Decline of Labour's Local Party Membership and Electoral Base 1945–79', in Dennis Kavanagh (ed.), *The Politics of the Labour Party*, Allen and Unwin, London 1982.

— *The Labour Party in Crisis*, Methuen, London and New York 1983.

Wilcox, Clyde, 'The Causes and Consequences of Feminist Consciousness Among West European Women', *Comparative Political Studies*, Vol. 23, no. 4, January 1991.

Wilensky, Harold L., *The Welfare State and Equality*, University of California Press, Berkeley 1975.

Wilensky, Harold L., 'Leftism, Catholicism, and Democratic Corporatism: The Role of Political Parties in Recent Welfare State Development', in Flora and Heidenheimer (eds), op. cit.

Wilkinson, Richard, 'Health, Redistribution and Growth', in Andrew Glyn and David Miliband (eds), *Paying for Inequality. The Economic Cost of Social Injustice*, IPPR/Rivers Oram Press, London 1994.

Wilks, Stephen, 'Liberal State and Party Competition: Britain', in Dyson and Wilks (eds), op. cit.

Williams, Beryl, 'Kollontai and After: Women in the Russian Revolution, in Reynolds (ed.) op. cit.

Williams, Geoffrey Lee and Alan Lee Williams, *Labour Decline and the Social Democrats' Fall*, Macmillan, London 1989.

Williams, Philip M., *Crisis and Compromise. Politics in the Fourth Republic*, Longman, London 1972.

— *Hugh Gaitskell*, Oxford University Press, Oxford 1982.

— and Martin Harrison, *Politics and Society in De Gaulle's Republic*, Longman, London 1971.

Williams, Raymond (ed.), *May Day Manifesto 1968*, Penguin, Harmondsworth 1968.

Williams, Shirley, *Politics is for People*, Penguin, Harmondsworth 1981.

— and Des Wilson, *People in Power. Why Constitutional Reform Matters to Everyone in Britain*, SDP–Liberal Alliance, Autumn 1986.

Willis, F. Roy, *Italy Chooses Europe*, Oxford University Press, Oxford 1971.

Wilson, Dorothy, *The Welfare State in Sweden. A Study in Comparative Social Administration*, Heinemann, London 1979.

Wilson, Frank L., *The French Democratic Left 1963–1969. Towards a Modern Party System*, Stanford University Press, Stanford CA. 1971.

Wilson, Harold, *The New Britain*, Penguin, Harmondsworth 1964.

Wilson, Harold, *The Labour Government 1964–70. A Personal Record*, Weidenfeld and Nicolson and Michael Joseph, London 1971

— *Final Term. The Labour Government 1974–1976*, Weidenfeld and Nicolson and Michael Joseph, London 1979.

Wise, Peter, 'A time for celebration and reflection', *Financial Times*, 22 February 1994.

Witherspoon, Sharon, 'Sex Roles and Gender Issues', in Roger Jowell and Sharon Witherspoon (eds), *British Social Attitudes. The 1985 Report*, Gower, Aldershot 1985.

Witherspoon, Sharon and Jean Martin, 'What Do We Mean by Green?', in Roger Jowell et al., *British Social Attitudes. The 9th Report*, SCPR/Dartmouth, Aldershot 1992.

Wittig, Monique, *The Straight Mind and Other Essays*, Harvester Wheatsheaf, Hemel Hempstead 1992.

Wohl, Robert, *French Communism in the Making 1914–1924*, Stanford University Press, Stanford CA 1966.

Wolfe, Alan, 'Has Social Democracy a Future?' *Comparative Politics*, Vol. 11, no. 1, October 1978.

Wolinetz, Steven B., 'Socio-economic Bargaining in the Netherlands: Redefining the Post-war Policy Coalition', *West European Politics*, Vol. 12, no. 1, January 1989.

— 'Reconstructing Dutch Social Democracy', *West European Politics*, Vol. 16, no.1, January 1993.

Wollstonecraft, Mary, *The Rights of Woman*, Dent, Everyman's Library, London 1977.

Woodhouse, C. M., *Karamanlis. The Restorer of Greek Democracy*, Clarendon Press, Oxford 1982.

Worsthorne, Peregrine, 'Beefing up the bosses', *Sunday Telegraph*, 30 January 1977.

Wright, A. W., *G. D. H. Cole and Socialist Democracy*, Clarendon Press, Oxford 1979.

Wright, Vincent and Howard Machin, 'The French Socialist Party in 1973: Performance and Prospects', *Government and Opposition*, Vol. 9, no. 2, 1974.

Yergin, Daniel, *Shattered Peace. The Origins of the Cold War and the National Security State*, Penguin, Harmondsworth 1977.

Young, John W., *France, the Cold War and the Western Alliance, 1944–49: French Foreign Policy and Post-war Europe*, Leicester University Press, Leicester and London 1990.

Zamagni, Vera, 'The Marshall Plan: An Overview of its Impact on National Economies', in Antonio Varsori (ed.), in *Europe 1945–1990s. The End of an Era?* Macmillan, London 1995.

Zeman, Z. A. B., *The Making and Breaking of Communist Europe*, Blackwell, Oxford 1991.

Zetkin, Clara, *Reminiscences of Lenin*, International Publishers, New York 1934.

— *Selected Writings*, ed. Philip S. Foner, International Publishers, New York 1984.

Ziebura, Gilbert, 'Léon Blum à la veille de l'exercice du pouvoir', in *Léon Blum chef du gouvernement 1936–37*, Cahiers de la Fondation Nationale des Sciences Politiques, Colin, Paris 1967.

Index